1996

VIETNAM LAOS & CAMBODIA HANDBOOK

SECOND EDITION

Editors **Joshua Eliot, Jane Bickersteth and John Colet**
Cartographer **Sebastian Ballard**

Everywhere, markets among the houses,
like an immense fresco,
No end of busy quarters, where purple jostles vermillion ...
Indeed it is
A rich, wonderful, royal city.
Nguyen Gian Thanh 1508, on Thang Long (Hanoi)

TRADE & TRAVEL
Handbooks

Trade & Travel Publications Ltd
6 Riverside Court, Lower Bristol Road, Bath BA2 3DZ, England
Telephone 01225 469141   Fax 01225 469461
Email 100660.1250@compuserve.com

©Trade & Travel Publications Ltd., September 1995

ISBN 0 900751 65 7   ISSN 1352-7878

CIP DATA: A catalogue record for this book is available from the British Library

In North America, published and distributed by

PASSPORT BOOKS
a division of *NTC Publishing Group*

4255 West Touhy Avenue, Lincolnwood (Chicago), Illinois 60646-1975, USA
Telephone 708-679-5500   Fax 708-679-2494   Email NTCPUB2@AOL.COM

ISBN 0-8442-8884-5

Library of Congress Catalog Card Number 95-69402

Passport Books and colophon are registered trademarks of NTC Publishing Group

IMPORTANT: While every endeavour is made to ensure that the facts
printed in this book are correct at the time of going to press, travellers
are cautioned to obtain authoritative advice from consulates, airlines,
etc, concerning current travel and visa requirements and conditions
before embarking. The publishers cannot accept legal responsibility for
errors, however caused, that are printed in this book.

Cover illustration by Suzanne Evans

Printed and bound in Great Britain by Clays Ltd., Bungay, Suffolk

CONTENTS

Xmas '95
Happy Trails...
Wherever they may be
Nigel

THE EDITORS

Joshua Eliot

Joshua has had a long-standing interest in Asia. He was born in Calcutta, grew up in Hong Kong, has a PhD on rural development in Thailand from the University of London, and lectures on Southeast Asia. He is the author of a book on the geography of the region and has written well over 30 papers and articles on Southeast Asia. He has lived and conducted research in Thailand, Sumatra and Laos and has travelled extensively in the region over a period of nearly 15 years. He speaks Thai, and some Lao and Indonesian.

Jane Bickersteth

Jane has worked on the guidebooks since the first edition in 1992. She has been visiting the region for over 10 years, spending a year there whilst she researched the first edition. Jane is an artist by training and is particularly inspired by the Khmer ruins of Thailand and the candis of Java and Bali.

John Colet

John is Head of Geography at St Paul's Girls' School in London, a post he formerly held at Eton College. He has written a number of papers, articles and book reviews on Vietnam and Southeast Asia. He is closely involved with the Saigon Children's Charity and has spent several months a year in Vietnam since 1988 working for the Charity and researching earlier editions of this *Handbook*.

The first edition

The first edition of this book was researched and written by Joshua Eliot, Jane Bickersteth, Georgina Matthews and Jonathan Miller.

Jonathan Miller

Jonathan is a journalist with the BBC World Service and based in Bangkok. Formerly he worked in London and Phnom Penh. He was raised in Malaysia and Singapore and before joining the BBC was a foreign correspondent in the region contributing pieces for such newspapers and magazines as *The Economist*, the *Asian Wall Street Journal*, *South*, and the *Daily Telegraph*.

Georgina Matthews

Georgina is a professional guidebook editor. She has published books for Nicholson and Dorling Kindersley and has a particular interest in Burma, Laos and Cambodia. She spent a year in the field researching the first edition of this guide.

PREFACE

The month of April 1975 was a momentous one in the modern history of Indochina, and April 1995 saw the celebration or remembrance of those events 2 decades ago. The 20th anniversary of the end of the Vietnam War fell on the 30 April 1995 and marches and festivities across the country marked the day. Just under 2 weeks earlier, the 17 April marked the 20th anniversary of another tragic slice of history – but one which was about to begin, not end. On 17 April 1975, the Cambodian capital, Phnom Penh, fell to the Khmer Rouge. Government soldiers, monks and officials were rounded up and marched away to their deaths. The Khmer Rouge then ordered everyone out of the city for 3 days, claiming that the Americans were about to unleash a bombing campaign. The 3 days were to turn into 3 years and 9 months of mass murder and economic madness. In Laos, meanwhile, the victories of Communist forces in Vietnam and Cambodia was a spur to the Pathet Lao who began their final and decisive advance in April 1975 – although the capital, Vientiane, was not to be declared fully liberated until the end of August.

In Laos there has been some loosening of travel restrictions. It is now possible to travel overland through much of the country, and permission to visit individual provinces does not have to be sought. Crossing into Laos from Thailand, China and Vietnam is now much easier, and mainland Southeast Asia is gradually emerging as an integrated region from the perspective of the traveller. Although overland travel in Laos and Vietnam may, at times, be arduous, it is at least possible.

In Cambodia, the security situation remains difficult. Although Phnom Penh, the capital, and Siem Reap (for Angkor) are considered safe, rural areas are not regarded as such, and overland travel is not advised. The murder of three western tourists by the Khmer Rouge in 1994 after they were abducted from a train in July (their bodies were only discovered in November), and slightly later the murder of an American tourist at Angkor, again by the Khmer Rouge, only served to illustrate the security risks that exist. Although Cambodia may have made the transition to some form of democracy, it is still not a stable or – over large areas – a safe country. Nonetheless, tourist arrivals in 1994 were 175,000, a considerable increase on 1993 and up from just 4,500 in 1991. Provided that visitors stick to the main tourist itineraries the country can be considered safe to visit as this guide went to press. (Prospective visitors should check with their embassies though.)

Vietnam continues to develop rapidly as a tourist destination. The number of tourists – not to mention business people – is growing rapidly, although there are times when the creaking tourist infrastructure appears almost on the verge of collapse. In early July 1995 the US and Vietnam, having partially normalized relations in 1994, agreed to full normalization of diplomatic and commercial relations. On the 28 July, Vietnam joined the Association of Southeast Asian Nations (ASEAN), marking the country's full rehabilitation into the international community.

During 1995, the editors visited Vietnam and the Cambodian capital, Phnom Penh. Duncan Shearer, our correspondent in Phnom Penh, fed us with much useful information on Cambodia, and Gill Henson, our correspondent in Vientiane, Laos, played an invaluable role in allowing us to update and substantially re-write the Laos section. We are grateful to both of them for their assistance.

We are also grateful to all those people who took the trouble to send us letters with their advice, views and criticisms, and they are acknowledged at the end of the appropriate *Information for visitors* section. However we would particularly like to thank the following for their help: Hilary Emberton, Chloe Gorman and Pilou Grenié for their extensive and meticulous notes on Laos and Vietnam; Julia Wilkinson for her material on Laos; Bob Samuels of Trailfinders for information on air travel to and within the region; and John H Stubbs of the World Monument Fund in New York for his help on the Angkor section.

The Editors
Bath

MAP SYMBOLS

International Border	~~~	State Capitals	▢
		Other Towns	○
State / Province Border	- - -	Bus Stations	**B**
		Hospitals	**H**
Cease Fire Line	-·-·-·-	Key Numbers	**27**
Main Roads (National Highways)	Rt 15	Post Office	**PO**
		Telephone/telegraph Office	☏
Other Roads	———	Tourist Office	❶
Jeepable Roads, Tracks, Treks, Paths, Ferries	- - -	Airport	✈
		Bridges	)(
One Way Street	→	Mountain Pass	)(
Railways, Stations	+—■—+	Mountains	⩗
Contours (approx)	≈	Waterfall	⋔
Rivers / Canals	*Mekong River*	National Parks, Wildlife Parks, Bird Sanctuaries	◆
Built Up Areas	▨	Archaeological Sites	▲
Lakes, Reservoirs, Tanks	▨	Hide	⌂
Seasonal Marshlands	▨	Camp site	Å
Sand Banks, Beaches	▨	Refuge	⌂
Stands of trees (Beach areas)	⁊	Lodge with facilities	⌂
National Parks, Gardens, Stadiums	▨	**Places of Worship & Religious Sites**	
		Pagoda	⛩
Fortified Walls	▲▲▲	Hindu Temple	♨
		Mosque	🕌
		Church/cathedral	♰

TB 0

INTRODUCTION AND HINTS

CONTENTS

General note The advice given below represents a regional summary of more detailed information provided in the *Information for visitors* sections of each country entry.

Before travelling

Documents

● **Passports**

Passports should be valid for at least 6 months from the day of entry. Visitors intending to stay for an extended period or those visiting a number of countries should ensure their passports are valid for even longer than this. Also ensure there is sufficient space for entry and exit stamps. Details of visa formalities are given in the relevant *Information for visitors* sections. Passports should be carefully looked after. Those travelling overland on a low budget, should keep their passport and other valuables in a money-belt, hidden beneath clothing. In hotels, keep valuables in a safe deposit box. In case of theft, keep a photocopy of your passport and other important documents in a separate place.

● **ISIC**

Anyone in full-time education is entitled to an International Student Identity Card (ISIC). These are issued by student travel offices and travel agencies across the world and offer special rates on all forms of transport and other concessions and services. The ISIC head office is: ISIC Association, Box 9048, 1000 Copenhagen, Denmark, T (45) 33 93 93 03.

When to go

● **Best time to visit**

The Thai authorities have recently announced that they no longer have an 'off-season' for tourism. This attempt to even-out arrivals has not, however, changed the pattern of the seasons. In general, the dry season extends from Nov to Mar, and the wet season from May/Jun to Oct (see rainfall chart, page 37). However, it is possible to travel throughout the year in most areas, and the low season for visitors has the advantage of discounted hotel rates.

EXCHANGE RATES (AUGUST 1995)

	US$	£	DM
Cambodia (riel)	2,300	3,627	1,604
Laos (kip)	729	1,150	508
Thailand (baht)	24.90	39.30	17.38
Vietnam (dong)	11,403	17,419	7,704

Climate

See page 37.

Health

See page 23.

Money

If travelling to the countries of Indochina, travellers' cheques denominated in US$ are most useful. In Thailand, travellers' cheques denominated in most major currency can be easily changed. Because transaction charges are often calculated per travellers' cheque, it is best to take mostly high value cheques (eg US$100). A small amount of cash (in US$) can also be useful in an emergency. Keep it separate from your travellers' cheques.

What to take

Travellers usually tend to take too much. If routing through Bangkok, Thailand's capital offers and has almost everything a visitor could need – and often at a lower price than in the West. But in Indochina the reverse is true: many goods are hard, if not impossible, to find and relatively expensive to buy. See the relevant section in the *Information for visitors* sections for more details on what to take to this second group of countries.

Suitcases are not appropriate if you are intending to travel overland by bus. A backpack, or even better a travelpack (where the straps can be zipped out of sight), is recommended. Travelpacks have the advantage of being hybrid backpacks-suitcases; they can be carried on the back for easy porterage, but they can also be taken into hotels without the owner being labelled a 'hippy'. Note however, that for serious hikers, a backpack with an internal frame is still by far the better option for longer treks.

In terms of clothing, dress in Southeast Asia is relatively casual – even at formal functions. Suits are not necessary except in a very few of the most expensive restaurants. There is a tendency, rather than to take inappropriate articles of clothing, to take too many of the same article. Laundry services are cheap, and the turn-around rapid.

● **Checklist**
Bumbag
Earplugs
First aid kit
Insect repellent and/or mosquito net, electric mosquito mats, coils
International driving licence
Photocopies of essential documents
Short wave radio
Spare passport photographs
Sun protection cream
Sunglasses
Swiss Army knife
Torch
Umbrella
Wipes (*Damp Ones*, *Baby Wipes* or equivalent)
Zip-lock bags

Those intending to stay in budget accommodation might also include:
Cotton sheet sleeping bag
Money belt
Padlock (for hotel room and pack)
Student card
Toilet paper
Towel

● **Health kit**
Antiacid tablets
Anti-diarrhoea tablets
Anti-infective ointment
Anti-malaria tablets
Condoms
Contraceptives
Dusting powder for feet
First aid kit and disposable needles
Flea powder,
Sachets of rehydration salts
Tampons
Travel sickness pills
Water sterilizing tablets

Getting there

Air

Bangkok has become the principal air travel hub for the countries of Indochina – Vietnam, Cambodia and Laos – although there are increasing numbers of direct flights to Hanoi and Saigon from outside the area. Availability is changing constantly so check with your travel agent for the latest information. There are direct flights from Bangkok to Hanoi and Ho Chi Minh City (Saigon), and to Vientiane, and Phnom Penh. Bangkok is also the easiest city to obtain visas for these countries: visas for Cambodia can also be obtained with ease in Ho Chi Minh City (Vietnam). There are also direct flights to Ho Chi Minh City (Saigon) from Taipei, Seoul, Kuala Lumpur, Hong Kong, Kaohsiung and Singapore; to Hanoi from Kuala Lumpur and Hong Kong; and to Phnom Penh from Kuala Lumpur.

Many airlines offer non-stop flights from European cities to Bangkok. The scheduled flying time from London to Bangkok is 12 hrs on non-stop flights, but may be up to 20 hrs on flights that stop. Many of the world's top airlines fly the Southeast Asian routes and standards are therefore high. Onward reservations should be reconfirmed at every stage. Within Southeast Asia there is a wide range of flight connections on internal airlines.

Direct flights Direct flights to Bangkok are readily available from Europe, Australasia and South Asia (Delhi, Karachi, Colombo, Dhaka and Kathmandu). From North America's west coast there are flights direct from Los Angeles and Vancouver. From Japan, Hong Kong and the Philippines there are frequent flights.

Stop-overs and round the world tickets It is possible to arrange several stop-overs in Southeast Asia on round the world (RTW) and other longer distance tickets. RTW tickets allow you to fly in to Bangkok and out from another international airport such as Singapore or Kuala Lumpur. Different travel agents organise different deals. *Trailfinders* of London, one of the world's biggest agencies, has a range of discounted deals. Contact at 194 Kensington High St, London W8 7RG, T (0171) 938-3939.

Tickets can be purchased locally, and paid for in local currency, but this is not a particularly cheap option.

● **Discounts**
It is possible to obtain significant discounts, especially outside European holiday times, most notably in London, even on non-stop flights. Shop around and book early. It is also possible to get discounts from Australasia, South Asia and Japan. All airlines have different seasonal rates – many using 8-10 bands. This means one airline's high season may not be another's. Generally, discounted fares have various restrictions on length of stay, whether they can be changed, and so on. It may even be cheaper buying intra-regional flights outside the region. For example, the Bangkok-Singapore full fare is £160; in London the ticket is discounted to £70.

● **Further information**
For more information on air travel to and within the countries of Indochina, see **Getting there** and **Getting around** sections within **Information for visitors** for each country. You are advised to check carefully with your travel agent before setting off for the latest schedules and best deals.

Airline security
International airlines vary in their arrangements and requirements for security, in particular, the carrying of equipment like radios, tape-recorders and laptop computers. It is advisable to ring the airline in advance to confirm their current regulations. **Note that internal airlines often have different rules from the international carriers.**

In this Handbook, further details on

MAPS OF MAINLAND SOUTHEAST ASIA

A decent map is an indispensable aid to travelling. Although maps are usually available locally, it is sometimes useful to buy a map prior to departure to plan routes and itineraries. Below is a select list of maps. Scale is provided in brackets.

Regional maps: Bartholomew Southeast Asia (1:5,800,000); Nelles Southeast Asia (1:4,000,000); Hildebrand Thailand, Burma, Malaysia and Singapore (1:2,800,000).

Country maps: Bartholomew Thailand (1:1,500,000); Bartholomew Vietnam, Laos and Cambodia (1:2,000,000); Nelles Thailand (1:1,500,000); Nelles Vietnam, Laos and Cambodia (1:1,500,000).

City maps: Nelles Bangkok.

Other maps: Tactical Pilotage Charts (TPC, US Airforce) (1:500,000); Operational Navigational Charts (ONC, US Airforce) (1:500,000). Both of these are particularly good at showing relief features (useful for planning treks); less good on roads, towns and facilities.

Locally available maps: maps are widely available in Thailand and many are given out free, although the quality of information is sometimes poor. In Vietnam, Laos and Cambodia maps are cheap although not always available beyond the capital cities; again, quality may be poor.

Map shops: in London, the best selection is available from Stanfords, 12-14 Long Acre WC2E 9LP, T (0171) 836-1321; also recommended is McCarta, 15 Highbury Place, London N15 1QP, T (0171) 354-1616.

air links to and from each country, arrival and departure regulations, airport taxes, customs regulations and security arrangements for air travel are outlined in the relevant *Information for visitors* sections.

Sea

Few people arrive in mainland Southeast Asia by sea. There are no regular passenger ships to Thailand, Vietnam or Cambodia. Laos is landlocked. Ships do dock in Singapore and there are regular ferries linking Thailand and Malaysia. For those interested in booking a passage on a cargo ship travelling to the region, contact the *Strand Cruise and Travel Centre*, Charing Cross Shopping Concourse, The Strand, London WC2N 4HZ, T (0171) 836-6363, F (0171) 497-0078.

Overland

There are road links between Thailand and Laos via the border crossing at Nong Khai (Northeastern Thai-land) to Vientiane and also from Nakhon Phanom to Tha Khaek, Mukdahan to Savannakhet, Chiang Khong to Huay Xai, and Chong Mek to Pakse. In April 1994 the first bridge over the lower reaches of the Mekong River opened near Nong Khai/Vientiane (see page 350). Note that in each case visitors wishing to cross into Laos at any one of these border posts must have the appropriate port of entry stamped in their passports. Overland links between Thailand and Cambodia are not yet open, although it is possible to travel by bus and taxi from Phnom Penh (Cambodia) to Ho Chi Minh City (Vietnam) – with occasional difficulties. The border between Vietnam and China has also recently opened. There are no overland links between Vietnam and Laos open to foreign visitors. See the relevant *Information for visitors* sections for further details.

On arrival

Appearance

Southeast Asians admire neatness and cleanliness. They find it difficult to understand how some Westerners – by definition wealthy – can dress so poorly and untidily. By dressing well, you will be accorded more respect and face fewer day-to-day difficulties. Women, particularly, should also dress modestly. Short skirts and bare shoulders are regarded as unacceptable except in beach resorts and one or two, more cosmopolitan, cities. Both men and women should be particularly sure to dress appropriately if visiting a religious site – a Buddhist monastery for example.

Confidence tricksters

Most common of all are confidence tricksters: people selling fake gems and antiques, informal currency exchange services offering surprisingly good rates, and card sharps. Confidence tricksters are, by definition, extremely convincing and persuasive. Time is cheap in Southeast Asia, and people are willing to invest long hours lulling tourists into a false sense of security. Be suspicious of any offer that seems too good to be true. That is probably what it is.

Drugs

Drugs (narcotics) are available in

TRAVELLING WITH CHILDREN & BABIES IN SOUTHEAST ASIA

Many people are daunted by the prospect of taking a child to Southeast Asia. Naturally, it is not something which is taken on lightly; travelling is slower and more expensive and there are additional health risks for the child or baby. But it can be a most rewarding experience, and with sufficient care and planning, it can also be safe. Children are excellent passports into a local culture. You will also receive the best service, and help from officials and members of the public when in difficulty.

Children in Southeast Asia are given 24-hr attention by parents, grandparents and siblings. They are rarely left to cry and are carried for most of the first 8 months of their lives – crawling is considered animal-like. A non-Asian child is still something of a novelty and parents may find their child frequently taken off their hands, even mobbed in more remote areas. This can be a great relief (at mealtimes, for instance) or most alarming. Some children love the attention, others react against it; it is best simply to gauge your own child's reactions.

Accommodation At the hottest time of year, air-conditioning may be essential for a baby or young child's comfort. This rules out many of the cheaper hotels, but a/c accommodation is available in all but the most out-of-the-way spots. When the child is bathing, be aware that the water could carry parasites, so avoid letting him or her drink it.

Transport Public transport may be a problem; trains are fine but long bus journeys are restrictive and uncomfortable. Hiring a car is undoubtedly the most convenient way to see a country with a small child. Back-seatbelts are rarely fitted but it is possible to buy child-seats in capital cities.

Food & drink The advice given in the health section on food and drink (**see page 30**) should be applied even more stringently where young children are concerned. Be aware that expensive hotels may have squalid cooking conditions; the cheapest street stall is often more hygienic. Where possible, try to watch food being prepared. Stir-fried vegetables and rice or noodles are the best bet; meat and fish may be pre-cooked and then left out before being re-heated. Fruit can be bought cheaply right across Southeast Asia: papaya, banana and avocado are all excellent sources of nutrition, and can be self-peeled ensuring cleanliness. Powdered milk is also available throughout the region, although most brands have added sugar. But if taking a baby, breast-feeding is strongly recommended. Powdered food can be bought in most towns – the quality may not be the same as equivalent foods bought in the West, but it is perfectly adequate for short periods. Bottled water and fizzy drinks are also sold widely. If your child is at the 'grab everything and put it in mouth' stage, a damp cloth and some *dettol* (or equivalent) are useful. Frequent wiping of hands and tabletops can help to minimize the chance of infection.

Sunburn NEVER allow your child to be exposed to the harsh tropical sun without protection. A child can burn in a matter of minutes. Loose cotton-clothing, with long sleeves and legs and a sun-hat are best. High-factor sun-protection cream is essential.

Disposable nappies These can be bought in Thailand, and in Vientiane, Laos, and in Saigon and Hanoi in Vietnam but are often expensive. If you are staying any length of time in one place, it may be worth taking Terry's (cloth) nappies. All you need is a bucket and some double-strength nappy cleanse (simply soak and rinse). Cotton nappies dry quickly in the heat and are generally more comfortable for the baby or child. They also reduce rubbish – many countries are not geared to the disposal of nappies. Of course, the best way for a child to be is nappy-free – like the local children.

Baby products Many Western baby products are now available in Southeast Asia: shampoo, talcum powder, soap and lotion. Baby wipes can be difficult to find.

Emergencies Babies and small children deteriorate very rapidly when ill. A travel insurance policy which has an air ambulance provision is strongly recommended. When planning a route, try to stay within 24 hours' travel of a hospital with good care and facilities. Many expatriats fly to Singapore for medical care, which has the best doctors and facilities in the region.

Suggested checklist:
Baby wipes
Child paracetamol
Disinfectant
First aid kit
Flannel
Immersion element for boiling water
Kalvol and/or *Snuffle Babe* or equivalent for colds
Instant food for under-one-year-olds
Mug/bottle/bowl/spoons
Nappy cleanse, double-strength
ORS/ORT (Oral Rehydration Salts or Therapy) such as *Dioralyte*, widely available in Thailand, and the most effective way to alleviate diarrhoea (it is not a cure).
Portable baby chair, to hook onto tables; this is not essential but can be very useful
Sarung or backpack for carrying child (and/or light weight collapsible buggy)
Sterilizing tablets (and an old baby-wipes container for sterilising bottles, teats, utensils)
Cream for nappy rash and other skin complaints such as *Sudocrem*
Sunblock, factor 15 or higher
Sunhat
Terry's (cloth) nappies, liners, pins and plastic pants
Thermometer
Zip-lock bags for carrying snacks, powdered food, wet flannel.

Suggested reading: Pentes, Tina and Truelove, Adrienne (1984) *Travelling with children to Indonesia and South-East Asia*, Hale & Iremonger: Sydney. Wheeler, Maureen *Travel with children*, Lonely Planet: Hawthorne, Australia.

Southeast Asia, particularly in Thailand. However, penalties are harsh. In Thailand there are scores of former tourists overstaying their visas in prisons across the country. Do not agree to take anything out of Thailand without knowing exactly what it is.

Etiquette

As a general rule, Southeast Asians admire a calm and considered approach to all aspects of life. Open anger or shows of temper should be avoided. Causing another person to 'lose face' is not recommended, and status – particularly in terms of age – should be accorded due respect.

Personal safety

So far as visitors are concerned, violence against the person is rare in Southeast Asia (but note above). If attacked, do not try to resist – firearms are widespread.

Theft is far more common than violence. Thieves favour public transport; confidence tricksters frequent popular tourist destinations. Personal valuables – money, travellers' cheques, passports, jewellery – should be kept safe. Do not leave valuables in hotel rooms; place them in a safe deposit box if possible, or keep them with you. A money-belt, concealed beneath clothing, is the safest way to carry valuables. Generally, the cheaper the mode or class of transport or hotel, the more likely thieves will be at work. Drugging of tourists on buses and trains by offering doped food does occur, particularly in Thailand. Simple common sense is the best defence.

Police

Report any incident that involves you or your possessions. Tourist Police operate in Thailand and are particularly geared to the problems of tourists. In the countries of Indochina there are no such dedicated tourist police. Nonetheless, report any incident. In general, police will act promptly and properly. Local people throughout

the region are proud of their country's reputation and are often all too willing to help a foreigner in trouble.

Prisoners Abroad

Prisoners Abroad is a charity dedicated to supporting UK nationals in prison abroad. As the charity writes: "Arrest, trial and imprisonment are devastating in a familiar environment, supported by family and friends. Abroad it is much worse." Young men and women caught with drugs may find themselves facing sentences of 10 years or more, often in appalling conditions. Volunteers can help Prisoners Abroad, and similar organizations, by becoming a pen pal, donating a magazine subscription, or sending books, for example. If you or a friend find yourself in the unfortunate position of being in jail, or facing a jail term, then contact the charity at: Prisoners Abroad, Freepost 82, Roseberry Avenue, London EC1B 1XB, UK, T 0171 833-3467, F 0171 833-3460 (if telephoning or faxing from abroad then the code is +44171-). Further information on the charity and its work can also be obtained from the above address.

Sensitive areas

In Thailand, visitors should be careful when visiting border areas in the North and West, and on the frontier with Cambodia. In Laos, tourists are constrained – although much less so than just a year or two ago – and it can be difficult reaching some areas without an official guide. Cambodia is also a country where travel is carefully controlled. It should be remembered that despite the peace agreement, clashes between the Khmer Rouge and government forces in Cambodia continue and mines are a menace in many areas. Of the countries of Indochina, independent travel is easiest in Vietnam. But, officials are still sensitive to foreigners travelling alone and tourists are commonly fined.

Tipping

Tipping is not customary except in more expensive hotels and restaurants. It is also common for a 10% service charge and government tax (usually of 10%-11%) to be added on to bills in more expensive hotels and restaurants.

Women travelling alone

Women travelling alone face greater difficulties than men or couples. The general advice given above should be observed even more carefully. Young Southeast Asian women rarely travel without a partner, so it is regarded as strange for Western women to do so. Western women are often believed to be of easy virtue – a view perpetuated by Hollywood and in local films, for example. To minimise the pestering that will occur, dress modestly. Comments, sometimes derogatory, will be made however carefully you dress and act; simply ignore them. Toiletries such as tampons are widely available in main towns and cities in Thailand, but not widely in Indochina.

Where to stay

Accommodation

In this book we do not quote prices for hotel rooms (or restaurants); we use price categories instead. This is not just to make it easier to update. A price gives an impression of permanency; yet room rates can double overnight. Kirman, an Indonesian tour guide, and restaurant and *losmen* (guesthouse) worker in Bali and Nusa Tenggara explains the difficulties with explicit prices in these terms "... people just believe the [guide] book – even if it's 5 years old – and then they fight about the prices with the local people. ... They want to be the winner and don't realize they are being rude to the local people."

In Vietnam, Loas and Cambodia first class hotels are only to be found in capital cities and one or two other towns. Service, facilities and value for money are generally poor in comparison to, say, Thailand. Budget accommodation likewise is limited although the range is expanding rapidly as tourism grows, and spreads to new areas. Some cheaper hotels may refuse to offer foreigners a room.

Bangkok, Thailand offers a wide range of accommodation. Some of the finest hotels in the world are to be found in the city, many moderately priced by Western standards for the facilities they offer. Mid-range and budget accommodation are also of a relatively good standard.

Camping

In Vietnam, Laos and Cambodia there are no camping grounds and few facilities.

HOTEL CATEGORIES

A brief summary of the facilities to be expected within each category of accommodation is given in the relevant *Information for visitors* sections for each country. Note that the categories are based on the cost of a double room for one night.

	US$	baht	dong	kip	riel
L	200+	+5,000	-	-	-
A+	100-200	2,500-5,000	-	70,000-140,000	-
A	50-100	1,250-2,500	-	35,000-70,000	-
B	25-50	625-1,250	-	17,500-35,000	57,500-115,000
C	15-25	375-625	150,000-250,000	10,500-17,500	34,500-57,500
D	8-15	200-375	80,000-150,000	5,600-10,500	18,400-34,500
E	4-8	100-200	<80,000	2,800-5,600	9,200-18,400
F	<4	<100		<2,800	<9,200

Food and drink

Food

Restaurants in Vietnam, Loas and Cambodia are limited in number and range. Simple local dishes are the best value and usually also the tastiest option. Although care regarding what you eat and where you eat it is obviously recommended, levels of hygiene are reasonable. The incidence of tourists suffering from serious stomach upsets is far less than, say, in South Asia. All towns have local restaurants and stalls serving cheap, tasty and nourishing dishes. Many towns will also have their requisite Chinese restaurant, so it is usually possible to order food that is not spicy-hot. Details on local cuisines are contained in each *Information for visitors* section.

In the capital cities and a handful of other major towns, the choice is reasonable. Generally, local dishes are excellent, but Western food is often poor. Ingredients – particularly meat – are sometimes of poor quality. Outside the main towns, restaurants can be few and far between, and the food inferior. Western food is not widely available. There are notable exceptions to this characterization, but it holds true over large areas of Indochina.

Across the region, fruit can be a lifesaver. It is varied, cheap, exotic, safe to eat (if peeled oneself) and delicious. A list of the more exotic Southeast Asian fruits is given below. More details on food and restaurants in each country are contained in the relevant *Information for visitors* sections.

Drink

In Vietnam, Laos and Cambodia, imported brand soft drinks can be bought in bigger towns but at a considerable mark-up. Locally made soft drinks are very sweet. Local beers are a better bet, and can be bought in most towns. Bottled water is either unavailable or imported, so it is expensive. Tea and coffee are available almost everywhere. It is not advisable to drink water straight from the tap.

Getting around

Air

Domestic airlines link major towns and cities. In Thailand, services are efficient and safe, although considerably more expensive than the overland alternatives. In Vietnam, Laos and Cambodia, services are reasonable although safety records are not up to international standards and flights are regularly overbooked. A spate of recent accidents in Vietnam has raised even more serious questions regarding maintenance and upkeep.

Train

Vietnam and Cambodia have passenger railways, but the networks are limited. Laos has no passenger railways. In Cambodia use of railways by tourists was not recommended until recently; reports are that since the election in 1993 safety (attacks by Khmers Rouges) is less of an issue, but visitors are advised to check on arrival. Travelling third class is often the cheapest way to get from A to B, while first class (a/c) is more comfortable (and safer) than travelling by bus (although usually slower). Rail travel makes good sense in Vietnam,

	US$	baht	dong	kip	riel
◆◆◆◆	15+	375+	150,000+	10,500	54,500
◆◆◆	5-15	125-375	50,000-150,000	3,500-10,500	17,500-54,500
◆◆	2-5	50-125	20,000-50,000	1,400-3,500	7,000-17,500
◆	<2	<50	<20,000	<1,400	<7,000

RESTAURANT CATEGORIES

DISTINCTIVE FRUITS OF SOUTHEAST ASIA

Custard apple (or sugar apple) Scaly green skin, squeeze the skin to open the fruit and scoop out the flesh with a spoon. Season: Jun-Sept.

Durian (*Durio zibethinus*) A large prickly fruit, with yellow flesh, about the size of a football. Infamous for its pungent smell. While it is today regarded by many visitors as simply revolting, early Europeans (16th-18th centuries) raved about it, possibly because it was similar in taste to Western delicacies of the period. Borri (1744) thought that "God himself, who had produc'd that fruit". But by 1880 Burbridge was writing: "Its odour - one scarcely feels justified in using the word 'perfume' - is so potent, so vague, but withal so insinuating, that it can scarcely be tolerated inside the house". Banned from public transport in Singapore and hotel rooms throughout the region, and beloved by most Southeast Asians (where prize specimens can cost a week's salary), it has an alluring taste if the odour can be overcome. Some maintain it is an addiction. Durian-flavoured chewing gum, ice cream and jams are all available. Season: May-Aug.

Jackfruit Similar in appearance to durian but not so spiky. Yellow flesh, tasting slightly like custard. Season: Jan-Jun.

Mango (*Mangifera indica*) A rainforest fruit which is now cultivated. Widely available in the West; in Southeast Asia there are hundreds of different varieties with subtle variations in flavour. Delicious eaten with sticky rice and a sweet sauce (in Thailand). The best mangoes in the region are considered to be those from South Thailand. Season: Mar-Jun.

Mangosteen (*Garcinia mangostana*) An aubergine-coloured hard shell covers this small fruit which is about the size of a tennis ball. Cut or squeeze the purple shell to reach its sweet white flesh which is prized by many visitors above all others. In 1898, an American resident of Java wrote, erotically and in obvious ecstasy: "The five white segments separate easily, and they melt on the tongue with a touch of tart and a touch of sweet; one moment a memory of the juiciest, most fragrant apple, at another a remembrance of the smoothest cream ice, the most exquisite and delicately flavoured fruit-acid known - all of the delights of nature's laboratory condensed in that ball of *neige parfumée*". Southeast Asians believe it should be eaten as a chaser to durian. Season: Apr-Sept.

Papaya (*Carica papaya*) A New World Fruit that was not introduced into Southeast Asia until the 16th century. Large, round or oval in shape, yellow or green-skinned, with bright orange flesh and a mass of round, black seeds in the middle. The flesh, in texture and taste, is somewhere between a mango and a melon. Some maintain that it tastes 'soapy'. Season: Year round.

Pomelo A large round fruit the size of anything from an ostrich egg to a football, with thick, green skin, thick pith, and flesh not unlike that of the grapefruit, but less acidic. Season: Aug-Nov.

Rambutan (*Nephelium lappaceum*) The bright red and hairy rambutan - *rambut* is the Malay word for 'hair' - with its slightly rubbery but sweet flesh is a close relative of the lychee of southern China and tastes similar. The Thai word for rambutan is *ngoh*, which is the nickname given by Thais to the fuzzy-haired Negrito aboriginals in the southern jungles. Season: May-Sept.

Salak (*Salacca edulis*) A small pear-shaped fruit about the size of a large plum with a rough, brown, scaly skin (somewhat like a miniature pangolin) and yellow-white, crisp flesh. It is related to the sago and rattan trees.

Tamarind (*Tamarindus indicus*) Brown seedpods with dry brittle skins and a brown tart-sweet fruit which grow on a tree introduced into Southeast Asia from India. The name is Arabic for 'Indian date'. The flesh has a high tartaric acid content and is used to flavour curries, jams, jellies and chutneys as well as for cleaning brass and copper. Elephants have a predilection for tamarind balls. Season: Dec-Feb.

as most major destinations are on the rail network. **NB** Security can be a problem on long-distance train journeys.

Road

Road is the main mode of transport in the region. **Buses** link nearly all towns, however small. Roads are still generally poor, despite continuing upgrading, and travel can be slow and painful. More express a/c minibuses ply the main routes, a trend that will continue as tourism expands, but the level of facilities and range of services does not begin to compare with, say, Thailand. Tourists are sometimes, and in some places constrained and/or discouraged from using buses, although limited use is possible (see relevant *Information for visitors* sections). In Vietnam, local transport was made much more freely available to overseas visitors in 1993, and conditions in Laos are also improving. **NB** Security can be a problem on long-distance bus journeys.

Car hire

Cars for self-drive hire are not available except very exceptionally. Far more common than self-drive, is for visitors to hire a car and driver. This is possible in all the countries covered in this book.

Hitchhiking and cycling

Hitchhiking is not common. However there are increasing numbers of visitors who tour Vietnam by **bicycle** – or at least with a bicycle. In Vietnam, bicycles can be used in towns to get around, and carried on buses between towns.

Boat

Boats are not a mode of transport frequently used by visitors – although rivers are important arteries of communication. Ferries link Saigon with towns in the Mekong Delta, and also run between Haiphong and Halong Bay in north Vietnam. There is also some river transport – for example on the Mekong in Vietnam, Cambodia, and Laos.

Communications

Language

In Indochina, English is not widely spoken except in Ho Chi Minh City (Saigon), although a few older people do still speak some French.

Southeast Asia on the Internet

Listed below are Internet addresses which access information on Asia generally, the Southeast Asian region, or individual countries within Southeast Asia. **Newsgroups** tend to be informal talking shops offering information from hotels and sights through to wide-ranging discussions on just about any topic. **Mailing Lists** have a more academic clientele, and probably are not worth plugging into unless you have a specific interest in the subject concerned. **Web sites** offer a whole range of information on a vast variety of topics. Below is only a selection.

Newsgroups on USENET with a Southeast Asian focus

Newsgroups are discussion fora on the USENET. Not every computer linked to the Internet has access to USENET – your computer needs Net News and a News reader. Newsgroups are informal fora for discussion; they are occasionally irreverent, usually interesting.

● *Asia general*
alt.asian.movies
alt.buddha.short.fat.guy
rec.travel.asia
soc.religion.eastern
talk.religion.buddhism

● *Southeast Asia*
soc.culture.asean

● *Cambodia*
soc.culture.cambodia

● *Laos*
soc.culture.laos

● *Vietnam*
soc.culture.vietnamese

Mailing lists

These are discussion groups with a more academic content; some may be moderate – ie the content of messages is checked by an editor. Mailing lists communicate using E-mail. The focus of the groups are in square brackets.

● *Asia general*

actmus-1@ubvm.bitnet [Asian Contemporary Music Discussion Group]

apex-1@uhccvm.bitnet [Asia-Pacific Exchange]

buddha-1@ulkyvm.bitnet [Buddhist Academic Discussion Forum]

● *Southeast Asia*

seanet-1@nusvm.bitnet [Southeast Asian Studies List]

seasia-1@msu.bitnet [Southeast Asia Discussion List]

● *Vietnam*

vietnam@uscvm.bitnet [Vietnmanese Discussion List]

Southeast Asia on the World Wide Web – Web sites

Web sites are on the World Wide Web. They can now be browsed using a graphical mouse-based hypertext system. The two in use are Mosaic and the newer, Netscape. They allow the user to browse through the WWW easily. Note, however, that images (especially) take time to download and if on the Web during the time of the day when the US is alive and kicking expect to spend a very long time twiddling your thumbs. The subject of the web site is in square brackets after the address.

● *Asia general*

http://none.coolware.com/infoasia/ [run by Infoasia which is a commercial firm that helps US and European firms get into Asia]

http://www.city.net/regions/asia [pointer to information on Asian countries] http://www.branch.com:80/silkroute/ [information on hotels, travel, news and business in Asia]

http://www.singapore.com/pata [Pacific Asia Travel Association – stacks of info on travel in the Pacific Asian region including stats, markets, products etc]

● *Southeast Asia*

http://emailhost.ait.ac.th/asia/asia. html [clickable map of mainland Southeast Asia with pointer to sources of other information on the region]

http://www.leidenuniv.nl/pun/ubhtm/ mjkintro.htm [library of 100 slides of Pagan (Burma), Thailand (Phimai, Chiang Mai, Lamphun), Cambodia (Angkor) and Vietnam (Myson)]

Terms

E-mail = Electronic mail

WWW = World Wide Web or, simply, the Web

HTML = Hypertext Markup Language

Source: the above was collated from *Internet news* published in the *IIAS Newsletter* [International Institute for Asian Studies Newsletter], Summer 1995.

SHORT WAVE RADIO GUIDE

British Broadcasting Corporation (BBC, London) *Southeast Asian service* 3915, 6195, 9570, 9740, 11750, 11955, 15360; *Singapore service* 88.9MHz; *East Asian service* 5995, 6195, 7180, 9740, 11715, 11750, 11945, 11955, 15140, 15280, 15360, 17830, 21715. **Voice of America (VoA, Washington)** *Southeast Asian service* 1143, 1575, 7120, 9760, 9770, 15185, 15425; *Indonesian service* 6110, 11760, 15425. **Radio Beijing** *Southeast Asian service (English)* 11600, 11660. **Radio Japan (Tokyo)** *Southeast Asian service (English)* 11815, 17810, 21610.

HEALTH INFORMATION

CONTENTS

The following information has been compiled by Dr David Snashall, Senior Lecturer in Occupational Health, United Medical Schools of Guy's and St Thomas' Hospitals and Chief Medical Adviser, Foreign and Commonwealth Office, London.

The traveller to Southeast Asia is inevitably exposed to health risks not encountered in North America, Western Europe or Australasia. All of the countries have a tropical climate; nevertheless the acquisition of true tropical disease by the visitor is probably conditioned as much by the rural nature and standard of hygiene of the countries concerned than by the climate. There is an obvious difference in health risks between the business traveller who tends to stay in international class hotels in large cities and the backpacker trekking through rural areas. There are no hard and fast rules to follow; you will often have to make your own judgements on the healthiness or otherwise of your surroundings.

The quality of medical care is highly variable. In recently devastated countries such as Cambodia it is at a very low level indeed and away from the main cities in Vietnam and Laos it can be equally poor. In Bangkok, medical care is adequate (and rapidly improving) for most exigencies, although Singapore and Hong Kong offer the best facilities for serious illness. In Indochina doctors may speak French, but the likelihood of finding this and a good standard of care diminishes very rapidly as you move away from the big

cities. In some of the countries – and especially in rural areas – there are systems and traditions of medicine wholly different from the Western model and you may be confronted with less orthodox forms of treatment such as herbal medicine and acupuncture. At least you can be sure that local practitioners have a lot of experience with the particular diseases of their region. If you are in a city it may be worthwhile calling on your embassy to provide a list of recommended doctors.

If you are a long way away from medical help, a certain amount of self administered medication may be necessary and you will find many of the drugs available have familiar names. However, always check the date stamping (sell-by date) and buy from reputable pharmacists because the shelf life of some items, especially vaccines and antibiotics, is markedly reduced in hot conditions. Unfortunately, many locally produced drugs are not subjected to quality control procedures and so can be unreliable. There have, in addition, been cases of substitution of inert materials for active drugs. With the following precautions and advice you should keep as healthy as usual. Make local enquiries about health risks if you are apprehensive and take the general advice of European, Australian or North American families who have lived or are living in the area.

Before travelling

Take out medical insurance. You should also have a dental check-up, obtain a spare glasses prescription and, if you suffer from a long-standing condition, such as diabetes, high blood pressure, heart/lung disease or a nervous disorder, arrange for a check-up with your doctor who can at the same time provide you with a letter explaining details of your medical disorder. Check the current practice for malaria prophylaxis (prevention) for the countries you intend to visit.

Inoculations

Smallpox vaccination is no longer required. Neither is cholera vaccination, despite the fact that the disease occurs – but not at present in epidemic form – in some of these countries. Yellow fever vaccination is not required either, although you may be asked for a certificate if you have been in a country affected by yellow fever immediately before travelling to Southeast Asia. The following vaccinations are recommended:

Typhoid (monovalent) One dose followed by a booster 1 month later. Immunity from this course lasts 2-3 years. An oral preparation is also available.

Poliomyelitis This is a live vaccine generally given orally but a full course consists of three doses with a booster in tropical regions every 3-5 years.

Tetanus One dose should be given, with a booster at 6 weeks and another at 6 months. 10 yearly boosters thereafter are recommended.

Meningitis and Japanese B encephalitis (JVE) There is an extremely small risk of these rather serious diseases; both are seasonal and vary according to region. Meningitis can occur in epidemic form; JVE is a viral disease transmitted from pigs to man by mosquitos. For details of the vaccinations, consult a travel clinic.

Children should, in addition to the above, be properly protected against diphtheria, whooping cough, mumps and measles. Teenage girls, if they have not had the disease, should be given a rubella (German measles) vaccination. Consult your doctor for advice on BCG inoculation against tuberculosis: the disease is still common in the region.

Infectious hepatitis (jaundice)

This is common throughout Southeast Asia. It seems to be frequently caught by travellers. The main symptoms are stomach pains, lack of appetite, nausea, lassitude and yellowness of the eyes and skin. Medically speaking there are two types: the less serious but more common is *hepatitis A* for which the best protection is careful preparation of food, the avoidance of contaminated drinking water and scrupulous attention to toilet hygiene. Human normal immunoglobulin (gammaglobulin) confers considerable protection against the disease and is particularly useful in epidemics. It should be obtained from a reputable source and is certainly recommended for travellers who intend to travel and live rough. The injection should be given as close as possible to your departure and as the dose depends on the likely time you are to spend in potentially infected areas, the manufacturers' instructions should be followed. A vaccination against hepatitis A has recently become generally available and is safe and effective. Three shots are given over 6 months and confer excellent protection against the disease for up to 10 years. Eventually this vaccine is likely to supersede the use of gammaglobulin.

The other, more serious, version is *hepatitis B* which is acquired as a sexually transmitted disease, from a blood transfusion or an injection with an unclean needle, or possibly by insect bites. The symptoms are the same as hepatitis A but the incubation period is much longer.

You may have had jaundice before or you may have had hepatitis of either type before without becoming jaundiced, in which case it is possible that you could be immune to either hepatitis A or B (or C or a number of other letters). This immunity can be tested for before you travel. If you are not immune to hepatitis B already, a vaccine is available (3 shots over 6 months) and if you are not immune to hepatitis A already, then you should consider having gammaglobulin or a vaccination.

AIDS

This is increasingly prevalent in Southeast Asia. Thus, it is not wholly confined to the well known high risk sections of the population ie homosexual men, intravenous drug abusers, prostitutes and the children of infected mothers. Heterosexual transmission is probably now the dominant mode of infection and so the main risk to travellers is from casual sex. The same precautions should be taken as when encountering any sexually transmitted disease. In some Southeast Asian countries, Thailand is an example, almost the entire population of female prostitutes is HIV positive and in other parts intravenous drug abuse is common. The disease has not yet had the impact

---

MODELLING AIDS IN SOUTHEAST ASIA

There has been a tendency to assume that there is a single AIDS 'pandemic'. However in reality it seems that there are possibly three different patterns to the spread of AIDS – one is characteristic of Europe and North America, the second of Sub-Saharan Africa, and a third of Asia. This third pattern, described by Tim Brown and Peter Xenos of the East-West Population Institute in Hawaii, is different in a number of important respects. Furthermore, they argue that these differences are likely to make the disease both more serious and more intractable. The pattern is based on the experience of Thailand, and it is assumed that the Thai experience will soon be seen reflected in other countries in Asia.

It seems that the possibility of transmission per exposure, whether that be through sexual relations or needle sharing, is higher in Asia than in Europe and North America because of the high incidence of sexually transmitted diseases, especially among sex workers. Furthermore, a significant proportion of the male population of the countries of the region visit prostitutes for sex, meaning that the population 'at risk' is also very high. Therefore, in Thailand – and by implication also soon in many other countries of Asia – AIDS quickly made the cross-over from the homosexual and drug-using populations, to the heterosexual population. Thailand's first AIDS case was reported in 1984. By the end of 1988, 30% of addicts visiting methodone treatment centres were HIV positive. 5 years later, by the end of 1993, levels of infection among sex workers had similarly reached 30%. Now, nearly 2% of women visiting pre-natal clinics are testing HIV positive. Thus, in the space of less than 10 years – far faster than in Europe and North America, and even faster than in Africa – AIDS has spread from homosexuals and drug addicts to the wives and babies of heterosexual men.

In Aug 1994, at a major international conference on AIDS in Asia, James Allen of the American Medical Association likened AIDS to the Black Death in Europe. The costs to Asia of the disease are likely to be truly staggering: McGraw-Hill have put a figure of US$38-52bn on the social and economic costs of AIDS in the region.

Southeast Asia: potential for the spread of AIDS/HIV
Rapidly increasing: Burma; Cambodia; Thailand
Potential for rapid increase: Indonesia; Laos; Malaysia; Vietnam
Increasing: Singapore
Not classified: Brunei

on Vietnam, Laos and Cambodia as it has on Thailand (but see box). The AIDS virus (HIV) can be passed via unsterile needles which have been previously used to inject an HIV positive patient, but the risk of this is very small indeed. It would, however, be sensible to check that needles have been properly sterilized or disposable needles used. The chance of picking up hepatitis B in this way is much more of a danger. Be wary of carrying disposable needles. Customs officials may find them suspicious. The risk of receiving a blood transfusion with blood infected with the HIV virus is greater than from dirty needles because of the amount of fluid exchanged. Supplies of blood for transfusion are supposed to be screened for HIV in all reputable hospitals so the risk should be small. Catching the virus which causes AIDS does not necessarily produce an illness in itself; the only way to be sure if you feel you have been put at risk is to have a blood test for HIV antibodies on your return to a place where there are reliable laboratory facilities. However, the test does not become positive for many weeks.

Common problems

Heat and cold

Full acclimatization to tropical temperatures takes about 2 weeks and during this period it is normal to feel relatively apathetic, esp-ecially if the humidity is high. Drink plenty of water (up to 15 litres a day are required when working physically hard in the tropics). Use salt on your food and avoid extreme exertion. Tepid showers are more cooling than hot or cold ones. Large hats do not cool you down but do prevent sunburn. Remember that, especially in highland areas, there can be a large and sudden drop in temperature between sun and shade and between night and day so dress accordingly. Loose-fitting cotton clothes are best for hot weather.

Warm jackets and woollens are often necessary after dark at high altitude.

Intestinal upsets

Practically nobody escapes intestinal infections, so be prepared for them. Most of the time they are due to the insanitary preparation of food. Do not eat uncooked fish, vegetables or meat (especially pork), fruit without the skin (always peel fruit yourself), or food that is exposed to flies (particularly salads). Tap water may be unsafe, especially in the monsoon seasons and the same goes for stream water or well water. Filtered or bottled water is usually available and safe but you cannot always rely on it. If your hotel has a **central** hot water supply, this is safe to drink after cooling. Ice should be made from boiled water but rarely is, so stand your glass on the ice cubes instead of putting them in the drink. Dirty water should first be strained through a filter bag (available from camping shops) and then boiled or treated. Bringing the water to a rolling boil at sea level is sufficient. In the highlands, you have to boil the water a bit longer to ensure that all the microbes are killed (because water boils at a lower temperature at altitude). Various sterilizing methods can be used and there are proprietary preparations containing chlorine or iodine compounds. Pasteurised or heat-treated milk is now fairly widely available as is ice cream and yoghurt produced by the same methods. Unpasteurised milk products, including cheese, are sources of tuberculosis, brucellosis, listeria and food poisoning germs. You can render fresh milk safe by heating it to 62°C for 30 mins followed by rapid cooling or by boiling. Matured or processed cheeses are safer than fresh varieties.

Fish and shellfish are popular foods in mainland Southeast Asia but can be the source of health problems. Shellfish which are eaten raw will transmit food poisoning or hepatitis if they have been living in contaminated water. Certain fish accumulate toxins in their bodies at certain times of the year, which give rise to illness when they are eaten. The phenomenon known as 'red tide' can also affect fish and shellfish which eat large quantities of tiny sea creatures and thereby become poisonous. The only way to guard against this is to keep as well informed as possible about fish and shellfish quality in the area you are visiting. Most countries impose a ban on fishing in periods when red tide is prevalent, although this is often flouted.

Diarrhoea is usually the result of food poisoning, but can occasionally result from contaminated water. There are various causes – viruses, bacteria, protozoa (like amoeba), salmonella and cholera organisms. It may take one of several forms coming on suddenly or rather slowly. It may be accompanied by vomiting or severe abdominal pain, and the passage of blood or mucus (when it is called dysentery).

All kinds of diarrhoea, whether or not accompanied by vomiting, respond favourably to the replacement of water and salts taken as frequent small sips of some kind of rehydration solution. There are proprietary preparations consisting of sachets of oral rehydration electrolyte powder which are dissolved in water, or you can make up your own by adding half a teaspoonful of salt (3.5 grams) and 4 tablespoons of sugar (40 grams) to a litre of boiled water. If it is possible to time the onset of diarrhoea to the minute, then it is probably viral or bacterial and/or the onset of dysentery. The treatment in addition to rehydration is Ciprofloxacin (500 mgs every 12 hours). The drug is now widely available as are various similar ones.

If the diarrhoea has come on slowly or intermittently, then it is more likely to be protozoal, i.e. caused by amoeba (amoebic dysentery) or giardia, and antibiotics

will have no effect. These cases are best treated by a doctor as should any diarrhoea continuing for more than 3 days. If there are severe stomach cramps, the following drugs may help: Loperamide (*Imodium,Arret*) and Diphenoxylate with Atropine (*Lomotil*). The drug usually used for giardia or amoeba is Metronidazole (*Flagyl*) or Tinidazole (*Fasigyu*).

The lynchpins of treatment for diarrhoea are rest, fluid and salt replacement, antibiotics such as Ciprofloxacin for the bacterial types, and special diagnostic tests and medical treatment for amoeba and giardia infections. Salmonella infections and cholera can be devastating diseases and it would be wise to get to a hospital as soon as possible if these were suspected. Fasting, peculiar diets and the consumption of large quantities of yoghurt have not been found useful in calming travellers' diarrhoea or in rehabilitating inflamed bowels. Oral rehydration has, especially in children, been a lifesaving technique and as there is some evidence that alcohol and milk might prolong diarrhoea they should probably be avoided during, and immediately after, an attack. There are ways of preventing travellers' diarrhoea for short periods of time when visiting these countries by taking antibiotics but these are ineffective against viruses and, to some extent, against protozoa. This technique should not be used other than in exceptional circumstances. Some preventatives such as Enterovioform can have serious side effects if taken for long periods.

Insects

These can be a great nuisance. Some, of course, are carriers of serious diseases such as malaria, dengue fever or filariasis and various worm infections. The best way of keeping mosquitos away at night is to sleep off the ground with a mosquito net and to burn mosquito coils containing Pyrethrum. Aerosol sprays or a 'flit gun' may be effective as are insecticidal tablets which are heated on a mat which is plugged into the wall socket (if taking your own, check the voltage of the area you are visiting so that you can take an appliance that will work; similarly, check that your electrical adaptor is suitable for the repellent plug; note that they are widely available in the region).

You can, in addition, use personal insect repellent of which the best contain a high concentration of diethyltoluamide (DET). Liquid is best for arms and face (take care around eyes and make sure you do not dissolve the plastic of your spectacles). Aerosol spray on clothes and ankles deter mites and ticks. Liquid DET suspended in water can be used to impregnate cotton clothes and mosquito nets. The latter are now available in wide mesh form which are lighter to carry and less claustrophobic to sleep under.

If you are bitten, itching may be relieved by cool baths and anti-histamine tables (take care with alcohol or when driving), corticosteroid creams (great care – never use if any hint of septic poisoning) or by judicious scratching. Calamine lotion and cream have limited effectiveness and anti-histamine creams have a tendency to cause skin allergies and are therefore not generally recommended. Bites which become infected (a common problem in the tropics) should be treated with a local antiseptic or antibiotic cream such as Cetrimide, as should infected scratches. Skin infestations with body lice, crabs and scabies are unfortunately easy to pick up. Use gamma benzene hexachloride for lice and benzyl benzoate for scabies. Crotamiton cream alleviates itching and also kills a number of skin parasites. Malathion lotion is good for lice but avoid the highly toxic full strength Malathion which is used as an agricultural insecticide.

Malaria

Malaria is prevalent in Southeast Asia and remains a serious disease and you are advised to protect yourself against

mosquito bites as above and to take prophylactic (preventative) drugs. Start taking the tablets a few days before exposure and continue to take them 6 weeks after leaving the malarial zone. Remember to give the drugs to babies and children, pregnant women also.

The subject of malaria prevention is becoming more complex as the malaria parasite becomes immune to some of the older drugs. Nowhere is this more apparent than in Southeast Asia – especially parts of Laos and Cambodia. In particular, there has been an increase in the proportion of cases of falciparum malaria which are resistant to the normally used drugs. It would not be an exaggeration to say that we are near to the situation where some cases of malaria will be untreatable with presently available drugs.

Before you travel you must check with a reputable agency the likelihood and type of malaria in the countries which you intend to visit. Take their advice on prophylaxis but be prepared to receive conflicting advice. Because of the rapidly changing situation in the Southeast Asian region, the names and dosage of the drugs have not been included. But Chloroquine and Proguanil may still be recommended for the areas where malaria is still fully sensitive; while Doxycycline, Mefloquine and Quinghaosu are presently being used in resistant areas. Quinine, Halofantrine and tetracycline drugs remain the mainstay of treatment.

It is still possible to catch malaria even when taking prophylactic drugs, although this is unlikely. If you do develop symptoms (high fever, shivering, severe headache, and sometimes diarrhoea) seek medical advice immediately. The risk of the disease is obviously greater the further you move from the cities into rural areas, with primitive facilities and standing water.

Sunburn and heat stroke

The burning power of the tropical sun

is phenomenal, especially in highland areas. Always wear a wide-brimmed hat, and use some form of sun cream or lotion on untanned skin. Normal temperate zone suntan lotions (protection factors up to 7) are not much good. You need to use the types designed specifically for the tropics or for mountaineers or skiers, with a protection factor between 7 and 15 or higher. Glare from the sun can cause conjunctivitis so wear sunglasses, particularly on beaches.

There are several varieties of heat stroke. The most common cause is severe dehydration. Avoid this by drinking lots of non-alcoholic fluid, and adding salt to your food.

Snake and other bites and stings

If you are unlucky enough to be bitten by a venomous snake, spider, scorpion, centipede or sea creature, try (within limits) to catch or kill the animal for identification. Reactions to be expected are shock, swelling, pain and bruising around the bite, soreness of the regional lymph glands, nausea, vomiting and fever. If in addition any of the following symptoms should follow closely, get the victim to a doctor without delay: numbness, tingling of the face, muscular spasms, convulsions, shortness of breath or haemorrhage. Commercial snake-bite or scorpion-sting kits may be available but these are only useful against the specific type of snake or scorpion for which they are designed. The serum has to be given intravenously so is not much good unless you have had some practice in making injections into veins. If the bite is on a limb, immobilize it and apply a tight bandage between the bite and the body, releasing it for 90 seconds every 15 minutes. Reassurance of the victim is very important because death from snake bite is very rare. Do not slash the bite area and try to suck out the poison because this sort of heroism does more harm than good. Hospitals usually hold stocks of snake-bite serum. The best precaution is not walk in long grass with bare feet, sandals, or in shorts.

When swimming in an area where there are poisonous fish such as stone or scorpion fish (also called by a variety of local names) or sea urchins on rocky coasts, tread carefully or wear plimsolls/trainers. The sting of such fish is intensely painful. This can be relieved by immersing the injured part of the body in water as hot as you can bear for as long as it remains painful. This is not always very practical and you must take care not to scald yourself, but it does work. Avoid spiders and scorpions by keeping your bed away from the wall, look under lavatory seats and inside your shoes in the morning. In the rare event of being bitten, consult a doctor.

Other afflictions

Remember that **rabies** is endemic in many Southeast Asian countries. If you are bitten by a domestic or wild animal, do not leave things to chance. Scrub the wound with soap and water and/or disinfectant, try to have the animal captured (within limits) or at least determine its ownership where possible and seek medical assistance at once. The course of treatment depends on whether you have already been satisfactorily vaccinated against rabies. If you have (and this is worthwhile if you are spending lengths of time in developing countries) then some further doses of vaccine are all that is required. Human diploid cell vaccine is the best, but expensive: other, older kinds of vaccine such as that derived from duck embryos may be the only types available. These are effective, much cheaper and interchangeable generally with the human derived types. If not already vaccinated then anti-rabies serum (immúnoglobulin) may be required in addition. It is wise to finish the course of treatment whether the animal survives or not.

CHILDREN AND BABIES

Younger travellers seem to be more prone to illness abroad, but that should not put you off taking them. More preparation is necessary than for an adult and perhaps a little more care should be taken when travelling to remote areas where health services are primitive. This is because children can become more rapidly ill than adults (they often recover more quickly however). For more practical advice on travelling with children and babies **see page 14**.

Diarrhoea and vomiting are the most common problems so take the usual precautions, but more intensively. Make sure all basic childhood **vaccinations** are up to date as well as the more exotic ones. Children should be properly protected against diphtheria, whooping cough, mumps and measles. If they have not had the disease, teenage girls should be given rubella (german measles) vaccination. Consult your doctor for advice on BCG inoculation against tuberculosis: the disease is still common in the region. Protection against mosquitos and drug prophylaxis against malaria is essential. Many children take to "foreign" food quite happily. Milk in Southeast Asia may be unavailable outside big cities. Powdered milk may be the answer; breast feeding for babies even better.

Upper respiratory infections such as colds, catarrh and middle ear infections are common – antibiotics could be carried against the possibility. **Outer ear infections** after swimming are also common – antibiotic ear drops will help.

The treatment of **diarrhoea** is the same as for adults except that it should start earlier and be continued with more persistence. Children get dehydrated very quickly in the tropics and can become drowsy and uncooperative unless cajoled to drink water or juice plus salts. Oral rehydration has been a lifesaving technique in children.

Protect children against the sun with a hat and high factor tanning lotion. Severe sunburn at this age may well lead to serious skin cancer in the future.

Dengue fever is present in most of the countries of Southeast Asia. It is a viral disease transmitted by mosquito and causes severe headaches and body pains. Complicated types of dengue known as haemorrhagic fevers occur throughout Asia but usually in persons who have caught the disease a second time. Thus, although it is a very serious type it is rarely caught by visitors. There is no treatment, you must just avoid mosquito bites.

Intestinal worms are common and the more serious ones, such as hook worm can be contracted by walking barefoot on infested earth or beaches.

Influenza and **respiratory diseases** are common, perhaps made worse by polluted cities and rapid temperature and climatic changes – accentuated by air-conditioning.

Prickly heat is a very common itchy rash, best avoided by frequent washing and by wearing loose clothing and is helped by the use of talcum powder, allowing the skin to dry thoroughly after washing.

Athlete's foot and other **fungal infections** are best treated by sunshine and a proprietary preparation such as Tolnaftate.

Returning home

On returning home, remember to take anti-malarial tablets for 6 weeks. If you have had attacks of diarrhoea, it is worth having a stool specimen tested in case you have picked up amoebic dysentery. If you have been living rough, a blood test may also be worthwhile to detect worms and other parasites.

Further health information

Information regarding country-by-country malaria risk can be obtained from the World Health Organization (WHO) or in Britain from the Ross Institute, London School of Hygiene and Tropical Medicine, Keppel Street, London WC1E 7HT which also publishes a highly recommended book: *The preservation of personal health in warm climates*. The Centres for Disease Control (CDC) in Atlanta, Georgia, USA will provide equivalent information. The organization MASTA (Medical Advisory Service for Travellers Abroad) also based at the London School of Hygiene and Tropical Medicine (T 0171 631-4408) will provide up-to-date country-by-country information on health risks. Further information on medical problems overseas can be obtained from the new edition of *Travellers health, how to stay healthy abroad*, edited by Richard Dawood (Oxford University Press, 1992). This revised and updated edition is highly recommended, especially to the intrepid traveller. A more general publication, with hints on health and much more besides, is John Hatt's new edition of *The tropical traveller* (Penguin, 1993).

SOUTHEAST ASIAN REALM

MAINLAND & ISLAND SOUTHEAST ASIA

A name to conjure with

Since the end of the second World War, the term 'Southeast Asia' has come to be widely used to describe that portion of the world that lies between India, China and Australasia. Early Chinese and Japanese traders and mariners referred to the area as *Nanyang* or *Nangyo* (both meaning the 'Southern Seas'), while Indian texts talked of a *Suvarnabhumi* ('Land of Gold') or *Suvarnadvipa* ('Island of Gold'), and Persian and Arab accounts of *Zir-e Bad* (the lands 'Below the Wind(s)'). However all the terms employed are loose and indistinct. In the first two cases, the terms merely describe Southeast Asia with respect to its geographical position vis à vis China and Japan. *Suvarnabhumi* and *Suvarnadvipa* – the El Dorados of the East – meanwhile probably only related to the Malay Peninsula, Sumatra, and possibly Java and parts of Burma. *Zir-e Bad* just made reference to the lands sailors arrived at by sailing E on the monsoon winds.

During the colonial period, Southeast Asia graduated to the status of a region – albeit still loose and ill-defined – virtually by default. To the Western colonial powers, it was that area which lay between the two cultural superpowers of China and India. The terms used to describe it indicate that it was viewed very much as a residual region: Further India, Chin-India, Little China, Indochina, the Indian Archipelago, the Far Eastern Tropics, and the Tropical Far East. In this way, Southeast Asia became defined either as an appendage of India, or as a tropical extension of China and Japan. The terms also indicate the extent to which the region has been overshadowed by its more illustrious neighbours, India and China.

The first use in English of the term 'Southeast Asia' may have been when the Reverend Howard Malcolm, an American from Boston, published a book with the title *Travels in South-Eastern Asia* in 1839. He describes the area covered by his book as including 'all the region

HEAT AND LUST: COLONIAL IMPRESSIONS

Many colonial visitors were tempted to see a link between the hot climate and the Southeast Asian character. In 1811, John Joseph Stockdale, a British publisher, ascribed what he saw as the "wantonness" of Javanese women to the warm temperatures. The British administrator William Marsden wrote in the same year that the Sumatran tradition of polygamy was based on the "influence of a warm atmosphere upon the passions of men" and the "cravings of other disordered appetites". Nor were the judgemental links between climate and activity restricted purely to people: Robert Mac Micking a British traveller who visited the Philippines in the mid 19th century wrote that because of the heat the Filipino dog did not have the same "strength or swiftness, nor is he of equal courage, sincerity and gentleness of character" to those faithful hounds back home.

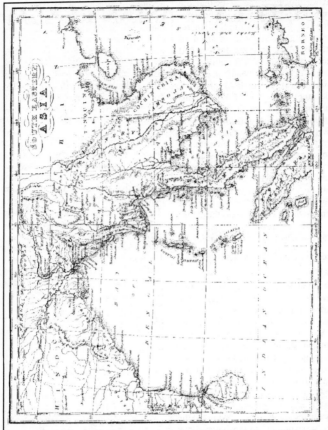

The map of 'South Eastern Asia' in Howard Malcolm's *Travels in South Eastern Asia* published in 1839. Note the coverage of the region.

between China and the Bay of Bengal, southward of the Thibet Mountains'. Although Malcolm, as well as a handful of anthropologists and other scholars, began to write about 'Southeast Asia' towards the middle of the 19th century, the colonial period prevented the further evolution of a Southeast Asian 'identity'. As Portugal, Britain, France, Holland and Spain (and later the United States) divided the region between themselves, leaving only Thailand with its independence, so the countries of the region became orientated toward one or other of the colonial powers. Economically, politically and to an extent, culturally, the countries' concerns and interests were focused outwards, beyond the region, postponing, for nearly a century, the development of a Southeast Asian regional identity.

It was not until the 1940s that the term Southeast Asia began to be more widely used again in English. In response to the Japanese invasion of Southeast Asia, wartime British and American leaders Churchill and Roosevelt created the South-East Asia Command (SEAC) in 1943, placing it under the leadership of Lord Louis Mountbatten. The creation of SEAC brought the term Southeast Asia into widespread and general usage. This was greatly accentuated by the onset of the Second Indochinese War in Vietnam in 1965, and growing US involvement in that war. The media coverage of the 'War in Southeast Asia', and particularly television coverage, brought the region to the attention of the public across the globe.

LAND AND LIFE

A region that has lost its heart to the sea

It is not so much the land, but the sea, which dominates Southeast Asia. At the heart of the region are the shallow waters of the South China Sea. During the last Ice Age, 15,000 years ago (when sea levels were considerably lower than they are today), much of this would have been exposed, linking the islands of Sumatra, Java and Borneo, and forming a Southeast Asian continent. In a quite literal sense therefore, Southeast Asia lost its heart to the sea. But the drowning of the once sprawling land mass has had one important side-effect: it has made the region uniquely accessible by sea. The region has a longer coastline than any other area of comparable size. It is no accident therefore that Southeast Asia's early history is one based upon maritime empires and trade.

The geological evolution of Southeast Asia

Originally, the world consisted of just two supercontinents: Gondwanaland to the S, and Laurasia to the N. Through a process of 'continental drift' whereby the earth's continental plates slide over or under each other, sections of Gondwanaland and Laurasia have broken away and ploughed across the oceans to take up their present positions. In the case of Southeast Asia this 'rifting' has been particularly complex. Over a period of 350 million years, successive fragments of Gondwanaland have detached themselves and drifted northwards eventually to collide with the other supercontinent, Laurasia. This process explains the peculiar spider-like shape of the Indonesian island of Sulawesi which consists of two halves that did not collide until the Miocene (15 million years ago).

Each fragment of Southeast Asia became a 'Noah's Ark' of plants and animals isolated from outside disturbance. The effect of this isolation can be seen reflected in the remarkable change in the fauna of the region from the Indo-Malayan zoological realm in the N, to the Austro-Malayan in the S. The point of change from one to the other is known as Wallace's Line. This runs approximately N to S between the Indonesian islands of Bali and Lombok and then through the Makassar Strait, and is named after one of Victorian England's greatest naturalists, Alfred Russel Wallace. It was Wallace, working in the former Dutch East Indies, who encouraged Charles Darwin to publish his seminal *Origin of species by means of natural selection*. For, independently of Darwin, Wallace too arrived at a theory of natural selection and coincidentally sent the paper outlining his ideas to Darwin in England. Darwin was appalled that his work might be eclipsed, but nevertheless acted entirely properly. Papers by both men were presented to a meeting of the Linnean Society in London in 1858, where they provoked surprisingly little reaction. 1 year later, in 1859, The *Origin of species* was published. Despite Southeast Asia's complex geological origins, it is clearly demarcated from the regions that surround it. To the N are the highlands of Burma, Thailand, Laos and Vietnam which form a natural barrier with China and India. Running from western Burma southwards through Sumatra and Java and finally northwards to Sulawesi and the Philippines, the region is bounded by a series of deep-sea trenches. These mark the point at which the earth's plates plunge one beneath the other and are zones of intense volcanic activity. Indonesia alone has about 300 volcanoes, of which 200 have been active in historical times, and 127 are active today. The volcanic activity of the area was most dramatically displayed when Krakatau (Krakatoa), located in the Sunda Straits between Java and Sumatra, erupted in 1883. Today, Anak Krakatoa (Child of Krakatoa) and the other remaining islands, are a reserve where scientists have been able to record the recolonization by plants and animals of an island that had effectively died.

FIELDS IN THE FOREST – SHIFTING CULTIVATION

Shifting cultivation, also known as slash-and-burn agriculture or swiddening, as well as by a variety of local terms, is one of the characteristic farming systems of Southeast Asia. It is a low-intensity form of agriculture, in which land is cleared from the forest through burning, cultivated for a few years, and then left to regenerate over 10-30 years. It takes many forms, but an important distinction can be made between shifting field systems where fields are rotated but the settlement remains permanently sited, and migratory systems where the shifting cultivators shift both field (swidden) and settlement. The land is usually only rudimentarily cleared, tree stumps being left in the ground, and seeds sown in holes made by punching the soil with a dibble stick.

For many years, shifting cultivators were regarded as 'primitives' who followed an essentially primitive form of agriculture and their methods were contrasted unfavourably with 'advanced' settled rice farmers. There are still many government officials in Southeast Asia who continue to adhere to this mistaken belief, arguing that shifting cultivators are the principal cause of forest loss and soil erosion. They are, therefore, painted as the villains in the region's environmental crisis, neatly sidestepping the considerably more detrimental impact that commercial logging has had on Southeast Asia's forest resources.

Shifting cultivators have an intimate knowledge of the land, plants and animals on which they depend. One study of a Dayak tribe, the Kantu' of Kalimantan (Borneo), discovered that households were cultivating an average of 17 rice varieties and 21 other food crops each year in a highly complex system. Even more remarkably, Harold Conklin's classic 1957 study of the Hanunóo of the Philippines – a study which is a benchmark for such work even today – found that the Hanunóo identified 40 types and subtypes of rocks and minerals when classifying different soils. The shifting agricultural systems are usually also highly productive in labour terms, allowing far more leisure time than farmers using permanent field systems.

But shifting cultivation contains the seeds of its own extinction. Extensive, and geared to low population densities and abundant land, it is coming under pressure in a region where land is becoming an increasingly scarce resource, where patterns of life are dictated by an urban-based élite, and where populations are pressing on the means of subsistence.

Climate

At sea level, **temperatures** are fairly uniform, both across the region and through the year. With the exception of the NE corner of Vietnam, annual average sea-level temperatures are close to 26°C. Travelling N and S from the equator, seasonal variations do become more pronounced. Therefore, while Singapore, virtually on the equator, has a monthly average temperature which varies by a mere 1.5°C, Sittwe (Akyab) in Burma which is 2,600 km to the N – has a monthly average which ranges across 7°C. The sea can also have a significant moderating effect. For example, Mandalay, on the same latitude as Sittwe but over 400 km inland, has a monthly average which spans 10°C. But these figures are monthly averages: before the onset of the SW monsoon in Apr or May, temperatures during the day in the Dry Zone of Burma and in Northeastern Thailand can reach a debilitating 40°C or more. At times like this nothing moves; even the farmers remain in the shade.

Altitude has the greatest effect on tem-

SOUTHEAST ASIA:
MONTHLY RAINFALL AND TEMPERATURE

		Jan	Feb	Mar	Apr	May	Jun	Jul	Aug	Sep	Oct	Nov	Dec
Singapore	°C	25.5	26	26.5	27	27	27	27	27	26.5	26.5	26	26
1°N, 104°E, 10m	mm	216	155	165	175	183	170	172	216	180	208	254	264
Cameron Hgh	°C	18.5	18.5	19.5	19.5	19.5	19	19	19	19	18.5	18.5	18
5°N, 101°E, 4500m	mm	152	132	162	312	267	127	122	198	213	328	307	246
Sittwe	°C	21	22.5	26	28.5	29	28	27	27	27.5	27.5	25.5	22
20°N, 93°E, 20m	mm	3	5	13	50	348	1255	1364	1080	625	294	127	15
Rangoon	°C	25	26	29	30.5	29	27	26.5	26.5	27	27.5	26.5	25
17°N, 93°E, 18m	mm	5	5	7	35	307	467	546	500	381	178	71	7
Saigon	°C	26	27	29	29.5	29	28	27	28	27	27	26.5	26
11°N, 107°E, SL	mm	17	2	15	48	221	333	307	282	343	272	114	63
Kupang	°C	25.5	26	26.5	26.5	26.5	25	24.5	25.5	26	26.5	26	26.5
10°S, 124° E, 48m	mm	572	361	107	41	2	43	2	2	2	180	104	266
Hanoi	°C	16.5	16.5	19.5	22.5	26.5	28.5	28.5	28.5	27	25.5	21.5	19
21°N, 106°E, SL	mm	30	40	46	71	193	244	289	317	305	111	61	30
Lashio	°C	15.5	17	21.5	24	25	25	24.5	24.5	24.5	22.5	19	16
23°N, 98°E, 2802m	mm	8	8	15	56	175	249	305	323	198	144	68	22
Luang Prab'ng	°C	20.5	22.5	25.5	28	29	28.5	28	28	28	26	23	21
20°N, 102°E, 942m	mm	15	17	30	109	162	155	231	300	165	78	30	13

denotes hot season   denotes wet season

Temperatures are in degrees Celsius, rainfall in mm. Note that the 'rainy' and 'hot' seasons are relative to the prevailing climate in each area. Near the equator the distinction between 'wet' and 'dry' seasons is less pronounced.

perature, and in the highlands of the region it can become distinctly cool. It is not surprising that the colonial powers built hill retreats in these areas: in the Cameron Highlands and at Fraser's Hill on the Malay Peninsula, at Brastagi in Sumatra (Indonesia), at Maymyo in Burma, and Dalat in southern Vietnam. In the Cameron Highlands, with its rose gardens, afternoon teas and half-timbered houses and log fires, it is easy to believe you are in rural England.

Patterns of **rainfall** in the region are more complex. They vary considerably both across the region and through the year, and seasonality – both for the farmer and the visitor – is linked to rainfall, not to temperature. The pattern of rainfall is intimately related to the monsoons, a term which is taken from the Arabic word *mawsim*, meaning 'season'.

Much of island Southeast Asia experiences what is termed an 'equatorial monsoon' climate. Annual rainfall usually exceeds 2,000 mm and can be as high as 5,000 mm. Close to the equator rainfall *tends* to be distributed evenly through the year, and there is no marked dry season. However, travelling N and S from the equator, the dry season becomes more pronounced, and rainfall is concentrated in one or two seasonal peaks. This pattern of rainfall is determined by two monsoons: the NE and the SW monsoons. The NE monsoon, prevails from Nov/Dec to Feb/Mar and forms the wet season. While the SW monsoon, extends from Jun to Aug/Sep and brings dry conditions to the area.

In mainland Southeast Asia, rainfall tends to be less than in the archipelago (less than 1,500 mm) and more seasonally concentrated, with the dry season in many places extending over 5 or 6 months. In comparison with island Southeast Asia, the seasons on the mainland are generally reversed. The NE monsoon from Nov to Mar brings cool, dry air to Thailand, Burma and much of Indochina. During this period rainfall

may be very low indeed. Just before the SW monsoon arrives in Jun, the heating of the land can lead to torrential thunderstorms – referred to in Burma and Thailand as 'mango rains'. The SW monsoon corresponds with the period of heaviest rainfall, and over much of the mainland 80%-97% of the year's rain falls between the months of May and Oct.

It should be emphasized that local wind systems and the shadowing effects of mountains often distort this generalized pattern of rainfall. Nonetheless, like the English, Southeast Asians talk endlessly about the weather. The seasons – and this means rain – determine the very pattern of life in the region. Rice cultivation, and its associated festivals, is dependent in most areas on the arrival of the rains, and religious ceremonies are timed to coincide with the seasons. Kampoon Boontawee in his novel *Luuk Isan* (Child of the Northeast) about village life in the Northeastern region of Thailand writes: "When Koon and Jundi and their fathers arrived at the *phuyaiban*'s [headman's] house, the men were talking about what they always talked about – the lack of rain and the lack of food in the village".

The Southeast Asian landscape

On the mainland, mountains, valleys and rivers run N-S. The great rivers of the region are found here: the Irrawaddy, Sittang, Salween, Chao Phraya, Mekong and the Red rivers. It is along these river valleys that people have settled in the greatest numbers, exploiting the rich alluvial soils and the abundance of water by cultivating wet rice. Except for narrow bands of lowland – for example, along the Vietnamese coast – much of the remainder of the mainland is mountainous. Here, tribal peoples such as the Hmong of N Thailand and Laos, and the Karen of Burma support themselves through shifting cultivation.

One of the challenges facing the region is how to protect these people and their way of life – and the forests themselves – when population pressure is growing and commercialization spreading.

In island Southeast Asia there are few favourable areas for human settlement. Much of the lowland in places such as eastern Sumatra and southern Borneo is swamp, and rivers are short, offering only limited scope for rice cultivation. The highland areas are cloaked in forest, and their traditional inhabitants such as the Dayaks of the island of Borneo and the tribes of Irian Jaya practise shifting cultivation like their brothers on the mainland. But, the islands are not entirely devoid of areas with significant agricultural potential. The fertile volcanic soils of central Java for example have supported a large population for hundreds of years. Today Java's population is nearly 110 million, and agricultural population densities in some areas exceed 2,000 people/sq km. Taking advantage of the abundance of rain and the rich soils, farmers grow up to three crops of rice each year.

Tropical forests

Across Southeast Asia from N Burma through the arc of the Indonesian islands eastwards to Irian Jaya, tropical rainforest – of which there are 13 different types – predominates. Southeast Asia supports the largest area of tropical rainforest in the world outside Latin America. The core areas, located on the islands of Borneo and New Guinea and in Peninsular Malaysia, are possibly the most diverse of all the world's terrestrial ecosystems. In a single hectare of Malayan rainforest there may be as many as 176 species of tree with a diameter of 10 cm or more, and island Southeast Asia as a whole contains 25,000 species of flowering plant – 10% of the world's flora. It is because of this bewildering diversity that environmentalists claim the forest resource must be preserved. And not just because mankind has a moral duty, but also because the forests are an invaluable genetic and pharmaceutical warehouse. Currently over 10% of all prescription drugs are derived from tropical forest products, and the great majority of species have yet to be named and recorded, let alone chemically investigated.

Water for life: wet rice cultivation

Rice probably spread into Southeast Asia from a core area which spanned the highlands from Assam (India) to N Vietnam. Some of the earliest evidence of agriculture in the world has been uncovered in and around the village of Ban Chiang in Northeastern Thailand, and also from Bac-son in N Vietnam. However archaeologists are far from agreed about the dating and significance of the evidence. Some believe that rice may have been cultivated as early as 7,000 BC; others say it dates back no further than 3,000-2,000 BC.

By the time the first Europeans arrived in the 15th century the crop was well-established as the staple for the region. Only on the dry islands of Timor and N Maluku (in Indonesia) did the environment preclude its cultivation. Today other staples such as taro (a root crop) and sago (produced from the sago palm) are frowned upon, being widely regarded as 'poor man's food'. The importance of rice can be seen reflected in the degree to which culture and crop have become intermeshed, and in the mythology and ceremony associated with its cultivation. The American anthropologist DeYoung, who worked in a village in Central Thailand in the late 1950s, writes that the farmer:

> "...reverences the crop he grows as a sentient being; he marks its stages of growth by ceremonies; and he propitiates the spirit of the soil in which it grows and the good or evil spirits that may help or harm it. He considers rice to possess a life spirit (*kwan*) and to grow much as a human being grows; when it bears grain, it has become 'pregnant'

like a mother, and the rice is the seed or child of the Rice Goddess".

Wet rice, more than any other staple crop, is dependent on an ample and constant supply of water. The links be-tween rice and water, wealth and pov-erty, and abundance and famine are clear. Throughout the region, there are numerous rituals and songs which hon-our the 'gift of water' and dwell upon

THE CYCLE OF WET RICE CULTIVATION

There are an estimated 120,000 rice varieties. Rice seed – either selected from the previous harvest or, more commonly, purchased from a dealer or agricultural extension office – is soaked overnight before being sown into a carefully prepared nursery bed. Today farmers are likely to plant one of the Modern Varieties or MVs bred for their high yields.

The nursery bed into which the seeds are broadcast (scattered) is often a farmer's best land, with the most stable water supply. After a month the seedlings are up-rooted and taken out to the paddy fields. These will also have been ploughed, puddled and harrowed, turning the heavy clay soil into a saturated slime. Traditionally buffalo and cattle would have performed the task; today rotavators, and even tractors are becoming more common. The seedlings are transplanted into the mud in clumps. Before transplanting the tops of the seedlings are twisted off (this helps to increase yield) and then they are pushed into the soil in neat rows. The work is back-breaking and it is not unusual to find labourers – both men and women – receiving a premium – either a bonus on top of the usual daily wage or a free meal at midday, to which marijuana is sometimes added to ease the pain.

After transplanting, it is essential that the water supply is carefully controlled. The key to high yields is a constant flow of water, regulated to take account of the growth of the rice plant. In 'rain-fed' systems where the farmer relies on rainfall to water the crop, he has to hope that it will be neither too much nor too little. Elaborate ceremonies are performed to appease the rice goddess and to ensure bountiful rainfall.

In areas where rice is grown in irrigated conditions, farmers need not concern themselves with the day-to-day pattern of rainfall, and in such areas 2 or even 3 crops can be grown each year. But such systems need to be carefully managed, and it is usual for one man to be in charge of irrigation. In Bali he is known as the *klian subak*, in North Thailand as the *hua naa muang fai*. He decides when water should be released, organizes labour to repair dykes and dams and to clear channels, and decides which fields should receive the water first.

Traditionally, while waiting for the rice to mature, a farmer would do little except weed the crop from time to time. He and his family might move out of the village and live in a field hut to keep a close eye on the maturing rice. Today, farmers also apply chemical fertilisers and pesticides to protect the crop and ensure maximum yield. After 90-130 days, the crop should be ready for harvesting.

Harvesting also demands intensive labour. Traditionally, farmers in a village would secure their harvesters through systems of reciprocal labour exchange; now it is more likely for a harvester to be paid in cash. After harvesting, the rice is threshed, sometimes out in the field, and then brought back to the village to be stored in a rice barn or sold. It is only at the end of the harvest, with the rice safely stored in the barn, that the festivals begin. As Thai farmers say, having rice in the barn is like having money in the bank.

the vagaries of the monsoon. Water-throwing festivals, designed to induce abundant rainfall, are widespread, and if they do not have the desired effect villagers will often resort to magic. The struggle to ensure a constant supply of

THE UNIVERSAL STIMULANT – THE BETEL NUT

Throughout the countryside in Southeast Asia, and in more remote towns, it is common to meet men and women whose teeth are stained black, and gums red, by continuous chewing of the 'betel nut'. This, though, is a misnomer. The betel 'nut' is not chewed at all: the three crucial ingredients that make up a betel 'wad' are the nut of the areca palm (*Areca catechu*), the leaf or catkin of the betel vine (*Piper betel*), and lime. When these three ingredients are combined with saliva they act as a mild stimulant. Other ingredients (people have their own recipes) are tobacco, gambier, various spices and the gum of *Acacia catechu*. The habit, though also common in South Asia and parts of China, seems to have evolved in Southeast Asia and it is mentioned in the very earliest chronicles. The lacquer betel boxes of Burma and Thailand, and the brass and silver ones of Indonesia, illustrate the importance of chewing betel in social intercourse. Galvao in his journal of 1544 noted: "They use it so continuously that they never take it from their mouths; therefore these people can be said to go around always ruminating". Among Westernized Southeast Asians the habit is frowned upon: the disfigurement and ageing that it causes, and the stained walls and floors that result from the constant spitting, are regarded as distasteful products of an earlier age. But beyond the elite it is still widely practised.

water can also be seen reflected in the sophisticated irrigation systems of Northern Thailand, Bali and Java. Less obvious, but no less ingenious and complex, farmers without the benefits of irrigation have also developed sophisticated cultivation strategies designed to maintain production through flood and drought.

People and land

An Indian king is reported to have said to a man boasting about the extent of the lands ruled by the King of Siam: "It is true, I admit, that they are greater in extent than mine, but then the King of Golconda is a king of men, while your king is only king of forests and mosquitoes". Southeast Asia has always been relatively land-rich when compared with India and China. In 1600 the population of the region was probably about 20 million, and even by 1800 this had only increased to 30 million. Except for a few areas such as the island of Java and the Red River Delta of Vietnam, the region was sparsely populated. Forests and wildlife abounded, and the inhabitants at times had great trouble maintaining their small areas of 'civilized space'. Even today local words for 'forest' also often imply 'wild' and 'uncivilized'.

The wealth of forest resources has meant that most buildings – even those of the richest nobles and merchants – have always been constructed of wood, bamboo and other forest products. The only exception to this rule was in the construction of religious edifices. In these, stone and brick were used, no doubt signifying the permanence of faith, and the impermanence of men. Today the building skills of the early civilizations of Southeast Asia can be seen reflected in the temples of Prambanan and Borobudur (Java), Angkor (Cambodia), Champa (Vietnam), Sukhothai and Ayutthaya (Thailand), and

Pagan (Burma). In most cases the temples stand stark and isolated, which accentuates their visual impact. However, when they were built they would have been surrounded by wooden houses, shops and the bustle and infrastructure of an ancient ceremonial city. These have now rotted away in the region's humid climate.

The abundance of land in Southeast Asia during historical times meant that people were very highly valued. A king's wealth was not measured in terms of the size of his kingdom, but the number of people that came under his control. Land was not 'owned' in the usual sense; ownership was transitory and related to utilization. When a farmer stopped cultivating a piece of land it would revert to the ownership of the sultan or king, but ultimately to God. The value of people becomes clear in the art of warfare in the region. In general, the objective was not to gain land, but to capture prisoners who could then be carried off to become slaves on the victorious king's land. This principle held true for the great kingdoms of Burma, Siam and Cambodia and the remotest tribes of Borneo. At times entire villages would be transported into captivity. Battles rarely led to many casualties. There was much noise, but little action, and the French envoy Simon de la Loubère in his 17th century account of Siam wrote: "Kill not is the order, which the King of Siam gives his troops, when he sends them into the field".

IN SIDDHARTHA'S FOOTSTEPS: A SHORT HISTORY OF BUDDHISM

Buddhism was founded by Siddhartha Gautama, a prince of the Sakya tribe of Nepal, who probably lived between 563 and 483 BC. He achieved enlightenment and the word *buddha* means 'fully enlightened one', or 'one who has woken up'. Siddhartha Gautama is known by a number of titles. In the W, he is usually referred to as *The Buddha*, ie the historic Buddha (but not just Buddha); more common in Southeast Asia is the title *Sakyamuni*, or Sage of the Sakyas (referring to his tribal origins).

Over the centuries, the life of the Buddha has become part legend, and the Jataka tales which recount his various lives are colourful and convoluted. But, central to any Buddhist's belief is that he was born under a *sal* tree (*Shorea robusta*), that he achieved enlightenment under a bodhi tree (*Ficus religiosa*) in the Bodh Gaya Gardens, that he preached the First Sermon at Sarnath, and that he died at Kusinagara (all in India or Nepal).

The Buddda was born at Lumbini (in present-day Nepal), as Queen Maya was on her way to her parents' home. She had had a very auspicious dream before the child's birth of being impregnated by an elephant, whereupon a sage prophesied that Siddhartha would become either a great king or a great spiritual leader. His father, being keen that the first option of the prophesy be fulfilled, brought him up in all the princely skills (at which Siddhartha excelled) and ensured that he only saw beautiful things, not the harsher elements of life.

Despite his father's efforts Siddhartha saw four things while travelling between palaces – a helpless old man, a very sick man, a corpse being carried by lamenting relatives, and an ascetic, calm and serene as he begged for food. These episodes made an enormous impact on the young prince, and he renounced his princely origins and left home to study under a series of spiritual teachers. He finally discovered the path to enlightenment at the Bodh Gaya Gardens in India. He then proclaimed his thoughts to a small group of disciples at Sarnath, near Benares, and continued

PRE-COLONIAL HISTORY

Prehistory

Histories are never simple, cut and dried affairs, and Southeast Asia's prehistory must rank among the most confused. Not only is the evidence available to archaeologists fragmentary and highly dispersed (partly because the humid conditions promote rapid decay), but it has also been subject to multiple interpretations. At the core of the debate, is the question as to whether Southeast Asia was a cultural 'receptacle' or a 'hearth' of civilization in itself. In other words, have people, technologies and cultures diffused into the region from the outside, or has Southeast Asia evolved a 'personality' independent of such influences? Ultimately the answer must be one of degree, not of kind.

Racial groups and migrations

The bulk of Southeast Asia's population are Southern Mongoloid. However there are small numbers of Negritos and Melanesians still living in the region; the Semang and Sakais of Malaysia, for example. However, these true indigenous inhabitants of Southeast Asia have been overwhelmed and marginalized by more recent arrivals. First, from about 5000 BC, there began a gradual southerly migration of Southern Mongoloids from southern China and eastern Tibet. This did not occur in

---

to preach and attract followers until he died at the age of 81 at Kusinagara.

In the First Sermon at the deer park in Sarnath, the Buddha preached the Four Truths, which are still considered the root of Buddhist belief and practical experience. These are the 'Noble Truth' that suffering exists, the 'Noble Truth' that there is a cause of suffering, the 'Noble Truth' that suffering can be ended, and the 'Noble Truth' that to end suffering it is necessary to follow the 'Noble Eightfold Path' – namely, right speech, livelihood, action, effort, mindfulness, concentration, opinion and intention.

Soon after the Buddha began preaching, a monastic order – the *Sangha* – was established. As the monkhood evolved in India, it also began to fragment as different sects developed different interpretations of the life of the Buddha. An important change was the belief that the Buddha was transcendent: he had never been born, nor had he died; he had always existed and his life on earth had been mere illusion. The emergence of these new concepts helped to turn what up until then was an ethical code of conduct, into a religion. It eventually led to the appearance of a new Buddhist movement, Mahayana Buddhism which split from the more traditional Theravada 'sect'.

Despite the division of Buddhism into two sects, the central tenets of the religion are common to both. Specifically, the principles pertaining to the Four Noble Truths, the Noble Eightfold Path, the Dependent Origination, the Law of Karma and nirvana. In addition, the principles of non-violence and tolerance are also embraced by both sects. In essence, the differences between the two are of emphasis and interpretation. Theravada Buddhism is strictly based on the original Pali Canon, while the Mahayana tradition stems from later Sanskrit texts. Mahayana Buddhism also allows a broader and more varied interpretation of the doctrine. Other important differences are that while the Thervada tradition is more 'intellectual' and self-obsessed, with an emphasis upon the attaining of wisdom and insight for oneself, Mahayana Buddhism stresses devotion and compassion towards others.

a great wave, as at one time postulated, but as a slow process of displacement and replacement. Later, during the early centuries of the Christian era, the political consolidation of the Chinese empire displaced increasing numbers of Deutero-Malays, as well as Tais, Khmers, Mons, Burmans, Viets and the various hill tribes of the mainland. These groups, the ancestors of the present populations of Thailand, Burma, Indochina, Malaysia and Indonesia, used the great river valleys of the region – the Mekong, Irrawaddy, Salween and Chao Phraya – as their routes S.

Southeast Asia has therefore represented a fragmented land bridge between Asia and Australasia into and through which successive racial groups have filtered. The original inhabitants of the region have all but disappeared. Most have been absorbed into the racial fabric of more recent arrivals; many others have been displaced into the highlands or out of the region altogether. The Melanesians for example now inhabit islands in the Pacific including New Guinea, while remnant Proto-Malays include the forest-dwelling Dayaks of Borneo and the Bataks of Sumatra.

Not only did these more recent migrants physically displace the earlier inhabitants, they also displaced them culturally. They brought with them knowledge of metallurgy, rice cultivation, the domestication of livestock, and new religious beliefs. But these cultural elements were not incorporated wholesale and unchanged. The nature of the Southeast Asian environment, the abundance of land and food, and the passage of time, have all served to allow the development of a distinctly Southeast Asian cultural heritage.

The historic period: water for communication

Southeast Asia's fragmented geography has made the region remarkably accessible. Winds tend to be moderate and the abundance of wood close to the shoreline has enabled ship-building to flourish. This has had two effects: on the one hand, it has meant that Southeast Asia has felt the effects of successive seaborne invasions, and on the other that different parts of the region have been in surprisingly close contact with one another. This is reflected in commonalities of language, particularly in the archipelago, and in the universality of cultural traits such as the chewing of betel nut. During the historic period there have been five major infusions of culture and technology into Southeast Asia – all of which have left their imprint on the region: Indianization, Chinese influences, Buddhism, Islam and Westernization.

1. The Indianization of Southeast Asia

From the beginning of the 1st century AD, the allure of gold and spices brought Indian traders to the region. Although they were not on a proselytizing mission – they came to make money – this resulted in the introduction of Hindu-Buddhist culture and the so-called 'Indianization' of Southeast Asia. 'Indianization' was the result not of the immigration of large number of Indians; rather the gradual infusion of an Indian cultural tradition introduced by small numbers of traders and priest-scholars. Given the nature of the contact, it is not surprising that the Indian influence was geographically uneven. Northern Vietnam – then under Chinese suzerainty – was never affected. Elsewhere however, kings quickly adopted and adapted elements of the Indian cultural tradition. For example, the cult of the *deva raja* – or 'god king'- in which the ruler claimed to be a reincarnation of Siva or Vishnu (or to be a Bodhisattva – a future Buddha) was used to legitimate kingship. Pagan (Burma) and Angkor (Cambodia), two of the greatest archaeological sites in the world, bear testament to the power and influence of these 'Indianized' empires.

2. Chinese influences

At the same time as this 'Indianization' was underway, Imperial China was also beginning to intensify its links with the region. This was prompted in the 5th century AD by the Jin Dynasty's loss of access to the central Asian caravan routes which brought luxury goods from the West. In response, maritime trading routes through the Southeast Asian archipelago were developed by the Chinese. Tribute-bearing missions from the states of Southeast Asia to the Chinese court became more common and the settlement of Chinese in the region increased as the area grew in commercial importance. In turn, the cultural impact of China also became more pronounced. Chinese medical theory, technology, cloth, games, music, and calligraphy were all assimilated to a greater or lesser degree. The Chinese diplomat Chou Ta-kuan who visited the city of Angkor in 1296 notes in his journal the large number of his countrymen who had arrived in the city and were gradually being absorbed into the social fabric of the kingdom:

> "The Chinese who follow the sea as a profession take advantage of their being in this country to dispense with wearing clothes. Rice is easy to obtain, women are easy to find, the houses are easy to run, personal property is easy to come by, commerce is easy to engage in. Thus there are constantly those who direct themselves towards this country".

3. Buddhism

By the early part of the second millennium the elitist cult of the god-king had become corrupt and degenerate, and was in decline on the mainland. At the same time a third infusion of culture was underway. During the early part of the 12th century, Burmese Buddhist monks travelled to Ceylon and came in contact with Theravada Buddhism (the 'Way of the Elders'). They returned to Burma with news of this populist faith and aggressively spread the word. Un-

like the deva raja cult it was an inclusive, rather than an exclusive religion, and it found a willing and receptive audience among the common people. By the 15th century Theravada Buddhism was the dominant religion across much of the mainland – in Burma, Thailand, Laos, and Cambodia.

Buddhism shares the belief, in common with Hinduism, in rebirth. A person goes through countless lives and the experience of one life is conditioned by the acts in a previous one. This is the Law of Karma (act or deed, from Pali *kamma*), the law of cause and effect. But, it is not, as commonly thought in the West, equivalent to fate.

For most people, nirvana is a distant goal, and they merely aim to accumulate merit by living good lives and performing good deeds such as giving alms to monks. In this way the layman embarks on the Path to Heaven. It is also common for a layman to become ordained, at some point in his life (usually as a young man), for a 3 month period during the Buddhist Rains Retreat.

Monks should endeavour to lead stringently ascetic lives. They must refrain from murder, theft, sexual intercourse, untruths, eating after noon, alcohol, entertainment, ornament, comfortable beds and wealth. They are allowed to own only a begging bowl, three pieces of clothing, a razor, needle, belt and water filter. They can only eat food that they have received through begging. Anyone who is male, over 20, and not a criminal can become a monk.

Theravada Buddhism (Hinayana)

The 'Way of the Elders', is believed to be closest to Buddhist as it originally developed in India. It is often referred to by the term 'Hinayana' (Lesser Vehicle), a disparaging name foisted onto Theravadans by Mahayanists. This form of Buddhism is the dominant contemporary religion in the mainland Southeast Asian countries of Thailand,

THE PRACTICE OF ISLAM: LIVING BY THE PROPHET

Islam is an Arabic word meaning 'submission to God'. As Muslims often point out, it is not just a religion but a total way of life. The main Islamic scripture is the Koran or Quran, the name being taken from the Arabic *al-qur'an* or 'the recitation'. The Koran is divided into 114 *sura*, or 'units'. Most scholars are agreed that the Koran was partially written by the Prophet Mohammad. In addition to the Koran there are the hadiths, from the Arabic word *hadith* meaning 'story', which tell of the Prophet's life and works. These represent the second most important body of scriptures.

The practice of Islam is based upon five central tenets, known as the Pillars of Islam: Shahada (profession of faith), Salat (worship), Zakat (charity), *saum* (fasting) and Haj (pilgrimage). The mosque is the centre of religious activity. The two most important mosque officials are the *imam* – or leader – and the *khatib* or preacher – who delivers the Friday sermon.

The **Shahada** is the confession, and lies at the core of any Muslim's faith. It involves reciting, sincerely, two statements: 'There is no god, but God', and 'Mohammad is the Messenger [Prophet] of God'. A Muslim will do this at every **Salat**. This is the daily prayer ritual which is performed five times a day, at sunrise, midday, mid-afternoon, sunset and at night. There is also the important Friday noon worship. The Salat is performed by a Muslim bowing and then prostrating himself in the direction of Mecca (in Indonesian *kiblat*, in Arabic *qibla*). In hotel rooms throughout Indonesia, Malaysia and Brunei, there is nearly always a little arrow, painted on the ceiling – or sometimes inside a wardrobe – indicating the direction of Mecca and labelled kiblat. The faithful are called to worship by a mosque official. Beforehand, a worshipper must wash to ensure ritual purity. The Friday midday service is performed in the mosque and includes a sermon given by the *khatib*.

A third essential element of Islam is **Zakat** – charity or alms-giving. A Muslim

---

Cambodia, Laos and Burma.

In Theravadan Buddhism, the historic Buddha, Sakyamuni, is revered above all else and most images of the Buddha are of Sakyamuni. Importantly, and unlike Mahayana Buddhism, the Buddha image is only meant to serve as a meditation aid. In theory, it does not embody supernatural powers, and it is not supposed to be worshipped. But, the popular need for objects of veneration has meant that most images *are* worshipped. Pilgrims bring flowers and incense, and prostrate themselves in front of the image. This is a Mahayanist influence which has been embraced by Theravadans.

Mahayana Buddhism

In the 1st century AD a new movement evolved in South India. Initially the differences between this and the 'original' Theravada tradition were not great. But in time the two diverged, with the 'new' tradition gaining converts at the expense of its rival. Eventually, a new term was coined – Mahayana Buddhism or the Greater Vehicle. Although the schism is usually presented as a revolutionary development, a gradual evolution is more accurate. The most important difference between Mahayana and Theravada Buddhism is that the principal aim of Mahayana Buddhism should not be to attain enlightenment only for oneself, but to reach Bodhisattvahood (someone who embodies the essence of enlightenment) and then to remain on earth to assist others in their quest for nirvana.

is supposed to give up his 'surplus' (according to the Koran); through time this took on the form of a tax levied according to the wealth of the family. In Indonesia there is no official Zakat as there is in Saudi Arabia, but good Muslims are expected to contribute a tithe to the Muslim community. In Bahasa Indonesia, *zakat* is translated as 'obligatory alms'.

The fourth pillar of Islam is **saum** or fasting. The daytime month-long fast of Ramadan is a time of contemplation, worship and piety – the Islamic equivalent of lent. Muslims are expected to read one-thirtieth of the Koran each night. Muslims who are ill or on a journey have dispensation from fasting, but otherwise they are only permitted to eat during the night until "so much of the dawn appears that a white thread can be distinguished from a black one".

The **Haj** or Pilgrimmage to the holy city of Mecca in Saudi Arabia is required of all Muslims once in their lifetime if they can afford to make the journey and are physically able to. It is restricted to a certain time of the year, beginning on the 8th day of the Muslim month of Dhu-I-Hijja. Men who have been on the Haj are given the title *Haji*, and women *hajjah*.

The Koran also advises on a number of other practices and customs, in particular the prohibitions on usury, the eating of pork, the taking of alcohol, and gambling. In Indonesia, these are not strictly interpreted. Islamic banking laws have not been introduced, drinking is fairly widespread – although not in all areas – and the national lottery might be interpreted as a form of gambling. There is quite a powerful Islamic revival in Malaysia – as well as in Brunei and Indonesia – which is attempting to change what is perceived as the rather lax approach to Islamic prohibitions. For example, there is an effort to have the national lottery abolished.

The use of the veil in its most extreme form is not common in Indonesia but is becoming *de rigeur* in Brunei and in areas of Malaysia. The Koran says nothing about the need for women to veil, although it does stress the necessity of women dressing modestly.

Mahayana Buddhism was a response to a popular appeal for a more approachable and accessible religion – in India, at the time, the Hindu gods Siva and Vishnu were attracting substantial numbers of followers and Buddhism had to respond in some way. Monks were no longer required to retire from everyday life in their ultimately selfish quest for nirvana; they were to lead active lives in the community. And, no longer was there just one distant historic Buddha to look up to; there was a pantheon of Buddhas and Bodhisattvas, all objects of veneration, worship and prayer. Now, Buddhas and Bodhisattvas such as the Buddhas Amitabha, Vajrapani, Vairocana and Avalokitsvara (all various reincarnations of the Buddha) could actively intervene

in the world for the betterment of mankind. Within Mahayana Buddhism there was a vast growth in doctrine (contained in the *sutras*) which accompanied this dramatic growth in the numbers of Buddhas and Bodhisattvas.

Mahayana Buddhism became the dominant form of Buddhism practiced in Northern Asia (China and Japan), and also in ancient Cambodia and Indonesia. Today, in Southeast Asia, it is most widely practiced in Vietnam where it has, in most instances, fused with the Chinese 'religions', Taoism and Confucianism.

4. Islam

In island Southeast Asia, a similar displacement of an elitist Hindu-Buddhist religion by a popular religion was underway. In this case however it was Arab and Indian traders who introduced Islam to the area, and this religion has always had strong links with coastal locations and maritime trading routes. Like Theravada Buddhism on the mainland, Islam spread rapidly and by the time the Spanish had begun to colonize the Philippines during the mid- to late-16th century it had diffused northwards as far as the Philippine island of Mindanao.

5. Western cultural influences

The fifth cultural infusion, and one that continues, was that associated with the colonization of Southeast Asia by Portugal, Spain, Holland, Great Britain, France and the United States. Their activities also created the conditions that would promote the immigration of large numbers of Chinese (and to a lesser extent Indians) from the end of the 19th century and into the 20th. In the 1890s for example, up to 150,000 Chinese were arriving annually in Singapore alone. Today the Chinese in Peninsular Malaysia make up a third of the total population. Much of Southeast Asia has been so integrated into the world economy that it comes as a genuine surprise to many first-time visitors. Words like Coca-Cola, Pepsi, Marlboro and Levi's all enter a Southeast Asian's vocabulary at an early age. Many Thais believe that 'supermarket' is a word of Thai origin; while everywhere advertisements entice Southeast Asians to buy Western consumer goods. Even in isolated Indochina and Burma, Western products are highly prized and a mark of success: Johnny Walker Red Label whisky and 555 cigarettes in Burma, jeans in Vietnam, cassette recorders and Western music in Cambodia.

Local genius

Because of these successive cultural infusions over the past 2,000 years, there has been a tendency to emphasize the degree to which the inhabitants of Southeast Asia have been moulded by external cultural influences. They have; but foreign cultural elements have also been adapted and tailored to meet the needs and preferences of the people. Islam in Central Java, for example, includes many elements of Buddhism, Hinduism and Sufi mysticism – religious precursors to Islam on the island. The same is true of Theravada Buddhism in Thailand, which incorporates a large number of essentially animist and Brahmanical elements. The important role of women in Southeast Asian society for example, reflects a tradition which has survived the diffusion of different religions – where women are accorded lesser roles – into the region. Historically at least, this was most clearly reflected in the role of women in sexual relations (see box).

The major empires

Southeast Asia has witnessed the development of dozens of states since the turn of the Christian era. In several cases their power and artistic accomplishments can still be seen reflected in the magnificence of the buildings that have survived. There can be few regions in the world offering the visitor such varied and glorious reminders of past civilizations. The Victorian naturalist Joseph Jukes on seeing the Hindu temples at Malang in East Java, and in a characteristically long Victorian sentence, records:

> "The imagination became busy in restoring their fallen glories, in picturing large cities, adorned with temples and palaces, seated on the plain, and in recalling the departed power, wealth and state of the native kingdom that once flourished in a land so noble, so beautiful, and so well-adapted for its growth and security" (1847).

A broad – although rather simplistic – distinction can be drawn between those Southeast Asian empires which drew their power and their wealth from maritime trade, and those which were founded on agricultural production.

PENIS BALLS AND SEXUAL ROLES IN HISTORICAL SOUTHEAST ASIA

One notable feature of Southeast Asian society is the relative autonomy of women. This is most clearly illustrated in sexual relations. As the historian Anthony Reid writes in his book *Southeast Asia in the age of commerce 1450-1680*: "Southeast Asian literature of the period leaves us in little doubt that women took a very active part in courtship and lovemaking, and demanded as much as they gave by way of sexual and emotional gratification". He then goes on to describe the various ways – often involving painful surgery – that men would try to satisfy their partners. Metal pins, for example, were inserted into the penis, and wheels, studs and spurs attached as accessories to increase the female's pleasure. Alternatively, metal balls or bells, sometimes made of gold or ivory, would be inserted beneath the skin of the penis. Numerous early European visitors expressed their astonishment at the practice. Tome Pires, the 16th century Portuguese apothecary observed that Pegu lords in Burma "wear as many as 9 gold ones [penis bells], with beautiful treble, contralto and tenor tones, the size of the Alvares plums in our country; and those who are too poor...have them in lead...Malay women rejoice greatly when the Pegu men come to their country... [because of] their sweet harmony". Whereas in Africa, genital surgery was, and is, often intended to suppress pleasure for women or increase it for men, in Southeast Asia the reverse was the case. The surgery described above was also widely practiced – in Burma, Siam, Makassar, among the Torajans of Sulawesi, and Java.

Maritime empires

Southeast Asia straddles the trade route between East and West. From the early years of the Christian era through to the colonial period, a succession of indigenous empires exploited these trade links with Europe, the Middle East, China and Japan, deriving wealth, power and prestige from their ability to control maritime trade. Foremost among them were Funan (Cambodia, 1st-6th century), and Srivijaya (Sumatra, 7th-13th century).

With its capital near Palembang in SE Sumatra, Srivijaya was in a strategic location to control trade through the two most important straits in Southeast Asia: the Strait of Melaka between the Malay peninsula and Sumatra, and the Sunda Strait between Sumatra and Java. Palembang offered seafarers an excellent harbour and repair facilities. The kings also used their wealth to build an impressive fleet with which they suppressed piracy in the Strait of Melaka. Srivijaya's empire expanded so fast that by the 9th century it included much of Sumatra, western Java, the Malay peninsula and the eastern portion of Borneo. In total, Srivijaya was the dominant power in the area for 350 years, from 670 AD to 1025.

Trade not only brought wealth to these maritime states. It also resulted in a fusion of Indian and Southeast Asian cultural traditions, a fact reflected in the legend of Funan's origins. Local legend records that a great Indian Brahmin with the name Kaundinya, acting on the instructions of a dream, sailed to the coast of Vietnam carrying with him a bow and arrow. On arriving, he shot the arrow and where it landed, he established the future capital of Funan. Following this act, Kaundinya married the princess Soma, daughter of the local King of the Nagas. The legend symbolizes the union between Indian and local cultural traditions – the *naga* representing indigenous fertility rites and customs (see page 494), and the arrow, the potency of Hinduism.

MAKING SPACE

Western historians like to think of kingdoms 'controlling' territory. In Southeast Asia such cut-and-dried spatial categorization made little sense until the early 20th centuries. This led the historian OW Wolters to suggest the word *mandala* to describe the manner in which Southeast Asian kingdoms controlled territory:

A *mandala* "...represented a particular and often unstable political situation in a vaguely defined geographical area without fixed boundaries and where smaller centres tended to look in all directions for security. *Mandalas* would expand and contract in concertina-like fashion. Each one contained several tributary rulers, some of whom would repudiate their vassal status when the opportunity arose and try to build up their own network of vassals."

Land-based empires

In addition to Funan and Srivijaya, Southeast Asia also witnessed the development of empires whose wealth was based upon the exploitation of the land, and in particular the cultivation of wet rice. Angkor (Cambodia, 9th-15th century), and the Sailendra Dynasty (Java, mid 8th-10th century) are both examples of such empires.

Angkor's power was derived from a coincidence of environmental wealth, human genius, and religious belief. The location of Angkor, close to the Tonle Sap or Great Lake meant that it had access to sufficient water to grow a surplus of rice large enough to support an extensive court, army and religious hierarchy. At the same time, it is also usually claimed that the kings of Angkor built an irrigation network of immense complexity – able to irrigate over 5 million ha of land, and producing three to four crops of rice each year. This is now subject to dispute, with scholars arguing that the tanks at Angkor were not for agricultural, but for urban use. The third element contributing to Angkor's success was the legitimacy provided to its kings by the deva raja cult. As long as the king was accepted as divine, as a *chakravartin* or ruler of the universe, by all his subjects and the vassal states and princes under his control, then the empire would remain stable. This was the case from the 9th to the 15th centuries: for over 600 years Angkor lay at the centre of the grandest empire in Southeast Asia. King Jayavarman VII

(1181-1219) for example built the famous Bayon, as well as around 200 hospitals and rest houses, and 20,000 shrines. There were an estimated 300,000 priests and monks. It is said that Ta Phrom – just one of the temples in the complex at Angkor – required 79,365 people from 3,140 villages to build it. In 1864 the French explorer Henri Mouhot declared Angkor to be "grander than anything of Greece or Rome".

Like the rulers of Angkor, the kings of the Sailendra Dynasty in island Southeast Asia, derived their wealth and power from agriculture. Exploiting the year-long rains, warmth, and fertile volcanic soil of Java, a substantial surplus of rice was produced. This fed a large court and a series of impressive monuments were built. The Sailendras were patrons of Buddhism, and they attracted Buddhist scholars from all over Asia to their court. It also seems that the kings were linked through marriage with the rulers of Srivijaya.

Of all the monuments of the Sailendra period none is more imposing than Borobudur built between 778 AD and 824 – to many the single greatest temple in all of Southeast Asia. This colossal monument, located on the Kedu Plain, represented the cosmological and spiritual centre of Sailendra power. Along its terraces, in row upon row of superbly executed reliefs (some 2,000 of them), the Sailendra world order is depicted: the nine previous lives of the Gautama Buddha, princes and carpenters, dancers and fishermen. Borobudur was a religious

Locals bringing nutmeg to sell to Dutch factors in Banda, the Moluccas, 1599.

justification for Sailendra rule, and at the same time gave the kings religious authority over Srivijaya. Johann Scheltema, a German traveller, on seeing Java's monuments wrote at the beginning of this century that they were: "...eloquent evidence of that innate consciousness which moves men to propitiate the principle of life by sacrifice in temples as gloriously divine as mortal hand can raise".

COLONIAL HISTORY

Early European contact: the allure of spices (16th-18th century)

During the course of the 15th century, the two great European maritime powers of the time, Spain and Portugal, were exploring sea routes to the E. Two forces were driving this search: the desire for profits, and the drive to envangelize. At the time, even the wealthy in Europe had to exist on pickled and salted fish and meat during the winter months (fodder crops for winter feed were not grown until the 18th century). Spices to flavour what would otherwise be a very monotonous diet were greatly sought after and commanded a high price. This was not just a passing European fad. An Indian Hindu wrote that: "When the palate revolts against the insipidness of rice boiled with no other ingredients, we dream of fat, salt and spices".

Of the spices, cloves and nutmeg originated from just one location, the Moluccas (Maluku) – the Spice Islands of eastern Indonesia. Perhaps because of their value, spices and their places of origin were accorded mythical status in Europe. The 14th century French friar Catalani Jordanus claimed for example that the clove flowers of Java produced an odour so strong it killed "every man who cometh among them, unless he shut his mouth and nostrils".

It was in order to break the monopoly on the spice trade held by Venetian and Muslim Arab traders that the Portuguese began to extend their possessions eastwards. This finally culminated in the capture of the port of Melaka by the Portuguese seafarer Alfonso de Albuquerque in Jun 1511. The additional desire to spread the Word of God is clear in the speech that Albuquerque made before the battle with the Muslim sultan of Melaka, when he exorted his men, stressing:

"...the great service which we shall perform to our Lord in casting the Moors out of this country and of quenching the fire of the sect of Mohammet so that it may never burst out again hereafter".

From their base in Melaka, the Portuguese established trading relations with the Moluccas, and built a series of forts across the region: at Bantam (Banten), Flores, Ternate, Tidore, Timor and Ambon (Amboyna).

As the Portuguese were sailing E to Southeast Asia, the Spanish, from their possessions in South America, were sailing W. It was in order to prevent clashes between the two powers that a Papal Bull of 1493 divided the world along a line just W of the Azores: everywhere to the W of this line was left for the Spanish, and everything to the E of it for the Portuguese. Unfortunately, the Pope remained convinced that the earth was flat and never envisaged the two powers meeting in Southeast Asia. This occurred when Ferdinand Magellan arrived in the Philippines in 1521 having crossed the Pacific – in a remarkable feat of seamanship. After a short period of conflict, the two protagonists settled their differences, the Portuguese leaving the Philippines to the Spanish, and the Spanish agreeing not to interfere in the Moluccas.

By the late 16th century, Portuguese influence in Southeast Asia was waning. Their empire was over-extended, and the claim that Portuguese seafarers were helping to introduce Christianity to the infidels of the region sat uneasily next to the barbaric methods they employed. Francis Xavier, the canonized Catholic missionary, is said to have been so appalled by the debauchery and vice of

Melaka that when he left he shook the sand from his shoes, vowing never to return to the cursed city again. The Portuguese were supplanted by the Dutch in the region who, by 1616, had established 15 trading posts and gained control of the spice trade.

But despite these advances, in many respects the European presence was peripheral. The motivation was to secure spices and to make money, not to extend territorially. The stupendous lost city of Angkor in Cambodia for example, was not extensively reported upon until the French naturalist Henri Mouhot published the diary of his 1861 visit 3 years later.

Intensification of the European presence (19th-20th century)

At the beginning of the 19th century, a number of developments markedly increased European interest in the colonization of Southeast Asia. Most important, was the region's new-found economic potential. Europe's industrial revolution led to increased demand for industrial raw materials, while at the same time companies were looking for markets for their manufactured goods. Southeast Asia was in a position to provide the first of these at the beginning, and as the region's development proceeded, the second too. Allied to these developments, there were also a number of technological advances which considerably shortened the journey to Southeast Asia. The opening of the Suez canal in 1869 precluded the dangerous trip around Cape of Good Hope, while the development of the steamship slashed days off the journey. The active spread of Christianity was once again firmly on the agenda, and European governments found it hard not to interfere when zealous missionaries and their converts were persecuted by local leaders. This was especially true in Vietnam where missionaries had been periodically persecuted from the early 17th century. This reached its height during the reigns of the Vietnamese emperors Minh Mang (1820-41), Thieu Tri (1841-47) and Tu Duc (1847-83). Minh Mang, for example, issued a decree in 1833 ordering churches to be destroyed and made profession of the Catholic faith a capital offence. French ecclesiastical magazines contained vivid accounts of the torture and murder of French missionaries, and the clamour raised by the French public ultimately led to the invasion and colonization of Vietnam by France.

The effect of these developments was that over a relatively short space of time – about 45 years, between 1825 and 1870 – all of Southeast Asia with the exception of Siam (the old name for Thailand) fell under European control. More detailed discussion about the final subjugation of the region is contained in the introductory sections dealing with the individual countries. In essence however, there were two sets of rivalries: between the French and the British on the mainland, and between the Dutch and the British in the archipelago. The local empires had neither the economic power, military might nor, in many cases, the political skills to withstand the Europeans.

The impact of the colonial period in Southeast Asia

The impact of the colonial period extended far beyond mere political domination. Southeast Asia was irreparably affected economically, socially, culturally, even physically. More to the point, these effects are still visible today in the region's economic and social fabric.

The principal effect of the colonial period was to alter the economic basis of life in Southeast Asia. In brief, a process of commercialization was set in train. Huge areas of land were cleared in the river deltas of the region and planted to rice. Along the Irrawaddy in Burma for example, the area under rice cultivation

increased from 400,000 ha in 1855, to 4 million ha by 1930. This process was pioneered by large numbers of individual peasants responding to the new economic opportunities provided by the presence of the colonial powers. This was even the case in independent Thailand, where the king could do little to constrain the economic influence of the West.

Even more dramatically, Western-financed estates growing plantation crops such as rubber and coffee were widely established. In Malaysia, the area planted to rubber – a crop which was only introduced to the region in the late 19th century – increased from a paltry 137 ha in 1897, to 1.4 million ha by 1939. These estates used immigrant labour, imported machinery, they were managed by Europeans, financed by foreign capital, and exported all their production. They formed 'enclaves', completely separate from the local, traditional, economy.

Nor did the economic effects of the colonial period merely affect agriculture. The Western powers also needed minerals and timber to fuel their industrial revolutions. Most spectacularly, tin-mining expanded. The introduction of the steam chain-bucket dredge, steam pumps, and new drilling methods revolutionized the tin industry. By the later 1930s, Indonesia, Thailand and Malaya were supplying 60% of the world's tin.

Not surprisingly, this process of commercialization deeply affected the inhabitants of the region. Farmers were inexorably drawn into the cash economy. Seeds and fertilizers were purchased in increasing quantities, money was borrowed, labour hired, land rented and surplus production sold. The process of commercialization not only undermined the traditional self-sufficiency of the Southeast Asian village, it also affected the social fabric of the village. People became dependent on economic developments in the international economy. This was thrown into stark perspective during the Great Depression of the early

1930s when the price of rubber halved, and then halved again, between 1929 and 1932. Rice farmers had their land repossessed as money lenders foreclosed on their loans. Riots broke out across the region as dispossessed peasants demonstrated their anger and frustration.

The exploitation of Southeast Asia's natural resources entailed the improvement of communications and transport infrastructure. As a result, a network of roads and railways were built. However these did not serve all areas equally. Mainly they linked areas of export commodity production with the outside world. In the same way, although the colonial presence led to a dramatic growth in the number and size of urban settlements, these occupied different locations and had different *raisons d'être* from their indigenous precursors. The great port cities of Singapore, Georgetown (Penang), Batavia (Jakarta), Rangoon, Saigon, even Bangkok developed in order to funnel export commodities out of the region, and manufactured imports in. Likewise, many inland towns owed their existence to the export commodities that were produced in the surrounding areas such as Taiping and Sungei Ujong (now Seremban), both Malayan towns that grew on the back of the tin trade.

Another feature of modern Southeast Asia, which has its roots in the colonial period, is their multi-racial make-up. These groups, although they lived (and continued to live) in close proximity to one another, rarely mixed. The most striking example of a plural society is Malaysia where 32% of the population of Peninsular Malaysia are Chinese, 8% Indian, and nearly 60% Malay. The explanation for this heterogeneous population lies in the demand for labour during the colonial period. For the colonial authorities found it extremely hard to recruit sufficient local labour to work on the plantations, in the tin mines, and in the other export industries. The logical solution was to import labour from abroad. From the end of the 19th century, hundreds of thousands of Chinese and Indians arrived in Malaya. It was usually these immigrants' intention to return to their mother countries, but many stayed on – sometimes because they were too poor to leave, sometimes because they wished to keep an eye on the wealth that they had accumulated. The immigration of 'indentured' labourers was greatest in British Malaya: between 1909 and 1940 some 16 million Indians and Chinese arrived in Malaya. Today Malaysia's total population is only 18 million.

The Second World War and the Japanese interregnum

Prior to the outbreak of WW2, the strains of commercialization, domination by foreign powers, and the often heavy-handed and insensitive behaviour of colonial officials had engendered only a limited reaction from the local populations. Nationalist movements lacked focus, and charismatic leaders were needed to add coherence and direction to nascent independence movements. Rather ironically, this was provided by a Western-educated Southeast Asian elite. Men such as Sukarno of Indonesia and Ho Chi Minh of Vietnam, travelled abroad for their further education, were introduced to notions of self-government and nationhood, and read works by Marx, Lenin, Locke and Rousseau. But even with the establishment of a handful of nationalist parties prior to the outbreak of WW2, they were regarded as only a minor irritation by the colonial powers. Few would have dreamt that within so short a space of time – less than a decade in most cases – the countries of Southeast Asia would have achieved independence.

The war changed the nature of the relationship between the colonial powers and the people that they ruled. In the space of less than 6 months, virtually the entire region was over-run by Japanese forces. In Dec 1941, the Japanese landed in Northern Malaya, having already taken control of French Indochina; on 11 Jan, Kuala Lumpur fell; on 15 Feb, Singapore capitulated; on 7 Mar, Rangoon was abandoned; and on 8 Mar, the Dutch surrendered in Indonesia. This was the darkest period of the entire war for the Allies. However, not only did the Japanese demonstrate the military fallibility of the colonial powers in a style that could not have been more compelling; they were also Asian. The war made independence inevitable – and sooner rather than later. The colonial powers were drained and exhausted; they had lost much of their credibility; and they returned to find that the fragmented nationalist parties of the pre-war years had grown in size, influence and authority. Burma was granted independence in 1948, Indonesia in 1949, Cambodia in 1953, North Vietnam and Laos in 1954, South Vietnam in 1955, Malaya in 1957, and Singapore in 1963. Brunei only attained full independence in 1984.

MODERN SOUTHEAST ASIA

From the end of the Vietnam War until, roughly, 1992, the Southeast Asian region was effectively divided into two groups of countries. On the one hand there were the market economies of the Association of Southeast Asian Nations (ASEAN). Until 1995, these included Thailand, Malaysia, Indonesia, Singapore and Brunei, as well as the Philippines. And on the other there were the Communist/socialist countries of Indochina – Vietnam, Laos and Cambodia – and Burma. These two sets of countries embraced contrasting economic and political ideologies. The countries of ASEAN followed – simplistically-speaking – the Western, capitalist, consumer-orientated path to economic success, although they have tended to look to Japan, rather than to Europe or America, as their role model. At the same time they have tended to side with the West politically. In contrast, the countries of Indochina and Burma embraced a socialist or Communist vision of reconstruction and development. They supported the former Soviet Union or China in the East-West conflict, except Burma which followed a policy of non-alignment and self-sufficiency.

This neat division of Southeast Asia into two blocs, always somewhat dubious, has gradually broken down since the late 1980s, so that today it is increasingly hard to sustain in any meaningful sense. Vietnam and Laos may remain explicitly 'Communist', but beneath the vacant terminology the differences are narrowing month-by-month. Politically too, the countries of ASEAN and Indochina have undergone a significant process of rapprochement. Whereas a mere 5 years ago, the Vietnamese were lobbing shells onto Thai territory to attack Khmers Rouges forces barracked there, the countries now exchange business delegations and senior ministers. And whereas the Lao and Thai armies fought a vicious little war in 1987-88 over some disputed territory near Ban Rom Khlao in the north of Thailand, 1994 saw the opening of the first bridge over the upper reaches of the Mekong River by the King of Thailand and the President of Laos (see page 350). In short, for the first time in recent history, there is the possibility that the Southeast Asian region might be a 'united' area of 400 million people. Former Thai prime minister Chatichai Choonhaven referred to this massive potential market as *Suwannaphume* or a 'Golden Land'. In so doing he was harking back to an earlier era when the great trading ports of the Malay Archipelago – places like Meleka (Malacca) and Aceh – were critical conduits in the fabulously wealthy trade in spices from the Moluccas, silks from China, camphor and ivory from the forests of Southeast Asia, and gold, silver and gemstones from Burma and the Spanish Main. The first substantive development on this path to a united Southeast

THE ASIAN WAY

There has been a great deal of debate recently about the so-called 'Asian Way'. The low crime levels in Singapore are favourably contrasted with the war zones that constitute the centres of some US cities, and it has been asked whether the West in general has allowed the rights of individuals to undermine those of wider society to such an extent that the protection of the majority has been ignored. In short, an abstract principle has got in the way of common sense.

The inability to stop, let alone reverse, the seeming inexorable rise in crime in the West is contrasted with the apparent peaceful situation in Asia. Have Asians got it right? Is the West, as former Prime Minister of Singapore Lee Kuan Yew appears to believe, decadent and rotten to its very core? It is on this basis that Asian values are promoted and a great deal of collective navel gazing has ensued.

Asian values – often thought to be Confucianist – are seen to embody such things as respect for elders and the law, hardwork, and recognition that the needs of society may transcend those of the individual. Former Singapore Prime Minister Lee Kuan Yew, for example, has explained: " A Confucianist view of order between subject and ruler – this helps in the rapid transformation of society ... in other words, you fit yourself into society – the exact opposite of the American rights of the individual." These values are reflected, so the argument goes, in rapid economic growth, low crime rates, stability and rising prosperity. Unfortunately, or perhaps fortunately, this view of Asia, and of the Asian success story, is hugely simplistic.

First, Asia is so diverse that to talk about a single set of Asian values is nonsense. Even 'Confucianism' as currently presented bears little relation to the sage's *The Analects* written in the 5th century BC. When Asian politicians try to summarize what Asian Values are all about they risk descending into pronouncements of such crassness as to be almost embarrassing. Second, Asia is not crimeless. Singapore has a low crime rate (Asian commentator Ian Buruma defines the city state as a "huge tropical boarding school", easy to police by the 'nanny' state

Asia came in the middle of 1995 when Vietnam joined the ranks of ASEAN and formerly ended the division of the region into competing geopolitical blocs.

Southeast Asia in the world economy

In a special report in 1993, *The Economist* predicted that "It is now likelier than not that the most momentous public event in the lifetime of anybody reading this survey will turn out to have been the modernisation of Asia". A rate of economic growth unprecedented in human history is transforming not just Asia, but the balance of global economic power, and by extension political and military power. The countries of Southeast Asia are a central component in this global transformation. Those that comprise the Association of Southeast Asian Nations are among the fastest-growing economies in the world. Since 1965 they have achieved average annual rates of growth of over 6%, and they are seen by many analysts to represent a second tier of 'dragons' or 'tigers': countries which are basing their success on aggressive, export-orientated industrial growth in the way Japan, South Korea, Taiwan and Hong Kong did before them. Although the countries of Indochina – Vietnam, Laos and Cambodia – are currently among some of the poorest in the world, they too, and particularly Vietnam, are per-

there), but the murder rate in Thailand is, in fact, higher than in the US While at the same time countries like China, Hong Kong and Japan face organised crime syndicates that are far more influential than any which operate in Europe, and corruption is endemic in some countries. Ian Buruma argues that in some of Asia's authoritarian states murder, theft, torture and larceny are institutionalised: rather than individuals doing these things to other individuals, the state does it to those members of its population who try and buck the trend. Events in Burma in 1988, and in Indonesia and Thailand in 1991 go to show, in Buruma's view, that "crime" has become a "state enterprise". Although this does not mean that the Asian experience should be rejected out of hand as fraudulent, all is not roses in the Asian garden and many Americans would find it suffocating to live in Singapore, for example, where the press is lack-lustre and one-dimensional in the extreme and chewing gum is outlawed for its supposed anti-social tendencies. As Buruma wrote, referring to the caning of American 18-year-old Michael Fay in Singapore in 1994, "the firm smack of discipline always sounds sweeter when it lands on someone else's bum."

Despite the claims that Asia is different, some Asian politicians are actively trying to prevent Westernization occurring. At the end of May 1994, the Singapore parliament debated the Maintenance of Parents Bill which would allow parents to sue their children if they did not support them financially in retirement. As the *Straits Times* put it in an editorial supporting the Bill, there is a danger that the younger generation "will grow up self-absorbed, middle-class and very likely, Westernized in reflex. In that milieu, financial support for parents as a time-honoured tradition would whither". There are many other signs that Asia is not impervious to the social trends evident in the West: divorce, crime, drug addiction and so on are all on the rise, just as incomes, level of education and life expectancy are too. Nonetheless, the government of Singapore may have taken some comfort from a survey of 700 Singaporean schoolchildren which revealed that they viewed the most important values to be, in order, filial piety, honesty, responsibility, and self-control.

ceived to be on the brink of a potential economic 'miracle'. From the Italian roof-top restaurants of Singapore, the clubs of Bangkok or the manicured golf greens of Malaysia, it is hard to believe that a mere 30 years ago these countries had incomes which put them on a par with India and the countries of Africa. Now, in terms of purchasing power parity (i.e. what average incomes are worth in real terms), they eclipse – or seem about to eclipse – such developed countries as Spain and Ireland. The economic success of Asia has altered the way people perceive the countries concerned and the process of development. What, for example, does the 'Third World' mean if some of the countries that comprise this Third World have higher standards of living than countries in the First World? In short, the ideology of Third Worldism, at least over large areas of Asia, is dead. Nor are the countries and their leaders willing meekly to follow the lead of the West. Individuals like Prime Minister Mahathir Mohamad of Malaysia confront assumptions about their and their countries' place in the world almost monthly, attacking the West for its cultural imperialism, latent superiority, and remnant colonial assumptions. With the Malaysian economy, and others in the region, growing so rapidly, Mahathir finds he is in a strong position to lecture to the West. China's rejection

THE ASIAN MIRACLE: WHY IT HAPPENED – THE STORY ACCORDING TO THE WORLD BANK

In 1993, the World Bank published a study which tried to make sense of the Asian economic success story, with the title *The East Asian miracle: economic growth and public policy*. The unprecedented rate of economic growth in Asia, including in a number of Southeast Asian countries, demanded an explanation so that other, less fortunate regions of the world might also embark on this road to fortune. Of course, not everyone is so sanguine about Asia's success, past or future. These critics point to, for example, human rights violations, poor working conditions, widening rural-urban disparities, environmental degradation on a monumental scale, the exploitation of child labour, and corrupt and corrosive government.

Although the World Bank study begins by pointing out that there is no 'recipe' for success, it does highlight a number of critical elements which countries and governments need, in their view, to get right. As the World Bank puts it, the so-called High Performing Asian Economies or HPAEs (including Singapore, Malaysia, Thailand and Indonesia) "achieved high growth by getting the basics right". Not all the below can be applied to all the countries in question all of the time; nonetheless, they represent a checklist of 'right' policies and government.

● **The principle of shared growth**: although the countries of Asia are not, in most cases, democracies, their governments have tried to ensure that the fruits of development have been relatively widely shared. This is particularly true in the case of the 'dragons' (including Singapore) where rapid growth has been achieved with relative equity. This has helped to establish the legitimacy of their governments and usually won the support of the populations at large – despite the fact that those governments may still be authoritarian in complexion.

● **Investment in physical capital**: the countries of Asia have, in general, been saving and investing a greater proportion of their total wealth than countries in any other region of the world. This includes both private and public investment,

in 1994 of US President Bill Clinton's attempts to link the renewal of Most Favoured Nation trading status (MFN) with human rights is the most obvious example of the waning power of the West to dictate terms, and the growing confidence of Asia. It is hard to believe that any Chinese leader would have 'lost face' so completely.

Asian drama

This optimism among the countries of Asia is remarkable when set against the landscape of the 1960s. In 1965 the Swedish economist and Nobel Prize winner Gunnar Myrdal wrote a massive, 2,200 page, two-volume study of Asia entitled *Asian drama*. It is a down-beat and depressing study, which predicted famine and revolution rather than growth and prosperity. Although it is now too easy to reject this seminal work as excessively pessimistic, at the time the volumes seemed prescient to most people, and were lauded as such. In Southeast Asia, the Vietnam War was escalating, Thailand was facing its own growing insurgency problem, Indonesia had experienced revolution and a bloodbath, Burma's formerly vibrant economy was in disarray, populations were growing out of control, and most people were mired in poverty.

The first country in Southeast Asia to break this mould was **Singapore** (along with the other newly industrialising

but is most dramatic in terms of private investment (the World Bank, as one might expect, views private investment as more efficient and effective in promoting growth).

●**Investment in human capital**: although the proportion of spending allotted to education is not very much higher in Asia than elsewhere in the developing world, this money has been primarily allocated to primary and secondary schooling, not to higher education. Among developing countries, the families of most of those entering higher education can pay for it anyway, and need little government support; the best way to improve general levels of education is by targetting primary and secondary schooling. Asian governments have also tended to educate girls nearly as well as boys.

●**Allowing the market to determine prices**: as one might expect from the World Bank, the report also highlights the importance of allowing the market to determine the price of labour, capital and goods. The Bank skipped around the tendency for Asian governments to intervene in economic decision-making (with the exception of Hong Kong) by arguing that this was judicious intervention which reinforced, rather than tried to buck, the market.

●**That vital intangible**: Lee Kuan Yew, former prime minister of Singapore, visited Vietnam – one of the poorest countries in the world with a per capita income of US$220 – and pronounced that the country's prospects were bright because it had that 'vital intangible'. Economists talk rather less poetically in terms of Total Factor Productivity (TFP). In effect, this is what cannot be explained in a country's growth by looking at such variables as investment in physical and human capital. The former Soviet Union, on paper, should have grown as fast as Singapore and South Korea. As is now abundantly clear, it did not. The problem is identifying this ghostly missing catalyst.

● **Creating a business-friendly environment**: the countries have usually welcomed foreign investment and have sought to create the conditions in which foreign companies can thrive. They have also created a cadre of efficient technocrats to manage the economy.

economies of East Asia, Taiwan, South Korea and Hong Kong). When the island-state achieved self government in 1959, it was in a woeful condition with high unemployment, a decaying urban core, political unrest and no manufacturing base to speak of. Today Singapore is one of the wealthiest countries in the world. Average per capita incomes exceed US$12,000 and far-sighted planning has given the city a futuristic feel.

Thailand, Indonesia and Malaysia have had to support sizeable poor rural populations and have enjoyed rather less stratospheric rates of economic growth. Nonetheless, they have still progressed at a speed which would be the envy of many Latin American and African coun-

tries. The proportion of the population living in absolute poverty has decreased from 60% to 15% between 1970 and 1990 in Indonesia, and from 26% to 16% over the same period in the case of Thailand. These four countries of Southeast Asia – Singapore, Malaysia, Thailand and Indonesia – were among the world's 13 most successful developing countries in the years 1965-1990 (four of the others were also Asian, namely Taiwan, Hong Kong, South Korea and China). The rates of growth achieved led to an 8-fold increase in real GDP, a doubling of output every 8 years.

The countries of **Indochina and Burma** may be part of the same region as those of ASEAN, but until the late 1980s

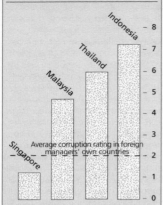

Source: Political & Economic Risk Consultancy, adapted from *The Economist*, 1995.

In 1995, the Hong Kong-based firm *Political and Economic Risk Consultancy* asked managers working in the Asian region – mainly of European and North American nationality – how they rated levels of corruption in Asian countries compared with their own, on a scale from 0–10. Although corruption levels were significantly higher – with the notable exception of Singapore – they are probably not quite as high as popular rumour would have it. Apparently, it is rare for firms to have to pay more than 5% of a contract in bribes and back-handers.

they belonged to a different world. They pursued a path to development which aped the experience of the other command economies, and like the others largely failed in the attempt. In the space of 15 years, Vietnam declined from being the greatest military power in the region, to become an economic disaster. The countries of Indochina and Burma are now having to contend with an entirely new global landscape. They have responded to economic stagnation and the general failure of their socialist programmes of development by introducing increasingly reformist economic policies. In Laos, the government talks of *chin thanakan mai* or 'new thinking', while in Vietnam there is *doi moi* or 'renovation' – both Southeast Asian equivalents to the former Soviet Union's *perestroika*. This new outlook embraces the market, foreign investment, incentives and private ownership. Even Burma, still a maverick state, has had to turn to outside investment and expertise to revitalize its moribund economy, even declaring 1996 Visit Myanmar Year in an effort to increase its foreign exchange earnings. But it would be wrong to see Vietnam, Laos, Cambodia and Burma as just a short step behind Malaysia, Indonesia, Thailand and Singapore. As *The Economist* put it in 1993:

> "The reality that can be seen, touched, heard and on occasion sniffed is that the average Vietnamese, Lao, Cambodian or Burmese is dirt-poor. Bangkok's street vendors peddle fake designer watches to foreign tourists; Hanoi's mend odd bits of ancient machinery for other townsfolk, or give them shaves and haircuts in front of cracked pieces of mirror."

Many westerners tend to equate 'free' markets with 'free' people, arguing that because these countries are allowing greater private enterprise there will inevitably be greater political freedom. This may well be wishful thinking and it is possible to argue that there is no latent contradiction. As the *Far Eastern Economic Review* put it in an editorial marking the 20th anniversary of the end of the Vietnam War on 30 April 1995: "Communism in practice, after all, has always had far more to do with Leninist prescriptions for holding power than Marxist notions about economic production."

The city and countryside

Development in the West has been evolutionary rather than revolutionary. In Southeast Asia the reverse has been the case. Progress has been bewilderingly fast and has resulted in the uneven distribution of wealth. The contrast between city and countryside provides tangible evidence of this. For the visitor, the capital cities of the region can be thoroughly exhausting, with hot and humid climates, noise and bustle, and often appalling traffic conditions. Away from the cities in the countryside, landscape and life tend to be much more in keeping with the popular view of Southeast Asia – rice, buffaloes, tropical forests, traditional festivals and ceremonies. Superficially, rural life seems to reflect traditional patterns and processes. But, in the same way that the modern cities embody many traditional elements, so the traditional countryside is rapidly modernizing. Beneath the surface, the technology of agriculture and the aspirations and outlook of farmers have changed dramatically. Improving communications in the form of better roads and transport, and radio and television, have meant that farmers are aware of developments in the wider world. Today they wish to provide for their families the benefits of modern health care and education, and this has necessitated that they embrace the cash economy.

But, the process of development has not always been devoid of tensions and frictions. In the forested areas of Southeast Asia, tribal groups such as the Hmong of Thailand and the upriver Dayak tribes of Sarawak have suffered both economically and culturally as a dominant, Western-style consumer culture has impinged on their lives. Some groups have tried to fight the process of commercialization, often in league with foreign environmentalist groups. A large segment of the population has also become economically marginalized – despite the rapid economic growth. In the cities, there are millions of slum dwellers and squatters, living without clean water, medical care and education and subsisting in the informal sector. In rural areas, farmers have been pushed off their land as population has begun to press upon the land resource, and as the commercialization of producton has led to the accumulation of land in the hands of a small number of wealthy landowners. The resulting army of landless peasants have been forced to work for wages of perhaps a dollar a day on other people's fields.

The politics of economic success

Although the countries of Southeast Asia may represent object lessons in 'how to build a successful market economy', there is much more debate over the political systems which underline the gloss of economic success. Thailand now has a democratically elected prime minister and government, and President Suharto of Indonesia seems to accept that greater pluralism in the political system is inevitable. But for groups like the New York-based *Human Rights Watch Asia* (formerly, *Asia Watch*) there is much to decry in terms of human rights violations and freedom of expression. They point, for example, to Singapore's heavy-handed government and attempts at social engineering, to Indonesia's 'genocide' in East Timor and control over political opposition, and to Malaysia's treatment of its tribal peoples not to mention its control over the press and muzzling of opposition politicians. The countries of Indochina (but not Burma, which is widely viewed as a gangster state), have not received the same human rights attention as those of ASEAN (minus Vietnam), perhaps due to a legacy of guilt over the war in Indochina. Pushing such guilt aside, it is clear that although market-orientated economic reform or *perestroika* may have been embraced with alacrity, there has been litte concomitant *glasnost* in the political system. With the exception of Cambodia, the ruling parties have retained a tight hold on the reins of power. They appear unwilling to allow greater plurality of political expression, and outspoken critics are quickly silenced. Whether these countries will be able to maintain the delicate balancing act of allowing greater economic freedom while denying their people any significant political freedom is a moot point.

This last sentence highlights a major difference in opinion between the West and Asia. There seem to be two key issues here, which are almost irreconcileable. First, many Asians, and particularly its political leaders, maintain that Western human rights pressure groups are trying to impose Western cultural values on Asia. They argue that these values are inappropriate in the Asian cultural context, and that this is just another form of imperialism (see box, page 56). The sanctity of the individual, so important in the West, is replaced in Asia by the group (or wider society). The second bone of contention concerns whether democracy really is the answer. It has been argued that the West's problem is that democracy stifles government by giving multitudes of special interest groups too much say. The result is that government cannot govern, and that good government is replaced by the government of appeasement. Lee Kuan Yew, former prime minister of Singapore and a key spokesman for the Asian realm was quoted at the end of 1993 as saying: "Americans believe that out of contention, out of the clash of different ideas and ideals, you get good government. That view is not shared in Asia."

Strategic threats in the post-Cold War era

Before the end of the Cold War, the principal worry was that there might be a clash between the Communist and Capitalist countries of the region, a clash brought on by competing ideologies and by the identification of the former countries with the Soviet Union and People's Republic of China, and the latter with the United States. South-

east Asia would become, in other words, a stage on which the Cold War could become 'hot' as client states of the West and East came to blows. This occurred in Indochina during the Vietnam War, and continued during the civil war in Cambodia when the Vietnamese, with Soviet backing, shored-up the Hun Sen government, and the West supplied the rebel factions fighting it with lethal and humanitarian assistance.

Today these fears, both real and prospective, have faded. Instead the current greatest worry is China, and it is one which almost all the countries of the region share. With a partial US withdrawal from the region following the closure of massive American naval and airforce installations in the Philippines in 1992, an increasingly assertive, self-confident and powerful People's Republic of China is filling the vacuum. The most likely flashpoint is the Spratly Islands, an archipelago of tiny islands and atolls in the South China Sea. Not only do the islands occupy a strategically important position on the sea lanes between east and west, but it is widely thought that the area is rich in oil. The islands are also claimed by six nations: China, the Philippines, Taiwan, Vietnam, Malaysia and Brunei. This brings together a potent mix of economic incentive, security fears, historical animosity, and national ego. In 1988, China seized six coral atolls, and in the process sunk two Vietnamese patrol craft. More recently, in Mar 1995, China occupied the appropriately named Mischief Reef, which lies within the Philippines' 200-mile zone, and built a rather rudimentary military base there – to add to the seven other outposts scattered across the archipelago. When, in May 1995, a Philippine patrol ship took 39 local and foreign journalists to Mischief Reef to show how aggressively the Chinese were defending their claims, they were almost run down by two Chinese 'fishing' vessels, closely supported by two frigates. After the confrontation, the Chinese issued a warning, stating that another such infringement of Chinese sovereignty could result in "serious consequences", adding "We advise the other side not to misinterpret Chinese restraint..." In claiming the reefs, Beijing may be in a position to argue that they constitute Chinese land. If so, then it could claim the area as being in its territorial waters – and the resources that might lie beneath the sea bed.

In Apr, Indonesia and China disagreed regarding sovereignty over the area covered by the Natuna gas field. China's growing blue water fleet is encroaching further S and ASEAN is beginning to be more openly concerned about China's intentions in this highly sensitive area. Security analysts, however, see little chance that ASEAN will prevent further Chinese encroachment. The Association has always been slow to respond to external threats – their one success in this regard was over the Vietnamese occupation of Cambodia – and most commentators doubt that the Association will muster the collective will to force China to back down.

TOURISM: COUNTING THE COSTS

"Tourism is like fire. It can either cook your food or burn your house down". This sums up the ambivalent attitude that many people have regarding the effects of tourism. It is the largest foreign exchange earner in countries like Thailand, and the world's largest single industry; yet many people in receiving countries would rather tourists go home. Tourism is seen to be the cause of polluted beaches, rising prices, loose morals, consumerism, and much else besides.

The word 'tourist' is derived from 'travail', meaning work or torment. Travail, in turn, has its roots in the Latin word *tripalium*, which was a three-pronged instrument of torture. For many people struggling through the back of beyond in countries like Vietnam or Indonesia this etymology should strike a chord. And yet, as *The Economist* pointed out in a survey of the industry in 1991:

> "The curse of the tourist industry is that it peddles dreams: dreams of holidays where the sun always shines, the children are always occupied, and where every evening ends in the best sex you have ever had. For most of its modern life, this has been matched by a concomitant dreaminess on the part of its customers. When asked, most tourists tell whopping lies about what they want on holiday..." (Economist, 1991).

Most international tourists come from a handful of wealthy countries. Half from just five countries (the USA, Germany, the UK, Japan and France) and 80% from 20 countries. This is why many see tourism as the new 'imperialism', imposing alien cultures and ideals on sensitive and unmodernised peoples. The problem, however, is that discussions of the effects of tourism tend to degenerate into simplifications – culminating in the drawing-up of a checklist of 'positive' and 'negative' effects, much like the one on page 67. Although such tables may be useful in highlighting problem areas, they also do a disservice by reducing a complex issue to a set of plusses and minusses. Different destinations will be affected in different ways; these effects are likely to vary over time; and different groups living in a particular destination will feel the effects of tourism in different ways and to varying degrees. At no time or place can tourism (or any other influence) be categorised as uniformly 'good' or 'bad'. Tourism can take an Australian backpacker on US$5 a day to villages in the Northern hills of Thailand, an American tourist to luxury hotels in the city state of Singapore where a room can cost over US$200 a night, and a Malaysian Muslim to the southern Thai cities of Hat Yai and Songkhla on a long weekend.

Searching for culture

Southeast Asia is one of the richest cultural areas in the world, and many tourists are attracted to the region because of its exotic peoples: the hill 'tribes' of Northern Thailand, the Hindu Balinese, and the Dayaks of Borneo, for example. When cultural erosion is identified, the tendency is to blame this on tourists and tourism. Turner and Ash have written that tourists are the "suntanned destroyers of culture", while Bugnicourt argues that tourism:

"...encourages the imitation of foreigners and the downgrading of local inhabitants in relation to foreign tourists; it incites the pillage of art work and other historical artefacts; it leads to the degeneration of classical and popular dancing, the profanation and vulgarization of places of worship, and the perversion of religious ceremonies; it creates a sense of inferiority and a cultural demoralization which 'fans the flames of anti-development' through the acquisition of undesirable cultural traits" (1977).

The problem with views like this is that they assume that change is bad, and that indigenous cultures are unchanging. It makes local peoples victims of change, rather than masters of their own destinies. It also assumes that tourism is an external influence, when in fact it quickly becomes part of the local landscape. Cultural change is inevitable and on-going, and 'new' and 'traditional' are only judgements, not absolutes. Thus new cultural forms can quickly become key markers of tradition. Tourists searching for an 'authentic' experience are assuming that tradition is tangible, easily identifiable and unchanging. It is none of these.

Thai hill people wearing American baseball caps are assumed to have succumbed to Western culture. But such changes really say next to nothing about an individual's strength of identity. There are also problems with identifying cultural erosion, let alone linking it specifically with tourism, rather than with the wider processes of 'modernisation'. This is exemplified in the case of Bali where tourism is paraded by some as the saviour of Balinese culture, and by others as its destroyer. Michel Picard in his paper "'Cultural tourism' in Bali" (1992) writes:

"No sooner had culture become the emblematic image of Bali [in the 1920s] than foreign visitors and residents started fearing for its oncoming disappearance. ...the mere evocation of Bali suggested the imminent and dramatic fall from the 'Garden of Eden': sooner of later, the 'Last Paradise' was doomed to become a 'Paradise Lost'" (Picard, 1992: 77).

Yet the authorities on Bali are clearly at a loss as to how to balance their conflicting views:

"...the view of tourism held by the Balinese authorities is blatantly ambivalent, the driving force of a modernisation process which they welcome as ardently as they fear. Tourism in their eyes appears at once the most promising source of economic development and as the most subversive agent for the spread of foreign cultural influences in Bali" (Picard, 1992: 85).

Tourist art: fine art, degraded art

Tourist art, both material (for instance, sculpture) and non-material (like dances) is another issue where views sharply diverge. The mass of inferior 'airport' art on sale to tourists demonstrates, to some, the corrosive effects of tourism. It leads craftsmen and women to mass-produce second rate pieces for a market that appreciates neither their cultural or symbolic worth, nor their aesthetic value. Yet tourism can also give value to craft industries that would otherwise be undermined by cheap industrial goods. The geographer Michael Parnwell has argued that in the poor Northeast of Thailand, the craft tradition should be allied with tourism to create vibrant rural industries. The corrosive effects of tourism on arts and crafts also assumes that artists and craftsmen are unable to distinguish between fine pieces and pot-boilers. Many produce inferior pieces for the tourist market while continuing to produce for local demand, the former effectively subsidising the latter.

Some researchers have also shown how there is a tendency for culture to be 'invented' for tourists, and for this to then become part of 'tradition'. Michel Picard has shown in the case of Bali how dances developed for tourists are now paraded as paragons of national cultural heritage. The same is true of art, where the anthropologist Lewis Hill of the Centre for South-East Asian Studies at the University of Hull has demonstrated how objects made for the tourist market in one period are later enthusiastically embraced by the host community.

Environment and tourism

The environmental deterioration that is linked to tourism is due to a destination area exceeding its 'carrying capacity' as a result of overcrowding. But carrying capacity, though an attractive concept, is notoriously difficult to pin down in any exact manner. A second dilemma facing those trying to encourage greater environmental consciousness is the so-called 'tragedy of the commons', better described in terms of Chinese restaurants. When a group of people go to a Chinese restaurant with the intention of sharing the bill, each customer will tend to order a more expensive dish than he or she would normally do - on the logic that everyone will be doing the same, and the bill will be split. In tourism terms, it means that hotel owners will always build those few more bungalows or that extra wing, to maximise their profits, reassured in the knowledge that the environmental costs will be shared among all hotel

---

TOURISM DEVELOPMENT GUIDELINES

● Tourism should capitalise on local features (cultural and natural) so as to promote the use of local resources.

● Attention should be given to the type of tourist attracted. A mix of mass and individual will lead to greater local participation and better balance.

● Tourist development should be integrated with other sectors. Coordination between agencies is crucial.

● Facilities created should be made available to locals, at subsidised rates if necessary.

● Resources such as beaches and parks must remain in the public domain.

● Different tourists and tourist markets should be exploited so as to minimize seasonal variations in arrivals and employment.

● A tourist threshold should be identified and adhered to.

● Environmental impact assessments and other surveys must be carried out.

● Provision of services to tourists must be allied with improvements in facilities for locals.

● Development should be focused in areas where land use conflicts will be kept to a minimum.

● Supplies, where possible, should be sourced locally.

● Assistance and support should be given to small-scale, local entrepreneurs.

owners. So, despite most operators appreciating that over-development may 'kill the goose that lays the golden eggs', they do so anyway. Pattaya, the beach resort on Thailand's eastern seaboard, is a classic example. By the late 1980s, the sea off the resort's beaches was too polluted to swim safely. In short, tourism contains the seeds of its own destruction.

But many developing countries have few other development opportunities. Those in Southeast Asia are blessed with beautiful landscapes and exotic cultures, and tourism is a cheap development option. Other possibilities cost more to develop and take longer to take-off. It is also true that 'development', however it is achieved, has cultural and environmental implications. For many, tourism is the least environmentally corrosive of the various options open to poor countries struggling to achieve rapid economic growth.

The 'post-tourist' and the traveller

In the last few years a new tourist has appeared; or at least a new type of tourist has been identified – the 'post-tourist'. The post-tourist is part of the post-modern world. He or she is aware that nothing is authentic; that every tourist experience is new and different; that tourism begins at home, in front of the television. The whole globe is a stage on and in which the post-tourist can revel; the crass and crude is just as interesting and delightful as the traditional and authentic to the post-tourist. He – or she – is abundantly aware that he is a tourist, not a brave and inquisitive searcher for culture and truth; just another sunburnt, probably overweight, almost certainly ignorant foreigner spending money to have a holiday (not a travel 'experience') in a foreign country. Paradoxically this lack of apparent discernment is what is seen

to identify the post-tourist as truly discerning. Feifer, in 1985, stated that the post-tourist is well aware he is "not a time-traveller when he goes somewhere historic; not an instant noble savage when he stays on a tropical beach; not an invisible observer when he visits a native compound. Resolutely 'realistic', he cannot evade his condition of outsider". Of course, all this could be discounted as the meaningless meanderings of a group of academics with little better to do than play with words and ideas. But, there is something akin to the post-tourist of the academic world beginning to inhabit the real world of tourism. These people might have once been described as just cynics, marvelling in the shear ironies of life. They are tourists for whom tourism is a game to be taken lightly; people who recognize that they are just another 'guest', another consumer of the tourist experience. No-one, and nothing, special.

The 'traveller' in contrast to the post-tourist finds it hard even to think of him or herself as a tourist at all. This, of course, is hubris built upon the notion that the traveller is an 'independent' explorer somehow beyond the bounds of the industry. Anna Borzello in an article entitled 'The myth of the traveller' in the journal *Tourism in Focus* (No 19, 1994) writes that "Independent travellers cannot acknowledge – without shattering their self-image – that to many local people they are simply a good source of income. ...[not] inheritors of Livingstone, [but] bearers of urgently needed money". Although she does, in writing this, grossly underestimate the ability of travellers to see beyond their thongs and friendship bracelets, she does have a more pertinent point when she argues that it is important for travellers realistically to appraise their role as tourists, because: "Not only are independent travellers often frustrated by the gap between the way they see themselves and the way they are treated, but unless they acknowledge that they are part of the tourist industry they will not take responsibility for the damaging effects of their tourism."

Guide books and tourism

Guide books themselves have been identified by some analysts as being part of the problem. They are selective in two senses. First, they tend to selectively pick destination areas, towns and regions. This is understandable: one book cannot cover all the possibilities in a country. Then, and second, they selectively pick sights, hotels and restaurants within those places. Given that many travellers use guide books to map out their journey, this creates a situation where books determine the spatial pattern of tourist flows. As John McCarthy writes in *Are sweet dreams made of this? Tourism in Bali and Eastern Indonesia* (1994, IRIP: Victoria, Australia):

A Tourism Checklist	
Costs	**Benefits**
vulnerable to external developments - e.g. oil price rises, 1991 Gulf War	diversifies an economy and is usually immune to protectionism
	requires few technical and human resources and is a 'cheap' development option
	requires little infrastructure
erodes culture by debasing it; strong cultures overwhelm sensitive ones (often tribal)	gives value to cultures and helps in their preservation
leads to moral pollution with rising crime and prostitution	changing social norms are not due solely, or even mostly, to tourism
often concentrated in culturally and environmentally sensitive areas, so effects are accentuated	helps to develop marginal areas that would otherwise 'miss out' on development
lack of planning and management causes environmental problems	poor planning and management is not peculiar to tourism and can be rectified
foreigners tend to dominate; costs of involvement are high so local people fail to become involved and benefit	costs of involvement can be very low; tourism is not so scale-dependent as other industries
tourism increases local inequalities	
jobs are usually seasonal and low-skilled	
economic leakages mean revenue generated tends to accrue to foreign multi-nationals	leakage is less than with many other industries; local involvement generally greater and value added is significant
tourism is not sustainable; tourism ultimately destroys tourism because it destroys those attributes that attracted tourists in the first place	tourism is not monolithic; destination areas evolve and do not have to suffer decay

"Such is the power of guide books that, unless they are carefully written, one writer's point of view can determine the commercial success or failure of a hotel or restaurant for years after. Even when the enterprise changes, the loathing or love of a travel writer who passed through a village 3 years ago remains too potent a testimony" (page 93).

There are no easy answers to this. If guide books were more diverse; if travellers really were more independent; and if guide books were not so opinionated and subjective, then this would all help in spreading the tourism phenomenon. But none of these is likely: guide books exist to 'guide'; humans are by nature subjective; and the notion of the free spirit 'traveller' has always, in the most part, been a mirage brought on by a romantic collective sense of what tourism *should* be. One answer is for books to become more specialist, and certainly one identifiable trend is towards guide books covering sub-national regions – Eastern Indonesia, Northern Thailand, and Kuala Lumpur, for example. It seems that people are now more willing to spend an extended period of time exploring one area, rather than notching up a large number of 'must do's'. Although even such specialist books also tend to suffer from the dangers of selectivity noted above, those people who do spend a longer period of time in an area are in a position to be more selective themselves, and to rely more on their own experiences rather than those of a guide book writer who may have visited a town in a bad mood 3 years previously.

In the opening page to his *Illustrated guide to the Federated Malay States*, Cuthbert Woodville Harrison wrote:

"It has become nowadays so easy and so common a venture to cross the world that the simple circum-navigation of the globe 'merely for wantonness' is very rapidly ceasing to be in fashion. But as the rough places of the earth become smooth to the travellers, and they no longer fear 'that the gulfs will wash us down', there is growing amongst them a disposition to dwell awhile in those lands whose climate and inhabitants most differ from ours. The more completely such places are strange to us the more do they attract us, and the more isolated they have lived hitherto, the more do we feel called upon to visit them now."

Cuthbert Woodville Harrison's book was published in 1923.

Suggested reading and tourism pressure groups

In the UK, **Tourism Concern** aims to "promote greater understanding of the impacts of tourism on host communities and environments", "to raise awareness of the forms of tourism that respect the rights and interests of [local] people", and to "work for change in current tourism practice". Annual membership is £15.00 which includes subscription to their magazine *In Focus*. Tourism Concern, Froebel College, Roehampton Lane, London SW15 5PU, T (081) 878-9053.

The most up-to-date book examining tourism in Southeast Asia is: Hitchcock, Mike *et al.* (edits.) (1993) *Tourism in South-East Asia*, Routledge: London.

Another recent book, rather more populist in tone and specifically on Eastern Indonesia is McCarthy, John (1994) *Are sweet dreams made of this? Tourism in Bali and Eastern Indonesia*, Indonesia Resources and Information Programme (IRIP): Victoria, Australia.

SUGGESTED READING AND LISTENING

Magazines

Asiaweek (weekly). A light weight *Far Eastern Economic Review*; rather like a regional *Time* magazine in style.

The Far Eastern Economic Review (weekly). Authoritative Hong Kong-based regional magazine; their correspondents based in each country provide knowledgeable, in-depth analysis particularly on economics and politics, sometimes in rather a turgid style (although a change of editor has meant some lightening in style).

Books

Buruma, Ian (1989) *God's dust*, Jonathan Cape: London. Enjoyable journey through Burma, Thailand, Malaysia and Singapore along with the Philippines, Taiwan, South Korea and Japan; journalist Buruma questions how far culture in this region has survived the intrusion of the West.

Cambridge History of Southeast Asia (1992). Two volume edited study, long and expensive with contributions from most of the leading historians of the region. A thematic and regional approach is taken, not a country one, although the history is fairly conventional. Published by Cambridge University Press: Cambridge.

Caufield, C. (1985) *In the rainforest*, Heinemann: London. This readable and well-researched analysis of rainforest ecology and the pressures on tropical forests is part-based in the region.

Clad, James (1989) *Behind the myth: business, money and power in Southeast Asia*, Unwin Hyman: London. Clad, formerly a journalist with the *Far Eastern Economic Review*, distilled his experiences in this book; as it turned out, rather disappointingly – it is a hotch-potch of journalistic snippets.

Conrad, Joseph (1900) *Lord Jim*, Penguin: London. The tale of Jim, who abandons his ship and seeks refuge from his guilt in Malaya, earning the sobriquet Lord.

Conrad, Joseph (1915) *Victory: an island tale*, Penguin: London. Arguably Conrad's finest novel, based in the Malay Archipelago.

Conrad, Joseph (1920) *The rescue*, Penguin: London. Set in the Malay Archipelago in the 1860s; the hero, Captain Lingard, is forced to choose between his Southeast Asian friend and his countrymen.

Dingwall, Alastair (1994) *Traveller's literary companion to South-east Asia*, In Print: Brighton. Experts on Southeast Asian language and literature select extracts from novels and other books by western and regional writers. The extracts are annoyingly brief, but it gives a good overview of what is available.

Dumarçay, Jacques (1991) *The palaces of South-East Asia: architecture and customs*, OUP: Singapore. A broad summary of palace art and architecture in both mainland and island Southeast Asia.

Fenton, James (1988) *All the wrong places: adrift in the politics of Asia*, Penguin: London. British journalist James Fenton skilfully and entertainingly recounts his experiences in Vietnam, Cambodia, the Philippines and Korea.

Fraser-Lu, Sylvia (1988) *Handwoven textiles of South-East Asia*, OUP: Singapore. Well-illustrated, large-format book with informative text.

Higham, Charles (1989) *The archaeology of mainland Southeast Asia from 10,000 BC to the fall of Angkor*, Cambridge University Press: Cambridge. Best summary of changing views of the archaeology of the mainland.

Keyes, Charles F (1977) *The golden peninsula: culture and adaptation in mainland Southeast Asia*, Macmillan: New York. Academic, yet readable summary of the threads of continuity and change in Southeast Asia's culture.

King, Ben F and Dickinson, EC (1975) *A field guide to the birds of South-East Asia*, Collins: London. Best regional guide to the birds of the region.

Miettinen, Jukko O (1992) *Classical dance and theatre in South-East Asia*, OUP, Singapore. Expensive, but accessible survey of dance and theatre, mostly focusing on Indonesia, Thailand and Burma.

Osborne, Milton (1979) *Southeast Asia: an introductory history*, Allen & Unwin: Sydney. Good introductory history, clearly written, published in a portable paperback edition.

Rawson, Philip (1967) *The art of Southeast Asia*, Thames & Hudson: London. Portable general art history of Cambodia, Vietnam, Thailand, Laos, Burma, Java and Bali; by necessity, rather superficial.

Reid, Anthony (1988) *Southeast Asia in the age of commerce 1450-1680: the lands below the winds*, Yale University Press: New Haven. Perhaps the best history of everyday life in Southeast Asia, looking at such themes as physical well-being, material culture and social organization.

Reid, Anthony (1993) *Southeast Asia in the age of commerce 1450-1680: expansion and crisis*, Yale University Press: New Haven. Volume 2 in this excellent history of the region.

Rigg, Jonathan (1991) *Southeast Asia: a region in transition*, Unwin Hyman: London. A thematic geography of the ASEAN region, providing an insight into some of the major issues affecting the region today.

SarDesai, DR (1989) *Southeast Asia: past and present*, Macmillan: London. Skilful but at times frustratingly thin history of the region from the 1st century to the withdrawal of US forces from Vietnam.

Savage, Victor R (1984) *Western impressions of nature and landscape in Southeast Asia*, Singapore University Press: Singapore. Based on a geography PhD thesis, the book is a mine of quotations and observations from Western travellers.

Sesser, Stan (1993) *The lands of charm and cruelty: travels in Southeast Asia*, Picador: Basingstoke. A series of collected narratives first published in the *New Yorker* including essays on Singapore, Laos, Cambodia, Burma and Borneo. Finely observed and thoughtful, the book is an excellent travel companion.

Steinberg, DJ *et al* (1987) *In search of Southeast Asia: a modern history*, University of Hawaii Press: Honolulu. The best standard history of the region; it skilfully examines and assesses general processes of change and their impacts from the arrival of the Europeans in the region.

Wallace, Alfred Russel (1869) *The Malay Archipelago: the land of the orang-utan and the bird of paradise; a narrative of travel with studies of man and nature*, Macmillan: London. A classic of natural history writing, recounting Wallace's 8 years in the archipelago and now reprinted.

Waterson, Roxana (1990) *The living house: an anthropology of architecture in South-East Asia*, OUP: Singapore. Illustrated, academic book on Southeast Asian architecture, fascinating material for those interested in such things.

Young, Gavin (1991) *In search of Conrad*, Hutchinson: London. This well-known travel writer retraces the steps of Conrad; part travel-book, part fantasy, it is worth reading but not up to the standard of his other books.

Radio

The BBC World Service's *Dateline East Asia* provides probably the best news and views on Asia. Also with a strong Asia focus are the broadcasts of the ABC (Australian Broadcasting Corporation).

VIETNAM

CONTENTS

MAPS

INTRODUCTION

The Socialist Republic of Vietnam (SRV) was born from the ashes of the Vietnam War on 2 July 1976 when former North and South Vietnam were reunified. Hanoi was proclaimed as the capital of the new country. But few Vietnamese would have guessed that their emergent country would be cast by the US in the mould of a pariah state for almost 18 years. First President George Bush, and then his successor Bill Clinton, eased the US trade embargo bit by bit in a dance of appeasement and procrastination, as they tried to comfort American business clamouring for a slice of the Vietnamese pie, while also trying to stay on the right side of the vociferous lobby in the US demanding more action on the MIA issue. Appropriately, the embargo, which was first imposed on the former North in May 1964, and then nationwide in 1975, was finally lifted a few days before the celebrations of Tet, Vietnamese New Year, on 4 February 1994.

On the morning of the 30 April 1975, just before 1100, a T-54 tank crashed through the gates of the Presidential Palace in Saigon, symbolically marking the end of the Vietnam War. Twenty years later, the same tank – number 843 – became a symbol of the past as parades and celebrations, and a good deal of soul searching, marked the anniversary of the end of the War. To many Vietnamese, in retrospect, 1975 was more a beginning than an end: it was the beginning of a collective struggle to come to terms with the War, to build a nation, to reinvigorate the economy, and to excise the ghosts of the past. Two decades after the armies of the South laid down their arms and the last US servicemen and officials frantically fled by helicopter to carriers waiting in the South China Sea, the Vietnamese government is still trying, as they put it, to get people to recognize that 'Vietnam is a country, not a war'. A further 20 years from now, it may seem that only in 1995 did the War truly end. It was not until 1986 that the economic reforms enshrined in *doi moi* were formally adopted; not until Sep 1989 that Vietnamese forces withdrew from the tragedy of Cambodia; not until Feb 1994 that the US finally lifted its trade embargo of Vietnam; and not until Jul 1995 that Vietnam joined the Association of Southeast Asian Nations (ASEAN). In one of those twists of fate, which the concerns of the present tend to obscure, in joining ASEAN Vietnam became part of an organization that was initially established to counteract the Communist threat of Vietnam itself.

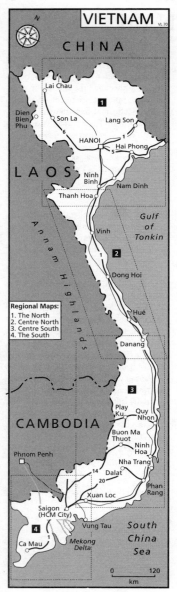

VIETNAM VL.20

CHINA

Lai Chau

Dien Bien Phu

Son La

Lang Son

HANOI

6

Hai Phong

5

Ninh Binh

Nam Dinh

Thanh Hoa

LAOS

Gulf of Tonkin

Vinh

1

Dong Hoi

Huế

Danang

Play Ku

Quy Nhon

Buon Ma Thuot

Ninh Hoa

CAMBODIA

Nha Trang

Phnom Penh

Dalat

14

20

Phan Rang

Xuan Loc

Saigon (HCM City)

Vung Tau

Ca Mau

Mekong Delta

South China Sea

0　120
km

Regional Maps:
1. The North
2. Centre North
3. Centre South
4. The South

Vietnam is almost schizophrenic in complexion: it has adroitly reformed its economy and has some of the most liberal foreign investment laws in Asia; yet the Communist Party maintains an almost Stalinist grip on political dissent. It consists of two halves which, for 20 years developed along diverging paths and appear to be diverging once more as the reforms bite. Northerners and Southerners often have little time for one another and have been characterized, respectively as temperamentally 'temperate' and 'tropical' – reflecting the environments of the N and S. In short, Vietnam is almost two countries in one.

Isolated from the Western world both economically and diplomatically since 1975, and so far as the N is concerned since 1954, Vietnam has an ambience and character not matched by any of the more Westernized nations of Southeast Asia. Many visitors find it difficult to disassociate the country from the Vietnam War – a conflict which managed to wreak such destruction in this corner of Asia, while traumatizing not one but two nations. But Vietnam has far more to offer than this sequence of recent historical events: there are the impressive temples of the ancient Kingdom of Champa, verdant rice paddys (during the wet season), palm fringed tropical beaches, and the former imperial palace at Hué. For those with revolutionary predilections, there are agricultural co-operatives and communes, innovative drug rehabilitation centres, and ideologically sound carpet factories – although such is the pace of economic reform that these may not last much longer. Vietnam is changing almost before one's eyes. Although the war may be ever-so-slowly fading from the memory (and from the landscape) there are, as journalist Lincoln Kaye writes "places where the fixed enormity of past horrors inexorably glares through the banal ephemera of the present."

But to talk of Vietnam as a single, unified country disguises the deep differences which divide the N from the S, and the cities from the countryside. The brash, bright, vital and economically energetic city of Saigon could not be further removed from the grave, elegant and romantically decrepit city of Hanoi over 1,500 km to the N. Between the two stretches a succession of cities remembered largely for their role in a war which in Vietnamese history occupies only a small slice of a centuries-long battle against outsiders: Nha Trang, Danang, Hué, Khe Sanh, Vinh and Dong Hoi.

The common view of Vietnam as one of the last bastions of Communism is already obsolete. The country is undergoing a fundamental reform of its economic system – known locally as *doi moi* or 'renovation'. In the S, the effects of these changes are already very much in evidence. New private businesses spring up almost overnight, foreign investors are moving in, and the bureaucracy is waking from its 15-year slumber. But although economic reform and market economics may be at the top of the government's agenda, political reform – in other words, *glasnost* to go with the *perestroika* – is actively discouraged. Journalists, novelists and academics who dare to question the supremacy of the Party are quickly silenced. It is uncertain how long the government will be able to maintain this balancing act.

Despite the visible signs of wealth in Saigon, or Ho Chi Minh City as it is officially known (see page 245), Vietnam is still among the poorest countries in the world. The government may be able to mobilize the world's fifth largest army, but producing consumer goods for its long-suffering population seems to be beyond its capabilities. *Doi moi* is reaping results, but it is still not clear whether this will create more than just small pockets of wealth among an otherwise destitute and increasingly dissatisfied population. Average incomes are still only US$230/year, nearly half of children aged less than five are malnourished, and there are a mere four television sets/100 people.

In economic terms, there are three Vietnams. There is Saigon, where most things are available – for a price: fax facilities, photocopying, hamburgers, imported beers and soft drinks. Then Hanoi, where some things are available. And then there is the rest of the country, where it is difficult to change money, buy anything beyond life's basic necessities and where English is rarely spoken.

Land and life

The regions of Vietnam

The name Vietnam is derived from that adopted in 1802 by Emperor Gia Long: Nam Viet. This means, literally, the Viet (the largest ethnic group) of the S (Nam), and substituted for the country's previous name, Annam. The country is 'S' shaped, covers a land area of 329,600 sq km and has a coastline of 3,000 km. The most important economic zones, containing the main concentrations of population, are focused on two large deltaic areas. In the N, there are the ancient rice fields and settlements of the Red River, and in the S, the fertile alluvial plain of the Mekong. In between, the country narrows to less than 50 km wide, with only a thin ribbon of fertile lowland suited to intensive agriculture. Much of the interior, away from the coastal belt and the deltas, is mountainous. Here minority hilltribes (Montagnards), along with some lowland Vietnamese resettled in so-called New Economic Zones since 1975, eke out a living on thin and unproductive soils. The rugged terrain means that only a quarter of the land is actually cultivated. Of the remainder, somewhere between about 20% and 25% is forested and some of this is heavily degraded.

VIETNAM - PROVINCES
VL 73

Provinces:
1. Hanoi
2. Hà Tay
3. Hai Phong
4. Thái Bình
5. Nam Ha
6. Ninh Bình
7. TP Ho Chi Minh
8. Ba Ria-Vung Tau
9. Dong Tháp
10. Vinh Long
11. Tien Giang

Geography

Vietnam consists of five major geographical zones. In the far N are the **northern highlands** which ring the Red River Delta and form a natural barrier with the People's Republic of China. The rugged mountains on the W border of this region – the Hoang Lien Son – exceed 3,000m in places. The tributaries of the Red River have cut deep, steep-sided gorges through the Hoang Lien Son, which are navigable by small boats and are important arteries of communication. The E portion of this region, bordering the Gulf of Tonkin, is far less imposing; the mountain peaks of the W have diminished into foothills, allowing easy access to China. It was across these hills that the Chinese mounted their successive invasions of Vietnam, the last of which occurred as recently as 1979.

The second region lies in the embrace of the hills of the N. This, the **Red River Delta**, can legitimately claim to be the cultural and historical heart of the Viet nation. Hanoi lies at its core and it was here that the first truly independent Vietnamese polity was established in 939 AD by Ngo Quyen. The delta covers almost 15,000 sq km and extends 240 km inland from the coast. Rice has been grown on the alluvial soils of the Red River for thousands of years. Yet despite the intricate web of canals, dykes and embankments, the Vietnamese have never been able to completely tame the river, and the delta is the victim of frequent and sometimes devastating floods. The area is very low-lying, rarely more than 3m above sea level, and often less than 1m. The high water mark is nearly 8m above the level of the land in some places. During the monsoon season, the tributaries of the Red River quickly become torrents rushing through the narrow gorges of the Hoang Lien Son, before emptying into the main channel which then bursts its banks. Although the region supports one of the highest agricultural population densities in the world, the inhabitants have frequently had to endure famines – most recently in 1989.

South of the Red River Delta region, lie the central lowlands and the mountains of the Annamite Chain. The **Annam Highlands**, now known as the **Truong Son Mountain Range**, form an important cultural divide between the Indianized nations of the W and the Sinicized cultures of the E. Its northern rugged extremity is in Thanh Hoa Province. From here the Truong Son stretches over 1,200 km S, to peter out 80 km N of Saigon. The highest peak is Ngoc Linh Mountain in Kon Tum Province at 2,598m. The Central Highlands form an upland plateau on which the hill resorts of **Buon Ma Thuot** and Dalat are situated. On the plateau, plantation agriculture and hill farms are interspersed with stands of bamboo and tropical forests. Still rich in wildlife, the plateau was a popular hunting ground during the colonial period.

To the E, the Annamite Chain falls off steeply, leaving only a narrow and fragmented band of lowland suitable for settlement – the **central coastal strip**. In places the mountains advance all the way to the coast, plunging into the sea as dramatic rockfaces and making N-S communication difficult. At no point does the region extend more than 64 km inland, and in total it covers only 6,750 sq km. The soils are often rocky or saline, and irrigation is seldom possible. Nonetheless, the inhabitants have a history of sophisticated rice culture and it was here that the Champa Kingdom was established in the early centuries of the Christian era. These coastal lowlands have also formed a conduit along which people have historically moved. Even today, the main road and rail routes between the N and S cut through the coastal lowlands.

Finally, there is the **Mekong Delta**. Unlike the Red River Delta this region

WILD WATER: MANAGING NATURE

People living in the N and S of Vietnam have been building sea and river defences for over 1,000 years. In total, there are an estimated 5,000 km of river dykes and 2,000 km of sea dykes protecting some of the country's richest rice lands from salt water incursion and flooding. Today, many of these ancient defences are at risk of imminent collapse. They have been built higher and higher in an effort to keep up with the pace of river sedimentation, but now, it seems, the limits of the possible have been reached. In Hanoi the course of the Red River is, in some places, several metres above ground level.

Traditionally, farmers would allot 20 free days of labour a year to the maintenance of dykes in an act of communal solidarity against the elements. Now, *doi moi* – economic reform – has led to the gradual disintegration of the group work ethic. People may be willing to donate money or rice, but their time is too precious. The Asian Development Bank (ADB) is spearheading an effort to modernize dyke construction and maintenance, replacing stone and bamboo structures with concrete and steel. But some people fear that this technological approach to dyke construction and management will only store up an even greater problem for a few years time, while also substantially increasing costs. The technology is imported, the skills are foreign and the methods are not geared to Vietnam's economic situation.

is not so prone to flooding, and consequently rice production is more stable. The reason why flooding is less severe lies in the regulating effect of the Great Lake of Cambodia, the Tonlé Sap. During the rainy season, when the water flowing into the Mekong becomes too great for even this mighty river to absorb, rather than overflowing its banks, the water backs-up into the Tonlé Sap, which quadruples in area. The Mekong Delta covers 67,000 sq km and is drained by five branches of the Mekong, which divides as it flows towards the sea. The vast delta is one of the great rice bowls of Asia producing nearly half of the country's rice, and over the years has been cut into a patchwork by the canals that have been dug to expand irrigation and rice cultivation. Largely forested until the late 19th century, the French supported the settlement of the area by Vietnamese peasants, recognizing that it could become enormously productive. The deposition of silt by the rivers that cut through the delta, means that the shoreline is continually advancing – by

up to 80m each year in some places. To the N of the delta lies **Saigon** or **Ho Chi Minh City**.

The French sub-divided Vietnam into three regions, administering each separately: *Tonkin* or **Bac Ky** (the N region), *Annam* or **Trung Ky** (the central region) and *Cochin China* or **Nam Ky** (the S region). Although these administrative divisions have been abolished, the Vietnamese still recognize their country as consisting of three regions, distinct in terms of geography, history and culture. Their new names are **Bac Bo** (N), **Trung Bo** (centre) and **Nam Bo** (S).

Climate

Vietnam stretches over 1,800 km from N to S and the weather patterns in the two principal cities, Hanoi in the N and Saigon in the S, are very different (for best time to visit, see page 283. Average temperatures tend to rise the further S one ventures, while the seasonal variation in temperature decreases. The exceptions to this general rule of thumb are in the interior highland areas where the altitude means it is considerably colder.

TEMPERATURE AND RAINFALL: SELECTED TOWNS			
	Annual Rainfall (mm)	Mean Annual Temp (°C)	Mean Annual Variation (°C)
Hanoi	1,680	23.4	12.4
Hué	3,250	25.1	9.0
Danang	2,130	25.4	7.8
Nha Trang	1,562	26.4	4.2
Dalat	1,600	19.1	3.4
Saigon	1,980	26.9	3.1
Sapa	2,750	13.0	10.0

North Vietnam The seasons in the N are similar to those of S China. The winter stretches from Nov to Apr, with temperatures averaging 16° C, and little rainfall. The summer begins in May and lasts until Oct. During these months it can be very hot indeed, with an average temperature of 30° C, along with heavy rainfall and the occasional violent typhoon.

Central Vietnam Central Vietnam experiences a transitional climate, half way between that in the S and in the N. Hué has a reputation for particularly poor weather: it is often overcast, and an umbrella is needed whatever the month – even during the short 'dry' season between Feb and Apr. The annual rainfall in Hué is 3,250 mm (see page 194 for best time to visit).

South Vietnam Temperatures in the S are fairly constant through the year (25° C-30° C) and the seasons are determined by the rains. The dry season runs from Nov to Apr (when there is virtually no rain whatsoever) and the wet season, from May to Oct. The hottest period is during Mar and Apr, before the rains have broken. Typhoons are quite common in coastal areas between Jul and Nov.

Highland Areas In the hill resorts of Dalat (1,500m), Buon Ma Thuot and Sapa nights are cool throughout the year, and in the 'winter' months between Oct to Mar it can be distinctly chilly with temperatures falling to 4° C. Even in the hottest months of Mar and Apr the temperature rarely exceeds 26° C.

Flora and fauna

The Vietnam War not only killed many people, but also decimated the country's flora and fauna. Communist soldiers killed game for food, while the American bombing campaign and the extensive use of defoliants – over 72 million litres – destroyed huge swathes of forest. Such was the degree of destruction that studies talk of 'ecocide'. With over 20 million bomb craters and the loss of 2.2 million ha of forest, it is easy to see why. In 1943, 44% of the country was forested. In 1990 the figure was about 19%. Although there can be no doubt that the Vietnam War did massive damage to the country, it also, in a strange sense, protected Vietnam's environment. For 50 years, people were usually too concerned with fighting to pollute and ravage the environment, and the more remote and wild areas of the country were simply out of bounds to all but the foolhardy or those in uniforms. But the government has been in no position to direct funds towards maintaining the integrity of the country's national parks and little is known about the status of many rarer animals and birds.

In the early 1990s a small herd of Javan rhinoceros, the rarest large mammal in the world, was discovered in Vietnam. This was followed by the astonishing discovery of two completely new species of mammal. In 1992 British scientist Dr John MacKinnon discovered the skeleton of an animal now known as the **Vu Quang ox** (*Pseudoryx nghetinhensis*) but known to locals as *sao la*. The Vu Quang ox was the first new large mammal species to be found in 50 years; scientists were amazed that a large mammal could exist on this crowded planet without their knowledge. In Jun

1994 the first live specimen (a young calf) was captured and shortly afterwards a second sao la was caught and taken to the Forestry Institute in Hanoi. Sadly, both died in captivity but in early 1995 a third creature was brought in alive. The animals look anything but ox-like, and have the appearance, grace and manner of a small deer. The government responded to the discovery by extending the Vu Quang Nature Reserve and banning hunting of sao la. Local hilltribes, who have long regarded sao la as a tasty and not uncommon beast, have therefore lost a valued source of food and no longer have a vested interest in sao la's survival. Sao la must rue the day they were 'discovered'. In 1993 a new species of deer which has been named the giant muntjac was also found in the Vu Quang Nature Reserve. The scientists have yet to see the beast alive but villagers prize its meat and are reported to trap it in quite large numbers.

Large rare mammals are confined to isolated pockets where the government does its best to protect them from hunters. On Cat Ba Island, the national park is home to the world's last wild troops of white-headed langur. In North Vietnam tigers are hunted to extinction and further S territorial battles rage between elephants and farmers. Rampaging elephants sometimes cause loss of life and are in turn decimated by enraged villagers.

Given the difficulty of getting to Vietnam's more remote areas, the country is hardly a haven for amateur naturalists. Professional photographers and naturalists have been escorted to the country's wild areas, but this is not an option for the average visitor. Getting there requires time and contacts. A wander around the markets of Vietnam reveals the variety and number of animals that end up in the cooking pot: deer, bear, snakes, monkeys, turtles etc. The Chinese penchant for exotic foods (such gastronomic wonders as tigers' testicles and bear's foot) has also become a predilection of the Vietnamese, and most animals are fair game.

The greening of Vietnam

However, the picture should not be entirely shaded in sombre tones. In particular, there is some evidence that the

---

FARMERS VERSUS FORESTS

In an attempt to conserve what is left of Vietnam's forest cover the government is encouraging swidden or shifting cultivators (see page 36) to practise sedentary (settled) farming. Since 1968 a total of 1.9 million ethnic minority people have been resettled as part of this expensive and culturally disruptive programme. Commentators seem undecided whether this is a fair response to the problem of disappearing forest land or just another reprehensible expression of ethnic rivalry and Kinh domination. The UN Food and Agriculture Organisation would appear to support the government; it has said that pressure on the highlands is so intense that shifting cultivation is no longer a sustainable form of food production. Fallow periods, which allow the soil to recover and forest to regrow, are too short. Consequently the soil is degraded and eroded and the forests do not get the opportunity to grow back. In Lao Cai province, for example, forest cover has fallen from 240,000 ha 15 years ago to 123,000 ha today; three quarters of this loss is attributed to hill farmers. In an attempt to reduce forest cover by logging, the government, in early 1992, introduced a ban on the export of raw logs and sawn timber. Unfortunately, the vested interests of local officials make it likely that the timber export ban will be less rigidly enforced than measures against minority farmers.

birth, or arguably rebirth, of environmentalism in other countries in Southeast Asia, most notably Thailand, is also emerging in Vietnam.

Together with overseas conservation agencies such as WWF, Vietnamese scientists have, in recent years, been enumerating and protecting their fauna and flora. The establishment of nature reserves began in 1962 with the gazetting of the Cuc Phuong National Park. Today there are a total of 87 reserves covering 3.3% of Vietnam's land area. However, some of them are too small to sustain sufficiently large breeding populations of endangered species and many parks are quite heavily populated. For instance 80,000 people live, farm and hunt within the 22,000 ha Bach Ma National Park.

In 1993 concerned residents in Saigon established the Green Club – among the first flowerings of an environmental movement in the country. The motivation behind the Green Club lay in the failure to stop a Taiwanese company from building a golf course in the protected Tu Duc National Park, 12 km from the city. In Hanoi, much of the effort has been focused on the protection of the city's architectural heritage (see page 146), but nonetheless the motivation is the same – the 'environmental' fear of uncontrolled economic growth. This led to the passage of Vietnam's first environmental bill through parliament in Dec 1993 – the Law on Environmental Protection. The country's environmental 'crisis' has also spilled out onto the international arena. Plans to build a dam on the Black River in Son La province to the NW of Hanoi, for example, has provoked considerable controversy. The dam is intended to provide power for Vietnam's industrialization, but it will also displace an estimated 130,000 Thai Den – the Black Thai, one of Vietnam's minorities – and flood large areas of their ancestral lands. The Tai Solidarity International, a group comprising mainly foreign resident ethnic Tai, is campaigning against the dam, claiming that it will be an environmental disaster and a human and cultural tragedy.

Birds have, in general, suffered rather less than mammals from overhunting and the effects of the war. There have been some casualties however: the eastern sarus crane of the Mekong Delta – a symbol of fidelity, longevity and good luck – disappeared entirely during the war. However, in 1985 a farmer reported seeing a single bird, and by 1990 there were over 500 pairs breeding on the now pacified former battlefields. A sarus crane reserve has been established in Dong Thap Province. Among the more unusual birds are the snake bird (named after its habit of swimming with its body submerged and only its snake-like neck and head above the surface), the argus pheasant, which the Japanese believe to be the mythical phoenix, the little bastard quail of which the male hatches and rears the young, three species of vulture, the osprey (sea eagle), and two species of hornbill (the pied and great Indian). Vietnam also has colonies of the endangered white-winged wood duck, one of the symbols of the world conservation movement. The Vietnamese, or Vo Quy, pheasant which was thought to be extinct was recently rediscovered in the wild and two males are now held in captivity in Hanoi zoo.

An animal inventory

Among the **larger mammals**, there are small numbers of tiger, leopard, clouded leopard, Indian elephant, Malayan bear, Himalayan black bear, sambar deer, gibbon and gaur (wild buffalo). These are rarely seen, except in zoos. The larger reptiles include two species of crocodile, the estuarine (*Crocodilus porosus*) and Siamese (*C. siamensis*). The former grows to a length of 5m and has been reported to have killed and eaten humans. Among the larger snakes are the reticulated python (*Python reticulatus*) and the smaller Indian python (*Python molurus*), both non-venomous constrictors. Venomous snakes include two species of cobra (the king cobra and common cobra), two species of krait, and six species of pit viper.

History

Prehistory

The earliest record of humans in Vietnam is from an archaeological site on Do Mountain, in the northern Thanh Hoa Province. The remains discovered here have been dated to the Lower Palaeolithic (early Stone Age). So far, all early human remains have been unearthed in North Vietnam, invariably in association with limestone cliff dwellings. Unusually, tools are made of basalt rather than flint, the more common material found at similar sites in other parts of the world.

Archaeological excavations have shown that between 5,000 and 3,000 BC, two important Mesolithic cultures occupied North Vietnam: these are referred to as the Hoa Binh and Bac Son cultures after the principal excavation sites in Tonkin. Refined stone implements and distinctive hand axes with polished edges (known as Bacsonian axes) are characteristic of the two cultures. These early inhabitants of Vietnam were probably small and dark-skinned, probably of Melanesian or Austronesian stock.

There are 2,000 years of recorded Vietnamese history and another 2,000 years of legend. The Vietnamese people trace their origins back to 15 tribal groups known as the **Lac Viet** who settled in what is now North Vietnam at the beginning of the Christian era. Here they established an agrarian kingdom known as Van-lang which seems to have vanished during the 3rd century BC.

A problem with early **French archaeological studies** in Vietnam was that most of the scholars were either Sinolo-

gists or Indologists. In consequence, they looked to Vietnam as a receptacle of Chinese or Indian cultural influences, and spent little time uncovering those aspects of culture, art and life that were indigenous in origin and inspiration. The French archaeologist Bezacier for example, expressed the generally held view that 'Vietnamese' history only began in the 7th century AD. Such sites as Hoa Binh, Dong Son and Oc-eo, which predate the 7th century, were regarded as essentially Chinese or 'Indonesian', their only 'Vietnameseness' being their geographical location. This perspective was more often than not based on faulty and slapdash scholarship, and reflected the prevailing view that Southeast Asian art was basically derivative.

Pre-colonial history

The beginning of Vietnamese recorded history coincides with the start of **Chinese cultural hegemony** over the N, in the 2nd century BC. The Chinese dominated Vietnam for over 1,000 years until the 10th century AD, and the cultural legacy is still very much in evidence, making Vietnam distinctive in Southeast Asia. Even after the 10th century, and despite breaking away from Chinese political domination, Vietnam was still overshadowed and greatly influenced by its illustrious neighbour to the N. Nonetheless, the fact that Vietnam could shrug off 1,000 years of Chinese subjugation and emerge with a distinct cultural heritage and language says a lot for Vietnam's strength of national identity. Indeed, it might be argued, as William Duiker does, that the Vietnamese nation "has been formed in the crucible of its historic resistance to Chinese conquest and assimilation".

The **Ly Dynasty** (1010-1225) was the first independent Vietnamese dynasty. Its capital, Thang Long, was at the site of present-day Hanoi and the dynasty based its system of government and social relations closely upon the Chinese

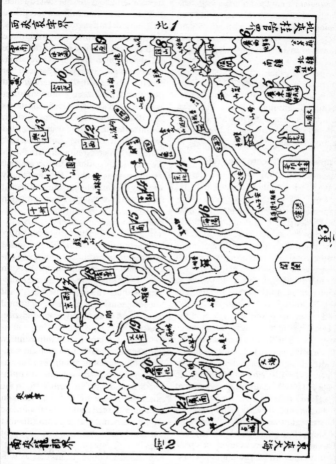

Map of Vietnam under the Lê Dynasty, taken from a manuscript dated 1490 and entitled *Geography of Hong Duc*. The orientation given is North (1), South (2), East (3), West (4); one can distinguish in the N, Kouang-tong (5), Kouang-si (6) and in the S, Champa (7). Between these two limits Vietnamese provinces are shown: from N to S and E to W: Lang Son (8), Thái Nguyên (9), Tuyên Quang (10), Kinh Bác (11), Son Tây (12), Hung Hoá (13), Trung Dô (14), Son Nam (15), Hai Durong (16), Tây Kinh (17), Thanh Hoá (18), Nghè An (19), Thuân Hoá (20), Quáng Nam (21).

Confucianist model (see page 119). The Vietnamese owe a considerable debt to the Chinese (government, philosophy and arts) but they have always been determined to maintain their independence. Vietnamese Confucianist scholars were unsparing in their criticism of Chinese imperialism. Continuous Chinese invasions, all ultimately futile, served to cement an enmity between the two countries, which is still in evidence today – despite their having normalized diplomatic relations in Oct 1991.

Funan (1st-6th centuries AD)

According to Chinese sources, Funan was a Hindu kingdom founded in the 1st century AD with its capital, Vyadhapura, close to the Mekong River near the border with Cambodia. A local legend records that Kaundinya, a great Indian Brahmin, acting on a dream, sailed to the coast of Vietnam carrying with him a bow and arrow. When he arrived, Kaundinya shot the arrow and where it landed he established the capital of Funan. Following this act, Kaundinya married the princess Soma, daughter of the local King of the Nagas (giant water serpents). The legend symbolizes the union between Indian and local cultural traditions – the *naga* representing indigenous fertility rites and customs (see page 494), and the arrow, the potency of the Hindu religion.

Funan built its wealth and power on its **strategic location** on the sea route between China and the islands to the S. The large port city of **Oc-eo** (see page 276) offered a safe harbour for merchant vessels and the revenues generated enabled the kings of the empire to expand rice cultivation, dominate a host of surrounding vassal states as far away as the Malay coast and S Burma, and build a series of impressive temples, cities and irrigation works. Although the Chinese chronicler K'ang T'ai records that the Funanese were barbarians – "ugly, black, and frizzy-haired" – it is clear from Chi-

nese court annals that they were artistically and technologically accomplished. It is recorded for example that one Chinese emperor was so impressed by the skill of some visiting musicians in 263 AD that he ordered the establishment of an institute of Funanese music.

Funan went into decline during the 5th century AD when improving maritime technology made Oc-eo redundant as a haven for sailing vessels. No longer did merchants hug the coastline; ships were now large enough, and navigation skills sophisticated enough, to make the journey from S China to the Malacca Strait without landfall. By the mid-6th century, Funan, having suffered from a drawn out leadership crisis, was severely weakened. Neighbouring competing powers took advantage of this crisis, absorbing previously Funan-controlled lands. Irrigation works fell into disrepair as state control weakened, and peasants left the fields to seek more productive lands elsewhere. Funan, having lost both the economic wealth and the religious legitimacy on which its power had been based, was ultimately conquered by the Cham.

What is interesting about Funan is the degree to which it provided a model for future states in Southeast Asia. Funan's wealth was built on its links with the sea, and with its ability to exploit maritime trade. The later rulers of Champa, Langkasuka (Malaya), Srivijaya (Sumatra), and Malacca (Malaya) repeated this formula.

Champa (2nd century AD – 1720)

In South Vietnam, where the dynastic lords achieved hegemony only in the 18th century, the kingdom of Champa – or Lin-yi as the Chinese called it – was the most significant power. The kingdom evolved in the 2nd century AD and was focused on the narrow ribbon of lowland that runs N-S down the Annamite coast, with its various capitals near the present-day city of Danang. Chinese sources record that in 192 AD a local official, Kiu-lien, rejected Chinese authority and established an independent kingdom. From then on, Champa's history was one of conflict with its neighbour: when Imperial China was powerful, Champa was subservient and sent ambassadors and tributes in homage to the Chinese court; when it was weak, the rulers of Champa extended their own influence and ignored the Chinese.

Like Funan, Champa built its power on its position on the **maritime trading route** through Southeast Asia. During the 4th century, as Champa expanded into previously Funan-controlled lands, they came under the influence of the Indian cultural traditions of the Funanese. These were enthusiastically embraced by Champa's rulers who tacked the suffix '-varman' onto their names (eg Bhadravarman) and adopted the Hindu-Buddhist cosmology. Though a powerful trading kingdom, Champa was geographically poorly endowed. The coastal strip between the Annamite highlands to the W, and the sea to the E, is narrow and the potential for extensive rice cultivation limited. This may explain why the Champa Empire was never more than a moderate power: it was unable to produce the agricultural surplus necessary to support an extensive court and army, and therefore could not compete with either the Khmers to the S nor with the Viets to the N. But the Cham were able to carve out a niche for themselves between the two, and to many art historians, their art and architecture represent the finest that Vietnam has ever produced (see page 212). Remains litter the central Vietnamese coast from Quang Tri in the N, to Ham Tan 800 km to the S.

For over 1,000 years the Cham resisted the Chinese and the Vietnamese. But by the time Marco Polo wrote of the Cham, their power and prestige were much reduced: "The people are idolators

and pay a yearly tribute to the Great Kaan which consists of elephants and nothing but elephants. ... In the year of Christ 1285... the King had, between sons and daughters, 326 children. There are a very great number of elephants in that country, and they have lignaloes (eagle wood) in great abundance. They have also extensive forests of the wood called Bonús, which is jet black, of which chessmen and pencases are made. But there is nought more to tell, so let us proceed." After 1285, when invading Mongol hoardes were repelled by the valiant Viets, Champa and Dai Viet enjoyed an uneasy peace maintained by the liberal flow of royal princesses South across the Col des Nuages (Hai Van Pass) in exchange for territory. During the peaceful reign of Che A-nan a Franciscan priest, Odoric of Pordenone, reported of Champa "'tis a very fine country, having a great store of victuals and of all good things". Of particular interest, he refers to the practice of suti, writing "When a man dies in this country, they burn his wife with him, for they say that she should live with him in the other world also". Clearly, some of the ancient Indian traditions continued.

Champa saw a late flowering under King Binasuos who led numerous successful campaigns against the Viet, culminating in the sack of Hanoi in 1371. Subsequently, the treachery of a low-ranking officer led to Binasuos' death in 1390 and the military eclipse of the Cham by the Vietnamese. The demographic and economic superiority of the Viet coupled with their gradual drift S contributed most to the waning of the Cham Kingdom, but finally, in 1471 the Cham suffered a terrible defeat at the hands of the Vietnamese. 60,000 of their soldiers were killed and another 36,000 captured and carried into captivity, including the King and 50 members of the royal family. The kingdom shrank to a small territory in the vicinity of Nha Trang which survived until 1720 when surviving members of the royal family and many subjects fled to Cambodia to escape from the advancing Vietnamese.

Le Dynasty and the emergence of Vietnam

During its struggle with the Cham, nascent Dai Viet had to contend with the weight of Ming Chinese oppression from the N, often in concert with their Cham allies. Despite 1,000 years of Chinese domination and centuries of internal dynastic squabbles the Viet retained a strong sense of national identity and were quick to respond to charismatic leadership. As so often in Vietnam's history one man was able to harness nationalistic sentiment and mould the country's discontent into a powerful fighting force: in 1426 it was Le Loi. Together with the brilliant tactician Nguyen Trai (see box below), Le Loi led a campaign to remove the Chinese from Vietnamese soil. Combining surprise, guerrilla tactics and Nguyen Trai's innovative and famous propaganda, designed to convince defending Ming of the futility of their position, the Viet won a resounding victory which led to the

enlightened and artistically distinguished Le period. Le Loi's legendary victory lives on in popular form and is celebrated in the tale of the restored sword in water puppet performances across the country.

The expansion of the Vietnamese state, under the Le, S from its heartland in the Tonkin Delta, followed the decline of the Cham Kingdom at the end of the 15th century. By the early 18th century the Cham were extinct as an identifiable political and military force and the Vietnamese advanced still further S into the Khmer-controlled territories of the Mekong Delta. This geographical over-extension and the sheer logistical impracticability of ruling from distant Hanoi, disseminating edicts and collecting taxes, led to the disintegration of the – ever tenuous – imperial rule. The old adage 'The edicts of the emperor stop at the village gate' was particularly apt more than 1,000 km from the capital. Noble families, locally dominant, challenged the emperor's authority and the Le Dynasty gradually dissolved into internecine strife and regional fiefdoms, namely Trinh in the N and Nguyen in

---

NGUYEN TRAI

"Our country, Dai Viet, has long been
A land of ancient culture,
With its own rivers and mountains, ways and customs,
Different from those of the North"
(Opening lines of *'Proclamation of victory over the invaders'*)

Nguyen Trai, mandarin, poet and nationalist rose to prominence as an adviser to Le Loi during the 10-year campaign to eject the Ming from Dai Viet. His famous counsel "better to win hearts than citadels" (which mirrors similar advice during a war over 5 centuries later) was heeded by Le Loi who aroused patriotic fervour in his compatriots to achieve victory on the battlefield. It was on Nguyen Trai's suggestion that 100,000 defeated Ming troops were given food and boats to make their way home. After the war Nguyen Trai accepted and later resigned a court post. He was a prolific composer of verse, which is considered some of the finest in the national annals. On an overnight visit to Nguyen Trai, Emperor Le Thai Tong (Le Loi's son and heir) died unexpectedly. Scheming courtiers were able to fix the blame on Nguyen Trai who in 1442, along with three generations of his family, were executed, a punishment known as *tru di tam tôc*.

VIETNAMESE DYNASTIES

Dynasty	Dates	Capital (province)
Hong Bang Dynasty (legendary)	2876-258 BC	Phong Chau (Son Tay)
Thuc Dynasty	257-208 BC	Loa Thanh (Vinh Phu)
Trieu Dynasty	207-111 BC	Phien Ngung (S. China)
(under Chinese domination 111 BC-23 AD)		
Trung Sisters	40-43 AD	Me Linh (Son Tay)
(under Chinese domination 25-589)		
Early Ly Dynasty	544-602	various (Hanoi)
(under Chinese domination 622-938)		
Ngo Dynasty	939-965	Co Loa (Vinh Phuc)
Dinh Dynasty	968-980	Hoa Lu (Ninh Binh)
Early Le Dynasty	980-1009	Hoa Lu (Ninh Binh)
Ly Dynasty	1010-1225	Thang Long (Hanoi)
Tran Dynasty	1225-1400	Thang Long (Hanoi)
Ho Dynasty	1400-1407	Dong Do (Hanoi)
Post Tran Dynasty	1407-1413	
(under Chinese domination 1414-1427)		
Le Dynasty	1427-1788	Thang Long (Hanoi)
Mac Dynasty	1527-1592	
Northern Trinh	1539-1787	Hanoi
Southern Nguyen	1558-1778	Hué
Quang Trung	1787-1792	
Nguyen of Tay Son	1788-1802	Saigon
Nguyen Dynasty	1802-1945	Hué

Note: from the 16th-18th centuries there were up to 4 centres of power in Vietnam. For a list of Nguyen Emperors **see page 195**.

the S, a pattern that was to reassert itself some 300 years later. But although on paper the Vietnamese – now consisting of two dynastic houses, Trinh and Nguyen – appeared powerful, the people were mired in poverty. There were numerous peasant rebellions in this period, of which the most serious was the Tay Son rebellion of 1771 (see page 225). One of the three Tay Son brothers, Nguyen Hue, proclaimed himself Emperor Quang Trung in 1788, only to die 4 years later.

The death of Quang Trung paved the way for the establishment of the **Nguyen Dynasty** – the last Vietnamese dynasty

French colonial troops and a wealthy Vietnamese mandarin flee from a victorious band of nationalist peasant rebels in this 1930s cartoon. The victors are shouting "Wipe out the gang of imperialists, mandarins, capitalists and big landlords!"

Source: Archives Nationales de France

– in 1802 when Emperor Gia Long ascended to the throne in Hué. Despite the fact that this period heralded the arrival of the French – leading to their eventual domination of Vietnam – it is regarded as a golden period in Vietnamese history. During the Nguyen Dynasty, Vietnam was unified as a single state and Hué emerged as the heart of the kingdom.

The Colonial Period

One of the key motivating factors that encouraged the **French** to undermine the authority of the Vietnamese emperors was their treatment of **Roman Catholics**. Jesuits had been in the country from as early as the 17th century – one of them, Alexandre-de-Rhodes, converted the Vietnamese writing system from Chinese characters to romanized script (see page 121) – but persecution of Roman Catholics began only in the 1830s. Emperor Minh Mang issued an imperial edict outlawing the dissemination of Christianity as a heterodox creed in 1825. The first European priest to be executed was

François Isidore Gagelin who was strangled by six soldiers as he knelt on a scaffold in Hué in 1833. Three days later, having been told that Christians believe they will come to life again, Minh Mang had the body exhumed to confirm the man's death. In 1840 Minh Mang actually read the Old Testament in Chinese translation, declaring it to be 'absurd'.

Yet, Christianity continued to spread as Buddhism declined, and there was a continual stream of priests willing to risk their lives proselytizing. In addition, the economy was in disarray and natural disasters common. Poor Vietnamese saw Christianity as a way to break the shackles of their feudal existence. Fearing a peasants' revolt, the Emperor ordered the execution of 25 European priests, 300 Vietnamese priests, and 30,000 Vietnamese Catholics between 1848 and 1860. Provoked by these killings, the French attacked and took Saigon in 1859. In 1862 Emperor Tu Duc signed a treaty ceding the three southern provinces to the French, thereby creating the colony of Cochin China. This treaty of 1862 effectively paved the way for the eventual seizure by the French of the whole kingdom. The French, through weight of arms, also forced the Emperor to end the persecution of Christians in his kingdom. In retrospect, although many Christians did die cruelly, the degree of persecution was not on the scale of similar episodes elsewhere: Minh Mang's successors Thieu Tri (1841-1847) and Tu Duc (1847-1883), though both *fervently* anti-Christian, appreciated French military strength and the fact that they were searching for pretexts to intervene.

The French conquest of the N was motivated by a desire to control trade and the route to what were presumed to be the vast riches of China. In 1883 and 1884, the French forced the Emperor to sign treaties making Vietnam a French protectorate. In Aug 1883 for example, just after Tu Duc's death, a French fleet appeared off Hué to force concessions. François Harmand, a native affairs official on board one of the ships, threatened the Vietnamese by stating: "Imagine all that is terrible and it will still be less than reality ... the word 'Vietnam' will be erased from history." The emperor called on China for assistance and demanded that provinces resist French rule; but the imperial bidding proved ineffective, and in 1885 the Treaty of Tientsin recognized the French protectorates of Tonkin (North Vietnam) and Annam (Central Vietnam), to add to that of Cochin China (South Vietnam).

Resistance to the French: the prelude to revolution

Like other European powers in Southeast Asia, the French managed to achieve military victory with ease, but they failed to stifle Vietnamese nationalism. After 1900, as Chinese translations of the works of Rousseau, Voltaire and social Darwinists such as Herbert Spence began to find their way into the hands of the Vietnamese intelligentsia, so resistance grew. Foremost among these early nationalists were Phan Boi Chau (1867-1940) and Phan Chau Trinh (1871-1926) who wrote tracts calling for the expulsion of the French. But these men and others such as Prince Cuong De (1882-1951) were traditional nationalists, their beliefs rooted in Confucianism rather than revolutionary Marxism. Their efforts and perspectives were essentially in the tradition of the nationalists who had resisted Chinese domination over previous centuries.

Quoc Dan Dang (VNQDD), founded at the end of 1927, was the first nationalist party, while the first significant Communist group was the **Indochina Communist Party (ICP)** established by **Ho Chi Minh** in 1930 (see profile, page 88). Both the VNQDD and the ICP organized resistance to the French and there were numerous strikes and uprisings, particularly during the harsh years of the Great Depression. The Japanese 'occupation' from Aug 1940 (Vichy France permitted the Japanese full access to military facilities in exchange for allowing continued French administrative control) saw the creation of the **Viet Minh** to fight for the liberation of Vietnam from Japanese and French control.

The Vietnam War

The First Indochina War (1945-1954)

The Vietnam War started in Sep 1945 in the S of the country, and in 1946 in the N. These years marked the onset of fighting **between the Viet Minh and the French** and the period is usually referred to as the First Indochina War. The Communists, who had organized against the Japanese, proclaimed the creation of the Democratic Republic of Vietnam (DRV) on 2 September 1945 when Ho Chi Minh read out the Vietnamese Declaration of

HO CHI MINH: "HE WHO ENLIGHTENS"

Ho Chi Minh, one of a number of pseudonyms Ho adopted during his life, was born Nguyen Sinh Cung, or possibly Nguyen Van Thanh (Ho did not keep a diary during much of his life, so parts of his life are still a mystery), in Nghe An Province near Vinh on the 19 May 1890, and came from a poor scholar-gentry family. In the village, the family was aristocratic; beyond it they were little more than peasants. His father, though not a revolutionary, was a dissenter and rather than go to Hué to serve the French, he chose to work as a village school teacher. Ho must have been influenced by his father's implacable animosity towards the French, although Ho's early years are obscure. He went to Quoc Hoc College in Hué, and then worked for a while as a teacher in Phan Thiet, a fishing village in S Annam.

In 1911, under the name Nguyen Tat Thanh, he travelled to Saigon and left the country as a messboy on the French ship *Amiral Latouche-Tréville*. He is said to have used the name 'Ba' so that he would not shame his family by accepting such lowly work. This marked the beginning of 3 years of travel during which he visited France, England, America (where the skyscrapers of Manhattan both amazed and appalled him) and North Africa. Seeing the colonialists on their own turf and reading such revolutionary literature as the French Communist Party newspaper *L'Humanité*, he was converted to Communism. In Paris he mixed with leftists, wrote pamphlets and attended meetings of the French Socialist Party. He also took odd jobs: for a while he worked at the Carlton Hotel in London and became an assistant pastry chef under the legendary French chef Georges Escoffier.

Gradually Ho became an ever-more-committed Communist, contributing articles to radical newspapers and working his way into the web of Communist and leftist groups. At the same time he remained, curiously, a French cultural chauvinist, complaining for example about the intrusion of English words like 'le manager' and 'le challenger' (referring to boxing contests) into the French language. He even urged the French Prime Minister to ban foreign words from the French press. In 1923 he left France for Moscow and was trained as a Communist activist – effectively a spy. From there, Ho travelled to Canton where he was instrumental in forming the Vietnamese Communist movement. This culminated in the creation of the Indochina Communist Party in 1930. His movements during these years are scantily documented: he became a Buddhist

Independence in Hanoi's Ba Dinh Square. Ironically, this document was modelled closely on the American Declaration of Independence. The French, although they had always insisted that Vietnam be returned to French rule, were in no position to force the issue. Instead, in the S, it was British troops (mainly Gurkhas) who helped the small force of French against the Viet Minh. Incredibly, the British also ordered the Japanese, who had only just capitulated, to help fight the Vietnamese. When 35,000 French reinforcements arrived, the issue in the S – at least superficially – was all but settled, with Ca Mau at the southern extremity of the country falling on 21 Oct. From that point, the war in the S became an underground battle of attrition, with the N providing support to their southern comrades.

In the N, the Viet Minh had to deal with 180,000 rampaging Nationalist Chinese troops, while preparing for the

HO CHI MINH PSEUDONYMS

Born 1890:	Nguyen Sinh Cung or Nguyen Van Thanh (Vinh)
1910:	Van Ba (South Vietnam)
1911:	Nguyen Tat Thanh (Saigon)
1913:	Nguyen Tat Thanh (London)
1914:	Nguyen Ai Quoc (Paris)
1924:	Linh (Moscow)
1924:	Ly Thuy (Moscow)
1925:	Wang (Canton)
1927:	Duong (Paris)
1928:	Nguyen Lai, Nam Son, Thau Chin (Siam)
1942:	Ho Chi Minh

monk in Siam (Thailand), was arrested in Hong Kong for subversive activities and received a 6 month sentence, travelled to China several times, and in 1940 even returned to Vietnam for a short period – his first visit for nearly 30 years. Despite his absence from the country, the French had already recognized the threat that he posed and sentenced him to death in absentia in 1930. He did not adopt the pseudonym by which he is now best known – Ho Chi Minh – until the early 1940s.

Ho was a consummate politician and, despite his revolutionary fervour, a great realist. He was also a charming man, and during his stay in France between Jun and Oct 1946, he made a great number of friends. Robert Shaplen in his book *The Lost Revolution* (1965) talks of his "wit, his oriental courtesy, his savoir-faire... above all his seeming sincerity and simplicity". He talked with farmers and fishermen, and debated with priests; he impressed people wherever he travelled. He died in Hanoi at his house within the former governor's residence in 1969 (see page 154).

Since the demise of communism in the former Soviet Union, the Vietnamese leadership have been concerned that secrets about Ho's life might be gleaned from old comintern files in Moscow by nosy journalists. To thwart such an eventuality, they have, reportedly, sent a senior historian to scour the archives. To date, Ho's image remains largely untarnished – making him an exception amongst the tawdry league of former communist leaders. But a Moscow-based reporter has unearthed evidence implying Ho was married, challenging the official hagiography that paints Ho as a celibate who committed his entire life to the revolution. It takes a brave Vietnamese to challenge established 'fact'. In 1991, when the popular Vietnamese *Youth* or *Tuoi Tre* newspaper dared to suggest that Ho had married Tang Tuyet Minh in China in 1926, the editor was summarily dismissed from her post.

imminent arrival of a French force. Unable to confront both at the same time, and deciding that the French were probably the lesser of two evils, Ho Chi Minh decided to negotiate. He is said to have observed in private, that it was preferable to 'sniff French shit for a while than eat China's all our lives'. To make the DRV government more acceptable to the French, Ho proceeded cautiously, only nationalizing a few strategic industries, bringing moderates into the gov-

ernment, and actually dissolving the Indochinese Communist Party (at least on paper) in Nov 1945. But in the same month Ho also said:

> "The French colonialists should know that the Vietnamese people do not wish to spill blood, that it loves peace. But if it must sacrifice millions of combatants, lead a resistance for long years to defend the independence of the country, and preserve its children from slavery, it will do so. It is certain the resistance will win."

In Feb 1946, the French and Chinese

signed a treaty leading to the withdrawal of Chinese forces, and shortly afterwards Ho concluded a treaty with French President de Gaulle's special emissary to Vietnam, Jean Sainteny in which Vietnam was recognized as a 'free' (the Vietnamese word *doc lap* being translated as free, but not yet independent) state within the French Union and the Indochinese Federation.

It is interesting to note that in negotiating with the French, Ho was going against the wishes of most of his supporters who argued for confrontation. But Ho, ever a pragmatist, believed at this stage that the Viet Minh were ill-trained and poorly armed and he appreciated the need for time to consolidate their position. The episode that is usually highlighted as the flash-point that led to the resumption of hostilities was the French government's decision to open a customs house in Haiphong at the end of 1946. The Viet Minh forces resisted and the rest, as they say, is history. It seems that during the course of 1946 Ho changed his view of the best path to independence. Initially he asked: "Why should we sacrifice 50 or 100,000 men when we can achieve independence within 5 years through negotiation?", but he later came to the conclusion that it was necessary to fight for independence. The customs house episode might, therefore, be viewed as merely an excuse. The French claimed that 5,000 Vietnamese were killed in the ensuing bombardment, as against five Frenchmen; the Vietnamese put the toll at 20,000.

In a pattern that was to become characteristic of the entire 25-year conflict, while the French controlled the cities, the Viet Minh were dominant in the countryside. By the end of 1949, with the success of the Chinese Revolution and the establishment of the Democratic People's Republic of Korea (North Korea) in 1948, the US began to offer support to the French in an attempt to stem the 'Red Tide' that seemed to be sweeping across Asia. At this early stage, the odds appeared stacked against the Viet Minh, but Ho was confident that time was on their side. As he remarked to Sainteny "If we have to fight, we will fight. You can kill 10 of my men for every one I kill of yours but even at those odds, I will win and you will lose". It also became increasingly clear that the French were not committed to negotiating a route to independence. A secret French report prepared in 1948 was obtained and then published by the Viet Minh in which the High Commissioner, Monsieur Bollaert wrote: "It is my impression that we must make a concession to Viet-Nam of the term, independence; but I am convinced that this word need never be interpreted in any light other than that of a religious verbalism".

Dien Bien Phu (1954) The decisive battle of the First Indochina War was at Dien Bien Phu in the hills of the NW, close to the border with Laos. At the end of 1953 the French, with US support, parachuted 16,000 men into the area in an attempt to protect Laos from Viet Minh incursions and to tempt them into open battle. The French in fact found themselves trapped, surrounded by Viet Minh and overlooked by artillery. There was some suggestion that the US might become involved, and even use tactical nuclear weapons, but this was not to be. In May 1954 the French surrendered – the most humiliating of French colonial defeats – effectively marking the end of the French presence in Indochina. In Jul 1954, in Geneva, the French and Vietnamese agreed to divide the country along the 17th parallel, so creating two states (for a fuller account of the battle see page 174). The border was kept open for 300 days and over that period about 900,000 – mostly Roman Catholic – Vietnamese travelled S. At the same time nearly 90,000 Viet Minh troops along with 43,000 civilians, went N, although many Viet Minh remained in the S to continue the fight there.

The Second Indochina War (1954-1975)

The Vietnam War, but particularly the American part of that war, is probably the most minutely studied, reported, analysed and recorded in history. Yet, as with all wars, there are still large grey areas and continuing disagreement over important episodes. Most crucially, there is the question of whether the US might have won had their forces been given a free hand and were not forced, as some would have it, to fight with one hand tied behind their backs. This remains the view among many members of the US military.

At the time of the partition of Vietnam along the 17th parallel, the government in the S was chaotic and the Communists could be fairly confident that in a short time their sympathizers would be victorious. This situation was to change with the rise of Ngo Dinh Diem. Born in Hué in 1901 to a Roman Catholic Confucian family, Diem wished to become a priest. He graduated at the top of his class from the French School of Administration and at the age of 32 was appointed to the post of Minister of the Interior at the court of Emperor Bao Dai. Here, according to the political scientist William Turley "he worked with uncommon industry and integrity" only to resign in exasperation at court intrigues and French interference. He withdrew from political activity during the First Indochina War and in 1946 Ho Chi Minh offered him a post in the DRV government – an offer he declined. Turley describes him as a man who was, in many respects, a creature of the past:

"For Diem, the mandarin, political leadership meant rule by example, precept, and paternalism. His Catholic upbringing reinforced rather than replaced the Confucian tendency to base authority on doctrine, morality and hierarchy. Utterly alien to him were the concepts of power-sharing, and popular participation. He was in fact the heir to a dying tradition, member of an elite that had been superbly prepared by birth, training, and experience to lead a Vietnam that no longer existed."

In Jul 1954 Diem returned from his self-imposed exile at the Maryknoll Seminary in New Jersey to become Premier of South Vietnam. It is usually alleged that the US administration was behind his rise to power, although this has yet to be proved. He held two rigged elections (in Oct 1955, 450,000 registered voters cast 605,025 votes) which gave some legitimacy to his administration in American eyes. He proceeded to suppress all opposition in the country. His brutal brother, Ngo Dinh Nhu, was appointed to head the security forces and terrorized much of Vietnamese society.

During the period of Diem's premiership, opposition to his rule, particularly in the countryside, increased. This was because the military's campaign against the Viet Minh targeted – both directly and indirectly – many innocent peasants. At the same time, the nepotism and corruption that was endemic within the administration also turned many people into Viet Minh sympathizers. That said, Diem's campaign was successful in undermining the strength of the Communist Party in the S. While there were perhaps 50,000-60,000 Party members in 1954, this figure had declined through widespread arrests and intimidation to only 5,000 by 1959.

The erosion of the Party in the S gradually led from 1959, to the N changing its strategy towards one of more overt military confrontation. The same year also saw the establishment of Group 559 which was charged with the task of setting up what was to become the Ho Chi Minh Trail, along which supplies and troops were moved from the N to the S (see page 209). But, even at this stage, the Party's forces in the S were kept from open confrontation and many of its leaders were hoping for victory without having to resort to open warfare. There was no call for a 'People's War' and armed resistance was left largely to guerrillas belonging to the Cao Dai (see page 121) and Hoa Hao (Buddhist millenarian) sects. The establishment of the National Liberation Front of Vietnam in 1960 was an important political and organizational development towards creating a credible alternative to Diem – although it did not hold its first congress until 1962.

The escalation of the armed conflict (1959-1963)

The armed conflict began to intensify from the beginning of 1961 when all the armed forces under the Communists' control were unified under the banner of the People's Liberation Armed Forces (PLAF). By this time the Americans were already using the term **Viet Cong** (or **VC**) to refer to Communist troops. They reasoned that the victory at Dien Bien Phu had conferred almost heroic status on the name Viet Minh. American psychological warfare specialists therefore invented the term Viet Cong, an abbreviation of *Viet-nam Cong-san* (or Vietnamese Communists), and persuaded the media in Saigon to begin substituting it for Viet Minh from 1956.

The election of **John F. Kennedy** to the White House in Jan 1961 coincided with the Communists' decision to widen the war in the S. In the same year Kennedy dispatched 400 special forces troops and 100 special military advisers to Vietnam – in flagrant contravention of the Geneva Agreement. With the cold war getting colder, and Soviet Premier Nicolae Khrushchev confirming his support for wars of 'national liberation', Kennedy could not back down and by the end of 1962 there were 11,000 US personnel in South Vietnam. At the same time the NLF had around 23,000 troops at its disposal. Kennedy was still saying that "In the final analysis, it's their war and they're the ones who have to win or lose it". But just months after the Bay of Pigs debacle in Cuba, Washington set out on the path that was ultimately to lead to America's first large-scale military defeat.

The bungling and incompetence of the forces of the S, the interference which US advisers and troops had to face, the misreading of the situation by US military commanders, and the skill – both military and political – of the Communists, are most vividly recounted in Neil Sheehan's massive book, *A bright shining lie* (see Recommended reading, page 303). The conflict quickly escalated from 1959. The N infiltrated about 44,000 men and women into the S between then and 1964, while the number recruited in the S was between 60,000 and 100,000. In Aug 1959, the first consignment of arms was carried down the **Ho Chi Minh Trail** into South Vietnam. Meanwhile, Kennedy began supporting, arming and training the Army of the Republic of Vietnam (ARVN). The US however, shied away from any large-scale, direct confrontation between its forces and the Viet Cong.

An important element in Diem's military strategy at this time was the establishment of '**strategic hamlets**', better-known simply as 'hamleting'. This strategy was modelled on British anti-guerrilla warfare during Malaya's Communist insurgency, and aimed to deny the Communists any bases of support in the countryside while at the same time making it more difficult for Communists to infiltrate the villages and 'propagandize' there. The villages which were ringed by barbed-wire were labelled 'concentration camps' by the Communists, and the often brutal, forced relocation that peasants had to endure probably turned even more of

VIETNAM WAR

V 74

CHINA

NORTH VIETNAM

○ Dien Bien Phu

HANOI □

○ Haiphong

LAOS

Sam Neua ○

○ Luang Prabang

Phonsavanh ○

Plain of Jars

Mekong

VIENTIANE □

Gulf of Tonkin

CHINA

THAILAND

Ho Chi Minh Trail

Demilitarized zone (22-7-54)

Khe Sanh ○

Hamburger Hill

○ Hué

○ Danang

○ My Lai

N

CAMBODIA

○ Pleiku

Ia Drang Valley

Qui Nhon ○

SOUTH VIETNAM

Ho Chi Minh Trail

Mekong

○ Dalat

Cam Ranh Bay

PHNOM PENH □

Tay Ninh ○

○ Cu Chi

Bien Hoa ○

SAIGON ○

○ Ap Bac

Sihanoukville ○

Gulf of Thailand

Camau ○

South China Sea

them into Communist sympathizers. Of the 7,000-8,000 villages sealed in this way, only a fifth could ever have been considered watertight.

In Jan 1963 at Ap Bac, not far from the town of My Tho, the Communists scored their first significant victory in the S. Facing 2,000 well armed ARVN troops, a force of just 300-400 PLAF inflicted heavy casualties and downed five helicopters. After this defeat, many American advisers drew the conclusion that if the Communists were to be defeated, it could not be left to the ARVN alone – US troops would have to become directly involved. As John Vann, a key American military adviser, remarked after the debacle when lambasting South Vietnamese officers: "A miserable fucking performance, just like it always is". In mid-1963 a Buddhist monk from Hué committed suicide by dousing his body with petrol and setting it alight. This was the first of a number of self-immolations, suggesting that even in the early days the Diem regime was not only losing the military war but also the 'hearts and minds' war (see page 251). He responded with characteristic heavy-handedness by ransacking suspect pagodas. On 1 December 1963, Diem and his brother-in-law Nhu were both assassinated during an army coup.

The American War in Vietnam

America's decision to enter the war has been the subject of considerable disagreement. Until recently, the received wisdom was that the US administration had already taken the decision, and manufactured events to justify their later actions. However, the recent publication of numerous State Department, Presidential, CIA, Defence Department and National Security Council files – all dating from 1964 – has shed new light on events leading up to American intervention (these files are contained in the United States Government Printing Office's 1,108 page-long *Vietnam 1964*).

By all accounts, **Lyndon Johnson** was a reluctant warrior. In the 1964 presidential campaign he repeatedly said "We don't want our American boys to do the fighting for Asian boys". This was not just for public consumption. The files show that LBJ always doubted the wisdom of intervention. But he also believed that John F. Kennedy had made a solemn pledge to help the South Vietnamese people – a pledge that he was morally obliged to keep. In most respects, LBJ was completely in agreement with Congress, together with sections of the US public, who were disquietened by events in South Vietnam. The Buddhist monk's self-immolation, broadcast on prime-time news, did not help matters.

It has usually been argued that the executive manufactured the **'Gulf of Tonkin Incident'** to force Congress and the public to approve an escalation of America's role in the conflict. It was reported that two American destroyers, the *USS Maddox* and *USS C. Turner Joy*, were attacked without provocation in international waters on the 2 August 1964 by North Vietnamese patrol craft. The US responded by bombing shore installations while presenting the Gulf of Tonkin Resolution to an outraged Congress for approval. Only two Congressmen voted against the resolution and President Johnson's poll rating jumped from 42% to 72%. In reality, the *USS Maddox* had been involved in electronic intelligence-gathering while supporting clandestine raids by South Vietnamese mercenaries – well inside North Vietnamese territorial waters. This deception only became apparent in 1971 when the *Pentagon papers*, documenting the circumstances behind the incident, were leaked to the *New York Times* (the *Pentagon papers* were commissioned by Defence Secretary McNamara in Jun 1967 and written by 36 Indochina experts).

But these events are not sufficient to argue that the incident was manufac-

THE WAR IN FIGURES

Vietnamese:		Australians:	
Killed (soldiers of the North)	1,100,000	Killed	423
Killed (soldiers of the South)	250,000	Wounded	2,398
Vietnamese civilians	2,000,000	At height of the war:	
Americans:		Bombs dropped	1.2 m tonnes/yr
Served	3,300,000	Cost of bombs	US$14bn/yr
Killed	57,605	Area defoliated	2.2 million ha
Captured	766 (651 returned)		(1962-71)
Wounded	303,700	US air attacks	400,000/yr
MIA	4,993 (121 returned,	Refugees	585,000/yr
	4,872 declared dead)	Civilian casualties	130,000/month

tured to allow LBJ to start an undeclared war against North Vietnam. On 4 Aug, Secretary of State Dean Rusk told the American representative at the United Nations that: "In no sense is this destroyer a pretext to make a big thing out of a little thing". Even as late as the end of 1964, the President was unconvinced by arguments that the US should become more deeply involved. On 31 Aug, McGeorge Bundy wrote in a memorandum to Johnson: "A still more drastic possibility which no one is discussing is the use of substantial US armed forces in operation against the Viet Cong. I myself believe that before we let this country go we should have a hard look at this grim alternative, and I do not at all think that it is a repetition of Korea".

But events overtook President Johnson, and by 1965 the US was firmly embarked on the road to defeat. In Mar 1965, he ordered the beginning of the air war against the N perhaps acting on Air Force General Curtis LeMay's observation that "we are swatting flies when we should be going after the manure pile". **Operation Rolling Thunder**, the most intense bombing campaign any country had yet experienced, began in Mar 1965 and ran through to Oct 1968. In 3½ years, twice the tonnage of bombs was dropped on Vietnam (and Laos) as during the entire Second World War. During its peak in 1967, 12,000 sorties were being flown each month – a total of 108,000 were flown throughout 1967.

North Vietnam claimed that 4,000 out of its 5,788 villages were hit. Most terrifying were the B-52s which dropped their bombs from such altitude (17,000m) that the attack could not even be heard until the bombs hit their targets. Each aircraft carried 20 tonnes of bombs. By the end of the American war in 1973, 14 million tonnes of all types of munitions had been used in Indochina, an explosive force representing 700 times that of the atomic bomb dropped on Hiroshima. As General Curtis LeMay explained on 25 November 1965 – "We should bomb them back into the Stone Age". In the same month that Rolling Thunder commenced, marines landed at Danang to defend its airbase, and by Jun 1965 there were 74,000 US troops in Vietnam. Despite President Johnson's reluctance to commit the US to the conflict, events forced his hand. He realized that the undisciplined South Vietnamese could not prevent a Communist victory. Adhering to the domino theory, and with his own and the US's reputation at stake, he had no choice. As Johnson is said to have remarked to his press secretary Bill Moyers: "I feel like a hitchhiker caught in a hail storm on a Texas highway. I can't win. I can't hide. And I can't make it stop."

Dispersal of the North's industry In response to the bombing campaign, industry in the N was decentralized and dispersed to rural areas. Each province

A WAR GLOSSARY

Agent Orange	herbicide used to defoliate forests
APC	armoured personnel carrier
ARVN	Army of the Republic of Vietnam; the army of the South
Body Count	the number of dead on a field of battle
BUFF	nick-name for the B-52 bomber; stands for Big Ugly Fat Fellow or, more usually, Big Ugly Fat F*****
COIN	counterinsurgency
DMZ	de-militarized zone; the border between North and South Vietnam at the 17th parallel
Dust-off	medical evacuation helicopter
DZ	parachute drop zone
FAC	forward air controller, airborne spotter who directed bombers onto the target
Fire base	defence fortification for artillery to support Infantry from
Fragging	to kill or attempt to kill with a fragmentation grenade; better known as the killing of US officers and NCOs by their own men. In 1970 one study reported 209 fraggings
Gook	slang, derogatory term for all Vietnamese
Grunt	slang for a US infantryman; the word comes from the 'grunt' emitted when shouldering a heavy pack
Huey	most commonly used helicopter, UH1
LZ	helicopter landing zone
Napalm	jellified fuel, the name derives from two of its constituents, naphthenic and palmitic acids. To be burnt by napalm after an attack was terrible and one of the most famous photo images of

was envisaged as a self-sufficient production unit. The economic effect of this strategy was felt at the time in a considerable loss of productivity; a cost judged to be worth paying to protect the N's industrial base. In order to protect the population in the N, they too were relocated to the countryside. By the end of 1967 Hanoi's population was a mere 250,000 essential citizens – about a quarter of the pre-war figure. The same was true of other urban centres. What the primary US objective was in mounting the air war remains unclear. In part, it was designed to destroy the N's industrial base and its ability to wage war; partly to dampen the people's will to fight; partly to sow seeds of discontent; partly to force the leadership in the N to the negotiating table; partly, perhaps, to punish those in the N for supporting their government. By Oct 1968 the US realized the bombing was having little effect and they called a halt. The legacy of Operation Rolling Thunder, though, would live on. Turley writes:

"...the bombing had destroyed virtually all industrial, transportation and communications facilities built since 1954, blotted out 10 to 15 years' potential economic growth, flattened three major cities and 12 of 29 province capitals, and triggered a decline in per capita agricultural output".

But, it was not just the bombing campaign which was undermining the N's industrial and agricultural base. Socialist policies in the countryside were labelling small land owners as 'landlords' – in effect traitors to the revolutionary cause – thus alienating many farmers. In the cities, industrial policies were no less short sighted. Though Ho's policies in the battlefield were driven by hard-headed pragmatism, in the field of eco-

	the war (taken by Nick Ut) showed a naked local girl (Kim Phuc) running along a road at Trang Bang, NW of Saigon after being burnt; the girl survived the attack by South Vietnamese aircraft and now lives in Canada
NLF	National Liberation Front
PAVN	People's Army of Vietnam
Phoenix	counter-insurgency programme established by the US after the Tet Offensive of 1968 (see page 101)
PLAF	People's Liberation Armed Forces; the army of the Communist North
POW/MIA	prisoner of war/missing in action
Pungi stakes	sharpened bamboo stakes concealed in VC pits: accounted for 2% of US combat wounds
Purple Heart	medal awarded to US troops wounded in action
R&R	Rest & Recreation; leave
ROE	rules of engagement
Rome Plow	20 tonne bulldozer designed to clear forest. Equipped with a curved blade and sharp protruding spike it could split the largest trees
Tunnel Rats	US army volunteers who fought VC in the Cu Chi tunnels
VC, Charlie	Viet Cong (see page 92); US term for Vietnamese Communist; often shortened to Charlie from the phonetic alphabet, Victor Charlie
Viet Minh	Communist troops – later changed to Viet Cong (see above and page 92)
WP, Willy Pete	White phosphorous rocket used to mark a target

nomic development they were informed – tragically – by revolutionary fervour.

William Westmoreland, the general appointed to command the American effort, aimed to use the US's superior firepower and mobility to 'search and destroy' PAVN forces. North Vietnamese bases in the S were to be identified using modern technology, jungle hideouts revealed by dumping chemical defoliants, and then attacked with shells, bombs, and by helicopter-borne troops. In 'free-fire zones' the army and airforce were permitted to use whatever level of firepower they felt necessary to dislodge the enemy. 'Body counts' became the measure of success and collateral damage – or civilian casualties – was a cost that just had to be borne. As one field commander famously explained: 'We had to destroy the town to save it'. By 1968 the **US** had more than 500,000 troops in Vietnam, while **South Korean**, **Australian**, **New Zealand**, **Filipino** and **Thai** forces contributed another 90,000. The ARVN officially had 1.5 million men under arms (100,000 or more of these were 'flower' or phantom soldiers, the pay for whom was pocketed by officers in an increasingly corrupt ARVN). Ranged against this vastly superior force were perhaps 400,000 PAVN and National Liberation Front forces.

1964-1968: who was winning?

The leadership in the N tried to allay serious anxieties about their ability to defeat the American-backed S by emphasizing human over physical and material resources. **Desertions** from the ARVN were very high – there were 113,000 from the army in 1965 alone (200,000 in 1975) – and the PAVN did record a number of significant victories.

The Communists also had to deal with large numbers of desertions – 28,000 men in 1969. By 1967 world opinion, and even American public opinion, appeared to be swinging against the war. Within the US, **anti-war demonstrations** and 'teach-ins' were spreading, officials were losing confidence in the ability of the US to win the war, and the President's approval rating was sinking fast. As the US Secretary of Defense, Robert McNamara is quoted as saying in the *Pentagon papers*:

"...the picture of the world's greatest superpower killing or seriously injuring 1,000 noncombatants a week, while trying to pound a tiny, backward nation into submission on an issue whose merits are hotly disputed, is not a pretty one".

But although the Communists may have been winning the psychological and public opinion wars, they were increasingly hard-pressed to maintain this advantage on the ground. Continual American strikes against their bases, and the social and economic dislocations in the countryside, were making it more difficult for the Communists to recruit supporters. At the same time, the fight against a vastly better-equipped enemy was also taking its toll in sheer exhaustion. Despite what is now widely regarded as a generally misguided US military strategy in Vietnam, there were notable US successes (for example the Phoenix Programme, see page 101). American GIs were always sceptical about the 'pacification' programmes which aimed to win the 'hearts and minds' war. GIs were fond of saying, 'If you've got them by the balls, their hearts and minds will follow'. At times, the US military and politicians appeared to view the average Vietnamese as inferior to the average American. This latent racism was reflected in General Westmoreland's remark that Vietnamese "don't think about death the way we do" and in the use by most US servicemen of the derogatory name "gook" to refer to Vietnamese.

At the same time as the Americans were trying to win 'hearts and minds', the Vietnamese were also busy indoctrinating their men and women, and the population in the 'occupied' S. In Bao Ninh's moving *The sorrow of war* (1994), the main character, Kien, who fights with a scout unit describes the indoctrination that accompanied the soldiers from their barracks to the field:

"Politics continuously. Politics in the morning, politics in the afternoon, politics again in the evening. 'We won, the enemy lost. The enemy will surely lose. The N had a good harvest, a bumper harvest. The people will rise up and welcome you. Those who don't just lack awareness. The world is divided into three camps.' More politics."

By 1967, the war had entered a period of military (though not political) **stalemate**. As Robert McNamara writes in his book *In retrospect: the tragedy and lessons of Vietnam*, it was at this stage that he came to believe that Vietnam was "a problem with no solution". In retrospect, he argues that the US should have withdrawn in late 1963, and certainly by late 1967. Massive quantities of US arms and money were preventing the Communists from making much headway in urban areas, while American and ARVN forces were ineffective in the countryside – although incessant bombing and ground assaults wreaked massive destruction. A black market of epic proportions developed in Saigon, as millions of dollars of assistance went astray. American journalist Stanley Karnow once remarked to a US official that "we could probably buy off the Vietcong at US$500 a head". The official replied that they had already calculated the costs, but came to "US$2,500 a head".

The Tet Offensive, 1968 – the beginning of the end

By mid-1967, the Communist leadership in the N felt it was time for a further escalation of the war in the S, to regain

THE ANZACS IN VIETNAM

In Apr 1964, President Johnson called for "more flags" to help defend South Vietnam. Among the countries that responded to his call were Australia and New Zealand. Australia had military advisers in Vietnam from 1962, but in Apr 1965 sent the 1st Battalion Royal Australian Regiment. Until 1972, there were about 7,000 Australian combat troops in Vietnam, based in the coastal province of Phuoc Tuy, not far from Saigon. There, operating as a self-contained unit in a Viet Cong controlled zone, and with the support of two batteries of 105 mm artillery (one New Zealand), the Australians fought one of the most effective campaigns of the entire war. As General Westmoreland said: "Aggressiveness, quick reaction, good use of firepower, and old-fashioned Australian courage have produced outstanding results".

Of the battles fought by the Australians in Phuoc Tuy, one of the most significant was **Long Tan**, on 18 August 1966. Although caught out by the advance of 4,000 Viet Cong, the Australians successfully responded to inflict heavy casualties: 17 dead against about 250 VC. Following this they managed to expand control over large areas of the province, and then win the support of the local people. Unlike the Americans who adopted a policy of 'search and destroy', the Australians were more intent on 'hearts and minds' (COIN – counter insurgency). Through various health, education and other civic action programmes, the Australians gained the confidence of many villagers, making it much harder for the VC to infiltrate rural areas of Phuoc Tuy.

This policy of gaining the support of the local population was complemented by the highly effective use of small **Special Air Service** (SAS) teams – who worked closely with the US Special Forces. Many of these men were transferred after fighting in the jungles of Borneo during the *Konfrontasi* between Malaysia and Indonesia. They came well trained in the art of jungle warfare and ended the war with the highest kill ratio of any similar unit: at least 500 VC dead, against none of their own to hostile fire. The Australians left Phuoc Tuy in late 1971 – having lost 423 men. The ARVN were unable to fill the vacuum, and the Viet Cong quickly regained control of the area.

the initiative. They began to lay the groundwork for what was to become known as the Tet (or New Year) Offensive – perhaps the single most important series of battles during the American War in Vietnam. During the early morning of 1 February 1968, shortly after noisy celebrations had welcomed in the New Year, 84,000 Communist troops – almost all Viet Cong – simultaneously attacked targets in 105 urban centres. Utterly surprising the US and South Vietnamese, the Tet Offensive had begun.

Preparations for the offensive had been laid over many months. Arms, ammunition and guerrillas were smuggled and infiltrated into urban areas, and detailed planning was undertaken. Central to the strategy was a 'sideshow' at Khe Sanh. By mounting an attack on the marine outpost at **Khe Sanh** (see page 208), the Communists successfully convinced the American and Vietnamese commanders that another Dien Bien Phu was underway. General Westmoreland moved 50,000 US troops away from the cities and suburbs to prevent any such humiliating repetition of the French defeat. But, Khe Sanh was just a diversion; a feint designed to draw attention away from the cities. In this the Communists were successful; for days

PATRIOT GAMES: VIETNAMESE STREET NAMES

Like other countries that have experienced a revolution, the Vietnamese authorities have spent considerable time expunging street names that honour men and women who lack the necessary revolutionary credentials. Most obviously, Saigon had its name changed to Ho Chi Minh City following reunification. But although all official literature uses the new name, the inhabitants of the city still stubbornly insist on calling it Saigon (see page 245). Most towns have the same street names, and most are in memory of former patriots:

Dien Bien Phu: site of the Communists' famous victory against the French (see page 173).
Duy Tan: 11th Nguyen emperor (1907-16) until exiled to Réunion by the French for his opposition to their colonial rule. Killed in an aircrash in Africa in 1945 his remains were interred in Hué in 1987.
Hai Ba Trung: the renowned Trung sisters who led a rebellion against Chinese overlords in 40 AD (see page 157).
Ham Nghi: the young emperor who joined the resistance against the French in 1885 at the age of 13 and thus gave it legitimacy.
Hoang Van Thu: leader of the Vietnamese Communist Party, executed by the French in 1944.
Le Duan: Secretary-General of Lao Dong from 1959.
Le Lai: brother-in-arms of Emperor Le Loi. Le Lai saved Viet forces by dressing in the Emperor's clothes and drawing away surrounding Chinese troops.
Le Loi: (**Le Thai To**) leader of a 15th century revolt which, in 1426, resulted in the liberation of Vietnam from Ming Chinese overlords. Born into a wealthy family he had a life-long concern for the poor. Founder of the Le Dynasty, he ruled 1426-33.
Le Thanh Ton(g): a successor to Le Loi, ruled 1460-1498, poet king, and cartographer he established an efficient administration on strict Confucian lines and an enlightened legal code; literature and the arts flourished.
Ly Thuong Kiet: military commander who led campaigns against the Chinese and Chams during the 11th century, and gained a reputation as a brilliant strategist. He died at the age of 70 in 1105.

after the Tet offensive, Westmoreland and the South Vietnamese President Thieu thought Khe Sanh to be the real objective and the attacks in the cities the decoy.

The most interesting aspect of the Tet Offensive was that although it was a strategic victory for the Communists, it was also a considerable tactical defeat. They may have occupied the US embassy in Saigon for a few hours but, except in Hué (see page 194), Communist forces were quickly repulsed by US and ARVN troops. The government in the S did not collapse, nor did the ARVN. Cripplingly high casualties were inflicted on the Communists – cadres at all echelons were killed – morale was undermined and it became clear that the cities would not rise up spontaneously to support the Communists. Tet, in effect, put paid to the VC as an effective fighting force. The fight now had to be increasingly taken up by the NVA. Walt Rostow wrote in 1995 that "Tet was an utter military and political defeat for the Communists in Vietnam", but adding "yet a political disaster in the United States". But this was not to matter; Westmoreland's request for more troops was turned down, and US public support for the war slumped further as horrified Americans watched the US embassy it-

Nguyen Du (1765-1820): Ambassador to Peking, courtier and Vietnam's most famous poet, wrote *The Tale of Kieu* (see page 123).

Nguyen Hue: Tay Son brother who routed the Chinese at the Battle of Dong Da. Later became Emperor Quany Trung (see below and page 225).

Nguyen Thai Hoc: leader of the Vietnam Quoc Dan Dang Party (VNQDD) (see page 87) and the leader of the Yen Bai uprisings; he was captured by the French and guillotined on 17 Jun 1930 at the age of 28.

Nguyen Trai: Emperor Le Loi's advisor and also a skilled poet, he advised Le Loi to concentrate on political and moral struggle: "Better to conquer hearts than citadels."

Nguyen Van Troi: Viet Cong hero who in 1963 tried, unsuccessfully, to assassinate Robert McNamara by blowing up a bridge in Saigon. He was executed.

Phan Boi Chau: a committed anti-colonialist from the age of 19, he travelled to China and Japan to organize resistance to the French. Captured in Shanghai in 1925 he was extradited to Hanoi and sentenced to life imprisonment. Public pressure led to his amnesty in the same year and he spent the rest of his life in Hué where he died in 1940.

Quang Trung: leader of the Tay Son peasant rebellion of 1771; defeated both the Siamese (Thais) and the Chinese (see page 225).

Ton Duc Thang: became President of the Socialist Republic of Vietnam; he took part in a mutiny aboard a French ship along with other Vietnamese shipmates in the Black Sea in support of the Russian Revolution.

Tran Hung Dao: 13th century hero who fought and defeated the Yuan Chinese (see page 180). He is not only regarded as one of Vietnam's great military leaders and strategists, but was also a man of letters writing the classic *Binh Thu Yeu Luoc* in 1284.

Tran Nguyen Han: a 15th century general who fought heroically against the Ming Chinese occupiers.

Tran Phu: the first Secretary General of the Communist Party of Indochina, killed by the French in 1931 at the age of 27.

30 Thang 4 Street: commemorates the fall of Saigon to the Communists on 30th April 1975.

---

self over-run. Those who for years had been claiming it was only a matter of time before the Communists were defeated appeared to be contradicted by the scale and intensity of the offensive. Even President Johnson was stunned by the VC's successes for even he had believed the US propaganda.

The Phoenix Programme, established in the wake of the Tet Offensive, aimed to destroy the Communists' political infrastructure in the Mekong Delta. Named after the Vietnamese mythical bird the Phung Hoang, which could fly anywhere, the programme sent CIA-recruited and trained Counter Terror Teams – in effect assassination units – into the countryside. The teams were ordered to try and capture Communist cadres; invariably they fired first and asked questions later. By 1971, it was estimated that the programme had led to the capture of 28,000 members of the VCI (Viet Cong Infrastructure), the death of 20,000, and the defection of a further 17,000. By the early 1970s the countryside in the Mekong Delta was more peaceful than it had been for years; towns which were previously strongholds of the Viet Cong had reverted to the control of the local authorities. Critics have questioned what proportion of

A NATION AT SEA: THE BOAT PEOPLE

One of the most potent images of Vietnam during the 1970s and 80s was of foundering, overloaded vessels carrying 'boat people' to Hong Kong, Thailand, Malaysia and the Philippines. Beginning in 1976, but becoming a torrent from the late 1970s, these boat people initially fled political persecution. More recently, most have been 'economic' migrants in search of a better life.

Escaping the country was not easy. Many prospective boat people were caught by the authorities (often after having already paid the estimated US$500-US$3,000 to secure a place on a boat), and sent to gaol or to a re-education camp. Of those who embarked, it has been estimated that at least a third died at sea – from drowning or dehydration, and at the hands of pirates. The boats were usually small and poorly maintained, hardly seaworthy for a voyage across the South China Sea. Captains rarely had charts (some did not even have an experienced sailor on board), and most had never ventured further afield than the coastal waters with which they were familiar.

By 1977, the exodus was so great that some freighters began to stop heaving-to to pick up refugees – a habit which, until then, had been sacrosanct among sailors. Malaysia instructed their coastal patrol vessels to force boats back out to sea and in the first 6 months of 1979 they did just that to 267 vessels carrying an estimated 40,000 refugees. One boat drifted for days off Malaysia, with the passengers drinking their own urine, until they were picked up – but not before two children had died of dehydration. The Singapore and Malaysian governments adopted a policy of allowing boats to replenish their supplies, but not to land – forcing some vessels to sail all the way to Australia before they were assured of a welcome (over 8,000 km). Cannabalism is also reported to have taken place; one boy who had only just survived being killed himself told a journalist: "After the body [of a boy] had been discovered, the boatmaster pulled it up out of the hold. Then he cut up the body. Everyone was issued a piece of meat about two fingers wide".

As numbers rose, so did the incidence of piracy – an age-old problem in the South China Sea. Pirates, mostly Thai, realizing that the boats often carried families with all their possessions (usefully converted into portable gold) began to target the refugee boats. Some commentators have estimated that by the late 1970s, 30% of boats were being boarded, and the United Nations High Commissioner for Refugees (UNHCR) in 1981 reported that 81% of women had been raped. Sometimes the boats were boarded and plundered, the women raped, all the passengers murdered, and the boats sunk. Despite all these risks, Vietnamese continued to leave in huge numbers: by 1980 there were 350,000 awaiting resettlement in refugee camps in the countries of Southeast Asia and Hong Kong.

Most of these 'illegals' left from the S of Vietnam; identified with the previous regime, they were systematically persecuted – particularly if they also happened to be ethnic Chinese or _Hoa_ (the Chinese 'invasion' of 1979 did not help matters). But as conditions worsened in the N, large numbers also began to sail from Ha

those killed, captured and sometimes tortured were Communist cadres, but even Communist documents admit that it seriously undermined their support network in the area. In these terms, the

Phoenix Programme was a great success.

The costs The Tet Offensive concentrated American minds. The costs of the war by that time had been vast. The US budget deficit had risen to 3% of GNP

Long Bay and Haiphong. Soon the process became semi-official, as local and regional authorities realized that fortunes could be made providing boats and escorts. Large freighters began to carry refugees – the *Hai Hong* (1,600 tonnes) which finally docked in Malaysia was carrying 2,500 passengers who claimed they had left with the cognizance of the authorities.

The peak period of the crisis spanned the years from 1976-1979, with 270,882 leaving the country in 1979 alone. The flow of refugees slowed during 1980 and 1981 to about 50,000, and until 1988 averaged about 10,000 each year. But in the late 1980s the numbers picked up once again – with most sailing for Hong Kong and leaving from the N. It seems that whereas the majority of those sailing in the first phase (1976-1981) were political refugees, the newer exodus has been driven by economic pressures. Daily wage rates in Vietnam at that time were only 3,000 dong (US$0.25) – so it is easy to see the attraction of leaving for healthier economic climes. With more than 40,000 refugees in camps in Hong Kong, the Hong Kong authorities began to forcibly repatriate (euphemistically termed 'orderly return') those screened as economic migrants at the end of 1989 when 51 were flown to Hanoi. Such was the international outcry as critics highlighted fears of persecution, that the programme was suspended. In May 1992, an agreement was reached between the British and Vietnamese governments to repatriate the 55,700 boat people living in camps in Hong Kong; by Jan 1993, 26,580 had been returned home. Only a few thousand are likely to be classified as political refugees and allowed to stay. (As part of their deal with China, the British government has agreed to empty the camps before the hand-over date in 1997.) There were even some 'double-backers' – migrants who had voluntarily returned home, received their UN allowance of US$440, and then returned again to Hong Kong in the hope of striking lucky once more.

Ironically, the evidence is that those repatriated are doing very well – better than those who never left the shores of Vietnam – and there is no convincing evidence of persecution, despite the fears of such groups as Amnesty International. With the European Community and the UN offering assistance to returnees, they have set up businesses, enroled on training courses and become embroiled in Vietnam's thrust for economic growth. The effect of the agreement is reflected in the fact that in 1992 only 55 boat people left Vietnam and in 1993, 777. The message has obviously got through. It is planned that the 50,000 Vietnamese boat people still scattered in camps across Asia at the end of 1994, will have been repatriated or settled elsewhere by the end of 1995. The difficulty is that those who are left are the least attractive to receiving countries. As Jahanshah Assadi of the UNHCR put it at the end of 1994, "Our Nobel Prize winners left a long time ago for the West", adding "What we have now is the bottom of the barrel." The criminal element grows by the month. There are many who doubt whether the targets set can be met. Even should thousands return to Vietnam in this way, there are thousands more leaving the country under the auspices of the UN Orderly Departure Programme – some 100,000 in 1992.

by 1968, inflation was accelerating, and thousands of young men had been killed for a cause which, to many, was becoming less clear by the month. Before the end of the year President Johnson had ended the bombing campaign and had begun to withdraw troops. Negotiations began in Paris in 1969 to try and secure an honourable settlement for the US. Although the last American combat troops were not to leave until Mar 1973, the Tet Offensive marked the beginning of the end. It was from that date that the Johnson administration began to search seriously for a way out of the conflict. The illegal bombing of Cambodia in 1969, and the resumption of the bombing of the N in 1972 (the most intensive of the entire conflict), were only flurries of action on the way to an inevitable US withdrawal.

The Paris Agreement (1972)

US Secretary of State **Henry Kissinger** records the afternoon of 8 October 1972, a Sun, as the moment when he realized that the Communists were willing to agree a peace treaty. There was a great deal to discuss, particularly whether the treaty would offer the prospect of peaceful reunification, or the continued existence of two states – a Communist N, and non-Communist S. Both sides tried to force the issue: the US mounted further attacks and at the same time strengthened and expanded the ARVN. They also tried to play the 'Madman Nixon' card, arguing that **President Richard Nixon** was such a vehement anti-Communist that he might well resort to the ultimate deterrent, the nuclear bomb. It is true that the PAVN was losing men through desertion and had failed to recover its losses in the Tet Offensive. Bao Ninh in his book *The sorrow of war about Kinh, a scout with the PAVN*, writes:

"The life of the B3 Infantrymen after the Paris Agreement was a series of long suffering days, followed by months of retreating and months of counter-attacking, withdrawal, then counter-attack. Victory after victory, withdrawal after withdrawal. The path of war seemed endless, desperate, and leading nowhere."

But the Communist leadership knew well that the Americans were committed to withdrawal – the only question was when, and so they felt that time was on their side.

By 1972, US troops in the S had declined to 95,000, the bulk of whom were support troops. The N gambled on a massive attack to defeat the ARVN and moved 200,000 men towards the demilitarized zone that marked the border between N and S. On 30 Mar the PAVN crossed into the S and quickly over-ran large sections of Quang Tri province. Simultaneous attacks were mounted in the W highlands, at Tay Ninh and in the Mekong Delta. For a while it looked as if the S would fall altogether. The US responded by mounting a succession of intense bombing raids which eventually forced the PAVN to retreat. The spring offensive may have failed, but like Tet, it was strategically important, for it demonstrated that without US support the ARVN was unlikely to be able to withstand a Communist attack.

Both sides, by late 1972, were ready to compromise. Against the wishes of South Vietnam's President Nguyen Van Thieu, the US signed a treaty on 27 January 1973, the ceasefire going into effect on the same day. Before the signing, Nixon ordered the bombing of the N – the so-called Christmas Campaign. It lasted 11 days from 18 Dec (Christmas Day was a holiday) and was the most intensive of the war. With the ceasefire and President Thieu, however shaky, both in place, the US was finally able to back out of its nightmare and the last combat troops left in Mar 1973. As J. William Fulbright, a highly influential member of the Senate and a strong critic of the US role in Vietnam, observed: "We [the US] have the power to do any damn fool thing we want, and we always seem to do it."

The final phase, 1973-1975

The Paris Accord settled nothing – it simply provided a means by which the Americans could withdraw from Vietnam. It was never going to resolve the deep-seated differences between the two regimes and with only a brief lull, the war continued, this time without US troops. Thieu's government was probably in terminal decline even before the peace treaty was signed. Though ARVN forces were at their largest ever and, on paper, considerably stronger than the PAVN, many men were weakly committed to the cause of the S. Corruption was endemic, business was in recession, and political dissent was on the increase. The North's Central Committee formally decided to abandon the Paris Accord in Oct 1973; by the beginning of 1975 they were ready for the final offensive. It took only until Apr for the Communists to achieve total victory. ARVN troops deserted in their thousands, and the only serious resistance was offered at Xuan Loc, less than 100 km from Saigon. President Thieu resigned on 27 Apr. ARVN generals, along with their men, were attempting to flee as the PAVN advanced on Saigon. The end was quick: at 1045 on 30 Apr a T-54 tank (number 843) crashed its way through the gates of the Presidential Palace, symbolizing the end of the Second Indochina War. For the US, the

aftermath of the war would lead to years of soul searching; for Vietnam, to stagnation and isolation. George Ball, a senior State Department figure reflected afterwards that the war was "probably the greatest single error made by America in its history".

Legacy of the Vietnam War

The Vietnam War (or 'American War' to the Vietnamese) is such an enduring feature of the West's experience of the country that most visitors are constantly on the look-out for legacies of the conflict. There is no shortage of physically deformed and crippled Vietnamese. Many men were badly injured during the war, but large numbers also received their injuries while serving in Cambodia (1979-1989). It is tempting to associate deformed children with the enduring effects of the pesticide Agent Orange (1.7 million tonnes had been used by 1973), although this has yet to be proven 'scientifically' –

American studies claim that there is no significant difference in congenital malformation. Certainly, local doctors admit that children and babies in the S are smaller today than they were before 1975. But this is more likely to be due to malnutrition than defoliants.

Bomb damage is most obvious from the air: well over 5 million tonnes of bombs were dropped on the country (N and S) and there are said to be 20 million bomb-craters – the sort of statistic people like to recount, but no one can legitimately verify. Many craters have yet to be filled in and paddy fields are still pockmarked. Some farmers have used these holes in the ground to farm fish and to use as small reservoirs to irrigate vegetable plots; they may also be partially to blame for the dramatic increase in the incidence of malaria. War scrap is one of the country's most valuable exports and shell casings, PSS (perforated steel sheeting) and other remnants can be seen piled high by roadsides – although even Vietnam is running out of accessible scrap. The cities in the N are surprisingly devoid of obvious signs of the bombing campaigns – Hanoi remains remarkably intact. Hué however, formerly Vietnam's greatest historical treasure, is a tragic sight. The Citadel and Forbidden Palace were extensively damaged during the Tet offensive in 1968 and are still being repaired (see page 197). In response to the American bombing campaign, the North Vietnamese leadership ordered the dispersal of industrial activities to the countryside. Though effective in protecting some of the N limited industrial base, this strategy created an inefficient pattern of production – a factor which even today hinders the N efforts at promoting growth.

Even harder to measure, is the **effect of the war on the Vietnamese psyche**. Bao Ninh in *The sorrow of war* writes of a driver with the PAVN who, talking with Kien the book's main character, observes: "I'm simply a soldier like you who'll now have to live with broken dreams and with pain. But, my friend, our era is finished. After this hard-won victory fighters like you, Kien, will never be normal again. You won't even speak with your normal voice, in the normal way again." Later in the book, Kien muses about the opportunities that the war has extinguished. Although the book is a fictional story, the underlying tale is one of truth:

"Still, even in the midst of my reminiscences I can't avoid admitting there seems little left for me to hope for. From my life before soldiering there remains sadly little. ... Those who survived continue to live. But that will has gone, that burning will which was once Vietnam's salvation. Where is the reward of enlightenment due to us for attaining our sacred war goals? Our history-making efforts for the next generations have been to no avail."

The Vietnamese Communist Party leadership still seem to be preoccupied by the conflict, and school children are routinely shown War Crimes Museums, War Museums and Ho Chi Minh Memorials. But despite the continuing propaganda offensive, people harbour surprisingly little animosity towards America or the West. Indeed, of all Westerners, it is often Americans who are most warmly welcomed, even in the N. During the Gulf conflict of 1991 young Vietnamese were rooting for the Americans and their allies, not for Saddam Hussein. But it must be remembered that about 60% of Vietnam's population has been born since the US left in 1973, so have no memory of the American occupation.

The deeper source of antagonism is the continuing divide between the N and S. It was to be expected that the forces of the N would exact their revenge on their foes in the S – and many were relieved that the predicted blood bath did not materialize. But few would have thought that this revenge would be so long-lasting. The quarter of a million Southern dead are not mourned or honoured, or even acknowledged. Former soldiers are denied jobs, and the government does not seem to accept any need for national reconciliation.

This is the multiple legacy of the War on Vietnam and the Vietnamese. The legacy on the US and Americans is more widely appreciated. The key question which still occupies the minds of many, though, is, was it worth it? Walt Rostow, Lee Kuan Yew and others would probably answer 'yes'. If the US had not intervened, communism would have spread farther in Southeast Asia; more dominoes, in their view, would have fallen. In 1973, when US withdrawal was agreed, Lee Kuan Yew observed that the countries of Southeast Asia were much more resilient and resistant to communism than they had been, say, at the time of the Tet offensive in 1968. The US presence in Vietnam allowed them to reach this state of affairs. Yet Robert McNamara in his book *In retrospect: the tragedy and lessons of Vietnam*, and one of the architects of US policy, writes:

"Although we sought to do the right thing – and believed we were doing the right thing – in my judgment, hindsight proves us wrong. We both overestimated the effects of South Vietnam's loss on the security of the West and failed to adhere to the fundamental principle that, in the final analysis, if the South Vietnamese were to be saved, they had to win the war themselves."

Art and architecture

Art

The first flourishing of Vietnamese art occurred with the emergence of the Dongson culture (named after a small town near Thanh Hoa where early excavations were focused) on the coast of Annam and Tonkin between 500 and 200 BC. The inspiration for the magnificent bronzes produced by the artists of Dongson originated from China: the decorative motifs have clear affinities with earlier Chinese bronzes. At the same time, the exceptional skill of production and decoration argues that these pieces represent among the first, and finest, of Southeast Asian works of art. This is most clearly evident in the huge and glorious **bronze drums** which can be seen in museums in both Hanoi and Saigon (see box).

If there was ever a 'golden' period in Vietnamese art and architecture, it was that of the former central Vietnamese **kingdom of Champa**, centred on the Annamite coast, which flowered in the 10th and 11th centuries. Tragically however, many of the 250 sites recorded in historical records have been pillaged or damaged and only 20 have survived the intervening centuries in a reasonable state of repair. Most famous are the sites of My Son and Dong Duong, S of Danang (see page 215). Many of the finest works have been spirited out of the country to private collections and foreign museums; others destroyed by bombing and artillery fire during the Vietnam War. Nonetheless, the world's finest collection – with some breathtakingly beautiful work – is to be found in Danang's Cham Museum (see page 214).

The earliest Cham art belongs to the Mi Son E1 period (early 8th century). It shows stylistic similarities with Indian Sanchi and Gupta works, although even at this early stage in its development Cham art incorporated distinctive indigenous elements, most clearly seen in the naturalistic interpretation of human form. By the Dong Duong period (late 9th century), the Cham had developed a unique style of their own. Archaeologists recognize 6 periods of Cham art:

Mi Son E1 – early 8th century
Hoa Lai – early 9th century
Dong Duong – late 9th century
Tra Kieu – late 9th-early 10th century
Thap Mam – 12th-13th century
Po Klaung Garai – 13th-16th century

The Cham Kingdom was ethnically and linguistically distinct, but was over-run by the Vietnamese in the 15th century. It might be argued, then, that their monuments and sculptures have little to do with 'Vietnam' *per se*, but with a preceding dynasty.

More characteristic of Vietnamese art and architecture are **the pagodas and palaces at Hué** (see page 193) and in and around Hanoi (page 147). But even this art and architecture is not really 'Vietnamese', as it is highly derivative, drawing heavily on Chinese prototypes. Certainly there are some features which are peculiarly Vietnamese, but unlike the other countries of mainland Southeast Asia, the Vietnamese artistic tradition is far less distinct. Vietnamese artistic endeavour was directed more towards literature than the plastic arts. In his art history of Indochina, French art historian Bernard Groslier – better known for his work on Angkor – writes, rather condescendingly:

'From 1428 to 1769 Vietnamese art is bogged down in formulas. Despite the absorption of Champa, no foreign influence, save that of China, affected them. However execution and technique greatly improved, so that some of the works take an honourable place among Chinese provincial products' (1962: 227)

The Vietnamese pagoda

The pagoda or *chua* is a Buddhist temple, and shows clear affinities with its Chinese equivalent (see page 118 for a background to Vietnamese Buddhism). But a Vietnamese pagoda is not a many-tiered tower – it is usually a single-storeyed structure. Most will have a sacred pond (often with sacred turtles), bell tower, and yard. The main building – the pagoda itself – usually consists of a number of rooms. At the front are three main doors which are opened only for special festivals. Behind these doors are the front hall, central hall and the main altar hall, the former being at the lowest level, the altar hall at the highest. At the back

---

MODERN VIETNAMESE ART

Contemporary art in Vietnam, as elsewhere in Southeast Asia, has recently benefited from an upsurge in interest from young Asian collectors with plenty of money and a preference for arts oriental to arts occidental. Exhibitions in New York, Paris and London have helped bring Vietnamese art to a wider public. Galleries have opened in all the major cities of Vietnam and although much of the work displayed is purely commercial, artists now have an opportunity to exhibit pictures which until recently were considered subversive. Vietnam has three art colleges in Saigon, Hué and the School of Fine Arts in Hanoi, which was founded by the French in 1925.

Although most Vietnamese painting is still conservative in subject, idiom and medium, some painters of the younger generation, including Dao Hai Phong, Tran Trong Vu and Truong Tan, are experimenting with more abstract ideas and, in the more liberal artistic clime of the nineties, their work is more expressive and less clichéd than that of 10 or 20 years ago. Even established artists such as Ly Quy Chung, Tran Luu Hau and Mai Long are taking advantage of their newly found artistic freedom to produce exciting experimental work; Trinh Cung and Tran Trong Vu are noted for their abstract paintings. Among the most respected artists of the older generation are Professor Nguyen Thu, Colonel Quang Tho and Diep Minh Chau, whose work draws heavily on traditional Vietnamese themes, particularly rural landscapes, but also includes recent history: the battle of Dien Bien Phu, life under American occupation and pencil sketches of Ho Chi Minh. Such traditional art forms as watercolour paintings on silk and lacquerwork are still popular and impact even to modern art a distinctive Vietnamese feel.

of the pagoda are living quarters for monks and nuns, as well as gardens and other secular structures. Monks and nuns never serve in the same pagoda. Particularly large pagodas are known as *dinh*.

Common pagoda characters and iconography

Avalokitesvara: the compassionate male Boddhisattva, usually depicted in an attitude of meditation with his attributes, a water flask and lotus. The figure is sometimes represented with four arms, in which case his attributes are a rosary and book, as well as the lotus and waterflask.

Bodhisattvas: enlightened beings or future Buddhas who have renounced nirvana to remain on earth. They are in theory countless, although just a handful are usually represented, most easily recognisable to the devotee. Boddhisattvas are usually depicted as princes with rich robes and a crown or headdress.

Buddha (Sakyamuni): the Buddha, or the historic Buddha; usually depicted seated on a throne or thrones (often a lotus) in one of the *mudras* (see page 332), and clothed in the simple dress of an ascetic. Among the Buddha's features are elongated ear lobes, the *urna* or third 'eye' in the centre of the forehead, and tightly curled hair.

Buddha of the Past (Amitabha): central to the Pure Land faith. Adherents chant the Amitabha sutra, and on their death are transported to the Western Paradise where they are guided to nirvana.

Dragon (long/rong): not the evil destructive creature of Western mythology but divine and beneficial. Often associated with the emperor.

Quan Am: Chinese Goddess of Mercy (Kuan-yin), often all-white, and usually depicted holding her adopted son in one arm and standing on a lotus leaf (the symbol of purity). Quan Am's husband is occasionally depicted as a parakeet (see page 154). Quan Am is sometimes represented as a man, and as a Bodhisattva – Avalokitesvara – the two are fused in a single representation.

Quan Cong and companions: usually red-faced and green-cloaked and accompanied by his two trusty companions, General Chau Xuong and the Mandarin Quan Binh, and sometimes also with his horse and groom.

Swastika: running either left to right or vice versa, it is often complicated by various additions. The motif symbolizes the 'heart of the Buddha', 'long life' and 'ten thousand'. In Buddhist and Cao Dai temples, swastikas run in opposite directions. Cao Dai believers argue that

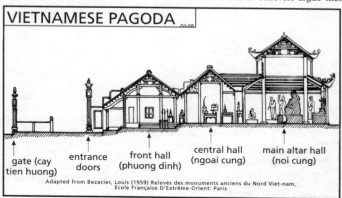

VIETNAMESE PAGODA

gate (cay tien huong) | entrance doors | front hall (phuong dinh) | central hall (ngoai cung) | main altar hall (noi cung)

Adapted from Bezacier, Louis (1959) *Relevés des monuments anciens du Nord Viet-nam,* Ecole Française D'Extrême-Orient: Paris

'their' direction is in harmony with the movement of the universe.

Thien Hau Thanh Mau: goddess of the sea and protector of sailors.

Yin-yang symbol: the Taoist symbol (see page 120); a circle divided by an 'S' line, splitting the circle into dark and light halves and symbolizing the dualism of the world.

Culture and life

People

Vietnam is home to a total of 54 ethnic groups including the Vietnamese themselves. The ethnic minorities vary in size from the Tay, with a population of about 1.3 million, to the O-du who number only 100 individuals. Life has been hard for many of the minorities who have had to fight not only the French and Vietnamese but often each other in order to retain their territory and cultural identity. Traditions and customs have been eroded by outside influences such as Catholicism and Communism although some of the less alien ideas have been successfully accommodated. Centuries of Viet population growth and decades of warfare have taken a heavy toll on minorities and their territories; increasingly, population pressure from the minority groups themselves poses a threat to their way of life.

BRILLIANCE IN BRONZE: RAIN DRUMS OF DONGSON

Of the artefacts associated with the Dongson culture, none is more technologically or artistically impressive than the huge bronze kettle drums that have been unearthed. Vietnamese archaeologists, understandably, have been keen to stress the 'Vietnamese-ness' of these objects, rejecting many of the suggestions made by Western scholars that they are of Chinese or Indian inspiration. As Professor Pham Huy Thong of the Academy of Sciences writes in a recent book, Western studies are "marked by insufficient source material, prejudices and mere deductions", and that their "achievements [in understanding the drums] remain insignificant". He supports the view that these magnificent objects were products of the forebears of the Viet people. The jury on the issue remains out.

The squat, waisted, bronze Dongson drums show their makers to have been master casters of the first order. They can measure over one metre in height and width and consist of a decorated tympanum, a convex upper section, waisted middle, and expanding lower section. Decoration is both geometric and naturalistic, most notably on the finely incised drum head. An area of continuing debate concerns the function of the drums. They have usually been found associated with human remains and other precious objects, leading archaeologists to argue that they symbolized power and prestige, and were treasured objects in the community. Also known as 'rain drums', they are sometimes surmounted with bronze figures of frogs (or toads). It is thought that the drums were used as magical instruments to summon rain – frogs being associated with rain. Other decorative motifs include dancers (again, possibly part of rain-making rites) and boats with feather-crowned passengers (perhaps taking the deceased to the Kingdom of the Dead). Other Dongson drums have been found as far east as the island of Alor in Nusa Tenggara, Indonesia, indicating trade links between northern Vietnam and the archipelago.

As if to emphasise the nationalist symbolism of the drums an image of an ornate tympanum is used as an icon by Vietnamese television, and Vietnam Airlines prints the motif on their tickets.

Highland peoples: the Montagnards of Vietnam

The highland areas of Vietnam are among the most linguistically and culturally diverse in the world. In total, the highland peoples number 6-8 million. As elsewhere in Southeast Asia, a broad distinction can be drawn in Vietnam between the peoples of the lowlands and valleys, and the peoples of the uplands.

DONGSON DRUM   TIB 302

0   5cm

Dongson drum and mantle, bronze (79cm in width, 63cm high).
Unearthed, Northern Vietnam 1893-94.

The former tend to be settled, cultivate wet rice, and are fairly tightly integrated into the wider Vietnamese state: in most instances they are Viet. The latter are often migratory, they cultivate upland crops often using systems of shifting cultivation (see page 36), and are comparatively isolated from the state. The generic term for these diverse peoples of the highlands is *Montagnard* (from the French, 'Mountain People'), in Vietnamese *nguoi thuong* ('highland citizen') or, rather less politely, *moi* ('savage' or 'slave'). As far as the highland peoples themselves are concerned, they identify with their village and 'tribal' group, not as part of a wider 'highland citizens' grouping.

The French attitude towards the Montagnards was often inconsistent. The authorities wanted to control them and sometimes succumbed to the pressure from French commercial interests to conscript them into the labour force, particularly on the plantations. But some officials were positively protective, one, Monsieur Sebatier refused missionaries access to the territory under his control, destroyed bridges to prevent access, and had three tribal wives. He recommended total withdrawal from their lands in order to protect their cultural integrity. In *A dragon apparent*, Norman Lewis provides a wonderful account of the Montagnard and their way of life, and perceptively examines the relationship between them and the French.

Relations between the minorities and the Viet have not always been as good as they are officially portrayed. Recognizing and exploiting this mutual distrust and animosity, both the French and American armies recruited from among the minorities. In 1961 US Special Forces began organising Montagnards into defence groups to prevent Communist infiltration into the Central Highlands from the N. Since 1975 relations between minorities and Viet have improved but there is still hostility, particularly in areas of heavy logging. Official publications embellish the nature of the relationship between Viet and minority peoples with a brazen contempt for history: thus we read "successive generations of Vietnamese, belonging to 54 ethnic groups, members of the great national community of Vietnam, have always stood side by side with one another, sharing weal and woe, shedding sweat and blood to defend and build up their homeland...". The government is keen to stress its role in promoting health care and introducing cash-cropping among the minorities but fails to discuss motive and effect, namely the narrowing, blunting and elimination of cultural differences.

But potentially a more serious threat to the minorities' way of life is tourism. A great deal has been written about cultural erosion by tourism (see pages 63 and 113) and any visitor to a minority village should be aware of the extent to which he or she contributes to this process. Traditional means of livelihood are quickly abandoned when a higher living standard for less effort can be obtained from the tourist dollar. Long-standing societal and kinship ties are weakened by the intrusion of outsiders. Young people may question their society's values and traditions which may seem archaic, anachronistic and risible by comparison with those of the modern, sophisticated tourist. And dress and music lose all cultural significance and symbolism if they are allowed to become mere tourist attractions.

Nevertheless, this is an unavoidable consequence of Vietnam's decision to admit tourists. Perhaps fortunately however, for the time being at least, many of the minorities are inaccessible to the average traveller. Visitors can minimize their impact by acting in a sensitive way (it is, for example, perfectly obvious when someone does not want their photograph taken). (See box for general advice on visiting minority villages.)

VISITING THE MINORITIES: HOUSE RULES

Etiquette and customs vary between the minorities. However, the following are general rules of good behaviour that should be adhered to whenever possible.

1. Dress modestly and avoid undressing/changing in public.
2. Ask permission before photographing anyone (old people, pregnant women and mothers with babies often object to having their photograph taken).
3. Only enter a house if invited.
4. Do not touch or photograph village shrines.
5. Do not smoke opium.
6. Avoid sitting or stepping on door sills.
7. Avoid excessive displays of wealth and be sensitive when giving gifts (for children, pens are better than sweets).
8. Avoid introducing Western medicines.

But the minority areas of Vietnam are fascinating places and the immense variety of colours and styles of dress add greatly to the visitor's enjoyment. Minority architecture and agriculture are highly distinctive and can produce whole landscape assemblages which sometimes owe more to the hand of man than God.

The peoples of the hills

Ba-na (Bahnar) A Mon-Khmer-speaking minority group concentrated in the central highland provinces of Gia Lai-Kon Tum and numbering about 150,000. Locally powerful from the 15th-18th centuries, they were virtually annihilated by neighbouring groups during the 19th century. Roman Catholic missionaries influenced the Ba-na greatly and they came to identify closely with the French. Some conversions to Catholicism were made but Christianity, where it remains, is usually just an adjunct to Ba-na animism. Ba-na houses are built on stilts and in each village is a communal house, or *rông*, which is the focus of social life. When a baby reaches his first full month he has his ears pierced in a village ceremony equivalent to the Vietnamese *day thang* (see box 'Rite of passage', page 116); only then is a child considered a full member of the community. Their society gives men and women relatively equal status. Male and female heirs inherit wealth, and marriage can be arranged by the families of either husband or wife. Ba-na practice both settled and shifting cultivation.

Co-ho (also Kohor, with small local groups the **Xre, Chil** and **Nop**) Primarily found on the Lam Dong Plateau in Lam Dong Province (Dalat) with a population of about 100,000. Extended family groups live in longhouses or *buon*, sometimes up to 30m long. Unusually, society is matrilineal and newly-married men live with their wives' families. The children take their mother's name; if the wife dies young her smaller sister will take her place. Women wear tight-fitting blouses and skirts. Traditional shifting cultivation is giving way to settled agriculture.

Dao (also **Man**) The Dao live in northern Vietnam in the provinces bordering China particularly Lao Cai and Ha Giang. They number, perhaps, half a million in all and include several sub-groupings notably the Dao Quan Chet (Tight Trouser Dao), the Dao Tien (Money Dao) and the Dao Ao Dai (Long Dress Dao). As these names suggest, Dao people wear highly distinctive clothing although sometimes only on their wedding day. Apart from the trousered Dao, women wear dresses which they embellish with embroidery or strings of coins. Head gear is equally elaborate and includes a range of shapes (from square to conical), fabrics (waxed hair to dried pumpkin fibres) and colours.

Dao wedding customs are as complex as Dao clothing and vary with group. Apart from parental consent, intending marriage partners must have compatible birthdays, and the groom has to provide the bride's family with gifts worthy of their daughter. If he is unable to do this a temporary marriage can take place but the outstanding presents must be produced and a permanent wedding celebrated before *their* daughter can marry.

The Dao live chiefly by farming: those in higher altitudes are swidden cultivators growing maize, cassava and rye. In the middle zone shifting methods are again used to produce rice and maize, and on the valley floors sedentary farmers grow irrigated rice and rear livestock.

Spiritually the Dao have also opted for diversity: they worship *Ban Vuong*, their mythical progenitor as well as their more immediate and real ancestors. The Dao also find room for elements of Taoism, and in some cases Buddhism and Confucianism, in their elaborate metaphysical lives.

E-de (also Rhade) Primarily concentrated in the Central Highlands province of Dac Lac and numbering nearly 200,000, they came into early contact with the French and are regarded as one of the more 'progressive' groups, adapting to modern life with relative ease. Traditionally the E-de live in longhouses on stilts; accommodated under one roof is the matrilineal extended family or commune. The commune falls under the authority of an elderly, respected woman known as the *khoa sang* who is responsible for communal property, especially the gongs and jars, which feature in important festivals. In E-de society it is the girl's family that selects a husband, who then comes to live with her (ie society is matrilocal). Wealth and property are inherited solely by daughters. Shifting cultivation is the traditional subsistence system, although this has given way in most areas to settled wet rice agriculture. Spiritually the E-de are polytheist: they number animism (recognizing the spirits of rice, soil, fire and water especially) and Christianity among their beliefs.

Gia rai (also **Zrai**) Primarily found in Gia Lai and Kon Tum provinces (especially near Play Ku) and numbering 260,000, they are the largest group in the Central Highlands. They are settled cultivators and live in houses on stilts in villages called *ploi* or *bon*. The Gia-rai are animist and recognize the spiritual dimension of nature; ever since the 7th century they have had a flesh and blood King of Fire and King of Water whose spirit is invoked in rain ceremonies.

Hmong (also **Meo**, **Mieu**, **Miao**) Widely spread across the highland areas of the country, but particularly near the Chinese border down to the 18th parallel. The Hmong number about 750,000 (over 1% of Vietnam's population) and live at higher altitudes than all other hill people – above 1,500m. Comparatively recent migrants to Vietnam, the Hmong began to settle in the country during the 19th century, after moving S from China. They have played an important role in resisting both the French and the Vietnamese. Living at such high altitudes they tend to be one of the most isolated of all the hill people. Their way of life does not normally bring them into contact with the outside world which suits them well – the Hmong traders at Sapa are an exception (see page 176). High in the hills, flooding is not a problem so their houses are built on the ground, not raised up on stilts. The Hmong practise slash and burn cultivation growing maize and dry rice. Although fields are often cleared on very steep and rocky slopes, the land is not terraced. There are a number of different groups among the Hmong including the White, Black, Red and Flower Hmong which are distinguishable by the colour of the women's clothes. Black Hmong wear almost entirely black clothing with remarkable pointed black turbans. White Hmong women wear white skirts and the Red Hmong tie their heads in a red scarf while the Flower Hmong wrap their hair (with hair extensions) around their head like a broad-brimmed hat.

Muong (also **Mol**) Numbering almost 1 million the Muong are one of the largest ethnic minorities in Vietnam. They live in the area between northern Thanh Hoa Province and Yen Bai but predominantly in Hoa Binh Province. It is thought that the Muong are descended from the same stock as the Viets: their languages are similar, and there are also close similarities in culture and religion. But whereas the Vietnamese came under strong Chinese cultural influence from the early centuries of the Christian era, the Muong did not. Culturally the Muong are akin to the Thai and live in stilt houses in small villages called *quel*, groupings of from three to 30 *quel* form a unit called a *muong*. Muong society is feudal in nature with each *muong* coming under the protection of a noble family (*lang*). The common people are not deemed worthy of family names so are all called Bui. Each year the members of a *muong* are required to labour for 1 day in fields belonging to the *lang*.

Marriages are arranged: girls, in particular, have no choice of spouse. Muong cultural life is rich, literature has been translated into Vietnamese and their legends, poems and songs are considered particularly fine.

Nung Concentrated in Cao Bang and Lang Son provinces, adjacent to the Chinese border, the Nung number approximately 1 million. They are strongly influenced by the Chinese and most are Buddhist, but like both Vietnamese and Chinese the Nung practise ancestor worship too. In Nung houses a Buddhist altar is placed above the ancestor altar and, in deference to Buddhist teaching, they refrain from eating most types of meat. The Nung are settled agriculturalists and, where conditions permit, produce wet rice; all houses have their own garden in which fruit and vegetables are grown.

Tày (also Tho) The Tày are the most populous ethnic minority in Vietnam; they number about 1.3 million and are found in the provinces of NW Vietnam stretching from Quang Ninh E to Lao Cai. Tày society was traditionally feudal with powerful lords able to extract from the free and semi-free serfs obligations such as *droit de seigneur*. Today Tày society is male dominated with important decisions being taken by men, and eldest sons inheriting the bulk of the family's wealth.

Economically the Tày survive by farming and are highly regarded as wet rice cultivators. They are also noted for the production of fruits, herbs and spices. Diet is supplemented by animal and fish rearing and incomes by the production of handicrafts.

Tày culture is in many respects similar to the Kinh and they follow the three main religions of Buddhism, Confucianism and Taoism in addition to ancestor worship and animist beliefs. Tày literature has a long and distinguished history and much has been translated into Vietnamese.

Thai (also **Tày** and **T'ai**) Numbering over 1 million this is the second largest ethnic minority in Vietnam and ethnically distinct from the Thais of modern-day Thailand. There are two main sub-groups, the Black (Thai Den) and the White Thai (Thai Don) and many others, including the Red Thai (Thai Do). The use of these colour-based classifications has usually been linked to the colour of their clothes, particularly the colour of women's shirts. However there has been some confusion over the origins of the terms and there is every reason to believe that it has nothing to

---

RITE OF PASSAGE: FROM BABY TO INFANT

In a poor country like Vietnam staying alive for long enough to see one's own first birthday has not always been easy. Fortunately, infant mortality levels have fallen dramatically (from 156/1,000 in 1960 to 49/1,000 in 1990) but remain high by Western standards. Perhaps not surprisingly therefore, Vietnamese families celebrate two important milestones in the early lives of their babies.

Day thang, or full month, is celebrated exactly one month after birth. Traditionally, the mother remained in bed with her heavily-swaddled baby for the first month keeping him away from sun, rain and demon spirits. At one month the child is beyond the hazardous neo-natal stage and the mother would leave her bed and go out of the house to introduce her baby to the village. Today, the parents hold a small party for friends and neighbours.

Thoi noi is celebrated at the end of the first year; it marks the time the baby stops sleeping in the cot and, having reached a full year, it is also a thanksgiving that the child has reached the end of the most dangerous year of life. At the party the baby is presented with a tray on which are various items such as a pen, a mirror, scissors, some soil and food; whichever the baby takes first indicates his character and the job he is likely to get: scissors for a tailor, pen for a teacher, soil for a farmer and so on. Babies are normally weaned at about this time: some Vietnamese mothers use remarkably unsubtle but effective means for turning the baby from the breast, smearing the nipple with charcoal dust or Tiger Balm!

---

do with the colour of their attire, and is possibly linked to the distribution of the sub-groups near the Red and Black rivers. The confusion of names becomes even more perplexing when the Vietnamese names for the sub-groups of Thai people are translated into Thai. Some scholars have taken Thai Den (Black Thai) to be Thai Daeng – *daeng* being the Thai word for red, thereby muddling up the two groups.

Being so numerous they cover a large part of NW Vietnam, in particular the valleys of the Red River and the Da and the Ma rivers, spilling over into Laos and Thailand. They arrived in Vietnam probably during the 4th century from southern China and linguistically they are part of the wider T'ai linguistic grouping.

The Thai tend to occupy lowland areas and they compete directly with the Kinh (ethnic Vietnamese) for good quality, irrigable farmland. They are masters of wet rice cultivation producing high yields and often two harvests each year. Their irrigation works are ingenious and

incorporate numerous labour-saving devices including river-powered water wheels that can raise water several metres. Thai villages (*ban*) consist of 40-50 houses on stilts; they are architecturally attractive, shaded by fruit trees and surrounded by verdant paddy fields. Being, as they are, so often located by rivers one of the highlights of a Thai village is its suspension footbridge. The Thai are excellent custodians of the land (particularly by comparison with some other minority peoples) and their landscapes and villages are invariably most scenic.

Owing to their geographical proximity and agricultural similarities with the Kinh it is not surprising to see cultural assimilation – sometimes via marriage – and most Thai speak Vietnamese. Equally it is interesting to note the extent to which the Thai retain a distinctive cultural identity, visibly most noticeable in their dress.

When a Thai woman marries, her parents-in-law give her a hair extension (*can song*) and a silver hair pin (*khat pom*) which she is expected to wear (even in bed) for the duration of the marriage. There are two wedding ceremonies, the first at the bride's house where the couple live for 1 to 3 years, followed by a second when they move to the husband's house.

Xo-dang Concentrated in Gia Lai and Kon Tum provinces and numbering about 100,000, the Xo-dang live in extended family longhouses and society is patriarchal. The Xo-dang practise both shifting agriculture and the cultivation of wet rice. A highly war-like people, they almost wiped out the Ba-na in the 19th century. Xo-dang thought nothing of kidnapping neighbouring tribesmen to sacrifice to the spirits; indeed the practice of kidnapping was subsequently put to commercial use and formed the basis of a slave trade with Siam (Thailand). Xo-dang villages, or *ploi*, are usually well defended (presumably for fear of reprisal) and are surrounded by thorn hedges supplemented with spears and stakes. Complex rules designed to prevent in-breeding limit the number of available marriage partners which sometimes results in late marriages.

Other Groups with populations of over 50,000 population *Hre* – Quang Ngai and Binh Dinh provinces, 94,000. *Mnong* – Dac Lac and Lam Dong provinces, 65,000. *Xtieng* – Song Be province 50,000.

Kinh (also Viet) The 1989 census revealed that 87% of Vietnam's population were ethnic Vietnamese. But with a well-run family planning campaign beginning to take effect in urban areas and higher fertility rates among the ethnic minorities it is likely that this figure will fall. The history of the Kinh is marked by a steady southwards progression from the Red River basin to the southern plains and Mekong Delta. Today the Kinh are concentrated into the two great river deltas, the coastal plains and the main cities. Only in the central and northern highland regions are they outnumbered by ethnic minorities. Kinh social cohesion and mastery of intensive wet rice cultivation has led to their numerical, and subsequently political and economic dominance of the country. Ethnic Vietnamese are also found in Cambodia where some have been settled for generations; recent Khmer Rouge attacks on Vietnamese villages have, however, caused many to flee to Vietnam.

Cham (also **Chiem**) With the overrunning of Champa in 1471 (see page 82) Cham cultural and ethnic identity was diluted by the more numerous ethnic Vietnamese. The Cham were dispossessed of the more productive lands and found themselves in increasingly marginal territory. Economically eclipsed and strangers in their own land, Cham artistic creativity atrophied, their sculptural and architectural skills, once the glory of Vietnam, faded and decayed like so many Cham temples and towers. It is estimated that there are, today, 99,000 Cham people in Vietnam chiefly in central and southern Vietnam in the coastal provinces extending S from Qui Nhon. Small communities are to be found in Ho Chi Minh City. They are artistically the poor relations of their forebears but skills in weaving and music live on.

The Cham of the S are typically engaged in fishing, weaving and other small scale commercial activities; urban Cham are poor and live in slum neighbourhoods. Further N the Cham are wet or dry rice farmers according to local topography; they are noted for their skill in wet rice farming and small scale hydraulic engineering.

In southern Vietnam the majority of Cham are Muslim, a comparatively newly acquired religion although familiar from earlier centuries when many became acquainted with Islamic tenets through traders from India and the Indonesian isles. In central Vietnam most Cham are Brahminist and the cult of the linga remains an important feature of spiritual life. In these provinces, away from the influence of Islam, vestiges of matriliny remain.

The *Hoa* and the *Viet-kieu*: ethnic Chinese and overseas Vietnamese

There are nearly 1 million ethnic Chinese or *Hoa* in Vietnam, 80% living in the S of the country. Before reunification in 1975 there were even more: persecution by the authorities and the lack of economic opportunities since the process of socialist transformation was initiated, encouraged hundreds of thousands to leave. There are now large Vietnamese communities abroad, particularly in Australia, on the W coast of the US, and France. It has been estimated that the total Viet-kieu population numbers some 2 million.

With the reforms of the 1980s, the authorities' view of the Chinese has changed – they now appreciate the crucial role they played, and could continue to play, in the economy. Before 1975, the *Hoa* controlled 80% of industry in the S and 50% of banking and finance. Today, ethnic Chinese in Vietnam can own and operate businesses and are once again allowed to join the Communist Party (although only 1,000 out of 2 million are members), the army, and to enter university. The dark days of the mid to late 1970s seem to be over.

Since 1988, overseas Vietnamese or *Viet-kieu* (most of whom are of Chinese extraction) have been allowed back to visit their relatives, spreading stories of untold wealth in the US, Australia and elsewhere. In 1990, 40,000 returned to visit. There are now over 2 million *Viet-kieu*. Many are former boat people, others have left the country as part of the UN-administered Orderly Departure Programme which began in earnest in the late 1980s. Having discovered some measure of prosperity in the West, the Vietnamese government is anxious to welcome them back – or rather, welcome their money. It is investment from the *Viet-kieu* which is helping to turn the Saigon area into a capitalist enclave.

Religion

Vietnam supports adherents of all the major world 'religions', as well as followers of religions that are peculiarly Vietnamese: Theravada and Mahayana Buddhism, Protestant and Catholic Christianity, Taoism, Confucianism, Islam, Cao Daism, Hoa Hao and Hinduism. In addition, spirit and ancestor worship (*Tò Tien*) are also practised. Confucianism, although not a formal religion, is probably the most pervasive doctrine of all. Nominal Christians and Buddhists will still pay attention to the moral and philosophic principles of Confucianism and it continues to play a central role in Vietnamese life.

Following the Communist victory in 1975, the authorities moved quickly to curtail the influence of the various religions. Schools, hospitals and other institutions run by religious organizations were taken over by the state and many clergy either imprisoned and/or sent to re-education camps. The religious hierarchies were institutionalized, and proselytizing severely curtailed. Since the late 1980s however, the government has allowed greater of freedom of action and expression to the clergy, and Buddhist pagodas, Christian churches and Cao Dai temples are beginning to fill up again as fears of persecution diminish. At the beginning of 1993, General Secretary of the Vietnamese Communist Party Do Muoi even went so far as to make a pair of official visits – to a Buddhist monastery and a Catholic church.

Mahayana Buddhism

Although there are both Theravada (also known as Hinayana) and Mahayana Buddhists in Vietnam, the latter are by far the more numerous (for background see page 45). Buddhism was introduced into Vietnam in the second century AD: Indian pilgrims came by boat and brought the teachings of Theravada Buddhism, while Chinese monks came by land and introduced Mahayana

Buddhism. In particular, the Chinese monk Mau Tu is credited with being the first person to introduce Mahayana Buddhism in 194/195 AD.

Initially, Buddhism was very much the religion of the elite, and did not impinge upon the common Vietnamese man or woman. It was not until the reign of Emperor Ly Anh Tong (1138-1175) that Buddhism was promoted as the State Religion – nearly 1,000 years after Mau Tu had arrived from China to spread the teachings of the Buddha. By that time it had begun to filter down to the village level, but as it did so it became increasingly syncretic: Buddhism became enmeshed with Confucianism, Taoism, spirituality, mysticism and animism. In the 15th century it also began to lose its position to Confucianism as the dominant religion of the court.

There has been a resurgence of Buddhism since the 1920s. It was the self-immolation of Buddhist monks in the 1960s which provided a focus of discontent against the government in the S (see page 251), and since the Communist victory in 1975, monks have remained an important focus of dissent – hence the persecution of Buddhists during the early years following reunification. Mahayana Buddhists are concentrated in the centre and N of the country, and the dominant sect is the Thien (Zen) meditation sect. Of the relatively small numbers of Theravada Buddhists, the majority are of Cambodian stock and are concentrated in the Mekong Delta. In Vietnam, Buddhism is intertwined with Confucianism and Taoism.

Confucianism

Although Confucianism is not really a formal religion, the teachings of the Chinese sage and philosopher Confucius (551-479 BC) form the basis on which Vietnamese life and government were based for much of the historic period. Even today, Confucianist perspectives are, possibly, more strongly in evidence than Communist ones. Confucianism was introduced from China during the Bac Thuoc Period (111 BC-938 AD) when the Chinese dominated the country. The 'religion' enshrined the concept of imperial rule by the mandate of heaven, effectively constraining social and political change.

In essence, Confucianism stresses the importance of family and lineage, and the worship of ancestors. Men and women in positions of authority were required to provide role-models for the 'ignorant', while the state, epitomized in the emperor, was likewise required to set an example and to provide conditions of stability and fairness for his people. Crucially, children had to observe filial piety. This set of norms, which were drawn from the experience of the human encounter at the practical level, were enshrined in the Forty-seven Rules for Teaching and Changing first issued in 1663. A key element of Confucianist thought is the Three Bonds (*tam cuong*) – the loyalty of ministers to the emperor, the obedience of children to their parents, and the submission of wives to their husbands. Added to these are mutual reciprocity among friends, and benevolence towards strangers. Not surprisingly the Communists are antipathetic to such a hierarchical view of society although ironically Confucianism which inculcates respect for the elderly and authority unwittingly lends support to a politburo occupied by old men. In an essay entitled 'Confucianism and Marxism', Vietnamese scholar Nguyen Khac Vien explains why Marxism proved an acceptable doctrine to those accustomed to Confucian values: "Marxism was not baffling to Confucians in that it concentrated man's thoughts on political and social problems. By defining man as the total of his social relationships, Marxism hardly came as a shock to the Confucian scholar who had always considered the highest aim of man to be the fulfilment of his social obligations ... Bourgeois individualism, which puts personal interests ahead of those of society and petty bourgeois anarchism, which allows no social discipline whatsoever, are alien to both Confucianism and Marxism."

Taoism

Taoism was introduced from China into Vietnam at about the same time as Confucianism. It is based on the works of the Chinese philosophers Lao Tzu (circa 6th-5th century BC) and Chuang Tzu (4th century BC). Although not strictly a formal religion, it has had a significant influence on Buddhism (as it is practised in Vietnam) and on Confucianism. In reality, Taoism and Confucianism are two sides of the same coin: the Taoist side is poetry and spirituality; the Confucianist side, social ethics and the order of the world. Together they form a unity. Like Confucianism, it is not possible to give a figure to the number of adherents of Taoism in Vietnam: it functions in conjunction with Confucianism and Buddhism, and also often with Christianity, Cao Daism and Hoa Hao.

Central to Taoist belief is a world view based upon *yin* and *yang*, two primordial forces on which the creation and functioning of the world are based. To maintain a balance, a harmony, in life it is necessary that a proper balance be maintained between *yin* (female) and *yang* (male). This is believed to be true both at the scale of the world and the nation, and also for an individual – for the human body is the world in microcosm. The root cause of illness is imbalance between the forces of *yin* and *yang*. Even foods have characters: 'hot' foods are *yang*, 'cold', *yin*. Implicit in this is the belief that there is a natural law underpinning all of life, a law upon which harmony ultimately rests. Taoism attempts to maintain this balance, and thereby harmony. In this way, Taoism is a force promoting inertia, maintaining the status quo. Traditional relationships between fathers and sons, between siblings, within villages, and between the rulers and the ruled, are all rationalized in terms of maintaining balance and harmony. Forces for change – like Communism and democracy – are resisted on the basis that they upset this balance.

Christianity

Christianity was first introduced into Vietnam in the 16th century by Roman Catholic missionaries from Portugal, Spain and France. The first Bishop of Vietnam was appointed in 1659, and by 1685 there were estimated to be 800,000 Roman Catholics in the country. For several centuries Christianity was discouraged, and at times, outlawed. Many Christians were executed and one of the reasons that the French gave for annexing the country in the late 19th century was religious persecution (see page 86). Today, 8-10% of the population are thought to be Catholic, some 6 million people; less than 1% are Protestant.

Following reunification in 1975, many Catholics in the former S were sent to re-education camps. They were perceived to be both staunchly pro-American and anti-Communist, and it was not until 1988 that many were returned to normal life. Today, Catholics are still viewed with suspicion by the state and priests felt to be drifting from purely religious concerns into any criticism of the state are detained. Indicative of this 'fear' of Christianity is the fact that the last Archbishop of Hanoi died in 1989 and the church is still waiting for permission to appoint a replacement. Similarly the Vatican is still awaiting government permission to appoint a prelate of Hué, a post viewed with distaste by the authorities as it was last held by the worldly brother of former president Ngo Dinh Diem.

Islam and Hinduism

The only centres of Islam and Hinduism are among the Cham of the central coastal plain and Chau Doc, a province in the Mekong Delta. The Cham were converted to Islam by Muslim traders. There are several mosques in Saigon and Cholon – some of them built by Indians from Kerala.

Cao Daism

Cao Dai took root in southern Vietnam during the 1920s after Ngo Van Chieu, a civil servant, was visited by 'Cao Dai' or the 'Supreme Being' and was given the tenets of a new religion. Ngo received this spiritual visitation in 1919 on Phu Quoc Island. The Cao Dai later told Ngo in a seance that he was to be symbolized by a giant eye. The religion quickly gained the support of a large following of dispossessed peasants. It was both a religion and a nationalist movement. In terms of the former, it claimed to be a synthesis of Buddhism, Christianity, Taoism, Confucianism and Islam. Cao Dai 'saints' include Joan of Arc, the French writer Victor Hugo, Sir Winston Churchill, Sun Yat Sen, Moses and Brahma.

Debates over doctrine are mediated through the spirits who are contacted on a regular basis through a strange wooden contraption called a *corbeille-à-bec* or planchette. The five Cao Dai commandments are: do not kill any living creature; do not covet; do not practise high living; do not be tempted; and do not slander by word. But, as well as being a religion, the movement also claimed that it would restore traditional Vietnamese attitudes, and was anti-colonial and modestly subversive. Opportunist to a fault, Cao Dai followers sought the aid of the Japanese against the French, the Americans against the Viet Minh, and the Viet Minh against the S. Following reunification in 1975, all Cao Dai lands were confiscated and their leadership emasculated. The centre of Cao Daism remains the Mekong Delta where – and despite the efforts of the Communists – there are thought to be perhaps 2 million adherents and perhaps 1,000 Cao Dai

temples. The Cao Dai Cathedral or Great Temple is in the town of Tay Ninh, 100 km from Saigon (see page 258).

Hoa Hao

Hoa Hao is another Vietnamese religion which emerged in the Mekong Delta. It was founded by Huynh Phu So in 1939, a resident of Hoa Hao village in the province of Chau Doc. Effectively a schism of Buddhism, the sect discourages temple-building and worship, maintaining that simplicity of worship is the key to better contact with God. There are thought to be perhaps 1 to 1.5 million adherents of Hoa Hao, predominantly in the Chau Doc area.

Language and literature

Language

The Vietnamese language has a reputation for being fiendishly difficult to master. Its origins are still the subject of dispute – at one time thought to be a Sino-Tibetan language (because it is tonal), it is now believed to be Austro-Asiatic and related to Mon-Khmer. During the 9th century, when Vietnam was under Chinese domination, Chinese ideograms were adapted for use with the Vietnamese language. This script – *chu nho* ('scholars script') was used in all official correspondence and in literature right through to the 20th century. Whether this replaced an earlier writing system is not known. As early Vietnamese nationalists tried to break away from Chinese cultural hegemony in the late 13th century, they devised their own script, based on Chinese ideograms but adapted to meet Vietnamese language needs. This became known as *chu nom* or 'vulgar script'. So, while Chinese words formed the learned vocabulary of the intelligentsia – largely inaccessible to the man on the street or in the paddy field – non-Chinese words made up a parallel popular vocabulary.

Finally, in the 17th century, European missionaries under the tutelage of

Father Alexandre-de-Rhodes, created a system of romanized writing – *quoc ngu* or 'national language'. It is said that Rhodes initially thought Vietnamese sounded like the 'twittering of birds' (a view interestingly echoed by Graham Greene in *The Quiet American*: "To take an Annamite to bed with you is like taking a bird: they twitter and sing on your pillow") but had mastered the language in 6 months. The first *quoc ngu* dictionary (Vietnamese-Portuguese-Latin), *Dictionarium Annamiticum Lusitanum et Latinum*, was published in 1651. *Quoc ngu* uses marks – so-called diacritical marks – to indicate tonal differences. Initially it was ignored by the educated unless they were Catholic, and it was not until the early 20th century that its use became a mark of modernity among a broad spectrum of Vietnamese. Even then, engravings in the mausolea and palaces of the royal family continued to use Chinese characters. The first *quoc ngu* newspaper, *Gia Dinh Bao* (Gia Dinh Gazette), was published in 1865 and *quoc ngu* was adopted as the national script in 1920.

Literature

In ancient Vietnam, texts were reproduced laboriously, by scribes, on paper made from the bark of the mulberry tree (*giay ban*). Examples exist in Saigon, Paris, Hanoi and Hué. Printing technology was introduced in the late 13th century, but unfortunately, because of the hot and humid climate no early examples exist.

Vietnam has a rich folk literature of **fables, legends, proverbs and songs**, most of which were transmitted by word of mouth. In the 17th and 18th centuries, satirical poems and, importantly, verse novels (*truyen*) appeared. These were memorized and recited by itinerant story-tellers as they travelled from village to village.

Like much Vietnamese art, Vietnamese literature also owes a debt to China.

Chinese characters and literary styles were duplicated and although a tradition of *nom* literature did evolve (*nom* being a hybrid script developed in the 13th century), Vietnamese efforts remained largely derivative. One exception was the scholarly Nguyen Trai (see box on page 84) who bridged the gap; he excelled in classical Chinese *chu nho* as well as producing some of the earliest surviving, and very fine, poetry and prose in the new *chu nom* script. An important distinction is between the literature of the intelligentsia (essentially Chinese) and that of the people (more individualistic). These latter *nom* works, dating from the 15th century onwards, were simpler and concerned with immediate problems and grievances. They can be viewed as the most Vietnamese of literary works and include *Chinh Phu Ngam* (Lament of a Soldier's Wife), an anti-war poem by Phan Huy Ich (1750-1822). The greatest Vietnamese literature was produced during the social and political upheavals of the 19th century – *Truyen Kieu* (The Tale of Kieu) written by Nguyen Du (1765-1820) is a classic of the period. This 3,254-line story is regarded by most Vietnamese as their cultural statement *par excellence*. Nguyen Du was one of the most skilled and learned mandarins of his time, and was posted to China as Vietnam's Ambassador to the Middle Kingdom. On his return, Nguyen Du wrote the *Truyen Kieu* (or *Kim Van Kieu*), a celebration of Vietnamese culture, in the lines of which can be traced the essence of Vietnamese-ness.

French influence, and the spread of the Romanized Vietnamese script, led to the end of the Chinese literary tradition by the 1930s and its replacement by a far starker, freer, Western-derived style. Poetry of this period is known as *Tho Moi* (New Poetry). The Communist period has seen restrictions on literary freedom, and in recent years there have been numerous cases of authors and poets, together with journalists, being

KIEU: ORIENTAL JULIET OR PROTOTYPE MISS SAIGON?

The Tale of Kieu is a story of pure love corrupted by greed and power. It also offers a fascinating glimpse into the Vietnamese mind and Vietnamese sexual mores. Kieu is in love with the young scholar Kim and early on in the story she displays her physical and moral qualities:

> *"A fragrant rose, she sparkled in full bloom,*
> *bemused his eyes, and kindled his desire.*
> *When waves of lust had seemed to sweep him off,*
> *his wooing turned to wanton liberties.*
> *She said: "Treat not our love as just a game –*
> *please stay away from me and let me speak.*
> *What is a mere peach blossom that one should*
> *fence off the garden, thwart the bluebird's quest?*
> *But you've named me your bride – to serve her man,*
> *she must place chastity above all else."*

But the overriding theme of the story is the ill-treatment of an innocent girl by a duplicitous and wicked world unopposed by Heaven. Unmoved by Kieu's sale into prostitution the fates actively oppose her wishes by keeping her alive when she attempts to kill herself.

Any respite in her tale of woe proves short-lived and joy turns quickly to pain. The story illustrates the hopelessness of women in a Confucianist, male-dominated world: Kieu likens herself to a raindrop with no control over where she will land. Early on in the story when Kim is away attending to family matters Kieu has to choose between Kim, to whom she has pledged herself, and her family. Such is the strength of family ties that she offers herself to be sold in marriage to raise money for her kith and kin:

> *"By what means could she save her flesh and blood?*
> *When evil strikes you bow to circumstance.*
> *As you must weigh and choose between your love*
> *and filial duty, which will turn the scale?*
> *She put aside all vows of love and troth –*
> *a child first pays the debts of birth and care."*

Kieu gets married off to an elderly 'scholar' called Ma who is in fact a brothel keeper; but so as not to arouse Kieu's suspicion before removing her from her family he deflowers her. Kieu is now commercially less valuable but Ma believes he can remedy this:

> *"One smile of hers is worth pure gold – it's true.*
> *When she gets there, to pluck the maiden bud,*
> *princes and gentlefolk will push and shove.*
> *She'll bring at least three hundred liang, about*
> *what I have paid – net profit after that.*
> *A morsel dangles at my mouth – what God*
> *serves up I crave, yet money hate to lose.*
> *A heavenly peach within a mortal's grasp:*
> *I'll bend the branch, pick it, and quench my thirst.*
> *How many flower-fanciers on Earth*
> *can really tell one flower from the next?*
> *Juice from pomegranite skin and cockscomb blood*
> *will heal it up and lend the virgin look.*
> *In dim half-light some yokel will be fooled:*
> *she'll fetch that much, and not one penny less."*

Kieu's sorrows deepen; she becomes a concubine of a married brothel patron, Thuc. After a year of happiness together with Thuc his spurned wife, Hoan, decides to spoil the fun. Kieu ends up as a slave serving Thuc and Hoan. She laments her fate knowing full well the reason for it:

> "I've had an ample share of life's foul dust,
> and now this swamp of mud proves twice as vile.
> Will fortune never let its victims go
> but in its snares and toils hold fast a rose?
> I sinned in some past life and have to pay:
> I'll pay as flowers must fade and jade must break."

She later commits her only earthly crime stealing a golden bell and silver gong from the shrine she is charged with keeping, and flees to seek sanctuary in a Buddhist temple. But when her crime comes to light she is sent to live with the Bac family which, again on the pretext of marriage, sells her to another brothel. This time she meets a free-spirited warlord Tu Hai:

> "A towering hero, he outfought all foes
> with club or fist and knew all arts of war.
> Between the earth and heaven he lived free...."

who rescues her from the brothel. They become soul- and bed-mates until, after 6 months, Tu Hai's wanderlust and urge to fight take him away from her. He returns a year later victorious in battle. At this stage the story reaches a happy (and false) ending; Tu Hai sends his Captains out to round up all those who have crossed Kieu's path.

> "Awesome is Heaven's law of recompense –
> one haul and all were caught, brought back to camp.
> Under a tent erected in the midst,
> Lord Tu and his fair lady took their seats.
> No sooner had the drumroll died away
> than guards checked names, led captives to the gate.
> "Whether they have used you well or ill," he said,
> "pronounce yourself upon their just deserts."

Those who have shown Kieu kindness are rewarded while those who have harmed her are tortured horribly. The only exception is Hoan who, cruel though she was, Kieu releases (after torture, of course) in a show of mercy following Hoan's plea "I have a woman's mind, a petty soul, and jealousy's a trait all humans share" – Kieu had, after all, been living with Hoan's husband for a year.

All is well for 5 years until another warlord, Lord Ho, flatters Kieu encouraging her to persuade Tu to put down his sword and make peace with the emperor. Guileless Kieu does so and "Lord Tu lets flags hang loose, watch-drums go dead. He slackened all defence – imperial spies / observed his camp and learned of its true state." All is lost: Tu is killed, Kieu has betrayed her hero and she is married off to a tribal chief. She throws herself into a river but yet again fails to die. Eventually Kieu, is reunited with Kim and her family:

> "She glanced and saw her folks – they all were here:
> Father looked quite strong, and Mother spry;
> both sister Van and brother Quan grown up;
> and over there was Kim her love of yore."

Kieu and Kim hold a wedding feast and share a house but not a bed; Kim has sons by Van, Kieu's sister, and they all settle down to an untroubled life overseen by a more benevolent Heaven.

Huynh Sang Thong's translation (see recommended reading) is considered the finest and is accompanied by excellent notes which explain the Vietnamese phrasing of the original and which set the story in context. Translation and commentary will bring Truyen Kieu to a wider and, one hopes, appreciative audience and help shed some light on what many Vietnamese regard as their most important cultural statement.

imprisoned owing to the critical nature of their work.

A Vietnamese account of the 'American' War

Most visitors to Vietnam, if they were not involved in the war themselves, gain their views from literature and films made by Westerners, for Westerners. It is rare for people to have access to Vietnamese literary perspectives on the war, partly because most that do exist are untranslated and because, in comparison to the torrent of especially American accounts, there have been comparatively few written by Vietnamese. One of these few is Bao Ninh's moving and poetic *The sorrow of war* which was first published in Vietnamese in 1991 under the title *Thân Phân Cua Tinh Yêu*. In Vietnam it was a huge success, no doubt prompting its translation into English by Frank Palmos. The English edition was published in 1994 and it is now available in paperback (in the UK under the Minerva imprint). This is not a romantic vision of war; nor a macho account relishing the fight; nor once revelling in victory. It is a deeply sad and melancholic book. Perhaps this is because Bao Ninh is recounting his story from the position of one who was there. He served with the Glorious 27th Youth Brigade, joining-up in 1969 at the age of 17. Of the 500 who went to war with the Glorious 27th, he was one of just ten to survive the conflict. For those who want an alternative perspective, the book is highly recommended.

Drama

Classical Vietnamese theatre, known as *hat boi* (hat = to sing; boi = gesture, pose), shows close links with the classical theatre of China. Emperor Tù Duc had a troupe of 150 female artists and employed stars from China via a series of extravagent productions. Since the partition of the country in 1954, there has developed what might be termed 'revolutionary realist' theatre and classical Vietnamese theatre is today almost defunct. However, the most original theatrical art form in Vietnam is *mua roi nuoc* or **water puppet theatre**. This seems to have originated in Northern Vietnam during the early years of this millennium when it was associated with the harvest festival (at one time scholars thought water puppet theatre originated in China before being adopted in Vietnam). An inscription in Nam Ha province mentions a show put on in honour of King Ly Nhan Ton in 1121. By the time the French began to colonize Vietnam at the end of the 19th century it had spread to all of the major towns of the country.

As the name suggests, this form of theatre uses the surface of the water as the stage. Puppeteers, concealed behind a bamboo screen symbolizing an ancient village communal house, manipulate the characters while standing in a metre of water. The puppets – some over half a metre tall – are carved from water resistant *sung* wood which is also very lightweight and then painted in bright colours. Most need one puppeteer to manipulate them, but some require three or four. Plays are based on historical and religious themes: the origins of the Viet nation, legends, village life, and acts of heroism. Some include the use of fireworks – especially during battle scenes – while all performances are accompanied by folk opera singers and traditional instruments. Performances usually begin with the clown, Teu, taking the stage and he acts as a linking character between the various scenes.

The most famous and active troupe is based in Hanoi, (see page 167), although in total there are about a dozen groups. Since the 1980s Vietnamese writers have turned their attention from revolutionary heroes to commentary on political and social issues of the day. Consequently, many plays have failed to see the light of day and those that have,

have often been badly mauled by the censoring committee's scissors; references to corrupt officials and policemen seldom make the transition from page to stage. Much of Vietnam's literature is allegorical (which the people readily understand); this reflects a centuries-old intolerance of criticism by the mandarinate and royal family. Although the Communist party might be expected to approve of anti-royal sentiment in literature it seldom does, fearing that the Party itself is the true object of the writer's scorn.

Crafts

True Vietnamese influence is best seen in the 'lower' arts – the crafts.

Lacquerware (*son mai*) The art of making lacquerware is said to have been introduced into Vietnam after Emperor Le Thanh Ton (1443-1459) sent an emissary to the Chinese court to investigate the process. Lacquer is a resin from the son tree (*Rhus succedanea* or *R. vernicifera*) which is then applied in numerous coats (usually eleven) to wood (traditionally teak), leather, metal or porcelain. Prior to lacquering, the article must be sanded and coated with a fixative. The final coat is highly polished with coal powder. The piece may then be decorated with an incised design, painted, or inset with mother-of-pearl. If mother-of-pearl is to be used, appropriately shaped pieces of lacquer are chiselled out and the mother-of-pearl inset. This method is similar to that used in China, but different from Thailand and Burma. The designs in the N show Japanese influences, apparently because Japanese artists were employed as teachers at the École des Beaux Arts in Hanoi in the 1930s.

Non la conical hat This cone-shaped hat is one of the most common and evocative sights in Vietnam's countryside. Worn by women (and occasionally men), it is usually woven from latania leaves. The poem hats of Hué are the best known examples (see page 210).

Ao dai The garment that exhibits more conspicuously what it was intended to hide. National women's costume of Vietnam, literally, but prosaically, 'long dress'. *Ao dai* consists

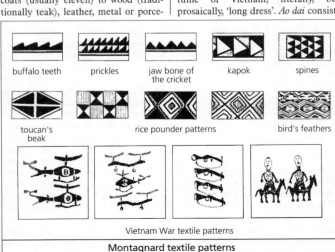

buffalo teeth	prickles	jaw bone of the cricket	kapok	spines

toucan's beak	rice pounder patterns	bird's feathers

Vietnam War textile patterns

Montagnard textile patterns

(After Dournes, Boulbert, Huard and Maurice and *France Asie*.)

of a long flowing tunic of diaphanous fabric worn over a pair of loose-fitting white pants; the front and rear sections of the tunic are split from the waist down. The modern design was created by a literary group called the *Tu Luc Van Doan* in 1932 based on ancient court costumes and Chinese dresses such as the chong san. In traditional society, decoration and complexity of design indicated the status of the wearer (eg gold brocade and dragons were for the sole use of the emperor; purple for higher-ranked mandarins). The *ao dai's* popularity has spread worldwide and the annual Miss *Ao Dai* pageant at Long Beach attracts entrants from all over the US. Today *ao dai* is uniform for hotel receptionists and many office workers, particularly in Saigon but less so in cooler Hanoi. French designer Elian Lille: "The first thing most people see when they come to Vietnam is the young students wearing a white *ao dai*, with their long hair clipped back and sitting very straight on their bicycles. It is exquisite."

Montagnard crafts There are over 50 different hill peoples, so their crafts are highly diverse. Textiles, jewellery and basketwork are the most widely available. The finely worked clothing of the Muong (with Dongson-derived motifs) and indigo-dyed cloth of the Ba-na are two examples of Montagnard crafts.

Silk Chinese style bivoltine or 'smooth' silks.

Modern Vietnam

Politics

The Vietnamese Communist Party (VCP) was established in Hong Kong in 1930 by Ho Chi Minh, and arguably has been more successful than any other such party in Asia in mobilizing and then maintaining support. While others have fallen, the VCP has managed to stay firmly in control. In 1986 at the sixth party congress the VCP launched its economic reform programme known as *doi moi* – a momentous step in ideological terms (see below). However, although the programme has done much to free-up the economy, the party has ensured that it retains ultimate political power. 'Reformers' such as Premier Vo Van Kiet have had to pay heed to the concerns of 'conservatives' in the leadership, and in 1989 restrictions on the press were tightened and talk of political pluralism tightly circumscribed. A year later for example, in an unprecedented move, politburo member Tran Xuan Bach was sacked following a speech in which he called for greater openness. In this sense, while economic reforms run apace – particularly in the S – there is a very definite sense that the limits of political reform have been reached, at least for the time being. To many Westerners the pronouncements of the leadership may seem contradictory. But to most Vietnamese there is nothing strange about Do Muoi's comment that economic reform is the keystone of party policy while the party remains unshakably determined to follow the path of socialism. The new constitution approved in Apr 1992 merely re-emphasizes this point by bluntly stating that the VCP will continue to be the only political player in the country.

How long the VCP can maintain the charade, along with China, while other Communist governments fall, is a key question. Despite the reforms, the leadership is still divided over the road ahead: it is common to hear and read of 'conservatives' and 'pragmatists' or 'radicals'. The labels themselves probably mean little, but they suggest that there is continuing disagreement over the necessity for political reform, and the degree of economic reform that should be encouraged. But as one provincial cadre was quoted as saying in 1989: "We cannot live on [socialist] theories". The crux is, how long the population of Vietnam will continue to accept a standard of living among the lowest in the world. This will become even more pertinent as *doi moi* brings wealth for a few, but leaves most people in poverty. This has pre-occupied Vietnam's leaders in recent years. In Jan 1992, the reformist Premier Vo Van Kiet in an interview in the party daily *Nhan Dan* said that the "confrontation between luxury and misery, between cities and country" could cause problems and talked of the need to "establish a new order of sharing" (see box "The bottom of the pile", page 133). As Party General Secretary Do Muoi put it with great understatement at the Special Party Conference held at the beginning of 1994, there are "complicated factors" with which the leadership will have to contend.

In terms of international relations, Vietnam's relationship with the countries of the Association of Southeast Asian Nations (Asean) have warmed markedly since the dark days of the early and mid 1980s. Indeed, Vietnam itself is due to join the Association – probably in Jun 1995 as this book goes to press. No longer is there a deep schism between the capitalist and Communist countries of the region, either in terms of ideology or management. The main potential flashpoint concerns Vietnam's long-term historical enemy – China. The enmity and suspicion which underlies the relationship between the world's last two real Communist powers stretches back over 2,000 years.

China and Vietnam, along with Malaysia, Taiwan, Brunei and the Philippines all claim part (or all) of the South China Sea's Spratly Islands. These tiny islands, many no more than coral atolls, would have caused scarcely an international relations ripple, were it not for the fact that they are thought to sit above huge oil reserves. He who claims the islands, so to speak, lays claim to this undersea wealth. Over the last decade

China has been using its developing blue water navy to project its power southwards. This has led to skirmishes between Vietnamese and Chinese forces, and to diplomatic confrontation between China and just about all the other claimants. Although the parties are committed to settling the dispute without resort to force, most experts see the Spratly Islands as the key potential 'flashpoint' in Southeast Asia – and one in which Vietnam is seen to be a central player.

Rapprochement with the US One of the keys to a lasting economic recovery (see below) was, and remains, rapprochement with the US. From 1975 until early 1994 the US made it largely illegal for any American or American company to have business relations with Vietnam. The US, with the support of Japan and other Western nations, also black-balled attempts by Vietnam to gain membership to the IMF, World Bank and Asian Development Bank, thus cutting-off access to the largest source of cheap credit. In the past, it has been the former Soviet Union and the countries of the Eastern Bloc which have filled the gap, providing billions of dollars of aid (US$6bn 1986-1990), training, and technical expertise. But in 1990 the Soviet Union halved its assistance to Vietnam, making it imperative that the government look to improving relations with the West and particularly the US.

In Apr 1991 the US opened an official office in Hanoi (to assist in the search for MIAs), the first such move since the end of the war, and in Dec 1992 allowed US companies to sign contracts to be implemented after the US trade embargo had been lifted. In 1992, both Australia and Japan lifted their embargoes on aid to Vietnam, and the US also eased restrictions on humanitarian assistance. Support for a full normalization of relations was provided by French President Mitterand during his visit in Feb 1993 – the first by a Western leader since the end of the war. He said that the US veto on IMF and World Bank assistance had "no reason for being there", and applauded Vietnam's economic reforms. He also pointed out to his hosts that respect for human rights was now a universal obligation – which did not go down quite so well. Nonetheless he saw his visit as marking the end of one chapter, and the beginning of another. This inexorable movement towards a full lifting of the trade embargo reached its logical conclusion on the 4 February 1994 when President Bill Clinton announced the normalization of trade relations.

The progress towards normalization was so slow because many Americans still harbour painful memories of the war. With large numbers of ordinary people continuing to believe that servicemen shot down and captured during the war languished in jungle gaols, presidents Bush and Clinton had to tread exceedingly carefully. In a sense, it was recognized long ago that the embargo no longer served American interests; it was just that the public were not yet ready to forgive and forget. In Apr 1993, the *New York Times* revealed the existence of a document – unearthed by Australian researcher Stephen Morris in a Soviet archive – which appeared to indicate that the Vietnamese had been deceiving the US about the number of American POWs it held during the war. The MIA lobby in Washington pounced on the revelation, claiming it was the 'smoking gun' which proved the Vietnamese had been lying all along, calling on President Clinton to break off negotiations. Since then, careful scrutiny of the document has revealed a series of inconsistencies and most commentators and experts now believe it to be a fake. Nonetheless, it is thought that its discovery set the normalization process back by several months.

Even though the embargo is now a thing of the past, there are still the families of 2,238 American servicemen listed as Missing in Action who continue to hope that the remains of their loved ones might, some day, make their way back to the United States. It was this, among other legacies of the war, which made progress towards a full normalization of diplomatic and commercial relations such a drawn-out business. It was only at the beginning of 1995 that Washington opened a 'liaison' office in Hanoi, and even then, in a very un-American show of modesty, there was no US flag flying from the building. As one American diplomat explained to a journalist from the *Economist*, "Washington would very much like this to be an invisible office". This diplomacy-at-a-snail's-pace frustrated many American businessmen who were clamouring for fanfare and celebration, not the slightly embarrassed shuffling of diplomats. Full normalization finally occurred on 11 July 1995 and in Aug Warren Christopher became the first US Secretary of State to visit Hanoi since 1970. This does not mean that everyone in America is cheered by the news – and certainly not the Republican Right.

In his book *Vietnam at the crossroads*, BBC World Service commentator Michael Williams asks the question: "Does communism have a future in Vietnam?". He answers that "the short answer must be no, if one means by communism the classical Leninist doctrines and central planning". Instead some bastard form of Communism is in the process of evolving. As Williams adds, "Even party leaders no longer appear able to distinguish between communism and capitalism...". There is certainly political opposition and disenchantment in Vietnam. At present this is unfocused and dispersed. Poor people in the countryside, especially in the N, resent the economic gains in the cities, particularly those of the S. But this rump of latent discontent has little in common with those intellectual and middle class Vietnamese itching for more political freedoms; or those motivated entrepreneurs pressing for accelerated economic reforms; or those

Buddhist monks and Christians demanding freedom of expression and re-

FOREIGN INVESTMENT IN VIETNAM

The economic reforms of the 1980s led to a surge in foreign investment in Vietnam. The largest portions originating from Taiwan, Hong Kong, France, Singapore, UK and Australia. The Foreign Investment Code (1987) is one of the most liberal in the region, allowing 100% foreign ownership and up to 99% equity participation in joint ventures.

By the end of 1994 US$10.9bn of investment capital had been pledged since the relaxation of investment laws in 1988. The value of proposed investments rose sharply in 1993 and 1994, to US$2.8bn and US$3.7bn respectively, while the mean size of investment has also grown from US$3.5mn in 1988-90 to US$9.9mn in 1993 (excluding oil-related investments).

The sectors which have attracted most overseas interest are oil, tourism and manufacturing: in 1988-90 32% of investment was in oil and gas and 21% in hotels; since 1991 manufacturing has increased its share of the total. The bulk of this money (63%) has gone into joint ventures and although before 1991 most money headed towards Saigon and the S, since then Hanoi and the N has received almost half of the incoming investment funds. European companies (particularly BP and Burmah (Castrol lubricating oil)) have gained a strong position in the oil sector; Asian companies have focused on hotels and manufacturing; and Viet Kieu (overseas Vietnamese – see page 118) have concentrated on smaller scale investments such as garment factories, hotels, tour companies and other services.

But of the funds invested, the majority is accounted for by a small number of oil corporations. Other companies, though attracted by Vietnam's cheap labour and large domestic market, have been hindered by the tortuous and often corrupt bureaucracy. Competition between different levels and ministries, all hoping to grab a slice of the lucrative foreign investment cake, has confused investors. Added to this are problems of poor physical infrastructure, an embryonic financial system, an inadequately developed legal system, labyrinthine bureaucracy, and the continued reluctance among some cadres and government officials to countenance the capitalist penetration of their country. The former General Secretary of the VCP, who devised the 'open door' policy, noted at the time that when "one opens the door, dust and flies also come in". So, despite the attractions of Vietnam and its cheap labour, the unforeseen costs – financial and otherwise – of establishing and running a company are often more than in Thailand, Malaysia or elsewhere. Reflecting this, the 'realization rate' of proposed investment is one of the lowest in the region.

TOP INVESTORS, 1994

	US$mn
1. Singapore	598
2. Hong Kong	547
3. Switzerland	453
4. Taiwan	365
5. Japan	328
6. S Korea	265
7. USA	220
8. France	150
9. Malaysia	122
10. Cayman Islands	121

NB In Hanoi and Saigon locally produced English language books outlining the Foreign Investment Law can be obtained cheaply. Far more comprehensive at 900 pages, but also expensive is *Foreign Investment Laws of Vietnam*, Law Printer: Melbourne (US$295); published in 1991.

spect for human rights. Unless and until this loose broth of opposition groups coalesces, it is hard to see a coherent opposition movement evolving. Nonetheless, each year a small number of brave, foolhardy or committed individuals challenge the authorities. Nine Vietnamese, including four Buddhist monks, were arrested for 'creating social disorder' and later sentenced to prison terms of between 6 months and 4 years in Nov 1993 following a protest they staged in Hué. A pro-democracy conference scheduled to begin on 27 November 1993 in Ho Chi Minh City was pre-empted by the expulsion of one of its American promoters and the detention of three Vietnamese organizers. There is always the possibility that cataclysmic, and unpredictable, political change will occur. As one veteran, but anonymous, Central Committee member said in an interview at the end of 1991: "If the CPSU [Communist Party of the Soviet Union], which had been in power for 74 years, can fall to pieces in 72 hrs, we have at least to raise that possibility in Vietnam". Major General Tran Cong Man highlighted these fears when he remarked that:

"the collapse of the Soviet Union was a devastating blow for [Vietnam]...[It] was our support, ideologically and psychologically, also militarily and economically. It was our unique model. Now we find it was a false model."

The tensions between reform and control were evident in the run-up to the special mid-term Conference of the Vietnamese Communist Party held at the end of Jan 1994. Intellectuals mounted attacks on the tenets of Marxist-Leninism in Vietnam and even questioned the role and ideals of Ho Chi Minh. Lu Phuong, a southern intellectual, authored a pamphlet which was unofficially circulated, but never published, in which he wrote that Ho had "borrowed Leninism as a tool" and never imagined that it would "turn intelligent people into foolish ones,

turn people with ideals into degenerate ones and bog down the nation in stagnation." Other tracts echoed similar sentiments. The leadership silenced these questioning minds, and the new press law which came into effect on 26 July 1993 makes it clear that the government aims to keep a tight rein on debate. The law prohibits the publication of works "hostile to the socialist homeland, divulging state or [Communist] party secrets, falsifying history or denying the gains of the revolution". Ly Quy Chung, a newspaper editor in Saigon, described the Vietnamese responding to the economic reforms "like animals being let out of their cage". But, he added, alluding to the tight control the VCP maintains over political debate, "Now we are free to graze around, but only inside the fences".

Economy

Partition and socialist reconstruction 1955-1975

When the French left North Vietnam in 1954 they abandoned a country with scarcely any industry. The N remained predominantly an agrarian society, and just 1.5% of 'material output' (the Socialist equivalent of GDP) was accounted for by modern industries. These employed a few thousand workers out of a population of about 13 million. The French added to the pitiful state of the industrial sector by dismantling many of the (mostly textile) factories that did exist, shipping the machinery back to France.

With independence, the government in the N embraced a socialist strategy of reconstruction and development. In the countryside, agricultural production was collectivized. Adopting Maoist policies, land reform proceeded apace. Revolutionary cadres were trained to spot 'greedy, cruel and imperialist landlords', farmers of above average wealth who might themselves have owned tiny plots. Leaders of land reform brigades applied Chinese-inspired rules through people's tribunals and summary justice.

TOURISM IN VIETNAM

The Vietnamese government nominated 1990 'Visit Vietnam Year'. Although it did not have the razzmatazz of the Visit Thailand (1989), Malaysia (1990) or Indonesia (1991) years, the authorities hope that tourism will become a significant foreign exchange earner in the future. In 1989, 60,000 tourists visited the country, of which a quarter were overseas Vietnamese and a further 10% were from former Eastern Bloc countries. In 1990 the figure was 187,000, of whom 40,000 were overseas Vietnamese, and in 1993, 670,000 tourists were said to have visited the country. The target is now 3 million visitors by the year 2000. Clearly, the authorities have identified tourism as a lucrative money spinner for a country short of dollars.

The problem facing the tourist industry as it attempts to expand, is a glaring lack of hotel rooms – the whole country has a paltry 7,500 international standard hotel beds and a total of 22,000 rooms in all (counting hotels and guesthouses): by comparison, Bangkok alone can boast 25,000. There is also a shortage of trained guides, hotel managers and other personnel to service the industry. This should change: after offshore oil exploration, hotel construction is the largest area for foreign investment. At the end of 1993, it was estimated there were 30 hotel projects planned for Saigon alone. Many may not get further than the drawing board; whether they do or not will depend on political and economic developments.

An estimated 10,000 people died; Ho Chi Minh was opposed to the worst excesses and, although he failed to curb the zealots, land reform in Vietnam was a much less bloody affair than it was in China. In industry, likewise, the means of production were nationalized, cooperatives were formed, and planning was directed from the centre. Although evidence is hard to come by, it seems that even as early as the mid-1960s both the agricultural and industrial sectors were experiencing shortages of key inputs and were suffering from poor planning and mismanagement. The various sectors of the economy were inadequately linked, and the need for consumer goods was largely met by imports from China. But it was just at this time that the US bombing campaign 'Rolling Thunder' began in earnest (see page 95), and this served to obscure these economic difficulties. It was not until the late 1970s that the desperate need to introduce reforms became apparent. The bombing campaign also led to massive destruction and caused the government in the N to decentralize activity to the countryside in order to protect what little industry there was from the American attacks.

Economic development since reunification, 1975-1995

With the reunification of Vietnam in 1975, it seems that most leaders in the N thought that the re-integration of the two economies, as well as their re-invigoration, would be a fairly straightforward affair. As one of the Party leadership tellingly said during the Sixth Plenum at the end of 1979: "In the euphoria of victory which came so unexpectedly, we ... somewhat lost sight of realities; everything seemed possible to achieve, and quickly". This is understandable when it is considered that the N had just defeated the most powerful nation on earth. But the war disguised two economies that were both chronically inefficient and poorly managed. The tragedy was that just as this fact was becoming clear, the Vietnamese government embarked on another military adventure –

THE BOTTOM OF THE PILE: POVERTY AND INEQUALITY

Except in the sense that a starving person is poor wherever he or she happens to live, poverty is relative. With an average per capita income of barely US$230 most Vietnamese, by Western standards, are poor. But less than 10 years of serious economic reform and two years of 8% economic growth have already created deep divisions between the haves and have nots. In Thanh Hoa Province in the N, foreign relief agencies estimate that well over a third of children under three years old are malnourished, and this is probably also true over large swathes of the country. Luong Xuan Hoang, a farmer from Quang Trang Province was quoted in the *Far Eastern Economic Review* as saying "Our lives haven't improved much under renovation" and his son had to drop out of school because the family couldn't pay the fees of 5-6,000 dong/month (about US$0.50). The bicycles, restaurants and electronic goods of Hanoi and Saigon are a world away from the grinding poverty of the countryside, and that world seems to be drifting further and further from the grasp of most farmers. Vietnam's leaders have already acknowledged that the 'politics of envy' is a cause for concern – both political and moral.

The preliminary results of Vietnam's first substantive poverty survey show what might have been guessed: that incomes in Saigon and its surrounds are 2.7 times higher than the national average; that nine-tenths of the poor live in the countryside; that two-thirds of the richest are city dwellers; and that incomes in the Red River Delta are half those in the Mekong Delta. A World Bank study released in 1995 told the same story: rural poverty running at 57%, urban poverty at 27%. The question is what to do about it. The pressure to continue the process of reform and to make the country attractive to foreign investers will almost certainly cause inequalities to widen further in the short to medium term. Hoang, like poor people the world over, strives for his children rather than for himself: "I hope the lives of my children will be different from my life. I want their futures to be the same as those of rich families' children", he explains. His son is not well placed to achieve this wish.

VIETNAM GDP

VL 72

HANOI

Haiphong

N

Da Nang

GDP per capita in Dong (By province)

☐ Below 350,000
☐ 350 - 450,000
▨ 450 - 750,000
▨ Over 1.1 million

Ho Chi Minh City (Saigon)

WASTE NOT, WANT NOT

Men fashioning spare parts from scrap metal, boys busily collecting tins and cans, women sewing sandals from care tyres, mechanics cannabilizing cars; these are some of the most potent images of Vietnam to Western visitors. In a country where labour is abundant, time is cheap, and where resources are scarce, almost all scrap has value. Michael DiGregorio of the East-West Center in Hawaii estimates that in Hanoi 6,000 people earn a living scavenging for scrap, feeding 250 tonnes of 'garbage' from the waste economy back into the productive economy every day, constituting over a third of the 830 tonnes of refuse produced daily in the capital. This informal process of recycling reduces waste, helps to limit environmental degradation, and provides a living for the poor.

this time the invasion and subsequent occupation of Cambodia in Dec 1978. Shortly afterwards, Hanoi had to deploy troops again to counter the Chinese 'invasion' in 1979. As a result, the authorities never had the opportunity of diverting resources from the military to the civilian sectors.

Conditions in the S were no better than in the N. The US had been supporting levels of consumption far above those which domestic production could match, the shortfall being met through massive injections of aid. Following the Communists' victory, this support was ended – overnight. The Americans left behind an economy and society deeply scarred by the war: 3 million unemployed, 500,000 prostitutes, 100,000 drug addicts, 400,000 amputees and 800,000 orphans. Nor did many in the S welcome their 'liberation'. The programme of socialist transition which began after 1975 was strongly resisted by large sections of the population, and never achieved its aims. As resistance grew, so the government became more repressive, thus leading to the exodus of hundreds of thousands of 'boat people' (see page 102). Even as late as 1978, with the economy close to crisis, sections of the leadership were still maintaining that the problems were due to poor implementation, not to the fact that the policies were fundamentally flawed. The key problem was the characteristic of 'bureaucratic centralism': if a factory

wished to transport umbrellas from Tay Ninh to Saigon, less than 100 km, it was required to go through 17 agencies, obtain 15 seals, sign five contracts, and pay numerous taxes.

Economic reform

In a bid to re-invigorate the economy, the Vietnamese government – like others throughout the Communist and former Communist world – has been introducing economic reforms. These date back to 1979 when a process of administrative decentralization was set in train. Farmers signed contracts with their collectives to deliver produce in return for access to land and inputs like fertilizers and pesticides, thereby returning many aspects of decision-making to the farm-level. Surplus production could be sold privately. Factories were made self-accounting, and workers' pay was linked to productivity. The reforms of 1979 also accepted a greater role for the private sector in marketing, agriculture and small-scale industry.

Unfortunately these reforms were generally unsuccessful in stimulating Vietnam's moribund economy. Agriculture performed reasonably, but industry continued to decline. Cadres at the regional and local levels often ignored directives from the centre, and critical inputs needed to fuel growth were usually unavailable. Both national income and per capita incomes continued to shrink. The reform process is referred to as *doi moi* or 'renovation', the Vietnamese equiva-

LOOKING BACK ON 20 YEARS OF PEACE

The 20th anniversary of the end of the Vietnam War fell on the 30 April 1995. The celebrations in Saigon raised the issue of whether political reunification had served merely to disguise a continuing sharp divide between the North and the South. Many southerners resent the fact that their graves go unmarked, their losses of 225,000 unacknowledged, and their former lives demeaned. Many find jobs hard to come by, and veterans – unlike those from the army of the former North – receive no pensions.

At the end of the war, 200,000 former southern politicians, soldiers and functionaries were sent to re-education camps – many never returned. One senior northerner remarked to Nayan Chanda, who was himself in Saigon during the final days of the war, that "After 20 years there is no sign of reconciliation ... Our press is still celebrating victory over the Saigon army. Mothers of northern heroes have been decorated and given rewards but mothers of Saigon troops have only humiliation." Despite the attempt to play down the victory for American consumption – who need to be placated for their dollars – in Vietnam the chasm between the two regions remains.

Nor is it clear, to some at least, from what it was that the former South was liberated. James Webb, a Marine in Vietnam, author of *Fields of fire*, and an apologist for the American presence in the country, wrote on the occasion of the 20th anniversary that "Oddly, Vietnam seems to be emerging into what might have occurred if the war had indeed ended in a negotiated stalemate: an authoritarian, Western-oriented, market economy." These sentiments are echoed by Gabriel Kolko, an anti-war activist and a man with very different views from those of Webb, and with a very different agenda. He wrote, also on the anniversary of the end of the war:

> "The irony of Vietnam today is that those who gave and suffered the most, and were promised the greatest benefits, have gained the least. The Communists are abandoning them to the inherently precarious future of a market economy which increasingly resembles the system the US supported during the war. For the majority of Vietnam's peasants, veterans, and genuine idealists, the war was a monumental tragedy – and a vain sacrifice."

lent of Soviet *perestroika*. Implementation of *doi moi* has not been easy. In Neil Sheehan's recent book *Two cities: Hanoi and Saigon* he asked one manager of a state enterprise: "What was worse ... fighting the French in Interzone Five ... or directing a state factory during *doi moi*?" The answer: "It was easier in Interzone Five".

Recognizing that the limited reforms of 1979 were failing to have the desired effect, the VCP leadership embraced a further raft of changes following the Sixth Congress in 1986. At the time, the Party daily, *Nhan Dan* wrote that never had "morale been so eroded, confidence

been so low or justice been so abused". Subsidies on consumer goods were reduced and wages increased partially to compensate. There was also limited monetary reform, although prices were still centrally controlled. In late 1987 the central planning system was reformed. The net effect of these changes was to fuel inflation which remained high from 1986-1988 – in 1988 it was running at well over 100%.

Again, appreciating that the reforms were not having the desired effect, and with the advice of the IMF, a third series of changes were introduced in 1988 and 1989. The market mechanism was to be fully employed to determine wages, output and prices for the great majority of goods. The domestic currency, the dong, was further devalued to bring it into line with the black market rate and foreign investment actively encouraged (see box).

Reforms have been so sweeping that the IMF views the country as almost a role model in structural adjustment. Nonetheless, the demands of economic transformation have required the government to continue with this process of liberalization. One raft of reforms seems to create the economic conditions which demand yet another, and so on. In 1993 government salary differentials were widened to better reflect responsibilities. Whereas under the old system the differential between the highest and lowest paid workers was only 3.5 to one, the gap is now 13 to one. Gone are the ideals of equality, and in their place have been instituted incentive structures and such like. Do Van Nhan, the director of a formerly state-owned shipping agency, and the first state company to be privatized in 1993, told Murray Hiebert of the *Far Eastern Economic Review*: "I see our staff working harder, because they want to make a profit for themselves. Everyone is trying to find new clients for our company."

In the 1980s about 250,000 Vietnamese were sent as migrant workers to Eastern Europe and the former Soviet Union to ease unemployment and to pay off Vietnam's rouble debt. These workers faced discrimination and racism. Following the collapse of Communism in Europe, the Vietnamese government became worried that the political reforms might rub-off on their own countrymen. Many have now returned home, some on the insistence of their host governments: some 63,000 workers in former East Germany for example have had their contracts terminated and been sent home. In exchange, the German government gave DM110mn to help with their resettlement. This does not mean, though, that the era of Vietnam

as a worker-exporting nation is over. Rather, the government is looking for new opportunities for workers to earn hard currency. In early 1994, 2,000 migrant workers travelled to Libya as part of this effort.

Given the changes in the world order, the Vietnamese economy has done well to escape disaster. The collapse of aid and assistance from the former Soviet Union (which has only been partially compensated by aid from Russia) and the corresponding precipitous decline in trade from US$1.8bn (admittedly at the then unrealistic rouble exchange rate) in 1990 to US$85mn in 1991, illustrates the extent to which Vietnam has had to re-orientate its economy. No longer able to rely on the Soviet Union to bail it out (although even before then the Vietnamese would lament that the Soviets were 'Americans without dollars'), the Vietnamese government took the drastic step of banning the import of all luxury consumer goods in Oct 1991 in an attempt to save valuable foreign exchange. Japan – not the Soviet Union – is now Vietnam's largest trading partner, and foreign interest and investment has been growing by leaps and bounds.

STATE OF THE ECONOMY, 1993-1994		
	1993	1994
GDP growth	8%	8.5%
Trade deficit (US$mn)	890	900
Exports (US$bn)	3	3.6
Inflation		14%
Leading exports*		
Crude oil (US$mn)	861	976
Rice (US$mn)	350	406
Coal (US$mn)	84	115
Textiles (US$mn)	350	550
Sea products (US$mn)	370	480
Leading imports*		
Oil products (mn tonnes)	3.33	
Fertilizers (mn tonnes)	1.26	
Steel (mn tonnes)	0.23	
Trade deficit (US$)		1.4bn
(* = Ministry of Trade)		

AIDS IN VIETNAM

Like the other countries of Southeast Asia, Vietnam is thought to have the potential for 'rapid increase' in the HIV/AIDS epidemic. As of the end of Jun 1994 there were 106 reported AIDS cases in Vietnam, and 9% of intravenous drug users were HIV-infected in 1993. This comparatively low level of infection probably reflects the absence of research, rather than the absence of a problem. It is thought that the epidemic will soon (if it has not done so already) cross over from the drug-using population into the heterosexual population, and has the potential of becoming almost as serious a problem as it currently is in Thailand. In 1994 Vietnam's National AIDS Committee estimated that by the year 2000 there will be between 200,000 and 300,000 AIDS cases in the country. The highest rates of infection are in the S – in Saigon and An Giang province bordering Cambodia.

By the end of 1994, cumulative authorized foreign investment since 1988 totalled US$10bn. The rate of investment appears, taking approved investment figures, to be picking up – US$2.8bn in 1993; US$3.7bn pledged for 1994. The problem with inferring from these figures that Vietnam is on the verge of foreign investment-driven export-led growth, is that it seems very little of the approved investment is, as the economists say, actually realized. In 1995 it was reported in the *Financial Times* that disbursement for 1994 was just US$400mn – a realization rate of a little over 10% (the rate for Indonesia, by comparison, is over 50%). These sorts of discrepancies lend support to the view that Vietnam has a very long way to go before it 'takes off'.

Economic challenges

The fact that Vietnam appears to have survived relatively unscathed the economic and political collapse of the former Soviet Union, has led some commentators to argue that the economy is more resilient than it looks. Although in terms of per capita income the country may be one of the 12 poorest in the world, Vietnam does have a well-educated population, good access to world markets and, as former Singapore Prime Minister Lee Kuan Yew has put it, that "vital intangible" necessary for NIC-style rapid economic growth. Eco-

nomic advisers are recommending an accelerated transition to a market economy, fearing that any delay will lead to increased social and political resistance. A number of recent events seems to indicate that the leadership have accepted these recommendations. At the end of 1991, foreign exchange dealing markets were opened in both Saigon and Hanoi, and in 1992 a policy of privatization of state-owned enterprises was announced, leading to the sale of General Forwarding & Agency Co in Oct 1993. Perhaps even more significantly, at least in a metaphorical sense, the massive portrait of Ho Chi Minh was lowered from the top of the state bank in Hanoi in 1991 while the roof was being repaired; whether it will ever be replaced is not clear.

But it is too easy to assume that Vietnam is set to become yet another Asian economic success story. Just because it happens to occupy a piece of Asian geographical space, does not mean that economic vitality and growth are pre-ordained. The country still faces enormous challenges. The population is growing rapidly in a country where there are 900 people for every sq km of agricultural land. As the World Bank has pointed out, this means "the country will have to develop on the basis of **human resources** rather than natural resources". But the human resources

FROM COLD WAR TO COLA WAR

The lifting of the US trade embargo at the beginning of Feb 1994 marked the full and final end of the Vietnam War but heralded the start of another war: the Cola War. PepsiCo erected a giant Pepsi can outside Reunification Palace in Saigon to celebrate the end of the embargo and had their bottles rattling off the production line the same evening, while rival Coca-Cola replied by inflating two outsized Coke bottles outside the Opera House in Hanoi. These brazen and somewhat insensitive stunts made longtime US residents shrink with embarrassment.

The rivalry is intense and unmissable: one of the first things visitors will notice on arrival in Vietnam, whether Hanoi or Saigon, are the Pepsi-Cola airport buses which ferry passengers from aircraft to terminal. At the end of the first year Pepsi would appear to have its nose in front, claiming a 55% share of the market to Coca-Cola's 39%. Coke has faced a series of problems licensing its bottling factory but looks set to narrow the gap: the new war is hotting up.

themselves need substantial 'upgrading': malnutrition is widespread and poverty in the countryside over large areas of the N and interior uplands, the norm rather than the exception (see box "The bottom of the pile" and map page 133). Education and health facilities also require massive investment, not to mention the physical infrastructure including roads and power. Unemployment is becoming an increasing cause for concern, while corruption, smuggling, mismanagement and wastage sap valuable dollars from the economy. In the first 10 months of 1993, 918 corruption cases were uncovered involving US$28.5mn, more than double the figure for the same period of the previous year.

In addition, and despite the much publicized reforms, there is still an extremely large, inefficient and unprofitable **state sector**. As in China, what to do about this part of the economy is proving the most intractable of the government's challenges. In 1995 there were still some 7,000 state-owned enterprises employing 1.5 million workers – admittedly down from 12,000 and some 2.5 million workers in 1990. But the 5,000 that have been closed-down or sold-off have been the smaller and/or more profitable firms – the big enterprises remain in place, sapping scarce funds. The government is forcing these state shibboleths to borrow money from the commercial sector, while cutting subsidies and introducing new, more stringent, bankruptcy laws. But Hanoi seems unwilling to contemplate either large-scale privatization or widespread closure. Instead it is opting for a tighter system of accountability in an attempt to bring the enterprises into line with the private sector. Foreign analysts say it is extremely hard to know the exact position of these public enterprises because of appalling book-keeping and a general lack of information. Managers and workers in state-owned enterprises are often resistant to changes, fearing the consequences of market 'discipline'. Workers expect to have a 'job for life', irrespective of profitability. The social consequences of the government forcing a change in this assumption are too great to contemplate, so instead state enterprises are being allowed to engage in joint ventures with foreign companies in the forlorn hope that either the problem will simply go away, or become less significant as other parts of the economy grow.

The numbers of **unemployed** are also

being boosted by the reduction in the size of the army – which celebrated its 50th anniversary in 1995. About 500,000 soldiers have been, or are in the process of being, demobilized. Preparation for civvy life seems perfunctory to say the least. As one former soldier, now a cyclo driver, recounted to a journalist from the *Economist*, "When I joined, I was told they would help me find a job later. But when I left, all they gave me was a set of clothes, a piece of cloth and a paper that said that I had fulfilled my requirements."

Foreign investors also worry about the **lack of legal, banking and accounting systems**, and are put off by the **archaic physical infrastructure** when compared to such other Southeast Asian countries as the Philippines and Indonesia. The fact that, for example, nearly three-quarters of law students were sent to the former Soviet Union and Eastern Europe for their training, explains the lack of expertise in some crucial areas. At the end of 1994, Le Dang Doanh of Hanoi's Central Institute of Economic Management plainly stated that many of the new laws introduced since the late 1980s to deal with the economic reforms 'are words, not really laws'. Commercial law, for instance, barely exists in Vietnam, and some foreign companies are unwilling to throw money into a country which is, in legal terms, the equivalent of a black hole. But less understandable are the bureaucratic horror stories of a more mundane type that can be picked up from almost any of the foreign businessmen drinking off their day's troubles in the bars of Hanoi and Saigon. A 1994 issue of the *Vietnam Investment Review* quoted the head of the Organization and Cadre Committee, Minister Phan Ngoc Tuong as saying that "three out of four civil servants are incompetent" – in other words, 800,000 out of 1.1 million. Although wage rates may be low and levels of education relatively high, countries like Thailand with much higher wages are keeping themselves competitive by streamlining investment procedures and making the investment 'climate' attractive in other ways. It is significant that of some US$10bn in approved investment between 1988 and 1994, US$734mn has been cancelled.

The country's **export base** is also still alarmingly narrow: oil, coal and rice accounted for well over half Vietnam's exports in 1994. It has been estimated that to just double incomes from their current derisory US$230/head by the year 2000 will require US$20bn in external funding.

In addition, the very success of the economic reforms has brought its own set of problems – in the same way that has occurred in China. **Inequalities**, both spatial and personal, are widening as some areas and people benefit, while others do not. Growth in agriculture is down to 3-4%, while industry is expanding at an annual rate of 12%. So, while the economies of Hanoi and Saigon are both growing at an annual rate of about 20%, the countryside is stagnating or, at best, growing slowly. Nationally, the World Bank estimates that 51% of the population live in poverty; in the cities the figure is 27%. This is drawing people in from the countryside, creating urban problems of both a social (for instance, unemployed people living in poor conditions and a lack of educational facilities) and economic (such as strains on the physical infrastructure) nature. These inequalities are likely to widen further in the short to medium term with the on-going process of reform. A World Bank report published in 1995 calculated that given sustained 8% growth in the economy, poverty in Saigon will be eradicated by the end of the 1990s. But by the same date, 68% of the population in the country's poorest rural provinces will remain mired in poverty.

Widening inequalities are also raising political challenges. Local and provincial governments in wealthy areas are beginning to resent financing poorer parts of the country, and are showing a greater inclination to 'go it alone', ignoring directives from Hanoi. This feeds back to foreign investors who find that they have to deal with different sets of regulations in different parts of the country. Ministers are ever warning of the dangers of so-called 'peaceful evolution' – meaning fundamental social and economic change. It seems that despite the enmity between Beijing and Hanoi, these fears have their origins in China's experience, which also provides the inspiration for their mitigation. It was reported that at the mid-term conference of the CPV at the end of Jan 1994, that Chinese pamphlets discussing such tensions were being widely distributed among delegates.

The gradual rapprochement between the US and Vietnam since 1993 has already yielded results for Vietnam. In Sep 1993, 15 countries including France and Japan agreed to provide US$140mn to enable Vietnam to clear its arrears with the IMF. As a result, in Oct 1993, the IMF, World Bank and the Asian Development Bank resumed lending to Vietnam, approving loans amounting to US$528mn to finance irrigation, education and infrastructural projects. A month later, international donors pledged assistance worth US$1.86bn for 1994, praising Vietnam's "impressive" reform programme. Key donors were Japan, Britain, South Korea and France. Finally, at the end of 1993, the Paris Club of Western creditors agreed to reschedule Vietnam's US$4.5bn hard currency debt.

VIETNAM: FACT FILE

Geographic

Land area	331,688 sq km
Arable land as % of total	17.5%
Average annual rate of deforestation	0.6%
Highest mountain, Fan Si Pan	3,143m
Average rainfall in Hanoi	1,680 mm
Average temperature in Hanoi	23.4°C

Economic

GDP/person (1993)	US$230
PPP* (1992)	US$1,250
GDP growth (1993)	8.0%
GDP growth (1994)	8.5%
% labour force in agriculture	67%
Total debt (% GNP)	n.a.
Debt service ratio (% exports)	n.a.
Military expenditure (% GDP)	4.8%

Social

Population	72.4 million
Population growth rate (1960-91)	2.2%
Adult literacy rate	89%
Mean years of schooling	4.9 years
Tertiary graduate as % of age group	n.a.
Population in absolute poverty	54%
Rural population as % of total	77%
Growth of urban population (1960-92)	3.6%/year
Urban population in largest city (%)	24%
Televisions per 1,000 people	39

Health

Life expectancy at birth	63 years
Population with access to clean water	50%
Calorie intake as % of requirements	102%
Malnourished children under 5 years old	3.8 million
Contraceptive prevalence rate‡	53%

* PPP = Purchasing Power Parity (based on what it costs to buy a similar basket of goods and services in different countries).
‡% of women of childbearing age using a form of modern contraception.

Source World Bank (1994) *Human development report 1994*, OUP: New York; and other sources.

HANOI

Hanoi is the capital of the Socialist Republic of Vietnam and lies nearly 100 kilometres from the sea on the Red River. The name means 'within a river bend' (*ha* = river, *noi* = in). It is a city of tree-lined boulevards, weathered colonial buildings, elegant squares, and the occasional bomb shelter. The history of the city must be the most confusing of any capital in Southeast Asia: established as a defensive citadel in the 8th century, it has had at least seven names since then.

The original village on the site of the present city was located in a district with the local name of **Long Do**. The community seems to have existed as a small settlement as early as the 3rd century AD, although the early history of the Red River Delta largely passed it by. At the beginning of the 8th century a general named Lu Yu became so enchanted with the scenery around the village of **An Vien** (close to Long Do), that he decided to move his headquarters there.

Here he built a shrine to the Emperor Hsuan Tsung, erected an inscribed tablet, and dedicated a statue of the local earth spirit on which was inscribed a poem extolling the beauty of the spot.

The origins of Hanoi as a great city lie with a temple orphan: Ly Cong Uan. Ly rose through the ranks of the palace guards to become their commander and in 1010, 4 years after the death of the previous King Le Hoan, was enthroned, marking the beginning of the 200 year-long Ly Dynasty. On becoming king, Ly Cong Uan moved his capital from Hoa Lu to Dai La, which he renamed **Thang Long** or 'Soaring Dragon'. Thang Long is present day **Hanoi**. During the Ly Dynasty the heart of Thang Long was the king's sanctuary in the Forbidden City (Cam Thanh). Drawing both spiritual and physical protection, as well as economic well-being from their proximity to the king and his court, a city of commoners grew-up around the walls of Cam Thanh. The Ly kings established a Buddhist monarchical tradition which mirrored other courts in Southeast Asia. A number of pagodas were built at this time. Most have since disappeared, although the One Pillar Pagoda and the

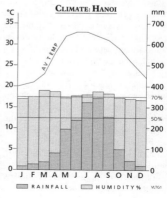

CLIMATE: HANOI

Tran Vu Temple both date from this period (see below).

Thang Long, renamed **Tay Do** (Western Capital), was to remain the capital of Vietnam until 1400 when the Ho Dynasty (1400-1407) established a new capital at Thanh Hoa. But soon afterwards, the focus of power shifted back to Thang Long which, in turn, was renamed **Dong Kinh** (Eastern Capital) and **Bac Thanh** (Northern Citadel). It is from Dong Kinh that the French name for Northern Vietnam – Tonkin – is derived. The present name of the city dates from 1831 when the Nguyen Emperor Tu Duc (1847-1883) made it the capital of the province of Hanoi.

During the period of French expansion into Indochina, the Red River was proposed as an alternative trade route to that of the Mekong. Francis Garnier was dispatched to the area in 1873 to ascertain the possibilities of establishing such a route. Despite having only a modest force of men under arms, when negotiations with Emperor Tu Duc failed in 1882, Garnier attacked and captured the citadel of Hanoi under the dubious pretext that the Vietnamese were about to attack him. Recognizing that if a small expeditionary force could be so successful, then there would be little chance against a full-strength army, Tu Duc acceded to French demands.

From 1882 onwards, Hanoi, along with the port city of Haiphong, became the focus of French activity in the N. Hanoi was made the capital of the new colony of Annam, and the French laid out a 2 sq km residential and business district, constructing mansions, villas and public buildings incorporating both French and Asian architectural styles. Many of these buildings still stand to the S and E of the Old City and Hoan Kiem Lake – almost as if they were grafted onto the older Annamese city. In the 1920s and 1930s, with conditions in the countryside deteriorating, there was an influx of landless and dispossessed labourers into the city.

In their struggle to feed their families, many were willing to take jobs at subsistence wages in the textile, cigarette and other industries that grew up under French patronage. Before long, a poor underclass, living in squalid, pathetic conditions, had formed. At the end of WW2, with the French battling to keep Ho Chi Minh and his forces at bay, Hanoi became little more than a service centre. By 1954 there were about 40,000 stallholders, shopkeepers, peddlars and hawkers operating in the city – which at that time had a population of perhaps 400,000. It has been calculated that one family in two relied on the informal sector for their livelihoods.

After the French withdrew in 1954, Ho Chi Minh concentrated on building up Vietnam and in particular Hanoi's industrial base. At that time the capital had only eight, small, privately-owned factories. By 1965, more than 1,000 enterprises had been added to this figure. However, as the US bombing of the N intensified with Operation Rolling Thunder in 1965, so the authorities began to evacuate non-essential civilians from Hanoi and to disperse industry into smaller, less vulnerable, units of operation. Between half and three-quarters of a million people were evacuated between 1965 and 1973: 75% of the inner city population. When hostilities ended in 1973, one Soviet reporter estimated that a quarter of all buildings had been destroyed. Nevertheless, the cessation of hostilities led to a spontaneous migration back into the capital. By 1984 the population of the city had reached 2.7 million, and today it is in excess of 3 million.

The physical damage wreaked upon the city during the war – much of which has yet to be repaired (although it is surprisingly difficult to spot) – means that there is a grave shortage of housing and office space. Western companies opening up offices in the capital have found, to their surprise, that rents in one of the poorest countries in the world are approaching those in Tokyo and Hong Kong. Prime sites near Hoan Kiem Lake cost US$40-70 per sq metre per month. Food supply is also a problem. Inefficient distribution, and the generally poor performance of agriculture in the N, means that there are still shortages. As Nigel Thrift and Dean Forbes in their account

The French officer and hero Francis Garnier was killed in an assault on Hanoi's citadel on 21 December 1873. He was killed by a volley of bullets from Black Flag mercenaries, and not speared, as depicted here. Only 35 years old at his death, he became a symbol of courage and Gallic fortitude in France.

Source: Petit, M. (n.d.) *La France au Tonkin et en Chine.*

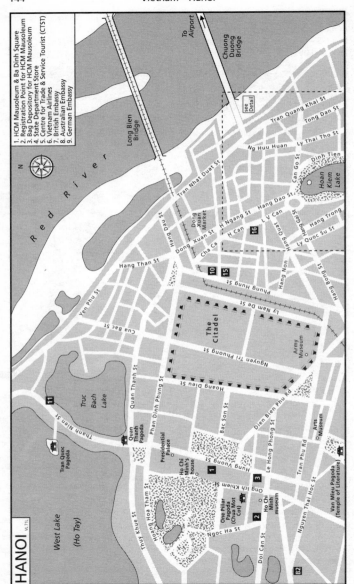

HANOI

1. HCM Mausoleum & Ba Dinh Square
2. Registration Point for HCM Mausoleum
3. Bag Depository for HCM Mausoleum
4. State Department Store
5. Centre for Trade & Service Tourist (CTST)
6. Vietnam Airlines
7. British Embassy
8. Australian Embassy
9. German Embassy

Red River

N

To Airport

Chuong Duong Bridge

Long Bien Bridge

See Detail

Tran Quang Khai St
Tong Dan St
Ng Huu Huan
Ly Thai Tho St
Can Go St
Dinh Tien
Hoan Kiem Lake
Hang Dao St
H Ngang St
L V Can
Hang Gai St
Hang Trong
Hang Bac St
Ly Quoc Su St
H Can
16
Dong Xuan Market
Dong Xuan St
Cha Ca
Hang Dau St
Tran Nhat Duat St
Hang Ngang
Hang Non
Hang Bong St

Hang Than St

10 15
Phung Hung St
Ly Nam De St

The Citadel

Nguyen Tri Phuong St
Hoang Dieu St
Army Museum

Yen Phu St
Cua Bac St
Truc Bach Lake
Quan Thanh St
Phan Dinh Phung St
11
Quan Thanh Pagoda
Bac Son St
Dien Bien Phu Rd
Arts Museum

Thanh Nien St
Tran Quoc Pagoda

West Lake (Ho Tay)

Hoang Hoa Tham St
Thuy Khue St
Presidential Palace
Ho Chi Minh's house
1
Hung Vuong St
Le Hong Phong St
Tran Phu Rd

One Pillar Pagoda (Chua Mot Cot)
Ong Ich Khiem St
3
Ho Chi Minh museum
Nguyen Thai Hoc St
Van Mieu Pagoda (Temple of Literature)

Doi Can St
Ngoc Ha St
2

B2

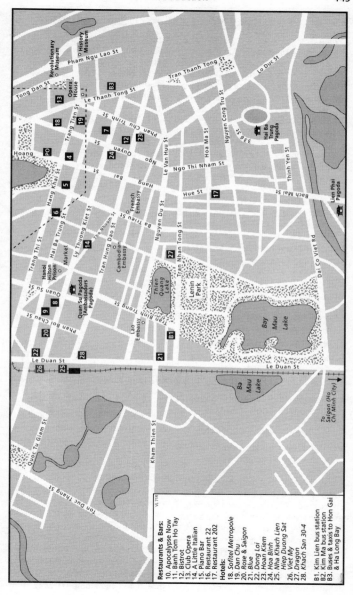

Restaurants & Bars:
10. Apocalypse Now
11. Banh Tom Ho Tay
12. Bistrot
13. Club Opera
14. A Little Italian
15. Piano Bar
16. Restaurant 22
17. Restaurant 202

Hotels:
18. Sofitel Metropole
19. Dan Chu
20. Rose & Saigon
21. Blue
22. Dong Loi
23. Hoa Kiem
24. Hoa Binh
25. Nha Khach Lien Hiep Duong Sat
26. Viet My
27. Dragon
28. Khach San 30-4

B1. Kim Lien bus station
B2. Kim Ma bus station
B3. Buses & taxis to Hon Gai & Ha Long Bay

BEAUTIFUL HANOI NEEDS A MIRACLE, SAYS BRITISH MP

When the French were unceremoniously bundled out of Vietnam in 1954 they did not leave much behind in the way of infrastructure, but they did leave Hanoi – one of the world's most beautiful cities. Built around more than twenty lakes, Hanoi consists of avenues lined with tamarind trees, elegant villas and magnificent public buildings. Decades of war and years of economic stagnation brought terrible decay, but not destruction. Hanoi has survived almost intact.

Alas the end is nigh. The arrival of the free market means that the planners now have the resources to succeed where the B-52 bombers failed. Unless a miracle occurs, Hanoi is about to be destroyed.

Already concrete monstrosities are rising in the most unlikely places. By Hoan Kiem lake in the city centre a ghastly confection of concrete and marble now dominates the skyline amid the yellow stucco and green wooden shutters of the public buildings left by the French. it is the new city hall. In this building dwell the very planners whose job is to regulate the development of the city. It is hard to think of a more ominous portent.

There is much worse to come. A consortium from Singapore has been given approval for a massive commercial development on the site of the old 'Hanoi Hilton' prison. It is to have 24 storeys in an area where there is nothing over five.

Nothing is sacred. A South Korean company is said to be pressing the Hanoi authorities to be allowed to build in a park which presently contains the city zoo. It would be wrong, however, to blame the impending disaster entirely on foreigners. Many Vietnamese, tired of long years of poverty and backwardness, are understandably enthusiastic about the arrival of the free market. Indeed, if there was ever a country urgently in need of a dose of market forces, it was Vietnam. In the past two or three years the living standards of many Vietnamese

---

of Vietnamese urbanization write:

"...there is considerable social tension in what is still an austere and disciplined city between the wishes of the state for ideological rectitude and the desire of some of the population (especially the young) for a more colourful life, stimulated by the unification with the S and the growth of a market in consumer goods" (1986:151).

Although Saigon has attracted the lion's share of Vietnam's foreign inward investment, Hanoi, as the capital, also receives a large amount. But whereas Saigon's investment tends to be in industry, Hanoi has received a great deal of attention from property developers, notably in the hotel and office sectors. Unfortunately, much of the proposed development is in prestigious and historical central Hanoi.

British MP Chris Mullin has written an impassioned attack on the hideous and architecturally utterly incongruous schemes (see box) and drawn attention to the developers' blatant disregard for truth (such as a claim by Peter Purcell of Dragon Properties that a 20 storey office block will be "in total harmony with the character of the surrounding neighbourhood" of Hoan Kiem Lake) and Vietnamese politicians' disturbing haste to sell off prime, historical sites to overseas developers. In late 1994, the Chief Architect's Office proposed height limits on new development in the vicinity of Hoan Kiem Lake but failed to define the area this would apply to.

A major development, the so-called Song Hong (Red River) City, is under construction between West Lake and the Red River. At a cost of US$260mn a Singaporean company is building luxury accommodation for 10,000, a 26-storey office, hotels and a hospital. Song Hong

have risen significantly. No sensible person will begrudge that.

Like all converts, however, Vietnam has gone from one extreme to the other. From a society where virtually all productive activity was paralysed by bureaucracy to one where almost everything goes. Being poor gave Vietnam one advantage. Its leaders could have learned from the mistakes of their neighbours. They were not obliged to repeat the urban disasters of Bangkok, Taipei, Manila – or for that matter, Los Angeles. Yet that is exactly where they are headed.

There is no better illustration than the coming of private motor cars. When I first visited the city in 1980 the bicycle was the only form of transport for all but a handful of high officials and foreign diplomats. (It was not unknown for ambassadors to travel by bicycle.) In a country of rice farmers with a per capita annual income of around US$200 the private motor car has no relevance to the lives of 99% of the population, except in so far as it poses a threat to their lives. Hanoi, or at least the old city, could still be saved, but time is running out.

What is most lacking is not funds but political will. Government and local authority leaders pay lip service to the preservation of old Hanoi, but there has been little in the way of action. A ban on private cars in the old city would be a good start. Strict controls over new building would be another.

If the political will existed, it would not be hard to generate foreign support. "There is not one of my colleagues who has not raised this with the Vietnamese Government", an ambassador wrote to me. Another said, "I say to the Vietnamese, when you can demonstrate the will to preserve your city, I will find funds to pay for a consultant to advise how it might be done."

What irony. A country that has suffered so much at the hands of rapacious foreigners is now on the point of surrender to a culture at least as foreign and at least as destructive as that which it paid such a high price to defeat.

Source: Extracted from an article written by Chris Mullin, MP, for the *Vietnam Investment Review* – March

City will be built on the dyke that protects Hanoi from flooding. Interestingly 250 new houses built on the dyke illegally or with 'irresponsible licences' have just been torn down by the authorities because of the serious damage they have caused this ancient flood protection measure.

Pollution levels in Hanoi have soared as a result of the construction boom: dust from demolition, piling, bricks and tiles and sand blown from the back of trucks add an estimated 150 cubic metres of pollutants to the urban atmosphere every day. But while asthmatics may wheeze, Hanoi's army of builders grows daily ever stronger. Hundreds of farmers join the urban job market each week and one can see bands of men standing around at strategic points waiting to be recruited; on Duong Thanh St, for example, carpenters with their tool boxes wait patiently for the call to a day's work.

Places of interest

Most visitors see the sights of Hanoi with the aid of tour guides. This is undoubtedly the quickest and easiest way. However, as tourism expands, so it is becoming increasingly easy to explore the city oneself – either by bicycle, cyclo or on foot. The buses will probably remain a complete mystery, except to the long-term visitor. Much of the charm of Hanoi, and indeed of the rest of Vietnam, lies not so much in the official 'sights' (some of which can be decidedly uninspired) but in the unofficial and informal: the traffic, small shops, stalls, the bustle of pedestrians, clothing, parents treating their children to an ice cream and evening visit to Hoan Kiem Lake ... Like China when it was 'opening-up' to Western tourists in the late 1970s, the primary interest lies in the novelty of exploring a city (and country) which, until recently, has opted for a firmly socialist road to development and has been insulated from the West. The city is charming, little changed from the French period, with tamarind-lined boulevards, wonderful provincial architecture, and streets which are still comparatively free of traffic. When Joleaud-Barral visited the city at the end of the 19th century he referred to it as a 'ville Française' and was of the opinion that whereas "at Saigon, one exists; at Hanoi, one *lives*". Humourist PJ O'Rourke describes the city along the same lines, if in a rather different style, in his book *Give war a chance*: "On first impression it seemed like Sixties America – not pot, war and hirsute aggravation ... but the madras-clad, record hop, beach-bunny nation of my school days ... there was a doo-ron-ron in the air". Sadly, the twentieth century is catching up quickly with Hanoi and arguably more lasting damage to Hanoi's fabric has occurred in almost a decade of *doi moi* than in 8 years of US bombing (see box above).

Hanoi's sights are centred in two main areas: around Hoan Kiem Lake, where many of the more expensive hotels are also located, and in the vicinity of Ho Chi Minh's Mausoleum. There are also some sights which fall outside these two areas.

Hoan Kiem Lake and Central Hanoi

Hoan Kiem Lake (the Lake of the Restored Sword) is named after an incident that occurred during the 15th century. Emperor Le Thai To (1428-1433), following a momentous victory against an army of invading Ming Chinese, was sailing on the lake when a golden turtle appeared from the depths to take back the charmed sword which had secured the victory and restored it to the lake from whence it came. Like the sword in the stone of British Arthurian legend, Le

Thai To's sword assures Vietnamese of divine intervention in time of national crisis and the story is graphically portrayed in water puppet theatres across the country. There is a modest and rather dilapidated tower (the *Tortoise Tower*) commemorating the event on an islet in the southern part of the lake. In fact, the lake does contain large turtles; one captured in 1968 was reputed to have weighed 250 kg. The park that surrounds the lake is used by the residents of the city every morning for jogging and tai chi (Chinese shadow boxing) and is regarded by locals as one of the city's beauty spots. When the French arrived in Hanoi at the end of the 19th century, the lake was an unhealthy lagoon surrounded by so many huts that it was impossible to see the shore.

The NE corner is *the* place to have your photo taken, preferably with the **Ngoc Son (Jade Hill) Pagoda** (see diagram) in the background. The pagoda was built in the early 19th century on a small island and is linked to the shore by a red, arched wooden bridge (the **The Huc** – Sunbeam – **Bridge**) constructed in 1875. The temple is dedicated to Van Xuong, the God of Literature, although the 13th century hero Tran Hung Dao, the martial arts genius Quan Vu and the physician La To are also worshipped here. Shrouded by trees and surrounded by water, the pagoda's position is its strongest attribute. Admission 12,000d.

Stretching N from the lake is the **Old City**. Previously, it lay to the E of the

HANOI'S NAMES (200 AD - PRESENT)	
Long Bien	200 AD
Dai La	900-1010
Thang Long	1010-1400
Dong Do	1400-1428
Dong Kinh	1428-1789
Bac Thanh	1789-1831
Hanoi	1831-

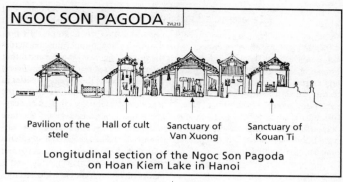

NGOC SON PAGODA ZVL213

Pavilion of the stele
Hall of cult
Sanctuary of Van Xuong
Sanctuary of Kouan Ti

Longitudinal section of the Ngoc Son Pagoda on Hoan Kiem Lake in Hanoi

citadel, where the emperor had his residence, and was squalid, dark, cramped and disease-ridden. This part of Hanoi has survived surprisingly intact, and today is the most beautiful area of the city. Narrow streets, each named after the produce that it sells (Basket St, Paper St, Silk St etc), create an intricate web of activity and colour. Another name for the area is '36 Streets': by the 15th century there were 36 short lanes here, each specializing in a particular trade and representing one of the 36 guilds. Among them, for example, were the Phuong Hang Dao or Dyers' Guild, and the Phuong Hang Bac, the Silversmiths' Guild. Some of this past is still in evidence: at the S end of Hang Dau St, for example, is a mass of stalls selling nothing but shoes while Tin St is still home to a community of tinkers. Generally however, the crafts and trades of the past have given way to new activities – but it is remarkable the extent to which the streets still specialize in the production and sale of just one type of good. The dwellings in this area are known as 'tube houses' (*nha ong*); they are narrow, with shop fronts sometimes only 3m wide, but can be up to 50m long. The house at No 97 Hang Dao St, for example, is a mere 1.6m wide. In the countryside the dimensions of houses were calculated on the basis of the owner's own physical dimensions; in urban areas no such regulations existed and tube houses evolved so that each house owner could have an, albeit very small, area of shop frontage facing onto the main street. The houses tend to be interspersed by courtyards or 'wells' to permit light into the house and allow some space for outside activities like washing and gardening. As geographers Brian Shaw and R Jones note in a paper on heritage conservation in Hanoi, the houses also had a natural air conditioning system: the difference in ambient temperature between the inner courtyards and the outside street created air flow, and the longer the house the greater the velocity of the flow. The older houses tend to be lower; commoners were not permitted to build higher than the Emperor's own residence. The structures were built of bricks 'cemented' together with sugar-cane juice.

A fear among conservationists is that this unique area – untouched since before WW2 – will be destroyed as residents who have made small fortunes with the freeing-up of the economy, redevelop their houses insensitively. The desire is understandable: the tube houses are cramped and squalid, and often without any facilities. In an attempt to protect and renovate Hanoi's heritage an international foundation – the Friends of Hanoi Heritage – was established at the beginning of 1993 to

---

TEARAWAYS TERRORIZE TOWNSFOLK

A recent trend in contemporary society has manifested itself in the form of young male Hanoians racing each other on powerful motorbikes around the city streets. Up to 400 racers take part and, to add to the frisson, the more reckless cut their brake cables. The participants are drawn chiefly from the families of the *nouveaux riches*, some the sons of senior party members. A number of racers and spectators have died and police have so far proved unable to prevent the clandestinely organized events. Now a team of police riders equipped with fast bikes, guns and electric cattle prods has been assembled to maintain order. The Hanoi People's Committee has (a little naïvely) put forward the suggestion of building a special race track — presumably with the hope that legalizing and managing the 'sport' will help to control it.

---

raise funds to thwart the "bulldozers [that] wait in the wings to raze its heritage to the ground". Time, as they say, is very short. For information contact: Friends of Hanoi Heritage, Level 9, 287 Elizabeth St, Sydney, NSW, Australia 2000.

Venturing further N, is the large and varied **Dong Xuan Market**, on Dong Xuan St. This large covered market was destroyed in a disastrous fire in Jul 1994. Stall holders lost an estimated US$4.5mn worth of stock and complained bitterly at the inadequacy of the fire services; one fire engine arrived with no water. The market is being rebuilt. **48 Hang Ngang St** is the spot where Ho Chi Minh drew up the Vietnamese Declaration of Independence in 1945, unashamedly and ironically modelled on the US Declaration of Independence (Hang Ngang St is at the N end of Hang Dao St, before it becomes Hang Duong St). The Old City is also a good area to eat, with a multitude of small and cheap eating houses (see page 164). Just to the E of the Dong Xuan market is the Red River, bridged at this point by the Cau Long Bien and Cau Chuong Duong. The former of these two bridges was built by the French in 1902 and named **Paul Doumer Bridge** after the Governor General of the time. Over 1.5 km in length, it was the only river crossing in existence during the Vietnam War, and suffered repeated attacks from US

planes only to be quickly repaired. The Chuong Duong Bridge was completed at the beginning of the 1980s.

To the S and E of Hoan Kiem Lake is the proud French-era **Municipal Theatre** or **Opera House**. It was built in 1911 and is one of the finest French colonial buildings in Hanoi. The exterior is a delightful mass of shutters, wrought iron work, little balconies and a tiled frieze. Inside, there are dozens of little boxes and fine decoration evocative of the French era (ask the doorman to let you in). Just in front of the Opera House is the **Revolutionary Museum** (Bao Tang Cach Mang) at 25 Tong Dan St. It is not a revolutionary museum as such, but a museum of the Vietnamese revolution, tracing the struggle of the Vietnamese people to establish their independence. The rooms are arranged chronologically beginning on the 1st floor, and as the first recounts the story of the destruction of the Mongol Chinese fleet at the mouth of the Bach Dang River in the autumn of 938 (see Ha Long Bay, page 182), it becomes clear that the American involvement in Vietnam has been just one episode in a centuries-long struggle against foreign aggressors. Also on display is a French guillotine (in the back passage on the 1st floor – one recent visitor was physically sick on seeing it), and an interesting room on the ground floor tracing the anti-war movement in

SYNDICATED LOANS KEEP THE SHARKS AWAY

Throughout Vietnam, and indeed across the world wherever there are large numbers of Vietnamese, one will find *hui* in operation. *Hui* is a credit circle of 10 to 20 people who meet every month; the scheme lasts as many months as there are participants. In a blind auction the highest bidder takes home that month's capital. Credit is expensive in Vietnam, partly because there are no banks to make personal loans, so in time of crisis the needy have to borrow from money-lenders at crippling rates of interest. Alternatively they can join a *hui* and borrow at more modest rates.

It works like this: the *hui* is established with members agreeing to put in a fixed amount, say 100,000d, each month. Then each month the members bid according to their financial requirements entering a zero bid if they need no cash. If, in month one, Mr Nam's daughter gets married he will require money for the wedding festivities and, moreover, he *has* to have the money so he must bid high, maybe 25,000d. Assuming this is the highest bid he will receive 75,000d from each member (ie 100,000 less 25,000). In future months Mr Nam cannot bid again but must pay 100,000d to the 'winner'. Towards the end of the cycle several participants (those whose buffalo have not died and those whose daughters remain unmarried) will have taken nothing out but will have paid in 100,000 (minus x) dong each month; they can enter a zero bid and get the full 100,000d from all participants and with it a tidy profit.

There is, needless to say, strategy involved and this is where the Vietnamese love of gambling ("the besetting sin of the Vietnamese" – Norman Lewis) colours the picture. One day, Mr Muoi wins 1 million dong on the Vinh Long lottery. He lets it be known that he intends to buy a Honda Dream, but to raise the necessary purchase price he must 'win' that month's hui and will be bidding aggressively. In the same month Thuy, Mrs Phuoc's baby daughter, celebrates her first birthday so Mrs Phuoc needs money to throw a lavish *thoi noi* party (see box on page 116). She has heard of old Muoi's intentions but does not know if he is serious. In case he is, she will have to bid high. On the day, nice Mrs Phuoc enters a knock out bid of 30,000 but wily old Muoi was bluffing all along and he and the others make a lot of interest that month. But they all bring generous presents to baby Thuy's party.

the West. The final rooms show the peace and prosperity of reunification: bountiful harvests, the opening of large civil engineering projects, and smiling peasants. Admission 2,000d. Open 0800-1230, 1400-1700 Tues-Sun.

A short distance S of the Revolutionary Museum, at 1 Pham Ngu Lao St, is the **History Museum** (Bao Tang Lich Su). It is housed in a building which dates from the late 19th century, and which was originally an archaeological research institute. The museum is now a centre of general cultural and histori-

cal research. The collection is large and rather confusing for the visitor without a working knowledge of the Vietnamese language or a guide to help. But fortunately, the rooms do proceed chronologically; from the prehistoric through to WW2. Exhibits include fine Dongson drums (see page 107), prehistoric artefacts, and Nguyen Dynasty pieces. Many of the pieces, though, are copies (eg the large 'tortoise' stelae). The curators will sometimes give visitors personal tours of the museum (for a small gratuity). Admission 10,000d. Open

0800-1245, 1315-1700 Tues-Sun.

The **General Department Store**, just off the W end of Trang Tien St, vividly illustrates the deficiencies of the state in producing an adequate supply of decently made consumer goods. West from here on Hai Ba Trung St is the **Cho 19-12** – a market linking Hai Ba Trung with Ly Thuong Kiet St – and selling primarily fresh fruit, vegetables and meat (including dog). A block to the W of the market once stood the grim walls of the *Hoa Lo Prison* better known as the **Hanoi Hilton**, the prison where US POWs were incarcerated, some for 6 years, during the Vietnamese War. Up until 1969, prisoners were also tortured here. Two airforce officers Charles Tanner and Ross Terry, rather than face torture, concocted a story about two other members of their squadron who had been court-martialled for refusing to fly missions against the N. Thrilled with this piece of propaganda, visiting Japanese Communists were told the story and it filtered back to the US. Unfortunately for Tanner and Terry they had called their imaginary flyers Clark Kent and Ben Casey (both TV heroes). When the Vietnamese realized they had been made fools of, the two prisoners were again tortured. The final prisoners were not released until 1973, some having been held in the N since 1964. At the end of 1992 a US mission was shown around the prison where 2,000 inmates were housed in cramped and squalid conditions. The fate of Hoa Lo is indicative of the radical nature of change in society. Despite pleas from war veterans and party members, the site was sold to a Singapore-Vietnamese joint venture to build a 5-star hotel and shopping complex. A prison museum will be incorporated into the new 22 storey building.

Nearby at 73 Quan Su St is the **Quan Su** or **Ambassadors' Pagoda**. In the 15th century there was a guesthouse here for visiting Buddhist ambassadors. The current structure was built between 1936 and 1942. Chinese in appearance from the exterior, the temple contains some fine stone sculptures of the past, present and future Buddhas. It is very popular and crowded with pilgrims, beggars and incense sellers. The pagoda is one of the centres of Buddhist learning in Vietnam: at the back is a school room with a mural of the Buddha behind the teacher's desk. Open 0830-1145, 1300-1545 Tues-Sun.

A short distance S from the Ambassador's Pagoda, is **Thien Quang Lake** and **Lenin Park**. Not surprisingly, the park contains a statue of Lenin, together with the wreckage of a US B-52 bomber. You may be charged 1,000d admission. Nearby, on Le Duan St S of the railway station stalls sell a remarkable array of US, Soviet and Vietnamese army surplus kit.

Ho Chi Minh's Mausoleum and surrounding sights

Ho Chi Minh's Mausoleum (Lang Chu Tich Ho Chi Minh) is 2 km to the W of Hoan Kiem Lake. Before entering the Mausoleum, visitors must register at the office (*Ban To Chuc*) on the corner of Doi Can (which becomes Le Hong Phong St) and Ngoc Ha sts, a few minutes walk from the Mausoleum. Most cyclo drivers and locals will point it out. The official may ask for each visitor's passport before filling out a slip, which is then presented to another official. From the registration office, walk down Le Hong Phong St and then N onto Hung Vuong St – which leads onto **Ba Dinh Square** where Ho read out the Vietnamese Declaration of Independence on 2 September 1945 – and the Mausoleum. (Thereafter 2 Sep became Vietnam's National Day. Coincidentally 2 Sep was the date on which Ho died in 1969, although his death was not announced until 3 Sep in order not to mar people's enjoyment of National Day in the beleaguered North.) Visitors will be asked to deposit

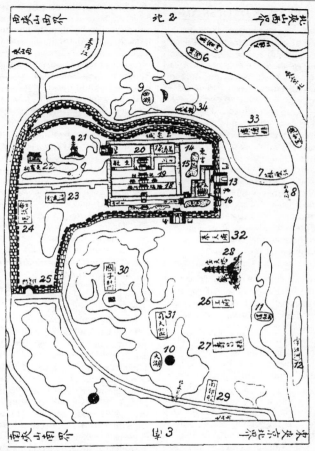

Map of Thang Long, former name of Hanoi, from *Hong Duc geography*, dated 1490.
The map is oriented N (2), S (3), E (4) and W (5). The citadel is protected by walls, double in the N. It is situated between the Red River in the E (6) and the Tô Lich River (7) in the W which forms a protective moat to the N and W. Two great lakes lie to the N and S of the citadel. The first still exists as the Hà Nôi or Western Lake (*Tây Hó*) (9); a major part of the second, the Great Lake or Dai Ho (10) has been filled in and built over. Hoàn Kiém Lake (11) is shown to the S of the citadel, and draining into the Red River near Phu Sa Island (12). The Eastern Gate (*Dông môn*) (13), leads to the Heir Prince's Palace (*Dông Cung*) (14) with a large pond (*trì*) (15). To the S of the Palace is the Emperor's ancestors temple (*Thái Miêu*) (16), while to the W is the Imperial Palace with its *Van Tho* Palace (17) and its various buildings aligned S-N: *Doan môn* (18) Gate, the Audiences' Hall, *Thân Triêu* (19), *Kinh Thiên* Palace (20). In the western portion of the citadel are 2 temples, *Khán Son* (21) and *Ling Lang* (22); while to the S is the Military Instruction Palace (*Giang võ diên*) (23) and the Literary Examination Camp (*Hôi thi duông*) (24). Outside the citadel's walls to the S (through the Bao Khanh Gate) (25) was the Lord Trinh's Palace (*Vuong phú*) (26), at Tho Xuong district (27). N of here and probably added to the map at a later date is the *Bao Thiên* Pagoda (28). Finally, to the NW of the Trinh's Palace was the College of State Sons (*Quôc Tu giám*) (30), present-day Van Miéu, and the Observatory in the W (*Tu Thiên Giám*) (31).

THE STORY OF QUAN AM

Quan Am was turned onto the streets by her husband for some unspecified wrong doing and, dressed as monk, took refuge in a monastery. There, a woman accused her of fathering, and then abandoning, her child. Accepting the blame (why, no one knows), she was again turned out onto the streets, only to return to the monastery much later when she was on the point of death – to confess her true identity. When the Emperor of China heard the tale, he made Quan Am the Guardian Spirit of Mother and Child, and couples without a son now pray to her. Quan Am's husband is sometimes depicted as a parakeet, with the Goddess usually holding her adopted son in one arm and standing on a lotus leaf (the symbol of purity).

their bags and cameras before marching in file to see Ho's embalmed corpse. In the rooms adjacent to the bag depository, short films are shown outlining the Great Man's life and work. The Vietnamese have made his body a holy place of pilgrimage. This is contrary to Ho's own wishes: he wanted to be cremated and his ashes placed in three urns to be positioned atop three unmarked hills in the N, centre and S of the country. He once wrote that "cremation is not only good from the point of view of hygiene, but it also saves farmland". Visitors must be respectful: dress neatly, walk solemnly, and do not talk. The **Mausoleum**, built between 1973 and 1975, is a massive, square, forbidding structure and must be among the best constructed, maintained and air-conditioned (for obvious reasons) buildings in Vietnam. Opened in 1975, it is a fine example of the Mausoleum genre and modelled closely on Lenin's Mausoleum in Moscow. Ho lies, with a guard at each corner of his bier. The embalming of

Ho's body was undertaken by the chief Soviet embalmer Dr. Sergei Debor who also pickled such Communist luminaries as Klenient Gottwald (President of Czechoslovakia), Georgi Dimitrov (Prime Minister of Bulgaria) and Forbes Burnham (President of Guyana), Debrov was flown to Hanoi from Moscow as Ho lay dying, bringing with him two transport planes packed with air conditioners (to keep the corpse cool) and other equipment. To escape US bombing, the team moved Ho to a cave, taking a full year to complete the embalming process. Russian scientists still check-up on their handiwork, servicing Ho's body regularly. Their embalming methods and the fluids they use are still a closely guarded secret, and in a recent interview, Debrov noted with pleasure the poor state of Mao's body, which was embalmed without Soviet help. "We had no part whatsoever in doing Mao", adding "I have heard reports that he is not in very good condition". Open 0730-1100 Tues-Thur, Sat and Sun. The Mausoleum is closed in Sep and Oct.

From the Mausoleum, visitors are directed to **Ho Chi Minh's house** built in the compound of the former **Presidential Palace**. The Palace, now a Party guesthouse, was the residence of the Governors-General of French Indochina and was built between 1900 and 1908. In 1954, when North Vietnam's struggle for independence was finally achieved, Ho Chi Minh declined to live in the palace, saying that it belonged to the people. Instead, he stayed in what is said to have been an electrician's house in the same compound. Here he lived from 1954-58, before moving to a new house built the other side of the small lake (Ho Chi Minh's 'Fish Farm', swarming with massive and well-fed carp). This modest house is airy and personal, and immaculately kept. Ho conducted meetings under the house which is raised up on wooden pillars (his books, slippers and telephones are still here), and slept and worked above. The typewriter on which it is said he typed the Declaration of Independence is on display. Built by the army, the house mirrors the one he lived in while fighting the French from his haven near the Chinese border. Behind the house is Ho's bomb shelter, and behind that the hut where he died in 1969. Open 0730-1130 Tues-Thur, Sat and Sun.

From Ho Chi Minh's house, visitors are directed to the **One Pillar Pagoda** (**Chua Mot Cot**), one of the few structures remaining from the original foundation of the city. It was built in 1049 by Emperor Ly Thai Tong, although the shrine has since been rebuilt on several occasions, most recently in 1955 after the French destroyed it before withdrawing from the country. Emperor Ly built the pagoda in a fit of religious passion after he dreamt that he saw the goddess *Quan Am* (Chinese equivalent Kuan-yin) sitting on a lotus and holding a young boy, who she handed to the Emperor. On the advice of counsellors who interpreted the dream, the Emperor built this little lotus-shaped temple in the centre of a water-lily pond and shortly afterwards his queen gave birth to a son. As the name suggests, it is supported on a single (concrete) pillar with a brick and stone staircase running up one side. The pagoda symbolizes the 'pure' lotus sprouting from the sea of sorrow. Original in design, with dragons running along the apex of the elegantly curved tiled roof, the temple is one of the most revered monuments in Vietnam.

Overshadowing the One Pillar Pagoda is the **Ho Chi Minh Museum** – opened in 1990 in celebration of the centenary of Ho's birth. Contained in a large and impressive modern building, it is the best arranged and most innovative museum in Vietnam. But, apart from newspaper clippings in French, everything is in Vietnamese. The display traces Ho's life and work from his early wanderings around the world to his death and final victory over the S. One

of the guides may speak English. Open 0800-1100, 1330-1600 Tues-Thur and Sat; 0730-1100, 1330-1600 Sun.

South from Ho Chi Minh's Museum on Nguyen Thai Hoc are the walls of the Temple of Literature. The entrance to the pagoda is at the S end of this long and narrow block on Quoc Tu Giam St. **The Temple of Literature** or **Van Mieu Pagoda** is the largest and probably the most important temple complex in Hanoi. It was founded in 1070 by Emperor Ly Thanh Tong, dedicated to Confucius who had a substantial following in Vietnam, and modelled, so it is said, on a temple in Shantung, China, the birthplace of the sage. Some researchers, while acknowledging the date of foundation, challenge the view that it was built as a Confucian institution pointing to the ascendancy of Buddhism during the Ly Dynasty. Confucian principles and teaching rapidly replaced Buddhism, however, and Van Mieu subsequently became the intellectual and spiritual centre of the kingdom as a cult of literature and education spread amongst the court, the mandarins and then among the common people. At one time there were said to be 20,000 schools teaching the Confucian classics in northern Vietnam alone.

The temple and its compound are arranged N-S, and visitors enter at the southern end from Quoc Tu Giam St. In the gateway two pavilions house stelae bearing the inscription *ha ma*, (climb down from your horse) a nice reminder that even the most elevated dignitaries had to proceed on foot. A path leads to the main *Van Mieu Gate* (*Van Mieu Mon*) adorned with 15th century dragons. Traditionally the large central gate was opened only on ceremonial occasions. The path leads through the *Dai Trung Mon* to a second courtyard and the *Khue Van Cac* Pavilion which was built in 1805 and dedicated to the Constellation of Literature. The roof is tiled according to the *yin-yang* principle.

Beyond lies the Courtyard of the Stelae at the centre of which is the rectangular pond or *Thien Quang tinh (Well of Heavenly Clarity)*. More important are the stelae themselves, 82 in all, on which are recorded the names of 1,306 successful examination scholars (*tien si*). Of the 82 that survive (30 are missing) the oldest dates back to 1442 and the most recent to 1779. Each stele is carried on the back of a tortoise, symbol of strength and longevity but they are arranged in no order; three chronological categories, however, can be identified. Fourteen date from the 15th and 16th centuries; they are the smallest and embellished with floral motifs and *yin-yang* symbols but not dragons (a royal emblem). Twenty five stelae are from the 17th century and ornamented with dragons (by now permitted), pairs of phoenix and other creatures mythical or real. The remaining 43 stelae are of 18th century origin; they are the largest and decorated with two stylized dragons, some merging with flame clouds. Passing was not easy: in 1733, out of some 3,000 entrants only eight passed the doctoral examination (*Thai Hoc Sinh*) and became Mandarins – a task that took 35 days. This tradition was begun in 1484 on the instruction of Emperor Le Thanh Tong, and continued through to 1878 – during which time 116 examinations were held. The Temple of Literature was not used only for examinations however: food was also distributed to the poor and infirm, 500 g of rice at a time. In 1880, the French Consul Monsieur de Kergaradec recorded that 22,000 impoverished people came to receive this meagre handout.

Continuing N, the *Dai Thanh Mon* or *Great Success Gate* leads on to a courtyard flanked by two buildings which date from 1954, the originals having been destroyed in 1947. These buildings were reserved for 72 disciples of Confucius. Facing is the *Dai Bai duong (Great House of Ceremonies)* which was built in the 19th century but in the earlier style of the Le Dynasty. The carved wooden friezes with their dragons, phoenix, lotus flowers, fruits, clouds and *yin-yang* discs are all symbolically charged, depicting the order of the universe and by implication reflecting the god-given hierarchical nature of human society, each in his place. It is not surprising the Communist government has hitherto

THE EXAMINATION OF 1875

The examinations held at the Temple of Literature and which enabled, in theory, even the most lowly peasant to rise to the exalted position of a Mandarin were long and difficult, and conducted with great formality. André Masson quotes Monsieur de Kergaradec, the French Consul's, account of the examination of 1875:

"On the morning of the big day, from the third watch on, that is around one o'clock in the morning, the big drum which invites each one to present himself began to be beaten and soon students, intermingled with ordinary spectators, approached the Compound in front of the cordon formed around the outer wall by soldiers holding lances. In the middle of the fifth watch, towards four or five o'clock in the morning, the examiners in full dress came and installed themselves with their escorts at the different gates. Then began the roll call of the candidates, who were thoroughly searched at the entrance, and who carried with them a small tent of canvas and mats, cakes, rice, prepared tea, black ink, one or two brushes and a lamp. Everyone once inside, the gates were closed, and the examiners met in the central pavilion of the candidates' enclosure in order to post the subject of the composition. During the afternoon, the candidates who had finished withdrew a few at a time through the central gate...the last ones did not leave the Compound until midnight."

THE TRUNG SISTERS

Vietnamese history honours a number of heroines, of whom the Trung sisters are among the most revered. At the beginning of the Christian era, the Lac Lords of Vietnam began to agitate against Chinese control over their lands. Trung Trac, married to the Lac Lord Thi Sach, was apparently of a 'brave and fearless disposition' and encouraged her husband and the other lords to rise up against the Chinese in 40 AD. The two sisters often fought while pregnant, apparently putting on gold plated armour over their enlarged bellies. Although an independent kingdom was created for a short time, ultimately the uprising proved fruitless; a large Chinese army defeated the rebels in 43 AD, and eventually captured Trung Trac and her sister Trung Nhi, executing them and sending their heads to the Han court at Lo-yang. An alternative story of their death has it that the sisters threw themselves into the Hat Giang River to avoid being captured, and turned into stone statues. These were washed ashore (surely not?), and placed in Hanoi's Hai Ba Trung Temple for worship.

had reservations about preserving a temple extolling such heretical doctrine. Inside is an altar on which sits tablets of Confucius and his closest disciples. Adjoining is the *Dai Thanh (Great Success)* Sanctuary which contains a statue of Confucius.

To the N once stood the first university in Vietnam, *Quoc Tu Giam*, which from the 11th to 18th centuries educated first the heir to the throne and later sons of mandarins. It was replaced with a temple dedicated to Confucius' parents and followers itself destroyed in 1947. Admission 12,000d. Open 0830-1600 Mon-Sun.

Not far from the northern walls of the Van Mieu Pagoda at 66, Nguyen Thai Hoc St is the **Arts Museum** (Bao Tang My Thuat) contained in a large colonial building with an oriental-style roof. It has a large collection of contemporary Vietnamese art, along with some handicrafts. Admission 10,000d. Open 0800-1200, 1300-1600 Tues-Sun.

A 5 mins walk E from the Arts Museum, situated at 30, Dien Bien Phu St is the **Army Museum** (Bao Tang Quan Doi). Across the road from the front entrance is a statue of Lenin. The museum displays military memorabilia – mostly contemporary. Tanks, planes and artillery fill the courtyard. Symbolically, an untouched Mig-21 stands at the museum entrance while the wreckage of B52s, F1-11s and Q2Cs is piled up at the back. The museum illustrates battles and episodes in Vietnam's fight for independence (for instance, the battle at Dien Bien Phu), but unfortunately, all explanations are in Vietnamese. In the precincts of the museum is a flag tower, the **Cot Co**, raised up on three platforms. Built in 1812, it is the only substantial part of the original citadel still standing. Admission to the museum 10,000d plus 2,000d for camera. Open 0800-1130, 1330-1630 Tues-Sun.

Outer Hanoi

North from the Old City is **Truc Bach (White Silk) Lake**. Truc Bach Lake was created in the 17th century by building a causeway across the SE corner of Ho Tay. This was the site of the 11th century **Royal Palace** which had, so it is said, 'a hundred roofs'. All that is left is the terrace of *Kinh Thien* with its dragon staircase, and a number of stupas, bridges, gates and small pagodas. Judging by the ruins, the palace must have been an impressive sight. At the SW corner of the lake, on the intersection of Hung Vuong, Quan Thanh and Thanh Nien sts is the **Quan Thanh Pagoda**, originally built in the early 11th century in honour of Huyen Thien Tran Vo (a genie) but since much remodelled. Despite renovation, it is still very beautiful. The large bronze bell was cast in 1677. Admission 5,000d.

The much larger **West Lake** or **Ho Tay** was originally a meander in the Red River. It is fast losing its unique charm as the redevelopment disease spreads. Nguyen Ngoc Khoi, director of the Urban Planning Institute in Hanoi estimates that the area of the lake has shrunk by 20%, from 500 to 400 ha, as residents and hotel and office developers have reclaimed land. The lake is also suffering encroachment by water hyacinths which are fed by organic pollutants from factories (especially a tannery) and untreated sewage. The **Tran Quoc Pagoda** can be found on an islet on the E shores of the lake, linked to the causeway by a walkway. It was originally built on the banks of the Red River before being transferred to its present site by way of an intermediate location. The pagoda contains a stele dated 1639 recounting its unsettled history. A few km N on the tip of a promontory stands **Tay Ho Pagoda**, notable chiefly for its setting. It is reached along a narrow lane lined with stalls selling fruit, roses and paper votives and a dozen restaurants serving giant snails with noodles (*bun oc*) and fried shrimp cakes.

South of the city centre, down Hue St, is the hub of motorcycle sales, parts and repairs. Off this street, for example along Hoa Ma, Tran Nhan Tong and Thinh Yen are numerous **stalls and shops**, each specializing in a single type of product: TVs, electric fans, bicycle parts and so on. It is a fascinating area to explore. At the intersection of Thinh Yen and Pho 332 people congregate to sell second-hand and new bicycles, as well as bicycle parts. Not far away is the venerable **Hai Ba Trung Temple** – the temple of the Trung Sisters – overlooking a lake. Ask for **Den Hai Ba Trung**. The temple was built in 1142, but like others, has been restored on a number of occasions. It contains crude statues of the Trung sisters (see box), Trung Trac and Trung Nhi which are carried in procession once a year during Feb. The pagoda is not always open. Until recently visitors had to obtain a permission slip from the district council; now they will sometimes let people in without one.

Further S still from the Hai Ba Trung, is another pagoda – **Chua Lien Phai**. This quiet pagoda which can be found just off Bach Mai St, was built in 1732, although it has since been restored.

Excursions

Hung Kings' Temples, Phong Chau
South of Yen Bai and approximately 100 km NW of Hanoi near the industrial town of Viet Tri in Vinh Phu Province is popular with Vietnamese visitors especially during the Hung Kings' Festival. In purely topographical terms the site is striking, most obviously an almost perfectly circular hill rising unexpectedly out of the monotonous Red River floodplain with two lakes at the bottom. Given its peculiar physical setting it is easy to understand how the site acquired its mythical reputation as the birthplace of the Viet people and why the Hung Vuong kings chose it as the capital of their kingdom.

In this place, myth and historical fact have become intertwined. Legend has it that the Viet people are the product of the union of King Lac Long Quan, a dragon, and his fairy wife Au Co. Au Co gave birth to a pouch containing 100 eggs which hatched to produce 50 boys and 50 girls. Husband and wife decided to separate in order to populate the land and propagate the race, so half the children followed their mother to the highlands and half remained with their father on the plains giving rise to the Montagnards and lowland peoples of Vietnam. Historically easier to verify is the story of the Hung kings (Hung Vuong). They built a temple in order to commemorate the legendary progenitors of the Vietnamese people. Subsequent dynasties and modern Vietnamese have added buildings, each in their own style.

From the car park a **museum** is reached up a flight of steps and through an old gatehouse to the right. Admission 1,000d. Open 0800-1130, 1300-1600, Mon-Sun. The museum is a hideous, Soviet inspired piece but upstairs there are on display numerous items excavated from the province. Exhibits include pottery, jewellery, fish hooks, arrow heads and axe heads (dated 1000-1300 BC) but of particular interest are the bronze drums dating from the Dongsonian period (see page 110). The Dongsonian was a transitional period between the neolithic and bronze ages and the drums are placed at around the 5th to the 3rd centuries BC. Photographs show excavation in the 1960s when these items were uncovered and models recreate village life. Unfortunately all labels are in Vietnamese only, but you may be lucky enough to find an English-speaking guide.

Ascending the hill, a track leads to a **memorial to Ho Chi Minh**. Ho said he hoped that people would come from all over Vietnam to see this historic site. Nearby is the **Low Temple** dedicated to Au Co, mother of the country and supposedly the site where the 100 eggs were produced. At the back of the temple is a statue of the Buddha of a thousand arms and a thousand eyes. Continuing up the hill is the **Middle Temple** where Prince Lang Lieu was crowned seventh Hung king and where the kings would play chess and discuss pressing affairs of state. Prince Lang Lieu was (like the English King Alfred) something of a dab hand in the kitchen and his most enduring creation is a pair of cakes, *banh trung* and *banh day*, which to this day (unlike Alfred's) remain popular delicacies, eaten at Tet. This temple has three altars and attractive murals.

Pressing on to the top of the hill is the **oath stone** on which the 18th Hung

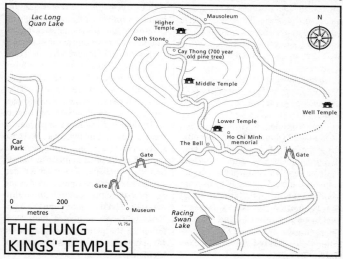

THE HUNG KINGS' TEMPLES

king, Thuc Phan, swore to defend the country from its enemies. Adjacent is the **Top Temple** dating from the 15th century. The roof is adorned with dragons and gaudily painted mural warriors stand guard outside. A not particularly ancient drum hangs from the ceiling but smoke rising from burning incense on the three altars helps add to the antiquity of the setting. Here it was that the kings would supplicate God for peace and prosperity.

Steps lead from the back right of this temple down the hill to the **mausoleum of the sixth Hung king**. These steps then continue down the far side of the hill to the **Well Temple** built in memory of the last princess of the Hung Dynasty. Inside is a well in the reflection of which this girl used to comb her hair. Today worshippers throw money in and, it is said, they even drink the water. Turn right to get back to the car park. Admission to the whole complex 2,000d.

Festivals: *Hung Kings' festival* (10th day of the third lunar month). A 2-week celebration when the temple site comes alive as visitors from all over Vietnam descend on the area, as Ho Chi Minh encouraged them to. The place seethes with vendors of all descriptions and food stalls and fairground activities spring up. There are racing swan boats on one of the lakes.

Getting there: turn off Highway 2 about 12 km N of Viet Tri: a morning or afternoon's excursion by car from Hanoi.

Thay Pagoda (Master's Pagoda), also known as Thien Phuc Tu Pagoda, lies 40 km SW of Hanoi in the village of Sai Son, Ha Son Binh Province. Built in the 11th century, the pagoda honours a herbalist, Dao Hanh, who lived in Sai Son village. It is said that he was reborn as the son of Emperor Le Thanh Tong after he and his wife had come to pray here. The pagoda complex is divided into three sections. The outer section is used for

ceremonies, the middle is a Buddhist temple, while the inner part is dedicated to the herbalist. The temple has some fine statues of the past, present and future Buddhas with gold faces and lacquered red garments, as well as an impressive array of demons. Water puppet shows are performed during holidays and festivals on a stage built in the middle of the pond at the front of the pagoda (see page 125). Dao Hanh, who was a water puppet enthusiast, is said to have created the pond. It is spanned by two bridges built at the beginning of the 17th century. There are good views from the nearby Sai Son Hill – a path leads upwards from the pagoda. *Getting there*: by tour or taxi (see Tourist offices, page 168).

Tay Phuong Pagoda is about 6 km from the Thay Pagoda in the village of Thac Xa. It may date back to the 8th century, although the present structure was rebuilt in 1794. Constructed of ironwood, it is sited at the summit of a hill and is approached by way of a long stairway. The pagoda is best known for its collection of 74 18th century *arhat* statues (statues of former monks). They are thought to be among the best examples of the woodcarver's art from the period. *Getting there*: by tour or taxi (see Tourist offices, page 168).

Perfume Pagoda (**Chua Huong** or Chua Huong Tich) is 60 km SW of Hanoi. Dedicated to Quan Am (see page 154), it consists of shrines and towers built amongst limestone caves and is regarded as one of the most beautiful spots in Vietnam. The stone statue of Quan Am in the principal pagoda was carved in 1793 after Tay Son rebels had stolen and melted down its bronze predecessor to make cannon balls. Emperor Le Thanh Tong (1460-1497) described it as 'Nam Thien de nhat dong' or 'foremost cave under the Vietnamese sky'. It is a popular pilgrimage spot, particularly during the festival months of Mar and Apr. Boat trips can be taken from one shrine to another through stunning scenery. *Getting there*: take a tour or charter a taxi. A taxi for the day can cost up to US$80 (0800-1900), a rowing boat takes 1 hr each way and costs 20,000d; organized tours are much cheaper.

Cuc Phuong National Park is about 160 km S of Hanoi, and is situated in an area of deeply-cut limestone scenery. Covering some 22,000 ha of humid tropical forest, it supports an estimated 1,880 species of flora including tall *parashorea*, *cinamomum* and *sandoricum* trees. However, the wildlife has been much depleted through hunting, only 64 mammal and 137 bird species are thought to remain. The park's 30,000 Muong minority people are being resettled elsewhere. Butterflies are reputed to swarm here during Apr and May. Neolithic remains have been unearthed in a cave in the park. **Accommodation** T 0130 66085, **B** 3 huts; one at the entrance, two in the centre. Each sleeps two people. Cheaper rooms also available, some very basic shared facilities, often no water. Guides available for hire at $3 a day. *Getting there*: only possible with a chartered car.

Keo Pagoda is 7 km outside the town of Thai Binh, which lies to the SE of Hanoi. This pagoda was built during the 11th century and is a fine example of Vietnamese provincial architecture. *Getting there*: by chartered car or on a tour.

Tam Dao is a rather run down French hill station 85 km N of Hanoi. There are some attractive colonial era buildings and the cool climate makes it a pleasant retreat from Hanoi. *Getting there*: by chartered car or on a tour.

Other possible day trips are excursions to **Haiphong** (see page 178), **Ha Long Bay** (see page 182), **Ninh Binh** (see page 188) and **Hoa Binh** (see page 172).

Tours

Day tours from Hanoi include visits to pagodas such as the **Tay Phuong**, **But Thap**, **Thay**, **Perfume**, **Tram Gian** and **Keo** and to the **Co Loa Citadel**, the 3rd century capital 20 km N of Hanoi, built by King An Duong with three rings of walls, the outer of which is 8 km in circumference. It is an important Bronze Age site and thousands of arrow heads and three bronze ploughshares have been excavated here. There are also tours to various Vietnamese **War sights** (like the wreckage of B-52s and the bomb-damaged Long Bien Bridge), **agricultural cooperatives**, **kindergartens**, **production enterprises**, **minority villages** and the Hanoi Railway Depot's collection of **steam locomotives** (mostly now withdrawn from service). Tour companies also organize day tours around **Hanoi's major sights**. Day tours are usually costed by the car, so it is cheaper to go in a group, see Tourist offices on page 168. The cost for a car, driver and guide is US$60-US$80.

Tour companies also organize 2-4 day trips to outlying cities and sights such as **Ha Long Bay**, **Haiphong**, **Do Son Beach**, **Hoa Binh**, **Dien Bien Phu**, **Lang Son**, **Sapa**, **Nam Dinh** and **Hoa Lu**. For a list of tour operators in Hanoi see Tourist offices, page 168.

Festivals

Jan/Feb: *Tet* (Vietnamese New Year, movable, see page 297) is celebrated in Hanoi, as in the rest of Vietnam, with great gusto and a range of events and festivities.

Jan/Feb: *Dong Da Hill festival* (5th day of Tet) celebrates the battle of Dong Da in which Nguyen Hue routed 200,000 Chinese troops. Processions of dancers carry a flaming dragon of straw.

Sep: *National Day* (2nd) parades in Ba Dinh Square, boat races on Hoan Kiem Lake.

Local information

● **Accommodation**

Price guide:

L	US$200+	C	US$15-25
A+	US$100-200	D	US$8-15
A	US$50-100	E	US$4-8
B	US$25-50	F	US$<4

There has been such a spate of hotel building and renovation in Hanoi that accommodation of all standards is readily available. Prices tend to be high and in some hotels service is poor and rooms badly maintained. Some of the cheaper hotels will still not take foreigners, although the number is decreasing. Popular business hotels are sometimes booked up weeks in advance: reserve and reconfirm; the most expensive offer a range of business services and have IDD and satellite TV.

City centre, S of Hoan Kiem Lake: L-A+ *Sofitel Metropole* (Thong Nhat), 15 Ngo Quyen St, T 266919, F 266920, restaurants, pool, business centre, Graham Greene stayed here in the 1950s, until renovation in 1991-92 by a French company it oozed character, still the only hotel in its class and usually packed, its prices reflect monopoly position and its clients' company credit cards rather than the intrinsic value of accommodation on offer; **A+ *Dan Chu***, 29 Trang Tien St, T 254937, F 266786, good restaurant, very pleasant, friendly hotel with clean and spacious rooms, some set well back from the street; **A+ *Hoa Binh***, 27 Ly Thuong Kiet St, a/c, T 253315, rambling old hotel with large rooms undergoing renovation, new extension now open; **A *Gold II***, 43C Ngo Quyen St, T 258863, F 250458, central, new, but very expensive, and rather charmless; **A-B *Bac Nam***, 20 Ngo Quyen St, T 257067, F 268998, new and friendly, good restaurant; **A-B *Hoan Kiem***, 25 Tran Hung Dao St, T 264204, a/c, big rooms, clean but overpriced; **A-B *Military Guesthouse***, 33 Pham Ngu Lao St, T 252896, F 259276, restaurant, quite pricey but popular; **B *Eden***, 78 To Nhuong St, T 245273, F 245619, good location and reasonable value; **B-D *Hotel 35***, 35 Trang Tien St, T 256115, some a/c, hot water, central, good value but always full and staff have a well deserved reputation for being unfriendly; **C *Bodega***, 57 Trang Tien St, T 252241, a/c, small hotel above restaurant and coffee shop and restaurant, well run, clean, rec, but some guests have reported unfriendliness (2 sister hotels have now opened nearby in Hang Bai St); **C *Sofia Guesthouse***, 6 Hang Bai St, T 266848, some

a/c, dirty, mouldy walls and beds, a classic and relic example of the old socialist system, nonchalant service and atrociously maintained, it is to be hoped the genre will soon become extinct.

Centre, N of Hoan Kiem Lake: A+ *Royal*, 20 Hang Tre, T 244233, F 244234, new, cheaper than the *Metropole* but service less good too; **A *Freedom***, 57 Hang Trong St, T 267119, F 243918, nr lake and cathedral; **A *Hoa Linh***, 35 Hang Bo St, T 243887, F 243886, in 36 Sts area, new mini hotel but traditional style with wood panelling; **A-B *Nam Phuong***, 16 Bao Khanh St, T 258030, F 258964, pleasant position nr Hoan Kiem Lake; **A-C *Phu Gia***, 136 Hang Trong St, T 255493, F 259207, some a/c, some rooms have views over Hoan Kiem Lake, cheaper rooms are good value; **B *Win***, 34 Hang Hanh St, T 267150, F 247448, like an increasing number of hotels in Hanoi has satellite TV; **B-C *Guest House Ma May***, 73 Ma May St, T 244425, friendly and clean; **C *Thanh Binh***, 81 Hang Dao St, T 244223, F 243970; **D *A Dong***, 46 Luong Ngoc Quyen St, T 256948, a/c; **D *Green Bamboo***, 42 Nha Chung St, T 268752, F 264949, cheaper rooms fan only, restaurant, bar and tour operator; **D *Hoa Long***, 94 Hang Trong St, T 269319, F 259228, good value with a/c and hot water and good restaurant; **D *Mai Phuong***, 32 Hang Be St, T 265341, cheaper rooms fan only and shared bathroom, friendly; **D *My Kinh***, 72-74 Hang Buom St, T 255726, a/c, fridge; **D *Tourist Café***, 6 To Tich St, T 243051, good value with a/c and hot water; **D-E *Darling Café***, 33 Hang Quat St, T 269386, F 256562, best known as a café but has a few cheap rooms; **D-E *Queen Café and Guest House***, 65 Hang Bac St, T 260860, shared bathrooms, fan rooms, basic but good, runs tours.

One pleasing development in Hanoi hotels is the advent of the *Especen Company*. It manages 11, small, private hotels all nr Hoan Kiem Lake which provide an excellent level of service with extraordinarily helpful multilingual staff (Especen = Esperanto centre). Several years on, however, it is a shame to see the company falling into the classic Vietnamese vice of failing to maintain rooms properly. Considering how little it pays its (still superb) staff this is inexcusable. The head office (see also Tourist offices) at 79E Hang Trong St, T 266856, F 269612 will make reservations at all 11 hotels which range **A-D**. *Especen 1*, 128 Hang Trong St, T 251347; *Especen 2*, 54 Hang Trong St, T 251346; *Especen 3*, 5 To Tich St, T 260879; *Especen 4*, 16 Trung Yen St,

T 261512; *Especen 5*, 10A Dinh Liet St,
T 253069; *Especen 6*, 28 Ta Hien St,
T 244182; *Especen 7*, 23 Hang Quat St,
T 251301; *Especen 8*, 21 Hang Hom St,
T 260880; *Especen 9*, 10B Dinh Liet St,
T 281160; *Especen 10*, 2 Hang Vai St,

T 281160; *Especen 11*, 28 Tho Xuong St,
T 244401.

Railway station area: A *Blue*, 209 Le Duan
St, T 263572, new, private and expensive; sister hotel, *Blue II*, at 6 Dinh Ngang St; **A** *Dong
Loi*, 94 Ly Thuong Kiet St, T 255721,

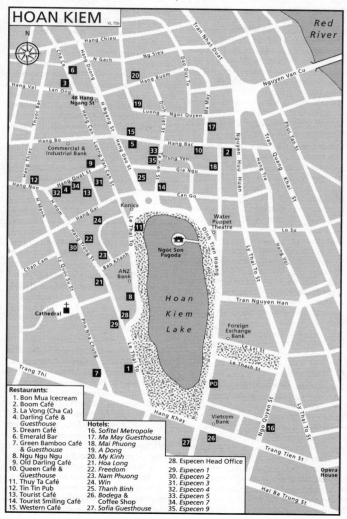

Restaurants:
1. Bon Mua Icecream
2. Boom Café
3. La Vong (Cha Ca)
4. Darling Café & Guesthouse
5. Dream Café
6. Emerald Bar
7. Green Bamboo Café & Guesthouse
8. Ngu Ngu Ngu
9. Old Darling Café
10. Queen Café & Guesthouse
11. Thuy Ta Café
12. Tin Tin Pub
13. Tourist Café
14. Tourist Smiling Café
15. Western Café

Hotels:
16. Sofitel Metropole
17. Ma May Guesthouse
18. Mai Phuong
19. A Dong
20. My Kinh
21. Hoa Long
22. Freedom
23. Nam Phuong
24. Win
25. Thanh Binh
26. Bodega & Coffee Shop
27. Sofia Guesthouse
28. Especen Head Office
29. Especen 1
30. Especen 2
31. Especen 3
32. Especen 4
33. Especen 5
34. Especen 7
35. Especen 9

F 267999, on the corner of Le Duan St, spectacular building but better value found elsewhere; **A** *Rose* (Hoa Hong), 20 Phan Boi Chau St, T 254439, a/c, new and comfortable but expensive for what it offers; **A** *Saigon*, 80 Ly Thuong Kiet St, T 268505, F 266631, newly renovated, expensive, business hotel; **A-B** *Dragon*, 57A Quang Trung St, T 259119, F 227871, overlooks Thien Quang Lake, over-priced; **B** *Nha Khach Lien Hiep Duong Sat*, 118 Le Duan St, T 243704, adjacent to station, expensive for what it offers but consolation of very friendly staff; **B-C** *Viet My III*, 84 Le Duan St, T 243035, new private hotel, clean, fair value, friendly; **D** *Khach San 30-4*, 115 Tran Hung Dao St, T 260807, F 252611, opp railway station, newly renovated but still cheap and good value, offers competitively priced tours; **D** *Nhat Phuong*, 39 Le Duan St, a/c, hot water, well priced, rec.

Out of town: L-A+ *Hanoi*, Giang Vo St, Ba Dinh District, T 254603, F 259209, newly refurbished, 11 storey and, for the time being, Hanoi's tallest building, Hanoi's chief fire officer has pointed out that his tallest ladders will reach only to the 8th flr, efficient but absurdly expensive and unfriendly business hotel, overlooks Giang Vo Lake; **A+-A** *Tay Ho*, Quang An, T 232380, F 232281, even further out of town, ruins a gorgeous position on West Lake with its three concrete stumps, pool and reasonable facilities; **A+-A** *Thang Loi*, Yen Phu, T 268211, F 252800, restaurant and pool, occupies a wonderful position on West Lake but unsympathetic Cuban architecture and inconvenient location 4 km N of town, mosquitoes are a problem; **A** *Dong Do*, Giang Vo St, nr National Exhibition Centre, T 343021, F 334228, has the *Sunset Pub* on its roof; **C-D** *Giang Vo*, Ngoc Khanh St, Giang Vo Lake, T 253407, venue of Classical Dancing Club.

● **Places to eat**

> **Price guide:** ♦♦♦♦*Over US$10* (100,000 dong); ♦♦♦*US$5-10* (50,000-100,000 dong); ♦♦*US$2-5* (20,000 -50,000 dong); ♦*Under US$2* (20,000 dong).

There has, over the last year or two, been a blossoming of eating places with the reawakening of the entrepreneurial spirit and the arrival of ex-pats and tourists sporting deep pockets and big bellies. Gone are the days when Western food was only to be had in dismal hotel restaurants with soiled tablecloths and surly service. Food of all descriptions is rapidly becoming one of Hanoi's greatest attractions but prices are escalating sharply. A few words of caution: dog (*thit chó* or *thit cau*) is an esteemed delicacy in the N, avoid or seek as taste and sensibility demand; second, old habits die hard: Communist ideals and recreational eating are uncomfortable bed-fellows and, inevitably, at some stage you will have inedible food ungraciously served in inhospitable surroundings; third, restaurants tend to close early, even by 2000 many will be shut. Western restaurants do, of course, stay open later.

Vietnamese: ♦♦♦♦*Indochine*, 16 Nam Ngu St, T 246097, excellent Vietnamese food served by elegantly attired staff; ♦♦♦*Restaurant 202*, 202 Hué St, Vietnamese and French menu, superb food at decent prices; ♦♦*Banh Tom Ho Tay*, Thanh Nien St, speciality is banh tom, shrimp cakes, nice location; ♦♦*Bodega*, 57 Trang Tien St, the ground floor is a popular coffee shop and ice-cream parlour, the first floor is a traditional restaurant with poor service and disappointing food; ♦♦*La Vong* (aka Cha Ca's), 14 Cha Ca St, serves one dish only, cha ca Hanoi, fried fish (see page 290) popular with visitors and ex-pats alike; ♦♦*Restaurant 22*, 22 Hang Can St, good menu, popular with Westerners but over-rated, quite good food but slow service; ♦♦*Sofia*, 6 Hang Bai St, in hotel of the same name, see comments above and avoid; ♦♦*Thuy Ta*, 1 Le Thai To St, nice setting on NW corner of Hoan Kiem Lake, popular meeting place for Vietnamese and travellers, ice creams and drinks.

International: ♦♦♦♦*A Little Italian*, 81 Tho Nhuom St (behind *Eden Hotel*), good pizzas; ♦♦♦♦*Club Opera*, 59 Ly Thai To St, T 268802, attractively restored colonial building, Vietnamese upstairs, western downstairs; ♦♦♦♦*Gustave*, 17 Trang Tien St, T 250625, named after the builder of a well-known landmark in Paris, restaurant upstairs, piano bar downstairs, Parisian decor but food doesn't quite match: expensive; ♦♦♦♦*Le Beaulieu*, 15 Ngo Quyen St (in *Sofitel Metropole Hotel*), T 266919, bland decor, French and Vietnamese menus, cold food and warm beer, could do much better; ♦♦♦*Bistrot*, 34 Tran Hung Dao St, T 266136, ever popular and deservedly so, highly erratic service but excellent French food; ♦♦♦*Five Royal Fish (Ngu Ngu Ngu)*, 16 Le Thai To St, terrace overlooks Hoan Kiem Lake, Vietnamese food and western; ♦♦♦*Piano Bar*, 50 Hang Vai St (nr intersection with Phung Hung), French and Vietnamese food, live music; ♦♦♦*Piano Bar and Restaurant*, 93 Phung Hung St, Western and Vietnamese food, live

BITES BUT NO BARK IN A VIETNAMESE RESTAURANT

Quang Vinh's restaurant was the ideal place for the ordeal to come. The palm-thatched house near the West Lake, on the outskirts of the Vietnamese capital Hanoi, was far from the accusing eyes of fellow-Englishmen.

It was dark outside. At one table, a Vietnamese couple were contentedly finishing their meal. At another, a man smoked a bamboo pipe. A television at the end of the room showed mildly pornographic Chinese videos.

But then came the moment of truth: could an Englishman eat a dog? Could he do so without his stomach rebelling, without his thoughts turning to labradors snoozing by Kentish fireplaces, Staffordshire bull terriers collecting sticks for children, and Pekinese perched on the laps of grandmothers?

One Englishman could: I ate roast dog, dog liver, barbecued dog with herbs and a deliciously spicy dog sausage, for it is the custom to dine on a selection of dog dishes when visiting a dog restaurant. The meat tastes faintly gamey. It is eaten with noodles, crispy rice-flour pancakes, fresh ginger, spring onions, apricot leaves and, for cowardly Englishmen, plenty of beer.

I had been inspired to undergo this traumatic experience – most un-British unless one is stranded with huskies on a polar ice cap – by a conversation earlier in the week with Do Duc Dinh, a Vietnamese economist, and Nguyen Thanh Tam, my official interpreter and guide.

They were much more anxious to tell me about the seven different ways of cooking a dog, and how unlucky it was to eat dog on the first 5 days of the month, than they were to explain Vietnam's economic reforms. "My favourite," began Tam, "is minced intestines roasted in the fire with green beans and onions." He remembered proudly how anti-Vietnamese protesters in Thailand in the 1980s had carried placards saying "Dog-eaters go home!"

During the Vietnam war, he said, a famous Vietnamese professor had discovered that wounded soldiers recovered much more quickly when their doctors prescribed half a kilogram of dog meat a day. Dinh insisted I should eat dog in Hanoi rather than Saigon. "I went to the S and ate dog, but they don't know how to cook it like we do in the N," he said. I asked where the dogs came from. "People breed it, then it becomes the family pet." And then they eat it? "Yes," he said with a laugh.

I told myself that the urban British, notorious animal lovers that they are, recoil particularly at the idea of eating dogs only because most of them never see the living versions of the pigs, cows, sheep and chickens that they eat in meat-form every day. And the French, after all, eat horses.

Resolutely unsentimental, we put aside our dog dinner and went to Vinh's kitchen. Two wire cages were on the floor; there was one large dog in the first and four small dogs in the second. 2 ft away, a cauldron of dog stew steamed and bubbled. Vinh told us about his flourishing business. The dogs are transported from villages in a nearby province. A 10 kg dog costs him about 120,000 Vietnamese dong, or just over US$10. At the end of the month – peak dog-eating time – his restaurant gets through about 30 dogs a day.

The restaurant, he said, was popular with Vietnamese, Koreans and Japanese. Squeamish westerners were sometimes tricked into eating dog by the Vietnamese friends, who would entertain them at the restaurant and tell them afterwards what it was they had so heartily consumed.

Source: Extracted from an article by Victor Mallet, *Financial Times*

music; ***Sunset Pub*, top of *Dong Do Hotel*, Giang Vo St, breezy setting in which to enjoy pizza, burgers, cocktails and ice cream in the company of several hundred clocks; ***The Emerald*, 53 Hang Luoc St, T 259285, Irish bar and restaurant without draught Guinness but still worth a visit; **Art Café*, 57 Hang Non St, good atmosphere, ideal for late night coffee and cocktails, open till after midnight; **Boom Café*, 29 Hang Mam, food, cocktails, art gallery open 0800-2400; **Café Pastry Shop*, 252 Hang Bong St, actually in Cua Nam St, excellent pastries, yoghurt and creme caramel, very popular for breakfast; **Dream Café*, 115 Hang Bac, good pastries and coffee; **Green Bamboo*, 42 Nha Chung St, café, bar and guesthouse (see also Tour companies); **Old Darling Café*, E on Hang Quat from its namesake, a breakaway café started up by disaffected staff, serves up the same old fare; **Real Darling Café*, 33 Hang Quat St (see also Tour companies), popular rendezvous with backpack fraternity, serves good snacks; **Tin Tin Pub*, 14 Hang Non St, Hergé may not have brought Tin Tin to Vietnam but he has become a local star, wide selection of beers and Tin Tin t-shirts; **Tourist Smiling Café*, S end of Dinh Liet, upstairs snacks and drinks; **Tourist Meeting Café*, 59B Ba Trieu St, for snacks and drinks, a good place to meet other travellers, next door is **Rendezvous Café*; *Bon Mua*, 38-40 Le Thai To St, popular ice-cream shop on the W bank of Hoan Kiem Lake; **Western Café*, 114 Hang Bac, western-style food, friendly; *35 Trang Tien*, the most popular ice-cream outlet in town, seething with people every evening; *Apocalypse Now*, 46 Hang Vai St, a bar rather than a restaurant but its status in travellers' folklore merits its inclusion.

Foodstalls: 36 Streets area is a good place to look around for cheap restaurants and foodstalls: To Tich St, between Hang Gai and Hang Quat sts, has special pho (*pho binh dan*) and other delights. Ta Hien St, N of Luong Ngoc Quyen St, offers an excellent selection of stalls and restaurants. The foodstall on the dead end street which runs off Tran Hung Dao St, 100m E of the railway station is rec. 2B Ly Quoc Su for excellent *pho*: queue, pay, eat. Night noodle and fried rice stalls on Hang Be St.

● **Airline offices**
Vietnam Airlines, 1 Quang Trung St, T 253842/250888; Vietnam Airlines is open 0700-1900 every day for both domestic and international bookings; **Air France**, 1 Ba Trieu St, T 253484, F 266694; **Aeroflot**, 4 Trang Thi St, T 252376; **Cathay Pacific**, 27 Ly Thuong Kiet (in *Hoa Binh Hotel*), T 267298 (Noi Bai, T 261113); **China Southern Airlines**, 27 Ly Thai To, T 269233; **Malaysian Airlines**, 15 Ngo Quyen St, T 268820; **Pacific Airlines**, 100 Le Duan, T 515356; **Singapore Airlines**, 15 Ngo Quyen St (*Hotel Sofitel Metropole*), T 268888, F 268666; **South Korea**, 29 Nguyen Dinh Chieu St, T 226677; **Thai**, 25 Ly Thuong Kiet St, T 266893, F 267934; **USA**, Liaison Office, 7 Lang Ha St, T 431500, F 350484.

● **Banks & money changers**
Banks, official money changers and black market operators are not as widespread as they are in Saigon. Major hotels will change US$ at poor rates. **ANZ Bank**, 14 Le Thai To St, T 258190, open 0830-1530 Mon-Fri and 0830-1200 Sat, provides full banking services including cash advances on credit cards; **Bank of Foreign Trade**, 47-49 Ly Thai To St, the bank will break US$100 notes into smaller bills but will not change dong back into US$; **Citibank**, 51 Ly Thai To St; **Commercial & Industrial Bank**, 37 Hang Bo St and 16 Phan Dihn Phung St; **Credit Lyonnais**, 10 Trang Thi St; **Foreign Exchange Centre**, 2 Le Lai St; **National Bank**, 10 Le Lai, open 0800-1100 and 1300-1600; **VID Public Bank**, 194 Tran Quang Khai St; **Vietcombank**, 50 Trang Tien St and 78 Nguyen Du St.

Black Market: Do **not** change money with the women who hang around outside the GPO: they are fraudsters. Black market rates are seldom better than official rates: if they are, beware. **NB** It is also possible to change dong back into US$ on Trang Tien St; it is impossible to use dong for anything except wallpaper outside the country.

● **Embassies & consulates**
Algeria, 15 Phan Chu Trinh St, T 253865; **Australia**, 66 Ly Thuong Kiet St, T 252763; **Belgium**, D1 Van Phuc Diplomatic Compound, T 252263; **Bulgaria**, 358 St, Van Phuc Diplomatic Compound, T 252908; **Cambodia**, 71 Tran Hung Dao St, T 253789; **Canada**, 31 Hung Vuong, T 235432; **Czech Republic**, 13 Chu Van An, T 254131; **China**, 46 Hoang Dieu St, T 253737; **Cuba**, 65 Ly Thuong Kiet St, T 254775; **Denmark**, 19 Dien Bien Phu, T 231888; **Egypt**, 85 Ly Thuong Kiet St, T 252944; **Finland**, B3b Qiang Vo Diplomatic Compound, T 256754; **France**, 49 Ba Trieu St, T 252719; **Germany**, 29 Tran Phu St, T 253836; **Hungary**, 47 Dien Bien Phu St,

T 252748; **India**, 58-60 Tran Hung Dao St, T 253409; **Indonesia**, 50 Ngo Quyen St, T 253353; **Iraq**, 66 Tran Hung Dao St, T 254141; **Israel**, Metropole Hotel, Room 111; **Italy**, 9 Le Phung Hieu St, T 256246; **Japan**, 61 Truong Chinh St, T 692600; **Laos**, 40 Quang Trung St, T 268724; **Libya**, Van Phuc Diplomatic Compound, T 253379; **Malaysia**, A3 Van Phuc Diplomatic Compound, T 253371; **Mongolia**, 39 Tran Phu St, T 253009; **Myanmar (Burma)**, A3 Van Phucw Diplomatic Compound, T 253369; **Netherlands**, 29 Trang Tien St, T 254937; **North Korea**, 23 Cao Ba Quat St, T 253008; **Philippines**, 27B Tran Hung Dao St, T 257873; **Poland**, 3 Chua Mot Cot St, T 252027; **Romania**, 5 Le Hong Phong St, T 252014; **Russia**, 58 Tran Phu St, T 254631; **Singapore**, 41-43 Tran Phu St, T 233966; **Sweden**, 2 358 St, Van Phuc Diplomatic Compound, T 254824; **Switzerland**, 77B Kim Ma St, T 232019; **Thailand**, 63-65 Hoang Dien St, T 256053; **UK**, 16 Ly Thuong Kiet St, T 252510, F 265762.

Visas from Hanoi to Russia – US\$10, allow 5 working days. 3 week visas available, stating date of entry and name of exit point.

● **Entertainment**
Evening entertainment in the traditional Western sense is virtually non-existent. Most restaurants shut by 2100-2200. *The Piano Bar*, *Apocalypse Now*, *Sunset Pub* tend to remain open slightly longer, but Hanoi is most definitely not a city for night owls.

Dance & theatre: the Municipal Theatre is housed in an impressive French-era building at the E end of Trang Tien St. Most performances are traditional or revolutionary. There is a newly opened foreign language cinema at the railway station end of Ly Thuong Kiet St.

Discos & dancing: always amusing, especially on Sat nights when the Hanoi trendies descend on the *Thang Loi Hotel*. Three of the more fashionable discos are *Queen Bee*, 42 Lang Ha St, *VIP Club*, 62 Nguyen Du, and *Palace Club*, 40 Nha Chung St.

Water puppet theatre (see page 125): at the Water Puppetry House 135, Truong Trinh St. Set up in 1956 by Ho Chi Minh, weekly performances have been staged almost continually since. In 1984 the Australian government provided the theatre with wet suits and water resistant paints, and in recent years the troupe has performed in Japan, Australia and Europe. Admission 20,000d. *Getting there*: by cyclo, by bicycle or by taxi; the theatre is some 7 km S of the centre.

A second water puppet theatre is at 57 Dinh Tien Hoang St at the NE corner of Hoan Kiem Lake. Fabulous performances, exciting music, the technical virtuosity of the puppeteers is astonishing. Performances every evening at 1830, 2000 and 2115 with live music (20,000d, camera 10,000d, video 50,000d).

● **Hospitals & medical services**
Hospitals: *AEA International*, 4th Flr, 4 Tran Hung Dao, T 213555; *Hospital Bach Mai*, Giai Phong St, T 522004, English speaking doctors; *Hospital K*, 43 Quan Su St, T 252143; *Friendship Hospital*, 1 Tran Khanh Du St, T 252231; *Swedish Clinic* opp Swedish Embassy, Van Phuc, T 252464; *Vietnam-German Hospital*, 40 Trang Thi, T 253531.

Dental treatment: at *Vietnam-German Hospital*, T 269723 and *Bach Mai Hospital*.

● **Post & telecommunications**
Central GPO: 85 Dinh Tien Hoang St.
DHL: in GPO and 49 Nguyen Thai Hoc St, T 267020.
International PO: 87 Dinh Tien Hoang St.
International telephone, telex and fax services: at the PO and from 66-68 Trang Tien St, 66 Luong Van Can St and in the PO on Le Duan next to the railway station.
TNT International Express: 23 Trang Thi St, T 265750; **UPS**, 4C Dinh Le St, T 246483.

● **Shopping**
Surprisingly – given the lack of consumer goods produced by Vietnam's moribund manufacturing sector – shopping is not a complete waste of time in Hanoi. One seasoned traveller was of the opinion that the city was a 'shopper's paradise' with cheap silk and good tailors, handicrafts and antiques.

Antiques: along Hang Khay and Trang Tien sts, S edge of Hoan Kiem Lake. Shops sell silver ornaments, porcelain, jewellery and carvings – much is not antique, not all is silver; bargain hard.

Art galleries: abound nr Hoan Kiem Lake, especially Trang Tien St and on Dinh Tien Hoang St at NE corner, try also *Mai Gallery*, 3B Phan Huy Chu St. Some oils but water colours on silk predominate.

Bicycles: from the *State General Department Store* on Hang Bai St (200,000-300,000d) or at the second-hand bike market at the intersection of Tinh Yen St and Pho 332, S of the city centre and on Ba Trieu St S of junction with Nguyen Du St.

Books: on Trang Tien St. For example, at No

61 is the *Foreign Language Bookshop* and No 40 is the *State Bookshop*. Private booksellers operate on Trang Tien St and have pavement stalls in the evening (bargain). *Xunhasaba*, the state book distributor, has a shop at 32 Hai Ba Trung; *The Gioi*, Publisher's bookshop is at 46 Tran Hung Dao.

Handicrafts: Hang Khay St, on southern shores of Hoan Kiem Lake, and Trang Tien St.

Maps: from stalls and shops along Trang Tien St and outside GPO.

Photo shops: processing (Japanese technology) and film on Hang Khay St, S shores of Hoan Kiem Lake, Konica at N shore of Hoan Kiem Lake. *Nang Thu*, 39 Hang Dan St, although slide film may occasionally be seen for sale it is strongly rec that you do not have it processed in Vietnam.

Silk: shops on Hang Gai St (eg No 109 Tan My); cheap tailoring services available. *State General Department Store* (Bach Hoa Tong Hop): Hanoi's equivalent of Harrods is on Hang Bai St. The window-dressing is terrible, and the goods are generally dismal in terms of both quality and range. But it is a good place to buy such things as North Vietnamese army hats, spectacles and measuring tapes.

● **Useful addresses**

Business Centre: Hanoi Business Centre, 51 Ly Thai To, T 268833, F 261222.
Hanoi People's Committee: 12 Le Lai St, T 253536.
Hanoi Police: 1 Hang Trong St, T 253131.
Immigration Dept: 40A Hang Bai St, T 260919.

● **Tour companies & travel agents**
With the expansion of tourism in Hanoi has come a welcome increase in the number and quality of tourist offices. Most noticeable is the rash of small private companies and although one or two may be operating at or beyond the limits of the law others offer decent services at very competitive rates. Virtually every hotel and café now claims to provide tourist services but usually they just act as agents for a company. One effect of this free market activity has been to force the state-owned companies into providing more imaginative tours at fairer prices. The private companies are generally limited to providing local tours or excursions to Ha Long Bay, Sapa or Dien Bien Phu at most; their geographical coverage does not yet match that of the state-owned companies. *CTST (Centre for Trade and Service Tourist)* have opened a large new office on

the corner of Hang Khay and Ba Trieu sts; *Darling Café* (sometimes the *Real Darling Café* to distinguish it from the schismatic branch), 33 Hang Quat St, T 269386, F 256562, a good range of tours to local destinations; *ECCO*, 74 Ba Trien St, (there have been numerous reports of the company demanding additional payments mid-journey, not recommended); *Especen*, 79E Hang Trong, T 266856, F 269612, although not infallible it is reliable and the staff make an effort; *Green Bamboo*, 42 Nha Chung, T 268752, F 264949; **Hanoi Tourism Service Company** (TOSERCO), 94 Ly Thuong Kiet St, T 255721; *OSC Travel*, 37 Nguyen Du St, T 258437, F 258883; *Saigontourist*, 55 Phan Chu Trinh, T 250953; *Vidotour*, 51 Phan Chu Trinh, T 265875; *Vietnamtourism*, 30A Ly Thuong Kiet St, T 264154, F 257583; *Vung Tau International Tourist Services*, 136 Hang Trong St (next to *Phu Gia Hotel*), T 252739.

● **Transport**
91 km from Ninh Binh, 103 km from Haiphong, 153 km from Thanh Hoa, 165 km from Ha Long Bay, 420 km from Dien Bien Phu, 658 km from Hué, 763 km from Danang, 1,710 km from Saigon.

Local The traffic in Hanoi is becoming more frantic – and lethal – as each month goes by. Bicycles, cyclos, mopeds, cars and Russian lorries fight for space with little sense of order, let alone a highway code. At night, with few street lamps and some vehicles without lights it can seem positively murderous. Pedestrians should watch out. **Bicycle**: this is the most popular form of local mass transport. Hiring a bike is an excellent way to get around the city; they can be hired from the *Sofia Guesthouse*, from the yoghurt and pastries shop at 252 Hang Bong St, from the *Tourist Meeting Café* at 59B Ba Trieu St, from 12 Trung Yen, just off Ta Hien St, from the little shops at 29-33 Ta Hien St, and from the *Phu Gia Hotel*. As demand increases, the number of outlets should likewise increase. Start by asking at your hotel or guesthouse. Expect to pay 6,000d/day. For those staying longer, it might be worth buying a bicycle (see Shopping above). **Bus**: there are limited city bus services. Routes are marked on some tourist maps. **Cyclos**: Hanoi's cyclo drivers must be among the most over-optimistic in Vietnam. They have obviously heard through the cyclo grapevine from Saigon that foreigners pay more than locals, but have taken this to extremes; prices quoted are usually 500% more than they should be. Drivers also have a

CONDENSED RAILWAY TIMETABLE (FROM HANOI)

		S1	S3	S5
		Mon–Thur	**Daily**	**Daily**
Hanoi	d	1900	1940	1000
Hué	a	0827	1044	0323
Danang	a	1140	1404	0700
Nha Trang	a	2206	0157	1925
Saigon	a	0700	1140	0600

FARES

From Hanoi to:		Hard Seat	Soft Seat	Hard Berth			Soft Berth
				High	**Middle**	**Low**	
S1	Hué		26	37	40	44	51
	Danang		30	42	46	50	59
	Nha Trang		54	76	83	91	106
	Saigon		65	91	99	108	127
S3	Hué	18	23	33	37	40	44
	Danang	20	26	38	42	46	50
	Nha Trang	36	47	69	76	83	90
	Saigon	42	56	82	91	99	107
S5	Hué	16	21	30	33	37	38
	Danang	18	24	34	38	42	44
	Nha Trang	33	43	61	69	76	79
	Saigon	39	51	73	82	91	94

HANOI TO LAO CAI

Dept Hanoi	Arr Lao Cai	Dept Lao Cai	Arr Hanoi
2020	0720	1730	0440
0510	1645	0925	2045
1350	1900	0525	1135

FARES

Hard Seat	Soft Seat	Hard Berth
7	10	16

All figures = US$. Fares and timings are liable to change. Tickets must be booked at least 3 days in advance.

ROAD TO NOWHERE

Wholly symptomatic of the government's Gadarene rush to 'modernize' the country is the new motorway between Hanoi and Noi Bai airport. It is both tragic and hilarious. Within days of its opening it was the scene of utter carnage as pedestrians, cyclists and buffalo exercised their right to cross the road on zebra crossings in front of speeding traffic. Huge road signs encourage motorists to execute U-turns in front of on-coming cars, while brazen hand-cart pushers obstinately cling to the fast lane swerving only to avoid the parked motorbikes of spectators squatting on the central reservation admiring the shambles. So appalling is the planning of the motorway that it takes longer to reach town than using the old road. Although motorists might touch speeds of over 100 kph they are deposited in such a remote and inaccessible part of Hanoi that it can take an hour to reach the city centre. Locals displayed their contempt for the scheme by hacking up the surface to excavate and sell the foundation sand and by cutting down and selling for scrap the metal handrails.

disturbing tendency to forget the agreed fare and ask for more: be firm, some travellers even ask that the price be written down if communication is a problem. A trip from the railway station to Hoan Kiem Lake should not cost more than 5,000d. **Taxi**: there are now metered taxis in Hanoi: *Hanoi Taxi*, T 535252, *Airport Taxi*, T 254250 and the much cheaper *PT Taxi*, T 533171. Private cars can be chartered from the major hotels, from outside the Vietnam Airlines Office at 1 Quang Trung St, from the *Toyota Service Station* at 5 Le Thanh Ton St, from 7 Dang Thai Than, T 254074 and from *Especen Hotel Co*, 79E Hang Trong, T 266856.

Air Hanoi's Noi Bai airport is 50 km from the city; about 1 hr's drive. **Transport to town**: a mini bus meets domestic arrivals at the front of the terminal building, taking Vietnamese into the city for $2, and foreigners for about $4. Minibuses leave for the airport from the Vietnam Airlines Office at 1 Quang Trung St, $4 for foreigners, service at regular intervals from 0415 but again, check bus departure times at the Vietnam Airlines office. A taxi takes 1 hr into Hanoi. Ensure the rate agreed is for the whole car and not pp. If travelling in a group, taxis organized by *Darling Café* cost $5 pp. Taxis can also be chartered from the Vietnam Airlines Office for the airport. Expect to pay about $16. Domestic air connections with Saigon (US$170), Danang (US$90), Nha Trang (US$130), Dien Bien Phu (US$60) and Hué (US$90). See timetable, page 293. Heli-Jet Vietnam offers charter helicopter services from Hanoi's Gia Lam Airport to Vinh, US$3,200; Dien Bien Phu, US$4,000; Ha Long, US$1,800

and other destinations. For reservations, *Hotel Sofitel Metropole*, T 266919 x 8046, F 250168.

Train The station (*Ga Hanoi*) is at 126 Le Duan St, at the end of Tran Hung Dao St (a 10-15 mins cyclo ride from the centre of town). Regular daily connections with Saigon (see timetable, page 293). Advance booking is required. There are four trains daily to Haiphong and also trains to the Chinese border at Lang Son and Lao Cai. Border opens 0700 Chinese time (1 hr ahead). Four trains a day to Kunming. Two trains for Thanh Hoa and Nam Dinh, and some for Vinh, leave from the Truong Tin station, 20 km S of the city. Buses for Truong Tin leave from the Kim Lien bus station.

Road Bus: Hanoi has a number of bus stations. The Kim Lien station is at the SW corner of Thien Quang Lake, on 100 Le Duan St. This serves destinations S of Hanoi: Saigon, Buon Ma Thuot, Vinh, Danang, Thanh Hoa, Nha Trang, Dalat, Qui Nhon, Ninh Binh and Nam Dinh. Express buses usually leave at 0500; advance booking is recommended. The Kim Ma station is on Nguyen Thai Hoc St (opp No 168), just past Giang Vo St, and serves destinations to the NW: Son Tay, Trung Ha, Phu To, Hat Lot, Moc Chau, Bat Bat, Tan Hong, Da Chong, Hoa Binh, Son La (en route to Dien Bien Phu) and Yen Bai. Minibuses to Haiphong leave regularly from the fountain at the northern tip of Hoan Kiem Lake opposite the Konica shop 2½ hrs (20,000d). Two buses leave at 0700 and 0800 for Hon Gai (Halong Bay) from outside the Toyota Service Station at 5 Le Thanh Tong St, 100m S of the Municipal Theatre 5 hrs (16,000d).

THE NORTH

CONTENTS

MAPS

The N encompasses the ancient rice lands of the Red River Delta, with Hanoi as its core, and the rugged mountains of the Hoang Lien Son which form a natural barrier to communications with Laos and China. This region represents the historic heart of Vietnam, and before the French unified the country in the late 19th century it was known as Tonkin.

HANOI TO DIEN BIEN PHU, LAI CHAU AND SAPA

The road from Hanoi to Dien Bien Phu winds its way for 420 km into the Annamite mountains that mark the frontier with the Lao People's Democratic Republic. From Hoa Binh the road dete-

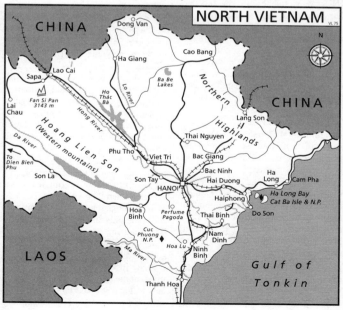

NORTH VIETNAM

riorates as it makes its way NW. Most people embark on this trek in order to visit the site of the historic Battle of Dien Bien Phu. From here it is possible to continue on to the delightful former French hill resort of Sapa, via Lai Chau. The area is inhabited mainly by minority hill peoples. Lao Cai, not far on from Lai Chau, is a flourishing border town and from here it is possible to continue on, back to Hanoi, following the valley of the Red River via the Hung King's Temples. The geology of much of NW Vietnam is limestone; the effect on this rock of the humid tropical climate and numerous streams and rivers is remarkable. Large cones and towers (hence tower karst) sometimes with vertical walls and overhangs rise dramatically from the flat alluvial plains. Dotted with bamboo thickets, this landscape is one of the most evocative in Vietnam; its hazy images seem to linger deep in the collective Vietnamese psyche and perhaps symbolize a sort of primaeval Garden of Eden, an irretrievable age when life was simpler and more innocent. It is certainly the most commonly reproduced image on calendars and greetings cards and artists professional and amateur are proud to paint what the cynical foreigner might consider a visual cliché.

Hoa Binh

Hoa Binh, on the banks of the Da River, marks the S limit of the interior highlands. Major excavation sites of the Hoabinhian prehistoric civilization (10,000 BC) were found in the province, which is its main claim to international fame. It is a possible stop-off point on the route to Dien Bien Phu, but since the construction of the huge dam and HEP station and the drowning of the valley much of its charm has been lost.

Excursions 70 km from Hoa Binh is **Mai Chau**, an attractive town with Black and White Thai villages nearby. **Accommodation** C *Mai Chau Guesthouse*, new but

pricey and already a bit scruffy.

Muong and Dao Minority villages are accessible from Hoa Binh. It is also possible to arrange a tour to the nearby **hydropower station**.

● **Accommodation** E *Hoa Binh I and II*, both on Route 6, 2 km towards Son La, T 52051.

● **Transport** 75 km from Hanoi. **Road Bus**: morning departures from Hanoi's Kim Ma terminal, 2 hrs.

Son La

Son La is the capital of the province of the same name which borders Laos. The surrounding highland area is home to a rich assortment of minority **hilltribes** (see page 113) including the Black Thai, Hmong, White Thai and Muong. It was only at the beginning of this century that the area was brought under the control of the central state – before then it was administered by the Black Thai ethnic minority. During the winter months it can be very cold.

What the road to Son La lacks in comfort is more than compensated for by the scenery and superb Black Thai villages. The road passes close to several particularly attractive villages each with a suspension footbridge and fascinating hydraulic works. Mini hydroelectric generators on the river supply houses with enough power to run a few lights and elsewhere water power is used to husk the rice.

The town itself is dusty and unremarkable; its chief function for the visitor is to provide an overnight stop en route for Dien Bien Phu.

It is a rough journey from Hanoi into the mountains that enclose much of the N of Vietnam; the road begins by running W past Ha Dong and Hoa Binh and gets steadily worse as it turns N. Son La is really just a stopping-off point two-thirds of the way to Dien Bien Phu. The only sight, if it could be thought of as such, is a **prison** built at the beginning of this century and found on a small hill in the centre of town, an elderly custodian charges 5,000d pp. Son La was the scene of a revolt against the French when the Thai minority people who live in the area took the town and killed the French administrator. When the French re-established control, their retribution is said to have been swift and merciless.

● **Accommodation B-D** Guesthouse a few hundred yards to the left of Route 6 on the way out of Son La to Dien Bien Phu, some a/c; **C-D** *Hoa Ban*, signposted from crossroads, T 52395; **C-D** *Son La Hotel*, some a/c, hot water, can be bargained down. Guesthouse to right of Route 6½ km further on.

● **Places to eat** Several eating places by a crossroads just E of the Do Rac Bridge, one offers goat dishes.

● **Transport** 310 km NW of Hanoi. **Road Bus**: connections with Hanoi's Kim Ma station nr the intersection of Nguyen Thai Hoc and Gianeg Vo sts.

Dien Bien Phu

Dien Bien Phu is a rapidly growing town. This reflects two things, first the recent decision to make it the provincial capital of Lai Chau Province and second its new function as a tourist destination. With increasing numbers of French and other tourists wishing to visit the battlefield a twice weekly air service from Hanoi has been inaugurated and the town's tourist infrastructure is growing to meet demand.

Dien Bien Phu was the site of the last calamitous battle between the forces of Ho Chi Minh's Viet Minh and the French, and was waged from Mar to May 1954. The French, who under Vichy rule had accepted the authority of the Japanese during WW2, attempted to regain control after the Japanese had surrendered. Ho, following his Declaration of Independence on 2 September 1945, thought otherwise, heralding nearly a decade of war before the French finally gave up the fight after their catastrophic

DIEN BIEN PHU VL76

The French Garrison, 13 March 1954 shortly before the siege began

GABRIELLE
Escarpment
Ford
Piste Pavie
Nam Yum River
Rt41
Ban Kéo
ANNE-MARIE
BEATRICE
HUGUETTE
DOMINIQUE
FRANCOISE
ELIANE
Phony Hill
Ban Ong Pet
CLAUDINE
Baldy Hill
Ban Hong Lech Cang
Ban Na Loi
Ban Papé
MARCELLE evacuated
Ban Palech
Ban Ten
Ban Bom La
Ban Nhong Nhai
Ban Kho Lai
Auxiliary airstrip
CLAUDINE - French strong points
Ban Hong Cum
● Villages
Barbed-wire systems
ISABELLE
WIEME
0   1
km

defeat here. The lessons of the battle were numerous, but most of all it was a victory of determination over technology. In the aftermath, the French people, much like the Americans 2 decades later, had no stomach left for a war in a distant, tropical and alien land.

On the battlefield **General** (as he was by the end of the battle) **de Castries' bunker** has been rebuilt (admission 2,000d) and eight of the 10 French tanks are scattered over the valley along with numerous US made artillery pieces. On **Hill A1** (known as Eliane 2 to the French and scene of the fiercest fighting) is a tank (*Grazielle*), a bunker, a war memorial and around the back is the entrance to a tunnel dug by coal miners from Hon Gai. Their tunnel ran several hundred metres to end beneath French positions and was filled with 1,000 kg of high explosives. It was detonated at 2300 on 6 May as a signal for the final assault.

THE BATTLE OF DIEN BIEN PHU

On 20 November 1953, after a series of French successes, Colonel Christian de Castries and six battalions of French and French-colonial troops were parachuted into Dien Bien Phu – a small heart-shaped basin 19 km long and 13 km wide. The location, in a narrow valley surrounded by steep wooded peaks, was chosen specifically because it was thought by the French strategists to be impregnable. From there, they believed, their forces could begin to harry the Viet Minh close to their bases as well as protect Laos from Viet Minh incursions. At the centre of the valley was the all-important airstrip – Colonel de Castries' only physical link with the outside world. In his history of Vietnam, Stanley Karnow writes of Castries: "Irresistible to women and ridden with gambling debts, he had been a champion horseman, dare-devil pilot and courageous commando, his body scarred by three wounds earned during World War II and earlier in Indochina".

In response, the famous Vietnamese General Giap moved his forces, some 55,000 men, into the surrounding area, manhandling heavy guns (with the help, it is said of a staggering 200,000 porters) up the impossibly steep mountainsides until they had a view over the French forces. The French commander still believed however that his forces would have the upper hand in any set-piece confrontation, and set about strengthening his position. He created a series of heavily fortified strongholds, giving them women's names: Anne-Marie, Françoise, Huguette, Beatrice, Gabrielle, Dominique, Claudine, Isabelle and Elaine. It is said that they were named after de Castries' numerous mistresses.

As it turned out, de Castries was not luring the Viet Minh into a trap, but creating one for himself and his men. From the surrounding highlands, Giap had the French at his mercy. The shelling started in the middle of March, and the strongholds fell one-by-one; Beatrice first and then Gabrielle and Anne-Marie by mid-March until de Castries' forces were concentrated around the airstrip. Poor weather, which prevented the French from using their air power, and human-wave attacks gradually wore the French troops down. By this time, de Castries had withdrawn to his bunker and command had effectively been taken over by his junior officers. A furious bombardment by the heavy guns of the Viet Minh from 1 May led to the final massed assault 5 days later. On the final night, the Viet Minh taunted the French defenders by playing the 'Song of the Partisans', the theme of the French Resistance, over the garrison's radio frequencies. De Castries' HQ fell on 7 May at 1730 when 9,500 French and French colonial troops surrendered. A small force of paratroopers at the isolated southern position, Isabelle, continued to resist for a further 24 hours.

This humiliation at Dien Bien Phu led the French to sue for peace at a conference in Geneva. On 20 July 1954, it was agreed that Vietnam should be divided into two along the 17th parallel: a Communist north and a capitalist south. In total, 20,000 Viet Minh and over 3,000 French troops were killed at Dien Bien Phu. The Geneva agreement set terms so that the dead from both sides would be honoured in a massive ossuary. But when Ngo Dinh Diem, the President of the Republic of South Vietnam, symbolically urinated over Viet Minh dead in the South rather than bury them with honour, Giap and Ho decided to leave the French dead to lie where they had fallen. Over the 9 years of war between the Viet Minh and the French, the dead numbered between a quarter and 1 million civilians, 200,000-300,000 Viet Minh and 95,000 French colonial troops. Who was to guess that another 20 years of warfare lay ahead?

The huge crater is still there.

The newly renovated **museum** (Bao Tang Chien Thang Lich Su Dien Bien Phu) has good collections of weapons and artillery from both sides in its grounds. Admission 5,000d. Open 0800-1100, 1400-1600 Mon-Sun. A guide from the museum can take you to visit the battle sights including **General Giap's newly rebuilt bunker** 8 km away at Ban Muong Phan. Opposite the museum and adjacent to hill A1 is the Viet Minh cemetery.

The road deteriorates from Son La to Dien Bien Phu, with the mountains rising up around the road as it snakes towards the border with Laos (the site of the battle is 16 km from the border). It is an arduous journey; 2 days each way from Hanoi, allow a minimum of 4 days for the whole trip. **Minority tribes** also inhabit the hills around Dien Bien Phu, among them Thai, Hmong, Phu La and Cong.

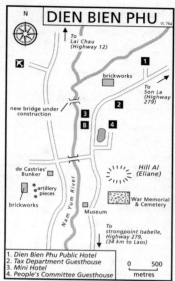

DIEN BIEN PHU

1. Dien Bien Phu Public Hotel
2. Tax Department Guesthouse
3. Mini Hotel
4. People's Committee Guesthouse

0 — 500
metres

Local information
● Accommodation
B-C *Dien Bien Phu Mini Hotel*, Be Van Dan St, T 122, new, central with restaurant; **B-D** *Dien Bien Phu Public Hotel*, 4 km from centre on Highway 279 coming in from Son La, friendly service no restaurant, some a/c.

C-D *People's Committee Guesthouse*, behind a pond nr bus station, unfriendly, unhelpful.

● Transport
110 km from Son La, 345 km from Hoa Binh, 420 km from Hanoi.

Air Vietnam Airlines flies every Tues and Fri from Hanoi. The 1 hr flight costs $130 return. The problem with this infrequent service is that it traps you in Dien Bien Phu for 3 to 4 days as it is very difficult to hire a car in Dien Bien Phu.

Road Bus: difficult. There are buses from Hanoi to Son La (see above), but no regular service from there to Dien Bien Phu. It is sometimes possible to hitch or cadge a lift. **Hire car/taxi**: roads are generally quite good (in the dry season) but so bad in places that a 4WD vehicle is required. Russian made army jeeps are ideal and can be hired with driver from hotels or tour operators in Hanoi (see page 168); prices vary but should be about US$300 for a 4 or 5 day round trip (1,200 km via Sapa), quite reasonable if split four ways.

Lai Chau

It is 104 km by road (Highway 12) from Dien Bien Phu to Lai Chau. The road was originally built by an energetic French district governor (Auguste Pavie) and was used by soldiers fleeing from the French garrison at Lai Chau to the safety of the garrison at Dien Bien Phu in 1953. Viet Minh ambushes along the Pavie Track meant that the French were forced to hack their way through the jungle and those few who made it to Dien Bien Phu found themselves almost immediately under siege again.

Today the journey is uncomfortable, scenically interesting but unspectacular. More diverting are the minority villages, Thai on the valley floors and Black and Red Hmong higher up. Lai Chau is strung out on both banks of the Da River and has no real centre. Like so many provincial towns it has little to offer other than accommodation and food but Lai Chau is not without charm and life proceeds at a very leisurely pace.

● **Accommodation D** *Nha Khach Uy Ban* (People's Committee Guesthouse), coming in from Dien Bien Phu turn left over the first bridge (Cau Uy Ban) and then up the zig-zag road, on the left, clean and comfortable some a/c. Further **E** in the main part of town are 2 guesthouses, one opp the bus station, both **F**.

● **Place to eat** *Nha Hang Thu Loan*, at the foot of the zig-zag road N of Cau Uy Ban, excellent food, highly rec.

● **Transport** 104 km from Dien Bien Phu. **Road** Highway 12 links Lai Chau with Dien Bien Phu. The route is best covered by taxi or hire car, preferably 4WD. The road continues on to Sapa and Lao Cai, and from there the railway runs to Hanoi, so it is possible to reach Lai Chau from either direction.

Tam Duong

Tam Duong is a little town some 80 km W of Sapa which some may find a helpful stopover. **Accommodation C** *Phuong Thanh Guesthouse*, pricey, clean and friendly; **D** *People's Committee Guesthouse* and **E** guesthouse at the bus station.

Sapa

Sapa is a delightful French hill station built in the early years of the century. Like Dalat in the S it served as a retreat for French administrators when the heat of the plains became unbearable. At 1,650m Sapa enjoys warm days and cool evenings in the summer but gets very cold in winter. Snow falls on average every couple of years and settles on the surrounding peaks of the Hoang Lien Son Mountains. Rain and cloud can occur at any time of year but the wettest months are May to Sep with nearly 1,000 mm of rain in Jul and Aug alone.

The huge scale of the Fan Si Pan Range gives Sapa an Alpine feel and this impression is reinforced by Haut Savoie vernacular architecture with steep pitched roofs, window shutters and chimneys. In an alluring blend of French and Vietnamese vegetation the gardeners cultivate foxgloves and apricot trees next to clumps of bamboo.

Distinctly oriental but un-Vietnamese in manner and appearance are the *Hmong, Dao* and other minorities who come to Sapa to buy and sell. Interestingly the Hmong have been the first to seize the commercial opportunities presented by Western tourists; they are engaging but persistent vendors of handloomed indigo clothing and handicrafts. Of the latter, notable is a little brass and bamboo musical instrument played like a jew's-harp. The other ethnic minorities hurry in and out of Sapa as quickly as business permits and appear anxious to have nothing to do with foreigners. For better or for worse, Sapa (like Hoi An) has rapidly established almost cult status among backpackers and is particularly crowded at weekends. With the huge influx of white faces the term 'ethnic minority' takes on a more literal meaning. The weekend trippers come on tours from Hanoi attracted by tales of the Saturday night bride market when young *Dao* men woo the unmarried *Dao* women. Sadly there have been reports of insensitivity on the part of some tourists.

Sapa is a pleasant place to relax and unwind, particularly after the arduous journey from Dien Bien Phu. Being comparatively new it has no important sights but several French buildings in and around are worth visiting. Most spectacular is the **ruined church** in the centre of Sapa built in 1930. The tower and nave still stand but the roof and interior were wrecked in 1952 by French artillerymen shelling the adjacent building in which Viet Minh troops were billeted. Inside the church stands a forlorn and headless Notre Dame de Lourdes and in the churchyard are the tombs of two former priests. A small rustic building nearby houses a little chapel and it is said the church will be rebuilt soon. Next to the church is the old French weather station, now abandoned.

Sapa was one of the places to be invaded by the Chinese in the 1979 border

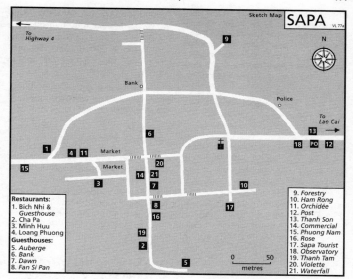

Restaurants:
1. Bich Nhi & Guesthouse
2. Cha Pa
3. Minh Huu
4. Loang Phuong

Guesthouses:
5. Auberge
6. Bank
7. Dawn
8. Fan Si Pan
9. Forestry
10. Ham Rong
11. Orchidée
12. Post
13. Thanh Son
14. Commercial
15. Phuong Nam
16. Rose
17. Sapa Tourist
18. Observatory
19. Thanh Tam
20. Violette
21. Waterfall

skirmish. Chinese soldiers found and destroyed the holiday retreat of Communist Party Secretary-General Le Duan, no doubt infuriated by such blatant hypocrisy and uncomradely display of bourgeois tendencies.

Excursions The remains of a French seminary are about 12 km from Sapa. This was ruined by militant Vietnamese suspicious of the true intentions of the order. They could not believe that so large a building in such a remote place lacked military or espionage capability. In reality the greatest threat to the Vietnamese way of life was Catholic proselytising. Beyond are **Dao and Hmong villages**, shy and reluctant people. *Getting there*: take the road 8 km to Lao Cai and a track left towards Ta Phim. Drivable with a brave and skilful driver and Russian army or Japanese jeep, but best walked.

Fan Si Pan, which at 3,143m is Vietnam's highest mountain, is a 2 to 3 day trek from Sapa; ask at Nha Hang Bich Nhi (see below) for route and guide. Also in the vicinity is a waterfall, **Thac Bac**

(Silver Falls). There are a number of trails around Sapa lasting 3 to 7 hrs and taking in minority villages Lao Chai, Sin Chai, and Chai Man (near which are some prehistoric rock drawings), rivers, waterfalls and views. They are described in a small book *Sapa*, edited by Leigh Stubblefield and published by The Gioi in Hanoi.

● **Accommodation** *C Forestry Guesthouse*, new and good with private bathrooms, and wonderful views, up a steep drive; *C-D Ham Rong Guesthouse*, T 71251, old style French building, views of Fan Si Pan, restaurant; *D Auberge Guesthouse*, T 721243, terrace for breakfast with good views, rent mountain bikes and jeeps and run tours, popular but some claims of unreliability (dormitory next door has US$2 beds); *D Dawn Guesthouse*, T 71222, hot water, clean, friendly, balcony; *D Fan Si Pan Guesthouse*, T 71290, private bathroom; *D Orchidée Guesthouse*, has a good restaurant, cheap, rec; *D Phuong Nam Guesthouse*, nice views and reasonable food; *D Post Guesthouse*, next to Post Office, T 71299, private bathrooms, balcony; *D-E Nha Khach Ngan Hang (Bank Guesthouse)*, more expensive rooms en suite bathrooms, hot water, cheaper ones share, friendly, rec; **E** *Nha Khach Thuong Nghiep (Commercial Guesthouse)*, **E** *Nha Nghi Du Lich Sapa (Tourist Guesthouse)*, T 71212, beyond the church through the gates, not welcoming; **E** *Rose Guesthouse*, rent jeeps and motorbikes, bus to Lao Cai; **E** *Thanh Son Guesthouse*, opp Post Office; **E** *Thanh Tam Guesthouse*, clean, friendly, French spoken; **E** *Waterfall Guesthouse*, T 71218, clean, friendly; **F** *Observatory Guesthouse*, very cheap dormitory accommodation, squeezes everyone in; **F** *Violette*, very cheap dormitory and shared accommodation, hot water.

● **Places to eat** ♦♦*Loang Phuong*, good food; ♦♦*Nha Hang Bich Nhi*, just beyond Minh Huu's, on the right, excellent food, popular with backpackers and a good place for exchange of news, arrange tours, also has rooms (**E**); ♦♦*Nha Hang Minh Huu*, down the steps, through the market, extensive menu, not so friendly; *Cha Pa*, cheap food and minibus to Lao Cai, 1300, US$2.5; *Orchidée Guesthouse*, restaurant is rec. Rice and noodle stalls in the market.

● **Banks & money changers** The bank used not to change money, most hotels will but at poor rates.

● **Transport** 38 km from Lao Cai. Most people visit Sapa on a tour from Hanoi. Tours cost about US$48 for 3 nights. **Road** Roads to and from Sapa are appalling, bumpy, rutted and pot-holed despite, and because of, the road builders. **Bus**: connections with Lao Cai usually 0600 and 1330 from *Rose Hotel*, US$3, 90 mins. It is also possible to drive to Lai Chau and from there to Dien Bien Phu. **Train** Trains leave Hanoi for Lao Cai at 0510, 1350 and 2020, journey time 6-12 hrs, cost 77,000-176,000d depending on comfort level. Honda om, jeep (US$3 pp) or local bus 20,000d from Lao Cai to Sapa.

Lao Cai

Lao Cai was badly damaged during the Chinese invasion in 1979; it is now a flourishing border crossing. Trade with China, mostly illegal, has turned this small town into a community of (dong if not dollar) millionaires. The crossing to China has quite recently opened to foreign tourists in both directions. Supply of accommodation has yet to match demand but Vietnamese entrepreneurship and the

building industry will, no doubt, rise to the occasion. Visas into Vietnam must be obtained in Hong Kong or Peking and specify the Lao Cai crossing; they normally take a week to process and are not obtainable at the border.

● **Accommodation** **D** *Song Hong*, nr border crossing; *Lao Cai Lottery Guesthouse*, kind and helpful manager.

● **Transport** 38 km from Sapa. **Train** A railroad runs along the steep-sided and spectacular upper reaches of the Red (Hong) River all the way from Hanoi to Lao Cai. Daily trains make the journey. **Road** Connections with Hanoi and also with Sapa (2 hrs).

International connections The border crossing with China is now open to foreigners. From China, catch a train from Kunming to Ha Khau (16 hrs), and then a ferry across the Red River to Lao Cai. From Vietnam to China, simply do this in reverse.

HANOI TO HAIPHONG AND HA LONG BAY

The 100 km road from Hanoi to Haiphong, the N's principal port, crosses the Red River and then passes through flood-prone riceland. The land along much of the route is below sea-level, and an elaborate network of dykes has been built over the years to protect the fields. Haiphong was heavily bombed during the Vietnam War, but still retains some of its French-era architecture. From Haiphong, regular ferries depart for Ha Long Bay – one of Vietnam's natural beauty spots. Set amidst spectacular limestone scenery, it is now a popular seaside resort. It is also possible to reach Ha Long Bay by bus or car direct from Hanoi – a 165 km journey which involves several river crossings.

Haiphong

The port of Haiphong was established in 1888 on the Cam River. It is the largest port and the second largest city in the N (with a population of 1.6 million). Highway 5, between Hanoi and Haiphong, begins by crossing the marvellous, rickety and cobbled-together Chuong Duong Bridge which spans the Red River. From the bridge the road passes through low-lying rice paddies, across railway bridges (when there are no trains they double-up as bridges for road transport alternating one-way flow – hence long delays) and through dour, grey villages.

Haiphong witnessed the initial arrival of the French in 1872 (they occupied Hanoi a year later) and, appropriately, their final departure from the N at 1500 in the afternoon on 15 May 1955. As the major port of the N, it was subjected to sustained bombing during the War. To prevent petrol and diesel fuel reaching the Viet Cong nearly 80% of all aboveground tanks were obliterated by American bombing in 1966. The US did not realize that the North Vietnamese, anticipating such an action, had dispersed much of their supplies to underground and concealed tanks. This did not prevent the city from receiving a battering, although Haiphong's air defence units are said to have retaliated by shooting down 317 US planes.

Places of interest

Much of outer Haiphong is an ugly industrial sprawl that will win no environmental beauty contests. But, considering the bombing the city sustained, there is still a surprising amount of attractive **colonial-style architecture** in the city centre. Much is run down and looks like most Vietnamese cities did 10 years ago. Central Haiphong is pleasantly green with tree-lined streets. Right

HAI PHONG VL 77

Cua Cam River

1. State Dept. Store
Hotels:
2. Ben Binh
3. Hong Bang
4. Bach Dang
5. de Commerce & Tourist Office
6. Cat Bi
B. Buses to Do Son

0 250
metres

THE BATTLES OF BACH DANG RIVER (938 AD AND 1288 AD)

The battles of Bach Dang River were both won in a style reminiscent of many battles fought against the US. In 938 AD, unable to confront the powerful Chinese fleet on equal terms, the Vietnamese General Ngo Quyen sunk sharpened poles tipped with iron into the bed of the river that the Chinese were about to sail up. When the Chinese fleet appeared off the mouth of the river, Quyen sent a small flotilla of shallow draught boats to taunt the Chinese. Rising to the bait they attacked and, as the tide fell, their heavy ships were impaled on the stakes that lay just below the surface. Over half the Chinese, including the Admiral Hung-ts'ao were drowned. In 1288, apparently not having learnt the lessons of history, another Mongol Chinese fleet of 400 ships appeared off the coast. This time the famous Vietnamese general Tran Hung Dao laid the trap, again luring the enemy onto sunken stakes. In both instances, the victories were so emphatic as to terminate the Chinese invasion plans.

in the heart of town, where Tran Hung Dao and Quang Trung sts meet, is the **Great Theatre**, built in 1904 of imported French materials, with a colonnaded front, facing a wide tree-lined boulevard. In Nov 1946 40 Viet Minh fighters died here in a pitched battle with the French, triggered by the French government's decision to open a customs house in Haiphong. The **museum** (Bao Tang Hai Phong), 66 Dien Bien Phu St, is an impressive colonial edifice in a wash of desert sand red, contains records of the city's turbulent past, open 0800-1100 and 1400-2130. The streets around the theatre support the greatest concentration of foodstalls, shops and restaurants. There are a number of **street markets** and **flower stalls** off Cao Dat St, which runs S from the theatre, along Tran Nhat Duat and Luong Khanh Thien sts. Sat market is to be found in the W quarter of town, at the end of Phan Boi Chau St. A market has stood on this site since 1876. In comparison with Hanoi, Haiphong seems a hotbed of economic enterprise with an abundance of street-sellers, hawkers and shops. A particular local favourite, sold on many street corners, are Siamese fighting-fish – for combat not for cooking. The **State Department Store** on the corner of Minh Khai and Dien Bien Phu sts offers the customer a paltry array of poorly made consumer goods. The port area off Ben Bach Dang St is not accessible to visitors.

2 km S of the city centre, at 121 Du Hang St, is the **Du Hang Pagoda**. Originally built in 1672 by wealthy mandarin turned monk Nguyen Dinh Sach, it has been renovated and remodelled several times since and is undergoing yet another restoration. Arranged around a courtyard, this small temple has some fine traditional woodcarving. Get there by cyclo, along a pot-holed road, past workers' houses. Also 2 km S of the centre is **Dinh Hang Kenh** (communal house) which dates back to 1856. The main building is supported by 32 columns of iron wood and the wood carvings in the window grilles are a notable feature. Near the centre of town at 51 Ngo Nghe St is the **Nghe Pagoda** built at the beginning of the 20th century. The pagoda is dedicated to the memory of Le Chan, heroine General, who fought with the Trung sisters against the Chinese. A festival is held on the 8th day of the 2nd lunar month to commemorate her birthday and offerings of crab and noodles, her favourite foods, are made.

Excursions

Do Son is a beach resort 21 km SE of Haiphong. Not exactly a 'Pattaya', but it does have sandy beaches and Vietnamese-style hotels. The Do Son Peninsula was originally developed as a resort by the French and it is currently experiencing a renaissance as joint ventures are signed, old hotels renovated and Haiphong Tourist cranks the marketing machine into action. The small *Den Ba De Temple* on Doc Mountain, at the N end of the peninsula, honours a young girl who threw herself to her death after spending a night with a courtier (this theme is a popular one in Vietnam – the idea of honourable maidens choosing death in preference to despoilation being highly romantic; although in this case she got both). Buffalo fights are held on the 9th day of the 8th lunar month at Do Son village to celebrate Nguyen Huu Cau who led an 18th century rebellion. **Accommodation B** *Do Son*, on the beach, run by *Haiphong Tourist*; **B** *Van Hoa* (formerly *Hotel de la Point*) occupies a superb location at the end of the peninsula, now renovated beyond recognition. Numerous other hotels and guesthouses, many in need of attention; not all will accept foreigners. *Getting there*: buses to the beach run down Lach Tray St, and leave from the corner of Nguyen Cong Tru and Lach Tray sts, 1 hr. Ferries also make the trip to the Do Son Peninsula. Heli-Jet Vietnam fly charter flights to the S tip of the Do Son Peninsula. Boats cross from Nghiem Wharf to Cat Ba Island (30 mins).

Ferry trip to Hon Gai (Ha Long Bay) takes 4 hrs through spectacular limestone scenery. It is a cramped but worthwhile experience (see page 186 and Transport).

Cat Ba National Park accounts for a small section of the island of Cat Ba, which covers an area of 120 sq km, much of it forested. The park is home to the world's last remaining troop of wild white-headed langurs. Most hotels rent out motorbikes which is the best means of visiting the National Park. The drive across the island is very pretty. Admis-

sion to the National Park: 10,000d, basic accommodation (**F**). The forests are rich in flora and fauna species but despite its status as a national park logging and firewood collection continue. The island has some fine beaches, two are near Cat Ba jetty and accessible via a tunnel, 5,000d. Cat Ba is the largest island in a coastal archipelago which includes over 350 limestone outcrops. Cat Ba is becoming a popular alternative base from which to explore. Ha Long Bay and new hotels are springing up to cater for this demand. **Accommodation E** *Cat Ba Hotel*, on right at the jetty, quiet but no hot water. **Places to eat** ♦♦*Hun Dung*, nr Family Hotel, friendly and good, rec; ♦*Cafeteria*, slow service, deafening karaoke but good food. *Getting there*: daily ferries leave at 1330 from the ferry dock on Ben Bach Dang St, 4 hr journey, 50,000d plus a wharf fee of 2,000d at either end; the 0835 train from Hanoi arrives in good time to make the connection. It is also possible to take the ferry to Cat Hai (2 hrs, 25,000d) on the mainland and from there a short ferry hop across to the island. A bus connects with Cat Ba town (15,000d). From Cat Ba to Ha Long catch the 0600 ferry to Haiphong and change at Cat Hai (2 hrs, 30,000d), take the connecting ferry to Hon Gai (2 hrs, 24,000d).

Local information
● **Accommodation**

Haiphong has a reasonable selection of hotels with better prices than Hanoi.

A *La Villa Blanche*, 5 Tran Hung Dao St, T 41113, F 42278, belongs to the Navy, foyer resembles Parisian brothel, mirrors and expensive looking ladies; **A-B** *Hong Bang*, 64 Dien Bien Phu St, T 42229, F 41044, colonial façade but 70s renovation.

B *Ben Binh*, 6 Ben Binh St (opp ferry dock), T 57260, a/c, villa with large and attractive rooms and bathrooms, rec; **B** *Dien Bien*, 67 Dien Bien Phu St, T 42264, F 42977, a/c; **B** *Hotel de Commerce* (formerly the *Huu Nghi*), 62 Dien Bien Phu St, T 42706, F 42560, a/c, restaurant, recently renovated and still atmospheric, attractive colonial style, large rooms;

B-D *Bach Dang*, 42 Dien Bien Phu St, T 42444, a/c, restaurant, rather run-down.

C *Thang 5*, 55 Dien Bien Phu St, T 42818, a/c;
C *Van Anh*, nr jetty, hot water.

D *Artex*, 56 Dien Bien Phu St, T 42945, set back from the road and through an art gallery;
D *Cat Bi*, 30 Tran Phu St, T 46306, a/c; **D** *Family Hotel*, next door, no hot water.

E *Hoa Binh*, 104 Luang Khanh Thien St, T 46907, rec; **E** *Mini Hotel*, in town, 500m walk from ferry, undergoing renovation, noisy karaoke, .

● **Places to eat**
Most eating places in Haiphong close by 2030 and few speak English. There are a number of cheap restaurants and foodstalls along Dinh Tien Hoang St and Quang Trung St, W of the theatre and on the streets that run off Quang Trung St. ♦♦*Binh Minh*, 60 Nguyen Duc Canh; ♦♦*Bong Sen*, 15-16 Nguyen Duc Canh, Asian and Vietnamese; ♦♦*Trong Khach*, 93 Nguyen Duc Canh, full menu including good seafood; *Thien Nhien*, 43 Quang Trung St (just W of the theatre), Vietnamese.

● **Banks & money changers**
Bank of Foreign Trade of Vietnam (Centre of Foreign Exchange), Quang Trung St (opp No 69, W of theatre), changes major international currencies, cash only, no TCs; **Vietcombank**, 11 Hoang Dieu.

● **Entertainment**
Dancing: at the *Bach Dang Hotel*.

● **Hospital & medical services**
Vietnam-Czech Friendship Hospital, 1 Nha Thuong St, T 46236.

● **Post & telecommunications**
GPO: 3 Nguyen Tri Phuong.
TNT International Express: T 47180.

● **Tourist offices**
Haiphong Toserco, 40 Tran Quang Khai, T 42288, F 42977; *Haiphong Tourist Office*, 87 Dien Bien Phu St, T 42709; *Vietnam Tourism*, 15 Le Dai Hanh St, T 42989, F 42674. All have cars for rent (with driver), and will organize boat charters to Ha Long Bay and Cat Ba National Park.

● **Transport**
103 km SE of Hanoi.

Air Daily flights to Saigon, US$170; flights to Danang Mon, Wed and Sat US$90. **Vietnam Airlines**, 30 Tran Phu St (Cat Bi Hotel),

T 46306.

Train The station is close to the intersection of Luang Khanh Thien and Pham Ngu Lao sts. Trains from Hanoi 0600 and 1600 daily and depart Haiphong for Hanoi 0900 and 1600, 2½-3 hrs (40,000d).

Road Bus: regular connections by minibus with Hanoi. They cruise around the theatre area picking-up fares, 2½ hrs (20,000d). In Hanoi, they leave from the fountain at the northern end of Hoan Kiem Lake, close to the Konica shop. Regular bus connections with Hon Gai (Ha Long Bay) 3 hrs.

Sea Boat: ferries leave from the dock on Ben Binh St for Hon Gai (Ha Long Bay). Three departures daily, 0600, 1100 and 1600, 4 hrs (8,000d). Ferries from Ha Long to Haiphong leave at the same times. The *Thong Nhat* leaves for Saigon every 10 days from the port 6 km to the E of the city centre; approx 60 hrs (US$20 and up).

Ha Long Bay

The route from Hanoi passes paddy fields and, after turning off the Hanoi-Haiphong road, dour mining villages with karst scenery in the background. Ha Long Bay is a coastal resort to the N of Haiphong and one of the N major tourist attractions. It is located in an area of spectacular, fragmented, limestone scenery – there are said to be over 3,000 islands, islets and rocky outcrops. The name Ha Long means 'descending dragon', and an enormous beast is said to have careered into the sea at this point, cutting the fantastic bay from the rocks as it thrashed its way into the depths. Vietnamese poets have traditionally extolled the beauty of this romantic area with its rugged islands that protrude from a sea dotted with sailing junks. Another local myth has it that the islands are dragons which were sent by the gods to impede the progress of an invasion flotilla. Historically more believable, if substantially embellished, the area was the location of two famous sea battles, in the 10th and 13th centuries (see box).

It was also at Ha Long that, arguably,

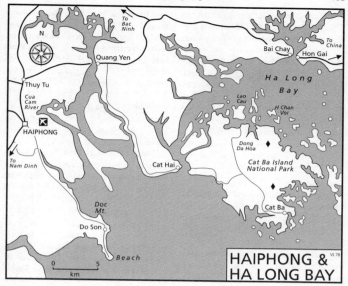

Ha Long Bay

To Bac
Ninh

N

Quang Yen

Bai Chay   Hon Gai

To China

Thuy Tu

Cua
Cam
River

Ha Long

Bay

HAIPHONG

Lao
Cau

H Chan
Voi

To
Nam Dinh

Cat Hai

Dong
Da Hoa

Cat Ba Island
National Park

Doc
Mt.

Do Son

Cat Ba

Beach

0   5
km

**HAIPHONG &
HA LONG BAY**

VL 78

Vietnam's fate under the French was sealed. In late 1882 Captain Henri Rivière led two companies of troops to Hon Gai to seize the coal mines for France. Shortly afterwards he was ambushed and killed and his head paraded on a stake from village to village. His death persuaded the French parliament to fund a full scale expedition to make all of Vietnam a protectorate of France. As the politician Jules Delafosse remarked at the time: "Let us, gentlemen, call things by their name. It is not a protectorate that you want, but a possession".

In 1994 the two towns of Bai Chay and Hon Gai were honoured with city status: 'Ha Long City' proclaim the road signs on the way into Bai Chay. The hotels in Ha Long are centred on Bai Chay and few tourists go beyond. Hon Gai is the main town and port of the province, it is 3 km and one short ferry crossing (500d) beyond Bai Chay. Ferries from Haiphong dock in Hon Gai.

Places of interest

Ha Long is surrounded by spectacular scenery although the beaches and swimming are poor, being both rocky and polluted. The resort is undeveloped by regional standards, with few activities to keep visitors entertained. The fact that Ha Long is a major coal mining area does not help the 'natural wonderland' image that Quang Ninh Tourism are trying to foster. But then foreign tourists do not come to Ha Long looking for another Pattaya, Phuket or Bali; it is a Vietnamese-style beach resort, and that in itself makes it interesting. The **port of Hon Gai** is busy with a good **market** – note the bamboo and resin coracles (*thung chai*) similar to those of Nha Trang. There is also a **pagoda** near the ferry dock. Hon Gai is a bustling and thriving little town usually overlooked in favour of 'glamorous' Bai Chay. For those who wish to stay longer than the standard 24 hrs package deal, Hon Gai offers everything Bai Chai does except a beach and hyper-inflated tourist prices. The 106m-high **Bai Tho Mountain** is so named following a visit in 1486 by King Le Thanh Tong who was so taken with the beauty of Ha Long Bay that he composed a poem celebrating the scenery and carved his verse into the rock. The mountain takes an hour to climb but it is not easy; ask for help in finding the path. 20 mins walk above Hon Gai is a **ruined colonial church** damaged by a bomb in 1972 but the site affords lovely views. About 1 km E of central Hon Gai is a small **museum** on Coc 3 St.

Excursions

Limestone outcrops and spectacular **caves** and grottoes characterize Ha Long Bay. The more famous caves have names like the Grotto of Wonders, Customs House Cave, Surprise Grotto and the Fighting Cocks. **Hang Manh Cave** extends for 2 km and tour guides will point out fantastic stalagmites and stalactites as well as other rock formations which, with imagination, become heroes, demons and animals. Many of the islets also have tiny, peaceful beaches. **Boats** can be booked through hotels, although it may be cheaper to try and organize the trip independently. Best value and what most people do is to book a Ha Long Bay excursion from Hanoi which includes accommodation and boat ride. However, the tour bus is not necessarily quicker or more comfortable than well-chosen local transport: some visitors have reported spending 2½ hrs driving around Hanoi picking up from hotels. The hotels provided in Bai Chay and the food have been criticized by some disgruntled punters who have paid to move to more agreeable accommodation. The tours are short and allow no time to explore Hon Gai. Because it takes about 1 hr to get into the bay proper, one long trip represents better value than two short ones. A tour of the bay including a cave or two and a swim needs 4-5 hrs. Price 40,000d/hour. Boats

can be hired overnight and food arranged (extra) for around 400,000d which, considering the saving on hotel bills, is a fairly economical option. **Boat hire**: ask in your hotel or try the Tourist Wharf, opposite *Van Hai Hotel*, in *Hon Gai Dac Tien Tourist Co*, Ben Doan St, T 46385, doubles as a hairdresser. **Microlight**: a French pilot offers aerial tours of the bay, US$100/1 hr, ask at the Hai Trang Hotel, T 46094 or T 46152 (see Tourist offices, page 168).

Cat Ba National Park Boats can be hired to visit the park (see page 181) and there are regular ferry connections. **Uong Bi** is about 1 hr drive from Ha Long on Highway 18. A hospital was built here by the Swedish and a holiday camp for Swedish aid workers. It is open to all-comers but has now been transferred into Vietnamese hands, and is in decline. The **Yen Tu Mountains** are 14 km NW of Uong Bi and climb to a maximum elevation of 1,068m. Peppered with pagodas from the 13th-16th centuries, much has been lost to the ravages of war and climate but stupas and temples of more recent foundation survive. The site has attracted pilgrims since the 13th century when King Tran Nhan Tong abandoned the throne in favour of a spiritual life. He washed the secular dust from his body in the Tam stream and entered the Cam Thuc (Abstinence) Pagoda. His 100 concubines traced him here and tried to persuade him of the folly of his ways but despite their undoubted allure he resisted all appeals and clung to his ascetic existence. Distraught by their failure, the poor women drowned themselves. Tran Nhan Tong later built a temple to their memory. Climbing the hills, visiting the temples and admiring the views can take a full day.

Local information
● **Accommodation**

The past couple of years has seen an explosion in the number of hotels and guesthouses in Bai Chay and Hon Gai; this reflects the popularity of Ha Long Bay as a destination for both Vietnamese and foreign visitors. The enthusi-

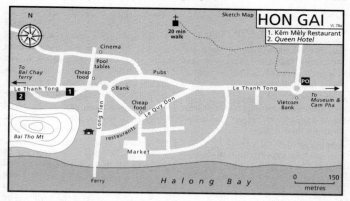

Sketch Map

HON GAI
VL 78a

1. Kêm Mêly Restaurant
2. Queen Hotel

N

20 min walk

To Bai Chay Ferry

Cinema

Pool tables

Cheap food

Pubs

Le Thanh Tong

Bank

Long Tien

Cheap food

Le Qui Don

restaurants

Market

Le Thanh Tong

PO

Vietcom Bank

To Museum & Cam Pha

Bai Tho Mt

Ferry

H a l o n g   B a y

0   150
metres

---

asm of the hotel builders has, for the time being at least, outstripped demand so owners are having to accept hard bargaining as an uncomfortable fact of life. Many of the newer hotels are badly built and, apart from the fact that some of the taller ones look structurally unsound, are hideously damp and musty; check the room first.

Hon Gai: **B-C** *Queen*, 70 Le Thanh Tong, central, disco; **C** *Khach San Hai Au*, halfway between Hon Gai centre and the ferry dock; **D** *Hien Cat*, left at ferry dock, excellent view, rec; **D** *Hoa Thuy Tien*, 193 Le Thanh Tong, a/c, clean, rec; **E** *Hon Gai Floating Hotel*, nr the ferry dock.

Bai Chay: there are two main groups of hotels, 2 km apart. Most are to be found at the W end, set back from the beach on the way in to town and includes Vuon Dao St composed entirely of new 5-8 rm mini hotels. 2 km further on nr the Bai Chay ferry dock (to Hon Gai) is a smaller group some of which have good views.

Ferry end: **B** *Bach Dang*, T 46330, a/c; **B** *Van Hai*, T 46403, F 46115, a/c, opp wharf, overlooking sea, probably the best run and most comfortable hotel in Ha Long, rec; **C** *Nha Nghi Son Hon*, T 46418; **D** *Minh Tuan*, T 46200, 50m to left before bus station.

West end: **B** *Bach Dang*, T 46285, facing on to the beach; **B** *Ha Long*, T 46320, a/c, tennis, elegant colonial structure, formerly a hospital, with spacious rooms; **B** *Hoang Long*, T 46318, a/c, recently renovated; **B** *Navy Guesthouse*, 2 colonial mansions with views over the sea, 3 rm in each house, bathrooms attached and shared sitting room; **B** *Post Office Hotel*,

on the corner with Vuon Dao St, T 46205, a/c, new, clean but characterless and sterile; **B** *Vuon Dao*, T 46427, F 46287, concrete, but spacious and airy; **C** *Thu Trang*, Vuon Dao St, T 46370, fan, runs tours of the bay (8 hrs US$40); **C-D** *Ha Long 2 & 3*, behind *Ha Long*, concrete blocks that cater mainly for Vietnamese holiday makers; **C-D** *Huong Tram*, Vuon Dao St, T 46365, views from top flr, helpful for boat trips and walks; **C-D** *Peace*, 5 rm, cheap rooms fan only; **C-D** *Thanh Nien*, 17 rm on the beach, T 46464, cheaper rooms fan only; **D** *Hai Trang*, Vuon Dao St, T 46094, small, a/c and fan rooms, ask here for microlight tours of the bay.

● **Places to eat**

The night market in Hon Gai sells good, fresh seafood and Le Qui Don St has good seafood restaurants. ◆◆*My Phuong*, Le Qui Don St, rec; *Kêm Mêly*, Le Thanh Tong St, sells delicious ice cream and western luxuries such as Pringles and Ritz biscuits. On the same street are popular open air pubs. In Bai Chay, opp the tourist wharf is a recommended restaurant; extending for several hundred metres along the beach nr Vuon Dao St are numerous restaurants, all much of a muchness.

● **Banks & money changers**

Hon Gai has three banks, **Vietcombank** on Le Thanh Tong St offers same rates as Hanoi. GPO also changes money.

● **Entertainment**

Discos: *Top Club* in Bai Chay, US$5 entry, and *Queen Hotel* in Hon Gai, US$2.

● **Hospitals & medical services**

Bai Chay Hospital, T 46566; *Hon Gai Hospital*,

T 25499.

● **Post & telecommunications**
Area code: 0133.
Post Office: in Bai Chay (opp the ferry dock), GPO in Hon Gai, Le Thanh Tong St open 0700-2000, international telephone (minimum 3 mins) and fax.

● **Shopping**
Quang Ninh traditional *coal sculpture* available in Hon Gai, also mother of pearl and lacquer goods, but cheaper in Hanoi.

● **Tourist offices**
Dac Tien Tourist Co, Ben Doan St, Hon Gai, T 46385; *Quang Ninh Tourism*, Bai Chay, T 46321. A promotional leaflet proclaims 'Honour to welcome and service you'.

● **Transport**
165 km from Hanoi.

Air Heli-Jet Vietnam which operates from *Sofitel Metropole* in Hanoi will charter a helicopter to Ha Long Bay for approximately US$1,000.

Road Bus: the Bai Chay station is on the waterfront road, by the PO. Regular connections with Hanoi's Gai Lam until early afternoon, 6 hrs and two ferry crossings (16,000d). Buses are slow, crowded and full of pickpockets. Regular connections with Danang (0630, 65,000d), Saigon (0700, 170,000d) and Nha Trang. Minibuses depart Bai Chay for Hanoi 0500 and 1100, 4-6 hrs, 40,000d. **Taxi**: quickest way (apart from helicopter) from Hanoi, US$50 return for a Russian car, US$60-80 for a Japanese car (see Local transport, Hanoi), 3 hrs.

Sea Boat: ferries leave from the dock in Hon Gai, 3 km from Bai Chay, for Haiphong at 0600, 1100 and 1600, 4 hrs (38,000d 'tourist price'). Ferries from Haiphong to Ha Long leave at the same times. The trip itself is worthwhile; the ferry is packed with local people and their produce and threads its way through the limestone islands and outcrops that are so characteristic of the area, before winding up the Cam River to the port of Haiphong. Ferries also connect with Cat Ba, via Cat Hai, 4 hrs, 54,000d.

THE NORTH EAST

Few visitors reach this remote corner of Vietnam. Rugged, but lacking the grandeur of mountainous NW Vietnam, the scenery consists of limestone hills deeply dissected by fast flowing streams – tributaries of the Red River – hurrying S with their burden of silt. Once densely wooded, centuries of slash and burn cultivation have taken their toll on the region and little tree cover remains. Hilltribe minorities Dao, Nùng and Tày are much in evidence. Localized landscapes draw admiration but extensive tracts are unremarkable. Facilities are sparse and the going tough. The three principal towns in the region, Ha Giang, Cao Bang and Lang Son offer a degree of provincial charm, however.

Lang Son

Lang Son, capital of Lang Son Province, is the gateway to SE China on the route to Macau and Hong Kong via Nanning. Lang Son's strategic position has given this little town an important place in the annals of Vietnamese history. In 1427 100,000 Ming Chinese reinforcements marched in to Vietnam; they were ambushed and decisively beaten by Le Loi's army at Chi Lang Pass, 30 km SW of Lang Son, effectively marking the end of 1,000 years of Chinese occupation. French troops garrisoned here were routed in 1885 and again in 1950. In Feb 1979, Chinese troops attacked once more, this time to punish Vietnam for its invasion of Cambodia and the overthrow of China's ally, the Khmer Rouge. Today Lang Son is a bustling staging post for imported Chinese manufacturers and a possible stopover for travellers. It is now possible to enter as well as leave Vietnam via the Huu Nghi (Friendship) crossing near Dong Dang, 20 km N of Lang Son. Note, however, that the necessary entry and exit visas must be secured beforehand in Hanoi or Beijing.

● **Accommodation** Nothing other than basic Vietnamese guesthouses have been reported.

● **Transport** 130 km from Hanoi, 20 km from Dong Dang. **Train** Daily connections with Hanoi. **Road Car or 4WD**: 4-5 hrs, this is Highway 1 at its worst. **Bus**: there are early morning departures from Hanoi's Long Bien terminal. Getting to and from Dong Dang is possible only by locally hired car or Honda. Huu Nghi border crossing is a further 3 km on.

Ba Be Lakes (Hô Ba Bê) are reached in some discomfort direct from Hanoi, from Cao Bang or even Ha Giang. Waters from the surrounding peaks have drowned this long narrow valley from where they drain into the river Gâm. Boat trips on the lake to visit caves and waterfalls can be arranged by guesthouses; expect to pay around US$3/hour. **Accommodation D** *Government Guesthouse*, nr the Ba Be Park gate, shared bathroom; **E** *Guesthouse* on the lake, primitive, but lovely setting, restaurant nearby.

Cao Bang is capital of the province of the same name. The road leading N from Cao Bang towards China passes through stunning scenery. About 15 km NW of Cao Bang is the Ma Phuc Pass, noted for its sugarloaf mountain landscape. **Accommodation** basic hotel.

Ha Giang, a small provincial town, lies near the confluence of two tributaries of the river Lô. Its remoteness and proximity to the Chinese border (no crossing) attract a few visitors but there have been reports of attempts by police to extort money from Western travellers. The road N from Ha Giang to Yen Minh and Dong Van reaches the northernmost tip of Vietnam almost touching the Tropic of Cancer. Visitors recently reported being turned back at Yen Minh for not having a permit. As is so often the case in Vietnam's remote, mountainous border areas tourists travel at the whim of underpaid local officials. The Dao minority people and their settlements (described on page 113) provide a splash of colour.

HANOI TO NINH BINH

From Hanoi, the route S runs through the rather grey, industrial towns of Nam Dinh and Ninh Binh. After Ninh Binh, Highway 1 passes into Vietnam's central region.

Nam Dinh

Nam Dinh is a large and diverse industrial centre, with a reputation for its textiles. The **Nam Dinh Textile Mill** was built here by the French in 1899, and is still operating (which says a lot for the state of Vietnamese industry and Vietnamese resourcefulness). The city is the third largest urban centre in the N with a population of about 250,000. This part of Vietnam was among the first to be influenced by Western missionaries: Portuguese priests were proselytizing here as early as 1627.

Excursions Thien Truong and Pho Minh Pagodas – both highly regarded – are to be found in the village of Tuc Mac (My Loc district), 3 km N of Nam Dinh. Also here are the few remains of the palaces of the Tran Dynasty. Thien Truong was built in 1238 and dedicated to the kings of the Tran family; Pho Minh was built rather later in 1305, and contains an impressive 13-storey tower. *Getting there*: on foot or by cyclo.

Doi Son and **Doi Diep Pagodas** are situated on two neighbouring mountains (Nui Doi Son and Nui Doi Diep). The former was originally built at some point during the early Ly Dynasty (544-602 AD). When the Emperor Le Dai Hanh (980-1005) planted rice at the foot of the mountain, legend has it that he uncovered two vessels, one filled with gold and the other with silver. From that season on, the area's harvests were always bountiful.

● **Accommodation** *Vi Hoang*, 115 Nguyen Du St, T 439362, some a/c.

● **Post & telecommunications Post Office**: Ha Huy Tap St.

● **Tourist offices** Ninh Binh Tourist Office, 115 Nguyen Du St.

● **Transport** 90 km from Hanoi. **Train**: Regular connections with Hanoi's Truong Tin station (20 km S of Hanoi) 4 hrs. See timetable, page 293. **Road Bus**: regular connections with Hanoi's Kim Lien bus station; other connections with Ninh Binh, Thanh Hoa and other major towns on the route S.

Ninh Binh

Ninh Binh is the capital of the densely populated province of Ha Nam Ninh, and is situated on the Day River. It marks the most southerly point of the northern region. The town has little to offer the tourist, although as it is located on both the main rail and road routes linking North and South Vietnam, it is a possible stopping-off point. Less than 10 km outside Ninh Binh is the site of the ancient capital of Vietnam, **Hoa Lu** (see below).

Excursions Hoa Lu lies about 13 km from Ninh Binh near the village of Truong Yen. It was the capital of Vietnam from 968 to 1010 AD, during the Dinh and Early Le dynasties. Prior to the establishment of Hoa Lu as the centre of the new kingdom, there was nothing here. But, the location was a good one in the narrow valley of the Hong River – on the 'dragon's belly', as the Vietnamese say. The passes leading to the citadel could be easily defended with a small force, and defenders could keep watch over the plains to the N and guard against the Chinese. The kings of Hoa Lu were, in essence, rustics. This is reflected in the art and architecture of the temples of the ancient city: primitive in form, massive in conception. Animals – elephants, rhinoceros, horses – were the dominant motifs, monumentally carved in stone. The inhabitants were not, by all accounts, sophisticated aesthetes.

Much of this former capital, which covered over 200 ha, has been destroyed, although archaeological excavations have revealed a great deal of historical and artistic interest. The two principal temples of Hoa Lu are those of King Dinh Tien Hoang (968-980) and King Le Hoan (980-1009). The **Temple of Dinh Tien Hoang** was originally constructed in the 11th century but was reconstructed in 1696. It is arranged as a series of courtyards, gates and buildings. The inscription on the pillar in the central temple, in ancient Vietnamese, reads 'Dai Co Viet', from which the name 'Vietnam' is derived. The temple also contains statues of various animals, often crude, which came to represent higher beings. The back room of the temple is dedicated to a far more colourful figure – King Dinh Bo Linh – whose statue occupies the central position, surrounded by those of his sons. In the 960s, Bo Linh managed to pacify much of the Hong River plain, undermining the position of a competing ruling family, the Ngos, who eventually accepted Bo Linh's supremacy. However this was not done willingly, and banditry and insubordination continued to afflict Bo Linh's kingdom. He responded by placing a large kettle and a tiger in a cage in the courtyard of his palace and decreed: 'those who violate the law will be boiled and gnawed'. An uneasy calm descended on Bo Linh's kingdom, and he could concern himself with promoting Buddhism and geomancy, arranging strategic marriages, and implementing administrative reforms. But, by making his infant son Hang Lang heir apparent, rather than Din Lien (his only adult son), he sealed his fate. History records that the announcement was followed by earthquakes and hailstorms, a sign of dissension in the court, and in 979 Lien sent an assassin to kill Hang Lang. A few months later in the same year, an official named Do Thich killed both Bo Linh and Din Lien as they lay drunk and asleep in the palace courtyard. When Do Thich was apprehended, it is said that he was executed and his flesh fed to the people of the city. The **Temple of King Le Hoan** is very similar to that of Dinh Tien Hoang, only smaller. The area is well worth exploring and scenically attractive. *Getting there*: take a local bus or charter a car signposted 6 km N on Highway 1. Admission 15,000d.

Bich Dong Pagoda or the 'Pagoda in the Mountains', is located about 11 km and 3 hrs by boat, considerably less by road, from Ninh Binh. The boat trip is well worthwhile. The small tributary of the Hoang Long River skirts past paddy fields and through water-filled limestone caves. From the landing spot it is a 15 mins walk to the 3-tiered pagoda. There are good views of the surrounding, rugged, landscape. *Getting there*: by boat (3 hrs), road or bicycle signposted 4 km S on Highway 1. Admission 10,000d.

Cuc Phuong National Park can be visited on a day trip from Ninh Binh (approx 45 km) (see page 161). *Getting there*: by chartered car. Admission US$5.

Tam Coc Cave, some 8 km S of Ninh Binh, is reached by road and boat. The boat ride is through stunning scenery and costs 15,000d. Admission 10,000d.

Phat Diem Church is 28 km SE of Ninh Binh. A striking architectural complex in the style of a Chinese pagoda. Services daily, 0730-1130 and 1430-1700, best to try and slip in towards the end. The journey takes in a number of more conventional churches, waterways and paddy fields.

● **Accommodation D** *Hoa Lu*, Huyen Hoa Lu (on Highway 1, towards Hanoi), a/c, hot water, friendly; **D** *Ninh Binh*, on Highway 1 (nr market), new; **D** *Sao Mai*, 30 Luong Van Tuy St, T 72190, friendly, clean and useful source of information, restaurant, rec.

● **Transport** 91 km from Hanoi. **Train** Regular local train connections with Hanoi. See timetable, page 293. **Road Bus**: regular connections with Hanoi's Kim Lien terminal, 3 hrs.

THE CENTRAL REGION

The Central Region extends over 1,000 km N to S. It includes the mountains of the Ammamite chain which form a natural frontier with Laos to the W and in places extend almost all the way to the sea, in the E. Most of Vietnam's hill peoples are concentrated in these mountains. The narrow coastal strip, sometimes only a few kilometres wide, supported the former artistically accomplished kingdom of Champa.

THANH HOA TO HUÉ

The narrow central region is traversed by a single road – Highway 1 – which runs all the way from Hanoi to Saigon. Along much of its route, the road runs close to the coast, passing through a succession of interesting, though rather unattractive, towns. These northern provinces – such as Nghe Tinh – are among the poorest in the country but their inhabitants are among the friendliest. Villagers here grow barely enough to feed themselves. 654 km S of Hanoi and 1,071 km N of Saigon, is the former imperial capital of Hué. Though devastated during the Vietnam War, the Imperial Palace and tombs represent the most impressive collection of historical sights in Vietnam.

Thanh Hoa

The **citadel of Ho** was built in 1397 when Thanh Hoa was the capital of Vietnam. Much of this great city has been destroyed, although the massive city gates are preserved. Art historians believe that they rival the finest Chinese buildings, and the site is in the process of being excavated. This town and province mark the most northerly point of the central region.

The 160m-long **Ham Rong Bridge** or 'Dragon's Jaw' which crosses the Ma River S of Thanh Hoa was a highly significant spot during the Vietnam War. The bridge, a crucial transport link with the S, was heavily fortified and the US lost 70 planes in successive abortive raids from 1965. Eventually, in 1972, they succeeded using laser-guided 'smart' bombs – at which point the Vietnamese promptly built a replacement pontoon bridge. Significantly however, during the attack in 1972, as well as one at the same time using the same technology against the Paul Doumer Bridge in Hanoi, no US aircraft were lost. 15 km E of Thanh Hoa lies the coastal resort of **Sam Son**, popular with Vietnamese but not yet geared to the demands of overseas tourists.

● **Accommodation** *Tourist*, 21A Quang Trung, T 298. *Khach San 25B* and *Khach San 25A*, Highway 1.

- **Tourist offices** Thanh Hoa Province Tourism, 21A Quang Trung St, T 298.

- **Transport** 153 km from Hanoi. **Train** Express trains to and from Hanoi and Saigon stop here, 4¼ hrs. See timetable, page 293. **Road Bus**: regular connections with Hanoi's Kim Lien bus station 4 hrs, Ninh Binh, Vinh and other towns on Highway 1.

Vinh

Vinh is a diversified industrial centre and capital of Nghe Tinh Province. It was damaged by the French before 1954, and then suffered sustained bombing by US and ARVN (Army of the Republic of Vietnam) aircraft from 1964 through to 1972. In the process it was virtually razed. Vinh lies at the important point where the coastal plain narrows, forcing roads and railways to squeeze down a slender coastal strip of land. The town has since been rebuilt with assistance from former East Germany, in startlingly unimaginative style. The dirty-brown apartment blocks make Vinh one of the most inhuman and uninspired cities in Vietnam. The province of Nghe Tinh also happens to be one of the poorest, and the mini-famine of 1989 struck hard.

There is nothing of historical interest here, unless socialist architecture can be thought of as such. The **Central Market**, at the S end of Gao Thang St (the continuation of Quang Trung St), is a bustle of colour and activity.

Excursions Chua village, 14 km W of Vinh, is the birthplace of Ho Chi Minh who was born here in 1890. **Sen** is another

village close to Chua, where Ho lived with his father from the age of six. Although the community and surrounding area were hardly wealthy, Ho was fortunate to be born into a family of modest means and his father was highly educated. The house where he lived (in fact a replica built in 1955) may be thatched and rude, but it was a great deal better than the squalor that most of his countrymen had to endure (see page 88 for a short account of Ho's life). The province of Nghe Tinh has a reputation for producing charismatic revolutionary leaders; not only Ho Chi Minh but also Phan Boi Chau – another fervant anti-colonialist – was born here (see page 101).

Cua Lo is a beach 20 km from Vinh. It boasts 8 km of white sandy beach and is a very popular (if slightly downmarket) holiday spot with the locals. **Accommodation** There are 15 hotels with more being built and finding a room during holiday time (Jan-Aug) can be tricky. **B** *Thai Binh Truc*, T 24164; *Cua Lo Hotel*, Cua Lo Beach.

● **Accommodation** Because so few visitors stay in Vinh, hotel rates can be bargained down considerably. **B-C** *Chuyen Gia Giao Te*, Thanh Ho St, T 4175, a/c, large and unattractive; **C** *Nghe Tinh Guesthouse*, Dinh Cong Trang St (E from the intersection with Le Mao St), T 3175, a/c; **E** *Nha Khach Xi Nghiep Dich Vu*, Le Loi St (not far from the intersection with Nguyen Si Sach St, E from the railway station), T 4705; **E** *Vinh*, Thong Nhat St; **E** *Vinh Railway Station Hotel*, Le Nin St (adjacent to the station).

● **Post & telecommunications Post Office**: Nguyen Thi Minh Khai St.

● **Tourist offices** Vinh Tourist Office, Quang Trung St (N of the cinema), T 4629.

● **Transport** 197 km from Dong Hoi, 291 km from Hanoi, 368 km from Hué. **Train** The station is in the W quarter of town, 3 km from the central market. Connections with Hanoi and all points S to Saigon; express trains stop here, 7 hrs from Hanoi, 34 hrs from Saigon. See timetable, page 293. **Road Bus**: the bus station is on Le Loi St. Express buses leave for Hanoi, Saigon and Danang at 0500.

Ngang Pass or **Porte d'Annam** Running between the Central Highlands and the coast is a small range of mountains, the Hoanh Son, which neatly divide the N from Central Vietnam. In French times the range marked the S limit of Tonkin and N limit of Annam. The mountains which reach up to 1,000m have a marked effect on climate blocking cold northerly winds in winter and receiving up to 3,000 mm of rain. During the reign of Minh Mang a gate was built, the Hoanh Son Quan. Subsequently, Emperor Thieu Tri on a visit N composed a poem which is inscribed on a nearby rock.

Dong Hoi

Travelling either S from Vinh towards Hué, or N to Vinh, there is little to entice the traveller to stop. Along this stretch of coastal plain, which crosses from the province of Nghe An to Ha Tinh to Quang Binh to Quang Tri to Thua Thien Hue, the inhabitants have been struggling against floods and encroaching sand dunes for years. During the Vietnam War, the area was pounded by bombs and shells, and sprayed with defoliants. Unexploded bombs still regularly maim farmers (1 million bombs have been unearthed since the end of hostilities), and it is claimed that the enduring effects of Agent Orange can be seen in the high rates of physical deformity in both animals and humans.

The town of Dong Hoi can be used as a stopping-off point on the way N or S. It was virtually annihilated during the war as it lies just N of the 17th parallel, marking the border between North and South Vietnam. Just S of the town is the **Hien Luong Bridge** which spans the Ben Hai River; the river forming the border between the two halves of former North and South Vietnam.

Excursions Khe Sanh and the Ho Chi Minh Trail lie to the S of Dong Hoi. 94 km S at Dong Ha, Highway 9 branches off the main coastal Highway 1 and proceeds to the border with Laos. Along this route is Khe Sanh (Huong Hoa) – one of the most evocative names associated with American involvement in Vietnam (see page 208). Close to Khe Sanh are parts of the famous Ho Chi Minh Trail along which supplies were ferried from the N to the S (see page 209). Highway 9 has been extensively improved in recent years to provide land-locked Laos with an alternative access route to the sea.

● **Accommodation**   **D** *Phuong   Nam*, T 23282, a/c, restaurant.

● **Transport** 522 km from Hanoi, 166 km from Hué, 197 km from Vinh. **Train** Regular connections with Hanoi and Saigon. See timetable, page 293. **Road** Buses travelling up Highway 1 linking Saigon with Hanoi pass through Dong Hoi.

Hué

A trip to Vietnam should, if possible, include a trip to Hué (population 350,000), 100 km S of the 17th parallel and built on the banks of the **Huong Giang** or Perfume River. The river is named after a scented shrub which is supposed to grow at its source.

Hué was the capital of Vietnam during the Nguyen Dynasty and is one of the cultural cores of the country. The Nguyen Dynasty ruled Vietnam between 1802 and 1945, and for the first time in Vietnamese history a single court controlled the land from Yunnan (southern China) southwards to the Gulf of Siam. To link the N and S – over 1,500 km – the Nguyen emperors built and maintained the Mandarin Rd (*Quan Lo*), interspersed with relay stations. Even in 1802 when it was not yet complete, it took couriers 13 days to travel between Hué and Saigon, and 5 days between Hué and Hanoi. If they arrived more than 2 days late, the punishment was a flogging. There cannot have been a better road in Southeast Asia, or a more effective incentive system.

The city of Hué was equally impres-

sive. George Finlayson, a British visitor in 1821-22 wrote that its "style of neatness, magnitude, and perfection" made other Asian cities look "like the works of children". Although the Confucian bureaucracy and some of the dynasty's technical achievements may have been remarkable, there was continual discontent and uprisings against the Nguyen emperors. The court was packed with scheming   mandarins,   princesses, eunuchs and scholars writing wicked poetry. The female writer Ho Xuan Huong, wrote of the court and its eunuchs:

"Why do the twelve midwives who cared for you hate each other? Where have they thrown away your youthful sexual passions? Damned be you if you should care about the twitterings of mice-like lovers, or about a bee-like male gallant caressing his adored one... At least, a thousand years from now you will be more able to avoid the posthumous slander that you indulged in mulberry-grove intrigues".

In 1883 a French fleet assembled at the mouth of the Perfume River, not far from Hué and opened fire. After taking heavy casualties, Emperor Hiep Hoa sued for peace, and signed a treaty making Vietnam a protectorate of France. As French influence over Vietnam increased, the power and influence of the Nguyen waned. The undermining effect of the French presence was compounded by significant schisms in Vietnamese society. In particular, the spread of Christianity was undermining traditional hierarchies. Despite the impressive imperial tombs and palace (see below), many scholars maintain that the Nguyen Dynasty was simply too short-lived to have ever had a 'golden age'. Emperor Tu Duc may have reigned for 36 years (1847-1883), but by then the imperial family had grown so large that he had to contend with a series of damaging attempted coups d'état as family members vied for the throne. Although the French, and then the Japanese during WW2, found it to their advantage to maintain the framework of Vietnamese imperial rule, the system became hollow and, eventually, irrelevant. The last Nguyen Emperor, Bao Dai, abdicated on 30 August 1945.

Unfortunately for art lovers, the relative peace which descended upon Hué at the end of WW2 was not to last. During the 1968 Tet offensive, Viet Cong soldiers holed-up in the Citadel for 25 days. The bombardment which ensued, as US troops attempted to root them out, caused extensive damage to the Thai Hoa Palace and other monuments, much of which has still to be repaired. During their occupation of Hué, the NVA forces settled old scores, shooting, beheading and even burning alive 3,000 people, including civil servants, police officers and anyone connected with, or suspected of being sympathetic to, the government in Saigon. This action lent support to the notion that should the N ever achieve victory over the S it would result in mass killings. The irony was that this series of atrocities went unremarked in the US: at the time the Western media were pre-occupied with the infamous My Lai massacre by American troops (see page 224).

Best time to visit

Hué has a bad reputation for its weather. The rainy season extends from Sep to Jan, and rainfall is particularly heavy between Sep and Nov; the best time to visit is therefore between Feb and Aug. However, even in the 'dry' season an umbrella is handy, especially when venturing out of town to the pagodas and

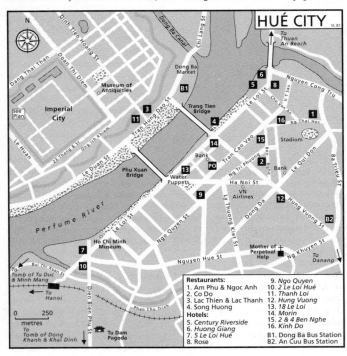

HUÉ CITY

Restaurants:
1. Am Phu & Ngoc Anh
2. Co Do
3. Lac Thien & Lac Thanh
4. Song Huong
Hotels:
5. Century Riverside
6. Huong Giang
7. 5 Le Loi Hué
8. Rose
9. Ngo Quyen
10. 2 Le Loi Hué
11. Thanh Loi
12. Hung Vuong
13. 18 Le Loi
14. Morin
15. 2 & 4 Ben Nghe
16. Kinh Do
B1. Dong Ba Bus Station
B2. An Cuu Bus Station

NGUYEN DYNASTY EMPERORS (1802-1945)	
Gia Long	1802-1819
Minh Mang	1820-1840
Thieu Tri	1841-1847
Tu Duc	1847-1883
Duc Duc	1883
Hiep Hoa	1883
Kien Phuc	1883-1884
Ham Nghi	1884-1885
Dong Khanh	1885-1889
Thanh Thai	1889-1907
Duy Tan	1907-1916
Khai Dinh	1916-1925
Bao Dai	1925-1945

tombs. Rainfall of 2,770 mm has been recorded in a single month.

Places of interest

The **Imperial City** at Hué is built on the same principles as the Forbidden Palace in Peking (Beijing). It is enclosed by 7-10m thick **outer walls** (Kinh Thanh), along with moats, canals and towers. Emperor Gia Long commenced construction in 1804 after geomancers had decreed a suitable location and orientation for the palace. The site enclosed the land of eight villages (for which the inhabitants received compensation), and covers 6 sq km; sufficient area to house the Emperor and all his family, courtiers, bodyguards and servants. It took 20,000 men to construct the walls alone. Ten gates pierce the four walls of the citadel, although many are in poor condition. Not only has the city been damaged by war and incessant conflict, but also by natural disasters such as floods which, in the mid 19th century, inundated the city to a depth of several metres.

Chinese custom decreed that the 'front' of the palace should face S (like the Emperor) and this is the direction from which visitors approach the site. Over the outer moat, a pair of gates pierce the outer walls: the **Hien Nhon** and **Chuong Duc** gates. Just inside are two groups of massive cannon; four

through the Hien Nhon Gate and five through the Chuong Duc Gate. These are the Nine Holy Cannon (Cuu Vi Than Cong), cast in 1803 on the orders of Gia Long from bronzeware seized from the Tay Son revolutionaries. The cannon are named after the four seasons and the five elements, and on each is carved its name, rank, firing instructions and how the bronze of which they are made was acquired. They are 5m in length, but have never been fired. Like the giant urns outside the Hien Lam Cac (see below), they are meant to symbolize the permanence of the empire. Between the two gates is a massive **flag tower**. The flag of the National Liberation Front flew here for 24 days during the Tet Offensive in 1968 – a picture of the event is displayed in Hué's Ho Chi Minh Museum.

Northwards from the cannon, and over one of three bridges which span a second moat, is the **Ngo Mon** (or Noon Gate), built in 1833 during the reign of Emperor Minh Mang. The ticket office is just to the right. The gate, remodelled on a number of occasions since its original construction, is surmounted by a pavilion from where the emperor would view palace ceremonies. Of the five entrances, the central one – the Ngo Mon – was only opened for the emperor to pass through. UNESCO has thrown itself into the restoration of Ngo Mon with vigour and the newly finished pavilion atop the gate now gleams and glints in the sun; those who consider it garish can console themselves with the thought that this is how it might have appeared in Minh Mang's time. On an upper floor are photographs showing Ngo Mon before and after restoration.

North from the Ngo Mon, is the **Golden Water Bridge** (again reserved solely for the emperor's use) between two tanks, lined with laterite blocks. This leads to the **Dai Trieu Nghi** (the Great Rites Courtyard) on the N side of which is the **Dien Thai Hoa Palace** (the Palace of Supreme Harmony) constructed by Gia Long in 1805 and used for his coronation in 1806. From here, sitting on his golden throne raised up on a dais, the emperor would receive ministers, foreign emissaries, mandarins and military officers during formal ceremonial occasions. In front of the palace are 18 stone stelae, which stipulate the arrangement of the nine mandarinate ranks on the Great Rites Courtyard: the upper level was for ministers, mandarins and officers of the upper grade; the lower for those of lower grades. Civil servants would stand on the left, and the military on the right. Only royal princes were allowed to stand in the palace itself, which is perhaps the best preserved building in the Imperial City complex. Its red and gold columns, tiled floor, and fine ceiling have been restored and the rear of the palace is now a tourist shop.

North of the Palace of Supreme Harmony is the **Tu Cam Thanh** (the Purple Forbidden City). This would have been reserved for the use of the emperor and his family, and was surrounded by 1m thick walls: a city within a city. Tragically, the Forbidden City was virtually

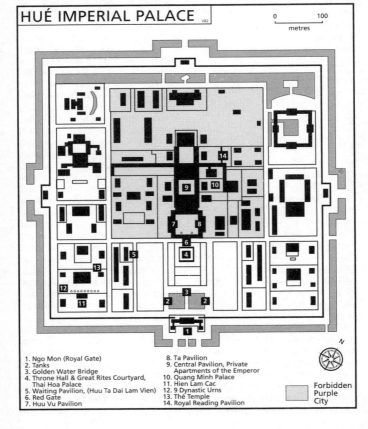

HUÉ IMPERIAL PALACE v82

0   100
metres

1. Ngo Mon (Royal Gate)
2. Tanks
3. Golden Water Bridge
4. Throne Hall & Great Rites Courtyard,
   Thai Hoa Palace
5. Waiting Pavilion, (Huu Ta Dai Lam Vien)
6. Red Gate
7. Huu Vu Pavilion
8. Ta Pavilion
9. Central Pavilion, Private
   Apartments of the Emperor
10. Quang Minh Palace
11. Hien Lam Cac
12. 9 Dynastic Urns
13. The Temple
14. Royal Reading Pavilion

N

Forbidden
Purple
City

destroyed during the 1968 Tet offensive. The two **Mandarin Palaces** and the **Royal Reading Pavilion** are all that survive.

At the far side of the Thai Hoa Palace, are two enormous **bronze urns** (Vac Dong) decorated with birds, plants and wild animals, and weighing about 1,500 kg each. To either side of the urns are the **Ta and Huu Vu Pavilions** – one converted into a souvenir art shop, the other a mock throne room in which tourists can pay US$5 to dress up and play the part of king for 5 mins. The Royal Reading Pavilion has been rebuilt but, needless to say, has no books. At least they still stand: much of the rest of the Forbidden City is a depressing pile of rubble with a few bullet marked walls, scrub and vegetable plots. It is an artistic tragedy. On the far side of the palace are the outer northern walls of the citadel and the N gate.

Most of the surviving buildings of interest are to be found on the W side of the palace, running between the outer walls and the walls of the Forbidden City. This part of the palace is easy to miss: they are to the left of the Thai Hoa Palace. At the SW corner is the well-preserved and beautiful **Hien Lam Cac**, a pavilion built in 1821, in front of which stand nine massive bronze urns cast between 1835 and 1837 on the orders of Emperor Minh Mang. It is estimated that they weigh between 1,500 kg and 2,600 kg, and each has 17 decorative figures, animals, rivers, flowers and landscapes representing between them the wealth, beauty and unity of the country. The central, largest and most ornate urn is dedicated to the founder of the empire, Emperor Gia Long. Next to the urns walking northwards is the **Thé Temple** (the Temple of Generations). Built in 1821, it contains altars honouring 10 of the kings of the Nguyen Dynasty (Duc Duc and Hiep Hoa are missing) behind which are meant to be kept a selection of their personal belongings. It was only in 1954, however, that

the stelae of the three Revolutionary Emperors Ham Nghi, Thanh Thai, and Duy Tan were brought into the temple. The French, perhaps fearing that they would become a focus of discontent, prevented the Vietnamese from erecting altars in their memory. North of the The Temple is **Hung Temple** built in 1804 for the worship of Gia Long's father, Nguyen Phuc Luan, the founder of the Nguyen Dynasty. The temple was renovated in 1951.

UNESCO began the arduous process of renovating the complex in 1983, but they have a very long way still to go: Vietnam at that time was still a pariah state due to its invasion of Cambodia in 1978-9 and the appeal for funds and assistance fell on deaf ears. It was therefore, fitting testimony to Vietnam's rehabilitation in the eyes of the world that in 1993 UNESCO declared Hué a World Heritage site. Although it is the battle of 1968 which is normally blamed for the destruction, the city has in fact been gradually destroyed over a period of 50 years. The French shelled it, fervent revolutionaries burnt down its buildings, typhoons and rains have battered it, thieves have ransacked its contents, and termites have eaten away at its foundations. In some respects it is surprising that as many as a third of the monuments have survived relatively intact. Admission to Imperial City: US$5, video cameras US$5 extra.

On the N bank of the river next to the Dong Ba bus station on Tran Hung Dao St is the covered **Dong Ba Market**. The **Bao Quoc Pagoda** (just off Dien Bien Phu St to the right, over the railway line), is said to have been built in the early 18th century by a Buddhist monk named Giac Phong. Note the 'stupa' that is behind and to the left of the central pagoda and the fine doors inscribed with Chinese and Sanskrit characters. Further along Dien Bien Phu St, at the intersection with Tu Dam St is the **Tu Dam Pagoda**. According to the Hué

Buddhist Association this was originally founded in 1690-1695 but has been rebuilt many times. The present day Pagoda was built shortly before WW2. In Aug 1963 the Diem government sent its forces to suppress the monks here who were alleged to be fermenting discontent among the people. The specially selected forces – they were Catholic – clubbed and shot to death about 30 monks and their student followers, and smashed the great Buddha image here.

Hué also has a number of museums. The best is the **Hué Museum of Antiquities** at 3 Le Truc St. Housed in the Long An Palace, the museum contains a reasonable (although unlabelled) collection of ceramics, furniture, screens and bronzeware. In the front courtyard are stone mandarins, gongs and giant bells. The building itself is worthy of note for its elegant construction, built by Emperor Thieu Tri in 1845 it was dismantled and erected on the present site in 1909. Directly opposite the museum is the **Royal College** established in 1803 and moved to this site in 1908. It is usually closed to visitors. Close by at 23 Thang 8 St (between Dinh Tien Hoang and Doan Thi Diem sts) is the **Military Museum**. Missiles, tanks and armoured personnel carriers fill the courtyard. Across the river at 7 Le Loi St is the requisite **Ho Chi Minh Museum** which displays pictures of Ho's life plus a few models and personal possessions. The 'tour' begins at the end of the corridor on the 2nd floor. Some interesting photographs (eg of Ho as a cook's assistant at the Carlton Hotel, London), but does not compare with the Ho Chi Minh Museum in Hanoi. Open 0730-1130, 1330-1630 Mon-Sun. The Perfume River is spanned by two bridges; downstream and currently under repair is the unfortunate **Trang Tien Bridge**, named after the royal mint that once stood at its northern end. It was built in 1896 and destroyed soon after by a typhoon; after having been rebuilt

it was then razed once more in 1968 during the Tet Offensive. Upstream is Phu Xuan bridge, built by the US Army in 1970.

The skyline of modern Hué is adorned by the striking pagoda-like tower of the **Church of Mother of Perpetual Help**. This 3-storeyed, octagonal steel tower is 53m high and an attractive blend of Asian and European styles. The church was completed in 1962 and marble from the Marble Mountain in Danang was used for the altar. The church lies at the junction of Nguyen Hue and Nguyen Khuyen sts.

Excursions

As the geographical and spiritual centre of the Nguyen Dynasty, Hué and the surrounding area is the site of numerous pagodas and seven imperial tombs, along with the tombs of numerous other royal personages. Few visitors will wish to see them all – some are extensively damaged – time and war have taken their toll.

Thien Mu Pagoda (the Elderly Goddess Pagoda), also known as the Thien Mau Tu Pagoda, and locally as the **Linh Mu Pagoda** (the name used on most local maps), is the finest in Hué. It is beautifully sited on the Perfume River, about 4 km upstream from the city. It was built in 1601 by Nguyen Hoang, the governor of Hué, after an old woman appeared to him and said that the site had supernatural significance and should be marked by the construction of a pagoda. The monastery is the oldest in Hué, and the 7-storey *Phuoc Duyen* (Happiness and Grace Tower), built later by Emperor Thieu Tri in 1844, is 21m high, with each storey containing an altar to a different Buddha. The summit of the tower is crowned with a water pitcher to catch the rain, water representing the source of happiness. Arranged around the tower are four smaller buildings one of which contains the *Great Bell* cast in 1710 under the orders of the Nguyen Lord, Nguyen Phuc Chu, and

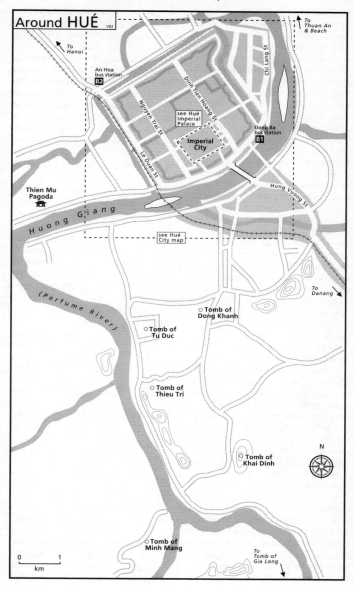

weighing 2,200 kg. Beneath another of these surrounding pavilions is a monstrous *marble turtle* on which is a 2.6m high stele recounting the development of Buddhism in Hué carved in 1715. Beyond the tower, the entrance to the pagoda is through a triple gateway patrolled by six carved and vividly painted guardians – two on each gate. The roof of the sanctuary itself is decorated with jataka stories. At the front of the sanctuary is a brass laughing Buddha. Behind that are an assortment of gilded Buddhas and a crescent-shaped gong cast in 1677 by Jean de la Croix. The first monk to commit suicide through self immolation, Thich Quang Duc, came from this pagoda (see page 251) and the grey Austin in which he made the journey to his death in Saigon is still kept here in a garage in the temple garden. In May 1993 a Vietnamese – this time not a monk – immolated himself at Thieu Mu. Why is not clear: some maintain it was linked to the persecution of Buddhists; others because of the man's frustrated love life. *Getting there*: it is an easy 3 km bicycle (or cyclo) ride from the city, following the river upstream (W).

Imperial Tombs After the Imperial Palace, the tombs of the former emperors which dot the countryside to the S of the city are Hué's most spectacular tourist attraction (see map). Each of the tombs follows the same stylistic formula, although at the same time they reflect the tastes and predilections of the emperor in question. The tombs were built during the lifetime of each emperor, who took a great interest in their design and construction; after all they were meant to ensure his comfort in the next life. Each mausoleum, variously arranged, has five design elements: a courtyard with statues of elephants, horses and military and civil mandarins (originally, usually approached through a park of rare trees), a stele pavilion (with an engraved eulogy composed by the king's son and heir), a Temple of the

Soul's Tablets, a pleasure pavilion, and a grave. They should also have a stream and a mountainous screen in front. The tombs faithfully copy Chinese prototypes, although most art historians claim that they fall short in terms of execution. Admission to each of the tombs US$5. An extra US$5 is charged for video cameras. **Getting to & around the Imperial Tombs**: is easiest by car/minibus as they are spread over a large area. Most hotels organize tours. A cyclo for the day should cost about 40,000-50,000d (with some walking up the hills), bicycle hire about US$1 (see Local transport). Set out early if bicycling; all the tombs are easily accessible by bicycle, with the exception of Gia Long's. It is also possible to go on the back of a motorcycle taxi (honda om). Finally, boats can be chartered to sail up the Perfume River – the most peaceful way to travel, but only a few of the tombs

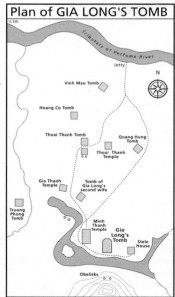

Plan of GIA LONG'S TOMB

Vi. 63b

Tributary of Perfume River

Jetty

N

Vinh Mau Tomb

Hoang Co Tomb

Thoai Thanh Tomb

Quang Hung Tomb

Thoai Thanh Temple

Gia Thanh Temple

Tomb of Gia Long's second wife

Truong Phong Tomb

Minh Thanh Temple

Gia Long's Tomb

Stele House

Obelisks

THE DEATH AND BURIAL OF EMPEROR GIA LONG (1820)

When the Emperor Gia Long died on 3 February 1820, the thread on the ancestors' altar (representing his soul) was tied. The following day the corpse was bathed and clothed in rich garments, and precious stones and pearls were placed in his mouth. Then a ritual offering of food, drink and incense was made before the body was placed in a coffin made of catalpa wood (*Bignonia catalpa*) – a wood impervious to insect attack. At this time, the crown prince announced the period of mourning that was to be observed – a minimum of three years. Relatives of the dead emperor, mandarins and their wives each had different forms and periods of mourning to observe, depending upon their position.

Three days after Gia Long's death, a messenger was sent to the Hoang Nhon Pagoda to inform the Empress, who was already dead, of the demise of her husband. Meanwhile, the new Emperor Minh Mang had the former ruler's deeds recorded and engraved on golden sheets which were bound together as a book. Then astrologers selected an auspicious date for the funeral, picking 27 May after some argument (11 May also had its supporters). On 17 May, court officials told the heaven, the earth, and the dynastic ancestors, of the details for the funeral and at the same time opened the imperial tomb. On 20 May the corpse was informed of the ceremony. Four days later the coffin left the palace for the three day journey to its final resting place. Then, at the appointed time, the coffin was lowered into the sepulchre – its orientation correct – shrouded in silk cloth, protected by a second outer coffin, covered in resin, and finally bricked-in. Next to Gia Long, a second grave was dug into which were placed an assortment of objects useful in his next life. The following morning, Emperor Minh Mang, in full mourning robes, stood outside the tomb facing east, while a mandarin facing in the opposite direction inscribed ritual titles on the tomb. The silk thread on the ancestors' altar – the symbol of the soul – was untied, animals slaughtered, and the thread then buried in the vicinity of the tomb.

(This account is adapted from James Dumarçay's *The palaces of South-East Asia*, 1991.)

can be reached in this way (see Tours). **Tomb of Emperor Gia Long** is rarely visited – it is accessible by bicycle (which can be taken by boat across the Perfume River) or by boat, with a long walk – but is well worth the effort. The tomb is overgrown with cassava bushes and several huge mango trees, and the pavilions are shoddily roofed with corrugated iron but the setting is quiet and peaceful. It was built between 1814 and 1820 (see box for an account of his burial). Gia Long's mausoleum follows the same formula as the other tombs: there is a surrounding lotus pond; a courtyard with five now headless mandarins, horses and elephants; steps leading up to a further courtyard with an ancestral temple at the rear; and to the right of this a double walled and locked burial chamber where Gia Long and his wife are interred (the Emperor's tomb is fractionally taller); the stele eulogizing the Emperor's reign is beyond the burial chamber. Ask the custodian for admittance to the burial chamber for which you should make a small contribution.

Nguyen Anh, or Gia Long as he was crowned in 1802, came to power with French support. Back in 1787 Gia Long's son, the young Prince Canh, had caused a sensation in French salon life when, with soldier/missionary Georges Pigneau de Béhaine, the two had sought military support against the Tay Son from Louis XVI. In return for Tourane

(Danang) and Poulo Condore the French offered men and weapons – an offer that was subsequently withdrawn. Pigneau then raised military support from French merchants in India and in 1799 Prince Canh's French-trained army defeated the Tay Son at Qui Nhon.

Gia Long's reign was despotic – to his European advisers who pointed out that encouragement of industry would lead to the betterment of the poor, he replied that he preferred them poor. The poor were virtual slaves – the price for one healthy young buffalo was one healthy young girl – and *vice versa*. Flogging was the norm; it has been described as the 'bamboo's golden age'. One study by a Vietnamese scholar estimated that there

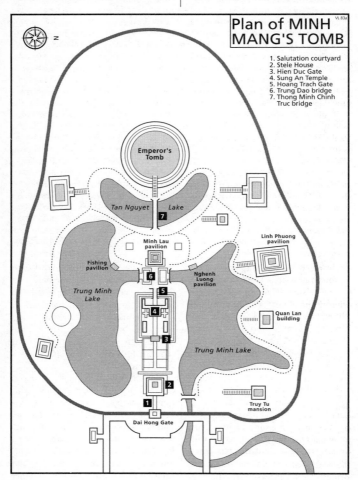

Plan of MINH MANG'S TOMB

1. Salutation courtyard
2. Stele House
3. Hien Duc Gate
4. Sung An Temple
5. Hoang Trach Gate
6. Trung Dao bridge
7. Thong Minh Chinh Truc bridge

Emperor's Tomb

Tan Nguyet Lake

Minh Lau pavilion

Linh Phuong pavilion

Fishing pavilion

Trung Minh Lake

Nghenh Luong pavilion

Quan Lan building

Trung Minh Lake

Truy Tu mansion

Dai Hong Gate

were 105 peasant uprisings between 1802 and 1820 alone. For this and the fact that he gave the French a foothold in Vietnam the Vietnamese have never forgiven Gia Long. Of him they still say "*cong ran can ga nha*" (he carried home a snake to kill the chicken). *Getting there*: from Minh Mang's tomb (see above for travel information) take the road SE for several kilometres through Minh Mang Village to a tributary of the Perfume River; a boat ferries travellers to the opposite bank (1,000d) where a single track path, which almost peters out in places, leads to the tomb after several more kilometres. The familiar twin pillars appear, miraculously, amidst the undergrowth. Ask directions along the way.

Tomb of Emperor Minh Mang is possibly the finest of all the imperial tombs. Built between 1841 and 1843, it is sited among peaceful ponds, about 12 km from the city of Hué. In terms of architectural poise and balance, and richness of decoration, it has no peer in the area. The layout is unusual in its symmetry along a single central and sacred axis (*Shendao*); no other tomb, with the possible exception of Khai Dinh, achieves the same unity of constituent parts, nor draws the eye onwards so easily and pleasantly from one visual element to the next. The tomb was traditionally approached through the **Dai Hong Mon** – today visitors pass through a side gate – a gate which leads into the *ceremonial courtyard* containing an array of statuary. Next is the stele pavilion in which there is a carved eulogy to the dead Emperor composed by his son, Thieu Tri. Continuing downwards through a series of courtyards there is, in turn, the **Sung An Temple** dedicated to Minh Mang and his Empress, a small garden with flower beds that once formed the Chinese character for 'longevity', and two sets of stone bridges. The first consists of three spans, the central one of which (**Trung Dao Bridge**) was for the sole use of the Em-

peror. The second, single, bridge leads to a short flight of stairs with naga balustrades at the end of which is a locked bronze door. The door leads to the tomb itself which is surrounded by a circular wall. *Getting there*: visitors must cross the Perfume River by boat. Costs vary enormously, from 20,000-55,000d return. Bargain hard. There are also boat tours to the tomb from Hué (see Tours).

Tomb of Thieu Tri (7 km SW of Hué in the village of Thuy Bang) was built in 1848 by his son Tu Duc, who took into account his father's wishes that it be 'economical and convenient'. Thieu Tri reigned for just 7 years and unlike his forebears did not start planning his mausoleum the moment he ascended the throne. Upon his death his body was temporarily interred in Long An Temple (now the Hué Museum of Antiquities). The tomb is in two adjacent parts, with separate tomb and temple areas; the layout of each follows the symmetrical axis arrangement of Minh Mang's tomb which has also inspired the architectural style.

Tomb of Tu Duc is 7 km from the city and was built between 1864 and 1867 in a pine wood. It is enclosed by a wall within which is a lake. The lake, with lotus and water hyacinth, contains a small island where the king built a number of replicas of famous temples – which are now rather difficult to discern. He often came here to relax, and from the pavilions that reach out over the lake, composed poetry and listened to music. The **Xung Khiem Pavilion** built in 1865 has recently been restored with UNESCO's help and is the most attractive building here (although it is usually overrun with Vietnamese picnickers). The tomb complex follows the formula described above: ceremonial square, mourning yard with pavilion, and then the tomb itself. To the left of Tu Duc's tomb are the tombs of his Empress, Le Thien Anh and adopted son, Kien Phuc. Many of the pavilions are crumbling and ramshackle – lending the tomb a rather

---

TU DUC'S LAMENT

Never has an era seen such sadness, never a year more anguish. Above me, I fear the edicts of heaven. Below, the tribulations of the people trouble my days and nights. Deep in my heart I tremble and blush, finding neither words or actions to help my subjects.

Alone, I am speechless. My pulse is feeble, my body pale and thin, my beard and hair white. Though not yet 40, I have already reached old age, so that I lack the strength to pay homage to my ancestors every morning and evening. Evil must be suppressed and goodness sought. The wise must offer their counsel, the strong their force, the rich their wealth, and all those with skills should devote them to the needs of the army and the kingdom. Let us together mend our errors and rebuild.

Alas! The centuries are fraught with pain, and man is burdened by fear and woe. Thus we express our feelings that they may be known to the world.

Taken from *Vietnam*, Karnow S

---

tragic air. This is appropriate: though he had 104 wives, Tu Duc fathered no sons. He was therefore forced to write his own eulogy, a fact which he took as a bad omen. The eulogy itself recounts the sadness in Tu Duc's life. A flavour of its sentiment can be gleaned from a confession he wrote in 1867 following French seizure of territory (see box). It was during Tu Duc's reign, and shortly after his death, that France gained full control of Vietnam.

Tomb of Duc Duc is the closest to Hué, 2 km S of the city centre on Tan Lang St. Despite ruling for just 3 days and then dying in prison, Emperor Duc Duc (1852-1883) has a tomb, built posthumously by his son, Thanh Thai, in 1889 on the spot where, it is said, the body was dumped by gaolers. Emperors **Thanh Thai** and **Duy Tan** are buried in the same complex. Unlike Duc Duc, though, both were strongly anti-French and were exiled for a period in Africa. Although Thanh Thai later returned to Vietnam and died in Vung Tau in 1953, his son Duy Tan was killed in an air crash in central Africa in 1945. It was not until 1987 that Duy Tan's body was repatriated and interred alongside Thanh Thai, his father. The tomb is in three parts: the Long An Temple; Duc Duc's tomb to the S; and Thanh Thai and Duy Tan's tombs adjacent to each other.

Tomb of Dong Khanh is 500m from Tu Duc's tomb: walk up the path on the other side of the road from the main entrance to Tu Duc's tomb – the path is partly hidden in amongst the stalls. Built in 1889, it is the smallest of the imperial mausoleums, but nonetheless one of the most individual. Unusually, it has two separate sections. One is a walled area containing the usual series of pavilions and courtyards and with an historically interesting collection of personal objects that belonged to the Emperor. The second, 100m away, consists of an open series of platforms. The lower platform has the honour guard of mandarins, horses and elephants along with a stele pavilion; the third platform is a tiled area which would have had an awning; and the highest platform, the tomb itself. The tomb is enclosed within three open walls, the entrance protected by a dragon screen (to prevent spirits entering).

Tomb of Khai Dinh is 10 km from Hué and was built between 1920 and 1932. It is the last of the mausoleums of the Nguyen Dynasty, and by the time Khai Dinh was contemplating the afterlife, brick had given way to concrete (which is beginning to deteriorate). Nevertheless, it occupies a fine position on the Chau Mountain facing SW towards a large white statue of Quan Am, also built by Khai Dinh. The valley, cultivated to cassava and sugar cane, and the pine-covered mountains, make this one of the most beautifully sited and peaceful of the tombs. Indeed, before construction could begin, Khai Dinh had to remove the tombs of Chinese nobles who had already selected the site for its beauty and auspicious orientation. 127 steep steps lead up to the Honour Courtyard with statuary of mandarins, elephants and horses. An octagonal Stele Pavilion in the centre of the mourning yard contains a stone stele with an eulogy to the Emperor. At the top of some more stairs, are the tomb and shrine of Khai Dinh, containing a bronze statue of the Emperor sitting on his throne and holding a jade sceptre. The body is interred 9m below ground level (see box describing Khai Dinh's interment). The interior is richly decorated with ornate and colourful murals (the artist incurred the wrath of the emperor and only just escaped execution), floor tiles, and decorations built-up with fragments of porcelain. It is the most elaborate of all the tombs and took 11 years to build. Such was the cost of construction that Khai Dinh had to levy additional taxes to fund the project. The tomb shows distinct European stylistic influences.

Hô Quyên (Amphitheatre) lies about 4 km upstream of Hué on the S bank of the Perfume River. It was built in 1830 by Emperor Minh Mang as a venue for the popular duels between elephants and tigers. This royal sport was in earlier centuries staged on an island in the Perfume River or on the river banks but by 1830 it was considered desirable for the

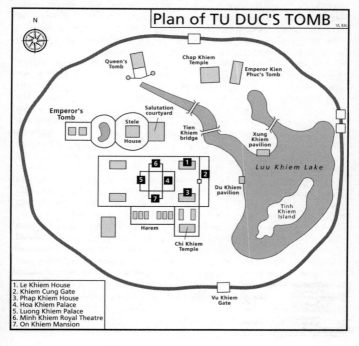

Plan of TU DUC'S TOMB

VL 83c

N

- Queen's Tomb
- Chap Khiem Temple
- Emperor Kien Phuc's Tomb
- Emperor's Tomb
- Stele House
- Salutation courtyard
- Tien Khiem bridge
- Xung Khiem pavilion
- *Luu Khiem Lake*
- Du Khiem pavilion
- Tinh Khiem Island
- Harem
- Chi Khiem Temple
- Vu Khiem Gate

1. Le Khiem House
2. Khiem Cung Gate
3. Phap Khiem House
4. Hoa Khiem Palace
5. Luong Khiem Palace
6. Minh Khiem Royal Theatre
7. On Khiem Mansion

THE FUNERAL OF A KING

On 6 November 1925, Dai-Hanh-Hoang-Khai-Dinh, King of Annam, 'mounted the dragon's back,' or, to put it briefly, died. Seven diamonds were put in the mouth of the corpse, which was washed, embalmed, dressed in state robes, placed in a huge red and gold lacquer coffin and covered over with young tea-leaves. Ten days later official mourning was inaugurated with the sacrifice of a bullock, a goat and a pig. A portrait of the late monarch, painted on silk, was placed on the throne. Paper invocations were burnt, massed lamentations rent the air 4 times daily for 60 days.

All Annam was in Hué, dressed in its best and brightest. Sampans swarmed about the bridge, packed with expectant people. Gay shrines lined the way, hung with flowers and paper streamers. Bunting, citron and scarlet, fluttered in the breeze. Route-keepers in green and red held the crowds in check, chasing small boys out of the way, swacking them over their mushroom hats—chastisement that produced a maximum of noise with a minimum of pain.

At the head of the column were 2 elephants, hung with tassels and embroidered cloths and topped with crimson howdahs and yellow umbrellas. Never have I seen animals so unutterably bored. They lolled against each other, eyes closed—and slumbered. But for an occasional twitch of an ear or tail they might have been dead. Their boredom was understandable when you came to think of it. An elephant is a long-lived beast. No elephant gets his photograph in the papers on reaching the century: it is far too common an occurrence. These two were full-grown; elderly, even. It is possible that they featured at the obsequies of Thieu-Tri, and there have been innumerable royal funerals since. At one period kings weren't stopping on the throne of Annam long enough to get the cushions warm. What was a very novel and splendid exhibition to me was stale stuff to these beasts.

"All very fine for you, mister", they might have said. "First time and all that. Can drop out and buy yourself a drink any time you like. All very well for you, Henry, in a feather-weight gent's suiting; but what about us, tight-laced front and back with about a ton of passengers, brollies, flags and furniture up top?"

An old bearded mandarin in a gorgeous coat of royal blue struck with a wooden hammer on a silver gong. The procession began to shuffle slowly forward—somebody in front had found means to rouse the elephants, apparently. 160 trained porters, clad in black and white, crouched under the red lacquer poles of the giant bier—slips of bamboo had been placed between their teeth to stop them from chattering.

Slowly, steadily, keeping the prescribed horizontal, the huge thing rose. Six tons it weighed and special bridges had to be built to accommodate it. Slowly, steadily it moved towards us, preceded by solemn-stepping heralds in white; flagbearers in sea-green carrying dragon banners of crimson and emerald, blue and gold.

The second day was spent in getting the coffin from Nam-Gio to the mausoleum and was a mere repetition of the first. The actual interment took place on the morning of the third day. In a few minutes the mourners were out in the daylight again and the vault doors were being sealed. The spirit of Khai-Dinh was on its way to the Ten Judgment Halls of the Infernal Regions, to pass before the Mirror of the Past wherein he would see all his deeds reflected, together with their consequences; to drink the Water of Forgetfulness, and pass on through transmigration to transmigration till he attained the Pure Land and a state of blessed nothingness. And Bao-Dai—weeping bitterly, poor little chap—reigned in his stead.

Adapted from *The Voyage from London to Indochina*, Crosbie Garstin

royal party to be able to observe the duels without placing themselves at risk from escaping tigers. The amphitheatre is said to have been last used in 1904 when, as usual, the elephant emerged victorious: 'The elephant rushed ahead and pressed the tiger to the wall with all the force he could gain. Then he raised his head, threw the enemy to the ground and smashed him to death.' The walls of the amphitheatre are 5m high and the arena is 44m in diameter. At the S side, beneath the royal box, is one large gateway (for the elephant) and to the N, five smaller entrances for the tigers. The walls are in good condition and the centre filled with immaculately tended rows of vegetables. *Getting there*: by cyclo or bicycle about 3 km W of Hué station on Bui Thi Xuan St.

Thuan An Beach is 13 km to the NE of Hué, about 4 km off the road to Danang. 6 km in length, it offers swimming in both a protected lagoon (into which flows the Perfume River) and in the South China Sea. *Getting there*: local buses leave for Thuan An from the Dong Ba bus station; boats can be chartered from the dock behind the Dong Ba Market, 1 hr (30,000-40,000d). **NB** Intermittent buses return from Thuan An village to Hué (16 km); an alternative would be to take bicycles on the boat and cycle back. At the main gate to the beach there is a bicycle park which charges 5,000d for a bicycle. **Accommodation** *Thuan An Hotel* is 100m from the beach, dirty and unhelpful; **C** *Dong Hai Hotel*, T 66115, about 1 km from the beach, new and clean.

DMZ

The incongruously named Demilitarized Zone (DMZ), scene of some of the fiercest fighting of the Vietnam War, lies along the Ben Hai River and the better known 17th Parallel. The DMZ was the creation of the 1954 Geneva Peace Accord which divided the country into two spheres of influence prior to elections that were never held. Like its counterpart in Germany the boundary evolved into a national border separating Communist from capitalist but unlike its European equivalent it was the triumph of Communism that saw its demise. A number of wartime sights can be seen on a single, rather gruelling, day's tour from Hué. **Getting to the sights of DMZ**: most visitors visit the sights of the DMZ, including Khe Sanh and the Ho Chi Minh Trail, on a tour. But buses do leave for the town of Khe Sanh from the An Hoa bus station; the site of the US base is 3 km from Khe Sanh Bus Station. From here it is possible to arrange transport to the Ho Chi Minh Trail and to other sights, but it is probably more trouble than it is worth. A 1 day tour of all the DMZ sights can be booked from a number of Hué hotels. Cost about US$19, depart early, return late.

Khe Sanh is the site of one of the most famous battles of the War. The battleground lies along Highway 9 which runs W towards Laos, to the N of Hué, and S of Dong Hoi and is 3 km from the village of the same name. There is not much to see here; it is of most interest to war veterans. The hardware used and abandoned during the battle still lies among the coffee bushes.

Ho Chi Minh Trail is another popular, but necessarily disappointing, sight given that its whole purpose was to be as inconspicuous as possible. Anything you see was designed to be invisible – from the air at least; rather an artificial 'sight' but a worthy pilgrimage considering the sacrifice of millions of Vietnamese porters and the role it played in the American defeat (see box below). A section runs close to Khe Sanh.

The tunnels of Vinh Moc served a similar function to the better known Cu Chi tunnels. They evolved as families in the heavily bombed village dug themselves shelters beneath their houses and then joined up with their neighbours.

THE BATTLE AT KHE SANH (1968)

Khe Sanh (already the site of a bloody confrontation in Apr and May 1967) is the place where the North Vietnamese Army (NVA) tried to achieve another Dien Bien Phu; in other words, an American humiliation. One of the NVA divisions, the 304th, even had Dien Bien Phu emblazoned on its battle streamers. Westmoreland would have nothing of it, and prepared for massive confrontation. He hoped to bury Ho Chi Minh's troops under tonnes of high explosive and achieve a Dien Bien Phu in reverse. But, the American high command had some warning of the attack: a North Vietnamese regimental commander was killed while he was surveying the base on 2 Jan and that was interpreted as meaning the NVA were planning a major assault. Special forces long-range patrols were dropped into the area around the base and photo reconnaissance increased. It became clear that 20,000-40,000 NVA troops were converging on Khe Sanh.

With the US Marines effectively surrounded in a place which the assistant commander of the 3rd Marine Division referred to as 'not really anywhere', there was a heavy exchange of fire in Jan 1968. The Marine artillery fired 159,000 shells, B-52s carpet-bombed the surrounding area, obliterating each 'box' with 162 tonnes of bombs. But, despite the haggard faces of the Marines, the attack on Khe Sanh was merely a cover for the Tet offensive – the commanders of the NVA realised that there was no chance of repeating their success at Dien Bien Phu against the US military. The Tet offensive proved to be a remarkable psychological victory for the NVA – even if their 77-day seige of Khe Sanh cost many 1,000s (one estimate is 10,000-15,000) of NVA lives, while only 248 Americans were killed (43 of those in a C-123 transporter crash). Again, a problem for the US military was one of presentation. Even Walter Cronkite, the doyen of TV reporters, informed his audience that the parallels between Khe Sanh and Dien Bien Phu were "there for all to see".

Later the tunnels developed a more offensive role when Viet Cong soldiers fought from them. Life for ordinary peasants in the battle zone just N of the DMZ was terrifying: some idea of conditions (for revolutionary peasants at least) can be gained from the 1970 North Vietnamese film *Vinh Linh Steel Ramparts*.

The Rock Pile is a 230m high limestone outcrop just S of the DMZ. It served as a US observation post. An apparently unassailable position, troops, ammunition, Budweiser and prostitutes all had to be helicoptered in. The sheer walls of the Rock Pile were eventually scaled by the VC but prove more of a challenge to faint-hearted tourists. The **Hien Luong Bridge** on the 17th parallel which marked the boundary between N and S (see page 192) is included in most tours.

Tours

The more expensive hotels organize bus and boat tours to the **Imperial Tombs**. It is also possible to charter boats to the tombs (the most romantic way to see them) and to **Thuan An Beach** (see Excursions). *DMZ Tours*, 26 Le Loi charges US$12 for a visit to Tien Ma Pagoda, Tu Duc and Minh Mang's Tombs and an additional US$3 for Gia Long's Tomb. Boats are available on the stretch of river bank between the *Huong Giang Hotel* and the Trang Tien Bridge, and also from the dock behind the Dong Ba Market. For Thuan An Beach, a 1 hr journey, expect to pay 30,000-40,000d. From Hué, there are also tours organized to some of the sights of the Vietnam War. DMZ Tours (see above) charge US$19 for a day's programme, taking in

LIFELINE TO THE SOUTH: THE HO CHI MINH TRAIL

The Ho Chi Minh Trail was used by the NVA to ferry equipment from the North to the South via Laos (**see page 394**). The road, or more accurately roads (there were 8 to 10 to reduce 'choke points') were camouflaged in places, allowing the NVA to get supplies to their comrades in the S through the heaviest bombing by US planes. Even the use of defoliants such as Agent Orange only marginally slowed the flow. The road was built and kept operational by 300,000 full-time workers and by another 200,000 part-time North Vietnamese peasant workers. Neil Sheehan, in his book *A bright shining lie*, estimates that at no time were more than one third of trucks destroyed, and by marching through the most dangerous sections, the forces themselves suffered a loss rate of only 10%-20%. Initially, supplies were man-handled (and woman-handled) along the trail on bicycles; later, as supplies of trucks from China and the Soviet Union became more plentiful, they were carried by motorized transport. By the end of the conflict the Ho Chi Minh trail comprised 15,360 km of all-weather and secondary roads. One Hero of the People's Army is said, during the course of the war, to have carried and pushed 55 tonnes of supplies a distance of 41,025 km – roughly the circumference of the world. The Ho Chi Minh Trail represents perhaps the best example of how, through revolutionary fervour, ingenuity, and weight of people (not of arms), the Viet Cong were able to vanquish the might of the US. But American pilots did exact a terrible toll through the years. Again, Sheehan writes: "Driving a truck year in year out with 20-25 to perhaps 30% odds of mortality was not a military occupation conducive to retirement on pension". The cemetery for those who died on the trail covers 16 ha, and contains 10,306 named headstones; many more died unnamed and unrecovered.

nine sights, depart 0600 return 2100, book in advance.

Local information
● **Accommodation**

Most hotels are to be found on, or just off, Le Loi St, a wide tree-lined boulevard that runs along the opp bank of the Perfume River to the Forbidden Palace. Accommodation is more expensive in Hué than in other provincial cities. Bargain. Most hotels are S of the river in the 'French' part of town, but there are now a couple in the old Vietnamese town.

A+-A Century Riverside Inn, 49 Le Loi St, T 23390, F 23399, opened in 1992, fabulous river views, Hué's classiest hotel; **A+-A Huong Giang** (*Perfume River Hotel*), 51 Le Loi St, T 22122, F 23424, some a/c, uninspired architecturally, but gorgeous position on the river, terraces and restaurants.

A-B Le Loi Hué, 5 Le Loi St, T 24668, a/c, large yellow wash and green shuttered villa on the river, expansive rooms, attractive ambience, romantic, rec; **A-B Thuan Hoa**, 7 Nguyen Tri Phuong St, T 22553, F 22470, restaurant and dancing.

B Hoa Hong (Rose), 46c Le Loi, T 24377, new, opp *Century Riverside*, popular; **B Hung Vuong**, 2 Hung Vuong St, T 23866, more expensive rooms in a villa, cheaper ones around a courtyard; **B Huong Giang Tourist Villa**, 3 Hung Vuong, T 26070, 8 rm, renovated villa but charmless interior; **B Kinh Do**, 1 Nguyen Thai Hoc St, T 23566, a/c, small rooms, comfortable and quiet.

C Villas on Ly Thuong Kiet St (nos 16, 18, 5), have rooms for rent, a/c, rooms are attractive and clean, run by the City Tourism Office; **C-D Ngo Quyen**, 11 Ngo Quyen, T 23278, cheaper rooms have fan and shared bathroom; **C-E Nha Khach Hué**, 2 Le Loi St, T 22153, consists of 6 blocks of differing comfort, money change, coach to Hanoi US$20, some a/c, clean and well-run, good value for Hué, rec.

D Khach San, 18 Le Loi St, T 23720, some a/c, upstairs light and pleasant, downstairs rather dark and musty; **D Nha Khach Ben Nghe**, 4 Ben Nghe St, T 23687, good value, rec; **D Nha Khach**, 2 Ben Nghe, attractively restored villa; **D-E Morin**, 2a Hung Vuong St, T 23866, restaurant, excellent hot water showers, huge rooms (but some complaints about damp, musty rooms), popular with backpackers, bikes for rent, good value, minibus to Danang US$8, Hoi An US$9, the hotel is due for renovation and it may not emerge as the backpacker's friend.

E *Hué Railway Station Hotel* (at the W end of Le Loi St, Vietnamese only for the time being); **E** *Tran Quang Khai Guesthouse*, 1 Tran Quang Khai St, T 23687, fan rooms and shared bathroom.

● **Places to eat**

Hué food is excellent and local restaurateurs are responding to the huge influx of tourists with raised standards and prices. Menus are often unpriced and charging policy seems to take into account the fact that diners are unlikely to return. Restaurants listed below are considered to offer reasonable value. Hué has a number of specialities: *banh khoai* (deep-fried egg batter filled with shrimps, pork and beansprouts – known as *banh xeo* in other parts of Vietnam) served with *nuoc tuong* (sesame sauce), *banh beo* (a rice pancake with shrimps and herbs), and *ram* (a rice pancake with pork). There are a number of cheap restaurants serving Hué specialities along Dinh Tien Hoang St. Huda is the light local beer brewed 'by Danish technology' see page 291 (a joint venture with the Danes).

♦♦♦*Century Riverside Inn*, 49 Le Loi, Hué specialties; ♦♦♦*Huong Giang Hotel*, 51 Le Loi St, Vietnamese and Western, surprisingly good food, frequented by officials (fancy dress 3rd flr Royal Dining Room where sad tourists can indulge their imperial fantasies); ♦♦*Am Phu (Hell)*, 35 Nguyen Thai Hoc, all types of Hué specialities, good value, rec; ♦♦*Café No 3*, 3 Le Loi St, close to railway station, good food, good information, bikes for rent for 10,000d/day and cheap boat tours organized, rec; ♦♦*Lac Thien*, 6 Dinh Tien Hoang St, very friendly and good value, rec; ♦♦*Ngoc Anh*, 29 Nguyen Thai Hoc, Vietnamese and western menus, very popular with travellers but is still good value; ♦♦*Ong Tao*, 134 Ngo Duc Ke, a second restaurant in grounds of Imperial Palace by the NE gate under a shady tree, good menu, rec; ♦♦*Song Huong*, Le Loi St (a floating restaurant just downstream from the Trang Tien Bridge), Vietnamese; ♦*Pho*, 6 Ha Noi St, good noodle soup and fried noodles. *Chinese bakeries*, 41 and 43 Tran Hung Dao St.

● **Airline offices**

Vietnam Airlines, 12 Hanoi St, T 23249.

● **Banks & money changers**

Industrial & Commercial, 2A Le Quy Don St (opp city theatre), 0700-1130 and 1330-1700, closed Thur pm; Vietcom Bank next to PO; PO also changes money.

● **Post & telecommunications**

Post Office: 8 Hoang Hoa Tham (international telephone), open 0630-2100.

● **Hospitals & medical services**

City Hospital, Kian Long, T 22280; *General Hospital*, 16 Le Loi, T 22325.

● **Shopping**

Non bai tho, or 'poem hats'. These are a form of the ubiquitous conical *non la* hat which are peculiar to Hué. Made from bamboo and palm leaves, love poetry, songs, proverbs or simply a design are stencilled onto them, which are only visible if the hat is held up to the light and viewed from the inside.

● **Tourist offices**

Tourist offices in Hué are not helpful for the independent traveller, but they can help to arrange a car, driver and guide. *DMZ Tours*, 26 Le Loi St, T 25242, competitive and helpful; Hué City Tourism, 9 Ly Thuong Kiet, T 23577; Hué Tourist Office, 15 Le Loi St, T 22369, F 24806.

● **Transport**

108 km from Danang, 166 km from Dong Hoi, 368 km from Vinh, 654 km from Hanoi, 1,071 km from Saigon.

Local Bicycle hire: from the hotels at 2 and 18 Le Loi St, Thanh Loi and *Morin Hotel* (1,000d/hour). **Boat hire**: from outside *Perfume River Hotel* (US$10/hour). **Bus**: local buses leave from the Dong Ba bus station on the river side of Tran Hung Dao St (see Transport, Hué). **Cyclos**: everywhere.

Air Flights to and from Hanoi twice daily, and Saigon twice daily (Tues, Thur, and Sun via Dalat). Hanoi is 2 hrs 20 mins (US$90) and Saigon is 2 hrs 50 mins (US$90). See timetable page 292. A bus service connects with Hué's Phu Bai Airport and town, 25 mins, US$1 or US$2 if being collected from your hotel, book at 12 Hanoi St in advance.

Train The station is at the W end of Le Loi St, and serves all stations S to Saigon and N to Hanoi. Advance booking, especially for sleepers, is recommended. The 4 hrs journey from

Danang is spectacular as the track runs along the sheer, rocky coast. Express trains stop here, 16 hrs from Hanoi, 24 hrs from Saigon. **S5**: daily, depart Hué 1525, arrive Nha Trang 1925, arrive Saigon 0600 + 1; **S3**: daily, depart Hué 1044, arrive Nha Trang 1347, arrive Saigon 1140 + 1; **S1**: Tues and Fri, depart Hué 0827, arrive Saigon 0700 + 1; **S6**: daily, depart Hué 1257, arrive Hanoi 0600 + 1, depart Hué 1952, arrive Hanoi 1140 + 1; **S2**: Tues and Fri, depart Hué 1655, arrive Hanoi 0700 + 1. **Fares**: this is a selection of prices, berths vary according to upper, middle, lower, with low berths being slightly cheaper: **To Nha Trang**: S5, 163,000d hard seat, 370,000d hard bed; S3, 232,000d soft seat, 404,000d soft bed; **To Saigon**: S5, 262,000d hard seat, 605,000d hard bed; S3, 376,000d soft seat, 662,000d soft bed; S1, 433,000d soft seat, 845,000d soft bed (2 berth cabin); **To Hanoi**: S6, 177,000d hard seat, 405,000d hard bed; S4, 253,000d soft seat, 480,000d soft bed; S2, 291,000d soft bed, 563,000d soft bed (2 berth cabin).

Road Bus: the An Cuu station at 43 Hung Vuong St serves destinations to the S of Hué, although tickets can also be bought here for destinations N of the city. Buses leave early, usually at 0500. Connections with Lang Co, Danang, Saigon, Qui Nhon, Buon Me Thuot, Dalat and Nha Trang. The An Hoa station at the NW corner of the walled city serves destinations N of Hué. Buses usually leave at 0500. Connections with Hanoi, Vinh, Dong Hoi, Khe Sanh and Dong Ha. Local buses leave from the Dong Ba station on the river side of Tran Hung Dao St, downstream from the Trang Tien Bridge. Buses leave from here for Thuan An, Cau Hai, Lang Co, Danang, An Lo, Bao Vinh, Cho No, Nong, Phu Luong, Dong Ha and Ban Thanh. Like the train journey, the road trip between Hué and Danang is spectacular.

HUÉ TO DANANG

Between Hué and Danang, the Truong Son Mountains extend all the way to the sea, making communication between N and S difficult. The pass marks the border between the provinces of Thua Thien (N) and Quang Nam (S), and in historic times marked the boundary between the kingdoms of Vietnam and Champa. The hills act as an important climatic barrier trapping the cooler, damper air masses to the

N. They also mark an abrupt linguistic divide with the Hué dialect to the N (the language of the royal court) and the source of bemusement to many southerners. The railway line closely follows the coastline – sometimes almost hanging over the sea – while Highway 1 winds its way through **Hai Van Pass** (*Deo Hai Van*); both routes are spectacular, see box (By Train from Hué to Danang). Deo Hai Van or 'Pass of the Ocean Clouds' (Col des Nuages) is admired by Vietnamese for its scenic beauty.

Travelling N to S the road passes through many pretty, red-tiled villages, compact in the local style and surrounded by clumps of bamboo and fruit trees which afford shade, shelter and sustenance. Of particular note is the *bougainvillea* which, through clever grafting, the villagers have succeeded in producing pink and white flowers on the same branch.

Just N of Hai Van Pass lies the idyllic fishing village of **Lang Co** (about 65 km S of Hué), which has a number of cheap but good seafood restaurants along the main road as well as the **D** *Nha Nghi Du Lich (Tourist Guesthouse)*, T 71248 (bargain hard, only 4 bedrooms, dirty, sporadic water and electricity supply). The beach here is excellent and usually deserted, but spoilt by high voltage power lines which run along its length. Shortly after the village, the road begins to climb steeply. The pass is about 20 km long and 497m high, dotted with abandoned pill boxes and crowned with an old French fort at the crest. From the top, before descending down towards Danang (30 km away), there are fine views over Danang Bay to the S and Lang Co to the N. A few km N of Danang Highway 1 passes through the village of **Nam Ô**, famous for firework manufacture. Pages of old school books are dyed pink, laid out in the sun to dry, rolled up and filled with gunpowder: children set about this task with peculiar relish. Red boxes of firecrackers are hung out in the street

By Train From Hué To Danang

The train journey from Hué to Danang is regarded as not just one of the most scenic in Vietnam, but in the world. Paul Theroux in his book *The Great Railway Bazaar* (Penguin) recounts his impressions as the train reached the narrow coastal strip, south of Hué and approaching Danang. The drizzle, so interminable in the former Royal Capital, gave way to bright sunshine and warmth; 'I had no idea,' I said. Of all the places the railway had taken me since London, this was the loveliest.

We were at the fringes of a bay that was green and sparkling in bright sunlight. Beyond the leaping jade plates of the sea was an overhang of cliffs and the sight of a valley so large it contained sun, smoke, rain, and cloud – all at once – independent quantities of colour. I had been unprepared for this beauty; it surprised and humbled me ... Who has mentioned the simple fact that the heights of Vietnam are places of unimaginable grandeur? Though we can hardly blame a frightened draftee for not noticing this magnificence, we should have known all along that the French would not have colonized it, nor would the Americans have fought so long, if such ripeness did not invite the eye to take it.

for sale. Like other pyrotechnical villages, Nam Ô has suffered from the government's severe restrictions on the sale of firecrackers at Têt. Danang was an important US military base during the Vietnam War and its museum has the finest collection of Cham art anywhere in the world. 32 km S of Danang is the historic town of Hoi An, architecturally one of the most distinguished in Vietnam.

Danang

Danang is yet another name to conjure with. It is a city with a history: originally Danang was known as **Cua Han** ('Mouth of the Han River'); when the French took control they renamed it Tourane, a rough transliteration of Cua Han. Then it acquired the title Thai Phien, and finally Danang. The city is sited on a peninsula of land at the point where the Han River flows into the South China Sea. An important port from French times, Danang gained world-wide fame when two US Marine battalions landed here in Mar 1965 to secure the airfield. They were the first of a great many more who would land on the beaches and airfields of South Vietnam.

Danang lies in a region of great his-torical significance. Fairly close to – but not often within particularly easy reach of – the city lie ruins of the powerful kingdom of Champa, one of the most glorious in ancient Southeast Asia (see page 82). The Cham were probably of Indonesian descent, and Chinese texts give the date 192 AD as the year when a group of tribes formed a union known as Lin-Yi, later to become Champa. The polytheistic religion of Champa was a fusion of Buddhism, Sivaism and local elements – and later Islam – producing

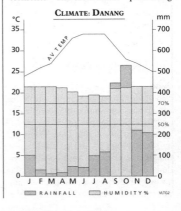

CLIMATE: DANANG

an abundance of religious (and secular) sculptures and monuments. The goddess Uroja is of central importance; the 'mother' of the nation, she is normally represented as a breast and nipple. Siva is represented as a linga. The kingdom reached its apogee in the 10th and 11th centuries, but unlike the Khmers, Champa never had the opportunity to create a capital city matching the magnificence of Angkor. For long periods the Cham were compelled to pay tribute to the Chinese, and after that they were dominated in turn by the Javanese, Annamese (the Vietnamese) and then the Khmers. The Cham 'nation' was finally eradicated in 1471, although there are still an estimated 90,000 Cham living in central Vietnam (mostly Brahmanists and Muslims). Given this turbulent his-

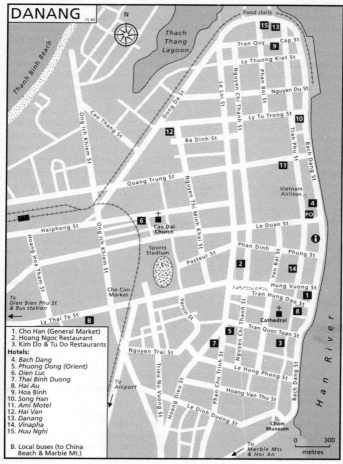

DANANG VL 84

N

Thach Thang Lagoon

Thanh Binh Beach

Food stalls

15 13

Tran Quy   9   Cap Ho

Ly Thuong Kiet St

Cao Thang St

Ong Ich Khiem St

Dong Da St

Nguyen Chi Thanh St

Phan Boi St

Nguyen Du St

Le Loi St

12

Ba Dinh St

Ly Tu Trong St

10

Tran Phu St

11

Bach Dang St

Quang Trung St

Vietnam Airlines

4

PO

Haiphong St

Ong Ich Khiem St

6
Cao Dai Church

Nguyen Thi Minh Khai St

Le Duan St

i

Hoang Hoa Tham St

Sports Stadium

Pasteur St

Phan Dinh

Phung St

2

Yen Bai St

14

Hung Vuong St

To
Dien Bien Phu St
& Bus station

Cho Con Market

Yersin St

Tran Hung Dao St

1

8

Cathedral

Ly Thai To St

B

Nguyen Chi Thanh St

Tran Quoc Toan St

3

1. Cho Han (General Market)
2. Hoang Ngoc Restaurant
3. Kim Do & Tu Do Restaurants
Hotels:
4. Bach Dang
5. Phuong Dong (Orient)
6. Dien Luc
7. Thai Binh Duong
8. Hai Au
9. Hoa Binh
10. Song Han
11. Ami Motel
12. Hai Van
13. Danang
14. Vinapha
15. Huu Nghi

B. Local buses (to China Beach & Marble Mt.)

Nguyen Trai St

5

7

Phan Chu Trinh St

Le Hong Phong St

Hoang Van Thu St

Han River

To
Airport

Trieu Nu Vuong St

Hoang Dieu St

Le Dinh Duong St

Cham Museum

0   300
metres

To
Marble Mts
& Hoi An

tory, it is perhaps surprising that the Cham found any opportunity for artistic endeavours. It should perhaps be added that since the demise of the kingdom, the number of Cham sculptures has grown enormously as forgers have carved more of the beautiful images.

Danang today has a population of 405,000 and is once more extending its influence as a commercial and trading city. Its position roughly equidistant between Hanoi and Saigon gives Danang strategic significance and its port facilities are being upgraded. Money has been invested in an Export Processing Zone which has yet to excite foreign interest but will no doubt do so when Saigon overheats.

Places of interest

The **Cham Museum** is at the intersection of Tran Phu and Le Dinh Duong sts. It was established by French academics, and contains the largest display of Cham art anywhere in the world (see page 107 and Excursions, below, to My Son and Dong Duong). The museum buildings alone are worth the visit: constructed in 1916 in a beautiful setting, the complex is open-plan in design, providing an environment in which the pieces can be exhibited to their best advantage. There are a number of rooms, each dedicated to a different period or style of Cham art, dating from the 4th to the 14th centuries. The Cham Period, spanning more than 1,000 years, produced abundant sculpture. Facial features on earlier works tend to be accentuated, and the bodies rather heavily sculpted. From the 10th century, under the influence of the Khmers, faces become less stylistic, more human, and the bodies of the figures more graceful and flowing. One problem with the display is the lack of any background information – not even dates are provided. The museum booklet (10,000d) has been written as an art history, not as a guide to the collection, and is of little help. The pieces are wonderful, but the visitor may

leave the museum rather befuddled by the display. Admission 10,000d (cameras 5,000d, videos 20,000d). Open 0700-1800 Mon-Sun.

Danang's **Cao Dai Church** is at 35 Haiphong St and is the second largest in Vietnam. The priest here is particularly friendly and informative – especially regarding Cao Dai-ism and its links with other religions. Services are held at 0600, 1200, 1800 and 2400 (see page 121). **Danang Cathedral**, single-spired with a pink sandstone coloured wash and built in 1923, can be found at 156 Tran Phu St. The stained glass windows were made in Grenoble, in 1927, by Louis Balmet who was also responsible for the windows of Dalat Cathedral. The city has a fair array of markets. There is a covered **general market** (**Cho Han**) in a new building at the intersection of Tran Phu and Hung Vuong sts. Another market, **Cho Con**, is at the intersection of Hung Vuong and Ong Ich Khiem sts. The stalls close by sell basketwork and other handicrafts. On Haiphong St, running E from the railway station, there is a **street market** selling fresh produce. Danang still retains some fine **French colonial architecture**, for instance, the house at 46 Tran Quoc Toan St.

Excursions

Hoi An is a beautiful, historic town (see page 219), situated 32 km S of Danang. Although a few years ago most visitors saw the town as an excursion from Danang, recently roles have been reversed, for some people prefer to stay here and make an excursion to Danang. *Getting there*: by bus from 350 Hung Vuong St, 1 hr; the last bus returns at about 1700.

Marble Mountain (or Ngu Hanh Son) overlooks the city of Danang and its airfield, about 12 km to the W. The name was given to these five peaks by the Nguyen Emperor Minh Mang (1820-1840) – although they are in fact limestone crags with marble outcrops. They are also known as the mountains of the five elements (fire, water, soil, wood and metal). An important religious spot for the Cham, the peaks became havens for Communist guerrillas during the war owing to their commanding view over Danang airbase. From here, a force with sufficient firepower could control much of what went on below, and the guerrillas harried the Americans mercilessly. The views from the mountain sides, overlooking Danang Bay, are impressive. On the Marble Mountains are a number of important sights, often associated with caves and grottoes which have formed through chemical action on the limestone rock.

At the foot of the mountains is a village with a number of shops selling marble carvings. From here, a circular route leads up the mountain and down again, finally ending up 200m further along the road towards China Beach. Of the mountains, the most visited is **Thuy Son**. The **Tam Thai Pagoda**, reached by a staircase cut into the mountain, is on the site of a much older Cham place of worship. Constructed in 1825 by Minh Mang, and subsequently rebuilt, the central statue is of the Buddha Sakyamuni (the historic Buddha) flanked by the Bodhisattva Quan Am (a future Buddha and the Goddess of Mercy), and a statue of Van Thu (symbolizing wisdom). At the rear of the grotto is another cave, the **Huyen Khong Cave**. Originally a place of animist worship, it later became a site for Buddhist pilgrimage. The entrance is protected by four door guardians. The high ceiling of the cave is pierced by five holes through which the sun filters and in the hour before midday it illuminates the central statue of the Buddha Sakyamuni. In the cave are various natural rock formations which, if you have picked up one of the young cave guides along the way, will be pointed out as being stork-like birds, elephants, an arm, a fish and a face. A few hundred metres further to the

S of the road on the right is a track leading to Chua Quan Thay Am which has its own grotto complete with stalactites, stalagmites and pillars. Local children will point out formations resembling the Buddha and an elephant.

Admission to Marble Mountain 10,000d. Guides, usually young boys, useful for pointing out the various caves dotted over the mountain. *Getting there*: 10 km from Danang, regular buses to Marble Mountain from Danang's local bus station opposite 350 Hung Vuong St, 25 mins or take a cyclo. Many travellers stop off at Marble Mountain on a day visit to Hoi An.

China Beach is a 1 km walk from Marble Mountain. Once a famous resort celebrated in rock songs, it is now a quiet sandy beach, with souvenir stalls, some surf and at times a strong cross current. It is unlikely to remain this way much longer, in mid 1994 a US company announced plans to build a multi-million dollar leisure complex: enjoy it while you can. **Accommodation B-C** *China Beach Hotel* or *Non Nuoc Seaside Resort*, Hoa Hai-Hoa Vang, T 21470, some a/c, breakfast included, comfortable. *Getting there*: regular buses from Danang's local bus station opposite 350 Hung Vuong St to Marble Mountain, 25 mins; walk the final 1 km.

My Son and **Dong Duong** are two centres of the former Cham Kingdom (see page 82) and, in theory, are among the main reasons to visit Danang. Unfortunately, reaching the sites is difficult: ask at your hotel to see whether any tours are available (and see Getting there, below). **My Son** is located about 60 km S of Danang (28 km W of Tra Kieu) and consists of over 70 monuments spread over a large area. The characteristic Cham architectural structure is the tower, built to reflect the divinity of the king: tall and rectangular, with four porticoes, each of which is 'blind' except for that on the W face. Because

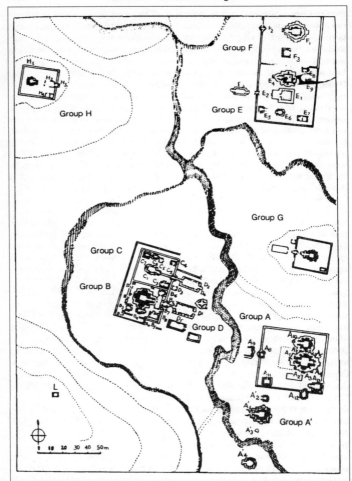

Plan of the My Son relics in the early part of the century. Although much has been destroyed some towers still stand (see text).

Cham kings were far less powerful than, say, the deva-rajas of Angkor, the monuments are correspondingly smaller and more personal. Orginally built of wood (not surprisingly, none remains), they were later made of brick, of which the earliest (7th century) are located at My Son. These are so-called Mi-Son E1 – the unromantic identifying sequence of letters and numbers being given, uncharacteristically, by the French archaeologists who initially investigated the monuments. Although little of these early examples remains, the temples seem to show similarities with post-Gupta Indian forms, while also embodying Chen-La stylistic influences. Bricks are exactly laid and held together with a form of vegetable cement. It is thought that on completion, each tower was surrounded by wood and fired over several days in what amounted to a vast outdoor kiln. Unfortunately, My Son was a Vietcong field headquarters and therefore located within one of the US 'free fire' zones and was extensively damaged – in particular, the finest sanctuary in the complex was demolished by US sappers.

60 km S of Danang and 20 km from My Son, **Dong Duong** supplanted My Son as the centre of Cham art and culture when King Indravarman II built a large Buddhist monastery there at the end of the 9th century. Artistically, little changed – the decoration of the towers simply became more ornate, flamboyant and involved, and the reliefs more deeply cut. Then, in the early 10th century, the focus of Cham art returned to My Son once again under the patronage of Indravarman III (so-called Mi-Son A1 style). Here, a new and far more elegant architecture, evolved. The towers became taller and more balanced, and the decoration purer and less crude.

Of the temple groupings, illustrated in the plan above, Groups A, E and H were badly damaged in the war. Groups B and C have largely retained their temples but many statues, altars and linga have been removed to the **Cham Museum** in Danang or by French collectors.

Getting to My Son: although officially a permit is no longer needed to visit My Son, visitors frequently report being stopped by police and 'mafia' who demand the journey be completed on their motorbikes. It is best to organize the trip through your hotel. From Danang, drive S on Highway 1 and turn right towards Tra Kieu after 34 km (some 2 km after crossing the Thu Bon River).

Drive through Tra Kieu to the village of Kim Lam. Turn left; the path to My Son is about 6 km further along this road. From here it is a short ferry crossing and a 2 km walk to My Son (pay the ferryman) although in the dry season it is possible to cycle across. Guides will help to lead visitors through the mines that are said to line the path. Take a hat, sun cream and water – it is hot and dry. My Son can be reached just as easily from Hoi An, 2 hrs each way by Honda Om (US$7) or by boat US$15, which takes all day. The boat will carry bicycles; negotiate with riverside restaurants in Hoi An. Admission 10,000d.

Local information
● Accommodation
A number of new hotels have opened and, together with renovated hotels, Danang now offers reasonable accommodation at a range of prices. Hotels are generally in one of two locations, the town centre or up to the N around Dong Da St. The latter tend to be cheaper and they are only a short walk from the centre.

A *Bach Dang Hotel*, 50 Bach Dang St, T 23649, F 21659, is new and rather cramped for the price, river views and quite a good restaurant, central; **A** *Phuong Dong (Orient)*, 93 Phan Chu Trinh St, T 21266, F 22854, a/c, still rather grand, good size rooms; **A-B** *Dien Luc*, 37 Haiphong St, T 21864, a/c, price incl breakfast, opened 1991 but doesn't look like it, a bit remote.

B *Hai Au*, 177 Tran Phu St, T 22722, F 24165, central, large rooms, friendly reception, indifferent restaurant; **B** *Hoa Binh*, 3 Tran Quy Cap, a/c, new hotel in a quiet street; **B** *Song Han*, 26 Bach Dang St, T 22540, some a/c and some river views; **B** *Thai Binh Duong (Pacific)*, 80 Phan Chu Trinh St, T 22137, a/c, central, rather characterless; **B-C** *Ami Motel*, 7 Quang Trung, T 24494, new, clean, friendly; **B-D** *Danang*, 3-5 Dong Da St, T 21986, some a/c, undergoing renovation, will be a little more expensive in 1996, restaurant and tour services, now merged with the old Marble Mountain hotel next door, cheap fan rooms.

C-D *Vinapha*, 80 Tran Phu St, T 25072, some a/c, owned by Pharmaceutical Company of Vietnam so it sells medicines, new, central, friendly.

D *Huu Nghi* (Friendship), 7 Dong Da St, T 22563; **D** *Thanh Thanh*, 54 Phan Chu Trinh St, some a/c, a bit run down but good location. **E** *Tu Do*, 65 Hung Vuong St.

● **Places to eat**
Seafood is good here, and Danang has its own beer, Da Nang 'Export'. There are a number of cafés and restaurants along Bach Dang St, overlooking the river. ✦✦*Bach Dang Hotel*, 50 Bach Dang St, informal, glimpses of river and decent food; ✦✦*Christies Harbourside Grill*, 9 Bach Dang, T 26645, mainly American fast food and giant burgers, some Vietnamese, paperback book exchange, rec; ✦✦*Hoang Ngoc*, 106 Nguyen Chi Thanh St, extensive menu, good food and welcoming atmosphere, popular with travellers; ✦✦*Kim Dinh*, 7 Bach Dang St, riverside restaurant, opp *Bach Dang Hotel*; ✦✦*Kim Do*, 174 Tran Phu St, Asian/Chinese, seafood and duck specialities, excellent food, rec; ✦✦*Thanh Lich*, 48 Bach Dang St, seafood, rec; ✦✦*Tu Do*, 172 Tran Phu St, extensive menu and excellent food, deservedly popular, rec; ✦*Huong Viet*, 41 Tran Quoc Toan St, Chinese. Dong Da St, at the N end of town has a number of good, cheap eating stalls opp the hotels.

● **Airline offices**
Vietnam Airlines Booking Office (domestic), 35 Tran Phu St, T 21130.

● **Banks & money changers**
VID Public Bank, 2 Tran Phu St; Vietcombank, 46 Le Loi St, will change most major currencies, cash and TCs.

● **Entertainment**
Dancing/Nightclub: *Cang Danang*, 1 Bach Dang St and under the *Bach Dang Hotel*.

● **Hospitals & medical services**
Hospital: 74 Haiphong St, T 22480.

● **Post & telecommunications**
Fax service: from *Phuong Dong Hotel*.
GPO: 210 Bach Dang St, corner of Bach Dang and Le Duan sts. Telex and telephone facilities here.
International telephone: calls can be made from the *Pacific* and *Phuong Dong* (Orient) hotels.
TNT International Express: T 21685/22582.

● **Shopping**
Marble carvings: from shops in town, but particularly from the stalls around the foot of Marble Mountain (see Excursions).

Silk: available for US$3/metre; *Thanh Nha Silk Shop*, Hung Vuong St offers the best selection; tailoring service available (as well as from other tailors on Hung Vuong St).

● **Tourist offices**
Danang Tourist Office, 68 Bach Dang St, T 21423, F 22854 – will arrange cars and guides; *Vietnamtourism*, 158 Phan Chau Trinh St, T 22990.

● **Useful addresses**
Immigration Police: Nguyen Thi Minh Khai St, opp Hai Van Hotel.

● **Transport**
108 km from Hué, 130 km from Quang Ngai, 965 km from Saigon, 759 km from Hanoi.

Local Bicycle hire: ask at your hotel or go to Tam and Lien opp the *Danang Hotel* or Mr Hai (see below); the *Danang Hotel* charges 8,000d/day. **Bus**: the local bus station is opp 350 Hung Vuong St. There are regular departures to Hoi An and Marble Mountain from here. **Car hire**: from the tourist office, or from Mr Hai who hangs about outside the Vietnam Airlines Office, 35 Tran Phu St, or at 6/8 Yen Bai St, T 24809. **Cyclos and Lambros**: around town. **Motorcycle hire**: from Tam and Lien opp the *Danang Hotel* (US$5/day).

Air The airport is 2.5 km SW of the city. Three flights daily to Hanoi (US$90) and Saigon (US$90); flight duration 1 hr 10 mins to Saigon and Hanoi. Connections with Nha Trang on Tues and Thur (US$50), Play Ku on Mon, Wed, Fri and Sun (US$50) and Quy Nhon on Mon, Wed and Sat (US$50). See timetable, page 292.

Train The station is at 120 Haiphong St, opp the intersection with Hoang Hoa Tham St. The 4 hrs trip from Nha Trang is spectacular, the track following the coast. Express trains stop here, $19^{1/2}$ hrs from Hanoi and $21^{1/2}$ hrs from Saigon. See timetable, page 293.

Road Bus: the long-distance bus station is at 8 Dien Bien Phu St, 2 km W of the city centre. Take Hung Vuong St W which becomes Ly Thai To St and then Dien Bien Phu St. Buses to Vinh, Hué, Haiphong, Quang Ngai and Hanoi. Express buses leave from Diem Ban Ve Xe Toc Hanh at 52 Phan Chu Trinh St (next to the *Thanh Thanh Hotel*) to Hanoi, Saigon, Haiphong, Buon Ma Thuot, Dalat, Vinh and Nha Trang. Daily express departures to most destinations at 0500. The local bus station, with regular departures to Hoi An and Marble

Mountain, is opp 350 Hung Vuong St. Like the train journey, the road trip N to Hué is spectacular (see page 211).

International connections It is possible to get a visa for Laos in Danang from the Laotian consulate here (US$25 for a 7-day transit visa).

Hoi An

The ancient town of Hoi An (formerly Faifo) lies 32 km S of Danang on the banks of the Thu Bon River. Originally a Champa port, the town has a distinct Chinese atmosphere with low, tiled-roof houses and narrow streets. The town is divided into five quarters or 'bangs', each of which would traditionally have had its own pagoda and supported one Chinese clan group. The Chinese, along with some Japanese, settled here in the 16th century and controlled trade between island Southeast Asia, East Asia (China and Japan) and India. Portuguese and Dutch vessels also docked at the port. During the Tay Son rebellion (1771-1788) the town was almost totally destroyed, although this is not apparent to the visitor. By the end of the 19th century the Thu Bon River had started to silt up and Hoi An was gradually eclipsed by Danang as the most important port of the area.

As we noted in last year's edition of the *Handbook*, Hoi An has emerged as one of the most popular tourist destinations in Vietnam and there has been no diminution in its status. Quite the reverse, walking along Tran Phu St one sees more Western than Vietnamese faces and every evening harassed hotel receptionists have to explain to tired and incredulous travellers that there really is no room in the inn – back to Danang!

Sadly, however, Hoi An's historic character is being submerged by the rising tide of tourism. Although remaining physically intact virtually every one of its fine historic buildings either markets some aspect of its own heritage or touts in some other way for the tourist dollar; increasingly it is coming to resemble the 'Vietnam' pavilion in a Disney theme park. Visitors to Hoi An are charmed by the gentleness of the people and the sedate pace of life. Although short on accommodation, Hoi An does have several highly praised restaurants and the nearby Cua Dai Beach.

Places of interest

Most of Hoi An's more attractive buildings and important pagodas and assembly halls (known as hoi quan) are found either on (or just off) Tran Phu St. Tran Phu stretches W-E from the Japanese Covered Bridge to the market, running parallel to, and one street in from, the river. The best way to explore this small, intimate town is on foot. People are friendly and will generally not mind inquisitive, but polite, foreigners. A day is needed to see the town properly.

At the W end of Tran Phu St is Hoi An's most famous landmark: the covered bridge – variously known as the Pagoda Bridge, the Faraway People's Bridge and, popularly, as the **Japanese Covered Bridge** (*Cau Nhat Ban*). The bridge was built in the 16th century, perhaps even earlier. On its N side there is a pagoda, Japanese in style, which protects sailors. At the W end of the bridge are statues of two dogs, and at the E end, of two monkeys – it is said that the bridge was begun in the year of the monkey and finished in the year of the dog. Some scholars have pointed out that this would mean a 2-year period of construction, an inordinately long time for such a small bridge; they maintain that the two animals represent points of the compass, WSW (monkey) and NW (dog). Father Benigne Vachet, a missionary who lived in Hoi An between 1673 and 1683 notes in his memoirs that the bridge was the haunt of beggars and fortune tellers hoping to benefit from the stream of people crossing over it. Its popular name – Japanese Covered Bridge – reflects a long-standing belief that it was built by the Japanese, al-

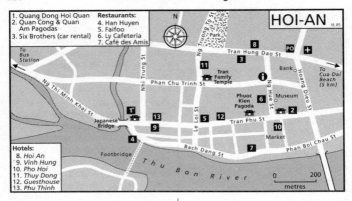

1. Quang Dong Hoi Quan
2. Quan Cong & Quan Am Pagodas
3. Six Brothers (car rental)

Restaurants:
4. Han Huyen
5. Faifoo
6. Ly Cafeteria
7. Café des Amis

HOI-AN VL 85

Hotels:
8. Hoi An
9. Vinh Hung
10. Pho Hoi
11. Thuy Dong
12. Guesthouse
13. Phu Thinh

though no documentary evidence exists to support this. One of its other names, the Faraway People's Bridge, is said to have been coined because vessels from faraway would moor close to the bridge.

Just S of the Covered Bridge is **Bach Dang St** which runs along the banks of the Thu Bon River. Here there are boats, activity and often a cooling breeze. The road loops round to the Hoi An Market (see below). One street inland from the river road is Nguyen Thai Hoc St where, at no 101 is **Tan Ky House**, a beautiful traditional house with a sumptuous Chinese/Japanese interior. The owner is welcoming. Admission 5,000d.

East from the Japanese Covered Bridge at 176 Tran Phu St is the **Quang Dong Hoi Quan**, or the **Assembly Hall for Maritime Commerce**. Since its establishment in the early 18th century this pagoda has gone through four name changes. The principal deity worshipped here was the goddess of the sea and protector of sailors, Thien Hau. Unusually for an assembly hall, it was a mutual aid society open to any Chinese trader or seaman, regardless of dialect or region of origin. Chinese vessels tended to visit Hoi An during the spring, returning to China in the summer. The assembly hall would help shipwrecked and ill sailors, and meet the costs of

burying merchants with no relatives in Hoi An. The pagoda with fine embroidered hangings, is in a cool, tree filled compound; a good place to rest. Admission 2,000d.

East from Quang Dong Hoi Quan on Tran Phu St are a number of distinguished **private houses**: for example at nos 74, 77, and 148. The house at no 140 is a weaving workshop. The **Phuoc Kien Pagoda** (also known as Phuc Kien Hoi Quan) at 46 Tran Phu St is a Fukien Pagoda (Vietnamese, *Phuoc Kien*) which was originally built around 1690. It was extensively rebuilt and extended in 1900 when the hall of worship was added. Chinese traders in Hoi An (like elsewhere in Southeast Asia) established self-governing 'dialect associations' or 'clan' houses (known as *kongsi*) which owned their own schools, cemeteries, hospitals and temples. There were four such associations in Hoi An: Fukien, Kwangtung, Teochiu and Hainan. The Phuoc Kien Pagoda is an intimate building within a large compound, and is dedicated to Thien Hau Thanh Mau (the goddess of the sea and protector of sailors). She is the central figure on the main altar, clothed in gilded robes. To the right of the sanctuary is a model of a Chinese war junk (which was repaired in 1875), and immediately on the right on entering the pagoda, is a mural depicting Thien Hau rescuing a sinking vessel. Behind the main altar, through an open courtyard, is a second altar. Admission 2,000d.

At the E end of Tran Phu St at No 24, close to the intersection with Nguyen Hue St, is the **Ong Hoi An Pagoda**. This temple is in fact two interlinked pagodas built back-to-back: *Chua Quan Cong*, and behind that *Chua Quan Am*. Their date of construction is not known, although both certainly existed in 1653. In 1824 Emperor Minh Mang made a donation of 300 luong (1 luong = 1.5 oz) of silver for the support of the pagodas. They are dedicated to Quan Cong and Quan Am respectively. Adjacent to Ong Hoi An Pagoda in Nguyen Hue St is Hoi An's **museum**, the Quan Yin Pagoda built in 1653. It contains a fine selection of artefacts relating to Hoi An's commercial past. Admission 5,000d.

Virtually opposite the Ong Hoi An Pagoda, is the **Hoi An Market** (*Cho Hoi An*). The market extends down to the river and then along the river road (Bach Dang St). At the Tran Phu St end is a covered market selling mostly dry goods, numerous cloth merchants and seamstresses will produce made-to-measure shirts in a few hours for US$5; along the river it becomes more interesting and colourful.

On the junction of Le Loi and Phan Chu Trinh sts stands the **Tran Family Temple** which has survived for 15 generations; the current generation has no son which means the lineage has been broken. The building exemplifies well Hoi An's construction methods and the harmonious fusion of Chinese and Japanese styles. It is roofed with heavy *yin* and *yang* tiling which requires strong roof beams; these are held up by a triple beamed support in the Japanese style (seen in the roof of the covered bridge). Some beams have ornately carved dragons of Chinese inspiration. The outer doors are Japanese, the inner are Chi-

nese. On a central altar rest small wooden boxes which contain the photograph or likeness of the deceased together with biographical details; beyond, at the back of the house is a small raised Chinese herb, spice and flower garden with a row of bonzai trees. Like all Hoi An's family houses guests are received warmly and courteously and served lotus tea and dried coconut; a small donation should be made.

Excursions

Cua Dai Beach, 5 km from Hoi An, E down Tran Hung Dao St, a pleasant 20 mins cycle ride. White sand and clear water. Refreshments available.

Local information
● **Accommodation**

The local authorities have regulated hotel building in Hoi An very carefully and do not permit foreigners to stay in private houses. As a result, in summer, rooms are like gold dust.

B-D *Hoi An*, 6 Tran Hung Dao St, T 61373, F 61636, attractive colonial building set well back from the road in spacious grounds, cheaper rooms have fan and shared bathroom; **B-C** *Vinh Hung*, 143 Tran Phu St, T 61621, cheaper rooms fan and shared bathroom, friendly.

C *Phu Thinh*, 144 Tran Phu St, T 61297, some a/c, private bathrooms, new; **C-D** *Guesthouse 92*, 92 Tran Phu St, very obliging and helpful, reluctant to turn anyone away hence often looks like a refugee camp; **C-D** *Huy Hoang*, 73 Phan Boi Chan St, T 61453, some a/c, bath, hot water; **C-D** *Pho Hoi*, 7/2 Tran Phu St, T 61633, nr market, some a/c, cheaper rooms share facilities; **C-F** *Thuy Dong*, 11 Le Loi St, T 61574, some a/c, some dormitory accommodation, friendly.

● **Places to eat**

A Hoi An speciality is *Cao Lau* – a special wanton soup made with water from one particular well. Fresh seafood is also readily available. There are new restaurants and cafés springing up all over town but especially on Tran Phu St. ◆◆*Café Can*, 74 Bach Dang St, good Vietnamese and Western menu, seafood specialities; ◆◆*Café des Amis*, 52 Bach Dang St, nr the river, fish and seafood, set menu changes daily, widely acclaimed food, excellent value, highly rec; ◆◆*Fukien*, 31 Tran Phu, family run Chinese; ♦♦*Han Huyen (Floating Restaurant)*, Bach Dang St, just E of footbridge, excellent seafood; ♦♦*Yellow River*, 38 Tran Phu St, good Hoi An family restaurant, fried wanton is rec, especially for Francophones; ♦*Fai Fo Restaurant*, 104 Tran Phu St, esp good for breakfast and ice cream; ♦*Ly Cafeteria 22*, 22 Nguyen Hue St, cheap and cheerful; ♦*Restaurant Cao Lau*, 42 Tran Phu St, for the best Cao Lau, rec.

● **Banks & money changers**
Hoi An Bank, 4 Hoang Dieu, only exchanges cash (US$).

● **Hospitals & medical services**
Hospital: 4 Tran Hung Dao St.

● **Post & telecommunications**
Post Office: 5 Tran Hung Dao St, next to *Hoi An Hotel* also has international telephone and fax service.

● **Tourist offices**
Hoi An Tourism Service, 6 Tran Hung Dao St, at the entrance of *Hoi An Hotel*; **Tourist Office**, 12 Phan Chu Trinh St, T 61276, car and minibus hire and services, bicycle hire 5,000d/day.

● **Transport**
32 km from Danang.

Road Bicycle/motorbike hire: most hotels offer services, also try 17 Tran Phu St. **Bus**: the bus station is about 1 km W of the centre of town. Regular connections with Danang's local bus station, 1 hr. If on a day's excursion from Danang, the last bus returns at about 1700. The road from Danang runs just inland from the coast and passes the skeleton of a former US Airforce base. This is an area of war scrap recycling. Further on towards Hoi An, the road becomes narrow, almost a rural lane, skirting past paddy fields, vegetable farms and cassava plots. Minibus to Hué, Nha Trang (US$10), Saigon (US$25), Hanoi (US$25) and Son My. **Taxi**: from Danang airport takes about 40 mins, US$15. **Six Brothers** operate from a house opp *Hoi An Hotel*, cars for rent, US$26 to take their most tortured vehicle to Danang.

QUANG NGAI TO PHAN RANG via Nha Trang

This 500 km stretch of Highway 1 runs along the coast, sometimes within sight of the sea. Areas of lowland suitable for rice cultivation are few, and the soils generally poor. The beach resort of Nha Trang is situated in the heartland of the former Cham Kingdom and along this stretch of Vietnam's central region are innumerable Cham towers, most unrestored and only rudimentarily studied. The former US Navy base at Cam Ranh Bay lies 50 km S of Nha Trang, and another 55 km S from here is the town of Phan Rang. Phan Rang is notable for the group of Cham Towers that lie just outside the town. From here the road divides: Highway 1 and the railway continue southwards to Phan Thiet and from there to Saigon, a total of 318 km; another road runs N-W to Dalat, 110 km.

Quang Ngai

Quang Ngai is a modest provincial capital on Highway 1, situated on the S bank of the Tra Khuc River. Most people don't stay here as it is only 130 km S of Danang. Its greatest claim to fame is its proximity to **Son My** – the site of the **My Lai massacre** (see below, Excursions). There is an extensive **market** running N from the bus station, along Ngo Quyen St (just E of Quang Trung St – Highway 1). Also in the city is a **citadel** built during the reign of Gia Long (1802-1819).

Excursions **Son My (My Lai)** lies 13 km from Quang Ngai. Just over 1 km N of town on Highway 1, soon after crossing the bridge over the Tra Khuc River, is a plaque indicating the way to Son My (My Lai). Turn right, and continue for 12 km to the subdistrict of Son My where one of the worst, and certainly the most publicized, atrocities committed by US troops during the Vietnam War occurred (see box). The massacre of innocent Vietnamese villagers is better known as the My Lai Massacre – after one of the four hamlets of Son My. In the centre of the village of Son My is a memorial and a military cemetery 400m beyond. There is an exhibition of contemporaneous US military photos of the massacre and a

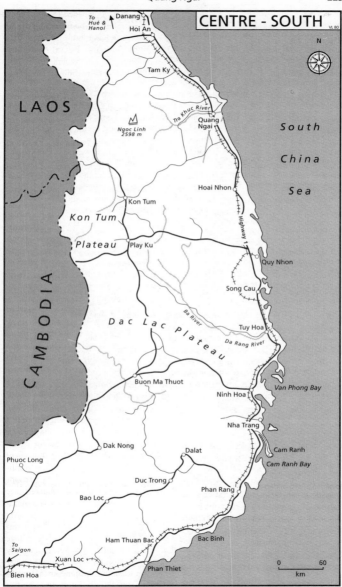

THE SON MY (MY LAI) MASSACRE

The massacre at Son My was a turning point in the American public's view of the war, and the role that the US was playing. Were American forces defending Vietnam and the world from the evils of communism? Or were they merely shoring-up a despotic government which had lost all legitimacy among the population it ostensibly served?

The massacre occurred on the morning of 16 March 1968. Units from the 23rd Infantry Division were dropped into the village of Son My. The area was regarded as an area of intense Communist presence – so much so that soldiers referred to the villages as Pinkville. Only 2 weeks beforehand, six soldiers had been killed after stumbling into a mine field. The leader of the platoon that was charged with the job of investigating the hamlet of My Lai was 2nd Lt. William Calley. Under his orders, 347 people, all unarmed and many women and children, were massacred. Some of Calley's men refused to participate, but nonetheless most did. Neil Sheehan, in his book *A bright shining lie*, writes:

> "One soldier missed a baby lying on the ground twice with a .45 pistol as his comrades laughed at his marksmanship. He stood over the child and fired a third time. The soldiers beat women with rifle butts and raped some and sodomized others before shooting them. They shot the water buffalos, the pigs, and the chickens. They threw the dead animals into the wells to poison the water. They tossed satchel charges into the bomb shelters under the houses. A lot of the inhabitants had fled into the shelters. Those who leaped out to escape the explosives were gunned down. All of the houses were put to the torch" (1989:689).

In total, over 500 people were killed at Son My; most in the hamlet of My Lai, but another 90 at another hamlet (by another platoon) in the same village. The story of the massacre was filed by Seymour Hersh, but not until 13 Nov – 8 months later. The subsequent court-martial only convicted Calley, who was by all accounts a sadist. He was sentenced to life imprisonment, but had served only 3 years before President Nixon intervened on his behalf (he was personally convicted with the murder of 109 of the victims). As Sheehan argues, the massacre was, in some regards, not surprising. The nature of the war had led to the killing and maiming of countless unarmed and innocent peasants; it was often done from a distance. In the minds of most GIs, every Vietnamese was a potential Communist; from this position it was only a small step to believing that all Vietnamese were legitimate targets.

---

reconstruction of an underground bomb shelter; the creek where many villagers were dumped after being shot has been preserved. A sign prohibits photos, but may be given by the informative English-speaking guide. There is no charge but visitors are invited to contribute to the upkeep of the memorial. The track to Son My from the main road is in poor condition (difficult except in a 4WD) but is under reconstruction.

● **Accommodation** B *Nha Khach Uy Ban*

Thi, Phan Boi Chau St (W of the Post Office), T 2109, a/c; **E** *Khach San So 2*, 41 Phan Boi Chau St.

● **Post & telecommunications Post Office**: intersection of Phan Dinh Phung and Phan Boi Chau sts (W of Quang Trung St – Highway 1).

● **Transport** 130 km from Danang, 174 km from Quy Nhon, 238 km from Hué, 411 km from Nha Trang, 888 km from Hanoi, 840 km from Saigon. **Train** The station is about 3 km W of town. Regular connections with Hanoi and Saigon and all stops between the two. See timetable, page 293. **Road Bus**: the bus

THE TAY SON REBELLION (1771-1788)

At the time of the Tay Son rebellion in 1771, Vietnam was in turmoil and conditions in the countryside were deteriorating to the point of famine. The three Tay Son brothers found a rich lode of dissatisfaction among the peasantry, which they successfully mined. Exploiting the latent discontent, they redistributed property from hostile mandarins to the peasants and raised a motley army of clerks, cattle-dealers, farmers, hill people, even scholars, to fight the Trinh and Nguyen lords. Brilliant strategists and demonstrating considerable skills of leadership, the brothers and their supporters swept through the country extending the area under their control S as far as Saigon and N to Trinh.

The Chinese, sensing that the disorder and dissent caused by the conflict gave them an opportunity to bring the entire nation under their control, sent a 200,000-strong army southwards in 1788. In the same year, the most intelligent (by all accounts) of the brothers, Nguyen Hue, proclaimed himself emperor under the name of Quang Trung and began to prepare for battle against the cursed Chinese. On the 5th day of Tet in 1789, the brothers attacked the Chinese near Thang Long catching them unawares as they celebrated the New Year. (The Viet Cong were to do the same during the Tet Offensive nearly 200 years later.) With great military skill, they routed the enemy, who fled in panic back towards China. Rather than face capture, one of the Chinese generals committed suicide. This victory at the Battle of Dong Da is regarded as one of the greatest in the annals of Vietnamese history. Quang Trung, having saved the nation from the Chinese, had visions of recreating the great Nam Viet Empire of the 2nd century BC, and of invading China. Among the reforms that he introduced were a degree of land reform, a wider programme of education, and a fairer system of taxation. He even tried to get all peasants to carry identity cards with the slogan 'the great trust of the empire' emblazoned on them. These greater visions were not to be however: Quang Trung died suddenly in 1792, failing to provide the dynastic continuity that was necessary if Vietnam was to survive the impending French arrival. As a postscript to the Tay Son rebellion, in 1802 the new Emperor Gia Long ordered his soldiers to exhume the body of the last of the brothers and urinate upon it in front of the deceased's wife and son. They were then torn apart by four elephants. Quang Trung and the other Tay Son brothers – like many former nationalist and peasant leaders – are revered by the Vietnamese and honoured by the Communists.

station is a short distance E of Quang Trung St (Highway 1), on Nguyen Nghiem St.

Quy Nhon

Quy Nhon, the capital of Binh Dinh Province, has a population of nearly 250,000 and is situated just off Highway 1. It can be used as a stopping-off point on the long journey N or S between Danang and Nha Trang. A seaside town, it has reasonable swimming off sandy **Quy Nhon Beach** and a number of sights in the vicinity. The **central mar-** ket (cho lon) is in the centre of town, near the intersection of Tang Bat Ho and 1 Thang 4 sts.

Excursions Thap Doi Cham towers are situated on the edge of town. The area around Quy Nhon was a focus of the Cham Empire, and a number of monuments (13, it is said) have survived the intervening years. These two impressive Cham towers are about 3 km from the centre of town. *Getting there*: walk or bicycle NW on Tran Hung Dao St, past the bus station, and after 2 km turn right onto Thap Doi St. The towers are a short distance along this street.

Tay Son District is about 50 km from Quy Nhon off Highway 19 running W towards Play Ku. It is famous as the place where three brothers led a peasant revolt in 1771 (see box). The Vietnamese have a penchant for celebrating the exploits of the poor and the weak, and those of the Tay Son brothers are displayed in the **Quang Trung Museum**. *Getting there*: take a bus from the station on Tran Hung Dao St.

Hoang De Citadel (also known as Cha Ban) is situated about 27 km N of Quy Nhon. Originally a Cham capital which was repeatedly attacked by the Vietnamese, it was taken over by the Tay Son brothers in the 18th century and made the capital of their short-lived kingdom. Not much remains except some **Cham ruins**, within the citadel walls, in the vicinity of the old capital. 50 km S of Quy Nhon is the small town of Song Cau, 2 km N of which is the *Sao Bien Restaurant*, rec for crab.

- **Accommodation** B *Quy Nhon*, 8 Nguyen Hue St, T 2401, a/c, on the beach, breakfast incl; E *Nha Khach Ngan Hang Dau*, 399 Tran Hung Dao St, T 2012; E *Thanh Binh*, 17 Ly Thuong Kiet St, T 2041, some a/c; E *Viet Cuong*, 460 Tran Hung Dao St, T 2434.

- **Banks & money changers** Vietcombank, 148 Tran Hung Dao St.

- **Post & telecommunications Post Office**: 127 Hai Ba Trung. **TNT International Express**: T 2193/2600.

- **Hospitals & medical services** *General Hospital*, 102 Nguyen Hue St.

- **Tourist offices** Binh Dinh Tourism Company, 4 Nguyen Hue St, T 2524.

- **Transport** 174 km from Quang Ngai, 223 km from Buon Ma Thuot, 238 km from Nha Trang, 304 km from Danang, 412 km from Hué. **Train** The station is just over 1 km NW of the town centre, on Hoang Hoa Tham St which runs off Tran Hung Dao St. Express trains do not stop here. To catch the express, the closest stop is Dieu Tri, 10 km away. See

timetable, page 293. **Road Bus**: the bus station is 1 km NW of the town centre, on Tran Hung Dao St (nr the intersection with Le Hong Phong St). Express buses leave at 0500 for Hanoi, Saigon, Nha Trang, Danang, Dalat, Hué.

Play Ku

Play Ku (Pleiku), with a population of 35,000, is located high on the Play Ku Plateau, one of many such structural features in the Central Highlands. It is the capital of Gia Lai Province which, with a population density of just 34/sq km, is one of the most sparsely inhabited areas of Vietnam. Historically, this was a densely forested part of the country and it remains home to a large number of hilltribes. Play Ku was HQ to II Corps, one of the four military tactical zones into which South Vietnam was divided during the American war. John Vann (see Neil Sheehan's *Bright shining lie* – recommended reading) controlled massive B52 bombing raids against the encroaching NVA from here and, in Jun 1972, he was killed in a helicopter crash just outside Play Ku.

Play Ku the town has little to offer the tourist; during the monsoon the streets turn into muddy torrents and chill damp pervades hotel rooms and bedding. The attractions of the area are excursions to **minority villages** and the nearby **Ya Ly Waterfalls**. These can be reached only by car – which cannot be hired in Play Ku. Some visitors to minority villages without an official Gia Lai Tourism guide have been fined.

Best time to visit The Central Highlands is miserable in the wet season (Apr-Oct), low cloud and mist obscure the views. Nov-Mar is cooler but largely free of rain.

- **Accommodation** B-C *Pleiku*, 124 Le Loi St, T 24296; B-C *Ya Ly*, 89 Hung Vuong St, T 24843, good restaurant and friendly staff, rec; *Hung Vuong*, 215 Hung Vuong St, cheaper but may not take Westerners.

- **Places to eat** ♦♦*Than Lich*, nr Pleiku Hotel, attentive hostesses, food rec.

● **Post & telecommunications Post Office**: 87 Hung Vuong St.

● **Tourist offices** Gia Lai Tourism, 124 Le Loi St, T 24891 in *Pleiken Hotel*, reported to be expensive, unhelpful and most unreliable, avoid if possible.

● **Transport** 186 km from Quy Nhon, 197 km from Buon Ma Thuot. **Air** Connections on Vietnam Airlines with Danang (US$30), Saigon (US$65) and Hanoi (US$110), all flights on Tues and Fri. **Road Bus**: regular connections with Quy Nhon and Buon Ma Thuot. Minibuses leave from the market.

Buon Ma Thuot

Buon Ma Thuot, the capital of Dac Lac Province with a population of 65,000, is inland from Nha Trang, not far from the Cambodian border. It is rarely visited by tourists as it is difficult to get to and lies off the main tourist route. The town is sited on the Daclac Plateau at an altitude of about 1,000m and has a population of less than 100,000.

Since reunification in 1975, areas of this part of Vietnam have been designated New Economic Zones. 'Excess' population from Saigon and from the overpopulated lands of the Red River Delta have been resettled in new villages, and the forest cleared. Many of the resettlement communities have been unsuccessful: the poor quality of the land was not fully appreciated and yields of crops have been disappointingly low. There has also been some friction between the settlers and the minority ethnic groups (mostly E-de) who live in the area, who have been discriminated against for many years. The town is an important commercial centre and the unofficial capital of the Central Highlands.

A **museum** at 1 Me Mai St, just across the road from the *Thang Loi Hotel*, displays artefacts of the various minority groups – 'Montagnards' – that live in the area, along with a E-de traditional house.

Excursions Tourists who manage to get to Buon Ma Thuot may be allowed to visit minority villages in the vicinity of the town. It is necessary to obtain permission from the local police. Among the various tribal groups are the E-de (or Rhade) and the M'nong. The latter number about 50,000 and are matriarchal. Visitors are usually taken to the E-de village *Buon* (meaning *village*) *Tuo*. The M'nong have been famed as elephant catchers for hundreds of years, and the forests around the town are still reputed to support a large population. The most frequently visited M'nong community is *Buon Don*, where elephants are trained.

There are some impressive **waterfalls** in the vicinity of the town, apparently all named after different types of synthetic fabric – Draylon, Draynour, Draysap and Drayling.

● **Accommodation** B-C *Tay Nguyen*, 106 Ly Thuong Kiet St; **B-C** *Thang Loi*, 1 Phan Chu Trinh St, T 2322, some a/c; **D** *Hong Kong*, 30 Hai Ba Trung St, T 2630, fan, cold water; **E** *Hotel 43*, 43 Ly Thuong Kiet St, fan, clean shared bathrooms. Few tourists reach Buon Ma Thuot so hard bargaining may be effective in reducing rates.

● **Places to eat** *My Canh*, by Thuong Kiet St, shrimp, beef or fish fondue is rec.

● **Tourist offices** Dac Lak Tourist Office, 3 Phan Chu Trinh St, T 2108.

● **Transport** 190 km from Nha Trang, 223 km from Quy Nhon, 396 km from Dalat, 1,427 km from Hanoi, 350 km from Saigon. **Road Bus**: regular connections with Hanoi, Saigon, Nha Trang, Quy Nhon, Dalat and most other provincial capitals.

Nha Trang

Nha Trang (pop 200,000) is an important port established in 1924 and known for its 6 km-long white-sand beach, warm sea and fine seafood. When US forces were based at nearby Cam Ranh Bay, the waters around the islands off Nha Trang were highly regarded by recreational scuba divers and fishermen.

Word has spread, and Nha Trang's

days as an undiscovered treasure are over. Nha Trang is a firmly established favourite of Vietnamese as well as foreign visitors and Nha Trangites of all backgrounds and persuasions endeavour to ease the dollar from the traveller's sweaty paw: clamouring beggars at Po Nagar; schoolgirls and toothless crones offering a massage on the beach (US$5 – nice work in a country where a teacher might earn only US$25 a month); hawkers of all kinds pestering sun bathers with sickly confections and postcards. But the beach is long and you do not have to walk far to escape the madding crowds.

The name Nha Trang is thought to be derived from the Cham word *yakram*, meaning bamboo river, and the surrounding area was a focal point of the Cham Kingdom – some of the country's best preserved Cham towers lie close by (see below). Nha Trang was beseiged for 9 months during the Tay Son rebellion of the late 18th century (see page 225), before eventually falling to the rebel troops. There are, in reality, two Nha Trangs: popular Nha Trang is a sleepy, sedate and genteel seaside town consisting of a long palm and casuarina-fringed beach, one or two streets running parallel to it, and a smattering of elegant colonial era buildings; commercial Nha Trang to the N of Yersin St is a bustling city with an attractive array of Chinese shop houses interspersed among the socialist – municipal architecture. Most Western tourists confine their acitivities to the former part of town, venturing N only to visit the Cham Ponagar Temple and S to see Bao Dai's Villa at Cau Da. Although, the best hotels are to be found in the seaside town, the best restaurants are undoubledly situated in the commercial district.

Places of interest

On a hill just outside the city is the **Cham Ponagar Temple complex**, known locally as Thap Ba. Originally the complex consisted of eight towers, four of which remain. Their stylistic differences indicate that they were built at different times between the 7th and 12th centuries. The largest (at 23m high) was built in 817 AD and contains a statue of Lady Thien Y-ana, also known as Ponagar (who was the beautiful wife of Prince Bac Hai) as well as a fine and very large lingam. She taught the people of the area weaving and new agricultural techniques, and they built the tower in her honour. The other towers are dedicated to gods: the central tower to Cri Cambhu (which has become a fertility temple for childless couples), the NW tower to Sandhaka (wood cutter and foster father to Lady Thien Y-ana), and the S tower to Ganeca (Lady Thien Y-ana's daughter). The best time to visit the towers is in the late afternoon, 1600-1700. Admission to temple complex 5,000d. **To get to the towers**: either walk or catch a cyclo. Take 2 Thang 4 St N out of town; Cham Ponagar is just over the second of two bridges, less than 1 km from the city centre. En route to the towers, the road crosses the **Cai River estuary** where there are mechanized fishing nets and a diversity of fishing craft – including coracles.

The best known pagoda in Nha Trang is the **Longson Pagoda**, built in 1963, which can be found on 23 Thang 10 St (the W extension of Yersin St). Inside the sanctuary is an unusual image of the Buddha, backlit with natural light (ask a monk for access if the building is closed). Murals depicting the jataka stories decorate the upper walls. To the right of the sanctuary, stairs lead up to a 9m high white Buddha, perched on a hill top, from where there are fine views. The pagoda commemorates those monks and nuns who died demonstrating against the Diem government. In particular those who, through their self-immolation, brought the despotic nature of the Diem regime and its human rights abuses to the attention of the American public.

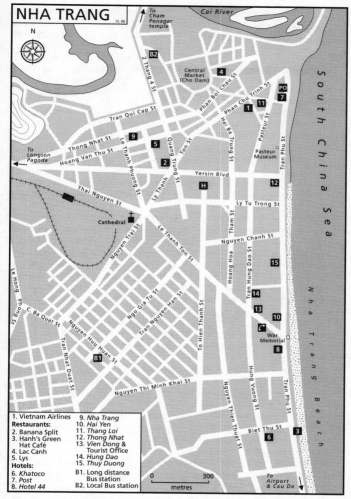

NHA TRANG VL 86

N

To
Cham
Ponagar
temple

Cai River

South China Sea

Central Market
(Cho Dam) 4

2 Thang 4 St B2

Phan Boi Chau St

Phan Chu Trinh St

Hai Ba Trung St

Pasteur St

PO 7

1 11

Tran Qui Cap St

Thong Nhat St 9

Hoang Van Thu St

Le Thanh Phuong St

5

Quang Trung St

Ly Thanh Ton St

2

Yersin Blvd

H

Pasteur Museum

Tran Phu St

12

To
Longson
Pagoda

Thai Nguyen St

Ly Tu Trong St

Cathedral

Nguyen Trai St

Le Thanh Ton St

Tham Ton St

Nguyen Chanh St

Hoang Hoa

Tran Hung Dao St

15

14

13

10

War Memorial

8

Le Hong Phong

15 Thang 6

C. Ba Quat St

Nguyen Huu Huan St

Ngo Gia Tu St

Tran Nguyen Han St

To Hien Thanh St

Hung Vuong St

Tran Phu St

B1

Tran Nhat Duat St

Nguyen Thi Minh Khai St

Nguyen Thien Thuat St

Biet Thu St

6

3

Nha Trang Beach

To
Airport
& Cau Da

1. Vietnam Airlines
Restaurants:
2. Banana Split
3. Hanh's Green Hat Café
4. Lac Canh
5. Lys
Hotels:
6. *Khatoco*
7. *Post*
8. *Hotel 44*
9. *Nha Trang*
10. *Hai Yen*
11. *Thang Loi*
12. *Thong Nhat*
13. *Vien Dong & Tourist Office*
14. *Hung Dao*
15. *Thuy Duong*
B1. Long distance Bus station
B2. Local Bus station

0   300
metres

Nha Trang Cathedral, granite-coloured (though built of concrete) and imposing, was built in 1933 on a small rock outcrop. The cathedral has a single, crenellated tower, with stained glass in the upper sections of its windows and pierced metal in the lower. The path to the cathedral runs off Nguyen Trai St. Daily mass is said here. The **Yersin Museum**, 8 Tran Phu St S from the Post Office, is contained within the colonnaded Pasteur Institute founded by the great scientist's protégé, Dr Alexander Yersin. Swiss-born Yersin first arrived in

Vietnam in 1891 and recommended that Dalat be developed as a hill resort. He was also a moving force behind the cul-tivation of rubber trees in Vietnam. Ask to be shown the museum by one of the staff, open Mon-Sat 0730-1100. The

---

"MARINE CONSERVATION IN VIETNAM": A PERSONAL VIEW

In the summer of 1992, I came to this fascinating country as a marine scientist. My first research vessel was a small 10m wooden boat hired from a local fisherman. For three days, we snorkelled around the scenic limestone islands of Halong Bay, investigating the life under the turbid water. Since then, I have travelled up and down the coast with Vietnamese scientists, searching for sites worthy of conservation.

Not surprisingly, all the sites we surveyed harbour a diversity of fish, coral and other invertebrates; some are frequented by turtles and dugongs. Sadly, all sites suffer a cocktail of human-induced threats. While much of Halong Bay remains spectacular above water, the corals beneath are smothered by silt washed down from deforested hillsides.

South on the Son Tra Peninsula, near Danang, are beautiful beaches where women, young and old, in their *non la* wade in the water harvesting seaweed and shells. Beneath the water the coral is dead, infested with tall seaweed. Back on shore are huge mounds of dead corals the height of a man, waiting for transport to nearby kilns and cement factories. Further S still is the famous seaside town of Nha Trang. Away from major rivers, Nha Trang is blessed with crystal blue sea where coral reefs with arrays of colourful fish, seastars and shells flourish. Here the country's first marine park was proposed in 1994. But as most of the nearby reefs have been dynamited by poverty-driven fishermen, more and more tourists crowd this tiny island and its surrounding waters throwing their devastating anchors and beer cans onto the previously undisturbed reefs. More subtle interference is taking place as the ornamental fish trade and aquarium business become lucrative.

But the tale is not entirely one of devastation. I did witness schools of jacks, barracuda and parrot fish on pristine reefs in some more remote areas. Two examples are the island groups of Con Dao some 200 km S of Ho Chi Minh City, and Phu Quoc, the 'wealthy kingdom' in the Gulf of Thailand. The two island groups remain blanketed in healthy forest and both areas support rich coral reefs. Con Dao, in particular, has escaped human pressure, thanks to its historical significance and low population. Until the ambitious development plans of the government materialize, Con Dao should remain relatively unspoilt. The coral reefs off the An Thoi Islands at the southern tip of Phu Quoc, are also in good condition, although certain species such as the highly priced groupers and sea cucumbers have been heavily exploited to satiate gourmands in Hong Kong and other Asian cities. There are more undisturbed areas, but for the sake of their safety, these locations will not be disclosed here.

The real encouragement lies not in discovering a new, pristine site, but in the growing awareness of my Vietnamese counterparts. The reward is the change from their cheers over trophies of dead squid and triton, to the vigorous criticism they now voice: "when we visited the island, the ranger offered us turtle eggs for tea, it's ridiculous!"

by Catherine Cheung

Khanh Hoa Museum is at 16 Tran Phu St. It contains a Dongson bronze drum and a palaeolithic stone xylophone. There is a room of ethnographics and, of course, a Ho Chi Minh room which contains several items of interest. English speaking curators will be pleased to show you around and should be tipped. The **Central Market** (*Cho Dam*) close to Nguyen Hong Son St is a good place to wander, although it is surrounded by rather unattractive mansion blocks. In the vicinity of the market, along **Phan Boi Chau St** for example, are some bustling streets with old colonial-style shuttered houses.

Excursions

Cau Da is a small fishing port 5 km S of Nha Trang, taking the beach road (Tran Phu St). Attractively sited on a small promontory outside Cau Da with magnificent views of Nha Trang harbour is a villa of former Emperor Bao Dai – now a hotel (see accommodation). On the Nha Trang edge of this village is the **Institute of Oceanography and Aquarium**. Built in 1922, it claims to be the first and only institute of its kind in Vietnam: it contains a small selection of poorly-displayed marine fauna including turtles, lion and puffer fish, lobsters and seahorses. Behind the aquarium is a museum of preserved marine life. Admission 5,000d. Open 0730-1130, 1330-1700 Mon-Sun. From the jetty at the far end of Cau Da, boats can be chartered to the **fish-rearing 'aquarium'** on **Mieu Island**. A 2-3 hrs trip should cost 30,000-40,000d. Near the jetty and perched on the decks of the fishing boats, can be seen bamboo and resin *thung chai*: small, circular boats akin to coracles. Similar boats can be seen elsewhere in Vietnam, for example at the port of Hon Gai. Cau Da has an array of souvenir stalls selling such environmentally unsound products as mounted horseshoe crabs, lobsters, sharks and turtles, along with many beautiful shells and shell jewellery. The limestone islands off Nha Trang are famous for the quality and quantity of birds' nests that they produce, used to make birds' nest soup (see page 291). Boats can also be hired from Cau Da Pier to visit some of these islands; expect to pay about US$30-40 for the day (1 boat, capacity 10 people). *Getting there*: either bicycle or take one of the lambros which regularly leave for the port from the Central Market (Cho Dam) in Nha Trang.

Hon Chong Beach and headland (Husband Rocks) is to be found 200m past the Cham Ponagar Towers; take a right turn down a track and walk for a further 1 km. The water of the crescent-shaped bay is clear and usually calmer than that of Nha Trang Beach, although the beach is rather dirty. The snorkelling is good. At the S end of the bay is the Hon Chong Promontory. The rock perched at the end of the promontory has a large, rather pudgy, indentation in it – said to have been made by the hand of a male giant. It looks more like a paw and is disfigured with graffiti. There are numerous beachfront cafés here. *Getting there*: by cyclo, walking the last 1 km, or a 3 km cycle ride from the centre of town. Admission 2,000d.

Ba Ho consists of a series of rapids and pools in a remote woodland area. Huge boulders have been sculpted and smoothed by the dashing stream. *Getting there*: 20 km N of Nha Trang along Highway 1 and a 2 km walk – usually accompanied by self-appointed 'guides', wear trainers.

Tours

Boats can be hired to visit the islands off Nha Trang. Recommended are the trips organized by the *Hai Yen Café* (*Hai Yen Hotel*) and *Hanh's Green Hat Café* on the beach, 400m S of the war memorial: both charge US$7 including snorkelling equipment and a bounteous seafood lunch. Book the night before. Boats leave early from the harbour beyond

Cau Da. Boats can also be hired at the harbour, 150,000d for the day (capacity 20 people, snorkelling equipment provided).Some visitors have reported being charged exhorbitant sums for seafood lunches on outlying islands. A French-Vietnamese company *Voiles Vietnam* offers very expensive diving cruises (2-4 days) in the islands and bays around Nha Trang. Book in Saigon, 17 Pham Ngoc Thach St, T 231589, or in Nha Trang, 36A Cau Da, next to pier, T 23966. The company also rents out diving equipment. Nha Trang Maritime Recovery, 44 Da Tuong St, T 22327, runs diving and snorkelling excursions at prices ranging from US$50 to US$7 (depending on numbers), experienced divers have questioned their safety.

Local information
● **Accommodation**
It can be hard finding a hotel to one's liking and many are the late arrivals who have spent a sleepless night fretting over the exhorbitant cost of the room necessity has compelled them to take. New hotels are springing up; the *Manila*, a 14-storey hotel which promises to be an oppressive concrete structure, will possibly help ease the situation, but at a high price to Nha Trang's distinguished sea front.

A-B Cau Da, Tran Phu St (just before Cau Da village), T 22449, F 21906, a/c, a villa of former Emperor Bao Dai, with magnificent views over the harbour and outlying islands, sited on a small promontory, with large elegant rooms, boat tours arranged (US$20), usually fully booked, but inefficient staff.

B Hang Hai (Maritime), 34 Tran Phu St, T 21969, F 21922, new, large concrete edifice whose architecture will win no prizes, some way S of town, quiet setting, glorious sea views from upper floors; **B-C Hotel 44**, 44 Tran Phu St, T 22445, large colonial mansion with spacious elegant, rooms overlooking the sea, cheaper bungalows at the back, rec; **B-C Nha Trang**, 129 Thong Nhat St, T 22347, a/c; **B-C Nha Trang**, 24 Tran Phu St T 22671, some a/c; **B-C Vien Dong**, 1 Tran Hung Dao St, T 21606, F 21912, some a/c, hot water, pool (open to outsiders for 5,000d), tennis, cheapest rooms are good value, most popular in Nha Trang, booked up weeks ahead; rec; **B-D Hai Au**, 177 Tran Phu St, T 22722, unlovely building but nice position overlooking beach; **B-D Hai Yen**, 40 Tran Phu St, T 22974, F 21902, some a/c, incl breakfast, large, characterless but comfortable and friendly with large rooms, sea view, access to *Vien Dong Hotel's* pool; **B-D Que Huong**, 60 Tran Phu St, T 25047, restaurant, clean, friendly, rec; **B-D Thang Loi**, 4 Pasteur St, T 22241, F 21905, some a/c, newly renovated, clean, friendly, with 'courtyard', rec; **B-D Thong Nhat**, 18 Tran Phu St, T 22966, some a/c, friendly staff, good large clean rooms, dorm beds available (**F**), rec.

D Hai Au II, 4 Nguyen Chanh, large but basic rooms, fan only, no hot water; **D Hai Quan** (Navy Guesthouse), 58 Tran Phu St, T 22997, nicely restored bungalow overlooks the beach, rather barrack-like block at the back, overpriced, often full; **D Hung Dao**, 3 Tran Hung Dao St, T 22246, friendly, but reports of thefts from rooms; **D 'Railway' Hotel**, 40 Thai Nguyen St, T 22298, some a/c, a little decrepit, but cheap; **D Thuy Duong**, 36A Tran Phu St, T 22534, a/c, good value, rec; **D-E Hotel 62**, 62 Tran Phu, T 21395, cheap, but reports suggest it may have been closed by police for immoral activities.

● **Places to eat**
There are a number of seafood restaurants and cafés along the beach front road. US$2 for a freshly cooked seafood platter. Sandwich stalls make good peanut butter sandwiches. **♦♦♦Vien Dong Hotel**, poolside restaurant, candle-lit at night, entertainment, a bit touristy but good food; **♦♦Cafe des Amis**, 16 Tran Phu St, good for breakfast, vegetarian and seafood dinners; **♦♦Lac Canh**, 11 Hang Ca St, serves excellent Chinese and Vietnamese food, with seafood specialities, best are the meats, squid and prawns barbecued at your table, smoky atmosphere and can be hard to get a table, rec; **♦♦Nha Hang 76**, 76 Tran Phu St; **♦♦Restaurant Lys**, 117A Hoang Van Thu St, Vietnamese and other Asian, rec; **♦♦Than Lan**, Le Thanh Ton, opp *Vien Dong Hotel*, nice garden setting and good food; **♦♦Thong Nhat Hotel Restaurant**, 18 Tran Phu St, Vietnamese, seafood, excellent spring rolls or 'rocket shrimps'; **♦♦Thuy Duong**, 36A Tran Phu St, seafood specialities in 60s-style diner building, service leaves a little to be desired; **♦♦Vietnam Restaurant**, 23 Hoang Van Thu St, excellent food; **♦Banana Split**, 58 Quang Trung St, excellent breakfasts, popular meeting place; **♦Hanh's Green Hat**, on beach 400m S of war memorial, popular; **♦Tu Quy**, 272 Thong Nhat St (at

the foot of big Buddha); *Austrian Pub*, 34 Tran Phu St, stays open late and serves food as well as cold beer; *Phuong Sang*, Hon Chong Bay (S end), Vietnamese, right on the beach.

● **Airline offices**
Vietnam Airlines, 26 Han Thuyen St, T 23797, open 0700-1100, 1330-1615.

● **Banks & money changers**
Vietcombank, 17 Quang Trung – will change most major currencies, cash, TCs, and cash advances on some credit cards. Gold shops nr Dam market will also change money.

● **Entertainment**
Ballroom dancing: at the *Hai Yen Hotel*, highly entertaining.

● **Hospital & medical services**
General Hospital, 19 Yersin St, T 22168.

● **Post & telecommunications**
Post Office: 2 Tran Phu St.
International telex and telephone: 50 Le Thanh Ton St (opp *Vien Dong Hotel*).
TNT International Express: T 21043.

● **Shopping**
Bookshop: 73 Thong Nhat St.
Local speciality: *Banh trang duong*; local sugar rock.
Seashells and shell jewellery: mounted marine life (lobsters, horseshoe crabs, turtles etc) – environmentalism and conservation are not words on the lips of many Vietnamese.

● **Sports**
Fishing: boats and equipment can be hired from Cau Da Pier (see Excursions); contact Khanh Hoa Tourism, 1 Tran Hung Dao St for more information.

● **Tourist offices**
Khanh Hoa Tourism, 1 Tran Hung Dao St, T 22753, F 24206.

● **Transport**
105 km from Phan Rang, 190 km from Buon Ma Thuot, 215 km from Dalat, 238 km from Quy Nhon, 445 km from Saigon, 1,299 km from Hanoi.

Local Bicycle hire: from some hotels, for example *Hai Duong* (10,000d/day), *Hai Yen* and *Vien Dong*. **Car hire**: from the *Vien Dong Hotel*, 1 Tran Hung Dao, or from the watch shop, 45 Le Thanh Ton, T 21858. Negotiate price. Also **cyclos**.

Air Connections on **Vietnam Airlines** with Saigon and with Hanoi. Saigon daily 0835 or 1230 (50 mins), US$60. Hanoi Tues, Thur and Sat 1600 (2½ hrs, US$130). Danang; Tues and Thur 0840 (65 mins, US$50).

Train The station is a yellow wash colonial building with blue shutters on Thai Nguyen St. The booking office is at 17 Thai Nguyen St, T 22113, open 0800-1430 Mon-Sun. Regular connections with Hanoi and Saigon and all stops between the two. (See timetable, page 293.) **Train times**: depart *Nha Trang*: 1700, arrive Saigon 0500; 0505, arrive Danang 1630, arrive Hué 1952, arrive Hanoi 1120 + 1; 2045, arrive Danang 0841 + 1, arrive Hué 1257 + 1, arrive Hanoi 0540 +2. **Fares**: **Saigon**: hard seat 110,000d, soft seat 142,000d, soft bed 255,000d. **Danang**: hard seat 138,000d, soft seat 178,000d, soft bed 322,000d. **Hué**: hard seat 163,000d, soft seat 211,000d, soft bed 385,000d. **Hanoi**: hard seat 359,000d, soft seat 470,000d, soft bed 865,000d.

Road Bus: the long distance bus station (*Ben Xe Lien Tinh*) is opp 212 Ngo Gia Tu St, close to the intersection with Nguyen Huu Huan St at the SW edge of town. Connections with Saigon, Phan Rang, Danang, Quy Nhon, Dalat, Hué and Vinh. The express bus ticket office is at 6A Hoang Hoa Tham St (*Diem Ban Ve Xe Du Lich*, T 22010); buses leave between 0430 and 0500, advance booking recommended. Express bus connections with Saigon, Hanoi, Quang Ngai, Danang, Dalat, Hué and Vinh. The local bus station is opp 115 2 Thang 4 St. Lambros run from the Central Market (Cho Dam) to Cau Da. Most hotels advertise minibus connections, depart for Saigon 0400 arrive 1300, US$11. For Danang depart 0500 arrive 1600, Hué depart 0500, arrive 1800, US$15. **Car**: cars and minibuses can be hired from **Khanh Hoa Tourism's** *Tourist Car Enterprise* at 1 Nguyen Thi Minh Khai St. Costs pp are about US$20 to Saigon, US$10 to Dalat, US$20 to Danang, US$20 to Hué and US$60 to Hanoi (prices are charged/vehicle and vary according to size), and see Car hire above.

Cam Ranh Bay

Cam Ranh Bay lies 50 km S of Nha Trang. Highway 1 skirts around this bay – one of the world's largest natural harbours – once an important US naval base and then taken over by the Soviets. In fact the Soviets, or at least the Russians, were here before the Americans: they used it for re-provisioning during the Russo-Japanese war of 1904, which they emphatically lost. After re-unification in 1975, the Vietnamese allowed the Soviets to use this fine natural harbour once again as part-payment for the support (political and financial) that they were receiving. However, from the late 1980s, the former Soviet fleet began to wind down its presence here as Cold War tensions in the area eased and economic pressures forced the former USSR to reduce military expenditure. Now the port is almost deserted. Cam Ranh is also a centre for Vietnam's salt industry; for miles around the scenery is white with salt pans (looking like wintry paddy fields) produce pure, crystalline sea salt. There is a modest **Cao Dai Church** near the intersection of Highway 1 and the road leading towards the Bay (Da Bac St). Contining E along Da Bac St, the road leads to a thriving fish market (down a pair of narrow alleys) and then to a busy boatyard producing small fishing vessels. At 120 Da Bac St is Chua Phuoc Hai, an attractive little Buddhist temple. **Accommodation** There is nowhere to stay in Cam Ranh, but following Highway 1 2 km S is *Hotel Restaurant Nguyen Quang*, which has two rooms on stilts over a lake. *Getting there*: by bus from the local station opp 115 2 Thang 4 St.

Phan Rang

Few tourists stop at Phan Rang, a small seaside town of about 50,000 and the capital of Ninh Thuan Province. Phan Rang was once the capital of Champa when it was known as Panduranga and there are a number of Cham temples nearby. The town and surrounding area are still home to a small population of **Cham**. In the centre of town at 305 Thong Nhat St (Highway 1) is a large salmon-pink **pagoda** with fine roof decoration. South from the pagoda, opposite 326 Thong Nhat St is the entrance to **Phan Rang Market** (*Cho Phan Rang*).

Excursions Po Klaung-garai is a group of Cham towers on the road towards Dalat, 6 km from Phan Rang. Built during the 13th century, they are located on a cactus and boulder-strewn hill with commanding views over the surrounding countryside. Raised up on a brick base, the towers have been extensively renovated. The central tower has a (new?) figure of dancing Siva over the main entrance and, inside, Siva's vehicle, the bull Nandi. *Getting there*: bicycle or take a cyclo or local bus towards Dalat; 2 km beyond the village of Thap Cham turn right when a concrete water tank comes into view. The towers are visible a short distance along this track. The temple complex has been looked after by a Cham caretaker since 1968.

Po Ro Me is another group of more recently constructed Cham buildings, which can be seen in the distance from Po Klaung-garai, rising up from the valley floor. Po Ro Me was the last king of independent Champa (1627-1651), and he died a prisoner of the Vietnamese. *Getting there*: it is not easy: drive S on Highway 1 from Phan Rang towards Saigon; the towers are a 5 km walk from the road. Ask for *Thap Cham Po Ro Me*.

Finally, there is a **third group of Cham towers**, in poor condition, 16 km from town right at the side of Highway 1 N to Nha Trang.

Tuan Tu is a small Cham village, about 5 km S of Phan Rang. To visit the community, special permission has to be obtained from the local police/district authorities. They may ask for a sizeable fee and may also insist that one of their men accompany any visitors.

● **Accommodation** C *Huu Nghi*, 1 Hung Vuong St (just off the road to Thap Cham, 200m from Highway 1), T 74, some a/c, 'At the service of country and foreign visitors'; **E** *Phan Rang*, 354 Thong Nhat St (Highway 1).

● **Places to eat** ♦♦*Huu Nghi*, 1 Hung Vuong St, Vietnamese.

● **Banks & money changers** Foreign Exchange Service, 334 Thong Nhat St.

● **Transport** 105 km from Nha Trang, 110 km from Dalat, 318 km from Saigon. **Train** The closest stop is Thap Cham, about 5 km W of town. See timetable, page 293. **Road Bus**: the long-distance bus station is 500m N of the centre of town opp 66 Thong Nhat St. Regular connections with Saigon, Dalat, Nha Trang and Danang. The local bus station is S of town, opp 428 Thong Nhat St.

PHAN RANG TO DALAT via the Ngoan Muc Pass

The 100 km trip between Dalat and Phan Rang is spectacular but sometimes excruciatingly uncomfortable by bus. The narrow strip of land between the highlands and the coast is an area of intensive rice, tobacco and grape cultivation. Winding upwards, the road passes under a massive pipe carrying water from the mountains down to the turbines of a hydropower plant in the valley. It then works its way through the dramatic Ngoan Muc Pass to the Dalat Plateau.

Dalat

Dalat is situated on a plateau in the Central Highlands, at an altitude of almost 1,500m, and has a population of 130,000. To the N are the five volcanic peaks of the Lang Biang mountains, rising to 2,400m. The town itself is centred on a lake – Xuan Huong – amidst rolling countryside. In the vicinity are forests, waterfalls, and an abundance of orchids and other temperate flora. As in other colonial possessions in Southeast Asia, the French developed this highland area as a hill resort to which hot and flustered colonial servants and businessmen and their families, could retire during the summer heat. The city was founded in 1897 after the site had been discovered by Dr. Alexander Yersin who recommended that it be developed as a hill resort. By 1935 a railway line had been laid linking it with Saigon, via Phan

Rang. The French built timber frame houses to remind them of Europe, and complained about the locals and the stinking heat of Saigon. It is still a resort town – but now for Vietnamese, rather than their former colonial masters.

Places of interest

More than other towns in Vietnam, Dalat has a distinctly French air with its lakeside cafés, Catholic church and the large colonial hotels. Along with the sedate pace of life, cool climate, good food and elegant hotels and villas, it is one of the most charming towns in Vietnam.

The central **Xuan Huong Lake** (originally the Grand Lake – renamed in 1954) was created in 1919 after a small dam was constructed at the W end of the valley. Boats can be hired from the *Thanh Tuy Restaurant* on the N shore. A road runs around the perimeter of the lake, a pleasant and easy bicycle ride. At the NE end of the lake is the **Dalat Flower Garden**. Established in 1966, it supports a modest range of temperate and tropical plants including orchids (in the orchid house), roses, camelias, lilies and hydrangeas. Admission 2,000d. Open 0730-1600 Mon-Sun.

Visible from the lake, and next to the *Dalat Hotel*, is the single-spired **Dalat Cathedral**. Construction began in 1931, although the building was not completed until the Japanese 'occupation' in the 1940s. The stained-glass windows, with their vivid colours and use of pure, clean lines, were crafted in France by Louis Balmet between 1934 and 1940. Lining the nave are blocks of woodcarvings of Jesus and the crucifixion. Mass is held twice a day at 0530 and 1715.

Many of the large **colonial villas** – universally washed in pastel yellow – are 1930s and 40s vintage. Some have curved walls, railings and are almost nautical in inspiration; others are reminiscent of houses in Provence. Many of the larger villas can be found along Tran Hung Dao St. They are now owned by

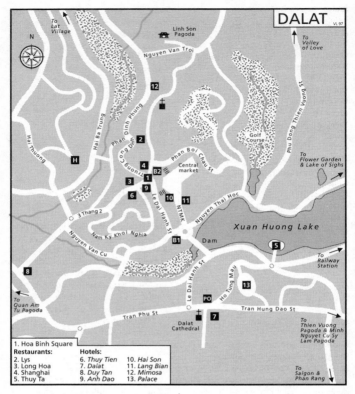

DALAT VL 97

To Lat Village

N

Linh Son Pagoda

To Valley of Love

Nguyen Van Troi

12

Hai Ba Trung

Phan Dinh Phung

Hai Thuong

Cong Dinh

2

4 B2

Phan Boi Chau St

Central market

Golf Course

Phu Dong Thien Vuong St

To Flower Garden & Lake of Sighs

H

3

1

9

6

10

11

Le Dai Hanh St

NTMK

Nguyen Thai Hoc

5

Xuan Huong Lake

3 Thang 2

Nam Ky Khoi Nghia

B1

Dam

To Railway Station

Nguyen Van Cu

8

To Quan Am Tu Pagoda

Le Dai Hanh St

Ho Tung Mau

13

PO

7

Dalat Cathedral

Tran Phu St

Tran Hung Dao St

To Thien Vuong Pagoda & Minh Nguyet Cu Sy Lam Pagoda

To Saigon & Phan Rang

1. Hoa Binh Square

Restaurants:
2. Lys
3. Long Hoa
4. Shanghai
5. Thuy Ta

Hotels:
6. *Thuy Tien*
7. *Dalat*
8. *Duy Tan*
9. *Anh Dao*
10. *Hai Son*
11. *Lang Bian*
12. *Mimosa*
13. *Palace*

the Provincial Tourism Authority and can be rented (see below), a wonderfully civilized way to stay in Dalat. Perhaps the largest and most impressive house is the **former residence of the Governor General** at 12 Tran Hung Dao St – now the *Hotel Dinh II*. 1930s in style, with large airy rooms and uncomfortable furniture, it occupies a magnificent position overlooking the town. The house is a popular place for domestic tourists to have their photographs taken with the requisite stuffed animals. Admission 2,000d. Open 730-1130, 1330-1630 Mon-Sun. North of here, in the valley and off Quang Trung St, is the **Dalat Railway Station**, a must for railway enthusiasts. It was opened in 1938, 5 years after the completion of the rack and pinion track from Saigon and was closed in 1976. In 1991 a 7 km stretch to the village of Trai Met was reopened and twice a day a small Russian-built diesel car makes the journey (see Excursions page 238). There is also a coal and oil-burning steam engine which is occasionally fired-up and an old Renault diesel car.

Quan Am Tu Pagoda (Lam Ty Ni Pagoda) is at 2 Chien My St. Unremarkable, save for a charming monk, Vien Thuc, who lives here. The main sanctuary was built in 1961 and contains an image of the Buddha with an electric halo. Vien Thuc arrived in 1968 and in 1987 he finished the gateway that leads up through a garden to the figure of Quan Am. He is hoping to construct an 8-storey pagoda to complement the gate. Vien Thuc also shows visitors around his small garden – which is almost Japanese in inspiration – behind the main sanctuary. He has named the garden An Lac Vien, or 'Peace Garden' and it features a miniature forest path. Vien Thuc is also an accomplished artist and sells his work at modest prices. The **Linh Son Pagoda** is at 120 Nguyen Van Troi St, just up from the intersection with Phan Dinh Phung St. Built in 1942 and still in good condition, the pagoda is reserved for men. Perched on a small hillock, the sanctuary is fronted by two dragon balustrades, themselves flanked by two ponds with miniature mountain scenes. To the right is a military-looking turret.

4 km from the centre of town, at the end of Khe Sanh St, is the **Thien Vuong Pagoda**. Begun in the 1950s, this stark pagoda has recently been expanded and renovated. In the main sanctuary are three massive bronze-coloured sandalwood standing figures with Sakyamuni, the historic Buddha, in the centre. Just before Thien Vuong St is another pagoda: **Minh Nguyet Cu Sy Lam**. The sanctuary is to the right of the main gates. These two pagodas, though in no way artistically significant, are popular with local visitors and stalls nearby sell local jams, artichoke tea, cordials and dried mushrooms.

Vietnam's last emperor, Bao Dai, had a **Summer Palace** on Le Hong Phong St, about 2 km from the town centre. Built on a hill with views on every side, it is Art Deco in style both inside and out, and rather modest for a palace. The stark interior contains little to indicate that this was the home of an emperor – perhaps many of Bao Dai's personal belongings have been removed. The impressive dining-room contains an etched glass map of Vietnam, while the study has Bao Dai's desk, a few personal ornaments and photographs, and a small collection of his books: Shakespeare's comedies, Voltaire, Brontë and the Bible. According to US reports, by 1952 Bao Dai was receiving an official stipend of US$4mn/year. Much of this was ferreted away in US and Swiss bank accounts – insurance against the day when his reign would end. The rest was spent on his four private planes – leaving little to lavish on his home. The palace is very popular with Vietnamese tourists who run riot lying on the beds, sitting in the chairs and having their photographs taken wherever they can. Admission 1,000d. Open 0700-1130, 1300-1630 Mon-Sun.

Dalat Market (*Cho Dalat*) is at the end of Nguyen Thi Minh Khai St and sells, to the eyes of an average lowland Vietnamese, a dazzling array of exotic fruits and vegetables grown in the temperate climate of the area: plums, strawberries, carrots, potatoes, loganberries, cherries, apples, onions and avocados. Fields of vegetables can be seen downstream from the Xuan Huong Dam.

Climate

Nights are cool throughout the year in Dalat, especially so from Oct to Mar. Temperatures range from 4°C in Dec and Jan, to 26°C in Mar and Apr. The rainy season stretches from May to Nov, with heaviest rains in Aug and Sep. Even during the warmest months it can be chilly in the evening.

Excursions

The area surrounding Dalat was a beautiful wilderness until fairly recently. It is still beautiful, but no longer a wilderness. It is said that during the War, US soldiers would come to hunt tiger, leopard, stag, bear and other game, only to find that they themselves were being hunted – not by the animals, but by the Viet Cong who lived and fought in the forests and mountains. Sadly, the authorities have not controlled deforestation in the Dalat area: the land on either side of the road up from Saigon is almost entirely cleared, except for a narrow band of pine forest around Dalat itself and on the steeper slopes.

The landscape around Dalat is characterized by fast-flowing rivers and waterfalls. **Cam Ly Waterfall** is the closest waterfall to Dalat, 2 km W of the town centre on Hoang Van Thu St. Tacky, but in a rather quaint 70s style, Dalat Tourism has its own posse of cowboys who lend the area a 'not really anywhere' feel. Open 0700-1800 Mon-Sun. **Dantania Falls** are along a track, 5 km out of town on the road towards Saigon. The path leads steeply downwards into a forested ravine; it is an easy hike there, but tiring on the return journey. The falls – really a cascade – are hardly spectacular, but few people come here except at weekends so it is usually peaceful. Admission 5,000d. **Prenn Falls** are also on the route to Saigon, next to the road, 15 km from Dalat. The falls were dedicated to Queen Sirikit of Thailand when she visited them in 1959. There is a restaurant here. Admission 5,000d (additional 3,000d for camera). *Getting there*: by bus en route towards Saigon.

Lake of Sighs lies 5 km NE of Dalat. The lake is said by some to be named after the sighs of the girls being courted by handsome young men from the military academy in Dalat. Another unlikely theory is that the name was coined after a young Vietnamese maiden, Mai Nuong, drowned herself in the lake in the 18th century. The story is that her lover, Hoang Tung, had joined the army to fight the Chinese who were mounting one of their periodic invasions of the country, and had thoughtlessly failed to tell her. Devastated, and thinking that Hoang Tung no longer loved her, she committed suicide in the lake. Not long ago the lake was surrounded by thick forest; today it is a thin wood. Souvenir shops, incredibly, sell stuffed tigers (no

environmental movement here), while Montagnard 'cowboys' with plastic guns and holsters lead horses along the forest trails. The area is busy at weekends. The **Valley of Love** or Thung Lung Tinh Yeu is 5 km due N of Dalat. Boats can be hired on the lake here, there is horse 'riding' and a few refreshment stands.

Getting to the waterfalls and lakes Because of the cool climate, the best way to reach the lakes, forests and waterfalls around Dalat is on foot or by bicycle.

Trai Met Village can be reached by train from Dalat. In 1991 a 7 km stretch of track from Dalat Railway Station to the village of Trai Met was reopened after 15 years of inoperation and every day at 0800 and 1400 a small Russian-built diesel car makes the return journey. The train can be hired at other times for a cost of around US$10. The journey to Trai Met village takes you near the Lake of Sighs and past immaculately tended vegetable gardens; no space on the valley floors or sides is wasted and the high intensity agriculture is a marvellous sight. Trai Met is a prosperous market village with piles of produce from the surrounding area. Walk 300m up the road and to the left a narrow lane leads down to Chua Linh Phuoc, an attractive Buddhist temple more than 50 years old. It is currently undergoing restoration and is notable for its huge Buddha and mosaic adorned pillars. The mosaics are made of broken rice bowls and fragments of beer bottle. *Getting there*: from the railway station off Quang Trung St.

In the vicinity of Dalat are a number of **villages**, both of **tribal minorities**, and of **migrants** who have been relocated here by the authorities – in some cases former inmates of re-education camps. The best-known group of such villages are the **Lat** communities, 10 km NW of town. At present, local officials are not keen to have foreigners visiting the villages. There have been numerous reports of fines being imposed – anything up to US$100 pp (one group managed to bargain their fine down from US$100 to US$15 pp). In theory, it should be possible to obtain a permit from the police in Dalat, although these are not always granted.

Local information
● **Accommodation**

Dalat has a large number of hotels and guesthouses, but some are reserved for Vietnamese and will not accept foreign visitors. Others charge exorbitant rates, sometimes higher than the equivalent accommodation in Saigon. Rooms can, therefore, be scarce. The provincial tourism authorities may ease this policy, allowing cheaper hotels to take foreign guests at realistic rates. Dalat can be cold at night and while most hotels charging room rates of US$10 upwards will have hot water, cheaper establishments, and cheaper rooms, may not. It is worth checking.

A *Dinh II Villa*, 12 Tran Hung Dao St, T 22092, former Governor General's residence, grand but full of noisy tourists for most of the day, unfriendly staff; **A** *Sofitel Dalat Palace*, 1 Tran Phu St, T 25444, F 25666, attractive colonial hotel overlooking lake, has undergone renovations in a joint venture with a Hong Kong company, a new wing has been added, should reopen late '95/early '96.

B *Anh Dao*, 50 Hoa Binh Sq, T 22384, newly renovated, smart, clean but expensive; **B** *Dalat*, 7 Tran Phu St, next to the cathedral, former grand colonial hotel, now undergoing renovation, should reopen in 1996, good location, good views; **B** *Hai Son*, 1 Nguyen Thi Minh Khai St, T 22379, dark and dingy, overpriced, noisy, price includes breakfast; **B-C** *Thuy Tien*, 7 3 Thang 2 St, T 21731, central, close to market and 5 mins from bus station, large rooms, with hot water; **B-C** *Tree House*, 3 Huynh Thuc Khang St, T 22070, 1 km out of town, curious house designed by woman architect incorporating cobwebs and a giraffe, 3,000d admission, some rooms with private bath and hot water too.

C *Duy Tan*, 83 3 Thang 2 St, T 2216, good location with average rooms, some dormitory beds (**E**); **C** *Xuan Huong*, Ho Xuan Huong St, T 22317, S side and overlooking lake; **C-D** *Cam Do*, 81 Phan Dinh Phung St, T 22732, friendly service but a bit noisy, restaurant.

D *Hoa Binh*, 64 Truong Cong Dinh St, T 22787, friendly, hot water, cheaper rooms have shared facilities; **D** *Langbian*, 6B Nguyen Thi Minh Khai St, T 22419, clean, hot water; **D** *Mimosa*, 170 Phan Dinh Phung St, T 22656, rather inconvenient location, hot water, helpful staff, car rental and bicycle hire, run tours, rec; **D** *Nha Khach Com*, 48 Phan Dinh Phung St, small and friendly, good value, restaurant; **D** *Pensée 6*, 6 3 Thang 4 St, T 22378, located on the road in from Saigon, 20 mins walk from Hoa Binh Sq, hot water, local branch of Sinh Café, Saigon, minibus to Saigon and Nha Trang (US$7); **D** *Thanh The*, 118 Phan Dinh Phung St, T 22180, hot water, large rooms, local tours, restaurant, helpful staff, popular.

E *Hoang Yen*, 90 Phan Dinh Phung St, T 23738, hot water, welcoming.

Villas: along Tran Hung Dao St and run by the provincial tourism company. A whole villa can be rented for US$15 (with bargaining) – very civilized, although slightly out of town. Either knock on the door or go to the Provincial Tourism Office.

● **Places to eat**

The cool climate allows a wide range of temperate fruits and vegetables to be cultivated; probably the best quality produce in Vietnam. Excellent vegetarian food is available in the market and good pastries and cakes from vendors on street corners. Cafés line Nguyen Thi Minh Khai St, leading to Dalat Market, and nearby Le Dai Hanh St which runs down from Hoa Binh Sq and the cinema. There are a number of lakeside restaurants which look romantic places to eat but are badly staffed, serve indifferent food, and are plagued with beggars.

Vietnamese: ♦♦*Do Yen*, 7 Hoa Binh Sq, food receives mixed reviews; ♦♦*Lys*, 98 Truong Cong Dinh, good Vietnamese and Chinese, rec; ♦♦*Palace*, 2 Tran Phu St, dine in moth-eaten splendour, also serves French food; ♦♦*Shanghai*, 8 Hoa Binh Sq, extensive Vietnamese, Chinese and European menu which includes 'the penis of beef steamed with tonic medicine of Chinese', goats testis and other delicacies, popular and good; ♦♦*Thanh Thanh*, 4 Tang Bat Ho St, just off Hoa Binh Sq, good soups and crab dishes; ♦♦*Thanh Thuy*, Nguyen Thai Hoc St (N side of the lake not far from the Dalat bus station), tables overlooking the lake; ♦♦*Thuy Ta*, lovely position overlooking the lake, below the *Palace Hotel*; ♦♦*Xuan Huong*, Ho Xuan Huong St (W end and overlooking the lake); ♦*Cam Do*, 81 Phan Dinh Phung St, good, cheap food; ♦*Dang A*, 82 Phan Dinh

Phung St, speciality dishes; ◆*Long Hoa*, 6 3 Thang 2, French/English speaking owner, great breakfast, good and cheap meals; ◆*Thanh Tra*, 67 3 Thang 2 St.

● **Airline offices**
Vietnam Airlines, 5 Truong Cong Dinh St, T 2895.

● **Banks & money changers**
There are two banks above the market; the **Industrial and Commercial Bank of Vietnam**, next to the *Anh Dao Hotel* on Hoa Binh Sq, offers a good rate of exchange and does exchange TCs, the other behind the cinema. *The Palace Hotel* also changes US$ cash but at disadvantageous rates.

● **Entertainment**
Dancing: at the *Dalat*, *Hai Son* and *Anh Dao* hotels. Also at the **Mini Star Dancing Club**, 6B Nguyen Thi Minh Khai St.

Jazz: *Duy Tan Hotel*, 83 3 Thang 2 St has a band which plays jazz and rock.

● **Post & telecommunications**
Post Office: 14 Tran Phu St (in front of *Dalat Hotel*).

● **Shopping**
Local delicacies: jams, artichoke tea, cordials and dried mushrooms. The artichoke tea is reputed to help in: 'liver well functioning; diuretic, increasing bile secretion; [and] lessening cholesterol and uremia'. Woodcarvings, stuffed animals (there can't be many left alive now).

● **Sports**
Golf: a course lies to the N side of Lake Xuan Huong. It is a joint venture with a Thai company.

Horse riding: really, horse leading. From around the *Palace Hotel*, Lake of Sighs and other popular tourist spots.

● **Tourist offices**
Lam Dong Provincial Tourist Office, 4 Tran Quoc Toan St, T 22125, F 22661. *Mimosa Hotel*, 170 Phan Dinh Phung, runs tours to local sites 0800-1600 daily (US$4) and to outlying destinations including the summit of Lang Biang Mountain, minority villages and waterfalls (US$8-25/day).

● **Transport**
110 km from Phan Rang, 210 km fron Nha Trang, 299 km from Saigon, 1,505 km from Hanoi.

Local Bicycle hire: from hotels, about 15,000d/day (rental charges are higher than elsewhere because the hilly terrain make accidents more frequent). Ask one of the employees if the hotel does not have any for rental. Also from a kiosk at the *Hai Son Hotel* end of the long distance bus station. **Car hire**: *Mimosa Hotel* and *Anh Dao Hotel*. **Motorcycle hire**: from some hotels. **Pony-drawn carriages**: around town.

Air Lien Khang airport is 30 km S of Dalat. There are connections with Saigon on Tues, Thur and Sun (50 mins, US$40).

Road Bus: Dalat has 2 bus stations, one long-distance, one local. But minibuses to Saigon and Hanoi (the fastest means of public transport) leave from both the local and the long-distance station. They are only 10 mins walk apart so it is easy enough to check which has the most convenient service. The **long distance bus station** (Ben Xe Dalat) is at the end of Nguyen Thi Minh Khai St, at the W extremity of Xuan Huong Lake and not far from the town centre. Express buses leave here in the early morning, about 0500, for Saigon, Nha Trang, Phan Rang, Hué, Quang Ngai, Buon Ma Thuot, Danang, Quy Nhon. The **local bus station** (Ben Xe Hoa Binh) is not far from Hoa Binh Sq, behind the cinema. Minibuses leave here at about 0500 for Hanoi, Vinh, Hué, Danang, Quy Nhon, and Nha Trang; and every hour from 0430 until about 1200 for Saigon. Most hotels advertise minibuses or cars, Saigon (US$10) and Nha Trang (US$8).

DALAT TO SAIGON

For the first 20 km out of Dalat on Highway 20 to Saigon the land is forested. But as the road descends on to the Bao Loc Plateau the forest is replaced by tea plantations and fruit orchards. Many of the farmers on the plateau settled here after fleeing from the N following partition in 1954. The plateau is dominated by the town of Bao Loc (180 km from Saigon, 120 km from Dalat), the capital of Lam Dong Province. There is a big, new hotel here, the *Seri Hotel*. The road then works its way down from the upland plateau through scrub bamboo forest towards the rolling landscape around Saigon, heavily cultivated with rubber and fruit trees. The road between Dalat and Saigon is good. At the important industrial centre of Bien Hoa, 26 km NE from Saigon, a road runs S to the beach resort of Vung Tau (113 km from Saigon).

Vung Tau

Vung Tau – formerly Cap-Saint-Jacques – is one of Vietnam's major ports and seaside resorts. It is situated on a promontory that juts out to sea, at the estuary of the Saigon River.

Before the 17th century, Vung Tau was under the control of the Khmer kings of Cambodia. A large dam and reservoir to the N of the city was built by one of the Cambodian kings to water his horses and elephants. In the 17th century, the Vietnamese annexed the surrounding territory, and later still the French gained control. The town began to develop as a seaside resort at the beginning of the 20th century when roads linking it with Saigon were constructed. It is now a popular resort town for (relatively) wealthy Vietnamese and foreign tourists. Vung Tau is one of the most prosperous cities in Vietnam, its wealth is based on oil, the port and tourism. It has also benefited from its new administrative role as provincial capital of newly created Ba Ria Vung Tau Province. Vung Tau is a popular bolt-hole with the expats from Saigon who drive down or take the hydrofoil at weekends. The fresh air and leisurely pace prove a relaxing contrast to the noisy metropolis which is, of course, exactly where the oilmen of Vung Tau head at the first opportunity.

Vung Tau is experiencing something of a building boom. Four or five large hotels are under construction or newly completed. But the town is unlikely to become another Bali or Pattaya for some time – even though recreational massage and prostitution do exist, and are on the increase. It is low key, quiet, and for the jaded Western tourist tired of run-of-the-mill beach resorts, rather charming – notwithstanding the appalling modern hotel architecture.

Places of interest

Being a beach resort one would expect good beaches but with the exception of Back Beach or Bai Sau, they are poor: narrow, with little or no sand, no coral and second-rate swimming. In the town itself is **Bai Truoc** or Front Beach, lined with kiosks and restaurants and really not a beach at all. Freighters moor offshore and fishing boats unload their catch at the S end of the bay, opposite the new *Hai Au Hotel*. South from town, taking the coast road (Ha Long St), is **Bai Dua** (formerly Roches Noires Beach) and a small collection of guesthouses. Again, the beach is poor. At Bai Dua there are two temples, one with a **large Buddha** looking out to sea, the other with an equally **large figure of Quan Am**. Also at Bai Dua is **Niet Ban Tinh Xa**, a pagoda built on a hill in 1971. It is said to be one of the largest temples in Vietnam, and contains a 5,000 kg bronze bell and a 12m-long reclining Buddha.

Around the headland is a small and peaceful cove with good surf – **Bai Nghinh Phong** (formerly Au Vents Beach); swimming can be dangerous here. Northeast from the headland, on Thuy Van St, and just past the **island pagoda of Hon Ba**, is the longest stretch of sand – **Bai Sau** (Back Beach). Bai Sau is about 2 km SE from town, taking Hoang Hoa Tham St. This is a beach in the usual sense of the word: 5 km of sand. It is exposed to the wind and the South China Sea and the surf is usually good, sometimes ferocious. A system of flags indicates whether swimming is safe: white (safe), red (unsafe). Swimming hours are 0700-1700. Regulations state: "People suffering from mental, blood pressure disorders and epilepsy must not bathe". Overlooking the South China Sea at the S end of Bai Sau is a

giant Jesus with arms outstretched. Behind the figure, on another hill, is a **lighthouse** built in 1910 which can be reached by path either from Ha Long St (near the *Hai Au Hotel*) or from the southern end of Bai Sau. Good views of the town, bays and sea.

North of town, at 12 Tran Phu St (the coast road) is **Bach Dinh** (Villa Blanche) built in the early part of this century and used by President Thieu. The gardens are open to visitors, but the house is closed. Open 0600-2100. **Bai Dau Beach** is 3 km NW of town along an appallingly rutted road at the fishing village of Ben Dinh (now geared primarily to the demands of domestic tourists). Again, the beach is nothing special, but it is the quietest spot on the peninsula. The pagoda on the hill here is called **Hung Tang Tu**.

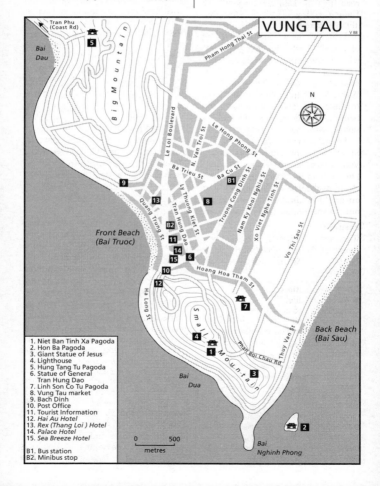

VUNG TAU

V.88

1. Niet Ban Tinh Xa Pagoda
2. Hon Ba Pagoda
3. Giant Statue of Jesus
4. Lighthouse
5. Hung Tang Tu Pagoda
6. Statue of General Tran Hung Dao
7. Linh Son Co Tu Pagoda
8. Vung Tau market
9. Bach Dinh
10. Post Office
11. Tourist Information
12. *Hai Au Hotel*
13. *Rex (Thang Loi) Hotel*
14. *Palace Hotel*
15. *Sea Breeze Hotel*

B1. Bus station
B2. Minibus stop

0   500
metres

Although there are numerous pagodas and churches in Vung Tau none is particularly noteworthy. At the S end of Tran Hung Dao Blvd is a massive and rather crude **statue of General Tran Hung Dao** who defeated a Chinese invasion force in the mid 13th century (see page 180). At 61 Hoang Hoa Tham St, on the way to Bai Sau, is the 100-year old **Linh Son Co Tu Pagoda**. Across the road from the Linh Son Pagoda is the **Lang Ca Ong** or 'Whale Dedication Temple, which – not surprisingly – is dedicated to the whale, the patron god of Vung Tau fishermen (worship of the whale was inherited from the Cham). It was built in 1911 and contains a number of whale skeletons displayed in cabinets. Whale and dolphin bones are brought to the temple and worshipped before being cremated: they are credited with saving drowning sailors and fishermen.

Vung Tau market is near Le Quy Don St. A number of visitors have forsaken Vung Tau in favour of *Long Hai*, a few km NE from Bai Sau. Long expanses of clean sand and beaches free from hawkers are the main attractions. There are one or two guesthouses and restaurants.

Festivals
Whale festival (16th day of the 8th lunar month), fishermen make offerings at the Lang Ca Ong (Whale) Temple on Hoang Hoa Tham St.

Local information
● **Accommodation**
Competition among the large, and rising, number of hotels helps ensure reasonable quality accommodation at sensible prices.

In town: **B** *Canadian*, 48 Quang Trung St, T 459852, F 459851, new, smart and comfortable, occupies a prime seafront site, some rooms have spectacular views; **B** *Hai Au*, 100 Halong St, T 452178, restaurant and small pool, opened mid-1990; **B** *Palace*, 11 Nguyen Trai St, T 452411, F 459878, offers a wide range of business and recreational services; **B** *Petro House*, 89 Tran Hung Dao St, T 52014, F 52015, new, central, satellite TV, business centre, French restaurant; **B** *Rex*, 1 Duy Tan St, T 452135, F 459862, set a short

way back from the beach but good views from the upper floors, good restaurant; **B** *Sea Breeze*, 11 Nguyen Trai St, T 452392, F 459856, popular with oilmen and other expats; **B-C** *Grand*, 26 Quang Trung St, T 452469, occupies a nice position overlooking the sea, offers the usual entertainments; **B-C** *Pacific*, 4 Le Loi Blvd, T 452279, large and sprawling with little character; **C** *Song Hong*, 12 Hoang Dieu St, T 452137, decent rooms, large downstairs restaurant; **C-D** *Sao Mai*, 93 Tran Hung Dao Blvd, T 452248, a/c, good value; **D** *Rang Dong*, 5 Duy Tan St, T 452133, utilitarian rather than comfortable; **D** *Song Han*, 3 Duy Tan St, T 452601, built with the undiscerning end of the Soviet package tour market in mind, fine for budget travellers.

Bai Dau: **C-D** Quiet, guesthouse-type accommodation along Tran Phu St, eg nos 28, 29, 47, 142 (about 6-7 of them), catering mostly to Vietnamese.

Bai Sau (Back Beach): **B-C** *Thang Muoi*, 46 Thuy Van St, T 452665, a/c, large restaurant, small pool (not always filled with water); **B-C** *Xay Dung*, Thuy Van St (N end of Bai Sau), a/c, large, clean and characterless; **C** *Club Thuy Duong*, Thuy Van St (behind Xay Dung), T 452635, a/c, pool (not always filled with water), tennis; **C** *Huu Nghi*, Thuy Van St (N end of Bai Sau), a/c, hot water, some character; **C-D** *Bimexco*, Thuy Van St (N end of Bai Sau), bungalows in casuarina-filled compound, rec; **C-D** *Cong Doan*, 15 Hoang Hoa Tham St, T 452300, large, friendly, but characterless; **D** *La Rose*, 39 Thuy Van St, some a/c, on beachfront, friendly and clean, rec.

Bai Dua: number of smaller hotels and guesthouses in this quiet, almost Mediterranean, enclave. **C** *Ha Long*, 48 Ha Long St, some a/c; **C** *Nha Nghi*, 50 Ha Long St.

● **Places to eat**
Restaurants in town tend to be associated with hotels. Two good seafood restaurants are: ♦♦♦*Frenchies* (*Grand Hotel*), French cuisine along with Chinese and Vietnamese dishes; ♦♦♦*Hue Anh*, 446 Truong Cong Dinh St, Chinese; ♦♦♦*Huu Nghi*, 14 Tran Hung Dao Blvd, rec; ♦♦*Hop Thanh*, 209 Ba Cu St, good Vietnamese dishes. There are a number of cafés along the seafront, eg *Thanh Nien*, 55 Quang Trung St.

On Bai Sau: there are numerous seafood restaurants, eg *Cua Hang*, 31 Thuy Van St (S end); *Dai Dung*, 27 Thuy Van St (S end); *Nha*

Hang, 11 Thuy Van St (S end); *Lam Thon Thung*, 79 Thuy Van St (N end); *Thuy*, 63/1 Hoang Hoa Tham, seafood specialities.

On Bai Dua: *Trung Tam*, 20 Ha Long St.

● **Banks & money changers**
Vietcombank, 27 Tran Hung Dao Blvd (closed Thur afternoon), changes TCs and cash in major currencies. Most major hotels will change US$ cash – eg *Hai Au* and *Rex*.

● **Entertainment**
Dancing: *Rex Hotel*, 1 Duy Tan St.

Inner tubes: can be hired on Bai Sau for fooling around in the surf.

Pool and drinking: at *Apocalypse Now*, 438 Truong Cong Dinh St.

● **Hospitals & medical services**
Hospital: *AEA International*, 1 Thanh Thai St, T 458776.

● **Post & telecommunications**
GPO: 4 Ha Long St (on the seafront, before the *Hai Au Hotel*).

● **Shopping**
Shells, shell ornaments and shell jewellery and stuffed lobsters are all to be found on the seafront along Quang Trung St.

● **Tourist offices**
Vung Tau Tourism, 59 Tran Hung Dao Blvd, T 452138.

● **Travel agents**
OTAS, 4 Le Loi St (*Pacific Hotel*), T 452279 – tours to surrounding sights.

● **Transport**
113 km from Saigon.

Local Bicycle: the best way to see the town is by bicycle. No bicycle rental places have opened yet, but hotels and guesthouses (or the people who work there) will sometimes rent out bicycles for about 5-8,000d/day. Also **cyclos**.

Road Bus: the station is on Ba Cu St, about 1 km from the centre of town. **Minibuses**: leave from the square on Tran Hung Dao Blvd and Ly Tu Trong St, and from the booth at 21 Tran Hung Dao Blvd. Minibuses leave every 30 mins for Saigon from 0400, 2-3 hrs; regular buses for Saigon take 3-4 hrs. **Taxi**: taxis can be chartered in Saigon to go to Vung Tau (see page 269).

Sea Boat: Dolphin Speed Lines operate hydrofoils from central Saigon to Vung Tau, quick (1 hr 20 mins) and cost 25,000-100,000d. The vessels are of Russian manufacture and quite uncomfortable. Saigon to Vung Tau on Mon, Tues, Thur, Fri depart 0730, Sat depart 0730, 1430, Sun depart 0830, 1630. Vung Tau to Saigon on Mon depart 0650, 1630, Tues, Thur, Fri, Sat depart 1630, Sun depart 0650, 1550, 1630.

SAIGON (HO CHI MINH CITY)

Saigon, Pearl of the Orient, is the largest city in Vietnam. It is also the nation's foremost commercial and industrial centre. Founded as a Khmer trading and fishing port on the W bank of the Dong Nai River it fell into Vietnamese hands in the late 17th century. Early in the 18th century the Nguyen emperors established Gia Dinh Citadel, destroyed by French naval forces in 1859. Rebuilt as a French colonial city it was named Saigon (Soai-gon – wood of the kapok tree). Officially Ho Chi Minh City since 1975, it remains to most the bi-syllabic, familiar, old 'Saigon'.

At the height of the War, as refugees spilled in from a devastated countryside, the population of Saigon rose to around 4.5 million. With reunification in 1975, the new Communist authorities pursued a policy of depopulation, believing that the city had become too large – that it was parasitic and was preying on the surrounding countryside. Certainly, most of the jobs were in the service sector, and were linked to the US presence. For example, Saigon had 56,000 registered prostitutes alone (and many, many, more unregistered 'amateurs') – most of them country girls. The population of the city today is an estimated 4 million and rising fast as the rural poor are lured by the tales of streets paved with gold.

Prior to the 15th century, Saigon was a small Cambodian village surrounded by a wilderness of forest and swamp. Through the years it had ostensibly been incorporated into the Funan and then the Khmer empires, although it is hard to believe that these kingdoms had any direct, long-term influence on the inhabitants of the community. The Khmers, who called the region *Prei Nokor*, used the area for hunting.

By 1623 Saigon had become an important commercial centre, and in the mid 17th century it became the residence of the so-called Vice-King of Cambodia. In 1698, the Viets managed to extend their control this far S and finally Saigon came under Vietnamese control. By 1790, the city had a population of 50,000 and before Hué was selected as the capital of the Nguyen Dynasty, Emperor Gia Long made Saigon his place of residence.

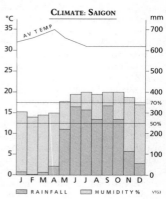

CLIMATE: SAIGON

RAINFALL   HUMIDITY %

SAIGON - 1930's

In the middle of the 19th century, the French began to challenge Vietnamese authority in the S of Vietnam and Saigon. Between 1859 and 1862, in response to the Nguyen persecution of Catholics in Vietnam, the French attacked and captured Saigon, along with the southern provinces of Vinh Long, An Giang and Ha Tien. The Treaty of Saigon in 1862 ratified the conquest and created the new French colony of Cochin China. Saigon was developed in French style: wide, tree-lined boulevards, street-side cafés, elegant French architecture, boutiques and the smell of baking baguettes. The map of French Saigon in the 1930s shows a city that owes more to Haussman than Vietnamese geomancers. And French insensitivity can be judged from the street names which include, astonishingly, a Cambodian King and minor French dignataries but not a single Vietnamese person, place or event.

Saigon is divided, administratively, into 12 urban precincts or *quan*, and six suburban districts. Each precinct and district has its own People's Committee, and the suburban areas have been developed into areas of food production to reduce the city's dependence on the countryside. The authorities claim that 100,000 ha of land in the suburbs is cultivated. A city-wide People's Committee, elected every 4 years, oversees the functioning of the entire metropolis.

With the 'freeing-up' of the Vietnamese economy and the influx of Westerners, con-men and touts have come out of the woodwork to plague visitors, as they did during the War. But crime is not yet the problem that it is elsewhere in Southeast Asia. Nonetheless, it is a good idea to be a little careful, especially if lulled into a false sense of security by the

CROSSING THE ROAD

Saigon's streets may look anarchic but they are not. A strict code of conduct applies: the main difference between Vietnam's roads and those of the West is that in Vietnam the individual abdicates responsibility for his personal safety and assumes an obligation to everyone else; it is the closest Vietnam has ever come to true communism! Watch Vietnamese cross a busy street: unlike Westerners they do not wait for a lull in the traffic but launch themselves straight into the flow, chatting and laughing with their friends, eyes ahead so as to avoid walking into a passing bicycle (their sole duty), no looking left and right, no ducking and weaving: responsibility for their safety rests entirely with the oncoming cyclists. In order to make it easier for cyclists not to hit them they walk at a steady, even pace with no deviation from a clearly signalled route, for any slight change in trajectory or velocity would spell certain disaster.

people of Hanoi. See the warning on Safety, page 287.

There are now so many bicycles and motorbikes on the streets of Saigon that intersections seem lethally confused. Miraculously, the riders miss each other (most of the time) while pedestrians safely make their way through waves of machines (see box, page 247). Another, rather more surprising, consequence of the reforms is the increasing popularity of the *ao dai* – the traditional tunic and loose trousers worn by women (see page 126).

Vietnam's economic reforms are most in evidence in Saigon (see page 132) and average incomes here at US$480 are over double the national average. It is here that the highest concentration of *Hoa* (ethnic Chinese) is to be found – 380,000 – and, although once persecuted for their economic success (see page 118), they still have the greatest economic influence, and acumen. Most of Saigon's ethnic Chinese live in the district of Cholon, and from there control two-thirds of small-scale commercial enterprises. The reforms have encouraged the *Hoa* to begin investing in business again. Drawing on their links with fellow Chinese in Taiwan, Hong Kong, Bangkok, and among the overseas Vietnamese, they are viewed by the government as crucial in improving prospects for the economy. The reforms

have also brought economic inefficiencies into the open: it was estimated at the end of 1991 that 230,000 people – mostly young – were unemployed in the city. Although the changes have brought wealth to a few, and increased the range of goods on sale, they have also created a much clearer division between the haves and the have nots.

In its short history Saigon has had a number of keepers. Each has flattened the existing structures and rebuilt in their own style. First the Khmer, then the Vietnamese, followed by the French who were succeeded by the Americans and the 'Puppet' Regime, and finally the Communist North who engineered society rather than the buildings, locking the urban fabric in a time-warp. Under the current regime, best described as international capitalist, the city is once more being rebuilt. Ever larger holes are being torn in the heart of central Saigon. Whereas two years ago it was common to see buildings disappear, now whole blocks fall to the wrecker's ball. In the holes left behind, concrete, steel and glass monuments emerge. There is, of course, a difference from earlier periods of remodelling of the city. Then, it was conducted on a human scale and the largest buildings, though grand, were on a scale that was in keeping with the dimensions of the streets and ordinary shophouses. French buildings in Dong Khoi St, for example, were consistent with the Vietnamese way of life: street level trading with a few residential floors above.

For the visitor and user of this *Handbook*, a practical consequence of all this activity is that when looking for that bijou restaurant, do not be surprised to find that not only is it missing but the entire street in which it once stood has been converted to a mountain of rubble.

Places of interest

Central Saigon

All the sights of Central Saigon can be reached on foot in no more than 30 mins from the major hotel areas of Nguyen Hue, Dong Khoi and Ton Duc Thang sts. Visiting all the sights described will take several days.

The *Rex Hotel*, a pre-Liberation favourite with US officers, stands at the intersection of Le Loi and Nguyen Hue

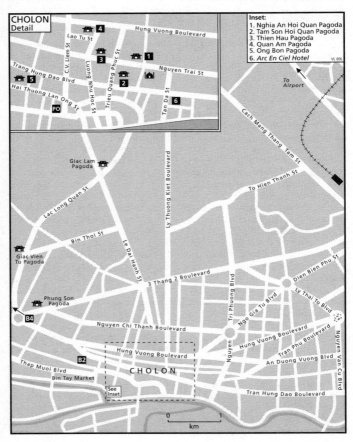

CHOLON Detail

Inset:
1. Nghia An Hoi Quan Pagoda
2. Tam Son Hoi Quan Pagoda
3. Thien Hau Pagoda
4. Quan Am Pagoda
5. Ong Bon Pagoda
6. *Arc En Ciel Hotel*

VL 89L

Hung Vuong Boulevard

Lao Tu St
C.V. Liem St
Luong Nhu Hoc St
Trieu Quang Phuc St
Trang Hung Dao Blvd
Hai Thuong Lan Ong St
Nguyen Trai St
Tan Da St
PO

To Airport

Cach Mang Thang Tam St

Giac Lam Pagoda

Lac Long Quan St

Ly Thuong Kiet Boulevard

To Hien Thanh St

Bin Thoi St

Le Dai Hanh St

3 Thang 2 Boulevard

Dien Bien Phu St

Ly Thai To Blvd

Giac Vien Tu Pagoda

Tri Phuong Blvd

Ngo Gia Tu Blvd

Phung Son Pagoda

B4

Nguyen Chi Thanh Boulevard

Hung Vuong Boulevard

Hung Vuong Boulevard

Nguyen

Tran Phu Boulevard

An Duong Vuong Blvd

Nguyen Van Cu Blvd

B2

CHOLON

Thap Muoi Blvd

Bin Tay Market

See Inset

Tran Hung Dao Boulevard

0   1
km

blvds. This was the scene of the daily 'Five O'clock Follies' where the military briefed an increasingly sceptical press corp during the Vietnam War. Fully renovated, the crown on the 5th floor terrace of the *Rex* (a good place to have a beer) is rotating once again after a number of years of immobility. Some maintain that it symbolizes Saigon's newly-discovered (or re-discovered) vitality. A short distance NE from the *Rex*, at the end of Le Loi Blvd, is the impressive French-era **Municipal Theatre**

which provides a varied programme of events; for example, traditional theatre, contemporary dance and gymnastics. On the green in front of the Theatre, Mr Hong makes remarkably realistic planes and helicopters from old drink cans. Based on the photographs in an old military identification manual, he can make anything from a Cessna to a Huey. Coffee grown on the highland plateau of Dalat is available on the terrace surrounding the theatre. At the NW end of Nguyen Hue Blvd, again close to the

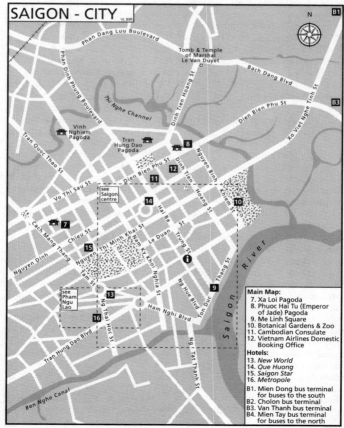

SAIGON - CITY

Main Map:
7. Xa Loi Pagoda
8. Phuoc Hai Tu (Emperor of Jade) Pagoda
9. Me Linh Square
10. Botanical Gardens & Zoo
11. Cambodian Consulate
12. Vietnam Airlines Domestic Booking Office

Hotels:
13. *New World*
14. *Que Huong*
15. *Saigon Star*
16. *Metropole*

B1. Mien Dong bus terminal for buses to the south
B2. Cholon bus terminal
B3. Van Thanh bus terminal
B4. Mien Tay bus terminal for buses to the north

Rex, is the yellow and white **City Hall** which overlooks a **statue of Bac Ho** (Uncle Ho) offering comfort, or perhaps advice, to a child. On weekend evenings literally thousands of young Saigon men and women cruise up and down Nguyen Hue and Le Loi blvds and Dong Khoi St (formerly the bar-lined Tu Do St, the old Rue Catinat) on bicycles and motorbikes; this whirl of people and machines is known as *chay long rong* or *song voi* – meaning 'living fast'.

North up Dong Khoi St is the imposing red, twin-spired **Catholic Cathedral of Notre Dame**, overlooking a grassed square. The cathedral was built between 1877 and 1880, and is said to be on the site of an ancient pagoda. Communion is celebrated here six times on Sun and three times on weekdays and Sat. Also facing onto the square, to the E, is the **General Post Office** built in the 1880s.

Northeast of the Cathedral on Le Duan St is the **French Consulate** and the **former US Embassy**. Vegetation grows up around the embassy buildings, almost like a latterday Angkor Wat. A plaque outside records the attack by Viet Cong special forces during the Tet offensive of 1968 and the final victory in 1975. The side entrance is sometimes open for those who want to take a closer look (ask the guard). On the other side of the road, a little further NE, is the former **British Embassy**, which will shortly be reinstated as the British Consulate General. At 2 Le Duan St is the **War Museum** (Bao Tang Quan Doi) with a tank and warplane in the front compound. It contains an indifferent display of photographs and articles of war. Open 0800-1130, 1330-1600 Tues-Sun.

At the end of Le Duan St are the **Botanical Gardens** which run alongside Nguyen Binh Khiem St at the point where the Thi Nghe channel flows into the Saigon River. The gardens were established in 1864 by French botanist Jean-Batiste Louis Pierre; by the 1970s they had a collection of nearly 2,000 species, and a particularly fine display of orchids. With the dislocations of the immediate post-war years, the gardens went into decline, a situation from which they are still trying to recover. In the S quarter of the grounds of the gardens is a mediocre **zoo** with a rather moth-eaten collection of animals which form a backdrop to smartly dressed Vietnamese families posing for photographs. The latest addition to the zoo is a life size family of Vietnamese speaking model dinosaurs. To popular dismay the local authorities have drawn up plans to drive a road through the site. Admission to gardens and zoo 10,000d.

More stimulating and impressive, at 2 Nguyen Binh Khiem St, just to the left of the main gates to the Botanical Gardens, is the **Historical Museum**, formerly the National Museum, and before that the Musée Blanchard de la Bosse (from 1929-1956). This elegant building was constructed in 1928 and is pagodaesque in style. It displays a wide range of artefacts from the prehistoric (300,000 years ago) and the Dongson periods (3,500 BC – 100 AD) through to the birth of the Vietnamese Communist Party in 1930. Particularly impressive are the Cham sculptures, of which the standing bronze Buddha from the 4th-6th century is probably the finest. There are also representative pieces from the Chen-la, Funan, Khmer, Oc-eo and Han Chinese periods, and from the various Vietnamese dynasties together with some hilltribe artefacts. Little of the labelling is in English and even the English booklet available from the ticket office is of little help. Water puppet shows (see page 125) are held here daily, 10,000d. Admission to the museum 10,000d. Open 0830-1130, 1330-1630 Tues-Sun. Opposite the Historical Museum is the **Memorial Temple**, constructed in 1928 and dedicated to famous Vietnamese. Open 0800-1130, 1300-1600 Tues-Sun.

The popular **Exhibition House of War Crimes** is on Vo Van Tan St, close to the intersection with Le Qui Don St.

THE BUDDHIST MARTYRS: SELF-IMMOLATION AS PROTEST

In Aug 1963 there was a demonstration of 15,000 people at the Xa Loi Pagoda, with speakers denouncing the Diem regime and telling jokes about Diem's sister-in-law, Madame Nhu (she was later on a speaking tour in the US to call monks "hooligans in robes"). Two nights later, ARVN special forces (from Catholic families) raided the pagoda, battering down the gate, wounding 30 and killing seven people. Soon afterwards Diem declared martial law. The pagoda became a focus of discontent, with several monks committing suicide through self-immolation to protest against the Diem regime. The first monk to immolate himself was 66-year-old Thich Quang Du, from Hué. On 11 June 1963, his companions poured petrol over him and set him alight as he sat in the lotus position. Pedestrians prostrated themselves at the sight; even a policeman threw himself to the ground in reverence. The next day, the picture of the monk in flames filled the front pages of newspapers across the world. Some 30 monks and nuns followed Thich's example in protesting against the Diem government and US involvement in South Vietnam. Two young US protesters also followed suit, one committing suicide by self-immolation outside the Pentagon and the other next to the UN, both in Nov 1968. Madame Nhu, a Catholic, is reported as having said after the monks' death: "Let them burn, and we shall clap our hands". Within 5 months Diem had been killed in a military coup. In May 1993 a Vietnamese man immolated himself at the Thien Mu Pagoda in Hué – the pagoda where the first monk-martyr was based (see page 198).

In the courtyard are tanks, bombs and helicopters, while in the museum itself are countless photographs, and a few exhibits, illustrating Man's inhumanity. The display covers the Son My (My Lai) massacre on 16 March 1968 (see box, page 224), the effects of napalm and phosphorous, and the after-effects of Agent Orange defoliation (this is particularly disturbing, with bottled malformed human foetuses). Understandably, there is no record of North Vietnamese atrocities to US and South Vietnamese troops. There is also a rather laughable exhibit of such latter-day Western atrocities as heavy metal music. This museum has gone through some interesting name changes in recent years. It began life as the Exhibition House of American and Chinese War Crimes. In 1990, 'Chinese' was dropped from the name, and in 1994 'American' was too. Admission 7,000d. Open 0730-1145, 1330-1645 Tues-Sun.

In total, Saigon has close to 200 pago-das – far too many to see. Many of the finest are in Cholon (see below), although there is a selection closer to the main hotel area in central Saigon. The **Xa Loi Pagoda** is not far from the War Crimes Museum at 89 Ba Huyen Thanh Quan St (see Saigon General map), surrounded by foodstalls. If the main gate is shut, try the side entrance on Su Thien Chieu St. Built in 1956, the pagoda contains a multi-storeyed tower which is particularly revered, as it houses a relic of the Buddha. The main sanctuary contains a large, bronze-gilded Buddha in an attitude of meditation. Around the walls is a series of silk paintings depicting the previous lives of the Buddha (with an explanation of each life to the right of the entrance into the sanctuary). The pagoda is historically, rather than artistically, important as it became a focus of dissent against the Diem regime (see box). Open 0630-1100, 1430-1700 Mon-Sun.

The **Presidential Palace**, now re-named **Reunification Hall**, or the

Thong Nhat Conference Hall, is in a large park to the SE of Nguyen Thi Minh Khai St, and SW of Nam Ky Khoi Nghia St. The residence of the French governor was built on this site in 1868, which was later renamed the Presidential Palace. In Feb 1962, a pair of planes took off to attack Viet Cong emplacements – piloted by two of the S's finest airmen – but they turned back to bomb the Presidential Palace in a futile attempt to assassinate Diem. The president escaped with his family to the cellar, but the palace had to be demolished and replaced with a new building. One of the most memorable photographs taken during the War was of a NVA tank crashing through the gates to the palace on 30 April 1975 – symbolizing the end of South Vietnam and its government. The President of South Vietnam, General Duong Van Minh, and his entire cabinet, were arrested in the Palace shortly afterwards. The hall has been preserved as it was found in 1975 and visitors can take a guided tour with an official who will probably speak only Vietnamese. In the *Vice President's Guest Room*, there is a lacquered painting of the Temple of Literature in Hanoi, while the *Presenting of Credentials Room* contains a fine 40-piece lacquer work showing diplomats presenting their credentials during the Le Dynasty (15th century). In the basement there are operations rooms, military maps, radios and other paraphernalia. In essence, it is a 60s-style building filled with 60s-style official furnishings. Visitors are shown a poorly made, but nonetheless interesting, film of the Revolution. Admission 40,000d. Open 0730-1030, 1300-1530 Mon-Sun. The guides are friendly, but their English is not always very good. **NB** The hall is sometimes closed for state occasions. The visitors' entrance is at 106 Nguyen Du St.

Close by, the **Revolutionary Museum** is at 65 Ly Tu Trong St. Like the equivalent in Hanoi, this is not a revolutionary museum but a museum of the revolution, with a display of photographs, a few pieces of hardware (helicopter, anti-aircraft guns) in the back compound, and some memorabilia. All the labelling is in Vietnamese, and the museum is usually filled with red-scarved school children. Open 0800-1130, 1330-1630 Tues-Sun. Opposite the museum is a small park with open-air cafés. Southeast from the Revolutionary Museum along Ly Tu Trong St is the centre of Saigon's 'fashion' industry. Not far away at 45 Truong Dinh St is the **Mariamman Hindu Temple**. Although clearly Hindu, with a statue of Mariamman flanked by Maduraiveeran and Pechiamman, it is largely frequented by *Hoa worshippers*, providing the strange sight of Chinese Vietnamese clasping incense sticks and prostrating themselves in front of a Hindu deity, as they would to a Buddha image. The Chinese have always been pragmatic when it comes to religions.

The **Cho Ben Thanh** – a large covered central market – faces a statue of Tran Nguyen Han at a large and chaotic roundabout which marks the intersection of Le Loi, Ham Nghi and Tran Hung Dao blvds. Saigon has a number of markets; this one and the Binh Tay Market in Cholon (see below) are the largest. Many of the markets are surprisingly well stocked for a country which a few years ago was close to economic collapse. The people of the S, and particularly the Chinese of Saigon, have not forgotten what it is like to conduct business, and with the economic reforms, private traders have reappeared on the streets to make a quick dong or buck. The market sells clothes, food, toys, household utensils, poor quality jewellery and is enjoyable to walk around, but has little to tempt the shopper except old watches and cheap T-shirts. **NB** Beware of pickpockets and 'steaming'.

South of the market, Le Thi Hong Gam St which runs off Pho Duc Chinh

St, is a centre of **furniture and shoe production and sale**. The **Art Museum** (*Bao Tang My Thuat*), in an impressive cream mansion at 97A Pho Duc Chinh St, displays work from the classical period through to socialist realist. Open 0800-1130, 1400-1700 Tues-Sun. At 338 Nguyen Cong Tru St is the **Phung Son Tu Pagoda**. This is a small temple built just after WW2 by Fukien Chinese; its most notable feature is the wonderful painted entrance doors

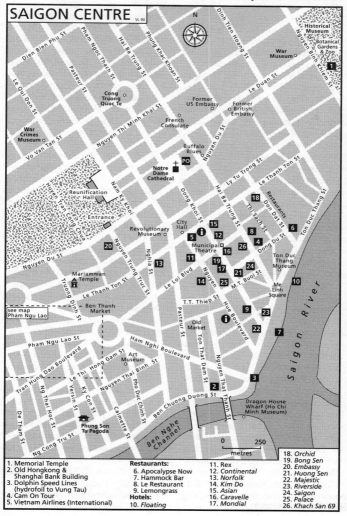

SAIGON CENTRE

1. Memorial Temple
2. Old Hongkong & Shanghai Bank Building
3. Dolphin Speed Lines (hydrofoil to Vung Tau)
4. Cam On Tour
5. Vietnam Airlines (International)

Restaurants:
6. Apocalypse Now
7. Hammock Bar
8. Le Restaurant
9. Lemongrass

Hotels:
10. Floating
11. Rex
12. Continental
13. Norfolk
14. Kim Do
15. Asian
16. Caravelle
17. Mondial
18. Orchid
19. Bong Sen
20. Embassy
21. Huong Sen
22. Majestic
23. Riverside
24. Saigon
25. Palace
26. Khach San 69

with their fearsome armed warriors. Incense spirals hang in the open well of the pagoda, which is dedicated to Ong Bon, the Guardian of Happiness and Virtue. The **War Surplus** or **Dan Sinh Market** is close to the Phung Son Tu Pagoda at 104 Nguyen Cong Tru St. Merchandise on sale includes dog tags and military clothing and equipment (not all of it authentic). The market is popular with Western visitors looking for mementoes of their visit, so bargain particularly hard.

The **Old Market** is on Ton That Dam St, running between Ham Nghi Blvd and Ton That Thiep St. It is the centre for the sale of black-market goods (particularly consumer electronics) – now openly displayed. There is also a good range of foodstalls and fruit sellers. Close by on Ben Chuong Duong St is the old **Hong Kong & Shanghai Bank building** which overlooks Saigon's **pet market**. Nguyen Tat Thanh St runs S from here over the Ben Nghe Channel to **Dragon House Wharf**, at the confluence of the Ben Nghe Channel and the Saigon River. The building has been converted into a **museum** (predominantly on the 1st floor) celebrating the life and exploits of Ho Chi Minh, mostly through pictures and the odd piece of memorabilia. School children are brought here to be told of their country's recent history, and people of all ages have their photographs taken with a portrait of Bac Ho in the background. Open 0800-1130, 1400-1800 Tues-Thur and Sat, 0800-1130, 1400-2000 Sun.

The **Floating Hotel**, unceremoniously dragged up from the Great Barrier Reef where it was losing money, floats like a massive lego toy at its berth next to Hero Square with its **statue** of the Vietnamese hero **Tran Hung Dao** who glares disapprovingly at the floating gin palace. A short distance N up Ton Duc Thang St is the rarely visited **Ton Duc Thang Museum**. Opened in 1989, it is dedicated to the life of Ton Duc Thang or Bac (Uncle) Ton. A comrade of Ho

Chi Minh with whom he fought, Bac Ton became President of Vietnam and died in 1980. The museum contains an array of photographs and other memorabilia. Open 0800-1100, 1400-1800 Tues-Sun.

Cholon

Cholon (*Cho lon* = big market) or **Chinatown** is, not surprisingly, an area inhabited predominantly by Vietnamese of Chinese origin. Since 1975, the authorities have alienated many Chinese, causing hundreds of thousands to leave the country. In making their escape many have died – either through drowning, as their perilously small and overladen craft foundered, or at the hands of pirates in the South China Sea (see page 102). In total, between 1977 and 1982, 709,570 refugees were recorded by the UNHCR as having fled Vietnam. By the late 1980s, the flow of boat people was being driven more by economic, than by political, forces; there was little chance of making good in a country as poor, and in an economy as moribund, as that of Vietnam. Today, although economic conditions have barely changed, the stream has dried to a trickle as the opportunities for claiming refugee status and gaining asylum have disappeared. Even with this flow of Chinese out of the country, there is still a large population of Chinese Vietnamese living in Cholon, an area which encompasses the 5th and the 6th precincts or *quan*, to the SW of the city centre. Cholon appears to the casual visitor to be the most populated, noisiest, and in general the most vigorous part of Saigon, if not of Vietnam. It is here that entrepreneurial talent and private funds are concentrated; both resources that the government are keen to mobilize in their attempts to reinvigorate the economy.

Cholon is worth visiting not only for the bustle and activity, but also because the pagodas found here are the finest in Saigon. The sights outlined below can be walked in half a day, although hiring a cyclo for a few hours is a more relaxing way to get around.

The **Nghia An Hoi Quan Pagoda** can be found at 678 Nguyen Trai St, not far from the *Arc en Ciel Hotel*, the best hotel in Cholon. A magnificent carved gold-painted wooden boat hangs over the entrance. To the left, on entering the pagoda, is a larger-than-life representation of Quan Cong's horse and groom. At the main altar are three figures in glass cases: the central red-faced figure with a green cloak is Quan Cong himself; to the left and right are his trusty companions, the General Chau Xuong (very fierce) and the mandarin Quan Binh respectively. On leaving the pagoda, note the fine gold figures of guardians on the inside of the door panels.

The **Tam Son Hoi Quan Pagoda** is nearby at 118 Trieu Quang Phuc St, just off Nguyen Trai St. The pagoda is frequented by childless mothers as it is dedicated to Chua Thai Sanh, the Goddess of Fertility, and was built in the 19th century by Fukien immigrants. It is an uncluttered, 'pure' example of a Chinese/Vietnamese pagoda; peaceful and quiet. Like Nghia An Hoi Quan, the temple contains figures of Quan Cong, his horse and two companions (see above).

The **Thien Hau Pagoda**, on 710 Nguyen Trai St, is one of the largest in the city. Constructed in the early 19th century, it is Chinese in inspiration and is dedicated to the worship of both the Buddha and to the Goddess Thien Hau Thanh Mau – the Holy Mother. She is the goddess of the sea and the protector of sailors. Two enormous incense urns can be seen through the main doors. Inside, the principal altar supports the gilded form of Thien Hau, with a boat to one side. Silk paintings depicting religious scenes decorate the walls. By far the most interesting part of the pagoda is the roof, which can be best seen looking up from the small open courtyard. It must be one of the finest and richly ornamented in Vietnam, with the high-relief frieze depicting episodes from the Legends of the Three Kingdoms. In the post 1975 era, many would-be refugees prayed here for safe deliverance before casting themselves adrift on the South China Sea. A number of those who survived the perilous voyage sent offerings to the merciful goddess and the pagoda has been well maintained since.

Close to Thien Hau, at 12 Lao Tu St (just off Luong Nhu Hoc St), is the **Quan Am Pagoda**, thought to be one of the oldest in the city. The roof supports four sets of impressive mosaic-encrusted figures, while inside, the main building is fronted with old gold and lacquer panels of guardian spirits. The main altar supports a seated statue of A-Pho, the Holy Mother. In front of the main altar is a white ceramic statue of *Quan Am, the Goddess of Purity and Motherhood* (Goddess of Mercy) (see page 154). The pagoda complex also contains a series of courtyards and altars dedicated to a range of deities and spirits. Outside, hawkers sell caged birds and vast quantities of incense sticks to pilgrims.

The **Binh Tay Market**, sandwiched between Thap Muoi Blvd and Ben Phan Van Khoe St, is one of the most colourful and exciting markets in Saigon, with a wonderful array of noises, smells and colours. It sprawls over a large area and is contained in what looks like a rather decayed Forbidden Palace. Beware of pickpockets here. A new high-rise market – the 5-storey **An Dong Market** – opened at the end of 1991 in Cholon. It was built with an investment of US$5mn from local ethnic Chinese businessmen.

A 25 mins walk from the Binh Tay Market and set back from the road at 1408 3 Thang 2 Blvd is the **Phung Son Pagoda**, also known as **Go Pagoda**. It was built at the beginning of the 19th century on the site of an earlier Cambodian structure and has been rebuilt several times. At one time, it was decided to move the pagoda, and all the temple valuables were loaded on to the back of a white elephant. The beast stumbled and the valuables tumbled out into the pond that surrounds the temple. This was taken as a sign from the gods that the pagoda was to stay where it was. In the sanctuary, there is a large seated gilded Buddha, surrounded by a variety of other figures from several Asian and Southeast Asian countries.

Outer Saigon

The **Phuoc Hai Tu (Emperor of Jade) Pagoda** can be found off Dien Bien Phu St at 73 Mai Thi Luu St, nestling behind low pink walls, just before the Thi Nghe Channel. Women sell birds that are set free to gain merit, and a pond to the right contains large turtles. The Emperor of Jade is the supreme god of the Taoists, although this temple, built in 1900, contains a wide range of other deities. These include the archangel Michael of the Buddhists, a Sakyamuni (historic) Buddha, statues of the two generals who tamed the Green Dragon (representing the E) and the White Dragon (representing the W) (to the left and right of the first altar) and Quan Am (see page 154). The Hall of Ten Hells in the left-hand sanctuary has reliefs depicting the 1,000 tortures of hell.

Not far from the Emperor of Jade Pagoda is the small **Tran Hung Dao Pagoda** at 34 Vo Thi Sau St. Built in 1932, it was dedicated to the worship of the victorious 13th century General Hung Dao, and contains a series of bas reliefs depicting the general's successes, along with weapons and carved dragons (see page 180). In the front courtyard is a larger-than-life bronze statue of this hero of Vietnamese nationalism. Open 0700-1100, 1430-1700 Mon-Sun.

To the W, on Nguyen Van Troi St, and just to the S of the Thi Nghe Channel is another modern pagoda, the **Vinh Nghiem Pagoda**. It was completed in 1967 and is one of the largest in Vietnam. Built in Japanese style, it displays a 7-storey pagoda in the classic style (only open on holidays) and a large, airy, sanctuary. On either side of the entrance are two fearsome warriors; inside is a large Japanese-style Buddha in an attitude of meditation, flanked by two goddesses. Along the walls are a series of scrolls depicting the jataka tales, with rather quaint (and difficult to interpret) explanations in English. Admission by donation. Open 0730-1130, 1400-1800 Mon-Sun.

A 10-15 mins cyclo ride across the Thi Nghe Channel and almost into the suburbs leads to the **Tomb and Temple of Marshal Le Van Duyet** at 126 Dinh Tien Hoang St. Le Van Duyet was a highly respected Vietnamese soldier who put down the Tay Son rebellion (see page 225) and died in 1831. The pagoda was renovated in 1937 – a plaque on the left lists those who made donations to the renovation fund. The main sanctuary contains a weird assortment of objects: a stuffed tiger, a miniature mountain, whale baleen, carved elephants, crystal goblets, spears and other weapons of war. Much of the collection is made up of the Marshal's personal possessions. In front of the temple is the tomb itself, surrounded by a low wall and flanked, at the front, by two guardian lions and two lotus buds. The pagoda's attractive roof is best seen from the tomb.

Giac Vien Tu Pagoda (Buddha's Complete Enlightenment) can be found at the end of a narrow 200m-long dirt road running off Lac Long Quan St (just after No 247), set among vegetable plots. It is similar in layout, content and inspiration to Giac Lam Pagoda (see below). Visiting just one of the two pagodas would be enough for most visitors. The Giac Vien Tu Pagoda was built in 1771 and dedicated to the worship of the Emperor Gia Long. Although restored, Giac Vien Tu remains one of the best preserved temples in Vietnam. It is lavishly decorated, with over 100 carvings of

REBIRTH OF A FOREST

25 km SE of Saigon, stretching down to the coast, lies the district of Can Gio. A low lying area, it is watered by the silty Saigon River and twice daily washed by the salty tides of the South China Sea. Conditions are ideal for mangrove forest, one of the most diverse and prolific of all woodland types, and the 30,000 ha forest in Can Gio is no exception. The forest visitors see today is, however, less than 16 years old, having been replanted by Vietnamese forestry workers to replace the dead stumps that remained after the US Air Force defoliated the old mangroves with herbicides, chiefly Agent Orange.

Ho Chi Minh's famous dictum "*Rùng là vàng, nêu ta biét bao vê, thi rung rât qúy*" (forests are gold, if we understand them we can be rich) was prescient; the great man understood environmental issues long before the 'greens' made them trendy. Happily the Can Gio mangrove swamps reflect the truth of Ho's words proving fertile spawning and nursery grounds for commercially valuable fish and crustacea stocks as well as providing habitat for numerous semi-aquatic and rare species such as otters. The *Rhizophora* tree species (distinguished by their stilt roots and 'flying buttresses') deliver a sustainable harvest of charcoal, building materials, fruit, edible leaves and tannin when carefully managed.

The Forestry & Environmental Protection Board of Ho Chi Minh City has allowed about 4,000 people back into the area and will increase the number as the forest further establishes itself. Not surprisingly, the provision of health and education facilities in the forest is inadequate and, working in cooperation with the Forestry Board and the local population, the *Saigon Children's Charity* has built three schools in the area and is providing a floating school to reach children in the remotest corners.

various divinities and spirits, dominated by a large gilded image of the Buddha of the Past (Amitabha). It is everything a pagoda should be: demons and gods jump out around every corner, a confusion of fantastic characters. With the smoke and smells, the richness of colour, and the darkness, it assaults the senses. Among the decorations, note the 'Buddha lamp', funerary tablets, and urns with photographs of the deceased.

The **Giac Lam Pagoda** (Forest of Enlightenment) is at 118 Lac Long Quan St, about 2 km NE from Giac Vien Tu Pagoda, through an arch and down a short track about 200m from the intersection with Le Dai Hanh St. Built in 1744, it is the oldest pagoda in Saigon. There is a sacred Bodhi tree in the temple courtyard and the pagoda is set among fruit trees and vegetable plots. Inside Giac Lam it feels, initially, like a rather cluttered private house. In one section, there are rows of funerary tablets with pictures of the deceased; a rather moving display of man's mortality. The main altar is particularly impressive, with layers of Buddhas, dominated by the gilded form of the Buddha of the Past. Note the 49-Buddha oil lamp. The monks are very friendly and will probably offer tea. Some have good English and French as well as detailed knowledge of the history of the pagoda. It is a small haven of peace. An unusual unique feature is the use of blue and white porcelain plates to decorate the roof and some of the small towers in the garden facing the pagoda.

Excursions

Cu Chi Tunnels are about 36 km NW of Saigon (see map, page 93). Cu Chi town is on the main road to Tay Ninh and the Cao Dai Cathedral, and both the tunnels and the cathedral can be visited in a single day trip. Dug by the Viet Minh who began work in 1948, they were later expanded by the VC and used for storage, and refuge, and contained sleeping quarters, hospitals and schools. The tunnels are too narrow for most Westerners, but a short section of the 200 km of tunnels has been especially widened to allow tourists to share the experience. Tall or large people might still find it a claustrophobic squeeze. Visitors are shown a somewhat antique but nevertheless interesting video and invited to a firing range to try their hand with equally ancient AK47s at a buck a bang. Cu Chi was one of the most fervently Communist of the districts around Saigon and the tunnels were used as the base from which the VC mounted the operations of the Tet Offensive in 1968. Communist cadres were active in this area of rubber plantations, even before WW2. Vann and Ramsey, two American soldiers, were to notice the difference between this area and other parts of the S in the early 60s: "No children laughed and shouted for gum and candy in these hamlets. Everyone, adult and child, had a cold look" (Sheehan 1989:539-40). When the Americans first discovered this underground base on their doorstep they would simply pump CS gas down the tunnel openings and then set explosives. Later, realizing that the tunnels might also yield valuable intelligence, they sent volunteer 'tunnel rats' into the earth to capture prisoners. Cu Chi district was a free fire zone and assaulted with the full battery of ecological warfare. Defoliants were sprayed and 20 tonne Rome Ploughs carved up the area in the search for tunnels. It was said that even a crow flying over Cu Chi district had to carry its own lunch. Admission US$4. *Getting there*: most visitors reach Cu Chi on a tour (*Saigontourist* charge US$30 pp but available cheaper from private tour operators – eg *Kim's Café* US$5), although it is also possible to charter a car in Saigon (about US$20-30/day, including a visit to Tay Ninh – see below) and split it between four passengers. Regular buses leave for Cu Chi town from the Mien Tay station (Cholon) and the Ham Nghi station; from Cu Chi it is necessary to charter a Honda Om (motorcycle taxi) to the tunnels, although some visitors report that the infrequent Ben Suc bus goes to the tunnels. It is also possible to take a Honda Om all the way from Saigon (US$10). Alternatively hire a bicycle for the day in Saigon and take it on the bus to Cu Chi, riding to the tunnels which are 2 km from town.

Tay Ninh is a town 96 km NW of Saigon and 64 km further on from Cu Chi town. It can be visited on a day trip from the city and can easily be combined with a visit to the tunnels of Cu Chi. The province of the same name borders Cambodia and, before the 17th century, was part of the Khmer Kingdom. Between 1975 and Dec 1978, soldiers of Pol Pot's Khmer Rouge periodically attacked villages in this province, killing the men and raping the women. Ostensibly, it was in order to stop these incursions that the Vietnamese army invaded Cambodia on Christmas Day 1978, taking Phnom Penh by Jan 1979 (see page 443). Tay Ninh town contains the idiosyncratic **Cao Dai Great Temple**, the 'cathedral' of the Cao Dai religion (see page 121 for background on Cao Daism) and is the main reason to visit the town. The cathedral is set within a large complex of schools and administrative buildings, all washed in pastel yellow. The twin-towered cathedral is European in inspiration but with distinct Oriental features. On the façade are figures of Cao Dai saints in high relief, and at the entrance to the Cathedral is a mural depicting Victor Hugo flanked by the Vietnamese poet Nguyen Binh Khiem and the Chinese nationalist Sun Yat Sen. The latter holds an inkstone, symbolizing, strangely, the link between

Confucianism and Christianity. Graham Greene in *The quiet American* called it "The Walt Disney Fantasia of the East". Monsieur Ferry, an acquaintance of Norman Lewis, described the cathedral in even more outlandish terms, saying it "looked like a fantasy from the brain of Disney, and all the faiths of the Orient had been ransacked to create the pompous ritual ...". Lewis himself was clearly unimpressed with the structure and the religion, writing in *A dragon apparent* that "This cathedral must be the most outrageously vulgar building ever to have been erected with serious intent".

After removing shoes and hats, women enter the cathedral through a door to the left, men to the right, and they then proceed down their respective aisles towards the altar, usually accompanied by a Cao Dai priest dressed in white with a black turban. During services they don red, blue and yellow robes signifying Confucianism, Taoism and Buddhism respectively. Two rows of pink pillars entwined with green dragons line the nave, leading up to the main altar which supports a large globe on which is painted a single staring eye – the divine, all seeing, eye. The roof is blue and cloud dotted, representing the heavens, and the walls are pierced by open, lattice-work, windows. Ceremonies are held each day at 0600, 1200, 1800 and 2400 and visitors can watch from the cathedral's balcony. **NB** Visitors should not enter the central portion of the nave – keep to the side aisles and also should not wander in and out during services. If you go in at the beginning of the service you must stay until the end (1 hr). Photography is allowed. About $\frac{1}{2}$ km from the cathedral (turn right when facing the main façade) is the *Doan Ket*, a formal garden. There is a café on the other side of the boulevard, close to the gardens.

Tay Ninh also has a good **market** and there are said to be some **Cham temples** 1 km to the SW of the town. *Getting there*: either go on a tour, or charter a car in Saigon (about US$40/day – combined with a visit to the Cu Chi Tunnels, see above). Regular buses leave for Tay Ninh, via Cu Chi, from Mien Tay station (2½ hrs).

Nui Ba Den (Black Lady Mountain) is 10 km to the NE of Tay Ninh and 106 km from Saigon. The peak rises dramatically from the plain to a height of almost 1,000m and can be seen in the distance, to the right, on entering Tay Ninh. The Black Lady was a certain Ly-thi Huong who, while her lover was bravely fighting the occupying forces, was ordered to marry the son of a local mandarin. Rather than complying, she threw herself from the mountain. Another version of this story is that she was kidnapped by local scoundrels. A number of shrines to the Black Woman are located on the mountain, and pilgrims still visit the site. Fierce battles were also fought here between the French and Americans, and the Viet Minh. There are excellent views of the surrounding plain from the summit.

Bien Hoa is a town 26 km from Saigon, on the road N. It is the capital of the province of Dong Nai and was established by Chinese migrants on the banks of the Dong Nai River in the late 17th century when the town was known by the name Dong Nai Dai Pho. During the war it was a massive US air base and although there is little to see today there are suggestions that it will replace Tan Son Nhat as Saigon's airport, owing to the latter's cramped site. Paul Theroux in *The Great Railway Bazaar* (Penguin) wrote of Bien Hoa:

"... out here in the suburbs of Bien Hoa, created by the pressure of American occupation, the roads were falling to pieces and cholera streamed into the backyards. Planning and maintenance characterize even the briefest and most brutish empire; apart from the institution of a legal system there aren't many more imperial virtues. But Americans weren't pledged to maintain. There is Bien Hoa Station, built fifty years ago. It is falling down, but that is not the point. There is no sign that it was ever mended by the Americans; even sagging under its corona of barbed wire it looks a good deal sturdier than the hangars at Bien Hoa airbase".

It is an important commercial centre, well connected with Saigon. *Getting there*: regular trains from Saigon station and buses from the Mien Dong terminal.

My Tho is another town it is quite possible to visit in a day. My Tho is on the Mekong Delta about 70 km from Saigon (see page 270).

Tours

As things 'free-up', so people are coming out of the woodwork to offer their services and set-up tour companies. Prices at the private (rather than the official) tour offices tend to be more competitive – shop around.

Day tours The most popular day tours are to the **Cu Chi Tunnels** and **Tay Ninh** (see page 257), and the **Saigon City Tour**. Another favourite is the **Drug Rehabilitation Centre** at Truong Giao Duc Lao which has treated, and continues to treat, many thousands of addicts. **The War** and the American presence created a drug problem of monumental proportions, and the centre was forced, through lack of funds, to rely in large part upon education and various psychological treatments to combat addiction. It is reputed to have a very high success rate in curing addicts. Other day tours include **Vung Tau** (see page 241), **Bien Hoa** (page 259), and **My Tho** (page 270). Through the state tour operations *Saigontourist* and *Vietnamtourism* these day tours cost US$80 (1 person), US$40-50 (3+ people); private tour companies charge considerably less (US$20-30).

Boat 'dinner' tours on the Saigon River Leave from the wharfs along Ton Duc Thang St, between the *Floating Hotel* and the end of Nguyen Hue Blvd. Most leave at 1930 and cruise for about 2 hrs. Good but expensive food and drink is available on board; there is also

dancing. Boat excursions to Binh Quoi Village include dinner and cultural evening 'in bucolic ambience', US$20, from *Saigontourist*.

Overnight tours Tours of more than a day are available from *Saigontourist* and *Vietnamtourism* to **Vung Tau** and destinations in the **Mekong delta** such as Vinh Long, Can Tho, Long Xuyen, Rach Gia and Ha Tien (see Mekong section, page 272). Rates are about US$50 pp/day. Longer tours N and to Cambodia can also be booked.

Overnight tours run by private companies

More imaginative, and considerably cheaper, are the overnight tours offered by companies that have sprung up to exploit on the one hand the wish of travellers to be at least partially independent, and on the other, the problems that foreigners face dealing with local officials, with the language and with the difficulties of transport. Often these consist of only a car or minibus and driver. Accommodation is not booked, and the group decide where they wish to stay. Costs vary, but a 21 day tour from Saigon to Hanoi is about US$400 (exclusive of board and lodging); *Saigontourist* covers the same ground in 14 days, in more style and inclusive of lodging, but for over US$1,000. Recommended companies can be found on page 268 under **Tour companies & travel agents.**

Local information

● **Accommodation**

Price guide:			
L	US$200+	C	US$15-25
A+	US$100-200	D	US$8-15
A	US$50-100	E	US$4-8
B	US$25-50	F	US$<4

Hotels in Saigon are the best in Vietnam. There is a good choice of reasonable places to stay, and many have been renovated. There are no bargains (which some people find difficult to understand for a country that is so poor), and although the better hotels are competitively priced by international standards, 'backpackers' accommodation is generally more expensive than the equivalent in cities such as Bangkok and Jakarta. At the beginning of 1994 there were 30 new hotel projects under discussion, so change is rapid. All of the larger hotels are owned by *Saigontourist* – the *Continental*, *Rex*, *Caravelle*, *Majestic* and *Palace*. They also have a share in the *Floating Hotel*.

Central Saigon: L-A+ *Century Saigon*, 68A Nguyen Hue Blvd, T 231818, F 292732, a/c, restaurant, coffee shop, friendly staff, business centre, health club, disco, central location but small, expensive rooms; L-A+ *Saigon Floating Hotel*, 1A Me Linh Sq, T 290783, F 290784, a/c, IDD, restaurants, pool, tennis courts, health club, nightclub, new Swiss management, regarded as the best run hotel in Vietnam with good business facilities and male staff in quaint sailors uniforms, but rooms are small and the hotel's future is in doubt – bitter feuding with Saigon's People's Committee which boils down to money, whatever the outcome hotel is due for overhaul in Singapore in 1998, very popular, book early and reconfirm, rec; L-A *Continental*, 132-134 Dong Khoi St, T 299201, F 290936, a/c, Graham Greene stayed here, the hotel features in the *Quiet American*, journalists' haunt – the *Continental Shelf* was a well known café terrace, Italian restaurant, bar, colonial splendour, large rooms, comfortable and very popular, book well in advance, rec; L-A *Norfolk Hotel*, 117 Le Thanh Ton St, T 223823, F 293415, a/c, nr Ben Thanh market and consequently quite noisy, business facilities, restaurant and excellent staff, popular with the business community, especially Australians; L-A *Rex* (Ben Thanh), 141 Nguyen Hue Blvd, T 292185, F 291469, a/c, restaurants, pool, good rooms with famous rooftop terrace bar, popular, book well in advance and reconfirm, new extension known as 'Mini Rex' with 10% discount, rec; A+ *Kim Do*, 133 Nguyen Hue Blvd, T 225914, F 225913, a/c, central, restaurant, old friends will not recognize the newly renovated hotel – stratospheric prices (+10% service) – what *is* the emperor wearing?; A+-A *Asian*, 146-150 Dong Khoi St, T 296979, F 297433, new, a/c, restaurant, central and popular; A+-A *Caravelle* (Doc Lap), 19-23 Lam Son Sq, T 293704, F 299902, a/c, central, 12th flr restaurant, superb breakfast incl, refurbished but still full of 60s atmosphere for nostalgophiles, former favourite with journalists; A+-A *Majestic* (Cuu Long), 1 Dong Khoi St, T 295515, F 291470, a/c, restaurant, large rooms, just

emerging from extensive renovation, exterior improved but still does not match its old grandeur, more expensive rooms have good river views, Jane March stayed here while filming *L'Amant*; A+-A *Riverside*, 19-20 Ton Duc Thanh St, T 297489, F 251417, a/c, the scaffolding has just been stripped away to reveal a neo-classical façade to this attractive colonial-era hotel, as the name implies more expensive rooms have river view, restaurant; A *Mondial*, 109 Dong Khoi St, T 296291, F 296324, a/c, roof restaurant, well managed, price incl breakfast, rec; A *Orchid*, 29A Don Dat St, T 231809, F 292245, a/c, just off centre, quiet area, surrounded by restaurants, rec; A-B *Bong Sen*, 117-119 Dong Khoi St, T 291516, F 299744, a/c, restaurant, price incl breakfast; A-B *Embassy*, 35 Nguyen Trung Truc St, T 291430, F 295019, restaurant, nightclub; the adjacent *Embassy II*, a windowless building (a failed brothel – in *Saigon*?), is cheaper; A-B *Huong Sen*, 70 Dong Khoi, T 291415, a/c, popular with tour groups; A-B *Palace* (Huu Nghi), 56-66 Nguyen Hue Blvd, T 292860, F 299872, a/c, restaurant, rooftop pool, dancing, price incl breakfast; A-B *Rose*, 123 Dong Khoi St, T 290613, F 298076, a/c, restaurant, price incl breakfast; B *Saigon Concert*, 7 Lam Son Sq, T 291299, F 295831, a/c, located in the back of the opera house, restaurant, helpful staff, rec; B *Viet Phuong Mini Hotel*, 105 Dong Khoi St, T 295429, a/c, located above a tailor's shop; B-C *Saigon*, 45-47 Dong Du St, some a/c, central, some rooms a bit dark and small, popular, clean and good value; C *Dong Du Guesthouse*, 26 Dong Du St, (next to *Cam On Tour*), T 230164, a/c, large rooms, some with sitting room attached, hot water, clean, rec; C-D *Khach San 69*, 69 Hai Ba Trung St, T 291513, some a/c, backs on to Saigon's Indian mosque, popular with Russian tour groups, seedy restaurant with female hostesses, clean rooms fairly priced; C-D *Mogambo*, 20 Thi Sach St, T 251311, a few rooms above this popular café bar; *Dong Khoi* (formerly Palace), 8 Dong Khoi St, an architectural treasure, currently undergoing extensive renovation; we hope the stained glass, marble staircase and vast suites will survive the ordeal but fear the worst.

Borders of Central Saigon: these hotels are a little out of the centre – a 10-30 mins walk or short cyclo/taxi ride. L-A+ *Omni Saigon*, 251 Nguyen Van Troi St, Q Phu Nhuan, T 449222, F 449200, opened early 1994, a/c, pool, health club, presidential suite, restaurants, full business facilities, probably the most opulent hotel in Vietnam, but inconvenient for

PHAM NGU LAO AREA

VL 92

Sketch Map

N

To Cholon

Pharmacy

Ben Thanh Market

Sacom Bank

Hotels:
9. Lé Lé
10. A Châu
11. Hoan Vu
12. Hoang Tu (Prince)
13. Huong Mini
14. Mercure
15. Linh Thu Guesthouse
16. Metropole
17. New World
18. Pham Ngu Lao
19. Phuong Lan Guesthouse
20. Thai Binh
21. Tran Thi Canh 2
22. Vien Dong
23. Windsor

1. Pacific Company Tours

Restaurants:
2. Kim Café
3. Long Phi Café
4. Que Huong Café
5. Mr Conehead Icecreams & Bookshop
6. Saivad Dee Thai
7. Sinh Café I & Tours
8. Sinh Café II

To Phung Son Tu Pagoda

---

town, a courtesy shuttle connects with Nguyen Hue Blvd; **L-A** New World, 76 Le Lai St, T 228888, F 230710, newly opened, a/c, pool, business facilities, 6 restaurants, Vietnam's largest hotel and proving quite popular; **A+** Metropole, 148 Tran Hung Dao Blvd, T 322021, F 322022, Saigontourist property, newly built, good position between Saigon and Cholon; **A+** Sol Chancery Saigon, 196 Nguyen Thi Minh Khai St, Q3, T 299152, F 251464, a/c, new, overlooks Lao Dong Sports Club, all rooms are suites, comfortable, good service, popular, rec; **A+** Windsor Saigon, 193 Tran Hung Dao Blvd, T 251503, F 251502, brand new, high quality finish, a/c, suites and studios, gym, restaurant and business facilities; **A+-A** Hotel Mercure, 79 Tran Hung Dao Blvd, T 242525, F 242602, now part of the French hotel group and will no doubt improve; **A+-A** Saigon Star, 204 Nguyen Thi Minh Khai St, Q3, T 230260, F 230255, a/c, business centre and secretarial facilities, a friendly, well run hotel overlooking Reunification Park; **A-B** International, 19 Vo Van Tan St, Q3, T 290009, F 290066, a/c, Chinese seafood restaurant and noodle shop, business centre; **B** Liberty (Que Huong), 167 Hai Ba Trung St, Q3, T 294227, F 290919, a/c, popular restaurant, good rooms but pricy for what it offers; **B** Nha Khach Quoc Te, 3 Cong Truong Quoc Te, T 290021,

F 231541, university guesthouse located behind university building (Vien Dai Hoc); **B** Sae Young (Festival), 31 Cao Thang St, Q3, T 390704, F 390559, a/c, dancing, numerous street restaurants in the vicinity; **B-C** Nhat Minh (Sunrise), 117 Tran Quang Khai St, T 438808, F 323866, small, clean, secluded hotel; **C-D** Architecture Guesthouse, 134 Nguyen Dinh Chieu St, T 225583, some huge rooms, a/c, quiet; **D** Khach San Ga Saigon (Station Hotel), 1 Nguyen Thong St, T 230105, overlooks the railway station, noisy area, rather run down; **D-F** Miss Loi's Guesthouse, 178/20 Co Giang St, T 352973, cheap and cheerful, well kept, some a/c, popular, rec; **E-F** Xuan Thu, 178/17 Co Giang St and other cheap guesthouses nearby.

Pham Ngu Lao area: most backpackers head straight for this bustling district, a 10 mins walk from downtown. There are countless hotels, guesthouses and rooms to rent which open, close or change hands with remarkable speed. Shared rooms can be had for as little as US$4-5/night but facilities and comfort levels at the bottom end are very basic. **A-D** Vien Dong, 275A Pham Ngu Lao St, T 393001, F 332812, newly refurbished, marble clad lobby, popular Cheers disco and a range of rooms; **C-D** Hoan Vu, 265 Pham Ngu Lao St, T 396522, some a/c, popular; **C-D** Huong Mini Hotel, 40/19 Bui

Vien St, T 322158, some a/c; **C-D** *Tran Thi Canh 2*, 211 Pham Ngu Lao St, T 352353, some a/c, clean, rooftop terrace; **D** *A Chau*, 92B Le Lai, T 331814, 6 rm above a pharmacy; **D** *Hotel 6*, 6 Pham Ngu Lao St, T 357120, a/c, bath; **D** *Lé Lé*, 269 De Tham St, T 322110, fan, shared bathroom; **D** *Linh Thu Guesthouse*, 72 Bui Vien St, T 330321, fan and bathroom; **D** *Phuong Lan Guesthouse*, 70 Bui Vien St, T 330569, fan and shared bathroom; **E** *Hoang Tu (Prince)*, 187 Pham Ngu Lao St, T 322657, now less popular with travellers as there is more choice, cheapest on the upper floors, rather noisy; **E** *Le Suong*, 94-96 Le Lai St, new and clean; **E** *Thai Binh*, 325 Pham Ngu Lao St.

Cholon: few people stay in Cholon, but it does have the best pagodas in Saigon and is only a short cyclo ride from the centre of town. **A** *Arc en Ciel (Thien Hong)*, 52-56 Tan Da St, Q5, T 552869, F 550332, a/c, restaurant, best in Cholon with rooftop bar, price incl breakfast; **D** *Phénix*, 411 Tran Hung Dao St (entrance is down a side street), T 556599, a/c.

Near airport: for most visitors, tourists and businessmen alike, these hotels are inconveniently located several km NW of the city centre. Prices tend to be marginally more competitive as a result. **A+-A** *Chains First Hotel*, 18 Hoang Viet St, Q Tan Binh, T 441199, F 444282, a/c, Wing A old and cheaper, Wing B new and pricier, free airport pickup and downtown shuttle, tennis court, business services; **A-B** *Airport*, 108 Hong Ha St, Q Tan Binh, T 445761, F 440166, closest to the airport and reasonable value. Just 100m E a café sits beneath the wings of a grounded Boeing 707; **B** *Cosevina*, 311 Nguyen Van Troi St, Q Phu Nhuan, T 442088, F 445898, a/c, comfortable with good restaurant; **B** *Mekong*, 261 Hoang Van Thu Blvd, Q Phu Nhuan, T 441322, F 444809, a/c, restaurant; **B-C** *Tan Son Nhat*, 200 Hoang Van Thu Blvd, Q Phu Nhuan, T 441079, F 442226, a/c, restaurant and pool.

● **Places to eat**

> **Price guide:** ✦✦✦✦*Over US$10* (100,000 dong); ✦✦✦*US$5-10* (50,000-100,000 dong); ✦✦*US$2-5* (20,000 -50,000 dong); ✦*Under US$2* (20,000 dong).

Several areas have established themselves as foci for lunchtime and evening eating. *Thi Sach St*, long a favourite with Vietnamese, is given over entirely to gastronomic pleasures and attracts increasing numbers of Westerners.

Pham Ngu Lao St adds daily to its already impressive number of nosh shops and cafés, tending towards the cheaper end of the market. Do not overlook street-side stalls whose staples consist of *pho* (noodle soup), *banh xeo* (savoury pancakes), *cha gio* (spring rolls) and baguettes stuffed with paté and salad – usually fresh and very cheap. At *binh dan* (popular) street restaurants the food is set out on a counter, and diners simply point to what they want. These places are frequented by shop and office workers at lunch time, and offer excellent value and normally very good food. Saigon restaurants are developing apace and new establishments are opening every month.

Vietnamese: ✦✦✦*Cung Dinh*, Pasteur St, adjacent to *Mini Rex Hotel* (part of *Rex Hotel*), serves specialities from all parts of Vietnam; ✦✦✦*La Bibliothèque (aka Madame Dai's)*, 84A Nguyen Du (unmarked), T 231438, also serves French food, Madame Dai was a member of the National Assembly of the former regime and a lawyer: customers eat in her study surrounded by law tomes, rather pretentious and the food is only average, book in advance; ✦✦✦*Lemon Grass*, 63 Dong Khoi St, T 298006, good Vietnamese food attractively served; ✦✦✦*Tu Do (Liberty)*, 80 Dong Khoi St, Vietnamese and Chinese and international, popular with young, monied Vietnamese, dancing upstairs; ✦✦✦*Vietnam House*, 93-95 Dong Khoi St, T 291623, attractively restored building, waiters and waitresses wear traditional Vietnamese costume and traditional music is played on an array of exotic instruments, excellent food, rec; ✦✦✦*VY*, 105 Yersin St, T 294567, Vietnamese specialities, highly regarded locally; ✦✦*Brodard*, corner of Dong Khoi and Nguyen Thiep sts, 60s decor; ✦✦*Caravelle Hotel*, 19-23 Lam Son Sq, the restaurant has a good reputation among hotels and has live music at lunch and dinner, also Chinese and French, rec; ✦✦*Cha Ca Hanoi*, 27 Nguyen Huu Canh St, a little way out of town and hidden down narrow streets but signposted and excellent cha ca (see page 290); ✦✦*Giac Duc*, 492 Nguyen Dinh Chieu, Q3, Vietnamese vegetarian restaurant; ✦✦*Givral*, 169 Dong Khoi, café, patisserie and convenient snacks and drinks in the city centre; ✦✦*13 Ngo Duc Ke*, fresh, well cooked food, open 0600-2400, popular with locals and travellers alike, one of the most successful restaurants in Saigon it has now taken over almost half the street, rec; ✦✦*Ngu Binh*, 82 Cu xa Nguyen Van Troi, Q Phu Nhuan, specializes in Hué dishes and closes early, some way out of town but very rewarding; **May Bon Phuong**, 335/5 Dien Bien Phu, Q3, tucked away between Bien Bien Phu and Nguyen Dinh Chieu sts, closed Tues, outstanding fish salad, popular with Vietnamese, rec; **Restaurant 95**, 95 Dinh Tien Hang St, spring rolls, fried noodles and crab soup; **Tib**, 187 Hai Ba Trung St, Q3, quiet, extensive menu; **Thanh Nien (Piano Bar)**, 11 Nguyen Van Chiem, popular with young Vietnamese, indoor and outdoor seating, live music, rec.

Other Asian: ****Lotus Court**, 251 Nguyen Van Troi St, (Omni Hotel), finest Cantonese cuisine; ****Ritz Taiwanese**, 333 Tran Hung Dao, superb food but expensive; ***Dynasty** (New World Hotel), 76 Le Lai St, Chinese dim sum; ***Ngan Dinh**, 2A Ton Duc Thang St, seafood, Chinese, Thai specialities, on the river front; ***Nihon Bashi**, 4-6 Le Loi (Rex Hotel), good, reliable Japanese; **Ashoka**, 17A-10 Le Thanh Ton St, a new and highly regarded Indian restaurant, rec; **Delhi Indian**, 68 Nguyen Hue Blvd, food a little disappointing but friendly service; **Korean Restaurant**, 213 Dong Khoi St, behind an ice cream parlour; **Seafood Palace**, 46A Nguyen Van Troi St, Chinese/seafood; **Seoul**, 37 Ngo Duc Ke St, T 294297, good Taiwanese food, popular with Korean businessmen.

International: ****La Cigale**, 158 Nguyen Dinh Chinh St, Q Phu Nhuan, T 443930, receives the highest acclaim for its French cuisine; ****Le Mekong**, 32 Vo Van Tan St, Q3, T 291277, excellent French cuisine but prices exclude all bar expense accounts; ***A**, 361/8 Nguyen Dinh Chieu St, Q3, T 359190, new Russian restaurant complete with authentic *Samovars*, run by a Russo-Vietnamese family; ***Annie's Pizzas**, 59 Cach Mang Thang Tam St, T 392577, nr *New World Hotel*, eat in, take away or free delivery service; ***Bavaria**, 20 Le Anh Xuan St, T 222673, nr *New World Hotel*, large German portions; ***Camargue**, 16 Cao Ba Quat St, T 243148, on the corner of Thi Sach, lovely open air terrace, *chic*, popular with diplomatic corps; ***Continental Hotel and Chez Guido**, 132-134 Dong Khoi St, good Vietnamese and French food and separate Italian restaurant (Chez Guido) which has good pizzas but is a bit overpriced; ***Floating Hotel**, 1A Me Linh Square, T 290783, choice of cafés and restaurants, check the latest promotion; ***Gartenstadt**, 34 Dong Khoi St, T 223623, excellent German food and draught German beer, crowded at lunchtime, rec, Mediterranean restaurant upstairs; ***Le

P'tit Bistrot**, 58 Le Thanh Ton St, T 230219, limited menu but excellent French food, rec; ***Le Restaurant**, 54 Hai Ba Trung St, T 906105, closed Mon, French, decline in quality noted over the last year; ***Maxim's**, 13-17 Dong Khoi St, T296676, massive menu; the food receives mixed reviews but the floorshows are widely acclaimed; 60s timewarp decor; ***Restaurant 180**, 180 Nguyen Van Thu St, T 251673, German management, ambitious European and Asian menu, large portions and excellent food, perennial favourite, rec; ***Rex Hotel**, 141 Nguyen Hue Blvd, top floor restaurant has good Western and Vietnamese food but the roof terrace has become increasingly crowded; ***Tex-Mex**, 24 Le Thanh Ton St, live blues, deep S and Mexican specialities; ***Thien Nam**, 53 Nam Ky Khoi Nghia St, was popular with US servicemen, its decor remains unaltered, a wide and varied menu; ***VY**, 164 Pasteur St, Western and Chinese specialities, less good than the Yersin branch; **Sapa**, 8A/8 Don Dat St, interesting and well cooked selection of Vietnamese and Swiss dishes, good value, rec; **Spago**, 158 Dong Khoi St, new restaurant café; *Kim Café**, 270 De Tham St, just off Pham Ngu Lao, range of food and drink, open from breakfast till late, popular with travellers; *Long Phi**, 163 Pham Ngu Lao St, bar, pool, music and decent food; *Mr Conehead**, 195 Pham Ngu Lao St, for all your ice cream requirements; *Sinh Café**, 6 Pham Ngu Lao St, good value food and drink all day; *Sinh Café II**, 1 Le Lai St, a second branch of the ever popular backpackers haunt.

Foodstalls: *A Phu**, 99 Pasteur St, tables set up alongside a parked bus serve good *ban xeo*; **Anh Thu**, 49 Dinh Cuong Trang St, and numerous other stalls nearby serve excellent *cha gio, banh xeo, bi cuon* and other Vietnamese street food, rec; **Nguyen Trai St** (extreme E end of, by the roundabout), late night *pho* can be had from the stalls in this area; **Tran Cao Van St**, E of Cong Truong Quoc Te, Q3, the restaurants and stalls here serve delicious noodles of all kinds; **362-376 Hai Ba Trung St**, these restaurants serve the best *com ga* (chicken rice); **144 Phan Dinh Phung St**, Q Phu Nhuan, is a long trek but noodle *aficionados* will be well rewarded.

● **Bars**

Along with the influx of foreigners and the freeing up of Vietnamese society has come a rapid increase in the number of bars in Saigon and they cater for just about all tastes – drink, music and company-wise. At one time hotel bars were just about the only safe and legal place for foreigners to drink but now, sadly, they are beginning to look much the same as hotel bars the world over. Bearing in mind the exciting things taking place outside the hotels, there is very little reason to stay in. The rooftop bar at the *Rex Hotel* is an exception, with its strange fish tanks, song birds, topiary, good views, cooling breeze, snacks and meals – and a link with history – rec; *Apocalypse Now*, 2C Thi Sach St, now in its third incarnation, larger premises, sticks to its roots (60s rock music and reasonably priced beer), pool, gets very busy after 2200. *Hard Rock Cafe*, 24 Mac Thi Buoi St, is quieter and clients concentrate more on the pool table. The *River Bar*, Ho Huan Nghiep (between Dong Khoi and Me Linh Sq), popular with expats; *Hammock Bar*, opp the *Majestic Hotel* occupies a nicely converted boat moored down river from the *Floating Hotel*, cool breezes, gentle motion, good food too, rec.

The most sophisticated of the bars is *Q Bar*, 7 Lam Son Sq, under the Opera House facing the *Caravelle Hotel*. Striking decor and Caravaggio murals, haunt of a wide cross-section of Saigon society, open till the small hours. On the other side of the City Opera House facing the *Continental Hotel* is *Saigon Headlines*; live music and serves food, popular with Asian businessmen. Nearby, at 74 Hai Ba Trung St is the new *Gecko Bar* which serves Saigon's latest tipple, chocolate vodka; N up Hai Ba Trung is *Buffalo Blues*, 72A Nguyen Du, live jazz and blues, draught Bass and food. Pham Ngu Lao area has a number of cheap bars, *Long Phi*, 163 Pham Ngu Lao St, *Sinh Café* opp, nearby *Kim Café*, 270 De Tham St, and many others are favourite meeting places for budget travellers.

A characteristic feature of Vietnamese nightlife is *bia om*, darkened bars with female hostesses whose job is to encourage clients to consume more beer than they had intended: this they do by rehearsing their English, or at least certain well-worn phrases and exercising plenty of charm. Bia om bars spring up like mushrooms and survive until the police close them down. Some remain in the downtown area, but most have moved further out. The girls should be tipped.

Vietnamese tend to prefer non-alcoholic drinks and huge numbers of cafés (both indoor and out) exist to cater for this market. Young romantic couples sit in virtual darkness listening to Vietnamese love songs while sipping coffee. The furniture tends to be rather small for the Western frame but these cafés are an agreeable way of relaxing after dinner in a more typically Vietnamese setting. There are one or two on Dong Khoi S of Ly Tu Trong St but dozens a little further out of the centre, for instance along Dien Bien Phu. The video café featuring kung fu films is an increasingly common phenomenon.

● **Airline offices**
Vietnam Airlines (international), 116-118 Nguyen Hue Blvd, T 292118; Vietnam Airlines (domestic), 45 Dinh Tien Hoang St, T 299980, T 255194; Aeroflot, 4B Le Loi St (opp the *Rex Hotel*), T 293489; Air France, 130 Dong Khoi St, T 290981, F 230190; Cathay Pacific, 58 Dongkhoi St, T 223203, 441895; Direct Flights, 24 Ly Tu Trong St, T 293257; EVA Air, 129 Dong Khoi St, T 224488; Garuda, 106 Nguyen Hue Blvd, T 293644; KLM, 244 Pasteur St, Q3, T 231990; Lufthansa, 132-134 Dong Khoi St, T 298529; MAS, 65 Le Thanh Ton St, T 292529; Pacific Airlines, 27B Nguyen Dinh Chieu, T 230930; Philippine Airlines, 4A Le Loi Blvd, T 292113; Qantas, Tan Son Nhat Airport, T 424950; Singapore Airlines, 6 Le Loi Blvd, T 231583, F 231554; Thai, 65 Nguyen Du St, T 223365.

● **Banks & money changers**
It is easy to change money in Saigon. Official rates are increasingly realistic. Foreign Exchange Bank, 101 Nam Ky Khoi Nghia St; Vietcombank: Nguyen Hue Blvd (opp the *Rex Hotel*); 123 Dong Khoi St; Tan Son Nhat Airport; Vietnam Export-Import Bank, 134 Calmette St, T 293938, F 298540 and Le Thi Hong Gam St. Although a number of foreign banks have opened branches in Saigon, few are retail or foreign exchange banks. Thai Military Bank, 11 Ben Chuong Duong St (good rates) and other foreign banks nearby; VID Public Bank, 15A Ben Chuong Duong; BFCE, 11 Me Linh Sq.

Black market: black market rates may be marginally more advantageous, but not always so. The chief advantage is that the process is sometimes quicker and banks are few and far between. Gold shops and some antique shops often change money. They may refuse to accept marked or scruffy US$ and they will not accept torn or sellotaped notes, but have no qualms in handing out filthy, torn and sometimes unrecognizable dong. Tourists should not change money on the streets (see page 283 for more details) or if approached unsolicited.

● **Church services**
Communion held six times on Sun and 3 times

on weekdays and Sat at the Cathedral at the N end of Dong Khoi St.

● **Entertainment**

Cinemas: there were 44 'picture houses' in Saigon at last count; Western films are beginning to be shown.

Dancing: at the *Rex, Caravelle, Majestic* and *Palace* Hotels. Also at some restaurants eg *Liberty*, 80 Dong Khoi St; *Maxim's* (from 2000, 15,000d).

Discos: entertaining to be a voyeur as well as a participant. *Cheers*, *Vien Dong Hotel*, rec; *Hoan Kiem*, 27 Ngo Duc Ke St (1730-2400); *Pub International*, 32-34 Ngo Duc Ke St (2100-2400); *Shangri La*, 1196, 3 Thang 2, Q11. The *Down Under* nightclub at the *Floating Hotel*, where Asian businessmen pick up prostitutes; *VIP*, Pham Ngoc Thach St, Q3, another pick up joint.

Karaoke: the Vietnamese may have proved hostile to foreign invaders but all resistance failed in the face of karaoke which has now established itself as a favourite pastime. The sight and sound of this latest assault on Vietnam's traditions would, one suspects have Ho Chi Minh turning in his mausoleum. For the incurable, *Queen Bee*, 106 Nguyen Hue Blvd, *Floating Hotel*, *Hotel Mercure* – and many others. A number of hotels now have private karaoke cubicles (tactfully known as VIP rooms) where punters can practice undisturbed with the girl of their choice.

● **Embassies & consulates**

Cambodian Consulate General, 41 Phung Khac Khoan St, T 294498; **Cuban Consulate General**, 23 Phung Khac Khoan St, T 295818; **Czech and Slovakian Consulate General**, 176 Tu Duc St, T 291475; **French Consulate General**, 102 Hai Ba Trung St, T 297231; **Indian Consulate General**, 49 Tran Quoc Thao St, T 294498; **Laotian Consulate General**, 181 Hai Ba Trung St, T 299262; **Malaysian Consulate**, 53 Nguyen Dinh Chieu, Q3, T 299023; **Polish Consulate**, 2 Tran Cao Van St, T 290114; **Russia**, 40 Ba Huyen Thanh Quan, Q3, T 292936; **Singapore Consulate**, 5 Phung Khac Khoan, T 225173; **UK Consulate General**, 261 Dien Bien Phu St, Q3, T 298433, F 225740.

● **Hospitals & medical services**

AEA International Clinic, 65 Nguyen Du St, T 298520, F 298551, comprehensive 24 hrs medical and dental service; *Cho Ray Hospital*, 201 Nguyen Chi Thanh Blvd, Q5, T 254137; *Emergency Centre*, 125 Le Loi Blvd, T 292071, 24 hr, some English and French speaking doctors; *Institut du Coeur*, 520 Nguyen Tri Phuong Blvd, Q10,

T 651586 – also has French doctors (expensive). **Dental treatment** available at *St Paul's Hospital*, 280 Dien Bien Phu St, Q3, T 225052.

● **Post & telecommunications**

Cholon Post Office: 26 Nguyen Thi St; fax and telex services.

Fax service: from Post Office at 230 Hai Ba Trung. To *receive* a fax use the Saigonfax number (010 84 8) 298540, make sure your name and address is at the top of the message and Saigonfax will deliver it for a few thousand dong.

GPO: 2 Cong Xa Paris (close to the Catholic Cathedral), open 0630-1930 Mon-Sun. Telex, telegram and international telephone services available. Long-distance calls between US$12 (Hong Kong, Thailand, Malaysia) and US$20 for the first 5 mins (UK call = US$20 for 5 mins). **DHL**: at GPO (T 231525) and 253 Hoang Van Thu, T 446268.

TNT International Express: 56 Truong Son St, T 446460.

● **Shopping**

Antiques: most shops are on Dong Khoi, Mac Thi Buoi and Ngo Du Ke sts (the latter two both run off Dong Khoi). For the knowledgeable, there are bargains to be found, especially Chinese and Vietnamese ceramics – the difficulty is getting them out of the country (see page 286, Export restrictions). Also available are old watches, colonial bric-a-brac, lacquerware and carvings etc.

Bicycles: from the State Department Store at the top of Nguyen Hue Blvd, from the stalls along Le Thanh Ton St close to the Ben Thanh market and Vo Thi Sau W of junction with Pham Ngoc Thach St 300,000-400,000d for a Vietnamese bike, 400,000-500,000d for a slightly better built Chinese one.

Books: *Lan Anh Bookshop*, 201 Dong Khoi St for second-hand books in French and English. Bookshop, at 20 Ho Huan Nghiep sells French, English and Vietnamese books including bound photocopies of volumes. Some old books have 'US Embassy Library' stamped in the front. It doubles as a café selling some of the tastiest ice cream in Saigon. *Hong Ha*, 40 Ngo Duc Ke St, and shops at 60-62 and 56 Le Loi Blvd and 40 Nguyen Hue Blvd sell English-Vietnamese dictionaries and phrase books and some books on Vietnam. *Mr Conehead*, 195 Pham Ngu Lao St, purveys fine ice creams as well as books.

Chinese ink drawings: 657 Nguyen Trai St, Cholon.

Foodstores: specializing in Western staples

HORSE RACES

The commencement was a race of 12 horses, or rather ponies; for, however great were the prizes for competition, the rivalship had not caused them to improve the breed of their cattle; a more meagre, dwarfish, crippled, puny lot of horses, I never before beheld. Chinese horses are bad enough, but these were ten times worse; and I think the best mode the Quong or the King could adopt to improve them would be, to have races twice or thrice a year, and give prizes to be run for, that would pay the natives to buy foreign horses, and mix the breed.

Well, these twelve animals started; but with all their whips, rattans, spurs, and shouting, they could not get more than a very slow canter out of the best of them. I pitied the poor beasts; they looked far more in want of a feed of corn, than fit to run a race. They made two or three more trials, but it was "no go"; I could have run faster myself, weak as I was. The poor brutes broke down before they got half-way round the course; and, out of the twelve that started, only three managed to come in anything at all like "racers".

Taken from *Cochin-China and my experience of it* by Edward Brown, London 1861.

(which, in Vietnam, seem suddenly luxurious) such as milk, cornflakes, peanut butter etc abound on Ham Nghi Blvd around number 62.

Handicrafts: there are a number of shops around the *Rex* and *Continental Hotels* and also along Dong Khoi St and Nguyen Hue Blvd. Handicrafts include lacquerware, mother-of-pearl inlaid screens and ceramics.

Lacquerware: Vietnamese lacquerware has a long history, and a reputation of sorts (see page 126). Visitors to the workshop can witness the production process and, of course, buy the products if they wish. Lacquerware is available from many of the handicraft shops on Nguyen Hue Blvd and Dong Khoi St. Also from the *Lamson Laquerware Factory*, 106 Nguyen Van Troi St (100m beyond the railway line going NW – they take Visa and Mastercard).

Linen: good quality linen table cloths, sheets, avaliable from shops on Dong Khoi St; bargain hard.

Maps: Saigon has the best selection in Vietnam; from the stalls around the intersection of Dong Khoi St and Nguyen Hue Blvd. Bargain hard – the bookshops listed above may well be cheaper.

Silk/Ao Dai (see page 126): Vietnamese silk and traditional dresses (*ao dai*) are to be found in the shops on Dong Khoi St and in Ben Thanh market.

War surplus: from Dan Sinh Market (see page 254).

Western newspapers and magazines: sold nr the main hotels, eg opp the *Rex*. Same day *Bangkok Post* and *The Nation* newspapers (English language Thai papers), and up-to-date *Financial Times*, *Straits Times*, *South China Morning Post*, *Newsweek*, *Economist*, *Far Eastern Economic Review*, and *Time* magazines plus fashion magazines such as *Elle*. Bargain hard; it is sometimes possible to get them cheaper than the cover-price because they are often second-hand, (presumably) they are taken from the hotels after a guest has left.

● **Sports**

Billiards: incredibly popular; every town has its billiard parlour (*bi da*) – there are many in Saigon.

Horse racing: the *Phu Tho Racecourse* (hardly an Ascot) stages races on Thur, Sat and Sun afternoons. Both the winner and the second horse have to be selected to collect. The course has been recently re-opened with financing from an interested Chinese entrepreneur but not a lot has changed since 1858 when Edward Brown recorded his impressions of Vietnamese racing, see box, page 267. He would be delighted to know of plans by fellow Britons to introduce new breeding stock to Vietnam. Admission to Turf Club 20,000d.

Swimming: some hotels (like the *Rex*, *Palace* and *New World*) allow non-residents to use their pool for a small charge. The Lao Dong Club (old Cercle Sportif) on the corner of Nguyen Thi Minh Khai and Huyen Tran Cong Chua St has a good size pool; the old US Embassy pool tends to be crowded but one can imagine the conversations that must have taken place there.

Tennis: courts at the *Floating Hotel*, *Rex Hotel* and *Huong Duong Hotel*, 150 Nguyen Thi Minh Khai St, for non-residents. Also at the Lao Dong Club in Van Hoa Park, behind Reunification Hall.

● **Tour companies & travel agents**
Ann Tourist, 58 Ton That Tung St, T 334356, F 323866 (generally excellent, knowledgeable guides); *Cam On Tour*, 32 Dong Du St, T 298443, F 298169 (not private – run by the Ho Chi Minh City People's Committee – but efficient, knowledgeable and friendly staff and helpful, English-speaking drivers); *Diethelm Travel*, 173B Nguyen Van Troi, Q Phu Nhuan, T 443370, F 443376; *Far East Tourist*, 61 Le Thanh Ton St, T 225187, F 295361; *Kim Café*, 270 De Tham, organize minibuses to Nha Trang, Dalat etc and tours of the Mekong, good source of information; *Oriental Pearls*, 2812 Cach Mang Thang Tam, Q Tan Binh, T 640500; *Pacific Tourist Agency*, 261 De Tham St, T 394407; *Peace Tour Co*, 60 Vo Van Tan, Q3, T 294416, F 294416; *Sinh Café*, 6 Pham Ngu Lao, organize tours of the S and minibuses further afield; *Vacation Planners*, 39/3 Tran Nhat Duat St, T 242807, F 299744, rec; *Vidotour*, Le Thanh Ton St, T 291438; *Youth Tourist Centre*, 51 Nguyen Dinh Chieu St, T 296743, F 290919. Extraordinarily expensive overnight cruises in the Mekong on the junk *Saigon River* are offered by *Voiles Vietnam*, 17 Pham Ngoc Thach, Q3, T 296750.

● **Tourist offices**
Cuu Long Tourist, 45 Dinh Tien Hoang St, T 293990 – for tours to Mekong Delta; **Saigontourist**, 49 Le Thanh Ton St, T 295834, F 224987, organize expensive tours, maybe useful for advice and a few useful handouts; **Vietnamtourism**, 69-71 Nguyen Hue Blvd, T 290772, F 290775, again, only helpful if booking one of their tours.

● **Useful addresses**
Business centres: *Rex Hotel*, 141 Nguyen Hue Blvd, *Floating Hotel*, 1A Me Linh Sq and *Century Saigon*, 68A Nguyen Hue Blvd, *Omni Hotel*, 25 Nguyen Van Troi St, among others for sorting out formalities, sending faxes etc. *Lotus Business Centre*, 71-73 Hai Ba Trung St, T 223053, F 298348 and *Saigon Business Centre*, 49-57 Dong Du St, T 298777, F 298155.
Chamber of Commerce and Industry: 171 Vo Thi Sau St, Q3, T 230301.

Foreign Affairs Service: 6 Thai Van Lung, T 224128.
Immigration Office: 161 Nguyen Du St, T 299398.
OSIC (import-export office): 8 Nguyen Hue Blvd.

● **Transport**
72 km from My Tho, 147 km from Vinh Long, 113 km from Vung Tau, 165 km from Can Tho, 250 km from Rach Gia, 299 km from Dalat, 338 km from Hatien, 445 km from Nha Trang, 965 km from Danang, 1,071 km from Hué, 1,710 km from Hanoi.

Local Bicycle: if staying in Saigon for any length of time (or intend travelling by bus with the bike) it might be a good idea to buy a bicycle (see Shopping, above and page 295). **Bicycle & motorcycle hire**: bicycles can be hired from some of the cheaper hotels and cafés; *Ann Tourist*, 58 Ton That Tung St (US$2/day); *Kim Cafeteria*, 270 De Tham St and *Sinh Café*, 6 Pham Ngu Lao both rent bicycles and Mr Nguyen Ngoc Ha at 49 Dong Khoi St (US$1/day); and from the magazine stall opp the *Rex Hotel* on Nguyen Hue St (by Ho's statue). Bicycling is the best way to get around town, and although there are not many places that hire out bikes this is likely to increase as tourism expands. Bikes are best parked in the roped-off compounds (*Gui xe*) that are all over town; they will be looked after for a small charge (500d by day, 1,000d after dark). Most hotels and restaurants have their own keepers. *Far East Travel* also rent out motorbikes (US$7/day with US$400 deposit), as does *Ann Tourist*. **Cyclo**: a good way to get around the city. They can be hired by the hour (approx US$2-3/hour) or to reach a specific destination (roughly 4-5,000d/km). Many drivers speak good English (especially the older cyclo drivers). Each tends to have his own patch which is jealously guarded – especially if it happens to be outside one of the more expensive hotels. Expect to pay more outside the major hotels – it is worth walking around the corner. Cyclos found waiting in tourist spots will often offer additional services such as money changing and taxi hire. Some visitors complain cyclo drivers in Saigon have an annoying habit of forgetting the agreed price (though it's not as bad as in Hanoi); ask for the agreed price to be written down to avoid confusion. For their part, locals complain that by paying US$2/journey, tourists are pushing-up the prices for locals. That said, there is still a 2-price tariff; one for locals and one for foreigners. **Motorcycle taxi** (*Honda Om*):

quickest way to get around town and only marginally more expensive than a cyclo; agree a price and hop on the back. **Taxi**: Saigon has quite a large fleet of meter taxis – rivalry between the two operators has forced fares down. Cheaper and more reliable is the yellow *Vinataxi* (T 442170, T 222990); the *Airport Taxi Co* (T 446666) (white cars) has banned *Vinataxi* from picking up at Tan Son Nhat Airport. Unmarked taxis can be chartered for most hotels for trips out to the airport or out of town. The drivers who hang around the tourist areas (Nguyen Hue and Le Loi blvds) are cheaper. Chartering a taxi for the day should be about US$30-40 (including petrol), which is a reasonably cheap form of transport if split four ways. It is also possible to charter cars from some tour companies (for instance, *Ann Tourist* and *Cam On Tour*).

Air Tan Son Nhat Airport is 30 mins NW of the city. **Transport to town**: taxis to city centre cost US$8-10). Vietnam Airlines bus, US$2. **Airport facilities**: include a branch of the **Vietcombank** for changing money, Post Office, airline offices and desks of **Vietnamtourism, Saigontourist** and **Cuu Long Tourist**. **NB** Luggage is always x-rayed on entry to the country. Domestic connections with Dalat (US$40), Danang (US$90), Hanoi (US$170), Haiphong (US$170), Hué (US$90), Nha Trang (US$60), Phu Quoc (US$65), Play Ku (US$65), Quy Nhon (US$65), Rach Gia (US$65) and Vinh (see timetable page 292). Vietnam Airlines, China Airlines, China Southern Airlines, Aeroflot, Air France, Philippine Airlines, Garuda, Thai, Lao Aviation and Royal Air Cambodge, KLM, Lufthansa, EVA Air, Malaysian Airlines, Singapore Airlines and Cathay Pacific all fly to Saigon.

Train The station (*Nha ga*) is 2 km from the centre of the city at the end of Nguyen Thong St. Much improved facilities for the traveller include a/c waiting room, Post Office and bank (not TCs). Regular daily connections with Hanoi and all points N. Express trains take between 41 and 47 hrs to reach Hanoi; hard and soft berths are available. Sleepers should be booked in advance. (See page 293 for more information on rail travel and a condensed timetable with selected fares.)

Road Bus: there are two main bus stations (see map for location). Buses N to Vung Tau, Dalat, Hué, Danang and all significant points on the road to Hanoi leave from the Mien Dong terminal, N of the city centre on Xo Viet Nghe Tinh St, before the road crosses the Saigon River. Buses S to Ca Mau, Rach Gia, Ha Tien, Long Xuyen, My Tho, An Long, Can Tho, Long Xuyen and elsewhere leave from the Mien Tay terminal, some distance SW of town on Hung Vuong Blvd (30 mins by cyclo). There is also a bus station in Cholon which serves destinations such as Long An, My Thuan, Ben Luc and My Tho. There are increasing numbers of express minibuses (some a/c) serving the more popular destinations, but offices change frequently. Ask at your hotel for updated information. The minibus office at 39 Nguyen Hue Blvd is one of the most central and popular; daily minibus departures to Dalat 6 hrs, Vung Tau, Nha Trang, Hué, Danang, and Quy Nhon. There are also offices at 89-91 Nguyen Du St. Also a bus station on Huyen Tran Cong Chua; buses to Mekong Delta only. Book tickets the day before.

Sea Boat: the *Thong Nhat* makes a trip from Saigon Port to Haiphong every 10 days, 60 hrs. The ship terminal is at 1A Nguyen Tat Thanh St, Q4. **Ferry**: daily afternoon ferries leave from the wharf on Ton Duc Thang St, at the end of Ham Nghi Blvd, for destinations in the Mekong Delta; eg My Tho 7 hrs, Can Tho 24 hrs, and Chau Doc 24 hrs+. Pay on boarding. **Hydrofoil**: Dolphin Speed Lines operate hydrofoils to Vung Tau from the Wharf at end of Ham Nghi Blvd in Central Saigon. Quick (1 hr 20 mins) but expensive (25,000-100,000d). One boat/day on week days. Four-five at weekends (see timetable on page 244). The vessels are of Russian manufacture and quite uncomfortable.

International connections Air Regular connections with Bangkok, Vientiane, Phnom Penh, Amsterdam, Berlin, Hong Kong and Taipei, Moscow, Manila, Paris, Jakarta, Kuala Lumpur and Singapore (see page 285). **Road** To Phnom Penh from the garage at 155 Nguyen Hue Blvd, next to the *Rex Hotel* every day except Sun at 0600, 10 hrs (approximately US$5 for non-a/c, US$12 for a/c). **NB** Most visitors have visas which preclude an overland journey to Cambodia (visas usually give the point of exit as Saigon or Hanoi airports). This can be changed however for about $25). *Immigration Office*, 254 Nguyen Trai St or *Ann Tourist*, 58 Ton That Tung St, *Cam On Tour*, 32 Dong Du St, and *Vacation Planners*, 39/3 Tran Nhat Duat St, can arrange a re-entry visa from Cambodia, and an exit stamp for overland travel to Phnom Penh via Moc Bai, but there may still be difficulties.

THE MEKONG DELTA

Formal sights are thin on the ground in the Mekong Delta area and travel can be slow, involving numerous ferry crossings. But the road SW has improved dramatically in recent years, and increasing numbers of Western visitors are venturing into the area. The towns, the countryside, and the inhabitants of the delta region offer a great deal to the traveller: beautiful scenery, excellent food and warm personalities. Remember that banks are few and far between – change sufficient money before setting out, and carry small US$ bills for unforeseen expenses along the way.

The Mekong Delta or *Cuu Long* (nine dragons), is Vietnam's rice bowl, and before the partition of the country in 1954, rice was traded from the S where there was a rice surplus, to the N where there was a rice deficit, as well as internationally. Even prior to the creation of French Cochin China in the 19th century, rice was being transported from here to Hué, the imperial capital. Since reunification in 1975 this pattern of trade has reasserted itself. The delta covers 67,000 sq km, of which about half is cultivated. Rice yields are in fact generally lower than in the N, but the huge area under cultivation and the larger size of farms means that both the region and individual households tend to produce a surplus for sale. In the Mekong Delta, there is nearly three times as much riceland pp as there is in the N. It is this which accounts for the relative wealth of the region.

The Mekong Delta was not opened-up to agriculture on an extensive scale until the late 19th and early 20th centuries. Initially it seems that this was a spontaneous process: peasants, responding to the market incentives introduced by the French, slowly began to push the frontier of cultivation southwards into this wilderness area. The process gathered pace when the French colonial government began to construct canals and drainage projects to open more land to wet rice agriculture. By the 1930s the population of the Delta had reached 4.5 million with 2.2 million ha of land under rice cultivation. The Mekong Delta, along with the Irrawaddy (Burma) and Chao Phraya (Thailand) became one of the great rice exporting areas of Southeast Asia, shipping over 1.2 million tonnes annually.

Travel in the Mekong Delta The road is relatively good from Saigon to Long Xuyen, Chau Doc, and Can Tho, but beyond these towns roads are narrow and pot-holed and travel is generally slow. The many ferry crossings slow travel down still further and if travelling by bus expect long delays waiting in queues (private cars go straight to the front).

My Tho

My Tho, the capital of Tien Qiang Province, is 71 km SW of Saigon on the banks of the My Tho River, a 'distributary' of the mighty Mekong and about 40 km from the South China Sea. The town has

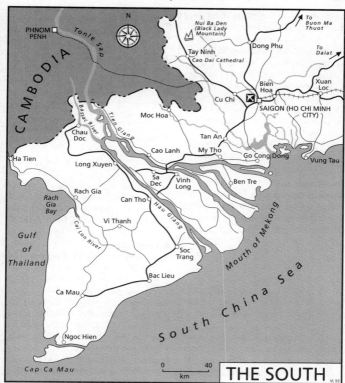

PHNOM PENH

CAMBODIA

Tonle Sap

N

Nui Ba Den (Black Lady Mountain)

Tay Ninh
Cao Dai Cathedral

Dong Phu

To Buon Ma Thuot

To Dalat

Bien Hoa

Xuan Loc

Cu Chi

SAIGON (HO CHI MINH CITY)

Moc Hoa

Chau Doc

Bassac River

Tien Giang

Tan An

My Tho

Go Cong Dong

Ha Tien

Long Xuyen

Cao Lanh

Sa Dec

Vinh Long

Ben Tre

Vung Tau

Rach Gia

Can Tho

Hau Giang

Mouth of Mekong

Rach Gia Bay

Vi Thanh

Cai Lon River

Soc Trang

Gulf of Thailand

Bac Lieu

Ca Mau

South China Sea

Ngoc Hien

Cap Ca Mau

0   40
km

THE SOUTH

VL 93

had a turbulent history: it was Khmer until the 17th century, when the advancing Vietnamese took control of the surrounding area. In the 18th century Thai forces annexed the territory, before being driven out in 1784. Finally, the French gained control in 1862.

Not far from My Tho is the hamlet of **Ap Bac**, the site of the Communists' first major military victory against the ARVN. The battle demonstrated that without direct US involvement the communists could never be defeated (see page 94).

Places of interest

Today, My Tho is an important riverside market town, 5 km off the main 'highway' to Vinh Long. On the corner of Nguyen Trai St and Hung Vuong Blvd, and a 5 mins walk from the central market, is **My Tho church**: yellow and white, with twin towers. The **central market** covers a large area from Le Loi Blvd, down to the river. The river – rather unromantically referred to as the Bao Dinh Channel – is the most enjoyable spot to watch My Tho life go by. By taking the bridge that crosses the river and then turning left down Nguyen An Ninh St the road leads, in the end, to **Vinh Trang Pagoda**: walk down the dirt track and then virtually straight over at the crossroads, onto Nguyen Trung Truc St. The temple is on the right, through a painted bamboo archway (No 60A). The entrance to the temple is through an ornate porcelain-encrusted gate. The pagoda built in 1849, and displays a mixture of architectural styles – Chinese, Vietnamese and colonial. The façade is almost fairytale in inspiration. The temple also has a small collection of animals that would be far happier elsewhere. Open 0900-1200, 1400-1700, Mon-Sun. **Getting to Vinh Trang Pagoda**: it is a long walk; best by bicycle or cyclo.

Excursions

Island of the Coconut Monk (or Con Phung) is about 3 km from My Tho. The 'Coconut Monk' established a retreat on this island shortly after the end of WW2 where he developed a new 'religion', a fusion of Buddhism and Christianity. He is said to have meditated for 3 years on a stone slab, eating nothing but coconuts (why, is not clear) – hence the name. Persecuted by both the South Vietnamese government and by the Communists, the monastery has fallen into disuse. *Getting there*: boats to the island can be chartered from the S end of Trung Trac St, at the ferry landing (expect to pay US$10-20, depending on the size of the boat).

Snake farm about 10 km from town at Dong Tam. The farm raises snakes for their medicinal qualities – not to remove their venom for use in serum, but because of the belief that their flesh and gall have strong healing powers. *Getting there*: take Highway 1 towards Vinh Long, at Dong Tam follow signs to *Trai Ran*. Admission US$1.

Tan Long Island is opposite My Tho and pleasant to wander the narrow paths. Tan Long is noted for its longan production. *Getting there*: either by tourist boat from the corner of 30 Thang 4 and Trung Trac sts (50,000d) or by ferry from the market in Le Thi Hong Gam St (1,000d).

Local information
● **Accommodation**

B *Song Tien* (used to be the *Grand*), 101 Trung Trac St, T 72009, overpriced and best avoided.

D *Huong Duong*, 33 Trung Trac St, T 72011, good river views.

E *Hotel 43*, 43 Ngo Quyen St, T 73126, good value, friendly, rec; **E** *Lao Dong*, corner of Le Loi and 30 Thang 4 sts, new, clean hotel with good views, rec; **E** *Rach Gam*, 33 Trung Trac St; **E** *Thanh Binh*, 44 Nguyen Binh Khiem St.

● **Places to eat**

A speciality of the area is *hu tieu my tho* – a spicy soup of vermicilli, sliced pork, dried shrimps and fresh herbs. The food at the friendly *Restaurant 43*, 43 Ngo Quyen St is good value and tasty; *Chi Thanh*, Trung Trac St, good fried noodles and shrimps, rec; *Nha Hang 52*, 52 Trung Trac St, excellent food at good prices; *Nha Hang 54*, 54 Trung Trac St, delicious ice cream.

● **Tourist offices**

Tien Giang Tourism, 66 Hung Vuong St, T 73154 (often shut).

● **Transport**

72 km from Saigon, 70 km from Vinh Long, 103 km from Can Tho, 179 km from Chau Doc, 182 km from Rach Gia, 272 km from Ha Tien.

Local Car hire: *Thuan Hung*, 130-156 Le Loi, T 72441, reasonable rates.

Road Bus: the bus station (*Ben Xe My Tho*) is 3-4 km from town on the road back towards Saigon and Vinh Long (continuation of Ap Bac St), ½ km past the city gates. Regular connections with Saigon's Mien Tay station (2 hrs); also buses to Vinh Long, Chau Doc, Can Tho and to other destinations in the Mekong Delta.

Sea Boat: daily afternoon ferries to My Tho leave from the wharf on Ton Duc Thang St, at the end of Ham Nghi Blvd in Saigon, 3 hrs (10,000d).

Vinh Long

Vinh Long is a rather ramshackle, but nonetheless clean and welcoming, riverside town on the banks of the Co Chien River and the capital of Vinh Long province. It was one of the focal points in the spread of Christianity in the Mekong Delta, and there is a **cathedral** and Catholic **seminary** in town. The richly stocked and well-ordered **Cho Vinh Long**, the central market, is on Hung Dao Vuong St, near the bus station. Vinh Long makes a reasonable stopping-off point on the road to Long Xuyen, Rach Gia and Ha Tien. There is a **Cao Dai church** not far from the second bridge leading into town from Saigon and My Tho, visible on the right-hand side.

Excursions Khmer Temples lie some distance S of town, in the district of Chau Thanh, and particularly around the town of Tra Vinh. *Getting there*: check at the *Cuu Long (A) Hotel* or the Cuu Long Tourist office for transport. Local boat rides organized by the Tourist office (expensive) or arrange with local boatmen (cheap).

● **Accommodation B-C** *Cuu Long (A)*, 1 1 Thang 5 St (ie No 1 1st May St), T 22494 (not far from the market, on the river), a/c, best in town, river views, price incl breakfast; **D** *Long Chau*, adjacent to Cuu Long (A), also lays claim to 1 1 Thang 5 St address, T 23611, incl breakfast, cheapest rooms have shared WC; **D-E** / *Cuu Long*, claims the same address, but is further up 1 Thang 5 St, set back from the river, rather run down; **E** *An Binh*, Hoang Thai Hieu St (behind bus station, opp Post Office), some a/c.

● **Places to eat** There are a number of restaurants and riverside cafés along 1 Thang 5 St, just beyond *Cuu Long (A) Hotel* incl *Phuong Thuy Restaurant*.

● **Post & telecommunications Post Office**: Doan Thi Diem St (behind bus station).

● **Tourist offices** Cuu Long Tourist, 1 Thang 5 St, T 23616, specialize in tours throughout the Delta, office in Saigon.

● **Transport** 70 km from My Tho, 32 km from Can Tho, 147 km from Saigon. **Road Bus**: the bus station is in the centre of town, close to the Post Office and central market on Hung Dao Vuong St. Regular connections, along a reasonable road, with Saigon's Mien Tay station (3½ hrs). Links with Can Tho, My Tho, Long Xuyen, Rach Gia and other Mekong Delta destinations.

Can Tho

Can Tho is a large commercial town of 200,000 situated in the heart of the Mekong Delta on the banks of the Can Tho or Bassac River, surrounded by canals and ricelands. It is the capital of Can Tho Province, the largest city in the Delta, and the region's principal transport hub, with roads and canals running to most other important towns. A small settlement was established at Can Tho at the end of the 18th century, although the town did not prosper until the French took control of the Delta a century later and rice production for export began to take-off. Can Tho was also an important US base. Paul Theroux in *The Great Railway Bazaar* writes:

"Can Tho was once the home of thousands of GIs. With the brothels and bars closed, it had the abandoned look of an unused fairground after a busy summer. In a matter of time, very few years, there will be little evidence that the Americans were ever there. There are poisoned rice fields between the straggling fingers of the Mekong Delta and there are hundreds of blond and fuzzy-haired children, but in a generation even these unusual features will change."

There is a university here and a teacher training college.

There is a bustling **market** on Hai Ba Trung St which runs along the banks of the river. The **Munirangsyaram Pagoda** at 36 Hoa Binh Blvd (SW from the post office) was built just after the war and is a Khmer Hinayana Buddhist sanctuary. The **Vang Pagoda** is on Hoa Binh Ave.

● **Accommodation B** *Hau Giang*, 34 Nam Ky Khoi Nghia, T 35537; **B** *International (Quoc Te)*, 12 Hai Ba Trung St (on the river), T 35973, a/c; **E** *Hoa Binh*, 5 Hoa Binh St, T 220537; **E** *Tay Do*, 61 Chau Van Liem St, T 21009, fan, shared WC, a bit grubby but cheap.

● **Places to eat** Several along the river on Hai Ba Trung St.

● **Entertainment Dancing**: *International Hotel*, 12 Hai Ba Trung St.

● **Post & telecommunications Post Office**: intersection of Hoa Binh Blvd and Ngo Quyen St.

● **Tourist offices** Hau Giang Tourism, 27 Chau Van Liem, T 20147.

● **Transport** 32 km from Vinh Long, 64 km from Long Xuyen, 103 km from My Tho, 115 km from Rach Gia, 120 km from Chau Doc, 165 km from Saigon, 206 km from Hatien. **Road Bus**: the station is about 2 km NW of town along Nguyen Trai St, nr the intersection with Hung Vuong St and route 4. Regular connections with Saigon's Mien Tay terminal, 4-5 hrs and other centres in the Mekong Delta. **Sea Ferries**: from Saigon dock 2½ km NW of town; vessels leave each day from the wharf on Ton Duc Thang St, at the end of Ham Nghi Blvd in Saigon, usually in the afternoon, 24 hrs (12,000d).

Long Xuyen

This is an airy, albeit rather shabby, town and the capital of An Giang Province. It is situated on the W bank of the Bassac River and has a population of 100,000. It falls slightly short, however, of the claims made by An Giang Tourism: "Travellers are invited to take a glimpse of Angiang's good decor. Elegant, comfortable hotels: particularly, perfect services with special dishes that are so delicious and fetching that hardly may another place be found out." The large **Catholic Cathedral** on Hung Vuong St is visible from out of town – two clasped hands form the spire. It was completed shortly before reunification in 1975. A short walk away at 8 Le Minh Nguyen St is the **Quan Thanh Pagoda**. It contains lively murals on the entrance wall and the figure of General Quan Cong and his two mandarin companions General Chau Xuong and Mandarin Quan Binh at the altar. Also on Le Minh Nguyen St, close to the intersection with Huynh Thi Huong St, is the **Dinh Than My Phuoc Pagoda**. Note the roof and the murals on the wooden walls near the altar. On the outskirts of town on Tran Hung Dao St travelling towards Chau Doc (just after the second bridge, about ½ km) is a **Cao Dai church**. This is worth visiting if unable to see the Cao Dai Cathedral at Tay Ninh (see page 258).

Excursions Chau Doc can be visited on a day trip (see page 274). *Getting there*: by bus from the station.

● **Accommodation B** *Cuu Long* (Mekong), 21 Nguyen Van Cung, T 52365, a/c, hot water, large rooms, clean; **B** *Long Xuyen*, 17 Nguyen Van Cung St, T 52927, a/c, hot water, newly repainted; **D** *Thai Binh*, 12 Nguyen Hue, T 52184, restaurant; **D** *Tien Thanh*, 240 Tran Hung Dao St, out of town on way in from Can Tho; **D** *Xuan Phuong*, 68 Nguyen Trai St, T 52041, a/c, clean.

● **Banks & money changers** Vietcombank, 1 Hung Vuong (at the junction of Hung Vuong and Nguyen Thi Minh Khai sts).

● **Post & telecommunications Post Office**: 101 Tran Hung Dao St (quite a way over the Hoang Dieu Bridge).

● **Tourist offices** An Giang Tourist Office, 6 Ngo Gia Tu St, T 52036.

● **Transport** 64 km from Can Tho, 126 km from My Tho. **Road Bus**: the station is 1½ km E of town on Tran Hung Dao St. Minibuses stop on Hung Vuong St, not far from the cathedral. Regular connections with Saigon's Mien Tay station 6-7 hrs, Chau Doc 1½ hrs, Can Tho, Vinh Long and other destinations in the delta. There are a number of private minibus companies in town offering a faster and more comfortable service than the regular buses; ask at the *An Giang Tourist Office*, 6 Ngo Gia Tu St.

Chau Doc

Chau Doc is an attractive bustling riverside town (formerly called Chau Phu) in An Giang Province on the W bank of the Bassac River (sometimes also called the Hau River) and bordering Cambodia. With a population of 80,000, it is an important trading and marketing centre for the surrounding agricultural communities. Until the mid-18th century this was part of Cambodia: it was given to the Nguyen lord, Nguyen Phuc Khoat, after he had helped to put down an insurrection in the area. The area still supports a large Khmer population, as well as the largest Cham settlement in the Delta. Cambodia's influence can be seen in the tendency for women to wear scarves instead of the *non la* conical hat, and in the people's darker skin,

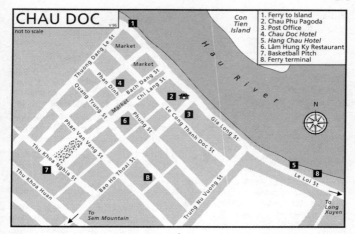

CHAU DOC v.96
not to scale

Con Tien Island

1. Ferry to Island
2. Chau Phu Pagoda
3. Post Office
4. Chau Doc Hotel
5. Hang Chau Hotel
6. Lâm Hung Ky Restaurant
7. Basketball Pitch
8. Ferry terminal

Hau River

Market
Market
Market

Thuong Dang Le St
Phan Dinh
Bach Dang St
Chi Lang St
Quang Trung St
Phan Van Vang St
Phung St
Le Cong Thanh Doc St
Gia Long St
Thu Khoa Nghia St
Bao Ho Thoai St
Thu Khoa Huan
Trung Nu Vuong St
Le Loi St

N

To Sam Mountain
To Long Xuyen

indicating Khmer blood. The Chau Doc district (it was a separate province for a while) is the seat of the Hoa Hao religion which claims about 1-1.5 million adherents and was founded in the village of Hoa Hao in 1939 (see page 121).

A large **market** sprawls from the riverfront down and along Le Cong Thanh Doc, Phu Thu, Bach Dang and Chi Lang sts. It sells fresh produce and black market goods smuggled in from Thailand. Near the market and the river, at the intersection of Gia Long and Bao Ho Thoai sts is the **Chau Phu Pagoda**. Built in 1926, it is dedicated to Thai Ngoc Hau, a former local mandarin: rather dilapidated, but with some fine carved pillars.

Excursions

Nui Sam or **Sam Mountain** lies about 5 km SW of town and is one reason to visit Chau Doc. This mountain was designated a 'Famed Beauty Spot' in 1980 by the Ministry of Culture. Rising from the flood plain, Nui Sam is a favourite spot for Vietnamese tourists who throng here, especially at festival time. The mountain, really a barren rock-strewn hill, can be seen at the end of the continuation of Bao Ho Thoai St. It is literally honeycombed with tombs, sanctuaries and temples. Most visitors come only to see Tay An Pagoda, Lady Chua Xu Temple, and the tomb of Thoai Ngoc Hau. But it is possible to walk or drive right up the hill for good views of the surrounding countryside: from the summit it is easy to appreciate that this is some of the most productive land in Vietnam. Admission 5,000d.

The **Tay An Pagoda** is at the foot of the hill, facing the road. Built originally in 1847, it has been extended twice and now represents an eclectic mixture of styles – Chinese, Islamic, perhaps even Italian. The pagoda contains a bewildering display of over 200 statues. A short distance on from the pagoda, past shops and stalls, is the **Chua Xu**. This temple was originally constructed in the late 19th century, and then rebuilt in 1972. It is rather a featureless building, though highly revered by the Vietnamese and honours the holy Lady Xu whose statue is enshrined in the new multi-roofed pagoda. On the other side of the road is the tomb of **Thoai Ngoc Hau** (1761-1829); an enormous head of the man graces the entranceway. The real reason to come here is to watch the pilgrims, rather than study the temples and tombs – which are rather poor – and to climb the hill. *Getting there*: either by bus (there is a stop at the foot of the mountain) or, more peacefully, by the local equivalent of the cyclo (about 5,000d one way).

Local information
● Accommodation
C *Hang Chau*, Le Loi St (on the river), T 66196, a/c, pool, restaurant, more expensive rooms have river view, attractive river view terrace, noisy nightclub – try to get rooms away from nightclub if you wish to sleep, best in town, rec; **C-D** *My Loc*, 51 Nguyen Van Thoai, T 66455, some a/c, friendly, incl breakfast, quiet area.

E *Chau Doc*, 17 Doc Phu Thu St, T 66484, friendly but grubby, popular and central; **E** *Hotel 777*, 47 Doc Phu Thu, T 66409, small but friendly; **E** *Nha Khach 44*, 44 Doc Phu Thu St, T 66540; **E** *Thai Binh*, 37 Nguyen Van Thoai, T 66221.

● Places to eat
Try the *Tourist* restaurant at the corner of Phan Dinh Phung and Doc Phu Thu sts (next to the *Chau Doc Hotel*) – cheap and cheerful. The *Hang Chau Hotel* has a good restaurant, popular with the local élite and Khmer businessmen. *Lam Hung Ky*, 71 Chi Lang, excellent freshly prepared and cooked food. There is a wide range of good foodstalls in the market area.

● Post & telecommunications
Post Office: corner of Gia Long and Bao Ho Thoai sts (on riverfront, opp the Chau Phu Pagoda).

● Transport
96 km from Ha Tien, 117 km from Can Tho, 179 km from Ho Chi Minh.

Road Bus: the station is SE of town on the S side of Le Loi St. 1-2 km from town centre, past the church; minibuses stop in town on Quang Trung St. Regular connections with Saigon's Mien Tay station (6-7 hrs), including two ferry crossings. Buses to Long Xuyen (1½ hrs), Can Tho, and other destinations in the delta. (There is no direct road from Chau Doc to Ha Tien; to get there by car involves driving along bad roads via Rach Gia (about 8 hrs).

Sea Ferries: leave Saigon daily from the wharf on Ton Duc Thang St, at the end of Ham Nghi Blvd. The journey takes over a day. There are also daily ferries along the canal to Ha Tien, journey time 10 hrs, a fascinating way to see village life, take plenty of water and food.

Rach Gia

Rach Gia is the capital of Kien Giang Province. The province is said to be one of the richest in Vietnam, its wealth based on rice and seafood. *Nuoc mam*, a renowned fish sauce, is produced here. The city is an important deep water port on the Gulf of Thailand with a population of 125,000. Already an entry point for goods, both smuggled and legal, from Thailand, it should grow in significance if Vietnam continues to follow the path of economic reform and rapprochement with the market economies of the region. The centre of the town is in fact an island at the mouth of the **Cai Lon** River.

Unfortunately, Rach Gia is a rather squalid and unpleasant little town, best known for its *bia om* bars and prostitution. Many hotels double as brothels. There are a number of pagodas in town including the **Phat Lon Pagoda**, which is on the mainland N of town just off Quang Trung St, and the **Nguyen Trung Truc Pagoda** which is not far away at 18 Nguyen Cong Tru St. The latter is dedicated to the 19th century Vietnamese resistance leader of the same name. Nguyen Trung Truc was active in Cochin China during the 1860s, and led the raid that resulted in the firing of the French warship *Esperance*. As the French closed in, he retreated to the island of Phu Quoc. From here, the French only managed to dislodge him after threatening to kill his mother. He gave himself up and was executed at the market place in Rach Gia on 27 October 1868. There is a small **museum** at 21 Nguyen Van Troi St in the heart of town and a **market** in the NE quarter of the island. The wharf area is interesting and the bustling fish market displays the wealth of the seas. Some attractive colonial architecture survives.

Excursions Oc-eo is an ancient city about 10 km inland from Rach Gia. It is of great interest and significance to archaeologists, but there is not a great deal for the tourist to view bar a pile of stones on which sits a small bamboo shrine. The site is overseen by an elderly custodian who lives adjacent. This port city of the ancient kingdom of Funan (see page 82) was at its height from 1st-6th centuries AD. Excavations have shown that buildings were constructed on piles and the city was inter-linked by a complex network of irrigation and transport canals. Like many of the ancient empires of the region, Oc-eo built its wealth on controlling trade between the E (China) and the W (India, Mediterranean). Vessels from Malaya, Indonesia and Persia docked here. No sculpture has yet been found, but a gold medallion with the profile of the Roman emperor Antonius Pius (152 AD) has been unearthed. *Getting there*: the site is near the village of Tan Hoi, and is only accessible by boat. Hire a small boat (the approach canal is very shallow and narrow) from the river front beyond the Vinh Tan Van Market, NE along Bach Dang St. The trip takes several hours expect to pay about US$12.

● **Accommodation** (all listed below are on the island) **B** *To Chau*, 41 Ho Chi Minh Ave (aka 41 Le Loi St), T 63718, a/c; **C-D** *1 Thang 5 (1 May Hotel)*, 38 Nguyen Hung Son, T 62103, reasonable; **E** *Binh Minh*, 48 Pham Hong Thai St may no longer accept Westerners, unpleasant; **E** *Thanh Binh*, 11 Ly Tu Trong St, shared WC but clean.

● **Places to eat** *Thien Nga*, 4A Le Loi St, kindly helpful owner, good freshly prepared food, tendency to undercharge.

● **Post & telecommunications Post Office**: Tu Duc St (on the mainland, N bank).

● **Tourist offices** Kien Giang Tourism, 12 Ly Tu Trong (on the island).

● **Transport** 92 km from Ha Tien, 115 km from Can Tho, 182 km from My Tho, 250 km from Saigon. **Air** Connections with Phu Quoc Island (Tues and Sat), 30 mins (US$40) and Saigon (via Phu Quoc), 2 hrs (US$65). **Road Bus**: the station is S of town on Trung Truc St. Regular connections with Saigon's Mien Tay terminal, (8 hrs). Also connections with Can Tho, Long Xuyen and Ha Tien. Express buses leave from an office at 33 30 Thang 4 St.

Ha Tien

This town of nearly 100,000 people is on the coast close to the Cambodian border and was part of the Khmer Kingdom until the beginning of the 18th century. During Pol Pot's reign of terror, Ha Tien became one of the Vietnamese towns harassed by Khmer Rouge troops. Much of the population fled, and it was these consistent incursions into Vietnamese territory which ultimately led to the invasion, or provided the excuse for the invasion (depending on which interpretation of history is being adhered to), of Cambodia by Vietnam on Christmas Day 1978 (see page 443).

There are a number of pagodas in town. The **Tam Bao Pagoda** at 328 Phuong Thanh St was founded in the 18th century, as too was the **Phu Dung Pagoda** which can be found not far away to the NW, just off Phuong Thanh St.

Lang Mac Cuu, the tomb of Mac Cuu, provincial governor under the waning Khmer who (in 1708) established a Vietnamese protectorate, sits on tomb mountain (nui lang) with others of the clan. Elsewhere, the tomb of Mac Cong Nuong, a descendant, has become an important shrine to locals seeking her divine intercession in time of family crisis.

Excursions Mui Nai lies about 5 km W of town. There are attractive beaches from which can be seen Phu Quoc Island and Cambodia. **Thach Dong Temple**, 3 km from Ha Tien, is dedicated to the goddess Quan Am; at the entrance to the cave temple is *Bia Cam Thu* (Monument of Hate – the Vietnamese don't mince their words) a memorial to the 130 slain by the Khmer Rouge in Mar 1978. Admission 5,000d, cameras 5,000d. A short distance beyond Thach Dong Temple is the **Cambodian border**: do not let the fact that it is permeable to locals and contraband of all sorts encourage you to follow, this is not an authorized crossing for foreigners.

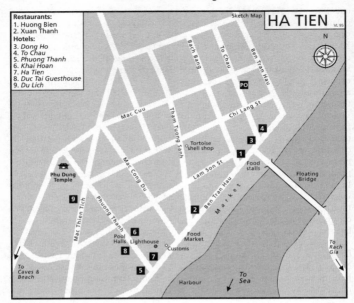

Restaurants:
1. Huong Bien
2. Xuan Thanh
Hotels:
3. Dong Ho
4. To Chau
5. Phuong Thanh
6. Khai Hoan
7. Ha Tien
8. Duc Tai Guesthouse
9. Du Lich

Hon Chong village is about 30 km E of Ha Tien, on a peninsula S of Highway 80 en route back to Rach Gia: its claim to fame is a holy grotto and the spectacular limestone formations, **Hon Phu Tu**, Father and Son Rocks which lie 100m offshore. Wander through Hai Son Tu Temple to the sandy white beach to hire a boat or just admire the view. **Accommodation E** *Hon Trem Guesthouse*.

Phu Quoc Island lies 45 km W of Ha Tien, it may be possible to charter a boat from Ha Tien to reach the island (see below).

● **Accommodation D-E** *Dong Ho*, Tran Hau St, T 52141, basic but clean, popular with Westerners; **D-E** *Du Lich*, Mach Thien Tich St, large fan rooms; **D-E** *Khai Hoan*, 239 Phuong Thanh St, T 52254, rec; **E** *Duc Tai Guesthouse*, Phuong Thanh St; **E** *Phuong Thanh*, Phuong Thanh St, old, fan only, may not accept Westerners; **E** *To Chau*, To Chau St, fan only, rundown.

● **Places to eat** Numerous food stalls along the river and Ben Tran Hau. ♦♦*Huong Bien*, Ben Tran Hau, not bad, but may run out of food; ♦♦*Khai Hoan*, 588 Ben Tran Hau, looks scruffy from the outside but food is good.

● **Post & telecommunications Post Office**: To Chau St.

● **Shopping** Ha Tien is known for its tortoise-shell products: carved fans, boxes, combs and other items made from the shells of specially bred tortoises, Tham Tuong Sanh St.

● **Transport** 92 km from Rach Gia, 96 km from Chau Doc, 206 km from Can Tho, 272 km from My Tho, 338 km from Saigon. **Road Bus**: the bus station is on the S edge of town, over the bridge that crosses the Chau To River. Buses from Saigon's Mien Tay station 10 hrs, regular connections with Rach Gia 5 hrs, and Can Tho. **Boat Ferry**: the ferry wharf is not far from the bridge on the To Chau River; there are ferries to Chau Doc (10 hrs, US$6) dep 0600.

Phu Quoc Island

Phu Quoc's northernmost tip lies just outside Cambodian territorial waters and, like other parts of present day Vietnam in this area, it has been fought over, claimed and reclaimed by Thai, Khmer and Viet. The island is today renowned for its *nuoc mam* (fish sauce, see page 289 for a description), which is exported globally. Fishing and pepper are mainstays of the local economy although smuggling provides a living for some of the island's 46,000 population. It seems unlikely that the tranquility of the island will last much longer: rival consortia of foreign developers have plans afoot to turn the island into a tropical playground for wealthy tourists. In 1995 a Canadian developer announced a US$1bn scheme to transform the island into an international financial centre, an idea greeted with scepticism by most commentators.

Historically, the island is renowned for its small part in the triumph of the Nguyen Dynasty. In 1765 Pigneau de Behaine was sent here as a young seminarist to train Roman Catholic missionaries; by chance he was on the island when Nguyen Anh (son of emperor-to-be Gia Long) arrived, fleeing the Tay Son. Pigneau's role in the rise of the Nguyen Dynasty is described more fully on page 201. Another link between the island and wider Vietnamese history is that it was here, in 1919, that the civil servant Ngo Van Chieu communed with the spirit world and made contact with the Supreme Being, leading to the establishment of the Cao Dai religion (see page 121).

● **Accommodation** *Duong Dong* and *Huong Bien* Hotels, Duong Dong.

● **Tourist offices** Phu Quoc Tourist Company, Duong Dong, T 46050/46113.

● **Transport Air** Connections with Saigon, 50 mins (US$65) and Rach Gia, 30 mins (US$40), Tues and Sat. **Sea Boat**: it may be possible to charter a boat from Ha Tien to Duong Dong, regular connections with Rach Gia.

INFORMATION FOR VISITORS

CONTENTS

General note Regulations for tourists and businessmen are in a constant state of flux. The advice given below was the latest available in 1995, but visitors must be ready for the possibility that new or altered regulations have come into force since then. Regulations are variously interpreted in different provinces and by different people, and however hard visitors try to remain within the letter of the law, this may be impossible. Some bureaucrats and policemen seem to view the fining of tourists as one of the perks of the job – irrespective of whether a crime or indiscretion has been committed. Most need second jobs to supplement their paltry salary, so perhaps this is unsurprising. Strange as it sounds, should visitors find themselves in the position of having to pay a fine 'on the road', bargain: a fine of US$100 should come down to US$25. Discretion and common sense will, of course, have to be used.

Before travelling

Entry requirements

● **Visas**

Valid passports with visas issued by a Vietnamese Embassy are required by all visitors, irrespective of citizenship. Visas are NOT available on arrival in Vietnam. Time needed to process a visa varies. Visitors booking a tour should allow about 10 days (longer for overseas Vietnamese), a little more if applying oneself. Visas state the port of entry and exit – usually Noi Bai (Hanoi Airport) and Tan Son Nhat (Saigon Airport). It is possible to have the port of exit changed: ask at a tour agent. Visas are usually only valid for entry by air (see page 285).

Visas for Vietnam are now easy to obtain even without booking a tour although this way they may cost more. Visas can now be obtained directly through Vietnamese embassies but this is not cheap. In Bangkok, numerous tour operators and travel agents will arrange a month-long visa for ฿1,300-1,500 (approx US$50-60), without requiring that the customer also books a tour. For a listing of agents in Bangkok specializing in Indochina, see page 594. This is expensive, but there is really little choice. Outside Bangkok (the main transit point for Vietnam), visas are harder to obtain unless booking a tour although it is gradually becoming easier. Specialist Vietnam tour operators in your own country (see listing on page 282) may also be able and willing to help arrange an independent visa but may require that you book a tour with them. **NB** Even though you have a visa in your passport you are still required to fill out a Visa Application Form (with photo) which is given to the Immigration Officer on arrival at the airport together with your Landing Card. You must keep your stamped landing card carefully until you leave the country.

● **Business visas**

Businessmen and women and officials from other governments or agencies (for example UN agencies) should have less difficulty arranging a visa, provided that their contact (ministry, company or institution) in Vietnam sends a letter, fax or telex to the Embassy where the visa is to be issued. It is advisable to make contact with the embassy well ahead of time, as there are considerable communication difficulties with Vietnam. If you have no links with an institution or company in Vietnam, contact the Vietnamese Chamber of Commerce in either Hanoi or Saigon (171 Vo Thi Sau, Q3, T 230301); they can provide details about relevant state-run organizations and help with visa formalities. **NB** It is not necessary to have the visa issued in the applicant's country of residence: a European businessman, for example, can have the letter of invitation sent to the Vietnamese Embassy in Bangkok, where it should only take 2 days to process the application for a visa. Remember to take all official correspondence along to the Embassy: it may help them track down the letter of invitation.

● **Visa extensions**

Many tour companies in Saigon and Hanoi will arrange visa extensions, including *Saigontourist* and *Vietnamtourism*, as well as the Immigration Police Office in Hanoi. Approach them 3-7 days before the visa expires; it costs US$10-20 for a 2 week extension, and the process takes about 3 days. This can be repeated three times, giving up to three additional months of travel. It has been reported that it is also possible to arrange visa extensions in Hué.

● **Visas for Cambodia**

Apply to the Cambodian Embassy in Hanoi or the Cambodian Consulate in Saigon. Applications take 5-7 days to process.

● **Visas for Laos**

Transit visas can be obtained from the Laotian Embassy in Hanoi; applications take 2 days to process. Tourist and transit visas also available from the Laotian Consulate in Saigon and Danang.

● **Visas for China**

Can be obtained from the Chinese Embassy in Hanoi; 3 days to process, valid for 1 month.

NB It is advisable to make several photocopies of your visa, passport, entry/exit card in case of theft. Hotels will need these to show to the immigration police and they are not always returned. Always try to keep the originals –

there have been reports of police in some towns holding onto the originals to extract payment. Cheaper hotels are notoriously forgetful at returning passports and visas. It is up to you to ask for documents back. Take at least four passport photographs into Vietnam – they are needed for various formalities.

● **Vaccinations**

No vaccinations required (but see Health, page 283).

● **Representation overseas**

Australia, 6 Timbara Crest, O'Malley, Canberra ACT, T 66059; **Cambodia**, Son Ngoc Minh Ave, Phnom Penh, T 25481; **Canada**, The Sandringham, 85 Range Rd, Suite 802, Ottawa, Ontario, T (613) 5652272, F (613) 5652595; **China**, 34 Guanghua Lu, Jianguo Dang Nghiem Hoanh, Menwai, Beijing, T 5321125; **CIS**, UL Nolshaia Piragovxkaia, 13 Nguyen Manh Cam, Moscow, T 2450925; **France**, 62-66 Rue Boileau, Paris 16e, T (452) 45063; **Germany**, Konstantin Strasse 37, 5300-Bonn 2, T 357021; **India**, 42 F South Extension, New Delhi, T 624586; **Indonesia**, 25 Jalan Teuku Umar, Jakarta, T 325347; **Italy**, 000187 Roman Piazza, Barberini 12, T 4755286; **Japan**, 50-11 Motoyoyogi-Cho, Shibuya-ku, Tokyo 151, T 446311; **Laos**, No 1, Thap Luong, Vientiane, T 5578; **Malaysia**, 4 Persisan Stonor, Kuala Lumpur, T 2484036; **Myanmar (Burma)**, 40 Komin Kochin Rd, Yangon (Rangoon), T 50361; **Philippines**, 54 Victor Cruz, Malate, Manila, T 500364; **Sweden**, Orbyslotsvag 26, 12578 Alvsjo, Stockholm, T 861214, F (010) 468 995713; **Switzerland**, 34 Chemin Francois Lehman, 1218 Grand Sacconnex, Geneva; **Thailand**, 83/1 Wireless Rd, Bangkok 10501, T 2517201; **UK**, 12-14 Victoria Rd, London W8 5RD, T (0171) 937 1912; **USA**, Liaison Office, 1233, 20th St NW, Washington DC 20036, T (202) 8610737, F (202) 8611397.

Tours

● **Tour operators in Vietnam**

The state tourism companies *Saigontourist* and *Vietnamtourism* have the greatest selection of tours from a day to 2 week-long tours. Prices are about US$100/day for 1 person, US$50/day pp for 3 people. This usually excludes food, but includes all transport, accommodation, a guide, and entrance charges to sights. In addition, they organize tours to Cambodia (Angkor) and Laos. These official tours are well run, clients tend to stay in the best hotels, but they are often unimaginative and expensive. For those on tighter budgets, much better are the tours run by private tour companies in Saigon and Hanoi. There is some freedom to design your own tour – which you can also do with the state-run agencies.

● **Overseas tour operators**

Thailand: the greatest number of tour companies outside Vietnam are to be found in Bangkok, the 'gateway' to Vietnam. They are concentrated on Khaosan Rd and Soi Ngam Duphli and, for the more up-market operations, on Sukhumvit and Silom roads (see page 594). There are also companies in the vicinity of the Vietnamese embassy. _Diethelm Travel_, Kian Gwan Building II, 140/1 Witthayu Rd, T 2559150, F 2560248; _MK Ways_, 57/11 Witthayu Rd, T 2545583, F 2545583/ 2802920; _BP Tour_, 17 Khaosan Rd, T 2815062, F 2803642; _Vista Travel_, 244/4 Khaosan Rd, T 2800348, F 2800348; _Exotissimo_, 21/17 Sukhumvit Soi 4, T 2835240, F 2547683 and 755 Silom Rd, T 2359196, F 2834885; _Marvel Holidays_, 279 Khaosan Rd, T 2829339, F 2813216; _Siam Wings Tours_, 173/1-3 Surawong Rd, T 2534757, F 2636808; _Educational Travel Centre_, Royal Hotel, 2 Rachdamnern Ave, T 2240043, F 2246930; _East-West Group_, 135 Soi Sanam Khli, Witthayu Rd, T 2530861, F 2536178.

UK: _Tour East_, King's Lodge, 28 Church St, Epsom, Surrey, KT17 42P, T 01372 739799, F 01372 739824; _Regent Holidays_, 15 John St, Bristol, BS1 2HR, T 0117 921-1711, F 0117 925-4866, tailor made holidays, rec; _Indochina Travel_, Chiswick Gate, 598-608 Chiswick High Rd, London W4 5RT, T 0181 995-8280, F 0181 994-5346, rec; _Explore Worldwide_, 1 Frederick St, Aldershot, Hants, GU11 1LQ, T 01252 344161, F 01252 343170.

France: _Vietnamtourism_, 4 Rue Cherubini 75002, Paris, T 42 86 86 37; _La Maison de L'Indochine_, 36 Rue des Bourdonnais, 75001 Paris, T 40 28 43 60; _Voyageurs Au Vietnam_, 55 Rue Sainte-Anne, 75002 Paris, T 42 86 16 88; _Nouvelles Frontières_, T 42 73 10 64.

Germany: _Lernidee Reisen_, Dudenstr 78, D-10965 Berlin, T (4930) 786 50 56.

USA: _Tour East_, 5120 West Goldleaf Circle, Suite 310, Los Angeles, California, 90056, T 213-2906500, F 213-2945531; _Kim's Travel_, 8443 Westminster CA 92682; _Mek-_

ong Travel, 151 First Ave, Suite 172, New York, T 212-5292891, F 212-5292891; *Viet Tours Holidays*, 8097 Westminster Av, Garden Grove, California, T 714-8952588.

Australia: *Tour East*, 99 Walker St, 12th floor, North Sydney, NSW 2060, T 9569303, F 9565340; *Intercontinental Travel*, 307 Victoria St, Abbotsford, Victoria 30567, T 42877849; *Tara International Travel*, Level 3, 427 George St, Sydney 2645811; *World Expeditions* T 2643366, run mountain biking tours from Hanoi to Hué.

Singapore: *Tour East*, Head Office, 70 Anson Rd, No 12-00, Apex Tower, Singapore 0207, T 2202200, F 2258119.

Hong Kong: *Vietnam Tours*, Friendship Travel, Houston Centre, 63 Moody Rd, Kowloon, T 3666862; *Skylion Ltd*, Suite D, 11 F Trust Tower, 68 Johnston Rd, Wanchai, T 8650363, F 8651306.

When to go

● **Best time to visit**

Hanoi and the north During the winter (Dec-Feb) it is grey and misty, though dry, with temperatures ranging from 10°C-15°C. The spring (Mar-Apr) is transitional, with tempera-

tures from 15°C-20°C. During the summer (May-Sep), it is hot and humid, with particularly heavy rain towards the end of the period and temperatures ranging from 27°C-33°C. Finally, autumn (Oct-Nov) is again transitional, with temperatures from 15°C-20°C.

Saigon and the south There are no great seasonal variations in temperature; ranging from 25°C-35°C throughout the year. Rainfall is concentrated from May-Oct.

For graphs of monthly rainfall and temperature see page 141 (Hanoi), page 212 (Danang) and page 245 (Saigon).

Health

● **Vaccinations**

None required, although cholera, polio, typhoid, hepatitis, rabies and tetanus are all recommended and Japanese encephalitis may be considered desirable if spending long in rural areas during the monsoon.

● **Malaria**

It is strongly advised that visitors take malaria tablets (see page 28).

● **Food and water**

In some cities (eg Saigon) the authorities maintain that it is safe to drink the water; even so, it is best to stick with bottled water.

● **Medical facilities**

Hospitals are listed under Hospitals & medical services in each town section. In general, hospitals are not up to international standards, although they can deal adequately with minor injuries and illnesses. The best Vietnamese hospitals in Hanoi and Saigon can deal well with quite serious accidents and illnesses and both now have foreign staffed international medical centres. Drugs are in short supply, equipment is obsolete, and doctors are few. For serious illness or injury it is advisable to fly to Singapore, Bangkok, Kuala Lumpur or Hong Kong (health insurance with emergency air ambulance provision is worthwhile). Pharmacies or chemists are usually poorly stocked except in Saigon and Hanoi, where Western prescription drugs are available over the counter.

Money

● **Cash**

Outside Hanoi and Saigon it is best to take US$ cash. Clean (ie unmarked US$ in poor condition may not be accepted in hotels and money changers) US$100 bills receive the best rates.

Small US$ bills are only useful for odd expenses. US$ can be changed at branches of the **Vietcombank**, in larger hotels (though rates are poorer) and on the black market (see above). But only expect to be able to change money in the more popular tourist destinations. The **Vietcombank** will also change other major currencies including Sterling, HK$, Thai baht, French francs, Swiss francs, A$, S$, C$, Yen and Deutschmarks. If possible, try to pay for everything in dong, not in US$; prices are usually less in dong, and in more remote areas people may be unaware of the latest exchange rate. Also, to ordinary Vietnamese 11,000d is a lot of money, while US$1 means nothing.

NB When leaving Hanoi or Saigon change sufficient money; it can be difficult to do so (though not impossible – see relevant sections) outside the two main centres.

● **Cost of living**
If staying in the better hotels expect to spend US$50-US$100/day; in cheaper establishments and using public transport, US$10-US$20/day.

● **Credit cards**
Visa, Mastercharge (Access) and JCB are accepted in Vietnam, mostly by hotels and restaurants in Saigon. In the N just Visa is accepted and then only in a few places. Larger bank branches only will give cash advances on credit cards.

● **Currency**
The unit of currency is the **dong**. Notes officially in circulation are in denominations of 200, 500, 1,000, 2,000, 5,000, 10,000, 20,000 and 50,000 dong (beware, 20,000 and 5,000 dong notes look very similar). The exchange rate in late 1995 was 10,500d=US$1 (in early 1991 it was 8,000d=US$1 and in 1989 it was 3,500d=US$1). The difference between the black market and official exchange rates has narrowed considerably in recent years, (it is usually near parity). It is hardly worthwhile changing money on the streets with the risks of being short changed. If the rates offered are too good to be true, be very suspicious – it is difficult to count out several hundred notes in a dark alley. If changing money on the black market try to do so in a shop; here it is far rarer for visitors to be cheated.

Any amount of foreign currency can be taken into or out of Vietnam, although amounts above US$?? must be declared on the customs form. If money has been declared, visitors should retain all hotel and other large receipts, as well as currency exchange slips, for inspection when leaving the country. These are then set against the initial sum declared on the customs form. In recent years, the customs authorities have shown less vigour in checking receipts and exchange slips, but it is a good idea to keep track of expenditure just in case.

● **Money transfer**
With the lifting of the US trade embargo, money can be transferred to foreign and Vietnamese banks in Vietnam. Vietnamese banks will probably require you open an account with them first and this is remarkably easy. Transfers are best denominated in US$ and cash can be withdrawn in US$.

● **Travellers' cheques**
Best denominated in US$, can only be changed in Hanoi and Saigon and major towns at the **Vietcombank**, **Cosevina** and **ANZ** for a 2% commission, TCs can be changed into US$ cash. When cashing TCs it is necessary to take passport and proof of purchase to the bank.

Getting there

Where to arrive: Saigon (Ho Chi Minh City) or Hanoi? Hanoi is the capital of Vietnam, yet Saigon is the main gateway into the country. There are a number of reasons why arriving in Saigon is advantageous. First, the authorities are more accustomed to tourists and especially to independent travellers. Second, Saigon has more hotels, restaurants, money changers – in general more facilities – than Hanoi. Third, Saigon has better international air links. And fourth, there are a greater number of independent (that is, not state-run) tour operators who can provide a wider array of tours. This does not mean that entering Vietnam via Hanoi is inadvisable; indeed, with each passing month the differential narrows.

Air

Regular connections from Bangkok to Hanoi and Saigon on Thai and Vietnam Airlines. Connections with Saigon and Hanoi on Air France from Paris. Connections with Saigon on KLM from Amsterdam, Philippine Airlines from Manila, Garuda from Jakarta, Lufthansa from Frankfurt, Taipei on EVA and China Airlines, Seoul on Korean Airlines, Kaohsiung on China Airlines and Pacific Airlines, Guangzhou on China Southern and fortnightly with Qantas from Sydney. MAS has connections from Kuala Lumpur to both Saigon and Hanoi, as does Cathay Pacific from Hong Kong and Singapore Airlines from Singapore. Vietnam Airlines connects Saigon with Bangkok, Berlin, Dubai, Guangzhou, Hong Kong, Kaohsiung, Kuala Lumpur, Los Angeles, Manila, Moscow, Paris, Phnom Penh, Seoul, Singapore, Taipei, and Vientiane and Hanoi with Bangkok, Guangzhou and Hong Kong. Region Air links Singapore and Vung Tau and Thai is introducing direct flights from Saigon to Phuket.

Train

There are currently no regular services between Vietnam and neighbouring countries. However, there are two lines running N from Hanoi across the border and into China, the first major stop in China being the city of Nam Ninh (Nanning) on the Lang Son line and Kunming on the Lao Cai line. These rail links were closed after the Chinese invasion of 1979. In late 1991 China and Vietnam normalized relations and eased border restrictions for Chinese and Vietnamese nationals and reopened the railway services. Foreigners can now enter and leave Vietnam overland across this northern border but the correct visas (both exit and entry) must be obtained from both Vietnamese and Chinese authorities. These cannot be obtained at the border. The train itself does not cross the border.

Road

There is a bus service between Phnom Penh (Cambodia) and Saigon (see page 269) but foreigners have experienced trouble crossing the border and are occasionally turned back. It seems to be easier to enter Vietnam by road from Cambodia than it is to leave. Tourists who have hired cars to make the trip from Saigon to Phnom Penh or *vice versa* are usually waved through; it is those on buses who seem to experience difficulties. The border closes to foreigners after dark so time your arrival in daylight hours. Note that visas usually have to be amended at the Vietnamese Embassy in Phnom Penh (US$25) to allow entry by road (visas usually state entry by air). From Vietnam to Cambodia ensure your visa is endorsed Moc Bai. Cambodian visas can be obtained from the Consulate in Saigon (US$20). There is now an overland route from Bangkok, through NE Thailand into Laos, and then from Laos via Highway 9 to Vietnam, the road running from Savannakhet (Laos), through Khe Sanh and reaching the coast N of Hué. The road was completed in 1989 with Soviet technical assistance, with the intention of reducing land-locked Laos' dependence on Thailand. In theory, the land crossing is open to foreigners, and it is possible to travel from Vientiane (Laos) to Vietnam which opens up a range of very exciting travel possibilities in Indochina. Travelling by land from Vietnam to Laos ensure your exit visit is endorsed Lao Bao which has been reported successfully obtained from the embassy in Bangkok. Visas can be amended in Hanoi (US$15), Saigon and Danang (US$20). The last bus from the border to Savannakhet depart 1500. A Lao visa is obtainable from the Lao Embassy in Hanoi (US$70 for 30 days) and from the Lao Consulate in Danang or Saigon (US$25 7 day transit visa).

In 1991 China and Vietnam normalized diplomatic relations and road border crossings are now open between the two countries. A number of roads run N from Hanoi and Haiphong, and into China (the mountains here are less imposing than those dividing Vietnam from Laos). Note that visas normally have to be amended to allow exit by road (US$15 at the Immigration office in Hanoi). However, latest information indicates that the journey across the border is difficult: there is no public transport to the border and the crossing involves a 10 km walk on the Chinese side. The flight to Nanning is US$60 from Hanoi, a much easier alternative.

Sea

Saigon, Haiphong, Vung Tau and Danang are international ports and visitors arriving by merchant ship might be able to enter the country in this way. Check with a Vietnamese embassy beforehand to ensure that documentation is in order. Yachtsmen who have tried to dock and land in Vietnam have been fined and turned away (sometimes incarcerated for a short time).

Customs

Visitors must complete two copies of a customs declaration form. The authorities are more relaxed than they were and it is no longer necessary to list the serial number of every piece of electronic equipment brought into the country. However, they are still awkward about video and cassette tapes. It is possible to import video tapes (blank and recorded) but they will be confiscated at the airport (the x-ray scanner will ensure that they are spotted) and you will be given a receipt enabling collection in 5 days time; in Saigon the office is at 179 Nam Ky Khoi Nghia, Q3. It is a kafkaesque experience: expect to wait at least an hour in crowded conditions for your name to be called out; you have to pay a fine. For overseas Vietnamese the same process applies to audio cassettes too. Keep one copy of your customs form which must be completed on departure.

● **Duty free allowance**
200 cigarettes or 50 cigars or 250 g of tobacco; 1 litre of spirits and 1 litre of wine, together with personal effects of a 'reasonable quantity'. The restriction on the number of rolls of film has now been lifted.

● **Export restrictions**
Goods of a commercial nature and articles of high value require export permits issued by the Customs Service. This can include antiques which may be confiscated (never to be seen again). Export licences for antiques can be obtained, in theory, from the Customs Service (see below). No dong (the domestic currency) are allowed out of the country. The Customs Service Headquarters in Saigon is at 21 Ton Duc Thang St, T 290912. The Hanoi General Customs Office is at 51 Nguyen Van Cu St, T 263951, and the Office for Cultural Import and Export Items (Ministry of Culture, Communication and Sports) is at 51 Ngo Luyen St, T 253231.

On arrival

● **Airport information**
Vietnam has two international airports, Saigon's Tan Son Nhat Airport (see page 269 for details) is the main international gateway for both businessmen and tourists. Hanoi's Noi Bai Airport (see page 170 for details) is used more often by people on official business who need to visit the capital.

Transport to town For details on Saigon's Tan Son Nhat Airport see page 269 and for Hanoi's Noi Bai Airport see page 170.

● **Airport tax**
US$8 departure tax (90,000d).

● **Clothing**
Vietnam has a relaxed attitude to dress – businessmen rarely wear suits, and ties are not required. Neatness, however, is expected and badly dressed travellers are liable to be treated poorly. In the N it is cold during the winter. In highland areas such as Dalat, Buon Ma Thuot and Sapa it is chilly at all times of year during the night; warm clothing is required. A waterproof can be very useful (they are available locally), particularly in Hué which is renowned for its rain.

● **Conduct**
Greetings Like the Thai *wai*, Vietnamese used to greet one another by clasping their hands, prayer-like, in front of their faces and bowing slightly. This charming custom has been replaced by the handshake. When trying to gain the attention of a Vietnamese, try not to point or gesture excessively. This is regarded as rude. Call out their name if possible, if not, beckon by using the whole hand, palm downwards. Again, as in the other countries of mainland Southeast Asia, do not touch people on the head which is regarded as spiritually the 'highest' part of the body. Expect to be the centre of attention outside Saigon, Hanoi and the main tourist centres; react accordingly.

Pagodas Visitors to pagodas or temples are expected (like Vietnamese) to put a small donation (several thousand dong) in the collection boxes.

An article in a Vietnamese language newspaper recently compared tourists (unfavourably) with cowboys. Tourists were described as badly dressed (walking around towns in shorts and dirty T-shirts) and arrogant; they went into places which they shouldn't and paid what they wanted rather than what they were asked. There is much truth in this: Vietnamese dress smartly in clean clothes and women may change 3 or 4 times a day; by comparison many tourists look distinctly scruffy and ill-dressed. Because tourists are accustomed to paying more for hotels and rail fares than local people they tend to assume that restaurants, bicycle hire and shops *et al* try to operate a dual-pricing system. Certainly, cyclo drivers will try to get as much as they can but in general Vietnamese are honest and fair.

● **Hours of business**
Offices: 0730-1630 Mon-Sat. **Banks**: 0800-1130, 1300-1600 Mon-Fri, 0800-1130, 1300-1500 Sat (on last working day of each month banks are open until 1100). Vietnamese banks close on the afternoon of the day before a public holiday.

● **Official time**
7 hrs ahead of GMT.

● **Overcharging**
The overcharging of foreigners is a problem. Foreigners already pay considerably more for

WHAT TO AND WHAT NOT TO TAKE

What to take:

● US$; take some small denomination US$ for incidental expenses and large denomination bills (US$100) for changing into the local currency (dong). Make sure bills are 'clean'/unmarked.

● Travellers' cheques together with proof of purchase.

● A stock of at least 4 passport photographs and completed Visa Application Form.

● A small first aid kit, including medicine for stomach disorders/diarrhoea (can be hard to find outside Saigon/Hanoi).

● Short-wave radio (there are no newspapers in English outside the 2 main cities).

● A torch can be useful for viewing caves, dark pagodas and during power cuts.

● Penknife.

● Photocopies of passport and visa (and entry permit, issued on arrival).

● Long-sleeved shirts for cool evenings, severely air-conditioned restaurants and to prevent sunburn.

● Reading material (little available, and journeys are long).

● Slide film (available in Saigon, but rarely elsewhere; print film is more widely sold) but do not get slides processed in Vietnam – poor quality.

● Mosquito coils and/or repellent.

● Warm clothing for upland areas in winter.

● Conserves, marmite, peanut butter or other to spread on French bread.

What not to take:

● Maps; cheap ones are available in Saigon and Hanoi.

● Dictionaries; many cheap ones on sale in larger towns.

● Foreign cigarettes for barter – they can be bought in Vietnam, sometimes even cheaper than in Thailand.

● Waterproof/umbrella for wet season: ubiquitous and cheap in Vietnam.

● Video tapes (see page 285).

hotels, trains, planes and other services and many Vietnamese seem to think they should pay more for everything else as well. Confirm prices before ordering a meal or venturing forth on a cyclo or in a taxi. Prices have an unnerving habit of increasing during a journey; insist on the agreed price. Some visitors even make sure that the fare or price is written down to prevent misunderstanding.

● **Prohibited items**

Weapons, explosives, inflammable goods, narcotics, live animals and cultural objects 'unsuitable to Vietnamese society' (for example, pornography, seditious material). In May 1993 a Hong Kong man was sentenced to death for drug smuggling: he was trying to import 11 lbs of heroin.

● **Registration**

Visitors no longer need to have their entry slip (issued at port of entry) stamped by the Immigration Police within 48 hrs of arrival. This process is now completed at the point of arrival by the immigration authorities.

● **Safety**

Vietnam is a safe country and visitors may be astonished at the warmth of the welcome they receive. If travelling away from the main centres of tourism, and particularly if travelling alone or in a small group, be aware of Vietnamese sensitivities regarding national security. Bridges and other strategic and military infrastructure **should not be photographed**. This could result in a fine and confiscation of film or imprisonment.

Personal safety is not generally a problem. However, as tourism expands, so thieves, pickpockets and confidence tricksters are becoming more common. In Saigon they are already quite a serious problem; no doubt they are resurrecting the skills they acquired during the war. Bag snatching by young men on motorbikes is now a serious menace. In Saigon the UK Consulate General recorded seven stolen passports lost in this way in just a 3 month period. Changing money on the street is not recommended (see below). Simple watchfulness and good sense is required, particularly at train and bus stations. Lock hotel rooms at night, preferably also bolting them. Valuables may be safer left hidden or locked away in hotel rooms than carrying them on the street; it is usually possible to judge the nature of the hotel and more expensive hotels tend to be safe. A concealed money belt is recommended for travellers taking long-distance buses and trains.

● **Shopping**
Vietnam is not a haven for shoppers in the same way that other countries in the region are. Locally produced goods are usually rather shoddy, although they can make novel gifts (for example the ubiquitous North Vietnamese Army helmet). Handicrafts, and traditional cloth and clothing, are good buys. Tailors are cheap and can produce shirts and skirts from patterns or photographs. Most fabrics tend to be synthetic, however, so a lot of visitors bring in material from Hong Kong and Europe. Antiques are available in most tourist centres, and often at very reasonable prices. A permit is often required to get them out of the country (which is difficult to get without contacts). Visitors taking antiques out of the country without a permit have had them confiscated at the airport.

● **Tipping**
It is customary to leave some small change. 10% is added to the bill in the more expensive hotels and restaurants. Good gifts to hand out include pens and balloons (for children). Foreign cigarettes are no longer a useful item of barter, but are good to give away. Every male seems to chain smoke.

● **Voltage**
In urban areas 220V/50 cycles is the norm, in rural areas 110V. Power surges are common and unprotected computers (eg without a surge regulator or protector) and other sensitive electronic equipment may be affected.

● **Weights and measures**
Metric.

Where to stay

● **Accommodation**
In general, hotels are poor and expensive by comparison with other poor Asian countries. Outside Saigon, Hanoi, Hué and Nha Trang the choice is limited, and many hotels are decrepit and poorly managed. More expensive establishments add 10% service to the bill and charge in US$; cheaper places usually expect payment in dong. Many hotels also include breakfast in the price of the room. New hotels are being built in the more popular tourist destinations, and others are being refurbished to emerge as smart, clean and pleasant places to stay. A shortage of cash and foreign partners means that the process is far from smooth and the supply of hotels remains inadequate by international standards. Only 1,565 of the 22,000 rooms are said to be 'acceptable'.

Like air and rail travel, foreigners may have to pay 2-3 times more than locals for the same facilities although price discrimination has disappeared in privately run hotels. In comparison with other countries of Southeast Asia, travellers' accommodation is expensive, but a/c rooms can be relatively cheap (less than US$10). Hotels, even of the same standard, vary a great deal in price, and rates are rising fast. Those in Saigon, particularly, and to a lesser extent in Hanoi offer some business services. But even in these cities, expect to be frustrated by the level of services. Outside these two cities expect nothing and you may be surprised. **NB** Some cheaper hotels still refuse to take foreigners, usually out of fear of being hounded by the authorities but such establishments are increasingly few and far between.

Despite the poor quality of most hotels, some do make up for this in charm. There are a handful of beautiful, atmospheric, though distinctly battered, French-era hotels – some beautifully restored. In some towns it is even possible to stay in attractive, rambling villas. Service tends to be enthusiastic rather than slick. If nothing else, staying in Vietnam makes

HOTEL CLASSIFICATION

L: US$200+ **Luxury:** one purposes-built but several others have pushed their prices into this category.

A+: US$100-200 **First class plus:** A number of refurbished hotels (eg *Saigon Century*) charge these prices but provide poor value for money.

A: US$50-100 **First class**: the hotels in the country that can be considered first class are chiefly found in Saigon. A number of others are under construction. Hotels in this category should offer reasonable business services, and a range of recreational facilities, restaurants and bars. A 10% service charge will be added to the bill, which must be paid for in US$.

B: US$25-50 **Tourist class:** all rooms will have air-conditioning and an attached bathroom with hot water. Other services should include one or more restaurants, a bar, and room service. Breakfast will often be included in the price. A 10% service will probably be added to the bill, which must be paid for in US$.

C: US$15-25 (150-250,000d) **Economy:** rooms should be air-conditioned and have attached bathrooms with hot water and 'Western' toilets. A restaurant and room service will probably be available. A 10% service charge may be added to the bill; it may be possible to pay in dong.

D: US$8-15 (80-150,000d) **Budget:** air-conditioning unlikely although they should have an attached bathroom. Toilets may be either Western-style or of the 'squat' Asian variety. Bed linen should be provided, towels perhaps. There is likely to be a restaurant. Bills can often be paid for in dong and most will not include a service charge.

E: Less than US$8 (P,000d) **Vietnamese:** fan-cooled rooms, often dirty, and in many cases with shared bathroom facilities. Toilets are likely to be of the 'squat' Asian variety. Bed linen should be provided, towels probably not. These hotels are geared to Vietnamese travellers; staff are unlikely to speak much English and managers are sometimes reluctant to take foreigners as guests. Bills can often be paid for in dong. No service charge.

a change from the run-of-the-mill hotels in the more Westernized countries of Southeast Asia.

The levels of service provided by hotels in different price categories is given below; but note that accommodation is highly variable. The rates are for double room.

Food and drink

Food

Although Vietnam has been culturally influenced by China for over 2,000 years, its cuisine (unlike its architecture) is no poor imitation of its mentor's. Vietnam has managed to maintain its culinary independence, and it is distinct and original. The roots of this distinctiveness lie in a number of ingredients which are not seen in Chinese cooking. *Nuoc mam*, or fish sauce (not unlike the Thai *nam plaa*), is the equivalent of soy sauce. It is used in cooking and is the basis for a key condiment, *nuoc cham* (see below). Nuoc mam is made from fresh anchovies and salt, layered together in barrels and allowed to ferment; the resulting clear salty liquid adds an entirely original dimension to Vietnamese food. The best *nuoc mam* comes from the first drawing-off and this is left to mature like a good claret. The test of a fine *nuoc mam* is if a grain of rice will float on the surface of the golden liquid, supported by the surface tension. Other ingredients which are very rarely seen in Chinese cooking, but which are regularly used in Vietnamese dishes are shallots, lemon grass and coriander. Another distinguishing feature, is that it is common to be offered plates of fresh vegetables and leaves (eg mint and coriander) to be eaten with a meal. Methods of cooking also vary: stir frying (when it is employed) uses only a minimum of oil, and boiling and simmering are more usual (in China the reverse is generally true). Finally, whereas the Chinese are great users of flavour enhancers and thickening agents such as MSG and cornstarch, the Vietnamese cook rarely uses them. In essence, Vietnamese cooking is a mixture of Thai and Chinese.

Vietnamese regional cooking can be divided, corresponding with the three major regions of the country: the N, centre, and S. The following brief characterization applies to restaurant food.

Cooking in the **north**, unsurprisingly, is most like that of China. Stir-frying is common and food is less spicy hot than that of the centre and S. In the **central region**, food is spicy hot and the chilli is used with great abandon. Perhaps reflecting its imperial roots, dishes are carefully arranged and served in small portions, like an Oriental equivalent of nouvelle cuisine. The **south** has a far wider array of fruit, vegetables, herbs and spices to draw upon than the centre and N. The influence of the other countries of mainland Southeast Asia, and even India, is also in evidence with curries and other dishes.

● **Eating in Vietnam**

Food in Vietnam ranges from the appalling to the good. Many restaurants have no name, and are identified by their number; for example *Nha Hang 49* means Restaurant 49, which would be found at No 49. Snacks like bags of cashews are often brought to the table unsolicited, and then added to the bill even if left unopened and uneaten; ask for them to be taken away and check the bill carefully. Towels provided for washing are also usually charged to the bill (1,000d). European-style breakfasts are only available in more expensive hotels where excellent French bread, cold meats and cheeses are served with strong coffee. Some regular visitors bring their own conserves, honey or peanut butter. Beyond such hotels, the usual breakfast fare is *pho*, pungent noodle soup infused with the taste of garlic and fresh coriander.

RESTAURANT CLASSIFICATION

Prices Stall food is very cheap – 1 dish costing perhaps 3,000d; a meal in an average restaurant might come to 20-30,000d per head. Restaurants are graded as follows:

◆◆◆◆	more than US$15
◆◆◆	US$5-15 (50-150,000d)
◆◆	US$2-5 (20-50,000d)
◆	less than US$2 (20,000d)

● **Popular dishes**

Pho (noodle soup, pronounced 'fir') is a cheap and usually delicious staple. If there is a national dish, it is *pho*. The broth is characteristically made from beef bones, and although the soup is available throughout the country, it has its roots in the N (and hence it is often known as *pho Hanoi*). Each restaurant or stall will serve their own variation but common ingredients include onion, ginger, beansprouts, fish sauce, noodles, lemon, a meat (usually beef), garlic, chillies and coriander. There are numerous other substantial noodle soups: *pho ga* is served with chicken; while *bun bo*, a spicy broth, uses pork; *hu tieu* is shrimp, chopped pork and pig's liver, a delicacy of the S; while Hué's *canh chua* is made from fish, fruit and herbs but eaten with rice, not noodles.

Com or *com trang* (steamed rice) is eaten at least once a day.

Banh xeo (sound pancakes) – a Vietnamese dosa; pancake stuffed with prawn, pork garlic, shallots, mushrooms and beansprouts and served with lettuce and a spicy sauce. A typical roadside meal. In the central region they are known as *banh khoai*.

Bi cuon (spring rolls) – transparent spring rolls with prawns, beansprouts and assorted vegetables.

Cha gio (spring rolls) – one of the most popular snacks in Vietnam; crisp, deep fried, rolled pancakes stuffed with noodles, pork, garlic, shallots and other ingredients. Smaller than the Chinese equivalent, wrapped with lettuce leaves and fresh herbs and dipped in a spicy sauce.

Nem nuong (barbecued skewered pork) – pounded pork combined with shallots, garlic and sugar, marinated, and then barbecued.

Bo vien (beef balls) – beef marinated in nuoc mam, sugar, and oil and then processed to a paste before being boiled and served with soup.

Gio lua – minced pork wrapped in banana leaves and boiled.

Muc don thit – squid stuffed with pork.

Com chay – stir-fried mixed vegetables.

Tom vo vien chien – shrimp paste shaped into cakes, deep fried, and served with rice and salad.

Cha ca Hanoi – fish marinated in nuoc mam, fried over an open fire in butter and dill, and then served with white noodles and condiments.

All meals, as far as the average Vietnamese is

BIRD'S NEST SOUP

The tiny nests of the brown-rumped swift (*Collocalia esculenta*), also known as the edible-nest swiftlet or sea swallow, are collected for bird's nest soup, a Chinese delicacy, throughout Southeast Asia. The semi-oval nests are made of silk-like strands of saliva secreted by the birds which, when cooked in broth, softens and becomes a little like noodles. Like so many Chinese delicacies, the nests are believed to have aphrodisiac qualities, and the soup has even been suggested as a cure for AIDS. The red nests are the most highly valued, and the Vietnamese Emperor Minh Mang (1820-1840) is said to have owed his extraordinary vitality to his inordinate consumption of bird's nest soup. This may explain why restaurants serving it are sometimes also associated with a plethora of massage parlours. Collecting the nests is a precarious but profitable business and in some areas mafias of concessionaires vigorously guard and protect their assets. The men who collect the nests on a piecework basis risk serious injury climbing rickety ladders to cave roofs in sometimes almost total darkness, save for a candle strapped to their heads.

concerned, would not be complete without the universal *nuoc mam*, fish sauce (see above). This is usually served as a condiment or dip in the form of *nuoc cham* which is *nuoc mam* mixed with garlic, chillies, lime and sugar (similar to the Thai *nam plaa prik*). In addition to noodles and rice, French bread (*banh mi*) is also widely available across the country. It is usually eaten with another French food – pâté.

Drink

Vietnamese cannot be described as big drinkers, average per capita annual consumption is 3 litres of beer and 1.2 litres of soft drink.

Locally-bottled drinks are sweet and usually involve an ingenious use of flavourings (close your eyes and the orange drink could be just about anything), but they are cheap (1,000d), just about universally available, and safe. Imported soft drinks (7-Up and Coke) are sold in the major cities and in smaller towns in the S (8,000-10,000d). Coconuts are a better thirst quencher than the sweet soft drinks (2,000d on the street). Local beers are good; 333 (*ba ba*) is the most widely sold, and there are also local brews in larger towns (eg *Saigon*, flat and weak) as well as draught beer (*bia hoi*). *Bia hoi*, is top fermented which allows most of the alcohol to escape. It is cheap and normally served warm; the Vietnamese drink it with ice. A bottle or can of local beer should cost about 6,000d. Imported beers such as Heineken, Sapporo, Tiger and San Miguel are available in the S, and in some places in the N (US$1). Chinese beer is available in the N and very cheap.

Several overseas brewers have set up in Vietnam. Tiger Beer, in a joint venture with Vietnam Breweries has built a brewery outside Saigon. Canned, bottled and now draught Tiger is delivered from here to bars and hotels in the S. BGI, a French company has a brewery down in Cuu Long from where it supplies excellent bottled and canned beer at very reasonable prices to the S. Huda, a joint Vietnamese-Danish beer has been on sale in Hué since 1991.

Coffee from upland areas such as Dalat and Buon Ma Thuot is filtered and strong; 'coffee with milk' usually means with sweetened, thick, condensed milk.

● **Water**

Outside major hotels it is best not to use ice, even though drinks, including beer, are usually drunk with ice. Some visitors travel for a month or more taking ice with their drinks wherever they stop, with no ill effects. Locally bottled water is now available (7,000d); imported brands are expensive (10,000-15,000d for a large bottle). Bottled water is difficult to find outside the main towns.

Getting around

Air

Vietnam Airlines, the national flag carrier, has a deservedly poor reputation both for safety and service – although progress is being made on both fronts. In Nov 1992 a plane crashed on a flight from Saigon to Nha Trang, killing all but a Dutch tourist; and in Sep 1992 an

VIETNAM AIRLINES CONDENSED TIMETABLE

Hanoi-Saigon			
Day	Flt	Dep	Arr
daily	VN741	0720	0920
3,4,7	VN211	0745	0945
7	VN215	0900	1100
1,2	VN217	1030	1230
1,2,4,5,6,7	VN219	1130	1330
2,3,4,6	VN221	1300	1500
2,3,4,6,7	VN223	1400	1600
1,6	VN225	1500	1700
daily	VN227	1615	1815
1,2,3,6	VN229	1715	1915
1,3,5	VN231	1800	2000
5,7	VN233	1830	2030

Hanoi-Danang			
daily	VN311	0700	0810
daily	VN313	1140	1250
daily	VN315	1400	1510

Hanoi-Hué			
1,2,3,4,5,7	VN249	0630	0750
1,3,5,6,7	VN247	1430	1550

Hanoi-Nha Trang			
2,4,6	VN269	1240	1510

Hanoi-Vinh			
1,5	VN271	1100	1140

Saigon-Hanoi			
1,2,3,4,5,6	VN210	0700	0900
1,4,7	VN212	0730	0930
1,2,3,4,5,6	VN214	0830	1030
2,7	VN216	0930	1130
1,3,4,6,7	VN218	1030	1230
2,5,6,7	VN220	1200	1400

3,5,7	VN222	1300	1500
2	VN224	1330	1530
1,4,5	VN226	1430	1630
5	VN228	1530	1730
daily	VN740	1630	1830
2,3,6	VN230	1800	2000

Saigon-Dalat			
2,4,7	VN466	1000	1050

Saigon-Danang			
daily	VN320	0720	0830
1,3,6	VN280	0900	1010
daily	VN322	1150	1300
2,4,5,7	VN324	1350	1500

Saigon-Haiphong			
daily	VN278	0830	1030

Saigon-Hué			
1,2,3,4,5,7	VN244	0630	0820
1,3,5,6,7	VN246	1000	1150

Saigon-Nha Trang			
daily	VN450	0705	0755
4,7	VN452	1440	1530

Saigon-Phu Quoc			
2,6	VN481	1130	1220

Saigon- Play Cu			
1,3,5,7	VN342	1120	1235

Saigon-Quy Nhon			
1,2,3,5,6	VN346	0700	0810

Symbols: 1=Mon, 2=Tues, 3=Wed, 4=Thur, 5=Fri, 6=Sat, 7=Sun.
Fares: One way Hanoi-Saigon, US$170; Hanoi-Danang, US$90; Hanoi-Hué, US$90; Hanoi-Nha Trang, US$130; Saigon-Dalat, US$40; Saigon-Danang, US$90; Saigon-Haiphong, US$170; Saigon-Hué, US$90; Saigon-Nha Trang, US$60; Saigon-Phu Quoc, US$65; Saigon-Play Cu, US$65.

CONDENSED RAILWAY TIMETABLE

		S2	S4	S6	S8
		Mon, Tues, Weds, Thur	Tues, Weds, Fri, Sat, Sun	Daily	Sat
Saigon	d	1900	1940	0800	2030
Nha Trang	a	0316	0517	1825	0623
Danang	a	1340	1637	0709	1950
Hué	a	1655	2004	1119	2340
Vinh	a	0034	0507	2116	1039
Hanoi	a	0700	1240	0530	1830

S2 = train number.

TRAIN FARES

S2	Soft seat	A/c 6 berth compartment			A/c 4 berth compart
From Saigon to:		High berth	Middle	Low berth	
Nha Trang	17	23	25	27	29
Danang	36	50	55	60	64
Hué	40	55	61	66	71
Hanoi	65	91	99	108	117

S4					
From Saigon to:	Soft seat	High berth	Middle berth	Low berth	Soft berth
Nha Trang	17	23	25	27	29
Danang	36	50	55	60	64
Hué	40	55	61	66	71
Hanoi	64	90	98	107	116

S6 and S8				
From Saigon to:	Seat	Soft seat	Medial berth	Soft berth
Nha Trang	13	15	23	27
Danang	27	32	50	60
Hué	29	35	55	66
Hanoi	48	56	91	108

All figures in US$. Fares and timings are liable to change. Tickets must be booked at least 3 days in advance so check the timings then.

overseas Vietnamese and former South Vietnamese airforce officer hijacked a flight from Bangkok to Saigon. He ordered the plane to swoop low over Saigon while scattering leaflets for the overthrow of the Communist government and afterwards parachuted from the plane before being arrested.

1995 did not start well for Vietnam Airlines: one plane crashed on landing at Dalat and another overran the runway in Phnom Penh; fortunately no one was seriously hurt in either of these accidents.

Vietnam Airlines has been transformed over the last couple of years with the acquisition of 5 Airbus A-320s, 2 Boeing 767s and five ATR-72s. The Airbus and Boeings are used on international flights and internal flights between Hanoi and Saigon with European and Vietnamese pilots. Now that the US trade embargo has been lifted, Vietnam Airlines can officially admit to possessing the planes and has repainted them in its livery. Tupolevs and Yaks, both Soviet-built aircraft, are being phased out either by design or by accident (ie by crash). But the dwindling band of survivors is still used on short haul flights. Despite their record it is undoubtedly quicker, more comfortable and safer to fly: it is a sobering fact that 100 people die on Vietnam's roads every week.

Vietnam Airlines flies from Hanoi to Saigon, Danang, Hué, Dien Bien Phu and Nha Trang; from Saigon to Hanoi, Danang, Hué, Dalat, Phu Quoc, Quy Nhon, Rach Gia, Nha Trang and Haiphong. Note that Vietnam Airlines also operates flights to more out-of-the-way spots. These are not always listed on official timetables: ask for further information. **NB** Flights to/from Hanoi and Saigon are often booked-up well in advance, but, passengers frequently do not turn up, so it is worth persevering. A second domestic airline, Pacific Airlines competes on several routes but it has been fraught with legal wrangles and looks financially unhealthy. The airline operates flights between Saigon and Hanoi, from Saigon to Taipei and from Saigon to Kaohsiung. On internal flights airport tax of 15,000d is payable, US$8 or 90,000d for international flights.

Train

A railway line links Hanoi with Saigon, passing through many of the towns and cities worth visiting, including Hué, Danang and Nha Trang. Other than going by air, the train is the most comfortable way to travel. *But*, this only applies to first class. Fares are not cheap. Locals pay about 25% of the price that foreigners are charged. The difference in price between first and second class is small and it is worth paying the extra. The express trains plying the Saigon-Hanoi route take between 36 and 46 hrs to make the full journey. First class travel is civilized; second class acceptable; for those in other classes it can be a nightmare – the sort of journey to tell one's grandchildren about. The buffet car on the Hanoi-Saigon service serves soups and simple but adequate rice dishes; it is a good idea to take additional food and drink on long journeys. First class long distance tickets include the price of meals. With overnight stays at hotels along the way to see the sights, a rail sight-seeing tour from Hanoi to Saigon, or vice versa, should take a minimum of 10 days. You must book sleepers at least 3 days in advance and you must take your passport to the station when booking. It is possible to book bicycles onto trains, but this must be done at least 2 days ahead (example of cost, Nha Trang to Danang US$4). Vietnam is one of the few countries where steam trains are still in operation although these are fast disappearing and run only in the N.

Bus

Buses, in general, are slow, old and cramped, but they usually (not always) arrive at their destination. The most common roadside enterprises are car (and bicycle) repair outfits. This is indicative of the appalling state of many of the roads and vehicles. It is not uncommon to see buses being totally disassembled at the side of the road and it is rare to travel through the country by public transport without experiencing several breakdowns/ punctures. Speeds average no more than 35 km/hour; public road transport can be a long and tiresome (sometimes excruciating) business but it is also fascinating and the best way to meet ordinary Vietnamese. A bewildering array of contraptions pass for buses, from old French jalopies, Chevrolet, Ford and DMC vans, to Soviet buses. Many (and this includes lorries) have ingenious cooling systems in which water is fed into the radiator from barrels strapped to the roof; along the route there are water stations to replenish depleted barrels (look for the sign *nuoc mui* or *do nuoc*). The roads in the S are generally reasonable by Vietnamese standards – those in the N are terrible. The driving is also often horrendous. As P. J. O'Rourke recently observed: "In America they drive on the right side of the road, in England they drive on the left side, and in Vietnam they drive on both sides... " Many travellers find that taking the train between Hué and Hanoi is the best idea (or flying from Danang), while using buses to explore the S.

Most bus stations are on the outskirts of town; in bigger centres there may be several stations. Long-distance buses invariably leave very early in the morning (0400-0500). Less comfortable but quicker are the minibus services (some a/c) which are beginning to ply the more popular routes. These are usually grossly overladen and driven by maniacs. Advance booking of express buses (1 day ahead of departure) is recommended. The final destination is usually marked on the front of the vehicle, with stops along the way listed on the side. Regular buses will stop to pick-up and drop-off anywhere, express buses may not. Buses are the cheapest form of transport, although sometimes foreigners find they are paying an unofficial foreigner's surcharge.

● **Example of fares by minibus**
Saigon-Dalat, US$7; Saigon-Nha Trang, US$; Saigon-Hué, US$.

Car hire

Self-drive car hire is not available. Cars with drivers can be hired, US$20-40/day in the larger cities.

Other local transport
● **Bicycle**
In cities and towns bicycles are the best way

EVERY MAN AND HIS PIG

"Vietnam is great ... except for the transport." This commonly voiced sentiment reflects the views of many visitors to Vietnam. The problem is a reflection of the run-down and underfunded public transport system and the large numbers of people needing to travel. It *may* be of some consolation to the modern day traveller to know that discomfort and overcrowding on Vietnam's buses is nothing new, the following account was written in 1928:

The bus was licensed for six first-class passengers and sixteen second. We started with five of the former and twenty-two of the latter, discarded nobody and picked up every suppliant. Besides the passengers was their luggage, and this did not mean a modest hand-bag apiece. It meant sleeping-mats, boxes, sacks, bales, furniture, crates of merchandise and poultry. In addition we carried a live pig and a bicycle, the latter hung outboard over the side like a life-boat in a steamer's davits. The second-class sufferers sat on each other, on the floor, on the piled-up luggage. The overflow mounted the already overburdened roof. One youth rode all day clinging to the running-boards, another to the step. How the topheavy vehicle contrived to keep its feet when hurtling round corners at top speed was nothing short of miraculous.

We passed out of cultivated country into desolate heaths again and climbing a hill beheld a strange procession racing along the sky-line to cut us off. It consisted of an Annamite and three French priests, skirts and umbrellas tucked up under their arms, mighty beards streaming in the breeze, galloping like colts, whooping like Cherokees. The native convert, being young and slender, reached the road first and executed a sort of war-dance in front of the oncoming bus. It stopped. The three missionaries arrived panting brokenly, sponging their foreheads. One was evidently fresh to the job. He was young, wore a cassock, and his beard was a mere tuft of struggling fluff, but the other two were old stagers, wearing native dress and beards of true tropical exuberance.

The bus by this time contained seven first-class passengers and thirty second. It was unthinkable that it would take in any more. But the driver never hesitated. The convert went up to join the throng (and the pig) on the roof. With a modesty commensurate with his beard, the young priest relegated himself to the second-class and the two elders hove their vast carcases in on top of us. On top of us literally. With a sunny smile, but without any warning or by your leave, the vaster of the pair sank ponderously and devastatingly upon my knees, apparently prepared to stop there all the way to Quang-Tri.

Extract taken from Crosbie Garstin (1928) *The voyage from London to Indochina*, Heinemann.

to get about. Sometimes hotels will hire out bikes, and there is always someone who is willing to lend their machine for a small charge (6,000-10,000d/day). Alternatively, it might be worth considering buying a bike on arrival in Hanoi (see page 167) or Saigon (see page 268) and then to take it around the country. Bicycles cost 400,000-500,000d. Buses and most trains will take bicycles on board (or on top), and there are countless cheap bicycle and puncture repair shops in every town. Bicycles are either Vietnamese or Chinese made (the latter are slightly better quality) and are poorly constructed with inferior components. The authorities are now more accustomed to the concept of long-distance bicycling; the flat coastal plains and delta regions are ideal bicycling country while the more intrepid pedal their machines up to Dalat. Note that some airlines will take bicyles in the hold (eg Air France). Components for Western-made bikes may not be available in Vietnam although usually Vietnamese resourcefulness and mechanical cunning will keep them on the road.

● **Bicycle taxi**
These exist in smaller towns; agree a fare before setting off and perch, precariously, on the back (2,000d for a short journey).

● **Cyclo**
Three-wheeled bicycle rickshaws. The driver sits behind while the passenger braves the traffic out in front. This is the cheapest form of local, short-haul, transport. They can be hired by the hour (US$1-2) or by trip (short journeys, 4,000d).

● **Hitchhiking**
There have been reports of travellers being picked-up by trucks for short, local trips. Long-distance hitchhiking is not a common way to travel in Vietnam and those trying are likely to be frustrated.

● **Lambro/Lambretta**
Small, usually packed, 3-wheeled 500cc vans which run short routes within and between local towns.

● **Motorcycle taxi**
Honda om are more common and considerably cheaper than sedan taxis ('om' means 'to cuddle'). They are also the fastest way to get around town; simply agree a price and climb aboard.

● **Taxi**
Taxis are rare outside Saigon and Hanoi; metered taxis have recently appeared on the streets of Saigon and Hanoi. About US$8 from Tan Son Nhat to town. Cars with drivers can be hired for the day (US$20-US$40, depending on mileage), or for a particular journey.

Boat

In the Mekong Delta, river transport is a common form of local travel, but really only used by tourists for sightseeing. There are ferries from Saigon to various towns in the delta (see page 269). There is also a ship which runs every 10 days between Saigon and Haiphong (60 hrs) (see pages 269 and **182**).

Communications

● **Language**
Outside the main tourist centres language can be a problem for those who have no knowledge of Vietnamese. However, most visitors arrive in the country on tours, and are chaperoned by tour guides, avoiding the need to communicate with the locals. Languages other than Vietnamese that are spoken include French (throughout the country, but usually by older people and then only the former educated élite), English (especially in the S), German, and Russian (particularly in Nha Trang, Vung Tau and Danang).

The Vietnamese language uses six tones, and has 12 vowels and 27 consonants. Like other tonal languages, one word can mean many things depending upon the tone used: 'ma', for example, can mean horse, cheek, ghost, grave and rice seedling. Vietnamese-English and English-Vietnamese dictionaries are cheap and widely available in Saigon and Hanoi (see page 266).

● **Postal services**
Most towns have a post office, often with facilities for sending telegrams and telexes. The postal service can be slow from provincial centres; from Saigon and Hanoi it is comparatively efficient. The rates for overseas destinations are also extraordinarily high (fraternal socialist countries have lower rates, but with the disintegration of the Soviet Union perhaps not for very much longer). DHL is available from general post offices in Hanoi and Saigon; there are TNT offices in Hanoi and Saigon with more due to open in Haiphong, Danang, Quy Nhon, Nha Trang and Vinh.

● **Telephone services**
Directory enquiries: 12 or 13. **Local**: from some post offices and better hotels; the

network is poor. **International**: better hotels in Saigon have International Direct Dialling. Calls can be booked through the general post offices in Saigon and Hanoi. **Fax**: General Post Offices in Saigon and Hanoi, Danang, Hué and Nha Trang and most of the major hotels in Hanoi and Saigon offer fax services. Fax rates are: UK US$11, USA US$12, Canada US$11, France, US$11, Hong Kong US$7.60, Malaysia US$7.60.

● **Tourist information**

All provincial capitals and important tourist destinations have a tourist office, but they are next to useless to the independent traveller. They will arrange tours, provide guides and hand out the occasional map.

Entertainment

Media

● **Newspapers**

There are three weekly English language newspapers in Vietnam: *Saigon Newsreader*, the *Vietnam Investment Review* and the *Saigon Times*. All three are useful for up-to-the-minute information, and are particularly geared to the needs and interests of foreign investors. A magazine in the same vein has also started up, *Vietnam Today* and *What's on in Saigon*, a monthly free glossy, keeps readers up to date with local events. *Vietnam News* is, as yet, the only daily English language newspaper. In Saigon and Hanoi international newspapers and magazines are available, 1 day old (see page 267).

● **Radio**

The only way to keep in touch with international events (except in Saigon) is by tuning in to short wave radio broadcasts (BBC, VoA etc). See page 22 for wave lengths.

Holidays and festivals

Jan: *New Year's Day* (1st: public holiday).

Feb: *Tet, traditional new year* (movable, 1st to the 7th day of the new lunar year – late Jan/early Feb: public holiday). The big celebration of the year, the word Tet is the shortened version of *tet nguyen dan* ('first morning of the new period'). Tet is the time to forgive and forget, and to pay off debts. It is also everyone's birthday – the Vietnamese do not celebrate each individual's birthday, everyone is 1 year older on Tet. Enormous quantities of food are consumed (this is not the time to worry about money), new clothes are bought, houses painted and repaired, and firecrackers lit to welcome in the new year. As a Vietnamese saying has it: 'Hungry all year but Tet 3 days full'. It is believed that during Tet the spirit of the hearth, Ong Tao, leaves on a journey to visit the palace of the Jade Emperor where he must report on family affairs. To ensure that Ong Tao sets off in good cheer, a ceremony is held before Tet, Le Tao Quan, and during his absence a shrine is constructed (Cay Neu) to keep evil spirits at bay until his return. On the afternoon before Tet, Tat Nien, a sacrifice is offered at the family altar to dead relatives who are invited back to join in the festivities. Great attention is paid to preparations for Tet, because it is believed that the first week of the new year dictates the fortunes for the rest of the year. The first visitor to the house on New Year's morning (beginning after 12 midnight) should be an influential, wealthy and happy person, so families take care to arrange a suitable caller. *Founding anniversary of the Communist Party of Vietnam* (3rd: public holiday).

Mar: *Hai Ba Trung Day* (movable, 6th day of 2nd lunar month). Celebrates the famous Trung sisters who led a revolt against the Chinese in 41 AD (see page 157).

Apr: *Liberation Day of South Vietnam and Saigon* (30th: public holiday); *Thanh Minh, New Year of the Dead* (5th or 6th, 3rd lunar month), or Feast of the Pure Light. People are supposed to walk outdoors to evoke the spirit of the dead and family shrines and tombs are cleaned and decorated.

May: *International Labour Day* (1st: public holiday); *Anniversary of the Birth of Ho Chi Minh* (19th: public holiday); *Celebration of the birth, death and enlightenment of the Buddha* (28th: public holiday).

Aug: *Trung Nguyen or Wandering Souls Day* (movable, 15th day of the 7th lunar month). One of the most important festivals. During this time, prayers can absolve the sins of the dead who leave hell and return, hungry and naked, to their relatives. The Wandering Souls are those with no homes to go to. There are celebrations in Buddhist temples and homes, food is placed out on tables, and money is burned.

Sep: *National Day* (2nd: public holiday). *President Ho's Anniversary* (3rd: public holiday).

USEFUL VIETNAMESE WORDS AND PHRASES

Vietnamese is a difficult language to learn. Like Thai or Lao, it is a mono-syllabic, tonal language, but in this case with six tones (rather than five). These are marked in Roman script using diacritical marks. Mid-tone (no tone mark), rising tone ('), falling tone (`), heavy glottal stop (.), falling-rising (?), and glottal stop rising (~). The one advantage for the Westerner that Vietnamese has over Thai or Lao, is that the language is written in Roman script

Vowel Sounds:

a	as in bar (but shorter)
ă	as in cut
â	as in hum
e	as in there
ê	as in sai
i	as in bin
y	as in be (but shorter)
o	as in saw (but shorter)
ô	as in so
ơ	as in blur (but without the r)
u	as in wheat
ư	as in mountain

Consonant Sounds:

ch	as in child
d	as in zip
đ	as in dad
g	as in gad
gi	as in zip
kh	as in the german Buch
ng	as in singer
nh	as in onion
ph	like an 'f'
r	like a 'z' in the north, 'r' in the south
th	as in tip
tr	as in child
x	like a 's'
-ch	as in eke (end position, e.g. ich)
-nh	as in singer (end position)

Greeting – hello or farewell:

to elderly people, both sexes	*chào cụ*
to people of over 40, both sexes	*chào bác*
to men	*chào ông*
to women	*chào bà*
to men of the same age or to young men	*chào anh*
to young women	*chào cô*
to children	*chào cháu*
How are you?	*ông/bà khỏe/... không?*
Thanks, I'm fine	*Cảm ơn, bình thường*
I'm glad to see you	*Hân hạnh được gặp ông*
What's your name?	*Tên ông/bà là gì?*
My name is John	*Tôi tên John*
How old are you?	*Ông/bà bao nhiêu tuổi?*
Are you married? (to a man)	*Ông có vợ không?*
(to a woman)	*Bà có chồng không?*
Do you have children?	*Ông/bà có con không?*
What is your job?	*Ông/ba làm nghề gì?*
Which country are you from?	*Ông ở nước nao?*
I am English	*Tôi la người Anh*
American	*Mỹ*
Australian	*Úc*
Austrian	*Áo*
Chinese	*Trung Quốc*
Dutch	*Hòa Lan*
French	*Pháp*
German	*Đức*
Indian	*Ấn đo*
Italian	*Ý*
Japanese	*Nhật*
Korean	*Triều tiên*

Swedish	*Thụy điển*
Swiss	*Thụy sĩ*
This is my first trip to Vietnam	*Đây là lần đầu tiên tôi đến Việt nam*
I'll go to Da Lat and then on to Hue	*Tôi đi Dà Lạt trước xong đi Huế*
I want to buy a street map	*Tôi muốn mua một bản đồ thành phố*
I want to see Mr Hai	*Tôi muốn gặp ông Hai*
Excuse me, what time is it?	*Xin lỗi, mấy giờ rồi?*
I must go at once	*Tôi phải đi ngay*
My flight is at:	*Chuyến bay tôi vào lúc*
9.00	*chín giờ*
9.15	*chín giờ mười lăm*
9.30	*chín giờ mười*
9.45	*chín giờ bốn mười lăm*
I'm rather tired	*Tôi hơi mệt*

Numbers

1	*một*	15	*mười lăm...etc*
2	*hai*	20	*hai mười*
3	*ba*	21	*hai mười một*
4	*bốn*	22	*hai mười hai...etc*
5	*năm*	30	*ba mười*
6	*sáu*	100	*một trăm*
7	*bảy*	101	*một trăm một*
8	*tám*	200	*hai trăm...etc*
9	*chín*	1,000	*một nghìn*
10	*mười or chuc*	10,000	*mười nghìn*
11	*mười một*	100,000	*trăm nghìn*
12	*mười hai*	1,000,000	*một triệu*

Days

Sunday	*chủ nhật*
Monday	*thứ hai*
Tuesday	*thứ ba*
Wednesday	*thứ tư*
Thursday	*thứ năm*
Friday	*thứ sáu*
Saturday	*thứ bảy*

Months

January	*tháng giêng*
February	*tháng hai*
March	*tháng ba*
April	*tháng tư*
May	*tháng năm*
June	*tháng sáu*
July	*tháng bảy*
August	*tháng tám*
September	*tháng chín*
October	*tháng mười*
November	*tháng mười một*
December	*tháng nười hai*

Morning	*sáng*
Noon	*trưa*
Afternoon	*chiều*
Evening	*tối*
This morning	*sáng nay*
Yesterday morning	*sáng hôm qua*
Last night	*đêm hôm qua*
Tomorrow morning	*sáng mai*
Tomorrow evening	*tối mai*
Yes	*vâng (N) phải(S)*
No	*không*
Thank you	*cảm ơn ông/bà/...*
Excuse me	*xin lỗi*

That's all right	*không dám*		
I'm sorry, I'm late	*xin lỗi, tôi đến chậm*		
It doesn't matter	*không sao*		
I want something to eat/drink	*tôi muốn ăn/uống*		
Could I have some tea please	*làm ơn cho tôi một ly tra*		
Agreed!	*đồng ý*		
I disagree	*tôi không đồng ý*		
Perhaps	*có lẽ*		
Certainly	*chắc chắn*		
I see	*tôi biết*		
I don't know	*tôi không biết*		

This is...	*cái này...*	dear/cheap	*đắt/rẻ*
good/bad	*tốt/xấu*	high/low	*cao/thấp*
beautiful/ugly	*đẹp/xấu*	heavy/light	*nặng/nhẹ*
old/new	*cũ/mới*	near/far	*gần/xa*
strong/weak	*mạnh/yếu*	hot/cold	*nóng/lạnh*
wide/narrow	*rộng/hẹp*	salty/unsalted	*mặn/nhạt*
long/short	*dài/ngắn*	delicious/not nice	*ngon/không ngon*
light/dark	*sáng/tối*		
fast/slow	*nhanh/chậm*		

I'm ill	*tôi ốm*
I need to see the doctor/dentist	*tôi cần gặp bác sĩ/nha sĩ*
I have a temperature/flu	*tôi bị sốt/cúm*
cold/cough	*cam lanh/ho*
diarrhoea	*đi rửa*
I have a pain in this hand	*toi bị đau tay*
toothache	*đau răng*
stomach-ache	*đau dạ dày*
I need some medicine	*cho tôi thuốc*
hospital	*bệnh viện*
pharmacy	*nhà thuốc*
I am hungry	*tôi đói*
I am full	*tôi no rồi*
Vietnamese dishes are very delicious	*món ăn Việt nam rất ngon*
What is this?	*đây là cái gì?*
What is that?	*kia là cái gì?*
I like chicken	*tôi thích thịt gà*
pork	*thịt lợn (N) heo (S)*
beef	*thịt bò*
goose	*thịt ngỗng*
frog	*thịt ếch*
goat	*thịt dê*
I like fish	*tôi thích cá*

crab	*cua*	dog	*chó (S) cầy (N)*
eel	*lươn*	fried noodles	*mì xào*
lobster	*tôm hùm*	shrimp	*tôm*
snail	*ốc*	spring rolls	*chả giò (S) nem (N)*

vegetable dishes	*các món ăn rau cải*
I don't want chilli	*đừng cho tôi ót*
yoghurt	*da ua*
ice cream	*kêm*
face cloth	*khăng lau mặt*
a pair of chopsticks	*một đôi đũa*
salad	*xà lát*
tomato	*cà tô mát (S) cà chua (N)*
apple	*trái bóm (S) trái táo (N)*
durian	*trái xàu riêng*

rambutan	*chôm chôm*
pineapple	*trái khóm (S) trái thơm (N)*
mango	*trái xoài*
banana	*chuối*
mangosteen	*măng cụt*
pawpaw	*đu đủ*
longan	*nhãn*
lychee	*vải*
custard apple	*na*
orange	*cam*
water-melon	*dưa hấu*
lemon	*chanh*
I'm thirsty	*tôi khát*
I want something to drink	*tôi muốn đồ giải khát*
A bottle of mineral water	*một chai nước xuối*
black coffee	*cà fê đen*
white coffee	*cà fê sữa*
iced coffee	*cà fê đá*
More ice	*thêm đá*
No ice	*không đa*
No sugar	*không đường*
A little sugar	*một chút đường*
A bottle of beer	*một chai bia*
lemonade	*nước chanh*
orange juice	*nước cam*
coconut milk	*nước dừa*
pineapple juice	*nước dứa*
hot tea/iced tea	*trà nóng/trà đá*
It is nice today	*hôm nay trời đẹp*
It is nasty	*trời xấu*
It is raining	*trời mưa*
It is sunny	*trời nắng*
Where is the toilet, please?	*nhà vệ sinh ở đâu*
Here it is	*ở đây*
It is over there	*ở đằng kia*
How far is it from here to Hué?	*từ đây đến Hué bao xa?*
Could you show me the way	*làm ơn chi cho tôi đường đi*
to the railway station?	*nha ga*
bus station	*bến xe*
market	*chợ*
post office	*buử điện*
restaurant	*nhà hàng*
Where does this road lead to?	*con đường này dẫn đến đâu?*
hotel	*khách sạn*
How much for a room?	*một phòng bao nhiêu?*
That's too expensive	*mắc quá*
cheap	*rẻ*
hot water	*nước nóng*
shower	*tắm*
soap	*xà bông*
towel	*khàng bàn*
Air conditioning/fan is broken	*máy lạnh/quạt máy bị hư*
The room is dirty	*phòng dở quá*
The room needs cleaning	*làm ơn chùi phòng*
Please wash these	*làm ơn rửa cái nầy*
iron	*bàn ủi*
power cut	*cúp điện*
1 cyclo, 2 people	*một xích lô, hai người*
Please wait one hour	*xin chờ một tiếng*

Trung Thu or *Mid Autumn Festival* (movable, 15th day of the 8th month). Particularly celebrated by children. Moon cakes are baked, lanterns made and painted, and children parade through towns with music and lanterns.

Nov: *Confucius' Birthday* (movable, 28th day of the 9th month).

Further reading

● Suggested reading

Beresford, Melanie (1988) *Vietnam: politics, economics and society*, Pinter: London. Academic account of social, economic and political developments to mid 1980s; too early to include much discussion of economic reform programme. Crawford, Ann Caddell (nd) *Customs and culture of Vietnam*, Charles Tuttle: Rutland, Vermont. Fenn, Charles (1973) *Ho Chi Minh: a biographical introduction*, Studio Vista: London. Duras, Marguerite (1964) *The lover*, Flamingo. Now a film starring Jane March; story of the relationship between an expat French girl and a Chinese from Cholon. Garstin, Crosbie (1928) *The Voyage from London to Indochina*: Heinemann. Hilarious, rather irreverent account of journey through Vietnam. Greene, Graham (1954) *The quiet American*, Heinemann: London. Features the Continental Hotel, Saigon. Greene, Graham (1980). *Ways of escape* (1980) Autobiographical. Grey, Anthony (1983) *Saigon*, Pan: London. Entertaining novel. Harris, George L. *et al* (1962) *US Army area handbook for Vietnam*, US Government Printing Office: Washington. Hejzlar, J (1973) *The art of Vietnam*, Hamlyn: London. The text is rather heavy going, but has numerous photographs. Hickey, Gerald (1964) *Village in Vietnam*, Yale University Press: New Haven; classic village study. Kemf, Elizabeth (1990) *Month of pure light: the regreening of Vietnam*, The Women's Press: London. Account of the attempts to overcome the aftereffects of US defoliation and regreen the Vietnamese countryside; more a light travelogue than an objective book. Lewis, Norman (1951) *A dragon apparent: travels in Cambodia, Laos and Vietnam*. One of the finest of all travel books; now reprinted by Eland Books. Nguyen Du (1983) *The tale of Kieu*, Yale University Press: New Haven, *tr.* Huynh Sanh Thong. Vietnamese early 19th century classic. Taylor, Keith Weller (1983) *The birth of Vietnam*, University of California Press: Berkeley. Academic history of early Vietnam from the 3rd century BC to 10th century. Theroux, Paul (1977) *The great railway bazaar*, Penguin: London. Two chapters describe a graphic account of one American's attempt to travel by rail between Saigon and Hué; Tin, Bui (1995) *Following Ho Chi Minh*, Hurst: London. Autobiographical account of a North Vietnamese Colonel's disillusionment with the Communist regime following Ho Chi Minh's death. Western readers may find it rather self-congratulatory in tone but nevertheless an interesting read; Turner, Robert F (1975) *Vietnamese Communism: its origins and development*, Hoover Institution Press: Stanford. Academic study of rise of Communism in Vietnam. Vu Tu Lap and Taillard, Christian (1994) *An Atlas of Vietnam*, Reclus – La Documentation Française. Marvellous summary of the population and economy of Vietnam in maps.

● Books on the Vietnamese War

There are more books on the Vietnam War than possibly any other conflict in global history. It has been examined in minute detail. Bao Ninh (1993) *The sorrow of war*, Secker & Warburg, London. Wartime novel by a young North Vietnamese soldier, wonderful account of emotions during and after the war. Cawthorne, Nigel (1992) *The bamboo cage*, Leo Cooper. The story of MIAs and POWs. Fall, Bernard B. (1966) *Street without joy*: Stackpole. Fall, Bernard B. (1967) *Hell in a very small place: the Siege of Dien Bien Phu*, Pall Mall Press. Fitzgerald, Francis (1972) *Fire in the lake*, Vintage Books: New York. Pulitzer prize winner; a well-researched and readable account of the US involvement. Harrison, James P. (1982) *The endless war: fifty years of struggle in Vietnam*, Free Press: New York. Herr, Michael (1977) *Dispatches*, Knopf: New York. An acclaimed 'account' of the war written by a correspondent who experienced the conflict first hand. Karnow, Stanley (1983 and 1991) *Vietnam: a history*, Viking Press: New York. A comprehensive and readable history; second edition published in 1991; the best there is. Lunn, Hugh (1985) *Vietnam: a reporter's war*, University of Queensland Press: St Lucia, Australia. Account of Australian reporter Hugh Lunn's year in Vietnam with Reuters between 1967 and 1968, including an account of his experiences during the Tet Offensive. McNamara, Robert S and Mark, Brian Van de (1995) *In retrospect: the tragedy and lessons of Vietnam*, Times/Random House: New York. McNamara was Secretary for Defense from 1961 to 1968 and this is his cathartic account of the war. Informed from the inside, he concludes that the war was a big mistake. Mangold, Tom and Penycate, John (1985), *The tunnels of Cu Chi*. Compelling account of the building of the tunnels and the VC who fought in them. Mason, Robert (1984) *Chickenhawk*, Penguin: Harmondsworth. Autobiography of a helicopter pilot, excellent. Sheehan, Neil (1989) *A bright shining lie*, Jonathan Cape: London. A meticulously researched 850-page account of the Vietnam War, based around the life of John Paul Vann; recommended. Sheehan, Neil (1992) *Two cities: Hanoi and Saigon* (in US *After the war was over*), Jonathan Cape: London. A short but fascinating book which tries to link the past with the present in a part autobiography, part travelogue, part contemporary commentary. SIPRI (1976) *Ecological consequences of the Second Indochina War*, Almqvist & Wiksell: Stockholm. Academic study of environmental side-effects of war. Thrift, Nigel and Forbes, Dean (1986) *The Price of war: Urbanization in Vietnam 1954-85*, Allen and Unwin: London. Turley, William S. (1986) *The Second Indochina War: a short political and military history 1954-1975*, Westview: Boulder. A clear, well-balanced academic account of the war. Williams, Michael C. (1992) *Vietnam at the crossroads*, Pinter: London. Most recent survey of political and economic reforms by a senior BBC World Service commentator; lucid and informed. Wintle, Justin (1991) *The Vietnam Wars*, Weidenfeld and Nicholson: London. Not just about *the War*, but about all of Vietnam's interminable conflicts. Young, Marilyn (1990) *The Vietnam Wars 1945-1990*, Harper Collins: New York. Good account of the origins, development and aftermath of the Vietnam wars.

● **Films**

Along with the better-known films on the Vietnamese War including *Apocalypse Now*, *Hamburger Hill*, *Good Morning Vietnam* and Oliver Stone's trilogy *Platoon*, *Born on the Fourth of July* and *Heaven and Earth*, three French films have nicely captured the atmosphere of Vietnam at peace: *Indochine* starring Catherine Deneuve and *The Lover* with Jane March adapted from Marguerite Duras' book. The little known but delightful *Scent of green papaya*, an account of family relationships and love, filmed entirely in a Paris studio.

● **Acknowledgements**

Tran Quoc Cong, Danang; Mark Allen, Ha Long City; Pilou Grenié, France; Derek Langley, Victoria, Australia; Andrew Mower, Kuala Lumpur; Angelika Teuschl, Vienna; Nils Meulemans, Holland; Martine Glasson, Switzerland; Nguyen Van Hue, Hué; Steven Pegrum, London; Heide Locke, USA; Mark Moriguchi, San Francisco; Patrich Aguillon, Sierentz; Nic Munro, Eton; Annand Mansouri, a Frenchman in SE Asia; Catherine Cheung, Hong Kong; Howard Gatiss, Saigon; Bui Kim Yen, Saigon; Tam Nguyen, London.

LAOS

INTRODUCTION

Authors of most guidebooks to most countries of Southeast Asia try to entice the reader with a familiar sequence of words: 'traditional', 'timeless', 'untouched', 'remote'... In the case of Laos, though, there is veracity in these adjectives. Crossing from the provincial town of Nong Khai in Northeastern Thailand, using the new Friendship Bridge, to Vientiane, the capital of Laos, feel like a journey of four decades, not a short hop of a few kilometres. Vientiane is sleepy, unsophisticated, quiet and small. It is also elegant, civilized and spiritually enriching. The same is true of the old royal capital of Luang Prabang, tucked into a rich valley and surrounded by the eastern-most peaks of the Himalayas. Barring a few other urban centres situated in the valley of the Mekong River, like Pakse, Savannakhet and Champassak, much of the country is remote and comparatively untouched by the forces of commercialization. In a country the size of the UK, there are less than 2,000 km of surfaced road, total exports amount to barely more than US$100mn, and per capita income is US$220. The average Lao is a farmer living in the countryside, posts one letter a year, shares a television with 150 other people, and stands a one in 500 chance of having visited a cinema during the previous 12 months. Few tourists come to Laos; some who do are disappointed, claiming there is 'nothing to do'. The wonder of Laos lies in its innocence, natural beauty and cultural charm: come here not to notch up sights, but to quietly savour a country without peer.

CONTENTS

MAPS

Laos is strategically sandwiched between China, Vietnam, Cambodia, Thailand and Burma. It has always been the landlocked, mountainous, underdeveloped backwater of Indochina. But its rich history, magnificent scenery, fragile culture and its years of isolation have left Laos an unexplored jewel in Southeast Asia. More than three-quarters of the population are subsistence farmers and only a tenth of its villages are anywhere near a road. One child in five dies before its fifth birthday and cars seem to have a longer life expectancy than people. The diet is inadequate, sanitation poor, and only a quarter of the population has access to safe drinking water. Dehabilitating and fatal diseases from malaria to bilharzia, are endemic

CHINA

VIETNAM

LAOS
VL 100

Phongsali

Ban
Boten

Louang
Namtha

BURMA

Ban
Houei Xai

Udom Xai

Pakmong

Sam
Neua

Dien Bien Phu

HANOI

N

Nam Ou

Nam Tha

Luang Prabang

Muang Kham

Rt 7

Nam Sam

Nam Neun

Sayaboury

Rt 13

Phonsavanh
Plain of Jars

Nong Het

Gulf
of

Tonkin

Vang Vieng

Nam Ngum

Xieng
Khouang

Paklai

Nam
Ngum
Res.

Rt 2

Paksane

VIENTIANE

Tha Dua

Khammuan
Plateau

Thakhek

Annamite Range

THAILAND

Savannakhet

Bolovens
Plateau

Muang
Khong Xedon

Saravan

Tha Teng

Ubon Ratchatani

Chongmek

Pakse

Rt 9

Sekong

Champassak

Paksong

Attapeu

Khong

Rt 6

Mekong

CAMBODIA

0   100
km

PROVINCES:
1. Phong Saly
2. Luang Nam Tha
3. Bokeo
4. Udom Xai
5. Luang Prabang
6. Houa Phan
7. Sayaboury
8. Vientiane
9. Préfecture de Vientiane
10. Xieng Khouang
11. Bolikhamsai
12. Khammouane
13. Savannakhet
14. Saravane
15. Sekong
16. Champassak
17. Attapau

in rural Laos while the health and education systems are limited. In N provinces the opium addiction rate is double the literacy rate. With per capita income of US$220, Laos is one of the poorest countries in the world.

Laos has also earned the distinction of being the most heavily-bombed nation on earth, per head of population – a record which even Iraq cannot match. During a 9-year secret war against the Communists, the United States dropped 6,300,000 tonnes of bombs on Indochina. About a third of them fell on Laos. In the 1960s and early-70s, more bombs rained on Laos than were dropped during WW2 – the equivalent of a plane load of bombs every 8 mins around the clock for 9 years. This cost American tax-payers more than US$2mn a day – but the cost to Laos was incalculable. But the B-52s were merely the climax of the final chapter in a centuries-long catalogue of warfare in which Laos has suffered from successive incursions by the Vietnamese, Siamese, Chinese, French and Japanese.

Now, after more than a decade of Soviet-inspired Marxism-Leninism, Laos is finally at peace and the septogenarian ex-guerrillas who head the Lao People's Revolutionary Party are tacitly conceding that their revolution has been an economic disaster. Communism's bamboo curtain has proved more resilient than its iron counterpart in Europe, but Party rhetoric is now deeply unfashionable. Just 15 years after the Marxists moved from their mountain caves to the capital's corridors of power, the capitalists began their advance on Vientiane. This time there is little doubt who will win.

While shying away from too much in the way of *glasnost*, the leadership has rubber-stamped the move from a centrally planned economy and embarked on a rapid transition to capitalism, known as *Chin Thanakan Mai* or 'New Thinking'. The hammer and sickle were discreetly painted out of the state emblem in 1991. Having watched the Eastern bloc crumble, the Politburo's Old Guard wants to go down looking good. President Kaysone Phomvihan, who died in Nov 1992, redeemed his regime's reputation by spearheading a series of economic reforms. With the demise of Soviet Communism, there will be no more handouts from Moscow or its erstwhile allies. As Vientiane turns to the W for investment, there is concern that the impoverished country, with no industrial infrastructure, could become a casualty of capitalism. Three-quarters of its intellectuals fled the country in advance of the Communist takeover in 1975 and thousands disappeared to jungle re-education camps, so Laos has few people experienced in managing a market economy.

At first the pace of change was what Laos call *koi koi bai* – slowly, slowly – but the momentum picked up in 1991 and now everything, it seems, is viable for privatization – from state enterprises to entire economic sectors. One of the first to fall to the capitalist onslaught has been tourism; as an easy foreign exchange earner it was an obvious target. In May 1991, the government began contracting out its regional tourism monopolies to private operators. An unwelcome invasion of backpackers in 1987 convinced the government that the Thai model for tourism development was not worth emulating. Laos now effectively means-tests its visitors: tours to Laos do not come cheap. The government is in no mood to accelerate the development of the Lao tourism industry mainly because it is acutely aware that the country's infrastructure is so inadequate.

The allure of capitalism, consumerism and westernism to many Lao is obvious. They do not want to be cultural artefacts forever, but with rapid change, it is easy to question the price of progress. At present rates, tourism alone will not destroy the gentle Lao spirit or the cultural treasure-trove which has remained intact despite years of war. But in downtown Vientiane, expectations are running high: Thai television, with its brash, materialist message, is beamed across the Mekong into Vientiane's front rooms and has already proved too much for party ideologues. Young Lao know what they want: stereos and motorbikes from Japan, rock music from Thailand, and Levi 501s from the USA.

Meanwhile, a steady stream of Thai businessmen has arrived to test the water on the other side of the Mekong. They have unleashed a capitalists' jamboree, rousing the Land of a Million Elephants from a long siesta and reintroducing corruption to Vientiane's legions of underpaid bureaucrats earning US$15–20 a month. Vientiane, although sleepy by the standards of other Southeast Asian capitals, is bustling with new businesses setting up every day.

Land and life

The regions of Laos

Laos is dominated by the Mekong River and the Annamite chain of mountains which both run SE towards the South China Sea. 1,865 km of the 4,000 km-long Mekong River flows along the borders of Laos and is the country's main thoroughfare. The lowlands of the Mekong valley form the principal agricultural areas, especially around Vientiane and Savannakhet, and these are home to the lowland Lao – sometimes argued to be the 'true' Lao. The Mekong has three main tributaries: the Nam Ou and Nam Tha from the N, and the Nam Ngum, which flows into Vientiane province.

Much of the N half of Laos is 1,500m or more above sea-level and its karst limestone outcrops are deeply dissected by steep-sided river valleys. Further S, the Annamite chain has an average height of 1,200m. Heavily forested, rugged mountains form a natural barrier between Laos and Vietnam. Most of the country is a mixture of mountains and high plateaux. There are four main plateaux: the Xieng

THE MEKONG: GREAT RIVER OF SOUTHEAST ASIA

The Mekong River is one of the 12 great rivers of the world. It stretches 4,500 km from its source on the Tibet Plateau in China to its mouth (or mouths) in the Mekong Delta of Vietnam. (On 11 April 1995 a Franco-British expedition announced that they had discovered the source of the Mekong – 5,000m-high, at the head of the Rup-Sa Pass, and miles from anywhere.) Each year, the river empties 475 billion m^3 of water into the South China Sea. Along its course it flows through Burma, Laos, Thailand, Cambodia and Vietnam – all of the countries that constitute mainland Southeast Asia – as well as China. In both a symbolic and a physical sense then, it links the region. Bringing fertile silt to the land along its banks, but particularly to the Mekong Delta, the river contributes to Southeast Asia's agricultural wealth. In former times, a tributary of the Mekong which drains the Tonle Sap (the Great Lake of Angkor and Cambodia), provided the rice surplus on which that fabulous empire was founded. The Tonle Sap acts like a great regulator, storing water in time of flood and then releasing it when levels recede.

The first European to explore the Mekong River was the French naval officer Francis Garnier. His Mekong Expedition (1866-1868), followed the great river upstream from its delta in Cochin China. Of the 9,960 km that the expedition covered, 5,060 km were 'discovered' for the first time. The motivation for the trip was to find a southern route into the Heavenly Kingdom – China. But they failed. The river is navigable only as far as the Lao-Cambodian border where the Khone rapids make it impassable. Nonetheless, the report of the expedition is one of the finest of its genre.

Today the Mekong itself is perceived as a source of potential economic wealth – not just as a path to riches. The Mekong Secretariat was established in 1957 to harness the waters of the river for hydropower and irrigation. The Secretariat devised a grandiose plan incorporating a succession of seven huge dams which would store 142 billion m^3 of water, irrigate 4.3 million hectares of riceland, and generate 24,200MW of power. But the Vietnam War intervened to disrupt construction. Only Laos' Nam Ngum Dam on a tributary of the Mekong was ever built – and even though this generates only 150MW of power, electricity exports to Thailand are one of Laos' largest export earners. Now that the countries of mainland Southeast Asia are on friendly terms once more, the Secretariat and its scheme have been given a new lease of life. But in the intervening years, fears about the environmental consequences of big dams have raised new questions. The Mekong Secretariat has moderated its plans and is now looking at less ambitious, and less contentious, ways to harness the Mekong River.

Khouang plateau in the N, the Nakai and the limestone Khammuan plateau in the centre and the 10,000 sq km Bolovens Plateau to the S. The highest peak is the 2,800m Bia Mountain, which rises above the Xieng Khouang plateau to the NE.

Geography

Laos stretches about 1,000 km from N to S, while distances from E to W range from 140 to 500 km. The country covers an area of 236,800 sq km – less than half the size of France and just a third of the size of Texas. Only 15% of the population live in towns and the country has the lowest population density in Asia with 17 people/sq km. The population is 4.5 million and is growing at 2.9% a year.

Rugged mountains cover more than three-quarters of the country and with few all-weather roads (there are just 2,000 km of sealed roads in the entire country), rivers are important communication routes. Historically, the Mekong River has been the country's economic artery. On its banks nestle Laos' most important cities: in the N the small, colourful former royal capital of Luang Prabang, further S the administrative and political capital of Vientiane, and farther S still the regional centres of Savannakhet, Pakse and Champassak.

Climate

The rainy season is from May through to Sep/Oct; the tropical lowlands receive an annual average rainfall of 1,250 mm a year. Temperatures during these months are in the 30s°C. In mountainous Xieng Khoung Province, it is cooler and temperatures can drop to freezing point in Dec and Jan. The first half of the dry season, from Nov to Apr, is cool, with temperatures between 10° and 20°C. This gives way to a hot, dry season from Mar to Jun when temperatures soar and are often in excess of 35°C. Average rainfall in Vientiane is 1,700 mm, although in N Laos and the highlands it is much wetter, with more than 3,000 mm each year. For the best time to visit, see page 409. Monthly temperature and rainfall for Vientiane are graphed on page 349.

Flora and fauna

Much of Laos is forested. The vegetation is rich and diverse: a mix of tropical and sub-tropical species. Grassy savanna predominates on plateau areas such as the Plain of Jars. In the forests, some hardwoods tower to over 30m in height, while tropical palms and mango are found in the settled lowlands and large stands of pine in the remote N hills.

About half the country is still covered in primary forest but this is being seriously threatened by logging which provides Laos with more than two-thirds of its export earnings. Officially, around 450,000 m^3 are felled each year for commercial purposes, although in reality this is probably an under-estimate owing to the voracious activities of illegal loggers – many of whom are Thai. A ban on the export of logs in 1988 caused official timber export earnings to slump 30% – but environmentalists claim that the ban has had little impact on the number of logs being exported. Another ban was imposed in late 1991. In addition, shifting cultivators clear an estimated 100,000 ha of forest a year (see page 36).

Government reforestation programmes far from compensate for the destruction. In Oct 1989 the Council of Ministers issued a decree on the preservation of forests of which the people appear to be blissfully unaware. There was a half-hearted propaganda campaign to 'teach every Lao citizen to love nature and develop a sense of responsibility for the preservation of forests'.

Mammals include everything from wildcats, leopards and tigers to bears, wild cattle and small barking deer. Laos is also home to the large Asian elk, rhinoceros, elephants, monkeys, gibbons and ubiquitous rabbits and squirrels. Ornithological life encompasses pheasants, partridges, many songbirds, ducks and some hawks and eagles – although in rural areas many birds (and other animals) have been killed for food (see Saravan's daily market, page 374). There is an abundant reptilian population, including cobras, kraits, crocodiles and lizards. The lower reaches of the Mekong River, marking the border between Cambodia and Laos, is the last place in Indochina where the rare Irrawaddy dolphin is to be found. However dynamite fishing is deminating the population, and today there are probably just 100 or 200 left. Another rare denizen of the Mekong, but one that stands a greater chance of survival, is the *pla buk* catfish (*Pangasianodon gigas*) which weighs up to 340 kg. This riverbed-dwelling fish was first described by western science only in 1930, although Lao fishermen and their Thai counterparts had been catching it for many years – as James McCarthy notes in the account of his travels through Siam and Laos published in 1900. The fish is a delicacy, and clearly has been for many years – its roe was paid as tribute to China in the late 19th century. Because of over-fishing, by the 1980s the numbers of *pla buk* had become severly depleted. However a breeding programme is having some success and young *pa buk* fingerlings are now being released into the Mekong.

There is an enormous problem of smuggling rare animals out of Laos, mainly to S Korea and China. In 1978, the gall bladder of a black bear from Laos was auctioned in Seoul for US$55,000. Teeth and bones of cats from Laos are in demand for Chinese medicine. In 1992 the English-language daily, *Khao San Pathet Lao*, published a report estimating that in 1992 more than 10 tonnes of protected wild animals had been slaughtered for export in the north-eastern province of Hona Phan alone.

History

Scholars of Lao history, before their even begin, need to decide whether they are writing a history a Laos; a history of the Lao ethnic group; or histories of the various kingdoms and principalities that have, through time, been encompassed by the present boundaries of the Lao People's Democratic Repubublic. Historians have tended to confront this problem in different ways without, often, acknowledging on what basis their 'history' is built. It is common to see 1365, the date of the foundation of the kingdom of Lan Xang, as marking the beginning of Lao history. But, as Martin Stuart-Fox points out, prior to Lane Xang the principality of Muang Swa, occupying the same geographical space, was headed by a Lao. The following account provides a brief overview of the histories of those peoples who have occupied what is now the territory of the Lao PDR.

Archaeological and historical evidence indicates that most Lao originally migrated S from China. This was followed by an influx of ideas and culture from the Indian subcontinent via Burma, Thailand and Cambodia – something which is reflected in the state religion, Theravada Buddhism.

Being surrounded by large, powerful neighbours, Laos has been repeatedly invaded over the centuries by the Thais (or Siamese) and the Vietnamese – who both thought of Laos as their buffer zone and backyard. They too have both left their mark on Lao culture. In recent history, Laos has been influenced by the French during the colonial era, the Japanese during WW2, the Americans during the Indochinese wars and, between 1975 and the early 1990s, by Marxism-Leninism.

The first kingdom of Laos

Myth, archaeology and history all point to a number of early feudal Lao kingdoms in what is now S China and N Vietnam. External pressures from the Mongols under Kublai Khan and the Han Chinese forced the Tai tribes to migrate S into what had been part of the Khmer Empire. The mountains to the N and E served as a cultural barrier to Vietnam and China, leaving the Lao exposed to influences from India and the W. There are no documentary records of early Lao history, although it seems probable that parts of present-day Laos were annexed by Lannathai (Chiang Mai) in the 11th century and by the Khmer Empire during the 12th century. But neither of these states held sway over the entire area of Laos. Xieng Khouang, eg was probably never under Khmer domination. This was followed by strong Siamese influence over the cities of Luang Prabang and Vientiane under the Siamese Sukhothai Dynasty. Laos (the country), in effect did not exist; although the Laos (the people) certainly did.

The downfall of the kingdom of Sukhothai in 1345 and its submission to the new Siamese Dynasty at Ayutthaya (founded in 1349) was the catalyst for the foundation of what is commonly regarded as the first truly independent Lao Kingdom – although there were smaller semi-independent Lao *muang* (city states) existing prior to that date.

The **kingdom of Lane Xang** emerged in 1353 under Fa Ngoum, a Lao prince who had grown up in the Khmer court of Angkor. Lane Xang – the land of a million elephants – is portrayed in some accounts as stretching from China to Cambodia, and from the Khorat Plateau in present-day NE Thailand to the Annamite mountains in the E. But it would be entirely wrong to envisage the kingdom controlling all these regions. Lane Xang probably only had total control over a comparatively small area of present-day Laos, and parts of NE Thailand; the bulk of this grand empire would have been contested with other surrounding kingdoms. In addition,

the smaller *muang* and principalities would themselves have played competing powers off, one against another, in an attempt to maximize their own autonomy. It is this 'messiness' which led scholars of Southeast Asian history to suggest that territories as such did not exist, but rather zones of variable control, termed *mandalas* by OW Wolters (see box, page 50).

Legend relates that Fa Ngoum was a descendant of Khoum Borom, "a king who came out of the sky from S China". Khoum Borom is credited with giving birth to the Lao people by slicing open a gourd in Muong Taeng (Dien Bien Phu, Vietnam) and his seven sons established the great Tai kingdoms. He returned to his country with a detachment of Khmer soldiers and united several scattered Lao fiefdoms. In those days, conquered lands were usually razed and the people taken as slaves to build up the population of the conquering group. The kings of Lane Xang were less philistine, demanding only subordination and allegiance as one part of a larger *mandala*.

Luang Prabang became the capital of the kingdom of Lane Xang. The unruly highland tribes of the NE did not come under the kingdom's control at that time. Fa Ngoum made Theravada Buddhism the official religion. He married the Cambodian king's daughter, Princess Keo Kaengkanya, and was given the gold **Phra Bang** (a golden statue and the most revered religious symbol of Laos) by the Khmer court.

It is common to read Lane Xang portrayed as the first kingdom of Laos; as encompassing the territory of present-day Laos; and as marking the introduction of Theravada Buddhism to the country. On all counts this portait is, if not false, then deeply flawed. As noted above, there were Lao states that predated Lane Xang; Lane Xang never controlled Laos as it currently exists; and Buddhism had made an impact on the Lao people before 1365. Fa Ngoum did not create a kingdom; rather he brought together various pre-existing *muang* (city states) into a powerful *mandala*. As Martin Stuart-Fox writes, "From this derives his [Fa Ngoum's] historical claim to hero status as the founder of the Lao Kingdom". But, as Stuart-Fox goes on to explain, there was no central authority and rulers of individual *muang* were permitted considerable autonomy. As a result the "potential for disintegration was always present..."

After Fa Ngoum's wife died in 1368, he became so debauched, it is said, that he was deposed in favour of his son, Samsenthai (1373-1416) who was barely 18 when he acceded the throne. He was named after the 1376 census, which concluded that he ruled over 300,000 Thais living in Laos: *samsen* means, literally 300,000. He set up a new administrative system based on the existing *muang*, nominating governors to each, that lasted until it was abolished by the Communist government in 1975. His death was followed by a period of unrest. Under King Chaiyachakkapat-Phaenphaeo (1441-1478), the kingdom came under increasing threat from the Vietnamese, culminating in the first of their incursions into Laos from Annam. On this occasion they sacked Luang Prabang but were driven out by Chaiyachakkapat-Phaenphaeo's son, King Suvarna Banlang (1478-1485). Peace was only fully restored under King Visunarat (1500-1520), who built Wat Visoun in Luang Prabang (see page 374).

Increasing prominence and Burmese incursions

Under King Phothisarath (1520-1548) Vientiane became prominent as a trading and religious centre. He married a Lanna (Chiang Mai) princess, Queen Yotkamtip, and when the Siamese King Ketklao was put to death in 1545, Pothisarath's son claimed the throne at Lanna. He returned to Lane Xang when his father died. Asserting his right as successor to the throne,

he was crowned Setthathirat in 1548 and ruled until 1571.

At the same time, the Burmese were expanding E and in 1556 Lanna fell into their hands. Setthathirat gave up his claim to that throne, to a Siamese prince, who ruled under Burmese authority. In 1563 Setthathirat pronounced Vieng Chan (Vientiane) the principal capital of Lane Xang. Seven years later, the Burmese King Bayinnaung launched an unsuccessful attack on Vieng Chan itself.

Setthathirat is revered as one of the great Lao kings, having protected the country from foreign domination. He built Wat Phra Kaeo (see page 355) in the middle of the city, in which he placed the famous Emerald Buddha brought from Lanna. Setthathirat mysteriously disappeared during a campaign in the S province of Attapu in 1574, which threw the kingdom into crisis. Vieng Chan fell to invading Burmese the following year and remained under Burmese control for 7 years. Finally the anarchic kingdoms of Luang Prabang and Vientiane were reunified under Nokeo Koumane (1591-96) and Thammikarath (1596-1622).

Disputed territory

From the time of the formation of the kingdom of Lane Xang to the arrival of the French, the history of Laos was dominated by the struggle to retain the lands it had conquered. Following King Setthathirat's death, a series of kings came to the throne in quick succession. King Souligna Vongsa, crowned in 1633, brought long awaited peace to Laos. The 61 years he was on the throne are regarded as Lane Xang's golden age. Under him, the kingdom's influence spread to Yunnan in S China, the Burmese Shan States, Isan in NE Thailand and areas of Vietnam and Cambodia.

Souligna Vongsa was even on friendly terms with the Vietnamese: he married Emperor Le Thanh Ton's daughter, and he and the Emperor agreed the borders

WARS OF THE ROSES?

Post World War II politics in Laos have been compared with the English Wars of the Roses: rival elements within one royal family, representing different political opinions, were backed by different foreign powers. By the early 1960s King Savang Vatthana was convinced that his centuries-old kingdom, now a pawn of conflicting superpower interests, was doomed to extinction. A speech made to the nation in 1961 reflects his despondency:

"Our country is the most peaceful in the world... At no time has there ever arisen in the minds of the Lao people the idea of coveting another's wealth, of quarrelling with their neighbours, much less of fighting them. And yet, during the past 20 years, our country has known neither peace nor security... Enemies of all sorts have tried to cross our frontiers, to destroy our people and to destroy our religion and our nation's aura of peace and concord... Foreign countries do not care either about our interests or peace; they are concerned only with their own interests."

between the two countries. The frontier was settled in a deterministic – but nonetheless amicable – fashion: those living in houses built on stilts with verandahs were considered Lao subjects and those living in houses without piles and verandahs were Vietnamese.

During his reign, foreigners first visited the country – the Dutch merchant Gerrit van Wuysthoff arrived in 1641 to assess trading prospects – and Jesuit missionaries too. But other than a handful of adventurers, Laos remained on the outer periphery of European concerns and influence in the region.

The three kingdoms

After Souligna Vongsa died in 1694, leaving no heir, dynastic quarrels and feudal rivalries once again erupted, undermining the kingdom's cohesion. In 1700 Lane Xang split into three: Luang Prabang under Souligna's grandson, Vieng Chan under Souligna's nephew and the new kingdom of Champassak was founded in the S 'panhandle'. This weakened the country and allowed the Siamese and Vietnamese to encroach on Lao lands. *Muang* which previously owed clear allegience to Lane Xang began to look towards Vietnam or Siam. Isan *muang* in present-day NE Thailand eg paid tribute to Bangkok; while Xieng Khouang did the same to Hanoi and,

later, to Hué. The three main kingdoms that emerged with the disintegration of Lane Xang leant in different directions: Luang Prabang had close links with China, Vieng Chan with Vietnam's Hanoi/Hué and Champassak with Siam.

By the mid-1760s Burmese influence once again held sway in Vieng Chan and Luang Prabang, and before the turn of the decade, they sacked Ayutthaya, the capital of Siam. Somehow the Siamese managed to pull themselves together, and only 2 years later in 1778 successfully rampaged through Vieng Chan. The two sacred Buddhas, the Phra Bang and the Phra Kaeo (Emerald Buddha) were taken as booty back to Bangkok. The Emerald Buddha was never returned and now sits in Bangkok's Wat Phra Kaeo (see page 547).

King Anou (an abbreviation of Anurutha) was placed on the Vieng Chan throne by the Siamese. With the death of King Rama II of Siam, King Anou saw his chance of rebellion, asked Vietnam for assistance, formed an army, and marched on Bangkok in 1827. In mounting this brave – some would say foolhardy – assault, Anou was apparently trying to emulate the great Fa Ngum. Unfortunately, he got no further than the NE Thai town of Korat where his forces suffered a defeat and were driven back. Nonetheless, Anou's rebellion is considered one of the most daring and ruthless rebellions in Siamese history and he was lauded as a war hero back home.

King Anou's brief stab at regional power was to result in catastrophe for Laos – and tragedy for King Anou. The first US arms shipment to Siam allowed the Siamese to sack Vieng Chan, a task to which they had grown accustomed over the years. (For those who are interested in such things, this marks America's first intervention in Southeast Asia.) Lao artisans were frog-marched to Bangkok and many of the inhabitants were resettled in NE Siam. Rama III had Chao Anou locked in a cage where he was taunted and abused by the population of Bangkok. He died soon afterwards. The cause of his death has been variously linked to poison and shame. One of his supporters is said to have taken pity on the king and bought him poison. Other explanations simply say that he wished himself dead. Whatever the cause, the disconsolate Anou, before he died, put a curse on Siam's monarchy, promising that the next time a Thai king set foot on Lao soil, he would die. To this day no Thai king has crossed the Mekong River. When the agreement for the supply of hydro-electric power was signed with Thailand in the 1970s, the Thai king was invited to officially open the Nam Ngum Dam, a feat he managed from a sandbank in the middle of the Mekong.

Disintegration of the kingdom

Over the next 50 years, Anou's Kingdom was destroyed. By the time the French arrived in the late 19th century, the virtually unoccupied city was subsumed into the Siamese sphere of influence. Luang Prabang also became a Siamese vassal state, while Xieng Khouang province was invaded by Chinese rebels – to the chagrin of the Vietnamese, who had always considered the Hmong mountain kingdom (they called it Tran Ninh) to be their exclusive source of slaves. The Chinese had designs on Luang Prabang too, and in order to quash their expansionist instincts, Bangkok dispatched an army there in 1885 to pacify the region and ensure the N remained firmly within the Siamese sphere of influence. This period was clearly one of confusion and rapidly shifting allegiances. In James McCarthy's book of his travels in Siam and Laos, *Surveying and exploring in Siam* (1900), he states that an old chief of Luang Prabang remarked to him that the city had never been a tributary state of Annam (N Vietnam) but had formerly paid tribute to China. He writes:

> "The tribute had consisted of 4 elephants, 41 mules, 533 lbs of nok (metal composed of gold and copper), 25 lbs of rhinoceros' horns, 100 lbs of ivory, 250 pieces of homespun cloth, 1 horn, 150 bundles of areca-palm nuts [for betel 'nut' chewing], 150 cocoanuts [sic], and 33 bags of roe of the fish pla buk [the giant Mekong cat fish, see page 309]."

The history of Laos during this period becomes, essentially, the history of only a small part of the current territory of the country: namely, the history of Luang Prabang. And because Luang Prabang was a suzerain state of Bangkok, the history of that kingdom is, in turn, sometimes relegated to a mere footnote in the history of Siam.

The French and independence

During this period following King Anu's death, Laos became the centre of Southeast Asian rivalry between Britain, expanding E from Burma, and France, pushing W through Vietnam. In 1868, following the French annexation of S Vietnam and the establishment of a protectorate in Cambodia, an expedition set out to explore the Mekong trade route to China. Once central and N Vietnam had come under the influence of the Quai d'Orsay in Paris, the French became increasingly curious about Vietnamese claims to chunks of Laos. In 1886, the French received Siamese approval to post a vice consul to Luang Prabang and a year later he persuaded the Thais to leave: so began the French colonial era.

Union of Indochina

In 1893 France occupied the left bank of the Mekong and forced Thailand to recognize the river as the boundary. The French Union of Indochina denied Laos the area which is now Isan, NE Thailand, and was the start of 50 years of colonial rule. Laos became a protectorate with a *resident-superieur* in Vientiane and a vice-consul in Luang Prabang. However, as Martin Stuart-Fox points out, Laos could hardly be construed as a 'country"during the colonial period. "Laos existed again", he writes, "but not yet as a political entity in its own right, for no independent sense of Lao political power existed. Laos was but a territorial entity within French Indochina." The French were not interested in establishing an identifiable Lao state; they saw Laos as a part, and a subservient part at that, of Vietnam, serving as a resource-rich appendage to Vietnam.

In 1904 the Franco-British convention delimited respective zones of influence. Only a few hundred French civil servants were ever in Vientiane at any one time and their attitude to colonial administration – described as 'benign neglect' – was as relaxed as the people they governed. To the displeasure of the Lao, France brought in Vietnamese to run the civil service (in the way the British used Indian bureaucrats in Burma). But for the most part, the French colonial period was a 50-year siesta for Laos. The king was allowed to stay in Luang Prabang, but had little say in administration. Trade and commerce was left to the omnipresent Chinese and the Vietnamese. A small, French-educated Lao elite did grow up, and by the 1940s they had become the core of a typically laid-back Lao nationalist movement.

Japanese coup

Towards the end of WW2, Japan ousted the French administration in Laos in a coup in Mar 1945. The eventual surrender of the Japanese in Aug that year gave impetus to the Lao independence movement. Prince Phetsarath, hereditary viceroy and premier of the Luang Prabang Kingdom, took over the leadership of the Lao Issara, the Free Laos Movement (originally a resistance movement against the Japanese). They prevented the French from seizing power again and declared Lao independence on 1 September 1945. 2 weeks later, the N and S provinces were reunified and in Oct, Phetsarath formed a Lao Issara government headed by Prince Phaya Khammao, the governor of Vientiane.

France refused to recognize the new state and crushed the Lao resistance. King Sisavang Vong, unimpressed by Prince Phetsarath's move, sided with the French, who had their colony handed back by British forces. He was crowned the constitutional monarch of the new protectorate in 1946.

The rebel government took refuge in Bangkok. Historians believe the Issara movement was aided in their resistance to the French by the Viet Minh – Hanoi's Communists.

Independence

In response to nationalist pressures, France was obliged to grant Laos ever greater self government and, eventually, formal independence within the framework of the newly reconstructed French Union in Jul 1949. Meanwhile, in Bangkok, the Issara movement had formed a government-in-exile, headed by Phetsarath and his half-brothers: Prince Souvanna Phouma and Prince Souphanouvong. Both were refined, French-educated men, with a taste for good wine and cigars. The Issara's military wing was led by Souphanouvong who, even at that stage, was known for his Communist sympathies. Within just a few months the so-called Red Prince had been ousted by his half-brothers and joined the Viet Minh where he is said to have been the moving force behind the declaration of the Democratic Republic of Laos by the newly-formed Lao National Assembly. The Lao People's Democratic Republic emerged – albeit in name only – somewhere inside Vietnam, in Aug 1949. Soon afterwards, the Pathet Lao – literally, 'the Lao nation' was born. The Issara movement quickly folded and Souvanna Phouma went back to Vientiane and joined the newly-formed Royal Lao Government.

By 1953, Prince Souphanouvong had managed to move his Pathet Lao headquarters inside Laos, and with the French losing their grip on the N provinces, the weary colonizers granted the country full independence. Retreating honourably, France signed a treaty of friendship and association with the new royalist government and made the country a French protectorate.

The rise of Communism

French defeat

While all this was going on, the king sat tight in Luang Prabang instead of moving to Vientiane. But within a few months of independence, the ancient royal capital was under threat from the Communist Viet Minh and Pathet Lao. Honouring the terms of the new treaty, French commander General Henri Navarre determined in late 1953 to take the pressure off Luang Prabang by confronting the Viet Minh who controlled the strategic approach to the city at Dien Bien Phu. The French suffered a stunning defeat which prestaged their withdrawal from Indochina (see page 174). The subsequent occupation of two N Lao provinces by the Vietnam-backed Pathet Lao forces, meant the kingdom's days as a western buffer state were numbered.

With the Geneva Accord in Jul 1954, following the fall of Dien Bien Phu in May, Ho Chi Minh's government gained control of all territory N of the 17th parallel in neighbouring Vietnam. The Accord guaranteed Laos' freedom and neutrality, but with the Communists on the threshold, the US was not prepared to be a passive spectator: the demise of the French sparked an increasing US involvement. In an operation that was to mirror the much more famous war with Vietnam to the E, Washington soon found itself supplying and paying the salaries of 50,000 royalist troops and their corrupt officers. Clandestine military assistance grew, undercover special forces were mobilized and the CIA began meddling in Lao politics. In 1960 a consignment of weapons was dispatched by the CIA to a major in the Royal Lao Army called Vang Pao – or VP, as he became known – who was destined to become the leader of the Hmong.

US involvement and the domino effect

Laos had become the dreaded 'first domino', which, using the scheme of US President Dwight D Eisenhower's famous analogy, would trigger the rapid spread of Communism if ever it fell. The time-trapped little kingdom rapidly became the focus of superpower brinkmanship. President Kennedy is said to have been too abashed to announce to the American people that US forces might soon become embroiled in conflict in a far-away flashpoint that went by the inglorious name of 'Louse'. For three decades Americans have unwittingly mis-pronounced the country's name as Kennedy decided, euphemistically, to label it 'Lay-os' throughout his national television broadcast.

Coalitions, coups and counter-coups

The US-backed Royal Lao Government of independent Laos – even though it was headed by the neutralist, Prince Souvanna Phouma – ruled over a divided country from 1951 to 1954. The

Communist Pathet Lao, headed by Prince Souphanouvong, emerged as the only strong opposition. The growth of the Pathet Lao had been overseen and sponsored by N Vietnam's Lao Dong party since 1949. By the mid-1950s, Kaysone Phomvihan, later Prime Minister of the Lao PDR, began to make a name for himself in the Indochinese Communist Party. Entrenched in the N provinces, Pathet Lao troops – supported by the Communist Viet Minh forces – made several incursions into central Laos and civil war erupted.

Government of National Union

Unable to secure cooperation with the Communists, elections were held in Vientiane in Jul 1955 but were boycotted by the Pathet Lao. Souvanna Phouma became Prime Minister in Mar 1956. He aimed to try to negotiate the integration of his half-brother's Pathet Lao provinces into a unified administration and coax the Communists into a coalition government. In 1957 the disputed provinces were returned to royal government control and in May 1958 elections were held. This time the Communists' Lao Patriotic Front clinched nine of the 21 seats in the Government of National Union. The Red Prince, Souphanouvong, and one of his aides were included in a coalition cabinet and former Pathet Lao members were elected deputies of the National Assembly.

Almost immediately problems which had been beneath the surface emerged to plague the government. The American-backed rightists were rather shaken by the result, and the much-vaunted coalition lasted just 2 months. The National Union fell apart in Jul 1958. Pathet Lao leaders were jailed and the right-wing Phoui Sananikone came to power. With anti-Communists in control, Pathet Lao forces withdrew to the Plain of Jars in Xieng Khouang province. A three-way civil war ensued, between the rightists, the Communists and the neutralists.

Civil war

CIA-backed strongman General Phoumi Nosavan thought Phoui's politics rather tame, and with a nod from Washington he stepped into the breech in Jan 1959, eventually overthrowing Phoui in a coup in Dec, and placing Prince Boun Oum in power. Confusion over Phoumas, Phouis and Phoumis led one American official to comment that it all "could have been a significant event or a typographical error".

Within a year, the rightist regime was overthrown by a neutralist coup d'état led by General Kong Lae, and Prince Souvanna Phouma was recalled from exile in Cambodia to become Prime Minister of the first National Union. Souvanna Phouma incurred American wrath by inviting a Soviet ambassador to Vientiane in Oct. With US support, Nosavan staged yet another armed rebellion in Dec and sparked a new civil war. Kong Lae backed down, Souvanna Phouma shuffled back to Phnom Penh and a new right-wing government was set up under Boun Oum.

Zurich talks and the Geneva Accord

The new Prime Minister, the old one and his Marxist half-brother finally sat down to talks in Zurich in Jun 1961, but any hope of an agreement was overshadowed by escalating tensions between the superpowers. A year later an international agreement on Laos was hammered out in Geneva by 14 participating nations and accords were signed, once again guaranteeing Lao neutrality.

By implication, the accords denied the Viet Minh access to the Ho Chi Minh Trail. But aware of the reality of constant N Vietnamese infiltration through Laos into S Vietnam, the head of the American mission concluded that the agreement was "a good bad deal".

Another coalition government of National Union was formed under the determined neutralist Prince Souvanna Phouma (as Prime Minister), with

Prince Souphanouvong for the Pathet Lao and Prince Boun Oum representing the right. It was no surprise when it collapsed within a few months and fighting resumed. This time the international community just shrugged and watched Laos sink back into the vortex of civil war. Unbeknown to the outside world, the conflict was rapidly degenerating into a war between the CIA and N Vietnamese jungle guerrillas.

The war that wasn't

With the Viet Minh denying the existence of the Ho Chi Minh Trail, while at the same time enlarging it, Kennedy dispatched an undercover force of CIA-men, Green Berets and US-trained Thai mercenaries to command 9,000 Lao soldiers. To the N, the US also supplied Vang Pao's force of 30,000 Hmong guerrillas, dubbed 'Mobile Strike Forces'. With the cooperation of Prince Souvanna Phouma, the CIA's commercial airline, Air America, ferried men and equipment into Laos from Thailand (and opium out). Owing to the clandestine nature of the military intervention in Laos, the rest of the world – believing that the Geneva settlement had solved the foreign interventionist problem – was oblivious as to what was happening on the ground. Right up until 1970, Washington never admitted to any activity in Laos beyond 'armed reconnaissance' flights over N provinces. Souvanna Phouma appropriately referred to it as "the forgotten war".

American bombing of the N Vietnamese Army's supply lines through Laos to S Vietnam along the Ho Chi Minh Trail in E Laos (see page 394) started in 1964 and fuelled the conflict between the Royalist Vientiane government and the Pathet Lao. The neutralists had been forced into alliance with the Royalists to avoid defeat in Xieng Kouang province. US bombers crossed Laos on bombing runs to Hanoi from air bases in Thailand, and gradually the war in Laos escalated. In his book *The Ravens* (1987), Christopher Robbins sets the scene:

"Apparently, there was another war even nastier than the one in Vietnam, and so secret that the location of the country in which it was being fought was classified. The cognoscenti simply referred to it as 'the Other Theater'. The men who chose to fight in it were hand-picked volunteers, and anyone accepted for a tour seemed to disappear as if from the face of the earth."

The secret war was conducted from a one-room shack at the US base in Udon Thani, 'across the fence' in Thailand. This was the CIA's Air America operations room and in the same compound was stationed the 4802 Joint Liaison Detachment – or the CIA logistics office. In Vientiane, US pilots supporting Hmong General Vang Pao's rag-tag army, were given a new identity as rangers for the US Agency for International Development; they reported directly to the air attaché at the US embassy. Robbins writes that they "were military men, but flew into battle in civilian clothes – denim cutoffs, T-shirts, cowboy hats, and dark glasses... Their job was to fly as the winged artillery of some fearsome warlord, who led an army of stone-age mercenaries in the pay of the CIA, and they operated out of a secret city hidden in the mountains of a jungle kingdom..." He adds that CIA station chiefs and field agents "behaved like warlords in their own private fiefdoms."

The most notorious of the CIA's unsavoury operatives was Anthony Posepny – known as Tony Poe, on whom the character of Kurtz, the crazy colonel played by Marlon Brando in the film *Apocalypse Now*, was based. Originally, Poe had worked as Vang Pao's case officer; he then moved to N Laos and operated for years, on his own, in Burmese and Chinese border territories, offering his tribal recruits one US dollar for each set of Communist ears they brought back. Many of the spies and pilots of this secret war have re-emerged in recent years in covert and illegal arms-smuggling rackets to Libya, Iran and the Nicaraguan Contras.

By contrast, the Royalist forces were reluctant warriors: despite the fact that civil war was a deeply ingrained tradition in Laos, the Lao themselves would go to great lengths to avoid fighting each other. One foreign journalist, reporting from Luang Prabang in the latter stages of the war, related how Royalist and Pathet Lao troops, encamped on opposite sides of the Nam Ou River, agreed an informal cease-fire over Pimay (Lao New Year), to jointly celebrate the king's annual visit to the sacred Pak Ou Caves, upstream from the royal capital (see page 376). Correspondents who covered the war noted that without the constant goading of their respective US and N Vietnamese masters, many Lao soldiers would have happily gone home. During the war, a US commander was quoted in a newspaper as saying that the Royalist troops were "without doubt the worst army I have ever seen," adding that they made the [poorly regarded] "S Vietnamese Army look like Storm Troopers."

Air Force planes were often used to carry passengers for money – or to smuggle opium out of the Golden Triangle. In the field, soldiers of the Royal Lao Army regularly fled when faced with a frontal assault by the NVA. The officer corps was uncommitted, lazy and corrupt; many ran opium-smuggling rackets and saw the war as a ticket to get rich quick. In the S, the Americans considered Royal Lao Air Force pilots unreliable because they were loath to bomb their own people and cultural heritage.

The air war

The clandestine bombing of the Ho Chi Minh Trail (see page 394) caused many civilian casualties – so-called collateral damage – and displaced much of the population in Laos' E provinces. By 1973, when the bombing stopped, the US had dropped 2,093,100 tonnes of bombs on Laos – equivalent to 300 kg of explosives pp. 580,994 bombing sorties were flown. The bombing intensified during the Nixon administration: up to 1969 less than half-a-million tonnes of bombs had been dropped on Laos; from then on nearly that amount was dropped each year. The war was not restricted to bombing missions – once potential Pathet Lao strongholds had been identified, fighters, using rockets, were sent to attempt to destroy them. Few of the villagers in Xieng Khouang province, the Bolovens Plateau or those living along the Ho Chi Minh Trail had any idea of who was bombing them or why. The consequences were often tragic as in the case of Tam Phiu Cave (see page 385).

In *The Ravens*, Robbins tells of how a fighter pilot's inauspicious dream would lead the commander to cancel a mission; bomber pilots hated dropping bombs, and when they did, aluminium canisters were carefully brought back and sold as scrap. After the war, the collection and sale of war debris turned into a valuable scrap-metal industry for tribespeople in Xieng Khouang province and along the Ho Chi Minh Trail. Bomb casings, aircraft fuel tanks and other bits and pieces that were not sold to Thailand have been put to every conceivable use in rural Laos. They are used as cattle troughs, fence posts, flower pots, stilts for houses, water carriers, temple bells, knives and ploughs.

But the bombing campaign has also left a more deadly legacy – of unexploded bombs and anti-personnel mines. Today, over two decades after the air war ended, people are dying in the fields and forests of provinces like Xieng Khouang. Anthropologist Grant Evans reported in the *Far Eastern Economic Review* that in 1993 100 people were killed in Xieng Khouang province alone; 30 more in the first half of 1994. The greatest irony of all perhaps, is that most of Xieng Khouang was not even a military target – pilots would simply dump their ordnance so that they would not have to risk landing with their bomb bays packed with high explosive. Making farming in this part a Laos a highly dangerous occupation was simply one of those 'accidents' of war.

The land war

Within Laos the war largely focused on the strategic Plain of Jars, in Xieng Khouang province, and was co-ordinated from the town of Long Tieng (the secret city), tucked into the limestone hills to the SW of the plain. Known as the most secret spot on earth, it was not marked on maps and was populated by the CIA, the Ravens (the air controllers who flew spotter planes and called in air strikes) and the Hmong.

The Pathet Lao were headquartered in caves in Sam Neua province, to the N of the plain. Their base was equipped with a hotel cave (for visiting dignatories), a hospital cave and even a theatre cave.

The Plain of Jars (coloquially known as the PDJ, after the French Plaine de Jarres) was the scene of some of the heaviest fighting and changed hands countless times, the royalist and Hmong forces occupying it during the wet season, the Pathet Lao in the dry. There was also fighting around Luang Prabang and the Bolovens Plateau to the S.

The end of the war

Although the origins of the war in Laos were distinct from those which fuelled the conflict in Vietnam, the two wars had effectively merged by the early 1970s and it became inevitable that the fate of the Americans to the E would determine the outcome of the secret war on the other side of the Annamite Range. By 1970 it was no longer possible for the US administration to shroud the war in secrecy: a flood of Hmong refugees had arrived in Vientiane in an effort to escape the conflict.

During the dying days of the US-backed regime in Vientiane, CIA agents

and Ravens lived in quarters S of the capital, known as Silver City. On the departure of the Americans and the arrival of the new regime in 1975, the Communists' secret police made Silver City their new home. Today, Laos still call military intelligence officers 'Silvers' – from time to time Silvers are even assigned as tour guides. Silver City however, 6 km from Vientiane, is now known just as KM-6, and its agents go by the same name – the Lao version of Britain's MI5.

Laos under Communism

A ceasefire was agreed in Feb 1973, a month after Washington and Hanoi struck a similar deal in Paris. Power was transferred in Apr 1974 to yet another coalition government set up in Vientiane under the premiership of the ever-ready Souvanna Phouma. The neutralist prince once again had a Communist deputy and foreign affairs minister. The Red Prince, Souphanouvong headed the Joint National Political Council. Foreign troops were given 2 months to leave the country. The N Vietnamese were allowed to remain along the Ho Chi Minh Trail, for although US forces had withdrawn from S Vietnam, the war there was not over. The Communists' final victories over Saigon (and Phnom Penh) in Apr 1975 were a catalyst for the Pathet Lao who advanced on the capital. Royalists and Vang Pao's men fled across the border into Thailand, where they lived in camps or left for exile in France and the USA. Vientiane was declared 'officially liberated' on 23 August 1975. The coalition government was dismissed and Souvanna Phouma resigned for the last time. All communications with the outside world were cut.

The People's Democratic Republic of Laos was proclaimed in Dec 1975 with Prince Souphanouvong as President and Kaysone Phomvihan as Secretary-General of the Lao People's Revolutionary Party (a post he had held since its formation in 1955). The king's abdication was accepted and the ancient Lao monarchy was abolished, together with King Samsenthai's 600-year-old system of village autonomy. But instead of executing their vanquished foes, the LPRP installed Souvanna and the ex-king, Savang Vatthana, as 'special advisers' to the politburo. On Souvanna's death in 1984, he was accorded a full state funeral. The king did not fare so well: he later died ignominiously while in detention.

Relations with Thailand, which in the immediate wake of the revolution remained cordial, deteriorated in late 1976. A military coup in Bangkok led to rumours that the Thai military, backed by the CIA, was supporting Hmong and other right-wing Lao rebels. The regime feared that Thailand would be used as a spring-board for a royalist coup attempt by exiled reactionaries. This prompted the arrest of King Savang Vatthana, together with his family and Crown Prince Vongsavang, who were all dispatched to a Seminar re-education camp in Sam Neua province. They were never heard of again. In Dec 1989 Kaysone Phomvihan admitted in Paris, for the first time, that the king had died of malaria in 1984 and that the queen had also died "of natural causes" – no mention was made of Vongsavang. The Lao people have still to be officially informed of his demise.

The re-education camps

Between 30,000 and 40,000 reactionaries who had been unable to flee the country were interned in remote, disease-ridden camps for 're-education'. The reluctant scholars were forced into slave labour in squalid jungle conditions and subjected to incessant political propaganda. Old men, released back into society after more than 15 years of 're-education' are cowed and subdued, some are prepared to talk in paranoid whispers about their grim experiences in Sam Neua.

It is unclear how many died in the camps, but at least 15,000 have been freed. Officials of the old regime, ex-government ministers and former Royalist air force and army officers, together with thousands of others unlucky enough to have been on the wrong side, were released from the camps during the 1980s. Most of the surviving political prisoners have now been reintegrated into society and it is not clear whether there are any still in captivity. Some work in the tourism industry and one, a former colonel in the Royal Lao Army, jointly owns the *Asian Pavilion Hotel* (formerly the *Vieng Vilai*) on Samsenthai Rd in downtown Vientiane. After years of being force-fed Communist propaganda he now enjoys full government support as an ardent capitalist entrepreneur.

The refugee camps

A total of 300,000 Lao – 10% of the population, and mostly middle class – fled the country's increasingly totalitarian regime between 1973 and 1975. From 1988, these refugees began to head back across the Mekong from camps in Thailand, and to asylum in the US and France. More than 2,000 refugees were also repatriated from Yunnan Province in China. For those prepared to return from exile overseas, the government offered to give them back confiscated property so long as they stay at least 6 months and become Lao citizens once again. Thailand's Lao refugee camps are now part of history. One of the best accounts of this period is Lynellyn D. Long's *Ban Vinai: the refugee camp*. As a Jesuit priest who worked at the camp explained to the author: "Before they [came to the camps the refugees] had a life revolving around the seasons... Here they cannot really work... Here people make only dreams".

Art and architecture

Lao art is well known for its wealth of ornamentation. As in other neighbouring Buddhist countries, the focus has been primarily religious in nature. Temple murals and bas-reliefs usually tell the story of the Buddha's life – the jataka tales. There has never been the range of art in Laos that there is in Thailand, as the country has been constantly dominated and influenced by foreign powers. Much of it has been destroyed over the centuries, as plundering neighbours ransacked towns and cities. The *Ramayana*, the Indian epic, has become part of the Lao cultural heritage and is known as the *Phra Lak Pralam* (see page 337). Many of the doors and windows of temples are engraved with scenes from this story, depicting the struggle between good and evil. Prime examples are the huge teak shutters at Wat Xieng Thong in Luang Prabang.

Lao sculpture

Sculpture in Laos is more distinctive in style; the best pieces originate from the 16th to 18th centuries. Characteristic of Lao Buddha images is a nose like an eagle's beak, flat, extended earlobes and tightly curled hair. The best examples are in Wat Phra Kaeo and Wat Sisaket in Vientiane.

The 'Calling for Rain' mudra (the Buddha standing with hands pointing towards the ground, arms slightly away from the torso) is distinctively Lao (see page 356). The 'Contemplating the Tree of Enlightenment' mudra is also uniquely Lao – it depicts a standing Buddha with hands crossed in front of the body. There are many examples in the Pak Ou Caves, on the Mekong, 25 km upstream from Luang Prabang (see page 376).

Lao architecture

Architecture reflects Laos' turbulent history and has strong Siamese/Thai, Bur-

mese and Khmer influences. Unfortunately, little has survived because many of the older structures were built of wood and were repeatedly ransacked by the Siamese/Thais, Chinese and Vietnamese and then bombed by the Americans. Religious buildings best exhibit the originality of Lao art and architecture.

Architectural styles

Lao wats are generally less ornate and grand than those in Thailand, although the temples of Luang Prabang are stunning, with their layered roofs that sweep elegantly towards the ground. There are three main styles of temple architecture in Laos: Luang Prabang, Vientiane and Xieng Khouang – the last of which has now been lost forever because of the destruction wrought on the city of Xieng Khouang during the war (see page 384).

The Vientiane style is influenced by the S Thai-style, with its high, pointed and layered roofs (usually an uneven number). Most of the main sanctuaries are rectangular and some, such as Wat Phra Kaeo in Vientiane, have a verandah around the entire building – a stylistic feature imported from Bangkok. Most of the larger sims have a verandah at the back. Vientiane's wats have higher roofs than those in Luang Prabang, the buildings are taller and the entrances more prominent. The steps leading up to the main entrance are often guarded by nagas or *nyaks*, while the doorways themselves are usually flanked by pillars and topped with intricately carved porticoes. That Luang, in Vientiane, historically provided a template for most Lao stupas and its unique shape is found only in Laos and some areas of N and NE Thailand. As in other Buddhist countries, many of the stupas contain sacred relics – bones of the Buddha, or the ashes of kings.

The Luang Prabang architectural style has been influenced by N Thai temples. The roofs of the main sanctuaries are very low, almost touching the ground – best exemplified by the magnificent Wat

Laos

THE LAO WAT

There is no English equivalent of the Lao word *wat*. It is usually translated as either monastery or temple, although neither is correct. It is easiest to get around this problem by calling them wats. They were, and remain to some extent, the focus of the village or town; they serve as places of worship, education, meeting and healing. Without a wat, a village cannot be viewed as a 'complete' community. The wat is a relatively new innovation. Originally, there were no wats, as monks were wandering ascetics. It seems that although the word 'wat' was in use in the 14th century, these were probably just shrines, and were not monasteries. By the late 18th century, the wat had certainly metamorphosed into a monastery, so sometime in the intervening 4 centuries, shrine and monastery had united into a whole. Although wats vary a great deal in size and complexity, there is a traditional layout to which most conform.

● Wats are usually separated from the secular world by **two walls**. Between these outer and inner walls are found the **monks' quarters** or dormitories (*kutis*), perhaps a **bell tower** (*hor rakang*) that is used to toll the hours and to warn of danger and, in larger complexes, schools and other administrative buildings. Traditionally the *kutis* were placed on the S side of the wat. It was believed that if the monks slept directly in front of the principal Buddha image they would die young; if they slept to the left they would become ill; and if they slept behind it there would be discord in the community of monks.

● The inner wall, which in bigger wats often takes the form of a **gallery** or cloister (*phra rabieng*) lined with Buddha images, represents the division between the worldly and the holy, the sacred and the profane. It is used as a quiet place for meditation. Within the inner courtyard, the holiest building is the **ordination hall** or **sim**, reserved for monks only. This is built on consecrated ground, and has a ring of eight stone tablets or boundary markers (*bai sema*), sometimes contained in mini-pavilions, arranged around it at the cardinal and subcardinal points and shaped like stylized leaves of the bodhi tree, often carved with representations of Vishnu, Siva, Brahma or Indra, or of nagas. Buried in the ground beneath the bai sema are stone spheres – and sometimes gold and jewellery. The bai sema mark the limit of earthly power. The ordination hall is characteristically a large, rectangular building with high walls and multiple sloping roofs covered in glazed clay tiles (or wood tiles, in the North). At each end of the roof are *dok sofa*, or 'bunches of flowers', which represent garuda grasping two nagas in its talons. Inside, often through elaborately carved and inlaid doors, is the main Buddha image. There may also be numerous subsidiary images. The inside walls of the sim may be decorated with murals depicting the Jataka tales or scenes from Buddhist and Hindu cosmology. Like the Buddha, these murals are meant to serve as meditation aids. It is customary for pilgrims to remove their shoes on entering any Buddhist building (or private house for that matter). Many complexes have secondary chapels, or **hov song phra** attached to the main sim.

● The other main building within the inner courtyard is the **assembly hall** (*viharn*), but not all wats have one, and some may have more than one. Architecturally this is often indistinguishable from the sim. It contains the wat's principal Buddha images. The main difference between the sim and the assembly hall is that the latter does not stand on consecrated ground, and can be identified by the absence of any *bai sema* – stone tablets – set around it. The assembly hall is for more general use than the sim. Both sim and assembly hall are supposed to face water, because the Buddha himself was facing a river when he achieved enlightenment under the bodhi tree. If there is no natural body of water, the monks may dig a pond.

Also found in the inner courtyard may be a number of other structures. Among the more common are *thats* (chedis), tower-like **relic chambers** which in Laos and parts of Northeastern Thailand (which is also Lao in terms of culture) take the distinctive lotus bud form. These can be built on a massive scale (such as That Luang in Vientiane, see page 349), and contain holy relics of the Buddha. More often, thats are smaller affairs containing the ashes of royalty, monks or pious lay people.

● Another rarer feature is the **library** or scripture repository (*hor trai*), usually a small, tall-sided building where the Buddhist scriptures can be stored safely, high off the ground. *Salas* are open-sided **rest pavilions** which can be found anywhere in the wat compound; the *sala kan parian* or **study hall** is the largest and most impressive of these and is almost like a sim or viharn without walls. Here the monks say their prayers at noon.

● Sometimes wats have a boat house to shelter the local boat used in the annual boat race.

● In rural villages wats often consist only of a sala, or meeting hall.

● It seems that wats are often short-lived. Even great wats, if they lose their patronage, are deserted by their monks and fall into ruin. Unlike Christian churches, they depend on constant support from the laity; the wat owns no land or wealth, and must depend on gifts of food to feed the monks and money to repair and expand the fabric of its buildings.

GENERALIZED PLAN OF A WAT

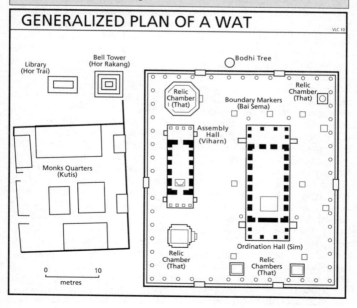

VLC 10

Library (Hor Trai)

Bell Tower (Hor Rakang)

Bodhi Tree

Relic Chamber (That)

Boundary Markers (Bai Sema)

Relic Chamber (That)

Assembly Hall (Viharn)

Monks Quarters (Kutis)

Relic Chamber (That)

Ordination Hall (Sim)

Relic Chambers (That)

0   10
metres

THE 'LOST WAX' PROCESS

A core of clay is moulded into the desired form and then covered in beeswax and shellac. Details are engraved into the beeswax. The waxed core is then coated with a watery mixture of clay and cow's dung, and built up into a thick layer of clay. This is then fired in a kiln, the wax running out through vents cut into the clay. Molten bronze is poured into the mould where it fills the void left by the wax and after cooling the mould is broken to reveal the image.

Xieng Thong in Luang Prabang. The pillars tend to narrow towards the top, as tree trunks were originally used for columns. The wats often have a verandah at the back and the front. The most famous wats in Luang Prabang and Vientiane were built with royal patronage. But most wats in Laos were, and are, constructed piece-meal with donations from the local community. Royal wats can be identified by the number of *dok sofa*: more than 10 'flowers' signifies that the wat was built by a king.

Culture and life

People

Laos is less a nation state than a collection of different tribes and languages. The country's enormous ethnic diversity has long been an impediment to national integration. In total there are more than 60 minority tribes which are often described as living in isolated, self-sufficient communities. (A summary of the origins, economy and culture of the major groups is provided on pages 327-334.) Although communication and intercourse may have been difficult – and remains so – there has always been communication, trade and inter-marriage between the different Lao 'worlds' and today, with even greater interaction, the walls between them are becoming more permeable still.

Laos' ethnically diverse population is usually – and rather simplistically – divided by ecological zone into three groups: the wet rice cultivating, Buddhist *Lao Loum* of the lowlands, who are politically and numerically dominant, constituting over half of the total population; the *Lao Theung* who occupy the mountain slopes and make up about a quarter of the population; and the *Lao Soung*, or upland Lao, who live in the high mountains and practice shifting cultivation, and who represent less than a fifth of Laos' total population. The terms were brought into general usage by the Pathet Lao who wished to emphasize that all of Laos' inhabitants were 'Lao', and to avoid the more derogatory terms that had been used in the past – such as the Thai word *kha*, meaning 'slave', to describe the Mon-Khmer *Lao Theung* like the Khmu and Lamet.

Although the words have a geographical connotation, they should be viewed more as contrasting pairs of terms: *loum* and *theung* mean 'below' and 'above' (rather than hillsides and lowland), while *soung* is paired with *tam*, meaning 'high' and 'low'. These two pairs of oppositions were brought together by the Pathet Lao into one three-fold division. Thus, the *Lao Theung* in one area may, in practice, occupy a higher location than *Lao Soung* in another area. In addition, economic change, greater interaction between the groups, and the settlement of lowland peoples in hill areas, means that it is possible to find *Lao Loum* villages in upland areas, where the inhabitants practice swidden, not wet rice agriculture. So, although it is broadly possible to characterize the mountain slopes as inhabited by shifting cultivating *Lao Theung* of Mon-Khmer descent, in practice the neat delimitation of people into discrete spatial units breaks down, and as the years go by is becoming increasingly untenable.

It has been noted that the Lao who have reaped the rewards of reform are the *Lao Loum* of T'ai stock – not the *Lao Theung* who are of Mon-Khmer descent or the *Lao Soung* who are 'tribal' peoples, especially Hmong but also Akha and Lahu. Ing-Britt Trankell in her book *On the road in Laos: an anthropological study of road construction and rural communities* (1993) writes that the *Lao Loum's* "sense of [cultural and moral] superiority is often manifested in both a patronizing and contemptuous attitude toward the Lao Theung and Lao Sung, who are thought of as backward and less susceptible to socio-economic development because they are still governed by their archaic cultural traditions".

During the 6th and 7th centuries the **Lao Loum** arrived from the S provinces of China. They occupied the valleys along the Mekong and its tributaries and drove the *Lao Theung* to more mountainous areas. The *Lao Loum*, who are ethnically almost indistinguishable from the Thais of the Isan region (the NE of Thailand), came under the influence of the Khmer and Indonesian cultures and sometime before the emergence of Lane Xang in the 14th century embraced Theravada Buddhism. The majority of Lao are Buddhist but retain many of their animist beliefs. Remote *Lao Loum* communities still usually have a *mor du* (a doctor who 'sees') or medium. The medium's job description is demanding: he must concoct love potions, heal the sick, devise and design protective charms and read the future.

Today, the *Lao Loum* are the principal ethnic group, accounting for just over half the population, and Lao is their mother tongue. As the lowland Lao, they occupy the ricelands of the Mekong and its main tributary valleys. Their houses are made of wood and are built on stilts

with thatched roofs – although tin is far more popular these days. The extended family is usually spread throughout several houses in one compound.

There are also several tribal subgroups of this main Thai-Lao group; they are conveniently colour-coded and readily identifiable by their sartorial traits. There are, eg the Red Tai, the White Tai and the Black Tai – who live in the upland valley areas in Xieng Khouang and Hua Phan provinces. That they live in the hills suggests they are *Lao Theung*, but ethnically and culturally they are closer to the *Lao Loum*.

The **Lao Theung**, consisting of 45 different sub groups, are the descendants of the oldest inhabitants of the country and are of Mon-Khmer descent. They are sometimes called *Kha*, meaning 'slave', as they were used as labourers by the Thai and Lao kings, and are generally still poorer than the *Lao Loum*. Traditionally, the *Lao Theung* were semi-nomadic and they still live mainly on the mountain slopes of the interior – along the whole length of the Annamite Chain from S China. There are concentrations of *Akha*, *Alak* and *Ta-Oy* on the Bolovens Plateau in the S (see page 395) and *Khamu* in the N.

Most *Lao Theung* still practise slash-and-burn, or shifting, agriculture and grow dry rice, coffee and tobacco. They would burn a small area of forest, cultivate it for a few years, and then, when the soil was exhausted, abandon the land until the vegetation had regenerated to replenish the soil. Some groups merely shifted fields in a 10-15 year rotation; others not only shifted fields but also their villages, relocating in a fresh area of forest when the land had become depleted of nutrients (see page 36). To obtain salt, metal implements and other goods which could not be made or found in the hills, the tribal peoples would trade forest products such as resins and animal skins with the settled lowland Lao. Some groups, mainly those living

PAPAVER SOMNIFERUM: THE OPIUM OF THE PEOPLE

The very name the Golden Triangle, is synonymous in many people's minds with the cultivation of the opium poppy (*Papaver somniferum* L). It is a favourite cash crop of the Lahu, Lisu, Yao and Hmong (the Akha only rarely grow it). The attractions of cultivating the poppy are clear: it is profitable, can be grown at high altitudes (above 1,500m), has low bulk (important when there is poor transport) and does not rot. Today, most opium is grown in Burma and Laos, and then often traded through Thailand to the world's drug markets.

The opium poppy is usually grown as part of a rotation, alternating with maize. It is sown in Sep/Oct (the end of the wet season) and 'harvesting' stretches from the beginning of Jan through to the end of Mar. Harvesting occurs after the petals have dropped off the seed heads. The 'pod' is then carefully scoured with a sharp knife, from top to bottom, allowing the sap to ooze through and oxidize on the surface of the pod. The next day, the brown gum is scraped off, rolled into balls, and wrapped in banana leaves. It is now ready for sale to the buyers who travel the hills.

Though a profitable crop, opium production has not benefited the hilltribes. It makes those who grow it criminals, and opium addiction is widespread – among the Hmong it is thought to be about 30% of the population. Efforts to change the ways of the hilltribes have focused upon crop substitution programmes (encouraging farmers to cultivate crops such as cabbages) and simple intimidation.

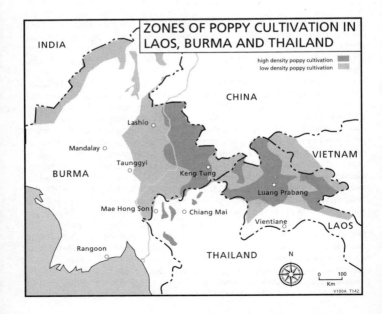

THE HILLTRIBE CALENDAR

	Hmong	Yao (Mien)	Akha
Jan	new year festival	embroidering	weaving
Feb	scoring poppies	scoring poppies	clearing fields
Mar	clearing field	clearing field	burning field
Apr	burning field	burning field	rice spirit ceremony
May	rice planting	rice and maize planting	rice planting
Jun	weeding	weeding	weeding
Jul	weeding	weeding	weeding
Aug	weeding	harvesting	swinging ceremony
Sep	poppy seeding	poppy seeding	maize harvest
Oct	thinning poppy field	rice harvest	rice harvest
Nov	rice harvest	rice harvest	rice harvest
Dec	new year festival	rice threshing	new year festival

Source: Tribal Research Institute, Chiang Mai University

closer to towns, have converted to Buddhism but many are still animist.

The social and religious beliefs of the *Lao Theung*, and their general outlook on health and happiness, are governed by their belief in spirits. The shaman is a key personality in any village. The *Alak*, from the Bolovens Plateau (see page 396) test the prospects of a marriage by killing a chicken: the manner in which it bleeds will determine whether the marriage will be propitious. Buffalo sacrifices are also common in *Lao Theung* villages and it is not unusual for a community to slaughter all its livestock to appease the spirits.

Viet Minh guerrillas and American B-52s made life difficult for many of the *Lao Theung* tribes living in E Laos, who were forced to move away from the Ho Chi Minh Trail. By leaving their birth places the *Lao Theung* left their protecting spirits, forcing them to find new and unfamiliar ones.

The **Lao Soung** began migrating to Laos from S China, Tibet and Burma, in the early 18th century, settling high in the mountains (some up to 2,500m). The *Hmong* (formerly known as the *Meo*) and *Yao* (also called the *Mien*) are the principal *Lao Soung* groups.

The Yao (or Mien)

The **Yao** mainly live around Nam Tha – deep inside the Golden Triangle, near the borders with Thailand, Burma and China. They are best-known as craftsmen – the men make knives, crossbows, rifles and high-quality, elaborately designed silver jewellery, which is worn by the women. Silver is a symbol of wealth among the Yao and Hmong.

The Mien or Yao, are unique among the hilltribes in that they have a tradition of writing based on Chinese characters. Mien legend has it that they came from 'across the sea' during the 14th century, although it is generally thought that their roots are in S China where they originated about 2,000 years ago.

The Mien village is not enclosed and is usually found on sloping ground. The houses are large, wooden affairs, as they need to accommodate an extended family of sometimes 20 or more members. They are built on the ground, not on stilts, and have one large living area and four or more bedrooms. As with other tribes, the construction of the house must be undertaken carefully. The house needs to be orientated appropriately, so that the spirits are not disturbed, and the ancestral altar installed on an auspicious day.

The Mien combine two religious beliefs: on the one hand they recognize and pay their dues to spirits and ancestors (informing them of family developments); and on the other, they follow Taoism as it was practised in China in the 13th and 14th centuries (see page 120). The Taoist rituals are expensive, and the Mien appear to spend a great deal of their lives struggling to save enough money to afford the various life cycle ceremonies, such as weddings, and death ceremonies. The Mien economy is based upon the shifting cultivation of dry rice, maize, and small quantities of opium poppy.

Material culture   The Mien women dress distinctively, with black turbans and red-ruffed tunics, making them easy to distinguish from the other hilltribes. All their clothes are made of black or indigo-dyed homespun cotton, which is then embroidered using distinctive cross-stitching. Their trousers are the most elaborate garments. Unusually, they sew from the back of the cloth and cannot see the pattern they are making. The children wear embroidered caps with red pompoms on the top and by the ears. The men's dress is a simple indigo-dyed jacket and trousers, with little embroidery. They have been dubbed "the most elegantly dressed but worst-housed people in the world".

The Akha (or Kaw)

The Akha have their origins in Yunnan, southern China, and from there spread into Burma (where there are nearly 200,000) and Laos, and rather later into Thailand.

The Akha are shifting cultivators, growing primarily dry rice on mountainsides but also a wide variety of vegetables. The cultivation of rice is bound up with myths and rituals: the rice plant is regarded as a sentient being, and the selection of the swidden, its clearance, the planting of the rice seed, the care of the growing plants, and finally the harvest of the rice, must all be done according to the Akha Way. Any offence to the rice soul must be rectified by ceremonies.

Akha villages are identified by their gates, a village swing and high-roofed houses on posts. They have no word for religion but believe in the 'Akha Way'. They are able to recite the names of all their male ancestors (60 names or more) and they keep an ancestral altar in their homes, at which food is offered up at important times in the year such as New Year, during the village swing ceremony, and after the rice harvest.

At the upper and lower ends of the village are gates which are renewed every year. Visitors should walk through them in order to rid themselves of the spirit of the jungle. The gates are sacred, and must not be defiled. Visitors must not touch the gates and should avoid going through them if they do not intend to enter a house in the village. A pair of wooden male and female carved figures are placed inside the entrance to signify that this is the realm of human beings. The two most important Akha festivals are the 4-day Swinging Ceremony celebrated during Aug, and New Year when festivities also extend over 4 days.

Material culture   Akha clothing is made of homespun blue-black cloth, which is appliquéd for decoration. Particularly characteristic of the Akha is their head-dress, which is adorned with jewellery. The basic clothing of an Akha woman is a head-dress, a jacket, a short skirt worn on the hips, with a sash and leggings worn from the ankle to below the knee. They wear their jewellery as an integral part of their clothing, mostly sewn to their head-dresses. Girls wear similar clothing to the women, except that they sport caps rather than the elaborate head-dress of the mature women. The change from girl's clothes to women's clothes occurs through four stages during adolescence. Unmarried girls can be identified by the small gourds tied to their waist and head-dress.

Men's clothing is much less elaborate. They wear loose-fitting Chinese-style black pants, and a black jacket which may be embroidered. Both men and women use cloth shoulder bags.

Today the Akha are finding it increasingly difficult to follow the 'Akha Way'. Their complex rituals set them apart from both the lowland Lao and from the other hilltribes. The conflicts and pressures which the Akha currently face, and their inability to reconcile the old with the new, is claimed by some to explain why the incidence of opium addiction among the Akha is so high.

The Hmong (or Meo)

Origins The Hmong, also known as the Meo, claim that they have their roots in the icy N. They had arrived in Laos by 1850 and by the end of the 19th century had migrated into the northern provinces of Thailand.

Economy and society The Hmong value their independence, and tend to live at high altitudes, away from other tribes. This independence, and their association with poppy cultivation and their siding with the US during the war, has meant that of all the hilltribes it is the Hmong who have been most severely persecuted. They are perceived to be a threat to the security of the state; a tribe that needs to be controlled and carefully watched. Like most hilltribes, they practise shifting cultivation, moving their villages when the surrounding land has been exhausted. The process of moving is stretched out over two seasons: an advance party finds a suitable site, builds temporary shelters, clears the land and plants rice, and only after the harvest do the rest of the inhabitants follow in their steps.

Hmong villages tend not to be fenced, while their houses are built of wood or bamboo at ground level. Each house has a main living area, and two or three sleeping rooms. The extended family is headed by the oldest male; he settles family disputes and has supreme authority over family affairs. Like the Karen, the Hmong too are spirit worshippers and believe in household spirits. Every house has an altar, where protection for the household is sought.

The Hmong are the only tribe in Laos who make batik; indigo-dyed batik makes up the main panel of their skirts, with appliqué and embroidery added to it. The women also wear black leggings from their knees to their ankles, black jackets (with embroidery), and a black panel or 'apron', held in place with a cummerbund. Even the youngest children wear clothes of intricate design with exquisite needlework. Traditionally the cloth would have been woven by hand on a foot-treddle/back-strap loom; today it is increasingly purchased from markets.

The White Hmong tend to wear less elaborate clothing from day to day, saving it for special occasions only. Hmong men wear loose-fitting black trousers, black jackets (sometimes embroidered), and coloured or embroidered sashes.

The Hmong particularly value silver jewellery; it signifies wealth and a good life. Men, women and children wear silver – tiers of neck rings, heavy silver chains with lock-shaped pendants, earrings and pointed rings on every finger. All the family jewellery is brought out at New Year and is an impressive sight, symbolizing the wealth of the family.

The Hmong in Laos: persecution and flight

The **Hmong** are probably the best-known tribe in Laos. In the 19th century, Chinese opium farmers drove many thousands of Hmong off their poppy fields and forced them S into the mountains of Laos. The Hmong did not have

---

VISITING THE HILLTRIBES: HOUSE RULES

Etiquette and customs vary between the hilltribes. However, the following are general rules of good behaviour that should be adhered to whenever possible.

1. Dress modestly and avoid undressing/changing in public.
2. Ask permission before photographing anyone (old people and pregnant women often object to having their photograph taken).
3. Ask permission before entering a house.
4. Do not touch or photograph village shrines.
5. Do not smoke opium.
6. Avoid sitting or stepping on door sills.
7. Avoid excessive displays of wealth and be sensitive when giving gifts (for children, pens are better than sweets).
8. Avoid introducing western medicines.

---

a written language before contact with Europeans and Americans, and their heritage is mainly preserved through oral tradition. Hmong mythology relates how they flew in from S China on magic carpets. Village story-tellers also like to propagate the notion that the Hmong are in fact werewolves, who happily devour the livers of their victims. This warrior tribe now mainly inhabits the mountain areas of Luang Prabang, Xieng Khouang and Sam Neua provinces where they practise shifting cultivation (see page 36).

Until a few years ago, other Lao and the rest of the world knew the Hmong as the *Meo*. Unbeknown to anyone except the Hmong, 'Meo' was a Chinese insult meaning 'barbarian' – conferred on them several millennia ago by Chinese who developed an intense disliking for the tribe. Returning from university in France in the mid-1970s, the Hmong's first highly qualified academic decided it was time to educate the world. Due to his prompting, the tribe was rechristened Hmong, their word for 'mankind'. This change in nomenclature has not stopped the Hmong from continuing to refer to the Chinese as 'sons of dogs'.

Nor has it stopped the *Lao Loum* from regarding the Hmong as their cultural inferiors. But, again, the feelings are reciprocated: the Hmong have an inherent mistrust of the lowland Lao – exacerbated by years of war – and *Lao Loum* guides reluctantly enter Hmong villages.

As animists, the *Hmong* believe everything from mountains and opium poppies to cluster bombs, has a spirit – or *phi* – some bad, some good. Shamans – or witchdoctors – play a central role in village life and decision making. The *phi* need to be placated incessantly to ward off sickness and catastrophe. It is the shaman's job to exorcise the bad *phi* from his patients. Until modern medicine arrived in Laos along with the Americans, opium was the Hmong's only palliative drug. Due to their lack of resistance to pharmaceuticals, the Hmong responded miraculously to the smallest doses of penicillin. Even Bandaids were revered as they were thought to contain magical powers which drew out bad *phi*.

In the dying days of the French colonial administration, thousands of Hmong were recruited to help fight the Vietnamese Communists. Vang Pao – known as VP – who would later command 30,000 Hmong mercenaries in the US-backed war against the Pathet Lao, was first picked out by a French colonel in charge of these *maquisards'* or 'native movements'. Later, the Hmong were recruited and paid by the CIA to fight the Pathet Lao. Under General VP, remote mountain villagers with no education were trained to fly T-28 fighter-bombers. It is said that when these US aircraft first started landing in remote villages, locals would carefully examine the undercarriage to see what sex they were.

An estimated 100,000 Hmong died during the war – even after the Pathet Lao's 'liberation' of Vientiane in 1975, Hmong refugees, encamped in hills to the S of the Plain of Jars, were attacked and flushed out by Vietnamese troops. Stories of chemical weapons being used against them (most notably 'yellow rain') were found to be US propaganda as the suspected biological agents, trichothecane mycotoxins, supposedly dumped on Hmong villages by the government, were identified as bee faeces. Swarms of over-flying bees have a habit of defecating simultaneously when they get too hot, showering the countryside with a sticky, yellow substance.

When the war ended in 1975 there was a mass exodus of Hmong and today more than 100,000 live in the US – mostly on the W coast and in Minnesota. A small group of Hmong, led by Vang Pao, is still optimistically fighting the Lao government, but they have lost much credibility in recent years and are widely regarded as bandits. VP is known to have extorted funds from *Hmong* in the US and regularly lobbies Republican politicians. His rebels' biggest public relations disaster came in 1989 when they shot dead several Buddhist monks while attacking a government convoy on the road to Luang Prabang. The Lao Air Force still carries out search-and-destroy missions against VP's bandits. The little-heard of United Front for the Liberation of the Lao People, under the command of another Hmong leader, Vang Shur, claimed in 1989 that their "10,000 resistance forces had scored many successes against the Vietnamese-backed Kaysone government" and controlled many villages in remote N Laos. Today this Hmong resistance movement

can be viewed as only a minor irritant to the government in Vientiane.

Following liberation, Hmong refugees continued to pour into Thailand, the exodus reaching a peak in 1979 when 3,000 a month were fleeing across the Mekong. Thousands also ended up in the US and France, fresh from the mountains of Laos: unsurprisingly they did not adapt easily. Various stress disorders were thought to have triggered heart attacks in many healthy young Hmong – a condition referred to as Sudden Unexplained Nocturnal Death Syndrome. In *The Ravens*, Robbins comments that "in a simpler age, it would have been said that the Hmong are dying of a broken heart".

There are three main groups of Hmong living in Laos – the Black, White and the Striped – identifiable, again, by their traditional dress and dialect. All the groups practise slash-and-burn agriculture and mainly grow dry hill rice and maize. They raise animals and also hunt and forage to supplement their diet. Opium poppies is the main cash crop for the Hmong and refined opium is exported on horseback to markets in Chiang Mai. They also export their embroidery to the tourist markets in Northern Thailand. They are well known for their appliqué (and reverse appliqué work) but these days, to produce saleable items quickly, some of the original patterns have been simplified and enlarged.

Other communities

The largest non-Lao groups in Laos are the Chinese and Vietnamese communities in the main cities. Many of the Vietnamese were brought in by the French to run the country and stayed. In more recent years, Vietnam also tried to colonize parts of Laos. The Vietnamese are not well-liked: one of the few rude words in the Lao language refers to them. The Chinese have been migrating to Laos for centuries and are usually traders, restaurateurs and shop-owners. With the relaxation in Communist policies in

MUDRAS AND THE BUDDHA IMAGE

An artist producing an image of the Buddha does not try to create an original piece of art; he is trying to be faithful to a tradition which can be traced back over centuries. It is important to appreciate that the Buddha image is not merely a work of art but an object of, and for, worship. Sanskrit poetry even sets down the characteristics of the Buddha – albeit in rather unlikely terms: legs like a deer, arms like an elephant's trunk, a chin like a mango stone and hair like the stings of scorpions. The Pali texts of Theravada Buddhism add the 108 auspicious signs; long toes and fingers of equal length, body like a banyan tree and eyelashes like a cow's. The Buddha can be represented either sitting, lying (indicating *paranirvana*), or standing, and occasionally walking. He is often represented standing on an open lotus flower: the Buddha was born into an impure world, and likewise the lotus germinates in mud but rises above the filth to flower. Each image will be represented in a particular *mudra* or 'attitude', of which there are 40. The most common are:

Abhayamudra – dispelling fear or giving protection; right hand (sometimes both hands) raised, palm outwards, usually with the Buddha in a standing position.

Varamudra – giving blessing or charity; the right hand pointing downwards, the palm facing outwards, with the Buddha either seated or standing.

Vitarkamudra – preaching mudra; the ends of the thumb and index finger of the right hand touch to form a circle, symbolizing the Wheel of Law. The Buddha can either be seated or standing.

Dharmacakramudra – 'spinning the Wheel of Law'; a preaching mudra symbolizing the teaching of the first sermon. The hands are held in front of the chest, thumbs and index fingers of both joined, one facing inwards and one outwards.

Bhumisparcamudra – 'calling the earth goddess to witness' or 'touching the earth'; the right hand rests on the right knee with the tips of the fingers 'touching ground', thus calling the earth goddess Dharani/Thoranee to witness his enlightenment and victory over Mara, the king of demons. The Buddha is always seated.

Dhyanamudra – meditation; both hands resting open, palms upwards, in the lap, right over left.

Buddha calling for rain – a common image in Laos but very rare elsewhere; the Buddha is depicted standing, both arms held stiffly at the side of the body, fingers pointing downwards.

Other points of note:

Vajrasana – yogic posture of meditation; cross-legged, both soles of the feet visible.

Virasana – yogic posture of meditation; cross-legged, but with the right leg on top of the left, covering the left foot (also known as *paryankasana*).

Buddha under Naga – a common image in Khmer art; the Buddha is shown seated in an attitude of meditation with a cobra rearing up over his head. This refers to an episode in the Buddha's life when he was meditating; a rain storm broke and Nagaraja, the king of the nagas (snakes), curled up under the Buddha (seven coils) and then used his seven-headed hood to protect the Holy One from the falling rain.

ZTB 201

Bhumisparcamudra – calling the earth goddess to witness.

Dhyanamudra – meditation.

Abhayamudra – dispelling fear or giving protection.

Vitarkamudra – preaching, "spinning the Wheel of Law" seated in the "European" manner.

Abhayamudra – dispelling fear or giving protection; subduing Mara position.

recent years, there has been a large influx of Thais; most are involved in business. In Vientiane there is also a small community of Indians running restaurants, jewellery and tailors' shops. The majority of the Europeans in Laos are embassy staff or involved with aid projects and oil prospecting companies and live on the S and E side of Vientiane.

Religion

Theravada Buddhism, from the Pali word *thera* ('elders'), means the 'way of the elders' and is distinct from the dominant Buddhism practiced in India, Mahayana Buddhism or the 'Greater Vehicle'. The sacred language of Theravada Buddhism is Pali rather than Sanskrit, Bodhisattvas (future Buddhas) are not given much attention, and emphasis is placed upon a precise and 'fundamental' interpretation of the Buddha's teachings, as they were originally recorded, see page 42. For a general account of Buddhism, see page 42.

The Lao often maintain that the Vientiane area converted to Buddhism at the time of the Moghul emperor Asoka. This seems suspiciously early and is probably untrue. The original stupa at That Luang was built to encase a piece of the Buddha's breastbone provided by Asoka. Buddhism was undoubtedly practised before Fa Ngoum united Lane Xang and created a Buddhist Kingdom in the mid-14th century. He was known as the Great Protector of the Faith and brought the Phra Bang, the famous golden statue – the symbol of Buddhism in Laos – from Angkor in Cambodia to Laos.

Buddhism was gradually accepted among the lowland Lao but many of the highland tribes remain animist. Even where Buddhism has been practised for centuries, it is usually interwoven with the superstitions and rituals of animist beliefs. Appeasing the spirits and gaining merit are both integral features of life. Most highlanders are animists and the worship of *phi* or spirits has remained central to village life throughout the revolutionary years, despite the fact that it was officially banned by the government. Similarly, the *baci* ceremony – when strings representing guardian spirits are tied around the wrists of guests – is still practised throughout Laos.

In the late 1500s, King Setthathirat promoted Buddhism and built many monasteries or *wats*. Buddhism was first taught in schools in the 17th century and prospered until the Thai and Ho invasions of the 18th and 19th centuries when many of the wats were destroyed. With the introduction of socialism in 1975 Buddhism was banned from primary schools and people prohibited from giving alms to monks. With the increasing religious tolerance of the regime it is now undergoing a revival and many of the wats are being rebuilt and redecorated. Males are expected to become monks for 3 months or so before marriage, usually during Buddhist Lent. All members of the priesthood are placed under the authority of a superior – the *Phra Sangharaja*– whose seat was traditionally in the capital of the kingdom.

In line with Buddhist tradition, materialism and the accumulation of personal wealth is generally frowned-on in Laos. Poverty is admired as a form of spirituality. This belief proved rather convenient for the Communist regime, when it was taken to extremes. Today, in the new capitalist climate, the traditional attributes of spirituality sit uncomfortably with Laos' increasingly bourgeois aspirations.

Growing religious tolerance has also rekindled Christianity. While many churches in provincial towns were turned into community centres and meeting halls after the revolution, Vientiane's Evangelical Church has held a Sun service ever since 1979. But Christians have only felt free to worship openly in recent years. In 1989 the first consultation between the country's Christian leaders (Protestant and

Punishments in the eight Buddhist hells commonly found on murals
behind the principal Buddha image in the *sim*.

Adapted from Hallet, Holt (1890) *A thousand miles on an elephant* in the Shan States,
William Blackwood: Edinburgh

Roman Catholic) was authorized by the government – it was the first such meeting since 'liberation'. Government representatives and two leaders of the Buddhist Federation were also invited to attend – ironically both were Hmong.

Foreign missionaries were ejected from Laos in 1975. But with indigenous priests and missionaries now operating in the countryside (many under the guise of non-governmental aid organizations), church leaders predict the rapid growth of Christianity – they say there are around 17,000 Christians in the country. Not many Buddhists have converted to Christianity but it seems to be growing among the animist hilltribes. The US Bible Society is currently working on a modern translation of the Bible into Lao, but tribal language editions do not yet exist. The shortage of bibles and other literature has prompted Christian leaders to 'offer unsolicited gifts' to the department of religious affairs to ease restrictions on the import of hymn books and bibles from Thailand.

Buddhism, as it is practised in Laos, is not the 'other-worldly' religion of western conception. Ultimate salvation – enlightenment, or *nirvana* – is a distant goal for most people. Thai Buddhists pursue the Law of Karma, the reduction of suffering. Meritorious acts are undertaken and demeritorious ones avoided so that life, and more particularly future life, might be improved. 'Karma' is often thought of in the W as 'fate'. It is not. It is true that previous karma determines a person's position in society, but there is still room for individual action – and a person is ultimately responsible for that action. It is the law of cause and effect.

It is important to draw a distinction between 'academic' Buddhism, as it tends to be understood in the W, and 'popular' Buddhism, as it is practiced in Laos. In Laos, Buddhism is a 'syncretic' religion: it incorporates elements of Brahmanism, animism and ancestor worship. Amulets are worn to protect against harm and are often sold in temple compounds. In the countryside, farmers have what they consider to be a healthy regard for the spirits (*phi*) and demons that inhabit the rivers, trees and forests. Astrologers are widely consulted by urban and rural dwellers alike. It is these aspects of Lao Buddhism which help to provide worldly assurance, and they are perceived to be complementary, not in contradiction, with Buddhist teachings.

Most Lao villages will contain a 'temple', 'monastery' or *wat* (the word does not translate accurately). The wat represents the mental heart of each community, and most young men at some point in their lives will become ordained as monks, usually during the Buddhist Rains Retreat, which stretches from Jul to Oct. Previously this period represented the only opportunity for a young man to gain an education and to learn how to read. An equally important reason for a man to become ordained is so that he can accumulate merit for his family, particularly for his mother, who as a woman cannot become ordained.

As in Thailand, Laos has adopted the Indian epic the *Ramayana* (see page 337), which has been the inspiration for much Lao art and sculpture. Complete manuscripts of the Lao *Ramayana* – known as the *Ramakien* used to be kept at Wat Phra Kaeo and Wat Sisaket.

Language and literature

The official language is Lao, the language of the ethnic majority. Lao is basically a monosyllabic, tonal language. It contains many polysyllabic words borrowed from Pali and Sanskrit (ancient Indian dialects) as well as words borrowed from Khmer. It has 6 tones, 33 consonants and 28 vowels. Lao is also spoken in NE Thailand and N Cambodia, which was originally part of the kingdom of Lane Xang. Lao and Thai, particularly the NE dialect, are mutually intelligible. Differences have mainly

THE LAO RAMAYANA AND MAHABHARATA

The *Ramakien* – literally "The Story of Rama" – is an adaptation of the Indian Hindu classic, the Ramayana, which was written by the poet Valmiki about 2,000 years ago. This 48,000 line epic odyssey – often likened to the works of Homer – was introduced into mainland Southeast Asia in the early centuries of the first millennium. The heroes were simply transposed into a mythical, ancient, Southeast Asian landscape.

In Laos, as in Thailand, the Ramakien quickly became highly influential. In Thailand this is reflected in the name of the former capital of Siam, Ayutthaya, taken from the legendary hero's city of Ayodhia. Unfortunately, these early Thai translations of the Ramayana, which also filtered into Laos, were destroyed following the sacking of Ayutthaya by the Burmese in 1767. The earliest extant version was written by Thai King Taksin in about 1775.

The Lao, and Thai, versions of the Ramayana, closely follow that of the original Indian story. They tell of the life of Ram (Rama), the King of Ayodhya. In the first part of the story, Ram renounces his throne following a long and convoluted court intrigue, and flees into exile. With his wife Seeda (Sita) and trusted companion Hanuman (the monkey god), they undertake a long and arduous journey. In the second part, his wife Seeda is abducted by the evil king Ravana, forcing Ram to wage battle against the demons of Langka Island (Sri Lanka). He defeats the demons with the help of Hanuman and his monkey army, and recovers his wife. In the third and final part of the story – and here it diverges sharply from the Indian original – Seeda and Ram are reunited and reconciled with the help of the gods (in the Indian version there is no such reconciliation). Another difference to the Indian version is the significant role played by the Thai Hanuman – here an amorous adventurer who dominates much of the third part of the epic.

Hanuman
Adapted from Hallet, Holt (1890) *A thousand miles on an elephant in the Shan States*
William Blackwood: Edinburgh

There are also numerous sub-plots which are original to the Ramakien, many building upon local myth and folklore. In tone and issues of morality, the Lao and Thai versions are less puritanical than the Indian original. There are also, of course, difference in dress, ecology, location and custom.

The stories that make up the epic **Mahabharata** centre on a long-lasting feud between two family clans: the Pandawas and the Korawas. The feud culminates in a frenzied battle during which the five Pandawa brothers come face to face with their 100 first cousins from the Korawa clan. After 18 days of fighting, the Pandawas emerge victorious and the eldest brother becomes king. The plays usually focus on one or other of the five Pandawa brothers, each of whom is a hero.

developed since French colonial days when Laos was insulated from developments of the Thai language. French is still spoken in towns – particularly by the older generation – and is often used in government but English is being increasingly used. Significant numbers of Lao have been to universities and colleges in the former Soviet Union and Eastern Europe, so Eastern European languages and Russian are spoken.

Many of the tribal groups have no system of writing and the Lao script is similar to Thai, to which it is closely related. One of the kings of the Sukhothai Dynasty, Ramkhamhaeng, devised the Thai alphabet in 1283 and introduced the Thai system of writing. Lao script is modelled on the early Thai script and is written from left to right with no spacing between the words. Lao literature is similar to Thai and influenced by the Indian epics, the *Ramayana* and the *Mahabharata* (see page 337). The first 10 jataka tales, recounting the former lives of the Gautama Buddha, are important Buddhist literature in Laos. As with traditional songs, much Lao poetry has been passed down the generations and remains popular. *Sin Xay* is one of the great Lao poems, and has been written down (although many have not) and is found in many temples.

In 1778 the Thais plundered Laos and along with the two most sacred Buddha images – the Phra Bang and the Phra Kaeo (Emerald Buddha) – they pillaged a great deal of Lao religious literature and historical documents. Most Lao manuscripts – or *kampi* – are engraved on palm leaves and are between 40 and 50 cm long, pierced with two holes and threaded together with cord. A bundle of 20 leaves forms a *phuk*, and these are grouped together into *mat*, which are wrapped in a piece of cloth.

There is very little modern literature compared with some other Asian countries; even the first novels were based on Buddhist texts.

Dance, drama and music

Lao music, songs and dances have much in common with those of the Thai. Instruments include bamboo flutes, drums, gongs, cymbals and pinched or bowed string instruments shaped like banjos. The national instrument is the *kaen*, a hand-held pipe organ. It is made from bamboo and is similar in appearance to the South American pan pipes. Percussion is an important part of a Lao orchestra and two of the most commonly used instruments are the *nang nat*, a xylophone, and the *knong vony*, a series of bronze cymbals suspended from a wooden frame. The *seb noi* orchestra – a consortium of all these instruments – is used to introduce or conclude vocal recitals. The *seb gnai* orchestra includes two big drums and a Lao-style clarinet as well; it was used in royal processions and still accompanies certain religious ceremonies.

Despite the lack of written notation, many epic poems and legends have survived to the present day as songs, passed, with the composition itself, from generation to generation. Early minstrels took their inspiration from folklore, enriched by Indian myths. Traditional Lao music can now only be heard during performances of the *Phra Lak Pralam*. Many of the monasteries have experts on percussion who play every Buddhist sabbath. There is also a strong tradition of Lao folk music, which differs between tribal groups.

In Vientiane and the provincial capitals, younger Lao tend to opt for western-style pop. To the raucous strains of the likes of *Joan Jett and the Blackhearts* – with the lyrics roughly translated into Lao – local bands entertain Levi-clad dancers well into the early hours in Vientiane's discos and nightclubs.

Classical Lao theatre and dance have Indian origins and were probably imported from the Cambodian royal courts in the 14th century. Thai influence has also crept in over the years.

Modern Laos

Politics

Laos underwent the political equivalent of an earth tremor in Mar 1991 at the Fifth Congress of the Lao People's Revolutionary Party (LPRP). Pro-market reforms were embraced and the politburo and central committee got a much-needed transfusion of new blood. At the same time, the hammer and sickle motif was quietly removed from the state emblem and enlightened sub-editors set to work on the national credo, which is emblazoned on all official documents.

This shift in economic policy and ideology can be traced back to the Party Congress of 1986, making Laos one of the very first countries to embrace 'perestroika'. As late General Secretary Kaysone Phomvihane stated at the Fourth Party Congress in 1986:

"In all economic activities, we must know how to apply objective laws and take into account socio-economic efficiency. At the present time, our country is still at the first stage of the transition period. Hence the system of economic laws now being applied to our country is very complicated. It includes not only the specific laws of socialism but also the laws of commodity production. Reality indicates that if we only apply the specific economic laws of socialism alone and defy the general laws pertaining to commodity production, or vice versa, we will make serious mistakes in our economic undertaking during this transition period" (General Secretary Kaysone Phomvihane, Fouth Party Congress 1986; quoted in Lao PDR 1989:9).

Under the horrified gaze of Marx and Lenin – their portraits still dominate the plenary hall – it was announced that the state motto had changed from "Peace, Independence, Unity and Socialism" to "Peace, Independence, Democracy, Unity and Prosperity". The last part is wishful thinking for the poorest country in Southeast Asia but it reflects the realization that unless Laos turns off the socialist road fast, it will have great difficulty digging itself out of the economic quagmire that 15 years' adherence to Marxism has created. In Aug 1991, at the opening of the People's Supreme Assembly, Kaysone Phomvihan, the late President, said: "Socialism is still our objective, but it is a distant one. Very distant." Now that the 'New Thinking' – or *Chin Thanakan Mai* – has begun to permeate, the floodgates have swung open.

President Kaysone died in Nov 1992, aged 71. (His right hand man, Prince Souphanouvong – the so-called Red Prince – died just over 3 years later on 9 January 1985.) As one obituary put it, Kaysone was older than he seemed, both historically and idealogically. He had been chairman of the LPRP since the mid-1950s and had been a prodigé and comrade of Ho Chi Minh, who led the Vietnamese struggle for independence from the French. After leading the Lao Resistance Government – or Pathet Lao – from caves in Sam Neua province in the N, Kaysone assumed the premiership on the abolition of the monarchy in 1975. But under his leadership – and following the example of his mentors in Hanoi – Kaysone became the driving force behind the market-orientated reforms. The year before he died, he gave up the post of Prime Minister for that of President. His death didn't change things much, as other members of the old guard stepped into the breach. Nouhak Phounsavanh – a sprightly 78-year-old former truck driver and hardline Communist – succeeded him as President. General Khamtai Siphandon – who had become Prime Minister the previous year – took over as head of the LPRP. Parliamentary elections were held the month after Kaysone's death. 154 officially recruited candidates stood for 85 seats and most of the country's 2 million voters prudently voted. Before the election, Party leaders said there would be no change after the election and the electorate got what they voted for.

In 1986, before *perestroika* had caught on in the former USSR, the Party introduced a New Economic Mechanism and embarked on the transition from a centrally planned economy to unbridled capitalism. Expectations are running high, but as in neighbouring Vietnam, economic liberalization has not really been matched by political *glasnost*. So far, the monolithic Party shows few signs of equating capitalism with democracy. While the Lao brand of Communism has always been seen as relatively tame, it remains a far-cry from political pluralism. Laos' first constitution since the Communists came to power in 1975, was approved in 1991. The country's political system is referred to as a 'popular democracy', yet it rejected any move towards multi-party reforms.

THE GOLDEN TRIANGLE – THE LAO CONNECTION

Since 1990, attempts have been made to combat the production and trafficking of illicit drugs – sizeable industries in Laos and one in which its mountain tribespeople excel. They contribute to the Golden Triangle's hard drugs output, providing at least 60% of the world's heroin supply. Laos is the third largest producer of opium after Burma and Afghanistan – 375 tonnes of it were produced in 1989 according to US figures. The opium trade was legal in Laos until US pressure forced the government to outlaw it in 1971. The French quietly bought and sold the Hmong opium crop to finance their war efforts against Vietnam's Communists and the Americans turned a blind eye to the trade and allegedly fostered it too. During the 1960s, the drugs trade was run by a handful of high-ranking Royalist officers who became very rich.

Today, in Laos' N provinces, the opium addiction rate of 50% in some villages is more than twice the literacy rate, and small *parakeets* (sachets) of opium have become an unofficial currency. A recent livestock survey in Luang Prabang province was an interesting pointer: most villages listed a few water buffalo, and a few hundred pigs and chickens. One Hmong village had none of these, but listed 214 ponies, which had just left for Chiang Mai when the survey team arrived.

In October 1990, following accusations from the US State Department that the Lao government and military authorities were actively involved in the narcotics trade network, Laos agreed to co-operate with the US in narcotics control and US aid is providing US$20mn to substitute cash crops – such as sesame, coffee and mulberry trees (for silk) – for *Papaver somnifera* (opium poppies) in the mountainous NE Houa Phan province. By signing up for the war against drugs, Laos has opened its empty coffers to a welcome flow of funds. Seizures of raw opium and heroin have increased and there have been reports of opium confiscated from traffickers being ceremonially burned. Traffickers are also being convicted in the Lao courts. The deputy foreign minister, Souban Salitthilat, who heads the National Committee for Narcotic Drugs Supression has been stressing to foreign governments that Laos is a signatory of the UN's Vienna Convention which proscribes production and trafficking.

But in the Golden Triangle area, bordering Burma and Thailand, anti-government insurgents finance their activities with opium smuggling and Vientiane reportedly wants to keep Washington's tendrils well away. There is also widespread suspicion that smuggled opium and heroin are countertraded for Thai consumer goods – everything from toothpaste to televisions have flooded the bustling markets of Vientiane and Luang Prabang.

On the dreamy streets of Vientiane, the chances of a Tiananmen-style uprising are remote, but the events of the late 1980s and early 1990s in Eastern Europe and Moscow have doubtless alarmed hard-liners – just as they did in Beijing. They can be reasonably confident, however, that in their impoverished nation, most people are more worried about where their next meal is going to come from than they are about the allure of multi-party democracy.

Foreign relations

The government has taken steps to improve its foreign relations – and Thailand is the main beneficiary. Historically, Thailand has always been the main route for international access to landlocked Laos. Survival instincts told the Vientiane regime that reopening its front door was of paramount importance. The 1990s began with an unprecedented visit by a member of the Thai royal family, Crown Princess Sirindhorn and in 1994 the Friendship Bridge officially opened (see page 350) linking Laos and Thailand. The border disputes with Thailand have now been settled, and the bloody clashes of 1987/88, when thousands on both sides lost their lives, are history.

Relations have also thawed with China. Laos and China have set up a bilateral trade agreement and the previous president, Kaysone, paid an official visit to Beijing in Oct 1991, returning a visit by Chinese Premier Li Peng to Vientiane in 1990. In 1993 the Lao and Chinese governments signed a defence cooperation agreement, and the Chinese are now important suppliers of military hardware to the Lao. This is causing some worries in Vietnam, which shares a 1,300 km-long border with Laos and historically has had poor relations with China. As the old men of the Lao Communist Party, who owed so much to the Vietnamese, die off so their replacements are looking elsewhere for invest-

ment and political support. Laos is also the only country in Indochina to have maintained relations with the US since 1975 – despite the fact that they never offered reparations or aid to the country. Washington even expected the Lao government to allocate funds to help locate the bodies of US pilots shot down in the war. When Vientiane pledged to co-operate with the US over the narcotics trade during Foreign Affairs Minister General Phoune Sipaseuth's meeting with US Secretary of State James Baker in Oct 1990, it agreed to step up the search for the 530 American MIAs still listed as missing in the Lao jungle.

In mid-1993, tri-lateral talks between Laos, Vietnam and the US allowed for greater cooperation in the search for MIAs. Many of the unaccounted-for servicemen are thought to have been airmen, shot down over the Ho Chi Minh trail which ran through Lao territory along the border with Vietnam. The MIA charity, based in Vientiane, assumed quite a high profile and, in the absence of other US aid organisations, has become a major conduit for humanitarian assistance to the Lao government. All this may eventually herald the return of the US Agency for International Development (USAID) – the organization that fostered dependence on the US when the French left, and provided useful cover for CIA agents. USAID was expelled in 1975. In Oct 1992, America's diplomatic presence in Laos was upgraded to ambassadorial status from chargé d'affaires. But, unwilling to put all its eggs in the basket of the superpower, Vientiane has also courted smaller western countries, particularly France, Germany and Australia. This, it refers to as its 'equilibrium policy'.

Japan is now Laos' biggest aid donor, following the signing of three economic aid agreements worth a total of US$11mn. These days Washington and Tokyo offer more in the way of hope for the embattled regime than Moscow: in

1991, 100 Soviet economic and technical advisers were pulled out of the dilapidated flats they occupied on the outskirts of Vientiane. There will be no more Soviet/Russian aid, although Laos has been given a few years' leeway before it has to pay back its 750-million rouble debt (three-quarters of Laos's total foreign debt). All purchases of military hardware from Russia now have to be paid for in hard currency.

As Laos turned to the W, Japan and Thailand for economic help, the government became more critical of its closest Communist ally, Vietnam. Following Vietnam's invasion of Cambodia in Dec 1978, thousands of N Vietnamese moved into N Laos as permanent colonizers and by 1978 there were an estimated 40,000 Vietnamese regulars in Laos. In 1987, 50,000 Vietnamese troops withdrew. With the death of President Kaysone Phomvihan in Nov 1992, another historical link with Vietnam was cut. He was half-Vietnamese and most of his cabinet owed their education and their posts to Hanoi's succour during the war years. In 1990 a Vientiane census found 15,000 Vietnamese living illegally in the capital, most of whom were promptly deported. That said, increased cooperation with Vietnam over the search for American MIAs is good for bilateral relations. Laos is the only land-locked country in Southeast Asia, and as with its dealings with western governments, Vientiane is keen to pursue a cooperative 'equilibrium' policy with all of them. Laos is in the tricky situation of having to play off China's military might, Thailand's commercial aggressiveness and Vietnam's population pressures, while keeping everyone happy. Perhaps the most incisive assessment of Laos was that of a western diplomat quoted by the French newspaper _Le Monde_ in 1993. He said: "This country's only hope is to become, within the next 10 or 20 years, a bridge between its powerful neighbours, while at the same time managing to avoid being engulfed by either of them".

Economy

If the world's financial markets crashed and international trade and commerce collapsed overnight, Laos would be blissfully immune from the catastrophe: it would be 'farming as usual' the next morning. Over the past few years, though, the government has gradually begun to tread the free-market path, veering off the old command economy system. Farms have been privatized and the state has to compete for produce with market traders at market prices. Many of the unprofitable state-owned business and factories have been leased or sold-off. Cutting credit to those old monoliths has helped bring the annual inflation rate down from nearly 80% in 1989 to less than 7% in 1994. Laos still receives in international aid more than double what it makes in export sales. But foreign investment is coming in, after a slow start – most in the garments sector. Economists say the country's greatest economic potential lies in its mineral resources – gold, precious stones, coal and iron. In 1993, Malaysian, Taiwanese and Chinese firms were awarded timber concessions in Laos – a big earner. Strict reafforestation commitments were written into the contracts.

Agriculture

Rice is the staple food crop – it is cultivated by 85% of the population – and nearly three-quarters of Laos' farmers grow enough to sell or barter some of their crop. Output has risen by 30% since 1985 and the country now produces 1.7 million tonnes of rice a year from nearly 600,000 ha of paddy land. More than half the rice is grown in the hills. In N Laos maize and cassava are often grown as substitutes. Northern provinces suffered a serious drought in 1992/93 however, prompting the UN's World Food Programme to provide about US$1mn in emergency assistance. The drought, followed by a long cold spell in the provinces of Luang Nam

AIDS IN LAOS

Like the other countries of Southeast Asia, Laos is thought to have the potential for 'rapid increase' in the HIV/AIDS epidemic. As of the end of Jun 1994, there were only 14 reported AIDS cases in Laos. However, a study undertaken in 1993 showed that 0.8% of blood donors were HIV-infected, and the low number of cases to date probably reflects a lack of research and the fact that the country is at a comparatively 'early' stage in the epidemic.

Tha, Phongsaly, Houa Phan and Xieng Khouang, cut rice production in some districts by 80%.

The main agricultural areas are on the Mekong's floodplains, especially around Vientiane and Savannakhet. The government has been successful in expanding the area capable of producing two rice crops a year. Cotton, coffee, maize and tobacco are the other main crops and the production of these and other 'industrial' crops such as soya and mung beans has increased in recent years. On the S Bolovens Plateau, rice, coffee and cardamom – 500 tonnes of the latter is produced a year – are grown. Fisheries and livestock resources are being developed – the cattle population has grown by about 30% in the past decade, as has the number of pigs.

While shifting cultivators continue to pose a problem in Laos, their numbers has dropped by about a third since 1985. This is reflected by the fact that they cut down 100,000 ha of forest a year now, compared with 300,000 in the early 1980s. The situation has improved dramatically since the mid-1970s when Hmong General Vang Pao complained to a *National Geographic* reporter that "In one year a single family will chop down and burn trees worth US$6,000 and grow a rice crop worth US$240". He demanded the Hmong get their share of fertile, irrigated land – a share they are still waiting for.

Centuries of war and 15 years of Communism had little impact on the self-reliant villages of rural Laos. Most families have enough to eat and barter with neighbouring villages and most now own the land they farm. The government's attempts at co-operativization proved unpopular and unworkable. Yet with per capita income around US$220, Laos is reckoned to be one of the 10 poorest countries in the world. The government says GDP increased 30% between 1985 and 1990, and growth topped 10% in 1990, but Laos remains the agricultural backwater of Southeast Asia.

Building up the economy

Tens of thousands of people work for the government in a top-heavy and often corrupt bureaucracy. Civil servants are doing well if they make US$15-20 a month and life is difficult for Laos' underpaid teachers, doctors, soldiers and civil servants. Junior government ministers earn around US$50 a month (far less than the US$100 a Vientiane trishaw pedlar can earn). Not surprisingly, official corruption and profiteering are on the increase – there is little else to explain the new houses and cars in the capital.

Major development constraints are the shortage of skilled workers and capital, an undeveloped communication system (10,000 km of road, only 20% of which is sealed), poor educational and health resources, rugged terrain and low population density. A piece in the *New Yorker* magazine, published in Aug 1990 and entitled 'Forgotten country', reported the experience of two aid workers as they struggled to travel to Phong Saly Province in the far N where they worked:

"When David Merchant and Lois Fochringer [two aid workers] visit Phong

Saly Province – the northernmost province of Laos, on the China border – they have to travel for 3½ days by boat and are then met by provincial authorities and given a jolting ride up the side of a mountain in a 4WD truck. The truck itself arrived by boat, having been cut into two pieces for the voyage. For 8 months or so of each year, Phong Saly Province is accessible only by helicopter, because the water level is too low for boat traffic" (Sesser 1990).

One of Laos' most important sources of foreign exchange is receipts from overflight rights, as the Bolovens Plateau lies on the flight path from Bangkok to Hong Kong and Tokyo. Around 80 international flights traverse Lao airspace every day, and the government receives US$300 for each one: a total of US$8.5mn a year. One of the country's biggest foreign exchange earners is hydro-electric power. Much of this comes from the Nam Ngum Dam, N of Vientiane and from the Xeset Dam in southern Laos. These generate not only electricity (the country's potential is estimated to be more than 18,000 MW), but more than US$20mn a year in exports to Thailand. Plans are afoot to further exploit the potential of the Mekong and its tributaries. The biggest proposed project is the Pa Mong Dam, 20 km upstream from the capital. If built, the resultant flooding would require the relocation of more than 6,000 people. The dam would cost about US$2.8bn. The decision to build the dam rests with the Mekong Committee, whose members include Laos, Thailand, Cambodia and Vietnam.

Former President Kaysone Phomvihan shouldered much of the blame for the miserable state of the economy, admitting that the Party had made mistakes. At the Congress in 1991 he set the new national agenda: Laos had to step up its exports, encourage more foreign investment, promote tourism and rural development, entice its shifting cultivators into proper jobs and revamp the financial system. In doing so he prioritized the problems but offered no solutions bar the loosening of state control and the promotion of private enterprise.

Since 1986, when economic reforms were first introduced, Laos has eliminated six of its seven official exchange rates to create a unified market-related rate and the kip has stabilized at around 700 to the dollar. The once-booming black market has all but disappeared. Although a non-convertible currency, the kip is now in as much demand in Laos as the US dollar and Thai baht. This helped put Laos on a more commercially-competitive footing. Now market forces are firmly in place as the central plank of economic planning, old-fashioned capitalism has taken root again.

Most of the new enterprise has been in the service sector – there is little evidence that the reforms have prompted a significant increase in manufacturing activity. Most industry in Laos is small scale – rubber shoes, matches, tobacco processing, brewing, and soft drinks and ice manufacturing. Saw-milling and timber processing account for the majority of factories – a toothpick plant is still a large source of manufactured export earnings. Pottery is produced at the cottage industry level. Altogether, industry employs only a few thousand people and accounts for a tiny fraction of the gross domestic product. However, this is changing: textile manufacturers have set up shop in the country and garments are now one of Laos' most valuable export (see below). Other important exports are raw timber, processed wood products and hydro-electricity.

With the odds stacked against it, the government cannot afford to be choosy when it comes to investment. No international bank will guarantee companies operating in Laos, which has a high risk rating. Nearly 300 foreign investment contracts have been approved since the government adopted a more liberal in-

FACING UP TO REALITY

In Mar 1995, the *Bangkok Post* reported the story of a new Lao face cream and the television commercial used to promote it. In the commercial, a woman using the cream is regarded by her friend with the exclamation "Wongdevan, you look so beautiful!", and then asked confidentially about the secret of her physical transformation. Laos subsequently began to greet friends looking rather the worse for wear with the stock phrase "My, Wongdevan, you look so beautiful!". Unfortunately, the actress in the commercial happened to be the girlfriend of an influential Lao, and in a fit of pique, no doubt believing the joke cast aspersions on his own taste in women, he had a new law introduced banning satirical jokes based on Lao TV commercials – with offenders liable to a fine of 2,500 kip or US$3.50. Latest reports are that the joke is more popular than ever, and sales of the face cream are sluggish.

vestment code in 1988, many of them textile factories and in the tourism sector. By the end of 1992 the latter had absorbed more than a fifth of all foreign investment in Laos. Unlike most of its Southeast Asian neighbours, Laos' embryonic garment industry is not subject to quotas from markets in the US and the European Community. The supposed 'flood' of foreign investment in this sector has been nothing more than blue-jeans and T-shirt manufacturers from Thailand, Hong Kong, Macao and France, relocating to avoid export restrictions. In 1993 garments became Laos' leading foreign exchange earner (US$35mn in 1993), although in the following year they were pushed into second place by wood products, a traditionally strong source of foreign exchange.

In an effort to make the business climate more attractive, the state bank now supplies credit to all sectors of the economy. Provincial banks have been told to operate as autonomous commercial banks. State enterprises have been warned that if their bottom line does not show a profit, they are out of business. Provinces are free to conclude their own trading agreements with private companies and neighbouring countries – which generally means Thailand.

Fears of dependency on Thailand
Thailand is Vientiane's lifeline to the outside world. Just 3 years after their last bloody border dispute in 1987/88, the old enemies patched up their differences and agreed to build the Mittaphab – or Friendship – bridge across the Mekong to Nong Khai in NE Thailand. The bridge was built with Australian assistance and opened in 1994 (see page 350). However, fears of Laos becoming a Thai commercial colony has led the government to extend an extremely cautious welcome to Thai proposals to build another bridge at Savannakhet in the southern 'panhandle', which would link NE Thailand with southern Vietnam. There is also talk of a bridge linking Chiang Khong in Thailand's N with Ban Huey Xai, allowing Thailand easier access to the rich market of Yunnan in southern China.

Following the visit of Thai Crown Princess Sirindhorn in early 1990 – the first visit by a member of the Thai royal family for 15 years – Thailand lifted a ban of the export on 200 'strategic goods' to Laos, which had been in place since 1975 and which covered everything from military equipment to food and bicycles. Most of these goods now go through the ports of Keng Kabao (near Savannakhet) and Tha Dua.

Thais have emerged as the biggest

foreign investors in Laos. Two way trade grew to US$233.4mn in 1993, with the balance heavily in Thailand's favour. Between 1988 (when a new foreign investment code was promulgated) and 1994 Thailand's investment in Laos totalled US$256mn. The second largest investor was the US with total investment over the period of just US$85mn. Trade is expected to surge now the Friendship Bridge is open.

Six Thai commercial banks have set up in Laos, along with businessmen, consultants and loggers. The warming of relations between Bangkok and Vientiane has raised some eyebrows: sceptics say Laos' wealth of unexploited natural resources is a tempting reward for patching things up. Laos has about 2 million ha of forest – 400,000 ha of which is teak and other high quality timber – and it is disappearing fast. But to its credit, Thailand has prioritized aid to Laos and has signed joint ventures in almost every sector – from science and technology to trade, banking and agriculture. One of the biggest joint ventures is the 65-year concession to the Thai Dusit Group to develop a resort at the Li Phi Waterfalls in the S of Laos. Thai businessmen have partially taken over the state beer and brewery, and the Thai conglomerate Shinawatra have been given telecommunications concessions. Nonetheless, Thai diplomats are only too aware of the poor reputation that their businessmen have in Vientiane. They are regarded as overbearing and superior in their attitude to the Lao, and rapacious, predatory and mercenary in their business dealings. The Thai government has even run courses to try and improve business behaviour. But Thai perceptions of their neighbours are deeply entrenched. As one Thai critic remarked in 1995: "Thai cultural diplomacy starts with the assumption that Thai culture is superior."

Thailand proposed, before the UN General Assembly, that Laos be admitted to ASEAN, along with Vietnam and Burma. Laos' export volume to Thailand has more than doubled since this process of rapprochement began. Young Lao who previously attended universities in the Soviet bloc are now being dispatched to Thai universities. The Vientiane government is acutely aware that skilled workers remain the country's number one limitation – three-quarters of its intellectuals left in 1975.

To understand Laos' fears of Thailand it is necessary to look back in history. Until the French absorbed Laos into Indochina, Laos came under Thai suzerainty, and indeed the Siamese saw Laos as a junior, rather primitive, colony of theirs. When the foolhardy King Anou of Vientiane tried to recreated the great 14th century Lao kingdom of Fa Ngoum and invaded Siam he was soundly thrashed in a battle at Korat, in NE Thailand, and then saw his capital Vientiane plundered, sacked and razed by Siamese forces. – a fact which explains why today this ancient city is so devoid of architecture pre-dating the French period. Needless to say, Thai and Lao history is at odds on this period of history: Thai accounts paint Anou as a rebel; those written by Lao historians characterize him as a national hero.

It is only with this background in mind that Lao fears of Thai commercial hegemony can be fully appreciated. When, in 1988, former Thai Prime Minister Chatichai Choonhaven expressed a desire to turn Indochina 'from a battlefield into a market place', this was viewed by many Lao – and some more thoughtful Thais – as tantamount to a threat of commercial invasion. (The theme was returned to in 1995 when a senior Thai diplomat, Suridhya Simaskul, remarked to the journalist Michael Vatikiotis, "We have passed the stage of turning battlefields into markets; now the market itself has become the battlefield.") Thailand, its own natural resources denuded through years of thoughtless exploitation, was hoping to pillage Laos' resource-rich larder. In Jul 1989, state run Radio Vientiane broadcast a commentary, presumably officially sanctioned, stating: "Having failed to destroy our country through their military might [referring to the Ban Rom Klao border conflict of 1987-88], the enemy has now employed a new strategy in attacking us through the so-called attempt to turn the Indochinese battlefield into a marketplace..." It is this fear of Thailand, and of over-dependence on Thailand, which has prompted the Lao government to do its utmost to try and diversify its commercial links. In a rather novel departure from the usual state of affairs, the Lao are also more scared of Thai cultural pollution, than western cultural pollution. The similarities between the two countries, and the fact that many Lao households watch Thai television, makes Thailand seem more of a risk. In 1993, former president and Pathet Lao veteran Phoumi Vongvichit warned against the dangers of prostitution, 'depraved' dancing and gambling. The source of these threats to pristine Lao culture was Thailand. Newspaper reports even dubbed the Mittaphaap Bridge the AIDS Bridge, because it is thought that it will bring prostitution and AIDS to the country.

Dependency on aid, and development aims

Laos depends heavily on imports – everything from agricultural machinery and cars to petrol products, textiles and pharmaceuticals – 75% of which are financed by foreign aid. Western bilateral donors are enthusiastically filling the aid gap left by the Socialist bloc. Countries and private donors are falling over each other to fund projects; NGOs are homing in and multi-lateral development banks are offering soft loans and structural adjustment programmes. As Laos' US$500mn foreign debt is mostly on highly concessional terms, it is not crippled by repayment schedules. But

with development banks accelerating their project-funding, fears are mounting that Laos is teetering on the edge of a debt trap.

At more than US$170mn a year, or US$39/head, external assistance now accounts for nearly one fifth of Laos' gross domestic product – over double the country's export earnings. By 1990, Vientiane's capacity to absorb this aid was swamped, its ministries overwhelmed by one of the highest per capita aid inflows in the developing world. While western economic advisers have been touting investment strategies, project co-ordination and quality have suffered in the rush. The country and its foreign strategists are looking for four distinct areas for future income. The first concentrates on mining and energy. Laos already has two HEP dams that generate power for export to Thailand and others are planned. South Korea's Daewoo group signed a contract for an HEP scheme in southern Laos. Mining rights to some of Laos' huge lignite reserves have been sold to Thai investors. Other untapped mineral resources include reserves of gold, gemstones and iron ore, while foreign companies have undertaken preliminary search for oil. The second area of interest is agriculture and forestry. Investors are looking at growing feed grains like soyabeans and maize for export to Thailand. Raw timber exports will be ended and replaced by processed wood industries. The third potential is tourism but the government is wary of Laos going the same way as Thailand. The fourth strategy, the most ambitious, is for Laos to be the 'service centre' between China, Vietnam, Cambodia and Thailand for everything from road, rail and river transport to power and telecommunications networks. Laos is perceived to be at the centre of what has been termed a 'golden quandrangle' and in a recent interview Deputy Prime Minister Khamphoui Keoboualapha stated as much when he said that "We want to become the link between Vietnam, China, Thailand, Burma and Cambodia".

The government claims its "programme for the basic elimination of illiteracy among the masses", launched in 1984 was "an outstanding success". Literacy rates are still low – 35% for women, 65% for men. Adult education has been expanded, schools upgraded and 62 classrooms built "for 1,600 tribal youths". But while the government has been busy building schools, the quality of education has slipped further: they cannot afford to pay teachers or buy textbooks.

Health care has suffered for the same reasons. Infant and under-five mortality rates are some of the highest in the world, the latter estimated at 193 per 1,000 live births. Half of those who do survive suffer malnutrition, nearly all contract malaria, diarrhoea, respiratory and intestinal diseases and few live beyond 50.

LAOS: FACT FILE

Geographic
Land area	236,800 sq km
Arable land as % of total	3.8%
Average annual deforestation rate	1.0%
Highest mountain, Bia	2,800m
Average rainfall in Vientiane	1,720mm
Average temperature in Vientiane	27°C

Economic
GNP/person (1991)	US$220
GDP/person (PPP*, 1991)	US$1,760
GNP growth (/capita, 1980-1990)	0.7%
% labour force in agriculture	76%
Total debt (% GNP)	110%
Debt service ratio (% exports)	7.6%
Military expenditure (% GDP) (1960 – latest available)	5.8%

Social
Population	4.5 million
Population growth rate (1960-92)	2.3%
Adult literacy rate	55%
Mean years of schooling	2.9 years
Tertiary graduate as % of age group	0.5%
Population in absolute poverty	n.a.
Rural population as % of total	80%
Growth of urban population (1960-92)	5.1%/year
Urban population in largest city (%)	48%
Televisions per 1,000 people	7

Health
Life expectancy at birth	50.3 years
Population with access to clean water	n.a.
Calorie intake as % of requirements	111%
Malnourished children under 5 years old	0.25 million
Contraceptive prevalence rate†	n.a.

* PPP = Purchasing Power Parity (based on what it costs to buy a similar basket of goods and services in different countries).
† % of women of childbearing age using contraception.

Source: World Bank (1994) *Human development report 1994*, OUP: New York; and other sources.

VIENTIANE

In 1563, King Setthathirat made the riverine city of Vientiane the capital of Laos – or, to be more historically accurate, Vieng Chan – or 'City of the Moon' – became the capital of Lane Xang. In those days it was a small fortified city on the banks of the Mekong with a palace and two wats, That Luang and Wat Phra Kaeo (built to house the Emerald Buddha). The city had grown prosperous from the surrounding fertile plains and taxes levied from trade going upriver. As Francis Garnier put it, this was the "former metropolis of the kingdom of Laos".

Vieng Chan remained intact until 1827 when it was ransacked by the Siamese – explaining why many of its wats are of recent construction. Francis Garnier in 1860 wrote of 'a heap of ruins', and having surveyed the 'relics of antiquity' decided that the "absolute silence reigning within the precincts of a city formerly so rich and populous, was ... much more impressive than any of its monuments ...". The city was abandoned for decades and only reconstructed by the French at the end of the 19th century, who built big colonial houses and wide tree-lined boulevards, befitting their new administrative capital, Vientiane. At the height of American influence it was reputed for its opium dens and sex shows.

Today Vientiane is a quiet capital city with a population of 400,000 – about 10% of the population of Laos (it has grown from 70,000 in 1960). It is the only Southeast Asian capital where pedestrians still rule the streets. Before 1970 there was only one set of traffic lights in the whole city and even with the arrival of cars and motorbikes from Thailand in recent years, the streets are a far-cry from the congestion of Bangkok – rush hour is a parade of bicycles. There are only scattered traces of French town planning – unlike Phnom Penh and Saigon – and the architecture is a mixture of E and W, with French colonial villas and traditional wooden Lao buildings intermingled with Chinese shophouses.

The capital is divided into *ban* or villages, mainly centred around their local wats, and larger *muang* or districts: **Muang Sikhottabong** lies to the W, **Muang Chanthabouli** to the N, **Muang Xaisettha** to the E and **Muang Sisattanak** to the S. Vientiane can be rather confusing for the first-time visitor as there are no street signs and most streets have two names – pre- and post-revolutionary. The names of major streets – or *thanon* – usually correspond to the nearest wat. Traffic lights and wats serve as directional landmarks.

Places of interest

Most of the interesting buildings in Vientiane are of religious significance. **That Luang**, on Thanon That Luang, is considered Vientiane's most important site. It looks impressive at the top of the hill, 3 km NE of the city. According to legend, a stupa was first built here in the 3rd century AD by emissaries of the

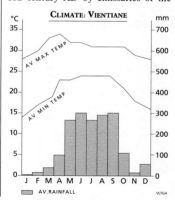

CLIMATE: VIENTIANE

AV. RAINFALL

Thai stamp commerorating the official opening of the Friendship Bridge in 1994

BRIDGING THE MEKONG

In April 1994, King Bhumibol of Thailand and the President of Laos, accompanied by Prime Ministers Chuan Leekpai of Thailand and Australia's Prime Minister Keating opened the first bridge to span the lower reaches of the Mekong River, linking Nong Khai in Northeast Thailand with Vientiane in Laos. The bridge has been a long time in coming. It was first mooted in the 1950s, but war in Indochina and hostility between Laos and Thailand scuppered plans until the late 1980s. Then, with the cold war ending and growing rapprochement between the countries of Indochina and Asean, the bridge, as they say, became an idea whose time had come

The 1.2 km-long Friendship Bridge, or Mittaphab has been financed with US$30 million of aid from Australia. It is a key link in a planned road network that will eventually stretch from Singapore to Beijing. For land-locked Laos, it offers an easier route to Thailand and through Thailand to the sea. For Thailand, it offers an entrée into one of the least developed countries in the world, rich in natural resources and potential. While for Australia, it demonstrated the country's Asian credentials. The Thais would like to build one, and maybe two, further bridges, possible at Mukdahan and Nakhon Pathom. The government of Laos is rather more circumspect, worrying that bridges not only bolster trade, but also bring consumerism, crime, prostitution and environmental degradation.

Moghul Emperor Asoka and it is supposed to have contained a relic of the Buddha. But excavations on the site have only located the remains of a 11th-13th century Khmer temple. It was built in its present form, encompassing the previous buildings, in 1566 by King Settathirat (his statue stands outside). Plundered by the Thais and the Chinese Ho in the 18th century, it was restored by King (Chao) Anou at the beginning of the 19th century. He added the clois-

The Buddha 'Calling for Rain'

ter and the Burmese-style pavilion containing the That Sithamma Hay Sok.

It was again carefully restored by l'Ecole Francaise d'Extreme-Orient – which also restored parts of Angkor Wat – at the beginning of this century. The stupa was rebuilt yet again in 1930, as many Lao disapproved of the French restoration. The reliquary is surrounded by a square cloister, with an entrance on each side, the most famous on the E. There is a small collection of statues in the cloisters including one of the Khmer king, Jayavarman VII. The cloisters are used as lodgings by monks who have travelled to Vientiane for the That Luang festival (see page 358).

The base of the stupa is a mixture of styles, Khmer, Indian and Lao, and each side has a *hor vay* or small offering

temple. The second tier is surrounded by a lotus wall and 30 smaller stupas, representing the 30 Buddhist perfections. Each of these originally contained smaller golden stupas but they were stolen by Chinese raiders in the 19th century. The 30m-high spire dominates the skyline and resembles an elongated lotus bud, crowned by a stylized banana flower and parasol. It was designed so that pilgrims could climb up to the stupa with walkways around each level. There was originally a wat on each side of the stupa but only two remain: **Wat Luang Nua** to the N and **Wat Luang Tai** to the S. That Luang is rather disappointing compared with Wat Sisaket and Wat Phra Kaeo (see below) but it is an important historical monument nonetheless and revered by the Lao. A booklet with more detail about the wat is on sale at the entrance. Admission 200 kip. Open 0800-1130, 1400-1630 Tues-Sun.

The **Revolutionary Monument** on Thanon Phon Kheng is visible from the parade ground, which resembles a disused parking lot, in front of That Luang. This spectacularly dull monument, a landmark on top of the hill, was built in memory of those who died during the revolution in 1975. The **Pathet Lao Museum**, to the NW of Wat That Luang, is only open to VIPs and never to the public. But there are a few tanks, trucks, guns and aircraft used in the war lying in the grounds, which can be seen from the other side of the fence.

At the end of Thanon That Luang and the top of Thanon Lane Xang is the oriental answer to Paris' Arc de Triomphe and Vientiane's best known landmark, the monstrous **Monument Anousavari**. It is called the Anou Savali, Pratuxai or Victory Gate, but is affectionately known as 'the vertical runway'. It was built by the former regime in memory of those who died in the wars before the Communist takeover, but the cement ran out before its completion. Refusing to be beaten, hundreds of tonnes of cement – part of a US aid package to help with the construction of runways at Vientiane's new Wattay Airport – were diverted up Thanon Lane Xang to finish off the monument in 1969. The top affords a birds-eye view of the leafy capital. The glittering golden dome in the distance is the expensive, Russian-built opera house, which is now only used during National Day celebrations.

The interior of the Monument Anousavari is reminiscent of a multi-storey car park, sporadically decorated with

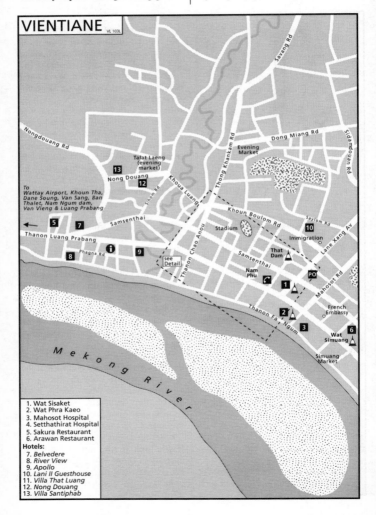

VIENTIANE VL 103L

To Wattay Airport, Khoun Tha, Dane Soung, Van Sang, Ban Thalet, Nam Ngum dam, Van Vieng & Luang Prabang

Nongdouang Rd

Talat Laeng (evening market)

Nong Douang

Khoua Luang

Thong Khankam Rd

Dong Miang Rd

Sidamouan Rd

Savang Rd

Evening Market

Khoun Boulom Rd

Saylom Rd

Lane Xang Av

Sihom Rd

Samsenthai

Thanon Luang Prabang

Phagna Rd

Thanon Chao Anou

Stadium

Samsenthai

That Dam

Immigration

Nam Phu

PO

Thanon Far Ngum

French Embassy

Wat Simuang

Simuang Market

Mahosot Rd

M e k o n g   R i v e r

1. Wat Sisaket
2. Wat Phra Kaeo
3. Mahosot Hospital
4. Setthathirat Hospital
5. Sakura Restaurant
6. Arawan Restaurant
Hotels:
7. *Belvedere*
8. *River View*
9. *Apollo*
10. *Lani II Guesthouse*
11. *Villa That Luang*
12. *Nong Douang*
13. *Villa Santiphab*

graffiti daubed on top of unfinished Buddhist bas-reliefs in reinforced concrete. The frescoes under the arches at the bottom represent mythological stories from the Ramakien. Until 1990 there was a bar on the bottom floor; today Vientiane's young hang out on the

parapet, listening to the *Lambada* in Lao. Admission 200 kip (30 kip to park a bike).

Further down Thanon Lane Xang is the **morning market** (see below under markets) and beyond, where Thanon Setthathirat meets Thanon Lane Xang, is one of the two national museums, **Wat**

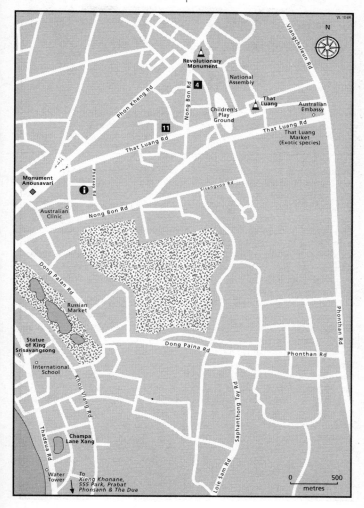

Cloisters at Wieng Chan
from the exterior

HWS

Wat Sisaket in Vientiane

McCarthy, James (1900) *Surveying and exploring in Siam with descriptions of Lao dependencies and of battles against the Chinese Haws*, John Murray: London. The pen and ink sketches are by H. Warrington Smyth, another chronicler of the Kingdom.

Sisaket. Built in 1818 during the reign of King Anou, it is one of the most important buildings in the capital. A traditional Lao monastery, the buildings survived the Thai sacking of the town in 1827 (perhaps out of deference to its having been completed only 10 years before the invasion), making it the oldest wat complex in Vientiane. The main sanctuary, or sim, with its sweeping roof has many stylistic similarities with Wat Phra Kaeo (see below): window surrounds, lotus shaped pillars and carvings of deities held up by giants on the rear door. The **sim** contains 2,052 Buddha statues (mainly terracotta, bronze and wood) in small niches in the top half of the wall. There is little left of the Thai-style jataka murals on the lower walls but the depth and colour of the originals can be seen from the few remaining pieces. The ceiling was copied from temples King Anou had seen on a visit to Bangkok. The standing image to the left of the altar is believed to have been cast in the same proportions as King Anou.

The sim is surrounded by a large court-yard, which originally had four entrance gates (3 are now blocked). The cloisters shelter 120 large Buddhas in the attitude of subduing Mara (see page 332) and thousands of small figures in niches, although many of the most interesting Buddha figures are now in Wat Phra Kaeo. The pile of broken Buddhas in the gateway were found during the French colonial period when they were reconstructing many of the local wats. Most of the statues are 16th-19th century, but there are some earlier images. The cloister walls were originally decorated with murals. Behind the sim is a large trough, in the shape of a naga, used for washing the Buddha images during the water festival (see page 422). An attractive Burmese-style library, or *hor trai*, stands on Thanon Lane Xang outside the courtyard. The large casket inside used to contain important Buddhist manuscripts but they have now been moved to protect them against vermin. Wat Sisaket is the home of the head of the Buddhist community in Laos, Phra Sangka Nagnok. Sadly Wat Sisaket is badly in need of restoration. Admission 200 kip. Open 0800-1130, 1400-1630 Tue-

Sun.

Just behind Wat Sisaket is an entire complex of superbly preserved colonial houses in a well maintained garden, where the French ambassador resides. The cathedral was built in 1928.

Almost opposite Wat Sisaket on Thanon Setthathirat is the other national museum, **Wat Phra Kaeo** (entrance on Thanon Mahosot). It was originally built by King Setthathirat in 1565 to house the Emerald Buddha (or *Phra Kaeo*), now in Bangkok. He brought the image from Chiang Mai where he had previously been king. Wat Phra Kaeo was never a monastery but was kept for royal worship. The Emerald Buddha was removed by the Thais in 1778 and Wat Phra Kaeo was destroyed by them in the sacking of Vientiane in 1827. Francis Garnier, the French explorer, who wandered the ruins of Vieng Chan in 1860 describes Wat Phra Kaeo "shin[ing] forth in the midst of the forest, gracefully framed with blooming lianas, and profusely garlanded with foliage". The building was expertly reconstructed in the 1940s and 1950s and is now surrounded by a garden.

The **sim** stands on three tiers of galleries, the top one surrounded by majestic, lotus-shaped columns. The tiers are joined by several flights of steps and guarded by nagas. The main door is an exquisite example of Lao wood sculpture with carved Buddhas surrounded by flowers and birds. This door, and the one at the rear, are the only notable remnants of the original wat. The sim now houses a superb assortment of Lao and Khmer art and some pieces of Burmese and Khmer influence, mostly collected from other wats in Vientiane.

Notable pieces: *3, 4, 17*: bronze Buddhas in typical Lao style; *294, 295*: Buddhas influenced by Sukhothai-style (Thailand), where the attitude of the walking Buddha was first created (see page 332); *354*: Buddha meditating – made of lacquered wood shows Burmese influence, 18th century; *372*: wooden, Indian-style door with erotic sculpture, dating back to the 16th century, originally from the Savannakhet region; *388*: copy of the Phra Bang, the revered statue associated with the origins of Buddhism in Laos (see page 310); *416*: a Khmer diety with 4 arms; *412, 414, 450*: also Khmer pieces; *415*: is a hybrid of Vishnu and Buddha; *430, 431*: are 18th century copies of the famous Khmer apsaras, the celestial nymphs of Angkor; *698*: this stone Buddha is the oldest piece of Buddhist art in Laos, 6th-9th century; *collection of stelae*: inscribed in Lao and Thai script, including one with a treaty delineating a 16th century agreement between Siam and Lane Xane. An unusual exhibit is the "Atom Struck Tile" found on the site of Sairenji Temple, Hiroshima. The *Vientiane Guide* is a worthwhile publication for getting around the city.

A short description of each exhibit is given in French and Lao. The garden has a small jar from the Plain of Jars (see page 382), which was helicoptered down to Vientiane. Admission 200 kip. Open 0800-1130, 1400-1630 Tue-Sat.

Adjacent to the museum is the **old royal palace**, today the presidential palace, closed to the public.

Travelling N on Chanta Koummane, the distinctive brick stupa of **That Dam** can be seen. It is renowned for the legend of the 7-headed dragon, which is supposed to have helped protect the city from Thai invaders. In the centre of town, on Thanon Samsenthai near the stadium, is the musty **Revolutionary Museum**. This distinctive white building houses a fascinating collection of artefacts and photographs depicting the 'fall' of the colonialists and their 'brutal ways'. Ironically it is housed in a French Colonial building, the Résidence Supérienre, the office of the highest-ranking French official in Laos. In Oct 1945, the Lao Issara government took it over and renamed it the Présidence du Conseil. Downstairs there is an exhibition of historic sights in Laos and Achievements of Communism. Admission 200 kip. Open 0800-1130, 1400-1630 Tue-Sun.

Parallel to Thanon Samsenthai is Thanon Setthathirat and **Wat Ong Teu** (with bright orange monks' quarters). Constructed by King Setthathirat, it houses one of the biggest Buddhas in Vientiane, which weighs several tons. The wat is also noted for its magnificent *sofa* and ornately carved wooden doors and windows with motifs from the Ramakien. The monastery runs one of the larger Buddhist schools in Laos and the Deputy Patriarch, Hawng Sangkharat, of the Lao monastic order lives here. The wat comes alive every year for the That Luang festival – originally a ceremony where nobles swore allegiance to the king and constitution, which amazingly has survived the Communist era (see page 358). Admission 100 kip.

A short walk away, on the banks of the Mekong (junction of Chao Anou and Fa Ngoum) is **Wat Chan**. Unfortunately, it was wrecked by the marauding Thais in 1827 – only the base of a single stupa remains in front of the sim. The stupa originally had Buddha images in the 'Calling for Rain' attitude on each side (see page 332); only one remains. Inside the reconstructed sim is a remarkable bronze Buddha from the original temple on this site. The wat is also renowned for its panels of sculpted wood on the doors and windows.

Further E of town on Thanon Simoung is **Wat Simoung**. It contains the town foundation pillar (*lak muang*), which was erected in 1563 when King Settharirat established Vientiane as the capital of the kingdom of Lane Xang. It is believed to be an ancient Khmer boundary stone, which marked the edge of the old Lao capital. The sim was reconstructed in 1915 around the foundation pillar, which forms the centre of the altar. In front of the altar is a Buddha, which is thought to have magical powers, and is often consulted by worshippers. 50 kip to leave a bike.

Just round the corner from Wat Simoung, where Thanon Settathirat and Thanon Samsenthai meet, is the **statue of the king**. The original statue was carved by a Lao sculptor, which apparently made the king look like a dwarf. Consequently was destroyed. It was replaced by the present statue (there's a copy of it in Luang Prabang) which was, peculiarly, donated by the Russians. Just as strangely, the statue survived the revolution. The *Vientiane Guide* is a worthwhile publication for getting around the city.

Excursions

Buses, trucks and pick-ups to destinations around Vientiane all leave from the station next to the Morning Market; it is also possible to hire a car (around US$45/day). Taxis can be hired for the day from the Morning Market or outside one of the main hotels and cost around 21,000 kip/day for excursions outside Vientiane. Also see **car hire**, page 366.

East/South

Garden of the Buddhas (Xieng Khonane) is a few km beyond **Tha Deua**, 25 km to the E of the capital (on Route 2), on the frontier with Thailand. It has been described as a Laotian Tiger Balm Gardens with reinforced concrete Buddhist and Hindu sculptures of Vishnu, Buddha, Siva etc. There's also a bulbous-style building with three levels containing smaller sculptures of the same gods. The garden was built in the late 1950s by a priest called Luang Pu, who combined the Buddhist and Hindu philosophies. He is very popular in Laos and N Thailand, where he now lives. He also built Wat Khaek in Nong Khai, just over the border in Thailand. Open Mon-Sun 0800-1700. Admission 200 kip. *Getting there*: 1 hr by bus (200 kip), the bus stops first at the border and then at

Xieng Khonane (1.5 km on). For returning to Vientiane, there is a bus stop in front of the Garden.

555 Park (Saam Haa Yai) are extensive, but rather uninspiring, gardens, with Chinese pavilions, a lake and a small zoo, 14 km down the Thanon Tha Deua (Route 2) from Vientiane. In the 1980s, a white elephant was captured in S Laos. Revered in this part of the world for their religious significance, it had to be painted to ensure it was not stolen on the way to the capital. Formerly kept in the Saam Haa gardens, it has since been moved to a secret location somewhere in Vientiane and is paraded in front of the crowds to marvel at during the That Luang festival. White elephants are not white; they are pink, if anything.

Lao Pako lies 50 km E of Vientiane, on the banks of the Nam Ngum River. There is a 'nature lodge' here, with river trips, treks, walks to Lao villages etc. **Accommodation** is in a Lao style longhouse **C-D** (**E** dorms) or in single bungalows overlooking the river, restaurant serves Lao and European food. For further information, contact Walter Pfabigan, c/o Burapha, 14 Thanon Fa Ngoum, Vientiane.

Tad Leuk waterfall is a 2 hr drive E in the direction of Paksane. There's a tarmaced road to Thabok (the waterfall sign is easily seen on the left) and then a dirt track for 1 hr. A good picnic spot, and it is possible to swim in the lake behind the waterfall.

Prabat Phonsanh, 80 km down the Paksane road, is built on a plug of volcanic rock, in the middle of a coconut plantation. It is known for its footprint of the Buddha and has a statue of a reclining Buddha – a mudra rarely seen in Laos. Houei Nhang Forest Reserve, on route 13 South, has a nature trail through lowland semi-evergreen forest. Mouse deer, porcupines and civet cats have been spotted here.

Friendship Bridge The observation area by the Mekong River makes a good picnic spot, or it would be possible to take lunch in Thailand for visitors with multi-entry visas. Forms need to be filled in and travel across the bridge is by minibus. Tuk-tuks wait at the other end.

North

Dane Soung is 30 km from Vientiane, on the Luang Prabang road. Turn left at the 22 km mark towards Ban Houa Khoua. Dane Soung is 6 km down the track, and is only accessible in the dry season. Large fallen rocks form a cave with Buddhist sculptures inside. On the left of the entrance is a footprint of the Buddha.

Nam Suong rapids and waterfall are 40 km N on Route 13, turn left at the Lao-Australian Livestock Project Centre and right before the bridge: there is an absurdly out-of-place, Surrey-style picnic spot by the lake. For the rapids and waterfall, turn left before the bridge along a precipitously narrow track – they are only impressive during the rainy season.

Ban Keun is about 50 km N of Vientiane on Route 10. There's a zoo here and a café and picnic area. Admission 1,000 kip for adults, free for children, pleasant trip.

Vang Sang, near the village of Houey Thone, 63 km up the road to Luang Prabang is home to the remains of the 11th century Mon sanctuary of Vang Sang. Five Buddha statues stand on what is said to be an old elephants' graveyard.

Ban Thalat and Nam Ngum Dam are 90 km from Vientiane on Route 13 to Luang Prabang.

The dam is the pride of Laos and figures prominently in picture postcards. It provides electricity for much of the country and exports to Thailand are the country's second biggest foreign exchange earner. No photographs are allowed at the dam wall or the HEP plant.

The lake is very picturesque and is dotted with hundreds of small islands. Huge semi-submerged tree-trunks pose an additional navigational hazard, as no one had the foresight to log the area before it was flooded. The untapped underwater cache of timber has been spotted by the Thais looking for alternative sources for their lucrative timber trade. Sub aqua chainsaws are used to take out the 'treasure'. For all their skills, it is necessary to bargain hard with boatmen before boarding to cross the lake. Boats from Nam Ngum Dam to Ban Pao Mo on the other side take around 2 hrs. Vang Vieng is 2 hrs ride from the dam. **Accommodation C** *Japanese Bungalows*, a/c, h/w; **D** *Done Dok Khounkham Resort*, on an island in the lake, bathrooms ensuite, basic but clean, restaurant across a small bay, boat tours and fishing trips organized, isolated and quiet; **D** *Floating Hotel*, Nam Ngum village, run by *Nam Ngum Tours*, a/c, h/w; **D** *Nam Ngum Dam Hotel* (on the right after the long bridge on the way to the dam), seafood restaurant in hotel; **E** *Santipab*, on island, rooms with bathrooms, tend to overcharge for the boat trip out there. **Places to eat** ♦♦*Lao Food Raft*, next to *Floating Hotel*, tasty food, friendly staff. *Getting there*: turn right at Phone Hong at the strategically-placed concrete post in the middle of the road. Then head left to the village of Ban Thalat – where the market is worth a browse – then right across the narrow bridge to the dam, about 4 km up the road. There is an alternative route through much prettier countryside on Route 10 out of Vientiane, across the Nam Ngum by ferry. Turn right at the end of the road for the dam. Buses and saamlors leave every 2 hrs from the Morning Market to Ban Thalat, 3 hrs (3,500 kip), and then a taxi on to Nam Ngum (400 kip). By taxi (US$30).

Vang Vieng is about 150 km N on the road to Luang Prabang (Route 13). The area is particularly picturesque, with its limestone caves and waterfalls, the caves are renowned in local mythology. The area is inhabited by the Hmong and Yao tribes. The best cave goes right under the mountain and is fed by a natural spring, perfect for an early morning swim (bring a waterproof torch). Most visitors either pay at the *Vang Vieng Resort* to swim in the pools (and into the caves) although it is possible to wade across the river (during the dry season) and arrive at them from a different point. **Accommodation D** *Vang Vieng Resort*, a new resort close to the caves, T/F 214743, bar and noodle restaurant, some chalets with bathrooms, the resort has control of Tham Chang, the cave, and have erected concrete steps and put lights inside, it's lost its natural beauty and visitors are charged to get into the resort, get into the cave, to take pictures etc; **E** *Saynamsong*, on the main square, by the market; **F** *Phou Bane*, close to the market and the bus station, restaurant (good), very friendly, convenient and manager speaks perfect French, nice garden to sit in, rec; **F** *Phabeng*, behind the Post Office; **F** *Siripanga*, nr the bus station, better value than *Phou Bane* as all rooms have clean bathroom attached, but not such a good atmosphere. *Getting there*: buses leave from the morning market 0630 and 1330, the road is new and in good condition, 4 hrs (1,500 kip). The road onto Luang Prabang from Vang Vieng is under construction. It is possible in the dry season, but still difficult in the rainy season.

Festivals

Oct: *Freedom of the French Day* (12th: public holiday) see page 422. *Boun Souang Heua* (Water Festival and boat races), full moon, end of Buddhist Lent. A beautiful event, with candles in all the homes and the landing of thousands of banana-leaf boats holding flowers, tapers and candles, after candle-lit processions around the wats and through the streets to the river. On the second day, boat races take place, with 50 or so men in each boat; they power up the river in perfect unison. An exuberant event, with plenty of merry-making.

Nov: *Boun That Luang* (movable), is celebrated in all of Vientiane's thats – but most of all in That Luang (the national shrine). Pilgrims pay homage to the Buddha, and there is a candlelit procession around the stupa. A week-long carnival surrounds the festival with fireworks, music and dancing.

Tours

The endearingly inefficient *Lao Tourism* (LNT) organizes excursions to Nam Ngum lake and Vientiane sightseeing tours (US$30 for car and guide, cheaper in a group). See also Tour companies & travel agents, page 366.

Local information

● **Accommodation**

Price guide:			
A+	US$100-200	D	US$8-15
A	US$50-100	E	US$4-8
B	US$25-50	F	US$<4
C	US$15-25		

Most hotels are centrally located on Samsenthai and Setthathirat but there are several about 1 km from the centre.

A *Lane Xang*, Thanon Fa Ngoum, T 214100, F 216854, a/c, international restaurant, pool, small suites available on the 3rd flr, payment in US dollars only, Government run, this monstrosity boasts Soviet architecture and interior design, complete with purple carpets, lime-green curtains and orange vinyl chairs, its flashing neon hammer and sickle remained in place long after the Lao People's Revolutionary Party disowned them; **A** *River View*, far W end of Thanon Fa Ngoum, T 216244, F 216232, a/c, international restaurant, more expensive rooms have a view of the Mekong, not central, no singles; **A** *Royal*, Lane Xang Ave, T 214455, F 214454, a/c, restaurant, brand new hotel; **A** *The Belvedere*, Thanon Samsenthai, nr the junction with Luang Prabang, T 213570, F 213572, a/c, restaurant, pool, price incl breakfast, but tax is on top, large international style hotel, best in town, gym, tennis court, sauna, Lao massage, disco etc; **A-B** *Tai-pan*, 2-12 François Nguin Rd, T 216906, F 216223, a/c, restaurant, ugly new 3-storey hotel with little charm but efficient service, discounts available for frequent visitors.

B *Ambassador*, Pang Kham, T 215259, F 2944800, a/c, international restaurant, large rooms, lacks atmosphere (an argument over who was paying for the hotel's redevelopment has meant that the jungle is beginning to take over); **B** *Apollo*, 69A Thanon Luang Prabang, T/F 213244, a/c, restaurant with live music every night; **B** *Asian Pavilion* (formerly *Vieng Vilai*), 379 Samsenthai, T 213430, F 213432, a/c, restaurant, standard rooms; **B** *Lani I*, 281 Setthathirat (set back from the road next to Wat Hay Sok), T/F 215639, a/c, restaurant (excellent Chinese, cooked by Lani's father on request), outside bar, clean and well run, set in a quiet garden, telex and fax service, used by long-term visitors, rec; **B** *Lao Paris*, 100 Thanon Samsenthai, T 216382, some a/c, private bathrooms with hot water; **B** *Samsenthai*, 15 Thanon Manthathurath, T 212116, some a/c, some private bathrooms, some h/w, bright, spacious rooms with polished wood floors, centrally located; **B** *Saysava*, Chao Anou, T 213580, a/c, restaurant, not as smart as it looks from the outside, *Victory disco* opens 2100-2330; **B** *Villa That Luang*, Thanon That Luang, a/c, restaurant with slow service (*Snake Bar* [sic]), large, clean rooms, friendly owners, but not central, hires out bikes; **B-C** *Anou*, 1-3 Heng Boun, T 213630, F 213635, some a/c, restaurant, impersonal; **B-E** *Ekkalath Metropole*, Samsenthai (not far from That Dam), T 213420, F 215628, some a/c, restaurant (European and Vietnamese), some up-market rooms with breakfast incl, lower priced rooms in guesthouse attached to hotel – very basic with no hot water but fairly clean, popular budget hotel.

C *Lani II*, 268 Thanon Saylom (set back from the road, entrance opp T junction), T 213022, some a/c, some private bathrooms, restaurant, clean, quiet and friendly, nice garden, just as good as *Lani I*, rec; **C** *Nong Douang*, 48 Thanon Nong Douang, T 5334, a/c, restaurant, Laotians returning from France/US often stay here; **C** *Settha*, 80/4 Samsenthai, T 213241, F 215995, a/c, private bathrooms and hot water; **C** *Sisavad*, 93/12 Sisavad Neua, T 217004, some a/c, restaurant, pool, ensuite bathrooms, big bedrooms, newly built guesthouse, N of town, nr the Monument, rooms around a courtyard, very friendly and helpful; **C** *Syri*, Quartier Chao Anou (nr the stadium), T 212682, F 217251, a/c, restaurant for breakfast and drinks only, some ensuite bathrooms, very hot water, clean sheets daily, relaxed at-

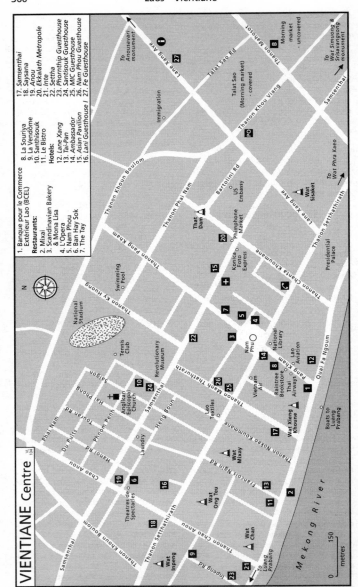

VIENTIANE Centre

1. Banque pour le Commerce Extérieur Lao (BCEL)

Restaurants:
2. Mixai
3. Scandinavian Bakery & Mona Lisa
4. L'Opera
5. Nam Phou
6. Ban Hay Sok
7. The Tay
8. La Souriya
9. La Vendôme
10. Santhisouk
11. Le Bistro

Hotels:
12. Lane Xang
13. Tai-Pan
14. Ambassador
15. Asian Pavilion
16. Lani Guesthouse

17. Samsenthai
18. Saysana
19. Anou
20. Ekkalath Metropole
21. Inte
22. Settha
23. Phonxaythip Guesthouse
24. Santisouk Guesthouse
25. MIC Guesthouse
26. Nam Phou Guesthouse
27. Fe Guesthouse

mosphere, family run and very friendly, bikes for hire, popular with backpackers; rec; **C** *Vientiane*, Thanon Luang Prabang, T 212929, some a/c, restaurant (downstairs from hotel).

D *Inte*, Fa Ngoum/Chou Anou, T 2881, a/c, restaurant, Thai owned hotel, recently upgraded, big rooms, excellent value for money; **D** *Mixai House*, 30/1 Fa Ngoum, T 216213, a/c, restaurant, 2 rm overlook the river, rest a bit dark and pokey, shared bath (same owners as the *Mekong*); **D** *Phornthip*, 72 Inpeng Rd, T 217239, some a/c, a quiet, family-run, very friendly guesthouse which is almost always full (pre-booking is rec), there's a courtyard at the back, but no garden, the grand-daughter tends to the business, whilst granny greets visitors and watches television, rec; **D** *Santisouk*, 77/79 Nokeo Koummane (above Santisouk restaurant), T 215303, a/c, some ensuite bathrooms and hot water, restaurant, laundry service available, clean; **D** *Villa Santiphab*, Thanon Nong Douang, a/c, restaurant (order meals, no menu), friendly and small hotel in an old villa, 1 room with attached bathroom (**C**), rec; **D-E** *Hua Guo*, 359 Samsenthai, T 216618, some a/c, some private bathrooms and hot water, Chinese guesthouse, bike for rent, bargaining possible; **D-E** *M.I.C. Guesthouse*, 67/11 Manthathurath Rd, fan rooms, some with bathroom attached, good value for money, dingy lobby and stairwell but rooms are fine, very popular with budget travellers; **D-E** *Nam Phou*, 69/5 Thanon Manthathurath, T 214738, some a/c and some ensuite bathrooms, friendly, but dirty.

E *Minister of Information and Culture Guesthouse (M.I.C.)*, 67/11 Thanon Manthathurath, T 212362, some ensuite bathrooms, friendly but very dirty; **E** *Sennesouk*, 100 Thanon Luang Prabang, T 215567, just before *Belvedere Hotel* on airport side, some a/c, some Western bathrooms, restaurant, clean, comfortable, friendly and good value if a little out of town.

Further out B *Vasana House*, Thanon Pouthan, T/F 3311, a/c, h/w, restaurant (Western and Lao), pool, reception room, quiet, garden, cars for hire, well out of town but free bikes for guests, rec.

C *Muang Lao*, Km 4 Thanon Tha Deua, T 2278, a/c, restaurant (Lao and Western), Chinese owned hotel, with good rooms, some with a view of the Mekong but a bit out of town; **C** *Thien Tong*, Sokpaluang, T 313782, F 312125, good food, nice garden, clean rooms with tiled shower room.

F *Fe Guesthouse*, Talat Sao St, the cheapest option in town.

● **Accommodation in wats**

It is possible to stay in monks' quarters at Wat Sisaket, Thanon Lane Xang in exchange for informal English lessons.

● **Places to eat**

> **Price guide:**
> ◆◆◆◆*Over US$10* (7,000 kip); ◆◆◆*US$5-10* (3,500-7,000 kip); ◆◆*US$2-5* (1,400 -3,500 kip); ◆*Under US$2* (1,400 kip)

Lao: ◆◆◆*Dao Vieng*, Heng Boun, large menu, good reputation, popular at lunchtime; ◆◆◆*Lane Xang*, quite smart, traditional live music and beautifully dressed dancers from 2000-2200, entrance on Pang Kham; ◆◆◆*Mekong*, Tha Deua, not far from the Australian Club, in bridge direction, T 312480, good food overlooking the Mekong, drinks on the balcony at sunset, Lao and international cuisine; ◆◆*Just for Fun*, 51/2 Phangkham Rd, opp *Lao Aviation*, good Lao food, excellent vegetarian selection and selection of coffees, teas and soft drinks, a/c with newspapers and comfy chairs (also sells textiles), rec; ◆◆*Mixai* (also known as the 'Russia Club'), Fa Ngoum, wooden restaurant overlooking the Mekong, selection of mainly Lao dishes, some international food, popular with expats, slow, inefficient service, but a good place to watch the sunset; ◆◆*Salongxay Garden* (part of *Lane Xang Hotel*), almost opp the hotel on Fa Ngoum, restaurant and garden bar, Lao specials, incl baked moose, grilled eel, baked turtle, also serves international dishes, see Entertainment; ◆◆*Sathaporn*, Don Palan, good Lao food; ◆◆*Somchan's Pob* (sic), Thanon Luang Prabang (opp Electro Vientiane), beware: menu incl a 'small intestine salad and hormones', international/Lao cuisine, singer/guitarist.

Thai: ◆◆*Pikun Thai Food*, Samsenthai (just beyond Russian Cultural Centre, has ox-cart outside), good food, incl excellent *tom kha kai* (coconut soup), rec; ◆*Saloon*, just off Samsenthai, has a wagon wheel outside and serves cheap, very good Thai dishes and more expensive European ones.

Chinese: there are a number of noodle shops in Chinatown along Khoun Boulom, Heng Boun and Chao Anou which all have a palatable array of vermicelli. ◆◆◆*Ban Hay Sok*, Heng Boun; ◆◆◆*Lani's*, 281 Setthathirat (set back from the road next to Wat Hay Sok), excellent Chinese cuisine, must pre-order; ♦♦♦–♦*Guang Dong*, 54 Chao Anou Rd.

Indian: ♦♦♦*The Taj*, 75/4 Pang Kham, a/c, good food; ♦*Noorjahan*, 370 Samsenthai (opp *Ekkalath Metropole*), delicious and cheap meat and vegetarian, great curries/thalis, rec.

Japanese: *Sakura*, Thanon Luang Prabang, Km 2/Soi 3.

Vietnamese: ♦*Chez Mo*, 352 Samsenthai, next to Vientiane Hospital, T 5766, home cooked food in the back of a pharmacy (Soviet medicine on hand should you suffer indigestion); Vietnamese food is also served in many of the stalls in the 'Chinatown' area.

International: ♦♦♦*La Souriya*, 31/2 Pang Kham (opp *Lao Aviation*), T 215887, French, Vientiane's classiest venue and tastiest menu with fillets and frogs' legs in sauces one dreams about, fine wines, Lao cuisine on request, owned by Hmong princess from Xieng Khouang and named after her son, closed Mon, rec; ♦♦♦*La Vendôme*, Soi Inpeng, as good as any 1* Michelin restaurant in France, a/c inside and an outside terrace, one of the best in town, good ambience, self-service salad bar, rec; ♦♦♦*Le Parasol Blanc*, behind National Assembly building, extensive (and good) French menu and some Lao dishes, incl Mekong fish, reasonably priced; ♦♦♦*L'Opera*, Nam Phon Place, T 215099, a/c Italian restaurant, with delicious ice-cream; ♦♦♦*Mona Lisa*, next door to *Scandinavian Bakery* on Pang Kham; ♦♦♦*Nam Phou*, Nam Phou Place, T 216248, French and Asian, Lao food on request, upmarket, rec; ♦♦♦*Scandinavian Bakery*, 74/1 Pangkham, on the Fountain Circle, delicious pastries, bread, cakes and sandwiches, one table outside and several more inside (a/c), friendly *farang* chef/baker, who made the cake for the President of Tanzania's daughter's wedding (photo to prove it), open 0700-1900 daily, rec; ♦♦♦*Win West*, opp Russian Cultural Centre by traffic lights, between Luang Prabang Rd and Setthathirat, quite good food, live music; ♦♦*Arawan*, 472-480 Samsenthai (not far from Wat Simoung/statue of king), the oldest French restaurant in Vientiane, run by a Corsican, good selection of cheeses ('flomages' [sic]) and wines – but a bit short on atmosphere and clientele, bar; ♦♦*Aspara*, 306 Samsenthai, pleasant interior, reasonable menu incl burger and chips; ♦♦*Inte*, Chao Anou (part of hotel), renowned for its steaks, Lao food on advance order; ♦♦*Santisouk* (also

known as *La Pagode*), entrance to stadium just off Samsenthai, extensive French menu, reasonably priced steaks, rec.

Breakfast: ♦♦*Le Bistro (de Mixay)*, 10/3 François Nguin Rd, opp *Taipan Hotel*, excellent café for breakfast and a full bar, camp decor and manager, but rec. **Home Sweet Home** (rec), *Kiang Kiang Bakery* and pavement cafés offering selection of freshly baked pastries, croissants, pain au chocolat, doughnuts and ice creams – best breakfasts in town, all open every day until 2330. *Scandinavian Bakery*, 74/1 Pangkham, good place for a leisurely breakfast, with English-language newspapers provided. *Venus Colour Photo/Café*, 94 Samsenthai (across from *Ekalath-Metropole*), good cheap breakfasts, passport pics while you wait, 500 kip. **Street food** For a Lao-style start to the day, stalls along Lane Xang Ave, next to Suzuki Bldg, sell the *khao ji pate*, a Lao pâté in French bread or ask for 'roti'.

● **Bars**

The bars of the debauched pre-revolutionary days have faded into legend: *The Purple Porpoise*, the *White Rose* pick-up joint and the renowned *Les Rendezvous des Amis*, run by Madame Lulu, which reportedly offered patrons "warm beer and oral sex". Lulu's ladies, exiled by the Communists to an island in the middle of Nam Ngum Lake, are now drifting back to town, having endured 15 years' re-education. The entertainment is all a little tamer these days, although red lights are going on again in some of the seedier bars along Quai Fa Ngoum. With enterprise culture now back in vogue, new bars are setting up to sell cheap revolutionary beer. Bars and clubs are expected to close at 2330 – but some contravene government regulations.

Champa Lane-Xang, Km 2 Thanon Tha Deua, outside bar overlooking lake – live music inside; *Creperie and Pub Belle-Ile*, 24 Lane Xang, open Thur-Sun 1700-2330 (or later unofficially), good music; *Hotel Inte*, Fa Ngoum/Chou Anou; *Nam Phou Place*, enter through the gate in the hedge around the fountain and drink in Vientiane's version of Piccadilly Circus: the fountain started spouting again in 1991 thanks to a Swedish joint venture (pricey drinks), serves Indian food and snacks; another expat hangout; *Nam Phou*, Nam Phou Place; *Salongxay Garden* (part of *Lane Xang Hotel*), almost opp the hotel on Quai Fa Ngoum, garden bar; *Sunset Bar*, Wattay airport end of Fa Ngoum (W end), open wooden house with good atmosphere, favourite meeting place of expats to watch the sunset; *Samlor Pub*, Setthathirat, opened by a Belgian in Jun 94, good ambience, popular meeting place for expats (good place for coffee after dinner), snooker, darts, pizza-type food; *Tai-pan Hotel*, 2-12 François Nguin Rd, lively bar.

● **Airline offices**
Lao Aviation, 2 Thanon Pang Kham (Fa Ngoum end) T 212051, F 212056, and at Wattay Airport, T 512028, agents for **Air France**, **Thai**, Thanon Pang Kham (in front of Lao Aviation), T 216143. **Vietnam Airlines**, c/o Air Lao Booking, 43/1 Thanon Sethathirat, T/F 216761.

● **Banks & money changers**
The best exchange rates are from the money changers in the Morning Market. **Banque Pour le Commerce Exterieur**, 1 Thanon Pang Kham. **Joint Development Bank**, 33 Thanon Lane Xang (opp market); **Sethathirat Bank**, Sethathirat Rd; **Thai Military Bank**, 69 Thanon Khoun Boulom; **Siam Commercial Bank**, Lane Xang, opp Post Office. **Mini Mart** on Samsenthai also changes cash, as do many shopkeepers in the capital.

● **Embassies & consulates**
Australia, Thanon Nehru, Quartier Phone Xay, T 413610. **NB** The British operate through the Australian Embassy; **Burmah (Myanmar)**, Thanon SokPhaluang, T 312439; **Cambodia**, Thanon Saphantong Neua, T 314952, F 312584; **Czechoslovakia**, Thanon Tha Deua, T 315291; **France**, Thanon Setthathirat, T 215258, F 215255; **Germany**, 26 Thanon Sokphaluang, T 312111; **Indonesia**, Thanon Phon Kheng, T 413910; **Malaysia**, Thanon That Luang, T 414205; **Sweden**, Sok-Phaluang, T 315018, F 315003; **Thailand**, Thanon Phon Kheng, T 214582 (consular section on Thanon That Luang): 2 month Thai visa costs ฿300 (baht only acceptable), it takes 2 days to process; **USA**, Thanon That Dam (off Samsenthai), T 212580, F 212584; **Vietnam**, Thanon That Luang, T 413400.

● **Entertainment**
Bands and discos: many hotels and restaurants have dance nights. *Anou Anou*, Thanon Heng Boun, great live music, friendly, crowded and loud, if you want to guarantee a seat, book a table and beer (draught Lao beer is the cheapest and sells out), most popular in town; *Champa Lane-Xang*, Km 2 Thanon Tha Deua, live band; *Dao Viang*, 40 Thanon Heng Boun, disco above

restaurant; *Feeling Well*, Thanon Dong Palane, live band and disco run by Douane Soharth of *Somchan's Pob* fame, one of the first returnees from France; *Manivan*, Thanon Luang Prabang, smells like an ash tray all day, but there's a live band at night; *Saysana Club*, *Saysana Hotel* (ground flr), Thanon Chao Anou; *Seng Aloune*, 138 Thanon Khou Viang, Lao and disco music; *Viengratry May*, Thanon Lane Xang, the *Stringfellows* of Vientiane with prices to match, where everyone dances the *Lam Wong* (the Lao National Dance), recently refurbished. **Live bands** at *Muang Lao Hotel*, Thanon Tha Deung; *Nokkeo Latrymai*, Thanon Luang Prabang; *Olympia*, *Lane Xang Hotel*, Thanon Fa Ngoum (weekends only); *Santiphab Hotel*, Thanon Luang Prabang; *Savsena Hotel*, Thanon Chou Anou (also disco); *Sukiyaki*, Thanon Fa Ngoum (opp *Lane Xang*), some taped music. **Dance**: *Natasin Lao School*, Thanon Phoun Hang, nr the stadium, traditional dance.

Cinema: Vientiane has a number of **Theatres de Spectacles** which are enthusiastically attended. Before 1975, Bruce Lee was in; now it's Indian idol Shashi Kapoor. Hindi epics are screened nightly. Lao voice-overs are dubbed in live every night by a team of skilled local dubbers who handle up to three voices each and try to put everything in the local context. There are considerable variations in the script from one show to another. During the screening of a western, eg one cowboy inquired of another "Wher've you ridden fram boy?" Reply: "Ah've come fram the Morning Market". For western films, the **Odeon**, off Talat Nong Douane (nr the evening market) shows occasional western films; the **American Embassy**, That Dam, shows a movie every Wed at 1830, US$5. The **French Embassy** run a film club and show movies twice a week, all in French. The **Australia Club**, in Tha Deua shows a film every other Sun evening, US$2.

Saunas and massage: many local wats have herbal saunas, which can be used by prior arrangement. After each session in the sauna one can sit on the verandha and sip tea provided by nuns. Donation in region of 1000 kip would be appreciated. Avoid washing for 4-5 hrs afterwards, to allow the herbs to soak in: *Wat Sokpaluang*, Thanon Sokpaluang (Sisattanak district): massage also available 1600-2200; *Wat Sri Amphorn*, Thanon Sri Amphorn. Good massage on Manthathurath nr Nam Phou, sign obvious.

Traditional dance: *Salongxay Garden Restaurant* provide excellent traditional dancers, accompanied by Lao musicians, while you eat.

Videos: in the bar of the *Ekkalath Metropole*, 1900.

● **Hospitals & medical services**

Clinics: *Australian Clinic*, Australian Embassy, Thanon Nehru, T 413603. *International Clinic*, Mahosat Hospital, Thanon Setthathirat, T 214018.

Hospitals: *Clinique Setthathirat*, next to That Luang. **NB** The Australian embassies have clinics for emergencies.

Pharmacies: Khoun Boulom and Samsenthai.

● **Places of worship**

Churches: *Vientiane Evangelical Church*, Thanon Luang Prabang, on way to airport. Sun services in Lao.

● **Laundry and dry cleaning**

101/3 Samsenthai, 1-day service.

● **Post & telecommunications**

Area code: 021.

International telephone office: Thanon Setthathirat, nr Nam Phou, telephone service open 24 hrs a day, fax service open 0730-2130.

Packers and shippers: *DHL*, Thanon Nokeo Khoummane; *Transpack Lao*, Thanon That Luang Tai; *State Enterprise for Construction and Shipping*, 105 Thanon Khoun. **Couriers**: *DHL*, 52 Nokeo Khoummane Rd.

Post Office: Thanon Khou Viang/Lane Xang (opp market). Poste restante, local and international telephone calls, and fax services (see page 418 for more detailed information).

● **Shopping**

The Chinese quarter is around Chao Anou, Heng Boun and Khoun Boulom and is a lively spot in the evenings.

Books: *Government Bookshop*, Nam Phou Place, mainly Russian literature. Also small selection of maps and books on Laos in the *Lane Xang Hotel* and at *Lani I. Raintree Books*, Thanon Pang Kham, opp Lao Aviation, first English-language bookshop in Laos, selection of coffee-table books, book exchange welcomed, glossy magazines available here. Books can also be found in some of the handicraft shops below.

Galleries: *Kuanming Art Gallery*, 265 Samsenthai; *Lao Gallery*, 108/2 Samsenthai, ex-

---

IKAT PRODUCTION

In the handicraft shops and at the morning market in Vientiane, it is possible to buy distinctively patterned cotton and silk ikat. Ikat is a technique of patterning cloth characteristic of Southeast Asia and is produced from the hills of Burma to the islands of Eastern Indonesia. The word comes from the Malay word *mengikat* which means to bind or tie. Very simply, either the warp or the weft, and in one case both, are tied with material or fibre so that they resist the action of the dye. Hence the technique's name – resist dyeing. By dyeing, retieing and dyeing again through a number of cycles it is possible to build up complex patterns. Ikat is distinguishable by the bleeding of the dye which inevitably occurs no matter how carefully the threads are tied; this gives the finished cloth a blurred finish. The earliest ikats so far found date from the 14th-15th centuries.

To prepare the cloth for dyeing, the warp or weft is strung tight on a frame. Individual threads, or groups of threads are then tied together with fibre and leaves. In some areas wax is then smeared on top to help in the resist process. The main colour is usually dyed first, secondary colours later. With complex patterns (which are done from memory, plans are only required for new designs) and using natural dyes, it may take up to 6 months to produce a piece of cloth. Today, the pressures of the market place mean that it is more likely that cloth is produced using chemical dyes (which need only one short soaking, not multiple long ones as with some natural dyes), and design motifs have generally become larger and less complex. Traditionally, warp ikat used cotton (rarely silk) and weft ikat, silk. Silk in many areas has given way to cotton, and cotton sometimes to synthetic yarns.

hibits local artists; **Champa Gallery**, nr That Dam (next to US Embassy), T 216299, a lovely converted French colonial house, with a gallery downstairs and Lao crafts upstairs.

Handicrafts and antiques: the main shops are along Setthathirat, Samsenthai and Pang Kham, the morning market is certainly worth a browse, with artefacts such as appliquéd panels, decorated hats, decorated sashes, basketwork – both old and new, small and large, wooden tobacco boxes, sticky-rice lidded baskets, axe pillows, embroidered cushions of Laos scenes. **Bouacham** (but no name outside), Setthathirat; **Vanxay Art Handicraft**, Samsenthai, antique and modern materials; **Phattana Handicraft**, 29/3 Pang Kham, mainly materials, some handicrafts; **Somsri Handicrafts**, 20 Setthathirat with a fair selection of crafts and antiques upstairs; **Lao Handicraft**, 72/5 Pang Kham, mainly wood carvings; **Union des Entreprises d'Artisanat Lao Export-Import**, Phon Kheng (about 500m N of the of the Monument Anousavari), large selection of materials from the N and the S; **Namsin Handicrafts**, Setthathirat, wooden objects; **Nang Xuan**, 385 Samsenthai, selection of opium pipes, Lao jewellery and Vietnamese trinkets; **Lao Culture and Antiquity Gallery**, 397 Samsenthai; **Nguyen Ti Selto**, 350 Samsenthai, Lao and Vietnamese antiques; **Phonethip Handicrafts and Ceramics**, 55 Thanon Saylom.

Jewellery: many of the stones sold in Vientiane are of dubious quality, but silver and gold are more reliable. Gold is always 24 carat, so darker in colour and softer, but is good value. Silver is cheap but not necessarily silver, nevertheless, the selection is interesting, with amusing animals, decorated boxes, old coins, ear-rings, silver belts cost 25,000 kip. Silver and gold shops on Samsenthai as well as in the Morning Market.

Markets: Vientiane has several excellent markets: the **Morning market** (Talat Sao) off Lane Xang is the best – although it's busiest in the mornings, it runs all day. It sells imported Thai goods, a good selection of handicrafts (see above), silk and cotton, and upstairs there are jeans (for 5,000 kip) and designer-label sportswear, silverware (incl beautiful silver betel nut holders) and local materials. There is also an interesting produce section (Talat Khua-Din) the other side of the bus stop. **Talat Thong Thum**, on the corner of Thanon Khoun Khum and Thanon Dong Miang, is the largest produce market. It is sometimes known as the evening market as it was built to replace the

evening market in Nong Douang but is busiest in the mornings. **Other markets**: Talat Simuang, Thanon Fa Ngoum/Thanon Simuang, **Talat That Luang**, S of parade ground, **Talat Dong Palane**, Thanon Dong Palane (nr the cinema).

Photographs: Konice Plaza, 110/5 Samsenthai.

Tailors: many Vietnamese tailors along Samsenthai and Pang Kham, about 4200-7000 kip/article depending on complexity, good at copying; **Queen's Beauty Tailor**, by the fountain, is quite good for ladies clothes, but leave at least a week; **Adam Tailleurs**, 72 Thanon Pang Kham; **La Fantasie**, 55 Thanon Pang Kham; **Nova**, 64 Samsenthai; **TV Chuong**, 395 Samsenthai.

Textiles: **Lao Women's Union Projects**, Nam Phou Place, handwoven cottons with traditional designs some made up into cushion covers, bags, dressing gowns; **Kanchana**, Chanta Koummane, handwoven silks and cottons; **The Textile Centre** (Lao Handicraft and Garment Co), Thanon Luang Prabang (next to the statue of the three elephants), pottery and textile, Government run and tends to be the stop off point for tour groups; **Lao Cotton**, on Luang Prabang Rd, out towards Wattay airport, approximately ¼ mile on right from Belvedere Hotel, good range of material, shirts, handbags and housecoats, ask to see the looms; **Lao Textiles** by Carol Cassidy, Nokeo Koummane, silk fabrics, including ikat (see box) with traditional Lao designs, run by an American, from a beautifully renovated colonial property, pricey, but many of the weavings are really museum pieces, dyeing, spinning, designing and weaving all done on premises, rec; **The Art of Silk**, Thanon Mathathurath, opp Samsenthai Hotel; every hue and design available in the Morning Market (Lao silk for 1,800 kip a metre).

Western goods Supermarkets: Phimphone Minimarket, Samsenthai, next to Ekkalath Metropole Hotel, good choice of bread, cheese, wine and other European food, as well as Russian caviar and almost opp on Samsenthai. Simuang Minimarket, Samsenthai, E end of Wat Simuang. Small minimarket next to bakeries on Chao Anou sells western goods; Aranan Charcutene, 472 Samsenthai, French foods; Friendship Intershop, 92/3 Samsenthai, alcohol and soft drinks; Foodland Minimarket, 117 Chou Anou; Lao Phanit Supermaket, 104 Khoun Boulom; Yoghurt

Shop, Thanon Heng Boun, makes fresh yoghurt daily. The vast supermarket in Morning Market building sells everything from pastries to Chinese bicycles.

● **Sports**

Snooker: *Kaonhot*, Thanon Sakarin; three full size snooker tables.

Swimming: *Lane Xang Hotel*, Fa Ngoum, 3,000 kip/day. *Australian Club*, Km 4 Tha Deua Rd, members only (monthly membership available, US$40), western food available, rec.

Tennis: *Vientiane Tennis Club*, next to the stadium. Equipment for hire, 2000 kip/hr, floodlight courts stay open until 2100, bar.

● **Tour companies & travel agents**

14 April (*Sip-sii Mesa*), 29/3 Pang Kham (opp Lao Aviation), T 212979, organizes independent travel to Luang Prabang, but for other provinces you have to take a guide or go on an official tour; *Diethelm Travel*, Nam Phou Square, Setthathirat, T 213833, F 217151; *Inter-Lao Tourism*, Nam Phou Square, Setthathirat, T 214232, F 216306; *Lane Xang Travels and Tour*, Thanon Pang Kham, T 212469, F 215777; *Lao National Tourism (Lanatour)*, 8/2 Lane Xang Ave, T 216671, F 212013; *Lao Travel Service*, 8/3 Lane Xang Ave, T 216603, F 216150; *Mixay Travel Service*, Thanon Fa Ngoum, T 216213, F 215445; *Phatana Khet Phoudoi*, 118/2 Thanon Luang Prabang, T 214673, F 216131; *Raja Tour*, 3 Thanon Heng Boun, T 213632, F 213635; *Sae Khong Guesthouse* (or *Mekhong Guesthouse*), Km 3 Tha Deua, T 215975, the Lao end of the Bangkok-based *Inter-Companion Group*; *SodeTour*, Thanon Fa Ngoum, T 216314, F 216313, upmarket travel agent, not particularly helpful to independent travellers; *That Luang Tour*, 28 Thanon Kham Khong, T 215809, F 215346.

● **Tourist offices**

Lao National Tourism, Thanon Setthathirat/Pang Kham, T 213134/213627; *Vientiane Tourist Office*, Thanon Sithan Nua Building II, Thanon Luang Prabang (ground flr of third Soviet apartment block on way to airport, almost opp the statue of the three elephants), T 214417/214041, F 215448/212892.

● **Useful addresses**

Business Centre: *Burapha*, 14 Thanon Fa Ngoum, T 215071/212604, F 212604. Fax, word processing and international calls.

Immigration: Thanon Phay Nam (morning market end). Open 0730-1130, 1400-1700 Mon, Tues and Thur-Sat, 0730-1130, 1400-1500 Wed.

Police Station: Thanon Setthathirat, in emergency, T 213352.

University: Dong-Dok, 10 km N on Route 10.

● **Transport**

Local Bicycle hire: for those energetic enough in the hot season, bikes are the best way to get around town. Some hotels have bikes for hotel guests only (eg *Lani I*, *Syri* and *Mekong Guesthouse*) but there is a bike hire shop attached to *Kanchana*, the handicraft shop opp the *Ekkalath Hotel*, on Chantha Koummane (the road going up to That Dam), 1,400 kip/day. **MiniMart**, Samsenthai, 1,000 kip/day. **Buses**: round central Vientiane and to outlying areas, most leave from the bus station by the Morning Market. Most trips cost 100 kip. **Car hire**: it is not essential to hire a driver but in the event of an accident it is always the foreigner's fault. **Burapha**, 14 Quai Fa Ngoum, T 216600, from US$21/day (Toyota) to US$37/day (Volvo Estate/Land Cruiser), plus US$5/day for a driver; **Jo Rumble Asia Vehicle Hire**, T 217493, Pandas and 4WD US$45-65; **Lane Xang Hotel**, Fa Ngoum, T 214100, US$6/hr or US$25/day. **Mr Seuth**, T 412785, US$20/day around town; **Samsenthai Hotel**, T 212116, US$20/day without a driver. **Motorbike hire**: Vientiane Motors, Thanon Setthathirat, US$10/day. **Taxis**: mostly found at the Morning Market or around the main hotels, 800 kip for first 2 km, 200 kip/km thereafter. A taxi for a day around Vientiane costs upwards of 7,000 kip; more to hire/day for going outside Vientiane. A taxi to Tha Deua costs 1,200 kip. **Tuk-tuks**: available around the fountain area until 2330.

Air Wattay Airport, 3 km W of town centre. Domestic flights several times a week between Vientiane and Luang Prabang (US$45), Pakse (US$95), Saravan (US$91), Phongsaly (US$87), Savannakhet (US$61) and less regularly to Xieng Khouang (US$37) and Luang Nam Tha (US$80), all prices are one way – double for return price. See timetable on page 416 for full list of destinations. **Transport to town**: no buses (except from the main road outside the airport) only taxis are allowed into the airport (3,000 kip to centre of town). Tuk-tuks can be taken from the main road (1,000 kip).

Road Many roads from Vientiane are under construction at present. **Bus/truck**: most leave from the Morning Market. Two-thirds of the road to Savannakhet is brand new, except the bridges which are still under construction. The last third is a bit of a mess. Daily connections, 12-15 hrs (7,000 kip). **Saamlor**: most leave from Morning Market, also outlying markets.

Sea Boats: to the S leave from S jetty and boats to the N leave from N jetty. The journey upriver to Luang Prabang takes 4½ days, with a change of boat at Paklai (it is possible to shorten the journey by taking a speedboat from Paklai – 5 hrs instead of 2 days and nights). The large boats for the first leg leave Luang Prabang most days, carrying passengers and cargo. Wooden boats are preferable to corrugated iron, as it gets very hot during the day. Take a blanket, warm clothes (cold at night) and *plenty* of food. There are shops in Paklai to restock (and some very basic guesthouses). There do not appear to be any boats travelling the entire distance from Vientiane to Luang Prabang at present.

The stretch from Paklai to Luang Prabang is quite rough and passengers are asked to walk along the bank for the particularly dangerous bits. The **speedboat** option is a noisy one (and for the fearless – everyone wears motorcycle helmets and life jackets). It carries about 6 people and not much baggage, and costs ₡1,000. The slow boat costs 5,200 kip for the first leg and 5,000 kip for the second leg. **NB** The boat navigator will take passports for stamping or just checking, in Vientiane and Paklai, pay about 500 kip if asked. There are buses from the small port to Luang Prabang, but they're not that frequent, 2-3 hrs (1,200 kip), or hitch a ride. Ask for the *Rama Hotel*, as it is well known and is in the centre of town.

LUANG PRABANG

Luang Prabang (in Lao, the 'r' is not pronounced) was established as the royal capital by Fa Ngoum, the first monarch of Lane Xang, the Land of a Million Elephants, in the 14th century. The city had already been the seat of local kingdoms for about 600 years. According to legend, the site of the town was chosen by two resident hermits and was originally known as Xieng Thong – literally 'copper tree city'. Interestingly, the ancient name for Luang Prabang was Chawa, which translates as Java.

Luang Prabang lies 300m above sea-level, on the upper Mekong, at its confluence with the Nam Khan. It is a sleepy town known for its magnificent temples, particularly the former royal Wat Xieng Thong and is dominated by Mt Phousi, which sits in the middle of the town. In the 18th century there were more than 65 wats in the city; many have been destroyed over the years but over 30 remain intact. The continuing splendour and historical significance of the town led UNESCO to designate it a World Heritage Site.

The English travel writer Norman Lewis described Luang Prabang in 1950 as:

"... a tiny Manhattan, but a Manhattan with holy men in yellow robes in its avenues, with pariah dogs, and garlanded pedicats carrying somnolent Frenchmen nowhere, and doves in its sky. Down at the lower tip, where Wall St should have been, was a great congestion of monasteries".

In some respects even more evocative than Lewis, James McCarthy, an otherwise rather plodding recorder of events and sights, wrote of Luang Prabang at the end of the 19th century:

"In a clear afternoon, Luang Prabang stood out distinctly. At evening the pagoda spires and the gilded mouldings of the wats, glancing in the light of the setting sun, added their effect to that of the natural features of the landscape – and caused in me a feeling of irresistible melancholy. Since my visit in Feb 1887, Luang Prabang had passed through much suffering. It had been ravaged by the Haw; its people had been pillaged and murdered or driven from their homes, and the old chief had only been rescued by his sons forcing him to a place of safety. The town seemed doomed to suffer, for within two months last past it had again been burned, and, more recently still, about 500 of its inhabitants had died of an epidemic sickness." Today it is an easy-going provincial city with about 20,000 inhabitants. Even the local attitude to crime and punishment is laid-back, as evidenced by the Nam Pha 'free-range' jail, where prisoners are reportedly reluctant to be released.

History

The town has been successively pillaged, razed and rebuilt over the years – the last invaders were the Chinese Ho in the mid-1880s. Virtually all traces of older

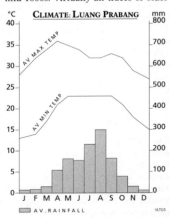

RIVER MONSTERS, REAL AND IMAGINED

It is said that the *pla buk*, the giant catfish of the Mekong, was only described by western science in 1930. That may be so, but the English explorer and surveyor, James McCarthy, goes into considerable detail about the fish in his book *Surveying and exploring in Siam* which was first published in 1900 and draws upon his travels in Siam and Laos between 1881 and 1893. He writes:

"The month of June in Luang Prabang is a very busy one for fishermen. Nearly all the boats are employed on fishing, each paying a large fish for the privilege. Two kinds of large fish, *pla buk* and *pla rerm*, are principally sought after. ... A *pla buk* that I helped to take weighed 130 lbs; it was 7 ft long and 4 ft 2 ins round the body; the tail measured 1 ft 9 ins. The fish had neither scales nor teeth, and was sold for 10 rupees. The roe of this fish is considered a great delicacy. The fish is taken in...Jun, Jul and Aug, when on its upward journey. Returning in Nov, it keeps low in the river, and a few stray ones only are caught."

McCarthy also recounts the story of a mythical river-serpent of the Mekong:

"It lives only at the rapids, and my informant said he had seen it. It is 53 ft long and 20 ins thick. When a man is drowned it snaps off the tuft of hair on the head [men wore their hair in this manner], extracts the teeth, and sucks the blood; and when a body is found thus disfigured, it is known that the man has fallen victim to the nguak, or river serpent, at Luang Prabang."

structures have disappeared as they were built of wood and susceptible to fire and the vagaries of climate.

King Setthathirat moved the capital to Vieng Chan (Vientiane) in 1563 – now the political hub of modern Laos. Luang Prabang's importance diminished in the 18th century, following the death of King Souligna Vongsa and the break-up of Lang Xang, but it remained a royal centre until the Communist takeover in 1975. Despite the demise of the monarchy (King Savang Vatthana and Crown Prince Vongsavang both died in the re-education camps) and years of revolutionary rhetoric on the city tannoy, its dreamy streets have somehow retained the aura of old Lane Xang.

Places of interest

The sights are conveniently close together in Luang Prabang. Most are walkable – the important ones can be covered leisurely within 2 days, but a bike is the best way to get around. When visiting the wats it is helpful to take a guide to obtain entry to all the buildings, which are often locked for security reasons.

The **Royal Palace** (also called the **National Museum**) is right in the centre of the city on the main road, Phothisarath which runs along the promontory. This allowed royal guests ready access from the Mekong. Unlike its former occupants, the palace survived the 1975 revolution and was converted into a museum the following year. The palace is not old: building started in 1904, during the reign of Sisavang Vong, and took 20 years. It replaced a smaller wooden palace on the same site. It is Khmer in style – cruciform in plan and mounted on a small platform of four tiers.

The museum contains a collection of 15th-17th century Buddha statues, including the famous Golden Buddha and artefacts from many of the wats in Luang Prabang such as the Khmer bronze drums from Wat Visoun. The palace itself is modest: its contents, spectacular.

On the right wing of the palace, as you face it, is the kings' private chapel, containing a copy of the **Phra Bang** – the Golden Buddha from whence the city

Luang Prabang

McCarthy, James (1900) *Surveying and exploring in Siam with descriptions of Lao dependencies and of battles against the Chinese Haws,* John Murray: London. The pen and ink sketches are by H. Warrington Smyth, another chronicler of the Kingdom.

derived its name. The Buddha is in the attitude of Abhayamudra or 'dispelling fear' (see page 332). The original image is reportedly kept in a bank vault. It is 90% solid gold, stands 83cm high and weighs around 50 kg. Originally from Ceylon (and said to date from 1st century), the statue was brought to Cambodia in the 11th century and was then taken to Lane Xang by King Fa Ngoum, who had spent some time in the courts of Angkor and married into Khmer royalty. The Phra Bang's arrival heralded the capital's change of name, from Xieng Thong to Nakhon Luang Prabang – 'The great city of the big Buddha'.

In 1563 King Setthathirat took the statue to Lane Xang's new capital at Vientiane. Two hundred years later in 1779 the Thais captured it but it was returned to Laos in 1839 and rediscovered in the palace chapel in 1975. The Phra Bang is revered in Laos as its arrival marked the beginnings of Buddhism in Lane Xang. The **Wat Ho Prabang** – whose untidy foundations are to the right of the entrance to the Royal Palace – was designed to house the statue but it was never completed (presently being restored). The chapel also contains four other Khmer Buddhas, ivories mounted in gold, bronze drums used in religious ceremonies and about 30 smaller Buddha images, surrounding the Prabang, which came from temples all over the city.

The main entrance hall of the palace was used for royal religious ceremonies, when the Supreme Patriarch of Lao Buddhism would oversee proceedings from his gold-painted lotus throne. The room to the immediate right of the entrance was the king's reception room, also called the Ambassadors' Room. It contains French-made busts of the last three monarchs, a model of the royal hearse (which is kept in Wat Xieng Thong) and a mural by French artist Alex de Fontereau, depicting a day in the life of Luang Prabang in the 1930s.

To the left of the entrance hall is the reception room of the king's secretary, and beyond it, the queen's reception room, which together house an eccentric miscellany of state gifts from just about every country except the UK. Of particular note are the moon rock presented to Laos by the US following the Apollo 11 and 17 lunar missions and a rifle inlaid with pearl – a present from Soviet premier Leonid Brezhnev in 1963. Also in this room are portraits of the last king,

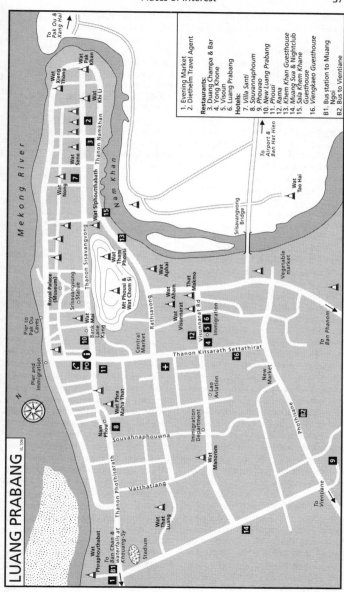

LUANG PRABANG

VL.106

Mekong River

Nam Khan

To Pak Ou &
Xang Hai

Wat Pak Khan

Wat Xieng Thong

Wat Khi Li

Wat Sene

Wat Nong

Thanon Namkhan

Wat Siphoutthabath

To Airport &
Ban Hat Hien

Wat Tao Hai

Srisavangyong Bridge

Wat Tham Phousi

Thanon Sisavangyong

Royal Palace (Museum)

Srisavangyong Statue

Mt Phousi & Wat Chom Si

Wat Aphai

That Makmo

Wat Aham

Wat Ban Mai

Lane Xang

Wat Visounarat

Rathsavong

Visunarat Rd

Immigration

Vegetable market

Pier to Pak Ou Caves

Pier and Immigration

Central Market

Thanon Kitsarath Settathirat

To Ban Phanom

New Market

Lao Aviation

Nam Phou

Wat Phra Maha That

To Vientiane

Immigration Department

Souvahnaphouwna

Wat Manorom

Phothisane

Wat Phraphouthabath

To Ban Chan & waterfalls at Khouang-Sy

Thanon Phothisarath

Vatthatlang

Wat That Luang

Stadium

1. Evening Market
2. Diethelm Travel Agent

Restaurants:
3. Duang Champa & Bar
4. Yong Khone
5. Visoun
6. Luang Prabang

Hotels:
7. Villa Santi
8. Souvannaphoum
9. Phouvao
10. New Luang Prabang
11. Phousi
12. Rama
13. Khem Khan Guesthouse
14. Muang Sua & Nightclub
15. Sala Khem Khane Guesthouse
16. Viengkaeo Guesthouse

B1. Bus station to Muang Ngoi
B2. Bus to Vientiane

Sisavong Vattana, Queen Kham Phouy and Crown Prince Vongsavang, painted by a Soviet artist in 1967.

The coronation room, to the rear of the entrance hall, was decorated between 1960 and 1970 for Sisavong Vatthana's coronation, which was postponed because of the war. The walls are a brilliant red with Japanese glass mosaics embedded in a red lacquer base with gilded woodwork and depict scenes from Lao festivals. To one side of the carved howdah throne, with its gold 3-headed elephant insignia, a huge candle, the same height as the king, stands guard; to the other, a tall pot to hold the crown. To the right of the throne, as you face it, are the ceremonial coronation swords and a glass case containing 15th and 16th century crystal and gold Buddhas, many from inside the 'melon stupa' of Wat Visoun. Because Luang Prabang was constantly raided, many of these religious artefacts were presented to the king for safekeeping long before the palace became a national museum.

In comparison, the royal family's private apartments behind are modestly decorated. They have been left virtually untouched since the day they left for exile in Sam Neua province. The king's library backs onto the coronation room: Savang Vatthana was a well-read monarch, having studied at the *Ecôle de Science Politique* in Paris. Behind the library, built around a small inner-courtyard are the queen's modest bedroom, the king's bedchamber and the royal yellow bathroom with its two regal porcelain thrones standing side by side. The remaining rooms include a small portrait gallery, the children's bedroom, dining room and a corridor containing the royal sedan chair which carried the king to religious ceremonies. Domestic rooms, offices and library are located on the ground floor beneath the state apartments. Admission: permission document from Tourist Office must be obtained to gain entry, US$3. Present this to the guide at the museum at 0830. Most visitors visit in a group.

Further down Phothisarath, next to the Royal Palace is **Wat May**. This temple was officially called Wat Souvanna Phommaram and was the home of the Buddhist leader in Laos, Phra Sangkharath. The royal building, inaugurated in 1788, has a 5-tiered roof and is one of the jewels of Luang Prabang. It took more than 70 years to complete. The façade is particularly interesting: a large golden bas-relief tells the story of Phravet (one of the last reincarnations of the Gautama or historic Buddha) with several village scenes. Inside are pillars similar to those in Wat Xieng Thong and Wat Visoun. The central beam at Wat May is carved with figures from Hindu mythology – the story of the birth of Ravanna and Hanuman. It was the home of the Phra Bang from 1894 until 1947. Admission 200 kip.

Directly opposite the Royal Palace, 328 steps wind up to **Mount Phousi**, a gigantic rock with sheer forested sides, in the centre of town, which affords a splendid panoramic view of Luang Prabang and its surrounding mountains. The Mekong lies to the N and W and the city to the SE. Near the anti-aircraft gun, a sign warns visitors not to point your camera towards the E; this is not for religious reasons, but because beyond the Nam Khan bridge lies Luang Prabang's secret weapon: the airport. Admission at western steps: 500 kip.

Apart from being a magnificent spot from which to watch the sun go down, Mt Phousi is culturally and symbolically very important. In the 18th century it was covered in monasteries and **Wat Chom Si**, built in 1804, still sits on the summit. Its shimmering gold-spired stupa rests on a rectangular base, ornamented by small metal Bodhi trees. Next to the stupa is a little sanctuary, from which a candle-lit procession descends at the Lao New Year festival, *Pimai*, accompanied by effigies of *Nang Sang*

Kham, the guardian of the new year, and *Naga*, protector of the city. The drum, kept in the small *hokong* on the E side of the hill, is used only on ceremonial occasions. The path going down from next to the ack-ack cannon leads to **Wat Tham Phousi**, which is more like a car-port than a temple, but which is home to a rotund Buddha, *Kaccayana* (also called Phra Ka Tiay). At the top of the steps leading out of the wat stand two tall cacti, planted defiantly in the empty shell casings of two large US bombs – the local monks' answer to decades of war.

Down a path to the N of Wat Tham Phousi is **Wat Siphouttabath**, just off the central road running along the promontory, which contains a 3m long footprint of the Buddha. Most of Luang Prabang's important wats are dotted along this main road, Phothisarath.

Wat Sene, further up the promontory, was built in 1718 and was the first sim in Luang Prabang to be constructed in Thai style, with a yellow and red roof, and lacks the subtlety of earlier Lao temples. Sene means 100,000 and the wat was built from a local donation of 100,000 kip. The donor is said to have discovered 'treasure' in the Nam Khan River – quite what this was is unclear.

Further N on Xienthong Rd is **Wat Xieng Thong**, set back from the road, and at the top of a flight of steps leading down to the Mekong. The striking buildings in the tranquil compound are decorated in gold and post-box red, with imposing tiled roofs, intricate carvings, paintings and mosaics – making this the most important royal wat in Luang Prabang. It was built by King Setthathirat in 1559, and is one of the few buildings to have survived the successive Chinese raids. It retained its royal patronage until 1975 and has been embellished and well-cared for over the years – even the crown princess of Thailand, Mahachakri Sirindhorn, has donated funds for its upkeep. The sim is a perfect example of the Luang Prabang-style, with its low, sweeping roofs in complex overlapping sections. The eight central wooden pillars have stencilled motifs in gold and the façade is finely decorated. At the rear of the sim is a mosaic representation of the Thong copper tree in glass inlay. This traditional technique can also be seen on the 17th century doors of Wat Ing Hang, near Savannakhet in S Laos. The interior of Wat Xieng Thong is decorated with rich frescoes and dharma wheels on the ceiling.

Behind the sim are two red *hor song phra* (side chapels): the one on the left houses a rare Lao reclining Buddha in bronze, dating from the construction of the monastery, which was shown at the 1931 Paris Exhibition. The red exterior mosaics on the hor song phra, which relate local tales, were added in 1957 to honour the 2,500th aniversary of the Buddha's birth, death and enlightenment. A small stone chapel with an ornate roof stands to the left of the sim.

The *hor latsalot* (chapel of the funeral chariot) is diagonally across from the sim. The grand 12m-high gilded wooden hearse, with its 7-headed serpent was built for King Sisavang Vong, father of the last sovereign, and carried his urn to the stadium next to Wat That Luang (see below) where he was cremated in 1959. It was built on the chassis of a 6-wheel truck by the sculptor, Thid Tun. The mosaics inside the chapel were never finished but the exterior is decorated with scenes from the Ramakien, sculpted in enormous panels of wood and covered with gold leaf. The *hor kong* at the back of the garden was constructed recently, and near it is the site of the copper tree after which Wat Xieng Thong took its name. Admission 250 kip.

At the far NE end of Phothisarath is **Wat Pak Khan**, which is not particularly noteworthy other than for its scenic location overlooking the confluence of the two rivers. It is sometimes called the Dutch Pagoda as the sculptures on the S door are of figures dressed in 18th and 19th century Dutch costume.

Wat Visunnarat is on the S side of Mt Phousi, next to the *Rama Hotel*. It is a replica of the original wooden building constructed in 1513. Destroyed by marauding Chinese tribes, it was rebuilt in 1898, although it is still very medieval looking. The sim is virtually a museum of religious art, with the numerous Buddha statues it exhibits: most are more than 400 years old and have been donated over the years by locals. It also contains the largest Buddha in the city and old stelae engraved with Pali scriptures (called *hiu chaluk*). The big stupa, commonly known as **That Makmo** (literally meaning "melon stupa"), was built by Queen Visounalat in 1504. It is of Sinhalese influence with a smaller stupa at each corner, representing the four elements. The arch on the NW side of the sim is original and the only piece remaining of the 16th century building.

Wat Aham, next door, was built by a relative of the king in 1823. The two Bodhi trees outside are important spirit shrines.

Wat Phra Maha That, close to *Hotel Phousi* on Phothisarath, is a typical Luang Prabang wat, built in the 1500s and restored at the beginning of this century. The ornamentation of the doors and windows of the sim merit attention with their graceful, golden figures from the *Ramakien*. The pillars, ornamented with nagas, are also in traditional Luang Prabang style. The front of the sim was renovated in 1991.

Behind the evening market at the far NW end of Phothisarath is **Wat Phra Bath** (or Phraphoutthabat Tha Phralak). The original wooden temple on this site dated back to the 17th century, but most of the present structure was built in 1959 by the local Chinese and Vietnamese community. It is worth a visit for its picturesque position above the Mekong. It is renowned for its huge Buddha footprint – '*bath*' is the Pali word for footprint.

Close by, behind the stadium, is **Wat**

That Luang. A royal wat, built in 1818 by King Manthaturat, it contains the ashes of the members of the royal family. Note the bars on the windows of the sim in wood and gold leaf, typical of Luang Prabang. The gold stupa at one end of the compound is the mausoleum of King Sisavang Vong, the last king. He is remembered fondly in Luang Prabang and many offerings are left at his stupa. The stone stupa contains relics of the Buddha and is the site of the Vien Thiene (candlelit) festival in May. There are also some traditional style *kuti*, or monks quarters, with carved windows and low roofs. When James McCarthy visited Wat Luang at the end of the 19th century, he was told of the ceremonies that were performed here on the accession of a new 'chief'. In his book *Surveying and exploring in Siam* (1900) he writes that the "... Kamus assembled and took the oath of allegiance, swearing to die before their chief; shot arrows over the throne to show how they would fight any of its enemies, and holding a lighted candle, prayed that their bodies might be run through with hot iron and that the sky might fall and crush them if they proved unfaithful to their oaths."

South of Wat That Luang (between Thanon Phu Wao and Thanon Kisarath Settathirat) is **Wat Manorom**. It was built by the nobles of Luang Prabang to entomb the ashes of King Samsenthai (1373-1416) and is notable for its large armless bronze Buddha statue, one of the oldest Laotian images of the Buddha, which dates back to 1372 and weighs 2 tonnes.

Wat Phra Phone Phao (Temple of Phao Tree Forest Hill) is 3 km out of town to the E, near Ban Phanom. Looking as though it is made of pure gold from a distance, this wat is rather disappointing close up. The small huts to the right of the entrance are meditation cells. The wat's construction, funded by donations from Lao living abroad and overseas Buddhist Federations, was started in 1959. But the building, modelled on the octagonal Shwedagon Pagoda in Rangoon, was only completed in 1988. The names of donors are inscribed on pillars inside. The inner walls are festooned with gaily painted gory frescoes of macabre allegories by a local equivalent of Hieronymus Bosch. Lurid illustrations depict the fate awaiting murderers, adulterers, thieves, drunks and liars who break the five golden rules of Buddhism. The less grotesque paintings document the life of Buddha and these extend right up to the 5th floor. On the second level, it is possible to duck through a tiny opening to admire the Blue Indra statues and the view of Luang Prabang. Open 0800-1000, 1300-1630 Mon-Sun.

Excursions

The **monasteries on the right bank** of the Mekong are accessible by boat from behind the old palace. **Wat Tham**, opposite Wat Xieng Thong, is a limestone cave temple with stairs and ballustrades cut out of the stone and the 3-tiered pinnacle has obvious Burmese influence. The interior is very dark but is worth exploring (a torch is recommended), as it is stacked with ancient, rotting Buddha images. **Wat Long Khoun**, to the E, was built in two parts. The oldest section is at the back and dates from the 18th century. The beautifully sculpted door was made in 1937. There are delightful frescoes. The kings of Lane Xang are said to have come on 3-day retreats to this spot, to prepare for coronation. Admission 200 kip.

Wat Chom Phet is on top of a small hill above the river – and is best-known as a scenic viewpoint. **Wat Xieng Mene** nearby dates from the last century. About 1 km downstream, in a clearing in the middle of the forest, is the **royal cemetery**. There are sculptures depicting members of the royal family who could not be cremated for religious reasons, eg

women, children who died as infants, and victims of contagious diseases. It is hard to find a local guide willing to take you there as most are terrified of ghosts.

Also on the right bank are two hills – **Phou Thao** and **Phou Nang**, named after the legend of two lovers. Thao Phouthasene and Nang Kang Hi died tragically and romantically only to find themselves transformed into rock and incorporated in the local landscape. The hills are said to look like a man and woman sleeping next to each other. On the edge of the village are several religious sanctuaries. The most important are **Wat Pa Nha Theup**, where many of the royal family and dignitaries were cremated, and **Wat Sangkhalock**, which was often visited by the kings during Pimay. *Getting there*: cross the river by boat (500 kip).

Ban Phanom (Tit Cliff Village) is 3 km E of Luang Prabang. This is a 300-year-old weaving village where shawls (*pha biang*) and sarongs (*pha sin*) are made from silk and cotton. The 100-odd families in Ban Phanom are members of the Lu minority who originated from Yunan in S China. They were traditionally the king's weavers, soldiers and palace servants. Because they have integrated with modern Lao society, they do not take kindly to being referred to as tribals. Although best known for its weavers, the village's main economic activity is rice cultivation. **NB** The women adopt hard-sell tactics at the first sight of a tourist.

Henri Mouhot's tomb is not far from Ban Phanom, between the village and the Nam Khan River. The French explorer Henri Mouhot stumbled across Angkor Wat in 1860 but succumbed to a malarial attack in Luang Prabang on 10 Nov the following year. Resident foreign aid workers spent months searching for the grave before rediscovering it in 1990. The French government has granted an allowance for its upkeep (it is still overgrown). The tomb – which was not constructed until 6 years after his death,

WEAVING

Women can distinguish themselves through excellence in weaving – a good weaver never has much problem finding a husband. Different ethnic groups have different styles of weaving, usually in strong, bold colours with striped patterns. Many of the northern groups embroider cloth, similar to some of the northern Thai tribal fabrics. In the northeast the patterns are intricate and the designs often symbolic. High-quality cloth is produced in the Luang Prabang area because of the previous royal patronage of weavers in this region. Central and southern Laos are best-known for their *mat mi* (ikat – **see page 364**) designs and the use of indigo dyes. The ikat-style silks produced in southern Laos are influenced by Cambodian designs.

in 1867 – is situated at the top of a grassy bank of the Mekong River and getting there is still not easy – the path is narrow and overgrown. It was designed by another French explorer, Doudart de Lagrée and in 1990 the town of Mouhot's birth, Montbéliard, donated a plaque inscribed, simply, 'Proud of Our Son'. *Getting there*: by saamlor to Ban Phanom (400 kip) or bus from the market (200 kip).

Ban Hat Hien is on the airport road, fork right before the terminal and at the end of the road is Luang Prabang's knife-making village. Residents beat scrap metal over hot stoves to make blades and tools. The flames are fanned by bellows, originally made from teak tubes and operated with plungers – but several craftsmen use old 155 mm Howitzer propellants and say their "little presents from the US come in very handy". One shed is stacked with hundreds of old car batteries from which the lead is extracted and poured into moulds for ball bearings and gunshot. From the nearby Nam Kham river, villagers harvest 'seaweed' – which is dried and eaten with sesame. *Khai pehn* from Luang Prabang is sold all over the country. *Getting there*: saamlor (500 kip).

Ban Chan is a few kilometres downstream from Luang Prabang or 4 km on the road beyond the evening market and a short crossing by boat. The village is known for its pottery industry and mostly produces *thongs* (large water storage jars) and salt pots. *Getting there*: by boat from

Luang Prabang (1500 kip) or cycle to Ban and pay a villager to paddle you across the river.

Pak Ou Caves (the lower caves are called Tham Thing, the upper, Tham Phum) are 25 km upstream, in the side of a limestone cliff and opposite the mouth of the Mekong's Nam Ou tributary. This is a popular outing and it is very easy to organize, as almost anyone will take you. Ensure you tell the driver you only want to see the caves and come back, otherwise village visits will be added, and the cost will rise. The two sacred caves, supposedly discovered by King Setthathirat in the 16th century, are studded with thousands of wood and gold Buddha statues; some are thought to be more than 300 years old. Many of the images are in the distinctive attitude of Buddha calling for rain (with arms by his side, palms turned inwards). For years the caves, which locals believe to be the home of guardian spirits, were inhabited by monks. The king visited them every new year and stayed at Pa Ou village, where there is a royal wat with beautiful old murals on the front gable. The caves are one of the main venues for Pimai in Apr, when hundreds make the pilgrimage upriver from Luang Prabang. During the dry season the river shrinks exposing huge sandbanks, which are improbable gold fields. Families camp out on the banks of the Mekong and pan for gold, most of which is sold to Thailand. Bring a torch. *Getting* *there*: boat from the base of Cat Steps, Luang Prabang, 2 hrs upstream, 1 hr down (whole boat – which can accommodate at least 8 people, approx 11,000 kip or US$6 pp). **NB** Take food and water.

Xang Hai is 20 km upstream, on the way to Pak Ou caves. The name of this village literally translates as 'making wine pots' and on the beach villagers brew *lau-lao*, a moonshine whisky. In the rainy season they grow glutinous rice and in the dry season they ferment it in water and yeast. The distilled 'wine' is sold illegally for 300 kip/litre in Luang Prabang. Villagers are delighted to give visitors a tasting session. **NB** Lao for 'Cheers': *Seung Dium*. *Getting there*: see Pak Ou Caves (above).

Waterfalls at Khouang-Sy are 30 km S on a tributary of the Mekong. Entrance fee: 700 kip. *Getting there*: travel agents run tours here, US$50 (incl lunch) or take a tuk-tuk, US$20.

Festivals

Apr: *Pimay* (movable: public holiday) is celebrated in Laos around 14 Apr. This festival has special significance in Luang Prabang, as it was the royal capital; certain traditions are celebrated in the city which are no longer observed in Vientiane. People from all over the province, and even further afield, descend on the city. The newly crowned Miss New Year (*Nang Sang Khan*) is paraded through town, riding on the back of the auspicious animal of the year. **Day 1**: morning market in the main street; sprinkling of the Buddha statues with water; construction of stupas in sand at Mong Khoum, next to Wat Xieng Mene; fireworks in the evening. **Day 2**: procession of the monks; dance of the masks of Pou Nheu Nha Nheu and Sing Kaeo Sing Kham; fireworks and festivities in the evening. **Day 3**: *baci* ceremony; procession of the bronzes; fireworks in the evening. **May**: *Vien Thiene* festival (movable) is the candlelit festival. **Aug**: *Boat races* (movable) celebrated in Luang Pra-

bang in Aug unlike other parts of the country, where they take place in Sep. Boats are raced by the people living in the vicinity of each wat.

Local information

● **Accommodation**
In early 1995 Luang Prabang had just nine hotels and guesthouses with a combined total of 204 rooms. Although new places are sprouting up, facilities are hardly abundant.

A *L'hotel Souvannaphoum*, Thanon Phothisarath, T 212200, a/c, restaurant (see places to eat), hot water, 2 newly restored villas, owned by a syndicate of French and Lao businessmen, set in attractive, large garden; *La Residence* has 20 twin rooms in French colonial style with big balconies, cool wooden floors, marble bathrooms and attractive decor; *La Villa* (more expensive) have two lovely suites but the other rooms are not so good; **A** *Villa Santi* (previously Villa de la Princesse), Rue Sakkdrine, T 212267 (opp Ecole Luang Prabang), restaurant, restored house of Princess Khampha, 10 rm, charming and well run, often booked up.

B *New Luang Prabang*, Sisavangvong Rd, T 212076, a/c, restaurant, 4 flrs and 15 rm in a rather ugly building, this is a new hotel set on a busy road, all rooms have hot water and a balcony, management is keen and friendly, rooms are clean, if a little sterile, restaurant serves Lao, Chinese and western food, boat available for trips; **B** *Phouvao*, Thanon Phuvao, T 7233, a/c, restaurant, pool, on a hillside, slightly out of town.

C *Muang Sua*, Thanon Phouvao, T 212263, some a/c, restaurant, bathrooms attached, new and clean, rather dodgy nightclub here – beware of being ripped off by the girls; **C** *Phousi*, Thanon Kitsarath Setthathirat, some a/c, restaurant, recently upgraded, good central location, bikes for hire US$3/day.

D *Khem Khan*, by the Nam Khan River, restaurant, 3 bamboo bungalows with a/c and hot water, very pleasant owner speaks French; **D** *Rama*, nr Wat Visunnarat, Visunnarat Rd, T 212247, hot water, basic but intending to renovate, range of room sizes, owner speaks good English, rec.

E *Vieng Kaeo*, Thanon Kitsarath Setthathirat (just round the corner from the *Rama*), T 212271. Fan rooms, rather basic, and shared bathrooms downstairs in courtyard (cold water and klong jars only), very comfortable beds with two blankets each. Lovely balcony with plenty of comfy chairs and water on the table all day, good place to recover and meet other travellers, friendly (if rather giggly) management. Also known as the 'Chinese Guesthouse', as it's a big old Chinese house.

● **Places to eat**

Luang Prabang produces a number of culinary specialities which make good souvenirs. They are, however, more likely to be found in the local market than in the restaurants. The most famous is *khai pehn*, dried 'seaweed', mainly from the Nam Khan, which is mixed with sesame and eaten nationwide. *Chao bong* – a mildly hot pimento purée is also popular throughout the country. Other delicacies incl: *phak nam*, a watercress which grows around waterfalls and is commonly used in soups and salads; *mak kham kuan*, tamarind jam and *Mak Nat Kuan*, pineapple jam.

◆◆◆◆–◆◆◆*L'Hotel Souvannaphoum*, Thanon Phothisarath, Lao dishes with French influence, good selection of wine, quite smart restaurant in a beautiful setting – covered verandah looking out over the garden; ◆◆◆*Phousi*, (in *Phousi Hotel*) Thanon Kitsarath Setthathirat, set menu, also bar food; ◆◆◆*Phouvao*, Thanon Phuvao, excellent international meals as well as a Lao menu (tailor food to your own requirements), no set menu – varies each day, but prices are fixed, breakfast 2800 kip, lunch/dinner 4200 kip; ◆◆◆–◆◆*Duang Champa*, Thanon Nam Khan, open 0900-2300, Lao and French food in a trendy restaurant, produce flown in (good range of cheeses), overlooks the Nam Khan River; ◆◆*Luang Prabang*, next to Wat Visunnarat, extensive menu, and an East German cuckoo clock, good vegetarian food, as well as specialities such as deer, spring rolls good here, clean, efficient and friendly, with tasteful decor – no neon lights and plenty of attractive Lao weaving, rec; ◆◆*Villa de la Princesse*, 1st flr, Rue Sakkdrine, traditional Lao and French menu; ◆*Khem Khan Food Garden*, cheap, OK food, good place for a sunset drink; ◆*Visoun*, opp *Rama Hotel*, good Chinese food; ◆*Yong Khoune*, diagonally across from *Rama*, Chinese dishes, delicious breakfasts (hot baguette with real butter and jam), good omelettes and salads, very popular, rec.

● **Bars**

La Villa (*L'Hotel Souvannaphoum*) has a very attractive bar area, with colonial rattan chairs and other lovely decor, dress reasonably smart; *Phousi* (in *Phousi Hotel*), Kitsarath Setthathirat, cheap and simple food; *Rama*, next to Wat Visunnarat, the only live band in town plays until midnight on Fri and Sat – be warned; *Visun Bar*, opp *Rama*, good selection of beer, Chinese and local wines and spirits.

● **Airline offices**

Lao Aviation, nr *Rama Hotel*.

● **Banks & money changers**

Lane Xang Bank, nr Wat May, changes US$ TCs into dollars or kip.

● **Entertainment**

Disco: Occasional disco at *Rama Hotel*.

Sauna: *Red Cross Sauna*, opp Wat Visunnarat, 3,000 kip.

● **Post & telecommunications:**

Area code: 071.

Post Office and Telephone Office: Phothisarath.

● **Shopping**

Antiques and weaving: a couple of shops opp Wat That, eg *Ban Wat That*, lovely old house. *Villa de la Princesse*, Rue Sakkdrine, Laotian artefacts and antiques.

Markets: *Morning market* in concrete market building in the middle of town (see map) where you can buy most Western goods. *Food market*, known as the *evening market*, in front of Wat Phra Bat where one of the former princesses, now used to doing her own shopping as a commoner, regularly shops. There is a good *vegetable market* a bit further out of town on the road to Ban Phanom.

Silver: One of Luang Prabang's traditional crafts is silversmithing. During the Communist era between 1975 and 1989 many silversmiths turned to other occupations, such was the lack of demand. However, with the rise in tourism and the economic reforms demand has increased and many silversmiths have returned to their craft. Most tourists buy their silver – and other crafts – from the main market in Luang Prabang. However, almost none of the pieces on sale here is from the Luang Prabang area – despite what the marketeers might say. Most are made instead in Vientiane and trucked to the royal capital. Expert silversmiths like Thithpeng Maniphone maintain that these Vientiane-made pieces are inferior, and certainly the finer engraving and silverwork does appear ruder. *Thit Peng*, signposted almost opp Wat That, workshop and small shop with jewellery and pots.

Woodcarving: *Art Gallery*, opp Wat Mai, makes coffins as well as traditional woodcarvings which are for sale.

● **Tour companies & travel agents**

Diethelm Travel, Phothisarath; *Lane Xang*, opp *Villa de la Princesse*, runs treks around Luang Prabang. *Luang Prabang Tourism*, Thanon Phothisarath.

● **Tourist offices**

Tourist information on the corner of Thanon Kitsarath Setthathirat and Sisavangvong. Two maps for sale, not very helpful.

● **Useful addresses**

Immigration office: opposite Rama Hotel on Visunnarat Rd. For people arriving by road, passports must be stamped here. Open Mon-Fri 0800-1200, 1400-1630. Visa extension is possible here for 700 kip or US$1/day.

● **Transport**

NB It is important to get passports stamped upon arrival in Luang Prabang, otherwise a fine is incurred upon departure. There are plans to develop the airport with Thai assistance to handle larger aircraft.

Local Bus: buses leave from the market and go to other nearby towns. **Saamlor and tuk-tuk**: lots around town, which can be hired to see the sights or to go to nearby villages. **Bicycles**: can be hired from some hotels, eg *Rama, Phousi*. **Boat**: boats can be hired from the bottom of the steps below the royal palace, but prices should be negotiated first.

Air Daily connections with Vientiane, 40 mins, US$46. Early morning departures are often delayed during the rainy season, as dense cloud makes Luang Prabang airport inoperable until about 1100. Flights to Phonsavanh on Wed and Fri, 0800, 30 mins (US$31), and connections with Ban Houei Xai, Udom Xai, Xieng Khouang and Luang Nam Tha. See timetable on page 416.

Sea Boat: boats downriver to Vientiane leave from below Luang Prabang's Royal Palace and those upriver from above the Palace. The trip to Vientiane takes 1 night/2 days (longer coming upriver). Larger boats only go in the rainy season but try local boatmen as most boats making the journey take passengers even if they are commercial. The price should be negotiated beforehand. Bring enough food and water (see page 366 for more details). There are also boats going upriver to Ban Houei Sai (see page 389).

Road Bus: the bus to Vientiane leaves from near the new market (see map). A truck-bus leaves every 2 days at 0900 and arrives in Vientiane at 0300 (18 hrs travelling, 6,500 kip). Buses to Phonsavanh go via Muang Ngoi, from the bus station on the junction of Thanon Phothisarath and Phuvao. No fixed departure time, but usually it's early morning. 8 hrs (4,000 kip) to Muang Ngoi (accommodation here **F** basic). From here there are pick-ups to Pakxeng and on to Phonsavanh via Muang Xiem. It might be possible to travel from Muang Ngoi to Phonsavanh in one day, if pick-ups (or lifts) are available. If not, there are basic places to stay in both Pakxeng (near the bridge) and in Muang Xiem. The road from Luang Prabang to Phonsavanh is adequate; the journey may seem arduous but the scenery is very rewarding, passing through many hilltribe villages.

X ieng Khouang province has a murky history – this remote area was incorporated into the kingdom of Lane Xang by King Fa Ngoum in the 14th century but was often ruled by the Vietnamese (who called it Tran Ninh) because of its proximity to the border.

Apart from the historic Plain of Jars, Xieng Khouang province is best-known for the pounding it took during the war. Many of the sights are battered monuments to the plateau's violent recent history. Given the cost of the return trip and the fact that the jars themselves aren't that spectacular, some consider the destination oversold. But for those interested in modern military history, it's fascinating, and the countryside – particularly towards the Vietnam frontier – is beautiful.

As the Lao Aviation Y-12 turbo-prop begins its descent towards the plateau, the meaning of the term 'carpet bombing' becomes clear. On the final approach to the main town of **Phonsavanh**, the plane banks low over the cratered paddy fields, affording a T-28 fighter-bomber pilot's view of his target, which in places has been pummelled into little more than a moonscape. Some of the craters are 15m across and 7m deep. During the secret war against the North Vietnamese Army and the Pathet Lao, Xieng Khouang province received some of the heaviest bombing. The Plain of Jars was hit by B-52s returning from bombing runs to Hanoi; excess bombloads were jettisoned before heading back to the US air base at Udon Thani in Thailand.

Tens of thousands of cluster bomb units (CBUs) were dumped on Xieng Khouang province in the 1960s and 1970s – as testified by the scrap metal trade in CBU casings. Each unit was armed with 150 anti-personnel plastic 'pineapple' bomblets, which still regularly kill children and cripple adults. Hundreds of thousands of these bomblets – and their equally lethal cousins, impact mines, which the Lao call *bombis* – remain buried in Xieng Khouang's grassy meadows. One aid worker relates how in the mid-1980s, a specially designed, armour-plated tractor was terminally disabled by *bombis* while attempting to clear them from the fields. Uncle Sam has, however, bequeathed to local people an almost unlimited supply of twisted metal. Bombshells and flare casings can frequently be seen in Xieng Khouang's villages where they are used for everything from cattle troughs and fences, to stilts for houses and water-carriers.

At 1,000m, the plateau area can be cold from Dec to Mar. The chief activity here is cattle rearing, although this has been much reduced by the after-effects of the war. Xieng Khouang also supported tea plantations before the war and many French colonial settlers took to the temperate climate. In the surrounding hills, the Hmong grew opium, which they traded to western pedlars in Xieng Khouang town. Phonsavanh is the main town of the province today, old Xieng Khouang having been flattened, and its small airstrip is a crucial transport link in this mountainous region. The old town of Xieng Khouang – now rebuilt and renamed Muang Khoune – has a population of 10,000 and Phonsavanh 6,000. The whole province has a population of only 170,000, a mix of different ethnic groups, predominantly Hmong.

Phonsavanh

The town offers little of interest other than the daily market, which is busy but rather undistinguished with the usual assortment of cheap Chinese bric-a-brac. The town still resembles a war-zone, with at least two ammunition dumps along the main street.

NB It is cold here from Nov-Mar; several jumpers and a thick jacket are required. Extra blankets can be obtained from *Mouang Phouane Hotel*. Also note that travel agents and airlines tend to refer to Phonsavanh as Xieng Khouang, which leads to a good deal of confusion.

Tours

The companies in town run tours to the Plain of Jars or to Xieng Khouang.

Excursions

Plain of Jars lies 10 km SE of Phonsavanh (see page 382). Further S still is the old city of **Xieng Khouang** (Muang Khoune) (see page 383). To the NE, route 7 runs to **Muang Khani** and the Vietnamese border (see page 384).

Festivals

Jan: *Hmong New Year* (movable) is celebrated in a big way in this area. Festivities centre around the killing of a pig and offering the head to the spirits. Cloth balls, *makoi*, are given by boys to girls they've taken a fancy to. **Dec**: *National Day* (2nd), horse-drawn drag-cart racing festival in Phonsavanh.

Local information
● **Accommodation**

B *Auberge de Plaine de Jarres*, 1 km from centre, on the hill overlooking town, restaurant, own bungalows with living room and fireplace, bathroom with hot water, clean and comfortable, good food, lovely views, the friendly owner speaks Lao, English and French.

D-E *Van Haloun*, some with bathroom, clean and friendly.

E *Dau Khoune*, new and clean, better value than *Van Haloun*; **E** *Dorkhone*, own bathroom, clean and friendly; **E** *Hay Hin*, basic, but toilet paper and soap is provided, very friendly, helpful people, upstairs, there is a nice balcony and a communal sitting area, with tea provided, jeep for hire can arrange trips to see the jars, or to Xieng Khouang, the manager does not speak English but is extremely enthusiastic; **E** *Moung Phouane*, in middle of town, restaurant, toilet and washbasin ensuite, hot water in a thermos flask, breakfast incl, extra blankets available; **E** *Phou Phieng Xieng Khouang*, 1 km E of Phonsavanh on Route 7, restaurant, new hotel, with pleasant views of surrounding hills; **E** *Vinh Thong*, cheaper rooms very small and shared bathrooms are dirty, karaoke bar here.

● **Places to eat**

♦♦♦*Auberge de Plaine de Jarres*, good; ♦♦♦*Muong Phuan*, also nr market, not much better than the *Hay Hin*.

♦♦*Daukham*, 500m past Chinese market, right going out of town, good local restaurant, but it's a long wait (or order food 1 hr in advance).

♦*Hay Hin*, nr market, restaurant, basic; ♦*Phonsavanh Service*, next to the airport on main street, serves whisky and good noodle soup if you can avoid swallowing the flies too; ♦*Sangah*, opp *Van Haloun Hotel*.

● **Banks & money changers**

No exchange, but hotels and shops will change money (the rate is not good).

● **Tour companies & travel agents**

Lane Xang, on road S from the market, very helpful but no English-spoken (other people in neighbouring shops may help interpret – eg the pharmacy); *Sode Tour*; *Hotel Plaine de Jarres* runs tours to San Neua.

● **Useful information**

Electricity available 1830-2130.

● **Useful addresses**

Police station: for entry and exit stamp is 2 km out of town on the road to the airport, in front of the Red Cross Hospital. Open 0700-1200, 1400-1630.

● **Transport**

Local Jeep hire: from *Hay Hin*, US$20-30/day. **Tuk tuk**: 5,000 kip return fare to Plain of Jars. **NB** It is not possible to walk from the airport to the Plain, as there is a military base in between.

Air Tuk tuk to airport, 3,000-5,000 kip, airport tax 300 kip. Daily connections with Vientiane, 40 mins and 2 a week with Luang Prabang.

Road Regular buses and trucks to Muang Kham or Vientiane. The road to Luang Prabang is out of bounds.

Plain of Jars

The 1,000m-high, 1,000 sq km undulating plateau of the Plain of Jars (also known as Plaine de Jarres or Thong Hai Hin) is about 50 km E to W. More than 300 jars survive, mainly scattered on one slope. Most are 1m to 2.5m high, around 1m in diameter and weigh about the same as three small cars. The jars have long presented an archaeological conundrum – leaving generations of theorists nonplussed by how they got there and what they were used for. Local legend relates that King Khoon Chuong and his troops from S China had a major party after their victory over the wicked Chao Angka and had the jars made to brew outrageous quantities of *lau-lao*.

However attractive the alcohol thesis, it is more likely that they are in fact 2,000 year-old stone funeral urns. The larger jars are believed to have been for the local aristocracy and the smaller jars for their minions. Some archaeologists speculate that the cave below the main site was hewn from the rock at about the same time as the jars themselves and that the hole in the roof possibly means the cave was used for cremation or that the jars were made and fired in the cave. But it's all speculation and their origins and function remain a mystery: the stone from which they are hewn doesn't even seem to come from the region. Tools, bronze ornaments, ceramics and other objects have been found in the jars indicating that a civilized society was responsible for them – but no one has a clue which one, as the artefacts bear no relation to those left behind by other ancient Indochinese civilizations. Some of the jars were once covered with round lids.

Over the years a few jars have been stolen and a number have been helicoptered down to Vientiane's Wat Phra Kaeo and the back yard of the Revolutionary Museum. Although it seems extremely improbable, local guides claim that despite four or five B-52 bombing raids every day for 5 years, the jars remained unscathed. During the heavy fighting on the Plain in the early 1970s, the Pathet Lao command set up their headquarters in the 'cave' next to the jars and then posed among the jars for photographs (which can be seen in the Revolutionary Museum in Vientiane).

The Plain occupies an important niche in modern Lao history as it became one of the most strategic battle-grounds of the war. For General Vang Pao's Hmong, it was the hearthstone of their mountain kingdom; for the royalist government and the Americans it was the Armageddon of the Orient; for Hanoi it was their back garden, which had to be secured to protect their rear flank. It was also the Pathet Lao's staging post in their march on the capital.

From the mid-1960s, neutralist forces were encamped on the Plain (dubbed 'the PDJ' after its French acronym). They were supported by Hmong, based at the secret city of Long Tieng, to the SW. US-backed and North Vietnamese-backed forces fought a bitter war of attrition on the PDJ; each time royalist and Hmong forces were defeated on the ground, US air power was called in to pummel from above. In mid-Feb 1970, American Strategic Air Command, on Presidential orders, directed that B-52 Stratofortress bombers should be used over the PDJ for the first time. Capable of silently dumping more than 100 500-pound bombs from 40,000 ft, they had a devastating effect on the towns and villages. Half-a-million tonnes of bombs had been dropped on the PDJ by the end of the war – not including the thousands jettisoned by bombers returning to bases in Thailand from Hanoi. But they had minimal effect on Communist morale. Even if the B-52s had managed to wipe out North Vietnamese and Pathet Lao forces, the US-backed troops were unable to reach, let alone hold, the territory. Hanoi had garrisons of reinforcements waiting in the wings.

On the Plain, the B-52 proved as in-

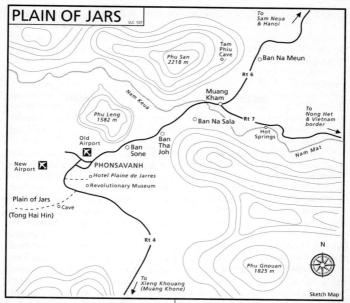

appropriate and ineffective a weapon as it later would on the Ho Chi Minh Trail. As the US bomber command increasingly turned its attention to the Trail, the Pathet Lao quickly seized the upper hand and retook the PDJ. The Communists were beaten back onto the surrounding hills and ridges a few more times by Vang Pao's forces and American bombers, but they kept swarming back. By Mar 1972, the North Vietnamese Army had seven divisions in Laos supporting the Pathet Lao. **Phu Kheng** ('Mountain of Courage' – the hill behind the new airport to the NW), was the scene of some particularly hard fighting. It was here that the royalists, encamped on Phu Kheng, were trapped on two fronts by the Communists. When the Pathet Lao retook Xieng Khouang for the last time in 1973, they consolidated their position and then began their march on Vientiane.

A vast aviation fuel depot was built next to the jars, early in the 1990s, to supply the huge new airbase just to the W. The base, designed by Soviet technicians, will be the new headquarters for the Lao Air Force. The Vientiane base was considered to be strategically unsuitable due to its proximity to Thailand. Admission fee to Plain of Jars: 1,000 kip.

● **Transport** Only accessible by jeep or tuk tuk from Phonsavanh (see local transport, page 381).

Xieng Khouang

The original, old town of Xieng Khouang was destroyed during the war along with the civilization that went with it. The town was founded by Chao Noi Muang and was a stronghold for the Xieng Khouang royal family. In 1832 the Hmong mountain state of Xieng Khouang was annexed by Vietnam and renamed Tran Ninh. The king was marched off to Vietnam and publicly executed in Hué while the population of

Xieng Khouang was forced to wear Vietnamese dress.

Many important temples were built here in the distinctive Xieng Khouang-style but these were completely obliterated by American bombs. The religious architectural style of the province was one of the three main styles of Laos (Luang Prabang and Vientiane styles being the other 2). The town was also the main centre for the French in this area during the colonial period and there are still remnants of French colonial architecture, including the hospital, patched together Lao-style, and the shell of a large house with its old tile floors.

Xieng Khouang was most heavily bombed during 1969 and 1970 when US air power was called in to reverse the success of the Communists' dry season offensive on the Plain of Jars. In his book *The Ravens*, Christopher Robins interviews several former US pilots who describe the annihilation of the town in which 1,500 buildings were razed, together with another 2,000 across the plain. Three towns, he says, "were wiped from the map. By the end of the year [1970] there would not be a building left standing".

The town was rebuilt after 1975 and renamed Muang Khoune, but today it holds little in the way of aesthetic charm, save for its magnificent position surrounded by mountains. Those visiting the wats must, for the most part, be content with piles of 16th century bricks.

There is virtually nothing left of the 16th century **Wat Phia Wat** (far end of town by the road), except the basement and several shrapnel-pocked Buddha statues. Two stupas perch on two hills above the town. **That Chompet** (also 16th century) is quite sizeable, with the centre hollow, making it possible to go inside. This stupa was built around a smaller one. **That Phuane** is smaller, with a square base. The centre of the stupa has been dug out by treasure hunt-

ers. **Wat Si Phoum** (opposite the market below the main road) was also destroyed by the war, but it is slowly being rebuilt by donations and the Buddha statue is being rehoused. There is a small monastery attached to the wat.

● **Transport Air** Connections with Vientiane and Luang Prabang. **Road Bus**: daily bus connections with Phonsavanh (sometimes it's a truck with seats). **NB** The bus leaves Phonsavanh from the station 1-2 km out of town (towards Highway 4), **not** the one by the market; take a tuk-tuk.

Route 7 and Muang Kham

Route 7 heads E from Phonsavanh towards Muang Kham and the border with Vietnam. Attractive rolling hills and grassy meadows in the wet season, but very barren in the dry season, especially where the bomb craters have pockmarked the landscape. 12 km E of Phonsavanh is the village of **Ban Sone** which lays claim to two famous daughters, Baoua Kham and Baoua Xi. These two heroines of the revolution are feted for having shot down a US B-52 with small arms fire. War historians are very sceptical about this claim, but a Lao popular song was nonetheless written about them. The ballad is said to characterize the women of Xieng Khouang, extolling their beauty and courage. On a roadside cutting just before the village lies a large unexploded US bomb which is given a wide berth by passing buses.

For the agriculturally-minded, the drive is an abject lesson in the potentially destructive nature of (some forms of) shifting cultivation. The figures are of dubious accuracy, but some authorities estimate that 100,000 ha of forest is destroyed each year in Laos by shifting cultivation. The government has had some success in reducing this from an estimated 300,000 ha in the 1970s, but it has been difficult to control. The difficulty in opportioning blame is that the Lao authorities would like to blame the minority shifting cultivation – especially the Hmong. Often swidden agriculturalists will cultivate land already logged-over by commercial timber firms – it is easier to cultivate. They are then blamed. Route 7 winds its way down off the plateau along the **Nam Keua**, a fertile area where Hmong villagers grow rice and maize.

About 30 km E of Phonsavanh is the roadside Hmong village of **Ban Tha Joh**. For those wishing to visit a more traditional Hmong village, **Ban Na Sala** is 3 km up the road. Leave your vehicle at Ban Na Sala Mai on the road, and walk S, up a very pleasant valley to the village. It is one of the best places to see the creative architectural and household application of war debris.

Muang Kham, 53 km E of Phonsavanh, is a small trading town in the centre of a large open valley on the route to Vietnam and China. It was devastated during the war, but now has a thriving economy dealing in Vietnamese and Chinese goods. The valley is an important fruit and rice growing area. There's a market early every morning in the centre of town.

More evidence of the dirty war can be seen. The intensity of the US bombing campaign under the command of the late General Curtis Le May was such that entire villages were forced to take refuge in caves. If discovered, fighter bombers were called in to destroy them. In the **Tam Phiu Cave**, overlooking the fertile valley near Muang Kham, 365 villagers from near-by Ban Na Meun built a 2-storey bomb shelter and concealed its entrance with a high stone wall. They lived there for a year, working in their rice fields at night and taking cover during the day from the relentless bombing raids which killed thousands in the area. On the morning of 8 March 1968 2 T-28 fighter-bombers took off from Udon Thani air base in neighbouring Thailand and located the cave mouth which had been exposed on previous sorties. It is likely that the US

forces suspected that the cave contained a Pathet Lao hospital complex.

The first rocket destroyed the wall, the second, fired as the planes swept across the valley, carried the full length of the chamber before exploding. There were no survivors and 11 families were completely wiped out. Local rescuers claim they were unable to enter the cave for 3 days, but eventually the dead were buried in a bomb crater on the hillside next to the cave mouth. Remains of their skulls, bones and teeth still litter the orange earth covering their makeshift grave. The interior of the cave was completely dug up by the rescue parties and relatives looking for their belongings and today there is nothing but rubble inside. It makes for a poignant lesson in military history, and locally it is considered a war memorial. *Getting there*: the cave is to the W of the Muang Kham-Sam Neua road, just after the 183 km post. A taxi from Muang Kham should cost about 2,500 kip. A rough track leads down to an irrigation dam, built in 1981. An unexploded bomb lies embedded in the stream by the dam and the cave mouth is directly above.

Not far from Muang Kham, off the Vietnam road are some **hot springs**, on the Nam Mat River. They are said to have enormous potential for geothermal power but this is hard to believe as they do not appear to be particularly active. Although they are disappointing, some do enjoy sitting in them and locally they are known for their curative properties.

Excursions
Nong Het is approximately 60 km from Muang Kham on the Vietnamese border. It is deep in Hmong country and is an important trading post with Vietnam, which is just a few kilometres down the road.

● **Transport Road** This area is accessible by truck, sometimes bus and sometimes songthaew.

Sam Neua

Hua Phan province is a mountainous region and access is therefore difficult. The limestone peaks are dramatic. The most obvious comparison is Guilin in China. The caves are derelict and there is little to see although historically the area is of significance as it was here, in the limestone caves that pockmark the cliffs, that the liberation movement was first based. The Lao Communist Party was formed in Sam Neua in 1955 and the Pathet Lao had their headquarters in the area as they confronted the Rightist government in Vientiane and the US. American planes tried to dislodge the Communists, but protected in their caves, they survived the onslaught. The population of Hua Phan province is small, only 210,000 and composed mostly of ethnic minorities: *Thai Dam* (Black Thai), *Thai Khao* (White Thai), *Thai Neua* (Northern Thai) and other Lao Seung minorities. This area has been greatly influenced by Vietnam. It is principally an agricultural area but is also known for its weaving.

● **Accommodation** **D-E** *Sam Neua Government Guesthouse*, spartan.

● **Transport Air** Rumours that flights to Sam Neua are to be revived, 2½ hrs. There are 2 flights a week on Lao Aviation between Vientiane and Vieng Xai. **Road Bus/truck**: there are irregular bus connections with the W (Muang Ngoy and Muang Khua), as well as connections with Phonsavanh.

THE NORTH

Sayaboury

Sayaboury is the capital of the five provinces of Laos on the right bank of the Mekong. It is not a spectacular town but an isolated, and therefore traditional, area. The village of **Ban Na La**, an ethnic Lao village, is 15 km from Sayaboury. The houses are indigenous and constructed from wood. The village is known for its weaving of scarves. **Ban Nam Phoui**, a pretty Hmong village, is next to the Mekong and not far from Sayaboury. Because of its proximity to Thailand this province is now being raped by Thai loggers.

● **Transport Air** Connections with Vientiane 3 times a week, 1½ hrs.

Nam Bak

The town of Nam Bak lies on the banks of the Nam Bak. It is a rather beautiful place and is worth an overnight stop, on the route N. The road on to Udom Xai is particularly beautiful, passing Blue Hmong villages.

● **Accommodation F** Big blue house with shutters, set on a hill in the centre of town, (the bus/truck driver will point it out), shared toilets, beautiful views, all Lao and Chinese customers.

● **Places to eat** Noodle shops.

● **Transport** 94 km from Udom Xai. **Road Bus/truck**: regular connections with Luang Prabang; the bus leaves from Luang Prabang when full (0700-0800) from just before the Srisavangvong Bridge, outside Wat Munna, 8 hrs (3,000 kip). The road runs parallel with the river for most of the journey; a dusty ride. From Nam Bak, buses to Udom Xai leave at 0900 from the main street, 3 hrs (2,000 kip), on a good road. From the intersection in Udom Xai, take a pick-up truck to Muang Khua (90 km), 4 hrs (2,000 kip).

Muang Ngoy

Muang Ngoy lies NE of Nam Bak and is a delightful little village on the banks of the Nam Ou, surrounded by limestone peaks. It is possible to swim in the river (women should wear longyis) or walk around the town or up the cliffs.

● **Accommodation F** Very basic hotel by the river, where the boats leave and songthaews stop. The toilet is a hut and you wash in the river, food available.

● **Transport Road Songthaew**: to Nam Bak or Udom Xai. **Truck**: it is possible to travel E from here on Highway I to Ko Kieng and from there either turn S down Highway 7 or continue E to Sam Neua. Trucks are infrequent, so be prepared to wait a long time. **Sea Boat**: to Luang Prabang, 5-6 hrs (3,500 kip).

Udom Xai

It is not worth staying in this rather ugly, hot and dusty town, but it makes a good stop off point N or S. The **market** here is second to none, with a huge variety of fresh goods – honeycombs, limes, lots of *kanom*, papayas etc. A good place to stock up on food and have lunch. The village of **Ban Ting**, behind Udom Xai is interesting to wander through and the wat just the other side of the stream has a ruined monastery.

● **Accommodation E-F** *Sai Xi*, by the market, some rooms with bathroom attached, a basic Chinese establishment with good views of the town and hills beyond from the roof. **F** There are several guesthouses opp the petrol station.

● **Transport Air** Daily connections on Lao Aviation with Luang Prabang. **Road Bus/truck/songthaew**: buses for the S to Muang Houn and Pakbeng leave from the main crossroads, nr the market. Departs at 1400 (2,000 kip). Attractive journey through a valley with paddy fields and many villages, on a good road. There are also connections E to Nam Bak (2,000 kip) and Muang Ngoy (2,500 kip).

Muang Khua

On arrival, officials will want to see your passport. Muang Khua is situated in the southern part of the province of Phonsali, where the Nam Phak converges with the Nam Ou. It's a small town with two 'hotels' and very few restaurants. What it lacks in restaurants, it makes up for in pool tables; very small children show a frightening aptitude. Be prepared to have an instant audience if you try your hand. There is usually a box in which you are expected to make a donation.

There is a 30m wood and iron pedestrian suspension bridge across the Nam Phak to a small village on the other side. Excellent views up and down the river but as the bridge tends to wobble, it is not for the vertiginous.

It is an attractive town to walk about, but be prepared for a group of children to join you on your saunter. The morning market sells fresh vegetables and meat, some Akha women come to the market. The goldsmith just off the main square is usually surrounded by a small group watching his very delicate work. There is a small new wat.

● **Accommodation F** 'Hotel', a white concrete house at the top of the new concrete steps going out of the main square, opp the official's hut, shared bathrooms, no electricity, blankets and mosquito nets provided, no food but adequate.

● **Places to eat**
Baguettes can be bought for a few hours in the morning from an old lady in the market, and again in the evening half way down the steep road to the Nam Ou. Next to this is the only place that sells hot coffee.

● **Transport Road** The road that parallels the river N to Phongsali is very rough and should be avoided. Another road which goes NW is also rough, but is rather beautiful as it goes through the mountains, at least 2 hrs (1,500 kip). From Muang Khua to Udom Xai, buses leave from the main square 0700-0800, 4 hrs (2,000 kip), the road is OK. **Sea Boat**: ferry boats travel N and S, leaving 0700-0800. To Phongsali in the N, approx 5 hrs (5,000 kip); a beautiful journey, especially for birdwatching, with kingfishers everywhere. It is quite shallow in places, and there is also quite a lot of white water. Take a blanket. Boats stop at

Hat Xa, just to the NE of Phongsali. A jeep or truck transports travellers to town, 20 km (1,500 kip).

Phongsali

High up in the mountains, this northern provincial capital provides beautiful views. The Chinese influence is very prominent here, mainly since the new road network linked the town with the border. The town has a very different feel to the southern towns, new Chinese shophouses are under construction and the roofs are mainly corrugated iron. It is possible to buy apples, pears and even potatoes here – the few restaurants along the only tarmaced road sell chips; a welcome relief after days of *feu*. The rice is steamed rather than sticky.

Many paths lead out of town over the hills; the walking is easy and the views are spectacular. It is not possible to hire bikes, tuk-tuks or even ponies; there is little to do other than walk. There are a few pool tables in town and a basketball pitch in the centre of town (play commences around 1700).

● **Accommodation E** *Seang Fa*, new Chinese monstrosity, very nr the *Phou Fa*; **F** *Lucksoon*, through town opp the new 3 storey Chinese shophouses, it is a 2-floored wooden house, with a good restaurant downstairs (groups of men come here to eat and drink every night – it is best to arrange dinner for earlier in the day, ask for chips in advance – they are worth it), 4 rm with 3 beds in each. Shared bathroom, no electricity, small balcony overlooks the street, the best of the 3, despite the mice and rats; **F** *Phou Fa*, up on the hill, overlooking town, good views but it looks and feels like a concentration camp, monkeys are chained up in the courtyard.

● **Post & telecommunications Post Office**: red roofed building at the end of the main road in town (heading towards China), no sign, but it is just past the new shophouses, on the other side of the road.

● **Transport Road Bus**: all buses leave early (0730-0800), from next to the *Lucksoon Hotel*. **Sea Boat**: take a truck to Hat Xa, boats leave in the morning for Muang Khua, 4-5 hrs (5,000 kip). It can be cold and wet – wear waterproofs if you have them.

Muang Houn

This is a new town (although it looks as old as any other), built in 1986 by the government to bring hill people down from the hills, in an attempt to stop them growing opium. There are a lot of Blue Hmong people in town.

● **Accommodation F** A 2-storey concrete house, with a little balcony upstairs, electricity in the evenings until 2200 (the hotel is rather proud of their electricity and there are fairy lights all over the place), no restaurant but good indoor bathroom to share, good value.

● **Places to eat** Two places in town, selling noodles, eggs and sticky rice.

● **Transport Road Bus**: regular buses to Pakbeng, 2 hrs (1,000 kip) from opp the main restaurant past the market.

Pakbeng

This long thin strip of village is perched half way up a hill, with fine views over the Mekong. There is not much to do here but it makes a stop-over point for the journey to Houei Say from Luang Prabang; the village is worth a visit for its traditional atmosphere and the friendliness of the locals. There's a good place to swim in the dry season, just downstream from the port – but be careful as the current is strong. **NB** Important to get stamped in and out at the Police Station (the station is open 0730-1200, 1400-1630 Mon-Fri).

● **Accommodation** Electricity is available from 1800-2300. **E** *Soukchareun Sarika*, a wooden hotel on the steep cliff overlooking the river, basic facilities, but rooms are clean, great toilet and shower area on the edge of the cliff – probably the best view from a bathroom in the whole of Laos; **F** *Phuvieng*, a little further up the road, basic, half wooden, half concrete house with shared bathrooms.

● **Places to eat**
Four or five places opp the hotel serving a good selection of Lao food (and a good range of beers and whiskys).

● **Transport Road Bus/songthaew**: buses leave from the jetty or the hotel for the route northwards to Muang Huan and Udom Xai in the mornings, 5-7 hrs (3,500 kip). There is no road between Pakbeng and Ban Houei Sai. **Sea Boat**: slow boat to Ban Houei Sai leaves at 0800 sharp from the port and takes all day (4,000 kip). Fast boats to Luang Prabang and to Ban Houei Sai.

Ban Houei Xai

Ban Houei Xai is in the heart of the Golden Triangle (see page 340) and is known for its poppy fields. Ban Houei Xai has a large ethnic mix of different minorities. The surrounding regions are very traditional and the way of life here cannot have changed much in the past few millennia. Ban Houei Xai has long been a wealthy town as it was on the heroin route to Chiang Mai in Thailand. Sapphires are also mined in this area. The town now mostly lives on timber exports to Thailand. **Wat Chom Kha Out Manirath**, in the centre of town, is worth a visit if only for its views. There is also a large French fort here called **Fort Carnot** now used by the Lao army (and subsequently out of bounds). **Ban Nam Keun**, a small traditional village on the high plateau not far from the main town, is worth a visit for its natural beauty.

● **Accommodation E** *Bokeo*, outside washing facilites; **E** *Houei Sai*, clean basic rooms with own bathroom, back rooms have a view of the Mekong; **E** *Manirath*, basic, but clean rooms with own bathroom, better than the *Houei Sai*.

F *Mung Da*, a few doors along from *Houei Sai*, Chinese guesthouse with good food.

● **Tour companies & travel agents** *Bokeo Travel*, next to *Bokeo Hotel*. English and French speaking, very helpful company with information on tours to villages and sapphire mines; *Lane Xang Travel* have international telephone service.

● **Transport Air** 6 weekly connections with Luang Prabang, 1½ hrs. **Sea Boat**: daily boats to Pakbeng (half way to Luang Prabang). The slow boat leaves between 0800 and 1100 from jetty 1½ km N of town (a charming journey through lovely scenery – worth sitting on the roof for), 6-7 hrs (US$6). Speedboats are a noisy, unrelaxing alternative, they leave from the jetty S of town, 2-3 hrs (US$12). These boats could be persuaded to continue on to Luang Prabang for a similar price and time.

International connections Boat: to Chiang Khong, Thailand Immigration open 0800-1200, 1400-1630 Mon-Fri (and the same the other end). **NB** It is important to get an exit stamp from the Immigration office before leaving town, otherwise a fine of US$5/day is charged.

THE SOUTH

Thakhek

Founded in 1911-12, Thakhek is also known by its old name, **Khammouane**. The recovery of commercial traffic has brought life back to this small settlement, although Thakhek remains a quiet town, set in beautiful countryside. **Boun Valley** is locally renowned for its beauty. **Wat Sikhotaboun**, 5 km to the S of Thakhek, was built by Chao Anou at the beginning of the 15th century on the banks of the Mekong, and restored in 1956. It contains, among other relics, the sceptre of Chao Sikhot, founder of the old town and son-in-law of Chao Anou. An immense wall surrounds the sanctuary and the viharn was built in 1970 by the last king.

Excursions
Nang Ang Cave and **Chiang Riap Cave** – beautiful drive through limestone scenery.

Local information
● **Accommodation**
D/E *Khammoan Hotel International* (known as *Hotel Inter*), a/c/fan, restaurant (Lao and English), proprietor has good English.

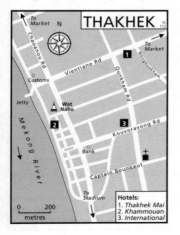

THAKHEK

To Market
N
Charoanou Rd
Vientiane Rd
Customs
Jetty
Wat Nabo
Mekong River
Ounkham Rd
Kouvoravong Rd
Bank
Captain Bounkeut
To Stadium

1
To Market
Xongbatham Rd
2
3

0   200
metres

Hotels:
1. Thakhek Mai
2. Khammouan
3. International

● **Post & telecommunications**
Area code: 051.

● **Transport**
Air Weekly connection with Vientiane, 1 hr. Also flights to 'Km 20'.

Road Bus/truck: connection with Vientiane twice a day, 8 hrs. Daily connection with Savannakhet.

Sea Boat: connections with Vientiane in rainy season, 10 hrs.

Savannakhet

On the banks of the Mekong, Savannakhet (pop 30,000) is an important river port town for trade with Thailand, and is the gateway for tourists to the S. At the starting point of the road to Danang in Vietnam (Route 9), it is very commercial with a large Chinese and Vietnamese population and is one of the only towns in Laos where there is still a sizeable Chinese population – most decided Communism did not sit well with their entrepreneurial instincts, and left. The town is of little interest to the tourist, apart from the colonial architecture (Thanon Khanthabuli, Thanon Simuang) and That Inheng stupa, on the route to Seno.

In 1989 US servicemen arrived in Savannakhet in their search for the remains of men missing in action (MIAs) and the whole town turned out to watch their arrival at the airport. Not realizing that the Lao bear absolutely no animosity towards Americans, the men kept their heads down and refused to disembark until the crowds dispersed. During the war against the Pathet Lao, Savannakhet was the headquarters of the Royal Lao Air Force.

The market just off Thanon Oudomsinh is worth a visit for its variety of products.

Excursions
The 16th century stupa of **That Inheng**

12 km N of Savannakhet, was built at the same time as That Luang in Vientiane. The wat is the site of an annual festival akin to the one celebrated at Wat Phou, Champassak (see below).

The area surrounding Savannakhet is beautiful, especially the village of **Kengkok**, 60 km from Savannakhet (and 3 hrs on a bus).

Ban Houan Hine 70 km S of Savannakhet on the road to Paksong there are some Khmer ruins. *Getting there*: by jeep or by boat.

Xepon is the nearest Hmong village to the Ho Chi Minh trail. *Getting there*: take a bus along Route 9 from Savannakhet, 5-6 hrs.

Trekking to the Ho Chi Minh trail

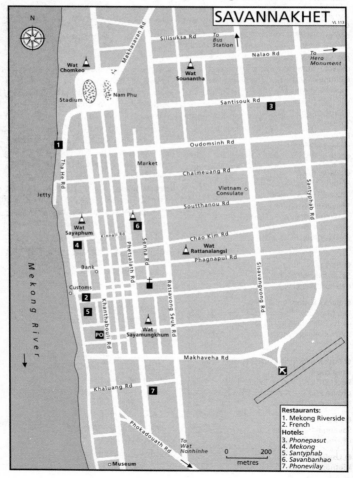

SAVANNAKHET VL 113

Restaurants:
1. Mekong Riverside
2. French
Hotels:
3. Phonepasut
4. Mekong
5. Santyphab
6. Savanbanhao
7. Phonevilay

0   200
metres

from Savannakhet can be done only with a guide, 2-3 days.

Festivals

Feb: *Than Ing Hang* (movable) similar to the festival at Wat Phou, Champassak (see page 403).

Local information
● Accommodation

C *Hoongthip*, Thanon Phetsarath, T 212262, 1 rm with a/c, bath, hot water, TV, very clean, also a tour company, car hire US$50/day, rec; **C** *Phonepasut*, Thanon Sisavang Vong, a/c, h/w, restaurant, pool (700 kip for visitors), best bet.

D-E *Savanbanhao*, Thanon Senna, nr the market, restaurant, some a/c, clean; **D-F** *Phonevilay*, 137 Thanon Phetsarath, T 242284, some a/c, restaurant, some rooms with bathrooms, clean.

E *Santyphab*, 100m from passenger pier to Thailand, basic and dirty.

F Guesthouse at the bus station, basic dorm rooms but useful for catching the Vietnam bus which leaves at 0200.

● Places to eat

Restaurant on riverside serving good food and beer.

✦✦*French/Vietnamese Restaurant*, diagonally opp *Santyphab Hotel*; ✦✦*Mekong Riverside*, Thanon Tha He, on a terrace overlooking Mekong, not to be confused with *Mekong Restaurant*, good food and nice position.

● Bars

Savanbanhao Night Club, across street from hotel of same name, open 2000-2400.

● Banks & money changers

Lao Mai Bank, Thanon Khanthabouli, branch in the Post Office. Exchange counters around the market, any currency accepted, and at pier (bad rate).

● Post & telecommunications

Area code: 041.
Post Office: Thanon Khanthabouli. **Telephone and fax service**: in Post Office, open Mon-Sun 0800-2200.

● Tourist offices

Savannakhet Tourism Co, *Savanbanhao Hotel*, Thanon Senna, T 212733, very helpful.

● Useful addresses

Vietnam Embassy/Consulate: open 0830-1200, 1400-1700, provides Vietnamese visas in 3 to 5 days, 2 photos and US$70 needed.
Immigration office: for exit to Thailand at passenger pier. Open 0830-1130, 1400-1600.

● Transport

Local Tuk-tuk: Khamphone Phachansitthy is an English-speaking man with a tuk-tuk and a motorbike, who will take tourists to local sights. He seems reliable and honest and quotes fair prices.

Air Daily connections with Vientiane. Some of these flights are in Antonovs which fly straight to Vientiane through Thai airspace. Others are on the Chinese-built Y-12s which, as they are not certified airworthy, have to stick to Lao airspace, following the dog-leg of the Mekong, which takes much longer. Also weekly connection with Saravan (US$22).

Road Truck/bus: daily connections with Vientiane, leaves Vientiane 0730, partly rough road, 10-14 hrs (7,000 kip), new road under construction. Daily connections with Pakse 7 hrs (3,200 kip), along a dusty track; be prepared to get very dirty. **NB** There are meant to be 2 buses a day from Savannakhet to Pakse, leaving at 0500 and 0600, but if the bus is full, then it leaves immediately.

Sea Boat: ferries to/from Vientiane once a week in rainy season.

International connections Bus: daily connections with Vietnam. Buses to different destinations leave on different days. Times, destinations and fares are all on a board outside the station office (tickets for sale in office). 5 hr trip to border on a rough track (2,800 kip). Exit fee 1,000 kip. **Boat**: to Thailand through the day, ¢30/850 kip. Exit fee 1,000 kip.

Ho Chi Minh Trail

Despite the herbicides, the mountainous region around the trail is still blanketed in dense tropical forest – much of it remarkably undisturbed. Because of its inaccessibility the forest has not been raided by the timber merchants. Many of the rare birds and animals found in the markets at Saravan are caught in this area. The Vietnam border area was more heavily populated before the war. Many of the tribal groups (mainly Lao Theung) were forced to move onto the Bolovens Plateau because of the heavy

THE HO CHI MINH TRAIL

Throughout the Vietnam War, Hanoi denied the existence of the Ho Chi Minh Trail and for most of it, Washington denied dropping 1,100,000 tonnes of bombs on it – the biggest tonnage dropped per square kilometre in history. The North Vietnamese Army (NVA) used the Trail, really a network of paths (trodden and cycled down by tens of thousands of men) and roads – some 2-lane carriageways, capable of carrying tanks and truck convoys – to ferry food, fuel and ammunition to South Vietnam. Bunkers beneath the trail housed cavernous mechanical workshops and barracks. Washington tried everything in the book to stem the flow of supplies down the trail.

By 1966, 90,000 troops were pouring down the 7,000 kilometres of Trail each year, and 4 years later, 150,000 infiltrators were surging southwards using the jungle network. Between 1966 and 1971, the Trail was used by 630,000 communist troops; over the same period, it was also the conduit for 100,000 tonnes of provisions, 400,000 weapons and 50,000 tonnes of ordnance. It was guarded by 25,000 troops and studded with artillery positions, anti-aircraft emplacements and SAM missiles.

The Trail wound its way through the Annamite mountains, entering Laos at the NE end of the 'Panhandle', and heading SE, with several access points into Cambodia and South Vietnam. The Viet Minh had used it as far back as the 1950s in their war against the French. The US airforce started bombing the Trail as early as 1964 in Operation Steel Tiger and B-52s first hit the Mu Gia pass on the Ho Chi Minh Trail in December 1965.

Carpet-bombing by B-52s was not admitted to by Lao Prime Minister Prince Souvanna Phouma until 1969, by which time the US was dispatching 900 sorties

bombing of the Ho Chi Minh Trail.

It is necessary to hire a Soviet jeep in order to cross the rivers because many of the bridges are broken and rivers are often impassable using other vehicles, especially during the rainy season. The trip can only be made in the dry season, Nov to Mar being the ideal time. The easiest access point to the Ho Chi Minh Trail is from Ban Tapung.

NB Warning nobody should go near the Trail without a guide – unexploded bombs abound.

● **Transport**
Road By hired jeep (around US$200).

Saravan and the Bolovens Plateau

The province is mainly populated by the Lao Loum and Lao Theung (see pages 324-334). The old French town of

Saravan was all but obliterated during the war – the only remaining colonial structure is the white post office. At the T-junction between Saravan's tiny airport and the market there is a bountiful harvest of rusting unexploded bombs, mortars and shells which were cleared from the runway when it was reconstructed. During the war, the town changed hands several times. It was located on a strategic flank of the Ho Chi Minh Trail.

When US airforce pilots bombed in Vietnam, their rules of engagement stated that airstrikes within 500m of a temple were illegal; in Cambodia, the margins were increased to 1 km; in Laos, rules did not apply. Like Xieng Khouang, Saravan had one of the most beautiful temples in the country, **Wat Chom Keoh**, which was destroyed in an air raid in 1968. (Philatelists should note

a day to hit the Trail. It is estimated that it took 300 bombs for each NVA soldier killed on the trail. The B-52 air strikes proved ineffective; they never succeeded in disrupting NVA supply lines for long.

In an effort to monitor NVA troop movements, the US wired the trail with tiny electronic listening devices, infra-red scopes, heat and smell-sensitive sensors, and locational beacons to guide fighter-bombers and B-52s to their target. The NVA carefully removed these devices from unused lengths of trail, urinated on them and retreated, while preparing to shoot down the bombers, which predictably arrived, on cue, from Clarke Field Air Base in the Philippines.

Creative US military technicians hatched countless schemes to disrupt life on the trail: they bombed it with everything from Agent Orange (toxic defoliant) to Budweiser beer (intoxicating inebriant) and dish-washing detergent (to make it into a frothing skid-track). In 1982 Washington finally admitted to dumping 200,000 gallons of chemical herbicides over the Trail between 1965 and 1966. The US also dropped chemical concoctions designed to turn soil into grease and plane-loads of Dragonseed – miniature bomblets which blew the feet off soldiers and the tyres off trucks. Nothing worked.

The US invasion of Cambodia in May 1970 forced Hanoi to further upgrade the Trail. This prompted the Pentagon to finally rubberstamp a ground assault on it, codenamed Lamson 719, in which South Vietnamese and US forces planned to capture the Trail-town of Tchepone, directly E of Savannakhet, and inside Laos. The plans for the invasion were drawn up using maps without topographical features.

In Feb 1971, while traversing the Annamite range in heavy rain, the South Vietnamese forces were routed, despite massive air support. They retreated leaving the Trail intact, 5,000 dead and millions of dollars-worth of equipment behind.

that the wat was commemorated on a postage stamp in the 1950s.) Today all that remains of the wat is two forlorn corner posts, one headless Buddha and a band of hapless monks who sit around on their pile of holy bricks and shattered tiles.

The **daily market** is worth a visit for its variety of flora and fauna.

Excursions around the Bolovens Plateau

The fertile farmland of the Bolovens Plateau has given Saravan province a strong agricultural base, supporting coffee and cardamom plantations. The road from Paksong to Pakse is known as the Coffee Rd.

Coffee was introduced to the area by French settlers in the 1920s and 30s who made a quick exit as the bombing escalated in the 1960s. It is mainly exported via Pakse to Thailand, Singapore and the USSR. Tea grown in this area is for local use. The Bolovens also has the perfect climate for durians, and villages (particularly on the road from Paksong to Pakse) are liberally dotted with durian trees. The fruit is exceptionally rich and creamy and in the peak season, between May and Jul, can be bought from roadside stalls for as little as 200 kip.

Given its fertility, the plateau is now rapidly repopulating and new farms are springing up everywhere. To claim land, settlers need only erect a territorial fence.

During the bombing of the Ho Chi Minh Trail (see box, page 394), to the E, many hilltribes and other ethnic minority groups migrated to the Bolovens, which consequently has become an ethnographic goldmine with more than 12 obscure minority groups, including the Katou, Alak, Ta-Oy, Ya Houne, Ngai and

Suk, living in the area. Most of the tribes are of Indonesian (or Proto-Malay) stock and have very different facial characteristics to the Lao; they are mainly animist (see page 325).

Ba Nom Buah, a beautiful lake near the source of the Xe Dong River, lies 15 km E of Saravan town. It is famed for its crocodiles which move into the river in the dry season (but remain out of sight). *Getting there*: by hired jeep.

About 40 km S from Saravan on the Bolovens Plateau is **Tha Teng**, a village that was levelled during the war. Before that it was the home of Jean Dauplay, the Frenchman who introduced coffee to Laos from Vietnam in 1920. Today the UNDP, in a joint venture with a private sector businessman, has set up a small wild-honey processing factory. Villagers are paid for the combs they collect from jungled hills around Tha Teng. The carefully labelled 'Wild honey from Laos' is exported to European health food shops. There are several ethnic minority villages in the area.

There are two villages, **Ban Khian** and **Tad Soung**, close to Tad Lo. They are an Austro-Indonesian, ethno-linguistic group and their grass-thatched huts with rounded roofs are not at all Lao in style and are distinct from those in neighbouring Lao Theung villages. But most fascinating is the Alaks' seeming obsession with death. The head of each household carves coffins out of hollowed logs for himself and his whole family (even babies), then stacks them, ready for use, under their rice storage huts. This tradition serves as a reminder that life expectancy in these remote rural areas is around 40 (the national average is 48) and infant mortality upwards of 120 per 1,000 live births; the number one killer is malaria.

The Ta-Oy village of **Ban Paleng**, not far from Tha Teng, is also fascinating – more so in Feb/Mar, when the animist Ta-Oy have their annual 3-day sacrificial festival. A water buffalo is donated by each family in the village – built in a circle around the *kuan* (the house of sacrifice). The buffalo have their throats

Around **SAVANNAKHET**

VL 114

To Thakhek
Xeno
Savannakhet
Lamphoy
Lamvay
Phin
Dong
Laobao
VIETNAM
Along Nam
Xenouan
Tangun Tai
Nadou Gnai
Salavan
Sekong River
Se dine
Mekong River
Thangbeng
THAILAND
Tad Lo
Tha Teng
Na Ngam
Sekong
Pakxong

0   30
km

cut and the blood is collected and drunk. The raw meat is divided among the families and surrounding villages are invited to come and feast on it. The head of each family throws a slab of meat into the *lak khai* – a basket hanging from a pole in front of the *kuan* – so that the spirits can partake too. The sacrifice is performed by the village shaman, then dancers throw spears at the buffalo until it dies. The villagers moved from the Vietnam border area to escape the war, yet Ban Paleng was bombed repeatedly: the village is still littered with shells and unexploded bombs. Ban Khan Nam Xiep on the Coffee Rd is also a Ta-Oy village.

Two hrs E of Tha Teng is **Xekhong**, a new town on the Xekhong River; not very interesting but it could be used as a stopping-off point on the way to Attapeu, further S. **Accommodation D** *SE Kong*, bathroom in room, clean, but rather pricey considering there is no electricity.

Attapeu, to the S, has an altogether different character from the Bolovens Plateau as the region is predominantly Lao-Loum rather than tribal. Attapeu is an attractive, leafy town positioned on a bend of the Xekhong River, at the confluence of the Xekaman River. It is an attractive place to walk around, with traditional wooden Lao houses with verandahs and some French buildings. The people are friendly and traffic is limited. Vegetables are grown on the banks of the river Xekhong. A ferry takes passengers across the river for 50 kip. **Accommodation E** *Government Guesthouse*, dusty and basic, with mosquito nets, there is a restaurant next door. *Getting there*: **Boat**: from Xekhong downriver (wet season only). **Truck/bus**: daily connections with Pakse, leaves from the market early morning, 7 hrs (4,000 kip). The road is little more than a track, but it's an experience. From Xekhong, there may be occasional trucks – it's a good journey, with excellent views of the Bolovens Plateau to the W. The road is

rough. A new road is being constructed to link Paksong with Attapeu.

The Katou villages such as **Ban Houei Houne** (on the Saravan-Pakse road) are famous for their weaving of a bright cloth used locally as *pha sin* – or sarongs. This village also has an original contraption to pound rice: on the river below the village are several water-wheels which power the rice pounders. The idea originally came from Sam Neua and was brought to this village by a man who had fought with the Pathet Lao.

The main town on the plateau is **Paksong**, a small market town (176 km from Pakse and 50 km from Tad Lo). It was originally a French agricultural centre, popular during the colonial era for its cooler temperature. Paksong was yet another catastrophe of the war and was virtually destroyed. The area is famous for its fruit and vegetables, even strawberries and raspberries can be cultivated here. **Accommodation E** *Paksong Guesthouse*, two houses in a green field by a river!

Not far from Paksong, 1 km off the road to Pakse, is **Tad Phan**, a dramatic 130m-high waterfall. Take a track to the left off the main road at Ban Pak Kud, Km 38, and at the end of the track a path leads down to a good view point half way down the horse-shoe shaped gorge. This, like many waterfalls in S Laos, is really spectacular. Saravan province also has a large hydroelectric power generating capacity – the Xeset River barrage, next to the largest of the river's three magnificent waterfalls, supplies power to Pakse and some is exported to Thailand.

NB It is not possible to drive across the Bolovens Plateau from Saravan to Attapeu. Even the new road being constructed from Paksong comes off the plateau.

Tours

Elephant trekking: from *Tad Lo Resort*. An excellent way to see the area as there are few roads on the plateau and elephants can reach areas inaccessible by car/jeep. **NB** The river water at Tad Lo is clean, safe and exhilarating to swim in.

Local information
● **Accommodation**

C-D *Tad Lo Resort*, Tad Lo, on the Pakse-Saravan road, 90 km and 2-3 hrs from Pakse, 30 km and 1 hr from Saravan, reception is at the restaurant (not at the bungalows), good restaurant producing plenty of Lao food, chalet-style accommodation built right on top of the waterfalls (Tad Hang, the lower, Tad Lo, the upper waterfall), it is an attractive location (during the wet season) and the accommodation is comfortable – cane rocking chairs on the balconies overlook the cascades on the left bank, elephant rides available, rec. *Getting there*: get off the bus at Ban Houak Houa Set, where a bridge crosses the river Seset. A blue signpost marks the way – 1 km S through a village. Daily buses and trucks ply the Saravan-Pakse route.

D *Saise Guesthouse*, 2 km from bus station (get there by tuk tuk), some a/c, restaurant (limited), some bathrooms, clean rooms, friendly management, who speak English and French and provide good information on the local area.

● **Places to eat**

Around the market area.

● **Banks & money changers**

Phak Tai Bank, nr the market.

● **Post & telecommunications**

Post Office: in modern yellow building opp the market. Local calls only from telephone exchange in same building.

● **Transport**

Air Connections twice a week with Vientiane and via Savannakhet (US$22).

Road Truck/Bus: regular connections with Pakse, 4 hrs (3,500 kip), daily connection with Muang Khong Xedon (and on to Savannakhet), 4 hrs (1,000 kip).

Pakse

The largest town in the S is strategically located at the junction of the Mekong and Xe Dong rivers, and has a population of 25,000. It is at the crossroads of routes to Vietnam and Cambodia and was the centre of the former kingdom, now province, of Champassak. It is a busy commercial town, built by the French early this century as an administrative centre for the S. The town has seen better days but the tatty colonial buildings lend an air of old world charm. Pakse is known locally for its large market. It is the jumping-off point for visiting the old royal capital of Champassak, famed for its pre-Angkor, 7th century Khmer ruins of Wat Phou (see below).

Places of interest

Boun Oum Palace, on the road N towards Paksong, is now a hotel; the town is dominated by what was a half-finished palace of the late Prince Boun Oum of Champassak, the colourful overlord of S Laos and a great collector of objets d'art. It was started in 1968 and was said to have more than a thousand rooms. The Prince was exiled to France, so never managed to complete this monstrosity.

Wat Luang, in the centre of town, is the oldest in Pakse. It was built in 1830, but the sim sports a kitsch pink and yellow exterior complete with gaudy relief work, since it was reconstructed and redecorated in 1990 at the cost of 27 million kip. The hefty doors were carved locally. The compound was originally much larger, but in the 1940s, the chief of Champassak province requisitioned the land to accommodate a new road. To the right of the main entrance stands a stupa containing the remains of Khatai Loun Sasothith, a former Prime Minister who died in 1959. To the right of the sim is the monks' dormitory, which dates from the 1930s; the wooden building behind the sim is the monastic school – the biggest in S Laos – and on the left of the entrance is the library, built in 1943. The compound backs on to the Xe Dong River.

Excursions

Wat Phou and Champassak See page 400.

Muang Khao lies on the opposite bank of the Mekong and was built before Pakse, but has now shrunk to a small village. *Getting there*: hire boats from the pier (2,000 kip return) also a ferry (100 kip).

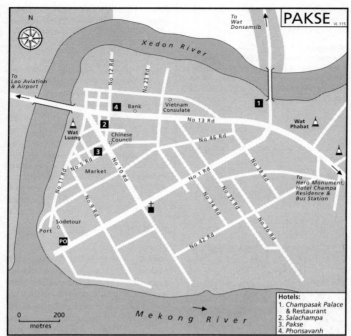

Ban Saphay, the local wat, 11 km N of Pakse, has a splendid statue of Ganesh, Indra and Parvati. Ban Saphay is a silk-weaving village, where they make silk ikat weavings and traditionally-designed *pha-sin*. *Getting there*: by taxi (3,000 kip).

Ban Pha Pho is 27 km from Ban Thang Beng on the road to Attapeu. Pha Pho is known of its working elephants. There are more than 90 in the area used to move hardwoods and to transport rice. *Getting there*: by jeep from Pakse.

Tours

The cruiser, *Croisieres du Mekong*, goes from Pakse to Khong Phapheng Falls (see page 406), 4 day trip (US$600), nicely decorated, good food.

Local information
● **Accommodation**

B *Champassak Palace*, T/F 4200034, a/c, bath-room, restaurant, right on the banks of the Xe Dong River, the rooms are big, but it has an institutional feel to it, due to its size.

C *Champa Residence*, beside stadium. Clean, quite nice; **C** *Salachampa*, old colonial house, with ensuite bathrooms; **C** *Souksam Lane*, some a/c, good restaurant, own bathrooms with hot water, clean small rooms, friendly staff.

D-E *Pakse*, nr the market, some a/c, bathroom attached, not very clean, basic, friendly.

E *Phonsavanh*, restaurant, dirty bathroom, friendly people.

● **Places to eat**

Vietnamese: ✦*Balian*, next door to *Souksam Lane Hotel*, no menu, but highly rec by locals as the best in town; ✦*Sedone*, next door to *Pakse Hotel*, good food.

● **Banks & money changers**

Phak Tai Bank changes TCs. There are money changers in the market. **Bank Pour le Commerce Exterier**, nr the market.

● **Post & telecommunications**
In town.
Area code: 031.

● **Shopping**
The main market, still called the *Morning Market* even though it goes on all day, is in the street parallel to *Pakse Hotel* and runs down to the confluence of the Xe Dong and Mekong rivers.

● **Tourist offices**
Sode Tour, nr the port, T 8056, a mine of information, even if not booking through them; **Lane Xang Travel and Tour Co**, *Souksamran Hotel*.

● **Transport**
Air Daily connections with Vientiane (US$170 return). **NB** We have been told that only kip is accepted here at present.

Road Truck/bus: the bus station is 2 km from the town centre. Tuk tuks there cost 300 kip.

Weft *ikat* textile designs from Pakse, southern Laos (after Fraser-Lu)

Daily connections from Vientiane with Savannakhet, 12 hrs (6,500 kip) and then a local bus on to Pakse, 2 hrs (2,500 kip). Regular connections with Champassak on a bad road, 2-3 hrs (1,000 kip) – stay on the bus for Wat Phou; it stops in a village 2 km from the wat. Connections with Saravan on a good road, 3 hrs (1,500 kip). Connections with Attapeu (**see page 397**) on a bad road.

International connections: It is possible to cross the border into Ubon Ratchathani via Chongmek from here. Obtain a departure permit from Pakse Police Station, stating date you intend to cross the border (100 kip for permit). Take a ferry across the Mekong, there may be taxis or pick-ups by the ferry. if not walk a km or so to a small village where shared taxis start. Very relaxed border control glances at papers and bags. Entry forms in Thailand and a pick-up truck and bus to Ubon Ratchathani.

Champassak and Wat Phou

The agricultural town of Champassak stretches along the right bank of the Mekong for 4 km. Chao Boun Oum began work on yet another rambling palace on the outskirts of Champassak, in 1970, but it was never finished as he was exiled to France in 1975. It is now the official residence of Champassak's squatter community. The Prince's brothers owned the two French-style houses along the main road S. Champassak is the nearest town to the fantastic archaeological sight of Wat Phou.

Excursions

The archaeological site of **Wat Phou** is at the foot of the Phou Passak, 8 km SW of Champassak. With its teetering, weathered masonry, it conforms exactly to the Western ideal of the lost city. The mountain behind Wat Phou is also called **Linga Parvata** as the Hindu Khmers thought it resembled a lingam – albeit a strangely proportioned one. The original Hindu temple complex is thought to have been built on this site 800 years ago because of the sacred phallic mountain symbol of Siva, the Hindu deity.

Today, Linga Parvata provides an imposing backdrop to the crumbling temple ruins, most of which date from the 5th and 6th centuries, making them at least 200 years older than Angkor Wat. At that time the Champassak area was the centre of power on the lower Mekong. The Hindu temple only became a Buddhist shrine in later centuries. The French explorer, Francis Garnier, discovered Wat Phou in 1866 and local villagers told him the temple had been built by "another race". Unfortunately, not much is known about Wat Phou's history. Ruins of a palace have been found next to the Mekong at Cesthapoura (half way between Wat Phou and Champassak – now an army camp) and it is thought the 6th century Chenla capital was based there. The old city wall crosses the main road just before the ravine on the return to Champassak. Archaeologists and historians believe most of the building was the work of the Khmer king, Suryavarman II (1131-1150) who was also responsible for starting work on Angkor Wat, Cambodia. The temple remained important for Khmer kings even after they had moved their capital to Angkor. They continued to appoint priests to serve at Wat Phou and sent money to maintain the temple until the last days of the Angkor Empire.

The king and dignitaries would originally have sat on the platform above the 'tanks' or baray and presided over official ceremonies or watched aquatic games. In 1959 a palace was built on the platform so the king had somewhere to stay during the annual Wat Phou festival (see below). The smaller house was for the king's entourage. A long avenue leads from the platform to the pavilions. The **processional causeway** was probably built by Khmer King Jayavarman VI (1080-1107), and may have been the inspiration for a similar causeway at Angkor Wat. The grand approach would originally have been flanked by statues of lions and mythical animals, but few traces remain.

The sandstone **pavilions**, on either side of the processional causeway, were

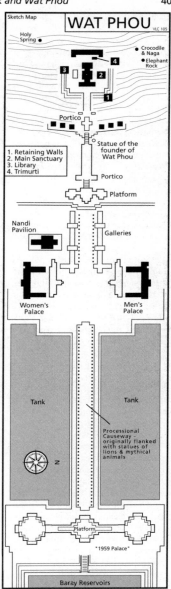

Sketch Map

WAT PHOU VLC 105

- Holy Spring
- Crocodile & Naga
- Elephant Rock

1. Retaining Walls
2. Main Sanctuary
3. Library
4. Trimurti

Portico

Statue of the founder of Wat Phou

Portico

Platform

Nandi Pavilion

Galleries

Women's Palace

Men's Palace

Tank

Tank

Processional Causeway originally flanked with statues of lions & mythical animals

N

Platform

"1959 Palace"

Baray Reservoirs

added after the main temple and thought to date from the 12th century (most likely in the reign of Suryavarman II). Although crumbling, with great slabs of laterite and collapsed lintels lying artistically around, both pavilions are remarkably intact, and as such are the most-photographed part of the temple complex. The pavilions were probably used for segregated worship for pilgrims, one for women (left) and the other for men (right). The porticoes of the two huge buildings face each other. The roofs were thought originally to have been poorly constructed with thin stone slabs on a wooden beam-frame and later replaced by Khmer tiles.

Only the outer walls now remain but there is enough still standing to fire the imagination – the detailed carving around the window frames and porticos is particularly well-preserved. The laterite used to build the complex was brought from Oup Moung, another smaller Khmer temple complex a few kilometres down river (see below), but the carving is in sandstone. The interiors were without partitions but it is thought they used rush matting. The furniture was limited, reliefs only depict low stools and couches. At the rear of the women's pavilion are the remains of a brick construction, believed to have been the queen's quarters. Brick buildings were very costly at that time. The original partitions were probably made of rush matting.

Above the pavilions is a small temple, the **Nandi Pavilion**, with entrances on two sides. It is dedicated to Nandi, the bull (Siva's vehicle) and is a common feature in Hindu temple complexes. There are three chambers, and each would originally have contained statues – but they have been stolen. As the hill begins to rise above the Nandi temple, the remains of six **brick temples** follow the contours, with three on each side of the pathway. All six are completely ruined and their function is unclear. Archaeologists and Khmer historians speculate that they may have

been Trimurti temples. At the bottom of the steps is a **portico** and statue of the founder of Wat Phou, Pranga Khommatha. Many of the laterite paving stones and blocks used to build the steps have holes notched down each side – these would have been used to help transport the slabs to the site and drag them into position.

The **main sanctuary**, 90m up the hillside and orientated E-W, was originally dedicated to Siva. The rear section (behind the Buddha statue) is part of the original 6th century brick building. Sacred spring water was channelled through the hole in the back wall of this section and used to wash the sacred linga. The water was then thrown out, down a shute in the right wall, where it was collected in a receptacle. Pilgrims would then wash in the holy water. The front of the temple is later – probably 8th-9th century – and has some fantastic carving: asparas, dancing Vishnu, Indra on a 3-headed elephant (the former emblem of the kingdom of Lane Xang).

Above the portico of the left entrance there is a carving of Siva, the destroyer, tearing a woman in two. The Hindu temple was converted into a Buddhist shrine (either in the 13th century during the reign of the Khmer king Jayavarman VII or when the Lao conquered the area in the 14th century), and a large Buddha statue now presides over its interior. Local legend has it that the Emerald Buddha – now in Bangkok – is a fake and the authentic one is hidden in Wat Phou; archaeologists are highly sceptical. There is also a modern Buddhist monastery complex on the site.

To the left of the sanctuary is what is thought to be the remains of a **small library**. To the right and to the rear of the main sanctuary is the **Trimurti**, the Hindu statues of Vishnu (right), Siva (central) and Brahma (left). Behind the Trimurti is the **holy spring**, believed by the Khmers to have possessed purificatory powers. Some of the rocks beyond the monks' quarters (to the right of the temple) have been carved with the figures of an elephant, a crocodile and a naga. They are likely to have been associated with human sacrifices carried out at the Wat Phou festival. It is said the sacrifice took place on the crocodile and the blood was given to the naga. Visitors in Feb (during the Wat Phou festival) should note that this practice has now stopped.

The UNDP and UNESCO have agreed to finance and assist the renovation of Wat Phou and to establish a museum to hold some of its more vulnerable artefacts. A team of archaeologists is based at the site. Admission to temple complex: 300 kip (goes towards restoration). Camera: 700 kip; video: 3,000 kip. Open 0800-1630 Mon-Sun. Foodstall on the gate. *Getting there*: catch a local bus from the terminal, tell the driver your destination and he should drop you close to the entrance. Bags can be left with the helpful (English-speaking) staff, whilst exploring the ruins.

Oup Moung is 1 km from Ban Noy on the Mekong or 2 km from Ban Phia Phay. It is accessible from the main road S from Pakse at Ban Thang Beng, Km 30, and can also be reached by jungle trail – it is about a ½-hr walk from the river. In colonial days, Oup Moung was a stopping point for ships travelling up river from Cambodia. But its main treasure is a 6th century temple complex built at roughly the same time as Wat Phou. The site is little more than an assortment of ruins, surrounded by jungle. A 7-headed sandstone naga greets you on arrival from the Mekong.

Like Wat Phou, the main temple is built of laterite and its carvings are in similar style to those of the bigger complex upriver. There are also remains of a second building, more dilapidated and moss-covered making it difficult to speculate about its function. Hidden amongst the jungle are also the remains of 2 baray. Oup Moung is not on the same scale and nowhere near as impressive as Wat Phou but stumbling across an unknown 6th century Khmer temple in the middle of the jungle is nonetheless a worthwhile diversion. With great slabs of laterite protruding from the undergrowth, and ancient sandstone carvings lying around the bushes, there is no doubt that a great deal lies undiscovered. Oup Moung is believed to be where the laterite blocks, used in the construction of Wat Phou, were taken from. Open Mon-Sun 0800-1630, admission 300 kip. Camera: 700 kip, video camera: 3,000 kip. *Getting there*: by boat from Champassak (10,000 kip), or by tuk-tuk, 30 mins (5,000 kip) or by hire car (30,000 kip) or boat from Pakse.

One hour downriver from Pakse is **Hao Pa Kho island**, where Chao Boun Oum had his weekend house, which has lain abandoned since his exile to France.

Festivals
Feb: *Wat Phou festival* (movable) lasts for 3 days with pilgrims coming from far and wide to leave offerings at the temple. In the evening there are competitions – football, boat racing, bull fighting.

Local information
● **Accommodation**
B *Auberge Sala Wat Phou*, clean rooms, most with bathrooms.

D On the Wat Phou side of the village, there is a local government resthouse straddling the road, rooms are basic but spotless, 2 local restaurants close by, early morning buses to Pakse can be hailed from outside the complex.

E *Than Bromlap*, behind the Centre de Archiology (not easy to find).

● **Places to eat**
⁺Champassak Restaurant, by the pier and market.

● **Transport**
Road Bus: Champassak and Wat Phou lie on the W bank of the Mekong River, whilst the main road is on the E bank. The ferry turning is 34 km from Pakse, the bus travels on the vehicle ferry, right into town. There are daily buses from Pakse.

Sea Boat: a ferry from Pakse leaves at 0900, 2 hrs (500 kip).

THE ISLANDS OF THE SOUTH

This area is locally known as *Sip Pan Done* 'The 4,000 Islands'. Don Khong and Don Khone are two of these many islands littered across the Mekong right at the S tip of Laos before the Cambodian border. Half these islands are submerged when the Mekong is in flood. Just before the river enters Cambodia it divides into countless channels. The distance between the most westerly and easterly streams is 14 km – the greatest width of the river in its whole 4,200 km course. The river's volume is swelled by the Kong, San Srepok and Krieng tributaries, which join just upstream. *Pakha* or fresh water dolphins, can sometimes be spotted in this area during Jan and Feb, when they come up river to spawn.

Don Khong

Don Khong is the largest island at 16 km long and 8 km wide, and the main village is **Muang Khong**, a small former French settlement. The island is worth exploring; there is a cyclable path around the perimeter of most of the island, providing great views of the Mekong, and attractive villages along the path. There is a *wat* at Muang Khong (a French-style building) and a large gold Buddha near the centre of town. Plans to build a 5-star hotel and casino on Don Khong are under way. A 2 lane highway will be constructed from here to Pakse and then from Pakse into Thailand at Ubon Ratchathani. Japanese money is going towards the construction of a bridge over the Mekong. What this will do to Don Khong does not bare thinking about.

Excursions

Don Khong Guesthouse organize motorbike trips to Khong Phapheng Falls (10-12,000 kip) and boat trips to Li Phi Falls (15,000 kip).

Local information
● **Accommodation**

B *Sala Done Khong*, to the left of the jetty, a/c, restaurant, spacious rooms, rec rooms on 1st flr with a balcony.

C *Auberge Sala Done Khong*, some rooms have ensuite bathrooms, restaurant is OK, boat for hire (21,000 kip/day).

D *Don Khong Guesthouse*, opp ferry landing, clean rooms, friendly management, bikes for hire (2,000 kip/day).

E *Souk Sun* (bungalows for **B**), organizes trips and has bikes for hire.

● **Places to eat**

There are several small *Lao restaurants nr the jetty. The one on the right, just off the road between the jetty and *Sala Done Khong* is rec. *Don Khong Guesthouse* produces good food.

● **Transport**

Air Lao Aviation have one flight a week between Muang Khong and Pakse.

Road Don Khong is approximately 150 km S of Pakse on Route 13. **Truck/bus**: buses leave daily from Pakse to the S (1,300 kip), tourists need permits to travel by bus (available from travel agents).

Sea Boat: from Ban Hat Xay Khoune it is possible to take a motorboat (1,000 kip) or, for a cheaper crossing, take the car ferries. The ferries, which spend most of their time transporting ancient Russian Zil trucks loaded with Cambodian rosewood across the Mekong, are made from two old US pontoon boats on either side of an ageing diesel river boat with a wooden pallet lying crossways over all 3 (100 kip). There are irregular connections to Champassak and Pakse from the W side of the island. Boats to Don Deth.

The Waterfalls, Don Khone and Don Deth

For those who have travelled on the upper reaches of the Mekong, where, for much of the year it is a slow, lazy river, huge roaring waterfalls might seem rather out of character. The area is well known for its impressive waterfall – Khone Falls. The name Khone is used loosely and there are in fact two impressive cascades in the area: **Li Phi** and **Khong Phapheng Falls** – the latter are the biggest in Southeast Asia. Lt. Francis Garnier was suitably impressed when he ascended the Khon cataract in 1860, his boatmen hauling their vessels "through a labyrinth of rocks, submerged trees, and prostrate trunks still clinging to earth by their many roots".

The best place to take a boat to Li Phi falls is from Ban Nakasong, downriver from Ban Hat Xay Khoune, the crossing point to Don Khong. The boat-trip down the fast-flowing channels between the many islands to **Don Khone** is very picturesque; the islands are covered in coconut palms, flame trees, stands of bamboo, kapok trees and hardwoods. The

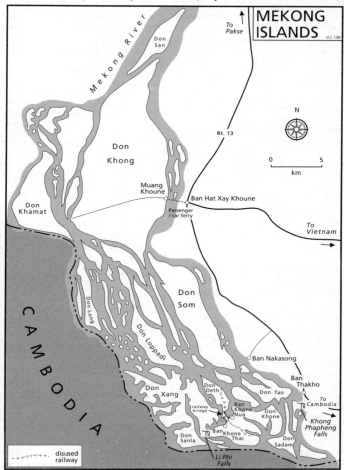

MEKONG ISLANDS
VLC 10B

To Pakse

Mekong River

Don San

Don Khong

Don Khamat

Muang Khoune

Rt. 13

Ban Hat Xay Khoune

Passenger / car ferry

To Vietnam

N

0 5
km

CAMBODIA

Don Long

Don Loppadi

Don Som

Don Xang

Don Deth

Don Tao

Ban Nakasong

Ban Thakho

To Cambodia

railway bridge

Ban Khone Nua

Don Khone

Don Sanla

Ban Khone Thai

Don Sadam

Khong Phapheng Falls

Li Phi Falls

⊢⊢⊢⊢⊣⊣⊣ disused railway

river is riddled with eddies and rapids and it demands a skilled helmsman to negotiate them. In the distance, a few kilometres to the S, are the Khong Hai Mountains which dominate the skyline and delineate the frontier between Laos and Cambodia.

Before putting into **Ban Khone**, the main settlement on Don Khone, **Don Deth** 'port' is on the right, with what remains of its steel rail jetty. In the late 19th and early 20th centuries Don Khone served as an important by-pass around the rapids for French cargo boats sailing upriver from Phnom Penh. Ports were built at the S end (Don Khone) and N end (Don Deth) of this string of rapids and cascades, and were linked by a 5 km stretch of railway track. This railway has the unique distinction of being the only line the French ever built in Laos. A colonial-style customs house still stands in the shadow of the impressive railway bridge at Ban Khone. On the S side of the bridge lie the rusted corpses of the old locomotive and boiler car.

From the bridge, follow the path through Ban Khone Thai and then wind through the paddy fields for 1½ km (20 mins walk) to **Li Phi** (also called **Somphamit** and **Khone Yai**) falls, which are more a succession of raging rapids, crashing through a narrow rocky gorge. In the wet season, when the rice is green, the area is beautiful – in the dry season, it is scorching. From the main vantage point on a jagged, rocky outcrop, the falls aren't that impressive, as a large stretch of the falls are obscured.

About 36 km S, the road down to **Khong Phapheng Falls** from Route 13 forks below Ban Thakho: one branch leads to a vantage point for a fantastic front-on view of the falls, the other leads down to the bank of the Mekong, 200m away, just above the lip of the falls. At this deceptively tranquil spot, the river is gathering momentum before it plunges over the edge. The 'front view' vantage point has a large wooden structure, built up on stilts, overlooking the cascades. When you see the huge volume of white water boiling and surging over the jagged rocks below, it is hard to imagine that there is another 10 km-width of river running through other channels. A perilous path leads down from the viewpoint to the edge of the water. Unsurprisingly, the river is impassable at this juncture, as an 1860s French expedition led by adventurers Doudart de Lagree and Francis Garnier discovered. Garnier wrote:

"There, in the midst of rocks and grassy islets, an enormous sheet of water leaps headlong from a height of 70 ft, to fall back in floods of foam, again to descend from crag to crag, and finally glide away beneath the dense vegetation of the forest. As the river at this point is about one thousand yards in width, the effect is singularly striking."

It was said that a tongue of rock once extended from the lip of the falls, and the noise of Khong Phapheng – literally 'the voice of the Mekong' – crashing over this outcrop could be heard many miles away. The rock apparently broke off during a flood surge, but the cascades still make enough noise to justify their name.

The principal settlement near Khone Falls, and the last Laotian town of any size before the Cambodian border, is Khinnak.

Excursions (from Don Khone)

It is possible to hire a boat for the day, and visit the islands and go fishing (15,000 kip/day).

Local information
● **Accommodation**

E *Sala Don Khone*, Ban Khone Nua, private bathroom, no electricity, good base from which to explore the area.

● **Places to eat**

Ban Nakasong (the jumping off point for Don Khone): there are two small thatched beachside ✦restaurants which serve good chicken noodle soup (*feu*), in the rainy season they move further up the bank.

● **Transport**

Sea Boat: from Ban Nakasong, 25 mins.

INFORMATION FOR VISITORS

CONTENTS

Before travelling

Regulations for tourists and businessmen are in a constant state of flux. The advice given below was checked in Jul 1994, but visitors must be ready for the possibility that new or altered regulations have come into force since then.

Entry requirements

● **Tourist Visas**

For the independent traveller, the visa is best obtained through a travel agent in Bangkok. The cost is US$100. If you know someone in Vientiane, they will be able to obtain a visa for you, which can be collected from the Lao Embassy in Bangkok for US$30. 'Lipco', T 215635 near Wattay Airport (manager Bounneua Douangpasenth) can organize it in 10 days for ₱500 (telex number sent through to Lao Embassy in Bangkok). With some difficulty it is possible to obtain a visa through the Ministry of Foreign Affairs in Vientiane; it is much cheaper at 8,000 kip but takes at least 6 weeks (telex number is then sent through to the Lao Embassy in Bangkok). If you know your entry dates, the easiest method of acquiring a visa may be through your home country Lao Embassy (if there is one).

Visas can also be obtained in Nong Khai, in the NE of Thailand, on the border with Laos for ₱3,000-3,500, but **be warned** – many of the travel agents here claim that they can obtain a visa within 24 hrs, but this is unlikely. One reliable set up for visas is *The Meeting Place*, 117 Soi Chuenchitt, T/F (042) 421223, run by an Australian couple. They claim that they can obtain a 15 day tourist visa within a few hours for ₱2,800. If you want to avoid any delay in Nong Khai, then phone or fax your name, nationality and passport number the day before you want to travel to *The Meeting Place*. **NB** The Laos Embassy does not operate at the weekend, so don't expect a Fri phone call to be processed by Mon.

It is considerably cheaper to obtain a visa from the Lao Embassy in Phnom Penh (Cambodia). It takes 2 days to process and costs US$20. The visa is valid from the date of issue, not the date of application, however they will agree to put a later date on it if you know when you will be getting to Laos. Cheap visas can also be obtained from the embassy in Rangoon (Burma), but they cannot be extended.

Visa Extension For overstaying a visa without extension, there will probably be a fine to pay. Some travel agents in Vientiane will arrange to go out of Laos on the Friendship Bridge and back in again to provide a new visa (not strictly legal), it costs around US$80.

NB It is useful to have several passport photographs for visas to get into Laos and to obtain permits.

A **Transit Visa** usually valid for 7 days, is offered to tourists with confirmed tickets en route to, or from, Thailand, Vietnam, Cambodia, Burma or the Soviet Union – or other destinations with air links to Vientiane. **NB** Transit visas are only valid for Vientiane prefecture and cannot be extended.

Business Visas for 30 days may be obtained from Laos' embassies or consulates, usually through the Bangkok Lao Embassy. The visa must be approved in Vientiane and requires a formal request from a business or governmental organization in Laos. Approval for issuing the visa is telexed to the appropriate embassy from Vientiane. The business requesting the visa should let the recipient of the visa know the number of the approval-telex sent from Vientiane, as this speeds up the process. A business visa allows travel throughout Laos, with multiple entries and exits. Business visas are renewable in Vientiane.

Visa extension Obtainable from the Ministry of Interior, US$1/day, should take 2 days to effect.

Visas for Thailand If you are going to Thailand overland or by river, when leaving Laos it is necessary to obtain a Thai visa from the embassy on Thanon Phon Kheng, Vientiane. A three month visa costs ฿300 and takes up to 3 days.

● **Vaccinations**
No vaccinations are required unless coming from an infected area; see page 410 for further details.

● **Entry/exit points**
The main port of entry, other than Vientiane's Wattay airport, is **Tha Deua** which can be reached by boat from Nong Khai in Thailand or via the Mittaphab Bridge. Visitors can also enter Laos at Thakhek, Savannakhet, Chongmek, Ban Houei Sai, Pakse (see page 400 for details), Lao Bao (from Vietnam) and Boten (from China). (See **Getting there** page 410.)

● **Representation overseas**
Australia: 1 Dalman Crescent, O'Malley, Canberra, T 2864535, F 2901910; **Burma**: A1 Diplomatic Headquarters, Fraser Rd, Rangoon; **Cambodia**: 15-17 Thanon Keomani, T 26441, F 85523; **China**: N23 Haigeng Rd, Rm 501, Kunming, T 4141678, F 2420344. 11 Sanlifun Dongsijie, Peking, T 5321224; **France**: 74 Raymond Poincare, T 45537047, F 47275789; **Germany**: Am Lessing 6, 53639, Koenigwinter, Bonn T 02223; **India**: E53 Panchsheel Park, T 6427447; **Indonesia**: Jn. KintmaniRaja, Keningan Timur, Jakarta, T 5202673; **Japan**: 3-21, 3-Chome, Nishi Azabu, Minato-ku, Tokyo, T 54112291, F 54112293; **Malaysia**: 108 Jln D'amal, Kuala Lumpur, T 2483895, F 2420344; **Thailand**: 193 Sathorn Tai Rd, Bangkok, T 213573, F 2873968; **USA**: United Nations, New York, T 8322734, F 7500039. 2222 S St, Washington, T 6670058; **Vietnam**: 22 Tran Binh Trong, Hanoi, T 252271. 181 Hai Ba Trung, Saiong, T 299272.

Tours

● **Costs**
The North (for single person tours): **Luang Prabang** 1 night US$250; 2 nights US$382; 3 nights US$477; 4 nights US$606. **Xieng Khouang/Plain of Jars** 1 night US$227; 2 nights US$300. **The South** (for 2 person tours): **Saravan/Pakse/Wat Phou** 3 nights US$540; **Khong Island/Pakse/Wat Phou/Saravan** 4 nights US$580; **Khong Island/Pakse/ Attopeu/ Saravan** 4 nights US$600.

● **Thailand based companies**
Those operating 'individual tours' to Laos, organize short, cheap packages to Vientiane for 1-2 nights to gain entry. Then travellers are left on their own to organize the rest of their stay in Laos. The problem is that these companies shut down as fast as they open up. *Asian Holiday Tour*, 294/8 Phayathai Rd, Bangkok, T 2155749; *Asian Lines Travel*, 755 Silom Rd, Bangkok, T 2331510, F 2334885; *Banglamphu Tour Service*, 17 Khaosan Rd, Bangkok, T 2813122, F 2803642; *Cham Siam*, 288 Surawong Rd, Bangkok, T 2555570; *Dee Jai Tours*, 2nd flr, 491/29 Silom Plaza Bldg, Silom Rd, Bangkok, T 2341685, F 2374231; *Diethelm Travel*, Kian Gwan Bldg II, 140/1 Witthayu Rd, Bangkok, T 2559150, F 2560248; *Dior Tours*, 146-158 Khaosan Rd, Bangkok, T 2829142; *East-West*, 46-1 Sukhumvit Soi Nana Nua, Bangkok, T 2530681; *Exotissimo*, 21/17 Sukhumvit Soi 4, Bangkok, T 2535240, F 2547683, and 755 Silom Rd, Bangkok, T 2359196, F 2834885; *Fortune Tours*, 9 Captain Bush Lane, Charoen Krung 30, Bangkok, T 2371050; *Inter Companion Group*, 86/4 Rambutri Rd, Banglamphu, Bangkok, T 2829400, F 2827316; *Kannika Tour*, 36/39 Srisatta Rd, Udon Thani, T (042) 241378; *M K Ways*, 18/4 Sathorn Tai Soi 3 (Saint Louis), Bangkok, T 2122532, F 2545583; *Magic Tours*, 59/63 Moon Muang Rd, Chiang Mai, T 214572, F 214749; *Pawana Tour and Travel*, 72/2 Khaosan Rd, Bangkok, T 2678018, F 2800370. Also try *Pangkaj Travel*, 625 Sukhumvit Soi 22, Bangkok 10110, T 2582440, F 2591261; *S I Tours*, 288/2 Silom Rd, Bangkok, T 2332631; *Siam Wings*, 173/1-3 Surawong Rd, Bangkok,

T 2534757, F 2366808; *Skyline Travel Service*, 491/39-40 Silom Plaza (2nd Flr), Silom Rd, Bangkok, T 2331864, F 2366585; *Spangle Tours*, 205/1 Sathorn Tai Rd, Bangkok, T 2121583, F 2867732; *Thai Indochina*, 4th flr, 79 Pan Rd, Silom, Bangkok, T 2335369, F 2364389; *Thai-Indochina Supply Co*, 4th flr, 79 Pan Rd, Silom, Bangkok, T 2335369, F 2364389; *Thai Travel Service*, 119/4 Surawong Rd, Bangkok, T 2349360; *Top Thailand Tour*, 61 Khaosan Rd, Bangkok, T 2802251, F 2823337; *Tour East*, Rajapark Bldg, 10th flr, 163 Asoke Rd, Bangkok, T 2593160, F 2583236; *Transindo*, 9th flr Thasos Bldg, 1675 Chan Rd, Bangkok, T 2873241, F 2873246; *Udorn Business Travel*, 447/10 Haisok Rd, Nong Khai, T 411393; *Vista Travel*, 244/4 Khaosan Rd, Bangkok, T 2800348; *Western Union*, branch in the foyer of *Atlanta Hotel*, 78 Sukhumvit Soi 2, Bangkok, T 2552151.

● **Tour companies outside the region**
Australia: *Orbitours*, 7th flr, 428 George St, Sydney (PO Box 3309), T 612 2217322, F 612 2217425. France: *KLV*, 67 Blvd de Belleville, 75011 Paris, T 4381080, F 43669188. UK: *Abercrombie and Kent*, Sloane Square House, Holbein Place, London SW1W 8NS,

T 0171 730 9600, F 0171 730 9376; *Explore Worldwide*, 1 Frederick St, Aldershot, Hants GU11 1LQ, T 01252 344161, F 01252 343170; *British Airways Holidays*, Atlantic House, Hazelwick Ave, Crawley, West Sussex RH10 1NP; T 01293 611611, F 01293 552319; *Regent Holidays*, 15 John St, Bristol, BS1 2HR, T 0117 9211711, F 0117 9254886 and 31a High St, Shanklin, Isle of Wight, T 01983 864212, F 01983 864197.

● **Tourist information**
Until independent privately-owned tour operators were set up in 1991, there was a tourist information vacuum in Laos. The official government-run **Lao National Tourism** is not renowned for its skills in information dissemination although **Vientiane Tourism** is more helpful. The best source of up-to-date information is from recent travellers, whose comments and advice is documented in scrap books in Nong Khai guesthouses. At the speed with which events are moving in Laos, these sources become outdated very quickly. Certain tour agencies in Bangkok also keep bulletin boards of up-to-date records and travellers' tips.

There is a local telephone directory, called *How to Call Us and Our Friends*, which lists the telephone numbers of expats living in Vientiane as well as aid agencies and embassies.

The Australian women's *Vientiane Guide* is very useful and full of up-to-date information and good maps. Another useful book is the *Guide to Wats in Vientiane*. There are maps of Vientiane and Luang Prabang available (produced by the state) but these are often in limited supply. Local maps and guides mentioned above are available at the *Lane Xang Hotel* shop and *Lani's Hotel* in Vientiane.

When to go

● **Best time to visit**
In the relatively cool winter months from Nov to Mar, during the dry season. Temperatures in high areas like the Plain of Jars and the Bolovens Plateau can drop to below freezing in winter. From Apr onwards, temperatures can exceed 40°C. See page 308 for more detail on climate.

● **Clothing**
Informal, lightweight clothing is all that is needed, although a sweater is vital for the highlands in the winter months. It is respectful for women to cover their arms and legs. An umbrella is useful during the rainy season.

Health

● **Vaccinations**

No innoculations are required except a cholera vaccination if coming from an infected area. It is advisable to take full precautions before travelling to Laos. Hospitals are few and far between and medical facilities are poor. Tetanus, polio, hepatitis, rabies, typhoid and cholera injections are recommended.

● **Staying healthy**

It is inadvisable to tangle with dogs as **rabies** is rife in Laos and if you're planning to visit rural areas it is advisable to have an anti-rabies jab. **Malaria**: malaria pills are strongly advised, about a third of the population contracts malaria at some stage in their lives. As a precaution wear long sleeved shirts and trousers, particularly at dusk and use insect repellent, a mosquito net, coils etc.

● **Food and water**

Urban areas have access to safe water, but all water should be boiled or sterilized before drinking. Cheap bottled water is available – as are fizzy drinks. Less than a third of rural areas have safe water. Do not swim in stagnant water for risk of bilharzia. Restaurant food is, on the whole, hygienically prepared, and as long as street stall snacks have been well grilled, they are usually fine.

● **Medical facilities**

Medical services are restricted by a lack of trained personnel and facilities and standards are poor – particularly at district and rural level. There is only one doctor to every 1,362 people. Emergency treatment is available at the Mahosot Hospital and Clinique Settathirath in Vientiane but better facilities are available in Thailand. The Australian and Swedish embassies have clinics – both charge a small fee – for smaller problems. Emergency evacuation to Udon Thani (Thailand) can be arranged at short notice. It is wise to carry a first aid pack in case of emergency. Pharmacies are usually poorly stocked.

Travelling with children: you will need to bring all essentials; it is not advisable outside Vientiane.

● **Further health information**

See main health section, page 23.

Money

● **Currency**

The kip is the currency unit: US$1 = 730 kip (mid-1995). Denominations in notes start at the diminutive – and useless – 1 kip. More commonly used notes are 10, 20, 50, 100 and 500; no coins. As the highest denomination note in normal circulation is worth about US$0.70, be prepared for your pockets to bulge with huge wads of kip.

La Banque pour Commerce Exterieur Lao and the **Lane Xang Hotel** exchange US dollars or TCs (1% commission charge) and most other major currencies. It is easier to carry US dollars cash in small denominations or Thai baht when travelling, changing them as you go (most shops and restaurants will give you kip for US dollars or baht). Since the government scrapped its multi-tier exchange rates there has been no black market, and everyone knows the bank rate.

More expensive items eg, tours, car hire, hotels etc are quoted in dollars (or baht) while smaller purchases are quoted in kip. Thai baht is readily accepted in most towns but it is advisable to carry kip in rural areas. It is quite normal to be quoted a price in kip, pay in US dollars and pick up the change in baht. Nor is it unheard of to pay for a meal in three different currencies.

The kip is non-convertible, so once you leave Laos any remaining notes are useless. It is illegal to enter the country with more than 100,000 baht without clearance.

● **Credit cards**

Only accepted in more up-market restaurants and hotels in Vientiane, although plans are afoot to introduce Visa, Mastercard and American Express payment facilities at hotels, shops, provincial commercial banks and other establishments servicing tourists.

● **Currency regulation**

There are no restrictions on the import or export of foreign currencies other than Thai baht: a maximum of ฿100,000 can be brought into Laos. The Lao kip is a non-convertible currency, but inside Laos it is now as much in demand as US dollars and baht.

Getting there

Air

● **From Thailand**

Bangkok is the main gateway to Vientiane. If you want to visit Bangkok as well as Laos, the best way is to include the Bangkok-Vientiane sector on your long-haul ticket at no extra cost.

This is a cheaper option than purchasing tickets separately in Bangkok. There are regular flights between Vientiane and Bangkok operated by **Thai Airways** (¢2,680/US$92 one way, US$184 return) and **Lao Aviation's** 50-seater Antonov-24 turboprops (same price as Thai Airways). At the beginning of 1995, *Lao Aviation* began a twice-weekly service between Chiang Mai, in Northern Thailand, and Vientiane. **NB** *Lao Aviations'* planes are not the safest in the world. The older aircraft have bald tyres which could lead to an accident.

● **From Vietnam**

There are 2 return flights a week between **Vientiane and Hanoi** – Tues, Lao Aviation, and Thur, Vietnam Airlines (US$90 one way, US$180 return) and flights to and from **Ho Chi Minh** (Saigon) via Phnom Penh once a week (US$172 one way). **China Southern Airlines** flies between Vientiane and **Kunming** and **Guangzhon** (Canton) once a week.

The **Vientiane-Phnom Penh** route has 1 return flight a week, Wed and Fri (US$120 one way, US$240 return), which drops in on Saigon en route.

NB With the reduction of trade with, and aid from, the CIS, Lao Aviation has found it difficult to stock enough spare parts to keep its ageing Antonovs in the air on the few routes it does operate. Services may be curtailed as planes are regularly grounded. **Thai Airways** is the agent for **Lao Aviation** in Bangkok: 491/17 Ground Flr, Silom Plaza, Silom Rd, Bangkok, T 2369822. Tickets bought in Bangkok on Lao Aviation are **not** refundable in Laos. The agent for Lao Aviation in Vietnam is **Hang Khong Vietnam**, 25 Trang Thi St, Hanoi, T (42) 253842 and 116 Nguyen Thi St, T (8) 292118 in Saigon, and in Cambodia, **Royal Air du Cambodge**, 62 Tou Samuth St, Phnom Penh, T (23) 25887.

Road

The **Thai-Lao Friendship Bridge** is now open (see page 350) and bus routes are planned between Northeastern Thailand and Vientiane. Crossing the border at Tha Deua is now very easy, open Mon-Sun 0800-1730. Immigration and customs are on both sides of the bridge and a bus transports visitors across (¢25 from Thailand, ¢10 from Laos). Tuk-tuks in Thailand wait for trade and attempt charging very high prices – bargain to ¢10-20 each. **NB** Do not travel with anybody else's belongings.

Boat

There is an official border post on the Mekong River, at the Thai town of **Nong Khai** with a crossing to **Tha Duea** (25 km from Vientiane) but this is only open for locals; tourists must use the bridge. There are regular ferries from 0800-1700, Mon-Fri and 0800-1200, Sat, across the Mekong at **Thakhek** to Nakhon Phanom (Thailand) (¢20).

Ferries run between Hua Wiang, 2 km N of Chiang Khong (Thailand) and **Ban Houei Sai** (¢20).

Regular ferries between **Savannakhet** and Mukdahan (Thailand) between 0830-1700, Mon-Fri, 0830-1230 Sat (¢30).

It is possible to cross the Mekong (100 kip) to Chongmek (Thailand) from **Pakse** (see page 400 for details).

From Vietnam, there is a crossing at **Lao Bao**, just NW of Hué. It is important to have Vietnamese visa stamped with Lao Bao as an exit point (could do this when applying for visa). For some reason, if the Lao visa is acquired in Phnom Penh, then they may not endorse a Lao Bao exit point. To change exit point costs US$15 in Hanoi (*Vietnam Tourism*), US$20 in Danang and US$8 in Saigon. Hué immigration will not change an exit point. From the border, travelling into Laos, the last bus to Savannakhet leaves at 1500, arriving 2400, with no food stops. Several other passes are now open from Vietnam: through **Deo Tay Chang Pass** from Dien Bien Phu, via Rt 6 to **Sam Neua**, from Hanoi, via Rt 7 to **Nong Het** through Barthelmy Pass from Vinh, via Rt 12 through **Mu Gia Pass** from Ha Tinh.

From Cambodia, the entry point is at **Muang Saen**, across the Mekong River from Phumi Khampong Sralan.

Customs

● **Duty free allowance**

500 cigarettes, 2 bottles of wine and a bottle of liquor. There is a small but well-stocked duty-free shop on the Lao side at Tha Duea – and at Wattay Airport.

● **Export restrictions**

Laos has a strictly enforced ban on the export of antiquities and all Buddha images. The last person to try stealing a Buddha caused the government to close the country to tourists for a year.

On arrival

● **Airport information**
Wattay International Airport is 3 km from Vientiane. Foreign exchange desk and duty free shop open for arrivals and departures. Flight information: T 212066.

Transport to town By bus: local buses operate from Thanon Luang Prabang outside the airport every 45 mins (200 kip). **By taxi**: fares payable in US$, baht or kip: 3,000 kip to centre of town (bargain hard). **By saamlor**: upwards of ₿50 (bargain).

● **Airport tax**
US$5 on departure for international flights; 300 kip on domestic departures.

● **Conduct**
Wats Lao monks are not as disciplined as Thai monks – probably owing to the effects of 15 years of Communism, but Buddhism is undergoing a resurgence. If talking to a monk your head should be lower than his. Avoid visiting a wat around 1100 as this is when the monks have their morning meal. It is considerate to ask the abbot's permission to enter the *sim* and shoes should be removed on entry. When sitting down, feet should point away from the altar and main image. Arms and legs should be fully covered when visiting wats. A small donation is often appropriate (kneel when putting it into the box).

Form of address Lao people are addressed by their first name, not their family name, even when a title is used.

Greeting *Wai* – remains the traditional form of greeting – with hands together and head bowed, as if in prayer (see page 602).

In private homes Remove shoes. When seated on the floor you should tuck your feet behind you. Do not pat children on the head, as it is the most sacred part of the body.

General Pointing with the index finger is considered rude.

● **Emergencies**
Police, ambulance or fire brigade: T 3590 (Vientiane).

● **Hours of business**
Government offices: 0800-1700 Mon-Fri but often closed for 2 hrs at lunchtime. **Banks**: 0800-1200, 1400-1500 Mon-Fri. **Shops**: 0900-1700 Mon-Sat and some on Sun.

● **Official time**
7 hrs ahead of GMT.

● **Photographs**
Sensitivity pays when taking photographs. Be very wary in areas that have (or could have) military importance – such as airports, where all photography is prohibited. Also be careful when photographing official functions and parades without permission. Always ask permission before photographing in a temple.

● **Safety**
Crime rates are very low but it is advisable to take obvious precautions. Most areas of Laos are safe except the road between Luang Prabang and Phonsavanh (Xieng Khouang), which is closed due to ambush. The road from Vang Vieng to Luang Prabang is also risky. The Golden Triangle area is unsafe because of the opium trade and foreigners can be mistaken for spies. Xieng Khouang province, the Bolovens Plateau and areas along the Ho Chi Minh Trail are littered with *bombis* – small anti-personnel mines and bomblets from cluster bomb units. There are also many large unexploded bombs all over Laos; in many villages they have been left lying around. They are very unstable so **DO NOT TOUCH**. Five to ten people are still killed or injured every month in Laos by inadvertently stepping on mines, or hitting 'pineapple' bomblets with hoes.

● **Shopping**
Best buys from Laos are hilltribe artefacts and textiles.

Antique textiles from N Laos are big business and they sell from US$40 upwards. It is hard to find old textiles in good condition as old ones are worn over new ones for work or bathing and so wear out quickly. There is a wide variety of modern materials which are used to make the *pha sin*, the Lao sarong, and *pha baeng*, or shawl, worn by Lao women. The latter became high-fashion in Bangkok in the early 1990s, after the Thai princess Mahacakri Sirindhorn took to wearing them on her return from Laos. The bridal *sin* is a popular buy; it is usually plain with a single motif repeated over most of the material and an elaborate border. Gold and silver thread, *tdinjok*, is often woven into the border pattern. Lao weavers have been isolated from external influences and have maintained many of their original patterns and styles. Most of the materials are sold in weaving villages or are available from markets in the main towns.

Making **silverware** is a traditional craft in Laos – most of it is in the form of jewellery and small silver pots (it may not be made of silver). Chunky antique tribal jewellery, bangles, pendants, belts and earrings, are often sold in markets in the main towns, or antique shops in Vientiane.

Craftsmen in Laos are still producing carvings for temples and coffins. Designs are usually traditional, with a religious theme. Craftsmen produce carved panels and statues for tourists, which are available in outlets in Vientiane.

● **Tipping**

It is not common practice, even in hotels but it is normal to tip guides.

● **Voltage**

220 volts, 50 cycles in the main towns. 110 volts in the country. 2 pin sockets are common so adaptors are required. For sensitive equipment it is essential to use a voltage regulator. Blackouts are common outside Vientiane.

● **Weights and measures**

Metric along with local systems of measurement.

Where to stay

● **Accommodation**

Rooms in Laos are rarely luxurious and standards vary enormously – you can end up paying double what you would pay in Bangkok. However, the hotel industry is expanding rapidly: many older buildings are under renovation, and new hotels are springing up – some in conjunction with Thai companies. Only the *Tai-pan, Royal, Belvedere* and *Lane Xang* in Vientiane and the *Villa Santi* and *L'Hotel Souvannaphoum* in Luang Prabang come in the 1st class bracket. *Transindo* (the Vientiane-based travel and tour company) now runs some beautifully renovated colonial houses and chalets in the S. There is a reasonable choice of hotels of different standards and prices in Vientiane and Luang Prabang.

The majority of hotels have fans and attached bathrooms, although more are installing air-conditioning where there is a more stable electricity supply; others are installing their own generators. Smaller provincial towns have only a handful of hotels and guesthouses – some of them quaint French colonial villas. In rural villages people's homes are enthusiastically transformed into bed and breakfasts on demand. Tourism infrastructure still has a long way to go before it approaches international standards. Expect to pay upwards of US$8 for a basic air-conditioned double room with attached bathroom in a Western-style hotel.

HOTEL CLASSIFICATIONS

A+ US$100-200 (70,000-140,000 kip) **International**: business services (fax, translation, seminar rooms etc), sports facilities (gym, swimming pool etc), Asian and Western restaurants, bars, and discotheques.

A US$50-100 (35,000-70,000 kip) **First class**: business, sports and recreational facilities, with a range of restaurants and bars.

B US$25-50 (17,500-35,000 kip) **Tourist class**: all rooms will have air-conditioning and an attached bathroom, swimming pool, restaurants and 24-hour coffee shop/room service. Cable films.

C US$15-25 (10,500-17,500 kip) **Economy**: air-conditioning, attached bathrooms. Restaurant and room service. No sports facilities.

D US$8-15 (5,600-10,500 kip) **Budget**: no air-conditioning, attached bathroom. Bed linen and towels, and there may be a restaurant.

E US$4-8 (2,800-5,600 kip) **Guesthouse**: fan-cooled rooms, shared bathroom facilities. 'Squat' toilets. Bed linen but no towels. Rooms are small, facilities few.

F US$<4 (<2,800 kip) **Guesthouse**: fan-cooled rooms, usually with shared bathroom facilities. Squat toilets. Variable standards of cleanliness.

Food and drink

Food

Expect to pay between US$2-10/head for a meal in main towns and less outside.

● **Cuisine**

There are many similarities between Lao and Thai food, although it is slightly influenced by the Chinese cuisine. Lao dishes are distinguished by the use of aromatic herbs (including marijuana) and spices such as lemon grass, chillies, ginger and tamarind. Coconut fat is used sparingly. Food takes a long time to prepare and does not keep well, which goes some way to explaining why many restaurants do not offer local dishes, or if they do, they demand advance warning. There are new restaurants springing up, especially in Vientiane, which offer Lao food, although it is more

RESTAURANT CLASSIFICATIONS

♦♦♦♦ Over US$15 (10,500 kip) for a meal. A 3-course meal in a restaurant with pleasant decor. Beers, wines and spirits available.

♦♦♦ US$5-15 (3,500-10,500 kip) for a meal. Two courses, reasonable surroundings.

♦♦ US$2-5 (1,400-3,500 kip) for a meal, probably only a single course, surroundings spartan but adequate.

♦ Under US$2 (under 1,400 kip). Single course, often makeshift surroundings such as a street kiosk with simple

usually found at roadside stalls and in the markets.

The staple Lao foods are glutinous rice (**khaaw niaw**) and fermented fish or **paddek** (the milder version is called **nam pa**). Being a landlocked country, most of the fish is fresh from the Mekong. Mutton (goat) is practically unheard of and beef (water buffalo) expensive, so most of the dishes are variations on two themes: fish and bird. But the Lao cookbook does not stop at chickens and turkeys (there are thousands of turkeys in Luang Prabang thanks to an esoteric aid project which farmed them). The rule of thumb is that if it has wings and feathers, it's edible. In some areas, such as Luang Prabang, the province's birds have long-since been eaten.

The most common vegetables are aubergines, tomatoes, cucumbers and lettuce, often cooked together, puréed and eaten with sticky rice. Soups are eaten at the middle or end of a meal but never at the beginning. They are usually a mixture of fish and meat infused with aromatic herbs.

Laap also meaning 'luck' in Lao, is a traditional ceremonial dish made from raw fish or meat crushed into a paste, marinated in lemon juice and mixed with chopped mint. It is said to be similiar to Mexican *cerviche*. It is called *laap sin* if it has a meat base and *laap pa* if it's fish based. Beware of *laap* in cheap street restaurants – sometimes it is concocted from raw offal and served cold, this should be consumed with great caution. **Phanaeng kay** stuffed chicken with pork, peanuts and coconut milk with a dash of cinnamon. *Kai ping* grilled chicken eaten with sticky rice. **Soup** there are several different types – **keng no may** (bamboo shoot soup), **keng khi lek** (vegetable and buffalo skin), **ken chut** (without pimentos) **keng kalami** (cabbage soup with fish or pork).

The Lao are also partial to **sweets**: sticky rice with coconut milk and black beans (which can be bought in bamboo tubes in the markets) and grilled bananas are favourites.

There is also a well-ingrained **Vietnamese** culinary tradition and **Chinese** food is never hard to find. *Feu* is the Lao version of Chinese noodle soup. Most restaurants outside the main towns do not have menus but will nearly always serve *feu* and *laap* or local specialities.

Laos has also inherited a sophisticated and tasty colonial legacy. **French** cuisine is widely available, with street cafés serving delectable fresh *croissants*, *baguettes*, *pain au chocolat* and a selection of sticky pastries, which can be washed down with a powerful cup of Lao coffee. The Lao however have a habit of eating *baguette* sandwiches with fish sauce sprinkled on top – these are available in Vientiane, Savannakhet and Pakse. Menus in many of Vientiane's restaurants still have a distinctly French flavour to them – frogs' legs included. Vintage Bordeaux and Burgundies occasionally emerge from the cellars of restaurants too. Hotels in main towns often provide international menus and continental breakfasts.

Drink

● Beer

Nam Saa, imported beer (mainly Heineken from Singapore), wines and spirits can be found in hotels, restaurants, bars and nightclubs but it is not particularly cheap. *Lao beer* (standard and '33' export brew) is palatable and reasonably priced. Russian champagne can be found in larger stores and restaurants – a few of which also offer a tempting (but extortionate) selection of French wines. The local brew is rice wine and is traditionally drunk from a clay jug with long straws. The white variety is called *lau-lao* – literally 'Lao alcohol' – and is made from fermented sticky rice. Red lau-lao – or **fanthong** – is fermented with herbs. **Be warned**: the water added to lau-lao is hardly ever boiled. Bottled lau-lao is also widely available – *Sticky Rice* brand is the best. Always ensure that the screw-top bottles are sealed as industrial alcohol is sometimes added, particularly in Vientiane.

● Soft drinks

Soft drinks are expensive – they are imported from Thailand. *Nam saa*, weak Chinese tea, is always served with strong coffee and is free.

FOOD GLOSSARY

apple	*mahk-appen*	orange	*mahk-kieng*
banana	*mahk-guay*	papaya	*mahk-huhng*
bean	*mahk-toua*	pineapple	*mahk-nuht*
beef	*seen nua*	pork	*seen moo*
bottled water	*nahm bolisut*	potato	*mahk-fal-ahng*
bread	*kao jee*	rice	*kao*
cabbage	*mahk galambee*	salt	*guea*
cake	*kanom*	salty	*kem*
chicken	*seen gai*	shrimp	*goong*
chilli	*mahk pet*	sour	*som*
Chinese rice	*hao tchao*	spicy hot	*pet*
coffee	*kah-fay*	sticky rice	*kao neo*
cold	*yin*	stir fry	*kua*
cucumber	*pahk-tehng*	sugar	*nahm daan*
egg	*kai*	sweetcorn	*mahk sa-lee*
egg, boiled	*kai dom*	tea	*nahm sa*
egg, fried	*kai dao*	vegetable	*pahk*
fish	*baa*	water	*nahm*
fruit	*mahk-my*	watermelon	*mahk-mo*
garlic	*pahk tiam*	**Street food**	
hot	*hawn*	deep fried ball	
hot tea	*nahm sa hawn*	of rice and meat	*nem*
ice	*nahm khon*	green papaya	
iced tea	*nahm sa yin*	salad (spicy hot)	*tam maak hung*
lemon	*mahk-naow*	hot noodle	*kao poun*
lemon juice	*nahm mahk naow*	lemon grass soup	*tom yam*
lettuce	*pahk sal-ad*	spring rolls	*kayo cuon*
lobster	*goong yai*	waffle	*roti*
mango	*mahk muang*	**Useful phrases**	
melon	*mahk maw*	breakfast	*kao sao*
milk	*nahm nome*	lunch	*kao tiang*
noodle soup	*me nahm* (Chinese)	dinner	*kao leng*
	feu (Vietnamese)	tasty	*saierb*
onion	*pahk bua yai*	too much	*lai pawd*

Getting around

Practicalities

Very few bus/truck/tuk-tuk or taxi drivers understand any foreign languages (except Thai). In order to travel to a particular destination, it is a great advantage to have the name written out in Lao. Spoken Lao will not be enough. Map reading is out of the question, and many people will not know road names – however, they will know where all the sights of interest are – eg thats, markets, monuments, waterfalls, etc.

In the N of Laos, it is still important to get your passport stamped in and out of any given town. In the S, this is no longer necessary. It is probably only a matter of time before this becomes unnecessary throughout the country.

Air

Many of the major towns are serviced by **Lao Aviation**. Tickets can be purchased from their office in Vientiane. **NB** Some of these aeroplanes leave a great deal to be desired, many have bald tyres and one wonders how they still fly. However, it is still the quickest and most convenient form of travel. For business travellers, there is an Australian helicopter charter service based at Wattay airport.

From Vientiane:	US$ (return)
Xieng Khouang	74
Nam Tha	160
Savannakhet	122
Saravan	182
Pakse	190
Luang Prabang	90

DOMESTIC AIR ROUTES: TIMETABLE

To	DAYS	Dep Time	Arr Time
FROM VIENTIANE			
Pakse	1,3,6	0700	0825
	2,4,7	1005	1130
	5	1400	1525
Savannakhet	1,3	1050	1155
	2,4,5,7	0700	0800
	6	1400	1505
Luang Prabang	1,2,3,4,6,7	1030	1110
	1,2,3,4,6,7	1230	1310
	1,2,3,4,6	1500	1540
	5	1000	1040
	5	1130	1210
	5	1430	1510
	7	1400	1440
Sayaboury	1,3,4	1005	1050
	6	1035	1120
Xieng Khouang	1,2,3,4,5,6,7	0830	0910
	1,2,3,7	1430	1515
	5	1200	1245
Namtha	1	1100	1220
	2,4,7	1400	1510
Km 20/Thakhek	2,4	1035	1140
	7	1010	1115
Vieng Xai	2,5	1100	1225
FROM LUANG PRABANG			
Ban Houei Xai	1,2,3,4,6	1130	1225
	5	1100	1155
Udom Xai	1,2,3,4,6	1400	1440
	7	1130	1210
Xieng Khouang	3	0900	0935
	5	1540	1615
Luang Nam Tha	3	1600	1640
	5	1330	1415
Vientiane	1,2,3,4,6,7	1130	1210
	1,2,3,4,6,7	1330	1410
	1,2,3,4,6	1600	1640
	5	1100	1140
	5	1240	1320
	5	1530	1610
	7	1500	1540
FROM PAKSE			
Savannakhet	1	1205	1300
	3	1100	1145
	6	1000	1055

To	DAYS	Dep Time	Arr Time
Attapeu	2,4	1300	1340
Muang Khong	6	1500	1530
Vientiane	1,3,6	0855	1020
	2,4,7	1200	1325
	5	1555	1720
FROM SAVANNAKHET			
Vientiane	1,3	1215	1320
	2,4,5,7	0825	0930
	6	1525	1630
FROM SAYABOURY			
Vientiane	1,3,4	1130	1155
	6	1140	1225
FROM XIENG KHOUANG			
Vientiane	1,2,3,4,5,6,7	0930	1010
	1,2,3,7	1535	1620
	5	1305	1350
Luang Prabang	3	0955	1030
	5	1635	1720
FROM LUANG NAM THA			
Vientiane	1	1240	1400
	2,4,7	1530	1640
FROM KM 20/THAKHEK			
Vientiane	2,4	1200	1305
	7	1135	1240
Pakse	1	1500	1720
	6	1235	1430
FROM VIENG XAI			
Vientiane	2,5	1245	1410
FROM BAN HOUEI XAI			
Luang Prabang	1,2,3,4,6	1245	1340
	5	1215	1310
FROM NAMTHA			
Luang Prabang	3	1700	1740
	5	1435	1520
FROM SAVANNAKHET			
Pakse	1	1320	1420
	3	1205	1250
	6	1115	1215
FROM ATTAPEU			
Pakse	2,4	1400	1440
FROM MUANG KHONG			
Pakse	6	1550	1620

NB: 1=Mon; 2=Tues; 3=Wed; 4=Thur; 5=Fri; 6=Sat; 7=Sun

Bus/truck

It is now possible to travel to most areas of the country by bus, truck or songthaew. The only areas to avoid are the road from Luang Prabang to Phonsavanh (Xieng Khouang) (closed due to ambush) and the road from Vang Vieng to Luang Prabang is supposed to be risky, although people have travelled on it. However, it is quite hard work; many roads are unsealed, buses are overloaded and breakdowns are frequent. For some connections you may need to wait days and some journeys can vary enormously in the length of time they take, depending on the weather conditions. Travellers can often negotiate a price if travelling by truck and it seems to be quite easy to hitch.

Car hire

Car hire is anything from US$40-80/day, depending on the vehicle, and first 150 km free, then US$10 every 100 km after that. Price includes a driver. *Jo Rumble (Asia Vehicle Rental)*, T 217493 or 314927 in Vientiane seems reliable. Drive on the right.

Other land transport

● Bicycle and motorcycle hire

Available in many towns and a cheap way to see the sights. Chinese bikes tend to be better than Thai ones. Many guesthouses own bikes for rent. There are a small number of motorcycles available too.

● Tuk-tuk/saamlor/trishaw

These can be hired in most towns – negotiate the price first, although the saamlor is now almost extinct in Vientiane. The majority of motorized three-wheelers are large motorbike taxis with two bench seats in the back.

● Taxi

Taxis are available, but they are unwilling to travel any distance on an unsealed road.

Boat

It is possible to take river boats up and down the Mekong and its main tributaries. The Mekong is navigable from Luang Prabang to Savannakhet during the rainy season (Jun-Oct), but there is no organized service. Boats leave at the last minute, and speaking Lao is definitely an advantage here. Boats are basic but cheap. Prices vary according to size of boat and length of journey. Downriver from Luang Prabang to Vientiane takes 4 days, travelling up to 10 hrs a day. There are plenty of boats available from Luang Prabang, travelling up or down river. The most common riverboats are the *hua houa leim*, with no decks, the hold being enclosed by side panels and a flat roof; the metal boats get very hot.

Communications

● Language

Lao is the national language but there are many local dialects. French is spoken by government officials and hotel staff, and many educated people over 40. There is also a small French-educated urban élite which has kept colonial connections alive. Russian is widely spoken (signs in Russian are still quite common) but these days everyone wants to learn English. Most government officials and many shop-keepers have some command of English.

● Postal services

International service: the outbound service is inexpensive but long-term foreign residents cast aspersions on its reliability; they prefer to have mail hand-delivered by people coming and going to Bangkok. Around 300 kip for a letter or card to Europe and the USA. When buying stamps, be sure to ask for big denominations as the state graphic design team has a penchant for vast postage stamps. Even domestic mail is plastered, back and front, with huge stamps celebrating the Lao PDR's various successes. Contents of outgoing parcels must be examined by an official before being sealed. In-going mail should use the official title, Lao PDR.

A telephone and **fax service** is available at the International Service Centre Settathirath, Vientiane, international telephone service open 24 hrs a day, fax service open daily 0730-2130 and faxes are received 24 hrs. Mark incoming faxes with telephone number and recipient will be informed immediately. **International operator**: T 170.

Poste restante: there is a poste restante at the post office in Vientiane.

● Telephone services

Local: all towns are now linked by phone and many places have fax facilities, particularly guesthouses and hotels. Call 178 in Vientiane for town codes.

International: possible from most big towns. Operator: 16.

Entertainment

● Newspapers

Vientiane Times is a weekly paper, costing 700 kip, which started in 1994. It provides querky

CALENDAR

The **Gregorian calendar** is the official calendar for administration, but many traditional villages still follow the lunar calendar. The **Lao calendar** is a mixture of Sino-Vietnamese and Thai-Khmer. It is based on the movement of the sun and moon and is different to the Buddhist calendar used in Thailand. New Year is in December, but is celebrated in April when the auspices are more favourable. As in China, each year is named after an animal. Weeks are structured on the waxing and waning of the moon and days are named accordingly.

pieces of information. *Discover Laos* is a monthly publication. *Newsweek* is available. The *Bangkok Post* (costing over ฿20) is the most recent addition to newstands which previously stocked only government-controlled Lao language newspapers and *Pravda* in Russian and French. The Lao Government *Khao San Pathet Lao News Bulletin* is produced daily in English and French and yields journalistic treats such as "Sayaboury province exceeds radish production forecast" and "Message of solidarity to Havana". They can be found blowing around hotel lobbies.

● **Radio**

The Lao National Radio broadcasts news in English. The BBC World Service can be picked up on shortwave on 11.955 MHz and 11.750 (25m band); 9.740 MHz (30m band); 7.145 MHz (41m band); 6.195 MHz (48m band) and 3.195 MHz (76m band). Voice of America also broadcasts (see page 22). Every day in many of the cities and towns loudspeakers blare out broadcasts of the municipal radio station. These days, socialist slogans have been replaced with commercials for soft drinks, washing powder and toothpaste.

● **Television**

This is becoming more popular as more towns and villages get electricity. Even Vientiane's poorest households boast forests of aluminium antennae orientated to receive signals from across the Mekong. The national TV station broadcasts in Lao but there is a distinct preference for Thai soaps and game shows. Channel 5 gives English sub-titles to overseas news. It is not possible to receive Lao TV broadcasts in Luang Prabang yet, but many homes have VCRs imported from Thailand, and the video cassette business is highly profitable.

Holidays and festivals

Being of festive inclination, the Lao celebrate New Year 4 times a year: the international New

Year in Jan, Chinese New Year in Jan/Feb, Lao New Year (Pimai) in Apr and Hmong New Year in Dec. The Lao Buddhist year follows the lunar calendar, so many of the festivals are movable. The first month begins around the full moon in Dec, although Lao New Year is celebrated in Apr. There are also many local festivals (see relevant sections).

The *Baci* ceremony is a uniquely Lao *boun* (festival) and celebrates any auspicious occasion – marriage, birth and achievement. The ceremony dates from pre-Buddhist times. It is centred around the *phakhouan*, a designer-tree made from banana leaves and flowers and surrounded by symbolic foods. The *mophone* hosts the ceremony and recites memorized prayers, usually in Pali, and ties cotton strips (*saisin*) around the wrists of guests symbolizing good health, prosperity and happiness. For maximum effect, these strings must have 3 knots in them. It is unlucky to take them off before 3 days have elapsed. All this is accompanied by a *ramvong* (traditional circle dance) which is accompanied by traditional instruments – flutes, clarinets, xylophones with bamboo crosspieces, drums, cymbals and the *kaen*, a hand-held pipe organ that is to Laos what the bagpipes are to Scotland.

Jan *New Year's Day* (1st: public holiday) celebrated by private *baci* throughout the country. *Pathet Lao Day* (6th: public holiday) parades in main towns. *Army Day* (20th: public holiday). *Boun Pha Vet* (movable) to celebrate King Vessanthara's reincarnation as a Buddha. Sermons, processions, dance, theatre. Popular time for ordination.

Feb *Magha Puja* (movable) celebrates the end of Buddha's time in the monastery and the prediction of his death. It is principally celebrated in Vientiane and at Wat Phou, near Champassak. *Chinese New Year* (movable, Jan/Feb) celebrated by Chinese and Vietnamese communities. Many Chinese and Vietnamese businesses shut down for 3 days.

USEFUL LAO WORDS AND PHRASES

Greetings

Yes/No	*men/baw*
thank you/no thank you	*kop jai/baw, kop jai*
hello/goodbye	*suh-bye-dee/lah-gohn*
what is your name? My name is...	*chow seu yang? koi seu....*
excuse me, sorry	*ko toat*
can/do you speak English?	*koy pahk pah-sah anhg-geet?*
a little, a bit	*noi, hoi*
where?	*you-sigh?*
how much is...?	*tow-dai?*
it doesn't matter, never mind	*baw penh yang*
pardon?	*kow toat?*
I don't understand	*kow baw cow-chi*
how are you? not very well	*chao suh-bye-dee-baw?/ baw suh-bye*

The hotel

what is the charge each night?	*kit laka van nuang taw dai?*
is the room air conditioned?	*hong me ai yen baw?*
can I see the room first please?	*koi ko beung hong dea?*
does the room have hot water?	*hong me nam hawn baw?*
does the room have a bathroom?	*me hang ap nam baw?*
can I have the bill please?	*koi ton han bai hap?*

Travel

where is the main station?	*sa ta ni lot phai yu sai?*
where is the bus station?	*sa ta ni lot mee yu sai?*
how much to go to...?	*khit la ka taw dai...?*
that's expensive	*pheng-lie*
will you go for...kip?	*chow ja pai...kip?*
what time does the bus/train leave for...?	*lot mea oak jay mong...?*
is it far?	*kai baw?*
turn left/turn right	*leo sai/leo qua*
go straight on	*pai leuy*

Restaurants

can I see a menu?	*kho beung lay kan arhan?*
can I have...?	*khoy tong kan...?*
I am hungry	*koy heo kao*
I am thirsty	*koy heo nahm*
I want to eat	*koh yahk kin kao*
where is a restaurant?	*lahn ah hai you-sigh?*
breakfast	*arhan sao*
lunch	*arhan athieng*
it costs....kip	*lah-kah ahn-nee...kip*

Time and days

in the morning	*muh-sao*	Monday	*Van Chanh*
in the afternoon	*thon-by*	Tuesday	*Van Ang Khan*
in the evening	*muh-leng*	Wednesday	*Van Pud*
today	*muh-nee*	Thursday	*Van Pa Had*
tomorrow	*muh-ouhn*	Friday	*Van Sook*
yesterday	*muh van-nee*	Saturday	*Van Sao*
		Sunday	*Van Arthid*

Numbers

1	*nung*	9	*cow*	100	*hoy*
2	*song*	10	*sip*	101	*hoy-nung*
3	*sahm*	11	*sip-et*	150	*hoy-hah-sip*
4	*see*	12	*sip-song*	200	*song-hoy*
5	*hah*	20	*sao*	1,000	*phan*
6	*hoke*	21	*sao-et*	10,000	*sip-phan*
7	*chet*	22	*sao-song*	100,000	*muun*
8	*pet*	30	*sahn-sip*	1,000,000	*laan*

Basic vocabulary

airport	*deune yonh*	island	*koh (or) hath*
bank	*had xay*	market	*ta lath*
bathroom	*hong nam*	medicine	*ya pua payad*
beach	*heva*	open	*peud*
beautiful	*ngam*	petrol	*nahm-mahn-eh-sahng*
bicycle	*loht teep*		
big	*nyai*	police	*lam louad*
boat	*quoi loth bath*	police station	*poam lam louad*
bus	*loht-buht*	post office	*hong kana pai sa nee*
bus station	*hon kay ya*		
buy	*sue*	restaurant	*han arhane*
chemist	*han kay ya*	road	*tha nonh*
clean	*sa ard*	room	*hong*
closed	*arte*	shop	*hanh*
cold	*jenh*	sick (ill)	*bo sabay*
day	*vanh (or) mua*	silk	*mai*
delicious	*sehb*	small	*noy*
dirty	*soka pox*	stop	*yoot*
doctor	*than mah*	taxi	*loht doy-sanh*
eat	*kinh*	that	*nahn*
embassy	*Satan Tood*	this	*nee, ahn-nee*
excellent	*dee leuth*	ticket (air)	*pee yonh*
expensive	*pheng*	ticket (bus)	*pee lot mea*
food	*ah-han*	toilet	*hong nam*
fruit	*mak-mai*	town	*nai mouang*
hospital	*hong moh*	very	*lai-lai*
hot (temp)	*hawn*	water	*nam (or) nah*
hotel	*hong*	what	*men-nyung*

Mar *Women's Day* (8th: public holiday). *People's Party Day* (22nd: public holiday). *Boun Khoun Khao* (movable) harvest festival, local celebration centred around the wats.

Apr *Boun Pimai* (movable: public holiday) to celebrate Lao New Year. The first month of the Lao New Year is actually Dec but festivities are delayed until Apr when days are longer than nights. By Apr it's also hotting up, so having hosepipes levelled at you and buckets of water dumped on you is more pleasurable. The festival also serves to invite the rains. Pimai is one of the most important annual festivals, particularly in Luang Prabang. Statues of the Buddha (in the 'calling for rain' posture) are ceremonially doused in water, which is poured along an intricately decorated trench (*hang song nam pha*). The small stupas of sand, decorated with streamers, in wat compounds are symbolic requests for health and happiness over the next year. It is celebrated with traditional Lao folksinging (*mor lam*) and the circle dance (*ramwong*). There is usually a 3-day holiday. Similar festivals are celebrated in Thailand, Cambodia and Burma.

May *Labour Day* (1st: public holiday) parades in Vientiane. *Visakha Puja* (movable) to celebrate the birth, enlightenment and death of the Buddha, celebrated in local wats. *Boun Bang Fai* (movable) or the rocket festival, is a Buddhist rain-making festival. Large bamboo rockets are built and decorated by monks and carried in procession before being blasted skywards. The higher a rocket goes, the bigger its builder's ego gets. Designers of failed rockets are thrown in the mud. The festival lasts 2 days.

Jun *Children's Day* (1st: public holiday). *Khao Phansa* (movable) is the start of Buddhist Lent and is a time of retreat and fasting for monks. These are the most usual months for ordination and for men to enter the monkhood for short periods before they marry. The festival starts with the full moon in Jun/Jul and continues until the full moon in Oct. It all ends with the *Kathin* ceremony in Oct when monks receive gifts.

Aug *Lao Issara* (13th: public holiday), Free Lao Day. *Liberation Day* (23rd: public holiday). *Ho Khao Padap Dinh* (movable) is a celebration of the dead.

Sep *Bouk ok Phansa* (movable) is the end of Buddhist Lent and the faithful take offerings to the temple. It is in the '9th month' in Luang Prabang and the '11th month' in Vientiane, and marks the end of the rainy season. Boat races take place on the Mekong River with crews of 50 or more men and women. On the night before the race small decorated rafts are set afloat on the river.

Oct *Freedom from the French Day* (12th: public holiday) which is only really celebrated in Vientiane.

Dec *Hmong New Year* (movable). *Independence Day* (2nd: public holiday), military parades, dancing, music.

NB This list is not exhaustive, but does include the most important festivals. There are many Chinese, Vietnamese and ethnic minority festivals which are celebrated in Laos and there are many regional variations.

Further reading

Grant Evans & Kelvin Rowley (1990) *Red Brotherhood at War, Vietnam Cambodia & Laos since 1975*, Verso; Grant Evans (1983) *Yellow Rainmakers: Are Chemical Weapons Being Used in Southeast Asia*, Verso; Grant Evans (1990) *Lao Peasants under Socialism*, Yale University Press; Rene de Berval (1959) *Kingdom of Laos*, France-Asie Publication; Christopher Robbins (1989) *The Ravens* Corgi; Cheeseman, Patricia (1988) *Ancient Symbols: Living Art* White Lotus; Alfred W McCoy (1991) *The Politics of Heroin: CIA Complicity in the Global Drugs Trade*, Lawrence Hill/Chicago Review Press. **Newsletters:** *Indochina Newsletter* (monthly) from Asia Resource Centre, c/o 2161 Massachusetts Ave, Cambridge, MA02140, USA.

● **Acknowledgements**

Angelika Teuschl (Austria), Hilary Emberton (UK), Chloë Gorman (UK), Pilou Grenié (France), Sandra Van Heel (France), Annand Mansouri (France), Derek Langley (Australia), Dave Gowlett (UK), Diana Wells (UK).

CAMBODIA

INTRODUCTION

Until the mid-19th century, the outside world knew almost nothing of the interior of Cambodia. From the 16th and 17th centuries, rumours began to surface in Europe – based on tales from Portuguese and French missionaries – about a magnificent city, hidden somewhere in the middle of the jungle. It is usually claimed that the ruins of Angkor were 'discovered' by the French naturalist and explorer Henri Mouhot in 1861. This is a travesty of history: Southeast Asians never forgot that Angkor existed. Truth, as they say, is determined by the powerful, and in this case the West determined that a westerner should 'discover' what was already known. In a sense, Angkor is a great weight on the collective shoulders of the Cambodian people. The usual refrain from visitors is: 'How could a people who created such magnificence have also nurtured Pol Pot and the Khmer Rouge?' The stark disjuncture between the glory of Angkor and the horrors of recent history are almost too sharp to countenance. As Elizabeth Becker wrote at the beginning of 1995:

"Cambodia's recent history is one of breath-taking tragedy; by comparison its immediate future looks small and venal. Today Cambodia resembles many of the striving, corrupt, developing nations trying to make up for time lost behind the iron curtain. ... The nation that bore the horrors of the Khmer Rouge seemed ready for a kinder if not a more prosperous transformation."

CONTENTS

MAPS

In his book *Sideshow*, the British journalist William Shawcross says the diplomats, journalists and tourists who visited Cambodia in the 1950s and 1960s described it as "an idyllic, antique land unsullied by the brutalities of the modern world". Paddy farmers laboured in their ricefields, mystical ruins lay hidden in the jungle, the capital had the charm of a French provincial town and pagodas dotted the landscape. "Such was the illusion," writes Shawcross, of "bucolic plenty, Buddhist serenity, neutralist peace". This was a fallacy because for centuries Cambodia has been in a state of continuous social and political upheaval. Since the demise of the Angkorian Empire in the 15th century, the country has been at the mercy of its much larger neighbours, Siam (Thailand) and Vietnam, and of various foreign powers –

China, France, the US and the former Soviet Union. This history of foreign domination is starkly overshadowed by the so called 'Pol Pot time'. Between 1975 and 1979, Cambodians suffered one of the worst human tragedies to afflict any country since WW2 – more than a million people died out of a total population of about 7 million. If the preceding period, during America's involvement in Indochina, is also taken into account, it is possible that up to a fifth of Cambodia's population was killed.

The relics and reminders of those days are now firmly on the tourist's sightseeing agenda. These include the chilling Tuol Sleng Genocide Museum, in the former high school where the Khmer Rouge tortured and killed at least 20,000 people and Choeung Ek, a series of mass graves, the 'Killing Fields', 15 km SW of Phnom Penh.

Land and life

Geography

Cambodia is all that remains of the once mighty Khmer Empire. Covering a land area of 181,035 sq km – about the size of England and Wales combined – the country is squeezed in between Thailand to the W, Vietnam to the E and Laos to the N. The **Mekong River** is as central to life in Cambodia as the Nile is to life in Egypt. The river runs through Cambodia for about 500 km, bisecting the E lowlands, N to S. It is navigable by cargo ships from the delta in Vietnam, right up to Phnom Penh and beyond. Near the centre of the country is the **Tonlé Sap** – the 'Great Lake' – the largest fresh water lake in Southeast Asia. It is connected to the Mekong via the short channel-like Tonlé Sap River. When the Mekong River floods between Jun and

THE TEARS OF THE GODS: RUBIES AND SAPPHIRES

Major deposits of two of the world's most precious stones are found distributed right across mainland Southeast Asia: rubies and sapphires are mined in Thailand, Burma, Vietnam, Cambodia and Laos. During the civil war in Cambodia, thousands of Thais were mining gems in Khmer Rouge controlled territory (especially around Pailin) – with the protection of the vilified Khmer Rouge and the support of the Thai Army. Bangkok has become the centre of the world's gem business and Thailand is the largest exporter of cut stones.

Rubies and sapphires are different colours of corundum, the crystalline form of aluminium oxide. Small quantities of various trace elements give the gems their colour; in the case of rubies, chromium and for blue sapphires, titanium. Sapphires are also found in a spectrum of other colours including green and yellow. Rubies are among the rarest of gems, and command prices four times higher than equivalent diamonds.

The colour of sapphires can be changed through heat treatment (the most advanced form is called diffusion treatment) to 1500-1600°C (sapphires melt at 2050°C). For example, relatively valueless colourless geuda sapphires from Sri Lanka, turn a brilliant blue or yellow after heating. The technique is an ancient one: Pliny the Elder described the heating of agate by Romans nearly 2,000 years ago, while the Arabs had developed heat treatment into almost a science by the 13th century. Today, almost all sapphires and rubies are heat treated. The most valued colour for sapphires is cornflower blue – dark, almost black, sapphires command a lower price. The value of a stone is based on the four 'C's: Colour, Clarity, Cut and Carat (1 carat = 200 mg). Note that almost all stones are heat treated to improve their colour.

Oct – sometimes these floods can be devastating, as they were in 1991 – the Tonlé Sap River reverses its flow and the floodwaters fill the Great Lake, which doubles in size, covering the surrounding countryside (see page 513).

North of Phnom Penh, the Mekong River is known as the Upper Mekong – or just the Mekong; downriver from the capital it divides into the Lower Mekong and the Bassac rivers. These two tributaries then swing to the SE across the fertile alluvial plain, towards the sprawling delta and the sea. The broad valley of the Mekong is a centuries-old trade route and its fertile central flood-plain is densely populated. The alluvial soils are irrigated but have an even greater potential for agricultural production than is presently being realized. Throughout most of its course in Cambodia the river averages more than 1.6 km in width. There are viscous rapids at Kratie, NE of Phnom Penh, and a succession of dramatic waterfalls – Li Phi and Khong Phapheng Falls – on the border with Laos (see page 406).

The **central lowlands** are surrounded by savanna; in S Cambodia these plains run all the way to the Vietnamese border. But to the N, E and W, Cambodia is enclosed by mountain chains: the Cardamom Mountains and Elephant Range to the W and SW, while the sandstone escarpment of the Dangrek Range forms a natural border with Thailand. The **Cardamom Mountains** (named after the spice) run in a gentle curve from just S of Battambang towards Phnom Penh. Phnom Aural, in the Cardamoms, is Cambodia's highest peak at 1,813m. The **Elephant Mountains** run along the S coastline. All these mountains are densely forested and sparsely inhabited, making them perfect operational bases for Cambodia's rebel guerrilla factions, who fought the Phnom Penh government throughout the 1980s. On the S coast around Kompong Som is a lowland area cut off from the rest of the country by mountains. Because the Mekong was a major thoroughfare, the **coastal region** never developed into a centre of trade until a road was built with American aid from Kompong Som to Phnom Penh in the 1960s.

Climate

The monsoons determine rainfall and temperature patterns in Cambodia. The SW monsoon, from May to Oct, brings heavy rain throughout the country. This period accounts for between 75% and 80% of the total annual rainfall. The NW monsoon blows from Oct to Apr and ushers in the dry season. In the mountain areas the temperature is markedly cooler and the dry season only lasts 3 months. Between the heat and rains there are transitional periods and the best time to visit the country is between Nov and Jan, before it gets too hot. Rainfall varies considerably from region to region. The Cardamom Mountains are the wettest. The mean temperature for Cambodia is 27.5°C. It is cooler – around 24°C – from Nov to Jan and hotter – around 32°C – between Feb and Apr. Humidity is generally high. For a table of monthly temperature and rainfall in Phnom Penh, see page 468).

Flora and fauna

The central plains are a predominantly agricultural area and are sparsely wooded but most of the rest of Cambodia – until recently – was still forested. In 1970, 73% of Cambodia's land area was thought to be forested; the figure in 1995 was less than 40%. In the SW, around the Cardamom and Elephant Mountains, there are still large tracts of primary forest where teak predominates. There are also tracts of virgin rainforest in the W and the NE. At higher elevations in these mountains there are areas of pine forest and in the N and E highlands, temperate forest.

Ly Thuch, Under-Secretary for State for the Environment told a meeting at the Foreign Correspondants Club in Phnom Penh that "the main destroyers of the environment are the Khmer Rouge and the rich and powerful". Thai logging companies, with the permission and connivance of the Khmer Rouge, have been logging large areas of valuable hardwood forest along Cambodia and Thailand's common border in the W – and generating revenue of US$10mn a month. Although the Thai government has consistently argued that Thai companies are not involved, and more to the point that the Thai army is not involved in this business, most independent commentators believe that the lucrative trade has been based upon a triangular relationship including the Khmer Rouge, Thai businessmen, and the Thai army. When government forces captured the town of Pailin in the gem-rich W from the Khmer Rouge in 1994, they discovered six Thai companies working there in league with the rebels. The figure rose to 16 by the end of 1994, with another 10 firms hoping to sign up with the Khmer Rouge soon. These reports flatly contradicted Thai government assurances that there were no Thai companies working in the area. The mining has devastated the area, with many of the rivers now filled with deep-red silt and poisoned with magnesium, potassium and iodine.

In 1995 the Cambodian government introduced a new Environment Law backed-up by further laws such as the Environmental Impact Assessments Law. Experts stated that the Environment Law should be seen as a first step – and not, in itself, as a comprehensive solution to the problems of environmental degradation and exploitation. The lack of transparency in many of the regulations that exist, and the ease with which companies and individuals with political and economic power can circumvent those regulations, makes environmental protection weak. In Mar 1995, for example, the UK-based environmental NGO Global Witness released a report accusing the Khmer Rouge, Thai companies, and the Cambodian government, of profiting from the booming illegal timber trade which, they claim, continues apace despite Cambodia's logging ban. The then Prime Minister of Thailand, Chuan Leekpai, responded to the report saying, "if we knew logs were coming from the Khmer Rouge, we would not allow them in", to which Global Witness Investigator Patrick Alley replied, "If it is so easy for us to visit border areas and see hundreds of trucks loaded with logs coming in from Cambodia, how is it they [the Thais] can't?".

Cambodia has a wide variety of fauna and, before war broke out in the 1970s, was on the international game-hunters' circuit; there were tigers (now an endangered species), buffalo, elephants, wild oxen, clouded leopards (also endangered) and bears including Malaysian sun bears. Even after all the fighting, game is still said to be abundant in forested areas, particularly in N-eastern provinces of Mondulkiri and Rattanakiri. Smaller animals include monkeys, squirrels, tree rats and shrews, flying foxes and numerous species of reptile, including several varieties of poisonous snake, the most common being Russell's viper, the banded krait, cobra and king cobra. The kouprey (meaning 'jungle cow') is Cambodia's most famous animal and a symbol of the Worldwide Fund for Nature. A wild ox, it was first identified in 1939 but is now virtually extinct worldwide. In 1963, King Sihanouk declared the animal Cambodia's national animal. Small numbers are thought to inhabit the more remote areas of the country, although some experts fear that the last specimens were either killed by guerrillas for meat or are being fatally maimed after treading on anti-personnel mines laid by the Khmer Rouge. An effort to capture and breed the kouprey is underway in Vietnam.

Even around Phnom Penh one can see herons, cranes, grouse, pheasant, wild duck, pelicans, cormorants and egrets. The Tonlé Sap area is particularly rich in fish-eating waterfowl.

The Tonlé Sap is also rich in marine life, and supports possibly the largest inland fisheries industry in the world. The lower reaches of the Mekong River, marking the border between Cambodia and Laos, is also the last place in Indochina where the rare Irrawaddy dolphin is to be found. Unfortunately, fishermen in the area have taken to fishing using dynamite and this threatens the survival of the mammal. Explosives are widely available, and evidently this method of fishing is quick and effective. It is also indiscriminate and wasteful, killing juvenile as well as mature fish, and animals like the dolphin which were hitherto left unharmed. The number of dolphins is put at between 100 and 200. It was also once found in Thailand's Chao Phraya River, but pollution put paid to that population years ago.

National parks

Towards the end of 1993, King Sihanouk signed a decree setting in motion a process that should lead to the creation of 23 protected areas, covering 15% of Cambodia's land area. These will include seven national parks and 10 wildlife sanctuaries (see map). The country's first new national park in 25 years is to open in the timber rich province of Kompong Speu.

It may be rather ironic, but the dislocations caused by Cambodia's long-running civil war have probably helped to protect the environment, rather than destroy it. Although larger animals like the kouprey may have suffered from the profusion of land mines that dot the countryside, other animals have benefit-

CAMBODIA'S NATIONAL PARKS (Proposed)

VL 121a

Natural Parks:
1. Kirirom Plateau (Kompong Speu, Koh Kong)
2. Bokor Mountain (Kampot)
3. Kep (Kampot)
4. Ream (Sihanoukville)
5. Botumsako (Sihanoukville)
6. Phnom Kulen Mountain (Siem Reap)
7. Virakcheay (Stung Treng, Ratanakiri)

Scenic Zones:
8. Angkor (Siem Reap)
9. Banteay Chmar (Banteay Mean Chey)
10. Preah Vihear (Preah Vihear)

Multi-Use Zones:
11. Dangpeng (Koh Kong)
12. Samlod (Battambang)
13. Tonle Sap (Kompong Chhnang, Kompong Thom, Siem Reap, Battambang, Pursat)

Wild Animal Sanctuaries:
14. Phnom Orall (Koh Kong, Pursat, Kompong Chhnang)
15. Pream Krasom (Koh Kong)
16. Phnom Samkok (Koh Kong)
17. Roneam Daun Som (Battambang)
18. Kulen, Promatep (Preah Vihear, Siem Reap)
19. Beong Per (Kompong Thom)
20. Lum Phat (Ratanakiri, Mondolkiri)
21. Phnom Prech (Mondolkiri)
22. Phnom Namlea (Mondolkiri)
23. Snoul (Kratie)

ted from the lack of development that has occurred. Unlike Thailand, and to a lesser degree Vietnam, forest has not been cleared for agriculture and many regions became 'no-go' areas except for the foolhardy and the well-armed. This created conditions in which wildlife could survive largely undisturbed by the forces of 'development'. Now wildlife experts and environmentalists are arguing that Cambodia has a unique asset that should be preserved at all costs – and not just because it might be the morally 'right' thing to do. In addition, the growth in eco-tourism world wide could create a considerable money-spinner for the country.

History

Archaeological evidence suggests that the Mekong Delta and the lower reaches of the river – in modern-day Cambodia – have been inhabited since at least 4,000 BC. But the wet and humid climate has destroyed most of the physical remains of the early civilizations. Excavated remains of a settlement at Samrong Sen on the Tonlé Sap show that houses were built of bamboo and wood and raised on stilts – exactly as they are today. Where these people came from is uncertain. Anthropologists believe there were two waves of migration; one from the Malay peninsula/Indonesia and a second from Tibet/China.

Rise of the Lunar and Solar dynasties

For thousands of years Indochina was isolated from the rest of the world and was virtually unaffected by the rise and fall of the early Chinese dynasties. India and China 'discovered' Southeast Asia early in the first millennium and trade networks were quickly established. The Indian influence was particularly strong in the Mekong basin area. The Khmers adopted and adapted Indian script as well as their ideas about astrology, religion (Buddhism and Hinduism) and royalty (the cult of the semi-divine ruler). Today, several other aspects of Cambodian culture are recognizably Indian in origin – including classical literature and dance. Religious architecture also followed Indian models. These Indian cultural influences which took root in Indochina gave rise to a legend to which Cambodia traces its historical origins. An Indian Brahmin called Kaundinya, travelling in the Mekong delta area, married Soma, daughter of the Naga (the serpent deity – see page 494), or Lord of the Soil. Their union, which founded the 'Lunar Dynasty' of Funan (a pre-Angkorian Kingdom), symbolized the fertility of the kingdom and occupies a central place in Khmer cosmology. The Naga, Soma's father, helpfully drank the floodwaters of the Mekong, enabling people to cultivate the land.

The kingdom of Funan – the forerunner of Kambuja – was established on the Mekong by tribal people from S China in the middle of the 3rd century AD and became the earliest Hindu state in Southeast Asia. Funan was known for its elaborate irrigation canals which controlled the Mekong floodwaters, irrigated the paddy fields and prevented the incursion of seawater. By the 5th century Funan had extended its influence over most of present day Cambodia, as well as Indochina and parts of the Malay Peninsula. Leadership was measured by success in battle and the ability to provide protection; in recognition of this fact, rulers from the Funan period onward incorporated the suffix – 'varman' (meaning protection) into their names. Records of a 3rd century Chinese embassy give an idea of what it was like: "There are walled villages, places and dwellings. The men ... go about naked and barefoot. ... Taxes are paid in gold, silver and perfume. There are books and libraries and they can use the alphabet." 20th century excavations suggest a seafaring people engaged in extensive trade with both India and China, and elsewhere.

CONFUSION IN THE NAME OF THE SONS OF KAMBU

The word Cambodia derives from 'Kambuja' meaning 'the sons of Kambu' – the ascetic who, according to Khmer legend, married a celestial nymph and founded the kingdom of Chenla, the forerunner to the great Khmer Empire.

Khmers called the country Kambuja; the English, Cambodia; and the French, Cambodge. Kampuchea is the usual transliteration of Kambuja – although political inferences crept into the usage of the term when the Khmer Rouge insisted on calling the country Kampuchea. In the 4 decades since Cambodian independence in 1953, the name has changed several times.

On independence in 1953, it was called the kingdom of Cambodia. In 1970, the country was renamed the Khmer Republic following the overthrow of Prince Sihanouk. Then, in 1975 it was renamed Democratic Kampuchea following the Khmer Rouge take-over. 4 years later, in 1979, the Hanoi-backed regime renamed the country the People's Republic of Kampuchea. Finally, in 1989, it was renamed the State of Cambodia or *Roet Kampuchea*.

MEKONG EXPLORATION – SLOWLY UP THE RAPIDS

In 1866, 3 years after Cambodia became a French protectorate, the first Resident in Cambodia, Doudart de Lagrée and a 23-year-old naval lieutenant, Francis Garnier, set out on an expedition to explore the interior of Indochina by following the Mekong River. One of their first stops was to visit the ruins of Angkor which had been made famous by Henri Mouhot just 5 years earlier, after which they pushed N, consuming legendary quantities of alcohol in an effort to ease the discomforts of the terrain, climate, mosquitoes and disease. They made their way up past the Kratie rapids and Khong falls, finally reaching Vientiane (Laos) in Apr 1867. A fortnight later, they were in the old royal Lao capital of Luang Prabang. From there they pushed further N into China, where Lagrée collapsed and died. Garnier made it back to Saigon with the other survivors, via Shanghai. He had surveyed about 6,500 km of uncharted territory; his maps were published in his landmark atlas of Indochina – *Atlas d'Explorations en Indo-Chine* – in 1873, the year he was ambushed and killed by Chinese bandits just outside Hanoi.

The 'Solar Dynasty' of Chenla was a tributary kingdom of Funan, probably first based on the Mekong at the junction with the Mun tributary, but rapidly grew in power. It was the immediate predecessor of Kambuja and the great Khmer Empire. According to Khmer legend, the kingdom was the result of the marriage of Kambu, an ascetic, to a celestial nymph named Mera. The people of Chenla – the Kambuja, or the sons of Kambu – lent their name to the country. Chenla, was centred in the area of present day S Laos. In 540 AD a Funan prince married a Chenla princess, uniting the Solar and Lunar dynasties. But the prince sided with his wife, turning against his own people and Funan was swallowed by Chenla. The first capital of this fusion of Chenla and Funan was at Sambor. King Ishanavarman (616-635) established a new capital at Sambor Prei Kuk, 30 km from modern Kompong Thom, in the centre of the country (the monuments of which are some of the best preserved of this period). His successor, Jayavarman I, moved the capital to the region of Angkor Borei near Takeo.

Quarrels in the ruling family led to the break up of the state in the 7th century: it was divided into 'Land Chenla', a farming culture located N of the Tonlé Sap (maybe centred around Champassak in Laos), and 'Water Chenla', a trading culture based along the Mekong River. Towards the end of the 8th century Water Chenla became a vassal of Java's powerful Sailendra Dynasty and members of Chenla's ruling family were taken back to the Sailendra court. This period, from the fall of Funan until the 8th century, is known as the pre-Angkorian period – it is a hazy period of Cambodian history. The Khmers remained firmly under Javanese suzerainty until Jayavarman II (802-850), who was born in central Java, returned to the land of his ancestors around 800 AD to change the course of Cambodian history.

Angkor and the god-kings

Jayavarman II, the Khmer prince who had spent most of his life at the Sailendra court, claimed independence from Java and founded the Angkor Kingdom to the N of the Tonlé Sap in 802, at about the same time as Charlemagne became Holy Roman Emperor in Europe. They were men cast in the same mould, for both were empire builders. Jayavarman won immediate political popularity on his return and, to consolidate and legiti-

HOW TO CROWN A GOD-KING

The coronation ceremony of a Cambodian god-king, dating back to the kings of Angkor is steeped in historical ritual. On coronation day, the crown prince traditionally took possession of the city by circumambulating in imitation of a mythical king who inherited the world by encircling the outermost shore of the outermost ocean. On his circumambulation, the would-be king used four different types of transport and changed his headdress four times, each time assuming the traditional costume and mount of one of the kings of the four cardinal points. Water also played an important role, symbolizing allegiance and vassaldom. At the courts of Phnom Penh – as in Bangkok – holy water was gathered from the principal rivers in the scattered provinces of the kingdom. This water was used to annoint the new monarch during the coronation ceremony.

mize his position, arranged his coronation by a Brahmin priest, declaring himself the first Khmer devaraja, or god-king. From then on, the reigning monarch was identified with Siva, the king of the Hindu gods. In the centuries that followed, successive devaraja strove to outdo their predecessors by building bigger and finer temples to house the royal lingam (the symbol of Siva and the devaraja). The god-kings commanded the absolute allegiance of their subjects, allowing them control of a vast pool of labour which was used to build an advanced and prosperous agricultural civilization. For many years historians and archaeologists maintained that the key to this agricultural wealth lay in a sophisticated hydraulic – ie irrigated – system of agriculture (see page 500) which allowed the Khmers to produce upto three harvests a year. However this view of Angkorian agriculture has come under increasing scrutiny in recent years and now there are many who believe that flood-retreat – rather than irrigated – agriculture was the key. Jayavarman II installed himself in successive capitals N of the Tonlé Sap, secure from attack by the Sailendras, and he ruled until 850. Indrapura was his first capital (to the E of Kompong Cham); later he moved his capital to Wat Phu (in S Laos) and the Roluos (Angkor).

Jayavarman III (850-877) continued

his father's traditions and ruled for the next 27 years. Indravarman (877-889), his successor, was the first of the great temple-builders of Angkor. At the end of the 9th century Yasovarman I (889-900) moved the capital from Roluos and laid the foundations of Angkor itself. He called his new capital Yasodharapura and copied the water system his father had devised at Roluos on an even larger scale, using the waters of the Tonlé Sap. In 921, Jayavarman IV set up a rival capital about 65 km from Angkor at Koh Ker (see page 515) but 30 years later, Rajendravarman moved the court back to Angkor, where the Khmer kings remained. Rajendravarman (944-968) is believed to have been a tolerant king and allowed the establishment of several Mahayana Buddhist temples at Angkor.

The formidable warrior King Suryavarman I (1002-1050), who may originally have come from the Malay peninsula, conquered the kingdom in the early 11th century and extended its influence as far as S Thailand and Laos. He continued the royal Hindu cult but also tolerated Mahayana Buddhism. Ta Keo (NW of Angkor Thom) and the Phimeanakas pyramid temples were Suryavarman's main contributions to Angkor's architectural heritage (see page 503). But on Suryavarman's death, the Khmer Kingdom began to fragment due to internal revolt. His three successors had short, troubled reigns and the

A CHINESE EMISSARY'S ACCOUNT OF HIS STAY AT ANGKOR (1296-1297)

One of the most interesting documents of the great empire of Angkor is the Chinese emissary Chou Ta-kuan's short account of his stay there entitled *Notes on the customs of Cambodia*. The book was written in the late 13th or early 14th century, shortly after he had returned to China after a sojourn at Angkor between 1296 and 1297. His book describes the last days of the kingdom and his role was as male companion to the Chinese ambassador.

The book is divided into 40 short 'chapters' dealing with aspects of everyday and royal life ranging from childbirth, to justice, to clothing. The account also details aspects of the natural environment (fish and reptiles, birds), the economy of the empire (agriculture, trade, products), and technology (utensils, boats and oars). What makes the account so useful and unusual is that it describes not just the concerns and actions of great men and women, but of everyday life too. The extracts below are just a sample of the insights into everyday Cambodian life during the waning days of the Angkorian Empire. For those intending to visit the site of Angkor, the book is highly recommended reading. It brings to life the ruins of a city, helping the visitor to imagine a place – now so empty – full of people and life.

Cambodian dwellings Out of the [royal] palace rises a golden tower, to the top of which the ruler ascends nightly to sleep. It is common belief that in the tower dwells a genie, formed like a serpent with nine heads, which is Lord of the entire kingdom. Every night this genie appears in the shape of a woman, with whom the sovereign couples. Not even the wives of the King may enter here. At the second watch the King comes forth and is then free to sleep with his wives and his concubines. Should the genie fail to appear for a single night, it is a sign that the King's death is at hand.

Straw thatch covers the dwellings of the commoners, not one of whom would dare place the smallest bit of tile on his roof.

Clothing Every man or woman, from the sovereign down, knots the hair and leaves the shoulders bare. Round the waist they wear a small strip of cloth, over which a large piece is drawn when they leave their houses. Many rules, based on rank, govern the choice of materials. ... Only the ruler may wear fabrics woven in an all over pattern.

The natives Generally speaking, the women, like the men, wear only a strip of cloth, bound round the waist, showing bare breasts of milky whiteness. ... As for the concubines and palace girls, I have heard it said that there are from three to five thousand of these, separated into various categories. ... When a beautiful girl is born into a family, no time is lost in sending her to the palace.

Childbirth Once a Cambodian woman's child is born, she immediately makes a poultice of hot rice and salt and applies it to her private parts. This is taken off in 24 hrs, thus preventing any untoward after-effects and causing an astringency which seems to renew the young mother's virginity. When told of this for the first time, my credulity was sorely taxed. However, in the house where I lodged a girl gave birth to a child, and I was able to observe beyond peradventure that the next day she was up carrying the baby in her arms and going with him to bathe in the river. This seems truly amazing!

Everyone with whom I talked said that the Cambodian women are highly sexed. One or 2 days after giving birth they are ready for intercourse: if a husband is not responsive he will be discarded. When a man is called away on matters of business, they endure his absence for a while; but if he is gone as much as 10 days, the wife is apt to say, "I am no ghost; how can I be expected to sleep alone?".

Slaves Wild men from the hills can be bought to serve as slaves. Families of wealth may own more than 100; those of lesser means content themselves with 10 or 20; only the very poor have none. ... If a slave should run away and be captured, a blue mark would be tattooed on his face; moreover, an iron collar would be fitted to his neck, or shackles to his arms or legs.

Cambodian justice Points of dispute between citizens, however trifling, are taken to the ruler. ... In dealing with cases of great seriousness, recourse is not had to strangulation or beheading; outside the West Gate, however, a ditch is dug into which the criminal is placed, earth and stones are thrown back and heaped high, and all is over. ... Lesser crimes are dealt with by cutting off feet or hands, or by amputation of the nose.

When a thief is caught red-handed, he may be imprisoned and tortured. Recourse is also had to another curious procedure. If an object is missing, and accusation brought against someone who denies the charge, oil is brought to boil in a kettle and the suspected person forced to plunge his hand into it. If he is truly guilty, the hand is cooked to shreds; if not, skin and bones are unharmed. Such is the amazing way of these barbarians.

Products of Cambodia Many rare woods are to be found in the highlands. Unwooded regions are those where elephants and rhinoceros gather and breed. Exotic birds and strange animals abound. The most sought-after products are the feathers of the kingfisher, elephants tusks, rhinoceros horns, and beeswax.

Trade In Cambodia it is the women who take charge of trade. For this reason a Chinese arriving in the country, loses no time in getting himself a mate, for he will find her commercial instincts a great asset.

Utensils For sleeping only bamboo mats are used, laid on the wooden floors. Of late, certain families have adopted the use of low beds, which for the most part are made by the Chinese.

A prodigy Within the Walled City, near the East Gate, a Cambodian man committed fornication with his younger sister. Their skin and their flesh were fused beyond the power of separating them. After 3 days passed without food, both parties died. My compatriot Mr Hsieh, who spent 35 years in this country declares he has known this to happen twice. If such be the case, it shows how well the Cambodians are policed by the supernatural power of their holy Buddha.

● Notes on the customs of Cambodia was originally translated from the Chinese original into French by Paul Pelliot. J Gilman d'Arcy Paul translated the French version into English, and the Siam Society in Bangkok have republished this version with colour photographs and reproductions of Delaporte's fine lithographs of the monuments. *The customs of Cambodia*, Siam Society: Bangkok, 1993.

Chams (Champa was a rural kingdom based in present day Vietnam) captured, sacked and razed the capital.

In 1080 a new kingdom was founded by a N provincial governor claiming aristocratic descent. He called himself Jayavarman VI (1080-1107). He never settled at Angkor, living instead in the N part of the kingdom. He left monuments at Wat Phou in S Laos (see page 401), and Preah Vihear (or Phra Viharn) and Phimai, both in Thailand. When Jayavarman VI died in 1107, the throne was protected by his brothers for his grand-nephew Suryavarman II (1131-1150), who asceded to the throne 6 years later. He was the greatest of Angkor's god-kings, during whose reign the temple of Angkor Wat was built. It was an architectural masterpiece and represented the height of the Khmer's artistic genius (see page 505). Under him, the Khmer Kingdom encompassed a large part of Thailand, S Vietnam, Laos and part of the Malay peninsula. A network of roads was built to connect regional capitals, one of the most important being Phimai in NE Thailand.

Suryavarman II deposed the King of Champa in 1145 but the Chams regained their independence in 1149 and the following year, Suryavarman died after a disastrous attempt to conquer Annam (northern Vietnam). In 1177 the Chams seized their chance of revenge and sacked Angkor. But when the 50-year-old Jayavarman VII – a cousin of Suryavarman – attained power in 1181, he hit back, attacking the Chams and seizing their capital, Vijaya. He expanded the Khmer Kingdom further than ever before; its suzerainty stretched from the Malay peninsula in the S to the borders of Burma in the W and the Annamite chain to the NE.

Jayavarman's VII's first task was to plan a strong, spacious new capital – Angkor Thom; but while that work was being undertaken he set up a smaller, temporary seat of government where he and his court could live in the meantime – Preah Khan meaning 'Fortunate City of Victory' (see page 509). He also built 102 hospitals throughout his kingdom, as well as a network of roads, along which he constructed resthouses. But because they were built of wood, none of these secular structures survive; only the foundations of four larger ones have been unearthed at Angkor.

Angkor's decline

Jayavarman VII's principal architectural legacy was his capital, Angkor Thom (*Thom* literally translates as 'great'), which was begun in 1200. The mysterious and visually powerful 12th century Bayon temple, was his most ambitious architectural feat. It is said that the Bayon was completed in 21 years and was the last of the fine monuments built at Angkor. Jayavarman took thousands of peasants from the rice fields to build it, which proved a fatal error, for rice yields decreased and the empire began its decline as resources were drained. Jayavarman VII adopted Mahayana Buddhism; Buddhist principles replaced the Hindu pantheon, and were invoked as the basis of royal authority. This spread of Buddhism is thought to have caused some of the earlier Hindu temples to be neglected, while others were converted to the new faith.

Jayavarman VII died in 1218 and the Kambujan Empire fell into progressive decline over the next 2 centuries. Territorially, it was eroded by the E migration of the Siamese. The Khmers were unable to prevent this gradual incursion but the diversion of labour to the military from temple building and rice farming helped seal the fate of Angkor. Another reason for the decline was the introduction of Theravada Buddhism in the 13th century, which undermined the prestige of the king and the priests. There is even a view that climatic change disrupted the agricultural system and led to Kambuja's demise. After Jayavarman VII, no king seems to have been able to unify the kingdom by force of arms or personality – internal dissent increased while the king's extravagance continued to place a crippling burden on state funds. With its temples decaying and its once-magnificent agricultural system in ruins, Angkor became virtually uninhabitable. In 1431 the royal capital was finally abandoned to the Siamese, who drove the Khmers out and made Cambodia a vassal of the Thai Sukhothai Kingdom.

Explaining Angkor's decline

Why the Angkorian Empire should have declined has always fascinated scholars in the W – in the same way that the decline and fall of the Roman Empire has done. Numerous explanations have been offered, and still the debate remains unresolved. As Anthony Barnett argued in a paper in the *New Left Review* in 1990, perhaps the question should be "why did Angkor last so long? Inauspiciously sited, it was nonetheless a tropical imperium of 500 years' duration."

There are essentially five lines of argument in the 'Why did Angkor fall?' game. First, it has been argued that the building programmes became simply so arduous and demanding of ordinary people that they voted with their feet and moved out, depriving Angkor of the population necessary to support the great empire. Second, some scholars have presented an environmental argument: that the great irrigation works silted-up, undermining the agricultural wealth on which the empire was based. (This line of argument conflicts with recent work that maintains that Angkor's wealth was never based on hydraulic – or irrigated – agriculture.) Third, there are those who say that military defeat was to be the cause – although that begs the question of why they were defeated in the first place. Fourth, historians with a rather wider view, have offered the opinion that the centres of economic activity in Southeast Asia moved from land-based to sea-based foci, and that Angkor was poorly located to adapt to this shift in patterns of trade, wealth and, hence, power. Lastly, some scholars have argued that the religion on which kings demanded labour of their subjects became so corrupt as to corrode the empire from within.

After Angkor – running scared

The next 500 years or so, until the arrival of the French in 1863, was an undistinguished period in Cambodian history. In 1434 the royal Khmer court under Ponheayat moved to Phnom Penh, where a replica of the cosmic Mt Meru was built. There was a short-lived period of revival in the mid-15th century until the Siamese invaded and sacked the capital again in 1473. One of the sons of the captured King Suryavarman drummed up enough Khmer support to oust the invaders and there were no subsequent invasions during the 16th century. The capital was established at Lovek (between Phnom Penh and Tonlé Sap) and then moved back to the ruins at Angkor. But a Siamese invasion in 1593 sent the royal court fleeing into Laos; finally, in 1603, the Thais released a captured prince to rule over their Cambodian vassal. There were at least 22 kings between 1603 and 1848.

Politically, the Cambodian court tried to steer a course between its powerful neighbours of Siam and Vietnam, seeking one's protection against the other. King Chey Chetta II (1618-1628), eg declared Cambodia's independence from Siam and in order to back up his actions he asked Vietnam for help. To cement the allegiance he was forced to marry a Vietnamese princess of the Nguyen Dynasty of Annam, and then obliged to pay tribute to Vietnam. His successors – hoping to rid themselves of Vietnamese domination – sought Siamese assistance and were then forced to pay for it by acknowledging Siam's suzerainty. Then in 1642, King Chan converted to

Islam, and encouraged Malay and Javanese migrants to settle in Cambodia. Considering him guilty of apostasy, his cousins ousted him – with Vietnamese support. But 50 years later, the Cambodian Ang Eng was crowned in Bangkok. This see-saw pattern continued for years; only Siam's wars with Burma and Vietnam's internal disputes and long-running conflict with China prevented them from annexing the whole of Cambodia, although both took territorial advantage of the fragmented state.

By the early 1700s the kingdom was centred on Phnom Penh (there were periods when the king resided at Ondong). But when the Khmers lost their control over the Mekong Delta to the Vietnamese in the late 18th century, the capital's access to the sea was blocked. By 1750 the Khmer royal family had split into pro-Siamese and pro-Vietnamese factions. Between 1794-1811 and 1847-1863, Siamese influence was strongest; from 1835-1837 the Vietnamese dominated. In the 1840s, the Siamese and Vietnamese armies fought on Cambodian territory devastating the country. This provoked French intervention – and cost Cambodia its independence, even if it had been nominal for several centuries. On 17 April 1864 (the same day and month as the Khmer Rouge soldiers entered Phnom Penh) King Norodom agreed to French protection as he believed they would provide military assistance against the Siamese. The king was to be disappointed: France honoured Siam's claim to the W provinces of Battambang, Siem Reap and Sisophon, which Bangkok had captured in the late 1600s. (They were only returned to Cambodia in 1907.) And in 1884, King Norodom was persuaded by the French governor of the colony of Cochin China to sign another treaty that turned Cambodia into a French colony, along with Laos and Vietnam in the Union Indochinoize. The establishment of Cambodia as a French protectorate probably saved the country from being apportioned between Siam and Vietnam.

The French colonial period

The French did little to develop Cambodia, preferring instead for the territory to pay for itself. The French only invested income generated from tax revenue to build a communications network. In the 1920s French private-sector investors planted out rubber estates in Kompong Cham in E Cambodia. From a Cambodian perspective, the only benefit of colonial rule was that the French forestalled the total disintegration of the country, which would otherwise have been divided up between its warring neighbours. French cartographers also mapped Cambodia's borders for the first time and in so doing, the French forced the Thais to surrender the NW provinces of Battambang and Siem Reap.

For nearly a century the French alternately supported two branches of the royal family, the Norodoms and the Sisowaths, crowning the 18-year-old schoolboy Prince Norodom Sihanouk in 1941. The previous year, the Nazis had invaded and occupied France; French territories in Indochina were in turn occupied by the Japanese – although Cambodia was still formally governed and administered by the French. It was at this stage that a group of pro-independence Cambodians realized just how weak the French control of their country actually was. In 1942 two monks were arrested and accused of preaching anti-French sermons; within 2 days this sparked demonstrations by more than 1,000 monks in Phnom Penh. These demonstrations marked the beginning of Cambodian nationalism. In Mar 1945 Japanese forces ousted the colonial administration and persuaded King Norodom Sihanouk to proclaim independence. Following the Japanese surrender in Aug 1945, the French came back in force; Sihanouk tried to negotiate independence from France and they responded by abolishing the absolute monarchy in 1946 – although the king remained titular head of state. A new constitution was introduced allowing political activity and a National Assembly elected.

Independence and neutrality

By the early 1950s the French army had suffered several defeats in the war in Indochina. Sihanouk dissolved the National Assembly in mid-1952, which he was entitled to do under the constitution, and personally took charge of steering Cambodia towards independence from France. To publicize the cause, he travelled to Thailand, Japan and the United States, and said he would not return from self-imposed exile until his country was free. His audacity embarrassed the French into granting Cambodia independence on 9 November 1953 – and Sihanouk returned, triumphant.

The people of Cambodia did not want to return to absolute monarchy, and following his abdication in 1955, Sihanouk became a popular political leader. But political analysts believe that despite the apparent popularity of the former king's administration, different factions began to develop at this time, a process which was the root of the conflict in the years to come. During the 1960s, eg there was a growing rift between the Khmer majority and other ethnic groups, between the city dwellers and the farmers, as well as among the urban élites themselves. Even in the countryside, differences became marked between the rice-growing areas and the remoter mountain areas where people practised shifting cultivation supplementing their diet with lizards, snakes, roots and insects. As these problems intensified in the late 1960s and the economic situation deteriorated, the popular support base for the Khmer Rouge was put into place. With unchecked population growth, land ownership patterns became skewed, landlessness more widespread and food prices escalated. The Chinese community was increasingly resented as Chinese businessmen emerged as loan-sharks.

Sihanouk managed to keep Cambodia out of the war that enveloped Laos and Vietnam during the late 1950s and 1960s by following a neutral policy – which helped attract millions of dollars of economic aid to Cambodia from both the W and the Eastern Bloc. But when a full scale civil war broke out in S Vietnam in the early 1960s, Cambodia's survival – and Sihanouk's own survival – depended on its outcome. Sihanouk believed the rebels, the National Liberation Front (NLF) – allied to the Communist regime in Hanoi – would win; he openly courted and backed the NLF. It was an alliance which cost him dear. In 1965-1966 the tide began to turn in S Vietnam, due to US military and economic intervention. This forced NLF troops to take refuge inside Cambodia (in 1966 half of Cambodia's rice supplies, normally sold abroad, were distributed to the NLF agents inside Cambodia). A peasant uprising in NW provinces in 1967 showed Sihanouk that he was sailing rather close to the wind; his forces brutally suppressed the rebellion by massacring as many as 10,000 peasants.

But slowly – and inevitably – he became the focus of resentment within Cambodia's political élite. He also incurred American wrath by allowing N Vietnamese forces to use Cambodian territory as an extension of the Ho Chi Minh Trail (see page 394), ferrying arms and men into S Vietnam. This resulted in his former army Commander-in-Chief, Marshal Lon Nol masterminding his removal as Head of State while Sihanouk was in Moscow in 1970. Lon Nol abolished the monarchy and proclaimed a republic. One of the most auspicious creatures in Khmer mythology is the white crocodile. The crocodile is said to appear above the surface at important times. A white crocodile was sighted near Phnom Penh just before Lon Nol took over.

KING NORODOM SIHANOUK: LATTERDAY GOD-KING

An uncomplimentary profile of Prince Norodom Sihanouk in *The Economist* in 1990 said that over the preceding 20 years, he "twisted and turned, sulked, resigned many times, [was] humiliated and imprisoned. In one thing, however, he [was] consistent: his yearning to recover the face he lost in 1970, and return to Phnom Penh in triumph". The following year, on 14 Nov, Prince Sihanouk did exactly that, arriving in his former royal capital to a rapturous welcome, after 13 years of exile. In Nov 1991, as in 1953 when he returned from exile at Independence, he represented the one symbol Cambodia had of any semblance of national unity.

Norodom Sihanouk was crowned King of Cambodia at the age of 18 in 1941. He owed his accession to the throne to a method of selection devised by the French colonial regime who hoped that the young, inexperienced Sihanouk would be a compliant puppet-king. But in the event he turned out to be something very different. Using his position to great advantage, he became a nationalist leader and crusaded for independence in 1953. But following independence, his royal title worked against him: the 1947 constitution restricted the role the monarch could play in politics. So, he abdicated in favour of his father, Norodom Suramarit, in 1955 and, as Prince Sihanouk, was free to enter politics. He immediately founded the *Sangkum Reastr Niyum* – the Popular Socialist Community (PSC). The same year, the PSC won every seat in the National Assembly – as it did in subsequent elections in 1958, 1962 and 1966.

The old king died in 1960, but Sihanouk side-stepped the problem of succession by declaring himself Head of State, without ascending to the throne. Michael Leifer, a British political scientist, writes: "As Head of State, Prince Sihanouk became literally the voice of Cambodia. He articulated its hopes and fears within the country and to the outside world... He appeared as a popular figure revered especially in the rural areas as the father figure of his country." He was a populist of the first order. In Someth May's autobiography *Cambodian Witness*, he describes Phnom Penh in the early 1960s:

"Sihanouk's portrait was everywhere around town: in uniform with a sword, in a suit, in monk's robes, dressed in white with a shaved head like an *achar*; on posters, on notebooks; framed in every classroom above the teacher's head; in the shops and offices. In the magazine that he edited himself we saw him helping a farmer

The third Indochina war and the rise of the Khmer Rouge

On 30 April 1970, following the overthrow of Prince Norodom Sihanouk, US President Richard Nixon officially announced Washington's military intervention in Cambodia – although in reality it had been going on for some time. The invasion aimed to deny the Vietnamese Communists the use of Sihanoukville port (present day Kompong Som) through which 85% of their heavy arms were reaching S Vietnam. The US Air Force had been secretly bombing Cambodia using B-52s since Mar 1969. In 1973, facing defeat in Vietnam, the US Air Force B-52s began carpet bombing Communist-controlled areas to enable Lon Nol's inept regime to retain control of the besieged provincial cities. Historian David P Chandler writes:

"When the campaign was stopped by the US Congress at the end of the year, the B-52s had dropped over half a million tons of bombs on a country with which the United States was not at war – more than twice the tonnage dropped on Japan during WW2.

dig an irrigation canal, reviewing the troops, shooting a film (for he was also a film-maker), addressing the National Assembly, giving presents to the monks, opening the annual regatta with his wife, Monique. On the radio we heard his speeches, and one year when he had a craze for singing you could hear his songs more than 10 times a day."

Sihanouk liked to run the show single-handedly and he treated his ministers like flunkies. In *Sideshow*, William Shawcross paints him as being vain – " a petulant showman who enjoyed boasting of his sexual successes. He would not tolerate criticism or dissent... At the same time he had enormous political skill, charm, tenacity and intelligence."

With an American-backed right-wing regime in power after the coup in 1970, the former king went into exile in China, where his supporters formed an alliance with his former enemies, the Khmer Rouge: the Royal Government of National Union of Cambodia – otherwise known as the Grunc. When the Khmer Rouge marched into Phnom Penh in 1975, they restored Prince Sihanouk as Head of State.

He resigned in Apr 1976 as he became increasingly marginalized, and the Grunc was dissolved. Sihanouk was kept under house-arrest until a few days before the Vietnamese army occupied Phnom Penh in Jan 1979, whereupon he fled to Beijing. There Sihanouk and his supporters once again joined forces with the Khmer Rouge in a tripartite coalition aimed at overthrowing the Hanoi-backed government.

The peace settlement which followed the eventual Vietnamese withdrawal in 1989 paved the way for Sihanouk's return from exile. His past association with the Khmer Rouge had tarnished the prince's image, but to many Cambodians, he represents one of their few hopes for a stable future. Following the elections of 1993, Sihanouk returned from Beijing to be crowned King on 24 Sep, thus reclaiming the throne he relinquished in 1955. Now an old man – he turned 73 in 1995 and suffers from cancer of the prostate – many commentators wonder whether he will ever see his country truly at peace. Who his successor might be, and what his role might be, is far from clear. The next king will be nominated by the fractious Royal Council to the Throne. Currently three of Sihanouk's sons are all in the frame.

"The war in Cambodia was known as 'the sideshow' by journalists covering the war in Vietnam and by American policy-makers in London. Yet the intensity of US bombing in Cambodia was greater than it ever was in Vietnam; about 500,000 soldiers and civilians were killed over the 4 year period. It also caused about 2 million refugees to flee from the countryside to the capital."

By the end of the war, the country had become totally dependent on US aid and much of the population survived on American rice rations. Confidence in the Lon Nol government collapsed as taxes rose and even children were drafted into combat units. At the same time, the Khmer Rouge increased its military strength dramatically and began to make inroads into areas formerly controlled by government troops. Although officially the Khmer Rouge rebels represented the Beijing-based Royal Government of National Union of Cambodia (Grunc), which was headed by the exiled Prince Sihanouk. Grunc's *de facto* leaders were Pol Pot, Khieu Samphan (who today is the public face of the Khmer Rouge), Ieng Sary (later foreign minister) and

POL POT – THE IDEALISTIC PSYCHOPATH

Prince Norodom Sihanouk once referred to Pol Pot as "a more fortunate Hitler". Unlike his erstwhile fascist counterpart, the man whose troops were responsible for the deaths of between 1 and 2 million fellow Cambodians has managed to get away with it. Pol Pot's real name is Saloth Sar – he adopted his *nom de guerre* when he became Secretary-General of the Cambodian Communist Party in 1963. He was born in 1928 into a peasant family in Kompong Thom, central Cambodia, and is believed to have lived as a novice monk for 9 months when he was a child. His services to the Democrat Party won him a scholarship to study electronics in Paris. But he became a Communist in France in 1949 and spent more time at meetings of Marxist revolutionary societies than in classes. In his 1986 book *Sideshow*, William Shawcross notes that at that time the French Communist Party, which was known for its dogmatic adherence to orthodox Marxism, "taught hatred of the bourgeoisie and uncritical admiration of Stalinism, including the collectivization of agriculture". Pol Pot finally lost his scholarship in 1953.

Returning to newly independent Cambodia, Pol Pot started working as a school teacher in Phnom Penh and continued his revolutionary activities in the underground Cambodian Communist Party (which, remarkably kept its existence a secret until 1977). In 1963, he fled the capital for the countryside, fearing a crack-down of the left by Sihanouk. There he rose to become Secretary-General of the Central Committee of the Communist Party of Kampuchea. He was trained in guerrilla warfare and he became a leader of the Khmer Rouge forces, advocating armed resistance to Sihanouk and his 'feudal entourage'. In 1975 when the Khmer

Son Sen (Chief of General Staff) – all Khmer Rouge men. By the time the American bombing stopped in 1973, the guerrillas dominated about 60% of Cambodian territory, while the government clung tenuously to towns and cities. Over the next 2 years the Khmer Rouge whittled away Phnom Penh's defence perimeter to the point that Lon Nol's government was only sustained by American airlifts into the capital.

Some commentators have suggested that the persistent heavy bombing of Cambodia, which forced the Communist guerrillas to live in terrible conditions – was in part, responsible for the notorious savagery of the Khmer Rouge in later years. Not only were they brutalized by the conflict itself, but they became resentful that the city-dwellers had no inkling of how unpleasant their experiences really were. This, writes US political scientist Wayne Bert, "created the perception among the Khmer Rouge that the bulk of the population did not

take part in the revolution, was therefore not enthusiastic about it and could not be trusted to support it. The final step in this logic was to punish or eliminate all in these categories who showed either real or imagined tendencies toward disloyalty." And that, as anyone who has watched *The Killing Fields* will know, is what happened.

The 'Pol Pot time': building year zero

On 1 April 1975 President Lon Nol fled Cambodia to escape the rapidly advancing Khmer Rouge. Just over 2 weeks later, on 17 Apr, the victorious Khmer Rouge entered Phnom Penh. The capital's population had been swollen by refugees from 600,000 to over 2 million. The ragged conquering troops wearing Ho Chi Minh sandals made of used rubber tyres – which were *de rigueur* for guerrillas in Indochina – were welcomed as heroes. None in the crowds that lined

Rouge marched into Phnom Penh, Pol Pot was forced out of the shadows to take the role of leader, 'Brother Number One'. Although he took the title of Prime Minister, he ruled as a dictator and set about reshaping Cambodia with his mentor, Khieu Samphan, the Head of State. Yet during the years he was in power, hardly any Cambodians – save those in the top echelons of the Khmer Rouge – had even heard of him.

The Vietnam-backed Hun Sen government, which took over the country after the overthrow of the Khmer Rouge in Dec 1978, calculated that by demonizing Pol Pot as the mastermind of the genocide, it would avert the possibility of the Khmer Rouge ever making a comeback. The Hun Sen regime showed no interest in analysing the complex factors which combined to bring Pol Pot to power. Within Cambodia, he has been portrayed simply as a tyrannical bogey-man. During the 1980s, 20 May was declared National Hate Day, when everyone reaffirmed their hatred of Pol Pot.

Pol Pot and what Hun Sen dubbed 'his genocidal clique' of close associates are thought still to control the movement, which continues to hold areas of rural Cambodia. In a review of David Chandler's biography of Pol Pot (*Brother Number One: A Political Biography of Pol Pot*, Westview Press, 1992), Peter Carey – the co-director of the British-based Cambodia Trust – was struck by what he called "the sinister disjunction between the man's evident charisma ... and the monumental suffering wrought by his regime". Carey concludes: "one is left with the image of a man consumed by his own vision, a vision of empowerment and liberation that has little anchorage in Cambodian reality".

the streets appreciated the horrors that the victory would also bring. Cambodia was renamed Democratic Kampuchea (DK) and Pol Pot set to work establishing a radical Maoist-style agrarian society. These ideas had been first sketched out by his longstanding colleague Khieu Samphan, whose 1959 doctoral thesis – at the Sorbonne University in Paris – analysed the effects of Cambodia's colonial and neo-colonial domination. In order to secure true economic and political independence he argued that it was necessary to isolate Cambodia completely and to go back to a self-sufficient agricultural economy.

It was Prince Norodom Sihanouk who had first coined the term 'Khmer Rouge' when he faced a peasant uprising in 1967; they called themselves *Angkar Loeu* – 'The Higher Organization'. Within days, the rubber sandalled revolutionaries had forcibly evacuated many of the inhabitants of Phnom Penh to the countryside. A second major displace-

ment was carried out at the end of the year, when hundreds of thousands of people from the area SE of Phnom Penh were forced to move to the NW. Prior to the Khmer Rouge coming to power, the Cambodian word for revolution had a conventional meaning: *bambahbambor* or 'uprising'. Under Pol Pot's regime, the word *pativattana* was used instead; it meant 'return to the past'. The Khmer Rouge did this by obliterating everything that did not subscribe to their vision of the past glories of ancient Khmer culture. Pol Pot wanted to return the country to 'Year Zero' – he wanted to begin again. One of the many revolutionary slogans was "we will burn the old grass and new will grow"; money, modern technology, education and newspapers were outlawed. Khieu Samphan, who became the Khmer Rouge Head of State, following Prince Sihanouk's resignation in 1976, said at the time: "No, we have no machines. We do everything by mainly relying on the strength of our people. We work completely self-sufficiently. This shows the overwhelming heroism of our people. This also shows the great force of our people. Though bare-handed, they can do everything".

Food was scarce under Pol Pot's inefficient system of collective farming and administration was based on fear, torture and summary execution. A veil of secrecy shrouded Cambodia and, until a few desperate refugees began to trickle over the border into Thailand, the outside world was largely ignorant of what was going on. Some academics initially viewed the revolution as an inspired, and brave, attempt to break the shackles of dependency and neo-colonial domination. But the stories of atrocities of the refugees turned the Khmer Rouge into international pariahs. During the Khmer Rouge's terrible 44-month reign of terror, over a million people died (some estimates are as high as 2-3 million). Some were shot, many starved, others died from disease – malaria was rife – and overwork. The Khmer Rouge transformed Cambodia into what the British journalist, William Shawcross, described as:

"a vast and sombre work camp where toil was unending, where respite and rewards were nonexistent, where families were abolished and where murder was used as a tool of social discipline... The manner of execution was often brutal. Babies were torn apart limb from limb, pregnant women were disemboweled. Men and women were buried up to their necks in sand and left to die slowly. A common form of execution was by axe handles to the back of the neck. That saved ammunition."

The Khmer Rouge revolution was primarily a class-based one, fed by years of growing resentment against the privileged élites. The revolution pitted the least-literate, poorest rural peasants against the educated, skilled and foreign-influenced urban population. Through a series of terrible purges, the members of the former governing and mercantile classes were liquidated or sent to work as forced labourers. But Peter Carey, Oxford historian and Chairman of the Cambodia Trust, argues that not all Pol Pot's victims were townspeople and merchants. "Under the terms of the 1948 Genocide Convention, the Khmer Rouge stands accused of genocide," he wrote in a letter to a British newspaper in 1990. "Of 64,000 Buddhist monks, 62,000 perished; of 250,000 Islamic Chams, 100,000; of 200,000 Vietnamese still left in 1975, 100,000; of 20,000 Thai, 12,000; of 1,800 Lao, 1,000. Of 2,000 Kola, not a trace remained." American political scientist Wayne Bert noted that: "The methods and behaviour compare to that of the Nazis and Stalinists, but in the percentage of the population killed by a revolutionary movement, the Khmer Rouge holds an unchallenged record."

It is still unclear the degree to which these 'genocidal' actions were controlled by those at the centre. Many of the killings took place at the discretion of local leaders, but there were some notably cruel leaders in the upper echelons of the Khmer Rouge and none can have been ignorant of what was going on. Ta Mok, who administered the region SW of Phnom Penh, oversaw many mass-executions eg. There is also evidence that the central government was directly involved in the running of the Tuol Sleng detention centre in which at least 20,000 people died. It has now been turned into the Cambodian version of Auschwitz, as a memorial to Pol Pot's holocaust (see page 475).

In addition to the legacy left by centres such as Tuol Sleng, there is the impact of the mass killings upon the Cambodian psyche. One of which is – to western eyes – the startling openness with which Khmer people will, if asked, matter-of-factly relate their family history in detail: this usually involves telling how the Khmer Rouge era meant they lost one or several members of their family. Whereas death is talked about in hushed terms in western society, Khmers have no such reservations, perhaps because it touched, and touches them all.

The Vietnamese invasion

The first border clashes over offshore islands between Khmer Rouge forces and the Vietnamese army were reported just a month after the Khmer Rouge came to power. These erupted into a minor war in Jan 1977 when the Phnom Penh government accused Vietnam of seeking to incorporate Kampuchea with an Indochinese federation. Hanoi's determination to oust Pol Pot only really became apparent however, on Christmas Day 1978 when 120,000 Vietnamese troops invaded. By 7 Jan (the day of Phnom Penh's liberation) they had installed a puppet government which proclaimed the foundation of the People's Republic of Kampuchea (PRK); Heng Samrin, a former member of the Khmer Rouge, was appointed president. The Vietnamese compared their invasion to the liberation of Uganda from Idi Amin – but for the western world it was an unwelcome Christmas present. The new government was accorded scant recognition abroad, while the toppled government of Democratic Kampuchea retained the country's seat at the United Nations.

But the country's 'liberation' by Vietnam did not end the misery; in 1979 nearly half Cambodia's population was in transit, either searching for their former homes or fleeing across the Thai border into refugee camps. The country reverted to a state of outright war again, for the Vietnamese were not greatly loved in Cambodia – especially by the Khmer Rouge. American political scientist Wayne Bert writes: "The Vietnamese had long seen a special role for themselves in uniting and leading a greater Indochina Communist movement and the Cambodian Communists had seen with clarity that such a role for the Viet-

namese could only be at the expense of their independence and prestige." Under the Lon Nol and Khmer Rouge regimes, Vietnamese living in Cambodia were expelled or exterminated. Resentment had built up over the years in Hanoi – exacerbated by the apparent ingratitude of the Khmer Rouge for Vietnamese assistance in fighting Lon Nol's US-supported Khmer Republic in the early 1970s. As relations between the Khmer Rouge and the Vietnamese deteriorated, the Communist superpowers, China and the Soviet Union, polarized too – the former siding with the Khmer Rouge and the latter with Hanoi. The Vietnamese invasion had the full backing of Moscow. While the Chinese and Americans began their support for the anti-Vietnamese rebels.

Following the Vietnamese invasion, three main anti-Hanoi factions were formed. In Jun 1982 they banded together in an unholy and unlikely alliance of convenience to fight the PRK and called themselves the Coalition Government of Democratic Kampuchea (CGDK), which was immediately recognized by the United Nations. The three factions of the CGDK were:

● The Communist **Khmer Rouge**, whose field forces had recovered to at least 18,000 by the late 1980s. Supplied with weapons by China, they were concentrated in the Cardamom Mountains in SW and were also in control of some of the refugee camps along the Thai border.

● The National United Front for an Independent Neutral Peaceful and Cooperative Cambodia (FUNCINPEC) – known by most people as the **Armée Nationale Sihanoukiste** (ANS). It was headed by Prince Sihanouk – although he spent most of his time exiled in Beijing; the group had under 15,000 well-equipped troops – most of whom took orders from Khmer Rouge commanders.

● The anti-Communist **Khmer People's National Liberation Front** (KPNLF),

---

CAMBODIAN REFUGEES

The Paris Peace Accord charged the UN's Transitional Authority in Cambodia (UNTAC) with overseeing one of the biggest population shifts in modern history. By May 1993 it resettled more than 360,000 Cambodian refugees – about 5% of the Cambodian population – from six refugee camps in Thailand at a cost of more than US$800mn. The resettlement programme was hailed as one of the most successful aspects of the UN's mission in Cambodia. It was supervised by the UN High Commissioner for Refugees (UNHCR) which organized the resettlement of up to 10,000 people a week between Mar 1992 and Apr 1993. The refugees moved to UN-built reception centres before being dispatched to their resettlement sites. The Geneva-based organization decided to let the refugees choose their resettlement location; it also promised that each should be given a plot of land, materials to build a house, land to farm, tools, cooking utensils and food for 1 year – until the first rice crop was harvested. But the UN soon discovered that it could not stand by its word; such a large area of farmland had been mined that there simply was not enough safe land to go round. Many went instead for cash handouts of US$300 each.

Like the country's physical infrastructure which lies in ruins, Cambodia's social infrastructure has been virtually destroyed by the years of civil war. Families have been split up and family members are often unaware of whether their parents, children, brothers or sisters are alive or dead. Even if they are still alive, they could be just about anywhere – in Cambodia, Thailand or the United States. The 360,000 refugees who have returned face a lengthy and difficult period of adjustment after nearly 14 years in camps on the Thai border. Observers note that the conditions in some of the Thai camps were markedly better than those in Cambodia, where banditry is rife, and land mines are everywhere. Nearly half of the returnees are under the age of 15 – most grew up in the Thai camps and have no experience of life outside them; their understanding of the outside world is limited. In 1991 a British newspaper report quoted a UNHCR official as saying: "Many of the children don't know that rice grows in paddies. They think it comes off the back of a lorry every Tuesday."

---

headed by Son Sann, a former prime minister under Sihanouk. Its 5,000 troops were reportedly ill-disciplined in comparison with the Khmer Rouge and the ANS.

The three CGDK factions were ranged against the 70,000 troops loyal to the government of President Heng Samrin and Prime Minister Hun Sen (previously a Khmer Rouge cadre). They were backed by Vietnamese forces until Sep 1989. Within the forces of the Phnom Penh government there were reported to be problems of discipline and desertion. But the rebel guerrilla coalition was itself seriously weakened by rivalries and ha-

tred between the different factions: in reality, the idea of a coalition was fiction. Throughout most of the 1980s the war followed the progress of the seasons: during the dry season from Nov to Apr the PRK forces with their tanks and heavy arms took the offensive but during the wet season this heavy equipment was ineffective and the guerrilla resistance made advances.

The road towards peace

In the late 1980s the Association of Southeast Asian Nations (ASEAN) – for which the Cambodian conflict had almost become its *raison d'être* – began steps to bring the warring factions to-

CAMBODIA 1953-1993

1953	Cambodian independence from France.
1965	Prince Sihanouk's government cuts links with the United States following deployment of US troops in Vietnam.
1966	Right-wing beats Sihanouk in the election; Lon Nol elected Prime Minister.
1967	Lon Nol toppled following left-wing demonstrations.
1969	Lon Nol becomes Prime Minister again.
1970	Lon Nol topples Sihanouk in US-backed coup; US bombs Communist bases in Cambodia.
1972	Lon Nol becomes first President of the Khmer Republic.
1975	Lon Nol flees as Khmer Rouge seizes power; Sihanouk made Head of Government.
1976	Cambodia renamed Democratic Kampuchea; Sihanouk resigns and Khieu Samphan becomes Head of State, with Pol Pot as Prime Minister. Government moves people from towns to labour camps in the countryside.
1978	Khmer Rouge government recognized by UN. Dec: Vietnam invades.
1981	Country renamed the People's Republic of Kampuchea (PRK).
1982	Coalition government-in-exile formed by anti-Hanoi resistance comprising Sihanoukists, Khmer Rouge and KPNLF. Sihanouk appointed President; Khieu Samphan, Vice-President and Son Sann, Prime Minister. Coalition backed by China and ASEAN.
1984	Vietnam gains rebel-held territory along Thai border; Vietnamese civilians settle in Kampuchea.
1989	Peoples Republic of Kampuchea renamed the State of Cambodia. Sep: last of the Vietnamese troops leave.
1991	International Conference on Cambodia leads to peace treaty and deployment of UN.
1993	In May elections were held under the auspices of the United Nations Transitional Authority in Cambodia. A coalition government was formed and Norodom Sihanouk was re-crowned King in Sep.

gether over the negotiating table. AS-EAN countries were united primarily in wanting the Vietnamese out of Cambodia. While publicly deploring the Khmer Rouge record, ASEAN tacitly supported the guerrillas. Thailand, an ASEAN member-state, which has had a centuries-long suspicion of the Vietnamese, co-operated closely with China to ensure that the Khmer Rouge guerrillas over the border were well-supplied with weapons.

After Mikhail Gorbachev had come to power in the Soviet Union, Moscow's support for the Vietnamese presence in Cambodia gradually evaporated. Gorbachov began leaning on Vietnam, as early as 1987, to withdraw its troops. Despite saying their presence in Cambodia was 'irreversible', Vietnam completed its withdrawal in Sep 1989, ending nearly 11 years of Hanoi's direct military involvement. The withdrawal led to an immediate upsurge in political and military activity, as forces of the exiled CGDK put increased pressure on the now weakened Phnom Penh regime to begin power-sharing negotiations (see page 455).

Art and architecture

The art of modern Cambodia is almost completely overshadowed by the greatness of its past. The influence of the Khmers at the height of the empire spread as far as the Malay peninsula in the S, to the Burmese border in the W and the Vietnamese frontier in the N and E. But ancient Khmer culture was itself inherited. Indian influence was particularly strong in the Mekong basin area and the Khmers accepted Indian ideas about astrology, religion and royalty – including the cult of the god-king (deva-raja). Other elements of Cambodian culture which are recognizably Indian in origin include classical literature and dance, as well as religious architecture. Hindu deities inspired the iconography in much of Cambodian (and Southeast Asian) art and Sanskrit gave the Khmers access to a whole new world of ideas, which were tailored and transformed to the Cambodian way of thinking. Cambodian influence is very strong in Thai culture as Siam's capture of a large part of the Khmer Empire in the 15th century resulted in many of Cambodia's best scholars, artists and craftsmen being transported to Siam (Thailand).

The richness of their culture remains a great source of pride for the Khmer people and in the past it has helped forge a sense of national identity. There has been an artistic revival since 1979 and the government has devoted resources to the restoration of monuments and pagodas. (Many local wats have been repaired by local subscription; it is estimated that one fifth of rural disposable income is given to the upkeep of wats.) The resurgence of Buddhism has been paralleled in recent years by a revival of traditional Khmer culture, which was actively undermined during the Pol Pot years. Today Phnom Penh's two Fine Arts Schools are flourishing again; one teaches music and dance, the other specializes in architecture and archaeology. There is a surprisingly good collection of artefacts in the National Museum of Arts even though huge quantities of treasure and antiques have been stolen and much of the remainder destroyed by the Khmer Rouge.

The height of Khmer art and architecture dates from the Angkor period. All the surviving monuments are built of stone or brick, and all are religious buildings. The culture and art of the early kingdoms of **Funan** and **Chenla** were central to the evolution of Angkorian art and architecture. Art historian Philip Rawson writes that these two kingdoms were the foundation of Khmer art, "just as archaic Greek sculpture was the foundation of later classical Greek art". Funan's centre was to the SW of the Mekong Delta but extended into present day Cambodia. The only remains that definitely came from the early kingdom of Funan are limited to four Sanskrit inscriptions and a few sculptures. The earliest surviving statues from Funan are at Angkor Borei and date from the 6th century; but by then Funan was a vassal of Chenla. The kingdom of Chenla – based at Sambor and later at Sambor Prei Kuk – expanded at the expense of Funan. It refined and developed Funan's earlier artistic styles.

Relics of the pre-Angkorian periods have been found all over S Cambodia and between the Mekong and the Tonlé Sap. The principal monuments are brick towers with square ground plans, false doors and mounting storeys of decreasing size. They were characterized by strong sculptural work, based on Indian ideas but carved in a unique style. Many of the statues from this era are in the National Museum of Arts at Phnom Penh (see page 473). Most of the art from the pre-Angkorian kingdoms is Hindu but it seems that Mahayana Buddhism was briefly introduced into the country as a number of images of Bodhisattvas have been found. In the late 8th century,

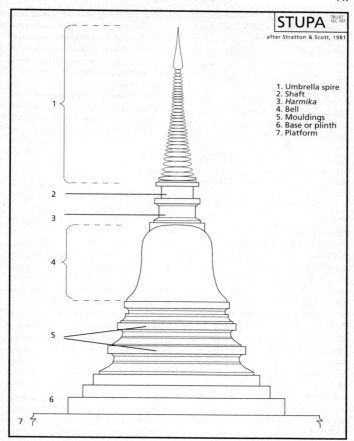

STUPA TBU 67 VLC 107

after Stratton & Scott, 1981

1. Umbrella spire
2. Shaft
3. *Harmika*
4. Bell
5. Mouldings
6. Base or plinth
7. Platform

the Chenla Kingdom collapsed and Jayavarman II, who had lived most of his life in the Sailendra court in Java, returned to declare himself devaraja in 802.

During the Angkor period, Javanese and neighbouring Champa architectural influences were incorporated into Khmer designs. The architecture and its decoration were governed by a series of mystical and religious beliefs. Temples were designed to represent the cosmic Mt Meru, surrounded by oceans. For a

detailed account of the typical design features and evolution of Angkor temple architecture, as well as the development of Khmer sculpture, see page 489.

Culture and life

People

Before 1975, Cambodia had a population of about 7.2 million; within 4 years this had dropped to around 6 million (some were the victims of genocide, others became refugees). The population topped 10 million in 1995. The Khmers are the dominant group and there are significant Chinese and Vietnamese minorities as well as a small percentage of tribal groups – most of whom suffered badly during the Pol Pot years.

Khmers

The Khmers are believed to have lived in the region from about the 2nd century AD but there is some argument as to from where they migrated. They may constitute a fusion of Mongul and Melanesian elements. The Khmers now constitute 85% of the population. They have been mainly influenced over the centuries by the powerful Indian and Javanese kingdoms.

Khmer Loeu

The Khmer Loeu, or Upland Khmer (divided into the Saoch, Pear, Brao and Kuy), are one of the main tribal groups and live in the forested mountain zones, mainly in the NE. The Saoch live in the Elephant Mountains to the SW; the Pear occupy the Cardamom Mountains to the W; while the Brao are settled along the Lao border to the NE. Traditionally the Khmer Loeu were semi-nomadic and practiced slash and burn agriculture. Like many tribal groups in Southeast Asia they were also mainly animist. In recent years, however, increasing number have turned to settled agriculture and adopted many of the customs of the lowland Khmers.

Chinese

In the 18th and 19th centuries large numbers of ethnic Chinese migrated to Southeast Asia, where most became involved in commerce. The Chinese settled in the countryside as well as in cities and towns. Until the Khmer Rouge takeover in 1975, the Chinese played a central role in the economy, controlling trade, banking and transport. As in neighbouring Thailand, they assimilated to a greater degree than in other parts of Southeast Asia. In recent decades, most of Cambodia's urban and governing élite has had at least some Chinese blood – Lon Nol, eg had a Chinese grandparent. The Chinese started leaving the country when civil war broke out in 1970 – and many of those who did not get out before 1975 were killed during the Pol Pot years. The few who survived the Khmer Rouge era emigrated during the first months of the pro-Vietnam PRK rule. There is a small Chinese population of about 100,000 in Cambodia today.

Vietnamese

The southern part of Cambodia, particularly along the Mekong River, has always had many inhabitants of Vietnamese descent as well as the area around Phnom Penh. The Vietnamese live very separate lives to the Cambodians due to centuries of mistrust and animosity between the two groups. They are known by the Khmers as 'youn', a derogatory term meaning 'people from the N'. The Cambodian Vietnamese can be distinguished from the Khmers by their typical two-piece pyjama suits of black cotton. Many of the Vietnamese population left following the takeover of the Khmer Rouge as they were a target of special persecution. A large percentage returned after 1979 with the Vietnamese military presence in the country. As in neighbouring Laos, the Hanoi government encouraged an active resettlement programme for Vietnamese in Cambodia. Most estimates currently put Cambodia's Vietnamese population at 6% of the total. Many Vietnamese have traditionally been businessmen and money changers; some work in skilled jobs and are tailors, mechanics and electricians but those living around the Tonlé Sap are mainly fishermen.

It is the Vietnamese in Cambodia who have suffered most in recent years, and who are most at risk. There are an estimated 200,000-500,000 in the coun-

PROSTITUTION AND AIDS IN CAMBODIA

A survey undertaken in mid-1994 found there to be 418 brothels in Phnom Penh with 1,444 **prostitutes**. This is, in all likelihood, a gross under-estimate. Most commentators would put the latter figures at 10,000, and 15,000-20,000 for the whole country. The going rate for intercourse is 10,000 riel or US\$4, while a night with a sex worker costs a client 50,000 riel (US\$20). Many of the women and girls working in these establishments are from poor farming families and it seems that most intend to return home with their savings, some to set up small businesses. There are also large numbers of Vietnamese women working in the industry.

On paper at least, the prostitution industry in Phnom Penh should now be history: in Aug 1994 the Mayor of Phnom Penh banned brothels from operating in the city, threatening a fine of 1 million riel (US\$200) to any brothel owners discovered ignoring the ban. However this edict has done little to stop prostitution, and many commentators saw it as just a wheeze so that the police could extort money from brothel owners, sex workers, and their clients. There were numerous reports of plainclothes policemen entering brothels, having sex, and then whipping out their police ID cards before illegally demanding a payment. Other stories tell of prostitutes being arrested by the police for illegally plying their trade, and then being 'sold' to another brothel. The going rate for a girl starts at around US\$40-60, but can be considerably more for an attractive girl. Health workers also fear that the banning of brothels will simply push the industry underground, creating an excellent environment for the unchecked spread of AIDS (see below). At the beginning of 1995 rumours were afoot in the capital that prostitution might be legalized such has been the failure of the 'crack down'.

Like other countries of Southeast Asia, Cambodia is thought to be on the verge of an **AIDS** epidemic. Although, as of the end of Jun 1994, not a single AIDS case had been reported in the country, the scale of HIV-infection is growing very rapidly. A study conducted in 1992 found that 9% of sex workers were HIV-infected, 3.5% of blood donors and 4% of those treated for other sexually transmitted diseases. But a more recent study conducted at the end of 1994 found that the rate of infection among sex workers had risen, alarmingly, to 69%. Most AIDS researchers believe that Cambodia could follow the path that Thailand has already forged – towards an AIDS epidemic of exceedingly serious proportions. (The Cambodia-Thailand border is porous and the employment of Cambodian women in Thai brothels is helping Thailand to 'export' its much more severe problem to Cambodia.) Towards the end of 1994, Dr Tea Phalla, the national AIDS programme manager in Cambodia warned that up to 2 million of the country's population of 9 million could die from AIDS. Cambodia already has a very high dependency ratio – every 1,000 people of productive age in Cambodia must support 1,144 dependents (old, very young or infirm/disabled people). In the industrialised world the ratio is 1,000:616. AIDS will only further worsen this already high dependency rate. The challenge facing Dr Phalla is the need to inform people of the dangers of unprotected sex and multiple partners when education levels and facilities are poor and his resources comparatively paltry. He is hoping to meet the challenge through inter-personal communication – encouraging wives to tell their husbands, men to tell their friends, fathers their sons, and so on. In Khmer this is known much more descriptively as the 'one crow tells 10 crows' method.

try, although the official figure is scarcely more than 100,000. Not only have they been specifically targetted by the Khmer Rouge, but it is hard to find a single Cambodian who has anything positive to say about Vietnamese settlers in the country. One human rights official was quoted as saying at the end of 1994 in the *Far Eastern Economic Review* that "Give a choice, alot of people in this country would expel every single Vietnamese". This dislike of the Vietnamese stems partly from historical fears – Vietnam absorbed large areas of the former Cambodian Empire in the 18th and 19th centuries; partly from Vietnam's role in Cambodia between 1979 and 1989; and partly from the shear size of Vietnam – some 70 million inhabitants – when set against Cambodia's population of 9 million. As a result anti-Vietnamese sentiment is mainstream politics in the country. Inventing fanciful stories about Vietnamese commandos infiltrating the country, or Vietnamese control of the economy, is never likely to do harm to a budding populist politician.

The possibility that the Vietnamese, as an ethnic group, might simply be legislated into exile seemed to come closer to reality when a controversial immigration law was passed by the National Assembly in Aug 1994. Some commentators saw the law as permitting the expulsion of ethnic Vietnamese residents.

Cham-Malays

There are about 500,000 Cham-Malays, descended from the Chams of the royal kingdom of Champa based in present day central Vietnam. They now constitute the single largest ethnic minority in the country. In the 15th century the Vietnamese moving S drove many of the Chams living in the lower Mekong area into Cambodia. They now mainly live along the Mekong, N of Phnom Penh. The Chams were badly persecuted during the Pol Pot years and their population more than halved, from about 800,000 during the rule of King Norodom Sihanouk to 350,000 by the end of the Khmer Rouge period. They are Muslim people and their spiritual centre is Chur-Changvra near Phnom Penh. They adopted their faith and script from Malays who settled in Kampot and interior regions on the invitation of the Muslim Khmer King Chan in 1642, after he had converted to Islam. The Chams are traditionally cattle traders, silk weavers and butchers – Theravada Buddhism forbids the Khmer to slaughter animals. Their batik sarongs are very similar to those found in Malaysia.

Although the Cham are now free to pursue their faith largely free from persecution, they still suffer from the stigma of being viewed, by many Cambodians, as second class citizens. Strangely perhaps, there is a close affinity between Christians and Muslims in Cambodia – in the face of an overwhelmingly dominant Buddhist faith.

Other groups

There are also a small number of Shans, Thai and Lao, most who live near Battambang, the descendants of miners and jewellers who came to work the ruby mines of Pailin during the French colonial era.

Religion

The god-kings of Angkor

Up to the 14th century Buddhism and Hinduism existed side-by-side in Kambuja. In the pre-Angkor era, the Hindu gods Siva and Vishnu were worshipped as a single deity, *Harihara*. The statue of Harihara from Phnom Da (8th century) is divided in half: the 'stern' right half is Siva (with wild curly hair) and the 'sublime' left half, Vishnu (who wears a mitre). The first city at Angkor, built by Jayavarman II in the early 9th century, was called Hariharalaya after this god. Early Angkor kings promoted various Hindu sects, mainly dedicated to Siva and Vishnu. During the Angkor period, Siva was the most favoured deity but by the 12th century Vishnu replaced him. Jayavarman VII introduced Mahayana Buddhism as the official court religion at the end of the 12th century. The constant chopping, changing and refining of state religion helped sustain the power of the absolute monarch – each change ushered in a new style of rule and historians believe refinements and changes of religion were deliberately imported to consolidate the power of the kings.

One reason the Khmer Empire was so powerful was its basis on the Hindu concept of the god-king or *devaraja*. Jayavarman II (802-850) crowned himself as a reincarnation of Siva and erected a Siva lingam (a phallic monument to the god) at Phnom Kulen, the source of power for the Khmer Dynasty. Siva-worship was not originally introduced by Jayavarman II however – it had been previously practised in the old kingdom of Funan (see page 82). The investiture of power was always performed by a Brahmin priest who also bestowed divinity on the king as a gift from Siva. This ceremony became an essential rite of kingship which was practised continuously – right into the 20th century. The king's spirit was said to reside in the lingam, which was enshrined in the centre of a monumental religious complex, representing the spiritual axis of the kingdom. Here, the people believed, their divinely ordained king communicated with the gods. Succeeding monarchs followed Jayavarman II's example and continued to install themselves as god-kings, evoking the loyalty of their subjects.

Very few of the statues of Vishnu and Siva and other gods left by the Khmer Empire were traditional representations of the deities. The great majority of the images were portraits of kings and princes and high dignitaries, each represented as the god into whom he would be absorbed at the end of his earthly existence. That the names given to the statues were usually a composite of the names of the man and the god, indicates that men were worshipped as gods.

The installation of the devaraja cult by Jayavarman II took place on the summit of Phnom Kulen. Under subsequent kings, it was transferred, in turn, to Bakong, Phnom Bakhen, Koh Ker and Phimeanakas. At the end of the 11th century, the Baphuon was constructed to house the golden lingam. The tradition of the god-king cult was so deeply rooted in the court that even Theravada Buddhism introduced in the 14th century bowed to its influence. Following the adoption of Buddhism in the second half of the 12th century, the god-king left his lingam to enter the statue of the Buddha. Jayavarman VII built the Bayon to shelter the statue of the Buddha-king in the centre of the city of Angkor.

Temple-mountains were built as microcosms of the universe, with Mt Meru, the home of the gods, at the centre, surrounded by oceans (followed most perfectly at Angkor Wat, see page 505). This concept was not invented by the Khmers but was part of an inherited tradition from India. At the summit of the cosmic mountain, located at the centre of the city, the king, embodied by his own sacred image, entered into contact with the world of gods. Each temple was the personal temple of an individual king, erected by him during his life. When, after his death, his ashes or remains were deposited there (to animate the statue and give the cult a living image), the temple became his mausoleum. His successor always built another sanctuary to house the image of the god-king. During the Angkor period the Khmers did not seem to question this system. It ordered their lives, regulating everything from agriculture to birth and death rites. But the temples were not the products of a popular faith, like Christian cathedrals – they were strictly the domain of royalty and high priests and were reserved for the worship of kings and members of the entourage deified in the form of one of the Hindu or Buddhist gods.

Theravada Buddhism

Despite the powerful devaraja cult, most Khmers also practised an amalgam of ancestor worship and animism. As Theravada Buddhism swept through Southeast Asia (well after the adoption of Mahayana Buddhism), propagated by missionary monks, its message of simplicity, austerity and humility began to undermine the cult of the god-king. As a popular religion, it held great attractions to a population which for so many centuries had been denied access to the élitist and extravagant devaraja cult. The Cambodian Buddhist clergy divided into two groups: the Mahanikay and Thommayuth (or Dhammayuttikanikay) orders. The latter was not introduced from Thailand until 1864, and was a reformist order with strong royal patronage. Theravada Buddhism remained the dominant and unchallenged faith until 1975.

It was a demonstration by Buddhist monks in Phnom Penh which first kindled Cambodian nationalism in the wake of WW2 (see page 436). According to historians, one of the reasons for this was the intensifying of the relationship between the king and the people, due to the founding of the Buddhist Institute in Phnom Penh in 1930. The Institute was under the joint patronage of the kings of Laos and Cambodia as well as the French. It began printing and disseminating Buddhist texts – in Pali and Khmer. American historian David P Chandler writes: "As the Institute's reputation grew, enhanced by frequent conferences, it became a rallying point for an emerging intelligentsia." The Institute's librarian founded a Khmer-language newspaper (*Nagaravatta* – or

'Angkor Wat') in 1936, which played a critical role in articulating and spreading the nationalist message.

Before 1975 and the arrival of the Khmer Rouge, there were 3,000 monasteries and 64,000 monks (*bonzes*) – many of these were young men who had become ordained to escape conscription – in Cambodia and rural life was centred around the *wat* (Buddhist monastery). Under Pol Pot, all monks were 'defrocked' and, according to some sources, as many as 62,000 were executed or died in the ricefields. Monasteries were torn down or converted to other uses, Pali – the language of Theravada Buddhism – was banned, and former monks were forced to marry. Ironically, Saloth Sar (Pol Pot) himself spent several years as a novice when he was a child. Buddhism was revived in 1979 with the ordination of monks by a visiting delegation of Buddhists from Vietnam; at the same time, many of the wats – which were defiled by the Khmer Rouge – were restored and reconsecrated. The two orders of Theravada Buddhism – the Thommayuth (aristocratic) and Mahanikay (common) – previously practised in Cambodia have now merged. The Hun Sen government has softened the position on Buddhism to the degree that it was reintroduced as the national religion in 1989 and young men were allowed to be ordained (previously restricted to men over 45, ie no longer able to serve in the army).

Cambodian Buddhism is an easy-going faith and tolerates ancestor and territorial spirit worship, which is widely practised. There are often small rustic altars to the guardian spirits or *neak ta* in the corner of pagodas. Cambodians often wear *katha* – or charms – which are believed to control external magical forces. Many Khmer communities have *achars*, who share in the spiritual guidance of people but do not compete with the monks. Most important ceremonies – weddings, funerals, coming of age – have both Buddhist and animist elements.

Other religions

There are around 60,000 Roman Catholics in Cambodia, mainly Vietnamese and about 2,000 Protestants. Islam, of the Sunni sect, is practised by many of the 500,000 Cham. During the Khmer Rouge period it has been reported that Chams were forced to eat pork while most Cham mosques were destroyed, and only now are they being slowly rebuilt. A new International Mosque in Phnom Penh, built with Saudi money, was opened in 1994. Almost all the Chinese in Cambodia are Taoist/Confucianist.

Language and literature

The Khmer language belongs to the Mon-Khmer family, enriched by the Indian Pali and Sanskrit languages and peppered with Thai and French influences. The use of Sanskrit in royal texts became more widespread after the introduction of Mahayana Buddhism in the 12th century (although there are inscriptions dating from the 6th century) and the Pali language spread into Cambodia via Siam with Theravada Buddhism. Khmer is related to languages spoken by hilltribe people of Laos, Vietnam and even Malaysia – but is very different to Thai or Lao. Khmer has no tones, no tenses, and words attached to the masculine or feminine genders. But Khmer does have 23 vowel-sounds and 33 consonants; it is also a very specific language – for instance, there are 100 different words for types of rice. The Khmer language is written from left to right with no separation between words. French was widely spoken by the intelligentsia before 1975 and is still spoken by a few elderly Cambodians. Today however, everyone seems to want to learn English, and there are informal pavement English schools setting up on Phnom Penh's streets.

Religious literature comprises works of religious instruction, derived from the Pali texts of the Theravada Buddhist canon, the Tripitaka. The Jataka tales are well known in Cambodia and several modern adaptations have been made from these texts. The two Khmer epics are the poem of Angkor Wat and the *Ramakerti*, derived from the Indian Ramayana (see page 337). Most of the early literature has been destroyed but there are surviving Sanskrit inscriptions on stone monuments dating from the 6th century. Historical literature consists largely of inscriptions from Angkor Wat as well as the Cambodian royal chronicles. Fictional literature is diverse in Cambodia and includes the *Ipaen* folk stories written in prose. French literature has had a large influence on modern Cambodian literature. Most of the recent Cambodian novels have been written by Cambodians living abroad – most writers and journalists were either killed by the Khmer Rouge or fled the country.

Dance, drama and music

There is a strong tradition of dance in Cambodia which has its origins in the sacred dances of the apsaras, the mythological seductresses of ancient Cambodia. **Classical dance** reached its height during the Angkor period; it was based on interpretations of the Indian epics, particularly the Ramayana. Dance also became a religious tradition, designed to bring the king and his people divine blessing. Dancers, nearly all of whom were well born, were central to the royal court and were protected as a separate part of the king's harem; only the god-king could touch them. The dancers became legendary even outside Cambodia: when Thailand invaded, the Khmer classical ballet dancers were part of their war booty and were taken to the Thai court. The decline of Angkor brought the decline of classical dance, although it continued to survive as an art form through the patronage of the royal Thai court. When the French colonialists revived Khmer ballet in the 20th century they initially imported dancers from Thailand.

The dances are very symbolic. Court dances are subject to a precise order, a strict form and a prescribed language of movements and gestures. Most of the dancers are women and the male and female roles are distinguished by costume. All the dancers are barefoot as the unimpeded movement of the feet is very important. The national dance is called the *lamthon* which is characterized by slow graceful movements of the hands and arms. The most highly trained lamthon dancers wear elaborate, tight-fitting costumes of silk and velvet that have to be sewn onto them before each performance.

Due to their close association with the royal family (they were based at the royal palace and right up to 1970, danced regularly for Prince Sihanouk), the once-famous and flourishing National Dance Group was a prime target for the Khmer Rouge regime of the mid-1970s. Many dancers were killed; others fled into exile. In 1981 the School of Fine Arts was opened to train new recruits, 80% of whom were orphans. Today the National Dance Group performs for some tour groups and made its first tour to the W in 1990.

Folk dancing has managed to survive the 1970s intact, although as a form of regular village entertainment, it has been undermined by the arrival of radios, televisions and videos. Unlike the court dances, folk dances are less structured, with dancers responding to the rhythm of drums. The dancers act out tales from Cambodian folk stories; folk dancing can often be seen at local festivals.

Folk plays and **shadow plays** are also a popular form of entertainment in the countryside. The latter are based on stories from the Ramayana, embroidered with local legends. The characters are cut out of leather and often painted. Wandering shadow puppeteers perform at local festivals.

Because of the importance of dance to the ancient royal Khmer court, **music** – which always accompanied dance routines – was also central to Cambodian court and religious life. Singers and musicians were often attached to specific temples. Cambodian music has evolved from Indian and Indonesian influences and, more recently, Thai. The traditional orchestra consists of three xylophones, *khom thom* (a horseshoe-shaped arrangement with 16 flat gongs), violins, wind instruments including flutes, flageolets and a Khmer version of bagpipes, as well as drums of different shapes and sizes. There are three types of drum: the hand drum, the *cha ayam* drum and the *yike* drum. The drummer has the most important role in folk music as he sets the rhythm. In 1938 a musical scholar estimated that only 3,000 melodies were ever employed in Khmer music. There is no system of written notation so the tunes are transmitted orally from generation to generation. There are five tones (compared to seven in western music) and no real harmony – the melodies are always simple.

Modern Cambodia

Politics

Since the mid-1960s Cambodian politics has been chaotic, with warring factions, backed by different foreign powers, and shifting alliances. The groups who battled for power following the Vietnamese invasion in 1979 are still in the political arena.

The Vietnamese withdrawal in Sep 1989 resulted in an escalation of the civil war as the rebel factions – comprised of the Khmer Rouge, the Sihanoukists and Son Sann's KPNLF (see page 445) – tried to take advantage of the supposedly weakened Hun Sen regime in Phnom Penh. The government committed itself to liberalizing the economy and improving the infrastructure in order to undermine the political appeal of the rebels – particularly that of the Khmer Rouge. Peasant farmers were granted life tenancy and collective farms were substituted with agricultural co-operatives. But because nepotism and bribery were rife in Phnom Penh, the popularity of the Hun Sen regime declined. The rebel position was further strengthened as the disparities between living standards in Phnom Penh and those in the rest of the country widened. In the capital, the government became alarmed; in a radio broadcast in 1991 it announced a crackdown on corruption claiming it was causing a "loss of confidence in our superb regime... which is tantamount to paving the way for the return of the genocidal Pol Pot regime".

With the Vietnamese withdrawal, the war followed the familiar pattern of dry season government offensives, and consolidation of guerrilla positions during the monsoon rains. Much of the fighting focused on the potholed highways – particularly Highway 6 which connects the capital with Battambang – with the Khmer Rouge blowing up most of the bridges along the road. Their strategy involved cutting the roads in order to drain the government's limited resources. Other Khmer Rouge offensives were designed to serve their own economic ends – such as their capture of the gem-rich town of Pailin.

The Khmer Rouge ran extortion rackets throughout the country, even along the strategic Highway four which ferried military supplies, oil and consumer goods from the port of Kompong Som to Phnom Penh. The State of Cambodia – or the government forces, known as SOC – were pressed to deploy troops to remote areas and allot scarce resources, settling refugees in more secure parts of the country. To add to their problems, Soviet and Eastern Bloc aid began to dry up.

Throughout 1991 the four warring factions were repeatedly brought to the negotiating table in an effort to hammer out a peace deal. Much of the argument centred on the word 'genocide'. The Prime Minister, Hun Sen, insisted that the wording of any agreement should explicitly condemn the former Khmer Rouge regime's 'genocidal acts'. But the Khmer Rouge refused to be party to any power-sharing deal which labelled them in such a way. Fighting intensified as hopes for a settlement increased – all sides wanted to consolidate their territory in advance of any agreement.

Rumours emerged that China was continuing to supply arms – including tanks, reportedly delivered through Thailand – to the Khmer Rouge. There were also accusations that the Phnom Penh government was using Vietnamese combat troops to stem Khmer Rouge advances – the first such reports since their official withdrawal in 1989. But finally, in Jun 1991, after several attempts, Sihanouk brokered a permanent ceasefire during a meeting of the Supreme National Council (SNC) in Pattaya, S Thailand. The SNC had been proposed by the United Nations Security Council in 1990 and formed in 1991, with an equal number of representatives from the Phnom Penh government and each of the resistance factions, with Sihanouk as its chairman. The following month he was elected chairman of the SNC, and resigned his presidency of the rebel coalition government in exile. Later in the year, the four factions agreed to reduce their armed guerrillas and militias by 70%. The remainder were to be placed under the supervision of the United Nations Transitional Authority in Cambodia (UNTAC), which supervised Cambodia's transition to multi-party democracy. Even more important was Heng Samrin's decision to drop his insistence that reference should be made to the former Khmer Rouge's "genocidal regime". It was also agreed that elections should be held in 1993 on the basis of proportional representation. Heng Samrin's Communist Party was promptly renamed the Cambodian People's Party, in an effort to persuade people that it sided with democracy and capitalism.

The Paris Peace Accord

On 23 October 1991, the four warring Cambodian factions signed a peace agreement in Paris which officially ended 13 years of civil war and more than 2 decades of warfare. The accord was co-signed by 15 other members of the International Peace Conference on Cambodia. There was an air of unreality about the whole event, which brought bitter enemies face to face after months of protracted negotiations. There was, however, a notable lack of enthusiasm on the part of the four warring factions. Hun Sen said that the treaty was far from perfect because it failed to contain the word 'genocide' to remind Cambodians of the atrocities of the former Khmer Rouge regime. Western powers obviously agreed. But in the knowledge that it was a fragile agreement, everyone remained diplomatically quiet. US Secretary of State James Baker was quoted as saying "I don't think anyone can tell you there will for sure be lasting peace, but there is great hope."

Political analysts ascribed the successful conclusion to the months of negotiations to improved relations between China and Vietnam – there were reports that the two had held secret summits at which the Cambodia situation was discussed. China put pressure on Prince Norodom Sihanouk to take a leading role in the peace process, and Hanoi's new understanding with Beijing prompted Hun Sen's participation. The easing of tensions between China and Moscow – particularly following the Soviet Union's demise – also helped apply pressure on the different factions. Finally, the United States had shifted its position: in Jul 1990 it had announced that it would not support the presence of the Khmer Rouge at the UN and by Sep US officials were talking with Hun Sen.

On 14 November 1991, Prince Norodom Sihanouk returned to Phnom Penh to an ecstatic welcome, followed, a few days later, by Son Sen, a Khmer Rouge leader. On 27 Nov Khieu Samphan, who had represented the Khmer Rouge at all the peace negotiations, arrived on a flight from Bangkok. Within hours mayhem had broken out, and a lynch mob attacked him in his villa. Rumours circulated that Hun Sen had orchestrated the demonstration, and beating an undignified retreat down a ladder into a waiting armoured personnel carrier, the bloodied Khmer Rouge leader headed back to Pochentong Airport. The crowd had sent a clear signal that they at least were not happy to see him back. There were fears that this incident might derail the entire peace process – but in the event, the Khmer Rouge won a small public relations coup by playing the whole thing down. When the Supreme National Council (SNC) finally met in Phnom Penh at the end of Dec 1991, it was unanimously decided to rubber-stamp the immediate deployment of UN troops to oversee the peace process in the run-up to a general election.

The UN peace-keeping mission

The UN mission "...conducted a brief, profound and very welcome social revolution [in Cambodia]" (William Shawcross (1994) *Cambodia's new deal: a report*).

The UN mission favoured "Phnom Penh's profiteers, the Khmer Rouge utopists, the Chinese businessmen of Southeast Asia, the annexationist neighbours..." (Marie Alexandrine Martin (1994) *Cambodia: a shattered society*).

Yasushi Akashi, a senior Japanese official in the United Nations, was assigned the daunting task of overseeing the biggest military and logistical operation in UN history. UNTAC, comprised an international team of 22,000 peacekeepers – including 16,000 soldiers from 22 countries; 6,000 officials as well as 3,500 police and 1,700 civilian employees and electoral volunteers. The first 'blue-beret' UN troops began arriving in Nov 1991, even before the SNC had agreed to the full complement of peace-keepers. The UN Advance Mission to Cambodia (UNAMIC) was followed 4 months later by the first of the main peacekeeping battalions. The odds were stacked against them. Shortly after his arrival, Akashi commented: "If one was a masochist one could not wish for more."

UNTAC's task

UNTAC's central mission was to supervise free elections ... in a country where most of the population had never voted and had little idea of how democracy was meant to work. The UN was also given the task of resettling 360,000 refugees from camps in Thailand and of demobilising more than a quarter of a million soldiers and militiamen from the four main factions. In addition, it was to ensure that no further arms shipments

CAMBODIA – THE BIGGEST MINEFIELD IN THE WORLD

Thanks to free-flowing supplies of military hardware to rebel factions throughout the 1980s, Cambodia became the most heavily mined war zone in the world. Conservative estimates suggest that there are 4-8 million mines in the country, mostly concentrated in the NW province of Battambang (a Khmer Rouge stronghold) as well as countless thousands close to the main roads. The upper figure would mean almost one mine for every man, woman and child. But statistics on the likely number of mines are irrelevant. Far more meaningful is the total area of land which cannot be used for anything because of the threat of the mines. One in every 236 Cambodians is an amputee, compared to one in 22,000 in the US. Every month, another 300 to 700 new mine injuries are added to the list. In 1993, an Australian Red Cross doctor said Cambodia's most obvious characteristic of national identity is the one-legged man. There are thought to be around 35,000 amputees inside the country.

A number of charities have been set up, where Cambodian craftsmen are trained to make cheap and simple prostheses, and many amputees have now been fitted with artificial limbs. UN troops, as well as private companies – such as the British-based charity, the Halo Trust – have been involved in delicate mine-clearance operations since 1990. At the beginning of 1995 the first Mine Awareness Day was declared. But, lifting a single mine costs between US$300 and US$900 and in the 24 months to the beginning of 1995 only 40,000 mines had been cleared – less than 1% of the total. The most common mine in Cambodia is the plastic-encased, Soviet-made PMN-2 mine, which mine clearance experts say guarantees above-the-knee amputation if triggered. Ba Bun Ra, a 29 year-old amputee and victim of a mine blast, is well aware of the challenges that face him: "I forgot my early dreams... I no longer have the capacity..." he was quoted as saying in 1994. Mines are the perfect weapon in a long war of attrition. They are designed not to kill, but to maim and thereby consume enemy resources in the evacuation, first aid, rehabilitaton and then support of the man, woman, girl or boy affected. They do not distinguish between men and women, children and the elderly, human beings and animals. Mines create dependents and, in turn, tend to create poverty. The civil war may end soon; the mine war will continue for years, perhaps decades to come – for mines do not respect the cessation of hostilities. It does not bode well for a country where the average life expectancy is already less than 50.

reached these factions, whose remaining forces were to be confined to cantonments. In the run-up to the elections, UNTAC also took over the administration of the country, taking over the defence, foreign affairs, finance, public security and information portfolios as well as ensuring respect for human rights.

By early 1993, UN electoral workers had successfully registered 4.7 million of roughly 9 million Cambodians – about 96% of the population above voting age. With a US$2bn price-tag, this huge operation was the most expensive mission ever undertaken by the UN. At the time, the UN was running 12 peacekeeping operations throughout the world, but two-thirds of its peacekeeping budget was earmarked for Cambodia. Over the months a steady stream of VIPs arrived to witness the operation – they included the UN Secretary-General, Boutros-Boutros Ghali, the Chinese Foreign Minister, Qian Qichen and President Francois Mitterrand of France.

UNTAC's job would have been easier if the different guerrilla factions and militias had stopped fighting once the Peace Accord was signed. In the months after their arrival UN troops had to broker successive ceasefires between government forces and the Khmer Rouge. During 1992, the Khmer Rouge refused to demobilize their fighters as required by the Accord and attempted to gain a foothold in the strategic central province of Kompong Thom in advance of the full deployment of UN peacekeeping forces. This prompted further scepticism among observers as to their commitment to the peace process. The Khmer Rouge – which was by then referred to (in politically neutral parlance) as the Party of Democratic Kampuchea, or the DK – made it as difficult as possible for the UN. It refused UN soldiers, officials and volunteers access to areas under its control. On a number of occasions in the months running up to the elections, UN military patrols were held hostage after entering Khmer Rouge-held territory.

The Khmer Rouge pulls out

At the beginning of 1993 it became apparent that the Khmer Rouge had no intention of playing ball, despite its claim of a solid rural support base. The DK failed to register for the election before the expiry of the UN deadline and its forces stepped up attacks on UN personnel. In Apr 1993 Khieu Samphan and his entire entourage at the Khmer Rouge compound in Phnom Penh left the city. It was at this stage that UN officials finally began expressing their exasperation and anxiety over the Khmer Rouge's avowed intention to disrupt the polls. The faction was well-known to have procured fresh supplies of Chinese weapons through Thailand – although there is no evidence that these came from Peking – as well as their having large arms caches hidden all over the country.

By the time of the elections, the group was thought to be in control of between 10% and 15% of Cambodian territory. Khmer Rouge guerrillas launched attacks in Apr and May 1993. Having stoked racial antagonism, they started killing ethnic Vietnamese villagers and settlers, sending up to 20,000 of them fleeing into Vietnam. In one particularly vicious attack, 33 Vietnamese fishermen and their families were killed in a village on the Tonlé Sap. The Khmer Rouge also began ambushing and killing UN soldiers and electoral volunteers.

The UN remained determined that the elections should go ahead despite the Khmer Rouge threats and mounting political intimidation and violence between other factions, notably the Cambodian People's Party and FUNCINPEC. But, it did not take any chances: in the week before the elections, 6,000 flak jackets and helmets were flown into the country and security was tightened. In the event, however, there were remarkably few violent incidents and the feared coordinated effort to disrupt the voting failed to materialize. Voters took no notice of Khmer Rouge calls to boycott the election. In fact, reports came in from several provinces of large numbers of Khmer Rouge guerrillas and villagers from areas under their control, turning up at polling stations and casting their ballots.

The UN-supervised elections

The voting was by proportional representation, province by province. The election was conducted under the aegis of 1,400 International Polling Station Officers from more than 40 countries. The Cambodian people were voting for a 120-member Constituent Assembly to write a new constitution.

The days following the election saw a political farce – Cambodian style – which, as Nate Thayer wrote in the *Far Eastern Economic Review* "might have been comic if the implications were not so depressing for the country's future". In just a handful of days, the Phnom Penh-based correspondent went on, Cambodia "witnessed an abortive secession, a failed attempt to establish a provisional government, a royal family feud and the manoeuvres of a prince [Si-

hanouk] obsessed with avenging his removal from power in a military coup more than 20 years [previously]". The elections gave FUNCINPEC 45% of the vote, the CPP 38% and the BLDP, 3% (see box, page 459). The CPP immediately claimed the results fraudulent, while Prince Norodom Chakrapong – one of Sihanouk's sons – announced the secession of the country's six eastern provinces. Fortunately, both attempts to undermine the election dissolved. The CPP agreed to join FUNCINPEC in a power sharing agreement while, remarkably, the Khmer Rouge was able to present itself as a defender of democracy in the face of the CPP's claims of vote-rigging. The new Cambodian consitution was ratified in Sep 1993, marking the end of UNTAC's involvement in the country. Under the new constitution, Cambodia was to be a pluralistic liberal-democratic country. 70-year-old Sihanouk was crowned King of Cambodia, reclaiming the throne he relinquished in 1955. His son Norodom Ranariddh was appointed First Prime Minister and Hun Sen, Second Prime Minister, a situation intended to promote national unity but leading, inevitably, to internal bickering and dissent.

PARTY-TIME: CAMBODIA'S NEW DEMOCRATS

● **FUNCINPEC** (Front Uni National pour un Cambodge Independent Neutre, Pacifique et Cooperatif). Founded by Prince Norodom Sihanouk to oppose the CPP, and run by his son, Prince Norodom Ranariddh. 58 seats.

● The **Cambodian People's Party** (CPP – formerly the Communist Party). Headed by Hun Sen and originally installed by Vietnam in 1979. The CPP's main election ticket in the 1993 elections was the crushing of the Khmer Rouge. 51 seats.

● **Buddhist Liberal Democratic Party** (BDLP). Led by octogenarian Son Sann, the pre-1970 Finance Minister and ex-leader of the Khmer People's National Liberation Front (KPNLF) from 1993, replaced by Information Minister Ieng Mouly in Jul 1995. 10 seats.

● **Liberal Democratic Party** (LDP), formed from the old military wing of the KPNLF. 1 seat.

WHITHER THE KHMER ROUGE?

The Khmer Rouge may have refrained from its promised systematic disruption of the May 1993 elections because it feared that it would drive people to vote for its sworn enemy, the CPP, instead. At the time, analysts said the guerrillas were probably keeping their options open. But that Cambodian voters ignored Khmer Rouge calls to boycott the election – and that in many instances Khmer Rouge soldiers actually voted – was a slap in the face for the group's leaders.

There is no doubt that militarily, the Khmer Rouge remains a force to be reckoned with – it is thought to have about 5-6,000 troops under arms. The organization's old leadership is also still intact – although in 1993 there were reports that Ieng Sary ('Brother Number Two') was dying of stomach cancer. That the Khmer Rouge is still a part of the Cambodian equation, western governments have themselves to blame. They did not intervene in 1979 when China began re-equipping the battered guerrillas – they wanted to signal their displeasure at the Vietnamese invasion. American policy reflected Washington's animosity towards Vietnam and, by extension, the former Soviet Union. US opposition to Hanoi's occupation, led it to support the Khmer Rouge-dominated exiled Coalition Government of Democratic Kampuchea for over a decade. Other western countries joined the US in backing the CGDK's claim to a seat at the United Nations. During the 1980s the Khmer Rouge worked hard to consolidate its territorial support base so that it became impossible to exclude it from the eventual peace negotiations.

Any scenario which accommodates the possibility of a Khmer Rouge come-back is unthinkable to many foreign observers. To some Cambodians the concept of the Khmer Rouge returning to power would be like the Nazis returning to power in post-war Germany. But while the parallel is emotive, it is also misleading. Margaret Scott writes: "The Nazis killed Jews because they were Jews; but the Khmer Rouge was made up of Cambodians who killed other Cambodians."

What many westerners find hard to understand is that the Khmer Rouge do still enjoy considerable popular support among Cambodians – despite the massacres and the torture they have meted out. UN officials working in Phnom Penh in 1992 and 1993 noted this disquietning phenomenon. In Jun 1994, the retiring Australian ambassador to Cambodia, John Holloway, in a leaked account of his $2\frac{1}{2}$ years in the country wrote:

> "I was alarmed in a recent dialogue with about 100 students from different groups at the University of Phnom Penh to hear them espousing a return to government by the Khmer Rouge. ... They estimated that 60% of the student body favoured Khmer Rouge participation in government... It is necessary for outsiders to understand, that for most Cambodians, the Vietnamese are a far more traumatic issue than the Khmer Rouge."

Nonetheless, these are signs that the Khmer Rouge may, at long last, be in decline. Partly this is due to the amnesty declared in 1994 (see page 461). Partly because Beijing has stopped supplying and supporting the organization, while revenue from logging and gem mining is drying up. It is also partly due to a loss of support in rural areas following indiscriminate attacks on local officials. But most importantly, perhaps, it is because the Khmer Rouge has nothing to fight for, and stands for nothing. It is, as Nate Thayer put it in 1995 some 20 years after the Khmer Rouge took Phnom Penh, waging a 'war without issues'.

Politics and the military struggle since the elections

Almost from day one of Cambodia's rebirth as an independent state espousing the principles of democracy and the market, cracks began to appear in the rickety structure that underlay these grand ideals. Rampant corruption, infighting among the coalition partners, political intrigue, murder and intimidation all became features of the political landscape. The Khmer Rouge spurned the offer of a role in government in return for a ceasefire; the civil war in the countryside began to gently simmer once more; and King Norodom Sihanouk continued to exasperate almost everyone.

In Jul 1994 there was another unsuccessful **coup attempt**, led by three former ministers: the troublesome Norodom Chakkrapong (a son of King Sihanouk), General Sin Song and Sin Sen. Sin Song and Norodom Chakkrapong had both been expelled from the government after alleged involvement in the attempted coup of Jun 1993. Norodom Chakkrapong managed to evade the authorities and fled the country while the two Sins – Sin Song and Sin Sen – were arrested (Sin Song later escaped from prison, to be rearrested in Thailand – a country with which Cambodia does not have an extradition treaty). Just to add some international spice to the coup attempt, the government also arrested 14 Thai citizens at Phnom Penh Airport – allegedly weapons experts flown in to assist in the coup. Their arrest led to a further outbreak of bickering, accusation and counter-accusation between the Cambodian and Thai governments. Who, and what purpose, lay behind the plot seemed to grow murkier by the month. Allegations emerged, for example, that vice prime minister Sar Kheng and 42 others had been involved in the coup attempt. Commentators took this as indicating a split in the Cambodian People's Party (CPP). Another rumour circulating in the capital was that the entire coup was faked by Hun Sen to undermine his CPP colleagues in the government.

Nor were the difficulties just between members, former members, and budding members of the Cambodian government. The Khmer Rouge continued – and still do – to pose a threat to the stability of the country. For much of 1994 the Khmer Rouge seemed to have the better of the military campaign. They retook their northern headquarters at Anlong Veng in Mar, which the government had seized just a month earlier. When government forces captured the Khmer Rouge headquarters at the strategic gem-mining centre of Pailin (which had been under Khmer Rouge control since late 1989), the Khmer Rouge once more were able to stifle the cries of victory by quickly retaking the town. In early May, the Khmer Rouge even came close to capturing the key city of Battambang after government forces were reported to have retreated without offering any resistance. It seemed, in mid-year, that the Khmer Rouge were gaining the upper hand. However a political decision – rather than brilliance on the battlefield – seems to have since swung the military balance decisively in favour of the government.

In Jun the government closed Khmer Rouge offices in the capital – to the annoyance of King Norodom Sihanouk who continued to argue that the rebel group simply could not be ignored and must be part of any political future. Shortly afterwards, the National Assembly outlawed the KR altogether, offering a 6 month amnesty to rank and file guerrillas. It was this latter act that seems to have most effectively undermined the Khmer Rouge's military strength. By the time the 6 months was up in Jan 1995, 7,000 Khmer Rouge had reportedly defected to the government, leaving somewhere between 5,000 and

6,000 hardcore rebels still fighting. One of these defectors was Sar Kim Lemouth, a French-trained economist, who was, in effect, the Khmer Rouge's Finance Minister. It is hoped that he may be able to reveal where the millions earned by the Khmer Rouge from its gem and logging operations are stashed. This may, in turn, allow the Cambodian government to freeze their assets and seriously to undermine the group. The associated fear, though, is that if the Khmer Rouge does come under increasing pressure then it will turn its back on finding a political solution, and return to an all-out military strategy.

The war in Cambodia, though in many ways a rather unimportant footnote to the Cold War, has reached the front pages of western newspapers – when, that is, westerners have been caught up in the maelstrom. In Apr 1994 two Britons and an Australian were **kidnapped** by the Khmer Rouge. 3 months later, three tourists (French, British and Australian) travelling on a train in Kompot province were also kidnapped. All were later reported murdered by the Khmer Rouge – for being 'spies'. The apparently cack-handed attempts on the part of the government to secure their release – the *Far Eastern Economic Review* called it a 'Theatre of the Absurd' – prompted harsh criticism from the British, French and Australian governments. The Australians even wanted to send their own special forces in – a plan which the British vetoed. When Chhouk Rin, the commander of the Khmer Rouge forces involved in the seizure of the three tourists, defected to the government and received amnesty from prosecution, anger turned to outrage. There were even rumours circulating that government forces had been involved in the train attack. Needless to say though, the murder of 17 Thai loggers by the Khmer Rouge in Preah Vihear province in Nov 1994 did not make news in the West.

Politics in Cambodia, to put in mildly, remains 'tainted' by corruption, incompetence, nepotism and cronyism. In Oct 1994 one of the few respected men in the Cambodian cabinet, Economy and Finance Minister Sam Rangsi, was replaced. Commentators interpreted this as a result of his tough anti-corruption stance, and significantly when the Minister for Foreign Affairs and International Cooperation, Prince Norodom Sereivut, resigned in solidarity with Rangsi he explained his actions by saying that "we must show...there are some honest people [in the government]". Although Cambodia is still a democracy, there are those who see the government putting on increasingly authoritarian airs. Journalists are worried that their freedom to report the news will be jeopardized by a press law approved by the National Assembly in Jul 1995, and opposition politicians are becoming more circumspect in broadcasting their criticisms of the government in the face of continued – and apparently state-organized – thuggery. At times the sensitivity of politicians has descended into farce. In Mar 1995, Cambodian newspaper editor Chan Rottana was sentenced to a year in gaol for writing a 'false and defamatory statement' that First Prime Minister Prince Norodom Ranariddh was 'three times more stupid' than Second Prime Minister Hun Sen. In mid-1995 former foreign minister Sam Rainsy summed up the state of political affairs in the country when he said:

"If you are satisfied with cosmetics, everything is OK, like some Americans tell me. But if you scratch a little bit below the surface, there is nothing democratic about the government. The parliament is a rubber stamp. The press is being killed ... The judiciary is far from independent."

Sam Rainsy is far from being an unbiased commentator on Cambodian affairs. Following his resignation as foreign minister, he was expelled from the ruling FUNCINPEC party and then, at the end of Jun 1995, expelled from Parliament. As the international community responded critically to the announcement – which was reached without a vote or a debate – there was speculation that aid might be cut in response. One senior UN official observed that "this is the clearest signal that the honeymoon for democracy is over [in Cambodia]".

There is no doubt that newspaper editors face severe repercussions should they print stories derogatory of the government and key ministers. In May, the *Khmer Ideal* newspaper was closed down and its publisher fined; in the same month, the editor of *New Liberty* was jailed for a year for penning an editorial entitled 'Nation of thieves', alluding to corruption in government ranks; a week later, the government began proceedings against the editor of the *Morning News* – a man who was jailed in 1994 for a previous offending article. Human Rights Watch Asia reported that this series of actions "represent one of the most serious assaults yet on freedom of expression". Yet the countries who bankrolled and supported the UN-administered move to democracy, namely Australia, France, Indonesia, and the US, are reluctant, apparently, to be too critical of the government. Partly, perhaps, this is because of the wish to present Cambodia as a UN 'success story' (there are notably few about), partly because they have invested considerable amounts of money and prestige in the country and fear that overt criticism might lead to instability. Whatever the reasoning, it does appear that Cambodia is becoming less democratic and less open as the government becomes increasingly defensive of its record.

Most commentators also see **King Norodom Sihanouk** as part of the problem, simply because he is so revered. He interferes in the political process, changes his mind constantly, and exasperates government ministers. Yet the respect held for him by his people means that he cannot be ignored, or easily contradicted or, for that matter, sacked. Nonetheless, the government does seem to be attempting to reduce his influence and role – perhaps with a view to permanently castrating the monarchy. At the beginning of 1995, police confiscated all copies of a booklet entitled *Only the King can save Cambodia* – reputed to call for a return of King Sihanouk to politics. Whether the monarchy can survive the buffeting is a moot point. The next King – Sihanouk is 73 and has cancer – must be nominated by the Royal Council to the Throne within 7 days of his death. But this council consists of a myriad of competing factions. It seems that Hun Sen would like Prince Yuvancath crowned as the next king (until 1994 he was a factory hand in Boston, in the US). As King Sihanouk was reported as saying in the *Far Eastern Economic Review* at the beginning of 1995:

"You know, they [Hun Sen and the Cambodian People's Party] want someone very flexible, a lamb, a lamb! A small cat! Very obedient, or an obedient dog to use as a king. And it is not good. It is not good at all."

Economy

1989 was a turning point for Cambodia; when the Vietnamese troops pulled out in Sep that year, the economy was in a sorry state. Hanoi had done what it could to restore some semblance of order after the mess left by the Khmer Rouge in 1979. But with the collapse of the Soviet Union, aid from Moscow and its erstwhile Eastern Bloc allies dried up. This deprived Phnom Penh of about US$100mn a year. The Hun Sen government also faced a total aid and trade boycott from the W, while the civil war against the resistance factions further sapped the regime's scant resources. But the Phnom Penh regime gradually shifted away from orthodox Communist ideology and central planning towards market economics. At first this was nothing more than paper policy, but deregulation and reform began to spark an upsurge in business activity.

Before, during and immediately after the elections of 1993, the economy was in dire straits. The value of the riel collapsed against the US dollar, inflation reached 340%, provincial towns were crowded with people subsisting by recycling rubbish or begging, and foreign investors were shying away from a country so wracked by manifold problems.

Today many of these problems have receded somewhat. Annual inflation was at a comparatively manageable 20% at the end of 1994 and at 10% during the first months of 1995 (in 1993 it was over 100%), and foreign investors are beginning to pluck up courage and put their money in the country. Malaysian, Singaporean, Thai, Taiwanese and other Asian companies are in the vanguard of this investment tide. Between Aug 1994 and Apr 1995 US$625mn in foreign investment was approved. The role of Malaysian investors is particularly striking – and surprising. In the last months of 1994 they took the lion's share of total approved investment. Various explanations have been presented to account for this. First, the Malaysians are not the Thais, which is an advantage given the ever-present friction between Thailand and Cambodia. (Thai journalists refer to Siem Reap – which means 'Victory over Siam' – as Siem Rap – 'Plains of Siam', just one of many annoyances, small and big, which divide the two countries.) Second, Malaysia is just far enough away so the two countries have no lingering territorial disputes, and there is little chance that an army of Malaysian workers will arrive in Phnom Penh to take jobs away from deserving Cambodians. Third, of course, Malaysia is a successful economy, at the early stages of beginning its own outward investment drive.

The intention is clearly to entice labour intensive manufacturing enterprises such as garment factories to set up shop, although to date most investment has been concentrated in the service sector. There has been speculation in land and property and hotels, bars and restaurants have been going up or are being refurbished – mainly in Phnom Penh, but also in S seaside towns like Kampot and in Siem Reap. Grant Evans, writing in *The Far Eastern Economic Review* in Mar 1993 noted that businessmen "have descended on the country like locusts in the atmosphere of frontier, tax-free capitalism. A few dollars trickle down to the Khmer." In Aug 1994 the National Assembly passed a new

BACK ON THE TOURIST TRACK

Between 1975, when the Khmer Rouge gained power, and the mid-1980s, Cambodia received virtually no tourists whatsoever. Since then, though, and linked with the peace settlement, numbers have picked up enormously, from 400 in 1986 to over 175,000 in 1994. In 1995, the Ministry of Tourism hopes to open offices in all of the country's 22 provinces (there are currently offices in 16) and the government clearly sees tourism as an easy way to generate foreign exchange. It was feared that the deaths in 1994 of a number of foreigners at the hands of the Khmer Rouge would deter travellers, although the effect seems to have been minimal.

Tourist arrivals

1986	400	1994	176,617
1991	4,500	2000	1 million (projected)
1993	118,183		

AN AMBASSADOR'S VIEW, CIRCA 1994

In Jun 1994, the retiring Australian ambassador to Cambodia, John Holloway, wrote a concluding 3,500 word summary of his 2½ years sojourn in the country. Although the cable was supposed to be secret, it was leaked to the *Sydney Morning Herald* and provides a frank – and none too laudatory – assessment of Cambodia, its politicians and prospects.

● **King Norodom Sihanouk**: "pathetically pursuing power although riddled with cancer, he has belittled the government, tried to cause splits in the ruling groups and thrown aside the government strategy to outlaw the Khmer Rouge... He has strutted around his small stage, erratic and emotive, continuing the negative influence he has wielded over the last 2 years"

● **Prime ministers Hun Sen and Norodom Ranariddh**: are unable to "exercise leadership, even when they are in the country."

● **Government ministries**: "most government ministries are barely working."

● **Civil servants**: "are only motivated to attend their offices at all by the possibility of making some extra money."

● **Corruption**: "every business deal must have a cut for the relevant minister."

● **Khmer Rouge**: "well disciplined, committed, and not engaged in petty corruption."

● **Army**: "people join the army to use their uniforms and their weapons as a meal ticket. ...government forces move through the countryside, unpaid and out of control, looting and committing a wide range of crimes ...the [state of the army] is deplorable".

● **The economy**: "...inefficient government, massive corruption, a hemorrhage of Khmer wealth caused by an influx of skilled Vietnamese...and a concentration of all development funds on the cities."

● **The countryside**: "out in the Cambodian countryside, where 80% of Cambodians live, it is difficult to find any progress. Very little, if any, new money has percolated into the countryside, and the life of rural dwellers is as brutish as ever."

investment law to make the country even more enticing, by providing foreign investors with tax exemption on profits for 8 years and allowing foreign investors to hold 100% equity.

Cambodia's future, to a considerable extent, rests in the hands of the international aid community, and especially the IMF and World Bank. Donors, operating through the International Conference for the Reconstruction of Cambodia, promised US$777mn for 1994-95 and until Sep 1994 were relatively reassured by progress. Since then

donors have become increasingly disenchanted with the government's management of its economic affairs. In Mar 1995 Cambodia asked for over US$1bn for 1995-96, but donors are not so keen to throw money at a country whose politicians are only concerned with lining their own pockets.

Cambodia's GDP is still estimated to be no higher than it was 25 years ago. Roads are potholed, bridges destroyed, power cuts are commonplace and there is a shortage of skilled managers to oversee reconstruction of the war-shattered economy. Paddy fields are littered with landmines, and marketing and distribution systems continue to be harpered by the civil war. In the district of Rattanak Mondal in the W of Battambang province, comprising some of the country's richest farmland, one adult male in seven has been killed or maimed by a mine between 1984 and 1994. The 1994/95 rice harvest was devastated by flood and drought – about a third was lost – and is not likely to be sufficient to meet the country's own needs (imports of 300,000 tonnes of rice in 1995 is one estimate). In short, there is a considerable gap between the macro-economic view from the windows of the Finance Ministry and that from the paddy field. (It needs to be remembered that 85% of the population still work on the land, and manufacturing accounts for just 17% of GDP.) Son Chhay, an MP representing Siem Reap, following the floods of 1994 said of the rescue efforts: "They [the government] probably spent three times more money on the reception for the prime minister than they are spending to help the flood victims."

The average monthly income of a medical officer in a Cambodian hospital – one of the busiest and most stressful jobs going – is about US$5 – plus a ration of rice and paraffin. These wages are paid 3 months late. Government soldiers earn a princely US$10 a month – but most of them have not been paid for 6 months. Most people consider themselves lucky to have jobs, however. It is hardly surprising that government soldiers, as well as Khmer Rouge rebels, sometimes resort to highway robbery to top up their meagre earnings. Bandits regularly hold travellers at gunpoint as they point torches into the eyes of long-distance taxi-drivers – who now build the extortion money into the cost of a trip.

In the past, resentment due to the huge discrepancies in wealth between city and countryside have been responsible for much of the political upheaval.

CAMBODIA: FACT FILE

Geographic

Land area	180,000 sq km
Arable land as % of total	16.5%
Average annual rate of deforestation	0.2%
Highest mountain Phnom Aoral	1,813m
Average rainfall in Phnom Penh	1,560mm
Average temperature in Phnom Penh	27.5°C

Economic

GNP/person (1991)	US$200
GDP/person (PPP*, 1991)	US$1,250
GNP growth (/capita, 1980-1988)	n.a.
GNP growth (/capita, 1965-1980)	0.6%
% labour force in agriculture	74%
Total debt (% GDP)	n.a.
Debt service ratio (% exports)	n.a.
Military expenditure (% GNP)	n.a.

Social

Population	8.8 million
Population growth rate (1960-92)	1.5%
Adult literacy rate	37.8%
Mean years of schooling	2 years
Tertiary graduate as % of age group	n.a.
Population in absolute poverty	n.a.
Rural population as % of total	88%
Growth of urban population (1960-92)	1.8%/year
Urban population in largest city (%)	n.a.
Televisions per 1,000 people	9

Health

Life expectancy at birth	50.4 years
Population with access to clean water	n.a.
Calorie intake as % of requirements	96%
Malnourished children under 5 years old	0.5 million
Contraceptive prevalence rate†	n.a.

*PPP = Purchasing Power Parity (based on what it costs to buy a similar basket of goods and services in different countries).

† % of women of childbearing age using contraception.

Source World Bank (1994) *Human Development Report 1994*, OUP: New York; and other sources.

Rampant corruption and the creation of private monopolies of national resources – particularly timber, rubber and gemstones – made a few people very wealthy. Foreign investors are concerned by the lack of 'transparency' in government affairs and the control that individuals have over some sections of the bureaucracy. If historical precedent is anything to go by, future governments are unlikely to learn from past governments' mistakes. As in many Southeast Asian countries, politics is a sure way of getting rich quick. Gemstones and timber both offer Cambodia's most lucrative possibilities. Thai logging companies have long brought timber from Khmer Rouge-controlled territory. In 1990 the Khmer Rouge built roads from their powerbase in W Cambodia into Thailand, to allow them to export timber and gemstones which help fund the organization. In the early 1990s these exports were thought to be worth around US$60mn a month, and the trade is likely to continue as long as the Khmer Rouge can maintain their hold on the borderlands with Thailand. The proceeds are said to be neatly divided between the Thai contractors (50%), the Thai military (5%) and the Khmer Rouge (45%).

PHNOM PENH

Legend has it that Cambodia's capital is named after Penh, a rich Khmer lady, who lived on the banks of the Mekong River. Floodwaters are said to have washed a tree onto the riverbank and Penh found four statues of the Buddha hidden inside. In 1372 she built a monastery to house the statues on a nearby hill – or 'phnom' in Cambodian. The people of Cambodia believed the statues were a sign from the gods that they wanted a new home. When the Thais invaded in 1431 and after the kingdom of Angkor later collapsed, the capital duly moved to Ondong and then to a site near the important temple of Phnom Penh. The city lies at the confluence of the Sap, Mekong and Bassac rivers and it quickly grew into an important commercial centre. The French called the junction 'Les Quatre Bras'; in Khmer it is known as the Chamean Mon.

Before 1970, the capital was the beguiling beauty of Indochina with its wide boulevards – laid out by the French – elegant colonial villas and Art Deco town houses. Only now, 25 years on, is the Phnom Penh of 1970 re-emerging. Energetic landscaping of the boulevards and promenades alongside the Tonlé Sap has much to do with this. Many of the buildings survive, although most are in a serious state of disrepair: the best-preserved colonial architecture is around Victory Monument.

Phnom Penh is more like a country town, than a capital city. The newest buildings still fail to top 10 storeys and Phnom Penh exudes a provincial charm, in stark contrast to its near neighbour, Bangkok. Rickety bamboo scaffolding is going up all over the city now that the country is more stable: residential and office properties are in heavy demand. Rents have come down from the UN-TAC – inflated era of 1992/93 but are still surprisingly high – a result of for-

eign businesses clamouring for a share in the new free market climate. Phnom Penh faces a housing crisis – two-thirds of its houses were damaged by the Khmer Rouge between 1975 and 1979. Apart from the sheer cost of building new ones and renovating the crumbling colonial mansions, there is a severe shortage of skilled workers in Cambodia: under Pol Pot 20,000 engineers were killed as well as nearly all the country's architects (three students survived within Cambodia).

The years of war have also taken a heavy toll on the city's inhabitants: Phnom Penh's population fluctuations in recent decades give some indication of the scale of social disruption. Refugees first began to flood in from the countryside in the early 1950s during the First Indochina War – the population grew from 100,000 to 600,000 by the late 1960s. In the early 1970s there was another surge as people streamed in from the countryside again, this time to escape US bombing and guerrilla warfare: on the eve of the Khmer Rouge takeover in 1975, the capital had a popu-

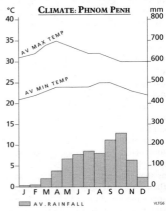

CLIMATE: PHNOM PENH

AV.RAINFALL

lation of 2 million. Phnom Penh then became a ghost town; on Pol Pot's orders it was forcibly emptied and the townspeople frog-marched into the countryside to work as labourers. Only 45,000 inhabitants were left in the city in 1975 and a large number were soldiers. In 1979, after 4 years of virtual abandonment, Phnom Penh had a population of a few thousand. People began to drift back following the Vietnamese invasion (1978/79) and as hopes for peace rose in 1991, the floodgates opened yet again: today the population is approaching 1 million. Most of the original population of Phnom Penh died during the Pol Pot era or are in exile and the population of the city is now more rural in character. In fact the population of the city tends to vary from season to season: in the dry season people pour into the capital when there is little work in the countryside but go back to their farms in the wet season when the rice has to be planted and the population drops to 750,000-800,000.

Public health facilities are woefully inadequate – the city's services are overstretched and there are problems with everything from water and electricity supplies to sewage and refuse disposal. The Khmer Rouge saw to it that the plumbing network was completely destroyed before they left. The capital's streets are potholed and in bad need of repair. A British newspaper correspondent, visiting the city in late 1991 noted that Phnom Penh boasted of the new urban phenomenon of traffic jams, regarding them as an indicator of economic development.

Phnom Penh has undergone an economic revival since the Paris Peace Accord was signed in 1991; there has been a frenzy of business deals in real estate (one of the most serious problems for residents is land disputes and expulsion as many do not possess title deeds to their property). Small businesses are springing up, Phnom Penh's river port which has recently been the recipient of

a US$30mn investment programme to renovate it by the Japanese – is bustling with traders from throughout the region – especially Singapore. Venture capitalists and aid organizations are homing in as evidenced by the presence of over 100 international non-governmental organizations. Thai investors have capitalized on their geographical proximity and linguistic advantage to develop a commanding position in the capital's reviving economy, and the Phnom Penh of 1995 is growing daily in manner and appearance, more like Bangkok. The Thai look is underscored by growing volumes of cars and pick-up trucks, lent added authenticity by their Bangkok registration plates; the majority of vehicles are smuggled over the border, many stolen. Other vices (not *necessarily* the preserve of Bangkok) are flourishing and Thai-style massage parlours are springing up, despite the departure of UNTAC. Monks' saffron robes are once again lending a splash of colour to the capital's streets, following the reinstatement of Buddhism as the national religion in 1989. But the amputees on street corners are a constant reminder of Cambodia's tragic story.

The Cambodian capital relies on the river. The Mekong provides the city's water supply. It is the only significant port on the Mekong above the delta and is navigable by ships of about 5,000-8,000 tons.

Finding your way around Phnom Penh can be very confusing. Most of the street names were changed in 1979 by the Vietnamese who decided that even urban nomenclature should be ideologically sound. However, since the elections of 1993 the street names have reverted to those used in the Sangkum era (1955-69): That said, street names have changed so many times in recent history that it is sometimes hard to establish the prevailing official name for a road. Maps and street signs commonly contradict. The majority of larger streets

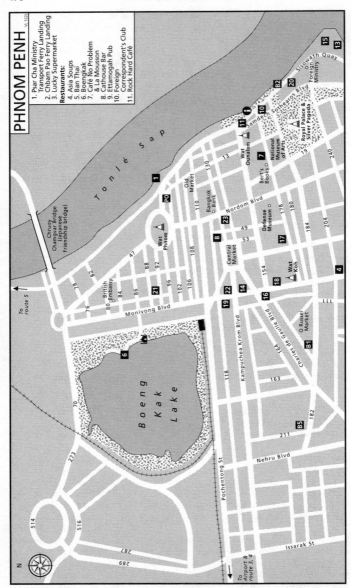

PHNOM PENH

VL 1321

1. Psar Cha Ministry
   Transport Ferry Landing
2. Chbam Pao Ferry Landing
3. Lucky Supermarket

Restaurants:
4. Asia Soups
5. Ban Thai
6. Boengkak
7. Café No Problem
   & La Mousson
8. Cathouse Bar
9. Ettamogah Pub
10. Foreign
    Correspondent's Club
11. Rock Hard Café

Tonlé Sap

Chruoy
Changvar Bridge
(Japanese
Friendship bridge)

To route 5

British
Embassy

Boeng Kak Lake

Pochentong St

To
Airport &
route 3, 4

Monivong Blvd

Wat Phnom

Old Market

PO

Bangkok
Bank

Nordom Blvd

Central
Market

Kampuchea Krom Blvd

Charles de Gaulle Blvd

Defense
Museum

Wat
Koh

Nehru Blvd

Issarak St

Wat
Ounalom

Bert's
Books

National
Museum
of Arts

Royal Palace &
Silver Pagoda

Samdech Sotheoros Blvd

Sisowath Quay

Foreign
Ministry

N

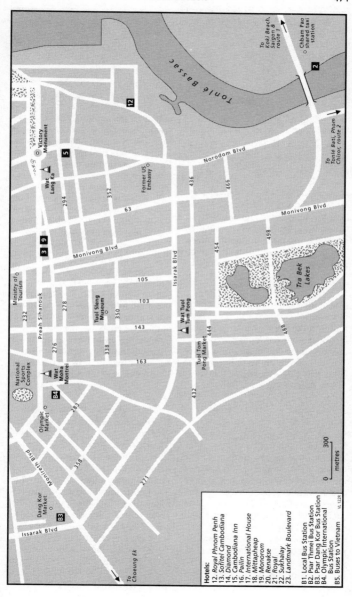

To Koki Beach,
Saigon & route 8

Chbam Pao
shared taxi
station

2

To Tonlé Bati, Phom
Chisor, route 2

Tonlé Bassac

12

Victory
Monument

5

Wat
Lang Ka

Norodom Blvd

Former US
Embassy

436

466

352

Monivong Blvd

294

63

498

Monivong Blvd

3 **9**

Ministry of
Tourism

454

Tra Bek
Lakes

105

232

278

103

350

Issarak Blvd

Preah Sihanouk

Tuol Sleng
Museum

Wat Tuol
Tum Pong

143

276

338

488

444

Wat
Moha
Montrei

163

Tuol Tom
Peng Market

National
Sports
Complex

432

B4

283

Olympic
Market

338

0   300
metres

Dang Kor
Market

211

B3

Monireth Blvd

Issarak Blvd

To
Choeung Ek

Hotels:
12. Royal Phnom Penh
13. Sofitel Cambodiana
14. Diamond
15. Cambodiana Inn
16. Pailin
17. International House
18. Mittapheap
19. Monorom
20. Renakse
21. Royal
22. Sukhalay
23. Landmark Boulevard

B1. Local Bus Station
B2. Psar Thmei Bus Station
B3. Psar Dang Kor Bus Station
B4. Olympic International
     Bus Station
B5. Buses to Vietnam

VL.1228

STREETS OF CONFUSION

Achar Mean = Monivong

Ton Samouth = Norodom

Lenin = Samdech Sothearos

Keo Mony = Issarak

Karl Marx = Sisowath

Sivutha = Preah Sihanouk

are named and the smaller streets numbered: as a rule, even numbered streets run E-W, odd numbered streets run N-S. The S is the royal quarter and the Khmer area; the N is the colonial quarter with the *Grand Hotel* and several large and dilapidated French buildings. Chinatown, the commercial quarter, surrounds the central covered market. The modern area, built after independence, is to the W of Monivong St.

Places of interest

One of the main sights in Phnom Penh is the Royal Palace, which, along with the Silver Pagoda, was closed to the public since its reinstatement as Prince Sihanouk's main residence. The Silver Pagoda is now open again but permits are required from the tourist office.

The **Royal Palace**, between 184 and 240 sts, was mainly built by the French in 1866 on the site of the old town. The entrance is on Samdech Sothearos Blvd via the Pavilion of Dancers (or Chan Chaya Pavilion). Opposite the entrance are the walls of the royal residence (closed to the public) and the stable of the white elephant (a highly auspicious and sacred animal treasured as a symbol of royal beneficence). The pagoda-style compound was built by the French, and since Nov 1991, has been home, once again, to Prince Norodom Sihanouk. In the weeks leading up to his return, there was a flurry of activity behind the royal residence's orange walls as decorators strove to give it as much regal opulence

as Cambodia could muster – despite the abolition of the monarchy in 1970.

The **Throne Room**, the main building to the left of the entrance, was built in 1917 in Khmer style; it has a tiered roof and a 59m tower, influenced by Angkor's Bayon Temple (see page 496). It was used for coronations and other official occasions such as the reception of foreign ambassadors when they presented their official credentials: scenes from the Ramayana adorn the walls. Inside stand the sacred gong and French-style thrones only used by the sovereign. There are two chambers for the king and queen at the back of the hall, which were used only in the week before a coronation when the royal couple were barred from sleeping together. The other adjoining room is used to house the ashes of dead monarchs before they are placed in a royal stupa. There are Buddha images in the left nave, at which the kings would pray before each day. Returning to his former abode in Nov 1991, Sihanouk must have found it much as he had left it – although many of the state gifts from the display cases have sadly been smashed or stolen. The chairs closest to the entrance were reserved for high officials and the others were for visiting ambassadors. The yellow chairs were used by visiting heads of state.

The **royal treasury** and the **Napoleon III villa** – or summerhouse – built in 1866, are to the S of the Throne Room. The latter was presented by Napoleon III to his Empress Eugenie as accommodation for the princess during the Suez Canal opening celebrations who later had it dismantled and dispatched it to Phnom Penh as a gift to the king. The prefabricated folly was renovated and refurbished in 1990 and its ersatz marble walls remarbled – all with French money. Next to the villa are rooms built in 1959 by Sihanouk to accommodate his cabinet. Beyond is the N gate and the Silver Pagoda enclosure.

The **Silver Pagoda** is often called the Pagoda of the Emerald Buddha or Wat Preah Kaeo after the statue housed here. The wooden temple was originally built by King Norodom in 1892 to enshrine royal ashes and then rebuilt by Sihanouk in 1962. The pagoda's steps are of Italian marble, and inside, its floor is comprised of more than 5,000 silver blocks which together weigh nearly 6 tonnes. All around are cabinets filled with presents from foreign dignitaries – the pagoda is remarkably intact, having been granted special dispensation by the Khmer Rouge, although 60% of the Khmer treasures were stolen from here. It is a magpie-style collection, as the writer Norman Lewis said in 1957: "One imagined the Queen, or perhaps a succession of queens, making a periodic clear out of their cupboards and then tripping down to the Silver Pagoda with all the attractive useless things that had to be found a home somewhere". In the centre of the pagoda is a magnificent 17th century emerald Buddha statue made of Baccarat crystal. In front is a 90 kg golden Buddha studded with 9,584 diamonds, dating from 1906. It was made from the jewellery of King Norodom and its vital statistics conform exactly to his – a tradition that can be traced back to the god-kings of Angkor. The gold Buddha image is flanked by bronze and silver statues of the Buddha. Under a glass cover is a golden lotus – a Buddhist relic from India. At the back of the room there is a marble Buddha (from Burma) and a litter used for coronations which required 12 porters to carry it.

The 600m-long wall enclosing the Silver Pagoda is galleried; its inward face is covered in frescoes, painted at the turn of the century, which depict epic scenes from the Ramayana – the story starts by the E gate. To the E of the Silver Pagoda is a **statue of King Norodom** on horseback (it is in fact a statue of Napoleon III with the head replaced with that of the Cambodian monarch) and a **stupa** containing the ashes of King Ang Duong (1845-59). Beyond the stupa, on the S wall, are **pavilions** containing a footprint of the Buddha (to the E) and a pavilion for royal celebrations (to the W). Next to **Phnom Mondap**, an artificial hill with a building covering the Buddha's footprint, in the centre of the S wall is a **stupa** dedicated to Sihanouk's favourite daughter who died of leukaemia in 1953. On the W wall is a stupa of King Norodom Suramarit with a bell tower in the NW corner. Beyond the bell tower on the N wall is the **mondap** or library, originally containing precious Buddhist texts.

NB Photography is not allowed inside the Silver Pagoda. Admission US$2. Camera US$2, video US$5. Open 0800-1100, 1400-1700 Tues-Sun. Pagoda is expected to close for renovation any time.

The **National Museum of Arts** (also called Musée des Beaux Arts) is the terracotta building just N of the palace (on 13 St between 178 and 184 sts). It was designed by a French archeologist and painter, George Groslier, in Khmer style in 1920 to exhibit works scattered throughout the country. The museum contains a collection of Khmer art – notably sculpture – throughout the ages (although some periods are not represented). Most of the exhibits date from the Angkor period but there are several examples from the pre-Angkor era (ie from the kingdoms of Funan, Chenla and Cham). The collection of Buddhas from the 6th and 7th centuries, includes a statue of Krishna Bovardhana found at Angkor Borei showing the freedom and grace of early Khmer sculpture. The chief attraction is probably the pre-Angkorian statue of Harihara, found at Prasat Andat near Kompong Thom. There is a fragment from a beautiful bronze statue of Vishnu found in the West Baray at Angkor, as well as frescoes and engraved doors. The library at the museum was one of the largest of its type in Southeast Asia but has now been dismantled and sold.

The shop attached to the museum sells reproductions of works from Angkor. The Fine Arts School, *École des Beaux Arts*, is behind the main building. French-speaking and English-speaking guides are available and most are excellent. Admission US$2. Camera US$2. Open 0700-1130, 1400-1730 Tues-Sun. Photographs only permitted in the garden.

Phnom Penh's most important wat, **Wat Ounalom**, is N of the museum, at the junction of 154 St and Samdech Sothearos Blvd, facing the Tonlé Sap. The first building on this site was a monastery, built in 1443 to house a hair of the Buddha. Before 1975, more than 500 monks lived at the wat but the Khmer Rouge murdered the Patriarch and did their best to demolish the capital's principal temple. Nonetheless it remains Cambodian Buddhism's headquarters. The complex has been restored since 1979 although its famous library was completely destroyed. The stupa behind the main sanctuary is the oldest part of the wat. The main sanctuary, which dates from 1952, now contains only the poorly-assembled fragments of a Burmese marble Buddha. On the first level there is a fine bust of the Buddha; frescoes on the second level represent scenes from the Buddha's life, painted in 1952.

Wat Phnom stands on a small, wooded hill at the end of Blvd Tou Samouth (in the N end of town, where it intersects 96 St) and is the temple from which the city takes its name. It was built by a wealthy Khmer lady called Penh (see page 468) in 1372. The sanctuary was rebuilt in 1434, 1890, 1894 and 1926. The main entrance is to the E, the steps are guarded by nagas and lions. The principal sanctuary is decorated inside with frescoes depicting scenes from Buddha's life and the Ramayana. At the front, on a pedestal, is a statue of the Buddha with four faces. There is a statue of Penh inside a small pavilion between the vihara and the stupa; the latter contains the ashes of King Ponhea Yat (1405-67).

Wat Phnom is a favourite with the Phnom Penhois and is often teeming with worshippers praying for a dose of good fortune. Vietnamese devotees flock to the shrine of the spirit Preah Chau, N of the main sanctuary. To the left of the image of Preah Chau is a statue of the Hindu god, Vishnu, 'the preserver', and the shrine is guarded by spirits wielding clubs. There are nice views down Phnom Penh's tree-lined avenues. On the slope behind the wat is an overgrown royal stupa.

King Sihanouk chose this wat to be the site of a new chedi – the **Preah Sakyamoni Chedei**. The chedi was to be built to house a bone of the Buddha himself, which is currently contained in the small, rather nondescript, Sakyamoni Chedei in front of the city's railway station. King Sihanouk no doubt thought that this was a far too insignificant, not to say noisy, shrine for such a relic and that the comparatively peaceful Wat Phnom a short way NE would be much more fitting. Construction of the new 50m-high chedi was begun on 14 July 1992 and was scheduled to have been completed within 18 months. The architects came up with a design which might be described as Art Deco Meets Angkor. Innovative perhaps, but the purists cannot be jumping for joy and the concrete piles already in place do not bode well for the finished product. However, and like many things Cambodian, funds dried up. Apparently, donations were dripping in at the princely sum of between US$1 and US$2 a day, hardly a king's ransom. But even this might be thought remarkable in a country as poor as Cambodia. Fearing his chedi might not be built in his lifetime, King Sihanouk donated US$900,000 in Oct 1994 from his own royal fund, arguing that his country would not see peace, unity and national reconciliation if the edifice was not completed. In Jun 1995 however, the building programme was curtailed, apparently because the foundations were too shallow to take the weight of the proposed 150-tonne structure. Instead, the chedi was to be converted into a museum housing Buddhist scriptures or *prey tray bedah*. How Cambodia happens to have a bone of the Buddha, is because at the death of the sage his bones were divided up and shipped to all Buddhist quarters of the world. Today there are far more bones housed in assorted shrines than even the Buddha is likely to have been endowed with.

The **French Embassy** which is being extensively rebuilt as a low concrete whitewashed complex for the French to occupy once again, was the building into which 800 expatriates and 600 Cambodians crowded when the Khmer Rouge first occupied the city in mid-Apr 1975, is on the intersection of Monivong Blvd and 76 St, N of Wat Phnom. Within 48 hrs of Pol Pot's troops arrival in Phnom Penh, the French vice-consul was informed that the new regime did not recognize diplomatic privilege. Cambodian women married to foreigners were allowed to stay in the Embassy, but all Cambodian men were ordered to leave. In *Sideshow*, William Shawcross says marriages were hastily arranged to safeguard the women. The foreigners were finally escorted out of Cambodia; everyone else was marched out of the compound. Many met their deaths in the killing fields.

South of the Royal Palace and Silver Pagoda on Samdech Sothearos Blvd (between 268 St and Preah Sihanouk Blvd) is **Victory Monument**. It was built in 1958 to commemorate independence but has now assumed the role of a cenotaph. The best colonial architecture is on roads 114 and 53, 178, Norodom Blvd and Samdech Sothearos Blvd.

Wat Lang Ka, just off Norodom Blvd (not far from the Victory Monument), was another beautiful pagoda that fell victim to Pol Pot's architectural holocaust. Like Wat Ounalom, it was restored in Khmer style on the direction of the Hanoi-backed government in the 1980s.

Further S, on 103 St (close to 350 St), is the **Tuol Sleng Museum** (or Museum of Genocide). After 17 April 1975 the classrooms of Tuol Svay Prey High School became the Khmer Rouge's main torture and interrogation centre, known as Security Prison 21 – or just S-21. More than 20,000 people were taken from S-21 to their executions at Choeung Ek extermination camp. Countless others died under torture and were thrown into mass graves in the school grounds. Only seven prisoners survived because they were sculptors and could turn out countless busts of Pol Pot. The school was converted into a 'museum of genocide' by the Vietnamese (with help from the East Germans who had experience in setting up the Auschwitz Museum) and exhibits, through the display of torture implements, photographs and paintings, the scale of the Khmer Rouge's atrocities. All their victims were methodically numbered and photographed; these pictures now cover the museum's walls. Admission US$2. Open 0800-1100, 1400-1700, closed Mon. Open Public Holidays 0800-1800.

Wat Tuol Tum Pong, next to a market of the same name (just off Issarak Blvd) is a modern pagoda – very bright, almost kitsch. Surrounded by a high wall, it has entrances with mythical animals associated with the Buddha.

There are several other wats worthy of a visit: **Wat Koh**, on Monivong Blvd (between 174 and 178 sts), is popular for its lake. **Wat Moha Montrel** on Preah Sihanouk Blvd (between 173 and 163 sts) was used as a rice storage depot by the Pol Pot regime. A second brick mosque on Chraing Chamres II, called **An-Nur an-Na'im Mosque**, is much smaller than the one which previously occupied the site: the original building, built in 1901 was destroyed by the Khmer Rouge.

The former **US Embassy**, now home to the Ministry of Fisheries, is at the intersection of Norodom and Issarak blvds. As the Khmer Rouge closed on the city from the N and the S in Apr 1975, US Ambassador John Gunther Dean pleaded with Secretary of State Henry Kissinger for an urgent airlift of embassy staff. But it was not until the very last minute, just after 1000 on 12 April 1975, with the Khmer Rouge firing mortars from across the Bassac River onto the football pitch near the compound that served as a landing zone, that the last US Marine helicopter left the city. Flight 462, a convoy of military transport helicopters, evacuated the 82 remaining Americans, 159 Cambodians and 35 other foreigners to a US aircraft carrier in the Gulf of Thailand. Their departure was overseen by 360 heavily armed marines. Despite letters to all senior government figures from the ambassador, offering them places on the helicopters, only one, Acting President Saukham Khoy, fled the country. The American airlift was a deathblow to Cambodian morale. Within 5 days, the Khmer Rouge had taken the city and within hours all senior officials of the former Lon Nol government were executed on the tennis courts of the embassy.

The **Defence Museum**, on Norodom Blvd, traces the phases of Cambodian history, notably the war against the USA and the Khmer revolution. Closed at the moment.

Excursions

It is often easier to hire your own transport (see page 483). Travel agents will also organize trips to surrounding sights.

Boat trips on the Mekong *Phnom Penh Tourism* own a boat which visitors can book to cruise the Mekong and see Mekong Island (famous for its silk production) fishing villages and 'river life'. A relaxing trip, includes lunch and cultural show. The boat is moored next to *Cambodiana Hotel* daily, depart 1100, return 1600. Contact Phnom Penh Tourism for more details (see below) US$28.

North

Nur ul-Ihsan Mosque, 7 km N of Phnom Penh on Route 5, was desecrated by the Khmer Rouge, who used it as a pig sty; it was reconsecrated in 1980. *Getting there*: take buses from the Olympic International bus station N towards Battambang or hire transport.

Oudong, 35 km N of Phnom Penh, was the royal capital between 1618 and 1866 – only the foundations of the ancient palace remain. At the top of the larger of two ridges, just S of Oudong itself, are the ruins of **Phnom Chet Ath Roeus**. The vihara was built in 1911 by King Sisowath to house a large Buddha image, but was destroyed by the Khmer Rouge. Beyond the wat to the NW is a string of viharas – now in ruins – and beyond them several stupas, including one (the middle one) intended to house the ashes of King Ang Douong (1845-1859) by his son, King Norodom. On the other side of the ridge stands a **memorial** to those murdered by the Khmer Rouge, whose remains were unearthed from mass graves on the site in the early 1980s. *Getting there*: N from Phnom Penh on Route 5, approximately 5 km after the Prek Kdam ferry, turn left (S) to Psar Dek Krom. Take buses from Olympic International bus station heading for Battambang or hire transport. **NB** This area is supposed to be mined – keep to well-trodden paths.

South

Choeung Ek, now in a peaceful setting surrounded by orchards and rice fields – was the execution ground for the torture victims of Tuol Sleng – the Khmer Rouge extermination centre, S-21 (see page 475). It is now the main 'tourist attraction' in Phnom Penh. Today a huge **glass tower** stands on the site, filled with the cracked skulls of men, women and children exhumed from 129 mass graves in the area (which were not discovered until 1980). It is estimated that around 40,000 Cambodians were murdered at Choeung Ek between 1975 and 1978. The haunting memorial is often featured in Western TV documentaries and newspaper articles, as its mountains of skulls have a forceful impact, and serve as a graphic reminder of the scale of the Khmer Rouge's atrocities. Cholung Ek is not for the squeamish – many of the graves have been exhumed and human remains can still be seen around the sight. *Getting there*: SW on Pokambor Blvd, about 9 km from the bridge. Hire transport from Phnom Penh – informal motorbike taxis are willing to make the return trip for about US$5.

Tonle Bati, 42 km S of Phnom Penh, is a popular weekend picnic site and beside the lake there is the added attraction of the temple of **Ta Phrom**. The temple dates from Jayavarman VII's reign (1181-1201) and, unusually, it is consecrated to both Brahma and the Buddha. There is a smaller temple, **Yeay Peau**, just N of Ta Phrom. Both temples have a number of fine bas-reliefs. The modern Wat Tonle Bati is nearby – it is another of the Khmer Rouge's architectural victims and a site of remembrance for the thousands who were murdered during the Pol Pot era. 10 km from Tonle Bati is a house belonging to Khmer royalty; locals climb the hill on Sun to make donations to the monks. *Getting there*: 33 km S of Phnom Penh on Route 2 and about 2.5 km from the main road. Take buses from Psar Dang Kor bus station heading for Takeo or hire transport.

Phnom Chisor, 62 km S of Phnom Penh, this phnom (or hill) is topped by a large rock platform on which many buildings from different eras have been built. The principal remaining sanctuary (originally called Suryagiri, literally meaning 'Sun Mountain') is dedicated to Brahma and dates from the 11th century. *Getting there*: 55 km S of Phnom Penh on Route 2, the turn off is marked by Prasat Neang

Khmau (the temple of the Black Virgin); Phnom Chisor is approximately 4 km from the main road. Take buses from Psar Dang Kor bus station heading for Takeo or hire transport.

West

Koki Beach is a riverside resort popular at weekends. Families bring picnics but there are several food stalls. Wooden huts on stilts over the river are for hire to shelter from the midday sun. There's an interesting wat close by and the surrounding villages are very traditional. *Getting there*: 12 km from Phnom Penh, turn off Route 1. Taxis leave from Chbam Pao shared taxi station or hire your own transport.

Tours

Most agents offer tours to surrounding sights, leaving early in the morning: Tonle Bati (US$17), Oudong (US$20).

Local information

● **Orientation**

Monivong and Norodom blvds are the main roads running N-S, and E-W is Kampuchea Krom Blvd. Sisowath Quay and Samdech Sothearos Blvd run parallel to the river, on the E side of the city. Most streets have numbers, rather than names. As a general rule even numbers run E-W, and low even numbers are in the N. Only main streets are signposted. Shops tend to have three numbers, a) number of the area, b) number of the street, c) number of the shop. These are not always in order so look for similar numbers to work out which street you are in.

● **Accommodation**

Price guide:			
L	over US$200	**C**	US$15-25
A+	US$100-200	**D**	US$8-15
A	US$50-100	**E**	US$4-8
B	US$25-50	**F**	<US$4

Visitors to Phnom Penh currently have a choice of accommodation at reasonable rates. A number of old hotels were renovated and new ones hurriedly put together to meet the needs of UNTAC. With the departure of the Blue

Berets space is relatively plentiful but the cheaper hotels tend to fill up astonishingly quickly. With the growing popularity of Phnom Penh as a tourist destination (176,617 visitor arrivals at Pochentong in 1994, 50% up from 1993) good hotel accommodation will soon become scarce. Most hotels are along Monivong Blvd.

L-A+ *Sofitel Cambodiana*, 313 Sisowath Quay, T 26288, F 26392, a/c, 2 restaurants, pool, also has tennis courts, health centre, boutique, US travel office (Sunrise) and business centre, originally built for Prince Sihanouk's guests (construction stopped in 1970), it was completed with funds from Cambodians living in Hong Kong and Singapore, and has well-maintained chalet-style accommodation overlooking the confluence of the Mekong, Sap and Bassac rivers; the *Cambodiana* is the best Phnom Penh has to offer, and is used by many tour groups, it is equivalent to any first class hotel in Bangkok but unfortunately is always overbooked, satellite TV, rec. Overseas reservations at: *Bangkok Vacation Planners (Thailand) Ltd*, T 2451897, F 2462821; *Singapore Cambodiana Investment*, T 2980733, F 2987022; *Hong Kong Express Holidays*, T 3678083, F 3113278.

A+ *Allson*, Monivong Blvd, T 62008, F 62018, a/c, new, central, restaurant; **A+** *Diamond*, 172-184 Monivong Blvd, T 26635, F 26636, a/c, restaurant, change TCs; **A+** *Juliana*, 152 St, T 810209, bungalow style accommodation, new and efficient; **A+** *Royal Phnom Penh*, Samdech Sothearos Blvd, T 60026, F 60036, a/c, restaurant, new deluxe hotel opened 1993 under Thai management; **A+** *Sheraton Hotel*, St 47 (behind Wat Phnom), T/F 61199, a/c, pool, business centre, newest of the city's hotels, the Sheraton opened in Nov 1994 with 112 rm in glitzy marble luxury, this is not a Sheraton, but is owned and operated by one of Cambodia's Sino-Khmer tycoons, the single lift means reaching the rooftop pool can be either a long wait, or an exhausting business; **A** *Cambodiana Inn*, Sisowath Quay, T 25059, F 26139, a/c, restaurant, next door to the *Cambodiana* but not under the same management, Cambodian style bungalows looking out onto the river, peaceful location, rec; **A** *Hotel International*, 84 St, T 27400, F 27401, a/c, restaurant, pool, new international-style hotel; **A** *Landmark Boulevard*, 63 Norodom Blvd, T 28461, F 28506, new '4-star' hotel with

rooftop garden restaurant and bar, discounts available mid-1995, few reports on quality though; **A-B** *La Paillote*, 234 St (nr central market), T 22151, F 26513, a/c, restaurant, good middle range hotel; **A-B** *Monorom*, 89 Monivong Blvd (corner of 118 St, nr the main railway station), T 26073, F 26149, a/c, restaurants, large rather shabby rooms, boutiques, noisy, run by *Phnom Penh Tourism*, the *Monorom* is the third main hotel for tour groups, journalists and aid workers, central location and helpful staff, business centre behind reception, IDD calls can be made from the manager's office, rooftop disco; **A-B** *Orchidée*, 262 Monivong Blvd, T 22659, F 26576, a/c, restaurant, modern hotel in the centre of town, opened late 1991, overflow for *Cambodiana* but not nearly as nice; **A-B** *Pailin*, Monivong Blvd/Charles de Gaulle Blvd (next door to the International Restaurant), T 22475, F 26376, restaurant, newly renovated.

B *Champs-Elysées*, 185 63 St, T 27268, French-speaking, helpful staff; **B** *Dusit*, T 22188, popular; **B** *Mittapheap*, 262 Monivong Blvd, T 23464, restaurant, average; **B** *Renakse*, opp the Royal Palace, T (IDD) 2326036 (local) 22457, F 26100, a/c, restaurant, French colonial building, well run, *Naga Diva Travel Tours* based here, accepts Visa, rec; **B** *Royal*, 92 St/Monivong Blvd (next to the library), a colonial style hotel built in 1910, used to be the Hotel le Phnom which was the journalists' headquarters during the war, undergoing renovation; **B** *Sukhalay*, Monivong Blvd, formerly Le Royal and a pre-1975 journalists' haunt, being renovated; **B** *The International House*, 35, 178 St, T/F 26246, restaurant, reasonably priced, simple but clean; **B-C** *L'Imprévu*, Route 1 (7 km out of the city), restaurant, pool, run by a French couple and their son and daughter who have escaped from Nice, charming wooden bungalows and good restaurant, peaceful, bicycles for hire, note that rates double over the weekend.

C *Asie*, 136 St, T 27825; **C** *Pasteur*, 60 51 St, a/c, small, family-run hotel, clean; **C** *Santepheap*, Monivong Blvd/136 St, T 23227, a/c, restaurant; **C** *Beauty Inn Hotel*, 537 Monivong Blvd, T/F 64505, a/c, clean rooms with attached bathrooms and fridge.

D *Timorda Guesthouse*, 128 St, a/c, restaurant.

E *Capitol Guesthouse I and II*, 182 St/107

St, T 64104, restaurant, centre for budget travellers and a good centre for information, bicycle hire (US$1/day), organizes trips to "Killing Fields" (US$5) and Siem Reap, IDD telephone service; **E** *Guesthouse No 50*, 50 125 St, good value rooms, shared facilities, with the added bonus of hiring out bicycles at US$1/day, good, cheap food and a wide 1st flr balcony to sit out on; **E** *Happy Guesthouse*, nr the *Capitol*, is run by the same owners and has similar facilities; **E** *Lotus Guesthouse*, 121 St, nr *La Paillote* restaurant and Central Market, some a/c, restaurant (good Indian food); **E** *Seng Sokhom's Guesthouse*, 111 St, motorbikes for hire; **E** *Sok Sin's Guesthouse*, on small dirt road between the old French Embassy and Calmette Hospital, Monivong Blvd, the owner is a fountain of knowledge on Cambodia, fan rooms, bikes and motorbikes for hire, restaurant. Other budget hotels close by.

● **Places to eat**

Price guide: ♦♦♦♦*Over US$10* (35,000 riel); ♦♦♦*US$5-10* (17,500-35,000 riel); ♦♦*US$2-5* (7,000 -17,500 riel); ♦*Under US$2* (7,000 riel)

Most places are relatively inexpensive – US$2-6/head. There are several cheaper cafés along Monivong Blvd, Kampuchea Krom Blvd (128 St) in the city centre and along the river as well as stalls by the main markets (see below). Generally the food in Phnom Penh is excellent and the restaurants surprisingly refined.

Asian: ♦♦♦♦*Dragon Court*, *Cambodiana Hotel*, new and expensive Chinese restaurant overseen by head Chinese-Singaporean Chef Lee Yan Hai, wide range of Chinese cuisine prepared incl Szechuan, Cantonese, Peking and 'Singaporean', stylish; ♦♦♦*Ban Thai 1*, 306 St, Thai, good menu and excellent service, try the delicious prawn and vegetable tempura, garden setting; ♦♦♦*Boung Thong*, Boeng Kak Lake, Thai food but some Khmer, Chinese and western, lovely outdoor setting on wooden jetties over the lake, however, despite the quantity of food, it is not up to much and the waiters are rather over-attentive; ♦♦♦*Chao Phra Ya*, attractive setting in the forecourt of a colonial French building (despite green galvanized sheeting), Thai cuisine (the restaurant is Thai-owned) but also serves Japanese and some western dishes, quality of food is a little disappointing but quantity is more than adequate; ♦♦♦*Chao Praya*, 67 Norodom Blvd, Thai buffet; ♦♦♦*Chiang Mai*, Samdech Sothearos

Blvd, a pavement café with, as the name suggests, an emphasis on Thai food – from simple one plate dishes like *phat Thai* (fried noodles with prawns, lime and nuts) to the famous fiery prawn soup *tom yang kung*, this restaurant and bar are run by a Thai, Madame Nui, from Surat Thani in S Thailand, opens 1100, happy hour 1600-1900, best Thai food in town; ♦♦♦*Coca*, Monivong Blvd/240 St, Thai and Chinese dishes; ♦♦♦*Hua Nam*, 753 Monivong Blvd, Thai, known for its shark soup; ♦♦♦*Midori*, 145 Norodom Blvd, authentic Japanese cuisine; ♦♦♦*New Wishing Well*, 9A, 163 St, Malay food and BBQ steaks, happy hours 1700-2100; ♦♦♦*Ponlok*, Sisowath Quay, Chinese, expensive but good shrimp dishes; ♦♦♦*Royal Bassac*, *Phnom Penh Hotel*, serves mainly Thai food but also other Asian and European cuisines, live music and dancing; ♦♦♦*Taj Mahal*, Norodom Blvd (S of Independence Monument), N Indian dishes; ♦*Asian International*, 118 St, cheap Malaysian cuisine; ♦*Asia Soups*, Monivong Blvd/204 St, excellent soups, roof terrace, rec.

Khmer: ♦♦*Little Boeng Kak*, Boeng Kak lake and amusement park off Monivong Blvd N of the city centre; ♦♦*Tonlé Sap 2* is at the junction of Sisowath Quay and 94 St, open air restaurant, reasonable; ♦♦-♦*Thmor Da*, Kampuchea Krom Blvd, opp Siam City bank, popular, Khmer and Vietnamese dishes; *Calmette*, Monivong Blvd, nr hospital, good soups.

International: several of the international restaurants are of a similar standard and offer Cambodian, Chinese, French and European dishes. Expect to pay US$3-5, some restaurants even stock champagne. ♦♦♦♦*La Mousson*, 55 178 St, T 27250, top French restaurant with prices to match, under same management as *Café No Problem*; ♦♦♦*Café No Problem*, 55, 178 St, opp National Museum, is in an immaculately restored colonial mansion and run by a Frenchman who imports cheese and wine from France, a landmark in Phnom Penh (closed Mon), happy hour 1800-1900, open 1100-2400, rec (especially the sandwiches) although we have received reports of surly service; ♦♦♦*Crackers*, 13 90 St, in colonial house, traditional French dishes; ♦♦♦*Déja Vu Café and Restaurant*, 22 240 St (sister restaurant to *Café Rendezvous* in Sihanoukville), relaxing upstairs restaurant with cushions and elegant chairs, art-deco style, the chef is English and the food is restrained bistro, quiche lorraine, pasta and Mediterranean, ice creams, one of the best places to round off an evening if peace and quiet is required, the music comprising Vivaldi and Albinoni sets the tone, excellent Sun breakfast, rec; **♦♦♦Foreign Correspondents Club (FCC)**, 363 Sisowath Quay, T 27757, superb colonial building, 2nd flr bar and restaurant overlook Tonlé Sap, programme of lectures and films, open to non-members, breezy, friendly service, burgers, cheap pasta dishes and a pool table; **♦♦♦La Paillotte**, 234 St, rated as the best restaurant in town because of its excellent predominantly French fare, good wines, elegant restaurant with good range of excellent cuisine, rather over-attentive service, rec; **♦♦♦Le Cordon Bleu**, Sihanouk Blvd, range of meat dishes, pasta and salad, delicious creme caramel; **♦♦♦L'Imprévu**, Route 1 (7 km out of the city), hotel and restaurant, run by a French couple and their son and daughter, this place consists of bungalows, pool, and restaurant serving good bistro food from pasta to salads to fish, non-residents can use the pool for US$3 (weekdays) or US$5 (weekends), a great place to escape to; **♦♦♦Trattoria del Gecko**, 114/61 St, decent pasta; **♦♦♦–♦♦Golden Eagle**, 144 St (just off Norodom Blvd), known for its bar but also has good menu; **♦♦♦–♦♦Monorom Hotel Restaurant**, 89 Monivong Blvd (corner of 118 St), 6th flr restaurant with good views of the city; **♦♦♦–♦♦Pailin Hotel**, 1st flr, Monivong Blvd (nr central market), quiet, good atmosphere, Vietnamese food; **♦♦♦–♦♦Cambodiana Hotel**, 313 Sisowath Quay, has 5 restaurants serving Asian and Western dishes incl the **Riverside Pool Terrace**, good lunchtime buffet from 1130-1400, high standards but tend to be pricey; **♦♦Bayon**, corner of Monivong Blvd/130 St; **♦♦California**, 55 Preah Sihanouk Blvd, trad American fare, open for breakfast; **♦♦Capitol**, 14 182 St, cheap and cheerful; **♦♦Chez Lipp**, Monivong Blvd, French fare, rec for steak; **♦♦Faculty of Medicine Restaurant**, Monivong Blvd/106 St, Asian and French; **♦♦Happy Neth's Pizza**, 295 Pochentong Blvd, T 60443, best pizza joint, known for its cheesecake, cook is from Chicago, free delivery; **♦♦La Pagode**, behind the **Monorom Hotel**, in a traditional Khmer building; **♦♦Lotus**, nr Central Market, pizzas, vegetarian and Indian dishes, popular; **♦♦McSam Burgers**, 13 St, opp Post Office; **♦♦Oasis**, 139 Monireth Blvd, home cooked European dishes; **♦♦Paksupie-abal**, 40 Monivong Blvd/84 St, rec by locals; **♦♦Sereipheap**, 76 Monivong Blvd/Kampuchea Krom Blvd (not far from the Monorom)**, serves almost every alcoholic drink as well as a mixture of Cambodian, Vietnamese and French dishes; **♦♦Tesphea Tonlé Sap Café**, Sisowath Quay/106 St.

Seafood: floating restaurants moored to the bank opp the old Royal Palace, nr the broken bridge: **♦♦Chaktomuk** and **Kong Kea** floating restaurants at Sisowath Quay; **Boengkak**, on Boeng Kak Lake, open air restaurant best known for its seafood, European and Asian dishes. (There is a second seafood restaurant here but it's not nearly as good.)

Boulangerie: Boucherie de Paris, 243 51 St; Cambodiana Hotel, more expensive than the Chefs Deli, but equally as good a selection; **Chefs Deli** (behind Pailin Hotel), a/c café with excellent breakfasts (newspapers provided) and a very good selection of patisseries, cakes, breads and biscuits.

Foodstalls: there are many Vietnamese stalls along Kampuchea Krom Blvd, Monivong Blvd and 117 St. Also some stalls between the railway station and Puchentong Blvd at night. **Central Market**, just off Monivong Blvd (at the intersection of 118 St and Charles de Gaulle Blvd); **O Russei Market**, 182 St; **Olympic Market**, 286 St; also good foodstalls around the Capitol Hotel on 182 St; **The Old Market**, between 13, 106 and 110 sts; **Tuol Tom Pong Market**, between 163, 432 and 450 sts, stalls in the centre of the market. Several Vietnamese stalls on 242 St. Numerous cheap stalls and eating places have sprung up along Route 6A, since the Japanese Friendship Bridge was opened in 1994.

● **Bars**

Ettamogah Pub, 154 Preah Sihanouk Blvd (next door to the Lucky Market), only opened in Aug 1994 but already popular with expat residents of Phnom Penh who maintain it serves the coldest beer in the capital, and the finest chips (fries), run by two Aussies, there is a small menu with the emphasis on things like steak and chicken served in baskets, opens 0700 for breakfast and closes late; **Heart of Darkness**, 51 St, value for money, good Bloody Mary's, run by the same owners as Apocalypse Now in Vietnam; bar at the Hotel Royal, 92 St, is a popular hangout; **Cathouse**, 51 St/81 St, good pool table (serves food until 1 am), satellite TV; **Foreign Correspondents Club (FCC)**, 363 Sisowath Quay, satellite TV, pool, Bangkok Post and The Nation both available for reading here; Le Bar, Preah Sihanouk, has a nice terrace; **Martini Pub**, 402 Issarak St, barbecue, video, fun, open till late; *Rock Hard Cafe* (nr *Foreign Correspondents Club*), backgammon sets kept behind the bar; *San Miguel*, Sisowath Quay, Filipino bands, lively atmosphere. Several restaurants also have good bars (see above): *Café No Problem*.

● **Airline offices**
Aeroflot, *Allson Hotel*, Monivong Blvd, T 62008; **Air France**, *Cambodiana Hotel*, T 26426; **Dragon Air**, 19 106 St, T 27665; **Lao Aviation**, 206 Norodom Blvd, T 25887; **Malaysian Airlines**, *Diamond Hotel*, 172-184 Monivong Blvd, T 26688; **Phnom Penh Airways**, *Hotel Dusit*, 118 St; **Royal Air Cambodge**, 206 Norodom Blvd, T 60154; **Silk Air**, *Palin Hotel*, Monivong Blvd, T 22236; **Thai**, 19 106 St, T 22335; **Transindo**, 16 Monivong Blvd, T 26298, represent **Bangkok Airways**; **Vietnam Airlines**, 537 Monivong, in *Beauty Inn Mini Hotel*, T 27426.

● **Banks & money changers**
There are several money changers at the central market. **Bangkok Bank**, 26 Norodom Blvd, T/F 26593; **Bank of Commerce of Kampuchea**, 26 Monivong Blvd; **Banque du Commerce Exterior du Cambodge**, 24 Norodom Blvd, **Foreign exchange bureau** changes TCs and accepts Visa; **Banque Indosuez**, 70 Norodom Blvd; **Banque Municipal de Phnom Penh**, 102 St/13 St; **Cambodian Commercial Bank**, Monivong Blvd, 118 St; **National Bank**, Norodom/118 St; **Silver/gold bazaar**, Grand Market is the best area for changing US dollars.

● **Embassies & consulates**
All the new diplomatic representatives are based in the *Cambodiana Hotel* at present. **Australia**, 11 254 St, T 26001; **China**, 256 Issarak Blvd, T 26271; **France**, 22 242 St, T 26278; **Germany**, 76 214 St, T 26193; **India**, 777 Monivong Blvd, T 22981; **Indonesia**, 179 51 St, T 26148; **Japan**, 75 Norodom, T 27161; **Laos**, 15 Issarak Blvd, T 26441; **Malaysia**, 161 51 St, T 26177; **Russia**, Samdech Sothearos Blvd, T 22081; **Thailand**, 4 Monivong Blvd, T 26182; **UK**, 27 75 St, T 27124; **USA**, 27 240 St, T 26436; **Vietnam**, Monivong Blvd/436 St (consular section on Monivong Blvd S of Issarak Blvd), T 27173.

● **Entertainment**
Casino: Singaporean-owned *Holiday International Hotel* opened the only casino in town in Nov 1994 – the first to begin operating since 1970. Roulette, black jack and usual entertainments provided.

Dance: folk and national dances are performed by the National Dance group at the National Museum of Arts, on 70 St in the N of the city. (Open to some tour groups.) Contact the National Museum of Arts directly or the Ministry of Information and Culture, 395 Monivong Blvd. Royal Pavilion, *Cambodiana Hotel*, has classical Khmer dancing every Fri 1900.

Disco: *Fantazia*, nr Olympic Stadium, new disco owned by 2 Los Angelinos, entrance is free; *New Wishing Well*, 9A, 163 St, new disco.

Films: *Foreign Correspondents Club*, 363 Sisowath Quay, shows films Tues (2000) and Sun (1730 and 2000) US$2 (very popular).

Music: the Lounge Bar at the *Cambodiana* is known for the Phnom Penh Blues Band – best avoided. The *Rock Hard Café* (nr *Foreign Correspondents Club*) 315 Sisowath Quay, has live music on Thur, Fri and Sat, plus a jam session on Sun afternoons. The *Cyclo Bar* has a band.

Nightclubs: the *Cambodiana Nightclub* tops the list – otherwise there are a plethora of seedy discos and bars which periodically open and close; the 7th flr of the *Monorom Hotel* is a popular spot with its balcony overlooking the city and a band which plays every night until 2300; *Royal Hotel*, 92 St has a restaurant with dancing, popular with Vietnamese 'taxi girls', ie prostitutes (closes 2300); *Martini Pub*, 402 Issarak St, bar, food, disco, favourite haunt of ex-pats and local and Vietnamese girls (closes 0300).

● **Hospitals & medical services**
Dentist: 195A Norodom Blvd, T 018812 055, European-run.

Hospital: *Access Medical Services*, 203 63 St, T 912100; *Calmette Hospital*, Monivong Blvd, T 23173, is generally considered the best, 24 hrs emergency. There is also a Western clinic at *SOS International Medical Centre*, 83 Issarak Blvd, T 9129645.

Opticians: *Royal Optic*, 220 Monivong Blvd (opp *Pailin Hotel*) and 136, 52 St.

● **Libraries**
National Library, 92 St (next to *Hotel Samaki*), T 23249. Most of the books were destroyed by the Khmer Rouge in the 1970s and the building was used as a pigpen for several years, open 0700-1130 and 1400-1730 Tues Sun.

● **Post & telecommunications**
Post Office: 13 St, it is possible to place

international telephone calls from here.

Shipping/courier services: *DHL*, Monivong Blvd, T 27726; *OCS* (express courier service), *Cambodiana Hotel*; *TNT*, 28 47 St, T 26694; *Transpeed Cargo*, 19 108 St, T 27633.

Telephone: easiest to make international calls from top hotels.

● **Shopping**

Art Galleries: *New Art Gallery*, 9 20 St, local artists.

Books/maps: Central Market, Tuol Tom Pong market and shops in some of the top hotels. *Berts Books*, No 63, 178 St (nr *Café No Problem*), said to have the largest selection of books in English, sells second-hand books and magazines; *Bookazine*, 228 Monivong Blvd, extensive collection of SE Asian books; *Hotel Cambodiana* has a selection of books, as does the *International Stationery and Book Centre* on Monivong Blvd.

Buddha images: the area on the E side of Norodom Blvd (not far from the Victory Monument) is packed with workshops making images to replace those destroyed between 1975 and 1979. There's also a shop opp the museum selling reproduction statues.

Handicrafts: many of the hotels have small boutiques selling local crafts; the National Museum of Arts, 19 St/184 St (behind the National Museum) also sells reproductions of Khmer statues, prints and frescoes of Angkor. Other recommended shops: *Banteay Srei*, 108 Monivong Blvd; *Ratana*, 118 St; *Vicheth Sal*, 121 Monivong Blvd, T 23137. *Kramas* (checked scarves) can be found in Central Market.

Markets: *Tuol Tum Pong* (in the middle of 155, 163, 440 and 450 sts, next to the pagoda of the same name) sells antiques (genuine articles and fakes) and jewellery – nearby is an antique furniture market as well as clothing and an immense variety of tobacco. There are also several foodstalls here. The *Central Covered Market*, just off Monivong Blvd, distinguished by its central dome (built 1937), is mostly full of stalls selling silver and gold jewellery, old coins and assorted fake antiques. Around the main building more mundane items are for sale, incl kramas. The *Old Market* or *Psar Cha* is between 13, 106 and 110 sts, and also sells jewellery. *O Russei Market* (Russian Market), 182 St, has a good selection of antiques – bargain hard. The 'new' *Olympic Market* is located located in a large 2-storey

building adjacent to the Olympic Stadium. It stocks reasonably priced electrical goods incl hi-fi's, there are no taxes to pay in Cambodia.

Rice paper prints: rubbings of bas reliefs from temples at Angkor, sold in museum shop and markets.

Silk: Koh Doch, a large island in the Mekong N of Phnom Penh is renowned for its silk.

Silverware & jewellery: old silver boxes, belts, antique jewellery along Monivong Blvd (the main thoroughfare), Samdech Sothearos Blvd, or *Tuol Tom Pong market*. The state jewellery shop, *Bijouterie d'Etat*, 13 St/106 St and the *Silver Shop*, 1 Monivong Blvd, are rec by tourists, also the 2 shops in *Cambodiana Hotel*. There are plenty of jewellery stalls in the central covered market. Most modern silverware is no more than 80% silver.

Supermarkets: *Lucky Supermarket*, Preah Sihanouk Blvd, opp Standard Chartered Bank, excellent French and Australian wine starting at US$5/bottle. (Cambodia has the cheapest wine in SE Asia.) *Lucky* sells *The European* and various English newspapers' weekly international editions. Also *Seven Seven Supermarket* on 90 St. *McSam's*, 20-22 13 St and *International Supermarket*, 35 178 St.

● **Sports**

Aerobics: *Hotel Sofitel Cambodiana*, US$2 Mon-Fri, 1800-1900.

Badminton/squash: *Hotel Sofitel Cambodiana*, US$10/hour for court hire.

Gym: *Hotel Sofitel Cambodiana*, US$10/day.

Running: Cinder track at the Olympic Stadium. Hash House Harriers meet 1500 Sun at the railway station.

Spectator sports: The 1960s Olympic Stadium is the centre of sport in Phnom Penh. Basketball (ablebodied and wheelchaired), volleyball and training sessions of Tai-kwondo can be watched. University and schools football league play from Nov-Apr as well as a league sponsored by business. The standard is good. Crowds reach several thousand for the big games.

Swimming: *Hotel Sofitel Cambodiana*, 20m pool, US$4 Mon-Fri, US$8 Sat, Sun. *International Youth Club*, 51/96 St, 50m pool, US$10.

Tennis: *Hotel Sofitel Cambodiana*, US$5-15/hr. *International Youth Club*, US$10/hr.

'Touch' rugby: Phnom Penh University every Sat from 1530.

● **Tour companies & travel agents**
Apsara Tours, 8 254 St, T 25408; *Aroon Tours*, 99 136 St, T 26300; *Cambodian-Australian Travel*, 6 222 St, T/F 26225; *Cams-Air Travel*, 187 Issarak Blvd, T 26739, F 26740; *Diethelm Travel*, 8 Samdech Sothearos Blvd, T 26648, F 26676; *East-West*, 17 114 St, T/F 26189; *Eurasie Travel*, 97 Monivong Blvd, T 23620; *Explotra*, 43 105 St, T/F 27973; *International Travel & Tours*, 339 Monivong Blvd, T/F 27248; *Khemara Travel*, 134 Preah Sihanouk Blvd, T/F 27434; *Naga*, *Renakse Hotel*, Samdech Sothearos Blvd, T 26288; *Orient Express Tour Company*, 19 106 St, T 26248, F 26313; *Peace Travel Agency*, 246 Monivong Blvd, T 24640, F 26533; *Phnom Penh Tourism*, 313 Sisowath Quay, T 24059, F 26043; *Preferred Indochina Travel*, *Monorom Hotel*, Monivong Blvd, T 25350, F 26625; *Skylink Travel*, 124 Tou Samouth Blvd, T 27010; *Sunrise Travel*, opp *Cambodiana Hotel*, Sisowath Quay, T/F 26762; *Suraya Voyages*, 17 294 St, T 60105, travel around Southeast Asia; *Transair Cambodia Travel*, 63 Norodom Blvd (ground floor of *Landmark Boulevard Hotel*), T 28323, F 26981; *Transindo*, 16 Monivong Blvd/84 St, T 26298, F 27119; *Transpeed Travel*, 19, 106 St, T/F 27633.

● **Tourist offices**
General Directorate of Tourism (Angkor Tourism or Cambodia Tourism), Monivong Blvd (at the junction with 232 St, T 25607, organizes tours and hires cars (US$25-30/day), friendly and helpful. **Phnom Penh Tourism**, 313 Susawath Quay (almost on the junction with Samdech Sothearos Blvd), T 23949/25349, open 0700-1100, 1400-1700 Mon-Sat, organizes tours, arranges trips around Phnom Penh as well as trips to Saigon. The 2 tourist offices don't communicate, which can be confusing for visitors.

● **Useful addresses**
Bureau d'Immigration: 5 Oknha Men St, T 23893.
Business centre: *Foreign Correspondents Club*, 363 Sisowath Quay Blvd; *Global*, 378 Preah Sihanouk Blvd, T 27397.
Minister of Information and Culture: Monivong Blvd/180 St, T 24769/24869.
Ministry of the Interior: 214 St/Norodom Blvd issues internal travel permits.
Press Office of the Foreign Ministry: Sisowath Quay (at the intersection of 240 St), T 22241.
Visa extensions: Foreign Ministry, Sisowath

Quay (at the intersection of 240 St), T 24641, takes 3 days, administration fee of US$10 is charged.

● **Transport**
Local Bicycle hire: from shops nr O Russei market or guesthouses. Bicycling is probably the best way to explore the city: it is mostly flat, so not too exhausting. **Bus**: most local buses leave from 182 St (next to O Russei market). Buses from here go to the Olympic Intercity bus station, the long distance terminal. Buses S leave from the Psar Thmei terminal, Charles de Gaulle Blvd/136 St (not far from central market). There are inexpensive buses around town. **Car**: chauffeur-driven cars are available at major hotels from US$30/day upwards, eg *Cambodiana*. Several travel agents will also hire cars. Prices increase if you're venturing out of town. **Cyclo** (French name for bicycle rickshaws): are plentiful but slow; fares are bargainable but cheap – Monorom to Cambodiana should be no more than 500CR. A few cyclo drivers speak English or French – they are most likely to be found loitering around the big hotels (US$0.25-0.35/hour), can also be hired for the day. **Ferry**: across the Tonlé Sap River leave from Psar Cha Ministry of Transport Ferry Landing but with the opening of the Japanese bridge in 1994, no longer necessary. Boats can also be chartered from Psar Cha (approx US$10-12/hour). **Motorcycle hire**: from 413 Monivong Blvd (US$5-15/day). **Motorbike taxi**: 'motos' are 50-100cc motorbikes; the fastest way to get around Phnom Penh. The moto driver is easily recognized by his sunglasses and baseball cap and will automatically approach anyone walking or standing by the road. Standard cost per journey is 500 Riel (short) 1,000 Riel (long) and 2,000 Riel after 2200. **Taxi**: from Psar Chbam Pao Shared-Taxi Station over Monivong Bridge on Route 1, nr the market of the same name (approx US$25/day, depending on where you want to go).

Air All domestic flights are with **Royal Air Cambodge**. There are 4 daily flights to Siem Reap – 2 early morning, 1 mid-morning and 1 afternoon (US$90 return). Also flights to Battambang 3 days a week (US$90 return); Koh Kong 3 days a week (US$100 return); Stung Treng 3 days a week (US$90 return). Rattanakiri 3 days a week (US$100 return) and Sihanoukville (Kompong Som) twice a week (US$75 return). Flights should be booked in advance, particularly at busy times of the year (ie Khmer New Year). **Transport to town**: a taxi from the airport costs US$5.

Train Station is between 106 and 108 Sts. Two main lines: one goes S to Kompong Som and the other N to Battambang. Travelling by train is definitely **not** recommended and is undertaken at a high personal risk. Three tourists were kidnapped and later killed travelling from Phnom Penh to Sihanoukville by train in late 1994. In addition to the dangers of Khmer Rouge kidnapping, the track is frequently blown up.

Road Bus: times and destinations of buses are in Khmer, so the only sure way to get the right bus is to ask. Most buses leave from the Olympic International bus station, 199 St (next to the Olympic Market). Those going S and SW of Phnom Penh leave from Psar Dang Kor bus station, Issarak Blvd (next to Dang Kor market). Travelling out of Phnom Penh by bus is hazardous – both because of extreme overloading (people and luggage) and because of your vulnerability to attack from Khmer Rouge or bandits. It is not recommended. **Shared taxi**: Psar Chbam Pao, nr Chbam Pao market on Route 1.

Sea Boat: ferries leave from Psar Cha Ministry of Transport Ferry Landing on Samdech Sothearos Blvd (between 102 and 104 Sts). Connections to Siem Reap (Angkor) Mon and Fri, Kratie, Stung Treng, Kompong Cham and Kompong Chhnang. Other ferries leave from Psar Cha Municipal Ferry Landing. Many NGOs prohibit their staff from travelling by any form of public transport incl the ferry due to the security risk.

International connections NB If travelling to Vietnam by road, ensure that your visa is appropriately stamped (*Moc Bai*), otherwise you may be turned back at the border, although it may be possible to offer a bribe (about US$50). **Road Bus**: buses to Saigon leave from the junction of 211 and 182 sts. The office is open 0700-1100, 1400-1900 Mon-Sun, US$5 (same price for a shared taxi), a/c bus Thur, Fri and Sat, US$15.

ANGKOR

Angkor, the ancient capital of the powerful Khmer Empire, is one of the archaeological gems of Asia and the spiritual and cultural heart of Cambodia. Henri Mouhot, the Frenchman, wrote that "it is grander than anything of Greece or Rome". Its mystical grandeur and architectural wonders are on a par with Peru's 'lost' Inca city of Machu Picchu. The huge complex of palaces and temples was built on the sprawling alluvial plain to the N of the Tonlé Sap.

Under Jayavarman VII, the Angkor complex stretched more than 25 km E to W and nearly 10 km N to S. For 5 centuries, the court of Angkor held sway over a vast territory. At its height, according to a 12th century Chinese account, Khmer influence spanned half of Southeast Asia, from Burma to the southernmost tip of Indochina and from the borders of Yunnan to the Malay peninsula. Khmer monuments can be found in the S of Laos and E Thailand as well as in Cambodia. The only threat to this great empire was a riverborne invasion in 1177, when the Chams used a Chinese navigator to pilot their war canoes up the Mekong. Scenes are depicted in bas reliefs of the Bayon temple.

Thai ascendency, and their eventual occupation of Angkor in 1431 led to the city's abandonment and the subsequent invasion of the jungle. 4 centuries later, in 1860, Henri Mouhot – a French naturalist – stumbled across the forgotten city, its monumental temple towers enmeshed in the forest canopy. Locals told him they were the work of a race of giant gods. Only the stone temples remained; all the wooden secular buildings had decomposed in the intervening centuries. Mouhot's diaries, published in the 1860s, with his accounts of 'the lost city in the jungle' fired the imagination of

archaeologists, adventurers and treasure-hunters in Europe. In 1873 French archaeologist Louis Delaporte removed many of Angkor's finest statues for 'the cultural enrichment of France'.

In 1898, the École Française d'Extrême Orient started clearing the jungle, restoring the temples, mapping the complex and making an inventory of the site. Delaporte was later to write the two-volume *Les Monuments du Cambodge*, the most comprehensive Angkorian inventory of its time, and his earlier sketches, plans and reconstructions, published in *Voyage au Cambodge* in 1880 are without parallel. Henri Parmentier was chief of the School's archaeological service in Cambodia until 1930. Public interest was rekindled in the 1920s when French adventurer and novelist André Malraux was imprisoned in Phnom Penh, charged with stealing sculptures from one of the temples, Banteay Srei at Angkor. He published a thriller, *The Royal Way*, based on his experiences. Today around 400 sandstone, laterite and brick-built temples, walls, tombs and other structures remain scattered around the site.

Colonial souvenir-hunters were not the first – or the last – to get their hands on Angkor's treasures. The great city's monuments were all subjected, at one time or another, to systematic plundering, mainly by the warring Chams (from S Vietnam) and Thais. Many temple pedestals were smashed to afford access to the treasure, hidden deep in pits under the central sanctuaries. Other looters knocked the tops off towers to reach the carefully concealed treasure chambers.

Centuries of entanglement in the jungle also took their toll on the buildings – strangler figs caused much structural damage and roots and vines rent roofs and walls asunder. In 1912, French writer Pierre Loti noted: "The fig tree is

FROM SOUVENIR-HUNTING TO ANTIQUITIES-SMUGGLING

An article in the *Far Eastern Economic Review* in March 1993 noted that the feeling of cultural disintegration that pervades Cambodia is epitomized by the hundreds of headless and limbless statues. Khmer Rouge guerrillas moved into Angkor Wat in 1971, lit fires in the galleries, installed rocket-launchers on Phnom Bakheng, looted temples and sliced the heads off sculptures. Like other guerrilla groups after them, they sold them on the black market in neighbouring Thailand to help finance their war efforts. From the mid-1970s, ancient Khmer sculptures began to resurface in private art collections in the West, and on the floors of leading auction houses. But much of the looting occurred during the year before the May 1993 elections.

In 1992 and 1993 there were reported thefts from many of the temples and from the conservation office in Siem Reap, where about 7,000 of the most valuable artifacts have been stored. Between February and April 1993, there was a series of carefully organized break-ins into the conservation office; many priceless statues were stolen. In the most dramatic raid, in February, thieves used machine guns to enter the conservation centre, shot one of the guards, fired a rocket-propelled grenade at the storeroom door and left with 11 of the most valuable statues. UN and local officials said they had been smuggled into Thailand. They also alleged that all four political factions were behind the thefts as well as soldiers "from a neighbouring country". And there was strong evidence that some of the thefts were orchestrated by the conservation office staff.

Today Angkorian antiquities can be viewed and purchased in the air-conditioned antique shops of Bangkok's River City complex or Singapore's Tanglin Shopping Centre. There has been growing evidence that wealthy, but unethical, Western art buyers have been able to place orders for busts and sculptures of their choice through some of these shops. There are persistent rumours pointing to the existence of 'catalogues', containing detailed photographs of Angkorian statues and bas-reliefs. River City shopkeepers will surreptitiously offer to 'organize' the acquisition of specific pieces.

Dealers in the antiquities-smuggling racket are reported to have links with organized crime. The underworld's labyrinthine networks – used in the trafficking of narcotics – facilitate the movement of statues around the world. 'Licences' for the illegal export of ancient works of art can be readily procured in Bangkok by dealers with good connections. Although Thailand does its best to prevent the smuggling of its own cultural treasures, it has refused to sign the UN's 1970 convention for preventing antiquities trafficking. This allows Bangkok dealers to trade Burmese and Cambodian pieces with impunity.

While many of the genuine pieces – there are plenty of fakes on the market – in Bangkok (and Singapore) are from Burma, Khmer sculpture is not uncommon. Having survived a thousand years of warfare and weather, many of Angkor's remaining statues are doomed to decapitation. The heads of the dancing Apsaras – the most famous motif of Angkor's temples – have disappeared, as have many of the heads from the western gate. Growing cultural consciousness – combined with uneasy consciences of some Western collectors – may allow for some of this invaluable loot to be returned in the years to come.

the ruler of Angkor today... Over the temples which it has patiently prised (presumably) apart, everywhere its dome of foliage triumphantly unfolds its sleek pale branches speckled like a serpent's skin." Even today, some roots and trees remain stubbornly tangled in the ancient masonry – affording visitors a Mouhot-style glimpse of the forgotten city. Between 1953 and 1970, the Angkor Conservancy – set up jointly by the French and Cambodian governments – maintained and restored the ruins. But when war broke out, the destructive forces of the Khmer Rouge – and other guerrilla factions – were unleashed on what the jungle had spared and the French archaeologists, such as Bernard Grosslier, had restored.

As if the conservation and protection of the complex was not already fraught with difficulties, a threat emerged in the mid-1980s, from the most unlikely of sources. The Vietnamese-backed administration enlisted the services of Indian archaeologists to begin where the Angkor Conservancy had left off. They were given a 6-year contract to clean and restore the galleries and towers of Angkor Wat itself. Prince Sihanouk is reported to have burst into tears when he heard that the Indians, using unskilled Cambodian workmen, had begun their concrete and chemical-assisted restoration effort.

The powerful cleaning agents stripped off the patina which for a millennium had protected the sandstone from erosion by the elements. Bas-reliefs depicting scenes from the Ramayana were scrubbed, scratched and scraped until some were barely discernable. Cement was used with abandon. Archaeologists around the world, who, since 1970, have only been dimly aware of the rape of Angkor, now consider the gimcrack restoration programme the last straw after 2 decades of pillage and destruction. A British journalist, visiting the complex in late 1990 wrote that after several centuries of abandonment in the jungle, "What is 20 years of neglect? The answer is: a lot."

However, whether the Indian team of archaeologists and conservators have really caused untold damage to the monuments of Angkor through insensitive restoration and the use of untested solvents is a source of some dispute. Generally, press reports in the W, as described above, have taken the latter line – that their work, rather than helping to restore and preserve the monuments, has helped to further ruin it. Cement has been used to fill in cracks, where western archaeologists would probably have left well alone. New stone have been cut and fitted where, again, other specialists might have been happy merely to have done sufficient restoration to prevent further degeneration. The Indian team also used chemical cleaning agents – an unorthodox and contentious approach to restoration. Although some of the methods used by the Indian team do seem rather crude and insensitive to the atmosphere of the place, the carping of some western archaeologists seems to have been motivated as much by professional envy as anything else. The Indians were called in by the government in Phnom Penh at a time when most western countries were boycotting the country, in protest at the Vietnamese occupation of the country. French archaeologists particularly, must have been pacing their offices in indignation and pique as a country with such 'primitive' skills took all the glory. Now, though, the French and the Japanese are back with their brushes and hammers, contributing to the preservation of Angkor.

In 1989 UNESCO commissioned a Japanese art historian to draw up an Angkor plan of action. The top priority in its restoration, he said, was to underpin the foundations of Angkor Wat, Bayon, Baphoun, Preah Khan, Neak Khan and Pre Rup. Once the Paris Peace agreements had been signed in 1991, the Ecole Française, the New York based World Monuments Fund and the Japanese started work. UNESCO is co-ordinating the activities of the various teams and Angkor was declared a world heritage sight. Some temples are closed for restoration work, check with guides. The agency has trained up police in order to counteract the greatest scourge, the organized theft of carvings. Many believe prompt action is the only way to protect Angkor from a post-peace settlement souvenir-hunters' free-for-all. Today however, would-be treasure hunters have to contend with horrors that even Mouhot could never have dreamt – minefields. Thousands of anti-personnel mines, the lethal legacy of the years of civil war, lie primed and buried in the undergrowth surrounding some temples – particularly the outer ones. **NB** Visitors are strongly advised to stick to the well-beaten track.

Documentation of Angkor

About 900 inscriptions have been found in Indochina that give a jigsaw set of clues to Angkor civilization. Those written in Sanskrit are largely poetic praises dedicated to gods and kings; Khmer-language ones give a much more focused insight into life and customs under the great kings. Some give a remarkably detailed picture of everyday life: one documents a ruling that pigs had the right to forage in ricefields, another dictates that ginger and honey should be used in the preparation of ritual foods. Most of the inscriptions have now been deciphered. Contemporary palm-leaf and paper documents which would have added to this knowledge have long since rotted away in the humid climate.

Bas-reliefs, carved in perpetuity into Angkor's temple walls also give a fascinating pictorial impression of life in the great city. Its citizens are shown, warring, hunting, playing and partying, and the reliefs present a picture which is often reassuringly normal in its detail... men played chess, old women read palms and people ate and drank and gossiped while local musicians provided live entertainment. Young men went hunting and young women evidently spent hours at the Angkorian equivalent of the hairdressers and boutiques.

The most complete eyewitness account of Angkor was written by Chou Ta-kuan, an envoy from the Chinese court, who visited Cambodia in 1296, around 75 years after the death of Jayavarman VII, the last great conqueror of the Angkor period. Chou Ta-Kuan wrote detailed accounts of his observations and impressions, and cast Angkor as a grand and highly sophisticated civilization, despite the fact that it was, by then, well past its heyday.

What the French archaeologists managed to do, with brilliance, was to apply scientific principles to deciphering the mysteries of Angkor. The French, and by extension the West, nonetheless managed to 'invent' Angkor for its own interests, moulding the Angkorian Empire and its art so that it fitted in with the accepted image of the Orient. (This notion that Europeans invented the Orient is most effectively argued in Edward Said's seminal book *Orientalism*, first published in 1978 and now widely available in paperback. It is a book that does not deal specifically with Angkor but much of the argument can be applied to the French appropriation of Angkor and the Khmers.) Much that has been written about the ruins at Angkor and the empire and people that built them says as much about what the French were trying to do in Indochina, as about the place and people themselves. What is perhaps ironic is that educated Cambodians then reappropriated the French vision and made it their own. Today, French invention and Cambodian 'tradition' are one and the same. Cambodia, lacking the cultural integrity to resist the influence of the French, became French; in so doing they took on board the French image of themselves and made it their own.

Art and architecture

The Angkor period encapsulated the greatest and best of Cambodia's art and architecture. Much of it shows strong Indian influence. The so-called 'Indianization' of Cambodia was more a product of trade than Hindu proselytism; there was no attempt made at formal conquest, and no great emigration of Indians to the region. In order to meet the Romans' demand for exotic oriental merchandise and commodities, Indian traders ventured into the South China Sea – well before the 1st century AD, it was discovered that monsoon winds could carry them to the Malay peninsula and on to Indochina and Cambodia. Because of their reliance on seasonal winds, Indian navigators were obliged to while away many months in countries with which they traded and the influence of their sophisticated culture spread.

But although Khmer art and architecture was rooted in Indian prototypes, the expression and content was distinctively Cambodian. Most of the art from the Angkor period is Hindu although Mahayana Buddhism took hold in the late 12th century. Some Buddhist figures have been dated to as early as the 6th century – the standing Buddhas were carved in the same style as the Hindu deities, minus the sensuous voluptuousness.

The ancient kingdoms of Funan (the Chinese name for the mercantile state encompassing the area SW of the Mekong Delta, in what is now S Vietnam and S Cambodia) and Chenla (a mountain kingdom centred on N Cambodia and S Laos) were the first to be artistically and culturally influenced by India. In his book *The Art of Southeast Asia*, Philip Rawson writes that the art-styles of Funan and Chenla were "the greatest phase of pre-Angkor Khmer art, and... we can treat the evolution under these two kingdoms together as a stylistic

unity. It was the foundation of classic Khmer art, just as archaic Greek sculpture was the foundation of later classical Greek art."

The only remaining traces of the kingdom of Funan – whose influence is thought to have spread as far afield as S Burma and Indonesia – are limited to four Sanskrit inscriptions on stelae and a few sculptures. The earliest surviving Funanese statues were found at Angkor Borei (see page 522) and have been dated to the 6th century. Most represent the Hindu god, Vishnu (patron of King Rudravarman) and their faces are distinctly Angkorian in style. Scattered remains of these pre-Angkorian periods are all over S Cambodia – especially between the Mekong and the Tonlé Sap. Most of the earliest buildings would have been made of wood and have consequently rotted away – there being a paucity of stone in the delta region.

The kingdom of Chenla, based at Sambor and later at Sambor Prei Kuk (see page 520), expanded at the expense of Funan, which gradually became a vassal state. Chenla inherited Funan's Indianized art and architectural traditions. Some buildings were built of brick and stone and typical architectural relics are brick towers with a square (or sometimes octagonal) plan: a shrine set atop a pedestal comprised of mounting tiers of decreasing size – a style which may have been structurally patterned on early Pallava temples in SE India. The

LATERITE

Many Khmer monuments in Cambodia and in the Northeastern region of Thailand (which formed part of the Khmer Empire) are made of laterite. This red, porous and pock-marked stone is actually an iron-bearing soil. The easily quarried soil was cut into large blocks and left to harden upon exposure to the air.

sculptural work was strongly rooted in Indian ideas but carved in a unique style – many of the statues from this era are in the museum at Phnom Penh (see page 473). Rawson writes: "Among the few great stone icons which have survived are some of the world's outstanding masterpieces, while the smaller bronzes reflect the same sophisticated and profound style."

In the late 8th century the Chenla Kingdom collapsed and contact with India came to an end. Chenla is thought to have been eclipsed by the increasingly important Sumatran-based Srivijayan Empire. Jayavarman II, who had lived most of his life in the Sailendra court in Java, but who was of royal lineage, returned to Cambodia in about 790 AD. Jayavarman II's reign marked the transition period between pre-Angkorian and Angkorian styles – by the 9th century the larger images were recognizably Khmer in style. From Jayavarman II onwards, the kings of Cambodia were regarded as god-kings – or devaraja (see page 430).

Jayavarman II established a royal Siva-lingam (phallic) cult which was to prove the inspiration for successive generations of Khmer kings. "He summoned a Brahmin learned in the appropriate texts, and erected a lingam... with all the correct Indian ritual,"

THE CHURNING OF THE SEA

The Hindu legend, the Churning of the Sea, relates how the gods and demons resolved matters in the turbulent days when the world was being created. The elixir of immortality was one of 13 precious things lost in the churning of the cosmic sea. It took a thousand years before the gods and demons, in a joint dredging operation – aided by Sesha, the sea snake, and Vishnu – recovered them all.

The design of the temples of Angkor was based on this ancient legend. The moat represents the ocean and the gods use the top of Mount Meru – represented by the tower – as their churning stick. The cosmic serpent offered himself as a rope to enable the gods and demons to twirl the stick. Paul Mus, a French archaeologist, suggests that the bridge with the naga balustrades which went over the moat from the world of men to the royal city was an image of the rainbow. Throughout Southeast Asia and India, the rainbow is alluded to as a multi-coloured serpent rearing its head in the sky.

Vishnu churning the sea
Source: Aymonier, Etienne (1901) *Cambodge*, Paris.

TRU 65
VLC 136

KHMER - style PRANG

basins – the oceans. The devaraja, or god-king, was enshrined in the centre of the religious complex, which acted as the spiritual axis of the kingdom. The people believed their apotheosized king communicated directly with the gods.

The central tower sanctuaries housed the images of the Hindu gods to whom the temples were dedicated. Dead members of the royal and priestly families were accorded a status on a par with these gods. Libraries to store the sacred scriptures were also built within the ceremonial centre. The temples were mainly built to shelter the images of the gods – unlike Christian churches, Moslem mosques and some Buddhist pagodas, they were not intended to accommodate worshippers. Only priests, the servants of the god, were allowed into the interiors. The 'congregation' would mill around outside in open courtyards or wooden pavilions.

The first temples were of a very simple design, but with time they became more grandiose and doors and galleries were added. Most of Angkor's buildings are made from a soft sandstone which is easy to work. It was transported to the site from Phnom Kulen, about 30 km to the NE. Laterite was used for foundations, core material, and enclosure walls, as it was widely available and could be easily cut into blocks (see box). The Khmer sandstone architecture has echoes of earlier wooden structures: gallery roofs are sculpted with false tiles, while balustred windows imitate wooden ones. A common feature of Khmer temples were false doors and windows on the sides and backs of sanctuaries and other buildings. In most cases there was no need for well-lit rooms and corridors as hardly anyone ever went into them. That said, the galleries round the central towers in later temples, such as Angkor Wat, indicate that worshippers did use the temples for ceremonial circumambulation when they would contemplate the inspiring bas-reliefs from the *Ramayana*

Rawson says. "This lingam, in which the king's own soul was held to reside, became the source and centre of power for the Khmer Dynasty. At the same time – and by that act – he severed all ties of dependence upon Indonesia." To house the sacred lingam each king in turn built a new temple, some of the mightiest and finest of the monuments of the Khmer civilization.

The temples at Angkor were modelled on those of the kingdom of Chenla, which in turn were modelled on Indian temples. They represent Mt Meru – the home of the gods of Indian cosmology. The central towers symbolize the peaks of Mt Meru, surrounded by a wall – representing the earth – and moats and

and *Mahabharata*.

In Europe and the Middle East, the arch and vault were used in contemporary buildings but at Angkor, architects used the false vault – known as a corbel stone. It was a fairly primitive vaulting system so the interiors of sanctuaries could never be very large. The stones were often laid without staggering the vertical joints and mortar was not used. The builders relied on the weight of the structure, gravity and a good fit between the stones to hold their buildings to-gether. This is why so many of the temples have collapsed.

Despite the court's conversion to Mahayana Buddhism in the 12th century (under Jayavarman VII) the architectural ground-plans of temples did not alter much – even though they were based on Hindu cosmology. The idea of the god-king was simply grafted onto the new state religion and statues of the Buddha rather than the gods of the Hindu pantheon were used to represent the god-king (see Bayon, page 504). One

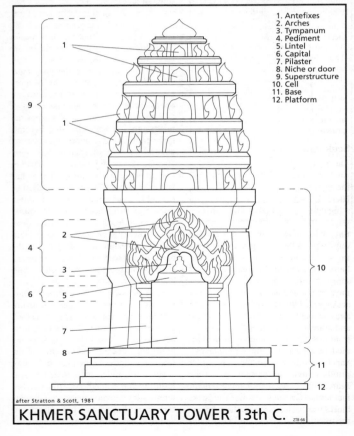

1. Antefixes
2. Arches
3. Tympanum
4. Pediment
5. Lintel
6. Capital
7. Pilaster
8. Niche or door
9. Superstructure
10. Cell
11. Base
12. Platform

after Stratton & Scott, 1981

KHMER SANCTUARY TOWER 13th C. ZTB 66

particular image of the Buddha predominated at Angkor in which he wears an Angkor-style crown, with a conical top which is encrusted with jewellery.

There are some scholars who maintain that Angkor has, perhaps, been over-praised. The label of 'genius' that has been attached to the architects that conceived the edifices, the builders that worked on them, and the empire that financed their construction, demands that Angkor be put in the highest division of human artistic achievement. Anthony Barnett in the *New Left Review* in 1990, for example, wrote:

"...to measure [Angkor's] greatness by the fact that it is nearly a mile square is to deny it a proper admiration through hyperbole. Thus the Church of Saint Sophia, to take one example, was for nearly a millennium the largest domed space in the world until St Peter's was constructed. Saint Sophia still stands in Istanbul. It was built 600 years before Angkor Wat, while Khmer architects never managed to discover the principles of the arch" (1990: 103).

Sculpture

The sculpture of the early temples at Angkor is rather stiff and plain, but forms the basis for the ornate bas-reliefs of the later Angkor Wat. Lintel-carving became a highly developed art form at an early stage in the evolution of Khmer architecture. The use of columns around doorways was another distinctive feature – they too had their antecedents in the earlier Chenla period. Frontons – the masonry covering originally used to conceal the corbeled end gables – were elaborate at Angkor. They were intricately carved and conveyed stories from the Ramayana and other great Hindu epics. The carved fronton is still used in temples throughout modern Thailand, Laos and Cambodia. Sanctuary doorways, through which priests would pass to enter the sacred heart of the temple, were an important site for icons. Ornately carved sandstone blocks were placed in front of and above the true lintel.

Angkor's most impressive carvings are its bas-reliefs, which, like the fronton, were devoted to allegorical depictions and mostly illustrate stories from the Hindu classics, the Mahabharata and Ramayana. The latter is best exemplified at the Baphuon (11th century). Details of the everyday lives of the Angkor civilization can be pieced together thanks to these bas-reliefs. Those on the Bayon illustrate the weaponry and armour used in battle, market scenes, fishing and cockfighting – probably the Khmers' favourite excuse for gambling. In contrast to the highly sculpted outer walls of the temples, the interiors were typically bare; this has led to speculation that they may originally have been decorated with murals.

Laterite, which is a coarse soft stone, found widely across Southeast Asia, was excavated to form many of the moats and barays at Angkor. Early structures such as those at Preah Ko in the Roluos group were built in brick. The brickwork was often laid with dry joints and the only mortar used was a type of vegetable-based adhesive. Bricks were sometimes carved in situ and occasionally plastered. In the early temples sandstone was only used for architectural embellishments. But nearly all of the later temples were built entirely of sandstone – with some blocks weighing over 4 tonnes. Most of the sandstone is thought to have been quarried from the northern hills around Kulen and brought by barge to Angkor.

The post-Angkor period was characterized by wooden buildings and fastidiously carved and decorated sculptures, but the humid climate has allowed little to survive. The contemporary art of 1990s Cambodia is still redolent of the grandeur of the Angkor era and today, Khmer craftsmen retain their inherent skills, and are renowned for their refined carvings. Art historians believe that the richness of Cambodia's heritage, and its incorporation into the modern artistic

MOTIFS IN KHMER SCULPTURE

● The **kala** – a jawless monster commanded by the gods to devour his own body – made its first appearance in lintels at Roluos. The monster represented devouring time and was an early import from Java.

● **Singhas** or lions appeared in stylized forms and are often guardians to temples. The lions lack realism probably because the carvers had never seen one.

● The **makara** was a mythical water-monster with a scaley body, eagles' talons and an elephantine trunk.

● The sacred snakes, or **nagas**, play an important part in Hindu mythology and the Khmers drew on them for architectural inspiration. Possibly more than any other single symbol or motif, the naga is characteristic of Southeast Asia. The naga is an aquatic serpent, the word being Sanskrit for snake, and is intimately associated with water (a key component of Khmer prosperity). In Hindu mythology, the naga coils beneath and supports Vishnu on the cosmic ocean. The snake also swallows the waters of life, these only being set free to reinvigorate the world after Indra ruptures the serpent with a bolt of lightning. Another version has Vishnu's servants pulling at the serpent to squeeze the waters of life from it (the so-called churning of the oceans, **see page 490**).

  The naga permeates Southeast Asian life from royalty to villager. The bridge across the bayon to Angkor Wat features nagas churning the oceans; men in Vietnam, Laos and Thailand used to tattoo their bodies with nagas for protection; water, the gift of life in a region where wet rice is the staple crop, is measured in Thailand in terms of numbers of nagas; while objects throughout Southeast Asia are decorated with the naga motif from boats, to water storage jars, to temples (gable ends, barge boards, finials), to musical instruments.

● The **garuda** appeared relatively late in Khmer architecture. This mythical creature – half-man, half-bird – was the vehicle of the Hindu god, Vishnu, and the sworn enemy of the nagas.

● The **apsaras** are regarded as one of the greatest invention of the Khmers. The gorgeous temptresses – born, according to legend, 'during the churning of the Sea of Milk' – were Angkor's equivalent of pin-up girls and represented the ultimate ideal of feminine beauty. They lived in heaven where their sole *raison d'être* was to have eternal sex with Khmer heroes and holy men. The apsaras are carved with splendidly ornate jewellery and, clothed in the latest Angkor fashion, they strike seductive poses and seemingly compete with each other like models on a cat-walk. Different facial features suggest the existence of several races at Angkor – it is possible that they might be modelled on women captured in war. Together with the 5 towers of Angkor Wat they have become the symbol of Khmer culture. The god-king himself possessed an apsara-like retinue of court dancers – who obviously impressed Chinese envoy Chou Ta-kuan sufficiently for him to write home about it in 1296. Before 1975 evening performances on the steps of Angkor Wat by traditional Cambodian dancers were commonplace.

psyche, has enabled Khmer artists to produce work which is reckoned to be aesthetically superior to contemporary carving and sculpture in Thailand.

Places of interest

The main cluster of monuments are about 7 km N of Siem Reap. The temples are scattered over an area in excess of 160 sq km. Two hills dominate the plain: Phnom Bakeng to the NW of Angkor Wat and Phnom Khrom at the N end of the Tonlé Sap.

The Royal City of Angkor Thom

Construction of Jayavarman VII's spacious walled capital, **Angkor Thom**, began at the end of the 12th century: he rebuilt the capital after it had been captured and destroyed by the Chams. Some stone buildings survived the sacking of the city, such as the temples of Phimeanakas and Baphuon, and these were incorporated by Jayavarman in his new plan. He adopted the general layout of the royal centre conceived by Suryavarman II.

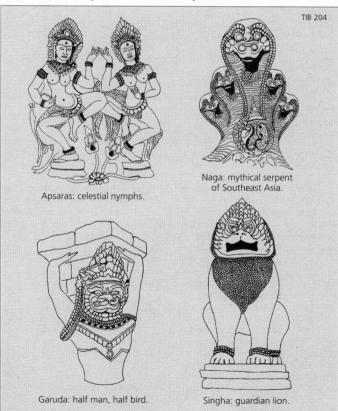

TIB 204

Apsaras: celestial nymphs.

Naga: mythical serpent of Southeast Asia.

Garuda: half man, half bird.

Singha: guardian lion.

THE KINGS OF ANGKOR AND THEIR CREATIONS

King	Monuments
JAYAVARMAN II (802-850) Founder of the Khmer Empire, he established his capital at Roluos. Instituted the linga cult of the god-king.	Ak Thom, Phnom Kulen, Banteay Chmar
JAYAVARMAN III (850-877)	
INDRAVARMAN I (877-889) Credited with presiding over the emergence of classical Khmer art. He also built the first baray (Lolei).	Bakong, Preah Ko
YASOVARMAN I (889-900) Built a new capital at Angkor called Yashodharapura.	Bakheng, Eastern Baray, Lolei
HARSHAVARMAN I (900-921)	Baksei Chamkrong, Prasat Kraven
ISHANAVARMAN II (c.921)	
JAYAVARMAN IV (921-941) Established his capital at Koh Ker, N of Angkor.	Prasat Thom
HASHAVARMAN II (941-944)	
RAJENDRAVARMAN (944-968) Moved the capital back to Angkor.	East Mebon, Pre Rup, started the Phimeanakas
JAYAVARMAN V (968-1001)	Continued building the Phimeanakas
UDAYADITYAVARMAN I (1001-1002)	

Angkor Thom was colossal: the 100m-wide moat surrounding the city – which was probably stocked with crocodiles as a protection against the enemy – extended more than 12 km. Inside the moat was an 8m-high stone wall, buttressed on the inner side by a high mound of earth along the top of which ran a terrace for troops to man the ramparts. Four great gateways in the city wall face N, S, E and W and lead to the city's geometric centre, the Bayon. The fifth, Victory Gate, leads from the royal palace (within the Royal Enclosure) to the E Baray. The height of the gates was determined by the headroom needed to accommodate an elephant and howdah, complete with parasols. The flanks of each gateway are decorated by three-headed stone elephants, and each gate-way tower has four giant faces, which keep an eye on all four cardinal points.

Five causeways traverse the moat, each bordered by sculptured balustrades of nagas gripped, on one side, by 54 stern-looking giant gods and on the other by 54 fierce-faced demons. The balustrade depicts the Hindu legend of the churning sea (see page 490).

Inside the walled city

The **Bayon**, Jayavarman VII's temple-mountain, stands at the centre of the royal city of Angkor Thom. The area within the walls was more spacious than that of any walled city in medieval Europe – it could easily have encompassed the whole of ancient Rome. Yet it is believed that this enclosure, like the Forbidden City in Peking, was only a

SURYAVARMAN I (1002-1050) The influence of Mahayana Buddhism spread; Buddhist sculpture became more common at Angkor.	Added to the Phimeanakas, Grand Plaza, N and S Kleangs, Ta Keo, Royal Enclosure, Terrace of the Elephants, Western Baray
UDAYADITAVARMAN II (1050-1066)	Baphuon, finished the Western Baray
HARSHAVARMAN III (1066-1080),	
JAYAVARMAN VI (1080-1107)	Phimai (Thailand), Preah Vihar, Wat Phou (Laos)
DHARANINDRAVARMAN I (1107-1113)	
SURYAVARMAN II (1131-1150)	Angkor Wat, Chan Say Tevoda, Banteay Samre, Thommanon
DHARANINDRAVARMAN II (c. 1160)	
YASOVARMAN II (1160-1165)	
TRIBHUVANADITYAVARMAN (1165-1177)	
JAYAVARMAN VII (1181-c.1200)	Angkor Thom, Bayon, Banteay Kdei, Preah Neak Pean, Preah Khan, Preah Palilay, Ta Prohm, Terrace of the Leper King, Sras Srang, Sras Srei, Ta Som added to Banteay Chmar
INDRAVARMAN II (c.1200-1243)	
JAYAVARMAN VIII (1243-1295)	

royal, religious and administrative centre accommodating the court and dignitaries. The rest of the population lived outside the walls between the two artificial lakes – the E and W barays – and along the Siem Reap River.

The **Royal Enclosure**, to the N of the Bayon, had already been laid out by Suryavarman I: the official palace was in the front with the domestic quarters behind, its gardens surrounded by a laterite wall and moat. Suryavarman I also beautified the royal city with ornamental pools. Jayavarman VII simply improved his designs. The jungle has now taken over where the royal landscapers left off.

In front of the Royal Enclosure, Suryavarman I laid out the first Grand Plaza with the recently renovated **Terrace of the Elephants** (also called the Royal Terrace) and the stately **North and South Kleangs** on the E side of the central square, which are thought to have provided accommodation for foreign envoys. The North Kleang was started by Jayavarman V; Jayavarman VII later added 12 laterite victory towers, called the **Prasat Suor Prat**. The Royal Terrace (also called the Terrace of the Elephants) was built by Suryavarman I and was originally the raised base of a hall of the palace complex. It is decorated with a bas-relief of elephants – depicting a hunting scene – and at the centre, where kings once sat in gold-topped pavilions, are rows of garudas, their wings lifted as if in flight. They were intended to give the impression that the god-king's palace was floating in the heavens, like the imagined flying celestial palaces of the gods.

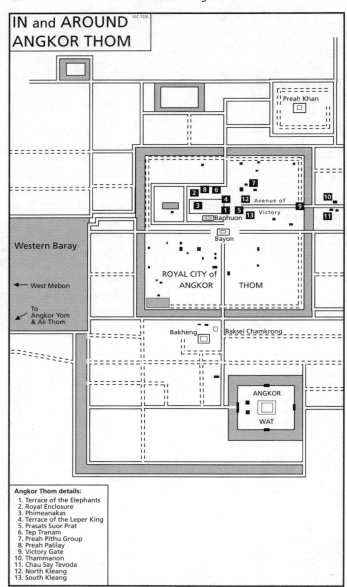

IN and AROUND ANGKOR THOM

VLC 123L

Preah Khan

Western Baray

← West Mebon

To Angkor Yom & Ak Thom

Avenue of Victory

Baphuon

Bayon

ROYAL CITY of ANGKOR THOM

Bakheng　　Baksei Chamkrong

ANGKOR WAT

Angkor Thom details:
1. Terrace of the Elephants
2. Royal Enclosure
3. Phimeanakas
4. Terrace of the Leper King
5. Prasats Suor Prat
6. Tep Tranam
7. Preah Pithu Group
8. Preah Palilay
9. Victory Gate
10. Thammanon
11. Chau Say Tevoda
12. North Kleang
13. South Kleang

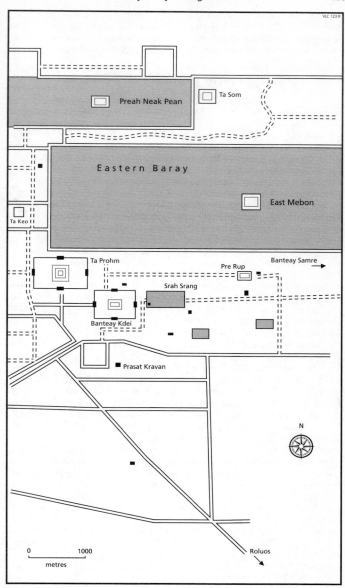

Preah Neak Pean

Ta Som

Eastern Baray

East Mebon

Ta Keo

Ta Prohm

Pre Rup

Banteay Samre

Srah Srang

Banteay Kdei

Prasat Kravan

N

0   1000
metres

Roluos

At the NE corner of the 'central square' is the 12th century **Terrace of the Leper King**, which may have been a cremation platform for the aristocracy of Angkor. The 7m-high terrace has bands of bas-reliefs, one on top of the other, with intricately sculptured scenes of royal pageantry and seated apsaras as

---

BARAYS AND THE JAYAVARMAN CONUNDRUM: THE CASE FOR IRRIGATION

By founding his capital at Roluos, just SE of Angkor, in the middle of an arid plain annually plagued by drought and flash floods, Jayavarman II bequeathed to archaeologists and other scholars a geo-climatic conundrum. What possessed him to site the nerve-centre of Khmer civilization at such an environmentally unfriendly spot and how did the great city sustain itself through the centuries? Archaeologists have postulated that the Khmers engineered a complex irrigation system to grow enough rice to feed the city's population. In this view, Angkor was a classic hydraulic society.

In *The Art of Southeast Asia*, Philip Rawson writes: "Angkor was a capital, filled with temples and supporting many inhabitants. But its nucleus was a splendid irrigation project, based on a number of huge artificial reservoirs fed by the local rivers and linked to each other by means of a rectangular grid system of canals." The *barays*, or man-made lakes, associated with the famous temples were used to feed an intricate network of irrigation channels. The first *baray* was Lolei, built by Indravarman at the city of Rolous. "The engineering involved at Angkor," Rawson says, "...was vaster and far more sophisticated than anything seen before in that part of the world." Lolei was more than 3.5 km long and 800m wide. The E Baray was twice the size of Lolei and the W Baray, built during Udayadityavarman II's reign, is thought to have held about 40 million cubic metres of water when full.

The barays were constructed by building up dykes above the level of the land, and waiting for the monsoon flood. Because the resultant reservoirs were higher than the surrounding agricultural lands, there was no need to pump the water to flood the paddy fields: a gap was simply cut in the dyke. The water stored in the barays would have been replenished by each monsoon, making it possible to irrigate the ricelands – even during the dry season. With their land being watered year-round, the Khmers would have been able to grow three crops of rice a year.

The barays were central to the health and vigour of Khmer civilization but because they were sitting targets for enemy saboteurs, they may also have played a part in its downfall. During successive Siamese invasions the fragile irrigation system would have been irreparably damaged and essential maintenance of the hydraulic works was neglected through a lack of manpower. The precarious – and artificial – balance between man and nature was disturbed and as the irrigation channels cracked and dried up, so did the mighty Khmer Empire.

Why Angkor should have gone into decline from about the 13th century has exercised the minds of historians for years. Apart from the destruction of the fragile irrigation system, several other explanations as to Angkor's downfall have been suggested: climatic change, the shift of trade from land to sea-based empires and the corruption of a system which, like the Roman emperors, made the king a demi-god. Some think the builder King Jayavarman VII bankrupted the empire with his vast building schemes.

well as nagas and garudas which frequented the slopes of Mt Meru. Above is a strange statue of an earlier date, which probably depicts the god of death, Yama, and once held a staff in its right hand. It is unusual because, unlike most Khmer statues, it is sexless. It does not represent a king as it does not wear a crown. The statue's naked, lichen-covered body gives the terrace its name – the lichen gives the uncanny impression of leprosy. Jayavarman VII may have suffered from leprosy, but this statue is not a representation of him.

BARAYS AND THE JAYAVARMAN CONUNDRUM: THE CASE AGAINST IRRIGATION

When the first Westerners stumbled upon the Khmer ruins at Angkor – the lost city in the jungle – in the middle of the 19th century, they judged it to be the finest example of a civilization based upon the massive control of water for irrigation. The sheer size of the monuments, the vast *barays* storing millions of gallons of water, all seemed to lend force to the notion that here was the finest example of state-controlled irrigation. In Karl Marx's words, the Khmer Kingdom was a society based upon the Asiatic mode of production. The upshot of this was that, by necessity, there needed to be a centralized state and an all-powerful king – leading, in Karl Wittfogel's famous phrase, to a system of 'Oriental Despotism'. Such a view seemed hard to refute – how could such enormous expanses of water in the baray be used for anything but irrigation?

But, in the past decade, archaeologists, irrigation engineers and geographers have challenged the view of the Khmer Kingdom as the hydraulic civilization *par excellence*. Their challenge rests on 4 main pillars of evidence. First, they point out that if irrigation was so central to life in Angkor, why is it not mentioned once in over 1,000 inscriptions? Second, they question the usual interpretation of Angkorian agriculture contained in the Chinese emissary Chou Ta-Kouan's account – *Notes on the customs of Cambodia* – written in 1312. This account talks of "three or four rice harvests a year" – which scholars have assumed means irrigated rice agriculture. However, the detractors put a different interpretation on Chou Ta-Kouan's words, arguing they in fact describe a system of flood retreat agriculture in which rice was sown as the waters of the Great Lake, the Tonlé Sap, receded at the end of the rainy season. Third, they note that aerial photographs show none of the feeder canals needed to carry water from the barays to the fields, nor any of the other irrigation structures needed to control water. Finally, the sceptics draw upon engineering evidence to support their case. They have calculated that the combined storage capacity of all the barays and reservoirs is 4 million m^3, sufficient to irrigate only 400 ha of riceland – hardly the stuff on which great civilizations are built.

The geographer Philip Stott maintains that flood retreat agriculture would have produced the surplus needed to feed the soldiers, priests and the court of the Khmer god-king, while postulating that the barays were only for urban use. He writes that they were "just like the temple mountains, essentially a part of the urban scene, providing urban symbolism, beauty, water for bathing and drinking, a means of transport, and perhaps a supply of fish as well. Yet, not one drop of their water is likely to have fed the rice fields of Angkor."

Today the E Baray is dry whereas the W Baray has been excavated for fish cultivation.

Opposite the Terrace of the Elephants, on the S side of the Terrace of the Leper King are the remains of an earlier wall, carved with bas-reliefs of demons. These reliefs were found by French archaeologists and had been intentionally concealed. This illustrates the lengths to which the Khmers went to recreate Mt Meru (the home of the Gods) as faithfully as possible. According to Hindu mythology, Mt Meru extended into the bowels of the earth; the bas-relief section below ground level was carved with weird and wonderful creatures to symbolize the mystical hidden depths of the underworld. The second

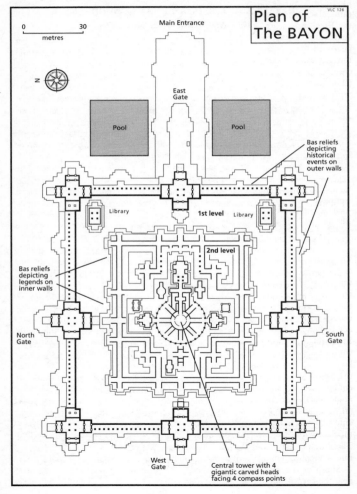

Plan of The BAYON

VLC 126

0 — 30 metres

Main Entrance

N

East Gate

Pool

Pool

Bas reliefs depicting historical events on outer walls

Library

1st level

Library

2nd level

Bas reliefs depicting legends on inner walls

North Gate

South Gate

West Gate

Central tower with 4 gigantic carved heads facing 4 compass points

layer of carving is the base of Mt Meru on earth. Flights of steps led through these to the lawns and pavilions of the royal gardens and Suryavarman's palace.

The **Phimeanakas** (meaning Celestial or Flying Palace in Sanskrit) inside the Royal Enclosure was started by Rajendravarman and used by all the later kings. Suryavarman I rebuilt this pyramidal temple when he was renovating the Royal Enclosure. It rises from the centre of the former royal palace. Lions guard all four stairways to the central tower. It is now ruined but was originally covered in gold, as the Chinese envoy, Chou Ta-kuan related in 1296:

"The king sleeps in the summit of the palace's golden tower. All the people believe that the tower is also inhabited by the Lord of the Sun, who is a nine-headed serpent. Every night the serpent appears in the form of a woman with whom the king sleeps during the first watch. None of the royal wives are allowed in the tower. The king leaves at the second watch to go to his wives and concubines. If the naga spirit does not appear one night, it is a sign that the king's death is imminent. Should the king fail to visit the naga for a single night, the welfare of the kingdom will suffer dire consequences."

The Phimeanakas represented a genuine architectural revolution: it was not square, but rectangular and on the upper terrace, surrounding the central tower, there was a gallery with corbelled vaults, used as a passageway. The **Celestial Palace** is now in a bad state of repair. The **Sras Srei**, or the women's bath – is also within the walled enclosure. Chou Ta-kuan, whose Chinese delegation appears to have enjoyed watching Angkor's womenfolk bathe, noted that women, even of noble families, would shamelessly take off their clothes to bathe in public. "To enter the water, the women simply hide their sex with their left hand," he wrote. The Phimeanakas is linked by the **Avenue of Victory** to the Eastern Baray.

South of the Royal Enclosure and near the Terrace of the Elephants is the **Baphuon**, built by Udayadityavarman II. The temple was approached by a 200m-long causeway, raised on pillars, which was probably constructed after the temple was built. The Baphuon is not well preserved as it was erected on an artificial hill which weakened its foundations. Only the three massive terraces of its pyramidal, Mt Meru-style form remain and these afford little indication of its former glory: it was second only to the Bayon in size. Chou Ta-kuan, the Chinese envoy, reported that its great tower was made of bronze and that it was "truly marvellous to behold". Most of the bas-reliefs were carved in panels and refer to the Hindu epics, in particular the stories of Rama and Krishna. Some archaeologists believe the sculptors were trying to tell stories in the same way as the shadow plays.

South of the Baphuon is one of Angkor's most famous sights, the **Bayon**. This was Jayavarman VII's own temple mountain, built right in the middle of Angkor Thom. Unlike other Khmer monuments, the Bayon has no protective wall immediately enclosing it. The central tower, at the intersection of the diagonals of the perfect square of the city walls, indicates that the city walls and the temple were built at the same time.

It is a pyramid temple with a 45m-high tower topped by four gigantic carved heads – images of Jayavarman VII as a Bodhisattva, facing the four compass points. They are crowned with lotus flowers, symbol of enlightenment, and are surrounded by 51 smaller towers each with heads facing N, S, E and W. When Pierre Loti, the French writer, first saw these towers in 1912 he was astounded: "I looked up at the tree-covered towers which dwarfed me, when all of a sudden my blood curdled as I saw an enormous smile looking down on me, and then another smile on another wall, then three, then five, then 10, appearing in every direction". The facial features are striking and the full lips, curling upwards at the corners, are known as 'the smile of Angkor'.

Even the archaeologists of the École Française d'Extrême Orient were not able to decide immediately whether the heads on the Bayon represented Brahma, Siva or the Buddha. There are many theories. One of the most plausible ones was conceived in 1934 by George Coedès – an archaeologist who spent many years studying the temples at Angkor. He postulated that the sculptures represented King Jayavarman VII in the form of Avaloketsvara, the Universal Buddha. If true, this would have meant that the Hindu concept of the god-king had been appended to Buddhist cosmology. Jayavarman VII, once a humble monk who twice renounced the throne and then became the mightiest of all the Khmer rulers, may be the smiling face, cast in stone, at the centre of his kingdom. The multiplication of faces, all looking out to the four cardinal points, may symbolize Jayavarman blessing the four quarters of the kingdom. After Jayavarman's death, the Brahmin priests turned the Bayon into a place of Hindu worship (confusing the archaeologists).

The Bayon underwent a series of reconstructions, a point first observed by Henri Parmentier – a French archaeologist who worked for the L'École Français d'Extrême Orient – in 1924 and later excavations revealed vestiges of a former building. It is thought that the first temple was planned as a two-tiered structure dedicated to Siva, which was then altered to its present form. As a result, it gives the impression of crowding – the towers rise right next to each other and the courtyards are narrow without much air or light. When Henri Mouhot rediscovered Angkor, local villagers had dubbed the Bayon 'the hide and seek sanctuary' because of its complex layout.

The bas-reliefs which decorate the walls of the Bayon all seem to tell a story but are much less imposing than those at Angkor Wat. The Bayon reliefs vary greatly in quality; this may have been because the sculptors' skills were being overstretched by Jayavarman's ambitious building programme. The reliefs on the outer wall and on the inner gallery differ completely and seem to belong to two different worlds: the relief on the outside depicts historical events; those on the inside are drawn from the epic world of gods and legends, representing the creatures who were supposed to haunt the subterranean depths of Mt Meru.

Two recurring themes in Angkor's bas-reliefs are the king and his might and the Hindu epics. Jayavarman is depicted in the throes of battle with the Chams – who are recognizable thanks to their unusual and distinctive headdress, which looks like an inverted lotus flower. The naval battle pictured on the walls of Banteay Chmar is almost identical. The bas-reliefs give a good idea of Khmer life at the time – the warrior elephants, ox-carts, fishing with nets, cockfights and skewered fish drying on racks. Other vignettes show musicians, hunters, chess-players, palm-readers and reassuringly down-to-earth scenes of Angkor citizens enjoying drinking sessions. In the naval battle scenes, the water around the war-canoes is depicted by the presence of fish, crocodiles and floating corpses. The sculpture work at the Bayon is, however, more naive and less sophisticated than the bas reliefs at Angkor Wat.

Preah Palilay, just outside the N wall of the Royal Enclosure was also built by Jayavarman VII. Just to the E of this temple is **Tep Tranam**, the base of a pagoda, with a pool in front of it. To the E of Tep Tranam and the other side of the Northern Ave is the **Preah Pithu Group**, a cluster of five temples.

South of Angkor Thom

Bakheng, Yasovarman's temple-mountain, stands on a natural hill (60m high) which affords good views of the plain of Angkor. It is just outside the S gate of Angkor Thom and was the centre of King Yasovarman's city, Yasodharapura – the 'City Endowed with Splendour'. A pyramid-temple dedicated to Siva, Bakheng was the home of the royal lingam and Yasovarman's mausoleum after his death. It is composed of five towers built on a sandstone platform. There are 108 smaller towers scattered around the terraces. The main tower has been partially demolished and the others have completely disappeared. It was entered via a steep flight of steps which were guarded by squatting lions. The steps have deteriorated with the towers. Foliate scroll relief carving covers much of the main shrine – the first time this style was used. This strategically placed hill served as a camp for various combatants, including the Vietnamese, and suffered accordingly. Today the hill is disfigured by a radio mast and the area is still not clear of mines.

Baksei Chamkrong was built by Harshavarman I at the beginning of the 10th century and dedicated to his father, Yasovarman I. It lies at the foot of Phnom Bakheng (between Bakheng and Angkor Thom), the centre of Yasovarman's city, and was one of the first temples to be built in durable material: brick on a stepped laterite base. An inscription tells of a golden image of Siva inside the temple.

Angkor Wat

To the S of Angkor Thom is the most famous of all the temples on the plain of Angkor: **Angkor Wat**. Angkor literally means 'city' or 'capital'. Probably the biggest religious monument ever built; it is certainly one of the most spectacular. The temple complex covers 81 ha and is comparable in size to the Imperial Palace in Beijing. Its distinctive five towers are emblazoned on the Cambodian flag and the

12th century masterpiece is considered by art historians to be the prime example of Classical Khmer art and architecture. It took over 30 years to build and is contemporary with Notre Dame in Paris and Durham Cathedral in England. The temple is dedicated to the Hindu god Vishnu, personified in earthly form by its builder, the god-king Suryavarman II, and is aligned E to W, as it is a funerial monument.

Like other Khmer temple mountains, Angkor Wat is an architectural allegory, depicting in stone the epic tales of Hindu mythology. The central sanctuary of the temple complex represents the sacred Mt Meru, the centre of the Hindu universe, on whose summit the gods reside. Angkor Wat's five towers symbolize Meru's five peaks; the enclosing wall represents the mountains at the edge of the world and the surrounding moat, the ocean beyond.

Angkor Wat was found in much better condition than most of the other temples in the complex because it seems to have been continuously inhabited by Buddhist monks after the Thais invaded. They were able to keep back the encroaching jungle. A giant stone Buddha was placed in the hall of the highest central tower, formerly sacred to the Hindu god, Vishnu. Three modern Buddhist monasteries flank the wat.

The temple complex is enclosed by a square moat – more than 5 km in length – and a high, galleried wall, which is covered in epic bas-reliefs and has four ceremonial tower gateways. The main gateway faces W and the temple is approached by a 475m-long road, built along a causeway, which is lined with naga balustrades (representing the rainbow bridge between heaven and earth). There are small rectangular barays on either side of the roadway. To either side of the balustrades are two isolated buildings, thought to have been libraries – there are two more pairs of them within the temple precincts on the first and second terraces.

At the far end of the causeway stands a **cruciform platform**, guarded by stone lions, from which the devaraja may have held audiences; his backdrop being the three-tiered central sanctuary. It is entered through the colonnaded processional gateway of the outer gallery. The transitional enclosure beyond it is again cruciform in shape. Its four quadrants formed galleries, once stocked full of statues of the Buddha. Only a handful of the original 1,000-odd images remain. Each gallery also had a basin which would originally have contained water for priests' ritual ablution. The second terrace, which is also square, rises from behind the Gallery of a Thousand Buddhas. It has a tower at each corner.

The cluster of central towers, 12m above the second terrace, is reached by 12 steep stairways, which represent the

---

ANTI-CLOCKWISE ROUND ANGKOR WAT'S BAS RELIEFS

1. West gallery, southern half represents a scene from the Mahabharata of a battle between the Pandavas (with pointed headdresses, attacking from the right) and the Kauravas. The 2 armies come from the 2 ends of the panel and meet in the middle. **NB:** The larger the figure the more important the person. The SW corner has been badly damaged – some say by the Khmer Rouge – but shows scenes from Vishnu's life.

2. South gallery, western half depicts Suryavarman II (builder of Angkor Wat) leading a procession. He is riding a royal elephant, giving orders to his army before leading them into battle against the Chams. The rank of the army officers is indicated by the number of umbrellas. The undisciplined, outlandishly dressed figures are the Thais helping the Khmers in battle against the Chams.

3. South gallery, eastern half was restored in 1946, it depicts the punishments and rewards one can expect in the after life. The damned are in for a rough ride: the chances of their being savaged by wild animals, seized by demons or having their tongues pulled out (or any combination thereof) are quite high.

4. Eastern gallery, southern half is the best-known part of the bas-relief – the churning of the sea of milk by gods and demons to make ambrosia (the nectar of the gods which gives immortality). In the centre, Vishnu commands the operation. Below are sea animals (cut in half by the churning close to the pivot) and above, apsaras. Shortly before Cambodia collapsed into civil war in 1970, French archaeologists, who were repairing the roof and columns of the E gallery dismantled the structure. Because they were unable to finish the job, the finest bas-reliefs have been left open to the elements.

5. Eastern gallery, northern half – this unfinished section represents a war between the gods for the possession of the ambrosia. The gate in the centre of the E gallery was used by Khmer royalty and dignitaries for mounting and dismounting elephants.

6. North gallery represents a war between gods and demons. Siva is shown in meditation with Ganesh, Brahma and Krishna. Most of the other scenes are from the Ramayana, notably the visit of Hanuman (the monkey god) to Sita.

7. Western gallery, northern half has another scene from the Ramayana depicting a battle between Rama and Ravana who rides on a chariot pulled by monsters and commands an army of giants.

precipitous slopes of Mt Meru. The five lotus flower-shaped sandstone towers – the first appearance of these features in Khmer architecture – are believed to have once been covered in gold. The eight-storey towers are square, although they appear octagonal, and give the impression of a sprouting bud.

Above the ascending tiers of roofs – each jutting gable has an elaborately carved pediment – the tower tapers into a circular roof. The towers are dominated by the central one, the Siva shrine and principal sanctuary, whose pinnacle rises more than 30m above the third level; 55m above ground level. This sanctuary

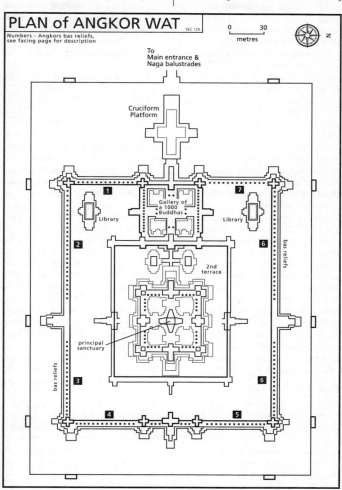

PLAN of ANGKOR WAT VLC 125

Numbers - Angkors bas reliefs,
see facing page for description

0   30
metres

N

To
Main entrance &
Naga balustrades

Cruciform
Platform

1   **7**

Library   Gallery of   Library
a 1000
Buddhas

2   **6**

bas reliefs

2nd
terrace

principal
sanctuary

bas reliefs

3   **6**

4   **5**

bas reliefs

would have contained an image of Siva in the likeness of King Suryavarman II, as it was his temple-mountain. But it is now a Buddhist shrine and contains statues of the Buddha.

The temple's greatest sculptural treasure is its 2m high **bas-reliefs**, around the walls of the outer gallery. It is the longest continuous bas-relief in the world. In some areas traces of the paint and gilt that once covered the carvings can still be seen. Most famous are the hundreds of figures of devatas and apsaras in niches along the walls. The apsaras – the celestial women – are modelled on the god-king's own bevy of bare-breasted beauties, and the sculptors' attention to detail provides an insight into the world of 12th century haute couture. Their hair is often knotted on the crown and bejewelled – although all manner of wild and exotic coiffures are depicted. Jewelled collars and hip-girdles also are common and bracelets worn on the upper arms. Sadly many of the apsaras have been removed in recent years.

The bas-reliefs narrate stories from the Ramayana and Mahabharata, as well as legends of Vishnu, and are reminiscent of Pallava and Chola art in SE India. Pious artisans and peasants were probably only allowed as far as Angkor Wat's outer gallery, where they could admire the bas-reliefs and pay hommage to the god-king. In the open courtyards, statues of animals enliven the walls. Lions stand on guard beside the staircases. There were supposed to be 300 of them in the original building. Part of the bas-reliefs were hit by shrapnel in 1972, and some of its apsaras were used for target practice.

East of Angkor Thom

There are a close group of temples just outside the E gate of Angkor Thom. **Chau Say Tevoda**, built by Suryavarman II is the first temple outside the E gate and is dwarfed by Ta Keo. The temple is dedicated to Siva but many of the carvings are of Vishnu. It is similar in plan to **Thammanon**, next door,

whose surrounding walls have completely disappeared, leaving only the gateways on the E and W ends and a ruined central tower. Originally both temples would have had a hall linked to the central tower, and enclosing walls with elaborate gateways. A library, to the S-E, is the only other building in the complex. There are repeated pediments above the doorways, which are more elaborate than those at Angkor Wat.

Ta Keo, begun during Jayavarman V's reign and left unfinished, stands E of the Royal Palace and just off the Avenue of Victory. The pyramid-temple rises over 50m: its five tower shrines are supported on a five-tiered pyramid. This temple was one of the first to be entirely built of sandstone. Previous tower sanctuaries had entrances only on the E side, but Ta Keo has openings on all four sides. It was originally surrounded by a moat.

The temple of **Ta Prohm**, to the S of Ta Keo, was consecrated in 1186 – 5 years after Jayavarman VII seized power. It was built to house the divine image of the Queen Mother. It underwent many transformations and an inscription gives detailed information on the complex. It contained 39 sanctuaries or prasats, 566 stone dwellings and 288 brick dwellings. Ta Prohm functioned as a monastery which was home to 18 abbots and 2,740 monks. By the 12th century, temples were no longer exclusively places of worship – they also had to accommodate monks, so roofed halls were increasingly built within the complexes. According to contemporary inscriptions, the temple required 79,365 people for its upkeep and relied on the income of 3,140 villages. The list of property it owned was on an equally impressive scale: it included 523 parasols, 35 diamonds, and 40,620 pearls. Ta Prohm is one of the most beautiful temples in the area, as it has been relatively untouched since it was discovered and retains much of its mystery.

For all would-be Mouhots and closet

Indiana Joneses, Ta Prohm is the perfect lost-temple-in-the-jungle: unlike most of the other monuments at Angkor, it has been only minimally cleared of its undergrowth, fig trees and creepers. It is widely regarded as one of Angkor's most enchanting temples. The French writer Elie Lauré wrote: "With its millions of knotted limbs, the forest embraces the ruins with a violent love".

The massive complex of **Banteay Kdei** is 3 km E of Angkor Thom and just to the SE of Ta Prohm. Some archaeologists think it may be dedicated to Jayavarman VII's religious teacher. It is a crowded collection of towers and connecting galleries on a flat plan, surrounded by a galleried enclosure. No inscriptions have been found here to indicate either its name or purpose, but it is almost certainly a Buddhist temple built in the 12th century, about the same time as Ta Prohm. The central tower was never finished. The artificial lake next to Banteay Kdei is called **Srah Srang** – 'the Pool of Ablutions' – which was doubtless used for ritual bathing. The steps down to the water face the rising sun and are flanked with lions and nagas.

Prasat Kravan, built in 921, means 'Cardamom Sanctuary' and is unusual in that it is built of brick. By that time brick had been replaced by laterite and sandstone. It consists of a row of five brick towers arranged in a line. In the central sanctuary is a bas-relief portrait of Vishnu and on the inner wall of the N tower his consort Lakshmi. In the early 10th century temples were commissioned by individuals other than the king; Prasat Kravan is one of the earliest examples.

Pre Rup, constructed in laterite with brick prasats, marks the centre of the royal city built by Rajendravarman (just NE of Srah Srang). Built in 961, it is larger and higher than its predecessor, the East Mebon, which it closely resembles. An important innovation at Pre Rup and East Mebon is that the sanctuary at the top is no longer a single tower – it is a group of five towers and is surrounded by smaller towers on the outer, lower levels. This more complicated plan reached its final development at Angkor Wat 150 years later. The group of five brick towers were originally elaborately decorated with plaster, but most of it has now fallen off. The shrine has fine lintels and columns on its doorways. Its modern name means 'turning the body' and, according to local legend, it is named after a cremation ritual in which the outline of a body was traced in the cinders one way and then the other.

The **Eastern Baray** – or Baray Orientale – was built by Yasovarman I and fed by the Siem Reap River. The four corners are marked by stelae. In the middle of the Eastern Baray, the flamboyant five towers of the **East Mebon** were finished in 952. Rajendravarman seems to have followed the Roluos trend and dedicated East Mebon to his parents. The East Mebon and Pre Rup were the last monuments in plaster and brick; they mark the end of a Khmer architectural epoch. The Siem Reap River is said to have been diverted while the temple was built.

North of Angkor Thom

Northeast of the walled city of Angkor Thom, about 3.5 km from the Bayon, is the rambling 12th century complex of **Preah Khan**. It was Jayavarman VII's first capital before Angkor Thom was completed and means 'Fortunate City of Victory'. It is similar in ground-plan to Ta Prohm (see page 508) but great attention was paid to the approaches: its E and W entrance avenues leading to ornamental causeways are lined with carved-stone boundary posts.

Holes in the inner walls of the central sanctuary of Preah Khan, suggest they may once have been decorated with brass plates – an obvious target for looters. The temple was built to shelter the statue of Jayavarman VII's father, Dharanindravarman II, in the likeness of Bodhisattva Avatokitsvara. The complex includes a 2-storey columnar pavilion and a generously sized hall built to accommodate the king's dancers – unusual Khmer architectural extras. A stele was discovered at the site glorifying the builder, Jayavarman VII and detailing what it took to keep the place ticking over. The inventory mentions that for Preah Khan's upkeep, it required the services of 97,840 men and women, 444 chefs, 4,606 footmen and 2,298 servants. A dharmasala (or resting house for monks) has been recently discovered at the site. The World Monuments Fund (WMF) has built a vernacular-style reception centre inside the W entrance of Preah Khan. Brochures and some guide books to Angkor are available. During the dry season, the WMF, based in New York, undertakes archaeological site conservation activities here.

To the E of Preah Khan and N of the Eastern Baray are two more Buddhist temples built by Jayavarman VII: **Preah Neak Pean** (the westernmost one) and the ruins of **Ta Som**. The exquisite temple of Neak Pean is also a fountain, built in the middle of a pool and representing the paradisiacal Himalayan mountain-

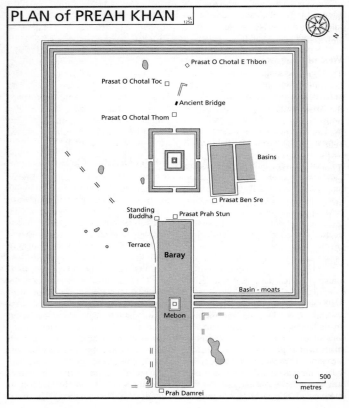

PLAN of PREAH KHAN

Prasat O Chotal E Thbon

Prasat O Chotal Toc

Ancient Bridge

Prasat O Chotal Thom

Basins

Prasat Ben Sre

Standing Buddha

Prasat Prah Stun

Terrace

Baray

Basin - moats

Mebon

Prah Damrei

0   500
metres

lake, Anaavatapta, from Hindu mythology. It is a small sanctuary on an island in the baray of Preah Khan. Two nagas form the edge of the island, and their tails join at the back. In modern Khmer it is known as the *Prea-sat neac pon* – the 'tower of the intertwined dragons'. The colossal image of the horse is the compassionate Bodhisattva who is supposed to save sailors from drowning. The temple pools were an important part of the aesthetic experience of Preah Khan and Neak Pean – the ornate stone carving of both doubly visible by reflection. Such basins within a temple complex were used for religious ritual, while the larger moats and barays were used for practical purposes of bathing, transport and possibly for irrigation.

West of Angkor Thom

The **Western Baray** was built by Udayadi-tavarman II, possibly to increase the size of the irrigated farmlands. In the centre is the **West Mebon**, where the famous bronze statue of Vishnu was discovered (now in the National Museum at Phnom Penh, see page 473).

Just S of the Western Baray is **Ak Thom**, which marks the site of Jayavarman II's earlier city. It is the oldest surviving temple in the Angkor region and although little remains, it is worth a visit. The central towers are constructed mostly of brick, with some stone features. The bricks were cemented together with a mortar of vegetable sap, palm sugar and termite soil.

Outlying temples

Depending on the political situation, transport availability and the state of the roads, it is possible to visit some of the other ancient Khmer sites dotted around the main temples at Angkor. Most of these temples can be reached by motos (motorbike taxi). It is reported that the years of war took a heavy toll on many of these monuments. These areas tend to be mined.

South-East

The **Roluos Group** is worth visiting if time permits. Jayavarman II built several capitals including one at Roluos, at that time called Hariharalaya. This was the site of his last city and remained the capital during the reigns of his three successors. The three remaining Hindu sanctuaries at Roluos are **Preah Ko**, **Bakong** and **Lolei**. They were finished in 879, 881 and 893 respectively by Indravarman I and his son Yashovarman I and are the best-preserved of the early temples.

All three temples are built of brick, with sandstone doorways and niches. The use of human figures as sculptural decoration in religious architecture developed around this time – examples of these guardian spirits can be seen in the niches of Preah Ko and Lolei. Other sculptured figures which appear in the Roluos group are the crouching lion, the reclining bull (Nandi – Siva's mount) and the naga (snake). The gopura – an arched gateway leading to the temple courtyards – was also a contemporary innovation in Roluos. Libraries – used for the storage of sacred manuscripts – also appeared for the first time, as did the concentric enclosures surrounding the central group of towers. Preah Ko and Lolei have characteristics in common: both, eg were dedicated to the parents and grandparents of the kings who built them. Neither temple has a pyramid centre like Bakhong as the pyramid temples were built exclusively for kings.

Preah Ko, meaning 'sacred ox', was named after the three statues of Nandi (the mount of the Hindu god, Siva) which stand in front of the temple. Orientated E-W, there is a cluster of six towers arranged in two rows on a low platform. The front row of towers was devoted to Indravarman's male ancestors and the second row to the female. The ancestors were represented in the image of a Hindu god. Only patches

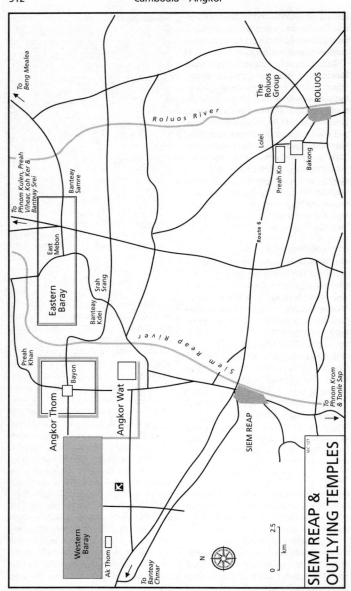

SIEM REAP & OUTLYING TEMPLES

remain of the once-magnificent stucco relief work, including a remnant of a kala – a motif also found on contemporary monuments in Java.

Indravarman's temple-mountain, **Bakong**, is a royal five-stepped pyramid temple with a sandstone central tower built on a series of successively receding terraces with surrounding brick towers. It may have been inspired by Borobudur in Java. Indravarman himself was buried in the temple. The central tower was built to replace the original one when the monument was restored in the 12th century and is probably larger than the original. The Bakong denotes the true beginning of classical Khmer architecture and contained the god-king's Siva lingam. The most important innovations of Indravarman's artists are the free-standing sandstone statues – such as the group of three figures, probably depicting the king with his two wives, who are represented as Siva with Uma and Ganga. The heads of all the figures are now missing but the simplicity of the sculpture is nonetheless distinctive; it is a good example of early Khmer craftsmanship. The statues are more static and stockier than the earlier statues of Chenla. There is now a Buddhist monastery in the grounds – originally it was dedicated to Siva.

Lolei was built by Yashovarman I in the middle of Indravarman's baray. The brick towers were dedicated to the king's ancestors, but over the centuries they have largely disintegrated; hardly any of the decoration remains.

South

On top of **Phnom Krom**, 12 km S of Siem Reap, is an 11th century temple overlooking the Tonlé Sap. Many of the statues have disappeared.

The **Tonlé Sap**, the Great Lake of Cambodia, is one of the natural wonders of Asia. Uniquely, the 100 km-long Tonlé Sap River, a tributary of the mighty Mekong, reverses its flow and runs up-hill for 6 months of the year. Spring meltwaters in the Himalayas coupled with seasonal rains increase the flow of the Mekong to such an extent that some is deflected up the Tonlé Sap River. From Jun the lake begins to expand until, by the end of the rainy season, it has increased in area ten-fold and in depth by some 12m. At its greatest extent, the lake occupies nearly a seventh of Cambodia's land area. From Nov, with the onset of the dry season, the Tonlé Sap River reverses its flow once more and begins to act like a regular tributary – flowing downhill into the Mekong. By Feb the lake has shrunk to a fraction of its wet season size.

This pattern of expansion and contraction has three major benefits. First, it helps to restrict flooding in the Mekong Delta in Vietnam. Second, it forms the basis for a substantial part of Cambodia's rice production. And third, it supports perhaps the world's largest and richest inland fisheries, yielding as much as 10 tonnes of fish per sq km.

Because of the dramatic changes in the size of the lake some of the fish, such as the 'walking catfish', have evolved to survive several hours out of water, flopping overland to find deeper pools. These *hok yue* – or elephant fish – are renowned as a delicacy well beyond Cambodia's borders. Large-scale commercial fishing is a major occupation during Feb to May and the fishing grounds are divided into plots and leased out. Although recent lack of dredging means the lake is not as deep as it was and fish are tending to swim downstream into the Mekong and Tonlé Sap rivers. The annual flooding covers the surrounding countryside with a layer of moist, nutrient-rich mud – which is ideal for rice-growing. Farmers grow a deepwater rice, long-stalked and fast growing – it grows with the rising lake to keep the grain above water and the stem can be up to 6m long. The lake also houses people and communities live in floating villages close to the shore. **Kompong Chhnang** is an important fishing and transportation centre near the lake and is known for its pottery. Boats for trips around the lake can be hired from fisheries police (fee negotiable).

The Tonlé Sap is said by some scientists to be facing an ecological calamity. Excessive forest clearance has undermined the annual cycle of renewal described above. The lake's level is lower than it has been for decades, and the life-giving inflow of silt which is so critical to the success of the fishing industry and rice cultivation, is much reduced due to excessive logging upstream.

East

Banteay Samre is much further to the E. It is a Hindu temple dedicated to Vishnu, although reliefs decorating some of the frontons (the triangular areas above arches) portray Buddhist scenes. It is thought to have been built by Suryavarman II and has many characteristics of Angkor Wat such as stone-vaulted galleries and a high central tower.

North

Banteay Srei is further away, about 25 km N of Angkor, but is well worth the trip. It was built by the Brahmin tutor to King Rajendravarman, Yajnavaraha, grandson of Harshavarman (900-921), and founded in 967. Covered terraces, of which only the columns remain, once lined both sides of the primary entrance (East). The layout was inspired by Prasat Thom at Koh Ker (see below). Three beautifully carved tower-shrines stand side by side on a low terrace in the middle of a quadrangle, with a pair of libraries on either side enclosed by a wall. Two of the shrines were dedicated to Vishnu and Siva, and both had libraries close by, with carvings depicting appropriate legends. The whole temple is dedicated to Brahma. Beyond this inner group of buildings was a monastery surrounded by a moat. One of the best-known statues from this site is a sculpture of Siva, sitting down and holding his wife, Uma, on his knee: it is in the National Museum of Arts in Phnom Penh (see page 473).

Having been built by a Brahmin priest, the temple was never intended for use by a king, which goes some way towards explaining its small size – you have to duck to get through the doorways to the sanctuary towers. Surprisingly, though, it contains some of the finest examples of Khmer sculpture. Finely carved and rare pink sandstone replaces the plaster-coated carved-brick decoration, typical of earlier temples. All the buildings are covered in carvings: the jambs, the lintels, the balustered windows. Banteay Srei's ornamentation is exceptional – its roofs, pediments and lintels are magnificently carved with tongues of flame, coiling serpents' tails, gods, demons and floral garlands. **NB** It was at Banteay Srei that an American tourist was killed at the end of 1994 by the Khmer Rouge. It was closed at the beginning of 1995.

Andre Malraux, who wrote the novel *The royal way* (1930) attempted to pillage Banteay Srei of its treasures. He apparently read in an issue of the *Bulletin de l'Ecole Francaise d'Extreme Orient* that the temple not only contained a series of brilliant carvings in excellent condition but also that the temple was unexcavated. Taking 'unexcavated' to mean 'abandoned', and assuming that it was then also unclaimed, he set out for Cambodia with a friend to loot the temple. He arrived in Cambodia, travelled to Angkor and proceeded to cut out one tonne of the finest statues and bas-reliefs. Fortunately, he was arrested trying to leave the country with the treasures and was sentenced to 3 years in prison (a term that he did not serve).

Phnom Kulen – or Mt Mohendrapura – 28 km NE of Angkor and 48 km from Siem Reap, is a sandstone plateau considered sacred by the Khmers. The site is the mythical birthplace of the Cambodian Kingdom. At the hill's summit is the largest reclining Buddha in the country – over 900 years old. Jayavarman II built his first brick pyramid temple mountain – to house the sacred golden Siva-lingam – here at the beginning of the 9th century. Today the temple is only visible in fragments although, over a millennium later, the phallic emblem is said to be still on display in the Phnom Kulen complex. The temple is best known for its elaborately carved lintels and bas reliefs. There are also some remains of 9th century Cham temples in the area. Today the hill is clothed in forest, and the nights here are cold and the days fresh and invigorating. Given that the area, until recently, was under Khmer Rouge control (see below) it is likely that the remains have suffered accordingly. Cutting through the area is the holy **River of a Thousand Lingas**. Cut into the sandstone bed of this river are some 1,000 lingas. Finnish journalist Teppo Turkki who visited the site for the *Phnom Penh Post* wrote at the beginning of 1995: "The lingas, some of which date back to the 9th century, are about 25 cm square and 10 cm deep and lined in a perfect grid pattern. The river runs over them, covering them with about 5 cm of pristine water." He continues: "The holy objects are designed to create a 'power path' for the Khmer kings." Further downstream, larger blocks of stone, also under water, are carved with apsaras, vishnus, and other figures. Altogether a wondrous and magical place. Note that until the beginning of 1995, Phnom Kulen was under the control of the Khmer Rouge and there are still occasional skirmishes in the area, so whether the site is open to visitors is far from clear. However, in Feb, a group of reporters were allowed to visit the area, and it is said to be being made ready for a pilgrimage trip by King Sihanouk.

Beng Mealea, a huge 12th century temple complex, 40 km E of the Bayon and about 7 km SE of Phnom Kulen, is completely ruined even though it was built at about the same time as Angkor Wat. Its dimensions are similar, but Beng Mealea has no central pyramid. Most of the Buddhist temples built under Jayavarman VII – Preah Khan, Banteay Kdei, Ta Som and Ta Prohm – were modelled after this complex.

Well over 100 km to the NE of Angkor is **Preah Vihear** (or Prasat Phra Viharn), which dates from the beginning of the 11th century but was added to by Suryavarman II. The temple dominates the plain from its prominent position in the Dangrek Mountains at an altitude of more than 700m and was only returned to Cambodia by a ruling of the International Court of Justice in the Hague in 1963 (previously it was occupied by the Thais). It is only possible to reach this temple from Thailand.

At the beginning of 1995 the Cambodian government appeared to be preparing to take the Preah Vihear temple complex from the Khmer Rouge. The temple's position at the summit of an escarpment means that it is most easily approached from Thai territory. The slopes of the escarpment are also strewn with mines. Whether the Thais will allow the Cambodian government to mount an assault through Thai territory is unclear. Many in Cambodia still feel that the Thai government and army offer support to the Khmer Rouge. In any case, the Khmer Rouge commander defending the capital is likely to be the feared, one-legged warrior, Ta Mok. The preferred option appears to be to starve the rebels into surrender or defection: in Mar about 3,000 Cambodian army men were dug in around the temple complex facing perhaps just 100 Khmer Rouge fighters.

Also to the NE, but closer to Angkor, is **Koh Ker**, the site of the old capital of Jayavarman IV. The main ruin here is

Prasat Thom. Its surrounding land was irrigated by baray, similar to but smaller than, the ones at Angkor.

Banteay Chmar, 61 km from Sisophon and to the NW of Angkor was one of the capitals of Jayavarman II. It was rebuilt by Jayavarman VII and dedicated to his son and four generals who were killed in battle repelling a Cham invasion in 1177. Banteay Chmar, because of its secluded location, is rarely visited. This remoteness has made the temple particularly vulnerable to looting, and in Jul 1994 valuable 12th century carvings were stolen from the site. Local officials say that Cambodian army units were involved in the looting, using trucks to pull statues from their pedestals and then transport them the short 30 mins journey across the Thai border for sale.

Site information

● **Tours**

Tours can be organized in Cambodia through **Phnom Penh Tourism** or through the **General Directorate of Tourism (GDT)** (see page 483 for addresses). There are daily flights to Siem Reap, but day tours allow only 3 hrs sightseeing before the return flight leaves for Phnom Penh. It takes at least 2 days to see Angkor's temples properly, preferably three. It costs US$100 for the first day's entrance to Angkor, including transport and guide, plus US$91 for the return airfare. For any further days **Angkor Tourism** hires out cars and drivers. The larger the group the cheaper the tour pp. Tours ask for a single room surcharge. Tour agencies in Siem Reap offer tours to outlying temples, eg Eurasie (opposite Pra Chea Chun Hospital).

● **Guides**

Guides are generally well trained by the head of Angkor Conservation. Guides will explain the history of the temples as well as the best way to get around them (US$20/day). They will meet visitors at the *Grand Hotel D'Angkor* and arrange visits to the sights including transport (car or minibus, depending on numbers). There are also children who will take you round the temples for a small fee.

● **Cost**

Temple fees: Angkor Wat (US$13), Bayon (US$5), Angkor Thom (US$15), Roluos (US$5), Bantheay Srei (US$5), grand circuit (US$11), all temples (US$71). Entry is free after 1615. For tours – **1 day**: US$100; **2 nights/3 days**: US$180; **3 nights/4 days**: US$270. Price includes accommodation at the *Grand Hotel*, meals, guide, police protection and transport around the sights (excluding air fare). Prices are slightly more expensive if you stay at the *Villa Apsara*. 1-day tours only give visitors a few hours to explore the sights.

● **Local transport**

There is no public transport around the sights. All transport for day trips is organized through Phnom Penh Tourism and organized tour companies and is usually included in the tour price. **Car hire**: from Angkor Tourism US$40/day with driver, plus US$20 for guide. Moped taxis are also available. It is difficult to reach some of the more remote sights as roads are bad – or non-existent – and deteriorate rapidly once the rains arrive. 4WD vehicles are needed to visit some of the sights. **Motorbikes**: from guesthouses (US$5/day). **Bicycle hire**: from the *Grand Hotel* and guesthouses.

● **Circuits of the Temples**

There are 3 so-called 'circuits'. The **Petit Circuit** takes in the main, central temples including Angkor Wat, Bayon, Baphuon and the Terrace of the Elephants. The **Grand Circuit** takes a wider route, including smaller temples like Ta Prohm, East Mebon and Neak Pean. The **Roluos Group Circuit** ventures further afield still, taking in the temples near Roluos – Lolei, Preah Ko and Bakong.

● **Safety**

All the temples are guarded and, on the Grand Circuit, there is a pill box every kilometre. However, though obvious, the security presence is not oppressive. Land mines have been planted on some outlying paths to prevent Khmer Rouge guerrillas from infiltrating the temples. They are more likely to be buried in the environs of the outer temples. The guides know which areas are dangerous. Stick to well used paths.

● **Snakes**

Be especially wary of snakes in the dry season. The very poisonous *Hanuman snake* – which is a lurid green colour – is fairly common in the area. There are also certain varieties of *centipede* which can give a nasty bite.

● **Angkor Conservation**

Just off the main road (not clearly signed) to Angkor and about 1 km from the *Grand Hotel*. Many statues, stelae and linga found at Angkor are stored here to prevent theft. Accessible by special appointment only.

Siem Reap

Before Cambodia's civil war it was a bustling town but has been considerably damaged by the constant fighting. This area was strategic to both sides and was a battle ground for 20 years. The growth of tourism to Angkor Wat may yet put Siem Reap back on its feet – certainly many new hotels have sprung up in the past year or so.

Local information
● **Accommodation**

Most hotels around Angkor did not survive the war intact but since 1991, entrepreneurs intending to cash in on the expected upturn in tourism, have been planning to build more hotels and upgrade existing ones. Other than the *Grand*, nearly all the hotels are run by Thais. Most serve Thai, Khmer and European food and sometimes Vietnamese. There is a concentration of cheaper guesthouses near the *Bayon Restaurant*. **NB** The electricity supply is unreliable but is available for most hours of the day, water supplies are similarly reliable. **NB** All telephone numbers listed here are mobile and need 015 prefix.

A *Banteay Srei*, on the road on the way in from the airport, 2 km from town, T 913839, new, a/c, restaurant, one of the most professionally managed places with reliable water and electricity supplies; **A** *Ta Prohm*, T 911783, a/c, restaurant, satellite TV, pleasant aspect, overlooking small park and river, attracts groups from Angkor Tourism and Phnom Penh Tourism, upmarket for Siem Reap but plastic and modern, Bangkok Post available in lobby; **A-B** *Grand Hotel d'Angkor*, this used to the **the** place to stay, 1920s colonial splendour, large rooms, run down but elegant, it is now under renovation by the Raffles group of Singapore – at a reputed cost of US$30mn, in the meantime, reports are that it is poor value for money and passé.

B *Baray*, Sangkat I (past *Grand Hotel* on right, on road to temples, before *Solid Rock Bar*), a/c, restaurant, 12 rm, prices negotiable; **B** *Bayon*, T 911769, further along the riverside road

from *Bopha Angkor*, a/c, restaurant, room prices negotiable; **B** *Bopha Angkor*, situated next to river in fairly quiet street, T 911710, a/c, restaurant, rather tacky and overpriced, old rooms cheaper; **B** *De La Paix*, Sivutha St, T 912322, a/c, restaurant, prices negotiable; **B** *Diamond*, Vithei Achasva Rd, T 910020, a/c, makeshift restaurant (serves breakfast in front of your villa), if no tourists in town half-price deals negotiable, opened '93, looks rather like motel with small villas; **B** *Golden Apsara*, Sivutha St, T 911292, a/c, clean, restaurant; **B** *Or Kan Sap* (behind *Grand*), a/c, no restaurant, fridge, mosquito net and big clean towels in every room, no English spoken, good bet as cheaper option; **B** *Prasat Sour*, Sivutha St, a/c, restaurant; **B-C** *Stung Siem Reap*, Wat Prom Rath St, T 914058, a/c, restaurant (even serves pizza and spaghetti), difficult to find, up a side street, but attractive old building, renovated but retains its character, nr a temple and in interesting part of town, rec.

C *Bakheng*, Sivutha St, a/c, 12 rm.

E-F *Mom's Guesthouse*, No 99 Wath Bo St (next to the *Bayon Restaurant*), T 914494, comes highly rec as a cheap place to stay, but with only 4 rm doesn't take much to fill up, 2 rm with shared facilities, 2 new rm en suite;

F *Dahomey*, the most popular of the budget hotels.

Guesthouses: tourists arriving at Siem Reap's airport will see many guesthouses signposted off the road into town; a number of them are nice-looking buildings. Few have eating facilities, but fridges are usually provided with bottled water. Most cost US$8-10 for a double room: *Sun Rise Guesthouse*, 592 Kroum 4, Phnom Wat Bou (towards market) friendly, and 54 Sivatha St (opp *Sky Palace*) and on same road as *Hotel de la Paix*), rooms simple and clean, mosquito nets provided, clean bathrooms; **E** *Apsara*, next to *Green House Kitchen*, clean and friendly, rooms with bathrooms, fans and mosquito nets. Travellers also rec **E** *Mahogany*, 593 Wath Bo St, friendly.

● **Places to eat**

Asian: ◆◆*Bayon*, nr guesthouses on Wath Bo St, serves excellent Thai food in a garden strung with fairy lights, welcoming, friendly service, delicious chicken curry and fish and seafood cooked in coconut; ◆◆*Green House Kitchen*, 6 St, on road to the airport, Khmer and Thai curries and soups; ◆*Arun*, opp bank of river to tourist information, good Cambodian nosh;

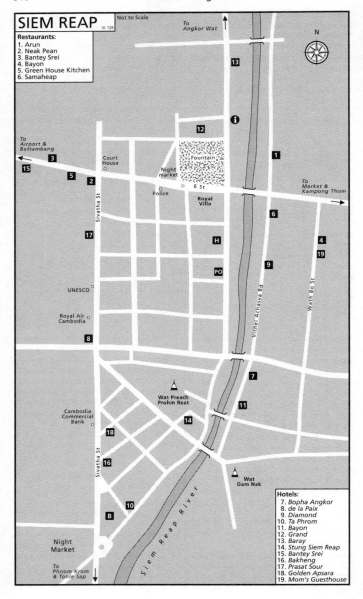

SIEM REAP
VL 128

Not to Scale

Restaurants:
1. Arun
2. Neak Pean
3. Bantey Srei
4. Bayon
5. Green House Kitchen
6. Samaheap

To Angkor Wat

To Airport & Battambang

To Market & Kampong Thom

Court House

Night market

Fountain

6 St

Police

Royal Villa

UNESCO

Royal Air Cambodia

Wat Preach Prohm Reat

Cambodia Commercial Bank

Wat Dam Nak

Sivatha St

Vithei Achava Rd

Wath Bo St

Siem Reap River

Night Market

To Phnom Krom & Tonle Sap

N

Hotels:
7. *Bopha Angkor*
8. *de la Paix*
9. *Diamond*
10. *Ta Phrom*
11. *Bayon*
12. *Grand*
13. *Baray*
14. *Stung Siem Reap*
15. *Bantey Srei*
16. *Bakheng*
17. *Prasat Sour*
18. *Golden Apsara*
19. *Mom's Guesthouse*

♦*Bayon Chinese Restaurant*, Route 6 (E of the river on the road to the Roluos Group before the central market); *Diamond Hotel*, by the river, Thai dishes.

International: ♦♦*Samaheap*, S of the *Grand Hotel* (just past the bridge), European, Chinese and Cambodian dishes; *Bantei Srei*, Airport Rd, 2 km from Siem Reap, clean, good international food, reliable water and electricity; *Neak Pean*, opp Courthouse, basic but cheap.

Foodstalls: on the main road S of the *Hotel de la Paix*, on E bank of the river just N of the bridge.

● **Airline offices**
Royal Air Cambodge, on the Roluos road (just over the bridge).

● **Entertainment**
Prassat Sonr, live music and dancing; *Nan-now*, Taiwanese-owned karaoke bar.

● **Post & telecommunications**
Post Office and **Telephone**: (*Samart*), satellite telephone service, W side of Siem Reap River (between bridges – across from *Samaheap Restaurant*).

● **Shopping**
Gifts: small gift shop in the *Grand Hotel* and shops opposite. There are small stalls at many of the main temples selling souvenirs.

Handicrafts: there are small stalls selling crafts at the main temple complexes.

Markets: central market is approximately 1.5 km E of Siem Reap on Route 6 (towards the Roluos Group). Many visitors say it has the best choice of Cambodian handicrafts- bamboo furniture, musical instruments etc. "Minders" charge 200 riel to watch motorbikes, while you wander round.

● **Tour companies & travel agents**
Diethelm, T 57524, F 57694; *Eurasie*, opp Pra Chea Chun hospital, organize day trips to Banteay Srei (US$80).

● **Tourist offices**
Angkor Tourism, next to *Villa Apsara*.

● **Transport**
Local Cars with driver/guides: available from major hotels, US$25/day. Depending on the political climate, it may soon be possible to visit the Angkor temples directly from Thailand – just 150 km to the W – without going via Phnom Penh. 314 km N of Phnom Penh. **Minibus and car tours**: arranged by Angkor Tourism. **Motorbikes & bicycle hire**: US$5/day from guesthouses nr the market and *Grand Hotel d'Angkor*. **Pillion tours on bikes**: around the temples US$5-10/day (prices negotiable).

Air Airport is 7 km from Siem Reap and 4 km from Angkor. Round trips 5 times daily between Phnom Penh and Siem Reap (US$110 return). Flights leave Phnom Penh early in the morning and return to Phnom Penh around 1600 – reserve return flight on landing. **Transport to town**: motorbike taxis (US$1) or cars (US$3-5).

Train To Sisophan and then shared taxi. Journey takes 2 days, take provisions.

Road Shared taxi: 10 hrs (US$6), but start early.

Sea Boat: boats upriver from Phnom Penh (Psar Cha Ministry of Transport Ferry Landing) leave Mon, Fri, 10 hrs (US$25), ask at Ministry of Tourism in Phnom Penh. **NB** Boat travel is **not** recommended by western embassies or the Cambodian government.

NORTH OF PHNOM PENH

Kompong Cham

Kompong Cham is a lively port on the banks of the Mekong, and has some good examples of colonial architecture. **Wat Nokor**, not far from town, is a well preserved 13th century monument. At **Phnom Pros** and **Phnom Srei**, to the N are the foundations of two early temples, as well as five mass graves in which thousands of victims of the Khmer Rouge are buried.

South of Kompong Cham is **Preah Theat Preah Srei**, the former capital of the Chenla kingdom in the 8th century. **Preah Nokor** to the SE was another ancient Khmer capital in the 7th century.

- **Accommodation** *Hotel Mekong*, on the river.

- **Transport Road Shared taxi**: regular connections with Phnom Penh from Olympic Market, 3 hrs (8,000 riel). **Sea Boat**: connections with Phnom Penh 5/6 hrs, (1,000 riels). Boats leave Phnom Penh from Sisowath Quay/106 St.

Kratie and area

Around the town of Kratie is the ancient capital of **Sambor**. The monuments are spread over an area of 1 sq km and were visited, in the mid-17th century, by Gerrit Van Wusthoff, the Dutch merchant-adventurer who also visited Laos. The most renowned stupa was built over the ashes of Princess Nucheat Khatr Vorpheak (who was killed by a crocodile in 1834) and the stupa became a pilgrimage site. Prince Sihanouk is supposed to have consulted a medium on matters of state here. Crocodiles are still supposed to inhabit the Mekong around Sambor. Below Sambor is the French colonial style town of Kratie and Kompong Cham, Cambodia's third largest city. It has some good examples of shophouse architecture common in Cambodian riverside towns. Tobacco and rubber, introduced by the French, are important local crops. **Transport Road Shared taxi**: regular connections with Phnom Penh from Olympic Market, 8 hrs (US$5). **Sea Boat**: connections with Phnom Penh, 2 days (3,000 riel).

Stung Treng

Stung Treng is a pretty town on the Mekong, only 40 km from Laos. The town has two busy, and interesting markets right next door to each other.

Excursions Some travellers have managed to reach Rattanakiri to the NE from here. The area is renowned for its tribal people, the Montagnards. It is possible to fly or go by car, 10 hrs (US$4).

- **Accommodation** *Sekong*, a/c, hot water. There are also a couple of cheaper but more basic options.

- **Transport Local** It is possible to hire boats for trips along the Mekong (about US$5/hour). **Air** Connections twice a week with Phnom Penh (US$45). **Road Shared taxi**: regular connections with Phnom Penh, via Kratie where you can pick up shared taxis to Stung Treng 6hrs, (US$4). **Sea Boat**: connections with Phnom Penh via Kratie, 4 days (40,000 riel).

Kompong Thom and area

Approximately 35 km from Kompong Thom is the important archaeological site of **Sambor Prei Kuk**, an ancient Chenla capital dating from the 7th century. The main temples are square or octagonal brick tower-shrines on high brick terraces with wonderful ornamentation in sandstone, especially the lintel stones. The idea of the jewel strings carved here is believed to be Indian in origin, as Indian donors used to literally hang their wealth on sacred trees or shrines. The temple in the group to the S is supposed to have contained a golden lingam.

- **Accommodation** Guesthouse on the lake, contact Mrs Kao Cheng Hour.

• **Transport Road Shared taxi**: regular connections with Phnom Penh.

Battambang

Cambodia's second city, lies 40 km W of the Tonlé Sap, on the route to Bangkok. Since 1979 Battambang has profited enormously from contraband trade with Thailand; it was also heavily fought-over during the civil war. In the past, it was a bread-basket – or, more accurately, a rice-basket – but it is now better known for its fishing industry (run by the Chinese), jute sack factory, industry making fishing nets as well as its rubber and sulphur processing plants. Rice production has been severely disrupted by the civil war. **Wat Ek**, 8 km N of Battambang, is an 11th century temple, built by Suryavarman. Having been used by the Khmer Rouge as a prison, the temple has fallen into disrepair. The **Prasat Sneng** temples, 22 km S of Battambang, were also ruined by the Khmer Rouge, who used the stones for the construction of their own buildings.

• **Accommodation** A number of new hotels were built to accommodate UNTAC, now possible to bargain on price. **B** *Angkor*, 1 St, a/c, hot water; **C** *Khemara*, 3 St, nr railway station, a/c, hot water; **C** *Paris*, 3 St, a/c, hot water; **C-D** *Victory* is also close to the railway station and has a small swimming pool, no a/c.

• **Transport Air** Connections 3 times a week with Phnom Penh (US$90). **Road Shared taxi**: regular connections with Phnom Penh from Central Market, 7 hrs (US$5), Siem Reap (US$5).

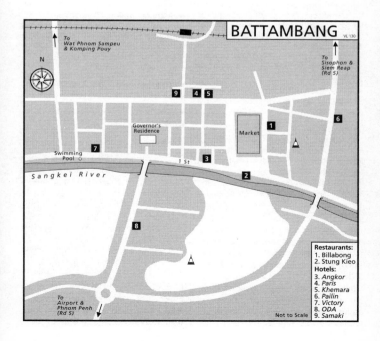

BATTAMBANG VL 130

To Wat Phnom Sampeu & Komping Pouy

To Sisophon & Siem Reap (Rd 5)

Governor's Residence

Market

Swimming Pool

Sangkei River

1 St

To Airport & Phnom Penh (Rd 5)

Restaurants:
1. Billabong
2. Stung Kieo

Hotels:
3. Angkor
4. Paris
5. Khemara
6. Pailin
7. Victory
8. ODA
9. Samaki

Not to Scale

SOUTH OF PHNOM PENH

(Kompong Som) Sihanoukville

Sihanoukville, or Kompong Som as it was previously called, has been rebuilt with Soviet aid and is now an important port. Opened in 1964 by Prince Sihanouk, its glory has somewhat faded and the beach is nothing to write home about.

Local information
● **Accommodation**

B *Bungalow Sokha*, Sokha beach; **B** *Hong Kong Motel*, Sokha beach, a/c, hot water; **B-C** *Seaside*, Ochateal Beach, attractive rooms, satellite TV, hot water and baths, large terrace.

C *Eagles Nest*, Ochateal Beach, c/o PO Box 974, Phnom Penh, T 015 914657, F 015 913864, was formerly named the *Villa Rendezvous* and run by Dominic Chappell and Kellie Wilkinson who were murdered by the Khmer Rouge in 1994, it was the warmest place in town, and Kellie is said to have acted as foster parent and the café as refuge for most of the local street children, Colin Jerram now runs the guesthouse, it has a rooftop bar, rooms with hot water bathrooms attached, satellite TV, Cambodian and Australian dishes incl an excellent cooked breakfast, and access to the beach and sea.

E *Sam's Hostel*, Sokha beach, run by an Englishman, Vic, an ex UN volunteer and Sam, a Cambodian.

● **Places to eat**

♦♦♦*Koh Pos*, Sokha beach, renowned for its deliciously fresh fish and seafood dishes, good Khmer salads with unusual leaves and fresh herbs, charming owner, very popular restaurant, rec; ♦♦*Sam's*, Sokha Beach, on the hill overlooking the beach, excellent fresh fish dishes and salads; *Crocodile Café* on the adjoining beach is run by the owners of *Koh Pos*.

● **Transport**

Local Fishermen will take visitors out to the islands (fee negotiable).

Air Royal Air Cambodge, 2 flights a week (US$75 return).

Train Connections every other day with Phnom Penh, 15 hrs.

Road Shared taxi: connections with Phnom Penh, 2/3 hrs.

The South Coast

There are plans to develop the S coast beaches like Kep. 'Kep-sur-Mer' was a fashionable French colonial resort, founded in 1908, just 90 km W of Kompong Som. The Khmer Rouge razed the resort to the ground in 1975. It was known as La Perle de la Cote d'Agathe and has beautiful offshore islands, including Ile du Pic and Ile Tonsay. In the past Sihanouk had his own private island here – Ile des Ambassadeurs – where he entertained guests. Kep has no town centre as such but the town follows a beautiful bay. The bay lacks the white sands of Sihanoukville.

Kampot is a pretty riverine town, only 5 km from the sea, and is also on the hit list for tourism development.

● **Accommodation** It is possible to stay with locals in Kep and Kampot. **Kep**: there's a hotel behind the hospital (**D**) and a guesthouse on the main road (**D**). **Kampot**: **B** *Phnom Khiew*; **D** *Kamchay*; **D** *Restaurant Hotel*, on riverside, popular with travellers.

● **Entertainment** *Hotel Kamchay* has live bands and dancing in the evening.

● **Transport Road Shared taxi**: from Kompong Som.

Takeo

Takeo is a small, relaxed town even though it is capital of the province of the same name. About 20 km E of Takeo is **Angkor Borei**, a 6th century monument. It was built in laterite by King Rudravarman of Funan (see page 489). His patron deity was Vishnu and many Hindu statues survive from this site. The images are carved from the front and back and have distinctly Indochinese faces (some are in the National Museum of Arts in Phnom Penh, see page 473). **Phnom Bayang**, 40 km from Takeo, is a 6th century monument, now badly damaged. **Transport Road Shared taxi**: regular connections with Phnom Penh.

Elephant Mountains

There are hill resorts in the Elephant Mountains, such as **Bokor** and **Kiriom**, which have been untouched for decades. There are plans to develop them for tourism.

● **Accommodation** *Bokor Mountain Club*, run by the owners of the Foreign Correspondents Club in Phnom Penh.

● **Transport** There's no direct transport from Phnom Penh. The easiest route is to go to Kompong Som and take a shared taxi from there.

INFORMATION FOR VISITORS

CONTENTS

Before travelling

Regulations for tourists and businessmen are in a constant state of flux. The advice given below was checked in 1994, but visitors must be ready for the possibility that new or altered regulations have come into force since then.

Entry requirements

● **Visas**

Visas for stays up to 14 days can be obtained on arrival at Pochentong airport, Phnom Penh. Fill in the application form in the arrival hall and hand over 1 photo, with your passport although *officially* free of charge you pay US$20.

Cambodia has a growing number of embassies abroad, so obtaining a visa abroad is getting easier. Bangkok and Saigon are the best places to obtain visas for independent travel (but leave a week to arrange). Nationals of most countries can join tours but citizens of the US, Israel, South Africa, China and South Korea must all have individual, rather than group visas, which takes longer to process.

Visa extensions can be secured through the Immigration Office, 5 Oknha Men St, takes 1 day. **Foreign Ministry** at the intersection of 240 St and Sisowath Quay, T 24641; **Ministry of Tourism**, 3 Monivong Blvd, T 26107; **Phnom Penh Tourism**, 313 Sisowath Quay, T 23949/25349 or a travel agency in Phnom Penh. Extensions cost US$20 for 1 week, US$40 for a month, US$100 for 6 months. You are fined US$3/day for not renewing your visa.

● **Vaccinations**

No vaccinations required except cholera if coming from an infected area. It is advisable to be vaccinated for typhoid, cholera, tetanus and hepatitis. Take all possible precautions against malaria (see page 526).

● **Representation overseas**

Australia, 5 Canterbury Cr, Deakin-ACT 2600, T 273 1259; **Bulgaria**, Mladost 1, Block Salvador Allende Residenzz, Sofia, T 757135; **China**, Dong Zhi Men Wai Dajio, 100600 Peking, T 5322101; **Cuba**, 7001 Sta Ave Esq, 70 Miramar, Havana, T 336400; **Czech Republic**, Na Habalec 1, 16900 Prague 6, T 352603; **France**, 11 Ave Charles Floquet, 75007, Paris, T 456 64023; **Germany**, Arnold Zweing Str 10, 13189 Berlin, T 711853; **Hungary**, Rath Gyorgyu 48, 1122 Budapest XII, T 155 5165; **India**, B47 Saomi Nagar, New Delhi 110017, T 642 3782; **Indonesia**, Panin Bank Plaza, Jln 52 Palmerrah Utara, Jakarta 11480, T 548 3716; **Japan**, 8.6.9. Akasaka, Minato Ku, Tokyo 107, T 3478 0861; **Laos**, Bane Saphanthong Noua, BP34, Vientiane, T 314951, it is not feasible to apply for a Cambodian visa in Vientiane as it takes more than 2 weeks to arrange, which is longer than the standard Lao visa – of 15 days – allows; **North Korea**, Rue de L'Universitie, Mounsou, Daedongang, Pyongyang, T 817 283; **Russia**, Starpuchenny Per 16, Moscow, T/F 956 6573; **Thailand**, 185 Rajadamri Rd, Bangkok 10500, T 254 6630; **USA**, 4500, 16th St, NW

Washington, DC20011, T (202) 726 7742, F (202) 726 8381; **Vietnam,** 71 Tran Hung Dao St, Hanoi, T 253789 or 41 Phung Khac Khoan St, Saigon, T 292751, it is possible to apply for a visa in Saigon and collect it in Hanoi and vice versa.

Travellers don't need permits to visit areas outside Phnom Penh. However it is wise to check with Ministry of Tourism, the Foreign Ministry or with guesthouses re the security situation before travelling outside Phnom Penh. Two Britons and an Australian were kidnapped at gunpoint in Apr 1994 on the road from Phnom Penh to Sihanoukville. Stretches of roads are often controlled by Khmer Rouge or bandits and travellers have been forced to pay large bribes. Visitors travelling by road, or river, are advised to join a convoy wherever possible. Do not travel at night under any circumstances, and for long distance road trips it is advisable to set off early in the day. The temples at Angkor lie near scenes of recent fighting between the Khmer Rouge and government troops. Up-market tour groups continue to visit Angkor, arriving by plane and touring by private bus but individuals are advised to check the situation. Facilities and transport are limited outside the capital. Travellers recommend taking shared taxis.

Tours

● **In Thailand**
Bangkok: *Diethelm*, Kian Gwan Bldg II, 140/1 Witthayu (Wireless) Rd, T 2559150, F 2560248. *Exotissimo*, 21/17 Sukhumvit Rd, T 2535240. *M K Ways*, 18/4 Saint Louis Soi 3, Sathorn Tai Rd, T 2122532, F 2545583. *Transindo Ltd*, 9th flr, Thasos Bldg, 1675 Chan Rd, T 2873241, F 2873245. This company operates the direct Bangkok-Phnom Penh air link, chartering Bangkok Airways planes daily. Rec. *Siam Wings*, 173/1-3 Surawong Rd, T 2354757, F 2366808. *Tour East*, Rajapark Bldg, 10th Flr, 163 Soi Asoke, T 2593160, F 2583236; *Vista Travel*, 244/4 Khaosan Rd, T 2800348, F 2800348.

   Chiang Mai: *Exotissimo*, 54-6 Tha Phae Rd, T 236237.

   Udon Thani: *Kannika Tour*, 36/9 Srisattha Rd, T 241378; *Thai-Indochina*, 79 Pan Rd, Silom, T 2335369, F 2364389; *Lucky Five*, 52/3 Pan Rd, Silom, T 2670389; *St Louis Travel*, 18/7 Soi St Louis 3, Sathorn Tai Rd, T 2113816, F 212583; *Lam Sam Travel*, 23/1 Sukhumvit Soi 4, Sukhumvit Rd, T 2522340, F 2558859.

● **In Vietnam**
Saigon Tourist, 49 Le Thanh Ton St, T 298914. Expensive short tours to the main sights (see page 260).

● **Outside the region**
UK: *Asia Voyages*, 230 Station Rd, Addlestone, Weybridge, Surrey, T 01932 820050; *Abercrombie and Kent*, Sloane Square House, Holbein Place, London SW1W 8NS, T 0171-730 9600; *Indochina Travel*, 598-608 Chiswick High Rd, London W4 5RT, T 0181 995 8280, F 0181 995 5346, rec; *Regent Holidays*, 15 John St, Bristol, BS1 2HR, T 0117-921-1711, F 0117-925-4866.

● **Tourist information**
Tourist information is virtually non-existent. There are 2 agencies in Phnom Penh: the **Ministry of Tourism** and **Phnom Penh Tourism** (see Phnom Penh section, page 483 for addresses). They both organize tours to Angkor Wat and rent out cars. Ministry of Tourism produce a small, but good brochure.

When to go

● **Best time to visit**
In the winter months, from Nov to Apr, temperatures average 25-32°C. The cool, dry NE monsoon blows during this period, which makes it a pleasant time to visit. The summer months, from May to Oct, are hot, wet and humid; the temperature hovers around 33°C and humidity is usually 90%. However, even in the wet season, it rarely rains heavily before lunch.

● **Clothing**
Women traditionally wear embroidered or patterned cotton sarongs, called *samphots*. Men also wear samphots but, these days, many prefer Western-style outfits. In the years when Pol Pot enforced 'social equality', everyone was forced to wear black. The *krama*, a checked cloth, worn as a turban or shawl is worn by most Khmers. Most kramas are black and white but the Khmer Rouge wear red and white checks. Take cool casual clothes. Cambodians are very modest and it is preferable for women to cover their arms and legs, particularly when visiting wats.

Health

● **Vaccinations**
No innoculations are required except a cholera vaccination if coming from an infected area. It is, however, advisable to take full precautions

before travelling to Cambodia. Tetanus, polio, hepatitis, rabies, typhoid and cholera injections are recommended.

● **Malaria**

Malarial drugs are a vital prerequisite for tourists in Cambodia. Much of the population is afflicted with malaria and there is little medicine available. **NB** A virulent malaria – resistant to all drugs, is present in Cambodia.

● **Food and water**

Avoid all but thoroughly boiled or sterilized water. It is advisable not to use ice. Beware of uncooked vegetables and fruit which cannot be peeled.

● **AIDS**

Prevalent among prostitutes, a survey in the western provinces found 60% of prostitutes HIV-positive, another in Sihanoukville revealed 39% HIV-positive, and an estimated 50% of Phnom Penh's prostitutes are affected. Of a sample of Phnom Penh's blood donors in Jan 1995, nearly 7% were HIV-positive. Locally purchased condoms are not considered to offer adequate or reliable protection.

● **Medical facilities**

Like most social institutions, health services were completely dismantled during the Pol Pot regime: 2 decades on, hospitals are still few and far between, medical facilities are poor and medicines are in short supply. Patients are often expected to buy their own medicines on the black market. Many of the pharmacies sell drugs which are well past their sell-by date or 'hot' pharmaceuticals – stolen from aid agencies. If you need emergency treatment, take the first plane to Bangkok. It is wise to carry a first aid pack.

● **Travelling with children**

Bring all essentials with you; it is not advisable outside Phnom Penh.

● **Further health information**

See main section on health, page 23

Money

● **Currency**

The riel (CR) is the official currency. In mid-1995 the government introduced new paper currency, printed in France, these notes are of larger denomination than the old, which are still in circulation. The new notes are 1,000, 2,000, 5,000, 10,000, 50,000 and 100,000. The old notes (50, 100, 200 and 500 riel) will be replaced by coins. In Jun 1995 US$1 = 2,300

riel. It is advisable to take small denomination US$ notes, which are easier to change; many services/goods can be paid for in dollars, although the government is trying to phase out their use. You should be able to change any major cash currency including Thai baht.

Cambodia operates strict currency controls. Riel cannot be taken out of the country.

● **Travellers cheques**

Are difficult to change – although it is possible at banks and the Diamond Hotel – and commission is high. It is possible to change US$, Sterling, French francs, TCs (American Express, Thomas Cook, Visa, Citicorp). Foreign Trade Bank charges 1%, Thai Farmers Bank 3%.

● **Credit cards**

Visa is now accepted at Banque du Commerce, 24 Norodom Blvd, but the bank charges US$30 for administration. Some of the top hotels also take Visa cards.

● **Black market**

Hard currency is traded openly but the rates are not that much better than the bank.

Getting there

Air

The vast majority of tourists arrive in Cambodia by air. All international flights land at Pochentong Airport, Phnom Penh. Due to the disbanding of the two incumbent Cambodian airlines (CIA and Kampuchea Airlines) in Dec 1994 in favour of a brand new national airline, **Royal Air Cambodge**, flight schedules have constantly changed during 1995. As a result of significant investment by Malaysian Airlines routes on offer have increased; there are connections with Bangkok, Saigon, Vientiane, Hong Kong, Singapore and Kuala Lumpur. There are several travel agents from which tickets can be purchased (Thai Airways, Malaysian Airlines, Vietnam Airlines and Singapore Airlines also work the routes. Subject to revision, there are daily connections with Saigon (US$75 one way), twice weekly connections with Hanoi (US$175 one way), weekly connections with Vientiane (US$322 one way), 4 flights a week with Kuala Lumpur (US$290 return), twice a week with Hong Kong on Dragon Air and Royal Air Cambodge (US$366 one way), 5 flights a week with Singapore on Silk Air (US$386 one way) and multiple daily connections with Bangkok (US$215). **Trans-**

port to town: a taxi from the airport cost US$5.

Road

It is possible to travel the 245 km from Saigon to Phnom Penh on Route 1, via the border crossing at Moc Bai. Buses leave from Saigon (next to the *Rex Hotel*) to Phnom Penh, 7-9 hrs, incl 2-3 hrs at the border. Buses leave from Phnom Penh from Psar Depot Market; non a/c buses leave on Mon, Tues, Wed (US$5) and a/c buses on Thur, Fri, Sat, 12 hrs (US$12). Shared taxis also go to the borders, 6 hrs (8-10,000 riel). There is no problem obtaining a visa for Vietnam in Phnom Penh (although it is more expensive (US$55). The border is only open from 0630 to 1800.

The road between Bangkok and Phnom Penh (via Poipet) is now open with foreign ministry approval. It takes 10 days to get a visa from the Phnom Penh office (US$20). Taxis cost ¢1,500 from Poipet to Phnom Penh. At present it is still not possible for tourists to enter Cambodia from Southern Laos.

Train and boat

The port and railways are not usually open to visitors. It is possible for yachts to harbour at Sihanoukville (Kompong Som) but contact a Cambodian Consulate first. There are plans afoot to open the Bangkok-Phnom Penh line.

Customs

Duty free allowance 200 cigarettes, 1 bottle of spirits and perfume for personal use.

On arrival

● **Airport information**
Phnom Penh's tiny Pochentong International Airport is 12 km from the city. The buildings have recently been redeveloped. The runway is being extended, to cater for the ever increasing number of visitors. Facilities include a good restaurant run by a Canadian-Cambodian couple. The menu includes traditional Khmer dishes, international food, delicious pastries and tropical fruit salads. There is also a helpful tourist information desk (who will make hotel reservations) and a foreign exchange counter.

Transport to town By taxi: (smart new red fleet of taxis operate into town) (US$10). **By motos**: (US$1-2). For pre-arranged tours or those who have hired guides there is a pick-up service.

● **Airport tax**
US$10 for international flights, US$5 for domestic.

● **Conduct**
Wats As in all Buddhist countries in the region, it is important to make sure your arms and legs are covered when visiting wats or religious sites. It is considerate to ask permission before entering the main sanctuaries – and take off your shoes. When sitting down, your feet should point away from the altar and the main image. If talking to a monk, one's head should be lower than his. A small donation is often appropriate.

Form of address Old men are addressed as *ta* (or, less commonly, *bang*) and old women *yeay* (or *bang srey*), but those of your own age can be called by name.

Greeting Cambodians use their traditional greeting – the 'wai', bowing with their hands held together. As a foreigner, shaking hands is perfectly acceptable.

In private homes It is polite to take your shoes off on entering a house and a small present goes down well if you are invited for a meal.

General Displays of anger or exasperation are considered unacceptable and therefore reflect very badly on the individual. Accordingly, even in adversity, Khmers (like the Thais) will keep smiling. Displays of affection are also considered embarrassing. Try not to pat children on the head. To beckon someone, use your hand with the palm facing downwards. Pointing is rude. (Also see page 601.)

● **Hours of business**
Government offices: 0730-1200, 1400-1800 Mon-Sat. **Banks**: 0730-1030, 1400-1600 Mon-Fri, 0730-1030 Sat. Some banks are closed Sat and Sun.

● **Official time**
7 hrs ahead of GMT.

● **Photography**
It is polite to ask permission before taking photographs; some people take offence. Stores in Phnom Penh only stock a few types of film.

It can be difficult to buy colour print and slide film so it is advisable to bring what you need. Some photo stores will also print film, but it's at your own risk.

● **Safety**
Tourists should be very cautious when walking

MINE SAFETY

Very few foreign visitors have been injured, maimed or killed by land mines in Cambodia. Most that have, were members of the UNTAC mission. However, mines do pose an ever-present danger (see the box on page 457) and as tourists venture further off the beaten track so the risks increase proportionately. The following is a short checklist of ways to avoid injury taken from a special supplement in the *Phnom Penh Post* published to coincide with Cambodia's first Mine Awareness day in Feb 1995:

● Ask local people whether mines are a problem in an area before venturing out by inquiring '*mian min teh*?'. It is worth asking the question of more than one local just to make sure.

● Stick to known safe paths.

● Use a guide wherever possible.

● Do not remove the mine warning signs (some tourists, incredibly, have taken to removing signs as souvenirs).

● Do not touch mines.

● If you find yourself in a mine field retrace your steps <u>exactly</u>, stepping into each of your foot marks.

in the countryside: land mines and other un-exploded ordnance is a ubiquitous hazard. **DO NOT TOUCH!** Take a guide in areas that have been heavily bombed or mined and stick to well-used paths, especially around Siem Reap. There are said to be more than 7 million anti-personnel mines buried around the country (see page 457). Tourists are advised not to travel after dark. It is advisable not to walk through Phnom Penh after dark, as many areas have no street lighting and frequent power cuts plunge the city into total darkness. Petty theft is a serious problem in Phnom Penh and other towns. Gangs of disabled people are forced to find a living on the streets, as they get no help from the government, and are well practised in the art of coercion. Shopkeepers are the usual victims, but tourists should be wary. Also see page 525.

On 11 April 1994 three westerners, two Britons and an Australian, were abducted on Route 4 SW of Phnom Penh and murdered by the Khmer Rouge. At the end of Jul, three more foreign tourists, this time a Briton, an Australian and a Frenchman were kidnapped by the Khmer Rouges while travelling by train in the southern province of Kompot and also murdered. Note that travelling off the main routes holds distinct dangers. Telephone your embassy before venturing off the beaten track, for the latest news and advice.

● **Shopping**

Cambodia is known for certain crafts: silver-ware, textiles, worked ivory, wooden sculptures, pottery and basketwork. Many of the hotels in Phnom Penh run small boutiques selling postcards and local handicrafts.

Textiles: The royal Cambodian court supported a vast retinue of weavers and wore sumptuous silk textiles, embellished with gold-patterned yarns in colours corresponding to the days of the week. They also wove beautiful scarves for the royal ballet troupe. *Samphots* (twice the size of a sarong, wrapped around the hips and pulled between the legs to form loose trousers) were traditionally woven in Cambodia. The same simple pictorial designs used on samphots were also woven into large banners for festivals. Banners for funerals have temple designs with a row of elephants underneath. *Matmii* – ikat – is also commonly found in Cambodia. It may have been an ancient import from Java) and is made by tie-dyeing the threads before weaving (see page 364). Matmii is also found in central and southern Laos and in Northeastern Thailand. The Cambodian civil war has levied a heavy toll on traditional crafts, such as weaving. *Kramas* – checked cotton scarves – can be found in local

កុំចាកចេញពីផ្ទះវុសុត្តិភាព

កុំ
ប៉ះពាល់
មីន

Illustration from *Support Ban Mine Campaign* poster

markets but little else is available.

Silverwork: Cambodian craftsmen are well known for their high-quality silver work, exemplified by betelnut boxes and jewellery. Dancers' anklets, decorated with tiny silver bells are popular buys.

Handicrafts: Other crafts include bamboo work, wooden panels with carvings of the Ramayana and temple rubbings. Stone and cement copies of Khmer sculptures are also popular buys. Many precious and semi-precious stones are for sale – although guarantees of authenticity are not so readily available.

● **Tipping**
Tipping is very rare and is only necessary if someone has given particularly good service. However, it is greatly appreciated as salaries are so low. A small present is often a good idea, rather than a tip.

● **Voltage**
220 volts, 60 cycles in Phnom Penh, 110 volts, 50 cycles in some other towns. Power cuts and power surges are commonplace – torches come in useful.

● **Weights and measures**
Metric system along with local systems of measurement.

Where to stay

● **Accommodation**
Many of Cambodia's hotels are run down and many lack basic amenities – don't visit Cambodia if you want luxury. Visitors have little choice of where to stay. In the past hotels were often full of officials and UN personnel, so rooms were difficult to get. That said, the peace agreement has sparked a flurry of hotel development in down-town Phnom Penh, and many new hotels have opened up. With the UN withdrawal, hoteliers are now crying out for custom and consequently rates are now lower. The *Cambodiana* in Phnom Penh and a few others including the *Royal Phnom Penh* are the only international standard hotels, the rest are well below par. Air-conditioned rooms are usually around US$20 upwards and fan-cooled rooms are about

HOTEL CLASSIFICATIONS

A+	US$100-200 **International**: business services (fax, translation, seminar rooms etc), sports facilities (gym, swimming pool etc), Asian and Western restaurants, bars, and discotheques.
A	US$50-100 **First class**: business, sports and recreational facilities, with a range of restaurants and bars.
B	US$25-50 (57,500-115,000 riel) **Tourist class**: most rooms will have a/c and an attached bathroom, swimming pool, restaurants and 24-hr coffee shop/room service. Cable films.
C	US$15-25 (34,500-57,500 riel) **Economy**: no a/c, attached bathrooms. Restaurant and room service. No sports facilities.
D	US$8-15 (18,400-34,500 riel) **Budget**: no a/c, attached bathroom. Bed linen and towels, and there may be a restaurant.
E	US$4-8 (9,200-18,400 riel) **Guesthouse**: fan-cooled rooms, shared bathroom facilities. 'Squat' toilets. Bed linen but no towels. Rooms are small, facilities few.
F	Less than US$4 (9,200 riel) **Guesthouse**: fan-cooled rooms, usually with shared bathroom facilities. Squat toilets. Variable standards of cleanliness.

NB The US$: riel exchange rate has been more volatile during 1995 and the riel equivalents are calculated from the Jun 1995 exchange rate.

US$10 and below. Hotels charge a 10% tax on all bills.

Food and drink

● Food

The Cambodian verb 'to eat', *sii bay*, translates literally as 'eat rice' – and rice is the central ingredient of any meal. Dried, salted fish is the most common accompaniment. Other than fish, Cambodians eat poultry, beef, pork and game. *An sam chruk* is a Cambodian favourite: a fat roll of sticky-rice filled with soybean cake and chopped pork. Local legend has it that *an sam chruk* was invented by the Buddha himself. *Khao phonne*, a noodle dish, is also a popular Cambodian meal.

A typical Cambodian meal consists of a bowl of fried or steamed rice, mixed with bits of fish and seasoned with chillies, mint or garlic. Most of the fish is fresh-water from the Tonlé Sap. Bits of fish are often eaten with *tuk trey*, a spicy sauce with ground peanuts. More elaborate meals include barbecued shrimp, roasted sunflower seeds and such delicacies as *pong tea kon* (duck eggs, which are eaten just before they hatch) and *chong roet* (crunchy cicadas). Soup accompanies most meals and is eaten at the same time as the main dishes.

The UN's presence in Phnom Penh resulted in many new restaurants opening and the selection has improved dramatically in the past few years. The choice of restaurants outside Phnom Penh is limited.

The French gastronomic influence is still in evidence – fresh French bread can be bought daily in Phnom Penh. Western food, as well as Khmer, Chinese and Vietnamese, is available at all the hotels and quite a few restaurants.

RESTAURANT CLASSIFICATIONS

♦♦♦♦ Over US$15 (54,500 riel) for a meal. A 3-course meal in a restaurant with pleasant decor. Beers, wines and spirits available.

♦♦♦ US$5-15 (17,500-54,500 riel) for a meal. Two courses, not including alcohol, reasonable surroundings.

♦♦ US$2-5 (7,000-17,500 riel) for a meal, probably only a single course, surroundings spartan but adequate.

♦ Under US$2 (under 7,000 riel). Single course, often makeshift surroundings such as a steet kiosk with simple benches and tables.

European style breakfasts are only available in the more expensive hotels otherwise you can eat a local breakfast of sliced roast pork, rice and a bowl of clear soup. Seafood is readily obtainable. Outside Phnom Penh, roadside stalls are the most you can expect. There are very few restaurants serving Cambodian food but plenty of stalls do (expect to pay about US$1) or 25 riel.

Food in Cambodia is relatively cheap. Expect to pay between US$2-6/head in most places.

● Drink

Tea is the national drink and is drunk without sugar or milk. Coffee is also available black or 'crème' with tinned milk. Ubiquitous coke is available as well as other soft, fizzy drinks imported soft drinks are available in the larger towns. Soda water with lemon, *soda kroch chhmar*, is a popular drink. Bottled water is widely available. Local and imported beers (the latter at no great mark up) are available. There is a limited selection of spirits in some of the main hotels.

Getting around

● Practicalities

It's best to travel up country by air. Roads are badly maintained and often blocked by bandits. The train network is constantly disrupted and is subject to attack. Check safety areas before leaving Phnom Penh.

Air

Air travel is becoming increasingly popular. Bookings should preferably be made at least 1 week in advance. Flights between Phnom Penh and Siem Reap (the nearest airport for those visiting Angkor) are often fully booked due to block bookings from travel groups. Flights are daily and there are also regular flights to Battambang, Sihanoukrille (Kompong Som), Rattanakiri, Koh Kong and Stung Treng. Schedules change regularly. All services are operated by Royal Air Cambodge. Tickets are available from travel agents and can be a cheaper and much faster way of purchasing a ticket than visiting the Airline. The baggage allowance for domestic flights is 10 kg pp.

From Phnom Penh:

	US$ Return	US$ One Way
Siem Reap	110	55
Battambang	90	45

Koh Kong	100	50
Stung Treng	90	45
Rattanakiri	100	55
Kompong Cham (Sihanoukville)	75	40

ROYAL AIR CAMBODGE TIMETABLE

DESTINATION	DAY
From Phnom Penh to:	
Siem Reap	Daily
Koh Kong	1,6
Battambang	1,3,5,6
Stung Treng	2,7
Rattanakiri	2,4,7
Sihanoukville	1,3,5,6
From Stung Treng to:	
Rattanakiri	2,7
From Siem Reap to:	
Battambang	3,5
From Koh Kong to:	
Sihanoukville	1,6
From Battambang to:	
Siem Reap	1,6
From Sihanoukville to:	
Koh Kong	3,5
From Rattanakiri to:	
Stung Treng	4
To Phnom Penh from:	
Siem Reap	Daily
Koh Kong	3,5
Battambang	1,3,5,6
Stung Treng	4
Rattanakiri	2,4,7
Sihanoukville	1,3,5,6

Timetable effective from 1 July 1995.

Note: 1= Mon; 2 = Tues; 3 = Wed; 4 = Thur; 5 = Fri; 6 = Sat; 7 = Sun.

Train

Cambodia's railway system is poorly developed. There are 2 main lines from Phnom Penh: one goes to the Thai border at Poipet and the other links with the coast at Kompong Som. Much of the rail network was destroyed during the civil war. The irregular services are unreliable and plagued with the problem of unexploded mines. **Travelling by train** The dangers of travelling by train in Cambodia are not difficult to see. In front of the engine are two 'mine clearing' flat bed cars. Those poor, brave or foolish enough to travel here are charged the reduced fare of 1,500 riel (notwithstanding the often quoted rumour, such passengers do not travel free). The cab of the locomotive itself is protected with 1 inch-thick plate steel, and a steel frame is welded onto the engine's buffers to deflect any obstructions on the line. Trains carry a force of 26 soldiers, but rarely are they able to repel attacks. One of the older engine drivers, 56-year-old Em Op, was quoted in the *Phnom Penh Post* recently as having survived no fewer than 12 attacks by Khmer Rouge gangs and marauding, ill-disciplined government forces. One of the most dangerous lines is the Kompot line which runs to Kompong Som or Sihanoukville. On 26 July 1994, 13 Cambodians were killed in a Khmer Rouge attack and three Western tourists taken hostage. The hostages were later found murdered. **NB** Most Western embassies recommend that visitors to Cambodia do not travel by rail.

Road

There is a basic road network, about 2,000 km in total. An extensive programme of road upgrading and maintenance is taking place. For example the Khmer-American Friendship Highway which runs from Phnom Penh to Kompong Som (first built in the 1960s) is now tarmac from start to finish. The Japanese in particular have put considerable resources into road building. However, bridges are often in a more perilous state being susceptible to Khmer Rouge attacks. The main roads are numbered 1-10 (see country map). Times from Phnom Penh to Pursat 3½ hrs; Pursat to Battambang 1½ hrs and Battambang to Sisophon 2½ hrs. From Sisophon to Aranyaprathet on the Thai border is 45 mins on a surfaced road. The road from Sisophon to Siem Reap is in an appalling condition and takes 3 hrs. As yet the road from Phnom Penh to Siem Reap is only surfaced as far as 20 km outside Phnom Penh. Again the Japanese are working on it. The main roads are generally tarmac or laterite.

The rainy season often makes many roads unpassable. There are buses and shared taxis to most parts of the country, although all services are unreliable. Shared taxis cost about 6,000 riel/100 km, and tend to leave early in the morning. Most travellers reckon shared taxi is the best way to get around.

There are often "road blocks" on routes out of Phnom Penh, where armed men oblige travellers to pay small fees of around 200 riel, or cigarettes, before proceeding. In a shared taxi the driver will take care of these additional costs.

Shared taxi fares from Phnom Penh:

Battambang	US$5
Kompong Cham	US$3
Kompong Som	US$3
Siem Reap	US$6
Kratie	US$5

Car hire

There are no taxis in Cambodia but cars can usually be hired from one of the government ministries (US$25-30/day) or from the *Cambodiana Hotel* (US$50/day).

Other local transport

● **Hitchhiking**

There are very few vehicles, so hitching is only on trucks ... but inadvisable at present because of bandits.

● **Cyclo**

It is customary to pay more for a cyclo in the mid-day heat. Cyclo and **moto** (motorcycle taxi) are the main form of transport in Phnom Penh. Cyclos can be hired for around (US$1/hour). Motos for US$5/day.

Boat

Boats are an important means of transport in Cambodia. The Mekong is navigable by small sea-going vessels as far as the capital and then by smaller boats up-river. Boats can be taken to Siem Reap (Angkor), Kratie, Stung Treng, Kompong Cham and Kompong Chhnang.

USEFUL CAMBODIAN (KHMER) WORDS & PHRASES

There are a number of sounds in Khmer, or Cambodian, which have no equivalent in English. The transcription given here is only an approximation of the sound in Khmer and is taken from David Smyth and Tran Kien's (1991) *Courtesy and survival in Cambodian*, School of Oriental & African Studies: London.

Consonants

bp	a sharp 'p', somewhere between 'p' and 'b' in English
dt	a sharp 't', somewhere between 't' and 'd' in English
j	as in 'jump'
g	as in 'get'
ng	as in 'ring'

Vowels

a	as in 'ago'	i		as in 'fin'
ah	as in 'car'	o		as in 'long'
ai	as in 'Thai'	oh		as in 'loan'
ao	as in 'Lao'	oo		as in 'boot'
ay	as in 'pay'	OO		as in 'cook'
ee	as in 'see'	u		as in 'run'
eu	as in 'uugh'			

Useful words and phrases

Yes	*baht* [male speakers]
	jah [female speakers]
No	*(ot) dtay*
Thank you (very much)	*or-gOOn (j'run)*
Hello	*jOOm ree-up soo-a*
Goodbye	*lee-a hai*
Excuse me/Sorry!	*som dto(h)*
Where's the..?	*...ai nah?*
How much is...	*...t'lai bpon-mahn?*
It doesn't matter, never mind, that's all right	*mun ay dtay*
I don't understand	*mun yoo-ul dtay*

There are check points on stretches, eg between Stung Tren and Kratie and foreigners are often expected to cough up dollars.

Boat fares from Phnom Penh:

Kompong Cham	1,000 riel
Kratie	3,000 riel
Siem Reap	10,000 riel

Communications

● **Language**
The national language is Khmer. Unlike other Southeast Asian languages it has no tones. The script is derived from the S Indian alphabet. English is used increasingly and French is widely spoken by the older generation. Outside Phnom Penh language can be a problem for those with no knowledge of Cambodian.

● **Postal services**
International service is slow, but it is reasonably priced and fairly reliable. Letters arrive and leave for Bangkok on Mon and Thur. Post from the UK takes between 5 and 15 days. It is recommended that mail be posted from the main Post Office in Phnom Penh, although there are post boxes everywhere.

International postal charge: 1,800 rielS for 20 kg airmail letter to Europe and the US.

Telegram and telex service and **Internal telephone service**: main Post Office in Phnom Penh.

● **Telephone services**
Local: poor service, but improving with

Travel			
That's expensive	t'lai na(h)		
Will you go for...riel?	...ree-ul bahn dtay?		
Is it far?	ch'ngai dtay?		
Turn left/right	bot dtoh kahng		
	ch'wayng/s'dum		
Go straight on	dtoh dtrong		
Time			
morning	bpreuk	today	t'ngai ni(h)
midday	t'ngai dtrong	tomorrow	sa-aik
night	yOOp	yesterday	m'serl mern
Numbers			
1	moo-ay	20	m'pay
2	bpee	30	sahm seup
3	bay	40	sai seup
4	boo-un	50	hah seup
5	bprum	60	hok seup
6	bprum moo-ay	70	jert seup
7	bprum bpee	80	bpait seup
	or bprum bpeul	90	gao seup
8	bprum bay	100	moo-ay roy
9	bprum boo-un	1,000	moo-ay bpohn
10	dop	10,000	moo-ay meun
11	dop moo-ay	100,000	moo-ay sain
12	dop bpee...etc	1,000,000	moo-ay lee-un
16	dop bprum moo-ay		
Basic vocabulary			
bank	ta-nee-a-gee-a	Khmer Rouge	k-mai gra-horm
day	t'ngai	market	p'sah
delicious	ch'ngun	post office	brai-sa-nee-ya-tahn
doctor	bpairt	toilet	borng-goo-un
food	m'hohp	water	dteuk
hospital	mOOn-dti-bpairt		

Australian help, there are now more than 60 pay phones in the capital; phonecards now on sale from hotels and restaurants – US$2, US$5, US$20, U$50 or US$100. Owing to the delays in having a telephone line connected many businesses use mobile phones – numbers prefixed 015 or 018 are mobile phones.

International: there are links to the rest of the world via Australia – it is sometimes possible to get straight through on this line but it is often a long wait. Most calls must be placed through the operator. It is not possible to place collect calls. A number of hotels (eg *Hotel Cambodiana*), restaurants (eg *Dejavu, Café No Problem, Capitol*) and bars (FCC) now have IDD service for telephone and fax. Overseas calls can also be made from the Post Office on 13 St, Phnom Penh. Both fax and telephone are charged at US$4.80/minute, Mon-Fri and US43.80/minute at the weekend. **NB** Charges for faxes are made, regardless of whether the call is connected or is busy.

Entertainment

● **News**

During the UN operation in 1992/93, a number of new titles appeared on Phnom Penh's streets. The circulation of the old Party newspaper, the *Pacheachun* (which was Cambodia's only daily), shrank drastically in 1991 due to the shortage of newsprint, formerly supplied by the Soviet Union. With the UN there as human rights guardians, a number of newsletters were produced by opposition parties, giving Cambodians their first taste of news from non-government sources in years. For a while, the Cambodian press was relatively free, although sadly this freedom proved short-lived: in Jul 1995 the National Assembly voted 90-4 in favour of legislation which allows the government to lock up its more outspoken critics.

The principal 3 English-language newspapers are the *Phnom Penh Post* (fortnightly), which is regarded as the best of the 3, the *Cambodia Daily*, published 5 times a week, it covers international and national news and the *Cambodiana Times*, the government newspaper, published weekly. Local journalist Khien Kannanarith brought out the *Kampuchea Weekly*. The centre pages of the *Phnom Penh Post* have a good city map. The *Cambodian Times* is published in English every week. *Bangkok Post* available from stalls in Phnom Penh.

● **TV**

Many of the large hotels have satellite TV.

Holidays and festivals

There are some 30 public holidays celebrated each year in Cambodia. Most are celebrated with public parades and special events to commemorate the particular holiday. The largest holidays also see many Khmers loosing off their guns, to the extent that red tracer fills the sky. The habit of firing weapons also extends to nights with a full moon and the onset of the rainy season. It is best to stay indoors at such times, as the concept of what goes up must come down does not seem to be recognized in Cambodia! A full list follows with details of the more important ones.

Jan: *Chinese and Vietnamese New Year* (movable), celebrated by the Chinese and Vietnamese communities (for more details see Vietnam section, page 297); *National Day* (7th: public holiday), celebration of the fall of the Khmer Rouge in 1979; *Anniversary of the last sermon of Buddha* (movable).

Mar: *Women's Day* (8th: public holiday), processions, floats and banners in main towns.

Apr: *Cambodian New Year* (13th), predictions are made for the forthcoming year, the celebration is to show gratitude to the departing demi-god and to welcome the new one, every household erects a small altar in front to welcome a new demi-god; *Independence Day* (17th: public holiday), celebrates the fall of the Lon Nol government (17 April 1975) floats and parades through Phnom Penh; *Chaul Chhnam* (movable), 3-day celebration, which involves an inevitable drenching, to welcome in the new year, a similar festival to *Pimai* in Laos and *Songkran* in Thailand (see page 422); *Visak Bauchea* (movable – full moon), most important Buddhist festival; a triple anniversary commemorating Buddha's birth, enlightenment and his Parenivana (state of final bliss).

May: *Labour Day* (1st: public holiday), no great event; *Genocide Day* (9th: public holiday), to remember the atrocities of the Khmer Rouge in which up to a million Cambodians lost their lives, the main ceremony is held at Choeng Ek.

Jun: *Anniversary of the Founding of the Revolutionary Armed Forces of Kampuchea* (19th), founded in 1951, main parades and celebrations are in Phnom Penh; *Anniversary of the founding of the People's Revolutionary Party of Cambodia* (28th), founded in 1951, again, the main parades and celebrations are in

Phnom Penh.

Jul: *Chol Vassa* – the start of the rainy season retreat – a Buddhist 'lent' – time for meditation.

Sep: *End of Buddhist 'Lent'* (movable), in certain areas it is celebrated with boat races; *Prachum Ben* (movable), in remembrance of the dead, offerings are made to ancestors.

Oct/Nov: *Water Festival, Bon Om Tuk* (movable) or *Festival of the Reversing Current* to celebrate the movement of the waters of the Tonlé Sap (see page 513), boat races in Phnom Penh, the festival dates back to the 12th century when King Jayavarman VII and his navy defeated water-borne invaders, most wats have ceremonial canoes which are rowed by the monks to summon the Naga King. Under the Cambodian monarchy, the king would command the waters to retreat, the festival was only revived in 1990; the festival coincides with *Ok Ambok* (The Pounding of Rice) – which stems from a myth of a female giant who can control the weather and Sampeah Preah Khai, dedicated to a rabbit who took his own life in a fire to feed a dying man, some celebrants look for the rabbit's figure drawn in the moon.

Further reading

Andersen, J & Pronzini, B (1983) *The Cambodia file*, Sphere; Chanda, Nayan (1986) *Brother Enemy: the war after the war*, Macmillan: New York. Exhaustive and engrossing account of 'the third Indochina war'; puts Cambodian conflict into regional perspective; vivid journalistic style. Coedès, George (1975) *Angkor*; Criddle, Joan & Butt Mam, T (1987) *To destroy you is no loss: the odyssey of a Cambodian family*, Doubleday; Elizabeth Becker (1986) *When the war was over*, Simon & Schuster; Chandler, David P (1991) *The Tragedy of Cambodian History: Politics, War and Revolution since 1945*, Yale University Press: New Haven; Chandler, David P (1992) *Brother Number One: A Political Biography of Pol Pot*, Westview Press: Colorado; Fitzsimmons, T (ed) (1959), *Cambodia, its people, its society, its culture*, HRAF Press: New Haven; Haing Ngor: *A Cambodian odyssey*; Jackson, K (ed) *Cambodia 1975-1978: Rendez-vous with Death*, Princetown University Press 1989; MacDonald, M (1958) *Angkor*, Cape: London; May, Someth (1986) *Cambodian witness*, Faber and Faber: London. Chilling personal account of the Pol Pot period; *National Geographic*, Vol 161, No 5, May 1982, pp548-623; Ponchaud, Francois (1978) *Cambodia year zero* (translation from French), Penguin: London; Shawcross, William (1984) *The quality of mercy: Cambodia, holocaust and modern conscience*, Fontana; Shawcross, William (1979; revised 1986) *Sideshow*, Chatto & Windus: London. Very readable investigative work on American involvement in the Cambodian 'sideshow' war; runs through to cover Pol Pot period; Shawcross, William (1994) *Cambodia's new deal*. Shawcross' new book examining the UN-brokered peace deal and progress since the elections. Var Hong Ashe (1975) *From Phnom Penh to paradise*, Hodder & Stoughton: London; Vickery, M (1984) *Cambodia 1975-1982*, George Allen & Unwin; Molyda Szymusiak (1987) *Stones cry out: a Cambodian childhood 1975-1980*, Jonathan Cape: London, *Phnom Penh – Then and Now*, Igont, M: Whitel Otus (1993).

● **Films**

The Killing Fields (based on The Life and Death of Dith Pran by Sydney Schanberg).

Acknowledgements

Duncan Shearer, Phnom Penh; John Stubbs, World Monument Fund, New York; Gill Henson, Vientiane; Hilary Emberton, Slough, UK.

BANGKOK

INTRODUCTION

This section on the Thai capital is included for the benefit of the many visitors to Indochina who need to travel through Bangkok. A full account of the whole of Thailand is given in Trade & Travel's *Thailand & Burma Handbook* in the same series.

CONTENTS

MAPS

BANGKOK HIGHLIGHTS

Temples Bangkok's best known sight is the temple of *Wat Phra Kaeo*, situated within the grounds of the *Grand Palace* (page 547). Other notable temples include *Wat Pho* (page 544), *Wat Arun* (page 559), *Wat Suthat* (page 555) and *Wat Traimitr* (page 558).

Museums Bangkok's extensive *National Museum* houses the best collection in the country (page 551); other notable collections include those in *Jim Thompson's House* (page 566), the *Suan Pakkard Palace* (page 565) and *Vimanmek Palace* (page 563).

Markets The sprawling *Chatuchak Weekend market* (page 568), *Nakhon Kasem* or Thieves' market (page 557), *Pahurat Indian market* (page 557) and Chinatown's *Sampeng Lane* (page 557).

Boat trip On *Bangkok's canals* (page 558).

Excursions Day trips to the former capital and ruins of *Ayutthaya* (page 571), the *Bridge over the River Kwai* outside Kanchanaburi (page 571), the massive *Nakhon Pathom* (page 571), and the *floating market at Damnoen Saduak* (page 570).

Bangkok is not a city to be trifled with: a population of 11 million struggle to make their living in a conurbation with perhaps the worst traffic in the world; a level of pollution which causes some children, so it is said, to lose four intelligence points by the time they are seven; and a climate which can take one's breath away. As journalist Hugo Gurdon wrote at the end of 1992: "One would have to describe Bangkok as unliveable were it not for the fact that more and more people live here". But, Bangkok is not just a perfect case study for academics studying the strains of rapid urban growth. There is charm and fun beneath the grime, and Bangkokians live life with a *joie de vivre* which belies the congestion. There are also numerous sights, including the spectacular Grand Palace, glittering wats (monasteries) and the breezy river, along with excellent food and good shopping.

The official name for Thailand's capital city begins Krungthep – phramaha – nakhonbawon – rathanakosin – mahin-thara – yutthayaa – mahadilok – phiphobnobpharaat – raatchathaanii – buriiromudomsantisuk. It is not hard to see why Thais prefer the shortened version – Krungthep, or the 'City of Angels'. The name used by the rest of the world – Bangkok – is derived from 17th century Western maps, which referred to the city (or town as it then was) as Bancok, the 'village of the wild plum'. This name was only superseded by Krungthep in 1782, and so the Western name has deeper historical roots.

Thonburi

In 1767, Ayutthaya, then the capital of Siam, fell to the marauding Burmese for the second time and it was imperative that the remnants of the court and army find a more defensible site for a new capital. Taksin, the Lord of Tak, chose Thonburi, on the western banks of the Chao Phraya River, far from the Burmese and from Phitsanulok, where a rival to the throne had become ensconsed. In 3 years, Taksin had established a kingdom and crowned himself king. His reign was short-lived, however; the pressure of thwarting the Burmese over three arduous years caused him to go

mad and in 1782 he was forced to abdicate. General Phraya Chakri was recalled from Cambodia and invited to accept the throne. This marked the beginning of the present Chakri Dynasty.

Bangkok: the new capital

In 1782, Chakri (now known as Rama I) moved his capital across the river to Bangkok (an even more defensible site) anticipating trouble from King Bodaw-paya who had seized the throne of Burma. The river that flows between Thonburi and Bangkok and on which many of the luxury hotels – such as *The Oriental* – are now located, began life not as a river at all, but as a canal (or *khlong*). The canal was dug in the 16th century to reduce the distance between Ayutthaya and the sea by shortcutting a number of bends in the river. Since then, the canal has become the main channel of the Chao Phraya River. Its original course has shrunk in size, and is now represented by two khlongs, Bangkok Yai and Bangkok Noi.

This new capital of Siam grew in size and influence. Symbolically, many of the new buildings were constructed using bricks from the palaces and temples of the ruined former capital of Ayutthaya. But population growth was hardly spectacular – it appears that outbreaks of cholera sometimes reduced the population by a fifth or more in a matter of a few weeks. An almanac from 1820 records that "on the 7th month of the waxing moon, a little past 2100 in the evening, a shining light was seen in the N-W and multitudes of people purged, vomited and died". In 1900 Bangkok had a population of approximately 200,000. By 1950 it had surpassed 1 million, and in 1992 it was, officially, 5,562,141. Most people believe that the official figure considerably understates the true population of the city – 11 million would be more realistic. By 2010, analysts believe Bangkok will have a population of 20 million. As the popu-

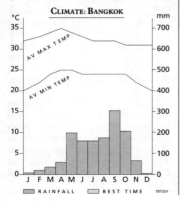

CLIMATE: BANGKOK

°C / mm

AV MAX TEMP

AV MIN TEMP

J F M A M J J A S O N D

RAINFALL   BEST TIME   TBTG01

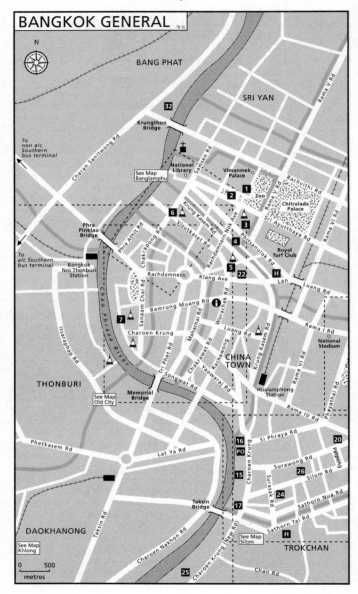

BANGKOK GENERAL

TB SL

N

BANG PHAT

SRI YAN

Rama V Rd

Krungthon Bridge

32

To non a/c Southern bus terminal

Charan Sanitwong Rd

National Library

See Map Banglamphu

Vimanmek Palace

Samsen Rd

Zoo

1

2

Rachvithi Rd

Rama V Rd

Chitralada Palace

Sri Ayutthaya Rd

Rama VI Rd

Rama VI Rd

6

Krung Kasem Rd

3

Phitsanulok Rd

Royal Turf Club

Visutkaset Rd

Rachdamnern Nok Ave

4

Phra Pinklao Bridge

To a/c Southern bus terminal

Bangkok Noi Thonburi Station

Phra Athit Rd

Chakrapong Rd

Rachdamnern

5

22

H

Lan

Luang Rd

Sanaam Chai Rd

Klang Ave

Bamrung Muang Rd

Worachak Rd

Luang Rd

Rama I Rd

National Stadium

Itsaraphap Rd

Chao Phraya River

7

Charoen Krung

Mahachai Rd

Chakrawat Rd

Rachawong

Krung Kasem Rd

CHINA TOWN

Rama VI Rd

Phayathai Rd

THONBURI

Tri Phet Rd

Songwat Rd

Yaowaraj Rd

Memorial Bridge

Hualamphong Station

Rama IV Rd

Phetkasem Rd

Lat Ya Rd

16

PO

15

Charoen Krung

Si Phraya Rd

Surawong Rd

26

Silom Rd

20

Sala Daeng

24

Surasak Rd

Taksin Rd

DAOKHANONG

See Map Khlong

0   500
metres

Taksin Bridge

17

Charoen Nakhon Rd

Charoen Krung (New Rd)

25

See Map Silom

Sathorn Nua Rd

Sathorn Tai Rd

H

TROKCHAN

Chan Rd

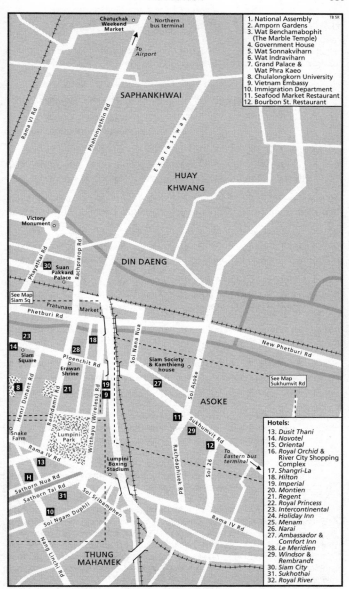

1. National Assembly
2. Amporn Gardens
3. Wat Benchamabophit (The Marble Temple)
4. Government House
5. Wat Sonnakviharn
6. Wat Indraviharn
7. Grand Palace & Wat Phra Kaeo
8. Chulalongkorn University
9. Vietnam Embassy
10. Immigration Department
11. Seafood Market Restaurant
12. Bourbon St. Restaurant

TB 5R

Hotels:
13. *Dusit Thani*
14. *Novotel*
15. *Oriental*
16. *Royal Orchid & River City Shopping Complex*
17. *Shangri-La*
18. *Hilton*
19. *Imperial*
20. *Montien*
21. *Regent*
22. *Royal Princess*
23. *Intercontinental*
24. *Holiday Inn*
25. *Menam*
26. *Narai*
27. *Ambassador & Comfort Inn*
28. *Le Meridien*
29. *Windsor & Rembrandt*
30. *Siam City*
31. *Sukhothai*
32. *Royal River*

lation of the city has expanded, so has the area that it encompasses: in 1900 it covered a mere 13.3 sq km; in 1958, 96.4 sq km; while today the Bangkok Metropolitan region extends over 1,600 sq km and the outskirts of the city sprawl into neighbouring provinces. Such is the physical size of the capital that analysts talk of Bangkok as an EMR or Extended Metropolitan Region.

Bangkok dominates Thailand

In terms of size, Bangkok is at least 23 times larger than the country's second city, Chiang Mai – 40 times bigger, using the unofficial population estimates. It also dominates Thailand in cultural, political and economic terms. All Thai civil servants have the ambition of serving in Bangkok, while many regard a posting to the poor NE as (almost) the kiss of death. Most of the country's industry is located in and around the city (the area contributes 45% of national GDP), and Bangkok supports a far wider array of services than other towns in the country. Although the city contains only 10% of the kingdom's population, its colleges of higher education graduate 71% of degree students, it contains 83% of pharmacists, and has 69% of Thailand's telephone lines. It is because of Bang-

kok's dominance that people often, and inaccurately, say 'Bangkok is Thailand'.

Bangkok began life as a city of floating houses; in 1864 the French explorer Henri Mouhot wrote that "Bangkok is the Venice of the East [in the process making Bangkok one of several Asian cities to be landed with this sobriquet] and whether bent on business or pleasure you must go by water". In 1861, foreign consuls in Bangkok petitioned Rama IV and complained of ill-health due to their inability to go out riding in carriages or on horseback. The king complied with their request for roads and the first road was constructed running S in the 1860s – Charoen Krung (New Rd). This did not initially alter Bangkok's watery character, for bridges to span the many canals were in limited supply. In addition, Charoen Krung was frequently under water during the monsoons. It was not until the late 19th century that King Chulalongkorn (Rama V) began to invest large sums of money in bridge and road building; notably, Rachdamnern Ave ('the royal way for walking') and the Makawan Rungsun Bridge, which both link the Grand Palace with the new palace area of Dusit. This avenue was used at the end of the century for cycling (a royal craze at the

---

RACING IN THE STREETS

In Bangkok, bored young men gain short-lived fame and money by racing through the darkened streets of the capital on motorcycles late at night on weekends. Gang members put their reputations on the line, and their lives, as they power down the wide and almost empty roads at over 160 kph. Large sums of money are gambled on the riders while 'rescue squads' wait to pick up the corpses that each night's racing produces. In Thai this dance with death is known as *sing* – from the English 'racing'. As journalist Gordon Fairclough explains: "Riders see themselves as members of an exclusive brotherhood, bound together by their willingness to risk death and dismemberment in the pursuit of thrills, notoriety and money". Although money is important, few of the riders are poor. Some even come from wealthy families. Critics of Thailand's climb into NIC-dom claim that the racing is a side-effect of the breakdown of traditional family life in the face of modernisation. The racers themselves tend not to engage in amateur sociology. They explain "It's fun. It's a high. We like the speed, and its better than taking drugs".

time) and later for automobile processions which were announced in the newspapers.

In the rush to modernize, Bangkok may have buried its roots and in so doing, lost its charm. But beneath the patina of modern city life, Bangkok remains very much a Thai city, and has preserved a surprising amount of its past. Most obviously, a profusion of monasteries (wats) and palaces remain. In addition, not all the khlongs have been filled in, and by taking a long-tailed boat through Thonburi (see page 558) it is possible to gain an idea of what life must have been like in the 'Venice of the East'.

Flooding

Bangkok is built on unstable land, much of it below sea-level, and floods used to regularly afflict the capital. The most serious was in 1983 when 450 sq km of the city was submerged. Each year the Bangkok Metropolitan Authority announced a new flood prevention plan, and each year the city flooded. The former populist Bangkok Governor, Chamlong Srimuang (see box), was perhaps the first politician seriously to address the problem of flooding. His blindingly obvious approach was to clear the many culverts of refuse, and some people believe that at last serious flooding is a thing of the past. This may be over-optimistic: like Venice, Bangkok is sinking by over 10 cm a year in some areas and it may be that the authorities are only delaying the inevitable.

First impressions

The immediate impression of the city to a first-time visitor is bedlam. The heat, noise, traffic, pollution – the general chaos – can be overwhelming. This was obviously the impression of Somerset Maugham, following his visit in 1930:

'I do not know why the insipid Eastern food sickened me. The heat of Bangkok was overwhelming. The wats oppressed me by their garish magnificence, making my head ache, and their fantastic ornaments filled me with malaise. All I saw looked too bright, the crowds in the street tired me, and the incessant din jangled my nerves. I felt very unwell...'

It is estimated that over 1 million Bangkokians live in slum or squatter communities, while average traffic speeds can be less than 10 km/hour. During peak periods the traffic congestion is such that 'gridlock' seems inevitable. The figures are sometimes hard to believe: US$500mn of petrol is consumed each year while cars wait at traffic lights; one day in Jul 1992 it took 11 hrs for some motorists to get home after a monsoon storm; and the number of cars on the capital's streets increases by 800 each day; while traffic speeds are snail pace – and expected to fall further. (In 1995 the singer Janet Jackson purposely avoided scheduling her concerts on Fri explaining, "With the traffic, who could make it on Fri?") For those in Bangkok who are concerned about their city and the environment, the worst aspect is that things will undoubtedly get worse before they get any better – despite the plethora of road building programmes the car and truck population is growing faster than the roads to accommodate them. The government of former Prime Minister Anand did give the go-ahead to a number of important infrastructural projects, but many would say a decade too late. As one analyst has observed: "Bangkok is only just beginning to happen". Even editorial writers at the *Bangkok Post* who, one might imagine, are used to the traffic find it a constant topic for comment. At the end of 1993 the newspaper stated: "Bangkok's traffic congestion and pollution are just about the worst in the world – ever. Never in history have people had to live in the conditions we endure each day".

Solutions to Bangkok's **traffic problem** have been suggested, devised, contracts drawn-up, shelved, cancelled and then revived since the early 1980s. The process of finding a solution is almost as

THE MOTHER OF ALL TRAFFIC JAMS

Bangkok's reputation for traffic congestion was already well-founded when, as the *Bangkok Post* put it, the Songkran exodus of 11-12 April 1995 created the 'mother of all traffic jams'. On Tues night, the capital saw the traditional mass movement of people to the provinces to celebrate Songkran. By late Wed afternoon, traffic on major routes was still heavily congested. One man telephoned a radio station to say that he had left his home in Bangkok at 2100 on Tues night and at 1100 on Wed had only made it to the Rangsit junction – barely out of the capital. One highway policeman remarked, perhaps with a touch of pride: "This is the first time in the 20-year history of the Vibhavadi Rangsit Highway that we have had traffic congestion for as long as 20 hours."

slow as the traffic itself. In addition to the failure to approach transport planning in a coordinated way, Bangkok has a number of characteristics which make it a special case. To begin with, Thailand was a city of canals; these have now been built over, but it means that the capital has a lower area of roads relative to its land area than any other capital – some 9% to New York's 24% and London's 22%. In addition, Bangkok is really Thailand's only city, making economic activity highly over-centralized. But there is more to it than just a series of historical accidents. Administration of roads is divided between numerous different agencies making coordination impossible. "It's like driving a bus with 16 hands on the wheel" one official is quoted as saying. The corruption that has accompanied many of the more grandiose projects, and the competition between various schemes – aerial railways, undergrounds, tollways, freeways – has meant that none got off the ground until recently. Even when one project was finished – the 20 km-long, US$800mn Bangkok Expressway which was completed in Mar 1993 – it didn't open to traffic until Sep that year. The government, under pressure from the public, tried to get the consortium to lower the agreed toll of ฿30. They refused, saying it would make the venture commercially unviable, so the city authorities gained a court order and opened the road themselves where upon

it promptly became snarled with traffic. Such actions on the part of the government threaten to scare away potential investors who require cast iron agreements if they are to undertake such BOT (Build, Operate, Transfer) projects. For more wealthy commuters, the solution to the traffic problem is to transform their cars into mobile offices, to leave home at un-godly hours and, in some cases, to move elsewhere – like Chiang Mai (which, partly as a result, is experiencing its own traffic problems). Taxi drivers have taken to 'chicken footing' – skipping through hotel car parks to short-cut intersections. Traffic optimists say that because the gridlock over which of the various competing projects will be approved has come to an end this will, in time, ease the gridlock on the roads. Certainly, frantic construction is underway on the elevated railway. But the need to dig up large sections of existing roads to put in the concrete supports for the railway is making things worse before they can get better.

With the traffic comes pollution. Traffic police stationed at busy intersections have 'respite booths' with oxygen tanks, wear face masks to protect them from the fumes, and are entitled to regular health checks. Even so, directing traffic can, apparently, drive you mad. At the end of 1993, Lance Cpl Suradej Chumnet blew a fuse and switched all the traffic lights to green at one of Bangkok's busiest intersections. He then danced a jig amidst the chaos. A recent study found that 34% of police officers suffered from loss of hearing, and 23% had lung disease. Sitting in an open-sided *tuk-tuk* at traffic lights can seriously damage your health – or it seems as much with the fumes swirling around. It is for this reason that the *tuk-tuk* as a mode of transport in the capital is rapidly losing out to the air-conditioned taxi. There is no sewerage system and most water gets pumped straight into the *khlongs* (canals) and waterways where it poses a health hazard before emptying into the Chao Phraya River which, in its lower stretches, is biologically dead.

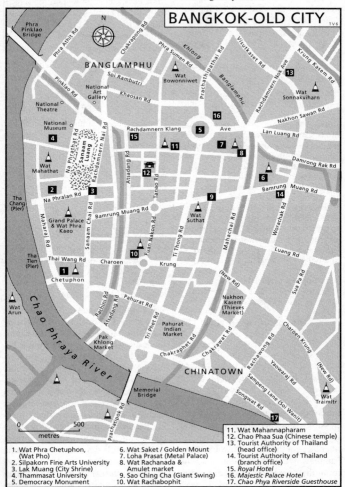

BANGKOK-OLD CITY

1. Wat Phra Chetuphon, (Wat Pho)
2. Silpakorn Fine Arts University
3. Lak Muang (City Shrine)
4. Thammasat University
5. Democracy Monument
6. Wat Saket / Golden Mount
7. Loha Prasat (Metal Palace)
8. Wat Rachanada & Amulet market
9. Sao Ching Cha (Giant Swing)
10. Wat Rachabophit
11. Wat Mahannapharam
12. Chao Phaa Sua (Chinese temple)
13. Tourist Authority of Thailand (head office)
14. Tourist Authority of Thailand (branch office)
15. *Royal Hotel*
16. *Majestic Palace Hotel*
17. *Chao Phya Riverside Guesthouse*

Despite the traffic conditions and pollution, Bangkok has a wealth of sights (even the traffic might be classified as a 'sight'): wats and palaces, markets and shopping, traditional dancing and Thai boxing, glorious food, *tuk-tuks* and water taxis. Ultimately, Bangkok and Bangkokians should win the affections of even the most demanding foreigner – although you may not be there long enough to get past the frustration phase. In Major Erik Seindenfaden's *Guide to Bangkok* published in 1928, the opening few sentences could be describing the city today:

'No other city in Southeastern Asia compares with Bangkok in the gripping and growing interest which leaves a permanent and fragrant impression on the mind of the visitor. It is difficult to set down in words, precisely whence comes the elusive fascination of Bangkok. With a wealth of imposing temples, beautiful palaces, other characteristic buildings and monuments, Bangkok offers a vista of fascinating views... In no other city is it possible to so often turn from the throng of the city street and find oneself, miraculously it would seem, in a little residential quarter... Even the most bitter misanthrope cannot but feel that in the very atmosphere of Bangkok, woven into all the stir and briskness of its daily life, is an impelling and pleasurable sense of more than mere contentment – of rare serenity and happiness everywhere.'

Places of interest

This section is divided into five main areas: the Old City, around the Grand Palace; the Golden Mount, to the E of the Old City; Chinatown, which lies to the S of the Golden Mount; the Dusit area, which is to the N and contains the present day parliament buildings and the King's residence; and Wat Arun and the khlongs, which are to the W, on the other bank of the Chao Phraya River in Thonburi. Other miscellaneous sights, not in these areas, are at the end of the section, under Other places of interest.

Getting around the sights

Buses, both a/c and non-a/c, travel to all city sights (see Local transport, page 594). A taxi or tuk-tuk for a centre of town trip should cost ฿50-100. Now that taxis are almost all metered visitors may find it easier, and more comfortable (they have a/c) – not to mention safer – than the venerable tuk-tuk, although a ride on one of these three-wheeled machines is a tourist experience in itself. If travelling by bus, a bus map of the city – and there are several, available from most bookshops and hotel gift shops – is an invaluable aid. The express river taxi is a far more pleasant way to get around town and is also often quicker than going by road (see map page 561 for piers, and box page 560).

The Old City

The Old City contains the largest concentration of sights in Bangkok, and for visitors with only one day in the capital, this is the area to concentrate on. It is possible to walk around all the sights mentioned below quite easily in a single day. For the energetic, it would also be possible to visit the sights in and around the Golden Mount. If intending to walk around all the sights in the old city start from Wat Pho; if you have less time or less energy, begin with the Grand Palace.

Wat Phra Chetuphon

(Temple of the Reclining Buddha) or **Wat Pho**, as it is known to Westerners (a contraction of its original name Wat Potaram), has its entrance on Chetuphon Rd on the S side of the complex. It is 200 years old and the largest wat in Bangkok, now most famous for its 46m long, 15m high gold-plated reclining Buddha, with beautiful mother-of-pearl soles (showing the 108 auspicious signs). The reclining Buddha is contained in a large viharn built during the reign of Rama III (1832).

The grounds of the wat contain more than 1,000 bronze images, rescued from the ruins of Ayutthaya and Sukhothai by Rama I's brother. The bot, or ubosoth, houses a bronze Ayutthayan Buddha in an attitude of meditation and the pedestal of this image contains the ashes of Rama I. Also notable is the 11-piece altar table set in front of the Buddha, and the magnificent mother-of-pearl inlaid doors which are possibly the best examples of this art from the Bangkok Period (depicting episodes from the Ramakien). The bot is enclosed by two galleries which house 394 seated bronze Buddha images. They were brought from the N during Rama I's reign and are of assorted periods and styles. Around the exterior base of the bot are marble reliefs telling the story of the Ramakien as adapted in the Thai poem the *Maxims of King Ruang* (formerly these reliefs were much copied by making rubbings onto rice paper). The 152 panels are the finest of their type in Bangkok. They recount only the second section of the Ramakien: the abduction and recovery of Ram's wife Seeda. The rather – to Western eyes – unsatisfactory conclusion to the story as told here has led some art historians to argue they were originally taken from Ayutthaya. Thai scholars argue otherwise.

A particular feature of the wat are the 95 chedis of various sizes which are scattered across the 20-acre complex. To the left of the bot are four large chedis, memorials to the first four Bangkok kings. The library nearby is richly decorated with broken pieces of porcelain. The large top-hatted stone figures, the stone animals and the Chinese pagodas scattered throughout the compound came to Bangkok as ballast on the royal rice boats returning from China. Rama III, whose rice barges dominated the trade, is said to have had a particular penchant for these figures, as well as for other works of Chinese art. The Chinese merchants who served the King – and who are said to have called him *Chao Sua* or millionaire – loaded the empty barges

WAT PHRA CHETUPHON (WAT PHO) ZT V6a

1 Sala kan parian or study hall
2 Viharn of the reclining Buddha
3 Enclosure of the royal chedis
4 Ubosoth (bot) or ordination hall
5 Cloister or phra rabieng

Source: adapted from a drawing by Kittisak Nualvilai based on aerial photographs and reproduced in Beek, Steve van and Tettoni, L. (1991) *The arts of Thailand*, Thames & Hudson: London

with the carvings to please their lord. Rama III wanted Wat Pho to become known as a place of learning, a kind of exhibition of all the knowledge of the time and it is regarded as Thailand's first university. Admission ¢10. Open 0800-1700 Mon-Sun. **NB** From Tha Tien pier at the end of Thai Wang Rd, close to Wat Pho, it is possible to get boats to Wat Arun (see page 558). Wat Pho is also probably Bangkok's most respected cen-tre of traditional Thai massage (see page 588), and politicians, businessmen and military officers go there to seek relief from the tensions of modern life. Most medical texts were destroyed when the Burmese sacked the former capital, Ayutthaya, in 1776 and in 1832 Rama III had what was known about Thai massage inscribed on stone and then had those stones set into the walls of Wat Pho to guide and teach. For Westerners wish-

THE THAI RAMAYANA: THE RAMAKIEN

The *Ramakien* – literally "The Story of Rama" – is an adaptation of the Indian Hindu classic, the Ramayana, which was written by the poet Valmiki about 2,000 years ago. This 48,000 line epic odyssey – often likened to the works of Homer – was introduced into mainland Southeast Asia in the early centuries of the first millennium. The heroes were simply transposed into a mythical, ancient, Southeast Asian landscape.

In Thailand, the Ramakien quickly became highly influential, as indicated by the name of the former capital of Siam, Ayutthaya. This is taken from the legendary hero's city of Ayodhia. Unfortunately, these early Thai translations of the Ramayana were destroyed following the sacking of Ayutthaya by the Burmese in 1767. The earliest extant version was written by King Taksin in about 1775, although Rama I's rather later rendering is usually regarded as the classic interpretation.

In many respects, King Chakri's version closely follows that of the original Indian story. It tells of the life of Ram (Rama), the King of Ayodhia. In the first part of the story, Ram renounces his throne following a long and convoluted court intrigue, and flees into exile. With his wife Seeda (Sita) and trusted companion Hanuman (the monkey god), they undertake a long and arduous journey. In the second part, his wife Seeda is abducted by the evil king Ravana, forcing Ram to wage battle against the demons of Langka Island (Sri Lanka). He defeats the

Hanuman
Adapted from Hallet, Holt (1890) *A thousand miles on an elephant in the Shan States*, William Blackwood; Edinburgh.

demons with the help of Hanuman and his monkey army, and recovers his wife. In the third and final part of the story – and here it diverges sharply from the Indian original – Seeda and Ram are reunited and reconciled with the help of the gods (in the Indian version there is no such reconciliation). Another difference to the Indian version is the significant role played by the Thai Hanuman – here an amorous adventurer who dominates much of the third part of the epic.

There are also numerous sub-plots which are original to the Ramakien, many building upon events in Thai history and local myth and folklore. In tone and issues of morality, the Thai version is less puritanical than the Indian original. There are also, of course, difference in dress, ecology, location and custom.

ing to learn the art, special 30-hrs courses can be taken for ฿3,000, stretching over either 15 days (2 hrs/day) or 10 days (3 hrs/day). The centre is located at the back of the Wat, on the opposite side from the entrance. A massage costs ฿100 for 30 mins, ฿180 for 1 hour. With herbal treatment, the fee is ฿260 for 1.30 hr. For other centres of Thai Traditional massage see page 594.

Grand Palace and Wat Phra Kaeo

About 10-15 mins walk from Wat Pho northwards along Sanaam Chai Rd is the entrance to the **Grand Palace** and **Wat Phra Kaeo**. (**NB** The main entrance is the Viseschaisri Gate on Na Phralan Rd.) The Grand Palace is situated on the banks of the Chao Phraya River and is the most spectacular – some might say 'gaudy' – collection of buildings in Bangkok. The complex covers an area of over 1.5 sq km and the architectural plan is almost identical to that of the Royal Palace in the former capital of Ayutthaya. It was started in 1782 and was subsequently added to. Initially, the palace was the city, the seat of power, surrounded by high walls and built to be self-sufficient.

The buildings of greatest interest are clustered around **Wat Phra Kaeo**, or the 'Temple of the Emerald Buddha'. On entering the compound, the impression is one of glittering brilliance, as the outside is covered by a mosaic of coloured glass. The buildings were last restored for Bangkok's bicentenary in 1982 (the Wat Phra Kaeo Museum shows the methods used in the restoration process). Wat Phra Kaeo was built by Rama I in imitation of the royal chapel in Ayutthaya and was the first of the buildings within the Grand Palace complex to be constructed. While it was being erected the king lived in a small wooden building in one corner of the palace compound.

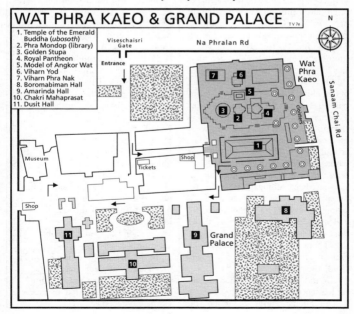

WAT PHRA KAEO & GRAND PALACE TV 7e N

1. Temple of the Emerald Buddha (*ubosoth*)
2. Phra Mondop (library)
3. Golden Stupa
4. Royal Pantheon
5. Model of Angkor Wat
6. Viharn Yod
7. Viharn Phra Nak
8. Boromabiman Hall
9. Amarinda Hall
10. Chakri Mahaprasat
11. Dusit Hall

Viseschaisri Gate
Na Phralan Rd
Entrance
Wat Phra Kaeo
Sanaam Chai Rd
Cloisters
Museum
Shop
Tickets
Shop
Grand Palace

THE EMERALD BUDDHA

Wat Phra Kaeo was specifically built to house the Emerald Buddha, the most venerated Buddha image in Thailand, carved from green jade (the emerald in the name referring only to its colour), a mere 75 cm high, and seated in an attitude of meditation. It is believed to have been found in 1434 in Chiang Rai, and stylistically belongs to the Late Chiang Saen or Chiang Mai schools. Since then, it has been moved on a number of occasions – to Lampang, Chiang Mai and Laos (both Luang Prabang and Vientiane). It stayed in Vientiane for 214 years before being recaptured by the Thai army in 1778 and placed in Wat Phra Kaeo on 22nd March, 1784. The image wears seasonal costumes of gold and jewellery; one each for the hot, cool and the rainy seasons. The changing ceremony occurs 3 times a year in the presence of the King.

Buddha images are often thought to have personalities. The Phra Kaeo is no exception. It is said, for example, that such is the antipathy between the Phra Bang in Luang Prabang (Laos) and Phra Kaeo that they can never reside in the same town.

The **ubosoth** is raised on a marble platform with a frieze of gilded figures of garudas holding nagas running round the base. Bronze singhas act as door guardians. The door panels are of inlaid mother-of-pearl and date from Rama I's reign (late 18th century). Flanking the door posts are Chinese door guardians riding on lions. Inside the temple, the Emerald Buddha (see box) sits high up, illuminated above a large golden altar. In addition, there are many other gilded Buddha images, mostly in the attitude of dispelling fear, and a series of mural paintings depicting the jataka stories. Those facing the Emerald Buddha show the enlightenment of the Buddha when he subdues the evil demon Mara. Mara is underneath, wringing out his hair, while on either side, the Buddha is surrounded by evil spirits. Those on one side have been subjugated; those on the other have not. The water from the wringing out of Mara's hair drowns the evil army, and the Buddha is shown 'touching ground' calling the earth goddess Thoranee up to witness his enlightenment. No photography is allowed inside the ubosoth.

Around the walls of the shaded cloister that encompasses Wat Phra Kaeo, is a continuous mural depicting the Ramakien – the Thai version of the Indian Ramayana. There are 178 sections in all, which were first painted during the reign of King Rama I but have since been restored on a number of occasions.

To the N of the ubosoth on a raised platform, are the **Royal Pantheon**, the **Phra Mondop** (the library), two gilt stupas, a model of Angkor Wat and the **Golden Stupa**. At the entrance to the Royal Pantheon are gilded kinarees. The Royal Pantheon is only open to the public once a year on Chakri Day, 6 Apr (the anniversary of the founding of the present Royal Dynasty). On the same terrace there are two gilt stupas built by King Rama I in commemoration of his parents. The Mondop was also built by Rama I to house the first revised Buddhist scriptural canon. To the W of the mondop is the large Golden Stupa or chedi, with its circular base, in Ceylonese style. To the N of the mondop is a model of Angkor Wat constructed during the reign of King Mongkut (1851-1868) when Cambodia was under Thai suzerainty.

To the N again from the Royal Pantheon is the **Supplementary Library** and two viharns – **Viharn Yod** and **Phra Nak**. The former is encrusted in pieces of Chinese porcelain.

To the S of Wat Phra Kaeo are the buildings of the **Grand Palace**. These are interesting for the contrast that they make with those of Wat Phra Kaeo. Walk out through the cloisters. On your left can be seen **Boromabiman Hall**, which is French in style and was completed during the reign of Rama VI. His three successors lived here at one time or another. The **Amarinda Hall** has an impressive airy interior, with chunky pillars and gilded thrones. The **Chakri Mahaprasart** (the Palace Reception Hall) stands in front of a carefully manicured garden with topiary. It was built and lived in by Rama V shortly after he had returned from a trip to Java and Singapore in 1876, and it shows: the building is a rather unhappy amalgam of colonial and traditional Thai styles of architecture. Initially the intention was to top the structure with a Western dome, but the architects settled for a Thai-style roof. The building was completed in time for Bangkok's first centenary in 1882. King Chulalongkorn (Rama V) found the overcrowded Grand Palace oppressive and after a visit to Europe in 1897, built himself a new home at Vimanmek (see page 563) in the area to the N, known as Dusit. The present King Bhumibol lives in the Chitralada Palace, built by Rama VI, also in the Dusit area. The Grand Palace is now only used for state occasions. Next to the Chakri Mahaprasart is the raised Dusit Hall; a cool, airy building containing mother-of-pearl thrones. Near the Dusit Hall is a museum, which has information on the restoration of the Grand Palace, models of the Palace and many Buddha statues. There is a collection of old cannon, mainly supplied by London gun foundries. Close by is a small café selling refreshing coconut drinks. All labels in Thai, but there are free guided tours in English throughout the day. Admission ฿100.

ADMISSION to the Grand Palace complex ฿125, ticket office open 0830-1130, 1300-1530 Mon-Sun except Buddhist holidays when Wat Phra Kaeo is free but the rest of the palace is closed. The cost of the admission includes a free guidebook to the palace (with plan) as well as a ticket to the *Coin Pavilion*, with its collection of medals and 'honours' presented to members of the Royal Family and to the Vimanmek Palace in the Dusit area (see page 563). **NB** Decorum of dress is required (trousers can be hired for ฿10 near the entrance to the Grand Palace) which means no shorts, and no singlets or sleeveless shirts.

Immediately opposite the entrance to the Grand Palace is **Silpakorn Fine Arts University**. It contains an exhibition hall. Open 0900-1900 Mon-Sun (see boards outside entrance for shows). Turn left outside the Grand Palace and a 5-mins walk leads to **Tha Chang pier and market**. The market sells fruit and food, cold drinks etc. There is also a small amulet (lucky charm) and second-hand section. From Tha Chang pier it is possible to get a boat to Wat Arun for about ฿150 return, or a water taxi (see page 559). To the N of the Grand Palace, across Na Phralan Rd, lies the large open space of the Pramane Ground (the Royal Cremation Ground) better known as **Sanaam Luang**. This area was originally used for the cremation of kings, queens and important princes. Later, foreigners began to use it as a race track and as a golf course. Today, Sanaam Luang is used for the annual **Royal Ploughing Ceremony**, held in May. This ancient Brahmanistic ritual, resurrected by Rama IV, signals the auspicious day on which farmers can begin to prepare their riceland, the time and date of the ceremony being set by Royal Astrologers. Bulls decorated with flowers pull a red and gold plough, while the selection of different lengths of cloth by the Ploughing Lord predicts whether the rains will be good or bad. Sanaam Luang is also used by the Thai public simply to stroll around – a popular pastime, particularly at weekends. **Kite-fighting** can be seen in the late afternoons between late-Feb and mid-Apr (the Kite Festival season). On Sun, salesmen and women sell kites for ฿15-20 on Sanaam Luang.

In the SE corner of Sanaam Luang opposite the Grand Palace is Bangkok's **Lak Muang**, housing the City Pillar and horoscope, originally placed there by Rama I in 1782. The original shrine deteriorated due to lack of maintainance and Rama VI erected a new pillar, with the horoscope of the city inscribed in gold. It is protected by an elaborate pavilion with intricate gold-inlay doors, and is set below ground level. The shrine is believed to grant people's wishes, so it is a hive of activity all day. In a small pavilion to the left of the main entrance, Thai dancers are hired by supplicants to dance for the pleasure of the resident spirits – while providing a free spectacle for everyone else. Open 24 hrs Mon-Sun. **NB** There is no entrance charge to the Lak Muang compound; touts sometimes insist there is. Donations can be placed in the boxes within the shrine precincts. At the NE corner of Sanaam Luang, opposite the *Royal Hotel*, is a small statue of the **Goddess of the Earth** erected by King Chulalongkorn to provide drinking water for the public.

Wat Mahathat

North along Na Phrathat Rd, on the river side of Sanaam Luang is **Wat Mahathat** (the Temple of the Great Relic), a temple famous as a meditation centre, which is tucked behind a façade of buildings and hard to find; walk under the archway marked 'Naradhip Centre for Research in Social Sciences' to reach the wat. For those interested in learning more about Buddhist meditation, contact monks in section five within the compound. The wat is a royal temple of the first grade and a number of Supreme Patriarchs of Bangkok have based themselves here.

The revision of the Tripitaka (the Buddhist Canon) took place at the

---

KITE FIGHTING

Kite fighting is a sport which is taken very seriously – perhaps because they were used as weapons of war during the Sukhothai Period, as well as being used to ward off evil spirits during Brahmanic rites. King Rama V was an avid kite-flyer and allowed Sanaam Luang to be used for the sport from 1899. There are usually two teams, each with a different kind of kite: the 'chula' or male kite is the bigger of the two and sometimes requires a number of people to fly it. The 'pukpao' or female kite is smaller and more nimble and opposes the chula. The field is divided into two and the aim of the contest is to land the opposition in your half of the field. Attached to the chula kite are a number of hooks (*champa*) with which the kite-flyer grapples the pukpao and forces it to land in the opposite side of the field. The pukpao meanwhile has a loop with which the flyer lassoes the chula – which then crashes to the ground.

---

temple in 1788, and an examination system was established for monks and novices after a meeting at the wat in 1803. In 1801 the viharn was burnt down during an over-enthusiastic fireworks display. In 1824 the future Rama IV began his 24 years as a monk here, and it was again reconstructed between 1844 and 1851. Both viharn and bot, crammed in side-by-side, are undistinguished. Note that there are only four *bai sema* (boundary stones), and they are affixed to the walls of the building – presumably because there is so little room. The main Buddha images in the viharn and ordination hall are of brick and mortar. In the mondop are 28 bronze Buddha images, with another 108 in the gallery around the ordination hall. Most date from the Sukhothai Period. Open 0900-1700 Mon-Sun.

Thammasat and National Museum

Attached to the wat is a fascinating daily market selling exotic herbal cures, amulets, clothes and food. It is worth a wander as few tourists venture into either the market or the wat. At weekends, the market spills out onto the surrounding streets (particularly Phra Chan Rd) and amulet sellers line the pavement, their magical and holy talismen carefully displayed. Further N along Na Phrathat Rd, is **Thammasat University**, the site of viciously suppressed student demonstrations in 1973. Sanaam Luang and Thammasat University remain a popular focus of discontent. Most recently, at the beginning of May 1992, massed demonstrations occurred here to demand the resignation of Prime Minister General Suchinda. The rally was led by former Bangkok Governor Chamlong Srimuang (see box, page 551).

Next to Thammasat lies the **National Museum**, reputedly the largest museum in Southeast Asia. It is an excellent place to view the full range of Thai art before visiting the ancient Thai capitals, Ayutthaya and Sukhothai.

Gallery No 1, the gallery of Thai history, is interesting and informative, as well as being air-conditioned, so it is a good place to cool-off. The gallery clearly shows Kings Mongkut and Chulalongkorn's fascination with Western technology. The other 22 galleries and 19 rooms contain a vast assortment of arts and artefacts divided according to period and style. If you are interested in Thai art, the museum alone might take a day to browse around. A shortcoming for those with no background knowledge is the lack of information in some of the galleries and it is recommended that interested visitors buy the 'Guide to the National Museum, Bangkok' for ฿50 or join one of the tours. Admission ฿20, together with a skimpy leaflet outlining the galleries. Open 0900-1600, Wed-Sun, tickets on sale until 1530. For English, French, German, Spanish and Portuguese-speaking tour information call T 2241333. They are free, and start at 0930, lasting 2 hrs (usually on Wed and Thur).

The **Buddhaisawan Chapel**, to the right of the ticket office for the National Museum, contains some of the finest Bangkok period murals in Thailand. The chapel was built in 1795 to house the famous Phra Sihing Buddha. Folklore has it that this image originated in Ceylon and when the boat carrying it to Thailand sank, it floated off on a plank to be washed ashore in Southern Thailand, near the town of Nakhon Si Thammarat. This, believe it or not, is probably untrue: the image is early Sukhothai in style (1250), admittedly showing Ceylonese influences, and almost certainly Northern Thai in origin. There are two other images that claim to be the magical Phra Buddha Sihing, one in Nakhon Si Thammarat and another in Chiang Mai. The chapel's magnificent murals were painted between 1795 and 1797 and depict stories from the Buddha's life. They are classical in style, without any sense of perspective, and the narrative of the Buddha's life begins to the right of the rear door behind the principal image, and progresses clockwise through 28 panels. German-speaking tours of the chapel are held on the third Tues of the month (0930).

Next to the National Museum is Thailand's **National Theatre**, a newish, large, Thai-style building on the corner of Na Phrathat and Phrapinklao Bridge rds. Thai classical drama and music are staged here on the last Fri of each month at 1730 as well as periodically on other days. Current programmes can be checked by telephoning 2210173, 0830-1630 Mon-Fri. Opposite the National Theatre is the **National Art Gallery** on Chao Fa Rd. It exhibits traditional and contemporary work by Thai artists. Admission ฿10. Open Tues-Thur, Sat and Sun 0900-1600.

The Golden Mount, Giant Swing and surrounding wats

The **Democracy Monument** is a 10-15 mins' walk from the N side of Sanaam Luang, in the middle of Rachdamnern Klang Ave. This rather stolid structure was completed in 1940 to commemorate the establishment of Siam as a constitutional monarchy. Its dimensions signify, in various ways, the date of the 'revolution' – the 24 June 1932. For example, the 75 buried cannon which surround the structure denote the Buddhist year (BE – or Buddhist Era) 2475 (1932 AD). In May 1992, the monument was the focus of the anti-Suchinda demonstrations, so brutally suppressed by the army. Scores of Thais died here, many others fleeing into the nearby *Royal Hotel*. From the Democracy Monument, across Mahachai Rd, at the point where Rachdamnern Klang Ave crosses Khlong Banglamphu can be seen the **Golden Mount** (also known as the Royal Mount), an impressive artificial hill nearly 80m high. The climb to the top is exhausting but worth it for the fabulous views of Bangkok. On the way up, the path passes holy trees, memorial plaques and Chinese shrines. The construction of the mount was begun during the reign of Rama III who intended to build the greatest chedi in his kingdom. The structure collapsed before completion, and Rama IV decided merely to pile up the rubble in a heap and place a far smaller golden chedi on its summit. The chedi contains a relic of the Buddha placed there by the present king after the structure had been most recently repaired in 1966. Admission ฿5. Open 0800-1800 Mon-Sun.

Wat Saket

This lies at the bottom of the mount,

Phak Palang Dharma – or Buddhist Force Party (wags rechristened the party the Palang Phak or Vegetable Force). His supporters see him as the Mahatma Gandhi of Thai politics, fighting a corrupt and degenerate system; his opponents, such as the former Prime Minister Kukrit Pramoj liken him to Ayatollah Khomeini.

In May 1992 he was the figurehead in the demonstrations against unelected prime minister General Suchinda Kraprayoon, which culminated in riots and the death of scores of demonstrators. His hunger strike during the midst of the crisis brought him to international prominence.

Although his party was a member of the ruling coalition under former PM Chuan Leekpai, he remains a maverick, on the outside of run-of-the-mill politics. He saw himself as the conscience of the government, making sure that other ministers mirrored his own high standards of moral rectitude in public life. Indeed, it was the withdrawal of the Palang Dharma Party from the coalition, in protest over a land reform scandal, which brought the government down in May 1995. But critics say they discern a tough operator beneath the surface. Political scientist Duncan McCargo has described him as "a Buddhist ascetic with authoritarian leanings". Following his party's disappointing performance in the Sep 1992 elections he retreated to manage a development project in Kanchanaburi province. But his backing of media tycoon Taksin Shinawatra as Foreign Minister brought condemnation as representing a return to 'money politics', and opposition from within the Palang Dharma Party to his leadership strengthened. Former Foreign Minister Prasong Soonsiri was quoted as saying that the party had "become nothing but rotten vegetables". After he brought down the government of Chuan Leekpai in 1995 he stepped down as leader of the Palang Dharma Party (the role of leader was filled by Taksin), and withdrew still further from politics. He remains, though, a considerable potential political force.

between it and Damrong Rak Rd – the mount actually lies within the wat's compound. Saket means 'washing of hair' – Rama I is reputed to have stopped here and ceremoniously washed himself before being crowned King in Thonburi (see Festivals, Nov). The only building of real note is the *library* (*hor trai*) which is Ayutthayan in style. The door panels and lower windows are decorated with wood-carvings depicting everyday Ayutthayan life, while the window panels show Persian and French soldiers from Louis XIV's reign. Open 0800-1800 Mon-Sun.

Also in the shadow of the Golden Mount but to the W and on the corner of Rachdamnern Klang Ave and Mahachai Rd lies Wat Rachanada and the Loha Prasat. Until 1989 these buildings were obscured by the Chalerm Thai movie theatre, a landmark which

Bangkok's taxi and tuk-tuk drivers still refer to. In the place of the theatre there is now a neat garden, with an elaborate gilded **sala**, which is used to receive visiting dignitaries. Behind the garden the strange looking **Loha Prasat** or Metal Palace, with its 37 spires, is easily recognizable. This palace was built by Rama III in 1846, and is said to be modelled on the first Loha Prasat built in India 2,500 years ago. A second was constructed in Ceylon in 160 BC, although Bangkok's Loha Prasat is the only one still standing. The palace was built by Rama III as a memorial to his beloved niece Princess Soammanas Vadhanavadi. The 37 spires represent the 37 Dharma of the Bodhipakya. The building, which contains Buddha images and numerous meditation cells, has been closed to visitors for many years, although it is possible to walk

MAGIC DESIGNS AND TOKENS: TATTOOS AND AMULETS

Many, if not most, Thai men wear amulets or *khruang*. Some Thai women do so also. In the past tattooing was equally common, although today it is usually only in the countryside that males are extensively tattooed – sometimes from the ankle to the neck. Members of secret societies and criminal gangs use tattoos to indicate their allegiance and for the power they bestow. Amulets have histories: those believed to have great powers sell for tens of thousands, even millions, of baht and there are several magazines devoted to amulet buying and collecting (available from most magazine stalls). Vendors keep amulets with their takings to protect against robbery, and insert them into food at the beginning of the day to ensure good sales. An amulet is only to be handled by the wearer – otherwise its power is dissipated, and might even be used against the owner.

Tattooing is primarily talismatic: magic designs, images of powerful wild beasts, texts reproduced in ancient Khmer script (*khom*) and religious motifs are believed to offer protection from harm and to give strength. (The word tattoo is derived from the Tahitian word *tattau*, meaning 'to mark'. It was introduced into the English language by Captain James Cook in 1769.) They are even believed to deflect bullets, should the tattoo be sufficiently potent. One popular design is the *takraw* ball, a woven rattan ball used in the sport of the same name. The ball is renowned for its strength and durability, and the tattoo is believed, magically, to have the same effect on the tattooed. The purpose of some tattoos is reflected in the use of 'invisible' ink made from sesame oil – the talismatic effects are independent of whether the tattoo can be seen. Most inks are commercial today (usually dark blue) although traditionally they were made from secret recipes incorporating such ingredients as the fat from the chin of a corpse (preferably seven corpses, taken during a full moon). Some Lao men, as a sign of their courage, would have themselves tattooed from the waist to just below the knees.

Amulets can be obtained from spirit doctors and monks and come in a variety of forms. Most common are amulets of a religious nature, known as *Phra khruang*. These are normally images of the Buddha or of a particularly revered monk. *Khruang rang* are usually made from tiger0's teeth, buffalo horn or elephant tusk and protect the wearer in very specific ways – for example from drowning. *Khruang rang plu sek* meanwhile are magic formulas which are written down on an amulet, usually in old Khmer script, and then recited during an accident, attack or confrontation. The tattooist is not just a artist and technician. He, like the tattoos he creates, is a man of power. A master tattooist is highly respected and often given the title *ajarn* (teacher) or *mor phi* (spirit doctor). Monks can also become well-known for their tattoos. These are usually religious in tone, usually incorporating sentences from religious text. The tattoos are always beneficial or protective and always on the upper part of the body (the lower parts of the body are too lowly for a monk to tattoo).

Tattoos and amulets are not only used for protection, but also for attraction: men can have tattoos or amulets instilled with the power to attract women; women, alternatively, can buy amulets which protect them from the advances of men. *Khruang phlad khik* are phallic amulets, worn around the wrist or the waist – not around the neck. Not surprisingly, they are believed to ensure sexual prowess, as well as protection from such things as snake bites.

around the outside.

Next to the Loha Prasat is the much more traditional **Wat Rachanada**. Wat Rachanada was built by Rama III for his niece who later became Rama IV's queen. The main Buddha image is made of copper mined in Nakhon Ratchasima province to the NE of Bangkok, and the ordination hall also has some fine doors. Open 0600-1800 Mon-Sun. What makes the wat particularly worth visiting is the **Amulet market** (see page 554) to be found close by, between the Golden Mount and the wat. The sign, in English, below the covered part of the market reads 'Buddha and Antiques Centre'. The market also contains Buddha images and other religious artefacts and is open every day.

Wat Suthat

A 5 min walk S of Wat Rachanada, on Bamrung Muang Rd, is the **Sao Ching Cha** or **Giant Swing**, consisting of two tall red pillars linked by an elaborate cross piece, set in the centre of a square. The Giant Swing was the original centre for a Brahmanic festival in honour of Siva. Young men, on a giant 'raft', would be swung high into the air to grab pouches of coins, hung from bamboo poles, between their teeth. Because the swinging was from E to W, it has been said that it symbolized the rising and setting of the sun. The festival was banned in the 1930s because of the injuries that occurred; prior to its banning, thousands would congregate around the Giant Swing for 2 days of dancing and music. The magnificent **Wat Suthat** faces the Giant Swing. The wat was begun by Rama I in 1807, and his intention was to build a temple that would equal the most glorious in Ayutthaya. The wat was not finished until the end of the reign of Rama III in 1851.

The viharn is in early-Bangkok style and is surrounded by Chinese pagodas. Its six pairs of doors, each made from a single piece of teak, are deeply carved with animals and celestial beings from

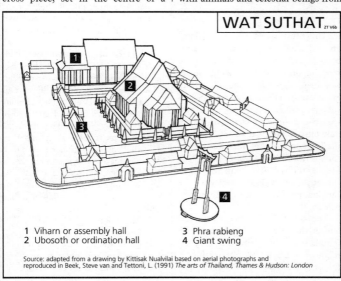

WAT SUTHAT ZT V6b

1 Viharn or assembly hall
2 Ubosoth or ordination hall
3 Phra rabieng
4 Giant swing

Source: adapted from a drawing by Kittisak Nualvilai based on aerial photographs and reproduced in Beek, Steve van and Tettoni, L. (1991) *The arts of Thailand*, Thames & Hudson: London

Engraving of the Sao Ching Cha from Henri Mouhot's *Travels in the central parts of Indo-China* (1864)

the Himavanta forest. The central doors are said to have been carved by Rama II himself, and are considered some of the most important works of art of the period. Inside the viharn is the bronze Phra Sri Sakyamuni Buddha in an attitude of subduing Mara. This image was previously contained in Wat Mahathat in Sukhothai, established in 1362. Behind the Buddha is a very fine gilded stone carving from the Dvaravati Period (2nd-11th centuries AD), 2.5m in height and showing the miracle at Sravasti and the Buddha preaching in the Tavatimsa heaven.

The bot is the tallest in Bangkok and one of the largest in Thailand. The murals in the bot painted during the reign of Rama III are interesting in that they are traditional Thai in style, largely unaffected by Western artistic influences. They use flat colours and lack perspective. The bot also contains a particularly large cast Buddha image. Open 0900-1700; the viharn is only open on weekends and Buddhist holidays 0900-1700.

Wat Rachabophit

The little visited Wat Rachabophit is close to the Ministry of the Interior on Rachabophit Rd, a few minutes walk S of Wat Suthat down Ti Thong Rd. It is recognizable by its distinctive doors carved in high relief with jaunty looking soldiers wearing European-style uniforms. The temple was started in 1869, took 20 years to complete, and is a rich blend of Western and Thai art forms (carried further in Wat Benchamabophit 40 years later, see page 564). Wat Rachabophit is peculiar in that it follows the ancient temple plan of placing the Phra Chedi in the centre of the complex, surrounded by the other buildings. It later became the fashion to place the ordination hall at the centre.

The 43m high gilded chedi's most striking feature are the five-coloured Chinese glass tiles which richly encrust the lower section. The ordination hall has 10 door panels and 28 window panels each decorated with gilded black lacquer on the inside and mother-of-pearl inlay on the outside showing the various royal insignia. They are felt to be among the masterpieces of the Rattanakosin Period (1782-present). The principal Buddha image in the ordination hall, in an attitude of meditation, sits on a base of Italian marble and is covered by the umbrella that protected the urn and ashes of Rama V. It also has a surprising interior – an oriental version of Italian Gothic, more like Versailles than Bangkok. Admission ฿10. Open 0800-1700 Mon-Sun.

North of Wat Rachabophit, on Tanao Rd is **Wat Mahannapharam**, in a large, tree-filled compound. A peaceful place to retreat to, it contains some good examples of high-walled, Bangkok Period architecture decorated with woodcarvings and mother-of-pearl inlay. Just S of here is the bustling **Chao Phaa Sua**, a Chinese temple with a fine tiled roof surmounted with mythological figures.

From Wat Rachabophit, it is only a short distance to the **Pahurat Indian Market** on Pahurat Rd, where Indian, Malaysian and Thai textiles are sold. To get there, walk S on Ti Thong Rd which quickly becomes Tri Phet Rd. After a few blocks, Pahurat Rd crosses Tri Phet Rd. **Pak Khlong Market** is to be found a little further S on Tri Phet Rd at the foot of the Memorial Bridge. It is a huge wholesale market for fresh produce, and a photographer's paradise. It begins very early in the morning and has ended by 1000.

Chinatown and the Golden Buddha

Chinatown covers the area from Charoen Krung (or New Rd) down to the river and leads on from Pahurat Rd Market; cross over Chakraphet Rd and immediately opposite is the entrance to Sampeng Lane. A trip through **Chinatown** can either begin with the Thieves Market to the NW, or at Wat Traimitr, the Golden Buddha, to the SE. An easy stroll between the two should not take more than 2 hrs. This part of Bangkok has a different atmosphere from elsewhere. Roads become narrower, buildings smaller, and there is a continuous bustle of activity. There remain some attractive, weathered examples of early 20th century shophouses. The industrious Sino-Thais of the area make everything from offertory candles and gold jewellery to metalwork, gravestones and light machinery.

Nakhon Kasem, or the Thieves Market, lies between Charoen Krung and Yaowaraj Rd, to the E of the khlong that runs parallel to Mahachai Rd. Its boundaries are marked by archways. As

its name suggests, this market used to be the centre for the fencing of stolen goods. It is not quite so colourful today, but there remain a number of second-hand and antique shops which are worth a browse – such as the *Good Luck Antique Shop*. Amongst other things, musical instruments, brass ornaments, antique (and not so antique) coffee grinders are all on sale here.

Just to the SE of the Thieves Market are two interesting roads that run next to and parallel with one another: Yaowaraj Road and Sampeng Lane. **Yaowaraj Road**, a busy thoroughfare, is the centre of the country's gold trade. The trade is run by a cartel of seven shops, the Gold Traders Association, and the price is fixed by the government. Sino-Thais often convert their cash into gold jewellery, usually bracelets and necklaces. The jewellery is bought by its 'baht weight' which fluctuates daily with the price of gold (most shops post the price daily). Should the owner need to convert his necklace or bracelet back into cash it is again weighed to determine its value. The narrower, almost pedestrian **Sampeng Lane**, also called Soi Wanit, is just to the S of Yaowaraj Rd. This road's history is shrouded in murder and intrigue. It used to be populated by prostitutes and opium addicts and was fought over by Chinese gangs. Today, it remains a commercial centre, but rather less illicit. It is still interesting (and cool, being shaded by awnings) to walk down, but there is not much to buy here – it is primarily a wholesale centre. It appears to have changed scarcely at all since James McCarthy wrote of it in his book *Surveying and exploring in Siam* published in 1900 (and since republished by the Bangkok-based publisher White Lotus): "The Chinaman is a born trader, and the country people prefer dealing with him. The consequence is the narrow streets of Sampeng, seen by few Europeans, are thronged with busy crowds, and the little shop-front awnings, meeting in the middle of the street, make the heat more stifling to the half-naked, happy-go-lucky passers-by".

The most celebrated example of the goldsmiths' art in Thailand sits within **Wat Traimitr**, or the **Temple of the Golden Buddha**, which is located at the E edge of Chinatown, squashed between Charoen Krung, Yaowaraj Rd and Traimitr Rd (just to the S of Bangkok's Hualamphong railway station). The Golden Buddha is housed in a small, rather gaudy and unimpressive room. Although the leaflet offered to visitors says the 3m-high, 700 year-old image is 'unrivalled in beauty', be prepared to be disappointed. It is in fact rather featureless, showing the Buddha in an attitude of subduing Mara. What makes it special, drawing large numbers of visitors each day, is that it is made of 5.5 tonnes of solid gold. Apparently, when the East Asiatic Company was extending the port of Bangkok, they came across a huge stucco Buddha image which they obtained permission to move. However, whilst being moved by crane in 1957, it fell and the stucco cracked open to reveal a solid gold image. During the Ayutthayan Period it was the custom to cover valuable Buddha images in plaster to protect them from the Burmese, and this particular example stayed that way for several 100 years. In the grounds of the wat there is a school, crematorium, food-stalls and, inappropriately, a money changer. Admission ฿10. Open 0900-1700 Mon-Sun. Gold beaters can still be seen at work behind Suksaphan store.

Between the river and Soi Wanit 2 there is a warren of lanes, too small for traffic – this is the Chinatown of old. From here it is possible to thread your way through to the River City shopping complex which is air-conditioned and a good place to cool-off.

RECOMMENDED READING Visitors wishing to explore the wonders of Chinatown more thoroughly, should buy Nancy Chandler's *Map of Bangkok*, a lively, detailed (but not altogether accurate) map of all the shops, restaurants and out of the way wats and shrines. ฿70 from most bookstores. Asia Books sell a very accurate map of Bangkok called *Bangkok, Central Thailand Travel Map*, published by Periplus Editions, ฿85.

Wat Arun and the khlongs

One of the most enjoyable ways to see Bangkok is by boat – and particularly by the fast and noisy *hang yaaws* (**long-tailed boats**). You will know them when you see them; these powerful, lean machines roar around the river and the khlongs at break-neck speed, as though they are involved in a race to the death. There are innumerable tours around the khlongs of Thonburi taking in a number of sights which include the floating market, snake farm and Wat Arun. Boats go from the various piers located along the E banks of the Chao Phraya River. The journey begins by travelling downstream along the Chao Phraya, before turning 'inland' after passing underneath the Krungthep Bridge. The route skirts past laden rice-barges, squatter communities on public land and houses overhanging the canals. This is a very popular route with tourists, and boats are intercepted by salesmen and women marketing everything from cold beer to straw hats. You may also get caught in a boat jam; traffic snarl-ups are not confined to the capital's roads. Nevertheless, the trip is a fascinating insight into what Bangkok must have been like when it was still the 'Venice of the East', and around every bend there seems to be yet another wat – some of them very beautiful. On private tours the first stop is usually the **Floating market** (*Talaat Nam*). This is now an artificial, ersatz gathering which exists purely for the tourist industry. It is worth only a brief visit – unless the so-called 'post-tourist' is looking for just this sort of sight. The nearest functioning floating market is at Damnoen Saduak (see excursions from

Bangkok, page 570). The **Snake Farm** is the next stop where man fights snake in an epic battle of wills. Visitors can even pose with a python. The poisonous snakes are incited, to burst balloon with their fangs, 'proving' how dangerous they are. There is also a rather motley zoo with a collection of crocodiles and sad-looking animals in small cages. The other snake farm in Central Bangkok is (appropriately) attached to the Thai Red Cross and is more professional and cheaper (see page 568). Admission ฿100, shows every 20 mins. Refreshments available. On leaving the snake farm, the boat will join up with Khlong Bangkok Yai at the site of the large **Wat Paknam**. Just before re-entering the Chao Phraya itself, the route passes by the impressive **Wat Kalaya Nimit**.

To the S of Wat Kalaya Nimit, on the Thonburi side of the river, is **Wat Prayoon Wong**, virtually in the shadow of Saphan Phut (a bridge). The wat is famous for its *Khao Tao* or turtle mountain. This is a concrete fantasyland of grottoes and peaks, with miniature chedis and viharns, all set around a pond teeming with turtles. These are released to gain merit and the animals clearly thrive in the murky water. To coin a phrase, rather grotty, but unusual. Also unusual is the large white chedi with its circular cloister surmounted with smaller chedis, and the viharn with a mondop at each corner, each containing an image of the Buddha. The bot adjacent to the viharn is attractively decayed with gold inlay doors and window shutters, and *bai sema* protected by large mondops. This wat is rarely visited by tourists. Khao Tao open 0830-1730. Getting there: can be reached by taking a cross-river shuttle boat from Tha Saphan Phut (฿1). The large white chedi of Wat Prayoon Wong is clearly visible from the Bangkok side of the river. A short walk (5 mins) upstream from here is **Santa Cruz Church**, facing the river. The church, washed in pastel yellow

with a domed tower, was built to serve the Portuguese community who lived in this part of Thonburi. **Getting there:** cross-river shuttles also stop at Tha Santa Cruz, running between here and Tha Rachini, close to the massive *Pak Khlong* fresh produce market.

Wat Arun

North on the Chao Phraya River is the famous Wat Arun, or the Temple of the Dawn, facing Wat Pho across the river. Wat Arun stands 81m high, making it the highest prang (tower) in Thailand. It was built in the early 19th century on the site of Wat Chaeng, the Royal Palace complex when Thonburi was briefly the capital of Thailand. The wat housed the Emerald Buddha before the image was transferred to Bangkok and it is said that King Taksin vowed to restore the wat after passing it one dawn. The prang is completely covered with pieces of Chinese porcelain and includes some delicate gold and black lacquered doors. The temple is really meant to be viewed from across the river; its scale and beauty can only be appreciated from a distance. Young, a European visitor to the capital, wrote in 1898: 'Thousands upon thousands of pieces of cheap china must have been smashed to bits in order to furnish sufficient material to decorate this curious structure....though the material is tawdry, the effect is indescribably wonderful'.

Energetic visitors can climb up to the halfway point and view the city. This is not recommended for people suffering from vertigo; the steps are very steep – be prepared for jelly-like legs after descending. Admission ฿10. Open 0830-1730 Mon-Sun. The men at the pier may demand ฿10 to help 'in the maintenance of the pier'. **NB** It is possible to get to Wat Arun by water-taxi from Tha Tien pier (at the end of Thai Wang Rd near Wat Pho), or from Tha Chang (at the end of Na Phralan near Wat Phra Kaeo) (฿1). The best view of Wat Arun is in the evening from the Bangkok side of the river when the sun sets behind the prang.

After visiting Wat Arun, some tours then go further upstream to the mouth of Khlong Bangkok Noi where the **Royal Barges** are housed in a hangar-like boat-house. These ornately carved boats, winched out of the water in cradles, were used by the king at 'krathin' (see OK Phansa festival, page 607) to present robes to the monks in Wat Arun at the end of the rainy season. The ceremony ceased in 1967 but the Royal Thai Navy restored the barges for the revival of the spectacle, as part of the Chakri Dynasty's bicentennial celebrations in 1982. The oldest and most beautiful

---

THE CHAO PHRAYA RIVER EXPRESS

One of the most relaxing – and one of the cheapest – ways to see Bangkok is by taking the Chao Phraya River Express. These boats (or *rua duan*) link almost 40 piers (or *tha*) along the Chao Phraya River from Tha Wat Rajsingkorn in the S to Tha Nonthaburi in the N. The entire route entails a journey of about 1¼-1½ hr, and fares are ₿4, ₿6 or ₿8. Adjacent to many of the piers are excellent riverside restaurants. At peak periods, boats leave every 10 mins, off-peak about every 15-25 mins. Note that boats flying red or green pennants do not stop at every pier; they also exact a ₿1 surcharge. Also, boats will only stop if passengers wish to board or alight, so make your destination known.

Selected piers and places of interest, travelling upstream

Tha Orienten By the *Oriental Hotel*; access to *Silom Road*.

Tha River City In the shadow of the *Royal Orchid Hotel*, on the S side and close to *River City* shopping centre.

Tha Ratchawong *Rabieng Ratchawong Restaurant*; access to *Chinatown* and *Sampeng Lane*.

Tha Saphan Phut Under the *Memorial Bridge* and close to *Pahurat Indian market*.

Tha Rachini *Pak Khlong Market*; just upstream, the *Catholic seminary* surrounded by high walls.

Tha Tien Close to *Wat Pho*; *Wat Arun* on the opposite bank; and just downstream from Wat Arun the *Vichaiprasit fort* headquarters of the Thai navy), lurking behind crenellated ramparts.

Tha Chang Just downstream is the *Grand Palace* peeking out above white-washed walls; *Wat Rakhang* with its white corn-cob prang lies opposite.

Tha Maharat *Lan The Restaurant*; access to *Wat Mahathat* and *Sanaam Luang*.

Tha Phra Arthit *Yen Jai Restaurant*; access to *Khaosan Road*.

Tha Visutkasat *Yok Yor Restaurant*; just upstream the elegant central *Bank of Thailand*.

Tha Thewes *Son Ngen Restaurant*; just upstream are *boatsheds* with royal barges; close to the *National Library*.

Tha Wat Chan Just upstream is the *Singha Beer* Samoson brewery.

Tha Wat Khema *Wat Khema* in large, tree-filled compound.

Tha Wat Khian *Wat Kien*, semi-submerged.

Tha Nonthaburi Last stop on the express boat route.

barge is the Sri Supannahong, built during the reign of Rama I (1782-1809) and repaired during that of Rama VI (1910-1925). It measures 45m long and 3m wide, weighs 15 tonnes and was created from a single piece of teak. It required a crew of 50 oarsmen, and two coxwains, along with such assorted crew members

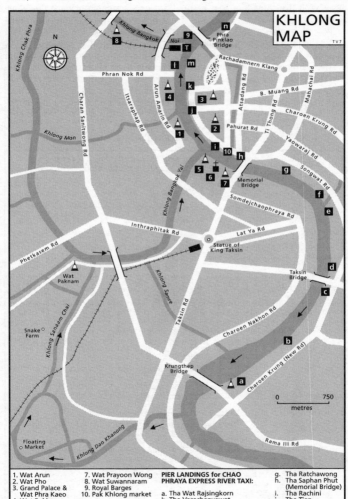

KHLONG MAP

TV7

1. Wat Arun
2. Wat Pho
3. Grand Palace & Wat Phra Kaeo
4. Wat Rakhang
5. Wat Kalaya Nimit
6. Santa Cruz Church
7. Wat Prayoon Wong
8. Wat Suwannaram
9. Royal Barges
10. Pak Khlong market
T. Bangkok Noi (Thonburi) Station

PIER LANDINGS for CHAO PHRAYA EXPRESS RIVER TAXI:

a. Tha Wat Rajsingkorn
b. Tha Vorachanyawat
c. Tha Sathorn
d. Tha Orienten (*Oriental Hotel*)
e. Tha Siphya (*Royal Orchid Hotel*)
f. Tha River City
g. Tha Ratchawong
h. Tha Saphan Phut (Memorial Bridge)
i. Tha Rachini
j. Tha Tien
k. Tha Chang
l. Tha Rot Fai
m. Tha Maharat
n. Tha Phra Arthit

as a flagman, a rhythm-keeper and singer. Its gilded prow was carved in the form of a *hamsa* (or goose) and its stern, in the shape of a *naga*. Admission ฿10. Open 0830-1630 Mon-Sun (see Festivals, Sep, page 572).

Two additional rarely-visited wats, are Wat Suwannaram and Wat Rakhang. The royal **Wat Rakhang** is located just upstream from Wat Arun, almost opposite Tha Chang landing, and is identifiable from the river by the two plaster sailors standing to attention on either side of the jetty. The original wat on this site dates from the Ayutthaya Period: it has since been renovated on a number of occasions including during the reign of King Taksin and Rama I. The **Phra Prang** in the grounds of the wat is considered a fine, and particularly well-proportioned example of early Bangkok architecture (late 18th century). The **ordination hall** (not always open – the abbot may oblige if he is available) was built during the reign of Rama III and contains a fine gilded Buddha image in an attitude of meditation, over which is the nine-tiered umbrella used to shelter the urn of Rama I during the Royal Cremation. Also here is a fine mural recording the 10 previous lives of the Buddha (note the trip to hell) painted

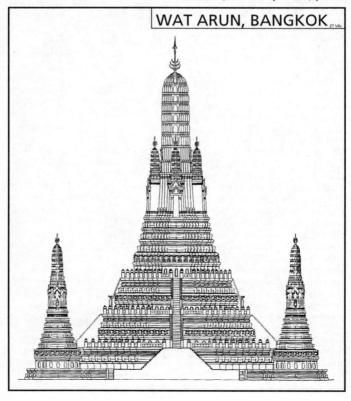

WAT ARUN, BANGKOK ZT V6c

by Phra Wannavadvichitre, an eminent monk-artist of the time. In 1995 the *bot* was undergoing extensive renovation. The beautiful red-walled wooden Tripitaka Hall (originally a library built in the late 18th century) to the left of the viharn and bot when facing away from the river, was the residence of Rama I while he was a monk (before he became king) and Thonburi was still the capital of Siam. Consisting of two rooms, it is decorated with faded but nonetheless highly regarded murals of the Ramakien (painted by a monk-artist), black and gold chests, a portrait of the king, and some odd bits of old carved door. It is one of the most charming buildings in Bangkok. The hall is towards the back of the complex, behind the large white prang, it is in excellent condition, having been recently restored. Admission ฿2. Open 0500-2100 Mon-Sun (the river ferry stops at the wat).

Wat Suwannaram is a short distance further on from the Royal Barges on Khlong Bangkok Noi, on the other side of the canal. The main buildings – which are particularly well proportioned – date from Rama I's reign (late 18th century), although the complex was later extensively renovated by Rama III. There was a wat on this site even prior to Rama I's reign, and the original name, Wat Thong (Golden Wat) remains in popular use. The ubosoth displays some fine woodcarving on the gable ends of the square pillared porches (Vishnu on his vehicle, Garuda), while the interior contains a series of murals, painted by two artists in professional competition with one another and commissioned by Rama III, and regarded by many as among the finest in Bangkok. The murals are in two 'registers'; the murals on the long walls between the windows show the Ten Lives of the Buddha. Entering the building through the right hand door (with the river behind), on the right hand wall, is a representation of a boat foundering with the crew being eaten by sharks and

sea monsters as they thrash about in the waves. Closer inspection shows that these unfortunates are wearing white skull-caps – presumably they are muslims returning from the haj to Mecca. The principal image in the bot is made of bronze and shows the Buddha calling the Earth Goddess to Witness. Sukhothai in style, it was presumably brought down from the old capital, probably in the first reign, although no records exist of its prior history. Next to the bot is the viharn abutted, unusually, by two cross halls at the front and rear. It was built during the reign of Rama IV. Wat Suwannaram is elegant and rarely visited and is a peaceful place to escape after the bustle of Wat Arun and the Floating Market.

Arranging a boat tour

Either book a tour at your hotel (see tours, page 571), or go to one of the piers and organize your own customized trip. The most frequented piers are located between the Oriental Hotel and the Grand Palace (see map, or ask at your hotel). The pier just to the S of the Royal Orchid Sheraton Hotel is recommended. Organizing your own trip gives greater freedom to stop and start when the mood takes you. It is best to go in the morning (0700). For the trip given above (excluding Wat Rakhang and Wat Suwannaram), the cost for a hang yaaw which can sit 10 people should be about ฿600 for the boat for a half-day. If visiting Rakhang and Suwannaram as well as the other sights, expect to pay about another ฿200-300 for the hire of a boat. Be sure to settle the route and cost before setting out.

The Dusit area

The Dusit area of Bangkok lies N of the Old City. The area is intersected by wide tree-lined avenues, and has an almost European flavour. The **Vimanmek Palace** lies off Rachvithi Rd, just to the N of the National Assembly. Vimanmek is the largest golden teakwood mansion in the world. It was built by Rama V in 1901 and designed by one of his brothers. The palace makes an interesting contrast to Jim Thompson's House (see page 566) or Suan Pakkard (page 565). While Jim Thompson was enchanted by Thai arts, King Rama V was clearly taken with Western arts. It seems like a large Victorian hunting lodge – but raised off the ground – and is filled with china, silver and paintings from all over the world (as well as some gruesome hunting trophies). The photographs are fascinating – one shows the last time elephants were used in warfare in Thailand. Behind the palace is the Audience Hall which houses a fine exhibition of crafts made by the Support Foundation, an organization set up and funded by Queen Sirikit. Support, rather clumsily perhaps, is the acronym for the Foundation for the Promotion of Supplementary Occupations and Related Techniques. Also worth seeing is the exhibition of the king's own photographs, and the clock museum. Dance shows are held twice a day. Visitors are not free to wander, but must be shown around by one of the charming guides who demonstrate the continued deep reverence for King Rama V (tour approx 1hr). Admission ฿50, ฿20 for children, tickets to the Grand Palace include entrance to Vimanmek Palace. Open 0930-1600 (last tickets sold at 1500) Mon-Sun. Refreshments available. Buses do go past the palace, but from the centre of town it is easier to get a tuk-tuk or taxi (฿50-60).

From Vimanmek, it is a 10-15 mins walk to the Dusit Zoo, skirting around the **National Assembly** (which, before the 1932 coup was the Marble Throne Hall and is not open to visitors). The route is tree-lined, so it is possible to keep out of the sun or the rain. In the centre of the square in front of the National Assembly stands an equestrian statue of the venerated King Chulalongkorn. To the left lie the **Amporn**

Gardens, the venue for royal social functions and fairs. Southwards from the square runs the impressive **Rachdamnern Nok Avenue**, a Siamese Champs Elysée. Enter the **Dusit Zoo** through Uthong Gate, just before the square. A pleasant walk through the zoo leads to the Chitralada Palace and Wat Benchamabophit. The zoo has a reasonable collection of animals from the region, some of which look rather the worse for wear. There is a children's playground, restaurants and pedal-boats can be hired on the lake. Admission ฿10, ฿5 children. Open 0800-1800 Mon-Sun.

From the Dusit Zoo's Suanchit Gate, a right turn down the tree-lined Rama V Rd leads to the present King Bhumibol's residence – **Chitralada Palace**. It was built by Rama VI and is not open to the public. Evidence of the King's forays into agricultural research may be visible. He has a great interest and concern for the development of the poorer, agricultural parts of his country, and invests large sums of his own money in royal projects. To the right of the intersection of Rama V and Sri Ayutthaya roads are the gold and ochre roofs of Wat Benchamabophit – about a 10 mins walk from the zoo.

Wat Benchamabophit

Or the **Marble Temple**, is the most modern of the royal temples and was only finished in 1911. It is of unusual architectural design (the architect was the king's half brother, Prince Naris), with carrara marble pillars, a marble courtyard and two large singhas guarding the entrance to the bot. Rama V was so pleased with the marble-faced ordination hall that he wrote to his brother: 'I never flatter anyone but I cannot help saying that you have captured my heart in accomplishing such beauty as this'. The interior is magnificently decorated with crossbeams of lacquer and gold, and in shallow niches in the walls are paintings of important stupas from all over the kingdom. The door panels are faced with bronze sculptures and the windows are of stained-glass, painted with angels. The cloisters around the assembly hall house 52 figures (both original and imitation) – a display of the evolution of the Buddha image in India, China and Japan. The Walking Buddha from the Sukhothai Period is particularly worth a look. The rear courtyard houses a large 80-year-old bodhi tree and a pond filled with turtles, released by people hoping to gain merit. The best time to visit this temple complex is early morning, when monks can be heard chanting inside the chapel. Admission ¢10. Open 0800-1700 Mon-Sun.

Government House is S of here on Nakhon Pathom Rd. The building is a weird mixture of cathedral gothic and colonial Thai. It is only open on Wan Dek – a once yearly holiday for children held on the second Sat in Jan. The little visited **Wat Sonnakviharn** is on Krung Kasem Rd, located behind a car park and schoolyard. Enter by the doorway In the far right-hand corner of the schoolyard, or down Soi Sommanat. It is peaceful, unkempt, and rather beautiful, with fine gold lacquer doors, and a large gold tile-encrusted chedi. Open Mon-Sun.

Other places of interest

In addition to the Vimanmek Palace, Bangkok also has a number of other beautiful Thai-style houses that are open to the public. **Suan Pakkard Palace** or Lettuce Garden Palace is at 352-354 Sri Ayutthaya Rd, S of the Victory Monument. The five raised traditional Thai houses (domestic rather than royal) were built by Princess Chumbhot, a great-grand-daughter of King Rama IV. They contain her fine collection of antiquities, both historic and prehistoric (the latter are particularly rare). Like the artefacts in the National Mu-

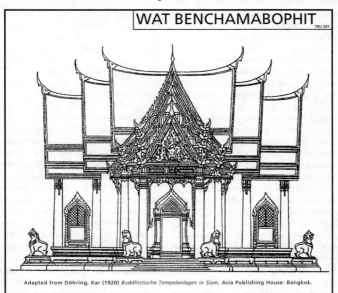

WAT BENCHAMABOPHIT

TBU 207

Adapted from Döhring, Kar (1920) *Buddhistische Tempelanlagen in Siam*, Asia Publishing House: Bangkok.

seum, those in Suan Pakkard are also poorly labelled. The rear pavilion is particularly lovely, decorated in black and gold lacquerwork panels. Prince Chumbhot discovered this temple near Ayutthaya and reassembled and restored it here for his wife's 50th birthday. The grounds are very peaceful. Admission ₿80 – including a fan to ward off the heat. Open 0900-1600, Mon-Sat. All receipts go to a fund for artists.

Jim Thompson's House is on the quiet Soi Kasemsan Song (2), opposite the National Stadium on Rama I Rd. It is an assemblage of traditional teak Northern Thai houses, some more than 200 years old, transported here and reassembled (these houses were designed to be transportable, consisting of five parts – the floor, posts, roof, walls and decorative elements constructed without the use of nails). Jim Thompson arrived in Bangkok as an intelligence officer attached to the United States' OSS (Office of Strategic Services) and then made his name by reinvigorating the Thai silk industry after WW2. He disappeared mysteriously in the Malaysian jungle on 27 March 1967, but his silk industry continues to thrive. (The *Jim Thompson Silk Company*, selling fine Thai silk, is at the NE end of Surawong Rd. This shop is a tourist attraction in itself. Shoppers can buy high-quality bolts of silk and silk clothing here – anything from a pocket handkerchief to a silk suit. Prices are top of the scale.) Jim Thompson chose this site for his house partly because a collection of silk weavers lived nearby on Khlong Saensaep. The house contains an eclectic collection of antiques from Thailand and China, with work displayed as though it was still his home. Shoes must be removed before entering; walking barefoot around the house adds to the appreciation of the cool teak floorboards. Bustling Bangkok only intrudes in the form of the stench from the khlong that runs behind the house. Compulsory guided tours around the house and no photography allowed. Admission ₿100 (profits to charity). Open 0900-1630, Mon-Sat. **Getting there**: bus along Rama I Rd, taxi or tuk-tuk.

A 10 mins' walk E along Rama I Rd is the shopping area known as **Siam Square** (or Siam Sa-quare). This has the greatest concentration of fast food restaurants, boutiques and cinemas in the city. Needless to say, it is patronized by young Thais. The land on which this chequerboard of shops are built is owned by **Chulalongkorn University** – Bangkok's, and Thailand's, most prestigious. While Thammasat University on Sanaam Luang is known for its radical politics, Chulalongkorn is conservative. Just S of Siam Square, on the campus itself (off Soi Chulalongkorn 12, behind the massive Mahboonkrong or MBK shopping centre; ask for 'sa-sin', the houses are nearby) is a collection of beautiful **traditional Thai houses**, newly built to help preserve Thai culture. Also on campus is the **Museum of Imaging Technology** with a few hands-on photographic displays. Occasional photographic exhibitions are also held here when it may be open other than on a Sat. Admission ₿100. Open 1000-1600 Sat. To get to the museum, enter the campus by the main entrance on the E side of Phaya Thai Rd and walk along the S side of the playing field. Turn right after the Chemistry 2 building and then right again at the entrance to the Mathematics faculty. It is at the end of this walkway in the Dept of Photographic Science and Printing Technology.

East of Siam Square is the **Erawan Shrine** on the corner of Ploenchit and Rachdamri rds, at the Rachprasong intersection. This is Bangkok's most popular shrine, attracting not just Thais but also large numbers of other Asian visitors. The spirit of the shrine, the Hindu god Thao Maha Brahma, is reputed to grant people's wishes – it certainly has little artistic worth. In thanks,

BANGKOK: ANIMAL SUPERMARKET OF THE WORLD

Thailand has few laws restricting the import of endangered species of wildlife – either alive or dead – and the country acts as a collection point for animals from Burma, Cambodia and Laos, as well as further afield. Tiger skins and penises (the latter much prized by the Chinese), ivory, rhino horns and nails, cayman skins (from Latin America), live gibbons and tiger cubs, clouded leopard skins, hawksbill turtle shells, and rare palm cockatoos are all available in Bangkok, a city which has been called the 'wildlife supermarket of the world'. This is nothing particularly new: in 1833, government records show that 50-60 rhinoceros horns were exported, along with 26,000 pairs of deer's antler and 100,000 deer hides.

But pressure on Thailand's natural environment means that the scale of the threat is different. In 1991 the World Wide Fund for Nature labelled Thailand as "probably the worst country in the world for the illegal trade in endangered species". Before the Olympic Games in Seoul, South Korea, in 1988 it is said that 200 Malayan sun bears were smuggled from Thailand to Korea so that local athletes could consume their energy-enhancing gall bladders and meat. Even Korean tourists are able to dine on bear meat in restaurants in Bangkok – the animals are reportedly lowered alive in cages into vats of boiling water.

Critics claim that the Thai government flagrantly violates the rules of the Convention on International Trade in Endangered Species (CITES) – which it has officially acceded to – and ignores blatant trading in both live and dead endangered species. In recent years there has been increasing pressure from conservationists and from other governments to try and force the Thai authorities to clean-up their act. This, at last, appears to be having some success although as recently as the end of 1994 a house was raided and discovered to contain piles of animal carcasses, frozen bears' paws, and live bears, monkeys and snakes – all destined for the cooking pot.

visitors offer garlands, wooden elephants and pay to have dances performed for them accompanied by the resident Thai orchestra. The popular *Thai Rath* newspaper reported in 1991 that some female devotees show their thanks by covorting naked at the shrine in the middle of the night. Others, rather more coy about exposing themselves in this way, have taken to giving the god pornographic videos instead. Although it is unlikely that visitors will be rewarded with the sight of naked bodies, the shrine is a hive of activity at most hours, incongruously set on a noisy, polluted intersection tucked into a corner, and in the shadow of the Sogo Department Store.

One other traditional house worth visiting is the home of the **Siam Society**, off Sukhumvit Rd, at 131 Soi Asoke. The Siam Society is a learned society established in 1904 and has benefitted from almost continual royal patronage. The **Kamthieng House** is a 120-year-old N Thai house from Chiang Mai. It was donated to the society in 1963, transported to Bangkok and then reassembled a few years later. It now serves as an ethnological museum, devoted to preserving the traditional technologies and folk arts of Northern Thailand. It makes an interesting contrast to the fine arts displayed in Suan Pakkard Palace and Jim Thompson's house. The Siam Society houses a library, organizes lectures and tours and publishes books, magazines and pamphlets. Admission ฿25, ฿10 for children. Open 0900-1200, 1300-1700, Tues-Sat, T 2583491 for information on lectures.

Wat Indraviharn is rather isolated from the other sights, lying just off

Visutkaset Rd. It contains a 32m-high standing Buddha encrusted in gold tiles that can be seen from the entrance to the wat. The image is impressive only for its size. The topknot contains a relic of the Buddha brought from Ceylon. Few tourists. Open Mon-Sun.

For those with a penchant for snakes, the **Snake Farm** of the Thai Red Cross is very central and easy to reach from Silom or Surawong rds. It was established in 1923, and raises snakes for serum production, which is distributed worldwide. The farm also has a collection of non-venomous snakes. During showtime (which lasts 30 mins) various snakes are exhibited, and venom extracted. Visitors can fondle a python. The farm is well maintained and professional. Admission ฿70. Open 0830-1630 Mon-Fri (shows at 1100 and 1430), 0830-1200 Sat/Sun and holidays (show at 1100). The farm is within the Science Division of the Thai Red Cross Society at the corner of Rama IV and Henri Dunant rds.

Slightly further out of the centre of Bangkok is the **Chatuchak Weekend Market** which is off Phahonyothin Rd, opposite the Northern bus terminal. Until 1982 this market was held at Sanaam Luang, but was moved because it had outgrown its original home and also because the authorities wanted to clean up the area for the Bangkok bicentenary celebrations. It is a huge conglomeration of 8,672 stallholders spread over an area of 28 acres, selling virtually everything under the sun, and an estimated 200,000 people visit the market over a weekend. It is probably the best place to buy handicrafts and all things Thai in the whole Kingdom. There are antique stalls, basket stalls, textile sellers, shirt vendors, carvers, painters ... along with the usual array of fish sellers, vegetable hawkers, butchers and candlestick makers. In the last couple of years a number of bars and food stalls geared to tourists and Thai yuppies have also

opened so it is possible to rest and recharge before foraging once more. Definitely worth a visit – and allocate half a day at least. In addition to the map below, Nancy Chandler's Map of Bangkok has an inset map of the market to help you get around. Believe it or not, the market is open on weekends, officially from 0900-1800 (although in fact it begins earlier). It's best to go early in the day. In 1994 plans were announced to transform the market by building a three-storey purpose-built structure with car parking and various other amenities. Such has been the outcry that the planners have retired to think again. But the fear is that this gem of shopping chaos will be re-organized, sanitized, bureaucratized and, in the process, ruined. **Beware pickpockets**. There is a tourist information centre at the entrance gate off Kamphaeng Phet 2 Rd,

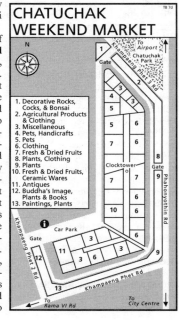

CHATUCHAK WEEKEND MARKET

1. Decorative Rocks, Cocks, & Bonsai
2. Agricultural Products & Clothing
3. Miscellaneous
4. Pets, Handicrafts
5. Pets
6. Clothing
7. Fresh & Dried Fruits
8. Plants, Clothing
9. Plants
10. Fresh & Dried Fruits, Ceramic Wares
11. Antiques
12. Buddha's Image, Plants & Books
13. Paintings, Plants

and the Clock tower serves as a good reference point should visitors become disoriented. **Getting there:** a/c buses 2 (from Silom Rd), 3, 10, 13 and 29 go past the market, and non-a/c buses 8, 24, 26, 27, 29, 34, 39, 44, 59, and 96. Or take a taxi or tuk-tuk. Also here, in the N section of Chatuchak Park is the **Railway Museum** with a small collection of steam locomotives. Open 0500-1200 Sun.

The **Science Museum and Planetarium** is just past Sukhumvit Soi 40, next to the Eastern bus terminal. It contains a planetarium, aeroplanes and other exhibits. Admission ฿10. Open 0900-2200 Wed-Sun. **Getting there:** bus (a/c 1, 8, 11, 13, non-a/c 2, 25, 38, 40, 48, 71, 119), taxi or tuk-tuk.

Excursions

Watery excursions

Apart from the khlong trips outlined on page 558, there are other places to go on the river. The cheapest way to travel the river is by regular water taxi. There are three types (not including the *hang yaaws*):

First, the **Chao Phraya Express River Taxi** (*rua duan*) which runs on a regular route from Wat Rajsingkorn (near Krungthep Bridge, at the S end of Charoen Krung) northwards to Nonthaburi. Fares range from ฿4-16 and the service operates every 8-25 mins depending on the time of day, 0600-1800 Mon-Sun (see map for stops). The boats are long and fast. There are also ferries which ply back and forth across the river, between Bangkok and Thonburi. The fare for these slower, chunkier boats is ฿1. Lastly, there are a number of other boat services linking Bangkok with stops along the khlongs which run off the main Chao Phraya River and into Thonburi. These are a good, cheap way of getting a glimpse of waterside life. Services from Tha Tien pier (by Wat Pho) to Khlong Mon, 0630-1800 Mon-Sun (every 30 mins) ฿4; from Memorial Bridge pier to Khlong Bang Waek, 0600-2130 Mon-Sun (every 15 mins) ฿10; from Tha Chang pier (by the Grand Palace) to Khoo Wiang floating market (market operates 0400-0700) and Khlong Bang Yai, 0615-2000 Mon-Sun (every 20 mins) ฿10; and from Nonthaburi's Phibun Pier (N of the city) to Khlong Om, 0400-2100 Mon-Sun (every 15 mins).

An interesting day trip by long-tailed boat takes visitors to a **traditional Thai house** 30 km from Bangkok, in Nonthaburi (see next entry). A day trip, including lunch costs ฿500. It is possible to stay here, as guests of the owner Mr Phaiboon (**A**), includes breakfast, fan rooms, outside bathrooms and no hot water. Call *Asian Overland Adventure*, T 2800740, F 2800741.

Nonthaburi

Nonthaburi is both a province and a provincial capital immediately to the N of Bangkok. Accessible by express river taxi from the city, the town has a provincial air that contrasts sharply with the overpowering capital: there are saamlors in the streets (now banished from Bangkok) and the pace of life is tangibly less frenetic. 30 mins walk away are rice fields and rural Thailand. A street market runs from the pier inland past the *sala klang* (provincial offices), selling clothes, sarong lengths, dried fish and unnecessary plastic objects. The buildings of the sala klang are early 19th century, wooden and decayed. Note the lamp posts with their durian accessories – Nonthaburi's durians are renowned across the kingdom. Walk through the sala klang compound (downriver) to reach an excellent riverside restaurant. Across the river and upstream (5 mins by long-tailed boat) is Wat Chalem Phra Kiat, a refined wat built by Rama III as a tribute to his mother who is said to have lived in the vicinity. The gables of the bot are encrusted in ceramic tiles;

the chedi behind the bot was built during the reign of Rama IV. Getting there: by express river taxi (45 mins) to Tha Nonthaburi or by Bangkok city bus (Nos 32, 64, 97 and 203).

Floating market at Damnoen Saduak

Ratchaburi Province, 109 km W of Bangkok. Sadly, it is becoming increasingly like the Floating Market in Thonburi, although it does still function as a legitimate market. Getting there: catch an early morning bus (No 78) from the Southern bus terminal in Thonburi – aim to get to Damnoen Saduak between 0800-1000, as the market winds down after 1000, leaving only trinket stalls. The trip takes about 1½ hrs. A/c and non-a/c buses leave every 40 mins from 0600 (฿30-49) (T 4355031 for booking).

The bus travels via Nakhon Pathom (where it is possible to stop on the way back and see the great chedi). Ask the conductor to drop you at Thanarat Bridge in Damnoen Saduak. Then either walk down the lane (1.5 km) that leads to the market and follows the canal, or take a river taxi for ฿10. There are a number of floating markets in the maze of khlongs – Ton Khem, Hia Kui and Khun Phithak – and it is best to hire a hang yaaw to explore the back-waters and roam around the markets, about ฿300/hour (agree the price before setting out). It is possible to combine a trip to Damnoen Saduak with a visit to the *Rose Garden* (see tours, page 571). Tour companies also visit the floating market.

Tours

Bangkok has innumerable tour compa-

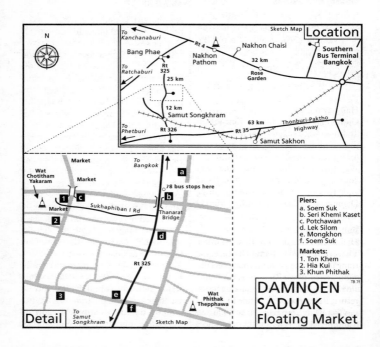

Piers:
a. Soem Suk
b. Seri Khemi Kaset
c. Potchawan
d. Lek Silom
e. Mongkhon
f. Soem Suk

Markets:
1. Ton Khem
2. Hia Kui
3. Khun Phithak

DAMNOEN SADUAK
Floating Market

nies that can take visitors virtually any-where. If there is not a tour to fit your bill – most run the same range of tours – many companies will organize one for you, for a price. Most top hotels have their own tour desk and it is probably easiest to book there (arrange to be picked up from your hotel as part of the deal). The tours given below are the most popular; prices per person are about ฿250-500 for a half day, ฿600-1,000 for a full day (incl lunch). A short list of com-panies is given at the end of the section; there are countless more.

Rose Garden

A Thai 'cultural village' spread over 15 ha of landscaped tropical grounds, 32 km W of Bangkok. Most people go for the cultural show – elephants at work, Thai classical dancing, Thai boxing, hilltribe dancing and a Buddhist ordi-nation ceremony. The resort also has a hotel, restaurants, a swimming pool and tennis courts, as well as a golf course close by. Admission ฿220. The cultural show is at 1500 Mon-Sun (Bangkok of-fice: 195/15 Soi Chokchai Chongcham-ron Rama III Rd, T 2953261). Daily tour from Bangkok, half day (afternoons only).

Half day tours

Grand Palace Tour; Temple Tour to Wat Traimitr, Wat Pho and Wat Benjamabo-phit; Khlong Tour around khlongs and to Floating Market, Snake Farm and Wat Arun (mornings only); Old City Tour; Crocodile Farm Tour; Rice Barge and Khlong Tour (afternoons only); Damnoen Saduak Floating Market Tour.

Full day tours

Damnoen Saduak and Rose Garden; Thai Dinner and Classical Dance, eat in traditional Thai surrounding and con-sume toned-down Thai food, ฿250-300, 1900-2200. Pattaya, the infamous beach resort; River Kwai, a chance to see the famous Bridge over the River Kwai and war cemeteries, as well as the great chedi at Nakhon Pathom; Ayutthaya and Bang Pa-In. There are also boat tours to Ayut-thaya and Bang Pa-In (see below).

Boat tours

The *Oriental Queen* sails up the Chao Phraya River daily from the *Oriental Hotel* to the old capital, Ayutthaya, re-turning to Bangkok by a/c bus, ฿1,200, 0800-1700 with lunch (T 2360400); *Ayutthaya Princess* operates from the *Shangri-La Hotel* pier or the *Royal Shera-ton* pier. The *Ayutthaya Princess* is a two-level vessel resembling a Royal Barge. Leaving at 0800 daily, there are daily cruises to Bang Pa-In, an a/c bus tour around Ayutthaya, returning to Bang-kok by coach at 1730. You can also do the reverse: coach to Ayutthaya and then a boat back to Bangkok, arriving at 1730, ฿1,100, including buffet lunch on board. (Kian Gwan Building, 140 Wireless Rd, T 2559200.)

Mekhala is operated by the *Siam Ex-clusive Tours* on the same route. The dif-ference is that *Mekhala* leaves Bangkok in the late evening and puts ashore for one night in Ayutthaya, supplying a ro-mantic dinner on deck. The *Mekhala* is a converted rice barge accommodating 12-16 passengers in six a/c cabins with attached bathrooms. The barge arrives in Ayutthaya at Wat Kai Tia in the eve-ning and departs the following morning for Bang Pa-In. To visit other sights, passengers are transferred to a long-tailed boat. An a/c minibus transports passengers back to Bangkok. The re-verse, proceeding by road up to Ayut-thaya/Bang Pa-In and returning on the rice barge, is also available ฿5,290 (sin-gle), ฿4,200 (twin). Book through travel agents or *Siam Exclusive Tours*, Bldg One, 7th Flr, 99 Witthayu Rd, T 2566153, F 2566665. Cheaper are the day boat tours to Bang Pa-In via Queen Sirikit's handicraft centre at Bang Sai and the stork sanctuary at Wat Phai Lom oper-ated by the *Chao Phraya Express Boat Company*. Tours leave on Sat and Sun only from the Maharaj and Phra Athit piers at 0800 and 0805 respectively, returning 1530, ฿180 or ฿240, T 2815564.

Train tours

The State Railway of Thailand organize day trips to Nakhon Pathom and the Bridge over the River Kwai and to Ayutthaya. Both trips run on weekends and holidays. The latter tour leaves Bangkok at 0630 and returns from Ayutthaya on the Chao Phraya River.

Dinner cruises

Chao Phraya, T 4335453; *Loy Nava*, T 4374932, ฿700. *Wanfah Cruise*, T 4335453, ฿650. *Ayutthaya Princess*, T 2559200, organizes Sun dinner cruise for ฿850.

International

For tours to Vietnam, Laos, Cambodia and Burma, see page 594.

Festivals and major events

Jan: *Red Cross Fair* (movable), held in Amporn Gardens next to the Parliament. Stalls, classical dancing, folk performances etc.

Feb: *Chinese New Year* (movable), Chinatown closes down, but Chinese temples are packed. *Handicraft Fair* (mid-month), all the handicrafts are made by Thai prisoners.

Mar-Apr: *Kite Flying* (movable, for 1 month), every afternoon/evening at Sanaam Luang there is kite fighting (see page 550). An *International Kite Festival* is held in late Mar at Sanaam Luang when kite fighting and demonstrations by kite-flyers from across the globe take place.

May: *Royal Ploughing Ceremony* (movable), this celebrates the official start of the rice-planting season and is held at Sanaam Luang. It is an ancient Brahman ritual and is attended by the king (see page 549).

Sep: *Swan-boat races* (movable), on the Chao Phraya River.

Nov: *Golden Mount Fair* (movable),

stalls and theatres set-up all around the Golden Mount and Wat Saket. Candles are carried in procession to the top of the mount. *Marathon* road race, fortunately at one of the coolest times of year.

Dec: *Trooping of the Colour* (movable), the élite Royal Guards swear allegiance to the king and march past members of the Royal Family. It is held in the Royal Plaza near the equestrian statue of King Chulalongkorn.

Local information

● **Accommodation**

Price guide		
	US$	Baht
L	200+	5,000+
A+	100-200	2,500-5,000
A	50-100	1,250-2,500
B	25-50	625-1,250
C	15-25	375-625
D	8-15	200-375
E	4-8	100-200
F	<4	<100

Bangkok offers a vast range of accommodation at all levels of luxury. There are a number of hotel areas in the city, each with its own character and locational advantages. Accommodation has been divided into five such areas with a sixth – 'other' – for the handful situated elsewhere. A new type of hotel which has emerged in Bangkok in recent years is the 'boutique' hotel. These are small, with immaculate service, and represent an attempt to emulate the philosophy of 'small is beautiful'.

NB For business women travelling alone, the *Oriental*, *Dusit Theni* and *Amari Airport* hotels allocate a floor to women travellers, with all-female staff.

Many of the more expensive places to stay are on the **Chao Phraya River** with its views, good shopping and access to the old city. Running eastwards from the river are **Silom** and **Surawong** rds, in the heart of Bangkok's business district and close to many embassies. The bars of Patpong link the two roads. This is a good area to stay for shopping and bars, but transport to the tourist sights can be problematic. A more recently developed area is along **Sukhumvit Rd** running E from Soi Nana Nua (Soi 3). The bulk of the accommodation here is in the **A-B** range, and within easy reach is a wide range of restaurants, 'girlie' bars, and reasonable shopping. But, the hotels are a long taxi or tuk-tuk ride from the sights of the old city and most of the places of interest to the tourist in Bangkok. In the vicinity of **Siam Square** are two deluxe hotels and several 'budget' class establishments (especially along Rama 1 Soi Kasemsan Nung). Siam Square is central, a good shopping area, with easy bus and taxi access to Silom and Sukhumvit rds and the sights of the old city. Guesthouses are to be found along and around **Khaosan Rd** (an area known as Banglamphu); or just to the N, at the NW end of Sri Ayutthaya Rd there is a small cluster of rather friendly places. **Soi Ngam Duphli**, off Rama IV Rd, is the other big area for cheap places to stay. These hotel areas encompass about 90% of Bangkok's accommodation, although there are other places to stay scattered across the city; these are listed under **Other**.

● **Silom, Surawong and the River**

L *Dusit Thani*, 946 Rama IV Rd, T 2360450, F 2366400, a/c, restaurants, pool, when it was built it was the tallest building in Bangkok, refurbished, still excellent, though disappointing pool, rec; L *Evergreen Laurel Hotel*, 88 Sathorn Nua, T 2669988, F 2667222, a/c, restaurants, pool, one of the new 'boutique' hotels with only 130 rm, Taiwanese-owned, all facilities and excellent service; L *Montien*, 54 Surawong Rd, T 2348060, F 2365219, a/c, restaurants, pool, one of the first high-rise hotels (opened 1967) with good location for business, shopping and bars, slick service, and continuing good reputation with loyal patrons; L *Oriental*, 48 Soi Oriental, Charoen Krung, T 2360400, F 2361939, a/c, restaurants, pool, one of the best hotels in the world, beautiful position overlooking the river, superb personal service despite size (400 rm), Joseph Conrad, Somerset Maugham and Noel Coward all stayed here at one time, good shopping arcade, good programme of 'cultural' events, and 6 excellent restaurants, some of the equipment and bathrooms could be said to be a little old, however it still comes highly rec; L *Royal Orchid Sheraton*, 2 Captain Bush Lane, Si Phraya Rd, T 2345599, F 2368320, a/c, restaurants, pool, at times strong and rather unpleasant smell from nearby khlong, lovely views over the river, close to River City shopping centre (good for antiques), rooms are average at this price but service is very slick; L *Shangri-La*, 89 Soi Wat Suan Plu, Charoen Krung, T 2367777, F 2368570, a/c, restaurants, lovely pool, great location overlooking river, sometimes preferred to *Oriental* but some consider it

dull and impersonal, recently upgraded and extended, rec; L-A+ *Sukhothai*, 13/3 Sathorn Tai Rd, T 2870222, F 2784980, a/c, restaurants (good Italian restaurant), pool, beautiful rooms and excellent service, in Thai postmodern style, clean and elegant, rec; L-A+ *Holiday Inn Crowne Plaza*, 981 Silom Rd, T 2384300, F 2385289, a/c, restaurants, pool, vast, pristine marble-filled hotel, all amenities, immensely comfortable, minimum atmosphere and character.

A+ *Menam*, 2074 Charoen Krung, T 2891148, F 2911048, a/c, restaurant, pool, good value for river-view rooms but inconvenient location, shuttle-boat makes sightseeing easier; A+ *Monarch Lee Gardens*, 188 Silom Rd, T 2381991, F 2381999, a/c, restaurants, pool, opened 1992, stark and gleaming high-tech high-rise, all facilities, still trying hard to attract custom, discounts available; A+ *Narai*, 222 Silom Rd, T 2370100, F 2367161, a/c, restaurant, pool, rather non-descript, with cold, marble-clad lobby; A+ *Tarntawan Place*, 119/5-10 Surawong Rd, T 2382620, F 2383228, a/c, restaurant, pool, good service and rooms, rec; A+ *Tawana Ramada*, 80 Surawong Rd, T 2360361, F 2363738, a/c, restaurant, pool, average hotel.

A *Mandarin*, 662 Rama IV Rd, T 2380230, F 2371620, a/c, restaurant, small pool, friendly atmosphere, comfortable rooms, popular nightclub; A *Manohra*, 412 Surawong Rd, T 2345070, F 2377662, a/c, coffee shop, small pool, unattractive rooms, mediocre service; A *Silom Plaza*, 320 Silom Rd, T 2368441, F 2367566, a/c, restaurant, small pool, caters mainly for East Asian tour groups, central but characterless, gently decaying; A *Silom Street Inn*, 284/11-13 Silom Rd, opp the junction with Pan Rd (between sois 22 and 24), T 2384680, F 2384689, a/c, restaurant, pool, small new hotel, small, comfortable, 30 well-equipped rm with CNN News, grubby rather seedy lobby, set back from road; A *Tower Inn*, 533 Silom Rd, T 2344051, F 2344051, a/c, restaurant, pool, simple but comfortable hotel, with large rooms and an excellent roof terrace, good value; A *Trinity Place*, 150 Silom Soi 5, T 2380052, F 2383984, a/c, restaurant, pool, attractive, small hotel.

B *Collins House (YMCA)*, 27 Sathorn Tai Rd, T 2872727, F 2871996, a/c, restaurant, large pool, clean, excellent value, friendly management; B *New Peninsula*, 295/3 Surawong Rd, T 2343910, F 2365526, a/c, restaurant, small pool, small rooms; B *River City Guesthouse*,

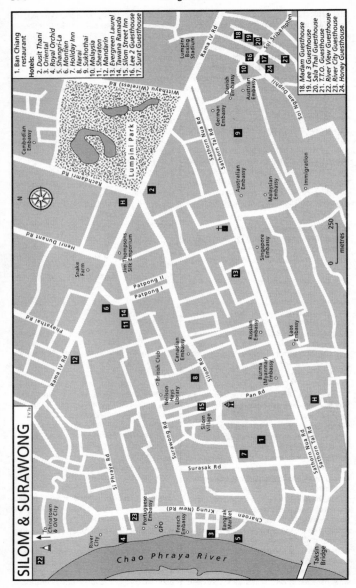

SILOM & SURAWONG [TV2b]

Ban Chiang restaurant

Hotels:
2. Dust Thani
3. Oriental
4. Royal Orchid
5. Shangri-La
6. Montien
7. Holiday Inn
8. Narai
9. Sukhothai
10. Malaysia
11. Sheraton
12. Mandarin
13. Tawana Ramada
14. Evergreen Laurel
15. Silom Street Inn
16. Lee 2 Guesthouse
17. Surat Guesthouse
18. Madam Guesthouse
19. Lee 3 Guesthouse
20. Sala Thai Guesthouse
21. T.T.O. Guesthouse
22. River View Guesthouse
23. River City Guesthouse
24. Honey Guesthouse

Chao Phraya River

11/4 Charoen Krung Soi Rong Nam Khang 1, T 2351429, F 2373127, a/c, not very welcoming but rooms are a good size and clean, good bathrooms, short walk to River City and the river; **B** *Rose*, 118 Surawong Rd, T 2337695, F 2346381, a/c, restaurant, pool, opp Patpong, favourite among single male visitors, but getting seedier by the month; **B** *Swan*, 31 Charoen Krung Soi 36, T 2348594, some a/c, great position, clean but scruffy rooms; **B** *Victory*, 322 Silom Rd, T 2339060, a/c, restaurant.

C *Chao Phya Riverside*, 1128 Songward Rd (opp the Chinese school), T 2226344, some a/c, old style house overlooking river, clean rooms, atmospheric, unusual location; **C** *River View Guesthouse*, 768 Songwad Soi Panurangsri, T 2345429, F 2375771, some a/c, the restaurant/bar is on the top floor and overlooks the river, food is mediocre, but the atmosphere is friendly, excellent hotel overlooking the river in Chinatown, rooms are large, clean, some with balconies, some hot water and friendly, professional management, Khun Phi Yai, the owner, is a pharmacist, so can even prescribe pills, highly rec.

● **Soi Ngam Duphli**

Soi Ngam Duphli is much the smaller of Bangkok's two centres of guesthouse accommodation. Locationally, the area is good for the shopping and bars of Silom Rd but inconvenient for most of the city's main places of interest in the old city. Guesthouses tend to be quieter and more refined than those of Khaosan Rd.

B *Malaysia*, 54 Rama IV Soi Ngam Duphli, T 2863582, F 2493120, a/c, restaurant, pool, once a Bangkok favourite for travellers.

C *TTO*, 2/48 Soi Sribamphen, T 2866783, F 2871571, a/c, well-run and popular, homely atmosphere, rooms a little small; **C-D** *Honey*, 35/2-4 Soi Ngam Duphli, T 2863460, some a/c, large rooms, in a rather rambling block, clean and good value, service can be rather surly, no hot water.

D *Sala Thai Guesthouse*, 15 Soi Sribamphen, T 2871436, at end of peaceful, almost leafy, soi, clean rooms, family run, good food, but shared bathroom, rec; **D-E** *Anna*, 21/30 Soi Ngam Duphli, clean rooms, some with bathrooms; **D-E** *Home Sweet Home*, 27/7 Soi Sribamphen (opp Boston Inn, down small soi, so relatively quiet, average rooms with attached bathrooms; **D-E** *Lee 3*, 13 Soi Saphan Khu, T 2863042, some a/c, wooden house with character, down quiet soi, rooms are clean but with shared bathrooms, rec; **D-E** *Madam*, 11 Soi Saphan Khu, T 2869289, wooden house, friendly atmosphere, attached bathrooms, no hot water, quiet, rec.

E *Lee 2*, 21/38-39 Soi Ngam Duphli, T 2862069, clean, friendly, rec; **E** *Lee 4*, 9 Soi Saphan Khu, T 2867874, spotless rooms and bathrooms, some with balconies and views over city, rec; **E** *Surat*, 2/18-20 Sribumphen Rd, T 2867919, some a/c, own bathroom, no hot water, clean and well-run, rec.

● **Siam Square, Rama I Road and Phetburi Road**

L *Grand Hyatt Erawan*, 494 Rachdamri Rd, T 2541234, F 2535856, the replacement hotel for the much-loved old *Erawan Hotel*, towering structure with grandiose entrance and a plastic tree-filled atrium plus sumptious rooms and every facility but has lost atmosphere in the process; **L** *Hilton*, 2 Witthayu Rd, T 2530123, F 2536509, a/c, restaurants, attractive pool, excellent hotel set in lovely grounds with a remarkable garden feel for a hotel that is so central, comparatively small for such a large plot and first class service; **L** *Novotel*, Siam Sq Soi 6, T 2556888, F 2551824, a/c, restaurant, pool, undistinguished but commendably comfortable; **L** *Siam Intercontinental*, 967 Rama I Rd, T 2530355, F 2532275, a/c, restaurants, small pool, relatively low-rise hotel, set in 26 acres of grounds, good sports facilities, excellent service; **L-A+** *Imperial*, 6-10 Witthayu Rd, (on the edge of Siam Sq area), T 2540023, F 2533190, a/c, restaurants, pool, lovely grounds but hotel seems rather jaded next to Bangkok's newer upstarts, 370 rm and numerous bars and restaurants where, apparently, it is possible to rub shoulders with the city's 'beautiful people', walls are very thin and recent visitors have been disappointed at how this hotel has declined in quality; **L-A+** *Regent Bangkok*, 155 Rachdamri Rd, T 2516127, F 2539195, a/c, restaurants (see Thai Restaurants, page 583), pool (although rather noisy, set above a busy road), excellent reputation amongst frequent visitors who insist on staying here, stylish and postmodern in atmosphere with arguably the best range of cuisine in Bangkok, rec.

A+ *Arnoma*, 99 Rachdamri Rd, T 2553411, F 2553456, a/c, several restaurants, pool, health club, business centre, 403 well-equipped rm, though much like any others in this price bracket, good location for shopping and restaurants; **A+** *Le Meridien President*,

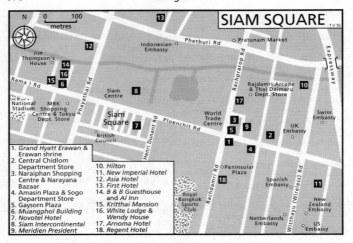

SIAM SQUARE TV 7b

N 0 100
metres

Jim Thompson's House

Indonesian Embassy
Phetburi Rd
Pratunam Market

Rama I Rd

Siam Centre

National Stadium

MBK Shopping Centre & Tokyu Dept. Store

Siam Square

British Council

Rajdamri Arcade & Thai Daimaru Dept. Store

World Trade Centre

Ploenchit Rd

UK Embassy

Swiss Embassy

Peninsular Plaza

Royal Bangkok Sports Club

Spanish Embassy

New Zealand Embassy

Netherlands Embassy

US Embassy

Phayathai Rd · Henri Dunant Rd · Rachdamri Rd · Witthayu (Wireless) Rd · Rachprarop Rd · Expressway

1. Grand Hyatt Erawan & Erawan shrine
2. Central Chidlom Department Store
3. Naraiphan Shopping Centre & Narayana Bazaar
4. Amasin Plaza & Sogo Department Store
5. Gaysorn Plaza
6. Muangphol Building
7. Novotel Hotel
8. Siam Intercontinental
9. Meridien President
10. Hilton
11. New Imperial Hotel
12. Asia Hotel
13. First Hotel
14. B & B Guesthouse and Al Inn
15. Kritthai Mansion
16. White Lodge & Wendy House
17. Arnoma Hotel
18. Regent Hotel

135/26 Gaysorn Rd, T 2530444, F 2537565, tranquil atmosphere, good service, excellent French food, a new sister hotel is being built next door – the luxury *President Tower*, due for completion in 1994, rec; **A+** *Siam City*, 477 Sri Ayutthaya Rd, T 2470120, F 2470178, a/c, restaurants, pool, another new hotel, with all facilities, tastefully designed.

A *Asia*, 296 Phayathai Rd, T 2150808, F 2154360, a/c, restaurant, pool, ugly hotel situated on noisy thoroughfare.

B *Kritthai Mansion*, 931/1 Rama I Rd, T 2153042, a/c, restaurant, situated on noisy thoroughfare; **B** *Florida*, 43 Phayathai Rd, T 2470990, a/c, restaurant, pool; **B** *Prince*, 1537/1 New Phetburi Rd, T 2516171, F 2513318, a/c, restaurant, pool, all facilities but no character.

C *A-1 Inn*, 25/13 Soi Kasemsan Nung (1), Rama I Rd, T 2153029, a/c, well run, intimate hotel, rec; **C** *Bed and Breakfast*, 36/42 Soi Kasemsan Nung (1), Rama 1 Rd, T 2153004, F 2152493, a/c, friendly efficient staff, clean but small rooms, good security, bright 'lobby', price includes breakfast, rec; **C** *Muangphol Building*, 931/9 Rama I Rd, T 2150033, F 2802540, a/c, pool, hot water, good sized rooms, reasonable rates; **C** *Wendy House*, 36/2 Soi Kasemsan Nung (1), Rama I Rd, T 2162436, F 2168053, a/c, spotless, but small rooms with eating area downstairs, hot water; **C** *White Lodge*, 36/8 Soi Kasemsan Nung (1), Rama I Rd, T 2168867, F 2168228, a/c,

hot water, airy, light reasonably sized rooms, rec; **C-E** *Alternative Tour Guesthouse*, 14/1 Rachaprarop Soi Rachatapan, T 2452963, F 2467020, friendly, excellent source of information, attached to *Alternative Tour Company*, promoting culturally and environmentally sensitive tourism, clean.

● **Sukhumvit Road**

L *Imperial Queen's Park*, Sukhumvit Soi 22, T 2619000, F 2619530, massive new 37-storey hotel with a mind boggling 1,400 rm, how service can, in any sense, be personal is hard to imagine, but all possible facilities, location is away from most sights and the main business district; **L** *Windsor Plaza Embassy Suites*, 8 Sukhumvit Soi 20, T 2580160, F 2581491, a/c, restaurants, pool, next door to the *Windsor Hotel*, 460 suites, health centre.

A+ *Delta Grand Pacific*, 259 Sukhumvit Rd, T 2544998, F 2552441, a/c, restaurants, pool, almost 400 rm in this large high-rise hotel, all facilities but characterless for the price; **A+** *Hotel Mercure*, 12/3 Sukhumvit Soi 22, T 2597420, F 2582862, medium-sized hotel with 90 rm, rather out of the way; **A+** *Rembrandt*, 15-15/1 Sukhumvit Soi 20, T 2617040, F 2617017, a/c, restaurants, pool, new hotel with lots of marble and limited ambience; **A+-A** *Somerset*, 10 Sukhumvit Soi 15, T 2548500, F 2548534, a/c, restaurant, tiny enclosed pool, small hotel, rather ostentatious, rooms are non-descript but comfortable, baths are designed for people of small stature.

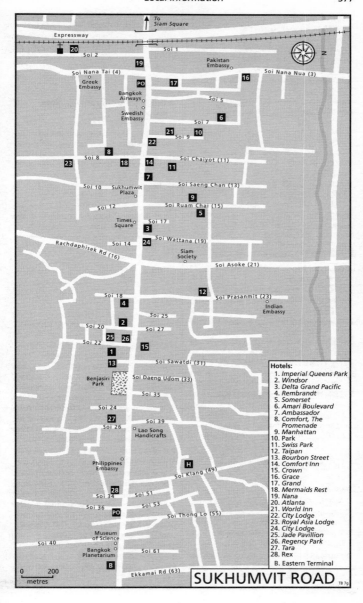

To Siam Square

Expressway

Soi 2
Soi 1

Soi Nana Tai (4)
Pakistan Embassy
Soi Nana Nua (3)
Greek Embassy
PO
Bangkok Airways
Soi 5
Swedish Embassy
Soi 7
Soi 9
Soi 8
Soi Chaiyot (11)
Soi 10
Sukhumwit Plaza
Soi Saeng Chan (13)
Soi 12
Soi Ruam Chai (15)
Times Square
Soi 17
Soi Wattana (19)
Rachdaphisek Rd (16)
Soi 14
Siam Society
Soi Asoke (21)
Soi 18
Soi Prasanmit (23)
Indian Embassy
Soi 20
Soi 25
Soi 27
Soi 22
Soi Sawatdi (31)
Benjasiri Park
Soi Daeng Udom (33)
Soi 35
Soi 24
Soi 39
Soi 26
Lao Song Handicrafts
Philippines Embassy
Soi Klang (49)
Soi 34
Soi 51
Soi 36
PO
Soi 53
Soi Thong Lo (55)
Museum of Science
Bangkok Planetarium
Soi 40
Soi 61
Ekkamai Rd (63)

0   200
metres

SUKHUMVIT ROAD

Hotels:
1. Imperial Queens Park
2. Windsor
3. Delta Grand Pacific
4. Rembrandt
5. Somerset
6. Amari Boulevard
7. Ambassador
8. Comfort, The Promenade
9. Manhattan
10. Park
11. Swiss Park
12. Taipan
13. Bourbon Street
14. Comfort Inn
15. Crown
16. Grace
17. Grand
18. Mermaids Rest
19. Nana
20. Atlanta
21. World Inn
22. City Lodge
23. Royal Asia Lodge
24. City Lodge
25. Jade Pavillion
26. Regency Park
27. Tara
28. Rex
B. Eastern Terminal

TB 7g

A *Amari Boulevard*, 2 Sukhumvit Soi 5, T 2552930, F 2552950, a/c, restauarant, pool; **A** *Ambassador*, 171 Sukhumvit Rd, T 2540444, F 2534123, a/c, restaurants, pool, large, impersonal rather characterless hotel, with great food hall (see restaurants); **A** *Comfort, The Promenade*, 18 Sukhumvit Soi 8, T 2534116, F 2547707, a/c, restaurant, small pool, fitness centre, rathe kitsch; **A** *Manhattan*, 13 Sukhumvit Soi 15, T 2550166, F 2553481, a/c, restaurant, pool, recently renovated high-rise, lacks character but rooms are comfortable and competitively priced although some are rather shabby so ask to inspect; **A** *Park*, 6 Sukhumvit Soi 7, T 2554300, F 2554309, a/c, restaurant, excellent service, peaceful oasis; **A** *Swiss Park*, 155/23-28 Sukhumvit Soi 11, T 2540228, F 2540378, a/c, restaurant, pool, another overbearing neo-classical hotel; **A** *Tai-pan*, 25 Sukhumvit Soi 23, T 2609888, F 2597908, a/c, restaurant, pool, tasteful new hotel; **A** *Windsor*, 8 Sukhumvit Soi 20, T 2580160, F 2581491, a/c, restaurant, pool, tennis.

B *Bourbon Street*, 29/4-6 Sukhumvit Soi 22 (behind Washington Theatre), T 2590328, F 2594318, a/c, small number of rooms attached to this Cajun restaurant, well run and good value, rec; **B** *China*, 19/27-28 Sukhumvit Soi 19, T 2557571, F 2541333, a/c, restaurant, a small hotel masquerading as a large one, but rooms are up to the standard of more expensive places, so good value; **B** *Comfort Inn*, 153/11 Sukhumvit Soi 11, T 2519250, F 2543562, a/c, restaurant, small hotel, friendly management, rec; **B** *Crown*, 503 Sukhumvit Soi 29, T 2580318, F 2584438, a/c, clean, good service; **B** *Grace*, 12 Sukhumvit Soi Nana Nua (Soi 3), T 2530651, F 2530680, a/c, restaurant, pool, *the* sex hotel of Bangkok now trying to redeem itself; **B** *Grand*, 2/7-8 Sukhumvit Soi Nana Nua (Soi 3), T 2533380, F 2549020, a/c, restaurant, small hotel with friendly staff, good value; **B** *Nana*, 4 Sukhumvit Soi Nana Tai (Soi 4), T 2520121, F 2551769, a/c, restaurant, pool, refurbished, good value.

C *Atlanta*, 78 Sukhumvit Soi 2, T 2521650, a/c, restaurant, large pool, left-luggage facility, poste restante, daily video-shows, good tour company in foyer, rec; **C** *Golden Palace*, Sukhumvit Soi 1, T 2525115, a/c, restaurant, pool, rec.

D *Chu's*, 35 Sukhumvit Soi 19, T 2544683, restaurant, one of the cheapest in the area, good food, rec; **D** *Happy Inn*, 20/1 Sukhumvit Soi 4, T 2526508, some a/c, basic rooms, cheerful management; **D** *SV*, 19/35-36 Sukhumvit Soi 19, T 2544724, some a/c, another cheap hotel in this area, musty rooms, shared bathrooms and poor service; **D-E** *Disra House*, 593/28 Sukhumvit Soi 33-33/1, T 2585102, some a/c, friendly and well run place which comes highly recommended, rather out-of-the-way but good value a/c rooms.

● **Banglamphu (Khaosan Road) and surrounds**

Khaosan Rd lies NE of Sanaam Luang, just off Rachdamnern Klang Ave, close to the Democracy Monument. It is continually expanding into new roads and sois, in particular the area W of Chakrapong Rd. The sois off the main road are often quieter, such as Soi Chana Songkhran or Soi Rambutri. Note that rooms facing on to Khaosan Rd tend to be very noisy. Khaosan Rd is not just a place to spend the night. Also here are multitudes of restaurants, travel and tour agents, shops, bus companies – almost any and every service a traveller might need. They are geared to budget visitors' needs and more than a few have dubious reputations.

A+ *Royal Princess*, 269 Lan Luang Rd, T 2813088, F 2801314, a/c, restaurants, pool, newish addition to Dusit chain of hotels, good facilities.

A *Majestic Palace*, 97 Rachdamnern Klang Ave (opp Democracy Monument), T 2805610, F 2800965, a/c, restaurant, pool, old hotel given half-hearted face-lift, good location but rooms overpriced and limited facilities; **A** *Royal*, 2 Rachdamnern Klang Ave, T 2229111, F 2242083, a/c, restaurant, pool, old (by Bangkok standards) hotel which acted as a refuge for demonstrators during the 1991 riots, rooms are dated and featureless; **A** *Viengtai*, 42 Tanee Rd, Banglamphu, T 2815788, a/c, restaurant, pool, rooms are very good, clean relatively spacious, with all the advantages of this area in terms of proximity to the Old City.

C *New World Apartment and Guesthouse*, 2 Samsen Rd, T 2815596, F 2815596, some a/c, good location for the Old City yet away from the hurly-burly of Khaosan Rd, rooms are clean and good value even if the overall atmosphere is rather institutional; **C-D** *7 Holder*, 216/2-3 Khaosan Rd, T 2813682, some a/c, clean, friendly; **C-D** *New Siam*, Phra Athit 21 Soi Chana Songkram, T 2824554, F 2817461, some a/c, good restaurant, modern and clean, friendly helpful staff, airy rooms, but featureless block, tickets and tour information, fax

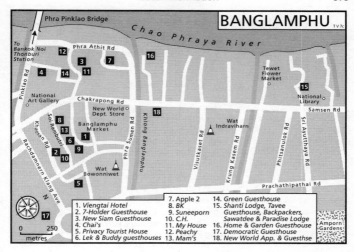

BANGLAMPHU TV7c

Phra Pinklao Bridge
Phra Athit Rd
Chao Phraya River
To Bankok Noi Thonburi Station
Pinklao Rd
National Art Gallery
Chakrapong Rd
New World Dept. Store
Banglamphu Market
Khaosan Rd
Soi Rambutri
Rachadamnern Klang Ave
Wat Bowonniwet
Phra Sumen Rd
Khlong Banglamphu
Visutkaset Rd
Wat Indraviharn
Krung Kasem Rd
Tewet Flower Market
National Library
Samsen Rd
Phitsanulok Rd
Sri Ayutthaya Rd
Prachathipatai Rd
Amporn Gardens
metres 0   250

1. Viengtai Hotel
2. 7-Holder Guesthouse
3. New Siam Guesthouse
4. Chai's
5. Privacy Tourist House
6. Lek & Buddy guesthouses
7. Apple 2
8. BK
9. Suneeporn
10. C.H.
11. My House
12. Peachy
13. Mam's
14. Green Guesthouse
15. Shanti Lodge, Tavee Guesthouse, Backpackers, Sawatdee & Paradise Lodge
16. Home & Garden Guesthouse
17. Democratic Guesthouse
18. New World App. & Guesthse

facilities, lockers available, overpriced; **C-E** *Chart*, 58 Khaosan Rd, T 2803785, restaurant, some a/c, small but clean rooms, some have no windows; **C-E** *Green House*, 88/1 Khaosan Soi Rambutri, T 2820323, some a/c, ask for rooms away from street, rec.

D *Chai*, 49/4-8 Chao Fa Soi Rongmai, T 2814901, F 2818686, friendly atmosphere, clean and colourful with borgainvillea growing from the balconies and in the restaurant, last house down Soi Rambhtri, so away from the others; **D** *Pra Suri*, 85/1 Soi Pra Suri, 5 mins from Khaosan Rd, fan, restaurant, own bathrooms (no hot water), clean and quiet, very friendly and helpful family-run guesthouse, rec; **D-E** *BK*, 11/1 Chakrapong Soi Sulaow, T 2815278, some a/c, in busy area of Banglamphu, but guesthouse is set back from road, so not too noisy, clean but dark rooms, shared bathrooms, good information; **D-E** *Buddy*, 137/1 Khaosan Rd, T 2824351, off main street, some a/c, rooms are small and dingy but it remains popular, large open restaurant area bustles with people exchanging information; **D-E** *CH*, 216/1 Khaosan Rd, T 2822023, some a/c, good reputation, left luggage (¢5/day, ¢30/week); **D-E** *Hello*, 63-65 Khaosan Rd, T 2818579, some a/c, popular; **D-E** *New Merry V*, 18-20 Phra Athit Rd, T 2803315, some a/c, good restaurant, clean but very small rooms, pleasant place to stay, friendly, good travel service, quiet at the back, safety deposit box and luggage room, books for rent; **D-E** *Privacy Tourist House*, 69 Tanow Rd, T 2827028, popular, quiet, rec.

E *Apple 2*, 11 Phra Sumen Rd, T 2811219, old-time favourite; **E** *Arunothai (AT)*, 90/1, 5, 12 Khaosan Soi Rambutri, T 2826979, friendly owner; **E** *Bonny*, 132 Khaosan Rd, T 2819877, quiet, off main road, reports of bed bugs; **E** *Chuanpis*, 86 Chakrapong Rd (nr intersection with Khaosan Rd, down small soi opp Wat Chanasongkhram), popular, geared particularly to Israeli visitors, good food, average rooms, often full; **E** *Democratic*, 211/8 Rachdamnern Ave, T 2826035, F 2249149, set back, opp the Democracy Monument, 4-storey concrete house with friendly management but small rooms and grubby stairwell; **E** *Dior*, 146-158 Khaosan Rd, T 2829142, small but clean rooms and bathrooms, quiet, as set back from road, 'family' atmosphere, rec; **E** *Emy*, 61 Chakrapong Soi Rambutri, T 2822737, friendly management; **E** *Home and Garden*, 16 Samphraya Rd (Samsen 3), T 2801475, away from main concentration of guesthouses, down quiet soi (quite difficult to find), good location for river taxi, rooms are small and basic but clean, well run and friendly, rec; **E** *Lek*, 90/9 Khaosan Soi Rambutri, T 2812775, popular; **E** *Mam's*, 119 Khaosan Rd, friendly, homely atmosphere, rec; **E** *Merry V*, 33-35 Phra Athit Soi Chana Songkram, T 2829267, some a/c, some rooms with bal-

KHAOSAN ROAD: A WORLD OF ITS OWN

Banglamphu, as the place for backpackers to stay, dates from the mid-1970s. The *Vieng Thai Hotel* opened in 1962, and as it gained a reputation for budget accommodation, so some local families began to rent out rooms to tourists. Most of these places were concentrated along Khaosan Road, which as Marc Askew has written in his study *The Banglamphu District: a portrait of change in inner Bangkok* (TDRI, 1993), soon became known as Thanon Farang Khaosan. As he explains, and which is evident from first sight: "There is nothing Thai about the character of Khao San Road: everything is for the Farang, from the clothing, the jewellery, to the food. Most local residents in surrounding neighbourhoods tend to keep the road at an arms length and do not claim a close familiarity with it...". Prior to this transformation Khaosan Road was an ordinary street of middle class Thai educated families, with a commercial specialization of dress-making and tailoring. Today, the tourist focus has spilt over into surrounding streets, particularly to the north and east. The Tourist Authority of Thailand in 1991 estimated that there were 83 guesthouses in the area and that 238,000 tourists stayed in the district each year. The irony perhaps is that the group of tourists which is usually perceived to live closest to the Thai way of living – backpackers – have helped to create a world which is wholly their own.

conies, lockers available; **E** *My House*, 37 Phra Athit Soi Chana Songkhram, T 2829263, post pick-up service, very popular; **E** *Nat*, 217 Khaosan Rd, brusque management but clean, larger than average rooms with fan, rec; **E** *PS*, 9 Phra Sumen Rd, T 2823932, spotlessly clean, rooms with no windows, but satellite TV and free tea and coffee, rec; **E** *Peachy*, 10 Phra Athit Rd, T 2816659, some a/c, recent visitors have reported a deterioration in quality and cleanliness, but still has pleasant restaurant area; **E** *Prakorb's House*, 52 Khaosan Rd, T 2811345, excellent restaurant with big choice of dishes, some international; **E** *Rose Garden*, 28/6 Phra Athit Soi Trok Rongmai, T 2818366, friendly; **E** *Siam*, 76 Chakrapong Rd, T 2810930, rooms facing onto the street are noisy, small rooms but good clean bathrooms; **E** *Suneeporn*, 90/10 Khaosan Soi Rambutri, T 2826887, popular; **E** *Sweety*, 49 Thani Rd, clean, rec; **E-F** *Bangkok Youth Hostel*, 25/2 Phitsanulok Rd (off Samsen Rd), T 2820950, N of Khaosan Rd, away from the bustle, dorms available.

F *KC*, 60-64 Phra Sumen Rd Soi Khai Chae, T 2820618, friendly management, clean rooms, rec.

● **Sri Ayutthaya Road**

Sri Ayutthaya is emerging as an 'alternative' area for budget travellers. It is a central location with restaurants and foodstalls nearby, but does not suffer the over-crowding and sheer pandemonium of Khaosan Rd.

D *Shanti Lodge*, 37 Sri Ayutthaya Rd, T 2812497, restaurant with extensive menu, very popular, rooms nicely done up, rec.

E *Backpackers Lodge*, 85 Sir Ayutthaya Rd, Soi 14, T 2823231, restaurant, rooms with fans, small patio, quiet and friendly, rec; **E** *Little Home*, 23/12 Sri Ayutthaya Rd, T 2821574, bit shabby, bigger garden and cheaper than *Backpackers*, but closer to main road; **E** *Paradise*, 57 Sri Ayutthaya Rd, T 2828673, some fans, small guesthouse, rooms with no outward-looking windows, friendly management; **E** *Sawatdee*, 71 Sri Ayutthaya Rd, T 2810757, Western menu, pokey rooms, popular with German travellers; **E** *Tavee*, 83 Sri Ayutthaya Rd, Soi 14, T 2801447, restaurant, fan, small garden, clean and pleasant, rec.

● **Others**

A+ *Central Hotel*, 1695 Phahonyothin Rd, T 5411234, F 5411087, a/c, restaurant, pool, out of town, close to w/e market, efficiently run, but inconveniently located and recently taken over by the Central Department Store group.

A+ *Marriot Royal Garden*, Riverside Resort, 257/1-3 Charoen Nakrom Rd, T 4760021, F 4761120, a/c, restaurant, excellent swimming pool, almost resort-like, very spacious surrounding, opp the *Oriental*, nr the Krung Thep Bridge, free shuttle-boat service every 30 mins between hotel and the *Oriental* and River City piers.

A *Amari Airport*, 333 Chert Wudthakas Rd, T 5661020, F 5661941, a/c, restaurants, pool, connected to airport by foot-bridge; rooms look onto attractive gardens, useful hotel for transit passengers; **A** *Rama Gardens*, 9/9 Vibhavadi Rangsit Rd, Bangkaen (nr the airport), T 561002, F 5611025, a/c, restaurants, two attractive, large pools, out of town on road to airport, inconvenient for most, but spacious grounds with fitness centre, tennis, squash, golf, putting; **A** *Sunroute Bangkok*, 288 Rama IX Rd, T 2480011, F 2485990, a/c, restaurants, pool, part of a Japanese chain, markets itself as the 'route to satisfaction', located away from most sights and shopping; Dusit Riverside, over Sathorn Bridge in Thonburi (opening late 1992); **A-B** *Ramada Renaissance Bridgeview*, 3999 Rama III Rd, T 2923160, F 2923164, a/c, numerous restaurants, pools, tennis, squash, new 476 room high-rise overlooking Chao Phraya River, all facilities, poor location for sights, shopping and business.

C-E *The Artists Club*, 61 Soi Tiem Boon Yang, T 4389653, some a/c, run by an artist, this is a guesthouse cum studio cum gallery in Thonburi (ie the other side of the river), clean rooms and a real alternative place to stay with concerts and drawing lessons, away from the centre of guesthouse activity.

● **Places to eat**

Price guide		
	US$	**Baht**
♦♦♦♦	15+	375+
♦♦♦	5-15	125-375
♦♦	2-5	50-125
♦	under 2	under 50

Bangkok has the largest and widest selection of restaurants in Thailand – everyone eats out, so the number of places is vast. Food is generally very good and cheap – this applies not just to Thai restaurants but also to places serving other Asian cuisines, and Western dishes. Roadside food is good value – many Thais eat on the street, businessmen and civil servants rubbing shoulders with factory workers and truck drivers. **NB** Most restaurants close between 2200 and 2230. For a fuller listing of places to eat see *Bangkok Metro Magazine* published monthly. Also good for bars, music venues, shopping etc.

Afternoon tea: *The Authors Lounge*, Oriental Hotel; the *Bakery Shop*, Siam Intercontinental Hotel; *The Cup*, second floor of Peninsula Plaza, Rachdamri Rd; *The Regent Hotel* lobby (music accompaniment), Rachdamri Rd; the *Dusit Thani Hotel* library, Rama IV Rd.

Bakery: *Jimmy*, 1270-2, nr Oriental Lane, Charoen Krung, a/c, cakes and ice creams, very little else around here, so it's a good stopping place; *Sweet Corner*, Siam Intercontinental Hotel, Rama I Rd, one of the best in Bangkok.

Chinese: most Thai restaurants sell Chinese food, but there are also many dedicated Chinese establishments. **Siam Square** has a large number, particularly those specializing in shark's fin soup. For shark's fin try the *Scala Shark's Fin* (reputed to be the best of the bunch), *Bangkok Shark's Fin*, and the *Penang Shark's Fin* all opp the Scala Cinema, Siam Square Soi 1. ♦♦♦♦-♦♦♦*Kirin*, 226/1 Siam Square Soi 2, over 20 years old, traditional Chinese decor, good atmosphere; ♦♦♦*Art House*, 87 Sukhumvit Soi 55 (Soi Thonglor), country house with traditional Chinese furnishings, surrounded by gardens, particularly good seafood; ♦♦♦*Chinese Seafood Restaurant*, 33/1-5 16 Wall St Tower, Surawong Rd, Cantonese and Szechuan; ♦♦♦*Joo Long Lao*, 2/1 Sukhumvit Soi 2, spacious, with wide choice of dishes, rec; ♦♦♦*Lung Wah*, 848/13 Rama III Rd, large restaurant, with good reputation, serves shark's fin and other seafood, also serves Thai; ♦♦♦*Pata*, 26 Siam Square Soi 3; ♦♦♦*Shangarila*, 154/4-7 Silom Rd, bustling Shanghai restaurant with dim sum lunch; ♦♦*Tongkee*, 308-314 Sukhumvit Rd (opp Soi 19), Kwangtung food, popular with Thais.

Fast Food: Bangkok now has a large number of Western fast food outlets, such as *Pizza Hut*, *McDonalds*, *Kentucky Fried Chicken*, *Mister Donut*, *Dunkin' Donuts*, *Shakey's*, *Baskin Robbins* and *Burger King*. These are located in the main shopping and tourist areas – Siam Square, Silom/Patpong rds, and Ploenchit Rd.

Foodstalls: scattered across the city for a rice or noodle dish, where a meal will cost ฿15-30 instead of a minimum of ฿75 in the restaurants. For example, on the roads between Silom and Surawong Rd, or down Soi Somkid, next to Ploenchit Rd, or opp on Soi Tonson.

International: ♦♦♦♦*Beccassine*, Sukhumvit, Soi Sawatdee, English and French home cooking, rec; ♦♦♦♦*Diva*, 49 Sukhumvit Soi 49, T 2587879, excellent French restaurant, with very good Italian dishes and crepe suzette which should not be missed, friendly service, attractive surroundings, good value, rec; ◆◆◆◆*La Grenouille*, 220/4 Sukhumvit Soi 1, T 2539080, traditional French cuisine, French chef and manager, small restaurant makes booking essential, French wines and French atmosphere, rec; ◆◆◆◆*Le Banyan*, 59 Sukhumvit Soi 8, T 2535556, excellent French food; ◆◆◆◆*L'Hexagone*, 4 Sukhumvit Soi 55 (Soi Thonglor), French cuisine, in 'posh' surroundings; ◆◆◆◆*L'Opera*, 55 Sukhumvit Soi 39, T 2585606, Italian restaurant with Italian manager, conservatory, good food (excellent salted baked fish), professional service, lively atmosphere, popular, booking essential, rec; ◆◆◆◆*Neil's Tavern*, Soi Ruamrudee, T 2515644, best steak in town, popular with expats; ◆◆◆◆*Paesano*, 96/7 Soi Tonson (off Soi Langsuan), Ploenchit Rd, T 2522834, average Italian food, sometimes good, in friendly atmosphere, very popular with locals; ◆◆◆◆*Wit's Oyster Bar*, 20/10 Ruamrudee Village, T 2519455, Bangkok's first and only Oyster Bar, run by eccentric Thai, one of the few places where you can eat late, good salmon fishcakes, international cuisine; ◆◆◆*Bei Otto*, 1 Sukhumvit Soi 20, Thailand's best known German restaurant, large helpings; ◆◆◆*Bobby's Arms*, 2nd Fl, Car Park Bldg, Patpong 2 Rd, British pub food; ◆◆◆*Bourbon Street*, 29/4-6 Sukhumvit Soi 22 (behind Washington Theatre), Cajun specialities including gumbo, jambalaya and red fish, along with steaks and Mexican dishes, served in a/c restaurant with VDOs and central bar – good for breakfast, excellent pancakes; ◆◆◆*Brussels Restaurant*, 23/4 Sukhumvit Soi 4, small and friendly, also serves Thai food; ◆◆◆*Chez Daniel Le Normand*, 1/9 Sukhumvit Soi 24, top class French restaurant; ◆◆◆*Classique Cuisine*, 122 Sukhumvit Soi 49, classic French cuisine; ◆◆◆*Den Hvide Svane*, Sukhumvit Soi 8, Scandinavian and Thai dishes, former are good, efficient and friendly service; ◆◆◆*Gino's*, 13 Sukhumvit Soi 15, Italian food in bright and airy surroundings, set lunch is good value; ◆◆◆*Gourmet Gallery*, 6/1 Soi Promsri 1 (between Sukhumvit Soi 39 and 40), interesting interior, with art work for sale, unusual menu of European and American food; ◆◆◆*Hard Rock Café*, 424/3-6 Siam Sq Soi 11, home-from-home for all burger-starved farangs, overpriced, videos, live music sometimes, and all the expected paraphernalia, a couple of Thai dishes have been included, large portions and good atmosphere. ◆◆◆*Haus*

Munchen, Sukhumvit Soi 15, German food in quasi-Bavarian lodge, connoisseurs maintain cuisine is authentic enough; ◆◆◆*Le Bordeaux*, 1/38 Sukhumvit Soi 39, range of French dishes; ◆◆◆*Le Café Français*, 22 Sukhumvit Soi 24, French seafood; ◆◆◆*Le Café de Paris*, Patpong 2, traditional French food, rec; ◆◆◆*Le Metropolitain*, 135/6 Gaysorn Rd, family French food; ◆◆◆*Longhorn*, 120/9 Sukhumvit Soi 23, Cajun and Creole food; ◆◆◆*Restaurant Des Arts Nouveaux*, 127 Soi Charoensuk, Sukhumvit Soi 55, art nouveau interior, top class French cuisine; ◆◆◆*Ristorante Sorrento*, 66 North Sathorn Rd, excellent Italian food; ◆◆◆*Robertos 18*, 36 Sukhumvit, Soi 18, Italian; ◆◆◆*Senor Pico*, Rembrandt Hotel, 18 Sukhumvit Rd, Mexican, pseudo-Mexican decor, staff dressed Mexican style, large, rather uncosy restaurant, average cuisine; ◆◆◆*Stanley's French Restaurant*, 20/20-21 Ruamrudee Village, good French food, special Sun brunch, closed Mon; ◆◆◆*Terrazzo*, Sukhothai Hotel, 13/3 South Sathorn Rd, T 2870222, stylish al fresco Italian restaurant overlooking the pool, wonderful Italian breads and good pasta dishes, rec; ◆◆◆*Tia Maria*, 14/18 Patpong Soi 1, best Mexican restaurant in Bangkok; ◆◆◆*Trattoria Da Roberto*, 37/9 Plaza Arcade, Patpong 2 Rd, authentic Italian setting; ◆◆◆*Vito's Spaghetteria*, Basement, Gaysorn Plaza, Ploenchit Rd (next to *Le Meridien Hotel*), bright and breezy pasta bar, make up your own dish by combining 10 types of pasta with 12 sauces and 29 fresh condiments, smallish servings but good for a hurried lunch; ◆◆*Caravan Coffee House*, Siam Sq Soi 5, large range of coffee or tea, food includes pizza, curry and some Thai food; ◆◆*Crazy Horse*, 5 Patpong 2 Rd, simple decor, but good French food, open until 0400; ◆◆*Harmonique*, 22 Charoen Krung, small elegant coffee shop with good music, fruit drinks and coffee. *La Brioche*, ground flr of Novotel Hotel, Siam Sq Soi 6, good range of French patisseries.

Other Asian cuisine: ◆◆◆◆*Pho*, Soi Phetburi, off Phetburi Rd, just before central Chidlom Dept Store, best Vietnamese in town in modern trendy setting, advise non-smoking area; ◆◆◆◆*Rang Mahal*, Rembrandt Hotel, Sukhumvit Soi 18, T 2617100, best Indian food in town, very popular with the Indian community and spectacular views from the roof top position, sophisticated, elegant and far...expensive; ◆◆◆*Akamon*, 233 Sukhumvit Soi 21, Japanese; ◆◆◆*Akbar*, 1/4 Sukhumvit Soi 3, Indian, Pakistani and Arabic; ◆◆◆*Bali*, 20/11 Ruamrudee Village, Soi Ruamrudee, Ploenchit Rd, only authentic Indonesian in Bangkok, friendly proprietress; ♦♦♦*Bane Lao*, Naphasup Ya-ak I, off Sukhumvit Soi 36, Laotian open-air restaurant (doubles as a travel agent for Laos), Laotian band, haphazard but friendly service; ♦♦♦*China*, 231/3 Rachdamri Soi Sarasin, Bangkok's oldest Chinese restaurant, serving full range of Chinese cuisine; ♦♦♦*Himali Cha Cha*, 1229/11 Charoen Krung, good choice of Indian cuisine, mountainous meals for the very hungry; ♦♦♦*Kobune*, 3rd Fl, Mahboonkrong (MBK) Centre, Rama 1 Rd, Japanese, Sushi Bar or sunken tables, rec; ♦♦♦*Le Cam-Ly*, 2nd Fl, 1 Patpong Bldg, Surawong Rd, Vietnamese; ♦♦♦*Le Dalat*, Sukhumvit Soi 23, same management as Le Cam-Ly, reputed to serve the best Vietnamese food in Bangkok, arrive early or management may hassle; ♦♦♦*Mandalay*, 23/17 Ploenchit Soi Ruamrudee, authentic Burmese food, most gastronomes of the country reckon the food is the best in the capital, rec; ♦♦♦*Moghul Room*, 1/16 Sukhumvit Soi 11, wide choice of Indian and Muslim food; ♦♦♦*Mrs. Balbir's*, 155/18 Sukhumvit Soi 11, Indian; ♦♦♦*Otafuku*, 484 Siam Sq Soi 6, Henry Dunant Rd, Japanese, Sushi Bar or low tables; ♦♦♦*Sweet Basil*, 1 Silom Soi Srivieng (opp Bangkok Christian College), Vietnamese; ♦♦*Ambassador Food Centre*, Ambassador Hotel, Sukhumvit Rd. A vast self-service, up-market hawkers' centre with a large selection of Asian foods at reasonable prices: Thai, Chinese, Japanese, Vietnamese etc, rec; ♦♦*Bangkok Brindawan*, 15 Sukhumvit Soi 35, S Indian, Sat lunch set-price buffet; ♦♦*Nawab*, 64/39 Soi Wat Suan Plu, Charoen Krung, N and S Indian dishes; ♦♦*New Korea*, 41/1 Soi Chuam Rewang, Sukhumvit Sois 15-19, excellent Korean food in small restaurant, rec; ♦♦*Saigon-Rimsai*, 413/9 Sukhumvit Soi 55, Vietnamese and some Thai dishes, friendly atmosphere; ♦*Samrat*, 273-275 Chakraphet Rd, Pratuleck Lek, Indian and Pakistani food in restaurant down quiet lane off Chakraphet Rd, cheap and tasty, rec; ♦*Tamil Nadu*, 5/1 Silom Soi (Tambisa) 11, good, but limited menu. There are 4 or 5 **Indian** restaurants in a row on Sukhumvit Soi 11.

Thai: ♦♦♦♦♦*Dusit Thani Thai Restaurant*, 946 Rama IV Rd, beautiful surroundings – like an old Thai palace, exquisite Thai food, very expensive wines; ♦♦♦♦♦*Spice Market*, Regent Hotel, 155 Rachdamri Rd, T 2516127, Westernized Thai, typical hotel decoration, arguably the city's best Thai food – simply delectable;

♦♦♦♦*Bussaracum*, 35 Soi Phiphat off Convent Rd, T 2358915, changing menu, popular, rec; ♦♦♦♦*D'jit Pochana Oriental* (aka *Sala Rim Nom*), in Thonburi, directly opp the *Oriental Hotel* (regular boat service from *Oriental* or *Royal Orchid Hotels*, free of charge), traditional Thai pavilion and excellent classic Thai cuisine; ♦♦♦♦-♦♦♦**there are several excellent restaurants in** *Silom Village*, a shopping mall, on Silom Rd (N side, opp Pan Rd), excellent range of food from hundreds of stalls, all cooked in front of you, enjoyable village atmosphere, rec; ♦♦♦♦-♦♦♦*Once Upon a Time*, 67 Soi Anumanrachaton, T 2338493, set in attractive traditional Thai house (between Silom and Surawong rds); ♦♦♦*Ban Chiang*, 14 Srivdieng Rd, T 2367045, quite hard to find – ask for directions, old style Thai house, large menu of traditionally-prepared food; ♦♦♦*Ban Khun Phor*, 458/7-9 Siam Square Soi 8, T 2501252, good Thai food in stylish surroundings; ♦♦♦*Ban Krua*, 29/1 Saladaeng Soi 1, Silom Rd, simple decor, friendly atmosphere, a/c room or open-air garden, traditional Thai food; ♦♦♦*Ban Thai*, Soi 32 or Ruen Thep, Silom Village, Silom Rd, with classical dancing and music; ♦♦♦*Banana Leaf*, Silom complex (basement floor), Silom Rd, T 3213124, excellent and very popular Thai restaurant with some unusual dishes, including *kai manaaw* (chicken in lime sauce), *nam tok muu* (spicy pork salad, Isan style) and fresh spring rolls 'Banana Leaf', booking recommended for lunch; ♦♦♦*Garden Restaurant*, 324/1 Phahonyothin Rd, open-air restaurant or the air-conditioned comfort of a wood panelled room, also serves Chinese, Japanese and International; ♦♦♦*Kaloang*, 2 Sri Ayutthaya Rd, T 2819228. Two dining areas, one on a pier, the other on a boat on the Chao Phraya River, attractive atmosphere, delicious food, rec.; ♦♦♦*Lemon Grass*, Sukhumvit Soi 24, T 2588637, Thai style house, rather dark interior, one step up from Cabbages and Condoms, rec; ♦♦♦*Moon Shadow*, 145 Gaysorn Rd, good seafood, choice of dining-rooms – a/c or open-air; ♦♦♦*Sarah Jane's*, 36/2 Soi Lang Suan, Ploenchit Rd, T 2526572, run by American lady, married to a Thai, best Thai salad in town and good duck, Isan food especially noteworthy, excellent value, rec; ♦♦♦*Seafood Market*, Sukhumvit Soi 24, this famous restaurant has recently moved to new premises, and is said to be both larger and better, "if it swims we have it", choose your seafood from the 'supermarket' and then have it cooked to your own specifications before consuming the creatures at the table, popular; ✦✦✦*Seven Seas*, Sukhumvit Soi 33, T 2597662, quirky 'nouvelle' Thai food, popular with young sophisticated and avant garde Thais; ✦✦✦*Side Walk*, 855/2 Silom Rd (opp Central Dept Store), grilled specialities, also serves French, rec; ✦✦✦*Tum Nak Thai*, 131 Rajdapisek Rd, 'largest' restaurant in the world, 3,000 seats, rather out of the way, classical dancing from 2000-2130; ✦✦✦*Whole Earth*, 93/3 Ploenchit Soi Lang Suan, T 2525574, Thailand's best known vegetarian restaurant, live music, ask to sit at the back downstairs, or sit Thai-style upstairs; ✦✦✦-✦✦*Ban Somrudee* 228/6-7 Siam Square Soi 2, T 2512085; ✦✦*Ban Bung*, 32/10 Mu 2 Intramara 45, Rachadapisek, well known garden restaurant of northern-style pavilions, row around the lake to build up an appetite; ✦✦*Ban Mai*, 121 Sukhumvit Soi 22, Sub-Soi 2, old Thai-style decorations in an attractive house with friendly atmosphere, good value; ✦✦*Cabbages and Condoms*, Sukhumvit Soi 12, Population and Community Development Association (PDA) restaurant so all proceeds go to this charity, eat rice in the Condom Room, drink in the Vasectomy Room, good *tom yam kung* and honey-roast chicken, curries all rather similar, good value, rec; ✦✦*Isn't Classic*, 154 Silom Rd, excellent BBQ, king prawns and Isan specialities like spicy papaya salad (*somtam*); ✦✦*Princess Terrace*, Rama I Soi Kasemsan Nung (1), Thai and French food with BBQ specialities served in small restaurant with friendly service and open terrace down quiet lane, rec; ✦✦*Puang Kaew*, 108 Sukhumvit Soi 23. Large, unusual menu, also serves Chinese; ✦✦*Rung Pueng*, 37 Saladaeng, Soi 2, Silom Rd, traditional Thai food at reasonable prices; ✦✦*Sanuk Nuek*, 397/1 Sukhumvit Soi 55 (Soi Thonglor), small restaurant with unusual decorations, live folk music; ✦✦*September*, 120/1-2 Sukhumvit Soi 23, art nouveau setting, also serves Chinese and European, good value for money; ✦✦*Suda*, 6-6/1 Sukhumvit Rd, Soi 14, rec; ✦✦*Wannakarm*, Sukhumvit Soi 23, T 2584241, well established, very Thai restaurant, grim decor, no English spoken, but rated food.

Travellers' food available in the guesthouse/travellers' hotel areas (see above). *Hello* in Khaosan Rd has been recommended, the portions of food are a good size and they have a useful notice board for leaving messages. Nearly all the restaurants in Khaosan Rd show videos all afternoon and evening. If on a tight budget it is much more sensible to eat in Thai restaurants and stalls where it should be possible to have a good meal for ฿10-20.

● **Bars**

The greatest concentration of bars are in the two 'red light' districts of Bangkok – Patpong (between Silom and Surawong rds) and Soi Cowboy (Sukhumvit). Patpong was transformed from a street of 'tea houses' (brothels serving local clients) into a high-tech lane of go-go bars in 1969 when an American made a major investment. In fact there are two streets, side-by-side, Patpong 1 and Patpong 2. Patpong 1 is the larger and more active, with a host of stalls down the middle at night (see page 589); Patpong 2 supports cocktail bars and, appropriately, pharmacies and clinics for STDs, as well as a few go-go bars. The *Derby King* is one of the most popular with expats and serves what are reputed to be the best club sandwiches in Asia, if not the world. Soi Cowboy is named after the first bar here, the *Cowboy Bar*, established by a retired US Airforce officer. Although some of the bars obviously also offer other forms of entertainment (something that quickly becomes blindingly obvious), there are, believe it or not, some excellent and very reasonably priced bars in these two areas. A small beer will cost ฿45-65, with good (if loud) music and perhaps videos thrown in for free. However, if opting for a bar with a 'show', be prepared to pay considerably more.

Warning Front men will assure customers that there is no entrance charge and a beer is only ฿60, but you can be certain that they will try to fleece you on the way out and can become aggressive if you refuse to pay. Even experienced Bangkok travellers find themselves in this predicament. Massages and more can also be obtained at many places in the Patpong and Soi Cowboy areas. **NB** AIDS is a significant and growing problem in Thailand so it is strongly recommended that customers practice safe sex (see page 25).

A particularly civilized place to have a beer and watch the sun go down is on the verandah of the *Oriental Hotel*, by the banks of the Chao Phraya River, expensive, but romantic; ✦✦✦*Basement Pub* (and restaurant), 946 Rama IV Rd, live music, also serves international food, open 1800-2400; ✦✦✦*Black Scene*, 120/29-30 Sukhumvit Soi 23, live jazz, also serves Thai and French food, open 1700-1300; ✦✦✦*Bobby's Arms*, 2nd Floor, Car Park Bldg, Patpong 2 Rd, English pub and grill, with jazz on Sun from 2000, open 1100-0100; *Gitanes*, 52 Soi Pasana 1, Sukhumvit Soi 63. Live music, open 1800-0100; *King's Castle*, Patpong 1 Rd, another long-standing bar with core of regulars; *Royal Salute*, Patpong 2 Rd, cocktail bar where local farangs end their working days.

Hemingway Bar and Grill, 159/5-8 Sukhumvit Soi 55, live jazz and country music at the w/e, plus Thai and American food, open 1800-0100; **Old West Saloon*, 231/17 Rachdamri Soi Sarasin, live country music, also serves international and Thai food, open 1700-0100. **Picasso Pub*, 1950-52 Ramkamhaeng Rd, Bangkapi. Live music, also serves Thai food, open 1800-0300; **Round Midnight*, 106/12 Soi Langsuan, live blues and jazz, some excellent bands play here, packed at weekends, good atmosphere and worth the trip, also serves Thai and Italian food, open 1700-0400; *Trader Vic's*, Royal Marriott Garden Hotel; **Trumpet Pub* (and restaurant), 7 Sukhumvit Soi 24, live blues and jazz, also serves Thai food, open 1900-0200.

Note For bars with live music also see *Music*, below, under **Entertainment**, page 586.

● **Airline offices**

For airport enquiries call, T 2860190. **Aeroflot**, Regent House, 183 Rachdamri Rd, T 2510617. **Air Canada**, 1053 Charoen Krung, T 2335900. **Air France**, Grd Flr, Charn Issara Tower, 942 Rama IV Rd, T 2339477. **Air India**, 16th Flr, Amarin Tower, 500 Ploenchit Rd, T 2569614. **Air Lanka**, Grd Flr, Charn Issara Tower, 942 Rama IV Rd, T 2369292. **Alitalia**, 8th Flr, Boonmitr Bldg, 138 Silom Rd, T 2334000. **American Airlines**, 518/5 Ploenchit Rd, T 2511393. **Bangkok Airways**, Queen Sirikit National Convention Centre, New Rajdapisek Rd, Klongtoey, T 2293434. **Bangladesh Biman**, Grd Flr, Chongkolnee Bldg, 56 Surawong Rd, T 2357643. **British Airways**, 2nd Flr, Charn Issara Tower, 942 Rama IV Rd, T 2360038. **Canadian Airlines**, 6th Flr, Maneeya Bldg, 518/5 Ploenchit Rd, T 2514521. **Cathay Pacific**, 5th Flr, Charn Issara Tower, 942 Rama IV Rd, T 2336105. **China Airlines**, 4th Flr, Peninsula Plaza, 153 Rachdamri Rd, T 2534241. **Continental Airlines**, CP Tower, 313 Silom Rd, T 2310113. **Delta Airlines**, 7th Flr, Patpong Bldg, Surawong Rd, T 2376438. **Egyptair**, CP Tower, 313 Silom Rd, T 2310503. **Finnair**, 6th Flr, Maneeya Bldg, 518 Ploenchit Rd, T 2515012. **Garuda**, 944/19 Rama IV Rd, T 2330981. **Gulf

Air**, Grd Flr, Maneeya Bldg, 518 Ploenchit Rd, T 2547931. **Japan Airlines**, Wall Street Tower, 33 Surawong Rd, T 2332440. **KLM**, Patpong Bldg, 2 Surawong Rd, T 2355155. **Korean Air**, Grd Flr, Kong Bunma Bldg, (opp *Narai Hotel*), 699 Silom Rd, T 2340846. **Kuwait Airways**, 159 Rajdamri Rd, T 2515855. *Lao Aviation*, 491 17 Ground Floor, Silom Plaza, Silom Rd, T 2369822. **Lufthansa**, Bank of America Bldg, 2/2 Witthayu Rd, T 2550370. **MAS**, 98-102 Surawong Rd, T 2364705. **Myanmar Airways**, Charn Issara Tower, 942 Rama IV Rd, T 2342985. **Pakistan International**, 52 Surawong Rd, T 2342961. **Philippine Airlines**, Chongkolnee Bldg, 56 Surawong Rd, T 2332350. **Qantas**, 11th Flr, Charn Issara Tower, 942 Rama IV Rd, T 2360102. **Royal Brunei**, 20th Flr, Charn Issara Tower, 942 Rama IV Rd, T 2340007. **Royal Nepal Airlines**, Sivadm Bldg, 1/4 Convent Rd, T 2333921. **Sabena**, CCT Bldg, 109 Surawong Rd, T 2332020. **SAS**, 412 Rama I Rd, T 2538333. **Saudi**, CCT Bldg, 109 Surawong Rd, T 2369355. **Singapore Airlines**, 12th Flr, Silom Centre, 2 Silom Rd, T 2360440. **Swissair**, 1 Silom Rd, T 2332935. **Thai**, 485 Silom Rd, T 2333810. **TWA**, 12th Flr, Charn Issara Tower, 942 Rama IV Rd, T 2337290. **Vietnam Airlines**, 584 Ploenchit Rd, T 2514242.

● **Banks & money changers**

There are countless exchange booths in all the tourist areas open 7 days a week, mostly 0800-1530, some from 0800-2100. Rates vary only marginally between banks, although if changing a large sum, it is worth shopping around.

● **Embassies**

Australia, 37 Sathorn Tai Rd, T 2872680. **Brunei**, 154 Ekamai Soi 14, Sukhumvit 63, T 3916017, F 3815921. **Burma** (Myanmar), 132 Sathorn Nua Rd, T 2332237. **Canada**, 12th Flr, Boonmitr Bldg, 138 Silom Rd, T 2341561/8. **Czechoslovakia**, Robinson Bldg, 16th Flr, 99 Witthayu Rd, T 2556063. **Denmark**, 10 Sathorn Tai Soi Attakarnprasit, T 2132021. **Finland**, 16th Flr, Amarin Plaza, 500 Ploenchit Rd, T 2569306. **France**, 35 Customs House Lane, Charoen Krung, T 2340950. (There is also a French consulate at 29 Sathorn Tai Rd, T 2856104.) **Germany**, 9 Sathorn Tai Rd, T 2132331. **Indonesia**, 600-602 Phetburi Rd, T 2523135. **Greece**, 79 Sukhumvit Soi 4, T 2542936, F 2542937. **Italy**, 399 Nang Linchi Rd, T 2872054. **Laos**, 193 Sathorn Tai Rd, T 2131203. **Malaysia**, 35 Sathorn Tai Rd,

T 2861390. **Netherlands**, 106 Witthayu Rd, T 2547701. **New Zealand**, 93 Witthayu Rd, T 2518165. **Norway**, 1st Flr, Bank of America Bldg, Witthayu Rd, T 2530390. **People's Republic of China**, 7 Ratchadapisek Rd, Dindaeng, T 2457032. **Philippines**, 760 Sukhumvit Rd, T 2590139. **Singapore**, 129 Sathorn Tai Rd, T 2862111. **South Africa**, 6th Flr, Park Place, 231 Soi Sarasin, Rachdamri Rd, T 2538473. **Spain**, 93 Witthayu Rd, T 2526112. **Sweden**, 20th Flr, Pacific Place, 140 Sukhumvit Rd, T 2544954. **UK**, Wireless Rd, Bangkok 10500, T 2530191/9. **USA**, 95 Witthayu Rd, T 2517201. **Vietnam**, 83/1 Witthayu Rd, T 2517201.

● **Entertainment**

Art galleries: *The Artist's Gallery*, 60 Pan Rd, off Silom, selection of international works of art. *The Neilson Hays Library*, 195 Surawong Rd, has a changing programme of exhibitions.

Buddhism: the headquarters of the World Fellowship of Buddhists is at 33 Sukhumvit Rd (between Soi 1 and Soi 3). Meditation classes are held in English on Wed at 1700-2000; lectures on Buddhism are held on the first Wed of each month at 1800-2000.

Classical music: at the Goethe Institute 18/1 Sathorn Tai Soi Attakarnprasit; check newspapers for programme.

Cinemas: most cinemas have daily showings at 1200, 1400, 1700, 1915 and 2115, with a 1300 matinee on weekends and holidays. Cinemas with English soundtracks include *Central Theatre 2*, T 5411065, *Lido*, T 2526729, *Pantip*, T 2512390, *Pata*, T 4230568, *Mackenna*, T 2517163, *Washington 1*, T 2582045, *Washington 2*, T 2582008, *Scala*, T 2512861, *Villa*, T 2589291. The *Alliance Française*, 29 Sathorn Tai Rd, T 2132122 shows French films. Remember to stand for the National Anthem, which is played before every performance. Details of showings from English language newspapers.

Cultural centres: British Council, 428 Siam Square Soi 8, T 2526136, for films, books and other Anglocentric entertainment; Check in 'What's On' section of *Sunday Bangkok Post* for programme of events; Alliance Française, 29 Sathorn Tai Rd; Goethe Institute, 18/1 Sathorn Tai Soi Attakarnprasit; Siam Society, 131 Soi 21 (Asoke) Sukhumvit, T 2583494, open Tues-Sat. Promotes Thai culture and or-

ganizes trips within (and beyond) Thailand.

Discos: *anas*, 3rd Flr, Oriental Plaza, Charoen Krung Soi 38; *Grand Palace*, 19th Flr, Rajapark Bldg, Sukhumvit Soi Asoke, 2100-0200.

Fortune tellers: there are up to ten soothsayers in the *Montien Hotel* lobby, Surawong Rd, on a regular basis.

Health club: *Phillip Wain International*, 8th Fl, Pacific Place, 140 Sukhumvit Rd, T 2542544. Open Mon-Sat 0700-2200.

Music: (see also **Bars**, page 584, for more places with live music): *Blues-Jazz*, 25 Sukhumvit Soi 53, open Mon-Sun 1900-0200, three house bands play really good blues and jazz, food available, drinks a little on the steep side. *Blue Moon*, 73 Sukhumvit 55 (Thonglor), open Mon-Sun 1800-0300, for country, rhythm, blues and jazz – particularly Fri and Sun for jazz – some food available. *Brown Sugar*, 231/20 Sarasin Rd (opp Lumpini Park), open Mon-Fri 1100-0100, Sat and Sun 1700-0200, five regular bands play excellent jazz, a place for Bangkok's trendies to hang out and be cool. *Cool Tango*, 23/51 Block F, Royal City Av (between Phetburi and Rama IX rds), open Tue-Sat 1100-0200, Sun 1800-0200, excellent resident rock band, great atmosphere, happy hour(s) 1800-2100. *Front Page*, 14/10 Soi Saladaeng 1, open Mon-Fri 1000-0100, Sat and Sun 1800-0100, populated, as the name might suggest, by journos who like to hunt in packs more than most, music is country, folk and blues, food available. *Hard Rock Café*, 424/3-6 Siam Sq Soi 11, open Mon-Sun 1100-0200, speaks for itself, burgers, beer and rock covers played by reasonable house band. *Magic Castle*, 212/33 Sukhumvit Plaza Soi 12, open Mon-Thu 1800-0100, Fri and Sat 1800-0200, mostly blues, some rock, good place for a relaxed beer with skilfully performed covers. *Picasso Pub*, 1950-5 Ramkhomhaeng Rd (close to Soi 8), open Mon-Sun 1900-0300, house rock band, adept at playing covers. *Round Midnight*, 106/12 Soi Langsuan, open Mon-Thu 1900-0230, Fri and Sat 1900-0400, jazz, blues and rock bands.

Magic Land, 72 Phahonyothin Rd. Amusement park with ferris wheel, roller coaster, etc. Admission ฿40 adults, ฿30 children. Open 1000-1800 Mon-Sun. **Getting there**: nr *Central Plaza Hotel* – ask for 'Daen Neramit'.

Safari World: 300 acre complex in Minburi, 9 km from the city centre, with animals and amusement park (T 5107295). **Getting**

there: bus No 26 from the Victory Monument to Minburi where a minibus service runs to the park.

Siam Park City: water world, theme park, zoo, botanical gardens and fair all rolled into one, 101 Sukhapibarn 2 Rd, Bangkapi, T 5171032, 30 mins E of town, or 1 hr by bus 26 or 27 from Victory Monument. Admission ฿200. Open 1000-1800 Mon-Fri, 0900-1900 Sat-Sun.

Thai Cookery Courses: the *Oriental Hotel* organizes a 5 day course, with different areas of cuisine covered each day, 0900-1200. ฿2,500/class or ฿11,500 for 5 classes. T 236 0400 ext 3456. *Wandee's Kitchen School*, 134/5-6 Silom Rd (on the 5th Fl, above the Dokya Book Shop), T 2372051, also offer a 5 day, 40 hour course from Mon-Fri but at the slightly cheaper rate of ฿5,200. Successful students emerge with a certificate and reeking faintly of chillies and *nam plaa*. There are also yet cheaper courses still run by Mrs Balbir every Fri 0930-1130, in which she instructs small classes of 10 or so, ฿100, 155/18 Sukhumvit Soi 11, T 2352281; and at *UFM Baking and Cooking School*, 593/29-39 Sukhumvit Soi 33, T 2590620 where classes hare held 0900-1000 Mon-Fri, again in groups of about 10.

Thai Performing Arts: classical dancing and music is often performed at restaurants after a 'traditional' Thai meal has been served. Many tour companies or travel agents organize these 'cultural evenings'. *National Theatre*, Na Phrathat Rd, (T 2214885 for programme). Thai classical dramas, dancing and music on the last Fri of each month at 1730 and periodically on other days. *Thailand Cultural Centre*, Rachdaphisek Rd, Huai Khwang, T 2470028 for programme of events. *College of Dramatic Arts*, nr National Theatre, T 2241391. *Baan Thai Restaurant*, 7 Sukhumvit Soi 32, T 2585403, 2100-2145. *Chao Phraya Restaurant*, Pinklao Bridge, Arun Amarin Rd, T 4742389; *Maneeya's Lotus Room*, Ploenchit Rd, T 2526312, 2015-2100; *Piman Restaurant*, 46 Sukhumvit Soi 49, T 2587866, 2045-2130; *Ruen Thep*, Silom Village Trade Centre, T 2339447, 2020-2120; *D'jit Pochana Coka Sala Rim Nam*, the *Oriental Hotel's* Thai restaurant, on the Thonburi side of the Chao Phraya River shuttle boat from the *Oriental*, Charoen Nakhon Rd, T 4376221; *Suwannahong Restaurant*, Sri Ayutthaya Rd, T 2454448, 2015-2115; *Tum-Nak-Thai Restaurant*, 131 Rachdaphisek Rd, T 2773828

2030-2130.

Thai traditional massage: see box. 126/2 Khaosan Rd, T 2826655.

● **Hospitals & medical services**

Bangkok Adventist Hospital, 430 Phitsanulok Rd, Dusit, T 2811422/2821100; *Bangkok Nursing Home*, 9 Convent Rd, T 2332610; *St. Louis Hospital*, 215 Sathorn Tai Rd, T 2120033. **Health clinics**: *Dental Polyclinic*, New Phetburi Rd, T 3145070; *Dental Hospital*, 88/88 Sukhumvit 49, T 2605000, F 2605026, good, but expensive; *Clinic Banglamphu*, 187 Chakrapong Rd, T 2827479. **Doctors**: Dr Philippe Balankura, 1 Nares Rd (not far from GPO), T 2361389, English, French and Thai speaking. Dr Vangvarothai Singhasivanon, Sathorn Hospital, 27/2 Soi Yommarat, Saladaeng, Silom Rd, T 2334706, French and English speaking.

● **Immigration**

Sathorn Tai Soi Suanphlu, T 2873101.

● **Language Schools**

Bangkok has scores. The best known is the AUA school at 179 Rachdomri, T 2528170.

● **Libraries**

British Council Library, 428 Rama I, Siam Sq, open Tue-Sat 1000-1930, membership library with good selection of English language books. *National Library*, Samsen Rd, close to Sri Ayutthaya Rd, open Mon-Sun 0930-1930; *Neilson Hays Library*, 195 Surawong Rd, T 2331731, next door to British Club. A small library of English-language books housed in an elegant building dating from 1922. It is a private membership library, but welcomes visitors who might want to see the building and browse; occasional exhibitions are held here. Open 0930-1600 Mon-Sat, 0930-1230 Sun. *Siam Society Library*, 131 Sukhumvit Soi 21 (Asoke), open Tue-Sat 0900-1700, membership library with excellent collection of Thai and foreign language books and periodicals (especially English) on Thailand and mainland south east Asia.

● **Massage**

See **Traditional Thai Massage**, below.

● **Meditation and Yoga**

The *Dharma Study Foundation*, 128 Soi Thonglor 4, Sukhumvit Soi 55, T 3916006, open 0900-1800 Mon-Fri and the *World Fellowship of Buddhists*, 33 Sukhumvit Rd (between sois 1 and 3), T 2511188, open 0900-1630 Mon-Fri, both offer classes in meditation and some religious discussions. Yoga classes available at

Sunee Yoga Centre, 2nd Fl, Pratunam Centre, 78/4 Rachprarop Rd, T 2549768, open 1000-1200 and 1700-1900 Mon-Sat.

● **Post & telecommunications**
Area code: 02.
Central GPO (*Praysani Klang* for taxi drivers): Charoen Krung, opp the *Ramada Hotel*. Open 0800-2000 Mon-Fri and 0800-1300 weekend and holidays. The money and postal order service is open 0800-1700, Mon-Fri, 0800-1200 Sat. Closed on Sun and holidays. 24 hrs telegram and telephone service (phone rates are reduced 2100-0700) and a packing service. **Post Office**: Tani Rd, closest for Khaosan Rd.

● **Places of worhsip**
Evangelical Church, Sukhumvit Soi 10 (0930 Sun service); the *International Church* (interdenominational), 67 Sukhumvit Soi 19 (0800 Sun service); *Baptist Church*, 2172/146 Phahonyothin Soi 36 (1800 Sun service); *Holy Redeemer*, 123/19 Wittayu Soi Ruam Rudee (Catholic, 5 services on Sun); *Christ Church*, 11 Convent Rd (Anglican – Episcopalian – Ecumenical) (3 Sun services at 0730, 1000 and 1800).

● **Shopping**
Most shops do not open until 1000-1100. Nancy Chandler's *Map of Bangkok* is the best shopping guide. Bangkok still stocks a wonderful range of goods, but do not expect to pick up a bargain – prices are high. Stallholders, entirely understandably, are out for all they can get – so bargain hard here. The traditional street market, although not dying out, is now supplemented by other types of shopping. Given the heat, the evolution of the air conditioned shopping arcade and air conditioned department store in Bangkok was just a matter of time. Some arcades target the wealthier shopper, and are dominated by brand name goods and designer ware. Others are not much more than street side stalls transplanted to an arcade environment. Most department stores are now fixed price.

Bangkok's main shopping areas are:

1. Sukhumvit: Sukhumvit Rd, and the sois to the N are lined with shops and stalls, especially around the *Ambassador* and *Landmark* hotels. Many tailors and made-to-measure shoe shops are to be found in this area.

2. Central: 2 areas close to each other centred on Rama I and Ploenchit rds. At the intersection of Phayathai and Rama I rds there is Siam Square (for teenage trendy Western clothing, bags, belts, jewellery, bookshops, some antique shops and American fast food chains) and the massive – and highly popular – Mah Boonkhrong Centre (MBK), with countless small shops and stalls and the Tokyu Department Store. Peninsular Plaza, between the *Hyatt Erawan* and *Regent* hotels is considered the smartest shopping plaza in Bangkok. For those looking for fashion clothes and accessories, this is probably the best area. A short distance to the E, centred on Ploenchit/Rachprarop rds, are more shopping arcades and large department stores, including the World Trade Centre, Thai Daimaru, Robinsons, Gaysorn Plaza (exclusive shopping arcade),

---

TRADITIONAL THAI MASSAGE

While a little less arousing than the Patpong-style massage, the traditional Thai massage or *nuat boroan* is probably more invigorating, using methods similar to those of Shiatsu, reflexology and osteopathic manipulation. It probably has its origins in India, and is a form of yoga. It aims to release blocked channels of energy and soothe tired muscles. A full massage should last 1-2 hrs and cost ¢150/hr. The thumbs are used to apply pressure on the 10 main 'lines' of muscles, so both relaxing and invigorating the muscles. Headaches, ankle and knee pains, neck and back problems can all be alleviated through this ancient art (a European visitor to the Siamese court at Ayutthaya noted the practise of Thai massage, 400 years ago). Centres of massage can be found in most Thai towns – wats and tourist offices are the best sources of information on where to go. In Bangkok, Wat Pho is the best known centre and murals on the temple buildings' walls help to guide the student. For Thais, this form of massage is as much a spiritual experience as a physical one – hence its association with monasteries and the Buddha (see page 544).

Naraiphan shopping centre (more of a market stall affair, geared to tourists, in the basement) and Central Chidlom. North along Rachprasong Rd, crossing over Khlong Saensap, at the intersection with Phetburi Rd is the Pratunam market, good for fabrics and clothing.

3. Patpong/Silom: Patpong is more of a night market (opening at 2100), the streets are packed with stalls selling the usual array of stall goods which seem to stay the same from year to year (fake designer clothing, watches, bags etc). **NB** Bargain hard. The E end of Silom has a scattering of similar stalls open during the day time, and Robinsons Department Store. Surawong Rd (at the other end of Patpong) has Thai silk, antiques and a few handicraft shops.

4. West Silom/Charoen Krung (New Rd): antiques, jewellery, silk, stamps, coins and bronzeware. Stalls set up here at 2100. A 15 min walk N along Charoen Krung (close to the *Orchid Sheraton Hotel*) is the River City Shopping Plaza, specializing in art and antiques.

5. Banglamphu/Khaosan Road: vast variety of low-priced goods, such as ready-made clothes, shoes, bags, jewellery and cassette tapes.

6. Lardphrao-Phahonyothin: some distance N of town, not far from the Weekend Market (see page 568) is the huge Central Plaza shopping complex. It houses a branch of the Central Department Store and has many boutiques and gift shops.

Department Stores: *Central* is the largest chain of department stores in Bangkok, with a range of Thai and imported goods at fixed prices; credit cards are accepted. Main shops on Silom Rd, Ploenchit Rd (Chidlom Branch), and in the Central Plaza, just N of the Northern bus terminal. Other department stores include **Thai Daimaru** on Rachdamri and Sukhumvit (opp Soi 71), **Robinson's** on corner of Silom and Rama IV rds, Sukhumvit (nr Soi 19) and Rachdamri rds, **Tokyu** in MBK Tower on Rama I Rd, **Sogo** in the Amarin Plaza on Ploenchit Rd, and **Zen**, World Trade Centre, corner of Rama I and Rajdamri rds.

Supermarkets: *Central Department Store* (see above), *Robinsons* – open until midnight (see above), *Villa Supermarket*, between Sois 33 and 35, Sukhumvit Rd – for everything you are unable to find anywhere else, *Isetan*, (World Trade Centre), Rachdamri Rd.

Markets: the markets in Bangkok are an excellent place to browse, take photographs and pick up bargains. They are part of the life blood of the city, and the encroachment of more organized shops and the effects of the re-developer's demolition ball are eating away at one of Bangkok's finest traditions. Nancy Chandler's map of Bangkok, available from most bookshops, is the most useful guide to the markets of the capital. The largest is the **Weekend Market** at Chatuchak Park (see page 568). The **Tewes Market**, nr the National Library, is a photographers dream; a daily market, selling flowers and plants. **Pratunam Market** is spread over a large area around Rachprarop and Phetburi rds, and is famous for clothing and fabric. Half of it was recently bulldozed for redevelopment, but there is still a multitude of stalls here. The *Bai Yoke Market* is next door and sells mostly fashion garments for teenagers – lots of lycra. **Nakhon Kasem** known as the **Thieves Market**, in the heart of Chinatown, houses a number of 'antique' shops selling brassware, old electric fans and woodcarvings (tough bargaining recommended, and don't expect everything to be genuine – see page 557). Close by are the stalls of **Sampeng Lane** (see page 557), specializing in toys, stationery, clothes and household goods, and the **Pahurat Cloth Market** (see page 557) – a small slice of India in Thailand, with mounds of sarongs, batiks, buttons and bows. **Bangrak Market**, S of the General Post Office, nr the river and the *Shangri-La Hotel*, sells exotic fruit, clothing, seafood and flowers. **Pak Khlong Market** is a wholesale market selling fresh produce, orchids and cut flowers and is situated nr the Memorial Bridge (see page 557). **Phahonyothin Market** is Bangkok's newest, opp the Northern bus terminal, and sells potted plants and orchids. **Banglamphu Market** is close to Khaosan Rd, the backpackers' haven, on Chakrapong and Phra Sumen rds. Stalls here sell clothing, shoes, food and household goods. The nearby **Khaosan Road Market** (if it can be called such) is much more geared to the needs and desires of the foreign tourist: CDs and cassettes, batik shirts, leather goods and so on. **Patpong Market**, arranged down the middle of Patpong Rd, linking Silom and Surawong rds, opens up about 1700 and is geared to tourists, selling handicrafts, T-shirts, leather goods, fake watches, cassettes and VDOs. **Penang Market**, Khlong Toey, situated under the expressway close to the railway line specializes in electronic equipment from hi-fis to computers, with a spattering of other goods as well. A specialist market is the **Stamp Market** next to the GPO on Charoen Krung which operates on Sun only. Collectors come here to buy or exchange stamps.

Specialist Shops Antiques: Chinese porcelain, old Thai paintings, Burmese tapestries, wooden figures, hilltribe art, Thai ceramics and Buddhist art. Be careful of fakes – go to the well-known shops only. Even they, however, have been known to sell fake Khmer sculpture which even the experts find difficult to tell apart from the real thing. Permission to take antiques out of the country must be obtained from the *Fine Arts Department* on Na Phrathat Rd, T 2214817. Shops will often arrange export licences for their customers. Buddha images may not be taken out of the country – although many are. A large number of the more expensive antique shops are concentrated in *River City*, a shopping complex next to the *Royal Orchid Sheraton Hotel* and an excellent place to start. More shops can be found in the Gaysorn area. *NeOld*, 149 Surawong Rd has a good selection of new and old objects, but it's pricey. *Peng Seng*, 942/1-3 Rama IV Rd, on the corner of Surawong Rd, has an excellent selection of antiques. *Thai House Antiques*, 720/6 Sukhumvit (nr Soi 28). *L'Arcadia*, 12/2 Sukhumvit Soi 23, Burmese antiques, beds, ceramics, carvings, doors, expensive but good quality. *Jim Thompson's*, Surawang Rd, for a range of antiques, wooden artefacts, furnishings and carpets.

NB Some of the more unscrupulous shops have allegedly 'obtained' works of art from Burma and Cambodia; customers can choose their piece from a brochure, and then it is 'removed' from the appropriate monument. Whether it is real or fake, this is NOT to be encouraged. Report offending shops to the *Fine Arts Department* or the Tourist Police. For the serious, see Brown, Robin (1989) *Guide to buying antiques and arts and crafts in Thailand*, Times Books: Singapore.

Books: *Asia Books* has the most extensive stock of books in Bangkok. They can be found at 221 Sukhumvit Rd, between Sois 15 and 17; 2nd floor Peninsula Plaza, Rachdamri Rd; Ground floor and 3rd floors, Landmark Plaza. Patpong has two book stores – *The Bookseller* (81, Patpong I) and *Bangkok Christian Bookstore*. *Chulalongkorn University Book Centre*, in University compound (ask for 'suun nang suu Chula') for academic, business and travel books. *DK (Duang Kamol) Books* in Siam Square and on the 3rd floor of the Mahboonkhrong Centre, is the best source of locally published books in English. They also have branches on the 3rd floor of the Mahboonkrong Centre (MBK), at the corner of Phoyathai and Rama I rds, and at 180/1 Sukhumvit (between sois 8 and 10). *Elite Used Books*, 593/5 Sukhumvit Rd, nr Villa Supermarket. Good range of secondhand books in several languages. *White Lotus*, 26 Soi Attakarnprasit, Sathorn Tai Rd, collectors books on Southeast Asia. *Kinokuniya*, 6th floor, Isetan Dept Store, World Trade Centre, Rachdamri Rd, selection of English language books. *Dokya*, 258/8-10 Soi Siam Sq 3. Books are also sold in the Central Department Stores, 1027 Ploenchit Rd, 1691 Pahonyothin Rd, and 306 Silom Rd. Second-hand books are also available at the *Chatuchak Weekend Market* (see page 568) in sections 22 and 25.

Bronzeware: Thai or the less elaborate Western designs are available in Bangkok. There are a number of shops along Charoen Krung, N from Silom Rd, eg Siam Bronze Factory at No 1250.

Celadon: distinctive ceramic ware, originally produced during the Sukhothai Period (from the late 13th century), and recently revived. *Thai Celadon House*, 8/8 Rachdapisek Rd, Sukhumvit Rd (Soi 16), also sells seconds, or from *Narayana Phand*, Rachdamri Rd.

Designer ware: clothing, watches, leather goods etc, all convincing imitations, can be bought for very reasonable prices from the many roadside stalls along Sukhumvit and Silom rds, Siam Square and in other tourist areas. Times Square, on Sukhumvit 14 has several 'designer clothing' shops.

Dolls: there is a Thai doll factory on Soi Ratchataphan (Soi Mo Leng) off Rachprarop Rd in Pratunam. The factory sells dolls to visitors and also has a display. Open 0800-1700 Mon-Sat (T 2453008).

Furniture: between Soi 43 and Soi 45, Sukhumvit Rd, is an area where rattan furniture is sold. *Rattan House*, 795-797 Sukhumvit Rd (between Soi 43 and 45); *Corner 43*, 487/1-2 Sukhumvit Rd (between Soi 25-27).

Gold: this is considerably cheaper than in USA or Europe; there is a concentration of shops along Yaowaraj Rd (Chinatown), mostly selling the yellow 'Asian' gold. Price is determined by weight (its so-called 'baht weight').

Handicrafts: the *State Handicraft Centre*,

BUYING GEMS AND JEWELLERY

More people lose their money through gem and jewellery scams in Thailand than in any other way (60% of complaints to the TAT involve gem scams). **DO NOT** fall for any story about gem sales, special holidays, tax breaks – no matter how convincing. **NEVER** buy gems from people on the street (or beach) and try not to be taken to a shop by an intermediary. **ANY** unsolicited approach is likely to be a scam. The problem is perceived to be so serious that in some countries, Thai embassies are handing out warning leaflets with visas. For more background to Thailand and Burma's gems see page 425.

Rules of thumb to avoid being cheated

● Choose a specialist store in a relatively prestigious part of town (the TAT will informally recommend stores).

● Note that no stores are authorized by the TAT or by the Thai government; if they claim as much they are lying.

● It is advisable to buy from shops who are members of the Thai Gem and Jewellery Traders Association.

● Avoid touts.

● Never be rushed into a purchase.

● Do not believe stories about vast profits from re-selling gems at home. They are lies.

● Do not agree to have items mailed ("for safety").

● If buying a valuable gem, a certificate of identification is a good insurance policy. The Department of Mineral Resources (Rama VI Rd, T 2461694) and the Asian Institute of Gemological Sciences (484 Rachadapisek Rd, T 5132112) will both examine stones and give such certificates.

● Compare prices; competition is stiff among the reputable shops; be suspicious of 'bargain' prices.

● Ask for a receipt detailing the stone and recording the price.

For more information (and background reading on Thailand) the *'Buyer's Guide to Thai Gems and Jewellery'*, by John Hoskin can be bought at Asia Books.

(*Narayana Phand*), 127 Rachdamri Rd, just N of Gaysorn, is a good place to view the range of goods made around the country. *House of Handicrafts*, *Regent Hotel*, 155 Rajdamri Rd; *House of Handicrafts*, 3rd floor, Amarin Plaza, 496-502 Ploenchit Rd.

Jewellery: Thailand has become the world's largest gem cutting centre and it is an excellent place to buy both gems and jewellery. The best buy of the native precious stones is the sapphire. Modern jewellery is well designed and of a high quality. Always insist on a certificate of authenticity and a receipt. *Ban Mo*, on Pahurat Rd, N of Memorial Bridge is the centre of the gem business although there are shops in all the tourist areas particularly on Silom Rd nr the intersection with Surasak Rd, eg *Mr Ho's*, 987 Silom Rd, *Uthai Gems*, 28/7 Soi Ruam Rudi, off Ploenchit Rd, just E of Witthayu Rd are rec. For western designs, *Living Extra* and *Yves Joaillier* are to be found on the 3rd floor of the Charn Issara Tower, 942 Rama IV Rd. Dedicated gem buildings are now under construction, eg *Gems Tower* opp Oriental Lane (completion due Mar 1993), while the Jewellery Trade Centre is under construction on the corner of Silom Rd and Surasak Rd, next door to the *Holiday Inn Crowne Plaza*. This is due to be finished Aug 1995 and will be an important gem centre and diamond house. (T 2373600 for information.)

Pottery: there are several pottery 'factories' on the LHS of the road on the way to the Rose Garden, nr Samut Sakhon (see page 571).

Shoes: the *Siam Bootery* is a chain of shops for handmade footwear.

Silk: beware of 'bargains', as the silk may have been interwoven with rayon. It is best to stick to the well-known shops unless you know what you are doing. Silk varies greatly in quality. Generally, the heavier the weight the more expensive the fabric. One ply is the lightest and cheapest (about ฿200/m), four ply the heaviest and most expensive (about ฿300-400/m). Silk also comes in three grades; grade one is the finest and smoothest and comes from the inner part of the cacoon. Finally, there is also 'hard' and 'soft' silk, soft being rather more expensive. Hand-made patterned silk, especially *matmii* from the NE region, can be much more expensive than simple, single coloured industrial silk – well over ฿10,000 per piece. There are a number of specialist silk shops at the top of Surawong Rd (nr Rama IV), including the famous *Jim Thompson's* (which is expensive, but has the best selection). Open 0900-2100 Mon-Sun. There are also a number of shops along the bottom half of Silom Rd (towards Charoen Krung) and in the Siam centre on Rama I Rd. *Anita Thai Silk*, 294/4-5 Silom Rd, slightly more expensive than some, but the extensive range makes it worth a visit. *Home Made (HM) Thai Silk*, 45 Sukhumvit Soi 35 (silk made on premises), good quality matmii silk. Village-made silks also available from *Cabbages and Condoms* (also a restaurant) on Sukhumvit Soi 12 and Raja Siam, Sukhumvit Soi 23. *Khompastr*, 52/10 Surawong Rd, nr *Montien Hotel*, distinctive screen-printed fabric from Hua Hin. Factory (industrial) silk available from *Shinawatra* on Sukhumvit Soi 31. Numerous stalls at the Chatuchak weekend market also sell lengths from Laos and NE Thailand (see page 568).

Spectacles: glasses and contact lenses are a good buy in Bangkok and can be made-up in 24 hrs. Opticians are to be found throughout the city.

Tailoring services: Bangkok's tailors are skilled at copying anything; either from fashion magazines or from a piece of your own clothing. Always request a fitting, ask to see a finished garment, ask for a price in writing and pay as small a deposit as possible. Tailors are concentrated along Silom, Sukhumvit and Ploenchit rds and Gaysorn Square. Indian tailors appear to offer the quickest service. *N and Y Boutique*, 11 Chartered Bank Lane (Oriental Ave), nr the *Oriental Hotel* (for ladies tailored clothes) and *Rajawongse*, 130 Sukhumvit Rd (near Sukhumvit Soi 4) have both been recommended. There are many other places, though.

Textiles: *Prayer Textile Gallery*, 197 Phayathai Rd, good range and excellent quality traditional and Laotian textiles.

● **Sports**

Facilities for sports such as badminton, squash or tennis are either available at the 4 to 5-star hotels or are listed in Bangkok's Yellow Pages.

Bowling: *PS Bowl*, 1191 Ramkamhaeng Rd, Huamark, 1000-0100 Mon-Thur, 1000-0200 Fri, Sat, Sun. *Sukhumvit Bowl*, 2 Sukhumvit Soi 63 (Ekamoi), open 1000-0100 Mon-Sun.

Diving: *Dive Master*, 110/63 Ladprao Soi 18, T 5121664, F 5124889, organize dive trips, NAVI and PADI courses and sell (or rent) diving equipment.

Golf: Most courses open at 0600 and play continues 'till dusk. Green fees vary from ฿400-2,000. Most also have clubs for hire. Telephone beforehand to check on availability. *Royal Thai Army*, 459 Ram Inthra Rd, Bangkhen, T 5211530, 25 mins from city centre, weekday green fee ฿400, 36 holes; *Krungthep Sports Golf Club*, 516 Krungthep Kritha Rd, Huamark, Bangkapi, T 3740491, 30 mins from city centre; *Railway Training Centre Golf Club*, Vibhavadi Rangsit Rd, Bangkhen, T 2710130, 15 mins from city centre; *Royal Thai Airforce Golf Club*, Vibhavadi Rangsit Rd, Bangkhen, T 5236103; *UNICO Golf Course*, 47 Mu 7, Krungthep Kritha Rd, Phra Khanong, T 3779038, 20 mins from city centre. Each has an 18-hole course and clubs can usually be hired for about ฿250. Green fees are usually double at weekends. Phone to check availability. *Rose Garden*, 4/8 Sukhumvit Soi 3, T 2953261, 45 mins from the city centre (green fees ฿300 weekdays, ฿600 weekends, club hire ฿200); *Royal Dusit*, Phitsanulok Rd, T 2814320 (green fees ฿320, weekdays ฿530 weekends, club hire ฿200; *Muang-Ake*, 34 Mu 7, Phahonyothin Rd, Amphoe Muang, Pathum Thani, T 5339336, 40 mins from city centre (green fees ฿300 weekdays, ฿600 weekends, club hire ฿300). Phone to check regulations for temporary membership. There are also a number of golf practice/driving ranges off New Phetburi and Sukhumvit rds. Check the Yellow Pages or *Bangkok Metro Magazine* for details.

Horse racing: at the *Royal Turf Club* and *Royal Sports Club* at the weekends, each card usually consists of 10 races. Check newspapers for details.

Kite flying: kites are sold at Sanaam Luang for ฿15-20 on Sun and public holidays during the 'season' (see page 550).

Spectator sports: Sanaam Luang, nr the Grand Palace, is a good place to sample traditional Thai sports. From late Feb to the middle of Apr there is a traditional Thai Sports Fair held here. It is possible to watch **kite-fighting**, and **takraw** (the only Thai ball game, a takraw ball is made of rattan, 5"-6" in diameter. Players hit the ball over a net to an opposing team, using their feet, head, knees and elbows – but not hands – and the ball should not be touched by the same team member twice in succession. Regions of Thailand tend to have their own variants of the sport; *sepak takraw* is the competition sport with a nationwide code of rules), **Thai chess, krabi** and **krabong** (a swordfighting contest).

Swimming: *NTT Sports Club*, 612/26 Soi Lao Lada, Phra Pinkklao Bridge Rd. Large pool open to public with sports centre, just N of Sanaam Luang, on the river (฿100). There are a number of other public pools as well as private pool which allow non-members/non-residents to swim for a small fee. For a full listing, see the capital's listing magazine *Bangkok Metro*.

Tennis: courts in many hotels. Public courts available at: *Central Tennis Club*, Sathorn Tai Soi Attakarnprasit, T 2867202, open 0700-2200 Mon-Fri, 1100-2100 Sat and Sun, ฿80-150/hour, 5 courts, showers, racket hire and food available; *Volvo Sports Club*, Ramkhamhaeng Soi 13 (near mall 3), T 3180322, open 0700-2200 Mon-Sun, ฿120/hr, good facilities, 6 courts, racket hire, hot showers.

Thai boxing: is both a sport and a means of self-defence and was first developed during the Ayutthaya Period, 1350-1767. It differs from Western boxing in that contestants are allowed to use almost any part of their body. Traditional music is played during bouts. There are two boxing stadiums in Bangkok – Lumpini (T 2804550) on Rama IV Rd, near Lumpini Park and Rachadamnern Stadium (T 2814205). At Lumpini, boxing nights are Tues (1800-2200), Fri (1800-2200) and Sat (1630-2400), up to and over ฿1,000 for a ringside seat (depending on the card); cheaper seats cost from about ฿150. At Rachdamnern Stadium, boxing nights are Mon and Wed (1800-2200), Thu (1700-2200), Sun (1400-2200), seats from ฿160-500.

● **Tour companies & travel agents**
Travel agents abound in the tourist and hotel areas of the city – Khaosan Rd/Banglamphu, Sukhumvit, Soi Ngam Duphli, and Silom (several down Pan Rd, a soi opp Silom Village). All major hotels will have their own in-house agent. Most will book airline, bus and train tickets, arrange tours, and book hotel rooms. Because there are so many to choose from, it is worth shopping around for the best deal. For those wishing to travel to Vietnam, Laos, Cambodia and Burma, specialist agents are recommended as they are usually able to arrange visas – for a fee. These agents are marked (I and B) in the listing below. *Alternative Tour*, 14/1 Soi Rajatapan, Rajaprarop Rd, T 2452963, F 2467020, offer excellent 'alternative' tours of the country, enabling visitors to see the 'real' Thailand, not just tourist sights; *Asian Holiday Tour*, 294/8 Phayathai Rd, T 2155749; *Asian Lines Travel* (I and B), 755 Silom Rd, T 2331510, F 2334885; *Banglamphu Tour Service* (I and B), 17 Khaosan Rd, T 2813122, F 2803642; *Dee Jai Tours*, 2nd flr, 491/29 Silom Plaza Bldg, Silom Rd, T 2341685, F 2374231; *Diethelm Travel* (I and B), Kian Gwan Bldg II, 140/1, Witthayu Rd, T 2559150, F 2560248; *Dior Tours* (I and B), 146-158 Khaosan Rd, T 2829142; *East-West* (I and B), 46/1 Sukhumvit Soi Nana Nua, T 2530681; *Exotissimo* (I and B), 21/17 Sukhumvit Soi 4, T 2535240, F 2547683 and 755 Silom Rd, T 2359196, F 2834885; *Fortune Tours*, 9 Captain Bush Lane, Charoen Krung 30, T 2371050; *Guest House and Tour* (I and B), 46/1 Khaosan Rd, T 2823849, F 2812348; *MK Ways* (I and B), 18/4 Sathorn Tai Soi 3 (Saint Louis), T 2122532, F 2545583; *Pawana Tour and Travel* (I and B), 72/2 Khaosan Rd, T 2678018, F 2800370; *Siam Wings*, 173/1-3 Surawong Rd, T 2534757, F 2366808; *Skyline Travel Service* (I and B), 491/39-40 Silom Plaza (2nd Flr), Silom Rd, T 2331864, F 2366585; *Thai Travel Service*, 119/4 Surawong Rd, T 2349360; *Top Thailand Tour* (I and B), 61 Khaosan Rd, T 2802251, F 2823337; *Tour East* (I and B), Rajapark Bldg, 10th flr, 163 Asoke Rd, T 2593160, F 2583236; *Transindo* (I and B), Thasos Bldg (9th Flr), 1675 Chan Rd, T 2873241, F 2873246; *Vista Travel* (I and B), 244/4 Khaosan Rd, T 2800348; *Western Union*, branch in the foyer of *Atlanta Hotel*, 78 Sukhumvit Soi 2, T 2552151, good all round service.

TOUR COMPANIES SPECIALIZING IN INDOCHINA AND BURMA

Bangkok is the world's centre for tour companies specializing in Indochina and Burma. Many of the cheaper outfits serving the backpacking market are concentrated in the Khaosan Rd area (Banglamphu); these will arrange independent visas as well as tours. The more expensive companies will usually only book tours (visa included). The cost of visas as of 1994 was approximately: ฿1,300-1,500 Vietnam (1 month, 5-7 days to arrange); ฿2,300-2,500 Laos (1 month, 5 days to arrange); ฿1,200-1,300 Cambodia (1 month, 2 days to arrange); ฿500-600 (2 weeks, 2 days to arrange) Burma.

● **Tourist offices**

Tourist Authority of Thailand (TAT), Rachdamnern Nok Ave. There is also a smaller office at 372 Bamrung Muang Rd, T 2260060. Open Mon-Sun, 0830-1630. **NB** The TAT is scheduled to move back into its renovated offices on Rachdamnern Nok Ave in mid-1995; the move may be delayed – if so, visit the temporary head office at 372 Bamrung Muang Rd. In addition there is a counter at Don Muang airport (in the Arrivals Hall, T 5238972) and offices at 1 Napralarn Rd, T 2260056, and the Chatuchak Weekend Market (Kampaeng Phet Rd). The main office is very helpful and provides a great deal of information for independent travellers – certainly worth a visit.

A number of good, informative, English language magazines providing listings of what to do and where to go in Bangkok have started up recently. The best is undoubtedly *Bangkok Metro*, published monthly (฿80). It is well designed and produced and covers topics from music and nightlife, to sports and fitness, to business and children. Less independent, and with less quality information, is the oddly named *Guide of Bangkok* or GoB. Its advantage is that it is free.

● **Tourist Police**

Unico House, Ploenchit Soi Lang Suan, T 1699 or 6521721. There are also dedicated tourist police offices in the main tourist areas.

● **Traditional Thai Massage**

Many hotels offer this service; guesthouses also, although most masseuses are not trained. The most famous centre is at Wat Pho (see page 547), a Mecca for the training of masseuses. Wat Pho specializes in the more muscular Southern style. The Northern-style is less exhausting, more soothing. Other centres offering quality massages by properly trained practioners include: *Marble House*, 37/18-19 Soi Surawong Plaza (opp Montien Hotel),

T 2353519, open 0100-2400 Mon-Sun, ฿300 for 2 hrs, ฿450 for 3 hrs and *Vejakorn*, 37/25 Surawong Plaza, Surawong Rd, T 2375576, open Mon-Sun 1000-2400, ฿260 for 2 hrs, ฿390 for 3 hrs.

● **Transport**

Local Bus: this is the cheapest way to get around town. A bus map marking the routes is indispensable. The *Bangkok Thailand* map and *Latest tours guide to Bangkok and Thailand* are available from most bookshops as well as many hotel and travel agents/ tour companies. Major bus stops also have maps of routes and instructions in English displayed. Standard non-a/c buses (coloured blue) cost ฿3.50. Beware of pickpockets on these often crowded buses. Red-coloured express buses are slightly more expensive, slightly less crowded, and do not stop at all bus stops. A/c buses cost ฿6-16 depending on distance. Travelling all the way from Silom Rd to the airport by a/c bus, for example, costs ฿14; most inner city journeys cost ฿6. There are also smaller a/c 'micro buses' which follow the same routes but are generally faster and less crowded because officially they are only meant to let passengers aboard if a seat is vacant. They charge a flat fare of ฿20. **NB** More people have their belongings stolen on Bangkok's city buses than almost anywhere else.

Car hire: approximate cost, ฿1000-1200/day, ฿6,000-8,000/week; Hertz and Avis charge more than the local firms, but have better insurance cover. **Not** recommended for use in Bangkok. **Avis**, 2/12 Witthayu Rd, T 2555300. **Central Car Rent**, 115/5 Soi TonSon, Ploenchit Rd, T 2512778. **Dollar Car Rent**, 272 Si Phraya Rd, T 2330848. **Grand Car Rent**, 233-5 Asoke-Din Daeng Rd, T 2482991. **Hertz**, 420 Sukhumvit Soi 71, T 3900341. **Highway Car Rent**, 1018/5 Rama IV Rd, T 2357746. **Inter Car Rent**, 45 Sukhumvit Rd, T 2529223. **Silver International**,

102 Esso Gas station, 22 Sukhumvit Rd, T 2596867. **SMT Rent-a-Car**, 931/11 Rama I Rd, T 2168020, F 2168039.

Express boats: travel between Nonthaburi in the N and Wat Rajsingkorn (nr Krungthep bridge) in the S. Fares are calculated by zone and range from ฿6-14. At peak hours boats leave every 10 mins, off-peak about 15-25 mins (see map, page 561 for piers, and page 569). The journey from one end of the route to the other takes 75 mins. Note that boats flying red or green pennants do not stop at all piers (they also exact a ฿1 express surcharge). Also, boats will only stop if passengers wish to board or alight, so make your destination known.

Ferries: small ferries take passengers across the Chao Phraya River, ฿1 (see map on page 561 for piers).

Khlong or long-tailed boats: can be rented for ฿200/hour, or more (see page 563).

Motorcycle taxi: a relatively new innovation in Bangkok (and now present in other towns in Thailand) they are the fastest, and most terrifying, way to get from A to B. Riders wear numbered vests and tend to congregate in particular areas; agree a fare, hop on the back, and hope for the best. Their 'devil may care' attitude has made them bitter enemies of many other road users. Expect to pay ฿10-20.

Taxi: most taxis are metered (they must have a/c to register) – look for the 'Taxi Meter' illuminated sign on the roof. There are a number of unmarked, unofficial taxis which are to be found around the tourist sites. Fares start at ฿35 for a journey of 2 km or less and it should cost ฿40-100 for most trips in the city. Sometimes taxis refuse to use the meter – insist they do so. Taxi drivers should not be tipped. For most tourists the arrival of the metered taxi has lowered prices as it has eliminated the need to bargain – check, though, that the meter is 'zeroed' before setting off.

Tuk-tuk: the formerly ubiquitous motorized saamlor is rapidly becoming a piece of history in Bangkok, although they can still always be found nr tourist sites. Best for short journeys: they are uncomfortable and, being open to the elements, you are likely to be asphyxiated by car fumes. Bargaining is essential and the fare must be negotiated before boarding, most journeys cost at least ฿40. Both tuk-tuk and taxi drivers may try to take you to restaurants or shops – do not be persuaded; they are often mediocre places charging high prices.

Long distance Bangkok lies at the heart of Thailand's transport network. Virtually all trains and buses end up here and it is possible to reach anywhere in the country from the capital. Bangkok is also a regional transport hub, and there are flights to most international destinations. For international transportation, see page 599.

Air Don Muang Airport is 25 km N of the city. Regular connections on **Thai** to many of the provincial capitals. For airport details see page 601. There are a number of Thai offices in Bangkok, Head Office for domestic flights is 89 Vibhavadi Rangsit Rd, T 5130121, but this is inconveniently located N of town. Two more central offices are at 6 Lan Luang Rd (T 2800070) and 485 Silom Rd. Tickets can also be bought at most travel agents. **Bangkok Airways** flies to Koh Samui, Hua Hin, Phuket, U-Tapao (Pattaya) and Mae Hong Son. Sukhothai is due to be added to their list of destinations. They have an office in the domestic terminal at Don Muang, and two offices in town: Queen Sirikit National Convention Centre, New Rachadapisek Rd, T 2293456; and llll Ploenchit Rd, T 2542903.

Train Bangkok has two main railway stations. The primary station, catering for most destinations, is Hualamphong, Rama IV Rd, T 2237010/ 2237020; condensed railway timetables in English can be picked up from the information counter in the main concourse. Trains to Nakhon Pathom and Kanchanaburi leave from the Bangkok Noi or Thonburi station on the other side of the Chao Phraya River. Sample destinations and fares: **Chiang Mai** (751 km) ฿537-121. **Ayutthaya** (71 km) ฿15-60. **Khon Kaen** (450 km) ฿77-333. **Kanchanaburi** (133 km) ฿28-111. **Phetburi** (167 km) ฿34-138. **Hat Yai** (945 km) ฿149-664.

Road Bus: there are three bus stations in Bangkok serving the N and NE, the E, and the S. Destinations in the Central Plains are also served from these terminals – places N of Bangkok from the northern bus terminal, SW of Bangkok from the southern terminal, and SE from the eastern bus terminal. The **North-**

ern bus terminal or *Mor Chit*, Phahonyothin Rd, T 2712961, serves all destinations in the N and NE as well as towns in the Central Plains that lie N of Bangkok like Ayutthaya and Lopburi. Getting to *Mor Chit* by public transport is comparatively easy as many a/c buses (Nos 2, 3, 9, 10, 29 and 39) and non-a/c buses travel along Phahonyothin Rd. The new **Southern bus terminal** is on Phra Pinklao Rd (T 4345557) nr the intersection with Route 338. Buses for the W (places like Nakhon Pathom and Kanchanaburi) and the S leave from here. A/c town bus No 7 travels to the terminal. The **Eastern bus terminal**, Sukhumvit Rd (Soi Ekamai), between Soi 40 and Soi 42, T 3912504 serves Pattaya and other destinations in the Eastern region.

Buses leave for most major destinations throughout the day, and often well into the night.

There are overnight buses on the longer routes – Chiang Mai, Hat Yai, Chiang Rai, Phuket, Ubon Ratchathani. Even the smallest provincial towns such as Mahasarakham have deluxe a/c buses connecting them with Bangkok. Note that in addition to the government-operated buses there are many private companies which run 'tour' buses to most of the major tourist destinations. Tickets bought through travel agents will normally be for these private tour buses, which leave from offices all over the city as well as from the public bus terminals listed above. Shop around as prices may vary. Note that although passengers may be picked up from their hotel/guesthouse therefore saving on the ride (and inconvenience) of getting out to the bus terminal the private buses are generally less reliable and less safe. Many pick-up passengers at Khaosan Rd, for example.

INFORMATION FOR VISITORS TO THAILAND

CONTENTS

This section provides information for visitors to Thailand who intend to stay in Bangkok. A fuller account, covering the whole country is given in Trade & Travel's *Thailand & Burma Handbook*, in the same series.

Before travelling

Entry requirements

● **Visas**

All tourists must possess passports valid for at least 6 months longer than their intended stay in Thailand. The regulations were changed in Feb 1995.

30 day visa exemptions No visa is required for tourists arriving by air, holding a confirmed onward air ticket and who intend to stay for up to 30 days (not extendable). Tourists are fined ฿100/day each day they exceed the 30 day limit. The same applies to tourists who arrive via the Thai-Malaysian border by sea, rail or road. This applies to nationals of the following countries: Argentina, Australia, Austria, Belgium, Brazil, Brunei, Burma, Canada, Fiji, France, Germany, Greece, Iceland, Indonesia, Ireland, Italy, Japan, Kenya, Luxembourg, Malaysia, Mexico, Netherlands, Papua New Guinea, Philippines, Portugal, Republic of Korea, Senegal, Singapore, Spain, South Africa, Switzerland, Turkey, UK, USA, Vanuatu, Western Samoa. Malaysian nationals arriving by road from Malaysia do not need evidence of onward journey.

Visas on arrival Nationals from most other countries can apply for entry visas at Don Muang, Chiang Mai, Phuket and Hat Yai airports. These are issued for 15 days.

3 month visa exemptions Nationals from South Korea, New Zealand, Sweden, Denmark, Norway and Finland visiting as a tourist do not require a visa for visits of up to 3 months, and those from Hong Kong for a visit of up to 15 days.

Tourist visas These are valid for 60 days from date of entry (single entry), transit visas for 30 days (single entry). **Visa extensions** are obtainable from the Immigration Department in Bangkok (see below) for ฿500. The process used to be interminable, but the system is now much improved and relatively painless. Extensions can also be issued in other towns, such as Koh Samui and Chiang Mai. Applicants must bring two photocopies of their passport ID page and the page on which their tourist visa is stamped, together with three passport photographs. It is also advisable to dress neatly. It may be easier to leave the country and then re-enter having obtained a new tourist visa. Visas are issued by all Thai embassies and consulates. **NB** There is now a new visa booth at Don Muang Airport itself, at customs control. Visitors without visas can have one issued here and there is even a photo booth to provide passport snaps. However, the desk only provides tourist visas valid for 15 days, which nationals of many countries do not require in any case (see above). The facility is only useful for nationals of those countries which are not exempted from having an entry visa. These number 82 in total. There are similar desks at Chiang Mai, Phuket and Hat Yai airports.

Passport control at Don Muang Airport during peak arrival periods (usually 1200-

1400) can be choked with visitors – be prepared for a wait of an hour or more before reaching the arrivals hall.

90-day non-immigrant visas These are also issued and can be obtained in the applicant's home country (about US$30). A letter from the applicant's company or organization guaranteeing their repatriation should be submitted at the same time.

In the UK there is now a visa information line, operating 24 hrs a day, T 01891 600 150.

● **Immigration Department**
Soi Suan Plu, Thanon Sathorn Tai, Bangkok 10120, T 2873101.

● **Vaccinations**
No vaccinations required, unless coming from an infected area (if visitors have been in a yellow fever infected area in the 10 days before arrival, and do not have a vaccination certificate, they will be vaccinated and kept in quarantine for 6 days, or deported. See health section below for details.

● **Representation overseas**
Australia, 111 Empire Circuit, Yarralumla, Canberra, ACT 2600, T (06) 2731149, 2732937; **Austria**, Weimarer Strasse 68, 1180 Vienna, T (0222) 3103423; **Belgium**, Square du Val de la Cambre 2, 1050 Brussels, T 2 6406810; **Canada**, 180 Island Park Drive, Ottawa, Ontario, K1Y 0A2, T (613) 722 4444; **Denmark**, Norgesmindevej 18, 2900 Hellerup, Copenhagen, T (31) 6250101; **France**, 8 Rue Greuze, 75116 Paris, T 47043222; **Germany**, Uberstrasse 65, 5300 Bonn 2, T (0228) 355065; **Greece**, 23 Taigetou St, PO Box 65215, Paleo Psychico 15452, Athens, T 6717969; **Italy**, Via Nomentana, 132, 00162 Rome, T (396) 8320729; **Japan**, 3-14-6, Kami-Osaki, Shinagawa-ku, Tokyo 141, T (03) 3441-1386; **Laos**, Route Phonekheng, PO Box 128, Vientiane, T 2508; **Malaysia**, 206 Jl Ampang, 50450 Kuala Lumpur, T (03) 2488222; **Myanmar**, 91, Pyay Rd, Rangoon, T 21713; **Nepal**, Jyoti Kendra Building, Thapathali, PO Box 3333, Kathmandu, T 213910; **Netherlands**, 1 Buitenrustweg, 2517 KD, The Hague, T (070) 3452088; **New Zealand**, 2 Cook St, PO Box 17-226, Karori, T 768618; **Norway**, Munkedamsveien 59B, 0270 Oslo 2, T (02) 832517-8; **Portugal**, Avenida Almirante Gago Coutinho 68A, 1700 Lisbon, T 805350; **Spain**, Calle del Segre, 29, 20 A, 28002 Madrid, T (341) 5632903; **Sweden**, Sandhamnsgatan 36 (5th Floor), PO Box 27065, 10251 Stockholm, T (08) 6672160; **Switzerland**, Eigerstrasse 60 (3rd Floor), 3007 Bern, T (031) 462281; **UK**, 29-30 Queens Gate, London, SW7 5JB, T 0171 589 0173 (there are also consulates in Birmingham, Glasgow, Liverpool, Cardiff and Hull); **USA**, 2300 Kalorama Rd NW, Washington, DC 20008, T (202) 4837200.

When to go

● **Best time to visit**
Nov to Feb when the rains have ended and temperatures are at their lowest. Although the rainy season brings thoughts of torrential daylong tropical rain to many people, this is rarely the case: heavy showers interspersed with clear skies is a more accurate description, and it is perfectly sensible to visit Thailand during the monsoon. Hours of daily sun average 5-6 hrs even during rainy season. Visitors will also benefit from lower hotel room rates.

Health

See page 23, main health section, details on health and health care.

Vaccinations: no vaccinations are required, but cholera immunization and a tetanus booster are advisable. A gamma globulin injection (against hepatitis) is also recommended. There is a vaccination clinic in the Science Division of the Thai Red Cross Society, at the corner of Rama IV and Henri Dunant rds, Bangkok, T 2520161.

Malaria: anti-malarial tablets are essential outside Bangkok, Chiang Mai, Phuket and Pattaya. Be sure to ask your doctor to recommend the appropriate type(s) – some particularly resistant strains are prevalent in Thailand and most are now resistant to Chloroquine. Mosquito coils, electronic mosquito 'Vapemats', repellents and nets are all worthwhile. Despite anti-malarial drugs, it is worth taking all possible precautions to avoid being bitten by mosquitoes – most bites occur between dawn and dusk, when protective clothing such as long-sleeved shirts and trousers should be worn. In general, the risk of malaria increases in direct proportion to the adventurousness of travel. In urban areas and main tourist areas there is little danger.

Heat exhaustion and dehydration: Thailand is hot and can be exhausting, so take care to avoid over-exertion. By perspiring profusely, loss of body fluids and salts can cause nausea, headaches and dizziness. This can be partially prevented by taking salt and by drinking lots of water. Sachets of electrolyte salts which can be dissolved in water are widely available in Thailand.

● **Medical facilities**

For full listing of hospitals, check the Yellow Pages, or listings under Useful addresses in each town. Hospitals in Bangkok and Chiang Mai are of a reasonable (Western) standard.

● **Food and water**

Tap water is not recommended for drinking. Cut fruit or uncooked vegetables from road-side stalls may not always be clean.

● **Travelling with children**

(For more information and a check-list, see the general introduction.) Disposable nappies are now widely available in Thailand, although they are expensive. Powdered milks and a good range of powdered foods are on sale in most supermarkets. Bottled water is available everywhere. Fruit is a good source of nutrition and is also widely available. Anti-malarials are recommended (quarter to half dosage) if travelling outside the main cities and tourist destinations.

Money

● **ATMs (cash dispensers)**

American Express can be used at Bangkok Bank, JCB at Siam Commercial Bank, Master Card at Siam Commercial, Visa at Bangkok Bank.

● **Credit cards**

Major credit cards such as American Express, Visa, Diners Club, Carte Blanche, Master Charge/Access are accepted in leading hotels, restaurants, department stores and several large stores for tourists. Visitors may have some problems upcountry where the use of credit cards is less common. **Notification of credit card loss**: American Express, IBM Bldg, Phahonyothin Rd, T 2730022; Diners Club, Dusit Thani Bldg, Rama IV Rd, T 2332645, 2335775; JCB T 2561361, 2561351; Visa and Master Card, Thai Farmers Bank Bldg, Phahonyothin Rd, T 2701801-10.

● **Cost of living**

Visitors staying in first class hotels and eating in hotel restaurants will probably spend a minimum of ฿1500/day. Tourists staying in cheaper air-conditioned accommodation, and eating in local restaurants will probably spend about ฿500-750/day. A backpacker, staying in fan-cooled guesthouses and eating cheaply, might expect to be able to live on ฿200/day. In Bangkok, expect to pay 20-30% more.

● **Currency**

The unit of Thai currency is the **baht** (฿), which is divided into 100 **satang**. Notes in circulation include ฿10 (brown), ฿20 (green), ฿50 (blue), ฿100 (red), ฿500 (purple) and new ฿1,000 (orange and grey). Coins include 25 satang and 50 satang, and ฿1, ฿5, and ฿10. **NB** There are different sized ฿1 and ฿5 coins, which can be confusing.

● **Exchange rates**

The exchange rate can be found in the daily newspapers. It is best to change money at banks or money changers which give better rates than hotels. First class hotels have 24 hrs money changers. There is a charge of ฿10/cheque when changing TCs (passport required). Indonesian Rupiah and Nepalese Rupees cannot be exchanged for Thai currency.

Getting there

Air

The majority of visitors arrive in Thailand through Bangkok's Don Muang airport. There are also international chartered flights to Chiang Mai in the N and to Phuket in the S (see below). More than 35 airlines and charter companies fly to Bangkok. **Thai International** is the national airline.

Train

Regular rail services link Singapore and Bangkok, via Kuala Lumpur, Butterworth and the major southern Thai towns. Express a/c trains take two days from Singapore, 34 hrs from Kuala Lumpur, 24 hrs from Butterworth (opp Penang). The *Magic Arrow Express* leaves Singapore on Sun, Tues and Thur, Bangkok-Singapore (฿899-1,965), Bangkok-Kuala Lumpur (฿659-1,432) and to Ipoh (฿530-1,145). An additional train from Butterworth departs at 1340, arriving Bangkok 0835 the next day. The train from Bangkok to Butterworth departs 1515, arriving Butterworth 1225 (฿457-1,147). All tickets should be booked in advance. The most luxurious way to journey by train to Thailand is aboard the *Eastern & Oriental (E&O) Express*. The a/c train of 22 carriages including a salon car, dining car, bar and observation deck and carrying just 132 passengers runs once a week from Singapore to Bangkok and back. Luxurious carriages, fine wines and food designed for European rather than Asian sensibilities make this not just a mode of transport but an experience. The journey takes 43 hrs with stops in Kuala Lumpur, Butterworth and Padang Besar. But such luxury is expensive: US$1,130-2,950. For information call Bangkok 2514862; London (071) 9286000; US (800) 5242420; Singapore (065) 2272068.

There are currently no other rail services available out of Thailand to Burma, Vietnam, Cambodia or Laos. There is talk of the railway to Phnom Penh via Battambang being reactivated, should political conditions improve.

Road

The main road access is to and from Malaysia. The principal land border crossings into Malaysia are nr Betong in Yala Province and from Sungei Golok in Narathiwat Province. In Apr 1994 the Friendship Bridge linking Nong Khai with Laos opened – and became the first bridge across the Mekong River. To cross into Laos here foreigners need to obtain a visa in Bangkok – although a consulate is due to open in Nong Khai. In 1992, an overland crossing to Burma opened at Mae Sai in the N, but only for forays into the immediate vicinity. The border at Saam Ong in the W can also be crossed by foreigners, but again only for day trips into Burma.

Boat

No regular, scheduled cruise liners sail to Thailand any longer but it is sometimes possible to enter Thailand on a freighter, arriving at Khlong Toey Port. For information on how to book a berth on a cargo ship, see page 13. The *Bangkok Post* publishes a weekly shipping post with details on ships leaving the kingdom.

There are frequent passenger ferries from Pak Bara, nr Satun, in Southern Thailand to Perlis and Langkawi Island, both in Malaysia. The passenger and car ferries at Ta Ba, nr the town of Tak Bai, S of Narathiwat, make for a fast border crossing to Pengkalan Kubor in Malaysia. An alternative is to hitch a lift on a yacht from Phuket (Thailand) or from Penang (Malaysia). Check at the respective yacht clubs for information.

Customs

● **Duty free allowance**

250 gr of cigars or cigarettes (or 200 cigarettes) and 1 litre of wine or spirits. One still camera with five rolls of film or one movie camera with three rolls of 8mm or 16mm film.

● **Currency regulations**

Non-residents can bring in up to ฿2,000 pp and unlimited foreign currency although amounts exceeding US$10,000 must be declared. Maximum amount permitted to take out of the country is ฿50,000 pp.

● **Prohibited items**

All narcotics; obscene literature, pornography; fire arms (except with a permit from the Police Department or local registration office).

Some species of plants and animals are prohibited, for more information contact the Royal Forestry Department, Phahonyothin Rd, Bangkok, T 5792776. Permission of entry for animals by air is obtainable at the airport. An application must be made to the Department of Livestock Development, Bangkok, T 2515136 for entry by sea. Vaccination certificates are required; dogs and cats need rabies certificates.

● **Export restrictions**

No Buddha or Bodhisattva images or fragments should be taken out of Thailand, except for worshipping by Buddhists, for cultural exchanges or for research. However, obviously many people do – you only have to look in the antique shops to see the abundance for sale. A licence should be obtained from the Department of Fine Arts, Na Prathat Rd, Bangkok, T 2241370, from Chiang Mai National Museum, T 221308 or from the Songkhla National Museum, Songkhla, T 311728. Five days notice is needed; take two passport photographs of the object and photocopies of your passport.

On arrival

● **Airport information**

Don Muang airport lies 25 km N of Bangkok. Facilities include: banks and currency exchange, post office, left luggage (฿20/item/day – max 4 months), hotel booking agency, airport information, airport clinic, lost and found baggage service, duty-free shops, restaurants and bars. **NB** Food is expensive here – cheap food is available across the footbridge at the railway station. The *Airport Hotel* is linked to the international terminal by a walkway. It provides a 'ministay' service for passengers who wish to 'freshen-up' and take a room for up to 3 hrs between 0800 and 1800 (฿400 T 5661020/1). **International flight information**: T 5351254 for departures, T 5351301 for arrivals. **Domestic flight information**: T 5351253. The new domestic terminal has a hotel booking counter, post office, currency exchange counters, restaurant and bookshop. An elevated walkway connects the international and domestic terminals; a shuttle bus is sometimes available, beware – taxis grossly overcharge for a drive of just 1 km.

Transport to town **By taxi**: official taxi booking service in the arrivals hall. There are two desks. One for the more expensive official airport taxis (newer, more luxurious vehicles); one for public taxis. The former cost ฿400 downtown; ฿300 to the northern bus terminal; ฿450 to the southern bus terminal; ฿1,500 to Pattaya. A public taxi to downtown should cost about half these prices – roughly ฿200 with ฿50 extra if using the new airport elevated expressway. Note that there are both metered and unmetered public taxis; the fare for the latter will be quoted when you state your destination at the desk. **Warning** There have been cases of visitors being robbed in unofficial taxis. The sedan service into town costs ฿500-650. Cars are newer, more comfortable and better maintained than the average city taxi. It takes 30 mins to 1 hr to central Bangkok, depending on the time of day and the state of the traffic. The new elevated expressway reduces journey time to 20 mins – ask the taxi driver to take this route if you wish to save time but note that there is a toll fee – ฿20 and ฿30 for the two sections of this elevated road. Also note that there have been some complaints about taxi drivers at the domestic terminal forming a cartel, refusing to use their meters and charging a fixed rate considerably above the meter rate.

By bus: cheapest and slowest way into town, 1½-3 hrs (depending on time of day) (฿7-15). The bus stop is 50m N of the arrivals hall. Buses are crowded during rush-hours and there is little room for luggage. Bus 59 goes to Khaosan Rd, bus 29 goes to Bangkok's Hualamphong railway station, via the Northern bus terminal and Siam Square. A/c bus 10 goes to Samsen Rd and Silom Rd via the Northern bus terminal, a/c bus 4 goes to Silom Rd, a/c bus 13 goes to Sukhumvit Rd and the Eastern bus terminal, a/c bus 29 goes to the Northern bus terminal, Siam Square and Hualamphong railway station. **By minibus**: ฿100 to major hotels, ฿60 shuttle bus to the *Asia Hotel* on Phayathai Rd. ฿50-80 to Khaosan Rd, depending on the time of day. Direct buses to Pattaya at 0900, 1200 and

1700, ฿180. **By train**: the station is on the other side of the N-S highway from the airport. Regular trains into Bangkok's Hualamphong station, ฿5. The State Railways of Thailand runs an 'Airport Express' 5 times a day, with a/c shuttle bus from Don Muang station to airport terminal, 35 mins (฿100). **Hotel pick-up services**: many of the more expensive hotels operate airport pick-up services if informed of your arrival ahead of time.

By ferry: a civilized way to avoid the traffic. If booked in the *Oriental, Shangri-la* or *Sheraton* Hotels it is possible to get a minibus from the airport to the ferry terminal on the river. Then take the hour long river crossing by long-tailed boat to the appropriate hotel.

● **Airport tax**

Payable on departure – ฿200 for international flights, ฿30 for domestic flights. **Tax clearance**: any foreign visitor who has derived income while staying in Thailand must pay income tax. In addition, all travellers who have stayed in Thailand for 90 days or more in any one calendar year must obtain a tax clearance certificate. To avoid delay at the airport, contact the Revenue Department, Chakrapong Rd, T 2829899.

● **Clothing**

In towns and at religious sights, it is courteous to avoid wearing shorts and singlets (or sleeveless shirts). Visitors who are inappropriately dressed may not be allowed into temples. Thais always look neat and clean. *Mai rieb-roi* means 'not neat' and is considered a great insult. Beach resorts are a law unto themselves – casual clothes are the norm, although nudity is still very much frowned upon by Thais. In the most expensive restaurants in Bangkok diners may well be expected to wear a jacket and tie.

● **Conduct**

Thais are generally very understanding of the foibles and habits of foreigners (*farangs*) and will forgive and forget most indiscretions. However, there are a number of 'dos and don'ts' which are worth observing:

Bargaining This is common, except in the large department stores (although they may give a discount on expensive items of jewellery or furniture) and on items like soap, books and most necessities. Expect to pay anything from 25-75% less than the asking price, depending on the bargainer's skill and the shopkeeper's mood. Bargaining is viewed as a game, so enter into it with good humour.

Common greeting *Wai*: hands are held together as if in prayer, and the higher the wai, the more respectful the greeting. By watching Thai's wai it is possible to ascertain their relative seniority. Again, foreigners are not expected to conform to this custom – a simple wai at chest to chin height is all that is required. When *farangs* and Thais do business it is common to shake hands.

Observant visitors will quickly notice that men and women rarely show open, public signs of affection. It is not uncommon however to see men holding hands – this is invariably a sign of simple friendship, nothing more. That said, in Bangkok traditional customs have broken down and in areas such as Siam Square it is common to see young lovers, hand-in-hand.

Heads, heart and feet More generally, try not to openly point your feet at anyone – feet are viewed as spiritually the lowest part of the body. At the same time, never touch anyone's head which is the holiest, as well as the highest, part. Among Thais, the personal characteristic of *jai yen* is very highly regarded; literally, this means to have a 'cool heart'. It embodies calmness, having an even temper and not displaying emotion. Although foreigners generally receive special dispensation, and are not expected to conform to Thai customs (all *farang* are thought to have 'hot hearts'), it is important to try and keep calm in any disagreement – losing one's temper leads to loss of face and subsequent loss of respect. An associated personal characteristic which Thais try to develop is *kreng jai*; this embodies being understanding of other people's needs, desires and feelings – in short, not imposing oneself.

A quality of *sanuk*, which can be roughly translated as 'fun' or *joie de vivre*, is important to Thais. Activities are undertaken because they are sanuk, others avoided because they are *mai sanuk* ('not fun'). Perhaps it is because of this apparent love of life that so many visitors returning from Thailand remark on how Thais always appear happy and smiling. However, it is worth bearing in mind that the interplay of *jai yen* and *kreng jai* means that everything may not be quite as it appears.

The monarchy Never criticize any member of the royal family or the institution itself. The monarchy is held in very high esteem and *lèse majesté* remains an imprisonable offence. In cinemas, the National Anthem is played before the show and the audience is expected to stand. At other events, take your lead from the crowd as to how to behave. A dying custom, but one which is still adhered to in smaller towns, is that everybody stops in their tracks at 0800, when the **National Anthem** is relayed by loudspeaker.

Monastery (*wat*) **etiquette** Remove shoes on entering, do not climb over Buddha images or have pictures taken in front of one. Wear modest clothing – women should not expose their shoulders or wear dresses that are too short (see below, clothing). Females should never hand anything directly to monks, or venture into the monks' quarters.

Smoking Prohibited on domestic flights, public buses and in cinemas.

Further reading A useful book delving deeper into the do's and don'ts of living in Thailand is Robert and Nanthapa Cooper's *Culture shock: Thailand*, Time Books International: Singapore (1990). It is available from most bookshops.

● **Emergencies**
Police 191, 123; **Tourist Police** 195; **Fire** 199; **Ambulance** 2522171-5. **Tourist Police head office**: Unico House, Ploenchit Soi Lang Suan, Bangkok, T 6521721-6. **Tourist Assistance Centre**, Rachdamnern Nok Ave, Bangkok, T 2828129.

● **Hours of business**
Banks: 0830-1530 Mon-Fri. **Currency exchange services**: 0830-2200 Mon-Sun in Bangkok and Pattaya, 0830-1930 in Phuket and 0830-1630 Mon-Fri in other towns. **Government offices**: 0830-1200, 1300-1630 Mon-Fri. **Tourist offices**: 0830-1630 Mon-Sun. **Shops**: 0830-1700, larger shops: 1000-1900 or 2100.

● **Official time**
7 hrs ahead of GMT.

● **Tipping**
Generally unnecessary. A 10% service charge is now expected on room, food and drinks bills in the smarter hotels as well as a tip for any personal service. Increasingly, the more expensive restaurants add a 10% service charge; others expect a small tip.

● **Tricksters**
Tricksters, rip-off artists, fraudsters, less than honest salesmen – call them what you will – are likely to be far more of a problem than simple theft. People may well approach you in the street offering incredible one-off bargains, and giving what might seem to be very plau-

sible reasons for your sudden good fortune. Be wary in all such cases and do not be pressed into making a hasty decision. Unfortunately, more often than not, the salesman is trying to pull a fast one. Favourite 'bargains' are precious stones, whose authenticity is 'demonstrated' before your very eyes. Although many Thais do like to talk to *farangs* and practice their English, in tourist areas there are also those who offer their friendship for pecuniary rather than linguistic reasons. Sad as it is to say so, it is probably a good idea to be suspicious.

● **Voltage**

220 volts (50 cycles) throughout Thailand. Most first and tourist class hotels have outlets for shavers and hair dryers. Adaptors are recommended, as almost all sockets are two pronged.

Food and drink

Food

Thai cuisine is an intermingling of Tai, Chinese, and to a lesser extent, Indian cuisines. This helps to explain why restaurants produce dishes which must be some of the (spicy) hottest in the world, as well as some which are rather bland. *Laap* (raw – now more frequently cooked – chopped beef mixed with rice, herbs and spices) is a traditional 'Tai' dish; *pla priaw waan* (whole fish with soy and ginger) is Chinese in origin; while *gaeng mussaman* (beef 'Muslim' curry) was brought to Thailand by Muslim immigrants. Even *satay*, paraded by most restaurants as a Thai dish, has been

RESTAURANT CLASSIFICATION

Prices A meal at a roadside stall will cost about ฿15-20; in a small, simple Thai restaurant, about ฿25-50. 'Traveller's' food will also usually cost less than ฿50 for a meal. In more sophisticated Thai restaurants, expect to pay up to ฿300, while restaurants in first class hotels (particularly if eating European food) can charge considerably more than this.

♦♦♦♦	฿375+
♦♦♦	฿125-375
♦♦	฿50-125
♦	under ฿50

introduced from Malaysia and Indonesia (who themselves adopted it from Arab traders during the Middle Ages).

Despite these various influences, Thai cooking is distinctive. Thais have managed to combine the best of each tradition, adapting elements to fit their own preferences. Remarkably, considering how ubiquitous it is in Thai cooking, the chilli pepper is a New World fruit and was not introduced into Thailand until the late 16th century (along with the pineapple and papaya).

When a Thai asks another Thai whether he has eaten he will ask, literally, whether he has 'eaten rice' (*kin khaaw*). Similarly, the accompanying dishes are referred to as food 'with the rice'. A Thai meal is based around rice, and many wealthy Bangkokians own farms up-country where they cultivate their favourite variety. A meal usually consists (along with the rice) of a soup like *tom yam kung* (prawn soup), *kaeng* (a curry) and *krueng kieng* (a number of side dishes). Generally, Thai food is chilli-hot, and aromatic herbs and grasses (like lemon grass) are used to give a distinctive flavour. *Nam pla* (fish sauce) and *nam prik* (nam pla, chillies, garlic, sugar, shrimps and lime juice) are two condiments that are taken with almost all meals. Food is eaten with a spoon and fork, and dishes are usually served all at once; it is unimportant to a Thai that food be hot. Try the open-air foodstalls to be found in every town which are frequented by middle-class Thais as well as the poor and where a meal costs only ฿15-20. Many small restaurants have no menus. Away from the main tourist spots, 'Western' breakfasts are commonly unavailable, so be prepared to eat Thai-style (noodle or rice soup or fried rice). Finally, due to Thailand's large Chinese population (or at least Thais with Chinese roots), there are also many Chinese-style restaurants whose cuisine is variously 'Thai-ified'. A popular innovation over the last 5 years or so has been the *suan a-haan* or garden restaurant. These are often on the edge of towns, with tables set in gardens, sometimes with bamboo furniture and ponds.

Tourist centres also provide good European, American and Japanese food at reasonable prices. Bangkok boasts some superb restaurants. Less expensive Western fastfood restaurants can also be found – McDonalds, Pizza Hut, Kentucky Fried Chicken and others.

Cuisine

It is impossible even to begin to provide a comprehensive list of Thai dishes. However (and at the risk of offending connoisseurs by omitting their favourites) popular dishes include:

● **Soups** (gaeng chud)

Tom yam kung – hot and sour prawn soup

Tom ka kai – chicken in coconut milk with laos (*ka*, or *laos*, is an exotic spice)

Khaaw tom – rice soup with egg and pork (a common breakfast dish). It is said that the soup can cure fevers and other illnesses. Probably best for a hangover.

Kwaytio – Chinese noodle soup served with a variety of additional ingredients, often available from roadside stalls and from smaller restaurants – mostly served up until lunchtime.

● **Rice and noodle-based dishes**

Single-dish meals served at roadside stalls and in many restaurants (especially cheaper ones).

Khaaw phat kai/mu/kung – fried rice with chicken/pork/prawn

Khaaw man kai – rice with chicken

Khaaw mu daeng – rice with red pork

Khaaw soi – a form of *Kwaytio*, with egg noodles in a curry broth

Phak sii-u – wide noodles, fried with egg, vegetables and meat/prawns

Phat thai – Thai fried noodles

Mee krop – Thai crisp-fried noodles

● **Curries** (gaeng)

Gaeng phet kai/nua – chicken/beef curry

Gaeng khiaw waan kai/nua/phet/pla – green chicken/beef/duck/fish curry (the colour is due to the large number of whole green chillies pounded to make the paste that forms the base of this very hot curry)

Gaeng mussaman – Muslim beef curry

● **Meat dishes**

Laap – chopped (once raw, now more frequently cooked) meat with herbs and spices

Kai/nua phat prik – fried chicken/beef with chillies

Nua priaw waan – sweet and sour beef

Mu waan – sweet pork

Kai/mu/nua phat kapow – fried meat with basil and chillies

Kai tort – Thai fried chicken

Kai tua – chicken in peanut sauce

Kai yang – garlic chicken

Priao wan – sweet and sour pork with vegetables

● **Seafood**

Pla priaw waan – whole fried fish with ginger sauce

Pla too tort – Thai fried fish

Haw mok – steamed fish curry

Pla nerng – steamed fish

Thotman plaa – fried curried fish cakes

Luuk ciin – fishballs

● **Salads** (yam)

Yam nua – Thai beef salad

Som tam – green papaya salad with tomatoes, chillies, garlic, chopped dried shrimps and lemon (can be extremely hot)

● **Vegetables**

Phak phat ruam mit – mixed fried vegetables

● **Sweets** (kanom)

Khaaw niaw sankhayaa – sticky rice and custard

Khaaw niaw mamuang – sticky rice and mango (a seasonal favourite)

Kluay buat chee – bananas in coconut milk

Kanom mo kaeng – baked custard squares

Kluay tort – Thai fried bananas

Leenchee loi mek – chilled lychis in custard

● **Fruits** (see page 19)

Chomphu – rose apple

Khanun – jackfruit. Season: Jan-Jun

Kluay – banana. Season: year round

Lamyai – longan; thin brown shell with translucent fruit similar to lychee. Season: Jun-Aug

Linchi – lychee. Season: Apr-Jun

Lamut – sapodilla

Makham wan – tamarind. Season: Dec-Feb

Malakho – papaya. Season: year round

Manaaw – lime. Season: year round

Mang khud – mangosteen. Season: Apr-Sep

Maprao – coconut. Season: year round

Majeung – star apple

Mamuang – mango. Season: Mar-Jun

Ngo – rambutan. Season: May-Sep

Noi na – custard (or sugar) apple. Season: Jun-Sep

Sapparot – pineapple. Season: Apr-Jun, Dec-Jan

Som – orange. Season: year round

Som o – pomelo. Season: Aug-Nov

Taeng mo – watermelon. Season: Oct-Mar

Thurian – durian. Season: May-Aug.

Drink

● **Drinking water**

Water in smaller restaurants can be risky, so many people recommend that visitors drink bottled water (widely available) or **hot tea**.

● **Soft drinks**

Coffee is also now consumed throughout Thailand (usually served with coffeemate or creamer). In stalls and restaurants, coffee come with a glass of Chinese tea. Soft drinks are widely available. Many roadside stalls prepare **fresh fruit juices** in liquidizers (*bun*) while hotels produce all the usual cocktails.

● **Alcohol**

Spirits Major brands of spirits are served in most hotels and bars, although not always off the tourist path. The most popular spirit among Thais is *Mekhong* – local cane whisky – which can be drunk straight or with mixers such as Coca-Cola. It can seem rather sweet to the Western palate but it is the cheapest form of alcohol.

Beer drinking is spreading fast. In 1987, beer consumption was 98 million litres; in 1992, 330 million litres.

The most popular local beer is *Singha* beer brewed by Boon Rowd. The company commands 89% of the beer market. It is said that the beer's distinctive taste is due to the formaldehyde that it contains. When the company removed the chemical (it was no longer needed as bottling technology had been improved) there was such an outcry from Thais that they quickly reincorporated it. Whether or not the story is true, an evening drinking *Singha* can result in quite a hangover. It's alcohol content of 6% must be partly to blame. Among expatriates, the most popular Thai beer is the more expensive *Kloster* brand (similar to a light German beer) with an alcohol content of 5.7%. *Singha* introduced a light beer called *Singha Gold* a few years ago which is quite similar to *Kloster*. *Amarit* is a third, rather less widely available, brand but popular with foreigners and brewed by the same company who produce *Kloster*. Between them, *Kloster* and *Amarit* control about 10% of the market. One new 'local' beer to enter the fray is *Carlsberg*. At the beginning of the 1990s they built a brewery N of Bangkok and had clearly done their homework. The beer is sweeter and lighter than *Singha* and *Kloster* but still strong with an alcohol content of 6%. The Carlsberg brew has made considerable inroads into the markets of the established brands – although in so doing they are said to have lost many millions of baht. In 1995 yet another local beer appeared on the shelves, although it appears to have only a very small segment of the market (as yet), and is hard to find: *Bier Chang* or *Elephant Beer*. Beer is relatively expensive in Thai terms as it is heavily taxed by the government. But it is a high status drink, so as Thais become wealthier, more are turning to beer in

preference to traditional, local whiskies. In a café expect to pay ฿30-50 for a small beer, in a coffee shop or bar ฿40-65, and in a hotel bar or restaurant, more than ฿60.

Communications

● **Language**

The Thai language is tonal and, strictly-speaking, monosyllabic. There are five tones: high, low, rising, falling and mid tone. These are used to distinguish between words which would otherwise be identical. For example: *mai* (low tone, new), *mai* (rising, silk), *mai* (midtone, burn), *mai* (high tone, question indicator), and *mai* (falling tone, negative indicator). Not surprisingly, many visitors find it hard to hear the different tones, and it is difficult to make much progress during a short visit (unlike, say, with Malaysian or Indonesian). The tonal nature of the language also explains why so much of Thai humour is based around homonyms – and especially when farangs say what they do not mean. Although tones make Thai a challenge for foreign visitors, other aspects of the language are easier to grasp: there are no marked plurals in nouns, no marked tenses in verbs, no definite or indefinite articles, and no affixes or suffixes.

Visitors may well experience two oddities of the Thai language being reflected in the way that Thais speak English. An 'l' or 'r' at the end of a word in Thai becomes an 'n', while an 's' becomes a 't'. So some Thais refer to the 'Shell' Oil Company as 'Shen', a name like 'Les' becomes 'Let', while 'cheque bill' becomes 'cheque bin'. It is also impossible to have two consonants after one another in Thai. If it occurs, a Thai will automatically insert a vowel (even though it is not written). So the soft drink 'Sprite' becomes 'Sa-prite', and the English word 'start', 'sa-tart'.

In general, English is reasonably widely spoken on the tourist trail, and visitors should be able to find someone to help. English is taught to all school children, and competence in English is regarded as a very useful qualification. Off the tourist trail making yourself understood becomes more difficult.

Despite Thai being a difficult language to pick up, it is worth trying to learn a few words, even if your visit to Thailand is short. Thais generally feel honoured that a *farang* is bothering to learn their language, and will be patient and helpful. If they laugh at some of your pronunciations do not be put off – it is not meant to be critical.

● **Postal services**

Local postal charges: ∅1 (postcard) and ∅2 (letter, 20 g). **International postal charges**: Europe and Australasia – ∅8 (postcard), ∅12.50 (letter, 10 g); US – ∅9 (postcard), ∅14.50 (letter, 10 g). Airletters cost ∅8.50. Poste Restante: correspondents should write the family name in capital letters and underline it, to avoid confusion.

Outside Bangkok, most post offices are open from 0800-1630 Mon-Fri and only the larger ones will be open on Sat.

Fax services: now widely available in most towns. Postal and telex/fax services are available in most large hotels.

● **Telephone services**

From Bangkok there is direct dialling to most countries. Outside Bangkok, it is best to go to a local telephone exchange for 'phoning outside the country.

Codes: local area codes vary according to province, they are listed under "Post & telecommunications" in each town; the code can also be found at the front of the telephone directory.

Directory inquiries: domestic long distance including Malaysia and Vientiane (Laos) – 101, Greater Bangkok BMA – 183, international calls T 2350030-5, although hotel operators will invariably help make the call if asked.

Callboxes cost ∅1, some boxes take the old coin, some take the new. All telephone numbers marked in the text with a prefix 'B' mean that they are Bangkok numbers.

Entertainment

● **Newspapers**

There are three major English language daily papers – the *Bangkok Post*, the *Nation Review* and the *Bangkok World* (an evening paper). The first two provide good international news coverage. There are a number of Thai language dailies and weeklys as well as Chinese language newspapers. The Thai press is one of the least controlled in Southeast Asia (although controls were imposed following the coup at the beginning of 1991 and during the demonstrations of May 1992), and the local newspapers are sometimes scandalously colourful, with gruesome annotated pictures of traffic accidents and murder victims. International newspapers and magazines are readily available in Bangkok, Chiang Mai, Pattaya and Phuket, although they are more difficult to come by upcountry.

● **Television and radio**

Five TV channels, with English language sound track available on FM. Channel 3 – 105.5 MHz, Channel 7 – 103.5 MHz, Channel 9 – 107 MHz and Channel 11 – 88 MHz. The *Bangkok Post* stars programmes where English soundtrack is available on FM. Shortwave radio can receive the BBC World Service, Voice of America, Radio Moscow and other foreign broadcasts, see page 22.

Holidays and festivals

Festivals with month only are movable; a booklet of holidays and festivals is available from most TAT offices.

Jan: *New Year's Day* (1st: public holiday).

Feb: *Magha Puja* (full-moon: public holiday) Buddhist holy day, celebrates the occasion when the Buddha's disciples miraculously gathered together to hear him preach. Culminates in a candle-lit procession around the temple *bot* (or ordination hall). The faithful make offerings and gain merit. *Chinese New Year* (movable, end of Jan/beginning of Feb) celebrated by Thailand's large Chinese population. The festival extends over 15 days; spirits are appeased, and offerings are made to the ancestors and to the spirits. Good wishes and lucky money are exchanged, and Chinese-run shops and businesses shut down.

Apr: *Chakri Day* (6th: public holiday) commemorates the founding of the present Chakri Dynasty. *Songkran* (movable: public holiday) marks the beginning of the Buddhist New Year. The festival is particularly big in the N (Chiang Mai, Lampang, Lamphun and Chiang Rai). It is a 3 to 5 day celebration, with parades, dancing and folk entertainment. Traditionally, the first day represents the last chance for a 'spring clean'. Rubbish is burnt, in the belief that old and dirty things will cause misfortune in the coming year. The wat is the focal point of celebrations. Revered Buddha images are carried through the streets, accompanied by singers and dancers. The second day is the main water-throwing day. The water-throwing practice was originally an act of homage to ancestors and family elders. Young people pay respect by pouring scented water over the elders heads. The older generation sprinkle water over Buddha images. Gifts are given. This uninhibited water-throwing continues for all 3 days (although it is now banned in Bangkok). On the third day birds, fish and turtles are all released, to gain merit and in remembrance of departed souls.

May: *Coronation Day* (5th: public holiday) commemorates the present King Bhumibol's crowning in 1950. *Ploughing Ceremony* (movable: public holiday) performed by the King at Sanaam Luang near the Grand Palace in Bangkok. Brahmanic in origin, it traditionally marks the auspicious date when farmers could begin preparing their riceland. Impressive bulls decorated with flowers pull a sacred gold plough.

Jun: *Visakha Puja* (full-moon: public holiday) holiest of all Buddhist days, it marks the Buddha's birth, enlightenment and death. Candlelit processions are held at most temples.

Aug: *The Queen's Birthday* (12th: public holiday). *Asalha Puja and Khao Phansa* (full-moon: public holiday) – commemorates the Buddha's first sermon to his disciples and marks the beginning of the Buddhist Lent. Monks reside in their monasteries for the 3 month Buddhist Rains Retreat to study and meditate, and young men temporarily become monks. Ordination ceremonies all over the country and villagers give white cotton robes to the monks to wear during the Lent ritual bathing.

Oct: *Ok Phansa* (3 lunar months after Asalha Puja) marks the end of the Buddhist Lent and the beginning of Krathin, when gifts – usually a new set of cotton robes – are offered to the monks. Particularly venerated monks are sometimes given silk robes as a sign of respect and esteem. Krathin itself is celebrated over two days. It marks the end of the monks' retreat and the re-entry of novices into secular society. Processions and fairs are held all over the country; villagers wear their best clothes and food, money, pillows and bed linen are offered to the monks of the local wat. *Chulalongkorn Day* (23rd: public holiday) honours King Chulalongkorn (1868-1910), perhaps Thailand's most beloved and revered king.

Nov: *Loi Krathong* (full-moon) a *krathong* is a small model boat made to contain a candle, incense and flowers. The festival comes at the end of the rainy season and honours the goddess of water. The little boats are pushed out onto canals, lakes and rivers. Sadly, few krathongs are now made of leaves: polystyrene has taken over and the morning after Loi Krathong lakes and river banks are littered with the wrecks of the night's festivities. **NB** The 'quaint' candles in flower pots sold in many shops at this time, are in fact large firecrackers.

Dec: *The King's Birthday* (5th: public holiday). Flags and portraits of the King are erected all over Bangkok, especially down Rachdamnern Ave and around the Grand Palace. *Constitution Day* (10th: public holiday). *New Year's Eve* (31st: public holiday).

NB Regional and local festivals are noted in appropriate sections.

TEMPERATURE CONVERSION TABLE

°C	°F	°C	°F	°C	°F	°C	°F	°C	°F
1	34	11	52	21	70	31	88	41	106
2	36	12	54	22	72	32	90	42	108
3	38	13	56	23	74	33	92	43	109
4	39	14	57	24	75	34	93	44	111
5	41	15	59	25	77	35	95	45	113
6	43	16	61	26	79	36	97	46	115
7	45	17	63	27	81	37	99	47	117
8	46	18	64	28	82	38	100	48	118
9	48	19	66	29	84	39	102	49	120

WEIGHTS AND MEASURES

Metric

Weight:
1 kilogram (kg) = 2,205 pounds
1 metric ton = 1.102 short tons
            = 0.984 long ton

Length:
1 millimetre (mm) = 0.03937 inch
1 metre = 3.281 feet
1 kilometre (km) = 0.621 mile

Area:
1 hectare = 2.471 acres
1 square km (km^2) = 0.386 sq mile

Capacity:
1 litre = 0.220 Imperial gallon
      = 0.264 US gallon
(5 Imperial gallons are approximately equal to 6 US gallons)

Volume:
1 cubic metre (m^3) = 35.31 cubic feet
                     = 1.31 cubic yards

British and US

1 pound (lb) = 454 grams
1 short ton (2,000lb) = 0.907 metric ton
1 long ton (2,240lb) = 1.016 metric tons

1 inch = 25.417 millimetres
1 foot (ft) = 0.305 metre
1 mile = 1.609 kilometres

1 acre = 0.405 hectare
1 square mile (sq mile) = 2,590 km^2

1 Imperial gallon = 4.546 litres
1 US gallon = 3.785 litres

1 cubic foot (cu ft) = 0.028 m^3
1 cubic yard (cu yd) = 0.765 m^3

GLOSSARY

C = Cambodia, **V** = Vietnam, **L** = Laos

A

Achar	Cambodian spiritual adviser (C)
Amitabha	the Buddha of the Past (see Avalokitsvara)
Amulet	protective medallion (see page 554)
Apsara	celestial dancers who entertain the gods and are sensual rewards of kings and heroes who die bravely; important in temple decoration, especially at Angkor (see page 494) (C)
Arhat	a person who has perfected himself; images of former monks are sometimes carved into arhat
Avadana	Buddhist narrative, telling of the deeds of saintly souls
Avalokitsvara	also known as Amitabha and Lokeshvara, the name literally means 'World Lord'; he is the compassionate male Bodhisattva, the saviour of Mahayana Buddhism and represents the central force of creation in the universe; usually portrayed with a lotus and water flask

B

Bai sema	boundary stones marking consecrated ground around a Buddhist bot (see page 322)
Ban	village; shortened from muban (L)
Baray	artificial lake or reservoir (C)
Batik	a form of resist dyeing
Ben Xe	bus station (V)
Bhikku	Buddhist monk
Bodhi	the tree under which the Buddha achieved enlightenment (*Ficus religiosa*)
Bodhisattva	a future Buddha. In Mahayana Buddhism, someone who has attained enlightenment, but who postpones nirvana to help others reach it.
Boun	Lao festival
Brahma	the Creator, one of the gods of the Hindu trinity, usually represented with four faces, and often mounted on a hamsa
Brahmin	a Hindu priest
Bun	to make merit

C

Cao Dai	composite religion of south Vietnam (see page 121)
Caryatid	elephants, often used as buttressing decorations
Champa	rival empire of the Khmers, of Hindu culture, based in present day Vietnam (see page 82)
Chao	title for Lao kings
Charn	animist priest who conducts the basi ceremony in Laos
Chat	honorific umbrella or royal multi-tiered parasol
Chedi	from the Sanskrit *cetiya* (Pali, *caitya*) meaning memorial. Usually a religious monument (often bell-shaped) containing relics of the Buddha or other holy remains. Used interchangeably with stupa

Chenla	Chinese name for Cambodia before the Khmer era
Chua	pagoda (see page 108) (V)
Cyclo	bicycle trishaw (V)

D

Deva	a Hindu-derived male god
Devata	a Hindu-derived goddess
Dharma	the Buddhist law
Dipterocarp	family of trees (*Dipterocarpaceae*) characteristic of Southeast Asia's forests
Doi moi	'renovation', Vietnamese perestroika
Dok sofa	literally, 'bucket of flowers'. A frond-like construction which surmounts temple roofs in Laos. Over 10 flowers signifies the wat was built by a king
Dtin sin	Lao decorative border on a tubular skirt
Dvarapala	guardian figure, usually placed at the entrance to a temple

F

Funan	the oldest Indianised state of Indochina and precursor to Chenla

G

Ganesh	elephant-headed son of Siva
Garuda	mythical divine bird, with predatory beak and claws, and human body; the king of birds, enemy of naga and mount of Vishnu (see page 494).
Gautama	the historic Buddha
Geomancy	the art of divination by lines and figures
Gopura	crowned or covered gate, entrance to a religious area

H

Hamsa	sacred goose, Brahma's mount; in Buddhism it represents the flight of the doctrine
Hinayana	'Lesser Vehicle', major Buddhist sect in Southeast Asia, usually termed Theravada Buddhism (see page 45)
Honda om	motorcycle taxi (*om* means 'to cuddle') (V)
Hor kong	a pavilion built on stilts where the temple drum is kept (L)
Hor latsalot	chapel of the funeral cart in a Lao temple
Hor song phra	secondary chapel in a Lao temple
Hor takang	bell tower (see page 322) (L)
Hor tray/trai	library where manuscripts are stored in a Lao or Thai temple (see page 322)
Hor vay	offering temple in a Lao temple complex

I

Ikat	tie-dyeing method of patterning cloth (see page 364)
Indra	the Vedic god of the heavens, weather and war; usually mounted on a 3 headed elephant

J

Jataka(s)	the birth stories of the Buddha; they normally number 547, although an additional 3 were added in Burma for reasons of symmetry in mural painting and sculpture; the last ten are the most important

K

Kala (makara)	literally, 'death' or 'black'; a demon ordered to consume itself; often sculpted with grinning face and bulging eyes over entranceways to act as a door guardian; also known as kirtamukha
Kambuja	Cambodia (C)
Kathin/krathin	a one month period during the eighth lunar month when lay people present new robes and other gifts to monks
Ketumula	flame-like motif above the Buddha head
Kinaree	half-human, half-bird, usually depicted as a heavenly musician
Kirtamukha	see kala
Koutdi	see kuti
Krishna	incarnation of Vishnu
Kuti	living quarters of Buddhist monks in a temple complex (L)

L

Lambro	small three-wheeled motorised van (V)
Laterite	bright red tropical soil/stone commonly used in construction of Khmer monuments (see page 489)
Linga	phallic symbol and one of the forms of Siva. Embedded in a pedestal shaped to allow drainage of lustral water poured over it, the linga typically has a succession of cross sections: from square at the base through octagonal to round. These symbolise, in order, the trinity of Brahma, Vishnu and Siva
Lintel	a load-bearing stone spanning a doorway; often heavily carved
Lokeshvara	see Avalokitsvara

M

Mahabharata	a Hindu epic text written about 2,000 years ago
Mahayana	'Greater Vehicle', major Buddhist sect (see page 46)
Maitreya	the future Buddha
Makara	a mythological aquatic reptile, somewhat like a crocodile and sometimes with an elephant's trunk; often found along with the kala framing doorways
Mandala	a focus for meditation; a representation of the cosmos
Mara	personification of evil and tempter of the Buddha
Matmii	Northeastern Thai and Lao cotton ikat
Mat mi	see matmii
Meru	sacred or cosmic mountain at the centre of the world in Hindu-Buddhist cosmology; home of the gods (see page 491)
Mondop	from the sanskrit, *mandapa*. A cube-shaped building, often topped with a cone-like structure, used to contain an object of worship like a footprint of the Buddha
Montagnard	'hill people', from the French (see page 111) (V)

Muang	administrative unit. In Laos, the system, based on local governors, was established by King Samenthai in the 14th century (L)
Muban	village, usually shortened to ban (L)
Mudra	symbolic gesture of the hands of the Buddha (see page 332)

N

Nak	Lao river dragon, a mythical guardian creature (see naga)
Naga	benevolent mythical water serpent, enemy of Garuda (see page 494)
Naga makara	fusion of naga and makara
Nalagiri	the elephant let loose to attack the Buddha, who calmed him
Nandi/nandin	bull, mount of Siva
Nirvana	release from the cycle of suffering in Buddhist belief; 'enlightenment'
Nyak	mythical water serpent (see naga) (L)

P

Pa kama	Lao men's all purpose cloth usually woven with checked pattern
paddy/padi	unhulled rice
Pagoda	a Mahayana Buddhist temple (V)
Pali	the sacred language of Theravada Buddhism
Parvati	consort of Siva
Pathet Lao	Communist party based in the north-eastern provinces of Laos until they came to power in 1975
Pha biang	shawl worn by women in Laos
Pha sin	tubular piece of cloth, similar to sarong (L)
Phi	spirit (see page 334)
Phnom/ phanom	Khmer for hill/mountain (C)
Phra sinh	see pha sin
Pra Lam	Lao version of the Ramayana (see Ramakien)
Pradaksina	pilgrims' clockwise circumambulation of holy structure
Prah	sacred
Prang	form of stupa built in Khmer style, shaped like a corncob
Prasada	stepped pyramid (see prasat)
Prasat	residence of a king or of the gods (sanctuary tower), from the Indian prasada (see page 489)

Q

Quan Am	Chinese goddess (Kuan-yin) of mercy (see page 154)

R

Rama	incarnation of Vishnu, hero of the Indian epic, the *Ramayana*
Ramakien	Lao version of the *Ramayana* (see page 337)
Ramayana	Hindu romantic epic (see page 337) (L)

S

Sakyamuni	the historic Buddha
Sal	the Indian sal tree (*Shorea robusta*), under which the historic Buddha was born
Sangha	the Buddhist order of monks

Sim/sima	main sanctuary and ordination hall in a Lao temple complex, equivalent to the bot in Thailand (see page 322) (L)
Singha	mythical guardian lion (see page 494)
Siva	the Destroyer, one of the three gods of the Hindu trinity; the sacred linga was worshipped as a symbol of Siva
Sofa	see dok sofa
Sravasti	the miracle at Sravasti when the Buddha subdues the heretics in front of a mango tree
Stele	inscribed stone panel
Stucco	plaster, often heavily moulded
Stupa	chedi (see page 489)

T

Tam bun	see bun
Taoism	Chinese religion (see page 120)
Tavatimsa	heaven of the 33 gods at the summit of Mount Meru
Thanon	street (L)
That	shrine housing Buddhist relics, a spire or dome-like edifice commemorating the Buddha's life or the funerary temple for royalty; peculiar to Laos and parts of Northeastern Thailand (L)
Theravada	'Way of the Elders'; major Buddhist sect also known as Hinayana Buddhism ('Lesser Vehicle') (see page 45)
Traiphum	the three worlds of Buddhist cosmology – heaven, hell and earth
Trimurti	the Hindu trinity of gods: Brahma, the Creator, Vishnu the Preserver and Siva the Destroyer
Tripitaka	Theravada Buddhism's Pali canon

U

Ubosoth	see bot
Urna	the dot or curl on the Buddha's forehead, one of the distinctive physical marks of the Enlightened One
Usnisa	the Buddha's top knot or 'wisdom bump', one of the physical marks of the Enlightened One

V

Vahana	'vehicle', a mythical beast, upon which a deva or god rides
Viet Cong	Vietnamese Communist troops (see page 92) (V)
Viet Minh	Vietnamese Communist troops (see page 87) (V)
Viharn	from Sanskrit *vihara*, an assembly hall in a Buddhist monastery; may contain Buddha images and is similar in style to the bot (see page 322)
Vishnu	the Protector, one of the gods of the Hindu trinity, generally with four arms holding a disc, conch shell, ball and club

614

INDEX OF ADVERTISERS

INDEX OF MAPS

TINTED BOXES

INDEX

Q

R

S

T

TRADE & TRAVEL
Handbooks

1996

Trade & Travel *Handbooks* are available worldwide in good bookshops. They can also be obtained by mail order directly from us in Bath (see below for address). Please contact us if you have difficulty finding a title.

South American Handbook

Mexico & Central American Handbook

Caribbean Islands Handbook

India Handbook

Thailand & Burma Handbook

Vietnam, Laos & Cambodia Handbook

Indonesia, Malaysia & Singapore Handbook

Morocco & Tunisia Handbook
with Algeria, Libya and Mauritania

East African Handbook
with Kenya, Tanzania, Uganda and Ethiopia

New in January 1996:
Egypt Handbook
Nepal & Tibet Handbook
Sri Lanka Handbook
Pakistan Handbook

Keep in touch. If you would like a catalogue or more information about the new titles please contact us at :
Trade & Travel, 6 Riverside Court, Lower Bristol Road, Bath BA2 3DZ. England
Tel 01225 469141   Fax 01225 469461   Email 100660.1250@compuserve.com